GENESIS 49 IN ITS LITERARY
AND HISTORICAL CONTEXT

OUDTESTAMENTISCHE STUDIËN

NAMENS HET OUDTESTAMENTISCH
WERKGEZELSCHAP IN NEDERLAND EN BELGIË

UITGEGEVEN DOOR

JOHANNES C. DE MOOR

KAMPEN

ADVISORY BOARD

WILLEM PRINSLOO †   MARC VERVENNE

PRETORIA   LEUVEN

DEEL XXIX

GENESIS 49 IN ITS LITERARY AND HISTORICAL CONTEXT

BY

RAYMOND DE HOOP

BRILL
LEIDEN · BOSTON · KÖLN
1999

BS
1235.2
.H65
1999

The investigations were supported by the Foundation for Research in the field of
Philosophy and Theology (SFT), which is subsidized by the Netherlands Organization
for Scientific Research (NWO).

This book is printed on acid-free paper.

Library of Congress Cataloging-in-Publication Data

Hoop, Raymond de.
   Genesis 49 in its literary and historical context / by Raymond de
Hoop.
      p.   cm. — (Oudtestamentische studiën, ISSN 0169–7226 ; d. 39)
   Includes bibliographical references and indexes.
   ISBN 9004109137 (alk. paper)
      1. Bible. O.T. Genesis XLIX—Criticism, interpretation, etc.
I. Title. II. Series.
BS1235.2.H65   1998
222'.1106—dc21   97–47628
                                                  CIP

Die Deutsche Bibliothek – CIP-Einheitsaufnahme

Hoop, Raymond de:
Genesis 49 in its literary and historical context / by Raymond de
Hoop. – Leiden ; Boston ; Köln : Brill, 1998
   (Oudtestamentische Studiën ; Deel 39)
   ISBN 90–04–10913 7

ISSN 0169-7226
ISBN 90 04 10913 7

PRINTED IN THE NETHERLANDS

To Louise, רַעְיָתִי

Contents

Preface

It has been ten years ago now, that professor Johannes de Moor asked me to work with him as a student-assistant in the project of "Poetic Fragments in the Pentateuch" at the Semitic Institute of the Theological University Kampen. My first assignment was to study Genesis 49 and this text has accompanied me during my studies ever since. It gives me great satisfaction to present this study on which I have worked under Johannes de Moor's guidance during the past five years. Even if we disagreed occasionally, I gratefully acknowledge my indebtedness to him "who put Kampen on the map of the international scholarly world" (John Day; Oslo, aug. '98). This study may bear testimony as to how I have enjoyed the "panorama" during his guided tour from Ugaritic religion, along Hebrew and Ugaritic verse, towards the *Rise of Yahwism*.

I also wish to thank Prof. Dr. C. Houtman, the co-supervisor of this project, who was so kind as to read the present study with a critical eye. His helpful comments are appreciated very much. It was a privilege to make use of his thorough knowledge of Pentateuchal research as established in his comprehensive work on *der Pentateuch*.

Dr. C.H.J. de Geus (Groningen) was willing to read the manuscript as a specialist on the *Tribes of Israel* and on the archaeology of ancient Israel. Yet he participated on this project far beyond his obligations as a referee and I wish to express my gratitude to him. His kind and stimulating, but nevertheless, critical remarks as well as his personal interest have meant a lot to me during the long way of preparing the present study.

Thanks are also due to Dr. F. Sepmeijer for his help with several problems concerning Arabic language and literature. Furthermore I wish to acknowledge my indebtness towards the staff of the library of our university, who were always ready to help with every request. It goes without saying that without their efficient assistance it would have been a difficult task to complete my investigations.

I wish to express my warmhearted gratitude to Mr. H. Blom (Koudum) who took the arduous task of correcting my English (or "Du-nglish"?) in the manuscript in a first draft. Although it concerned a subject outside his own specialism, he read the manuscript with great interest and prevented me from making bad mistakes. Dr. L. McFall (Cambridge) read the manuscript in a second draft and purged it with great speed and accuracy from remaining errors.

Most pages of this book have been written in the period I was privileged to work in one room with my colleagues Dr. Willem Smelik and Dr. Paul Sanders. I have taken full advantage of our many fruitful discussions in which friendship merged with critical scholarship. During the final year Willem and Marian Smelik frequently offered me hospitality, in that way enabling me to continue work during the weekends. In addition to them I wish to thank my colleagues Hennie Marsman and Bram van Putten (Utrecht) for their support during the final stage of my study. A special word of gratitude is due to Carolina Koops who accurately took care of the indices and helped me tidying up the manuscript in many respects.

Despite this highly appreciated help from various sides I alone bear full responsibility for the final result and for any errors I may have failed to weed out.

This study could not have been written without the support of my family. My parents have encouraged and supported me in the study of theology, and in this respect I owe a lot to them. During the long run of my study my parents-in-law have supported me and stimulated me and very often took care of my work at home in order to enable me to write this book. My daughters, Jitske, Flore and Mieke had to miss me several times at the moments they would have liked to see me.

My deepest feelings of gratitude concern her whose support goes beyond the conceivable. It is just a superfluous cliché to state that the present study could not have been written without her backing. Her confidence in me and in the result of my investigation have encouraged me to persevere and to row against every possible current. More than can be written on the pages of this book I owe to her. Therefore the book is dedicated to her, Louise Roersma, רֵעְיָתִי.

Kampen, October 1998   Raymond de Hoop

Chapter 1

Genesis 49: The *Status Quaestionis*

1.1 Introduction

In 1895 C.J. Ball wrote the following paragraph as an introduction to his article on Genesis 49:

> This ancient text has exercised a kind of fascination upon the mind of many scholars of the most varied gifts and acquirements. After all the pains, however, that have been lavished upon its interpretation, it still remains in many respects obscure and unintelligible. The dying patriarch who is the mouthpiece of the unknown poet, like the fabled Sphinx, propounds his ancient riddles anew to each succeeding generation of students. Yet there is no valid reason for assuming beforehand that the thoughtful labours of the competent will not eventually clear up the remaining obscurities, and produce out of materials, gathered from every possible source, a trustworthy text, and a self-coherent and harmonious interpretation which will carry conviction to the general apprehension.[1]

However, more than a century has passed since this was written and little has changed. Each new generation of students must face up to the difficulties in this enigmatic chapter. Even if Ball is rather optimistic about an eventual solution to the riddles, he has not succeeded in establishing an "interpretation which carries conviction to the general apprehension". The situation since his day has not got any easier and for that reason it may be appropriate to set out the difficulties that a student of this text will encounter.

The earliest interpretations of Genesis 49[2] were beset by difficulties inherent in the Hebrew text itself. Almost every saying[3] contains a problem to do with translation or interpretation. This can be demonstrated by using two of the most enigmatic passages in this chapter. The first example is the famous Shiloh-oracle (Gen. 49:10), rendered

---

[1]C.J. Ball, "The Testament of Jacob (Gen. xlix)", *PSBA* May 7 (1895) 164–91, esp. 164.

[2]Throughout this book "Genesis 49" will refer only to Gen. 49:1–28, or even more specifically to 49:3–27, where the "blessing" of the twelve sons is found. If the whole chapter is meant this will be indicated, *viz.* Gen. 49:1–33. The use of "blessing" for Genesis 49 is purely a literary device and is not a designation of its genre. The same applies to the term "saying".

[3]Cf. the preceding footnote.

in the *King James Version* as follows:

> The sceptre shall not depart from Judah, (10aA)
>   Nor a lawgiver from between his feet, (10aB)
> Until Shiloh come; (10bA)
>   And unto him shall the gathering of the people be. (10bB)

However, in the *Revised Standard Version* the text runs:

> The sceptre shall not depart from Judah, (10aA)
>   nor the ruler's staff from between his feet, (10aB)
> until he comes to whom it belongs; (10bA)
>   and to him shall be the obedience of the peoples. (10bB)

The translation of the *Jewish Publication Society*[4] offers the text with a remarkable difference:

> The sceptre shall not depart from Judah, (10aA)
>   Nor the ruler's staff from between his feet, (10aB)
> So that tribute shall come to him (10bA)
>   And the homage of peoples be his. (10bB)

Apart from some minor differences between these translations, it is clear that the Hebrew text in verse 10bA caused the translators many problems. The same can be seen in the following quotation from the *RSV* of the first part of the Joseph saying (Gen. 49:22):

> Joseph is a fruitful bough, (22aA)
>   a fruitful bough by a spring, (22aB)
>   his branches run over the wall. (22aC)

Compare this with the JPS version:

> Joseph is a wild ass, (22aA)
>   a wild ass by a spring, (22aB)
>   — wild colts on a hillside. — (22aC)

These two examples clearly demonstrate that the Hebrew of these two verses is equivocal. The differences between the translations are characteristic of the problems facing us when studying the Hebrew of this chapter.

However, translating the text is not the only problem one meets in this chapter; Genesis 49 occupies an important position in scholarly literature since the beginning of literary criticism. In 1753 J. Astruc in his *Conjectures* isolated Genesis 49 from its context on the

---

[4] *The Torah: The Five Books of Moses. A new translation of the Holy Scriptures according to the Masoretic text*, Philadelphia (PA) ²1962.

basis of different Divine names,[5] and this separation has survived up to the present day. This resulted, however, in a remarkable situation: Genesis 49 as well as its context (the Joseph Story, Genesis 37; 39–48; 49:29–50:26) became two completely independent entities which were discussed separately without taking the other into account.[6] C. Westermann in his commentary on Genesis, for example, discusses Gen. 49:1–28a only after he has finished the commentary on Genesis 37–48 and 49:28b–50:26.[7] N. Kebekus in his study of the literary and redactional criticism of Genesis 37–50 writes:

> A literary critical analysis of Gen. 49 might leave the tribal sayings in vv. 2–27 aside, because these were inserted only secondarily — probably with the addition of the introduction in v. 1b ... and the caption in v. 28abα ... — into the context of the chapter.[8]

On the other hand, studies on Genesis 49 do not take into consideration its present position in the Joseph Story, but take it for granted

---

[5] J. Astruc, *Conjectures sur les mémoires originaux dont il paraît que Moyse s'est servi pour composer le Livre de la Genèse: Avec des remarques qui appuient ou qui éclaircissent ces conjectures*, Bruxelles [Paris] 1753, 211–72, and esp. 263–7.

[6] H. Seebaß, *Geschichtliche Zeit und theonome Tradition in der Joseph-Erzählung*, Gütersloh 1978, 70, n. 23, remarks in this connection: "War es nicht eine Kuriosität der Quellentheorie, daß man 49,3–27 mit relativ großer Wahrscheinlichkeit und die Quelle J immerhin mit einer gewissen Wahrscheinlichkeit in die Zeit Salomos datierte, ohne zwischen ihnen eine gesicherte Verknüpfung zu sehen?"

[7] Westermann, *Genesis 37–50*, 243–78. Cf. also C. Westermann, *Genesis 12–50* (EdF, 48), Darmstadt 1975, where any reference to Genesis 49 is absent.

[8] N. Kebekus, *Die Joseferzählung: Literarkritische und redaktionsgeschichtliche Untersuchungen zu Genesis 37–50*, Münster 1990, 209: "Eine literarkritische Analyse von Gen 49 kann zunächst die Stammessprüche in V.2–27 unberücksichtigt lassen, die erst sekundär — wahrscheinlich unter Hinzufügung der Einleitung in V.1b ... und der Unterschrift in V.28abα ... — in den Zusammenhang des Kapitels eingebunden wurden"; cf. also *op.cit.*, 4. Similarly: L. Ruppert, *Die Josephserzählung der Genesis: Ein Beitrag zur Theologie der Pentateuchquellen* (StANT, 11), München 1965, 15–21; H.-C. Schmitt, *Die nichtpriesterliche Josephsgeschichte: Ein Beitrag zur neuesten Pentateuchkritik* (BZAW, 154), Berlin 1980, 73, with n. 305; L. Schmidt, *Literarische Studien zur Josephsgeschichte* (BZAW, 167), Berlin 1986, 127–8, 207. H. Schweizer, *Die Josefsgeschichte: Konstituierung des Textes*, Tl. I–II, Tübingen 1991, 332–3, n. 373 (cf. also his, *Joseph: Urfassung der alttestamentlichen Erzählung [Genesis 37–50]*, Tübingen 1993).
  Here the suggestion of I. Willi-Plein, "Historiographische Aspekte der Josefsgeschichte", *Henoch* 1 (1979) 305–331, 308, might be contrasted: "Allerdings wäre es grundsätzlich denkbar, dass cap. 49 ingesamt zur Josefsgeschichte gehörte. Der Verfasser hätte ja die Segenssprüche in sein Werk einbauen können, ebenso wie er auch in 48,15f. und 20 Segensworte in Bezug auf Josef bringt". However, the result here is that Genesis 49 is also regarded as independent from the context.

that this chapter was somehow inserted into it.[9] This separation is demonstrated very clearly in two volumes of the popular series *Die Schriften des Alten Testaments* by H. Gunkel and H. Greßmann. Whereas in Gunkel's volume on Genesis the discussion of Genesis 49 is absent,[10] Greßmann in his volume on Judges discusses our text together with Deuteronomy 33 just before Judges 5.[11]

In addition to the more *literary* critical approach of Astruc the *historical* critical approach started to question Genesis 49 as spoken originally by Jacob. The first to question this was J.G. Hasse in 1788, followed two years later by J.H. Heinrichs, but both scholars still considered the text as a coherent composition.[12] In 1855 E. Renan rest doubt on — together with the unity of Deuteronomy 33 — the unity of our chapter,[13] followed only three years later by J.P.N. Land, who took Genesis 49 to be a collection of oracles, only gradually reaching

---

[9]Cf. H.-J. Kittel, *Die Stammessprüche Israels: Genesis 49 und Deuteronomium 33 traditionsgeschichtlich untersucht*, Berlin 1959; H.-J. Zobel, *Stammesspruch und Geschichte: Die Angaben der Stammessprüche von Gen. 49, Dtn. 33 und Jdc. 5 über die politischen und kultischen Zustände im damaligen "Israel"* (BZAW, 95), Berlin 1965. Although H. Pehlke, *An Exegetical and Theological Study of Genesis 49:1–28*, Ann Arbor 1985, (cf. his p. 47. n. 1), does not share this view of a later insertion, he does not discuss the context of Gen. 49 (on pp. 46–51 he discussed Gen. 47:26–50:14 but only in order to refute someone's argument concerning these texts, not to position Gen. 49 in its literary context).

[10]H. Gunkel, *Die Urgeschichte und die Patriarchen (Das erste Buch Mosis) übersetzt und erklärt und mit Einleitungen in die fünf Bücher Mosis und in die Sagen des ersten Buches Mosis versehen* (SAT, I/1), Göttingen 1911, ²1921).

[11]H. Greßmann, *Die Anfänge Israels (Von 2. Mose bis Richter und Ruth) übersetzt, erklärt und mit Einleitung versehen* (SAT, I/2), Göttingen 1914, ²1922, 171–84.

[12]J.G. Hasse, "Neue Uebersetzung des Abschieds-gesangs Jakobs, 1 Mos. XLIX", *Magazin für die biblisch-orientalische Litteratur und gesammte Philologie* I. Theil, 1. Abschnitt (1788) 5–16; J.H. Heinrichs, *De auctore atque aetate capitis Geneseos XLIX commentatio*, Göttingen 1790 (according to J.P.N. Land, *Disputatio de carmine Jacobi Gen. XLIX*, Leiden 1858, 25, Heinrichs was the first to question the origin ["... primus, quantum scio..."]). The basic unity of Genesis 49 was neither disputed in the following century by K. Kohler, *Der Segen Jacob's mit besonderer Berücksichtigung der alten Versionen und des Midrasch kritisch-historisch untersucht und erklärt: Ein Beitrag zur Geschichte des hebräischen Altertums wie zur Geschichte der Exegese*, Berlin 1867, although he considered Genesis 49 to be *vaticinia ex eventu*. Cf. also W.M.L. de Wette, *Beiträge zur Einleitung in das Alte Testament*, II. *Kritik der Israelitischen Geschichte. Erster Teil: Kritik der mosaischen Geschichte*, Halle 1807 (repr. Darmstadt 1971), 164–5; F. Bleek, *Einleitung in die Heilige Schrift. Erster Theil: Einleitung in das Alte Testament*, J. Bleek, A. Kamphausen (hrsg.), Berlin ³1870, 260–1.

[13]E. Renan, *Histoire générale et système comparé des langues sémitiques*, Paris 1855, ⁴1863, 122–3, with n. 2. According to Zobel, *SuG*, 1, n. 4, Renan had already questioned this unity in the first impression of his book in 1855, p. 112.

its present form and in this way reflecting certain aspects of Israel's history.[14] But the theory concerning these oracles was developed more elaborately at the turn of the century, as H.-J. Zobel has pointed out.[15] This development was mainly the work of H. Greßmann some fourteen years after the turn of the century, while "in the preceding period the results of this research remained almost unnoticed".[16] Greßmann developed the theory of the "tribal saying", an independent saying in oral tradition, expressing something crucial concerning the tribe. These tribal sayings were added during the course of transmission in written form. As the quotation from Kebekus clearly demonstrates,[17] this classification became a cornerstone for literary critical considerations, which throughout the century helped to keep Genesis 49 separated from its context.

The questioning of Jacob's "authorship" consequently caused the next problem: when did the blessing,[18] with the different sayings it contains, come into being? Obviously the answer to this question depends partly on how the origin of its context, the Joseph Story, is seen. If one considers this context to be a rather late development, originated for example during the Exile,[19] it is possible that Genesis 49 had a long genesis, maybe until the Exile or even after it, before it was incorporated into its present position. However, if the Joseph Story is thought to have been compiled from several documents (J, E and P), the definition of the origin depends on its place within these documents. The framework of the blessing (Gen. 49:1a, 28b) is nowadays thought to belong to P, so this justifies once again a dating during, or after the Exile. However, if Genesis 49 belongs to J it might

---

[14]Land, *Disputatio de carmine Jacobi Gen. XLIX*, esp. 90–100.

[15]Zobel, *SuG*, 1–2; cf. also J.D. Heck, "A History of Interpretation of Genesis 49 and Deuteronomy 33", *BS* 147 (1990) 16–31, 17.

[16]Zobel, *SuG*, 1–2: "Nachdem zunächst im Laufe des 19. Jh. darin weitgehend Übereinstimmung erzielt worden war, daß Gen 49 und Dtn 33 als *vaticinia ex eventu* zu verstehen, mithin dem Jakob und Mose abzusprechen seien, konnte sich zu Beginn dieses Jahrhunderts die einst von E. Renan lediglich am Rande geäußerte, von J.P.N. Land nur für Gen 49 nachgewiesene und in den folgenden Jahrzehnten fast unbeachtet gebliebene Erkenntnis immer mehr durchsetzen, daß die Einheitlichkeit beider Stücke zugunsten der Annahme von Sammlungen ursprünglich unabhängig voneinander umlaufender Einzelsprüche aufzugeben sei." The importance of Greßmann is also stressed by those, who start immediately with Greßmann without any reference to earlier scholars; cf. Kittel, *Die Stammessprüche Israels*, 65; Pehlke, *Genesis 49:1-28*, 3.

[17]Cf. p. 3 above.

[18]Cf. p. 1, n. 2 above.

[19]Cf. *e.g.* A. Meinhold, "Die Gattung der Josephsgeschichte und des Esterbuches: Diasporanovelle, I", *ZAW* 87 (1975) 306–24; II, *ZAW* 88 (1976) 72–93.

go back to the period of David and Solomon.[20] But the problem is more complicated because an independent origin of Genesis 49, or at least parts of it, is almost commonly assumed: the text is compiled from different independent sayings and inserted by a redactor in its present position. If so, then a much earlier date for these sayings is possible. The saying on Issachar (49:14–15) for example, seems to reflect the period of settlement of this tribe:[21]

> Issachar is a strong ass, (14A)
>   crouching between the sheepfolds; (14B)
> he saw that a resting place was good, (15aA)
>   and that the land was pleasant; (15aB)
> so he bowed his shoulder to bear, (15bA)
>   and became a slave at forced labor. (15bB)

Thus it has become possible to date these sayings in the period of transition from Late Bronze to Early Iron I. On the other hand the well-known Shiloh-oracle (Gen. 49:10) is interpreted by E. Blum (taking שִׁילֹה as a reference to the LN "Shiloh") as reflecting the time of king Josiah, when he wanted to restore the correct religion and needed Shiloh as a symbol of the original religion.[22] The difference between these two datings is about seven- to eight hundred years, showing a gap which is almost impossible to narrow down.

Furthermore, the use of Biblical texts in connection with the history of Israel is nowadays strongly criticized by scholars.[23] The main reason for this approach is that, in their view, the Hebrew Bible reflects the post-Exilic period, and thus the post-Exilic view of Israel's history. In this way the use of the Hebrew Bible is played down as a source for the pre-Exilic period, not to mention the pre-Monarchic times. Hence, previous attempts to date Genesis 49 in the Monarchic

---

[20]Of course such dating depends on the dating of J. After the Exile a "late Jahwist" is found (H.-C. Schmitt); according to J. Van Seters an Exilic date is appropriate; whereas others date it any time between David and that period.

[21]See *e.g.* H. Donner, "The Blessing of Issachar (*Gen.* 49:14–15) as a Source for the Early History of Israel," in J.A. Soggin *et al.*, *Le Origini di Israele*, Rome 1987, 53–63; cf. also De Moor, *RoY*, 109–10 (with n. 39 for additional bibliographical references). Quotation from *RSV*.

[22]E. Blum, *Die Komposition der Vätergeschichte* (WMANT, 57). Neukirchen-Vluyn 1984, 262–3.

[23]Most prominent in this discussion are probably P.R. Davies, N.P. Lemche and T.L. Thompson. Cf. I.W. Provan, "Ideologies, Literary and Critical: Reflections on Recent Writing on the History of Israel", *JBL* 114 (1995) 585–606; T.L. Thompson, "A Neo-Albrightean School in History and Biblical Scholarship?", *JBL* 114 (1995) 683–98; P.R. Davies, "Method and Madness: Some Remarks on Doing History with the Bible", *JBL* 114 (1995) 699–705.

or pre-Monarchic period are open to suspicion and any discussion of historical aspects has to take these presuppositions into account.

From this we can conclude that the study of Genesis 49 is burdened with many problems of translation, literary criticism, historical criticism, and historiography. Now, in order to create a clear picture of the problems involved we will give a description of previous research. Such a description has to serve a twofold goal: Firstly, to present the work done so far and to set out the results of this research. Secondly, such a description will inevitably bring forward deficiencies within previous research and in this way it will help us to formulate the goal of the present study. In the present chapter we will focus exclusively on Genesis 49. In a later stage of our study we will return on the separation of Genesis 49 from its context; there we will consider the matter whether this *a priori* decision of separation is justified or not. Following now the order of this brief description of previous research we will approach the problems of Genesis 49 from the beginning, starting with the translation of Genesis 49.

1.2 The Translation of Genesis 49 and Hebrew Study

In the introductory section we noted that the differences between the English translations of Gen. 49:10 and 22 characterize the problems found in this chapter. The following chart shows the most enigmatic Hebrew words to be found in the text.

Verse	Name	Hebrew	Translation (RSV)
4	Reuben	פַּחַז כַּמַּיִם	unstable as water
		עָלָה	*you*[24] went up
5	Sim. & Levi	מְכֵרֹתֵיהֶם	their swords[25]
6		שׁוֹר	oxen[26]
10	Judah	שִׁילֹה	to whom it belongs[27]
13	Zebulun	לְחוֹף יַמִּים יִשְׁכֹּן	dwell at the shore of the sea[28]
14	Issachar	הַמִּשְׁפְּתָיִם	sheepfolds[29]
15		לְמַס־עֹבֵד	slave at forced labour
16	Dan	יָדִין	judge
			Continued on next page

---

[24]KJ: "he went up"; JPS: "he mounted".
[25]KJ: "their habitations"; JPS: "their weapons".
[26]KJ: "wall".
[27]KJ: "Shiloh"; JPS: "tribute to him".
[28]KJ: "haven of the sea".
[29]KJ: "two burdens".

Continued from previous page			
Verse	Name	Hebrew	Translation (RSV)
21	Naphtali	אַיָּלָה	hind
		אִמְרֵי	fawns[30]
22	Joseph	בֵּן פֹּרָת	fruitful bough[31]
		בָּנוֹת צָעֲדָה	his branches run[32]
		שׁוּר	wall[33]
23		וַרֹבּוּ	shot at him
		וַיְמָרֲרֻהוּ	harassed him sorely[34]
24		אֲבִיר	the Mighty One
		מִשָּׁם	by the name of[35]
		אֶבֶן יִשְׂרָאֵל	the Rock[36] of Israel
25		אֵל אָבִיךָ	the God of your father
		וְאֵת שַׁדַּי	by God Almighty[37]
26		הוֹרַי עַד־	eternal mountains[38]

It is impossible and unnecessary to list here all the suggestions that have been put forward to translate these difficult texts. In this paragraph we will give only a brief outline of the historical conditions which formed the background to some of these suggestions. The different proposals themselves will be listed, when relevant, in Chapter Two when discussing the translation of Genesis 49.

Already the ancient Versiones testify time and again to the difficulties confronting the exegetes. But history shows that the testimony of interpretating the problems in this chapter are not restricted to the period of the ancient translations but are already found in the Hebrew Bible itself. The aforementioned שִׁילֹה in Gen. 49:10bA seems to find an early interpretation in Ezek. 21:32, where the word is interpreted in the sense of a relative particle שֶׁ followed by the preposition לְ and a suffix 3.p. masc.sg. ה–, meaning something like "to whom it is"; an interpretation which occurs later on in the Versiones; but has also found its way into modern translations as the quotation from RSV

---

[30]KJ: "words".

[31]JPS: "wild ass".

[32]JPS: "wild colts".

[33]JPS: "hillside".

[34]RSV changed the sequence of the verbs and of the cola in this verse completely: v. 23b became v. 23a and vice versa, whereas the verbs in the former v. 23a also changed their order.

[35]KJ: "From thence"; JPS: "There, . . . ".

[36]JPS: "Rock".

[37]KJ: "by the Almighty"; JPS: "and Shaddai"; RSV states in a note that the Hebrew reads "*Ĕl Shăd'dăï*"!

[38]KJ: "my progenitors unto. . . "; JPS: "my ancestors, to. . . ".

above shows.[39]

After the period of consolidation of the different ancient translations, the interpretation of the *Hebrew* Bible appears to have been
restricted to the Jewish community. This situation continued until the
end of the Middle Ages. During this period the interpretation of the
text in the Jewish community found its way into official documents
like the Mishna, into commentaries, but also into linguistic studies by,
for example, Jonah Ibn Ḡanâḥ,[40] Solomon ben Isaac Rashi,[41] Abraham Ibn Ezra,[42] and the Kimchi's.[43] In linguistic studies, especially
those of Ibn Ḡanâḥ and Ibn Ezra, methods are applied which are still
practised in modern linguistic reference works, such as the comparative method, using other Semitic languages like Arabic[44] and Aramaic in order to elucidate difficult passages.[45] These medieval studies,
which are of general importance for the knowledge of Hebrew, sometimes contain unexpected solutions. In the saying on Reuben the expression פַּחַז כַּמַּיִם is found (Gen. 49:4). Exegetes have puzzled on the
meaning of the word פַחַז ever since the Versiones came into existence,
because the exact meaning was lost. However, in the lexicon of Ibn

---

[39]The description of the history of interpretation of Gen. 49:10bA would require
a large volume. An early attempt was made by A. Posnanski, *Schiloh: Ein Beitrag
zur Geschichte der Messiaslehre, Teil I: Die Auslegung von Genesis 49, 10 im
Altertume bis zu Ende des Mittelalters*, Leipzig 1904, which comprises only the
period before the Reformation and already contains more than 450 pages; the
second part was to cover the time from the Reformation until modern times but
it never appeared. Cf. also B. Zimmel, "Zur Geschichte der Exegese über den Vers
Gen. 49, 10", *MWJ* 18 (1890) 1–27, 261–79; *MWJ* 19–20 (1892–93) 56–78, 168–
80; the latter scholar died at the age of thirty-one, which is why his description
finishes at the twelfth century. See also J.J. Thierry, "'Totdat Silo komt'", in:
D.S. Attema *et al.*, *Schrift en Uitleg: Studies ... W.H. Gispen*, Kampen 1970,
206–21; and further the section on the translation of this verse below.

[40]For the life and work of Ibn Ḡanâḥ, cf. *EJ*, vol. 8, 1181–6.

[41]See *EJ*, vol. 13, 1558–65.

[42]See *EJ*, vol. 8, 1163–70.

[43]For Joseph Kimchi, the father, cf. *EJ*, vol. 10, 1006–7; for his son David
Kimchi, cf. *ibid.*, 1001–4; for the latter's brother, Moses Kimchi, cf. *ibid.*, 1007–8.

[44]This is especially clear in the work of Ibn Ḡanâḥ, who wrote in Arabic and
whose works were translated in Hebrew only later. Moreover, Ibn Ḡanâḥ made
abundantly use of the work of Arabian grammarians, from which he copied whole
sentences and passages; see: D. Becker, "Linguistic Rules and Definitions in Ibn
Janāḥ's *Kitāb al-Luma'* (*Sefer ha-Riqmah*) Copied from the Arab Grammarians",
JQR 86 (1996) 275–98. Cf. also J. Kaltner, *The Use of Arabic in Biblical Hebrew
Lexicography* (CBQ.MS, 28), Washington (DC) 1996.

[45]Cf. J. Barr, *Comparative Philology and the Text of the Old Testament*, Oxford 1968, 60–5; idem, "Hebrew Lexicography", in: P. Fronzaroli (ed.), *Studies
on Semitic Lexicography* (QuSem, 2), Firenze 1973, 103–26, 105; D. Cohen, "La
lexicographie comparée", *ibid.*, 183–208, 184–7.

Ḡanâḥ, dating from the early eleventh century, it is interpreted as meaning the same as בגד "to deceive", which might be correct.[46] Ibn Ezra was apparently unfamiliar with Ibn Ḡanâḥ's solution — or he did not agree with it — for in connection with Zeph. 3:4, referring to Gen. 49:4, he gave a different interpretation of the word ("empty"),[47] which is probably based on the passage in Judg. 9:4 where רֵיק "empty, futile" is juxtaposed with פֹּחַז. Knowledge of Hebrew among Christians was completely dependent on Jewish scholars; this was even the case with Jerome.[48] On the Jewish side it is, for example, Rashi, who was frequently consulted by Christian scholars, and after his death his works were used in Christian schools.[49]

The beginning of the sixteenth century is also the beginning of a new era in this respect. In the fifteenth century Humanism began to florish and one of the ideals of this movement was *trium linguarum gnarus*, a *homo trilinguus*, a man well acquainted with the three (classical) languages: Latin, Greek, and Hebrew.[50] This ideal arose because of the motto of Humanism: *ad fontes*, back to the sources, in order to answer the demand for absolute truth.[51] Because the knowledge of Hebrew was virtually absent among Christian scholars they had to turn to Jewish teachers,[52] but they quickly established their own tradition, forgetting that they once had been completely dependent

---

[46] A.M. Ibn Ḡanâḥ (R. Jona), *Sepher Haschoraschim: Wurzelwörterbuch der hebräischen Sprache*, Berlin 1896, 400. I owe the reference to this work to Dr. S.C. Reif, University of Cambridge. Cf. further R. de Hoop, "The Meaning of *PḤZ* in Classical Hebrew", *ZAH* 10 (1997) 16–26.

[47] T. Muraoka, Z. Shavitsky, "Abraham Ibn Ezra's Biblical Hebrew Lexicon: The Minor Prophets II", *AbrN* 29 (1991) 106–28, 115.

[48] Cf. H.F.D. Sparks, "Jerome as Biblical Scholar", in: P.R. Ackroyd, C.F. Evans (eds.), *The Cambridge History of the Bible, Volume I: From the Beginnings to Jerome*, Cambridge 1970, 510–41, 512; Barr, *Comparative Philology*, 65.

[49] H. Hailperin, *Rashi and the Christian Scholars*, Pittsburg (PA) 1963, 1–15, 103–34.

[50] B. Hall, "Biblical Scholarship: Editions and Commentaries; Biblical Humanism and Its Resources", in: S.L. Greenslade (ed.), *The Cambridge History of the Bible: The West from the Reformation to the Present Day*, Cambridge 1963, 38–48, 40.

[51] Cf. Hall, "Biblical Scholarship", 38–40; Barr, *Comparative Philology*, 66; H.J. Kraus, *Geschichte der historisch-kritischen Erforschung des Alten Testaments*, Neukirchen ³1982, 24–8; Houtman, *Der Pentateuch*, 28; R. Boon, *Hebreeuws Reveil: Wat bracht christen-theologen rond 1500 in de leerschool der rabbijnen?* Kampen 1983, 30–43. Further also W.J. Kooiman, *Luther en de Bijbel* (BBB), Baarn 1961, 61–5.

[52] The first Jewish teacher to mention here is Eliah ben Asher ha-Levi, better known as Elias Levita; cf. G.E. Weil, *Élie Lévita: Humaniste et massorete* (StPB, 7), Leiden 1963; Hall, "Biblical Scholarship", 45–6; Barr, *Comparative Philology*, 66; Boon, *Hebreeuws Reveil*, 30–3.

on the knowledge of Jewish grammar and lexicography.[53]

The seventeenth century is important as the era in which the vision on the Hebrew language as a human language as such, and not any longer as a sacred tongue alone, emerged, although this viewpoint was not expressed as such at that time. It was the view of the rabbis that a divine radiance rested on the Hebrew consonants and words[54] and this view was initially followed by Christian scholars, as can be derived from the title of J. Buxtorf's *Thesaurus grammaticus linguæ sanctæ hebræœ*,[55] one of the most important studies of that time. Buxtorf even defended the sacred character of the pointing of the text,[56] but soon different opinions were defended. L. Cappellus, for example, showed that the vocalisation of the Hebrew text was particularly young, but he also held the view that Hebrew was a poor, dark and equivocal language.[57] In the following century the knowledge of the Semitic languages, and especially Arabic, increased considerably, partly due to the appearance of several polyglot lexica, where related roots from the different Semitic languages were listed together.[58] These works formed the basis for comparative Semitic philology, which considered Hebrew to be just another Semitic dialect, even though the *lingua sacra* was still considered to be *primus inter pares*, if not *primus omnium*.[59]

It is the distinguished scholar A. Schultens who drew some radical conclusions from the studies of the preceding century.[60] Although he was at first inclined — as was common in those days — to consider Hebrew the oldest dialect, the mother-language of all other tongues,[61]

---

[53] Barr, *Comparative Philology*, 66.

[54] Kraus, *Geschichte*, 80-1.

[55] J. Buxtorfius, *Thesaurus grammaticus linguæ sanctæ hebræœ, duobus libris methodice propositus: querum prior, vocum singularum naturam & proprietates: alter vocum conjunctarum rationem & elegatiam universam, accuratissime explicat, adjecta, prosodia metrica, sive poeseos Hebræorum dilacida tractatio: lectionis Hebræo-Germanicæusus & exercitatio*, Basilæ 1609.

[56] Kraus, *Geschichte*, 81. This view might still be found with scholars who think that the Masoretes did not do much more than fixate the pronunciation of the text as it was transmitted to them, even when they did not understand the meaning completely; cf. J.P. Lettinga, *De 'Tale Kanaäns': Enkele beschouwingen over het Bijbels Hebreeuws*, Groningen 1971, 7-8, with n. 6.

[57] Barr, *Comparative Philology*, 67; Kraus, *Geschichte*, 81.

[58] Cf. Barr, *Comparative Philology*, 67; S. Segert, "Hebrew Bible and Semitic Comparative Lexicography", in: *Congress Volume : Rome 1968* (SVT, 17), Leiden 1969, 204-11, 204-5; Kraus, *Geschichte*, 81.

[59] Barr, *Comparative Philology*, 67; Kraus, *Geschichte*, 81.

[60] For an excellent description of his life and work in its historical and scholarly context, cf. J.C. de Bruïne, "Schultens, Albert", *BLGNP*, dl. 1, 330-3.

[61] This view is found in his *Disputatio de utilitate linguæ Arabicæ in interpre-*

in the course of his scholarly career he changed his mind and described Arabic as the purest and clearest of the Semitic languages, while acknowledging that there was a sister-relation between Hebrew and Arabic.[62] However, from the beginning he argued that Arabic was just as old as any other Semitic language and could therefore be applied to the understanding of Hebrew passages. When Arabic and Hebrew are considered to be equal languages, and find their origin in the same period, an important shift is made: the study of Hebrew was brought from the sacred into the historical — and thus human — realm.[63] Schulten's viewpoint and method, and after him J.D. Michaelis', were criticized by later scholars as a form of "hyperarabism",[64] but their work has been immensely important for the study of Semitic languages and especially of Hebrew.

It appears that the nineteenth century was less important for the study of the Hebrew language from the viewpoint of comparative philology, although the final two decades mark an important change in this respect. Meanwhile however, important lexica and grammars were published, stimulating the study of Hebrew enormously. The most important scholar to be mentioned in this respect is W. Gesenius, who published his *Thesaurus philologicus* between 1835 and 1853;[65] and his Hebrew grammar, which is still in use as a *vade mecum*.[66] However, as J. Barr describes this period, this increase of knowledge of Hebrew also produced very self-assured scholars, who could rely on what they knew:

---

tanda S. Scriptura, Groningen 1706 (= idem, *Opera Minora, Animadversiones ejus in Jobum, et ad varia loca V.T. nec non varias dissertationes et orationes, complectentia*, Lugduni Batavorum 1769, 487–510); but also in his inaugural lecture *Oratio de fontibus ex quibus omnis linguæ Hebrææ notitia emanavit horumque vitiis et defectibus*, Franeker 1714, where he called Arabic a daughter-language of Hebrew, and described at the same moment Arabic, Aramaic, Syriac and Ethiopic as sister-languages.

[62]He already defended this view in his *Oratio (prior) de linguæ Arabicæ antiquissima origine*, Franeker 1729; and elaborated it in his *Oratio altera de linguæ Arabicæ antiquissima origine*, Lugduni Batavorum 1732; and *Clavis mutationis elementorum, qua dialecti linguæ hebrææ ac praesertim arabica dialectus aliquando ab hebraicæ deflectunt*, Lugduni Batavorum 1733. Cf. Kraus, *Geschichte*, 83; De Bruïne, "Schultens, Albert", 331.

[63]Barr, *Comparative Philology*, 67; De Bruïne, "Schultens, Albert", 331; Kraus, *Geschichte*, 82.

[64]See Barr, *Comparative Philology*, 68; Cohen, "Lexicographie comparée", 188.

[65]W. Gesenius, *Thesaurus philologicus criticus linguæ Hebrææ et Chaldææ Veteris Testamenti*, I–III, Leipzig 1835–53.

[66]This characterization is found in JM §4c. The grammar of Gesenius is, after several improvements by E. Rödiger and E. Kautzsch: W. Gesenius, *Hebräische Grammatik*, völlig umgearbeitet von E. Kautzsch, Leipzig [28]1909.

if the text made no sense, one need no longer hide this fact, as the older exegesis had done, and one certainly need not try artificial explanations for the anomalies of the text. Rather let the text be emended to what it had been before careless scribes corrupted it, and the difficulties would be gone. In conjectural textual criticism the careless scribe plays a role somewhat analogous to the role of the clumsy redactor in source criticism.[67]

To give an example, we quote from C.J. Ball:

> We need not be afraid of emending a text which cries aloud for emenda-
> tion. The general laws of Hebrew syntax — apart from that extraord-
> inary mass of ingenious speculations by which it is sought to palliate
> improbable, and justify impossible constructions — must be steadily
> borne in mind. Continuity of thought must be expected, and, where not
> apparent, must be made the object of careful search in each distinct
> portion of the text.[68]

To achieve his goal he proposed numerous emendations. In the saying on Zebulun (Gen. 49:13) he takes the final colon וְיַרְכָתוֹ עַל־צִידֹן "and his border is at Sidon", to be "an explanatory gloss or interpolation ... as a local determination it is without parallel in the entire piece, and is, besides, thoroughly prosaic".[69] In the sayings on Naphtali and Joseph (Gen. 49:21-2) he changes אילה and אמרי in verse 21 into פרת in verse 22 because

1. "It is generally admitted that the utterance concerning Naphtali is corrupt as it stands in MT";[70]

2. LXX read in verse 21A στέλεχος, which is in two different places a rendering for פארה "branch", which LXX might have confused with פרת = פריה "a fruiting tree".[71]

3. In verse 21B LXX read γένημα, which is in ten other places the rendering for פרי "fruit".[72]

4. Verse 22 reads twice פרת (equivalent of פרה) which, connected with Akk. *parratu*, means "ewe" (since a "fruiting tree" does not fit in this context). Although בן פרת "son of a ewe" would fit

---

[67] Barr, *Comparative Philology*, 68.
[68] Ball, "Testament of Jacob", 164; cf. also his commentary on the book of Genesis.
[69] Ball, "Testament of Jacob", 167-8.
[70] Ball, "Testament of Jacob", 172.
[71] Ball, "Testament of Jacob", 172.
[72] Ball, "Testament of Jacob", 172-3.

for Joseph ben Rachel (רחל, "ewe"), a ewe standing alone at a spring is unlikely, as are archers shooting at sheep.[73] This might be expected of a "hart, hind" which is found in verse 21A: אילה. "This is far from being the only instance of such unfortunate transpositions of words by transcribers of the O.T. text."[74]

5. Concerning the final colon of verse 22, MT "starts with a grammatical anomaly, besides being discordant with what precedes and follows".[75] The LXX supposes (supported by Sam) בני צערי "my son, my little one". Further, שור might mean "lie in wait" as עלי is an easy corruption for עלו "going up", which "supplies the link of connection we desiderate": "they went up to lie in wait".[76] Now the preceding terms must qualify this statement, and the reading of LXX (with Sam) בני צערי suggests the correction מבצעדו "in his tracks", because a "broken ם might easily be read נ, and ד is constantly confused with ר."[77] Perhaps, he suggests, MT should rather be corrected במצעדה (ה– = ו–).[78]

The result of his transposition of the words in verses 21–22 is the following text:

Naphtali is a spreading vine (21A)	נפתלי פרת שלחה
that yieldeth beauteous fruit (21B)	הנתנת פרי שפר
A young hart is Joseph, (22A)	בן אילה יוסף
a young hart beside a spring; (22B)	בן אילה עלי עין
In his track they go up to lie in wait. (22C)	במצעדה עלו שור

This suggestion was followed by another proposal of T.K. Cheyne on verses 20–26, who reads in verse 22 the following text:[79]

Ephraim is an ornament for Joseph, (22A)	אפרים תפארת ליוסף
Manasseh a bracelet for Israel. (22B)	מנשה צעדה לישראל

This text is accompanied by the explanation that

---

[73] Ball, "Testament of Jacob", 173–4.

[74] Ball, "Testament of Jacob", 174.

[75] Ball, "Testament of Jacob", 174.

[76] Ball, "Testament of Jacob", 175.

[77] Ball, "Testament of Jacob", 175.

[78] Ball, "Testament of Jacob", 175.

[79] T.K. Cheyne, "The Blessing on Asher, Naphtali, and Joseph", *PSBA* June 6 (1899) 242–5. Cheyne introduces his note with the statement that, "two things seem to be necessary at the present moment for the study of the Old Testament; one is the zealous prosecution of Biblical archæology, and the other *the correction of the Massoretic text*" (italics, RdH).

Corrupt dittograms have much disfigured this verse. שֹׁפֶר (v. 21, end) comes from אפרים (א and שׁ are liable to be confounded); בֶן comes from רים, the second part of אפרים. פרת is a shrivelled up form of הפארת; cf. ברית, Isa. xlii, 6, xlix, 8, which probably comes out of תפארת. ... The second בֶן פרת is dittographed, and to be omitted. עלי־עין comes from לְיוֹסֵף (so read; cf. next line); the initial עׁ is dittographed; ס and עׁ, ף and ן are confounded. בנות is a bad corruption of מנשה (ס and ב, ה and שׁ confounded). עלי־שׁור comes out of לישראל; when the letters had been misarranged (a common source of misreadings) the editor tried to make some kind of sense; "upon the wall" is the strange result.[80]

This method of text emendation is still applied; the reading of אֶפְרַיִם "Ephraim" in verse 22 for example is still found, although now it replaces יוֹסֵף "Joseph" at the end of verse 22A.[81] Others who still take a rather critical stand concerning MT are M. Dahood in several articles on lexicography; F.M. Cross and D.N. Freedman in their work on *Ancient Yahwistic Poetry*; and S. Gevirtz in seven articles on the different sayings. They have proposed many emendations for Genesis 49 in MT, but find very few followers today.

The beginning of archaeology in the ancient Near East had an important impact on the study of the Hebrew Bible. It is a period — starting as far back as the seventeenth century — that travel stories from the ancient Near East and especially from Palestine were published; the geography, topography, social institutions, etc. of Palestine were now described and studied in the land itself.[82] The consequences

---

[80]Cheyne, "Blessing on Asher, Naphtali, and Joseph", 243–4.

[81]Zobel, *SuG*, 22; C.H.J. de Geus, *The Tribes of Israel: An Investigation into Some of the Presuppositions of Martin Noth's Amphictyony Hypothesis* (SSN, 12), Assen 1976, 90; Westermann, *Genesis 37–50*, 270; J. Sanmartín, "Problemas de textologia en las 'bendiciones' de Moises (Dt 33) y de Jacob (Gn 49)", in: V. Collado, E. Zurro (eds.), *El misterio de la Palabra: Homenaje ... D.L. Alonso Schökel*, Madrid 1983, 75–96, 86.

[82]Kraus, *Geschichte*, 163–5, 295–300; M.A. Beek, *Atlas van het Tweestromenland: Overzicht over de geschiedenis en beschaving van Mesopotamië van de steentijd tot de val van Babylon*, Amsterdam 1960, 19–28; K.M. Kenyon, *Archaeology in the Holy Land*, London ⁴1979, 1–18; K.A. Kitchen, *Ancient Orient and Old Testament*, London 1966, 15–25; E. Hornung, *Einführung in die Ägyptologie: Stand · Methoden · Aufgaben* (Die Archäologie), Darmstadt 1967, 9–14. Concerning the early stages of archaeology in Israel, cf. C.H.J. de Geus, "Archeologie van Palestina en andere Bijbelse landen: De ontwikkeling van de Palestijnse archeologie en haar betekenis voor de Bijbelwetenschap", *BijbH*, dl. I, 94–110, 94–9; V. Fritz, *Einführung in die biblische Archäologie* (Die Archäologie), Darmstadt 1985, 29–34; A. Mazar, *Archaeology of the Land of the Bible* (ABRL), New York (NY) 1990, 10–21; the contributions by Y. Hodson, E. Puech, P.J. King, A. Strobel, M. Piccirillo, A.G. Auld, R. Reich, in: A. Biran, J. Aviram (eds.), *Biblical Archaeology Today, 1990: Proceedings of the Second International Congress on Biblical*

of these studies were enormous: they influenced almost every level of
the study of the Hebrew Bible and may be characterized by the following quotation from Kraus:

> Between 1850 and 1900 a gradual but irrepressible revolution took
> place in Old Testament study. By the discoveries of the sources from
> the ancient Orient the environment of ancient Israel was uncovered and
> formerly unexpected connections were revealed. In particular in the fi-
> nal two decades of the nineteenth century, when historical and religious
> texts from Egypt and Mesopotamia were published, Old Testament re-
> search had to reorientate completely.[83]

The study of Hebrew also took advantage of these developments because many texts in "new" comparable languages were found.[84] From
the beginning of the nineteenth century Phoenician inscriptions were
found that had to be deciphered, whereas in 1860 the Moabite Mesa-
stele was discovered.[85] The most important language for the study
of Hebrew in that period, however, was Akkadian, an east-Semitic[86]
dialect of which an enormous number of texts were found, which —
also from a philological point of view — is important, because such
an amount permits a more precise description of grammar and meaning of words than when a small corpus is available. The discovery of
Akkadian considerably stimulated the comparative study of Hebrew
with other languages, because "it altered the perspective from which
Hebrew could been seen, and in particular provided a very different
angle of view from that which had been mainly informed by Arabic
and Aramaic".[87] Yet the danger of overestimating the value of the ma-

---

Archaeology Jerusalem, June–July 1990, Jerusalem 1993, 6–30.

[83]Kraus, *Geschichte*, 298: "Zwischen 1850 und 1900 vollzog sich langsam, aber
unaufhaltbar in der alttestamentlichen Wissenschaft eine umstürzende Wende.
Durch die Entdeckung der altorientalischen Quellen trat die Umwelt des alten
Israels ins Licht. Zusammenhänge, die man nie zuvor erahnte, taten sich plötzlich
auf. Insbesondere in den letzten zwei Jahrzehnten des 19. Jahrhunderts, in denen
historische und religöse Dokumente aus Ägypten und Mesopotamien bekannt wurden, mußte die alttestamentliche Forschung eine völlige Neuorientierung suchen."

[84]"New" is used here in comparison with Aramaic, Syrian, Persian, Arabic,
being "old" languages, because they had been known for a long time, although
they are sometimes "younger" than certain phases of these "new" languages.

[85]Kraus, *Geschichte*, 296. On the finding of this stele, cf. C.H.J. de Geus,
"Koninginscripties uit Moab uit de 9ᵉ eeuw v.Chr.", in: K.R. Veenhof (ed.), *Schrij-
vend Verleden: Documenten uit het oude Nabije Oosten vertaald en toegelicht*
(MEOL), Leiden 1983, 25–30; K.A.D. Smelik, *Writings from Ancient Israel: A
Handbook of Historical and Religious Documents*, Edinburgh 1991, 29–50.

[86]Cf. J.C. de Moor, "Schriftsystemen en talen in de wereld van de bijbel, A:
Schriftsystemen en niet-bijbelse talen", *BijbH*, dl. 1, 113–4; JM §2b; GAG §1.

[87]Barr, *Comparative Philology*, 70. Cf. also Kraus, *Geschichte*, 298.

terial was present on the "theological" or "religious historical" level,[88] as well as on the philological level. Several solutions for dark passages in Genesis 49 have been offered from Akkadian material:

- For מְכֵרֹתֵיהֶם (verse 5B) it has been suggested that we consider the first מ as an *enclitic mem*[89] belonging to the preceding word, whereas the remaining כֵרֹת could be analysed as a feminine plural noun reflecting a prior כְּרָת (with an appropriate case ending).[90] This word could be related to Sum.-Akk. (DUG.)KIR = *kirru/kīru*, "vessel", attested in plural *kirrātum* in the Amarna-texts. As this word would also appear in Akk. marriage-texts, כְּרָת should be read here too because of its link with Genesis 34.[91]

- It is suggested that שִׁילֹה (verse 10bA) could be related to Akk. *šēlu/šīlu* "lord, ruler";[92] a proposal which is in line with the

---

Of particular interest are the Amarna Letters, found in 1887/88 in *Tell el-Amarna*, Egypt: letters, written in Akkadian, containing the correspondence with the Egyptian court from (among others) the rulers of Canaanite city-states, vassals of Egypt. The historical value of these letters can not be discussed here, but reference can be made to their contribution to the knowledge of (proto-) Hebrew, since they contain elements of the "Canaanite" dialect; cf. A.F. Rainey, "Some Presentation Particles in the Amarna Letters from Canaan", *UF* 20 (1988) 209–20; Z. Cochavi-Rainey, "Canaanite Influence in the Akkadian texts Written by Egyptian Scribes in the 14th and 13th Centuries B.C.E.", *UF* 21 (1989) 39–46; idem, "Tenses and Modes in Cuneiform texts Written by Egyptian Scribes in the Late Bronze Age", *UF* 22 (1990) 5–23; W.L. Moran, *The Amarna Letters*, Baltimore (Ml) 1992, xxi–xxii; and especially nowadays: A.F. Rainey, *Canaanite in the Amarna Tablets: A Linguistic Analysis of the Mixed Dialect Used by Scribes from Canaan* (HO, 25), Leiden 1995. Yet, prudence is in order: JM, §2e, n. 3.

[88] Cf. Kraus, *Geschichte*, 305–14, and esp. 309–14.

[89] This assumption is based on a later development in the knowledge of west-Semitic languages, namely the discovery of the Ugaritic texts, where the *enclitic mem* is frequently found; cf. W.G.E. Watson, "Final *–m* in Ugaritic", *AuOr* 10 (1992) 223–52; J.A. Emerton, "What Light Has Ugaritic Shed on Hebrew?" in: G.J. Brooke *et al.* (eds.), *Ugarit and the Bible: Proceedings of the International Symposium on Ugarit and the Bible, Manchester, September 1992* (UBL, 11), Münster 1994, 53–69, esp. 60.

[90] D.W. Young, "A Ghost Word in the Testament of Jacob (Gen 49:5)?" *JBL* 100 (1981) 335–42.

[91] Young, "A Ghost Word", 340–1.

[92] P. Riessler, "Zum 'Jakobsegen'", *ThQ* 90 (1908) 489–503, 494; G.R. Driver, "Some Hebrew Roots and Their Meanings", *JThS* 23 (1922) 69–73; F. Nötscher, "Gen. 49,10: שִׁילֹה = akk. *šēlu*", *ZAW* 47 (1929) 323–5; E. Dhorme, *La Poésie biblique*, Paris 1931, 101 n. 3; J. Coppens, "La bénédiction de Jacob: son cadre historique à la lumière des parallèles ougaritiques", in *Volume du Congres Strassbourgh 1956* (SVT, 4), Leiden 1957, 97–115, 112–4. See also Barr, *Comparative Philology*, 120.

classical point of view that שִׁילֹה contains the subject of this clause.

- Since the classical and widespread rendering of יָדִין in verse 16A "he judges/will judge" causes some trouble for the interpretation,[93] it is suggested we derive the verb from the root דנן which is found in Akk. *danānu* "to be strong".[94]

Of course more examples could be given, but these will be discussed — together with those listed above — in Chapter Two. The relevance of the findings of Akk. texts for Hebrew philology cannot be doubted nor its contribution to the approach of the text. Barr refers in this connection to the work of Friedrich Delitzsch and of H.S. Nyberg, scholars who strongly opposed the "textual treatment" of problematic passages in MT.[95] Delitzsch warned against a too easy emendation of "unusual locutions or *hapax legomena*", because the text corpus of Hebrew is rather fragmentary and the original could inadvertently be removed by the emendation,[96] given that the Akkadian language could help to solve many of the enigmas, that previously remained unsolved.

Some fifty years later H.S. Nyberg published several studies on the Book of Hosea in which he criticized the "proneness to emendation in contemporary scholarship".[97] He argued that the transmission of the text, being live and oral, had never been mechanical nor consisted of mere guesses about the meaning of the text. Such was the prevailing point of view given that the understanding of the Hebrew Bible diminished very early in the Jewish community.[98] Secondly, according to Nyberg, there are distinct regional and temporal strata in the Hebrew Bible, so scholars can easily be deceived by the punctuation system of the Masoretes, which suggests a uniform grammar.[99] Thirdly, he

---

[93] Cf. H.M. Niemann, *Die Danieten: Studien zur Geschichte eines altisrae-litischen Stammes* (FRLANT, 135), Göttingen 1985, 204–6.

[94] J.A. Emerton, "Some Difficult Words in Genesis 49", in: P.R. Ackroyd, B. Lindars (eds.), *Words and Meanings: Essays . . . D.W. Thomas*, London 1968, 81–93, 90–1.

[95] Barr, *Comparative Philology*, 70–5.

[96] Barr, *Comparative Philology*, 70.

[97] Barr, *Comparative Philology*, 72.

[98] Barr, *Comparative Philology*, 72–3. The assumption that the text was transmitted mechanically is sometimes elaborated by those who think that the Masoretes fixed the pronunciation in the vocalisation even when they did not understand it; cf. p. 11, n. 56 above.

[99] Cf. also Lettinga, *'Tale Kanaäns'*, 7–10. However, this might argue against the assumption that the Masoretes sometimes fixed the pronunciation without understanding it (p. 11, n. 56 above).

held the view that within the realm of textual criticism each decision
has to be taken anew, instead of assuming that "MT was a late and
poor form of the text, and that better and earlier guidance was to
be found in the versions, and especially the LXX".[100] In this respect,
according to Nyberg, the MT has to be considered as seriously as all
other witnesses.[101]

Nyberg had somehow sensed the right of the MT to be taken
more seriously, which only a dozen years later was confirmed when
the Judean Desert revealed a treasure for the research of the history
of the Jewish community and its written documents at the beginning
of the common era: the so-called Dead Sea Scrolls.[102] Scores of Biblical manuscripts were found and these contributed strongly to our
knowledge of the transmission of the Biblical text. But at the same
time they also contribute to the value the MT may have as a textual
witness among the other witnesses.[103] On the other hand it has to be
emphasized that the findings also confirm the reliability of the ancient
translations, and especially the LXX, as readings and interpretations
of the Hebrew text which circulated within Judaism.[104] However, it
may be asked if we have to consider these different traditions as different "texts", as E. Tov prefers to call them,[105] or that they should
be considered as variant readings from one main stream preserved in
Temple circles.[106] As yet the findings in the Desert of Judah do not

---

[100]Barr, *Comparative Philology*, 73.

[101]Barr, *Comparative Philology*, 73; it is intriguing in this context that, as Barr
describes a page before, Nyberg argued that "if the text was really corrupt ...
then the honest thing was not to emend but abandon altogether the attempt at
interpretation."

[102]On Qumran and its finding, cf. J.N. Allegro, *The Dead Sea Scrolls: The story
of the recent manuscript discoveries and their momentous significance for students
of the Bible*, Harmondsworth 1956; J.P.M. van der Ploeg, *Vondsten in de Woestijn
van Juda* (Aula, 447), Utrecht ⁴1970; J. Murphy-O'Connor, "Qumran, Khirbet",
ABD, vol 5, 590–4; F.M. Cross, *The Ancient Library of Qumran*, Sheffield ³1995,
19–53. On the texts found, cf. Allegro, *op.cit.*, 50–74, 94–123; Van der Ploeg,
op.cit., 167–203; J.J. Collins, "Dead Sea Scrolls", *ABD*, vol. 2, 85–101.

[103]On the merit of the Scrolls, cf. E. Tov, "Tekstgetuigen en tekstgeschiedenis
van het Oude en Nieuwe Testament; A: De tekst van het Oude Testament", in
BijbH, dl. I, 217–62, 230–3, 254–6; idem, *Textual Criticism of the Hebrew Bible*,
Assen, Philadelphia 1992, 100–17; idem, "Textual Criticism (O.T.)", *ABD*, vol.
6, 393–412, 401–2.

[104]Cf. Tov, "De tekst van het Oude Testament", 233; idem, *Textual Criticism*,
117; idem, "Textual Criticism (O.T.)", 402.

[105]Tov, "De tekst van het Oude Testament", 251, 254–6; idem, *Textual Criticism*,
155–63; idem, "Textual Criticism (O.T.)", 404.

[106]This view is defended by A.S. van der Woude, *Pluriformiteit & Uniformiteit:
Overwegingen betreffende de tekstoverlevering van het Oude Testament*, Kampen

contribute very much to the textual criticism or translation of Genesis 49, except for some tiny fragments of the text,[107] or the occurrence of a difficult verb like פחז in extra-biblical texts.[108]

Before the findings in the Judean Desert in 1947, a similar coincidental discovery of some very old objects of value by a farmer in North Syria was the cause of the excavation of Ras Shamra in 1929. The tell appeared to cover the ancient city of Ugarit, known already from other documents, like the Amarna letters.[109] The most important findings during the excavations were the many clay tablets, written in an alphabetical cuneiform alphabet of 29 signs. Many tablets published to date,[110] contain mythological, cultic and legendary texts shedding light on "the gods of the Canaanites", as they are called in the Hebrew Bible, like Ba'al, Ashera, and El. But in addition to the occurrence of these gods, many of the religious concepts of the Hebrew Bible are found in Ugarit, suggesting that the religion of Israel was much more indigenous in the land of Canaan, than the Hebrew Bible suggests.[111] However, many similarities between these two

---

1992 (= idem, "Pluriformity and Uniformity: Reflections on the Transmission of the Text of the Old Testament", in: J.N. Bremmer & F. Garı́a Martı́nez (eds.), *Sacred History and Sacred Texts in Early Judaism* [CBET, 5], Kampen 1992, 151–69). The existence of a temple-tradition is also described by Tov, cf. his, *Textual Criticism*, 29–33, 193–7; the point is however, what weight should be given to such traditions and variants.

[107] E. Ulrich, F.M. Cross (eds.), *Qumran Cave 4 · VII: Genesis to Numbers* (DJD, 12), Oxford 1994, 17–8 (with plate I.15–16); 52 (with plate X.9).

[108] However, the occurrence of the verb does not result in an unequivocal rendering for Gen. 49:4; cf. J.C. Greenfield, "The Meaning of *pḥz*", in: Y. Avishur, J. Blau (eds.), *Studies in Bible and Ancient Near East ...S.E. Loewenstamm*, Jerusalem 1978, 35–41; De Hoop, "Meaning of *pḥz* in Classical Hebrew", 16–7.

[109] Cf. *e.g.* EA 89:51; 98:9; 151:55. See also A.S. Kapelrud, "Ugarit", *IDB*, vol. IV, 724–32; J.C. de Moor, "Ugarit", *IDBS*, 928–31; P.C. Craigie, *Ugarit and the Old Testament: The story of a remarkable discovery and its impact on Old Testament studies*, Grand Rapids (MI) 1983, 7–25; O. Loretz, *Ugarit und die Bibel: Kanaanäische Götter und Religion im Alten Testament*, Darmstadt 1990, 1–13; M. Yon, "Ugarit: History and Archaeology", *ABD*, vol. 6, 695–706.

[110] The most recent and complete edition of the texts is now *KTU²*: M. Dietrich, O. Loretz, J. Sanmartín, *The Cuneiform Alphabetic Texts from Ugarit, Ras Ibn Hani and Other Places (KTU: second, enlarged edition)* (ALASP, 8), Münster 1995. For an overview of the texts, see D. Pardee, P. Bordreuil, "Ugarit: Texts and Literature", *ABD*, vol. 6, 706–21.

[111] Many studies have appeared in which the religious concepts of both traditions have been studied and compared; the following titles form a (rather subjective) selection: A. van Selms, *Marriage and Family Life in Ugaritic Literature* (POS, 1), London 1954, 125–43; M.H. Pope, *El in the Ugaritic Texts* (SVT, 2), Leiden 1955; M.J. Mulder, *Ba'al in het Oude Testament*, 's-Gravenhage 1962; idem, *Kanaänitische goden in het Oude Testament*, Den Haag 1965; J. Gray, *The*

traditions are also found on the more formal level of philology and literature. In this respect Ugaritic and Hebrew studies have influenced each other.[112] The study of Hebrew poetry has considerably benefited by the findings of these texts,[113] whereas lexicography and grammar

---

Legacy of Canaan: The Ras Shamra Texts and their Relevance to the Old Testament (SVT, 5), Leiden ²1965; W.H. Schmidt, *Königtum Gottes in Ugarit und Israel* (BZAW, 80), Berlin ²1966; W.F. Albright, *Yahweh and the Gods of Canaan: A Historical Analysis of Two Contrasting Faiths*, London 1965 (repr. Winona Lake ²1978); J.C. de Moor, *New Year with Israelites and Canaanites* (KaCa, 21–22), Kampen 1972; J.M. Sasson, "Literary Criticism, Folklore Scholarship, and Ugaritic Literature", in: G.D. Young (ed.), *Ugarit in Retrospect: 50 Years of Ugarit and Ugaritic*, Winona lake (IN) 1981, 81–98; P.C. Craigie, "Ugarit and the Bible: Progress and Regress in 50 Years of Literary Study", *ibid.*, 99–111; M. Pope, "The Cult of the Dead at Ugarit", *ibid.*, 159–79; Craigie, *Ugarit and the Bible*, 67–90; C. Kloos, *Yhwh's Combat with the Sea: A Canaanite Tradition in the Religion of Ancient Israel*, Amsterdam, Leiden 1986; K. Spronk, *Beatific Afterlife in Ancient Israel and in the Ancient Near East* (AOAT, 219), Kevelaer, Neukirchen-Vluyn 1986; M.C.A. Korpel, *A Rift in the Clouds: Ugaritic and Hebrew Descriptions of the Divine* (UBL, 8), Münster 1990; Loretz, *Ugarit und die Bibel*, 13–28 (with on p. 13–4, n. 60 some additional studies); J.C. de Moor, *The Rise of Yahwism: The Roots of Israelite Monotheism* (BETL, 91), Leuven 1990; M.S. Smith, *The Early History of God: Yahweh and the Other Deities in Ancient Israel*, San Francisco 1990; J. Day, "Yahweh and the Gods and Goddesses of Canaan", in: W. Dietrich, M. Klopfenstein (Hrsg.), *Ein Gott allein? JHWH-Verehrung und biblischer Monotheismus im Kontext der israelitischen und altorientalischen Religionsgeschichte* (OBO, 139), Freiburg, Göttingen 1994, 181–96; O. Loretz, "Das 'Ahnen- und Götterstatuen-Verbot' im Dekalog und die Einzigkeit Jahwes. Zum Begriff des Göttlichen in altorientalischen und alttestamentlichen Quellen", *ibid.*, 491–527; many contributions in: G.J. Brooke *et al.* (eds.), *Ugarit and the Bible: Proceedings of the International Symposium on Ugarit and the Bible, Manchester, September 1992* (UBL, 11), Münster 1994; A. Caquot, "Une contribution ougaritique à la préhistoire du titre divin Shadday", in: J.A. Emerton (ed.), *Congress Volume: Paris 1992* (SVT, 61), Leiden 1995, 1–12; J.C. de Moor, "Ugarit and Israelite Origins", *ibid.*, 205–38; M. Dijkstra, "El, Yahweh and their Asherah on Continuity and Discontinuity in Canaanite and Ancient Israelite Religion", in: M. Dietrich, O. Loretz (hrsg.), *Ugarit: Ein ostmediterranes Kulturzentrum im Alten Orient: Ergebnisse und Perspektiven der Forschung*; Bd. I: *Ugarit und seine altorientalische Umwelt* (ALASP, 7), Münster 1995, 43–73; N. Wyatt, "The Significance of ṢPN in West Semitic Thought. A contribution to the history of a mythological motif", *ibid.*, 213–37; J.C. de Moor, "Standing Stones and Ancestor Worship", *UF* 27 (1995) 1–21.

[112] For the start of Ugaritic studies in which comparative philology played a leading role, cf. J.C. de Moor, "Ugaritic Lexicography", in: P. Fronzaroli (ed.), *Studies on Semitic Lexicography*, Firenze 1973, 61–102, 61–78. In addition, see: J.F. Healey, "Ugaritic Lexicography and Other Semitic Languages", *UF* 20 (1988) 61–8; O. Loretz, "Ugaritische Lexikographie", *SEL* 12 (1995) 105–20; W.G.E. Watson, "Ugaritic Lexical Studies in Perspective", *ibid.*, 217–28.

[113] Cf. J.C. de Moor, "The Art of Versification in Ugarit and Israel, I: The Rhythmical Structure", in: Y. Avishur, J. Blau (eds.), *Studies in Bible and the Ancient*

also profit of these findings.[114] Some of the proposals for the translation of Hebrew texts based on Ugaritic will illustrate the relevance of
Ugaritic for our understanding of Genesis 49:

- A grammatical feature is the so-called *enclitic mem*, one of the
  most confusing particles of Ugaritic because it is difficult to establish its precise meaning. It "is often added to the end of a
  word in Ugaritic, even a word in the construct state, without
  making an obvious change to meaning."[115] It has been used in
  several instances to solve a problem in Genesis 49 by considering
  the מ, which in MT forms the first consonant of the problematic
  word, as an *enclitic mem*, belonging in fact to the preceding
  word. In case of מכרתיהם (verse 5) Young's suggestion that the
  remaining כרת could be connected with a *kirtu*-ritual has already been mentioned.[116] Gevirtz suggested we read an *enclitic
  mem* in two instances in verse 5: at the end of אחים (which he re-
  vocalizes), followed by כלי from verse 5b, meaning "spent owls";

Near East Presented to S.E. Loewenstamm, Jerusalem 1978, 119–39; idem, "The
Art of Versification, II: The Formal Structure", *UF* 10 (1978) 187–217; idem,
"The Art of Versification, III: Further Illustrations of the Principle of Expan-
sion", *UF* 12 (1980) 311–5; Y. Avishur, *Stylistic Studies of Word-Pairs in Biblical
and Ancient Semitic Literatures* (AOAT, 210), Neukirchen-Vluyn 1984; M.C.A.
Korpel, J.C. de Moor, "Fundamentals of Ugaritic and Hebrew Poetry", *UF* 18
(1986) 173–212 (= *SABCP*, 1–61); W.G.E. Watson, *Classical Hebrew Poetry: A
Guide to its Techniques* (JSOTS, 26), Sheffield ²1986; O. Loretz, I. Kottsieper,
*Colometry in Ugaritic and Biblical Poetry: Introduction, Illustrations and Topical
Bibliography* (UBL, 5), Altenberge 1987; E. Zurro, *Procedimientos iterarivos en
la poesía ugarítica y hebrea* (BibOr, 43), Valencia, Roma 1987; D. Pardee, *Ugaritc
and Hebrew Poetic Parallelism: A Trial Cut ('nt I and Proverbs 2)* (SVT, 39),
Leiden 1988; W.G.E. Watson, *Traditional Techniques in Classical Hebrew Verse*
(JSOTS, 170), Sheffield 1994.

[114]For a brief overview of the grammatical aspects, see Emerton, "What Light
Has Ugaritic Shed on Hebrew?" 53–69. For the theoretical discussion of Ugaritic
lexicography, cf. J.C. de Moor, "Ugaritic Lexicography", 61–102. Since the latter
wrote already in 1973 (*art.cit.*, 72–3) "it is a sheer impossibility to review all
that literature here, even if I were bold enough to entertain the illusion that I
have seen a good deal of it" more than twenty years have passed and the present
author would not even dare to list a fragment of the relevant literature. Cf. De
Moor, *art.cit.*, 73–102; and further the annual *Ugarit Forschungen* 1– (1969–) in
which many relevant studies (including grammar) have appeared. Further: *RSP*,
vol. I–III; M. Dahood, *Psalms III: 101–150* (AB, 17A), Garden City (NY) 1970,
361–456.

[115]Emerton, "What Light Has Ugaritic Shed on Hebrew?" 60. Cf. now esp. J.A.
Emerton, "Are There Examples of Enclitic *mem* in the Hebrew Bible?" in: M.V.
Fox *et al.* (eds.), *Texts, Temples, and Traditions: A Tribute to Menahem Haran*,
Winona Lake (IN) 1996, 321–38.

[116]See p. 17, with n. 90 above.

whereas he rearranges verse 5b, taking the מ from מכרתיהם and adds it (together with a ת in front) to חמס, finally taking the הם as a personal pronoun.[117] In the saying on Issachar, he takes גרים as a active participle of גור, followed by an *enclitic mem*.[118]

- The accusation that Simeon and Levi had hamstrung a bull (שׁור; RSV: "oxen") causes some trouble in connection with Genesis 34, where no such act is reported. In Ugaritic *tr*, "bull" can be used as a title for "prince", and this could be meant here as well.[119]

- The problematic reading in Gen. 49:22 of פרת (verse 22AB) and עלי שׁור (verse 22C), which in several cases already led to the proposal to read an animal-metaphor here, was strengthened by Ugaritic. Verse 22C was reinterpreted reading עלי שׁור as "young bull"[120] or "towards the Bull",[121] taking "bull" here as a reference to the Canaanite deity *Ilu*, who has the epithet *tr*.

- The verb מרר in the pi'el also means "to strengthen, bless". This was established in several places in the Hebrew Bible[122] and is now also suggested in Gen. 49:23a, where it has the connotation of strengthening with offspring.[123]

---

[117]S. Gevirtz, "Simeon and Levi in 'The Blessing of Jacob' (Gen. 49:5–7)", *HUCA* 52 (1981) 93–128, 95.

[118]S. Gevirtz, "The Issachar Oracle in the Testament of Jacob", *ErIs* 12 (1975) 104*–12*, 105*.

[119]B. Vawter, "The Canaanite Background of Genesis 49", *CBQ* 17 (1955) 1–17, 4; P.D. Miller, "Animal Names as Designations in Ugaritic and Hebrew", *UF* 2 (1970) 177–86, 178–9, 185. Cf. also H.L. Ginsberg, "The Legend of King Keret", in *ANET*, 142–9, 148; *CML*[2], 92 n. 6; *TOML*, 543 n. x; *MLC*, 644, s.v.; *ARTU*, 208 n. 59.

[120]Vawter, "Canaanite background", 8. Comparable interpretations of עלי are found in J. Coppens, "La bénédiction de Jacob: son cadre historique à la lumière des parallèles ougaritiques", in *Volume du Congres Strassbourgh 1956* (SVT, 4), Leiden 1957, 97–115, 101; E. Testa, "La formazione letteraria della benedizione di Giacobbe (Gen. 49,2–27)", *SBF LA* 23 (1973) 167–205, 175.

[121]Korpel, *RiC*, 532, n. 60; the interpretation of these two words as "towards the bull" was already suggested in the nineteenth century by J.P. Peters, "Jacob's Blessing", *JBL* 6 (1886) 99–116, 111.

[122]Gordon, *UT*, 438; cf. further O. Loretz, "Weitere ugaritisch-hebräische Parallelen", *BZ* 3 (1959) 293; S. & S. Rin, "Ugaritic – Old Testament Affinities, II", *BZ* 11 (1967) 89; D. Pardee, "The Semitic Root *mrr* and the Etymology of Ugaritic *mr(r)/brk*", *UF* 10 (1978) 249–88; W.A. Ward, "Egypto-Semitic *mr* 'Be Bitter, Strong'", *UF* 12 (1980) 357–60; *ARTU*, 227, n. 23; see also Pardee, UB, 421.

[123]Korpel, *RiC*, 533, n. 61.

- For several terms in the following "blessings" connections with Ugaritic have been suggested. In verse 25aA אֵל אָבִיךָ is connected with *il ảbk* "Ilu, your father" and *ilib* "deified father",[124] and translated therefore with "God your Father". In verse 25bC שָׁדַיִם וָרָחַם "breasts and womb" are connected with the epithets of the Ugaritic goddesses Asherah and Anatu, and are therefore mostly rendered as names: "Breast-and-Womb".[125]

It is clear that Ugaritic has contributed considerably to the scholarly work on Hebrew in general and on the understanding of Genesis 49 in particular. Ugaritic has proved to be one of the most important languages, as it is most frequently referred to, in connection with Genesis 49. Remarkable in this connection is the fact that the Joseph-saying, containing the most problematic words[126] seems to profit most from the knowledge of the Ugaritic language and culture, since the majority of suggestions based on Ugaritic concern Gen. 49:22–26.

The use of Ugaritic for our understanding of Hebrew words certainly belongs to the etymological considerations of a translation. Nevertheless on the level of methodological considerations this approach is criticized because it sometimes obscured the specific meaning of a word within its context. It has therefore been argued that a semantical approach has to prevail over etymologizing. In this sense the appearance of two Hebrew dictionaries during the nineties[127] both refraining from offering the words from cognate languages, and the start of an international project, *the ESF-Network on the Semantics of Classical Hebrew*,[128] could be considered symptomatic for the approach preferred nowadays. Methodologically this approach gives preference to the orientation "toward the sentence or the unit of discourse", in contrast to the earlier concentration "on the word, the individual word, the meaning of the word".[129] Nevertheless, it can-

---

[124]Vawter, "Canaanite Background", 12; Coppens, Bénédiction de Jacob", 102; Van Selms, *Genesis, dl. II*, 281 (suggesting that it might be the required rendering); N. Wyatt, "The problem of the 'God of the Fathers'", *ZAW* 90 (1978) 101–4; D.N. Freedman, "Divine Names and Titles in Early Hebrew Poetry", in: idem, *Pottery, Poetry and Prophecy: Collected Essays on Hebrew Poetry*, Winona Lake (IN) 1980, 77–129, 86, 112; Korpel, *RiC*, 533; Smith, *Early History of God*, 16–7; De Moor, "Standing Stones", 19.

[125]Cf. Vawter, "Canaanite Background", 15; Testa, "Benedizione di Giacobbe", 179–80; Smith, *Early History of God*, 16–8.

[126]Cf. p. 8 above.

[127]*DBHE*; *DCH*, vol. I– .

[128]J. Hoftijzer, "The History of the Data-base Project", in: T. Muraoka (ed.), *Studies in Ancient Hebrew Semantics* (AbrN.S, 4), Leuven 1995, 65–85.

[129]*DCH*, vol. I, 26.

not be concluded that an etymological approach is nowadays abandoned, nor that it is considered to be superfluous. On the contrary, the eighteenth edition of the *Genenius*, where the words from cognate languages are still listed, as well as the recent continuation of the project by D. Cohen on the dictionary of Semitic roots, shows that this approach is still active.[130] However, in the introduction to the *Dictionary of Classical Hebrew* it is prefaced that,

> theoretically speaking ... data about the meaning of cognate words in Akkadian and Arabic, for example, are strictly irrelevant to the Hebrew language; and, practically speaking, there is evidence that the significance of the cognates has been systematically misunderstood by many users of the traditional dictionaries.[131]

Yet it appears that the general approach to Hebrew lexicography is best reflected in the statement of the editors of the new *Gesenius*:

> General experience teaches that etymological data are of little use to the beginner; for the advanced user they are nevertheless helpful, if not indispensable.[132]

The work of J. Barr, who vigorously criticizes wrong etymologizing, shows in this respect that a balanced approach is required, using words from cognate languages but giving prevalence to semantics.[133]

1.2.1 Recapitulation

1. Genesis 49 proves to contain many problems for the translator, most of which are found in the saying on Joseph (49:22–26).

---

[130] Ges[18], ix; D. Cohen, *Dictionnaire des racines Sémitiques ou attestée dans les langues sémitiques*, Fasc. 1–2, Paris 1970–76; Fasc. 3– , Leuven 1993– .

[131] *DCH*, vol. I, 17–8. T. Muraoka, "A New Dictionary of Classical Hebrew", in: T. Muraoka (ed.), *Studies in Ancient Hebrew Semantics* (AbrN.S, 4), Leuven 1995, 87–101, 90, considers that the "approach advocated by the *DCH* is probably overreacting to the notorious and inadmissible excess of etymologies in most of the current BH lexica".

[132] Ges[18], ix: "Nach aller Erfahrung nützen die etymologischen Angaben dem Anfänger wenig; für den fortgeschrittenen Benutzer aber sind sie hilfreich, wenn nicht unentbehrlich."

[133] Cf. J. Barr, *The Semantics of Biblical Language*, Oxford 1961; idem, *Comparative Philology and the Text of the Old Testament*, Oxford 1968; idem, "Hebrew Lexicography", 103–26; idem, "Etymology and the Old Testament", in: A.S. van der Woude (ed.), *Language and Meaning: Studies in Hebrew and Biblical Exegesis* (OTS, 19), Leiden 1974, 1–28. Furthermore: J.C. de Moor, "Ugaritic Lexicography", in: Fronzaroli, *Studies in Semitic Lexicography*, 61–102; J.C. Greenfield, "Etymological Semantics", *ZAH* 6 (1993) 26–37; B. Albrektson, "Response to J.C. Greenfield", *ZAH* 6 (1993) 38–43; J.A. Emerton, "Comparative Semitic Philology and Hebrew Lexicography", in: J.A. Emerton (ed.), *Congress Volume, Cambridge 1995* (SVT, 66), Leiden 1997, 1–24.

2. The study of Hebrew has always taken advantage of the use of cognate languages. This has been the case since the Middle Ages, when Arabic and Aramaic were used to elucidate obscure passages, while in later times Akkadian and several west-Semitic languages were added, of which Ugaritic is the most important.

3. The removal of Hebrew from the realm of the sacred to the secular, increased the understanding of Hebrew as a human language. Hebrew was now considered to be a language that had developed gradually and had its own (dialectic) peculiarities.

4. In attempts to translate difficult words or passages we should give semantics priority over etymology. The meaning of a word is created by its use within a certain context. However, the use of cognate languages is indispensable in cases of obscure passages and *hapax legomenon*.

1.3 The Origin of Genesis 49

1.3.1 Introduction: The "Tribal Saying"

The discussion on the origin of Genesis 49 is mainly centered around the definition of the genre of this text. The attempts to classify Genesis 49 as part of a certain document (J, E or P) have proved to be fruitless while, on the other hand, the definition of the genre of the text (going back to a pre-literary stage) has met with greater approval. Genesis 49 is almost generally viewed as a collection of independent "tribal sayings", brought together in this collection by an editor some time after their origin. The basis of this theory was first propounded by Renan and Land and was only gradually accepted within scholarly literature.[134] The view that Genesis 49 was not a unity but composed from more ancient separate couplets was defended — many years

---

[134]Cf. pp. 4–5, with nn. 13–14 above. This view of Genesis 49 is found in A. Kuenen, *Historisch-critisch onderzoek naar het ontstaan en de verzameling van de boeken des Ouden Verbonds*, dl. I/1: *De Hexateuch*, Leiden ²1885, 233–4, n. 16; D.C.H. Cornill, *Einleitung in das Alte Testament mit Einschluss der Apokryphen und Pseudepigraphen*, Leipzig ²1891, 68–9; G. Wildeboer, *De Letterkunde des Ouden Verbonds naar de tijdsorde van haar ontstaan*, Groningen 1893, ²1896, 42 (German tr.: *Die Litteratur des Alten Testaments nach der Zeitfolge ihrer Entstehung*, Göttingen 1895).

Cf. also C. Steuernagel, *Lehrbuch der Einleitung in das Alte Testament mit einem Anhang über die Apokryphen und Pseudepigraphen*, Tübingen 1912, 257–8, who also thinks that Genesis 49 contains independent sayings which did not come into being simultaneously. It was also suggested that the original song was expanded by some strophes; cf. E.I. Fripp, "Note on Gen. xlix, 24b–26", *ZAW* 11 (1891) 262–6.

later, but apparently independent from Renan and Land — by J.P. Peters.[135] However, the theory concerning these independant sayings as "tribal sayings" is commonly ascribed to H. Greßmann.[136] It is important to note, nevertheless, that Greßmann was partly dependent on H. Gunkel, who offered the theoretical background for Greßmann's work[137] in his study on Israelite literature and in his commentary on Genesis.[138] Since the theory concerning the "tribal sayings" has governed scholarly literature on Genesis 49 on a literary but as well as on a historical level, is seems appropriate to start our survey of previous research with a description of Gunkel's view on the origin of Israel's literature and more specifically of Genesis 49.

1.3.2 H. Gunkel

Gunkel's form-critical method is well known and does not need a very extensive discussion.[139] However, because this view is of fundamental

---

[135] J.P. Peters, "Jacob's Blessing", *JBL* 6 (1886) 99–116, 113.

[136] Cf. p. 5, n. 16 above.

[137] Of course Gunkel himself was also influenced by the time and culture he lived in and more specifically, he was dependent on other scholars like R. Lowth, K. Budde, and H. Zimmern, and on the developments in other disciplines such as Oriental Studies, Classics and Germanics, cf. in this respect M.J. Buss, "The study of Forms", in: J.H. Hayes (ed.), *Old Testament Form Criticism* (TUMSR, II), San Antonio 1974, 1–56, and especially 39–52; further: idem, "The Idea of Sitz im Leben — History and Critique", *ZAW* 90 (1978) 157–70, 160–5; A. Wolf, "H. Gunkels' Auffassung von der Verschriftlichung der Genesis im Licht mittelaltlicher Literarisierungsprobleme", *UF* 12 (1980) 361–74; Houtman, *Der Pentateuch*, 125, n. 58. This is in contrast to K. Koch, *Was ist Formgeschichte? Methoden der Bibelexegese*, Neukirchen-Vluyn 1964 (⁴1981), 37–8 (47), who writes: "Der Brückenschlag von der Gattungsbeobachtung zum Sitz im Leben war ein genialer Einfall Gunkels. Er scheint sich ihm völlig unabhängig von der allgemeinen Literaturwissenschaft, allein auf Grund des biblischen Materials aufgedrängt zu haben. So verwundert es nicht, daß die Verflechtung von Gattung und Lebensbereich ihm erst allmählich klar bewust wurde ...". This phrase was quoted with approval by W. Klatt, *Hermann Gunkel: Zu seiner Theologie der Religionsgeschichte und zur Entstehung der formgeschichtlichen Methode* (FRLANT, 100), Göttingen 1969, 144–5.

Cf. further also H.-J. Zobel, "Die Stammessprüche des Mose-Segens (Dtn 33,6–25) Ihr 'Sitz im Leben'", *KLIO* 46 (1965) 83–92, 83–4 (= idem, *Altes Testament — Literatursammlung und Heilige Schrift* [BZAW, 212], Berlin 1993, 19–30, 19–20); R. Smend, *Deutsche Alttestamentler in drei Jahrhunderten*, Göttingen 1989, 160–81.

[138] H. Gunkel, "Die israelitische Literatur", in: P. Hinneberg (Hrsg.), *Die Kultur der Gegenwart*, Tl. I, Abt. VII: *Die orientalischen Literaturen*, Leipzig 1906, 51–102; ²1925, 53–112; idem, *Genesis übersetzt und erklärt* (HK, I/1), Göttingen ²1902, ³1910.

[139] For a general survey of Gunkel's work, cf. in addition to Klatt, *Hermann Gunkel* also: J.A. Wilcoxen, "Narrative", in: J.H. Hayes (ed.), *Old Testament*

importance for the later interpretation of Genesis 49, it needs a short description.[140] To understand a literary text properly it is not sufficient to establish how it was composed and who was involved in its development, as was usual in Gunkel's time with literary critics. There has to be asked beyond the text (and the religious conceptions of the author), to investigate where the literary forms and genres (*Gattungen*) have their setting in life (*Sitz im Leben*), and where the patterns and themes in the literary composition came from (*Stoffgeschichte*). In order to achieve this purpose we have to go back in history to the era of oral tradition.[141] According to Gunkel, it is there that we can find the true origins of our literary texts:

> Every ancient literary genre has originally its own setting in Israel's public life at a very specific place. Just as today the sermon belongs to the pulpit, and fairy tales are told to children, so in ancient Israel the girls sing a victory song to the army marching in; the funeral song is sung by a wailer at the bier of the deceased; the priest preaches the Torah to the laity at the sanctuary; the judgement (*mišpaṭ*) is put forward by the judge at court to sustain his decision; the prophet raises his saying somewhere at the court of the temple; it is the proverb that delights the old at the gate; etc. Whoever wants to understand the genre, has to make the situation clear to himself and ask: who is talking? who are the listeners? what mood governs the situation? what effect is intended?[142]

Form Criticism (TUMSR, II), San Antonio 1974, 57–98, esp. 58–79; Kraus, *Geschichte*, 341–67, esp. 347–52; J.W. Rogerson, "Introduction", in: H. Gunkel, *The Folktale in the Old Testament* (HTIBS), Sheffield 1987, 13–8; Houtman, *Der Pentateuch*, 121–39 (with pp. 122, n. 49; 125–6, n. 58 for additional bibliographical references); H.-P. Müller, "Formgeschichte/Formenkritik", *TRE*, Bd. 11, 271–85, esp. 271–4.

[140] For a more elaborate description of the form-critical method, cf. the well-known work of Koch, *Was ist Formgeschichte?*, and also the following: G. Tucker, *Form Criticism of the Old Testament*, Philadelphia 1971; M.J. Buss, "The study of Forms", in: Hayes (ed.), *Old Testament Form Criticism*, 1–56; R. Knierim, "Old Testament Form Criticism", *Int* 27 (1973) 435–68; idem, "Criticism of Literary Features, Form, Tradition, and Redaction", in: D.A. Knight, G.M. Tucker (eds.), *The Hebrew Bible and Its Modern Interpreters*, Philadelphia (PA) & Chico (CA) 1985, 123–65, 136–50; A. Schoors, "De vormkritische methode", in A.S. van der Woude (red.), *De studie van het Oude Testament*, Kampen 1986, 143–58; J. Barton, "Form Criticism: Old Testament", *ABD*, vol. 2, 838–41.

[141] Houtman, *Der Pentateuch*, 123–4. According to Houtman, the presupposition of this method is that formerly literature was not a matter of great personalities but of the people.

[142] H. Gunkel, "Die Grundprobleme der israelitischen Literaturgeschichte", in his *Reden und Aufsätze*, Göttingen 1913, 29–38, 33 (originally published in *Deutsche Literaturzeitung* 27 [1906] 1797–800): "Jede alte literarische Gattung hat ur-

Accordingly the book of Genesis has to be described as a collection
of legends, oral stories transmitted by bard-like figures, which were
gathered only later by a collector (J or E).[143]

The sayings of Genesis 49 have to be understood as prophecies,
and some of them have the form of a "blessing" (Gen. 49:4, 7, 10–12,
17 and 25–26). A "blessing" was originally a part of a legend, telling
how it happened that this word was spoken. This is the case with the
blessings of Noah (Genesis 9) and Isaac (Genesis 27).[144] From these
blessings very soon an independent literary genre developed:

> The sayings of Balaam are already almost independent from the Ba-
> laam legend; the blessings of Jacob and Moses do not have a close
> relation with any legend and would according to their character sooner
> belong in a collection of songs than in a book of legends.[145]

But these blessings are all (including Genesis 9 and 27) "in verse and
under pseudonym; they are descriptions of the writer's present time
spoken by an ancestor: *vaticinia ex eventu* of the poet".[146] There is,
nevertheless, an important distinction between the early and later
blessings: the former are quite short, the latter much longer; further,

---

sprunglich ihren *Sitz im Volksleben* Israels an ganz bestimmter Stelle. Wie noch
heute die Predigt auf die Kanzel gehört, das Märchen aber die Kinder erzählt wird,
so singen im alten Israel die Mädchen das Siegeslied dem einziehenden Heere ent-
gegen; das Leichenlied stimmt das Klageweib an der Bahre des Toten an; der
Priester verkündet die Tora dem Laien am Heiligtum; den Rechtsspruch (*Mišpaṭ*)
führt der Richter vor Gericht zur Begründung seiner Entscheidung an; der Prophet
erhebt seinen Spruch etwa im Vorhof des Tempels; am Weisheitsspruch erfreuen
sich die Alten im Tore; usw. Wer die Gattung verstehen will, muß sich jedesmal
die ganze Situation deutlich machen und fragen: wer ist es, der redet? wer sind
die Zuhörer? welche Stimmung beherrscht die Situation? welche Wirkung wird
erstrebt?"

[143] Gunkel, *Genesis*, ²1902, xi–xvi; ³1910, vii–xiii.

[144] Gunkel, *Genesis*, ²1902, 419; ³1910, 475; for that reason, according to Gunkel,
those blessings are only intelligible in the context of such a legend ("daher nur im
Zusammenhang mit solcher Erzählung verständlich)."

[145] Gunkel, *Genesis*, ²1902, 419; ³1910, 475: "Die Bileamsprüche sind schon von
der Bileamsage fast unabhängig; der Segen Jaqobs und der des Moses haben zu
keiner einzelnen Sage mehr ein näheres Verhältnis und gehören ihrer Art nach
eher in eine Liedersammlung als in ein Sagenbuch." In view of this quotation, it
is significant that, as we wrote before (see p. 4, with nn. 10–11 above), in the
popular series *Die Schriften des Alten Testaments*, Genesis 49 was not discussed
in Gunkel's commentary on Genesis, but in the volume by Greßmann, *Von 2.
Mose bis Richter*, 171–84, in combination with Deuteronomy 33 in the context of
Judges 5 as a collection of *Stammeslieder*.

[146] Gunkel, *Genesis*, ²1902, 418; ³1910, 475: "... haben poetische Form und gehen
unter fremdem Namen; es sind Beschreibungen der Gegenwart des Verfassers aus
dem Munde eines Urvaters: vaticinia ex eventu von Dichtern."

the oldest — being part of a folk legend — are of popular origin, the younger work is "art poetry" (*Kunstpoesie*); and finally the blessings of Noah and Isaac concern the period of pre-Israelite conditions and are, therefore, Israel's most ancient traditions. The blessings of Jacob, Moses and Balaam concern historical Israel and are thus much younger.[147]

Regarding the evolution of ancient Israel's literature, Gunkel's view did not change very much between the second and third editions of his commentary on Genesis, as might be derived from the preceding description and quotations. However, his view concerning the origin of Genesis 49 changed considerably, causing sometimes rather contradictory references to his earlier work on Genesis 49.[148] In the second edition of 1902 Gunkel describes the origin of Genesis 49 after a short reference to the different length of the sayings (five sayings with one long verse, and Judah and Joseph with both nine long verses). According to Gunkel all these sayings were originally rather short and were later expanded; which is in accordance with the law of expansion, seen elsewhere in the history of Hebrew literature.[149] This is confirmed by the fact that several of the longer sayings do not constitute a cohesive unity but seem to be built up of several short sayings (Dan, probably Joseph, very clearly Judah). However, although several scholars are inclined to describe Genesis 49 as a composition of independent sayings from different times (Kuenen, Holzinger), "Genesis 49 is clearly intended to be a unity and without the context the shortest sayings are not even possible."[150] Concerning the origin of Genesis 49 Gunkel writes:

> To explain the given state of affairs we have to assume a long history: Such a song was sung by the singers of Israel since time immemorial and existed in Israel in many versions... the genesis of such a poem,

---

[147]Gunkel, *Genesis*, ²1902, 419; ³1910, 475–6. Cf. the fact that this way of reasoning is characteristic for Gunkel's method; he uses the same way of reasoning to give an outline of the development of the legends in Genesis, cf. *op.cit.*, xxxiii–xxxiv; see also Houtman, *Der Pentateuch*, 131, 137.

[148]Cf. *e.g.* A.H.J. Gunneweg, "Über den Sitz im Leben der sog. Stammessprüche: Gen 49, Dtn 33, Jdc 5", *ZAW* 76 (1964) 245–55, 246 (= idem, *Sola Scriptura: Beiträge zu Exegese und Hermeneutik des Alten Testaments*, Göttingen 1983, 25–35, 26); Wenham, *Genesis 16–50*, 469: Gunkel argues for an essential unity. On the other hand, see *e.g.* König, *Die Genesis*, 774–5, who refers to Gunkel for the assumption that the sayings functioned independently.

[149]Gunkel, *Genesis*, ²1903, 420; cf. also xxxiii–xxxiv.

[150]Gunkel, *Genesis*, ²1902, 420: "... Gen 49 ist deutlich als eine Einheit gedacht, und ohne die Verbindung mit dem Ganzen sind die kürzesten unter den Sprüchen gar nicht denkbar."

speaking of each tribe separately, can only be explained sufficiently from the days when the tribes lived independently, thus before the rise of the centralized state. Transmitted during a long period, the song gradually received new parts when the situation of the tribes changed and may finally, when the era had changed completely, have been modified considerably: in this way the difference in age of the sayings can be explained and also the relation of Genesis 49 to Deuteronomy 33: Deuteronomy 33 is a new edition of older material.[151]

Gunkel here still holds the view that Genesis 49 was a song which grew during the process of transmission and that there must have existed an earlier and thus a much shorter version of this text. It is not clear from his introduction if all the tribes had already been incorporated in this earlier version.

In the third edition of 1910 the mutual influence of Gunkel and Greßmann becomes clear.[152] The introduction to Genesis 49 was rewritten and elaborated, resulting in the following theory: the sayings in Genesis 49 are mainly descriptions of the present situation of that time, with remarkable, sometimes even literal resemblances to the song of Deborah.[153] In order to explain these two points (description of the present, resemblance with Judges 5) he writes:

> We have (*according to Greßmann's oral communication*) to explain these two phenomena as follows: there existed a literature of 'praising and rebuking sayings' concerning the tribes. Such 'sayings' were very likely recited publicly when several tribes gathered for a joint armed operation or a religious ceremony. The poets of Genesis 49 and Judges 5 adopted this style; the poet of Genesis 49 created a poem from sayings about all twelve tribes and dressed it in the guise of the patriarch's blessing.[154]

---

[151]Gunkel, *Genesis*, ²1902, 420–1: "Vielmehr hat man zur Erklärung des vorliegenden Tatbestandes eine ganze Geschichte anzunehmen: Ein solches Lied ist von den Sängern Israels seit uralter Zeit gesungen worden und bestand in Israel in manchen Rezensionen... die Entstehung einer solchen Dichtungsart, die über jeden Stamm besonders spricht, lässt sich doch nur recht aus einer Zeit erklären, wo die Stämme, jeder für sich, ein Sonderleben führen, also vor Entstehung des Einheitsstaates. Durch lange Zeit hindurch fortgepflanzt, hat das Lied allmählich, wenn die Situation der Stämme eine andere geworden war, neue Stücke bekommen und ist, wenn die Zeit sich ganz verändert hatte, auch wohl ganz umgearbeitet worden: so erklärt sich das verschiedene Alter der Sprüche von Gen 49 und das Verhältnis von Gen 49 zu Dtn 33: Dtn 33 ist eine neue Bearbeitung des alten Stoffs."

[152]On this fact, cf. Smend, *Deutsche Alttestamentler*, 168.

[153]Gunkel, *Genesis*, ³1910, 476–7.

[154]Gunkel, *Genesis*, ³1910, 477 (emphasis, RdH): "Wir werden (*nach Greßmanns mündlicher Mitteilung*) beides so zu erklären haben, daß es eine Liter-

Concerning the age of Genesis 49 Gunkel continues with an altered version of the previous edition; the omissions and changes are however sufficient to give a complete new view, which is already introduced by the previous quotation. Important is the fact that Gunkel omits the phrase concerning the unity of Genesis 49 and the impossibility of the independence of certain sayings.[155] Further, he changes the word "song" in the first large quotation above[156] into "saying":

> For the explanation of this variety of facts (*i.e.* the different ages of the sayings [RdH]) one has to remind himself of the origin of the genre. 'Sayings', such as adopted in Genesis 49, were sung by the singers of Israel since time immemorial and existed in Israel in many versions... the genesis of such a poem, speaking of each tribe separately, can only be explained sufficiently from the days when the tribes lived independently, thus before the rise of the centralized state.[157]

Also the omission of another phrase, "Transmitted during a long period, the song gradually received new parts...", is remarkable. It is a clear demonstration of the fact that Gunkel adopted Greßmann's view concerning the origin of Genesis 49. The method developed by Gunkel was apparently adopted by Greßmann, who mutually influenced Gunkel concerning the origin of the sayings in Genesis 49. The outlines of the development of the blessing-genre, given by Gunkel, were elaborated by Greßmann in his commentary on the "tribal songs" (*Stammeslieder*), where he gave a more specified description of his theory on the "tribal sayings" (*Stammessprüche*).

1.3.3   H. Greßmann

After the exegesis of Genesis 49 and Deuteronomy 33, Greßmann describes the different forms of sayings in both blessings. According to

---

atur von lobenden und tadelnden Sprüchen über die Stämme gegeben hat; solche Spruchgedichte werden öffentlich rezitiert worden sein, wenn ein gemeinsames kriegerisches Unternehmen oder etwa eine große gottesdienstliche Feier mehrerer Stämme vereinigte. Diesen Stil haben die Dichter von Gen 49 und Jdc 5 aufgenommen; der von Gen 49 hat ein Gedicht geschaffen aus Sprüchen über alle zwölf Stämme und ihnen das Gewand des Segens des Urvaters übergeworfen."

[155]Cf. n. 150 above.

[156]See p. 30 above.

[157]Gunkel, *Genesis*, ³1910, 477–8: "Zur Erklärung dieses mannigfaltigen Tatbestandes hat man sich an die Entstehung der Gattung zu erinnern: Sprüche, wie sie Gen 49 aufnimmt, waren von den Sängern Israels seit alter Zeit gesungen worden und bestanden in Israel in manchen Rezensionen... die Entstehung einer Dichtungsart, die über jeden Stamm besonders spricht, läßt sich doch nur recht aus einer Zeit erklären, wo die Stämme, jeder für sich, ein Sonderleben führen, also vor Entstehung des Einheitsstaates."

him three principal forms can be distinguished, appearing in two variant forms: a positive or a negative form. The first two principal forms are of the same period, while the third form originated some time later.[158]

1. The most simple form is the "descriptive form". Here the poet describes the conditions of his own time in the present tense, and sometimes refers in the narrative tense to events in the past. Such a description could be approving or disapproving. The poet either praises or rebukes a tribe in such sayings. The rebuke is sometimes faint, but the praise is clearly expressed and undoubtedly concerns the poet's own tribe.

2. The second form, just as simple and closely related to the first, is the "wish-form". When somebody is praised, he receives good wishes; in this manner the praise becomes a blessing. Is somebody rebuked, then bad wishes are his share; and thus a reprimand becomes a curse. Praise and rebuke are concerned with the present; blessing and curse refer to the future, but not in the future tense but in the optative. In such sayings the emotions of the poet are much more dominant. Derived from the blessing is the prayer, like Gen. 49:16, 18, 17 (Greßmann's order) and Deut. 33:7.

3. The final form is the oracle, representing the future, again distinguished in two groups: the praise and blessing correspond to the promise; the rebuke and curse to the threat. This form is the most difficult and could therefore be considered the youngest,[159] found in the blessings only twice, where Reuben is threatened and a promise is given to Judah. However, these oracles are in fact no oracles but fulfilled prophecies, not just describing the present but also explaining it. This nevertheless usually happens in mysterious words without names or the like: oracles are mysterious.

Concerning the contents and stylistic devices of the tribal sayings Greßmann argues that they contain almost exclusively the geographical location, whereas the general living conditions are also referred

---

[158]Greßmann, *Anfänge Israels*, 179–80. Cf. also Kittel, *Die Stammessprüche Israels*, 65–6; Pehlke, *Genesis 49:1–28*, 3–6. The following description of Greßmann's theory follows closely that of Pehlke.

[159]The youngest and not "the earliest" as Pehlke, *Genesis 49:1–28*, 4, writes; since the development in Gunkel's and Greßmann's genre criticism is from simple to difficult; short to long; primitive to developed.

to. The poet sometimes recalls historical events (Joseph fighting with archers), but more frequently applies legendary patterns (Reuben going up to Bilhah's bed). An eschatological notion is found only once: in the saying on Judah, the tribe from which the Messiah will come.[160] The stylistic devices, according to Greßmann, are characterized first by witty word plays, at times explicitly, other times implicitly and only discovered by the fantasy of the hearers and partly lost in the course of time.[161] Secondly, the use of animal figures is an important stylistic device, forming like the word plays, the precious stones of the poem. Finally, concrete proper names are almost absent and the poet prefers only to allude to certain matters and to describe them. Consequently, one does not know who the archers were, who fought Joseph (Gen. 49:23), or who is the one to come from Judah (Gen. 49:10).[162]

The original length of the sayings was very short and is still so in most cases. These short sayings can be considered folk poetry while the more extended sayings on Judah and Joseph can be looked upon as "art poetry" (*Kunstpoesie*).[163] The poets were bound to follow form and contents, so sayings could circulate for many decades without any change, before being fixed in written form. When a saying was adapted, this was more the result of chance than of a systematically applied process. In Genesis 49 only the saying on Judah was adjusted to the present at the moment of the collection, while others were inserted without any change.[164]

---

[160]Greßmann's reproduction of this eschatological motive in Gen. 49:8–12 is rather free and apparently inspired by New Testamentary expectations concerning the coming Messiah: "An eschatological motive is found only once, how from Judah the 'Messiah' will come, the ideal king of the last days, who will bring back paradise." ("Ein eschatologisches Motiv ist uns nur einmal begegnet, wie aus Juda der 'Messias', der Idealkönig der Endzeit, kommen und das Paradies zurückbringen soll." [Greßmann, *Anfänge Israels*, 180]).

[161]Greßmann, *Anfänge Israels*, 181.

[162]Greßmann, *Anfänge Israels*, 181.

[163]The same distinction is found with Gunkel; see: p. 30 above. Cf. also H. Greßmann, "Die neugefundene Lehre des Amen-em-ope und die vorexilische Spruchdichtung Israels", *ZAW* 42 (1924) 272–96, 289: "Die älteste Form der Spruchdichtung ist in allen Literaturen der kurze Einzelspruch gewesen, der niemals einen Zusammenhang weder mit dem Vorhergehenden noch mit dem Folgenden aufweist, da er selbständig (mündlich oder schriftlich) umläuft; von ihm muß daher die Interpretation ebenso wie die Literaturgeschichte ausgehen." Although Greßmann's statement initially concerns the sayings in the book of Proverbs, it illustrates his method as applied to our text.

[164]Greßmann, *Anfänge Israels*, 181. According to Pehlke, *Genesis 49:1–28*, 6, most of the sayings were in Greßmann's view, originally very short "and have been reworked little". But Pehlke's survey of Greßmann's theory is in this respect

The described theory concerning Genesis 49 and Deuteronomy 33 became of great importance in the following decades and was adopted by many scholars without any critical evaluation. Greßmann's work was only taken up critically and expanded almost fifty years later in the unpublished, but nevertheless well-known study of H.-J. Kittel, *Die Stammessprüche Israels*.[165]

1.3.4   H.-J. Kittel

After briefly introducing the problems of Genesis 49 and Deuteronomy 33 and presenting the translation and exegesis of these two chapters, Kittel discusses the form- and tradition-history of the individual sayings. He distinguishes four categories of sayings: 1. the short individual saying; 2. sayings consisting of several elements; 3. structured sayings; 4. editorially adapted sayings.[166] We will now reproduce these four forms and their subsequent categories.

1.   *The short individual sayings.*[167] This saying has no trace of revision and it is short and concise. The criterion to distinguish this genre is that the saying does not need a framework to make it understandable. Two main types, each divided into subcategories, can be discerned:

   (a) The comparisons:

   i.   Pure comparisons. According to Kittel the sayings on Judah, Naphtali and Benjamin (49:9, 21, 27)[168] are pure comparisons because in these sayings the typical behaviour of animals is utilized for the addressees; in these sayings this typical behaviour is the only topic (not the name of the animal).

   ii. Extended comparisons. The sayings on Issachar and Dan (49:14–15, 17)[169] are so-called extended comparisons. The typical behaviour of the animal is not the

---

beside the mark, because according to Greßmann most sayings are indeed very short, and were included *without any change* except for the saying on Judah: "In I. 49 (= I Mose 49 [RdH]) ist nur der Spruch über Juda umgestaltet und der damaligen Gegenwart angepast worden, während die übrigen blieben wie sie waren." (Greßmann, *Anfänge Israels*, 181).

[165]H.-J. Kittel, *Die Stammessprüche Israels: Genesis 49 und Deuteronomium 33 traditionsgeschichtlich untersucht*, Berlin 1959.

[166]Kittel, *Stammessprüche Israels*, 66.

[167]Kittel, *Stammessprüche Israels*, 66–79.

[168]Cf. also Dan in Deut. 33:22.

[169]Cf. the saying on Ishmael in Gen. 16:12.

only topic, but the saying is enlarged with a special situation. This specific situation and the typical behaviour of the animal illustrate why the tribe is compared with this specific animal.

   iii. Comparisons as part of the saying. A comparison is part of a larger context as is the case with the saying on Joseph (49:22).[170] These embedded comparisons illustrate according to Kittel his thesis that the typical behaviour of the animal is the reason for the comparison, not the name of the animal itself.

(b) The descriptions. For this category Kittel refers also to Judges 5, but some of these sayings are constructed literary so strongly within their context that they cannot be separated from it without being misunderstood.[171] Although he discerns typical sayings and sayings subjected to a situation, both are characterizations.

   i. Typical descriptions. The saying on Zebulun and on Naphtali (49:13, 20)[172] are not as expressive and pithy as the comparisons. However, despite the apparent geographical interest of these sayings, the description is subjected to the typical living conditions of the inhabitants of this particular area and their relations with others.

   ii. Descriptions subject to a situation. Although the saying on Gad (49:19)[173] is very close to the typical description it is hard to consider the distress of Gad as a permanent condition of the tribe.

   iii. Descriptions as part of the saying. As such the descriptions of Reuben, Simeon and Levi, and Joseph (49:3, 5, 23) might be considered;[174] these descriptions serve to emphasize the typical quality.

The *Sitz im Leben* of the sayings.[175] A large group of sayings is transmitted in a context with a concrete situation, for example,

---

[170]Cf. in Deut. 33:17a, 20, the saying on Joseph and Gad; further also Num. 24:8a, 9a.

[171]Kittel, *Stammessprüche Israels*, 71.

[172]See further Reuben and Naphtali in Deut. 33:6, 23; Gilead, Asher, Zebulun and Naphtali in Judg. 5:17–18.

[173]Cf. for this category the sayings on Reuben and Dan in Judg. 5:15b–16, 17.

[174]A description as part of a saying is, according to Kittel, also found in the saying on Joseph in Deut. 33:17b.

[175]Kittel, *Stammessprüche Israels*, 76–9.

the sayings in the Song of Deborah.[176] Two of these sayings are so strongly interwoven with their context, that they belong directly to the battle against Sisera. For that reason the event described in Judges 4–5 is a typical example of a situation which caused the origin of such sayings. In this respect Judges 4–5 show exemplarily the *Sitz im Leben* of the praising and blaming sayings: the (joint) battle against a (mutual) enemy. This is confirmed by the comparisons, originating in speech conditioned by certain situations, as was shown by the extended comparisons. Because all praising comparisons refer to predators (lion, snake, wolf; 49:9, 17, 26) and the blaming ones use other animals (Issachar as an ass, has to do compulsory labour, Gen. 49:14), this indicates that these sayings also originated in battle. At the same moment it is obvious, since these sayings are *tribal sayings*, that the tribes are the subject as well as the object.

2. *Sayings consisting of several elements.*[177] As the heading suggests, the most important characteristic is the inconsistency of the saying. The components have preserved their own characteristics in such a way that they are still discernible in the new context, but redactional activity is impossible to establish.

   (a) Organically grown sayings. An early stage in the process of growth is the extended comparison. Comparison and extension are immediately related: the extension is the justification for the use of the comparison: these sayings, consisting of several elements, mark a new stage in the history of the *Stammessprüche*. The complete saying on Joseph (49:22–26)[178] is such a grown saying, consisting of six independent components, which together became a new unity. However, the seams in the text are clearly recognizable, although each component can no longer be understood as an independent element.

   (b) Sayings consisting of disparate parts. In the previous section the unity had some consistency; here however the saying has grown out of disparate parts, of which the combination does not make sense. This type of saying is, however, not found in Genesis 49.[179]

---

[176] Kittel referred to these sayings in his descriptions of the different categories at several places; cf. nn. 172, 173 above.

[177] Kittel, *Stammessprüche Israels*, 79–88.

[178] The same applies to the saying on Joseph in Deut. 33:13–17.

[179] Cf. however the sayings on Levi, Zebulun and Issachar, and Asher in Deut.

3. *Structured sayings*.[180] These sayings have characteristic forms in which the artistic interest is evident. The preceding sayings, consisting of several elements, were the result of a process of tradition and expansion; the structured sayings have been composed in the present form.

   (a) Puns. Word-plays are found in the sayings on Reuben, Judah, Dan and Gad (49:3b–4a, 8, 16, 19). The main interest of these word-plays is not — as in the short individual sayings — a short typical saying, but the artistic playful joy of finding phonetically similar words: *l'art pour l'art*.

   (b) Sayings with the structure of a prophetic utterance. Prophetic oracles have certain typical characteristics. Such utterances consist of two elements: announcement and explanation/justification. These two elements each consist of two parts: the announcement speaks of God's intervention and the results; the explanation gives the accusation and the development.[181] The sayings on Reuben, Simeon and Levi, and Judah (49:3–4, 5–7, 10–12)[182] have the structure and characteristic features of the prophetic oracle.[183]

4. *Editorially adapted sayings*.[184] An editor has stripped the sayings from their individual character (if they had such a character) and subjected them to a theme, which was originally foreign to them. This adaptation is only intelligible with a view to the collection.

   (a) Sayings composed from several sayings. These are found in the sayings on Judah and Dan (49:8, 9, 10–12, 16, 17). These compositions are not a result of organic growth but of editorial work, because an editor, who wanted to pass on these two (or three) sayings, had only one place at his disposal. For that reason he combined these sayings into one, changing them as little as possible.

33:8–11, 18–19, 24–25.

[180] Kittel, *Stammessprüche Israels*, 88–97.

[181] Cf. also C. Westermann, *Grundformen der prophetischen Rede*, München 1960, 102–16; 141, with n. 18.

[182] Cf. the curse on Meroz, Judg. 5:23.

[183] Kittel, *Stammessprüche Israels*, 93, n. 1, admits that only one saying contains the characteristic Divine speech (for the prophetic oracle) in the 1st person (Gen. 49:7b).

[184] Kittel, *Stammessprüche Israels*, 97–104.

(b) Sayings connected with a frame story. The oldest layer of tradition of the tribal sayings does not allow an integration in a frame story, because the meaning of such sayings will be changed. This occurred, however, with a few sayings: they presume a frame. Separation of the frame and the sayings would result in the misunderstanding of both.[185] We find this kind of sayings in Gen. 49:3–4, 8, while the corresponding "frame", formed by the blessing of the sons by their father, is found in verse 2. The saying on Simeon and Levi interrupts the course of these verses, since in that saying there is no reference to verse 2. But as this saying is linked with an old tribal legend (Genesis 34) in the same way as the saying on Reuben (Gen. 35:22), it actually fits perfectly. Thus the sayings in Gen. 49:2–8 are closely related, and together form an aetiology, explaining how Judah rose to its leading position. The composition of Gen. 49:8–12, where, after v. 8, no reference to v. 2 is found any more, forms a shift from 49:2–8 to vv. 9–27. When this small composition in vv. 2–8 had been made the starting-point, we might have expected some more references to the father-son-conception; therefore vv. 2–8 are not the nucleus of the collection of sayings.[186]

(c) Deuteronomistic adapted sayings. This redactional activity is found solely in Deuteronomy 33, not in Genesis 49. Kittel assumes that this adaptation occurred in the sayings on Judah, Levi, Benjamin, Zebulun and Issachar, Gad, and Naphtali (vv. 7, 8–11, 12, 18–19, 20–21, 23). The common motive of all these sayings is their religious interest, which is undoubtedly of Deuteronomistic origin.

(d) Glosses. These are found in Gen. 49:6a, 13bA; the first to mitigate the curse, the second to explain Zebulun's relation with the sea as sailors. Formally Gen. 49:18 is not a gloss because no saying is involved.[187]

---

[185] Kittel, *Stammessprüche Israels*, 98–9, lists some parallels in other texts to demonstrate the phenomenon that sayings and story are strongly connected and that they cannot easily be separated: Gen. 3:14–9; 27:27–9, 39–40 (cf. however the fact that according to Gunkel, *Genesis*, ³1910, 475, this blessing originally belonged to the story); and further 48:15–6. In other cases saying and story are not so strongly related and the seams are still discernable: Gen. 9:18–27 (cf. once again Gunkel, *ibid.*) and Num. 22–24. With respect to Deuteronomy 33 Kittel considers all sayings adapted to fit the frame in v. 1.

[186] Kittel, *Stammessprüche Israels*, 99–100.

[187] Kittel, *Stammessprüche Israels*, 104, considers Deut. 33:9a to be a gloss, while

In this way Kittel describes the development of the tribal sayings from the shortest form ("short individual saying") to the collection placed in a frame story. After this description he discusses the problem of this collection of tribal sayings and the meaning of such collections in the Pentateuch and Deuteronomistic History; we will discuss this matter later.

1.3.5   A.H.J. Gunneweg

A.H.J. Gunneweg felt that some problems remained despite the general acceptance of the tribal saying as a genre as such and he was especially concerned with the correct definition of the *Sitz im Leben* of these sayings.[188] According to him the many different forms of these sayings neither suggest a common life setting nor an originally shared identity of the sayings.[189] Therefore he puts as *status quaestionis*, that the question about the correct life setting of the (collection of) sayings has not been answered yet, or has not even been put. In his view the question could not have been asked from a methodological point of view, or it was solely put in connection with a single saying as the smallest unity.[190]

Gunneweg argues that the life setting of the sayings was the theophany festival of the amphictyony, where, parallel to the self-predication and name revelation of Yhwh, the self-presentation of the tribes came into being. With this classification he follows a suggestion of Weiser, who was undoubtedly influenced by Noth's amphictyony hypothesis.[191] According to Gunneweg the sayings are based on word-

---

vv. 21, 23 could also contain glosses.

[188] A.H.J. Gunneweg, "Über den Sitz im Leben der sog. Stammessprüche: Gen 49, Dtn 33, Jdc 5", *ZAW* 76 (1964) 245–55 (= idem, *Sola Scriptura: Beiträge zu Exegese und Hermeneutik des Alten Testaments*, Göttingen 1983, 25–35).

[189] Gunneweg, "Über den Sitz im Leben", 245 (= *Sola Scriptura*, 25).

[190] Gunneweg, "Über den Sitz im Leben", 247 (= *Sola Scriptura*, 27): "Die Frage unseres Themas wurde entweder noch gar nicht gestellt, weil sie von den methodischen Voraussetzungen aus gar nicht gestellt werden konnte; oder aber man fragte nur nach dem Sitz im Leben der Einzelsprüche als der kleinsten Einheiten und machte dann die durchaus richtige Entdeckung, daß diese Frage aussichtslos ist."

[191] A. Weiser, *Einleitung in das Alte Testament*, Stuttgart 1939, 38; idem, *Die Psalmen* (ATD, 15), Göttingen ⁷1966, 320, n. 3. For Noth's amphictyony hypothesis see principally M. Noth, *Das System der zwölf Stämme Israels* (BWANT, 4/1), Stuttgart 1930; and furthermore De Geus, *The Tribes of Israel*, 1–68, esp. 40–2; O. Bächli, *Amphiktyonie im Alten Testament: Forschungsgeschichtliche Studie zur Hypothese von Martin Noth* (ThZ.S, 6). Basel 1977, 7–17; U. von Arx, *Studien zur Geschichte des alttestamentlichen Zwölfersymbolismus, I: Fragen im Horizont der Amphiktyoniehypothese von Martin Noth* (EHS.T, 397), Frankfurt aM./Bern 1990, 55–64.

plays or on animal comparisons, being the forms of self-presentation. Sayings not answering to this distinctive characteristic and not being explained by it, should be considered to be of more recent date (which might also be assumed because of their contents). This is the case with the saying on Reuben, Simeon and Levi, and Judah in v. 8.[192] As a tentative basis for this amphictyony he refers to the fact that in several contexts the "gathering" of the sons/tribes is mentioned in the frame (Gen. 49:1b), together with the theophany (Deuteronomy 33; cf. also Judges 5; Pss. 50:5; 68:25–35; 80:3).

With this solution he solves in his view two important problems of this discussion: the life-setting of the individual saying as well as of the collection.[193] In his proposal he follows previous solutions concerning the life-setting, namely the gathering of the tribes on certain occasions.[194] In this respect Gunneweg's study did not add new aspects to the discussion concerning the tribal sayings, albeit he focused attention on the question of the life-setting.

1.3.6   H.-J. Zobel

As is indicated in the title of H.-J. Zobel's monograph, *Stammesspruch und Geschichte*,[195] (a study of the historical and social background of the tribal sayings) Zobel presumes the existence of the genre "tribal saying". The theory that these chapters (Genesis 49, Deuteronomy 33, Judges 5) are composed of independently circulating sayings is in his view confirmed by the exegesis.[196] Before describing several important moments from the form- and tradition history, he offers some methodological considerations, in order to enable a more precise characterization of the historical context.

Because the tribe and its fate is the main interest of the sayings, it might be assumed that the origin of such sayings lies in the time of a vivid tribal awareness. This assumption is affirmed by Arabic poetry.[197] This allows a second presumption: in these tribal sayings a remnant of the nomadic past of Israel's tribes has survived a

---

The connection between Weiser's suggestion and Noth's hypothesis was observed by Zobel, "Stammessprüche des Mose-Segens", 83–4.

[192] Gunneweg, "Über den Sitz im Leben", 250–1 (= *Sola Scriptura*, 30–1).

[193] Gunneweg, "Über den Sitz im Leben", 253–5 (= *Sola Scriptura*, 33–5).

[194] Cf. Gunkel, p. 31, with n. 154 above; for Kittel, p. 36, with n. 175 above.

[195] H.-J. Zobel, *Stammesspruch und Geschichte: Die Angaben der Stammessprüche von Gen 49, Dtn 33 und Jdc 5 über die politischen und kultischen Zustände im damaligen "Israel"* (BZAW, 95), Berlin 1965 (= Zobel, *SuG*).

[196] Cf. Zobel, *SuG*, 2, 53. Zobel does not agree with Kittel in all respects with regard to the outlined tradition-history (*op.cit.*, 53, n. 4).

[197] Zobel, *SuG*, 54, n. 6. Cf. also below, section 3.2.1.

considerable time after Israel's settlement in Palestine. It cannot be
doubted that the change from nomadic to a more urbanized society,
caused mainly by the rise of the monarchy, pushed tribal life into the
background. The *terminus ad quem* of the vivid tribal awareness can
therefore be established in the time of David and Solomon or even
the time of Saul. Because the sayings are certainly no swan-songs but
date from the palmy days of the independent tribes, it is obvious that
we have to go back to the period of the Judges.

Zobel discerns three categories of sayings: 1. the profane sayings;
2. the "yahwisticized" sayings; 3. the disintegrating sayings:

1. *The profane sayings.*[198] A number of sayings, mainly found in
   Genesis 49, are of a profane character while others, mostly in
   Deuteronomy 33, are formed theologically. This is an important indication for the dating of these texts, because this final
   theological influence is absent in the sayings of Judges 5 and
   therefore a date for these profane sayings in the time of the
   battle against Sisera is plausible.[199]

   In this group we find the shortest sayings, being the original
   form of the genre, where the metaphor forms its nucleus (Gen.
   49:9, 14, 17, 21, 22, 27). In the applied metaphors (lion, snake,
   wolf) the poet uses images of the world he lives in, which according to Zobel is unquestionably the nomadic world. But in
   the saying on Joseph (49:22) the shift to settlement in cultiv-
   ated land can be recognized.[200] Some similar short sayings use
   as style the pun on the tribal name, not explaining the name
   but deriving the fate of the tribe from the name (Gen. 49:13,
   16, 19).[201] These "etymologizing" sayings should be dated in
   the period between the twelfth and the beginning of the tenth
   century BCE, on the basis of the appearance of etymologies in
   other texts of the Hebrew Bible and on the basis of the literary
   critical analysis.

   In addition there are two other groups of profane sayings. The
   first group is the saying making a direct statement about a
   tribe, instead of using a metaphor (Gen. 49:20).[202] The second

---

[198] Zobel, *SuG*, 55–8.

[199] Cf. also Kittel, *Stammessprüche Israels*, 76–9.

[200] Zobel, *SuG*, 21–2 translates the word פרת in Gen. 49:22 with "fruitful bough"
(*Fruchtrebe*); cf. the discussion on translation in Chapter Two.

[201] To these three texts we could add the pun on the name of Judah in Gen. 49:8.

[202] The other texts in which direct statements about tribes are given, are to be
found in Judg. 5:15b–18.

group is formed by verses not circulating independently, but amplifying and interpreting existing sayings, pushing them in a certain direction by leaving the metaphor behind and applying direct descriptions (Gen. 49:10–12, 15, 23–24).

2. *The "yahwisticized" sayings.*[203] These sayings — absent in Genesis 49 — are either dominated by a theophoric element or by the fact that they are defined completely by that element. The presentation of achieved conditions has been replaced by thanksgiving, and the wish by the prayer. These theophoric elements are missing in Judges 5 and therefore we have to date these yahwisticized sayings after the middle of the twelfth century. In this category we can distinguish two groups: the first group, where the original form has been preserved with an inserted theophoric element;[204] whereas the second contains the more elaborated forms of prayer and thanksgiving.[205]

3. *The disintegrating sayings.*[206] The final category is formed by those sayings which could not be included in the two preceding categories. In the sayings of those categories the addressees were unquestionably the tribes; there is, however, a group of sayings where the difference between tribe and ancestor is obscured (although not completely): the sayings on Simeon and Levi, and on Joseph, where "brothers" is used (Gen. 49:5, 26).[207]

The sayings in Gen. 49:3–4, 8 differ even more, because in the first saying Reuben is addressed in such a way that nobody would think of a tribe. The same in verse 8, where a picture of Judah is painted, being praised by his brothers. Another kind is the saying in which a curse is uttered on persons: Gen. 49:5–7. In this saying we find, on the one hand, individualisation, and on the other, the well-known twelve-tribe system, which seems to be an indication that the vision on the tribe makes way for individuals. Therefore a scheme was developed, where the twelve tribes were gathered as one nation, by means of a genealogy of their ancestors descending from one common forefather.

With this literary classification of sayings Zobel at the same time offers an outline for the historical setting of the sayings. After having

---

[203] Zobel, *SuG*, 58–9; idem, "Die Stammessprüche des Mose-Segens", 83–92.
[204] Cf. Deut. 33:8–10, 12, 13–15, 17, 23.
[205] These forms are found in Deut. 33:7, 11, 16, 18–19, 20–21, 24–25.
[206] Zobel, *SuG*, 59–61.
[207] Similarly in Deut. 33:13–16 (Joseph), and 24.

described the different kinds of sayings, he starts in a next chapter
of his study the discussion of the historical information preserved in
the tribal sayings, based to a large extent on these literary categories.
The studies by Greßmann, Kittel and Zobel, discussed above, had an
immense influence on the study of Genesis 49: the assumption of the
tribal sayings was almost generally accepted.

1.3.7   C. Westermann

The statement which closed the preceding section on the importance
of previous studies can be illustrated by C. Westermann's discussion
of Genesis 49.[208] Here Westermann begins his discussion of the genre
of Genesis 49 with the following words:

> Genesis 49 is a collection of tribal sayings. Despite all the differences of
> opinion on this chapter either in whole or in detail, there is agreement
> in this matter. ... The text of Genesis 49 (with its parallels [Deut. 33;
> Judg. 5:14–18]) leads us into a different world. It is neither an original
> part of the Patriarchal narratives nor of the Joseph Story; the parallels
> in Deuteronomy and Judges demonstrate this. It deals with Israel's
> tribes in the land of Canaan in the period of the Judges.[209]

According to Westermann the typical tribal saying is short, not longer
in average than the proverbs. In one or two lines it declares something
about a tribe. The sayings on Judah and Joseph must have been expanded in later times, because they are dealing with the rulers' tribes.
Like the sayings in the book of Proverbs, these sayings originated separately or in smaller groups. The number of twelve belongs solely to
the period of the collection and it is an independent element of the
tradition. "The single sayings are independent from the twelve; the
number twelve originated independently from the sayings".[210]

The short sayings are characterizations of a single tribe, by means
of an animal comparison or a pun. When Genesis 49 and Deuteronomy
33 are compared, it turns out that the sayings in Genesis 49 have

---

[208] C. Westermann, *Genesis. 3. Teilband: Genesis 37–50* (BKAT, I/3), Neukirchen-Vluyn 1982.

[209] Westermann, *Genesis 37–50*, 250: "Gn 49 ist eine Sammlung von Stammessprüchen; bei allen Differenzen der Beurteilung dieses Kapitels im ganzen und im
einzelnen ist man sich darin einig. ... Dieser Text Gn 49 (mit den Parallelen) führt
uns in eine andere Welt. Er ist weder ein ursprünglicher Bestandteil der Väter-
noch der Josepherzählung; das zeigen schon die Parallelen in Deuteronomium und
Richter. Er handelt von den Stämmen Israels im Lande Kanaan in der Zeit der
Richter."

[210] Westermann, *Genesis 37–50*, 250: "Die einzelnen Sprüche sind unabhängig
von der Zwölfzahl; die Zwölfzahl ist unabhängig von den Sprüchen entstanden".

preserved their original form, whereas in Deuteronomy 33 the form has become more developed and modified: in Genesis 49 the saying is profane, in Deuteronomy 33 it is theologized.[211]

The sayings have the function of praise or rebuke and at this point the question of the *Sitz im Leben* arises. A comparison of the different texts is in this respect helpful. The sayings in Judg. 5:14-18 are from a previous stage in the development of the tribal sayings, because they are an inseparable part of a larger context: the description of Deborah's battle. Judg. 5:14-18 demonstrates the original *Sitz im Leben* of the tribal sayings, not the battle itself (Kittel), but a subsequent gathering after the battle. They are a kind of military debriefing or manoeuvre critique, which is a usual event after a battle. However, this military character has disappeared in Genesis 49 and Deuteronomy 33, where the form is more general and not limited to a specific situation. The praise and rebuke have now a permanent validity and the circumstance where such sayings arise is not the gathering after the battle but the many other occasions on which the representatives of the tribes gathered (Joshua 24; Judg. 20:1).[212]

1.3.8   Other Proposals for the Genre of Genesis 49

1.3.8.1   Genesis 49 as a Testament

G. Dillmann wrote in 1892 concerning the designation of Genesis 49:

> Jacob's sayings on the future of his twelve sons or (v. 28) tribes. In verse 1 these are characterized as a pre-announcement; more often (vv. 4, 6-7, 17, 25-26) they are spoken in a commanding or a wishing sense, decreed in a paternal authority, so that they are better designated as the testament of Jacob. Less correctly the passage is called Jacob's blessing, for it also contains much that is detrimental to the tribes ...[213]

However, the view on Genesis 49 as a collection of "tribal sayings" has become prevalent since the studies of Gunkel and Greßmann appeared. Despite this, Dillmann's suggestion turned up again in 1940 from another direction and without any dependence on his work. Al-

---

[211]Westermann, *Genesis 37-50*, 250-1.

[212]Westermann, *Genesis 37-50*, 251.

[213]Dillmann, *Die Genesis*, 452: "*Die Sprüche Jacob's* über die Zukunft seiner 12 Söhne oder (V. 28) Stämme. Als eine Vorausverkündigung werden sie V. 1 charakterisirt; es wird öfters (4. 6f. 17. 25f.) darin befehls- oder wünschweise gesprochen, in väterl. Vollmacht verfügt, so daß man sie besser das Vermächtniss Jacob's nennt. Weniger gut nennt man das Stück den *Segen Jacob's*, denn es enthält auch gar viel nachtheiliges für die Stämme ... ". Cf. also Jacob, *Das erste Buch*, 929.

though C.H. Gordon was probably not that much concerned with the correct genre of Genesis 49, he suggested, on the basis of a comparison with texts from Nuzi, that the blessings of the Patriarchs were a kind of testament. A legal document found in Nuzi suggests that the final words of a dying father to his son had legal validity.[214] He states in this connection that

> ... however much the blessings themselves may have been shaped to fit subsequent history, their original function as testamentary wills is still preserved. Thus Isaac appoints his son to follow him as family chief... (Gen. 27:29), while Jacob designates Judah as his successor... (Gen. 49:8).[215]

The designation "testament"[216] is adopted by several other scholars, who consider it a better term for Genesis 49 than the term "blessing".[217]

1.3.8.1.1   E. von Nordheim

The definition of Genesis 49 as a testament is defended more systematically by E. von Nordheim. In his view Genesis 49 answers the general features of the genre "testament", as he describes them on the basis of his study of the different testaments from the Hellenistic and Roman period.[218] According to von Nordheim a testament has a

---

[214]C.H. Gordon, "Biblical Customs and the Nuzu Tablets", in: D.N. Freedman, E.F. Campbell (eds.), *Biblical Archaeologist Reader*, vol. 2, Garden City (NY) 1964, 21–33 (= *BA* 3 (1940) 1–12), 27–8; idem, "The Patriarchal Narratives", *JNES* 13 (1954) 56–9, 56. He was followed by E.A. Speiser, "'I Know Not the Day of My Death'", *JBL* 74 (1955) 252–6; idem, *Genesis*, 370; R.K. Harrison, *Introduction to the Old Testament with a Comprehensive Review of Old Testament Studies and a Special Supplement on the Apocrypha*, Grand Rapids (MI) 1969, 110–1.

[215]Gordon, "Biblical Customs", 27–8.

[216]Next to "testament" the term "farewell speech" is used in scholarly literature. This is mainly influenced by New Testament scholars, who studied the several farewell speeches in the N.T. (for example John 13–17; Acts 20:17–38) from a form-critical perspective; cf. E. von Nordheim, *Lehre der Alten I: Das Testament als Literaturgattung im Judentum der hellenistisch-römischen Zeit* (ALGHJ, 13), Leiden 1980, 5–7; Pehlke, *Genesis 49:1–28*, 23–36.

[217]W.F. Albright, *Yahweh and the Gods of Canaan: An Historical Analysis of Two Conflicting Faiths*, Garden City (NY) 1968, 265; Sarna, *Genesis*, 331; Wenham, *Genesis 16–50*, 468. Cf. also Koopmans, *Joshua 24*, 398. According to M. Philonenko, "Testament", *BHH*, Bd. IV, 1954–5, the literary genre "testament" has the following basic pattern: "before his death a man of God directs a farewell speech to his people with admonitions and premonitions". According to him Gen. 49 is a precursor of this genre.

[218]E. von Nordheim, *Die Lehre der Alten II: Das Testament als Literaturgattung*

fixed form containing three specific elements, which form the external stylistic criteria:

1. In the *opening frame* the title and the name of the (fictitious) author is usually found, also the addressees, a reference to the approaching death of the speaker, information on the age (with a comparable date), description of the situation in which the Patriarch deceased, and finally an introductory formula to the speech.[219]

2. The *middle section* contains at times a very long speech of the dying person to the gathered ones (children and grandchildren, friends, the people or their representatives). This speech has three characteristics: retrospective of the past, instructions how to behave, prediction of the future. The order of these three elements is free, while the elements can be repeated as well.[220]

3. The *closing frame* corresponds to the opening. Here the speech closing formula is found, followed or preceded by an instruction for the funeral. In all cases a note on the death of the Patriarch is given, sometimes followed by the remark that he was buried by his sons.[221]

In addition to these external characteristics, some internal criteria are listed for this genre:

1. The question of the *intention* has to clarify what effect on the reader is aimed at by the genre of the testament. This intention is found in "the appeal to the reader to behave in a certain manner, described before, which offers him support to come to terms with his life."[222]

---

im Alten Testament und im Alten Vorderen Orient (ALGHJ, 18), Leiden 1985, 29–51; his study of the different Testaments appeared in vol. I: idem, *Die Lehre der Alten I* (n. 216 above). In this study he discussed the following texts: the Testaments of the twelve Patriarchs; of 'Amram (4Q'Amram); of Job; of the three Patriarchs (Abraham, Isaac and Jacob); of Adam; of Solomon; of Moses (*Assumptio Mosis*); of Hezekiah (*Ascensio Isaiae*). Furthermore he studied the testaments embedded in the Slavonic Apocalypse of Enoch (2 Enoch 55–67) and in *Liber Antiquitatum Biblicarum* (Pseudo-Philo 33).

[219] Von Nordheim, *Lehre der Alten I*, 229.
[220] Von Nordheim, *Lehre der Alten I*, 229.
[221] Von Nordheim, *Lehre der Alten I*, 229–30.
[222] Von Nordheim, *Lehre der Alten I*, 233: "Die Intention der Gattung 'Testament' liegt also in dem Appell an den Leser, sich in bestimmten, vorher dargestellten Weise zu verhalten, die ihm eine Hilfestellung für die Bewältigung seines Lebens bieten will."

2. The way of *argumentation* is very rationalistic, not legal, even
   when it sometimes uses imperatives: it tries to persuade, convince, make cogent.[223] To corroborate the argument analogies
   are used, especially found in the life of the speaker. The retrospective aspect functions as a substantiation of the instructions
   for the behaviour and shows the consequences for the future on
   the basis of this experience in the past. Because we are dealing
   with a literary genre, it may be clear that the predictions are in
   fact a literary technique. They are used by the author to reach
   the readers in his own time and they are nothing but *vaticinia
   ex eventu.*[224]

3. The *motivation* of the genre: by what right is the instruction
   for the reader justified and explained? This right is found in the
   need to preserve the treasures of the ancients from being lost and
   in this way to make them advantageous to future generations.[225]

An important question is that of the function of the death of the
speaker within the testament. It is important to note that the decease itself is nowhere the focus of the testament: the testament is
meant as an *ars vivendi*, not as an *ars moriendi*; not the approaching
death of the Patriarch but the future life of the hearers (readers) is
important. The death functions as the decisive moment at which the
life of the famous person can be summarized and evaluated. It has no
other function than to legitimize emphatically the instructions on behaviour.[226] This definition excludes at the same moment a widespread
view that the state of dying is the appropriate moment for prophesy,
the so-called *divinare morientes*. The prediction is based on the experience of the speaker, this experience enables him to foretell what
will happen.[227]

The *Sitz im Leben* of the testament can be defined with the help of
external, stylistic and internal criteria. From a stylistic point of view
it is important that a father is speaking to his children, respectively
an older person to younger ones. Also the fact that the introductory
formula (*Lehreröffnungsruf*) and the final reminder — interpreting
the complete testament as an instruction; a recommendation for a
certain behaviour — are found in these texts, can be taken into the
definition of its *Sitz im Leben*. The internal criteria, however, offer

---

[223] Von Nordheim, *Lehre der Alten I*, 233–4.
[224] Von Nordheim, *Lehre der Alten I*, 234–5.
[225] Von Nordheim, *Lehre der Alten I*, 236.
[226] Von Nordheim, *Lehre der Alten I*, 237–8.
[227] Von Nordheim, *Lehre der Alten I*, 238.

the clearest indications, these are: the intention as a summons to influence future behaviour; the rationalistic way of arguing; and at last the motivation to safeguard the treasure of the ancients from obscurity for the benefit of future generations. All these indications suggest a sapiential basic character of the testament: the testament is a wisdom genre. It is closely related to the didactic and exhortation speech and differs mainly in this specific situation, the positioning in the hour of death,[228] and in the fact that it has to be considered a true *literary* genre.[229]

In order to trace back the genre in the Hebrew Bible and to find some forerunners in the Ancient Near East, von Nordheim offers some additional considerations concerning the term testament. In his view the term διαθήκη, which is a "heading-term" (*Überschriften-Begriff*) is not suitable as an indication of potential forerunners of the genre. He argues that:

1. Διαθήκη is not used in every text with testamental character.

2. The testamental genre appears within larger literary contexts and the heading διαθήκη is not to be expected here.[230]

3. Διαθήκη is actually a legal term and stands for a document which contains the last will concerning an estate.

The character of such a legal testament is absent in the analysed testaments and the term διαθήκη is probably connected only in a secondary manner to the testamental form without giving it a legal character.[231] This secondary character of the term might be based on the fact that διαθήκη sometimes was replaced by the more general λόγος, which seems to suggest that the term is not essential for the testamental form.[232] Because there are such clear differences between the legal and sapiential sphere it is unlikely that this Greek term belongs to the earliest history of the genre.[233] This argues also against

---

[228] Von Nordheim, *Lehre der Alten I*, 239.

[229] Von Nordheim, *Lehre der Alten I*, 240.

[230] Cf. von Nordheim, *Lehre der Alten I*, 220.

[231] Von Nordheim, *Lehre der Alten I*, 240–1.

[232] Von Nordheim, *Lehre der Alten I*, 89; cf. *e.g.* Test.Sim. 1:1; Test.Lev. 1:1; Test.Jud. 1:1; Test.Iss. 1:1; Test.Dan 1:1; Test.Benj. 1:1.

[233] Von Nordheim, *Lehre der Alten II*, 72–93, compares both genres, "testament" and "covenant-formula", which is important because the LXX rendered בְּרִית with διαθήκη; given that both forms are very similar, this makes the comparison even more necessary. The result was the already well-known differentiation of the *Sitz im Leben* into two genres known respectively as "sapiential" and "legal" life setting.

the assumption that the forerunners of the Israelite testaments have
been the Greek philosophers' testaments because these are all of a
proprietary nature and thus belong to the legal realm.[234]

Tracing back the history of the genre, von Nordheim in the second volume of his study discusses testaments in the apocryphal books,
the Hebrew Bible and the Ancient Near East. Because it is sometimes
suggested that the "Testaments of the Twelve Patriarchs" are shaped
after Genesis 49, von Nordheim gives special attention to this chapter. Genesis 49 is described according to the external criteria of a
testament as follows:[235]

1. Opening frame. In Genesis 49 Jacob calls his sons (v. 1a), and
   the speech is opened with an introductory formula (v. 2). The
   reference to his approaching death is missing, but this is corrected in the closing frame.[236]

2. Middle section. This middle section in Genesis 49 contains only
   "tribal sayings", while normally this section should contain a
   retrospect of the past, instruction how to behave and prediction
   of the future.[237] According to von Nordheim the tribal sayings
   have nothing in common with this form element: "without the
   framework nobody would have got the idea to consider this collection the middle section of a testament".[238] However, the short
   statement וַיְכַל יַעֲקֹב לְצַוֹּת "Jacob finished charging his sons... "
   (Gen. 49:33a) could be a hint that he has said more than just
   the instructions for his funeral.[239]

3. Closing frame. In this section the reference to the speaker's approaching death (which was missed in the opening frame) is

---

[234]Von Nordheim, *Lehre der Alten I*, 241–2.

[235]Von Nordheim, *Lehre der Alten II*, 33.

[236]Von Nordheim, *Lehre der Alten II*, 34, considers Gen. 49:1–28 forms a unity
(in its final form) with Gen. 49:29–33; 50:12–13. As he excluded Gen. 47:29–48:22,
he indeed misses the reference to the approaching death, which could be found
in 47:28 and 48:1. These two texts, however, belong to a different account in his
view: the latter to the blessing of Ephraim and Manasseh; the former to the report
contained in Gen. 47:29–31, 50:1–11, 14, but here the note on Jacob's death is
missing (von Nordheim, *op.cit*, 32).

[237]Von Nordheim, *Lehre der Alten I*, 229; idem, *Lehre der Alten II*, 33.

[238]Von Nordheim, *Lehre der Alten II*, 33.

[239]Von Nordheim, *Lehre der Alten II*, 34: "Diese sonderbare Stilform könnte
ein Fingerzeig sein, daß Jakob seinen Söhnen außer den Bestattungsanweisungen
noch weitere Aufträge gegeben habe, m.a.W. daß der Schlußrahmen die ganze
Rede Jakobs, auch die Aussprüche über die Stämme, als Verhaltensanweisung
stilisiert, was sie nun wirklich nicht sind."

made up; instruction for the funeral is given, and after the closing formula for direct speech, Jacob dies (v. 33).

According to von Nordheim, Genesis 49 has a very complicated tradition history. Also the form of a testament is just *one* stage in the
development of this kind of text and a rather late one.[240] But his definition of Genesis 49 as a testament does not exclude the possibility
that in the middle section tribal sayings could be included, because
in this instance the middle section of Genesis 49 does not meet the
general feature of a regular middle section and only contains tribal
sayings. The genre "testament" is rather a "large-scale genre" (*Großgattung*), which in this way can include other genres as well.[241]

1.3.8.1.2   N.M. Sarna; G.J. Wenham

A middle course is adopted by N.M. Sarna, who does not consider
Genesis 49 as a unity in origin but a collection of aphorisms about the
tribes.[242] The text contains "material of a very mixed nature: blessings
and curses, censure and praise, geographical and historical observations",[243] and for that reason a designation as "The Last Words of
Jacob" or "The Testament of Jacob" would suit better the context,
in his view. In its present form the poem is the product of "careful
design". The tribal order does not correspond to any of the lists of
names:

> The six sons of Leah are addressed first and the two of Rachel last.
> In between come the sons of the maidservants; the two sons of Zilpah,
> maid of Leah, are inserted between the two sons of Bilhah, maid of
> Rachel. This yields a deliberate chiastic arrangement:
>
> LEAH, Bilhah-Zilpah, Zilpah-Bilhah, RACHEL.
>
> Each group is presented in a descending order of seniority. The single
> exception is Issachar and Zebulun, reversed for historical reasons.[244]

The change in order of Issachar and Zebulun reflects in his view the
time when Zebulun was in the ascendancy. Here Issachar is clearly the
less energetic of the two.[245] Important for the moment, however, is

---

[240]Von Nordheim, *Lehre der Alten II*, 51.

[241]Von Nordheim, *Lehre der Alten I*, 240.

[242]Sarna, *Genesis*, 331. Interesting is that this was — according to Sarna —
recognized already by medieval Jewish exegetes.

[243]Sarna, *Genesis*, 331.

[244]Sarna, *Genesis*, 331. For a similar view view, see Jagersma, *Genesis 25–50*,
256–7.

[245]Sarna, *Genesis*, 338.

his view on the chiastic structure of the Testament, which is referred to with appreciation by Wenham in his commentary.[246]

The genre of Genesis 49 was discussed critically by G.J. Wenham in his commentary on Genesis 16–50.[247] As a general designation for Genesis 49 Wenham prefers the term "testament" to "blessing" because the last words of the patriarch contain curses as well as blessings.[248] In his discussion Wenham refers to the work of Longacre, who argues that Genesis 49 seems to be a high point of the *tōledôt* of Jacob, or even of the whole book of Genesis.[249] Longacre notices that Judah and Joseph are given more attention within Genesis 49 (ten verses of the twenty-five), reflecting the preeminence these tribes engaged later on and also in the surrounding narrative.[250]

Wenham elaborates Longacre's arguments referring to the fact that five other verses refer to two other important tribes in the Joseph Story: Reuben and Simeon; while six other tribes, who only make their appearance in lists, merit only eight verses: Zebulun, Issachar, Dan, Gad, Asher, and Naphtali.[251] He also mentions the relationship of the Testament with earlier parts of Genesis, such as the roughly corresponding order of the names with the birth narrative (Gen. 29:32–30:24, 35:18), the condemnations of Reuben, Simeon and Levi (Gen. 34; 35:22), the fact that there is a reference made to the name YHWH explaining the names of the four sons who play a key role in Genesis 29–50 (Gen. 29:32–35; 30:24). In his view these points show that Genesis 49 is well integrated into the book of Genesis.[252] The coherence of Genesis 49 with chapter 48 is also discussed by Wenham.[253] In his view this coherence matches the contents and sequence of that in Gen. 22:15–25:10 and 35:9–14, as does the repetition of the deathbed blessing occurs also in 28:2–6; also Noah's last words, as a prediction of his son's future (9:25–27), provide a parallel to Genesis 49.[254]

The assumption of independent tribal sayings is not cogent in

---

[246]Wenham, *Genesis 16–50*, 469.

[247]G.J. Wenham, *Genesis 16–50* (WBC, vol. 2), Dallas (TX) 1994, 468–71.

[248]Wenham, *Genesis 16–50*, 468. Cf. also Sarna, *Genesis*, 331.

[249]R.E. Longacre, *Joseph: A Story of Divine Providence; A Text Theoretical and Textlinguistic Analysis of Genesis 37 and 39–48*, Winona Lake (IN) 1989, 23. Cf. already his, "Who Sold Joseph into Egypt?" in: R.L. Harris *et al.* (eds.), *Interpretation and History: Essays ... A.A. MacRae*. Singapore 1986, 75–91; esp. 78–9. Similarly Sarna, *Genesis*, 331.

[250]Longacre, "Who Sold Joseph into Egypt", 79; idem *Joseph*, 54.

[251]Wenham, *Genesis 16–50*, 468; See also Jagersma, *Genesis 25–50*, 256–7.

[252]Wenham, *Genesis 16–50*, 469.

[253]Wenham, *Genesis 16–50*, 460–2.

[254]Wenham, *Genesis 16–50*, 469.

Wenham's view:

> The longer tribal sayings constitute more than two-thirds of the Testa-
> ment and are intimately linked to each other and to the wider context
> of Genesis. All presuppose that Jacob is the speaker (49:3–4, 6, 8–9,
> 25–26), mention relations between the brothers (49:4, 7, 10, 26), and
> concern major actors in the Jacob and Joseph stories. This makes it
> highly likely that these tribal sayings, at least in their present form, all
> belong together; they make less sense as isolated statements. And this
> is even more true of the other tribal sayings, e.g., about Gad, Asher,
> or Naphtali (vv. 19–21). In their present context, these tribal sayings
> make sense… but it is hard to envisage a situation where remarks such
> as "Asher has rich food; he will produce royal delicacies" (v. 20) would
> have a place by itself. It therefore seems most likely that this poem was
> from the start a substantial unity; this is not to rule out the probability
> that the poem developed with time, … [255]

The incorporation of the poem into the account of the patriarchal
period is widely accepted, but it is difficult to establish an earlier use
or its date of composition. The theory that Genesis 49 was used in a
national covenant festival (Gunneweg) he deems unlikely, especially
because of the curses on three tribes (Gen. 49:3–7). The tradition in
Genesis that dying patriarchs pronounce blessings, makes it likely,
in his view, that Genesis 49 was from the beginning associated with
Jacob.[256] A date of origin for Genesis 49 is rather difficult to determine
and Wenham does not attempt to give a firm date. He follows the
scholarly consensus that "we are dealing with one of the oldest parts
of the Bible".[257] With approval he refers to Gunkel, who claimed that
"for the earliest history of the tribes, Gen 49 is, next to Judg 5, the
most important chapter in the OT."[258]

1.3.8.2   Genesis 49 as a Blessing: H. Pehlke

In his dissertation on Genesis 49 H. Pehlke also discussed the previous
opinions regarding the genre of Genesis 49. He did not, however, agree
with the solutions offered. He rejected the testamental genre because
the identifying criteria were not sufficiently met (contra von Nord-

---

[255] Wenham, *Genesis 16–50*, 469–70. Wenham did not exclude the possibility of
a later development of the poem but he argues that "whether the stages of its
growth can be identified must be left to exegesis rather than decided in advance"
op.cit., 470.

[256] Wenham, *Genesis 16–50*, 470.

[257] Wenham, *Genesis 16–50*, 471.

[258] Gunkel, *Genesis*, ³1910, 478: "Für die älteste Geschichte der Stämme ist Gen
49 neben Jdc 5 das wichtigste Kap. im AT." Wenham, *Genesis 16–50*, 471.

heim).[259] First, the parallel with the Nuzi texts is doubtful (contra Gordon and Speiser);[260] and, secondly, the *Sitz im Leben* of the tribal sayings is not defined adequately (contra *inter alii* Westermann).[261] In opposition to these views he suggests that Genesis 49 is a blessing, which is suggested by the use of בְּרָכָה in verse 28.[262]

He answers the objections made against this view that curses (and not just blessings) occur within Genesis 49, whereas only in verses 22–26 is the root ברך used. Concerning the first objection, the use of curses, he argues that throughout the ancient Near East blessings and curses occur in the same context, similar to other "blessings" in Genesis (9:25–27; 21:1–3 with 17:20–21; 26:3–5, 24; 25:27–34). Further the בָּרוּךְ-formula is used analogous to אָרוּר, which seems to suggest that both had the same life setting.[263] The second objection, the use of ברך only in verses 22–26 is rejected because the *contents* of many sayings contain blessings, such as success, fertility, etc. Therefore a saying like Gen. 49:27 "can be called a blessing even though the word 'blessing' is not used in every saying because it harmonizes with the concept of blessing".[264] The argument that Gen. 49:28 belongs to P and thus is not part of the same document as the sayings does not convince Pehlke. If it were correct, P (or the editor) had some reason for placing these sayings in their present context, where they would receive the designation of "blessing", and the best reason seems to be that he considered Gen. 49:3–27 a blessing.[265] Finally, according to Pehlke, his solution offers an adequate *Sitz im Leben*, which is supported by

> other similar blessings having a comparable life setting; e.g. Genesis 27. The setting in life is the imminent death of the aged patriarch who passes on judgments and blessings to his sons as a continuation of the blessing of his ancestor Abraham (Gen. 12:1–3).[266]

The fact that there is a difference in the type of speech cannot be an indication of a change of circumstances because participants of a

---

[259] Pehlke, *Genesis 49:1–28*, 31–51.

[260] Pehlke, *Genesis 49:1–28*, 51–3.

[261] Pehlke, *Genesis 49:1–28*, 53–8.

[262] Pehlke, *Genesis 49:1–28*, 58; he refers to G. Wehmeier, *Der Segen im Alten Testament*, Basel 1970, 98, 114–45. Cf. also Aalders, *Genesis*, dl. 3, 193.

[263] Pehlke, *Genesis 49:1–28*, 59–60.

[264] Pehlke, *Genesis 49:1–28*, 61.

[265] Pehlke, *Genesis 49:1–28*, 61.

[266] Pehlke, *Genesis 49:1–28*, 62. Note that the term *Sitz im Leben* (which is a *general* description of the context of the genre) is confused here with the scene as the *specific* situation of this text.

scene can play more than one role and have multiple opportunities.[267]

1.3.9   The Provenance of Genesis 49

1.3.9.1   Introduction

The sayings in Genesis 49 are almost unanimously considered to be old. The form criticism of the Blessing, which described the text as a collection of tribal sayings, appears to be almost the only methodological basis to establish the early dating of the text. According to this theory Genesis 49 contains sayings which circulated independently in the period between approximately 1400 and 1000 BCE. Beside the form-critical arguments there are some historical arguments and linguistic peculiarities in the text, which may suggest a certain provenance. In the following sections we will deal with these two kinds of arguments.

1.3.9.2   Linguistic Arguments

It is obvious that in Genesis 49, which is assumed to contain ancient sayings, scholars have looked for elements of the archaic[268] language. In the quest for such archaic language the Ugaritic language was often the most important source of information,[269] next to the Canaanite glosses in the El-Amarna correspondence.[270]

Contrary to what one would expect, however, only a few examples of archaic traits in Genesis 49 were found. In his study of early Hebrew poetry, D.A. Robertson found only one example of what he considered

---

[267]Pehlke, *Genesis 49:1–28*, 62, with n. 1, where the source of this final statement is given in an equivalent quotation: M.J. Buss, "The Idea of Sitz im Leben — History and Critique", *ZAW* 90 (1978) 157–70.

[268]In the following chapter we will use the term "archaic language" for the language that is supposed to have been current in Canaan at the end of the second millennium BCE, say about 1200–1000 BCE, and which differs in certain respects in morphology, syntax and vocabulary from "standard" biblical Hebrew. For the most characteristic traits of "archaic biblical poetry", see E.Y. Kutscher, *A History of the Hebrew Language*, edited by R. Kutscher, Jerusalem, Leiden 1982, 79–80; A. Sáenz-Badillos, *A History of the Hebrew Language*, Cambridge 1993, 56–62. See also D.A. Robertson, *Linguistic Evidence in Dating Early Hebrew Poetry* (SBL.DS, 3), Missoula (MT) 1972, 7–9, and *passim*.

[269]Cf. *e.g.* B. Vawter, "The Canaanite Background of Genesis 49", *CBQ* 17 (1955) 1–17; J. Coppens, "La bénédiction de Jacob: son cadre historique à la lumière des parallèles ougaritiques", in: *Volume du Congres Strassbourgh 1956* (SVT, 4), Leiden 1957, 97–115.

[270]Robertson, *Linguistic Evidence*, 4–5; Kutscher, *History of the Hebrew Language*, 77–9; Sáenz-Badillos, *History of the Hebrew Language*, 33–4. The last-mentioned study offers a rather wide perspective for the historical background of our knowledge of the Hebrew language (*op.cit.*, 29–49).

an early form.[271] As a *morphologic* peculiarity he lists the ־י affixed to a singular noun in the construct state: בְּנִי אֲתֹנוֹ "his ass's colt".[272] According to Robertson the ־י strengthens the noun in the construct state.[273] It never occurs in "standard poetry" and therefore might be considered as evidence for an early date.[274] Robertson recognizes that in the case of Genesis 49 "use of this evidence must be tempered by the recognition that only one example is found".[275] As there is only one example in Genesis 49, this text belongs to "the vast majority of undatable poems[, that] resemble standard poetry in that they contain no more than two early forms, ... and exhibit one or more standard forms".[276]

However, next to the example Robertson found, some other features should be mentioned. In Gen. 49:11aA.bB, we find the suffix ־ה which might also be an archaic form,[277] and in 49:22a (MT) we find the primitive fem. ending ־ת in פֹּרָת.[278]

In addition to the archaic grammatical features, reference is made to the specific vocabulary found in Genesis 49 and the use of *hapax legomena*. In Gen. 49:11 we find the word סוּתֹה "his vesture", which occurs further only in Phoenician inscriptions.[279] In addition, we may mention here that reference has been made above to other specific words of which the usage is peculiar and which occur also in other

---

[271] D.A. Robertson, *Linguistic Evidence*, 138. Although it appears that he offers two examples in Genesis 49, he excluded one of these examples in his discussion concerning the ־י following a participle (*op.cit.*, 76).

[272] Robertson, *Linguistic Evidence*, 70. Similarly: Kutscher, *History of the Hebrew Language*, 79; Sáenz-Badillos, *History of the Hebrew Language*, 58. Robertson also discusses the ־י affixed to the participle, like אֹסְרִי (49:11aA), but his conclusion is that it cannot be considered an example of early poetry because the occurrence of this form is more frequent in standard poetry (*op.cit.*, 76).

[273] Robertson, *Linguistic Evidence*, 75.

[274] Next to Gen. 49:11aB, Robertson, *Linguistic Evidence*, 76, lists Deut. 33:16; Pss. 30:8; 110:4, where this morpheme occurs in comparable positions.

[275] Robertson, *Linguistic Evidence*, 76.

[276] Robertson, *Linguistic Evidence*, 138.

[277] Cf. Kutscher, *History of the Hebrew Language*, 79; I. Young, *Diversity in Pre-Exilic Hebrew* (FAT, 5), Tübingen 1993, 36, 105, 126; Sáenz-Badillos, *History of the Hebrew Language*, 57.

[278] G.A. Rendsburg, *Linguistic Evidence for the Northern Origin of Selected Psalms* (SBL.MS, 43), Atlanta (GA) 1990, 23, n. 28 regards this ending in many cases as a "northernism". In the case of Gen. 49:22, פֹּרָת (MT) he considers this form as "simply archaic poetic diction". He provides no arguments for this statement, however, which is quite remarkable, because in his view the "various tribal blessings which appear in Genesis 49 ... may also be assumed to be of northern provenance" (*op.cit.*, 11, with n. 49).

[279] Kutscher, *History of the Hebrew Language*, 80. Sáenz-Badillos, *History of the Hebrew Language*, 60.

texts, like those of Ugarit: שׁוֹר "bull, prince" (v. 6bB); פָּרָת "cow" (22aAB); שׁוֹר "Bull" (epithet, 22bA); מרר D-st.,"to strengthen" (23aB).[280] Also the epithets used in Gen. 49:25–26 (like אֵל אָבִיךָ "El, your Father" [25aA]) have led scholars to assume an early date for the poem.[281]

Besides an indication for the dating of the Blessing linguistic features may be used to determine the possible *geographical* provenance of Genesis 49. S. Gevirtz draws our attention to possible "northernisms" in Genesis 49,[282] namely the supposed occurrence of the word רשׁאת (49:3C, emendation)[283] and the relative particle שֶׁ (49:20, emendation)[284] and the "double plural" construct chain בַּעֲלֵי חִצִּים literally "masters of arrows" (49:23).[285] G.A. Rendsburg, apparently endorsing this localization of the poem's origin, regarded the occurrence of נָעֵמָה "pleasant" (v. 16), שֶׁפֶר "lovely" (v. 21), and אֲבִיר יַעֲקֹב "Strong One of Jacob" (v. 24) as evidence for the northern origin of certain psalms.[286] In his study of pre-Exilic Hebrew, discussing the Siloam Tunnel inscription, I. Young has suggested that the occurrence of different suffixes (ֹי– and ֹה–) in 49:11 may be due to dialectic influence in which the different spellings actually represent the pronunciation of two different suffixes.[287] The ה– could originally have represented -ahū, but, taking into account the "Aramaizing" tendency of archaic Biblical Hebrew, the ה– could also have been related to the Aramaic 3. masc.sg. suffix -ēh. This suffix may have occurred also in official Judean inscriptions, such as the Siloam Tunnel inscription in Young's discussion. Since his argument is not concerned with the provenance of Genesis 49, he does not relate this data to a probable origin of the sayings and no conclusion is reached in this matter.

---

[280]Cf. above, pp. 23.

[281]D.N. Freedman, "Divine Names and Titles in Early Hebrew Poetry", in: F.M. Cross (ed.), *Magnalia Dei: The Mighty Acts of God*, New York 1976, 55–107, 66 (= idem, *Pottery, Poetry, and Prophecy: Studies in Early Hebrew Poetry*, Winona Lake [IN] 1980, 77–129, 88). Cf. also above p. 24, for some other scholars, who assume corresponding Ug. epithets in Genesis 49.

[282]S. Gevirtz, "Asher in the Blessing of Jacob (Genesis xlix 20)", *VT* 37 (1987) 154–63, esp. 159–60.

[283]S. Gevirtz, "The Reprimand of Reuben", *JNES* 30 (1971) 87–98, esp. 90–1, with n. 27.

[284]Gevirtz, "Asher", 159. For the particle, see also Kutscher, *History of the Hebrew Language*, 32; Young, *Diversity in Pre-Exilic Hebrew*, 78, 115–6, 167–8.

[285]Gevirtz, "Asher", 160, with n. 20, referring to his study "Of Syntax and Style in the 'Late Biblical Hebrew'–'Old Canaanite' Connection", *JANES* 18 (1986) 25–9, esp. 28–9.

[286]Rendsburg, *Northern Origin of Selected Psalms*, 31, 87.

[287]Young, *Diversity in Pre-Exilic Hebrew*, 105.

1.3.9.3   Historical Arguments

According to the "tribal saying" theory, the sayings in Genesis 49 originated when the tribes were almost autonomous groups and the tribal consciousness was still strong. This period would be the pre-monarchic era, between approximately 1400 and 1000 BCE.[288] The scholarly world has been almost unanimous with regard to this dating and only a few dissenting voices are found, which concern mostly details. We will present some of the suggestions concerning the historical background of some of the sayings.

In his study *Stammesspruch und Geschichte*, Zobel considers the saying on Judah, for example, to have originated in three different stages:[289] first Gen. 49:9, then verse 10–12 and finally verse 8. The first stage (v. 9) concerns the pattern of the settlement of the tribe of Judah, a pattern which Zobel found also in other sayings. This description he relates to the events described in Judges 1, in which a certain independent development for Judah is significant (cf. also Genesis 38).[290] The second stage in the development (vv. 10–12) concerns the claim to the leadership in Israel, which Judah will find in Shiloh, according to Eissfeldt "the symbol of the highest national religious leadership in Israel".[291] The *terminus ad quem* is in this case the destruction of the village by the Philistines around the middle of the eleventh century BCE.[292] The *terminus a quo* has to be seen after the battle of Deborah, when the ark was brought to Shiloh as the cultic and political metropolis of the house of Joseph.[293] The final stage (v. 8) must be considered a *vaticinium ex eventu*, which is related to the time of the Davidic kingship.[294]

Also the saying of Issachar (vv. 14–15) is frequently attributed to the settlement of the tribe in the pre-monarchic period. In this case there are extra-biblical documents that are sometimes related to Issachar's history.[295] The saying presupposes the settlement of the tribe,

---

[288]Cf. esp. Zobel, *SuG*, 62–126.

[289]For Zobel's view on the development of the genre "tribal saying"; cf. above, pp. 41–4.

[290]Zobel, *SuG*, 73–4.

[291]O. Eissfeldt, "Silo und Jerusalem", in: *Volume du Congrès, Strasbourg 1956* (SVT, 4), Leiden 1957, 138–47, 141; Zobel, *SuG*, 75.

[292]Similarly Eissfeldt, "Silo und Jerusalem", 141.

[293]Zobel, *SuG*, 75–6.

[294]Zobel, *SuG*, 79.

[295]See A. Alt, "Neues über Palästina aus dem Archiv Amenophis' IV", *PJB* 20 (1924) 22–41 (= idem, *KS*, Bd. III, 158–75); Zobel, *SuG*, 85–7; H. Donner, "The Blessing of Issachar (*Gen.* 49:14–15) as a Source for the Early History of Israel", in: J.A. Soggin *et al.*, *Convegno sul tema: Le origini di Israele*, Rome 1987, 53–63.

which abandoned its freedom and became dependent on the lord of the land because of the "good" (טוֹב) land.[296] According to Donner the Issacharites were "nomads"[297] because "he was couching down between the sheepfolds", which were outside the cities and villages, while "between the sheepfolds" suggests the living in tents.[298] From the Amarna correspondence it is known that Biridiya, the dynast of Megiddo had $^{LU\text{-}ME\check{S}}massa^{ME\check{S}}$ "corvee workers" at work in the region of Shunem (EA 365).[299] It is generally accepted that Akk. *massu* and Hebr. מַס (in *e.g.* 49:15b) are cognate, and for that reason the identification of the tribe of Issachar with the *massu*-people of the Amarna correspondence seems obvious. Donner states in this case: "When the blessing was created, the Issacharites were — perhaps not exclusively, but mainly — *massu*-people under the control of Canaanite city-states in the plains of Jezreel and Beth-Shan".[300]

Concerning the saying on Joseph, Wellhausen suggested that the archers of Gen. 49:24 were the Aramaeans of Damascus, who had attacked the Northern Kingdom when "Joseph" was the "crowned one of his brothers" (Gen. 49:26).[301] Gunkel suggested the period of the Judges, when nomads from the desert crossed the Jordan and raided the land (*e.g.* Midianites). Archery in Gunkel's view belongs much more to the nomads (cf. Gen. 21:20), than to the Aramaeans.[302] Zobel related the saying to a possible war between Ephraim and Benjamin, which is reflected in Judges 19–20 and might even be concerned with the bringing of the ark from Bethel (probably Benjaminite) to Shiloh (Ephraimite).[303]

However, it is clear that today the value of the sayings in Genesis 49 as a source for historical information is decreasing. Whereas in many so-called classical "histories of Israel" references to the say-

---

[296]Zobel, *SuG*, 85. For a description of the general interpretation of the saying against the background of the classical historical models, cf. Donner, "The Blessing of Issachar", 53–6.

[297]Donner, "The Blessing of Issachar", 57–8, defines the term "nomad" in a quite wide sense "as unsettled inhabitants of tents in contrast to the settled inhabitants of houses, ... and nothing else".

[298]Donner, "The Blessing of Issachar", 56. He offers more arguments, like the use of the root שׁיב which is used more often in connection with cattle breeding, and the fact that מְנֻחָה is used several times as a contrast to unsettled life (*op.cit.*, 57).

[299]Alt, "Neues über Palästina", 169–74; Zobel, *SuG*, 87; Donner, "The Blessing of Issachar", 59–60.

[300]Donner, "The Blessing of Issachar", 59; see also p. 61.

[301]Wellhausen, *Composition*, 322–3.

[302]Gunkel, *Genesis*, ³1910, 485–6.

[303]Zobel, *SuG*, 117–9.

ings of Genesis 49 are found,[304] there is a strong tendency in recent "histories" to ignore them completely[305] or to deny them their value *expressis verbis*.[306] The denial of their value is connected with the fact that their location in the pre-monarchic period is no longer taken for granted. Sayings like those of Judah (49:9), Dan (49:16), and Benjamin (49:27) suggest warlike acts by independent tribes. However, according to V. Fritz,

> ... this antedating before the rise of the monarchy is by no means compelling, because in such comparisons the self-consciousness of the respective tribe could just as easily be expressed during the monarchy.[307]

Finally, the opinions concerning the process of collection, redaction and insertion into its present position have begun to differ considerably as well. The time of redaction, as distinct from the debate concerning the final editing of the Joseph Story, may lie between the time of the Yahwist, and that of the Priestly editor; and in some cases an Exilic or post-Exilic date cannot be positively excluded.

1.3.10   Recapitulation

1. Genesis 49 unlike most other parts of Genesis is not classified as a part of one of the Pentateuchal documents. It is considered a collection of "tribal sayings", inserted in its present position by an editor, probably R[P] at a certain moment during the long history of the book.

2. The classification as a collection of "tribal sayings" is based on form criticism, which was developed by H. Gunkel. The object

---

[304] Cf. the indices of *e.g.* H. Jagersma, *Geschiedenis van Israel in het oudtestamentisch tijdvak*, dl. I, Kampen 1979; H. Donner, *Geschichte des Volkes Israel und seiner Nachbarn in Grundzügen* (ATD.E, 4), Göttingen 1984–1986; J.M. Miller, J.H. Hayes, *A History of Ancient Israel and Judah* London 1986; J.A. Soggin, *An Introduction to the History of Israel and Judah*, London ²1993.

[305] Cf. the indices of *e.g.* G.W. Ahlström, *History of Ancient Palestine*; T.L. Thompson, *Early History of the Israelite People: From the Written and Archaeological Sources* (SHANE, 4), Leiden 1992; N.P. Lemche, *Die Vorgeschichte Israels: Von den Anfängen bis zum Ausgang des 13. Jahrhunderts v. Chr.* (BE, Bd. 1), Stuttgart 1996.

[306] V. Fritz, *Die Entstehung Israels im 12. und 11. Jahrhundert v. Chr.* (BE, Bd. 2), Stuttgart 1996, 57–8.

[307] Fritz, *Die Entstehung Israels*, 58: "... zwingend ist diese Rückdatierung vor die Entstehung des Königtums keineswegs, da in den Vergleichen auch das Selbstbewußtsein des jeweiligen Stammes während der Königszeit zum Ausdruck kommen kann."

of this method is to go back to the era of oral tradition in order
to discover the purest form and original setting of these literary
forms. The correct definition of the genre and of the life setting
(*Sitz im Leben*) is of vital importance for the understanding of
the text in its historical context.

3. After Gunkel had developed the concept of independent sayings
   as "blessings", his view was modified by H. Greßmann, who
   suggested that the sayings were really "tribal sayings". These
   sayings functioned independently and were recited at gatherings
   of the tribes against a common foe or for a religious event. Greßmann discerned a development within the tribal sayings from a
   short and descriptive form into a longer and predicting form.
   Whereas the shortest forms — built up of only one or two cola
   — are still folk poetry, the longer ones are more difficult and
   therefore "art poetry" (*Kunstpoesie*).

4. H.-J. Kittel described the development more meticulously from
   short individual sayings via sayings consisting of several elements and then structured sayings into editorially adapted sayings. Kittel defined the *Sitz im Leben* with the help of Judges
   4–5 as the battle, where the praising and blaming sayings have
   their origin.

5. Concerning Genesis 49 it may be concluded that these tribal sayings are not found in each "blessing", because it was pointed out
   (Kittel, Zobel) that Gen. 49:3–8 does not contain tribal sayings
   in the strict sense, using puns and metaphors in a short saying
   to give a typical description of the tribe. These verses could be
   considered an aetiology where the rise of Judah is explained by
   means of the legends in Genesis 34 and 35:22.

6. The original *Sitz im Leben* of tribal sayings is the element least
   know about in the description of this genre. Although Gunneweg
   tried to establish this matter definitely, defining it as part of
   the amphictyony festival, Westermann later returned to Kittel's
   position (cf. the preceding item).

7. Another definition of the genre is more concerned with the whole
   chapter than with the smaller parts. Genesis 49 is defined as a
   "testament". A twofold interpretation is found here, namely the
   interpretation of the testament as a legal document containing
   someone's last will concerning his estate; and the interpreta-

tion as a kind of farewell speech, which originated in sapiential circles.

8. It is also suggested that Genesis 49 is a "blessing". This is mainly based on the fact that the word בְּרָכָה is used in verse 28 to describe the sayings. In this case it is argued that the fact that curses also appear in the text does not contradict this statement because blessings and curses often occur in the same context and for many tribes the contents of the saying reflects "blessed" conditions.

9. The early date of Genesis 49 (1400–1000 BCE) is no longer taken for granted, later dates must also be taken into consideration.

1.4   The Genre of Genesis 49 Evaluated

1.4.1   Independent Sayings?

The form-critical analysis of Genesis 49 as a collection of tribal sayings is very seldom critically evaluated. Many scholars nowadays seem to be inclined to accept the genre "tribal saying" for these sayings. However, the theory that Genesis 49 is a collection of originally independent sayings has been questioned by scholars from different angles. It is worthwhile reviewing their objections here if only to clarify what is at stake.

The first in the twentieth century who objected to this theory was, as we have already seen, Gunkel himself. In contrast to Kuenen and Holzinger, whom he mentions explicitly, he regards Genesis 49 as a unity. In his opinion the shortest sayings were not even possible without any literary context.[308] He is followed by Skinner, though the latter also sees some historical differences between the sayings. Nevertheless he considers the poem

> to have existed as a traditional document whose origin dates from the early days of the Israelite occupation of Palestine, and which underwent successive modifications and expansions before it took final shape in the hands of a Judæan poet of the age of David or Solomon. The conception of Jacob as the speaker belongs to the original intention of the poem;
> . . .[309]

Further he writes that

---

[308] Gunkel, *Genesis*, ²1902, 420; cf. p. 30 with nn. 150–151 above.
[309] Skinner, *Genesis*, 509.

the inadequacy of the theory... that the poem consists of a number of fugitive oracles which had circulated independently among the
tribes... is seen when we observe that all the longer passages (Reuben,
Simeon-Levi, Judah, Joseph) assume that Jacob is the speaker, while
the shorter pieces are too slight in content to have any significance
except in relation to the whole.[310]

As we have seen, Wenham also argues in his commentary on Genesis
against the theory, mainly following the arguments of Gunkel and
Skinner.[311] However, his objections against this theory do not exclude
the possibility that there existed former stages in the transmission of
the sayings. In his view the sayings are strongly interrelated, which
makes it likely that at least in the present form they belong together.
Also the poetic structure of the present form of the text is generally
overlooked in scholarly studies. Sarna is an exception for, although
he assumes an independent origin of the sayings, his observation of
the chiastic structure of the text[312] argues for its unity and its impact
can only be countered by clear evidence of a dispersed origin. Form
criticism, with its focus on the "tribal saying" unit, has prevented
scholars from reading the text holistically in its present form. It tends
to read the chapter as a collection of disparate fragments.

In Wenham's view the sayings make less sense as isolated statements, especially the shorter sayings, since it is hard to envisage a
situation in which they would have had a place by themselves. His
criticism is quite fundamental, because no solution has been offered
by any author to the problem of what the meaning would be of such
an independent saying.[313] Of course, in every commentary an explanation is given, but *nowhere* in its supposed *Sitz im Leben*. This is the
main problem Gunkel, Skinner and Wenham pointed out: just one

---

[310]Skinner, *Genesis*, 510–1.

[311]Wenham, *Genesis 16–50*, 469–70; cf. the quotation from his commentary concerning these sayings on p. 53, with n. 255 above.

Wenham also refers to Seebaß, "Stammessprüche Gen 49", 333–50, as an author
who had argued "for the essential unity of the poem". However, Seebaß, *art.cit.*,
334 and *passim*, considers Genesis 49 a collection (*Sammlung*) of tribal sayings
(*Stammessprüche*; cf. the title of his article); further he argues (*art.cit.*, 339–44)
that four sayings reflect conditions previous to the song of Deborah, two sayings
reflect almost the same period as that song, while he is not able to establish a
date for three others.

[312]Sarna, *Genesis*, 331.

[313]Zobel, "Stammessprüche des Mose-Segens", 19–30, seems to be an exception.
However, his definition of the *Sitz im Leben* is almost identical to the described
situation in Deuteronomy 33, be it that not a dying leader (like Jacob or Moses)
pronounced the sayings, but that they originated at a cultic gathering (*Kultver-
sammlung*) and were spoken by a priest or at least a person functioning as such.

saying, like the one on Asher in Gen. 49:20, is difficult to understand without its present context and hardly seems to have any meaning when verbalized independently of it. This matter, which involves the "setting in life" was rightly exposed by Wenham and marks the transition to the next section.

1.4.2   The *Sitz im Leben*

Wenham's observation that it is hard to envisage a situation where short sayings such as the one on Asher, would have been meaningful,[314] was made as far back as Gunkel and Skinner. It is, in fact, a frontal attack on the supposed life-setting of the tribal sayings. When the life-setting of these sayings turns out to be incorrect, or does not provide the proper situation in which they arose, the genre definition may be at fault and probably also the literary analysis based upon it. As we saw above the question of the *Sitz im Leben* had already been brought forward by Gunneweg. However, his solution is almost identical with the answers given by Greßmann, Kittel, Zobel, and later Westermann, and therefore his study does not form a critical evaluation. Moreover, his presupposition is that the genre "tribal saying" does exist which makes him unable to evaluate the problem critically.[315]

The matter of the *Sitz im Leben* of the tribal sayings was touched upon by W. Richter, who discusses the methodology required to establish the *Sitz im Leben* of a genre.[316] In his view such an endeavour cannot possibly function without textual data. However, these data are usually not present in the investigated genre itself, but are mostly scattered in the literature, or they arise from other data. Here one has to be aware of the risk of circular reasoning because such data is sometimes not available and one has to draw conclusions from other data, or even from extant units of data belonging to the supposed genre. In that case we are dealing with conjectures which the exegete has to be careful to mark as such.[317] In this connection Richter refers to Gunneweg,[318] who

---

[314]Wenham, *Genesis 16–50*, 470.

[315]Cf. A.H.J. Gunneweg, "Über den Sitz im Leben der sog. Stammessprüche: Gen 49, Dtn 33, Jdc 5", *ZAW* 76 (1964) 245–55, 245–8 (= idem, *Sola Scriptura: Beiträge zu Exegese und Hermeneutik des Alten Testaments*, Göttingen 1983, 25–35, 25–8).

[316]W. Richter, *Exegese als Literaturwissenschaft: Entwurf einer alttestamentlichen Literaturtheorie und Methodologie*, Göttingen 1971, 145–8.

[317]Richter, *Exegese*, 146.

[318]Cf. p. 40–41 above.

worked substantially with two generalizations in which the word "self-" appears, on the assumption of their affinity along with the presupposition of the identity of representation and event. None of these assumptions were examined, and none of them would have passed examination.[319]

One such unproven assumption is the amphictyony,[320] which can be paralleled to the gathering of representatives of the tribes at certain events like a battle (cf. Judges 4–5), as was assumed by Greßmann, Kittel and Westermann. The problem with such a definition is that there is no data that would warrant such an assumption concerning Genesis 49 and Deuteronomy 33.[321]

In this case it is important to make a clear distinction between the sayings contained in Judg. 5:14–18 and those in Genesis 49 and Deuteronomy 33.[322] The sayings in Judges 5 are clearly reflections on events: the battle against Sisera, while the sayings in Genesis 49 and Deuteronomy 33 are intended as *predictions* (cf. Gen. 49:1).[323] Thus in Judges 5 the sayings are connected with a certain situation to which they refer. According to Westermann, they are a kind of military briefing or manoeuvre critique,[324] which is usual after a battle.

> Whereas Judg. 5:14–18 belongs to a certain situation in which participation or not is the main question, Genesis 49 and Deuteronomy 33 contain sayings on the tribes which are more general, and not connected with a definite situation.[325]

However, with the statement that the sayings in Genesis 49 and Deuteronomy 33 are not tied to a stated situation, he seems to break with the idea of *vaticinia ex eventu*, which is held by the majority of scholars. The sayings are formulated more generally than those contained in Judges 5; however, even as "tribal sayings" they are meant

---

[319]Richter, *Exegese*, 146, n. 56: "Er arbeitet also mit zwei inhaltlichen Verallgemeinerungen, bei denen das Wort 'Selbst-' vorkommt, mit der Annahme ihrer Verwandtschaft und mit der Voraussetzung der Identität von Darstellung und Vorgang. Keine dieser Annahmen wird überprüft, keine würde einer Überprüfung standhalten."

[320]Richter, *Exegese*, 146, n. 57.

[321]Similar Pehlke, *Genesis 49:1–28*, 55.

[322]Westermann, *Genesis 37–50*, 251.

[323]Of course these are *vaticinia ex eventu*. However, within their literary context they are not intended as such (see below).

[324]Westermann, *Genesis 37–50*, 251.

[325]Westermann, *Genesis 37–50*, 251: "Während aber Ri 5,14–18 in eine einmalige Situation gehören, sind die in Gn 49 und Dt 33 gesammelten Stammessprüche allgemeine, nicht an eine Situation gebundene Worte über die Stämme."

to refer to a specific situation. This is certainly the case in the present literary context, where they are meant as predictions and thus as a reference to a certain moment in history, which was recognized as such by the author/editor at least.[326] Therefore we have to maintain the assumption that these sayings are *vaticinia ex eventu*, and simultaneously we have to investigate whether the described *Sitz im Leben* and genre can be matched up.

Wenham doubts the correctness of this genre definition primarily because of the unlikeliness of the independent use of sayings, such as Gen. 49:20.[327] In our view this criticism could be applied to almost every saying in Genesis 49 — with the possible exclusion of verses 14–15 — because an almost complete new context for the saying has to be created before it would be understandable. A reference to the saying concerning Zebulun (Gen. 49:13) will illustrate the point here:[328]

> Zebulun shall dwell at the shore of the sea; (13aA)
> He shall become a haven for ships, (13bA)
> and his border shall be at Sidon; (13bB)

The *Sitz im Leben* of this saying, together with the others is described by Westermann: The places where these sayings (Genesis 49 and Deuteronomy 33) originated and were handed down, were occasions where representatives of several tribes met.

> Such meetings are mentioned in Josh. 24 and Judg. 20:1; which can have different functions. Here they inquired after each other, news was exchanged; here they talked about others, and in this way such sayings had their significance and their starting-point. From this starting-point and earliest transmission it becomes clear that each saying emerged separately, or in groups of several sayings; this appears from their function as praise or rebuke.[329]

However, the saying on Zebulun does not contain any praise or rebuke; it just seems to be a description of geographical conditions, no more

---

[326] Cf. in this connection also Wellhausen's dictum on the relation of the time of origin and the contents of a text, in: J. Wellhausen, *Prolegomena zur Geschichte Israels*, Berlin ²1883, 336 (⁶1905, 316) quoted below, in section 5.21.

[327] Cf. our quotation of Wenham above, on p. 53.

[328] Quoted from *RSV*.

[329] Westermann, *Genesis 37–50*, 251: "Solche Zusammenkünfte werden Jos 24; Ri 20,1 erwähnt; sie können zu ganz verschiedenen Zwecken abgehalten werden. Hier erkundigte man sich nach den anderen und tauschte Kunde aus, hier sprach man über die anderen, und dabei hatten solche Sprüche ihren Sinn und ihren Ort. Von diesem Ort des Entstehens und frühesten Tradierens her wird auch klar, daß jeder Spruch einzeln für sich entstand, oder in Gruppen zu mehreren Sprüchen; das geht schon aus ihrer Funktion als Lob oder Tadel hervor."

and no less. This is apparently recognized by Westermann:

> But what is the significance of the saying? Some exegetes consider it
> as just a designation of the location of Zebulun, but this does not
> suffice as a motive for the formation and handing down of a tribal
> saying.... H.-J. Kittel, however, understands it as a rebuke, especially
> with reference to Judg. 5:17b (Dan and Asher) .... These phrases in
> Judg. 5:17 are unequivocally meant as a rebuke. Therefore it has also
> to be assumed that in the saying on Zebulun the attraction for the sea
> with its commercial possibilities (ships, similar Deut. 33:20) and its
> leaning against Sidon (the back) was intended as a gentle rebuke.[330]

In our view this is a rather forced approach to maintain the supposed
genre and its *Sitz im Leben*, and this kind of argument could be classed
as circular reasoning in Richter's scheme.

In Gunneweg's opinion sayings are based on word-plays or on animal comparisons as a form of self-presentation. However, this saying
does not contain such a pun on the name as is supposed by *inter alii*
Gunneweg, since the meaning of זבל is not "to live" but "to raise".[331]
So it appears that neither a form of "self-presentation" (or passive
"being self-presented") in the amphictyony (Gunneweg), nor a rebuke
(Westermann) is present in this saying.

In discussing the genre and life setting of our text, it is safer not to
force the text in advance into the mould of a certain genre but to take
into consideration all the available data before defining the precise
genre. In the case of Genesis 49 form criticism seems to function
rather as the Procrustean bed in which the text and exegesis has to
be forced rather than as a supporting tool for exegesis. For that reason
the use of form criticism will be discussed in the following section.

1.4.3 Form Criticism and the Written Text

The basic assumption behind Gunkel's thesis is that we have to ask
certain questions above and beyond the written text in order to dis-

---

[330]Westermann, *Genesis 37–50*, 265: "Was aber ist der Sinn des Spruches? Einige
Ausleger sehen ihn einfach als Angabe der Lage Sebulons an, aber das wäre
für das Entstehen und Tradieren eines Stammesspruches kein ausreichendes Motiv.... HJKittel dagegen hört aus ihm einen Tadel, insbesondere unter Hinweis
auf Ri 5,17b (Dan und Aser) .... Diese Sätze in Ri 5,17 sind eindeutig im Sinn
eines Vorwurfs gemeint. Deswegen ist anzunehmen, daß auch im Sebulonspruch
das Streben zum Meer mit seinen Handelsmöglichkeiten (Schiffe, das sagt auch
Dt 33,19b) und das Sich-Anlehnen an Sidon (Rücken) als ein vielleicht gedämpfter
Tadel gemeint ist."

[331]זבל is often interpreted as "to live" (Gunkel; Skinner; Vawter; Gunneweg);
however the basic meaning is "to raise", found also in the folk etymology in Gen.
30:20; cf. *HAL*, 252.

cern its oral tradition, and this cannot be questioned here; nor is
the fact that there existed several literary patterns which belonged
to a certain setting. But the real stumbling-block is the relationship
between the oral stage and the written one.

According to Gunkel each genre had a specific setting in life, where
it originated in an oral form, not in a written one.[332] In his view writing determined literature less in ancient Israel than in our day, which
explains the paucity of such ancient productions. "The ancient Hebrew folk song comprised only one or maybe two long verses; the people
of that time were not able to grasp any more than that!"[333] Many of
these original genres were expanded which undoubtedly is connected
with the fact that the era became "literary" — a turning point in
the history of ancient literature. Genres, originally belonging to folk
life (*Volksleben*), were translated into a written form. First collections
arose. But in the new era of writing the "author" also comes into
being, who might be a singer, narrator or prophet, who applies the
folk genres to suit his own purposes. In this way the poetry of the
artists arose from folk poetry. In the Old Testament there are many
examples of ancient folk poetry, some of them classical creations, but
also dull imitations are preserved alongside each other.[334] The oldest
genres, still part of folk life, have always a pure form. In later times,
however, when people and conditions became more complicated, and
authors grasped the significance of genres, bending and blending took
place.[335]

> Particularly rich in form-blending are the prophets, who in their zeal to
> affect the people, took up a great many little used genres and merged
> and filled them with prophetic contents. In this way the prophets be-
> came poets, narrators and legislators.[336]

This, in brief, is Gunkel's interpretation of the development of Israel's
literature. His description is clearly the product of his era and an

---

[332] H. Gunkel, "Die Grundprobleme der israelitischen Literaturgeschichte", in:
idem, *Reden und Aufsätze*, Göttingen 1913, 29–38, 33 (originally published in
Deutsche Literaturzeitung 27 [1906] 1797–800).

[333] Gunkel, "Grundprobleme der israelitischen Literaturgeschichte", 33–4; quotation on p. 34: "Das älteste hebräische Volkslied umfaßt nur eine oder etwa zwei
Langzeilen; mehr vermochten die damaligen Menschen nicht zu übersehen!"

[334] Gunkel, "Grundprobleme der israelitischen Literaturgeschichte", 35.

[335] Gunkel, "Grundprobleme der israelitischen Literaturgeschichte", 36.

[336] Gunkel, "Grundprobleme der israelitischen Literaturgeschichte", 36: "Besonders reich an allerlei Stilmischungen sind die Propheten, die im Eifer, auf ihr Volk
zu wirken, eine fast unübersehbare Fülle von fremden Gattungen aufgenommen,
verschmolzen und mit prophetischem Inhalt erfüllt haben. So sind die Propheten
zu Dichtern, Erzählern und Gesetzgebern geworden."

evolutionistic view of the development is apparent, especially in his remark that "the people of that time were not able to grasp any more than that!" In the (oral) folk poetry the people did not bend or blend the genre(s), these genres had a constant form and setting. The bending and blending of genres was a later development during the era of writing in which longer compositions became much more frequent.

One of the more critical questions that arises from this is whether the ancients were indeed unable to handle texts longer than two poetic verses in oral tradition. This question is justified given the amount of data available concerning the oral tradition of long texts in Mesopotamia and Ugarit.[337] In the texts from Mesopotamia and Ugarit indications have been found that longer parts were learned off by heart and recited on special occasions. Such data makes the theory of linear development within Israel's literature untenable. Furthermore, the myths and legends of Ugarit show that the supposed short form of the legends in the Hebrew Bible is a fiction.[338] In these texts a mixture of genres is developed in a comparable way to in the literature of the prophets: in the myths and legends messenger formulas are found,[339] lamentations,[340] curses,[341] and blessings.[342] This justifies the question whether such a clear cut division between oral and written tradition is possible on the one hand; and on the other, whether a division between folk and art poetry is tenable. Is it possible that in oral/folk as well as in written/art literature the "writer" or "speaker" of such a text applied several genres in order to produce the effect he had in mind? This question was posed very forcefully by Muilenburg in his article on "form criticism and beyond".[343]

In his article Muilenburg pleads for a stricter use of form criticism and respect for other features in the text, which had been neglected in applying form criticism up until then. It is remarkable that Muilenburg draws attention to aspects in the text which were already pointed out by Gunkel.[344] According to Muilenburg

form criticism by its very nature is bound to generalize because it is con-

---

[337] Cf. E. Nielsen, *Oral Tradition: A Modern Problem in Old Testament Introduction* (SBT, 11), London 1954, 18–38; J.C. de Moor, *Mondelinge overlevering in Mesopotamië, Ugarit, en Israel*, Leiden 1965, 9–19; *ARTU*, 99, n. 481.

[338] Cf. also H.J. Kraus, *Psalmen* (BKAT, XV/1), Neukirchen ⁵1978, 287.

[339] Cf. KTU 1.2:i.17–18, 33–34.

[340] KTU 1.16:i.1–23; 1.16:ii.37–49.

[341] KTU 1.2:i.8–9; 1.16:vi.54–57.

[342] KTU 1.15:ii.19–iii.16; 1.17:i.34–53.

[343] J. Muilenburg, "Form Criticism and Beyond", *JBL* 88 (1969) 1–18.

[344] Gunkel, "Grundprobleme der israelitischen Literaturgeschichte", 33–6.

cerned with what is common to all the representatives of a genre, and
therefore applies an external measure to the individual pericope . . . .
Exclusive attention to the *Gattung* may actually obscure the thought
and intention of the writer or speaker . . . . It is the creative synthesis of
the particular formulation of the pericope with the content that makes
it the distinctive composition that it is.[345]

Muilenburg's criticism is not intended to dismiss form criticism,[346]
but to stress the point that there are other features in the text which
lie beyond the competence of the *Gattungsforscher*. In many texts
we find the literary genre in its pure form, but there are also many
instances where the literary genres are imitated. Therefore we have
to reckon with the fact that

in numerous contexts old literary types and forms are imitated, and,
precisely because they are imitated, they are employed with considerable fluidity, versatility, and, if one may venture the term, artistry. The
upshot of this circumstance is that the circumspect scholar will not
fail to supplement his form-critical analysis with a careful inspection of
the literary unit in its precise and unique formulation. He will not be
completely bound by the traditional elements and motifs of the literary
genre; his task will not be completed until he has taken full account of
the features which lie beyond the spectre of the genre.[347]

It is precisely these points, as formulated by Muilenburg, that are
important for a correct understanding of our text. A strong emphasis
has always been laid on the fact that in each saying a pronouncement
was made upon a certain tribe. This led to the conclusion that there
existed a genre of tribal sayings, functioning independently in the
supposed tribal society of Israel. The fact that the first three sayings
in Genesis 49 clearly function in their biblical setting to justify the
leading position of Judah, as is generally recognized by scholars, did
not lead to the question whether these "tribal sayings" were probably imitated in order to serve the view and aim of the writer or
speaker. Neither was the function of the literary context considered
in combination with the genre of these sayings, nor did form critics
give a clear definition of the genre of the literary context in which
these sayings were placed.[348] Finally, as the quotation from Kebekus

---

[345]Muilenburg, "Form Criticism and Beyond", 5.

[346]Muilenburg, "Form Criticism and Beyond", 4, denies such an idea explicitly.

[347]Muilenburg, "Form Criticism and Beyond", 7.

[348]Or we should have to consider "collection of tribal sayings" as a genre definition for Genesis 49 (cf. Coats, *Genesis*, 307–11). The designation "Jacob Death
Report" for Genesis 47–50 (*op.cit.*, 300) is too general to be of any use. In any
case the exact setting is not given.

demonstrates,[349] in order to isolate Genesis 49 from its context a *form-critical* observation is applied as the sole, but nevertheless, absolute and decisive argument in a *literary-critical* debate. This seems an intolerable entanglement of arguments and is even contradicted by the form-critical observations of Gunkel, and later Muilenburg, presented here above.

1.4.4 Other Genre Definitions for Genesis 49

The definition of Genesis 49 as a collection of "tribal sayings" does not not reflect a scholarly concensus, as we have seen. Genesis 49 is also described as a "testament" or as a "blessing". An extensive description of a "testament" was given by von Nordheim,[350] whose approach was strongly influenced by the fact that he developed the criteria for the genre on the basis of late wisdom texts. This may be concluded, for example, from the fact that he describes the middle section of a testament as the instructive part.[351]

It must be questioned, however, whether his approach is correct in this respect. As was noted above, he does not consider the Greek term διαθήκη to be appropriate to denote this genre, because the word is derived from Greek jurisprudence, whereas on the other hand the generally accepted term "testament" is correct in his view.[352] However, he ignores the fact that the term "testament" itself is also derived from the world of jurisprudence (testament < Lat. *testamentum* < *testor* "to witness; declare as witness"[353]) and has the same meaning as διαθήκη. For that reason it seems to be more appropriate to take into consideration a development from the "legal" testament into the "wisdom" testament as a literary genre.[354]

In fact the legal "testament" existed already before the name was applied to this kind of document. The existence of the official testaments (including witnesses) is attested abundantly in the literature of

---

[349]Quoted above, p. 3, with n. 8.

[350]For von Nordheim's point of view, cf. pp. 46–51 above.

[351]Von Nordheim, *Lehre der Alten I*, 230: "Nicht alle Formelemente müssen in jedem Testament erscheinen, obwohl einige in jedem Fall unverzichtbar sind: ... eine Rede, die auf die Todessituation bezug nimmt und in derem Zentrum Anweisungen für die Hinterbliebenen, den Nachfolger, das Volk stehen."

[352]Von Nordheim, *Lehre der Alten I*, 241–2.

[353]H. Georges, K.E. Georges, *Ausführliches Lateinisch-Deutsches Handwörterbuch*, Hannover [13]1972, 3087, 3091.

[354]Cf. J. Bergman, "Gedanken zum Thema 'Lehre — Testament — Grab — Name'", in: E. Hornung, O. Keel (Hrsg.), *Studien zu altägyptischen Lebenslehren* (OBO, 28), Freiburg, Göttingen 1979, 73–104, 76–85. On διαθήκη, cf. J. Behm, G. Quell, "διατίθημι, διαθήκη", *ThWNT*, Bd. II, 105–37; H. Hegermann, διαθήκη, ης, ἡ *diathēkē* Bund, Testament", *EWNT*, Bd. I, 718–25.

Emar,[355] but also in Egypt. Here we can find the so-called Imet-per
(*Jmjt-pr*), "what-is-in-the-house"(-document) where the appearance
of witnesses is usual.[356] As this kind of document is already attested
at the beginning of the Fourth Dynasty (2575–2465 BCE[357]), it can
be concluded that the development of "legal" testament" into a "wisdom" testament took place rather early, because the first sapiential
testament, namely the *Instruction for Merikare*, is attested later on
in the First Intermediate period (2134–2040 BCE[358]). Here Bergman's
description of the basic functions of a testament help to elucidate the
matter:

1. The testament has a twofold determination of time: in order to
   be valid it has to be written during the lifetime of the testator;
   on the other hand, the decisions are only valid after the death
   of the testator.

2. The testament establishes a close relation between a person who
   is designated by name, and one or more persons, who are the
   beneficiaries.

3. The testament is determined by the will to preserve the estate
   for the future; so the testament is an instrument of continuation
   of the tradition and, in case of a critical situation of the change
   of generations, to ensure the succession according the will of the
   older generation.[359]

These basic functions are not restricted to legal testaments, but are
also attested in sapiential testaments, the so-called "instructions"
as Bergman has demonstrated.[360] The "wisdom" of the instruction
may be regarded as the "spiritual" estate of the deceased, whereas
such a testament could contain both elements, "material" as well as
"sapiential" aspects. This might be derived from one of the most
ancient "testaments", the *Instruction for Merikare*, which is usually
described as a wisdom text giving instruction, but which, in fact, is
a (pseudepigraphic) testament concerning the deceased king's estate

---

[355]See D. Arnaud, *Recherches au Pays d'Aštata. Emar VI: Textes suménens
et accadiens*, Tm. 3: Texte (ERC.S, 18), Paris 1986, 11-3, 23–4, 41–7, 49–52, 55,
77–9, 117–9, 136–9, 188–208, 214–5. Cf. furthermore section 3.5 below.

[356]K.B. Gödecken, "Imet-per", *LdÄ*, Bd. III, 141–5.

[357]Dating according to E. Hornung, *Grundzüge der ägyptische Geschichte*
(Grundzüge, 3), Darmstadt ²1978, 18–29, 160.

[358]Dating acc. Hornung, *Grundzüge der ägyptische Geschichte*, 41–6, 161.

[359]Bergman, "Gedanken", 77.

[360]Bergman, "Gedanken", 77–9.

— the Egyptian empire.[361] It is therefore not necessary to consider the Greek philosophers' testaments as the forerunners of the Israelite testamental literature,[362] but they can be considered as examples of the same development in Greek literature as in Egyptian, and for that reason they may be both illustrative for the development of the genre.

The definition of Pehlke for Genesis 49 as a blessing cannot be rejected, but it's acceptance depends on how one wants to define "blessing" in this context. There are also curses contained in this "blessing" (Gen. 49:3–4, 5–6), as Pehlke readily admits; so the word "blessing" is not used in a completely positive sense. בְּרָכָה "blessing" might be considered here as a summarizing term for the whole pericope, which could also be applied to the "negative blessings" on Reuben, Simeon and Levi. A "negative blessing", parallel to a curse, does occur in Jer. 20:14:

Cursed be the day on which I was born,	אָרוּר הַיּוֹם אֲשֶׁר יֻלַּדְתִּי בּוֹ
The day when my mother bore me, let it not be	יוֹם אֲשֶׁר־יְלָדַתְנִי אִמִּי
blessed!	אַל־יְהִי בָרוּךְ

The close antithetical relationship of the roots ברך and ארר might justify indeed the designation in Gen. 49:28 as בְּרָכָה "blessing". This is strengthened by the fact that a "blessing is not merely the expression of a wish", but that "it actually provokes and initiates what it announces, similar in this to the prophetic oracle",[363] pointing in the direction of a strong, changeless word. However, the meaning which is usually attached to the English term "blessing" and its Western European cognates, does apparently not correspond completely with Hebr. בְּרָכָה,[364] and further discussion seems to be imperative.

The designation of Genesis 49 as a "blessing" comes closest to the understanding of others that this chapter should be considered a testament. Since the words of the patriarch are his last wish in which he laid down his final will concerning his succession by means

[361] M. Lichtheim, *Ancient Egyptian Literature*, vol. I: *The Old and Middle Kingdoms*, Berkeley (CA) 1973, 97; G. Posener, "Lehre für Merikare", *LdÄ*, Bd. III, 986–9; L.G. Perdue, "The Testament of David and Egyptian Royal Instructions", in: W.W. Hallo *et al.* (eds.), *Scripture in Context*, vol. II, Winona Lake (IN) 1983, 79–96, esp. 85–7; von Nordheim, *Lehre der Alten II*, 133.

[362] As was stated already by von Nordheim — though on other grounds; cf. his *Lehre der Alten I*, 241–2.

[363] K. van der Toorn, "From Patriarchs to Prophets. A Reappraisal of Charismatic Leadership in Ancient Israel", *JNSL* 13 (1987) 191–218, 200. Compare also J. Scharbert, "ברך, בְּרָכָה", *ThWAT*, Bd. I, 808–41, 836; Westermann, *Genesis 12–36*, 541–2.

[364] Scharbert, "ברך, בְּרָכָה", 835.

of a בְּרָכָה, it appears that "blessing" and "testament" are in this connection more related than is usually assumed.[365] However, since a "blessing" as such is not restricted to a deathbed scene or solely concerned with matters of succession and last will,[366] the definition of the chapter as a blessing might be too general and a more precise definition like "deathbed blessing" (which preserves the meaning of the "last will") might be more appropriate.

1.4.5   The Provenance of Genesis 49

1.4.5.1   Linguistic Arguments

Although the sayings in Genesis 49 are considered old, morphological peculiarities in the text are quite rare: consisting only of the "archaic" suffix ה–; the paragogic vowel י–, indicating the construct state in the singular; and the primitive fem. ending ת–. We will now consider to what extent these peculiarities might be regarded as reliable indications of "archaic" language, or whether these features can be found in other periods also.

Regarding the suffix ה–, it is remarkable that in 49:11, where this suffix is found, it alternates with וֹ–, which might be due to a deliberate variation in spelling (sometimes called "an archaizing tendency"), comparable to the use of suffix מוֹ– next to ם–.[367] Yet, it is very questionable if the suffix is indeed an indication of "archaic" language, because inscriptions show that the suffix ה– was used right down to the Exile. Moreover, several cases of these spellings are still found in Jeremiah.[368] For that reason the suffix ה– is by no means an exclusive feature of "archaic" texts.

The primitive fem. ending ת– (found in פֹּרָת, 49:22), is also found in Jer. 48:36: יִתְרַת "saving".[369] The ending occurs also in Moabite,

---

[365] Cf. also Genesis 27, where the "blessing" is strongly connected to the succession of the patriarch whereas this "blessing" is at the same time a kind of "testament", which cannot be changed.

[366] Scharbert, "בְּרָכָה, ברך", 837.

[367] See Robertson, *Linguistic Evidence*, 68; Sanders, *Provenance of Deuteronomy 32*, 50, n. 263.

J. Barr, *The Variable Spellings of the Hebrew Bible* (The Schweich Lectures, 1986), Oxford 1989, 203–4, doubts the deliberate use of archaic language and the possibility of "archaizing", because there is mostly no system in the use of "archaic" language; "archaisms" are not concentrated in "late" books, but sporadically scattered over a wide variety of texts; and they are usually a minority in them all.

[368] Jer. 2:21; 8:6; 15:10. See Barr, *Variable Spellings of the Hebrew Bible*, 208.

[369] Also in Isa. 12:2, which appears, however, to be an expression borrowed from Exod. 15:2 and is text-critically uncertain as well.

Phoenician and Ammonite inscriptions and in Samaritan ostraca.[370] In Samaritan ostraca and in the Mesha inscription we find the word שׁת "year"[371] instead of BHebr. שָׁנָה.[372] It appears therefore, as in the case of the suffix ה‑, that this trait is not confined to an early stage of biblical Hebrew.

The י‑ indicating the construct state of a singular noun is throughout the Hebrew Bible affixed to אָב and אָח in the construct state.[373] Also in singular nouns which have a possessive suffix, these suffixes follow after י‑, which is the old case ending (even though it functions now as a connecting vowel[374]). This might be due to the fact that this morpheme is indeed a remnant of archaic language and is in these cases a kind of "frozen" ending. But they might also indicate that this morpheme was used during a considerable period of the biblical era and for that reason left its traces in the biblical books. Robertson fails to consider this possibility, which is a substantial weakness in his argumentation. In some cases, where the morpheme seems to occur in "late texts", he even denies that we are dealing with a word in the construct state, like רַבָּתִי עָם (Lam. 1:1aB; see also 1:1bB.cA), considering the word to be in apposition, functioning as an adjective.[375] J. Renkema, however, recently argued that this interpretation of Lam. 1:1aB is unlikely and that רַבָּתִי עָם has to be rendered as "lady of the people".[376] If his interpretation is correct, it would demonstrate that the י‑ was used even during the Exile, thus showing that this grammatical feature was not restricted to archaic language. In our view the examples of the "archaic" morphological features in Genesis 49 and in later texts clearly demonstrate that these traits are not indisputably old and consequently unsuitable to date our text.

The argument of specific vocabulary is sometimes brought forward by scholars, but there are some serious objections against this suggestion. First, the use of *hapax legomenon* like סוּתֹה "his vesture" (v. 8) as an indication of the age of the poem is weak. It is a simple *argumentum e silentio* because no other usages are attested. Secondly, there are several *hapax legomena* in, for example, Deutero- and Trito-Isaiah where the meaning could be solved or clarified with the help of

---

[370] JM, §89m, n. 1.

[371] KAI 183:1; 184:1; 185:1; 186:1; 187:1.

[372] The Samaritan ostraca are discussed by Young, *Diversity in Pre-Exilic Hebrew*, 29, where he suggests that the spelling might be due to Phoenician influence.

[373] *HAL*, 1, 28; JM, §93l.

[374] Lett, §26e.

[375] Robertson, *Linguistic Evidence*, 73.

[376] J. Renkema, *Klaagliederen vertaald en verklaard* (COT), Kampen 1993, 68–9. See also Waltke, O'Connor, *IBHS*, 128, n. 1.

Ugaritic.[377] Moreover, Ugaritic lexicography itself has taken considerable advantage of Arabic,[378] even though the latter is in its oldest attestations at least a thousand years younger than the Hebrew Bible and more than two thousand years younger than the Ugaritic texts.

With regard to certain peculiarities being regarded as dialectic remnants, more specific "northernisms", Rendsburg based his argument on the geographical location of the tribes (excluding Judah, Simeon and Benjamin as the southern tribes) but especially on Gevirtz's suggestion that in some cases we might be dealing with "northernisms".[379] The location of the tribe concerned is, however, no argument for the geographical provenance of the saying, because the saying — especially where we are dealing with "tribal sayings" — would most likely have originated in the circles of another tribe. Regarding Gevirtz's suggestions: in two cases (49:3, 20) he proposed an emendation, which may be false, rendering his arguments unreliable.[380] The third case concerns the so-called double-plural construct chain, found in 49:23, and accepted by Rendsburg quite uncritically as a characteristic grammatical trait.[381] Gevirtz suggests in his study of the Asher-saying[382] (basing himself on a previously unpublished study of syntax and style in Judges 5, and Phoenician, Ugaritic and Amarna correspondence coming from Byblos[383]) that such a construct "need not to be identified as a feature of Late Biblical Hebrew only, but of northern Hebrew".[384] However, when the article referred to is studied, one may discover that — next to Judges 5 and some late examples (among others 1 Chr. 14:1) — he offers examples from Deut. 9:2; 1 Kgs. 9:27; and Ps. 123:2; and refers (in a footnote) to other examples in Isa. 2:19; 26:6; 45:3; 51:9; Ezek. 19:11; Pss. 29:2; 59:3; 95:4.[385] These examples suggest a Southern use as well as a Northern

---

[377] Cf. Isa. 41:10, 23, שתע and Ug. *ṯt'* "to fear"; Isa. 51:22, קבּעת and Ug. *qb't* "cup"; Isa. 66:11, מצץ and Ug. *mṣṣ* "to suck". See for many more examples of "late" *hapax legomena*, H.R. Cohen, *Biblical Hapax Legomena in the Light of Akkadian and Ugaritic* (SBL.DS, 37), Missoula (MA) 1978, 107–43.

[378] J.C. de Moor, "Ugaritic Lexicography", in: P. Fronzaroli (ed.), *Studies on Semitic Lexicography*, Firenze 1973, 61–102, 76. As an example, see: F. Renfroe, *Arabic-Ugaritic Lexical Studies* (ALASP, 5), Münster 1992.

[379] Rendsburg, *Northern Origin of Selected Psalms*, 11, n. 49.

[380] For more details, and if the emendations are correct, cf. our discussion *ad loc.*

[381] Rendsburg, *Northern Origin of Selected Psalms*, 35–6, with n. 2.

[382] Gevirtz, "Asher", 160, with n. 20.

[383] The study Gevirtz referred to, was at that time forthcoming, and has now appeared and was already referred to above: Gevirtz, "Of Syntax and Style", 28–9.

[384] Gevirtz, "Asher", 160.

[385] Gevirtz, "Of Syntax and Style", 29, with n. 19. Note that from the Psalms re-

one, and therefore the construct in question cannot be regarded as a "northernism". In our view Gevirtz's and Rendsburg's suppositions lack hard evidence and are based on presuppositions only.

Young's explanation of the suffix ה- as a possible Aram. −*ēh* in Gen. 49:11 could be correct. However, there are some objections to this, while another explanation is possible. There is no evidence that the suffix represented −*ēh*, where it is generally possible to follow the development of the suffixes in the different dialects. For that reason the other explanation he suggested — that the suffix reflects the pronunciation *ahū*[386] — seems more likely. Yet, beside the possibility of a variation in pronunciation we might consider a simple orthographic variation, which is also found in 49:1, where the root קרא I, "to call" is used next to the variant spelling of קרה, namely קרא II, "to happen". If the assumption that the spelling in the Hebrew Bible was revised is correct,[387] this variant spelling could be explained in several ways. The writer of the text used the variable spellings and a later editor preserved the variable spellings; or, the writer used indeed the archaic spellings for all the suffixes in verse 11, but the editor revised the spelling but some of the suffixes "escaped a revision";[388] or, the editor simply liked variation[389] and preserved some of the archaic spellings. In fact all of these suggestions are possible, next to Young' proposal, but none of them can be argued decisively.

1.4.5.2 Historical Arguments

The argumentation concerning the historical background of Genesis 49 is — as we have stated before — strongly connected with the idea of the tribal sayings. If the genre-definition of these sayings proves to be incorrect, it will at the same time affect the historical reconstructions based on this theory. However, on the other hand, historical identification of events laying behind a certain saying could be helpful to offer a chronological stratification of the text. If, for example, the identification of Issachar with the *massu*-people were correct and, on the other hand, we could prove the connection of certain parts of the Judah-saying with the period of David and Solomon, this would be extremely helpful in dating the different layers in the text. Yet it

---

ferred to, Rendsburg only discusses Ps. 29:2 as a psalm which probably originated in the north.

[386]Young, *Diversity in Pre-Exilic Hebrew*, 105.

[387]See *e.g.* Barr, *Variable Spellings in the Hebrew Bible* , 208; Young, *Diversity in Pre-Exilic Hebrew*, 105.

[388]Barr, *Variable Spellings in the Hebrew Bible* , 208.

[389]Barr, *Variable Spellings in the Hebrew Bible*, 194.

appears that this possibility of identification is problematic.

When we take into consideration the idiom applied to Issachar (Hebr. מַס) and the word applied to people living in the district of Issachar (Akk. *massu*), the correspondence is striking indeed. It might be asked, however, if this justifies Donner's identification that "the Issacharites were ... *massu*-people under the control of the Canaanite city-states in the plain of Jezreel and Beth-Shan".[390] This is possible, of course, but the Issachar-saying could also concern a later period. In 1 Kgs. 9:15, for example, it is told that Solomon levied forced labour (מַס) for the walls of *inter alii* Megiddo. In that region there were still at that time people who were subject to a king raising מַס. Consequently the saying could concern this period just as well. Or, it could be that the people who were called Issacharites were descendants from the *massu*-people in the Amarna period, and that יִשָּׂשׂכָר "Issachar", has been an old nickname for this group. The saying as such could thus have been composed in a later period, taking into consideration the history of the group concerned.

With regard to the Judah-saying it has to be asked if Zobel's description of the evolutionary development of the saying is compelling. The contents of verses 10–12 also point to the leadership of Judah and it might be asked why this could not concern a later period than the one Zobel assumed. Some scholars suggested particularly for verse 10 (as they did for verse 8) the period of David,[391] and this is quite feasible. Moreover, his dating of the text is based on the classical *crux interpretum* שִׁילֹה, which he renders with "Shiloh". If this rendering should prove to be incorrect, then his historical reconstruction would collapse as well.

1.4.5.3   Conclusion

For the moment we may conclude that the different arguments put forward to establish the date of Genesis 49 are quite weak. The form-critical classification of Genesis 49 has been questioned, which raises also some doubts about the dating of the text on the basis of such a classification. Arguments on the basis of the language of the text — morphology and lexicography — are questionable too, because it has been shown that those features — or comparable ones — did occur until the Exile. Historically, the dating of some of the sayings might be possible in other periods too and an early dating is by no means compelling.

---

[390]Donner, "The Blessing of Issachar", 59, see also p. 61.

[391]Cf. *e.g.* J. Lindblom, "The Political Background of the Shiloh Oracle", in: *Congress Volume, Copenhagen 1953* (SVT, 1), Leiden 1953, 78–87.

1.4.6 Recapitulation

1. Though the classification of "tribal saying" is almost generally accepted for the different sayings in Genesis 49, the independence of some smaller sayings is questionable. In several cases it is hard to envisage a situation where these sayings would have functioned independently.

2. Of crucial importance in form criticism is the definition of the *Sitz im Leben* for the genre. With regard to the genre of the tribal saying it has been shown that a satisfactory *Sitz im Leben* has not yet been defined for these sayings. Since such a definition is crucial, the reference to the genre "tribal saying" has to be handled cautiously.

3. The differentiation between oral and written tradition is artificial and similarly the supposed independent existence of the different genres in oral tradition. This distinction is based on an evolutionary view of the development of literature. Comparison with the texts of the *Umwelt* has shown that this view is no longer tenable.

4. The arguments in favour of the form-critical classification of the sayings in Genesis 49 as "tribal sayings" and in addition the isolation of this chapter from its context have never been systematically questioned. Other definitions than "tribal saying" are possible and have to be considered more seriously than has happened until now.

5. The isolation of Genesis 49 from its literary context is mainly based on a form-critical classification instead of on literary-critical arguments. Theoretically this is impossible because form criticism is not a method developed for this application, but, moreover, offers itself the arguments against such a literary-critical adoption.

1.5 Desiderata

From the foregoing chapter it can be deduced that Genesis 49 is a rather complicated text in many respects. The points that deserve further attention in the following chapters will be listed briefly.

1. A correct translation of Genesis 49 appears to be a *conditio sine qua non* for our understanding of this text. This translation will

be performed with the help of all available data from cognate languages, but semantics will take priority over etymologizing.

2. Since Genesis 49 is written in verse, the text's structure will be analysed. This analysis may give a first impression of the text's coherency (or the absence of it), which might be helpful for the diachronic analysis.

3. Since the definition of the sayings in Genesis 49 as "tribal sayings" has raised serious questions, despite the fact that this definition is widely accepted, it is necessary to go through the (ancient) Near Eastern literature to discover whether this genre is attested in extra-biblical texts. The findings of this search will be discussed in view of the pressing question about the correct genre of Genesis 49 and the diachronic analysis of the Deathbed Episode (Gen. 47:29–49:33).

4. Before performing a diachronical analysis the text will be interpreted at a synchronic level within the complete Deathbed Episode in order to describe the meaning of the text especially with regard to its possible ideological (theological and political) purpose. It may be expected that such an interpretation will also reveal certain inconsistencies in the text (if any), indicating a diachronic development.

5. A diachronic analysis of the complete Deathbed Episode will need to be performed in order to be able to describe the possible growth of the text to its present shape.

6. The results of the foregoing analysis will be interpreted with regard to the history of Israel: does the text in its (possible) different stages reflect certain historical situations? The answer to this question will have to take into account recent research into Israel's early history.

Chapter 2

Genesis 49: The Text, Translation and Structure

2.1 Introduction

2.1.1 Translation

In this chapter a translation of the text of Genesis 49 will be presented with an analysis of its poetic structure. Many attempts to translate some smaller part(s) of Genesis 49 have been made[1] whereas an integral translation is found only occasionally.[2] In this study a careful

---

[1]It is impossible to offer a complete bibliography of all published studies here, so we refer only to studies which offer a translation for one complete saying or more than one problem in Genesis 49: C. Armerding, "The Last Words of Jacob: Genesis 49", *BS* 112 (1955) 320–329; G. Beer, "Zur Geschichte und Beurteilung des Schöpfungsberichtes Gen 1,1–2,4a nebst einem Exkurs über Gen 49,8–12 und 22–26", in: K. Marti (Hrsg.), *Beiträge zur alttestamentliche Wissenschaft: Fs K. Budde* (BZAW, 34), Giessen 1920, 20–30; A. Caquot, "Le parole sur Juda dans le testament lyrique de Jacob (Genèse 49,8–12)", *Sem* 26 (1976) 5–32; idem, "Ben Porat (Genèse 49,22)", *Sem* 30 (1980) 43–56; idem, "Siméon et Lévi sont frères ... (Genèse 49,5)", in: J. Doré *et al.* (eds.), *De la Tôrah au Messie: Etudes ... H. Cazelles*, Paris 1981, 113–119; C.M. Carmichael, "Some Sayings in Genesis 49", *JBL* 88 (1969) 435–444; J. Coppens, "La bénédiction de Jacob: son cadre historique à la lumière des parallèles ougaritiques", in: *Volume du Congres Strassbourgh 1956* (SVT, 4), Leiden 1957, 97–115; J.A. Emerton, "Some Difficult Words in Genesis 49", in: P.R. Ackroyd, B. Lindars (eds.), *Words and Meanings: Essays ... D.W. Thomas*, London 1968, 81–93; S. Gevirtz, "The Reprimand of Reuben", *JNES* 30 (1971) 87–98; idem, "The Issachar Oracle in the Testament of Jacob", *ErIs* 12 (1975) 104–112; idem, "Of Patriarchs and Puns: Joseph at the Fountain, Jacob at the Ford", *HUCA* 46 (1975) 33–54; idem, "Simeon and Levi in 'The Blessing of Jacob' (Gen. 49:5–7)", *HUCA* 52 (1981) 93–128; idem, "Adumbrations of Dan in Jacob's Blessing on Judah", *ZAW* 93 (1981) 21–37; idem, "Naphtali in 'The Blessing of Jacob'", *JBL* 103 (1984) 513–521; idem, "Asher in the Blessing of Jacob (Genesis XLIX 20)", *VT* 37 (1987) 154–163; E.M. Good, "The 'Blessing' on Judah, Gen 49,8–12", *JBL* 82 (1963) 427–432; J.D. Heck, "Issachar: Slave or Freeman? (Gen 49:14–15)", *JETS* 29 (1986) 385–396; R. Martin-Achard, "A propos de la Bénédiction de Juda en Genèse 49,8–12(10)", in: J. Doré *et al.* (eds.), *De la Tôrah au Messie: Études ... H. Cazelles*, Paris 1981, 121–134; J. Sanmartín, "Problemas de textologia en las 'bendiciones' de Moises (Dt 33) y de Jacob (Gn 49)", in: V. Collado, E. Zurro (eds.), *El misterio de la Palabra: Homenaje ... D.L. Alonso Schökel*, Madrid 1983, 75–96; H. Seebaß, "Die Stammessprüche Gen. 49,3–27", *ZAW* 96 (1984) 333–350; E. Testa, "La formazione letteraria della benedizione di Giacobbe (Gen. 49,2–27)", *SBF LA* 23 (1973) 167–205; B. Vawter, "The Canaanite Background of Genesis 49", *CBQ* 17 (1955) 1–17.

[2]In addition to the commentaries on Genesis, where of course a translation of the text is given, integral translations can be found in: E. Burrows, *The Oracles of Jacob and Balaam* (The Bellarmine Series, III), London 1938, 8–43; Kittel,

rendering of the Hebrew text is indispensable in order to achieve a correct understanding of the possible historical context of Genesis 49.

Previous attempts to render the text of Genesis 49 have been marked by historical as well as etymological considerations. In many cases these diachronic considerations have led to the exclusion of certain solutions. Starting from a diachronic point of view, it is difficult to avoid such pitfalls. As a methodological starting point for the translation of Genesis 49, the text and its parts will therefore be approached at a synchronic level in a twofold sense: linguistic and literary.[3] These two approaches are closely related, but not identical. Linguistically, each word will be approached as part of the context from which they derive their meaning. In other words, in the translation semantics will be given prevalence over etymologizing.[4] But giving priority to semantics does not exclude a diachronic approach, because working on a synchronic level often involves the use of data found with the help of the diachronic approach.[5] The literary synchronic approach,[6] is used in this chapter as an auxiliary discipline to linguistics. The text is studied as a final product,[7] a *Letztgestalt*, where words have their meaning within the context of that final product, disregarding a possible diachronic process. Every word in the text received its po-

---

Stammessprüche Israels, 7–41; Cross, Freedman, *Ancient Yahwistic Poetry*, 69–93; Zobel, *SuG*, 4–26; Pehlke, *Genesis 49:1-28*, 108–243.

[3]Cf. J. Barr, "The Synchronic, the Diachronic and the Historical: A Triangular Relationship", in: J.C. de Moor (ed.), *Synchronic or Diachronic: A Debate on Method in Old Testament Exegesis* (OTS, 34), Leiden 1995, 1–14; cf. also J. Hoftijzer, "Holistic or Compositional Approach? Linguistic Remarks to the Problem", in: *ibid.*, 98–114, 98, with n. 2.

[4]Cf. J. Barr, *The Semantics of Biblical Language*, Oxford 1961; idem, *Comparative Philology and the Text of the Old Testament*, Oxford 1968; idem, "Hebrew Lexicography", in: P. Fronzaroli (ed.), *Studies on Semitic Lexicography* (QuSem, 2), Firenze 1973, 103–26; idem, "Etymology and the Old Testament", in: A.S. van der Woude (ed.), *Language and Meaning: Studies in Hebrew and Biblical Exegesis* (OTS, 19), Leiden 1974, 1–28. Furthermore: J.C. de Moor, "Ugaritic Lexicography", in: Fronzaroli, *op.cit.*, 61–102; J.C. Greenfield, "Etymological Semantics", *ZAH* 6 (1993) 26–37; B. Albrektson, "Response to J.C. Greenfield", *ZAH* 6 (1993) 38–43; J.A. Emerton, "Comparative Semitic Philology and Hebrew Lexicography", in: J.A. Emerton (ed.), *Congress Volume, Cambridge 1995* (SVT, 66), Leiden 1997, 1–24.

[5]Cf. Barr, "The Synchronic, the Diachronic and the Historical", 6–8.

[6]According to Barr, "The Synchronic, the Diachronic and the Historical", 9, the use of this term here is in fact "metaphorical", because the word is used in a different meaning than was meant, namely excluding every possible diachronic aspect of the text.

[7]Cf. Hoftijzer, "Holistic or Compositional Approach", 98, n. 2, who defines this approach as follows: "the approach which aims at the definition and description of the structure of a text in the final form it is handed down to us".

sition within the present context because of its (supposed) meaning, and thus the author or editor thought these words to have a meaning in the "Blessing".[8] Of course the possibility exists that later editors did not understand certain archaic words when they used these texts some centuries after their original composition.[9] However, as a principal point of departure it seems appropriate to approach the text as a coherent whole, to which a possible editor may have attributed some meaning. The contrary approach — a pious transmission of unintelligible text — can only be considered if it is evident from the tradition that they handed the text down without even understanding it. Accordingly, the problems related to the diachronic level (literary- and form-critical) will be discussed in Chapter Six.

2.1.1.1 Rendering the Verbal Tenses

The rendering of Hebrew verbal forms into languages other than Semitic poses great problems to the translator. One of the main problems involved is the fact that the *qatal* (and *w-qataltí* and *w-qatálti*) and *yiqtol* (and *wayyiqtol* and *w^e yiqtol*) conjugations, the so-called perfect and imperfect, are both able to express events in the past, present and future, whereas they can also express a certain aspect.[10]

---

[8] Cf. Hoftijzer, "Holistic or Compositional Approach", 99–100: "... the text presupposes a certain author/redactor who, writing/composing it, consciously or unconsciously had a certain readership in mind. ... Moreover the text usually belongs to a certain type of medium and will be influenced to a greater or lesser degree by the rules valid for that medium in the time and *Umwelt* in which it was written."

[9] For this possibility concerning *e.g.* Gen. 49; Deut. 33, cf. J.C. de Moor, "Poetic Fragments in Deuteronomy and the Deuteronomistic History", in: F. García Martínez *et al.* (eds.), *Studies in Deuteronomy ... C.J. Labuschagne* (SVT, 53), Leiden 1994, 183–96, 194–6. Use of unknown words in certain traditions is known from Mesopotamia but also from later Jewish tradition. For the transmission of texts in Mesopotamia, even when not completely understood, see J.C. de Moor, "Schriftsystemen en talen in de wereld van de bijbel: Schriftsystemen en niet-bijbelse talen", *BijbH*, dl. I, 113–72, 119–20; cf. J. Krecher, "Sumerische Literatur", in: W. Röllig (Hrsg.), *Neues Handbuch der Literaturwissenschaft: Altorientalische Literaturen*, Wiesbaden 1978, 101–50, 106–13.

[10] Almost every grammar will offer a discussion of the problems involved. The discussion of the rendering of the different forms in this chapter is mainly based on the following grammars: Lett, §§72–3; Waltke, O'Connor, *IBHS*, §§29–34; JM, §§111–22. For a survey of the problems involved, cf. next to these grammars: R. Meyer, "Das hebräische Verbalsystem im Lichte der Gegenwartigen Forschung", in: *Congress Volume: Oxford 1959* (SVT, 7), Leiden 1960, 309–17; J.P. Lettinga, *De 'Tale Kanaäns': Enkele beschouwingen over het Bijbels Hebreeuws*, Groningen 1971, 11–19; T.N.D. Mettinger, "The Hebrew Verb System: A Survey of Recent Research", *ASTI* 9 (1973) 64–84; J. Hoftijzer, *Verbale vragen*, Leiden 1974. For a thorough survey of the history of interpretation until 1954, see: L. McFall, *The*

These verbal forms also trouble us in Genesis 49 and for that reason in
each section on a saying we will present a short paragraph on the rendering of the verbal tenses. Following the usage in recent grammars,
we will use the terms "perfect" and "imperfect" in the paragraphs
dealing with the translation of the text, whenever this cannot lead
to misunderstanding. In the paragraphs where we are dealing especially with the rendering of the verbal tenses, however, we will avoid
these ambiguous terms and use the more neutral terms *qatal*, *yiqtol*,
etcetera.[11]

2.1.2   Analysis of the Poetic Structure

It is a commonly accepted fact that the wording of the sayings in Genesis 49 is in verse. To describe the structure of the text in its present
form we will analyse the strophic structure according to the method
applied by the so-called "Kampen School".[12] To determine the structural units we move from the smaller segments, like the "colon"[13] and
"poetic verse",[14] to the higher structural units, such as "strophes",[15]
"canticles"[16] and "(sub-)cantos".[17]

Enigma of the Hebrew Verbal System: Solutions from Ewald to the Present Day
(HTIBS, 2), Sheffield 1982.

[11]Cf. *e.g.* JM, §111b; though this grammar uses "future" instead of "imperfect".

[12]This method is extensively described in other studies, in particular: M.C.A.
Korpel — J.C. de Moor, "Fundamentals of Ugaritic and Hebrew Poetry," *UF*
18 (1986) 173-212 (= *SABCP*, 1-61); W. van der Meer, *Oude woorden worden
nieuw: De opbouw van het boek Joël*, Kampen 1989, 35-39; W.T. Koopmans,
Joshua 24 as Poetic Narrative (JSOTS, 93), Sheffield 1990, 165-180; J. Kim, *The
Structure of the Samson Cycle*, Kampen 1993, 118-127; and recently P. Sanders,
The Provenance of Deuteronomy 32 (OTS, 37), Leiden 1996, 99-102; 111-9; 132-
6. Cf. also P. van der Lugt, *Rhetorical Criticism & the Poetry of the Book of Job*
(OTS, 32), Leiden 1995, 31-49; 460-503.

[13]Unit of one to five feet (= a stressed segment), which could be recited or sung
in one breath. Cf. Korpel, De Moor, "Fundamentals", 4-14; Kim, *Samson Cycle*,
123-4; Sanders, *The Provenance of Deuteronomy 32*, 100-1.

[14]A unit consisting of one or more cola. Korpel, De Moor, "Fundamentals", 14-
29; Kim, *Samson Cycle*, 124. Usually the term "verse" or "verse-line" is used, but
"poetic verse" is more appropriate; see Sanders, *The Provenance of Deuteronomy
32*, 101.

[15]Usually considered the most important basic structural unit, comprising one
or more poetic verses. Cf. Korpel, De Moor, "Fundamentals", 29-38; Kim, *Samson
Cycle*, 124-5.

[16]A group of one or more strophes, belonging together; sometimes called
"stanza". Cf. Korpel, De Moor, "Fundamentals", 38-44; Kim, *Samson Cycle*,
125-7.

[17]The next higher structures are the sub-canto and canto. These units are
formed by one or more canticles, which belong together because of external parallelism and thematic progression. See Korpel, De Moor, "Fundamentals", 44-53;
Kim, *Samson Cycle*, 127.

In order to enable a controlled discussion of the analysis, formal criteria are used to discern the several units. The cola are determined with the help of the Masoretic accentuation, which, although itself a medieval tradition, certainly reflects ancient traditions.[18] The strophes are delimited with the help of "transition markers", distinguishing stylistic features such as emphatic particles, verbal forms and constructions (dividing elements)[19] and external parallelism between the poetic verses (binding element). Finally, larger units like canticles and (sub-)cantos are sometimes defined with the help of the *setumah* and *petuḥah*.[20] With the help of these formal criteria the text is structured and divided over the several structuring elements.

The use of *setumah* and *petuḥah* in Genesis 49 is of special importance since most sayings are discerned from each other by means of a *setumah* or *petuḥah* and form in this way a reliable help, in addition to the contents.[21] However, the delimitation of the first canticle in Genesis 49 is somewhat problematic. The saying on Reuben (Gen. 49:3–4) is not marked in front (before verse 3) with a *setumah* or *petuḥah*, but a *setumah* is placed before verse 1. Of course this can be interpreted as the marker for this pericope, as is usually done, since at least verse 1 is mostly considered to be prose. Another solution might be suggested nevertheless, namely the possibility that the introduction to the "Blessing" is part of the poem and perhaps written in verse too — be it so called "narrative poetry".[22] Since in other contexts introduction and direct oration are part of the same strophe[23]

---

[18]Cf. Sanders, *The Provenance of Deuteronomy 32*, 111–9. The system and syntax of these accents, including their "dividing" force, is described there, and in the context of the present study there is nothing to add to it. It is encouraging that the syntax of the Masoretic accents as described by Sanders, corresponds in all respects to the system that was described in my unpublished paper he referred to (*op.cit.*, 112, n. 47): R. de Hoop, *Kamper School en Masoretische Accenten: Evaluatie en Perspectief* (unpublished paper Theol. Univ. Kampen), Kampen 1993. This paper will be published in the near future, entitled "Hebrew Colometry and Masoretic Accents".

[19]Cf. Sanders, *The Provenance of Deuteronomy 32*, 261–3.

[20]Cf. J.M. Oesch, *Petucha und Setuma: Untersuchungen zu einer überlieferten Gliederung im hebräischen Text des Alten Testaments* (OBO, 27), Freiburg, Göttingen 1979. Cf. further also p. 93, n. 77 below.

[21]Only the transition from verses 17–19 is not marked in the BHS by these signs; cf. however the discussion *ad.loc.*

[22]Cf. the fact that for example Joshua 24 is also marked with a *petuḥah* before verse 1; see Koopmans, *Joshua 24*, 180, 190.

[23]The combination of introduction to direct speech and the beginning of a long speech is found in Josh. 23:2; cf. W.T. Koopmans, "The Poetic Prose of Joshua 23", in: *SABCP*, 83–118, 90, 93; at the end of a composition, it is found in Josh. 24:27–8; cf. Koopmans, *Joshua 24*, 189, 224 (str. II.v.3). For the frequent appear-

it is worthwhile considering the possibility that the introduction to Genesis 49 is part of the composition. For that reason Gen. 49:1–2 will be discussed in combination with the first saying.

2.2   Opening with Reuben (Gen. 49:1–4)

I.A.i.1   ס

And Jacob called to his sons (1A)	וַיִּקְרָא יַעֲקֹב אֶל־בָּנָיו
and said: "Gather that I may tell you (1B)	וַיֹּאמֶר הֵאָסְפוּ וְאַגִּידָה לָכֶם
what will happen to you in days hereafter. (1C)	אֵת אֲשֶׁר־יִקְרָא אֶתְכֶם בְּאַחֲרִית הַיָּמִים
Assemble and listen, sons of Jacob, (2A)	הִקָּבְצוּ וְשִׁמְעוּ בְּנֵי יַעֲקֹב
and listen to Israel your father. (2B)	וְשִׁמְעוּ אֶל־יִשְׂרָאֵל אֲבִיכֶם

I.A.i.2

Reuben, my firstborn are you, (3A)	רְאוּבֵן בְּכֹרִי אַתָּה
my might and the firstling of my strength, (3B)	כֹּחִי וְרֵאשִׁית אוֹנִי
superior in tallness, and superior in power; (3C)	יֶתֶר שְׂאֵת וְיֶתֶר עָז
deceptive like water — you shall have no superiority, (4A)	פַּחַז כַּמַּיִם אַל־תּוֹתַר
for you went up to your father's bed, (4B)	כִּי עָלִיתָ מִשְׁכְּבֵי אָבִיךָ
then you defiled the concubine's couch." (4C)	אָז חִלַּלְתָּ יְצוּעִי עָלָה פ

2.2.1   Translation

The opening of the "Testament of Jacob" does not pose any serious problem to the translator. The only expression causing some trouble is the expression בְּאַחֲרִית הַיָּמִים, "the days hereafter" in v. 1C, but this is more a matter of interpretation rather than translation. These words are considered by some scholars as a designation for the far future, the "end of days", as in the case of Dan. 10:14, and because of this late usage and interpretation of the expression, it is judged to be a later addition in other texts in the Hebrew Bible.[24] But this

---

ance of narration and direct oration throughout a whole text, cf. Kim, *Samson Cycle*, *passim.* See also R. de Hoop, "The Testament of David: A Response to W.T. Koopmans", *VT* 45 (1995) 270–9, 271–2; Sanders, *Provenance of Deuteronomy 32*, 203–204.

[24]Westermann, *Genesis 37–50*, 252–3. Gunkel, *Genesis*, 478, considers the word as a "Terminus der prophetischen Eschatologie: 'die letzte Zukunft, die der Prophet überhaupt schaut' (Dillmann)". Gunkel's quotation of Dillmann is somewhat misleading, because, according to Dillmann, this interpretation would not be at its right place ("die letzte Zukunft hat hier ... keine Stelle"); cf. Dillmann, *Die Genesis*, 436. Nevertheless, the assumption that this expression could be a later interpolation in the text is, according to Gunkel, "tendenziös und ganz unbeweisbar". Cf. also F.M. Cross, D.N. Freedman, *Studies in Ancient Yahwistic Poetry* (SBL DS 21), Missoula (MA) 1975, 72, 77, n. 1, considering v. 1C as a

expression could easily be meant to refer to the near future, the "days hereafter", (cf. esp. Num. 24:14; and even more so the clearly exilic texts Deut. 4:30; 31:29[25]), as both the Akkadian *ana aḥrāt ūmī* "in the future" and the Ugaritic *uḥryt* "future" suggest.[26]

In the introductory saying Reuben is addressed as the firstborn of Jacob (see Gen. 29:32). Speiser translated the pronoun אַתָּה in v. 3A appositional ("You, Reuben"), since predicative ("Reuben, you are") would be banal in this context.[27] However, because of the sharp contrast between v. 3 and v. 4, caused by the predicative use in v. 3A we should consider אַתָּה to be predicative.[28] The first-born was considered to be the strongest son according to the culture of the ancient world.[29]

V. 3C presents some translation problems. This is not the case with the construction itself: a substantive in the construct state expressing an adjectival thought can be found in biblical prose and poetry: מִבְחַר קְבָרֵינוּ, "the choicest of our graves", meaning "our best graves" (Gen. 23:6); רֹעַ מַעַלְלֵיכֶם, "the evil of your doings", meaning "your evil deeds" (Isa. 1:16).[30]

---

later addition to the poem.

[25] For the exilic dating of these texts, cf. Sanders, *The Provenance of Deuteronomy 32*, 348–52.

[26] Cf. H. Seebaß, "אַחֲרִית", *ThWAT*, Bd. I, 224–8. Further *HAL*, 35; *Ges*[18], 42; *DCH*, vol. I, 200–1; Dillmann, *Die Genesis*, 436; König, *Die Genesis*, 749–50; Skinner, *Genesis*, 513; Jacob, *Das erste Buch*, 891; Aalders, *Genesis, dl. III*, 194; Speiser, *Genesis*, 364; Van Selms, *Genesis, dl. II*, 273; Von Rad, *Erste Buch Mose*, 347; Sarna, *Genesis*, 332; Wenham, *Genesis 16–50*, 470; Th.C. Vriezen, "Prophecy and Eschatology", *Congress Volume, Copenhagen 1953* (SVT, 1), Leiden 1953, 203, with n. 2, 223–4; H. Kosmala, "At the End of the Days", *ASTI* 2 (1963), 27–37; E. Lipiński, "באחרית הימים dans les textes préexiliques", *VT* 20 (1970) 445–450. For Ugarit cf. J.C. de Moor, P. van der Lugt, "The Spectre of Pan–Ugaritism," *BiOr* 31 (1974) 3–26, 8.

[27] Speiser, *Genesis*, 364. Similarly S. Gevirtz, "The Reprimand of Reuben", *JNES* 30 (1971) 87–98, 88, who suggests reading אַתָּה as the subject of the following clause.

[28] Similarly: RSV; NBG; KBS; FB; LuthV; Buber; Dillmann, *Die Genesis*, 437; Gunkel, *Genesis*, 479; König, *Die Genesis*, 750–1; Skinner, *Genesis*, 513; Jacob, *Das erste Buch*, 892; Aalders, *Genesis, dl. III*, 189; Von Rad, *Erste Buch Mose*, 344; Westermann, *Genesis 37–50*, 253; Sarna, *Genesis*, 332; Wenham, *Genesis 16–50*, 454, 471.

[29] Cf. De Moor, *ARTU*, 140, n. 41.

F.I. Andersen, *The Hebrew Verbless Clause in the Pentateuch*, Nashville 1970, 37, 67, suggests we read here a broken construct chain, together with the first word of the next colon: רְאוּבֵן בְּכֹרִי אַתָּה כֹּחִי "Reuben, you are the fistborn of my strength". The usual rendering makes good sense however, therefore this suggestion is not followed here. Cf. JM, §129a, with n. 4 for Andersen's suggestion.

[30] Cf. GK §128.r. RSV offers in both texts a translation which is very close to

The usual translation of שְׂאֵת as "dignity, majesty" or the like is doubtful according to Gevirtz,[31] since the word-pair שְׂאֵת ‖ עַז is not known from elsewhere.[32] Therefore Gevirtz suggested we read יֶתֶר רְשָׁאוּת, "pre-eminent in authority" instead of יֶתֶר שְׂאֵת because of the possibility the ר was a "shared consonant" and in Phoen. the word-pair rš't ‖ 'z is found.[33] Although his proposal is not impossible,[34] there are several objections to it. Gevirtz did not discuss the possibility of simply accepting the usual meaning "dignity" for שְׂאֵת, and so omitted to give a valid reason for introducing a conjecture in the first place. The meaning of "elevation" > "dignity" for שְׂאֵת cannot be disputed.[35] Secondly, the use of "shared consonants" is not a common practice, as he suggests,[36] but is rather exceptional,[37] indeed,

---

the Hebrew text; cf. also StV.

[31] The word is used with this particular meaning in Hab. 1:7; Ps. 62:5; Job 13:11; 31:23. Cf. also Job 41:17 (E.T. 41:25); Gen. 4:7. Gevirtz, "Reprimand of Reuben", 89, n. 10, also refers to some commentaries, and to KBL, 913, which suggests only Hab. 1:7 and Job 31:23 have this meaning and the former could be deleted; the other two texts had to be emended. *HAL*, 1211, only takes an emendation for Ps. 62:5 into consideration. For the proposal to change the text, cf. H.-J. Kraus, *Psalmen: 2.Teilband, Psalmen 60–150* (BKAT, XV/2), Neukirchen-Vluyn ⁵1978, 595; M. Dahood, *Psalms II: 51–100; Introduction, Translation and Notes* (AB, 17), Garden City, N.Y. 1968, 92. According to J. Ridderbos, *De Psalmen vertaald en verklaard, II: Psalm 42–106* (COT), Kampen 1958, 149; N.A. van Uchelen, *Psalmen deel II: 41–80* (PredOT), Nijkerk 1977, 152, 155, this meaning does fit the text and a conjecture is therefore unnecessary.

[32] See however Deut. 28:50, where the root of both words is used in parallel; cf. further the analysis of the poetic structure below.

[33] Gevirtz, "Reprimand of Reuben", 90–1, with n. 27; cf. also *HAL*, 1206, listed s.v. רְשָׁאוּת.

[34] His suggestion was accepted by Y. Avishur, "Word-Pairs Common to Phoenician and Biblical Hebrew", *UF* 7 (1975) 13–47, 23. For the possibility of "shared consonants", cf. I.O. Lehman, "A Forgotten Principle of Biblical Textual Criticism Rediscovered", *JNES* 26 (1967) 93–101; W.G.E. Watson, "Shared Consonants in Northwest Semitic", *Bib* 50 (1969) 525–533. The possibility that shared consonants do occur was also accepted by A.R. Millard, "'Scriptio Continua' in Early Hebrew: Ancient Practice or Modern Surmise", *JSS* 15 (1970) 15, n. 4.

[35] שְׂאֵת < נשא is probably a substantivated infinitive; so *inter alia HAL*, 1213.

[36] Gevirtz, "Reprimand of Reuben", 90.

[37] An example is probably found in the Mesha Inscription. At line 8/9 we can find *wyš/bh*. Some scholars suggest to read the text as follows *wyšb.bh.kmš.bymy*, "And Chemosh lived there during my days". The *b* would have been left out because of lack of space at the end of line 8. This reading corresponds with the text at the start of line 8: *wyšb.bnh.ymh*, "And he (Omri) lived there during his days". A similar reading would be necessary in line 33. Cf. *inter alia* S. Segert, "Die Sprache der moabitischen Königsinschrift", *ArOr* 29 (1961) 210, 226; F.I. Andersen, "Moabite Syntax", *Or* 35 (1966) 99. Others suggest to read, however, *wyšbh.kmš.bymy*, "but Chemosh restored it in my days"; cf. *DISO*, 293; *DNWSI*,

the idea of this practice might even be false.[38] Thirdly, the absence of a word-pair in other texts, does not exclude the possibility that the words are paralleled in the text in question.[39] Finally, the sibilant of the two words differs, (namely שְׂאֵת and רְשָׁאוּת), which renders a connection with Phoen. *rš't* and mHebr. רְשׁוּת problematical.[40] We retain here the reading of MT and accept the usual translation.

In the following verse Reuben is rebuked for having laid with his father's concubine (Gen. 35:22). The first word of this rebuke is a *crux interpretum*. פַּחַז is a *hapax legómenon*, followed by a comparison כַּמַּיִם, "like water", that does not solve the riddle of the preceding פַּחַז immediately. The root פחז occurs in three other instances, Judg. 9:4; Jer. 23:32; Zeph. 3:4 and is used as a verb or as a substantive.[41] In these texts פחז is paired with רֵיק, "empty, futile"[42] שֶׁקֶר, "infidelity, lie"[43] and בגד, "to act unfaithfully".[44] Based on the use of פחז in these texts, it seems plausible פחז has a meaning like "deceptive, false". Combined with the use of these parallel words like בגד in connection with water(-sources) in Job 6:15:

My brothers are treacherous like a wadi, (15aA)   אַחַי בָּגְדוּ כְמוֹ־נָחַל

as freshets that pass away, (15aB)   כַּאֲפִיק נְחָלִים יַעֲבֹרוּ

and also Jer. 15:18:[45]

Truly, You are to me a deceitful brook, (18bA)   הָיוֹ תִהְיֶה לִי כְּמוֹ אַכְזָב

water, that is not trustworthy. (18bB)   מַיִם לֹא נֶאֱמָנוּ

the conclusion seems justified to interpret the root פחז as meaning "to deceive, act untrustworthy".[46] Reuben is thus described as a very

---

part 2, 1115; P.D. Miller, "A Note on the Mesaʿ Inscription", *Or* 38 (1969) 461–464; J.C. de Moor, "Narrative Poetry in Canaan", *UF* 20 (1988) 149–71, 151, n. 14; K.A.D. Smelik, *Converting the Past: Studies in Moabite and Israelite Historiography* (OTS, 28), Leiden 1993, 64, n. 10.

[38] Millard, " 'Scriptio Continua' in Early Hebrew", 14.

[39] Cf. also Pehlke, *Genesis 49:1–28*, 123, n. 4; and Gordon, *UT*, 131, n. 2.

[40] Cf. also *HAL*, 1206.

[41] *HAL*, 872–3. Reference is also made to Sir. 4:30; 8:2; 19:2; 41:17 (text uncertain). See n. 46 below for more details.

[42] *HAL*, 1146; RSV: "reckless"; R.G. Boling, *Judges: Introduction, Translation and Commentary* (AB, 6A), Garden City, N.Y. 1975, 171: "empty".

[43] *HAL*, 1519–20; M.A. Klopfenstein, "שׁקר", *THAT*, Bd. II, 1010–1019.

[44] *HAL*, 104; Ges¹⁸, 123–4; *DBHE*, 85; M.A. Klopfenstein, "בגד", *THAT*, Bd. I, 261–3.; cf. S. Erlandsson, "בגד", *ThWAT*, Bd. I, 508: "Das Verb drückt das unbeständige Verhältnis des Menschen zu einer bestehenden festen Ordnung aus und kann mit "treulos handeln" übersetzt werden."

[45] Cf. also Isa. 33:16; 58:11.

[46] For a more elaborated discussion of פחז, meaning "to deceive, act untrustworthy" in Gen. 49:4; Judg. 9:4; Jer. 23:32; Zeph. 3:4; Sir. 4:30; 19:2; 23:4; 41:17;

untrustworthy person, who, like water that can appear and disappear at any moment in the Near East, is someone on whom one cannot build.

Finally, at the end of v. 4C we have a problem with עלה. The Vrs took this word as a pf. 2.masc.sg. of the verb עלה (probably inspired by the verb עלה in the previous colon) and rendered with "when you went up (my bed)".[47] If עלה is to be derived from the verb עלה it must be a pf. 3.masc.sg. and not a pf. 2.masc.sg. Because the 3.p. does not fit in the context, the translators apparently choose for their rendering the 2.p. — a solution frequently followed by modern scholars.[48] Another proposal was offered by Dahood,[49] Gevirtz[50] and Reider,[51] who suggest we interpret יצועי as a construct-form, hence יְצוּעֵי and deriving עלה not from the root עלה, "to go up" but from a different root. Dahood suggested we read יְצוּעַ יַעֲלָה, rendering יַעֲלָה, "female mountain-goat, doe" in a metaphorical sense: "concubine" (with reference to Prov. 5:19, where the word is used for "wife").[52] However, this metaphor is not very likely in this context, despite the fact that animal-names are used throughout the chapter as metaphors.[53] Gevirtz interpreted עלה as a part.act.fem. of the root עול, "suckle", referring to Arab. ǧawala, "to suckle" used for women and animals, who often when nursing were already pregnant again. The root is used some five times in the Hebrew Bible for animals, but not for humans.[54] Gevirtz supposes Bilhah,

---

4Q 177:1–4:7; 184.1:2, 13, 15; see R. de Hoop, "The Meaning of *pḥz* in Classical Hebrew", *ZAH* 10 (1997) 16–26.

[47] עלה מִשְׁכָּב is an euphemism for sexual intercourse. Cf. M. Dijkstra, J.C. de Moor, "Problematical Passages in the Legend of Aqhâtu", *UF* 7 (1975) 171–215, 179; also J.W. Wevers, *Notes on the Greek Text of Genesis* (SCSt, 35), Atlanta (GA) 1993, 821–2. For עלה, see also Gen. 31:10; for מִשְׁכָּב, Gen. 19:32, 35; 30:15; 35:22; 39:12, 14; Deut. 29:30 (Q and the critical *apparatus* of BHS); 2 Sam. 13:5, 11, 14 and Isa. 57:7–8; Ezek. 23:8, 17. For some more examples, cf. *HAL*, 1378; M. Dahood, T. Penar, "Ugaritic-Hebrew Parallel Pairs (I)", *RSP*, vol. I, 294, 350.

[48] Skinner, *Genesis*, 514; Speiser, *Genesis*, 364; Zobel, *SuG*, 6, n. 4; Westermann, *Genesis 37–50*, 254; Alter, *Genesis*, 293. Others still prefer the reading of MT and render as an interogative clause "my bed he mounted"; cf. Sarna, *Genesis*, 333; Wenham, *Genesis 16–50*, 454, 457 (nn.), 472.

[49] M. Dahood, "Hebrew-Ugaritic Lexicography, III", *Bib* 46 (1965) 311–32, 319; J.M. Sasson, "Flora, Fauna and Minerals", *RSP*, vol. I, 420–1.

[50] Gevirtz, "Reprimand of Reuben", 98.

[51] J. Reider, "Etymological Studies in Biblical Hebrew", *VT* 4 (1954) 276.

[52] Dahood, "Hebrew-Ugaritic Lexicography, III", 319. Approved by Hamilton, *The Book of Genesis*, 645–6, n. 8.

[53] *Pace* Dahood, "Hebrew-Ugaritic Lexicography, III", 319.

[54] Gevirtz, "Reprimand of Reuben", 97; although he suspects עָלוֹת in Gen. 33:13 to refer to women. In our opinion, however, this is not very likely in the context of Gen. 33:13; which does not exclude the possibility that the root עול was used

the wife of Jacob, was pregnant again (with Naphtali) when she was still nursing Dan.[55] This suggestion is highly speculative and for this reason his solution remains questionable. In addition, the solution offered by Reider — also based on Arab. — is much more plausible. He refers to Arab. *'lh*, "concubine",[56] which would fit very well in our context and offers a very neat parallelism with the preceding colon. Moreover, Reider refers to the fact that this phrase is used, including the plural יְצוּעִי, "couches of ... ", in 1 Chr. 5:1, though עָלָה is replaced by אָבִיו, "his father" there. Perhaps the author of 1 Chr. 5:1 understood our text in a way similar to Reider.[57]

2.2.1.1　Rendering the Verbal Tenses

In Gen. 49:1A the pericope starts with a *wayyiqtol* form,[58] וַיִּקְרָא followed in the second colon by a similar form וַיֹּאמֶר translated as "and (he) called ... and said ...". The use of a *wayyiqtol* at the (relative) beginning of a narrative is not unusual and occurs even at the beginning of a book.[59] Whereas a free[60] *yiqtol*, like יִקְרָא "(it) will happen" (Gen. 49:1C) mainly refers to the future,[61] the free *wayyiqtol* mostly refers to the past.[62] These verbs are part of the narrative framework of the blessing and as such rendered in the past tense.

All the following verbs from verse 1B up to verse 27 are part of the direct speech of the dying patriarch. This becomes clear in the next verb in verse 1B, הֵאָסְפוּ "gather" and the verbs in verse 2AB, הִקָּבְצוּ וְשִׁמְעוּ "assemble and listen". These three verbs are imperative forms and therefore do not cause any trouble; even the final imperative וְשִׁמְעוּ with a juxtaposing וְ is a direct imperative.[63] In verse 1B the

---

for women. Derivatives of עול were also used for children; cf. *HAL*, 753–4. See also Ug. *'l* "to suck" and *'l* "child", cf. *CARTU*, 159.

[55] Gevirtz, "Reprimand of Reuben", 98.

[56] Cf. Lane, *Arabic–English Lexicon*, Book I, Part 6, 2124.

[57] His suggestion was accepted by several modern translations: NEB; KBS.

[58] As already noted, we will use these terms derived from the paradigma of the Hebr. verb. In the discussion of the different forms it will become clear that the European names, especially those for the *wayyiqtol* and *w-qatalti*, like "(im)perfect consecutive" (*e.g.* Lett, §72de) or "inverted forms" (*e.g.*, JM, §117a), are all based on only one main aspect of this form and are for that reason biased. Cf. M.S. Smith, *The Origins and Development of the Waw-Consecutive: Northwest Semitic Evidence from Ugarit to Qumran* (HSS, 39), Atlanta (Ga) 1991, 14–5.

[59] Lett, §72d1; JM, §118c, with n. 2; Lett¹⁰ 77d1.

[60] The term "free" for *e.g.* *yiqtol*, *wayyiqtol* is used to indicate that the verbal form is "freestanding", and as such not related to, or specified by another preceding verbal form.

[61] Lett, §72c; JM, §113b; Lett¹⁰, §77c.

[62] Lett, §72d1; JM, §118c–o; Lett¹⁰, 77d1.

[63] JM, §§114a; 116a.

imperative הֵאָסְפוּ is followed by a cohortative with ו: וְאַגִּידָה, expressing the notion of purpose and making the cohortative in this way into an indirect cohortative: "that I may tell you".[64] For יִקְרָא "(it) will happen" in verse 1C, we noted that a free *yiqtol* usually refers to the future. Of course other solutions are possible, like the present or even the past,[65] but by means of the expression בְּאַחֲרִית הַיָּמִים this *yiqtol* is explicitly placed in the future. In fact these words give the interpretative framework for all the other verbal forms in the following verses since they interpret the following words as predictions of the tribes' future.[66]

For the opening phrase of the saying on Reuben in Gen. 49:3 a nominal clause is used as in most of the other sayings.[67] This nominal clause is rendered here as a present, being the primary meaning of nominal phrases since they describe a certain state.[68] Verse 4A contains a jussive with the imperative negation אַל expressing the negative will of the speaker: אַל־תּוֹתַר "you shall have no superiority" in a negative optative clause.[69] This prohibition is followed by two explicative clauses introduced by כִּי in verse 4B. These clauses have verbs in the *qatal*: עָלִיתָ "you went up" and חִלַּלְתָּ "you defiled". Both are referring to events in the past (Gen. 35:22) and thus rendered according to this main usage of the *qatal* form of active verbs.[70]

2.2.2　Analysis of the Poetic Structure

2.2.2.1　The Strophic Structure

Strophe I.A.i.1

The opening strophe (Gen. 49:1–2) of the Testament is partly recognized as poetry by scholars: at least v. 2 was considered as such

---

[64] JM, §116a,b.

[65] JM, §113c–h.

[66] Cf. in this way C. Westermann, "Micha 5, 1–3", in: G. Eichholz (Hrsg.), *Herr, tue meine Lippen auf: Eine Predigthilfe*, Bd. 5: *Die alttestamentlichen Perikopen*, Wuppertal-Barmen ²1961, 54–9, 54–5. Contrast *e.g.* Holzinger, *Genesis*, 256, who excludes this possibility: "1ᵇ bezeichnet das folgende Stück als Weissagung, was es nicht ist; es ist auch kein Segen, sondern eine Revue der Stämme mit Lob und Tadel auf Grund von thatsächlichen Verhältnissen, mit Wünschen und Drohungen." Though it could be that Holzinger is correct, but such arguments should be considered only after the text has been carefully translated, not before. With regard to the priority of the synchronical approach, see above, section 2.1.1.

[67] Simeon and Levi (49:5AB); Judah (8aA, 9aA); Issachar (14A); Asher (20A); Naphtali (21A); Joseph (22a); Benjamin (27A).

[68] JM, §112a.

[69] JM, §§114g,i; 163a.

[70] Lett, §72b3.5; JM, §112b.

because of its parallelism,[71] while others included the preceding v. 1b
(our v. 1BC) as part of the direct speech in verse,[72] or even v. 1 as
a whole.[73] Although v. 1 is not built up on the traditional *parallelismus membrorum*, the use of many word-pairs in this poetic verse and
its strong connection with the following poetic verse[74] — as will be
demonstrated below — clearly marks this opening strophe as narrative poetry.[75] The Masoretic accents seem to favour here a division of
verse 1 into a unicolon, delimited by the *athnaḥ*, [2], and a bicolon,
delimited in the first colon by *zaqeph parvum*, [5], and in the second
by the *silluq*, [1]. Since this division would result in contra-indicative
markers of separation in the middle of the strophe (introduction to the
direct oration; imperative; cohortative), and because introductions to
direct speech are mostly part of the same poetic verse, as is also normally recognized by the Masoretes, we take v. 1 as a tricolon.[76]

Accents: [8]–2(?) | [10]–5 | [8]–1 ‖ [8]–2 | [8]–1.

Sep.↑: *petuḥah*;[77] tricolon; introduction to direct speech וַיֹּאמֶר; repet-

---

[71]Dillmann, *Die Genesis*, 436; Gunkel, *Genesis*, 478–9; König, *Die Genesis*,
749–50; Skinner, *Genesis*, 513; Speiser, *Genesis*, 361; Van Selms, *Genesis, dl. II*,
273; Von Rad, *Erste Buch Mose*, 344, 347; Cross, Freedman, *Ancient Yahwistic
Poetry*, 72, 77, n. 1 (who however placed v. 1B in front, thus forming a tricolon
together with v. 2); Westermann, *Genesis 37–50*, 252–3; Sarna, *Genesis*, 332.

[72]Jacob, *Das erste Buch*, 891 (cf. the lay-out); Lipiński, "בְּאַחֲרִית הַיָּמִים", 446–7
(the introduction to the direct speech was omitted as a redactional expansion,
originally Gen. 47:31b preceded 49:1B); Wenham, *Genesis 16–50*, 454, 471, referred to the parallelism of v. 2, but in the layout of the Testament, enclosed also
v. 1B. Cf. also the layout of BHK² and BHS, which seems to suggest v. 1BC, was
read as a tricolon by the editors.

[73]W.G.E. Watson, "The Hebrew Word-Pair *'sp ‖ qbṣ*", *ZAW* 96 (1984) 426–34,
429 (= idem, *Traditional Techniques in Classical Hebrew Verse* [JSOTS, 170],
Sheffield 1994, 301–312, 305); Koopmans, *Joshua 24*, 190, n. 80.

[74]Cf. here Sarna's remark, that the use of the fixed word-pair of Hebrew poetry
אָסַף ‖ קָבַץ is evidence that this introductory sentence is an organic part of the
whole composition (Sarna, *Genesis*, 332). However, in his view verse 1 is in prose,
not in poetry.

[75]Cf. J.C. de Moor, W.G.E. Watson, "General Introduction", *VANEP*, ix–xviii,
esp. p. xi, with nn. 13–20 for literature.

[76]Cf. also Deut. 31:7, where we find a similar phraseology, but a different accentuation; furthermore Josh. 24:24 and Koopmans, *Joshua 24*, 188; Judg. 13:15
and Kim, *Samson Cycle*, 198.

[77]For *petuḥot* and *setumot* as indicators of larger units such as canticles and
cantos in Hebr., see Korpel, De Moor, "Fundamentals", 201 (= *SABCP*, 43);
Koopmans, *Joshua 24*, 160, n. 33. For corresponding formal markers in Ug.
and Phoen., cf. De Moor, "Narrative Poetry in Canaan", 171; J.C. de Moor,
P. Sanders, "An Ugaritic Expiation Ritual and Its Old Testament Parallels", *UF*
23 (1991) 283–300, 283–4; for some Eg. material, cf. J. Assmann, "Die Rubren
in der Überlieferung der Sinuhe-Erzählung", in: M. Görg (Hrsg.), *Fontes atque*

itive parallelism[78] (rep.) ‑כֶם; imper. הֵאָסְפוּ.

Sep.↓: imper. הִקָּבְצוּ; rep. *and* imper. וְשִׁמְעוּ; vocative בְּנֵי יַעֲקֹב.[79]

Int. ||: **1**: הֵאָסְפוּ || וַיִּקְרָא || וַיִּקְרָא‑‑יִקְרָא[81] || וַיֹּאמֶר[80];וְאַגִּידָה || וְאַגִּידָה ... יִשְׂרָאֵל || בְּנֵי יַעֲקֹב || וְשִׁמְעוּ[84] **2**: הִקָּבְצוּ || וְשִׁמְעוּ || אֶתְכֶם[83] לָכֶם || יִקְרָא[82] אֲבִיכֶם.[85]

Pontes: Fs H. Brunner (ÄAT, 5), Wiesbaden 1983, 18–41.

[78] For this term, see M.C.A. Korpel, "The Literary Genre of the Song of the Vineyard", *SABCP*, 124, n. 32.

[79] בֵּן, "son" or בָּנִים, "sons" are used as vocative without particle; cf. JM §137.gc; for the use of several vocatives as markers of separation, cf. Van der Lugt, *SSBHP*, 510–7, where he lists only vocatives as far as it concerns invocations of God (see pp. 517–8): אֲדֹנָי, אֱלֹהִים, יָה and יהוה.

[80] The grouping of these three words occurs very frequently in so-called prose texts, cf. Gen. 27:42; Exod. 19:3; Judg. 9:7 (which is however written in verse, cf. n. 87 below); 2 Kings 6:11; 7:10; 22:10 (|| 2 Chr. 34:18); but also in the poetic text Jer. 4:5 (cf. the fact in this text also הֵאָסְפוּ is used; see W.T.W. Cloete, *Versification and Syntax in Jeremiah 2–25: Syntactical Constraints in Hebrew Colometry* [SBL DS, 117], Atlanta, Ga. 1989, 108, 146–7). The word-pair קרא || אמר is well-known; cf. Koopmans, *Joshua 24*, 425; Kim, *Samson Cycle*, 294, n. 282. The word-pair אמר || נגד, although in Gen. 49:1B in halfline parallelism, occurs also in poetic texts, cf. Kim, *op.cit.*, 194, n. 94. Finally, קרא || נגד occurs in Judg. 14:15; 16:18 (this pair was not listed by Kim, *op.cit.*, 254, 348, although he did list the prepositions with the object-suffixes as parallel); Isa. 44:7; 58:1; see also 1 Sam. 19:7; 2 Sam. 18:25; 2 Kings 7:11; cf. in addition 2 Sam. 14:33; Jer. 33:3; Dan. 2:2.

[81] Although these two words are not parallel as synonyms in this verse, נגד as derivative of the root נגד (*HAL*, 629) is used parallel with קרא II in the prose texts 1 Kings 20:27; 2 Kings 2:15.

[82] The parallelism יִקְרָא || וַיִּקְרָא is based on the homography of the roots of these verbs (*HAL*, 1053, 1055), which results of course in assonance. The parallelism יִקְרָא || הֵאָסְפוּ || וַיִּקְרָא is based on the one hand (קרא I) on the semantic coherence because of the aspect of convenance; cf. Josh. 24:1; Joel 1:14; 2:15–16 (in the latter text קבץ is also used parallel to אסף; see ext. par., below. Cf. also 2 Kings 10:18–19; Zeph. 3:8–9; further W. van der Meer, *Oude woorden worden nieuw: De opbouw van het boek Joël*, Kampen 1989, 54; Koopmans, *Joshua 24*, 190, n. 80). See also n. 80 above. On the other hand, אסף || קרא II is found in so-called prose text: Num. 21:23; 1 Sam. 17:2; 2 Sam. 10:17.

[83] In this parallelism the pronominal suffixes are of course parallel; for the parallelism of ל || את, cf. Josh. 24:3 and Koopmans, *Joshua 24*, 192, who parallels אוֹתוֹ || לוֹ. Cf. further also Josh. 24:4a, in which לְיִצְחָק is parallel to אֶת יַעֲקֹב וְאֶת עֵשָׂו, whereas Koopmans, *op.cit.*, 193, only lists the PNN as parallel.

[84] שׁמע || שׁמע occurs as pair in Isa. 28:23; 41:26; 43:9; 52:7; Zech. 7:13; Ps. 81:9; Qoh. 7:5; as ext. || : Isa. 34:1; 37:4, 9, 17; 48:6; see further Dahood, Penar, "Ugaritic-Hebrew Parallel Pairs", 363 (# 571).

[85] The word-pair בֵּן || אָב is listed by Van der Meer, *Oude Woorden*, 43; De Moor, "Narrative Poetry in Canaan", 156; Koopmans, *Joshua 24*, 194, n. 108. See for יִשְׂרָאֵל || יַעֲקֹב, vv. 7, 24. For a more extensive list, cf. Koopmans, *Joshua 24*, 194, n. 109, 310, n. 230; further Y. Avishur, *Stylistic Studies of Word-Pairs in Biblical and Ancient Semitic Literatures* (AOAT, 210), Neukirchen-Vluyn 1984, 238.

‎... וְאַגִּידָה | (1A) וַיִּקְרָא [86];(2A) הִקָּבְצוּ וְשִׁמְעוּ || (1B) הֵאָסְפוּ וְאַגִּידָה ||.Ext
‎בְּנֵי יַעֲקֹב || (1A) יַעֲקֹב אֶל בְּנָיו [87];(2B) וְשִׁמְעוּ | (2A) וְשִׁמְעוּ || (1B) וַיֹּאמֶר
‎(2A) | אֶל יִשְׂרָאֵל אֲבִיכֶם (2B).[88]

Strophe I.A.i.2

Accents: [10]–5 | [8]–2 | [8]–1 || [10]–5 | [8]–2 | [8]–1.

Sep.↑: vocative and emphatic position ‎רְאוּבֵן; אַתָּה‎; rep. ‎יֶתֶר‎.

---

[86] The parallelism of ‎אסף || קבץ‎ is discussed by Avishur, *Stylistic Studies*, 637, 642; Watson, "Hebrew Word-Pair *'sp* || *qbṣ*", 426–34 (= idem, *Traditional Techniques*, 301–12); Sarna, *Genesis*, 332. For the pair ‎נגד || שמע‎, see Isa. 43:9; 48:3, 5, 6, 14, 20; further Avishur, *op.cit.*, 147, 272, 293, 307. For the pairing of ‎קבץ, שמע‎ and ‎נגד‎, see Isa. 48:14 (see also vv. 13 and 15, where ‎קרא‎ and ‎דבר‎ are used).

[87] These words are paired at several levels: in groups of two, three and even all four roots in one text. Here we will discuss only the pairs which are formed by external parallelism. For ‎קרא || שמע‎ cf. Koopmans, *Joshua 24*, 200, n. 157, who offers an extensive list with occurrences. For ‎שמע || אמר‎ *ibid.*, 223, n. 298. ‎קרא || אמר || שמע‎ is discussed by L. Roersma, "The First-Born of Abraham: An Analysis of the Poetic Structure of Gen. 16", *VANEP*, 228, n. 56. Finally ‎קרא || אמר || נגד || שמע‎ occurs in Judg. 9:7, the "prose" introduction to Jotham's fable, which itself is in verse. De Moor, *RoY*, 182–97 discussed Jotham's fable extensively and defended its strophic structure, in which he included also Judg. 9:7b as poetry (cf. also BHS) and as part of the original fable. We agree with De Moor, *op.cit.*, 182–3 (with nn. 348–50 for literature), the fable does not fit in its present context (Judg. 6–9). But in our view it could be questioned whether the fable functioned originally as a completely independent text, as he assumes, with, among others, F. Crüsemann, *Die Widerstand gegen das Königtum* (WMANT, 49), Neukirchen 1978, 19–32; V. Fritz, "Abimelech und Sichem in Jdc. ix", *VT* 32 (1982) 129–44. V. 7b as an introduction requires for an introductory formula: who says so, when, where, and why? It seems justified to assume that the redaction of the narrative framework in the first instance obscured the polytheistic context of the fable, and that in the present context we find redactional expansions as well as the original context of the story. For the moment, however, it is important to note v. 7 as a whole forms a well composed introductory strophe to the fable, whether originally belonging to it or redactionally added afterwards:

And it was told to Jotham, and he went (7aA)	‎וַיַּגִּדוּ לְיוֹתָם וַיֵּלֶךְ‎
and he stood on the top of Mount Gerizim (7aB)	‎וַיַּעֲמֹד בְּרֹאשׁ הַר־גְּרִזִים‎
and he rose his voice and cried, (7aC)	‎וַיִּשָּׂא קוֹלוֹ וַיִּקְרָא‎
and he said to them: (7bA)	‎וַיֹּאמֶר לָהֶם‎
"Listen to me, o citizens of Shechem, (7bB)	‎שִׁמְעוּ אֵלַי בַּעֲלֵי שְׁכֶם‎
and the gods will listen to you!" (7bC)	‎וְיִשְׁמַע(וּ) אֲלֵיכֶם אֱלֹהִים‎

[88] For the parallelism of the nouns involved, cf. the preceding list of parallelisms; for ‎אֶל || אֶל‎, which are parallel because these two words are identical, cf. Judg. 13:3a and Kim, *Samson Cycle*, 176, with n. 4, although he only mentions the affixed objects to the prepositions, with reference to A. Berlin, *The Dynamics of Biblical Parallelism*, Bloomington (IN) 1985, 33; however, the grammatical parallelism as given by Berlin is determined by the parallel prepositions; cf. further on repetition of identical words, Berlin, *op.cit.*, 69–71.

Sep.↓: vocative פַּחַז כַּמַּיִם; prohibitive; כִּי; אָז;[89] *petuḥah.*

Hlfl.‖: **3C**: וַיֶּתֶר עָז ‖ יֶתֶר שְׂאֵת.[90]

Int. ‖: **3**: שְׂאֵת ‖ וְרֵאשִׁית ‖ עָז;[92] כֹּחִי ‖ עָז;[91] וְרֵאשִׁית אוֹנִי ‖ בְּכֹרִי ‖ -י ‖ -י (2×); כֹּחִי ‖ עָז;[92] שְׂאֵת ‖ וְרֵאשִׁית.[93] יְצוּעִי עָלָה ‖ מִשְׁכְּבֵי אָבִיךָ; חִלַּלְתָּ[95] ‖ עָלִיתָ ‖ עָלִיתָ ‖ חִלַּלְתָּ; חִלַּלְתָּ[94] ‖ תּוֹתַר ‖ עָלִיתָ; חִלַּלְתָּ[94] ‖ פַּחַז **4**:

Ext.‖: רְאוּבֵן (3A) ‖ אָבִיךָ (4B);[96] בְּכֹרִי (3A) ‖ אָבִיךָ (4B);[97] שְׂאֵת (3C) ‖ עָז (4B); —ךָ (4B);[96] יֶתֶר ... יֶתֶר (3C) ‖ תּוֹתַר (4A); אַתָּה (3A) ‖ וַיֶּתֶר (3C) ‖ אָז (4C) (assonance).

---

[89] For this marker of separation, see Van der Lugt, *SSBHP*, 511, and cf. *e.g.* Pss. 19:14; 40:8 with marker upwards; and Pss. 51:21; 69:5; 119:6 with marker downwards. Furthermore Ruth 2:7 and J.C. de Moor, "The Poetry of the Book of Ruth (II)", *Or* 55 (1986) 19.

[90] This colon was considered as an example of half-line parallelism by W.G.E. Watson, "Internal or Half-Line Parallelism in Classical Hebrew Again", *VT* 39 (1989) 44–66, 45, with n. 3 (= IDEM, *Traditional Techniques*, 163, with n. 268). The pair יֶתֶר ‖ יֶתֶר is found in Joel 1:4 as Van der Meer, *Oude Woorden*, 43 shows; further in Jer. 39:9; 52:15; Ezek. 34:18; Qoh. 2:13; and see furthermore Ex. 10:15; 12:10; 29:34; Lev. 10:12; Deut. 28:54; 1 Kings 20:30; 2 Kings 25:11; Jer. 27:19. In spite of the remark of Gevirtz, "Reprimand of Reuben", 89, the parallelism עָז ‖ שְׂאֵת would only occur in this text, we maintain this parallelism, because it is semantically possible that these words are used parallel. Moreover we referred already to Deut. 28:50 (n. 32 above), where the roots of both words were used in parallel:

A nation "of strong face", (50aA)	גּוֹי עַז פָּנִים
who shall not raise its face over the elder (50bA)	אֲשֶׁר לֹא־יִשָּׂא פָנִים לְזָקֵן
nor show favour to the younger. (50bB)	וְנַעַר לֹא יָחֹן

This Masoretic verse forms a very strong poetic unity by means of the word-pairs: פָּנִים ‖ פָּנִים ‖ לְזָקֵן; וְנַעַר ‖ לֹא‖לֹא; יִשָּׂא פָנִים ‖ יָחֹן. The final word-pair, in particular, has an interesting parallel in Num. 6:25–6, see M.C.A. Korpel, "The Poetic Structure of the Priestly Blessing", *JSOT* 45 (1989) 3–13, esp. 6. For this parallel she only refers to Mal. 1:9; in our text we have found a second parallel. For the expression נָשָׂא פָנִים, cf. *HAL*, 684.

[91] See Pss. 78:51; 105:36; and also Deut. 21:17. Cf. too Ezek. 44:30; Hos. 9:10 and 1 Chr. 26:10. For both terms cf. M. Tsevat, "בְּכוֹר", *ThWAT*, Bd. I, 644–50.

[92] See Job 26:2; Prov. 24:5.

[93] See for this word-pair: Isa. 2:2 ‖ Mic. 4:1; cf. Job 20:6.

[94] Cf. Zeph. 3:4 (external parallelism). The parallelism בגד ‖ פחז in this text suggests בגד and חלל are also parallel. This is confirmed in Mal. 2:10–11 (as well as int.- as ext. ‖). This strengthens the proposed meaning of פחז, "to deceive, act untrustworthy".

[95] These verbs do not occur in parallel, except in our text. For an analogous parallelism see Amos 2:7, where הלך, in the sense of "going to a woman" (cf. *HAL*, 237, comparable with בוא), is used in parallel with חלל.

[96] The parallelism is based upon the etymology of the name Reuben, "Behold, a son" (Gen. 29:32; cf. Westermann, *Genesis 12–36*, 577) and אָב. Concerning the word-pair אָב ‖ בֵּן cf. n. 85 above.

[97] For the parallelism of אָב ‖ בְּכוֹר see Jer. 31:9.

2.2.2.2   The Poetic Structure of Canticle I.A.i

Sep.↑: *petuḥah.*
Sep.↓: *petuḥah.*
Ext.‖: בָּנָיו (1A) | בְּנֵי (2A) ‖ בְּכֹרִי (3A);[98] אֲבִיכֶם (2B) ‖ אָבִיךָ (4B).[99]

2.3   Simeon and Levi (Gen. 49:5–7)

I.A.ii.1   פ

Simeon and Levi are brothers, (5A)	שִׁמְעוֹן וְלֵוִי אַחִים
weapons of violence are their knives. (5B)	כְּלֵי חָמָס מְכֵרֹתֵיהֶם[100]
My soul shall not enter in their company, (6aA)	בְּסֹדָם אַל־תָּבֹא נַפְשִׁי
My glory shall not rejoice in their gathering; (6aB)	בִּקְהָלָם אַל־תֵּחַד כְּבֹדִי

I.A.ii.2

For in their anger they slew a man, (6bA)	כִּי בְאַפָּם הָרְגוּ אִישׁ
in their wantonness they hamstrung a bull; (6bB)	וּבִרְצֹנָם עִקְּרוּ־שׁוֹר
cursed be their anger, for it is fierce, (7A)	אָרוּר אַפָּם כִּי עָז
and their wrath, for it is cruel, (7B)	וְעֶבְרָתָם כִּי קָשָׁתָה
I will divide them in Jacob, scatter them in	אֲחַלְּקֵם בְּיַעֲקֹב וַאֲפִיצֵם
Israel (7C) ס	בְּיִשְׂרָאֵל

2.3.1   Translation

The saying concerning Simeon and Levi has two main problems. The first problem is the translation of the word מְכֵרֹתֵיהֶם in verse 5B. The second is much more a matter of interpretation: Does this saying refer to the event narrated in Genesis 34, the revenge for Dinah's rape, or is this relation only ostensible? To solve the former problem — the translation of MT מְכֵרֹתֵיהֶם — the latter has to be answered first. Since we have to solve the problems of the text at a synchronical level, the question is relevant, because the preceding saying on Reuben contains a rebuke for a previous misbehaviour and we might expect the same here. Even if a diachronical distinction was possible in our text, the relation at the synchronical level determines the translation, because

---

[98]For the pair בֵּן ‖ בֵּן see Hos. 2:2 (E.T. 1:11); Joel 4:6, 8; Ps. 62:10; Prov. 10:1, 5; furthermore in ext. ‖ : Josh. 24:9; Isa. 51:18; Ezek. 23:23; Ps. 18:45–6; KTU 1.16:i.25–6; 1.17:i.19–21. Further Dahood, Penar, "Ugaritic-Hebrew Parallel Pairs (I)", 146 (# 112); Van der Meer, *Oude Woorden*, 94–5; Koopmans, *Joshua 24*, 200, n. 156. The parallelism of בֵּן ‖ בְּכֹר is not attested in poetic texts; cf. however the following texts, from which it can be concluded that בֵּן and בְּכֹר can be used in parallelism: Gen. 27:32; 35:23; 36:15; 46:8; Exod. 4:22–23; 1 Sam. 17:13; 2 Sam. 3:2; Job. 1:13, 18. Cf. also KTU 1.15:iii.16, where *bkr* is used in the context of a blessing for sons and daughters.

[99]For אָב ‖ אָב see Koopmans, *Joshua 24*, 191, n. 90 (with literature).

[100]Proposed vocalization: מְכֵרֹתֵיהֶם.

the text gained its position in the context on the basis of its meaning. Therefore we will deal in the present section with the problem to the extent that it concerns the translation/interpretation of the text of verses 5–7.

The main problem concerning the relation between these two texts subdivides into two other problems:

1. The description of the anger of the two brothers in vv. 5–7 does not match the description of the anger in Genesis 34. It is narrated they killed a man — even more than one — but in the story in Genesis 34 we do not find reference to hamstringing a bull. Indeed, the sons of Jacob led the cattle away.[101]

2. According to Nielsen, who compared both texts in his study of the traditions concerning Shechem, there are some more problems. In Genesis 34 Simeon and Levi are true Israelites, revenging an infamous action of Canaanite Shechem. Therefore the tenor is more against Shechem than against Simeon and Levi, contrary to Gen. 49:5–7, which has an anti-Simeonite and -Levite bias. In fact Shechem is not even mentioned in Gen. 49:5–7.[102] Furthermore there are some problems in Genesis 34 itself, the most important of which is the question whether Simeon and Levi originally belonged to the story or whether they were inserted later on during the process of tradition.[103]

In this section we will discuss the first problem mentioned above, the question concerning the bull- and cattle-episodes. Is the text and translation correct in Gen. 49:6b and what is the difference — if there is any — between this verse and Genesis 34?

In Gen. 49:6b Simeon and Levi are accused of having hamstrung a bull. However, in the story of Genesis 34 we do not find any reference

---

[101] E. Nielsen, *Shechem: A Traditio-Historical Investigation*, Copenhagen 1955, 282; W. Krebs, "'... sie haben Stiere gelähmt' (Gen 496)", *ZAW* 78 (1966) 359–61; W. Schottroff, *Der altisraelitische Fluchspruch* (WMANT, 30), Neukirchen-Vluyn 1969, 131–41; H. Seebaß, "Die Stammessprüche Gen. 49,3–27", *ZAW* 96 (1984) 333–50, 340.

[102] Nielsen, *Shechem*, 282.

[103] Cf. S. Lehming, "Zur Überlieferungsgeschichte von Gen 34", *ZAW* 70 (1958) 228–50; A. de Pury, "Genèse xxxiv et l'histoire", *RB* 76 (1969) 5–49; E. Otto, *Jakob in Sichem: Überlieferungsgeschichtliche, archäologische und territorialgeschichtliche Studien zur Entstehungsgeschichte Israels* (BWANT, 110), Stuttgart 1979, 170–5; N. Wyatt, "The Story of Dinah and Shechem", *UF* 22 (1990) 433–58; J.A. Soggin, "Genesis Kapitel 34: Eros und Thanatos", in: A. Lemaire, B. Otzen (eds.), *History and Traditions of Early Israel: Studies Presented to E. Nielsen* (SVT, 50), Leiden 1993, 133–5.

to such an event, a discrepancy which led to different solutions by various scholars. Nevertheless most scholars consider the saying in Gen. 49:5–7 as a rebuke for the event in Genesis 34, even when they have some trouble with the interpretation of v. 6bB.[104] This problem is already reflected in the Vrs (TO, Peš, TN, Vg), which tried to solve the discrepancy between the two texts by interpreting שׁוֹר as שׁוּר "wall" and עִקְּרוּ as "they uprooted".[105] However, with this interpretation the problem remains as frustrating as before, since there is no tradition of "uprooting" a wall. It seems, therefore, plausible to maintain the interpretation by MT and LXX of שׁוֹר, reading the word as שׁוֹר "bull". Jacob and Gevirtz suggested to interpret עִקְּרוּ in line with LHebr. "to tear out, wrench" and in our text the pi'el-form as an intensive: "to despoil, take away".[106] However, in LHebr. עקר denotes "to unfit, mutilate, hamstring, make barren" in connection with animals, but *nowhere* "taking away, despoil" in the sense Jacob and Gevirtz assume.[107] It seems, therefore, appropriate to maintain the usual interpretation of these words עִקְּרוּ שׁוֹר "they hamstrung a bull". If so,

---

[104]Gunkel, *Genesis*, 371 (acc. to G., Gen. 49:5–7 is referring to a third tradition, which existed alongside the two other traditions, J and E, preserved in Genesis 34); König, *Die Genesis*, 641, 753 (does not even discuss this problem!); Skinner, *Genesis*, 422, 516; Aalders, dl. III, 197–8 (A. tries to harmonize the difference: in their furious anger they started to hamstring the bulls, but when their anger abated they considered it preferable to take the cattle with them [34:28]); Van Selms, *Genesis, dl. II*, 274; Westermann, *Genesis 37–50*, 256–7 (similar to Gunkel); Von Rad, *Erste Buch Mose*, 348; Sarna, *Genesis*, 335; Wenham, *Genesis 16–50*, 474–5; E.M. Good, "The 'Blessing' on Judah, Gen 49,8–12", *JBL* 82 (1963) 429 with n. 14; C.M. Carmichael, "Some Sayings in Genesis 49", *JBL* 88 (1969) 435–44, 436; D.W. Young, "A Ghost Word in the Testament of Jacob (Gen 49:5)?", *JBL* 100 (1981) 335–42; E. Blum, *Die Komposition der Vätergeschichte*, 216–23.

[105]*HAL*, 827–8; T. Jansma, "Vijf teksten in de Tora met een dubieuze constructie", *NedThT* 12 (1957–58) 161–79, 168–70. Cf. Qoh. 3:2 (qal); Zeph. 2:4 (niph.). Jacob, *Das erste Buch*, 897, remarks that the use of עקר in Zeph. 2:4 could have been inspired by the word-play with the name of the town עֶקְרוֹן, and therefore should be considered an exception. Although the word-play is obvious, this statement does not seem to be correct, comparing the use of the qal in Qoh. 3:2. In Zeph. 2:4 עקר is used in a metaphorical way: the town will be uprooted like a plant; this kind of metaphor does not seem to fit for a wall. This rendering is also found in Alter, *Genesis*, 294.

[106]Jacob, *Das erste Buch*, 897; S. Gevirtz, "Simeon and Levi in 'The Blessing of Jacob' (Gen. 49:5–7)", *HUCA* 52 (1981) 93–128.

[107]Dalman, *Hw*, 321; Jastrow, *Dictionary*, 1108. It is striking that Jacob and Gevirtz both refer to this interpretation, but both with a different purpose: Jacob, *Das erste Buch*, 897, refers to this meaning, convinced that this rendering fits Gen. 34:28. Gevirtz, "Simeon and Levi", 111, first rejects the connection with Genesis 34 — following Lehming and De Pury (cf. n. 103 above) — and then proposes afterwards a rendering for עקר which would fit very well with Gen. 34:28!

the problem remains whether these words are related to the narrative of Genesis 34, and if so, how? Kimchi referred to Jacob b. Eliezer, who considered שׁוֹר to be a synonym of חֲמוֹר (literally "donkey"), the name of the ruler of Shechem.[108] Dillmann refers in amazement ("sonderbarerweise") to "modern" exegetes, who understand שׁוֹר "bull" as "hero, ruler" in connection with Deut. 33:17, Ps. 68:31.[109] These interpretations are more plausible, however, than both scholars could have known in their days. Vawter and Miller have drawn attention to the fact *ṯr* "bull" in the texts of Ugarit could be used in the sense of "prince".[110] The clearest example is found in KTU 1.15:iv.6–8 (cf. also iv.17–19):

ṣḥ . šb'm [.] *ṯry*	Call my seventy Bulls,
ṯmnym . ẓbyy	my eighty Gazelles,[111]
ṯr . ḫbr . [rb]t	the Bulls of Great Khuburu,
ḫbr [.] *ṯr* [*r*]*t*	of little Khuburu.

The context of this quotation is clear and scholars agree on the interpretation of the "bulls" and "gazelles" as dignitaries from Khuburu.[112] Miller has gathered considerable evidence for this kind of metaphorical language in Ug. as well as Hebr. texts,[113] which makes the example quoted above just an illustration of the wide-spread use of this

---

[108] Cf. Jacob, *Das erste Buch*, 898.

[109] Dillmann, *Die Genesis*, 439. This view was found already with J.G. von Herder, *Vom Geist der Ebraeischen Poesie: Eine Anleitung für die Liebhaber derselben und der ältesten Geschichte des menschlichen Geistes*, Tl. 2/2, Stuttgart 1783 (= Sämmtliche Werke, Tl. 3, Stuttgart 1827), 73, n. h.

[110] B. Vawter, "The Canaanite Background of Genesis 49", *CBQ* 17 (1955) 1–17, 4; P.D. Miller, "Animal Names as Designations in Ugaritic and Hebrew", *UF* 2 (1970) 177–186, 178–9, 185. Cf. also H.L. Ginsberg, "The Legend of King Keret", in *ANET*, 142–9, 148; *CML²*, 92 n. 6; *TOML*, 543 n. x; *MLC*, 644, s.v.; *ARTU*, 208 n. 59. Miller, *art.cit.*, 185 with n. 43, rightly corrects Vawter; *ṯr* does not simply mean a man, but a prince or a noble. Cf. also Carmichael, "Some Sayings", 436–7, who suggests to read "bull" in the sense of "leader", *viz.* Jacob, parallel to "a man", *viz.* Hamor. The rebuke of Simeon and Levi was because they killed a man (Hamor) and hamstrung a bull (Jacob): they made the house of Jacob vulnerable before the Canaanites and Perizzites. (This suggestion was recently repeated in C. Carmichael, "Forbidden Mixtures in Deuteronomy xxii 9–11 and Leviticus xix 19", *VT* 45 (1995) 433–48, 437).

[111] Ginsberg, *ANET*, 146; *CML²*, 92, render respectively "peers" and "dukes" for *ṯry* and "barons" for *ẓbyy*.

[112] Cf. n. 110 above.

[113] Miller, "Animal Names", 177–186. His conclusions are confirmed by various scholars, who refer to fewer examples than he does; cf. once again n. 110 above. Further see also M. Dahood, "*UT* 128 iv 6–7, 17–18 and Isaiah 23:8–9", *Or* 44 (1975) 439–41.

kind of metaphorical language. The quoted text illustrates clearly the metaphorical usage of the term "bull", which makes it possible to understand our text as a similar, metaphorical usage of the "bull"-terminology. "They hamstrung a bull" could be interpreted as "they hamstrung (= killed) a prince", which could form very well a reference to the narrated event in Genesis 34, that Simeon and Levi killed Shechem, the "bull/prince" after he was circumcised. Hamstringing of animals was nothing more than a postponed execution: the animal could not move any more to gather its water and food and thus had to die.[114] Though it may be objected that עקר is a technical term, the root is not only used for animals, but also for plants and, as in Gen. 49:6 in pi'el, even for chariots (רֶכֶב, 2 Sam. 8:4; 1 Chr. 18:4).[115] Finally the fact that אִישׁ "man" as well as שׁוֹר "bull" are both used in the singular seems to point at the fact that the main conflict in Genesis 34 was with the prince Shechem. It seems, therefore, correct to consider this saying as a reference to the event as it is narrated in the present form of Genesis 34.[116]

In view of the proposed solution for the relation of Gen. 49:5–7 to the event of Genesis 34, we now will discuss the problem of the translation of the final word in v. 5b: מְכֵרֹתֵיהֶם. The lemma is vocalized by the Masoretes as a plural noun with a *ma/miqtil*-formation, comparable with nouns like מְאֵרָה, "curse" and מְגֵרָה, "saw",[117] to which a suffix 3.p. masc.plur. was added. This vocalization is specific for ע"ע-roots, and probably for ע"וּ-roots[118] and ל"ה-roots,[119] which suggests the Masoretes understood מכרת as a part.act. of כרר, "to dance", כור, "to dig(?)"[120] or כרה, "to dig".[121] Examples of words, to which a מ-

---

[114]Cf. the Arab. practice of hamstringing a camel on the grave of its master (and other examples), mentioned in Krebs, "'... sie haben Stiere gelähmt'", 359–61.

[115]Cf. *HAL*, 827–8. Cf. also the fact that the derivatives of עקר seem to point at a suggestive pun here: עָקָר is used for "bareness" (*HAL*, 828; see Gen. 11:30; 25:21; 29:31, etc.), which might reflect in the context of the rape and circumcision in Genesis 34 a pun on the killing of Shechem.

[116]Whether the story of Genesis 34 was originally written in its present form, which makes its linking with Gen. 49:5–7 plausible, or whether it is the product of a later expansion, will be discussed below in Chapter Six.

[117]BL, §61.wζ; Pehlke, *Genesis 49:1–28*, 147.

[118]There is contamination of ע"ע-roots by ע"וּ-roots and *vice versa*; cf. JM, §82.o.

[119]There are no examples given of *ma/miqtil*-formations of ל"ה-roots, but their existence cannot be denied.

[120]*HAL*, 549, *s.v.* מְכוֹרָה; there are however no examples of *ma/miqtil*-formations of ע"וּ-roots. For ע"י-roots, compare מְרִיבָה, "strife"; מְלִיצָה, "allusive saying" and מְדִינָה, "province" with the following *ma/miqtil*-formations of the ע"ע-roots מְגִלָּה, "scroll"; מְזִמָּה, "deliberation, plan" and מְחִתָּה, "terror, ruins" (BL, §61.vζ–wζ).

[121]Pehlke, *Genesis 49:1–28*, 147, moves too quickly from these roots to the root

preformative was added without affecting the consonants, are easy to give,[122] therefore it is uncertain whether the vocalization must point to a weak verb, as described above; but the roots כרר and כור (> כרה??) are certainly *possibilities*.

Also the ancient Versions seem to have been troubled by the word: according to the official editions LXX translated ἐξ αἱρέσεως, "to their choice". However, as was indicated by Caquot,[123] mss. A and B read ἐξαιρέσεως[124] "taking out, extraction". Although Caquot simplifies the actual situation a little, mss. A and B *very likely* did read ἐξαιρέσεως instead of ἐξ αἱρέσεως. Because both mss. are so called majuscule-writings, with scriptio continua and without accents and breathings (this is certainly the case with ms. A; in ms. B accents and breathings were added later on[125]), the division into two words can be considered a wrong interpretation by the later correctors and copiers of the text. So the older text of the LXX apparently derived מְכֵרֹת from כרת "to cut", because this version uses ἐξαίρεω some twenty times for the root כרת.[126] Therefore it seems justified to suppose LXX

כרת proposed by Dahood; cf. for this proposal p. 108 below.

[122]See M. Cohen, *"mᵉkērōtēhem* (Genèse XLIX 5)", *VT* 31 (1981) 472–482, 474–5.

[123]A. Caquot, "Siméon et Lévi sont frères ... (Genèse 49,5), in: J. Doré *et al.* (eds.), *De la Tôrah au Messie. Etudes ... H. Cazelles*, Paris 1981, 113–9, 113–4.

[124]We used the following facsimile editions, for ms. A: F.G. Kenyon, *The Codex Alexandrinus in Reduced Photographic Facsimile*, part 1, London 1915; for ms. B: *Bibliorum Sanctorum Graecorum Codex Vaticanus 1209 (Cod. B) denuo phototypice expressus* (Codices e Vaticanis Selecti Phototypice Expressus, IV), pars prima: Testamentum Vetus, tm. I, Milano 1905. For these mss., cf. E. Würthwein, *Der Text des Alten Testaments*, Stuttgart ⁵1988, 84–5; E. Tov, *Textual Criticism of the Hebrew Bible*, Assen 1992, 138–9. To be exact, both mss. read EΞEPE-ΣEΩΣ. Codex B has a corrective AI placed at the left above the second *epsilon*. The interchange αι > ε occurred frequently in mss. after the second century and here it could have been due to the change of sound of the αι; cf. P. Walters, *The Text of the Septuagint: Its Corruptions and their Emendation*, Cambridge 1973, 58–64. It is remarkably that this variant is not mentioned in the Göttingen LXX-edition edited by J.W. Wevers, nor in his *Notes on the Greek Text of Genesis* (SCSt, 35), Atlanta (GA) 1993, 822.

[125]Cf. on this point J. Finegan, *Encountering New Testament Manuscripts*, Grand Rapids (MI) 1974, 128; Würthwein, *Text des Alten Testaments*, 84; K. & B. Aland, *Der Text des Neuen Testaments: Einführung in die wissenschaftliche Ausgaben sowie in Theorie und Praxis der moderne Textkritik*, Stuttgart 1981, 284–6. Cf. also Sanders, *Provenance of Deuteronomy 32*, 121–30, esp. 122–3, with n. 106.

[126]Cf. Hatch-Redpath, 485–6. That LXX derived מְכֵרֹת from כרת was suggested already by J.P. Peters, "Jacob's Blessing", *JBL* 6 (1886) 99–116, 102; similarly now: M. Rösel, "Die Interpretation von Genesis 49 in der Septuaginta", *BN* 79 (1995) 54–70, 59. Important to note is LXX used also ἀφαιρέω (*op.cit.*, 180: nine

read originally ἐξαιρέσεως instead of ἐξ αἱρέσεως.[127]

Also Vg understood מְכֵרֹת as a derivative from כרת, according to Caquot: *bellantia*.[128] Peš read *mn kynhwn* "according to their nature", probably inspired by the word מְכוּרָה (preceded twice by אֶרֶץ) in Ezek. 16:3; 21:35; and 29:14, which could be rendered by "origin".[129] The same reading seems to occur in TO, which also re-interpreted the negative חָמָס: אבדו גבור בארע תותבוחתהון "they performed mighty feats in the land of their sojourning".[130] TN unified both ("to cut" and "origin") traditions in one text: שמעון ולוי אחין תלימין מרי זיינה שנינה

---

times) and καθαιρέω (*op.cit.*, 697: once) for Hebr. כרת. According to Wevers, *Greek Text of Genesis*, 822 it is not certain from which Hebr. root LXX derived מְכֹרֹתֵיהֶם; but he too mentions כרת (next to כרה and כרר), whereas he does not use the reading of mss. A and B. In addition he suggests LXX could have read בחרת instead of כרת, misreading the כ as ב (but apparently also adding a ה to the word); notwithstanding the problems of the correct reading of the text of LXX, this could have been possible, cf. Hatch-Redpath, 36, 484.

According to Vawter, "Canaanite Background of Genesis 49", 3, Aq — who rendered מְכֵרֹתֵיהֶם with ἀνασκάφαι — also derived מְכֵרֹתֵיהֶם from כרת; however, ἀνασκάφαι is derived from ἀνασκάπτω, "to dig up" and thus refers to כרה, "to dig up" (*HAL*, 472; cf. Caquot, *art.cit.*, 115); Wevers, *op.cit.*, 822 n. 7. This could probably be linked with the interpretation of the vocalization of MT and with TO, cf. n. 130 below; depending, however, on the question from which root מְכוּרָה has to be derived: כור <(?) כרה (*HAL*, 549).

[127]It is, in case of ms. B, unclear whether the later corrector, who placed the accents and breathings, and who also placed the correction αι above the second *epsilon*, considered this αι as the begin of a new word, since the breathing — necessary here for the beginning of the new word — is not discernible.

[128]Caquot, "Siméon et Lévi", 114.

[129]*HAL*, 549.

[130]Translation by Grossfeld, *TOGen*, 158. Caquot, "Siméon et Lévi", 114, pointed out that TO seems to follow TJon in these verses in Ezekiel, because TJon translated מְכוּרָה in Ezekiel into תותבוחתא, similar to תותבוחתא in Gen. 49:5.

J. Maier, "Bemerkungen zur Fachsprache und Religionspolitik im Königreich Juda", *Jud* 26 (1970) 89–105, 89–91, interprets מְכוּרָה in Ezekiel the same as מְכֵרֹת in Gen. 49:5. He renders the word with "Depots, Pfründen" and senses in the use of this terminology a form of criticism of the incomes policy of the Levites (in the period of the Kings). He links this thought to 2 Kings 12:6, 8 (E.T. 12:5, 7), also a difficult text with a homophonous word מֶכֶר. In the view of the present writer, however, he overlooks several serious problems. He interprets Gen. 49:6b, like the preceding part of the saying, in connection with cruelties performed by the Levites during the period of the kings: gory pursuit and paralysing bulls, "*was immer dies letztere zu bedeuten hat*" (emphasis, RdH). Furthermore, the relation of Simeon and Levi in this saying remains unresolved (91). Leaving these two problems without any solution, he fails to give solid support for his proposal that this text should refer to the behaviour of the Levites in the First Temple period. For מֶכֶר in 2 Kings 12:6, 8, cf. L.S. Wright, "*mkr in 2 Kings xii 5–17 and Deuteronomy xviii 8*", *VT* 39 (1989) 438–448, who considers the word to be a derivative of מכר "to sell", which renders Maier's proposal very unlikely.

עבדי קרב מן טליותיהון בארע באלי דבביהון עבדו נצחני קרביהון, "Simeon and
Levi are twin brothers, masters of sharp arms, waging war from their
youth. In the land of their enemies they have wrought the victories of
their combats".[131] In short, it can be concluded that the Vrs did not
have a uniform tradition, but derived מְכֵרֹתֵיהֶם either from כרת, "to
cut" (LXX, Vg; TN) or from כור "to dig" (> מְכוּרָה, "origin") (MT,
TO, TN, Peš, Aq[?]).[132]

We will now discuss the proposals which do not consider מְכֵרֹת to
be some kind of weapon. A proposal is offered by Young, who tries to
interpret the word in the context of Genesis 34 using an Akk. word
to solve the problem. He supposes MT is the product of a faulty
word-division, suggesting the preceding מ was originally an *enclitic
mem* suffixed to חֲמָס.[133] The remaining כֵּרֹת could be analysed as a
feminine plural noun reflecting a prior כְּרֹת (with an appropriate case
ending). This word might be connected with Sum.-Akk. (DUG.)KIR
= *kirru/kīru*, "vessel", attested in plural *kirrātum* in Amarna-texts.

---

[131] According to Vawter, "Canaanite Background of Genesis 49", 4; Caquot,
"Siméon et Lévi", 114. Translation by McNamara, *TNGen*, 218. Vawter, "Canaanite Background of Genesis 49", 3–5, calls upon TN and Peš to emend MT. He
suggests the text had originally משרתיהם, and the other traditions (LXX, Sam,
TO, Aq) read for an original שׁ a כ, referring to the similarity of these two characters in the Phoen. script. The word משרתיהם has to be derived from Hebr. *שׁרה,
"originate", comparable to Ug. *trr*, "small"; Akk. *šerru*, "child"; Aram. *šerā/û*,
"begin(ning)"; and Hebr. שׁרוּת (K. in Jer. 15:11) from *שׁרה. See however the table
of Sem. alphabets in *ANEP*, 88, # 286; and also the discussion on palaeography
in *HAE*, Bd. II/1, 158–9, 202–3, where this supposed similarity of letters does not
seem to warrant a departure of MT כ to שׁ. Furthermore, J.A. Emerton, "Some
Difficult Words in Genesis 49", in: P.R. Ackroyd, B. Lindars (eds.), *Words and
Meanings: Essays ... D.W. Thomas*, London 1968, 81–93, 82, disagrees (among
other things) with Vawter because he does not consider whether the renderings of
TN and Peš could have been derived from the same consonants as MT, and they
translated our word with Ezek. 16:3; 21:35 and 29:14 in mind. This can be found
in GenRab. 49:7: "Some hold that mekerothehem means their habitations as in
the verse '*Thine origin* (mekurothayik) *and thy nativity*' (Ezek. xvi, 3)" (quoted
from H. Freedman, M. Simon (eds.), *Midrash Rabbah translated into English with
Notes, Glossary and Indices*, vol. II: Genesis, London 1931, 980). Cf. also Nielsen,
Shechem, 279.

Vawter's proposal was also rejected by J. Coppens, "La bénédiction de Jacob: son cadre historique à la lumière des parallèles ougaritiques", in *Volume
du Congres Strassbourgh 1956* (SVT, 4), Leiden 1957, 139; Caquot, "Siméon et
Lévi", 115; Pehlke, *Genesis 49:1–28*, 139; E. Testa, "La formazione letteraria della
benedizione di Giacobbe (Gen. 49,2–27)", *SBF LA* 23 (1973) 171.

[132] For other, later traditions of the text, cf. Caquot, "Siméon et Lévi", 114–115.

[133] D.W. Young, "Ghost Word", 335–6. On p. 336 n. 12, he refers to the possible
plural חֲמָסִים similar as in Ps. 140:2, 5 and Prov. 4:17; but he rejects this reading
in Gen. 49:5b, because it would "not explain why the text was eventually garbled,
if indeed it is." (emphasis, RdH).

Because this word would also appear in Akk. marriage-texts, he suggests this word should be read here too because of its link with Genesis 34.[134] In reply it should be noted, first, that the meaning of *kirru* in these texts is very unclear and sometimes the reading is even disputed.[135] Secondly, when the word has to be interpreted as a marriage ritual, it presents major problems in connection with Genesis 34; since — as Young admits — "we do not know whether a *kirru*-ritual was entailed". This is because the narrator "had no need to provide the details of the marriage rites except for the mass circumcision incorporated therein."[136] Nevertheless, if Gen. 49:5b should refer to this ritual, as implied in Genesis 34, according to Young, this could only have happened if the narrator had referred to a marriage-ritual. But according to the narrative the massacre took place before the wedding. This makes Young's solution very unlikely, because the poet would then refer to an event in Genesis 34, which did not yet take place in the narrative.[137]

Gevirtz offers another translation, also based on a reconstruction of MT.[138] He justifies his emendation of the text with several arguments. First, he denies the relation of our saying in vv. 5-7 with Genesis 34, mainly basing himself on the analysis by De Pury[139] and Lehming.[140] Secondly, he argues that the poetic style of the first part of the saying in the present form and translation is rather "clumsy".[141] Thirdly, the construct chain כְּלֵי חָמָס is not otherwise attested, and — of course — the unknown מְכֵרֹתֵיהֶם has resisted all attempts at decipherment. Finally, he thinks the commonly accepted meaning of אַחִים "brothers" to be suspect, because all sons of Jacob are brothers.[142] Furthermore, as an additional argument he refers to the fact

---

[134]Young, "A Ghost Word", 340-341; referring to S. Greengus, "Old Babylonian Marriage Ceremonies and Rites", *JCS* 20 (1966) 65.

[135]Cf. the fact that — as Young, "A Ghost Word", 340 n. 31 himself mentions — *AHw*, Bd. II, 918, does not discuss the word *s.v. kirru* but *s.v. qerrum*; while *CAD*, vol. G, 92-3, discusses the word *s.v. girru*, which was later corrected, in *CAD*, vol. K, 410. Cf. also Pehlke, *Genesis 49:1-28*, 144 n. 1.

[136]Young, "A Ghost Word", 341.

[137]Pehlke, *Genesis 49:1-28*, 144-5.

[138]Gevirtz, "Simeon and Levi", 93-128.

[139]De Pury, "Genèse xxxiv et l'histoire", 5-49.

[140]Lehming, "Überlieferungsgeschichte von Gen 34", 228-50.

[141]Gevirtz, "Simeon and Levi", 95: "Thus one notes here, in striking contrast to the precise parallelistic structure of the remainder of the poem, an absence of any clear or perceptible coupling of terms ... and the observation that the syntax of the phrase is poetically clumsy."

[142]Gevirtz, "Simeon and Levi", 96: "Clearly in need of revision also is the vocalization of אַחִים, for "brothers" cannot be right. All the "sons of Jacob" being

that six of the other sons of Jacob are typified as animals, which combined with the other problems in the text makes it attractive to him
to accept C.J. Ball's proposal אחים, "eagle-owl".[143] Furthermore, to
obtain a good parallelism, he moves כלי from v. 5B to v. 5A; adds a ת
at the beginning of חמס: תחמס; and supposes an *enclitic mem* suffixed
to אחים and תחממסם:[144]

| Simeon and Levi are spent owls, | שמעון ולוי אחי–ם כלי |
| Cashiered hawks are they. | <ת>חמס–ם כרתי הם |

However, Gevirtz's arguments must be called into question. First, his
argument concerning poetic style is not conclusive, because it happens
very frequently in undoubtably poetic passages like the Psalms that
two cola, forming together a bicolon, are not strictly parallel, simply
because they are forming so-called "synthetic parallelism".[145]

Secondly, his argument concerning the interpretation "brothers"
for אחים is void, because it is striking that in this saying two names
are mentioned, in contrast to the other sayings. The reference to the
brotherhood of Simeon and Levi would seem to justify their pairing.[146]
Furthermore, the Vrs do not differ in this tradition and this too is not
in favour of his suggestion.

Finally, although he is right in his suggestion that in six of the
other sayings animal-metaphors are used, this argument is not decisive concerning our text. The colon where אחים is used, is completely
intelligible and emendation is therefore superfluous.[147] Furthermore,

---

siblings, isolating two of them in this manner (in a poem in which all the brothers
come in for evaluation) can find little, if any, justification."

[143] Gevirtz, "Simeon and Levi", 96. Reference was to C.J. Ball, "The Testament
of Jacob", *PSBA* May 7 (1895) 164–91, 191, translating את as "hyena", since the
meaning of את is still not established. For את cf. *DBHE*, 33; Ges[18], 33; *HAL*, 28–9.
[144] Gevirtz, "Simeon and Levi", 95.
[145] Also known as "enjambment". Cf. the examples given, but also the criticism
on the terminology of synthetical parallelism by S.A. Geller, *Parallelism in Early
Biblical Poetry* (HSM, 20), Missoula, Ma. 1979, 375–85; W.G.E. Watson, *Classical
Hebrew Poetry: A Guide to its Techniques* (JSOTS, 26), Sheffield [2]1984, 332–5.
Furthermore, we could refer to the phenomenon of the unicolon; cf. De Moor,
"The Poetry of the Book of Ruth", 264 with n. 13; Watson, *op.cit.*, 12, 168–74.
[146] E. Meyer, 421, refers to 34:25(?). Sarna, *Genesis*, 334; Wenham, *Genesis
16–50*, 470, interpret אחים as "allies, confederates" and thus in a "non-literal
sense". Similarly already — although not always excluding a more literal meaning
— Dillmann, *Die Genesis*, 438; Gunkel, *Genesis*, 480; König, *Die Genesis*, 752;
Jacob, *Das erste Buch*, 896; Aalders, *Genesis, dl. III*, 196; Speiser, *Genesis*, 364;
Van Selms, *Genesis, dl. II*, 274.
[147] The argument of animal-metaphors could be decisive only if the text and the
words under study are incomprehensible and therefore in need of emendation; cf.
Gen. 49:22 below, which could also then be read without changing the consonantal

his starting point is that these verses are not to be connected with Genesis 34, a point of view he based on the analysis by De Pury and Lehming. However, as we have seen it remains to be seen whether a relation with Genesis 34 is really impossible. And finally, not every saying contains an animal metaphor which removes the justification for emendation of the text.

Another solution is offered by Ullendorff, who suggests we derive מְכֵרֹת from Aeth. mkr "to counsel".[148] However, "their counsels are weapons of violence" is not a very convincing rendering.[149] Speiser suggested we derive מְכֵרֹת from מכר I, "to trade".[150] Caquot, relating our text according to this rendering with Genesis 34, had to add an explanatory word in order to make the rendering intelligible: "their trade are objects (obtained) by violence".[151] However, the fact that a word has to be added, argues against its plausibility. The explanation by De Moor, that we could find here a reference to the early history of the tribes of Israel as a kind of ḥapiru[152] — mercenaries, doing corvée in peace-time — is an attractive explanation in itself, when treating this verse from a diachronical point of view, namely as a tribal saying. However, first of all it has to be rendered as a saying of the dying patriarch who rebukes his sons for a certain event. We have to look, therefore, for a solution which explains the morphological form as well as the meaning in the context of Genesis 49, and the book of Genesis as a whole. However, "their trade are weapons of violence" demands a special explanation, for there is no reference to any "trade" in Genesis 34, where the brothers are not described as "traders" but as "shepherds" acting violently.

Earlier exegetes — influenced by medieval Jewish exegetes[153] —

---

text.

[148] E. Ullendorff, "The Contribution of South Semitics to Hebrew Lexicography", *VT* 6 (1956) 190–98, 194; He refers to D.W. Thomas, *JThS* 1936 and 1952. This proposal is accepted in *HAL*, 551, "Plan, Ratschläge" (< מכר II); Von Rad, *Erste Buch Mose*, 344.

[149] Van Selms, *Genesis, dl. II*, 274.

[150] Speiser, *Genesis*, 365; furthermore A. Caquot, "Le parole sur Juda dans le testament lyrique de Jacob (Genèse 49,8–12)", *Sem* 26 (1976) 11; IDEM, "Siméon et Lévi", 117–8; Cross, Freedman, *Studies in Ancient Yahwistic Poetry*, 72, 78 n. 13; De Moor, *RoY*, 109 n. 38. For the terminology see E. Lipiński, "Sale, Transfer, and Delivery in Ancient Semitic Terminology", in H. Klengel (Hrsg.), *Gesellschaft und Kultur im alten Vorderasien* (SGKAO, 15), Berlin 1982, 173–85; idem, "מכר", *ThWAT*, Bd. IV, 869–75; Alter, *Genesis*, 293.

[151] Caquot, "Siméon et Lévi", 117: "Leurs marchandises (sont) des objets acquis par la violence", soit "ils font trafic d'objets mal acquis".

[152] Cf. De Moor, *RoY*, 109.

[153] Freedman, Simon (eds.), *Midrash Rabbah translated: Genesis*, 980; another

explained the puzzling מְכֵרֹת as a Gr. loan word: μάξαιρα, "knife, sword".[154] However, Dillmann already criticized this etymology, and this suggestion was not followed up in more recent lexica.[155] Yet, the context suggests a word which denotes instruments by which violent actions could be performed;[156] this results in many translations of the word, without any definitive solution.[157] Others still try to derive the word from a particular root to explain its etymology, and which are closely related to the Vrs: מְכֵרֹת < כרה (cf. Aq) "to hollow, dig";[158] or < כרר ה/ "originally: to be round(?)", pilp. "dance, skip".[159]

An attractive solution to the problem was offered by Dahood, who pointed to the fact that the root כרת, "to cut" is used in Exod. 4:25 for circumcision, which is one of the crucial elements in the story of Genesis 34.[160] The derivation from the root כרת leads to the meaning "cutting instrument", while the linking with circumcision makes it more particularly a "blade or knife for circumcision".[161] The pre-

---

tradition is found at *op.cit.*, 953; Hebr. text: J. Theodor, Ch. Albeck (Hrsg.), *Bereschit Rabba mit kritischen Apparat und Kommentar, Parascha LXXXVII-C*, Jerusalem ²1965, 1278. Cf. furthermore Cohen, "$m^e k\bar{e}r\bar{o}t\bar{e}hem$ (Genèse XLIX 5)", 472, 478 n. 2, for some additional bibliographical references.

[154] The following translations offer "swords, knives": RSV, KBS, FB; cf. furthermore Ges, *Thes*, 671v.; this view is defended by Böhl, *Genesis*, 49, 140; C.H. Gordon, "Homer and the Bible", *HUCA* 26 (1950) 43–108, 60; O. Margalith, "$mek\bar{e}r\bar{o}t\bar{e}hem$ (Genesis XLIX 5)", *VT* 34 (1984) 101–2.

[155] Dillmann, *Die Genesis*, 438. The result is however an explicit "ungedeutet"; cf. GB, 423, KBL, 523. The former refers only to a possible Akk. derivation. Speiser, *Genesis*, 365, rejects this etymology because of the anachronism. It is striking, furthermore, that LXX did not render מְכֵרֹת with μάξαιρα.

[156] Westermann, *Genesis 37–50*, 255.

[157] Van Selms, *Genesis, dl. II*, 274, "weapons"; Westermann, *Genesis 37–50*, 256, "Schwerter".

[158] Buber: "Karste"; NBG: "tools" ("gereedschappen"); NEB: "spades"; Gunkel, *Genesis*, 479–80: "ihre Fallen"; Skinner, *Genesis*, 516–7, "dagger" (מְכֵרֹת derived from כרה); Sarna, *Genesis*, 334 "weapons" < "a digging or piercing instrument". The rendering by Wenham, *Genesis 16–50*, 473, "they are equipped with weapons of violence", remains obscure since he discusses other proposals but does not explain his own rendering "equipped". But it is very likely close to the proposals listed in this note.

[159] Dillmann, *Die Genesis*, 438, "etwa 'Krummesser, Sichel' ".

[160] M. Dahood, "*mkrtyhm* in Genesis 49,5", *CBQ* 23 (1961) 54–56. The proposal to derive מכרתיהם from the root כרת can be found also in Bruno, *Genesis – Exodus*, 320. Cf. also Peters, "Jacob's Blessing", 102, who seems to follow this rendering of LXX.

[161] Dahood, "*mkrtyhm* in Genesis 49,5", 55. Dahood was followed by R.H. Moeller, "Four Old Testament Problem Terms", *BiTr* 13 (1962) 219–222, 219; P. Beauchamp, "Review of R. De Vaux, La Genèse (BJ²), Paris 1962, 373–4; E. Testa, "La formazione Letteraria della Benedizione di Giacobbe", *SBF LA* 23 (1973) 167–205; Pehlke, *Genesis 49:1-28*, 147–9.

formative מ/מַ is used very frequently to form names of instruments, "so that from the morphological point of view such a signification for *makrēt* (most probable vocalization) would not be exceptionable".[162] According to the story in Genesis 34 the demand for circumcision was a trap for the Shechemites and turned out to be an act of violence; therefore the translation offered by Dahood seems to be the best suggestion in this case, and is the one which follows closely LXX: "tools of violence are their circumcision-blades".[163] We would suggest, however, rendering the word in a more neutral way as the derivative of כרת "to cut" > מַכְרֵת "cutter" > "knife".

In v. 6aB there is a problem of translation (or better: vocalization) of כבדי, and the interpretation of the verb תֵחַד. The LXX interpreted כבדי, which was vocalized by the Masoretes as כְּבֹדִי, "my glory, honour",[164] as τὰ ἥπατά μου "my liver", corresponding to Hebr. כְּבֵדִי. This reading of LXX is followed by many scholars as the most likely interpretation.[165] According to Watson, כְּבֵדִי in connection with a verb in the 3.p.sg. has to be interpreted as a polite reference to oneself, similar to נַפְשִׁי with a verb in 3.p.sg.[166] Gevirtz objected to the reading of LXX, but also to the interpretation of MT כָּבֹ(וֹ)ד, "glory", there is a discrepancy in gender of the noun and verb, because both nouns are attested elsewhere as masc., and the verb is fem.[167] Rendsburg, however, suggests we consider תחד as a 3.masc.sg. impf., known from El Amarna and some other instances in the Hebr. Bible (among others Hab. 3:4).[168] This solution for the discrepancy of gender between noun

---

[162]Dahood, "*mkrtyhm* in Genesis 49,5", 55; For the vocalization מַכְרֵת he referred to BL, 492. Further, we can refer to the fact that another word for "knife" is formed similarly with the preformative *ma/mi* with the root, which determines the function of the instrument for its direct purpose: מַאֲכֶלֶת, "knife" < אכל, "to eat"; *HAL*, 44, 512.

[163]Dahood, "*mkrtyhm* in Genesis 49,5", 55.

[164]Cf. *HAL*, 436.

[165]Dillmann, *Die Genesis*, 459; Strack, *Genesis*, 169; Gunkel, *Genesis*, ³1910, 480; Skinner, *Genesis*, 517; J. Gray, *The Legacy of Canaan: The Ras Shamra Texts and Their Relevance to the Old Testament* (SVT, 5), Leiden ²1965, 282; *HAL*, 435; cf. furthermore, F. Nötscher, "Heisst *kābōd* auch 'Seele'?", *VT* 2 (1952) 358–362, 360–1; W.G.E. Watson, "Hebrew 'to Be Happy' — An Idiom Identified", *VT* 31 (1981) 92–95.

[166]Watson, "Hebrew 'to Be Happy'", 95 n. 8. Gevirtz, "Simeon and Levi", 100 n. 29, 110.

[167]Gevirtz, "Simeon and Levi", 101.

[168]Cf. G. Rendsburg, "Double Polysemy in Genesis 49:6 and Job 3:6", *CBQ* 44 (1982) 48–51, 50 (with n. 15, for relevant literature). This phenomenon is comparable to the 3.masc.pl. with preformative ת, cf. W.L. Moran, "The Hebrew Language in its Northwest Semitic Background", in G.E. Wright (ed.), *The Bible and the Ancient Near East: Essays ... W.F. Albright*, London 1961, 54–72, 62–

and verb is important in relation to another objection Gevirtz puts
forward in his study, namely, the fact that in several cases the meaning
"glory" for כָּבֹד is inappropriate, which has led to the change in interpretation as "soul" or to the emendation כָּבֵד, "liver": Pss. 7:6; 16:9;
30:13; 57:9; 108:2.[169] The verbs used in these cases (except for 7:6 [ob-
ject] and 108:2 [uncertain]) are masc., which would result in a reversed
problem: noun fem. and verb masc. The solution offered by Rendsburg seems to be the best explanation for MT as it does not require
any emendation.[170] Furthermore Gevirtz noted that the evidence of
LXX is inconsistent, for they rendered the noun כָּבֹוד by δόξα "glory"
(4×), γλῶσσά "tongue" (1×) and where MT reads כָּבֵד "liver", LXX
rendered δόξα "glory" (Lam. 2:11).[171] Therefore Gevirtz suggests we
assume, besides כָּבֹוד I, the existence of a noun כָּבֹוד II, which denotes
the front of the body, the "belly" and by extension of meaning the
"person, self, mind".[172] However, his references are not correct, because he only refers to the more problematical passages, mentioned
above, not to the other texts where MT reads כָּבֹוד. Weinfeld is right
in contradicting his statement, saying LXX is uniform with its translation.[173] Therefore, we have to be cautious with emendation of the
problematical passages in MT, as Weinfeld has counseled.[174] כָּבֹוד has
primarily the meaning "substance, being" whereby "honour, glory"
is derived from this meaning.[175] As in Akk. and Ug., Hebr. כָּבֹוד can
be taken as one noun with several meanings.[176] However, because the
words of the dying patriarch suggest that in the future his soul (נַפְשִׁי)
might enter the assemblies of his sons (סֹוד || קְהָל), this seems to re-
flect the belief that souls of died ancestors could communicate with

---

3; cf. however, J.A. Emerton, "What Light has Ugaritic Shed on Hebrew?" in:
G.J. Brooke *et.al.* (eds.), *Ugarit and the Bible: Proceedings of the International
Symposium on Ugarit and the Bible, Manchester, September 1992* (UBL, 11),
Münster 1994, 53–69, 63.

[169] For the objection against the interpretation of "soul", cf. Nötscher, "Heisst
kābōd auch 'Seele'?", 358–62; cf. for literature Gevirtz, "Simeon and Levi", 102,
nn. 35–6.

[170] *Pace* Watson, "Hebrew 'to Be Happy'", 92, 94 with n. 1, who takes כָּבֵד as
fem.; likewise M. Dahood, "A New Translation of Gen. 49.6a", *Bib* 36 (1955) 229.

[171] Gevirtz, "Simeon and Levi", 102.

[172] Gevirtz, "Simeon and Levi", 102.

[173] M. Weinfeld, "כָּבֹוד", *ThWAT*, Bd. IV, 23–40, 25: "Die Wiedergabe der LXX
ist eindeutig: es begegnen δόξα (177mal), mit den Wurzelverwandten ἔνδοξος
(3mal), δοξάζειν (2mal) und δόξις (1mal). Daneben begegnet τιμή (7mal); konkret-
inhaltlich orientierte Wiedergaben liegen vor in πλοῦτος (2mal), καλός und δύναμις
(je 1mal). Warscheinlich ist auch γλῶσσα (Ps 16,9) entsprechend zu werten."

[174] Weinfeld, "כָּבֹוד", 24–5.

[175] Weinfeld, "כָּבֹוד", 24–5.

[176] Weinfeld, "כָּבֹוד", 25.

their offspring. Important in this connection is the appearance of a
deity which is described as the occurence of the כָּבוֹד, which is mostly
rendered with "glory", and therefore we follow this rendering here
also. This text is rendered therefore: "my soul shall not enter in their
company; nor shall my glory rejoice in their gathering".[177]

Concerning the verb, Watson proposed we derive תֵּחַד from חדה I,
"to be happy, rejoice";[178] since the combination of this subject and
verb could be compared to similar expressions in Akk., where a corresponding form of the idiom is found.[179] The translation "In their
gathering my glory shall not rejoice" is therefore quite probable.

2.3.1.1　Rendering the Verbal Tenses

The nominal clauses opening the saying on Simeon and Levi in verse
5AB are here rendered in the present tense, as in the saying on
Reuben.[180] Like that saying these nominal clauses are followed by
a negation by means of אַל paired with the jussive in a negative optative clause:[181] אַל־תֵּחַד ... אַל־תָּבֹא "(it) shall not enter ... (it) shall not
rejoice". This negative will of the patriarch is — again like the saying of Reuben — followed by an explicative clause introduced with כִּי
"for". The similar structure of the saying on Reuben and on Simeon
and Levi is also another reason to render the *qatal* forms here as
forms referring to the past. This is reasonable because such a rebuke
(followed by אָרוּר "cursed") would be unintelligible if not founded on
events or facts justifying this curse. Therefore we do not follow the
rendering by Sarna and Wenham, who seem to interpret the *qatal* as a
"performative" perfect, based on an interpretation of בְּאַפָּם and וּבִרְצֹנָם

---

[177]J.C. de Moor, "Standing Stones and Ancestor Worship", *UF* 27 (1995) 1–20,
15–6. For the rendering "rejoice", cf. below.

[178]For this verb, cf. GB, 192; BDB, 292; *HAL*, 280.

[179]Cf. Watson, "Hebrew 'to Be Happy'", 93, 95, nn. 3–5, for relevant examples.
The same solution for תֵּחַד is offered independently by Rendsburg, "Double Polysemy", 48–51. Gevirtz, "Simeon and Levi", 107–9 agrees with these scholars and
offers some additional arguments for this rendering.
Rendsburg also proposes to derive תָּבֹא (v. 6aA) from אבה, "to want, desire",
which is neither likely nor necessary; cf. Isa. 56:7a (בוא [hi.] ‖ שמח [hi.]). For
another proposal for תֵּחַד, cf. M. Dahood, "A New Translation of Gen. 49.6a",
Bib 36 (1955) 229 (תֵּחַד < Hebr. חזה; cf. Ug. ḥdy); cf. also idem, "Hebrew-Ugaritic
Lexicography", *Bib* 45 (1964) 393–412, 407–8. His arguments are, however, refuted
by H.L. Ginsberg, "Lexicographical Notes", in: *Hebräische Wortforschung: Fs W.
Baumgartner* (SVT, 16), Leiden 1967, 71–73; O. Loretz, *Die Psalmen: Beitrag der
Ugarit-Texte zum Verständnis von Kolometrie und Textologie der Psalmen; Teil
II: Psalm 90–150* (AOAT, 207/2), Kevelaer, Neukirchen-Vluyn 1979, 497.

[180]References to relevant grammars are found on pp. 91–92 above.

[181]JM, §163a.

as temporal clauses:[182] "for when angry they slay men, and when pleased they maim oxen".[183] A temporal rendering seems to be unlikely, however, since the preposition בְּ must in that case be combined with an infinitive and not with a noun.[184]

In the final poetic verse (49:7) the first two cola (in the second colon ellipsis has taken place) both consist of two clauses. The first clause of verse 7A, אָרוּר אַפָּם is nominal and has an optative sense, because the passive participle is the predicate and precedes the subject.[185] The second clauses of verses 7A and 7B are explicative clauses with the very common conjunction כִּי,[186] followed by a *qatal*.[187] These clauses are rendered in the present tense because the *qatal* of a stative verb has primarily a present meaning.[188] The final colon contains two parallel clauses both with a *yiqtol*, refering to the future.[189]

2.3.2   Analysis of the Poetic Structure

2.3.2.1   The Strophic Structure

Strophe I.A.ii.1

Accents: [8]–2 | [8]–1 ‖ [10]–5 | [8]–2.

Sep.↑: *petuḥah*.

Sep.↓: emphatic בְּסֹדָם and בִּקְהָלָם; repetitive ‖ אַל, מַ, —בְּ, and יַ –.

Int. ‖: **5:** אָחִים ‖ הֵם–. **6a:** בְּסֹדָם ‖ בִּקְהָלָם;[190] אַל ‖ אַל;[191] נַפְשִׁי ‖ כְּבֹדִי.[192]

---

[182]Cf. on the "performative" perfect: JM, §112f,g; see also Lettinga, *De 'Tale Kanaäns'*, 18–9. For temporal clauses, cf. JM, §166.

[183]Sarna, *Genesis*, 334. Similarly Wenham, *Genesis 16–50*, 454.

[184]JM, §166l.

[185]JM, §§154e.II; 163b.

[186]JM, §170d.

[187]עֹז might be interpreted as the *qatal* of עזז, although it is usual to interpret it as a noun; cf. *HAL*, 760. In fact there is no difference, since עזז is a stative verb: a nominal clause with this noun or a *qatal* of the verb express both the same. See JM, §41b; 112a. However, because in the parallel clause the verbal form is used, it might be used here to interpret עֹז as a verb.

[188]Lett, §72b.1; JM, §112a; Lett[10], §77b.1.

[189]JM, §113b. Since the *yiqtol* of active verbs can have a present meaning with the aspect value of a repeated or a durative action, it is possible to render the *yiqtol* as a present with a similar aspect. However, "I divide them" or "I am dividing them" is rather unlikely and the future, in accordance with the interpretation of 49:1C, is the most probable tense.

[190]These two words are nowhere else used in parallel. Cf., however, Ps. 89:6, 8, where we find both words constructed with קְדֹשִׁים. For the parallelism of בְּ ‖ בְּ, see Dahood, Penar, "Ugaritic-Hebrew Parallel Pairs (I)", 134.

[191]Cf. Dahood, Penar, "Ugaritic-Hebrew Parallel Pairs (I)", 109.

[192]For this pair, cf. Ps. 7:6; Lam. 2:11–12. In the latter text the pair is used in external parallelism both connected with the verb שׁפך. This strengthens the

Ext.‖: אַחִים (5A) ‖ בִּקְהָלָם (6aB);[193] הֵם– (5B) ‖ ם– (6aA) | ם– (6aB).

Strophe I.A.ii.2

Accents: [10]–5 | [8]–1 ‖ [10]–5 | [8]–2 | [5]–[8]–1.

Sep.↑: כִּי; emphatic position בְּאַפָּם and וּבְרְצֹנָם; repetitive ‖ ם, –בְ.

Sep.↓: tricolon; אָרוּר;[194] repetitive ‖ suffix ם–; כִּי and בְ; *setumah*.

Hlfl.‖: **7C:** אֲחַלְקֵם ‖ וַאֲפִיצֵם; בְּיַעֲקֹב ‖ בְּיִשְׂרָאֵל.

Int. ‖: **6b:** בְּאַפָּם ‖ וּבְרְצֹנָם;[195] הָרְגוּ ‖ עִקְּרוּ;[196] אִישׁ ‖ שׁוֹר. **7:** –ם ‖ –ם ‖ –ם (2×); וְעֶבְרָתָם ‖ אַפָּם.[197]

Ext.‖: וּבִרְצֹנָם (6bB) ‖ וְעֶבְרָתָם (7B);[198] הָרְגוּ (6bA) ‖ קָשָׁתָה (7B).[199]

2.3.2.2 The Poetic Structure of Canticle I.A.ii

Sep.↑: *petuḥah.*

Sep.↓: *setumah.*

Ext.‖: הֵם– (5aB) ‖ ם– (6aA), ם– (6aB) ‖ ם– (6bA), ם– (6bB) ‖ ם– (7aA), ם– (7aB) ‖ ם– (7bA), ם– (7bB);[200] חָמָס (5aB) ‖ בְּאַפָּם (6bA) ‖ אַפָּם;[201] חָמָס (5aB) ‖ וּבִרְצֹנָם (6bB);[202] בִּקְהָלָם (6aB) ‖ בְּיִשְׂרָאֵל (7bB).[203]

---

arguments concerning the concentric structure in Lam. 2, by J. Renkema, "The Literary Structure of Lamentations (I)", *SABCP*, 307–9. Cf. furthermore Prov. 7:23. See also Avishur, *Stylistic Studies*, 65–6, 85–6.

[193] Cf. Ps. 22:23.

[194] This word, which is emphatically positioned, is not listed by Van der Lugt, *SSBHP*, 508–24, because of its absence in the book of Psalms. Cf. however the opposite אַשְׁרֵי, "happy, blessed"; see *op.cit.*, 513.

[195] Cf. Ps. 30:6. Furthermore Avishur, *Stylistic Studies*, 283.

[196] Cf. for the parallelism of these words, Qoh. 3:2–3 (ext. ‖).

[197] For אַף ‖ עֶבְרָה, cf. Amos 1:11; Hab. 3:8; Pss. 7:7; 78:49 (cf. v. 21, reversed and ext. ‖); 85:4; 90:11; for the reverse order: Isa. 14:6; see also 13:9. Cf. Avishur, *Stylistic Studies*, 157; De Moor, *RoY*, 129.

[198] See also Prov. 14:35.

[199] Cf. Exod. 13:15. See also Isa. 27:7–8. Although the parallelism קשה ‖ הרג in the latter text seems not convincing, we could point to the fact that the fierce hot east wind was considered a deadly enemy in Canaan. The god Motu is the god of the sirocco in Ugarit, cf. KTU 1.3:v.17–8; De Moor, *SPU*, 114–5, 173–5; De Moor, *ARTU*, 16 n. 87, 64 n. 288, 72 n. 335, 97 n. 470; J.C. de Moor, "The Seasonal Pattern in the Legend of Aqhatu", *SEL* 5 (1988) 61–78, 67–8; M.S. Smith, *The Early History of God: Yahweh and the Other Deities in Ancient Israel*, San Fransisco 1990, 53, 73 n. 80. Cf. also Hos. 13:14–5. Further reference could be made to the parallel between Isa. 27:1 and 8: בְּחַרְבּוֹ הַקָּשָׁה and בְּרוּחוֹ הַקָּשָׁה, which clarifies the parallelism הרג ‖ קשה in Gen. 49:6–7 and also Isa. 27:7–8.

[200] The whole canticle is linked by the use of suffixes 3.masc.plur.

[201] The verb חמס is paralleled to אף (in ext. ‖) in Jer. 51:45–6; Lam. 2:6.

[202] This parallelism is determined by the context in which חָמָס and רָצֹן are used. In Prov. 8:35–6 both words are used again in a similar context, but there they are used antithetically.

[203] קְהָל ‖ יִשְׂרָאֵל are used antithetically: the קְהָל of Simeon and Levi are scattered in later times in Israel. There is no parallel for this usage: furthermore קְהָל is used

2.4 Judah (Gen. 49:8–12)

I.B.i.1   ס

Judah are you, (8aA)	יְהוּדָה אַתָּה
your brothers shall praise you, (8aB)	יוֹדוּךָ אַחֶיךָ
Your hand shall be on your enemies' neck, (8bA)	יָדְךָ בְּעֹרֶף אֹיְבֶיךָ
your father's sons shall bow down to you. (8bB)	יִשְׁתַּחֲווּ לְךָ בְּנֵי אָבִיךָ

I.B.i.2

A lion's whelp is Judah, (9aA)	גּוּר אַרְיֵה יְהוּדָה
may you grow up, my son, from the prey; (9aB)	מִטֶּרֶף בְּנִי עָלִיתָ
If he stoops down, crouches as a lion, (9bA)	כָּרַע רָבַץ כְּאַרְיֵה
a "king's lion",[204] who will raise him? (9bB)	וּכְלָבִיא מִי יְקִימֶנּוּ

I.B.i.3

The sceptre shall not depart from Judah, (10aA)	לֹא־יָסוּר שֵׁבֶט מִיהוּדָה
nor the ruler's staff ever from between his feet, (10aB)	וּמְחֹקֵק מִבֵּין רַגְלָיו עַד(!)
For certain, let tribute come to him, (10bA)	כִּי־יָבֹא שִׁילֹה[205]
and may the obedience of the peoples be to him. (10bB)	וְלוֹ יִקְּהַת עַמִּים

I.B.i.4

May he bind his foal to the vine, (11aA)	אֹסְרִי לַגֶּפֶן עִירֹה
and his ass's colt to the choice vine; (11aB)	וְלַשֹּׂרֵקָה בְּנִי אֲתֹנוֹ
May he wash his garments in wine, (11bA)	כִּבֵּס בַּיַּיִן לְבֻשׁוֹ
and his vesture in the blood of grapes; (11bB)	וּבְדַם־עֲנָבִים סוּתֹה
His eyes shall be darker than wine, (12A)	חַכְלִילִי עֵינַיִם מִיָּיִן
his teeth whiter than milk. (12B) פ	וּלְבֶן־שִׁנַּיִם מֵחָלָב

2.4.1 Translation

The first long saying in Genesis 49 contains several problems, the
most notorious, no doubt, being the שִׁילֹה-oracle in v. 10bA. We will
start however with a problem of some minor importance for the interpretation of this saying. In v. 8aA a pun seems to have been made
on the folk etymology of the name יְהוּדָה, "Judah" (deriving the name
from ידה hiph., "to praise") and יוֹדוּךָ, "they shall praise you"; but this
folk-etymology is not without its difficulties.[206] In many studies ref-

---

in the Hebrew Bible for Israel alone; cf. Judg. 21:5, 8; 1 Kings 8:14, 22, 55, 65.

[204] Both Hebr. words אַרְיֵה and לָבִיא mean "lion", the exact difference between
them is unclear. For the latter word, cf. e.g. HAL, 491–2. With our rendering we
have tried to indicate the differences between the Hebrew words.

[205] Proposed reading: שַׁי לֹה.

[206] Cf. Jacob, Das erste Buch, 900; Von Rad, Erste Buch Mose, 237; H.-J. Zobel,
"יְהוּדָה", ThWAT, Bd. III, 514; Scharbert, Genesis 12–50, 204–5; C.H.J. de Geus,

erence is made to Gen. 49:8 for the etymology of the name "Judah",
it is, therefore, necessary to discuss the etymology of the name Judah
here first.

2.4.1.1   The Meaning of the Name "Judah"

The etymology of the name Judah is still disputed, mainly because of
the issue of the origin of the name "Judah" as a personal or as a geographical name.[207] Although the origin of a name as a geographical
or personal name in general is of great importance for the etymology,[208] a clear cut division cannot be made with names in the Sem.
languages, and esp. in the Hebrew Bible.[209] M. Noth and R. de Vaux

---

"Judah (Place)", *ABD*, vol. 3, 1033–36, 1034; M. Görg, "Juda — Namensdeutung
in Tradition und Etymologie", in: R. Bartelmus *et al.* (Hrsg.), *Konsequente Tra-
ditionsgeschichte: Fs K. Baltzer* (OBO, 126), Freiburg, Göttingen 1993, 79–87,
79.

[207] Of course an origin as a tribal or a divine name are also possible categories
of names; there is, however, no reason to consider Judah as a divine name. Tribal
names are mostly derivatives of personal or geographical names; see S.C. Layton,
Archaic Features of Canaanite Personal Names in the Hebrew Bible (HSM, 47),
Atlanta, Ga. 1990, 4, n. 15.

Cf. for the origin of the name "Judah" as a PN/TN: W.F. Albright, "The Names
'Israel' and 'Judah' with an Excursus on the Etymology of *Tôdâh* and *Tôrâh*",
JBL 46 (1927) 151–85, on Judah 168–78, 178; A.R. Millard, "The Meaning of the
Name Judah", *ZAW* 86 (1974) 216–8; De Moor, "The Twelve Tribes", 487–8;

For the origin as GN/TN, cf. A. Alt, "Die Gott der Väter", *KS*, Bd. I, 5, n. 1; M.
Noth, *Geschichte Israels*, Göttingen ²1954, 60–1; idem, *Die Welt des Alten Testaments: Einführung in die Grenzgebiete der alttestamentliche Wissenschaft*, Berlin
³1957, 47–51; R. Bach, "Juda", *RGG*, Bd. III, 963–4, 963; K. Elliger, "Judah",
IDB, vol. II, 1003–4, 1003; J. Hempel, "Juda", *BHH*, Bd. II, 898–900, 898; S. Mowinckel, *Tetrateuch — Pentateuch — Hexateuch* (BZAW, 90), Berlin 1964, 66; W.
Borée, *Die alten Ortsnamen Palästinas*, Hildesheim ²1968, 37, #34; De Vaux, *The
Early History of Israel*, vol. II, 547; E. Lipiński, "L'etymologie de 'Juda'", *VT*
23 (1973) 380–1; M.A. Cohen, "Judah, Formation of", *IDBS*, 498–9, 498; Zobel,
"יְהוּדָה", 514–6; H. Donner, *Geschichte des Volkes Israel und seiner Nachbarn in
Grundzügen* (ATD.Erg, 4/1), Göttingen 1984, 131; G.W. Ahlström, *Who Were
the Israelites*, Winona Lake (IN) 1986, 42–3; T.L. Thompson, *Early History of
the Israelite People: From the Written and Archaeological Sources* (SHANE, 4),
Leiden 1992, 140; De Geus, "Judah", 1033–4.

The question is left unanswered by Scharbert, *Genesis 12–50*, 204–5; Görg,
"Juda — Namensdeutung", 86–7.

[208] Cf. Lipiński, "L'etymologie", 380–1; and more general Borée, *Die alten Ortsnamen Palästinas*.

[209] Cf. *e.g.* יִזְרְעֶאל as PN and LN (*HAL*, 387); יֵשׁוּעַ PN and LN (cf. Neh. 11:26);
PNN יְהוּדִית and יְהוּדִי (resp. Gen. 26:34; Jer. 36:14) < GN / TN יְהוּדָה (cf.
J.J. Stamm, "Hebräische Frauennamen", in *Hebräische Wortforschung: Fs W.
Baumgartner*, [SVT, 16]. Leiden 1967, 301–339, 322 [= Stamm, *BHAN*, 118]).
See furthermore Borée, *Die alten Ortsnamen Palästinas*, 105–6, 20–32, ##13,
122, 141, 142, 153, 175, 197. Cf. also A.F. Rainey, "The Toponymics of Eretz-

(*inter alii*) have pointed out, that in the Hebrew Bible several traces are found, indicating that the name "Judah" was originally a geographical name or a territorial designation.[210] However, the fact that LNN and GNN are sometimes of the *yqtl*-type, comparable to PNN, and sometimes depending on PNN, causes us to look first for a root that in all likelihood could be used both in a PN and in a GN.

It is commonly acknowledged that in Gen. 29:35 and 49:8 an allusion is found to the folk etymology of יְהוּדָה, namely an impf. hoph. of ידה, "to praise", meaning "let NN be praised",[211] and which is probably reflected also in Ps. 45:18.[212] However, such a allusion cannot be considered as the final word in this case.[213] Van der Merwe writes in this connection:

> The fact that this word (ידה hiph.; RdH) is used in connection with the coronation ceremony, and the possibility that this word may indicate the public acknowledgment of the king,[214] may indicate that the con-

---

Israel", *BASOR* 231 (1978) 1–17, 4, who refers to geographical sentence names, which probably were originally PNN. Cf. furthermore Layton, *Archaic Features of Canaanite Personal Names*, 4, n. 16.

[210]Noth, *Welt des Alten Testaments*, 47–50; De Vaux, *The Early History of Israel*, 547. Cf. Josh. 20:7; Judg. 17:7, 9; 19:1; 1 Sam. 23:3; cf. also Judg. 1:16 and 1 Sam. 23:25; 26:2; 2 Chr. 20:20.

[211]Cf. *e.g.* Westermann, *Genesis 12–36*, 577: "Der Name Juda erhält ebenfalls eine 'ausgedachte' Deutung . . . "; *HAL*, 372, s.v. ידה, "Wortspiel". Most commentators agree: Dillmann, *Die Genesis*, 325; Gunkel, *Genesis*, 48; König, *Die Genesis*, 604, 755; Skinner, *Genesis*, 386; De Fraine, *Genesis*, 220, 326; Van Selms, *Genesis II*, dl. II, 274; W.H. Gispen, *Genesis 25:12–36:43* (COT), Kampen 1983, 83; Scharbert, *Genesis 12–50*, 293; Sarna, *Genesis*, 207, 365, n. 18; Wenham, *Genesis 16–50*, 244, 476. Scholars are sometimes ambiguous, however: Aalders, *Genesis*, dl. II, 213, states concerning the sayings in Gen. 29:31–35, that these are not meant to give an etymological explanation of the names but that they are made only because of the resemblance in sound of the names and the central words in the sayings. However, concerning Gen. 49:8 he thinks (Aalders, *Genesis*, dl. III, 201) that the wordplay in 49:8 is not only due to the resemblance in sound, but also because it is likely that the name Judah is etymologically connected with the Hebr. verb ידה.

[212]B.J. van der Merwe, "Judah in the Pentateuch", *ThEv(SA)* 1 (1968) 37–52, 38.

[213]Cf. the fact that in Gen. 49:8bA also a wordplay is made with יָדְךָ, which certainly does not give the etymology of the name; see Albright, "The Names 'Israel' and 'Judah'", 169; De Fraine, *Genesis*, 326; Wenham, *Genesis 16–50*, 476. For the theoretical problems, cf. J. Barr, "Etymology and the Old Testament", in *Language and Meaning: Studies in Hebrew Language and Biblical Exegesis* (OTS, 19), Leiden 1974, 1–28, esp. 15–16.

[214]Van der Merwe, "Judah in the Pentateuch", 38, n. 4, refers here to Kraus, *Psalmen*, Bd. I, 63, who writes (concerning Ps. 7:18): "הורה aber, das wir mit 'preisen' übersetzten, bedeutet eigentlich: 'bekennen', 'bejahen'". Van der Merwe continues then: "It is interesting to note that this word is often used to indicate

nection of the name Judah with the verb *hodah* (praise) is not merely a popular etymology but an allusion to the supremacy of the tribe of Judah and the Davidic kingship."[215]

The etymology could be right, nevertheless, although we have to reckon with a very unusual morphological form of the hoph. of the verb, since the ה in the impf. tense of the hiph./hoph.-forms is mostly elided.[216] However, the retention of the ה does appear sometimes, even in the hiph. of ידה, namely Ps. 28:7; 45:18; Neh. 11:17.[217] Nevertheless, if this etymology was correct it is likely that we would have found some forms of the name, where the ה was elided, like יוּדָה, יָדָה, יוּד or יָד; but these forms are completely absent.[218] Within the Hebrew Bible the only variant to be found for the name יְהוּדָה is LN יְהוּד, written in Josh. 19:45 as יְהֻד.[219] In EHebr. a larger amount of this variant is found: יהד is given six times against יהוד eight; where יהדה is given four times against יהודה only once.[220] In case of deriva-

---

the praising of Yahweh in public, cf. Ps. 18:50; 35:18; 57:10; 109:30; 111:1; 138:1. That the public acknowledgment of a king forms part of the coronation ceremonies is evident from 1 Sam. 10:24; 1 Kgs. 1:39, 40; 2 Kgs. 11:12." Cf. on the meaning of ידה: M.J. Boda, "Words and Meanings: ידה in Hebrew Research", *WTJ* 57 (1995) 277–297.

[215]Van der Merwe, "Judah in the Pentateuch", 4.

[216]Millard, 217; GK, §53ab; JM, §54a. This etymology is called "dubious" by BDB, 397; similar by R. Zadok, *The Pre-Hellenistic Israelite Antroponymy and Prosopography* (OLA, 28), Leuven 1988, 135 (§21369). Furthermore, Van Selms, *Genesis, dl. II*, 102, denies the possibility of deriving the name from הוֹדָה ("De naam Juda kan niet van het werkwoord *hōdā*, 'loven', afgeleid worden."); similar: Van der Merwe, "Judah in the Pentateuch", 38. Cf. also Lipiński, "L'étymologie de 'Juda'", 380; Görg, "Juda — Namensdeutung", 82. The latter argues that such usage ("El/JHWH möge gepriesen werden") is not testified either in BHebr., or in EHebr. He adds to this argument, that this is confirmed by the fact that such usage does not appear in the Hebr. nomenclature — although he does not want to overstress this argument, referring to Millard, "Meaning of the Name Judah", 217, who does not exclude the possibility of such usage (the hoph. of ידה, RdH), because of the high frequency of the hiph. of ידה (Görg, *art.cit.*, 82, n. 20). However, it cannot be denied that in case of the verb ידה the hoph. is not attested; whereas there is also no other example of a causative passive impf. (Zadok, *op.cit.*, 135). Moreover, the imper. hiph. of ידה is the most common form to express the wish that YHWH has to be praised; also in PN: הוֹדַוְיָהוּ / הוֹדַוְיָה (*HAL*, 231; Ezra 2:40; 3:9; Neh. 7:43; 1 Chron. 3:24; 5:24; 9:7).

[217]GK, §53q; BL, §25e′–h′; JM, §54b.

[218]*Pace* De Moor, "The Twelve Tribes", 486–7, who suggests we read the defective reading שָׂרֵי יָד "princes of Yûdah" for שָׂרִיד in Judg. 5:13. Since this appearance of יָד as the short form of יְהוּדָה is based on an emendation, it cannot be considered to prove the contrary.

[219]*HAL*, 376.

[220]Only the evident cases are considered here; cf. G.I. Davies, *Ancient Hebrew*

tion from יָדָה impf. hoph., this would be an inexplicable spelling, for
the ו is never elided in the impf. hiph./hoph.-forms, where retention
of the ה appears and just once in a part. hiph./hoph., and in that
case a very doubtful one: מְהֻקְצָעוֹת (Ezek. 46:22).[221] These data make
the derivation of the name יְהוּדָה from יָדָה impf. hoph. questionable.
M. Görg concluded, therefore, that the radicals ה־ד are the best attested in this name. For Görg — preceded already by E. Meier[222] —
this was reason enough to suggest another etymology for the name,
namely a root connected with the noun הוֹד "majesty, splendour".[223]
This root is found in several other PNN,[224] like אֲבִיהוּד, "Father is

---

Inscriptions: Corpus and Concordance, Cambridge 1991, 364–5. There is also a
PN יְדוֹ (*HAL*, 372; cf. Davies, *op.cit.*, 362), whose etymology is uncertain (< ידה II
or ידע (?), *HAL*, 372). But even if this name could be derived from the root ידה II,
it is certainly not a hiph./hoph.-form of יָדָה. However, the name is derived mostly
from ידע: Noth, *IPN*, 39, 181; B.J. Oosterhoff, *Israëlietische persoonsnamen* (Ex,
I/4), Delft 1953, 76; J.J. Stamm, "Der Name des Königs Salomo", *ThZ* 16 (1960)
285–297, 292 (= Stamm, *BHAN*, 52); Fowler, *TPN*, 158, 347.

Albright, "The Names 'Israel' and 'Judah'", 171, argues that LXX supported
the vocalization of an elided ה with Ιουδα(ς). This argument is however not valid,
first because Gr. does not have a corresponding consonant for Hebr. ה and would
thus almost automatically skip this consonant. This can be demonstrated on the
basis of Hebr. names with initial יְה־, which are written in LXX in a shortened form
with initial Iη–, Iου– or Iω–; cf. יְהוֹשׁוּעַ > Iησου(ς) (Deut. 3:21); יְהוֹאָחָז > Iωαχας
(2 Kgs. 10:35); יְהוֹאָשׁ > Iωας (2 Kgs. 12:1–3). Secondly, this can be demostrated
on the basis of Hebr. names with initial ה, which are not rendered uniformly by
LXX; cf. הוֹדִיָּה > Iδουιας (1 Chron. 4:19), and Ωδουια (Neh. 10:11 / 2 Ezra 20:11);
הוֹהָם > Aιλαμ (Josh. 10:3); הוֹשֵׁעַ > Aυση (Num. 13:8) and Ωσηε (2 Kgs. 15:30).
These examples show clearly that the testimony of the LXX for the vocalization
of names has to be used very critically, certainly in case of a name with a ה in it.

[221] GK, §53q. This word is text-critically uncertain (LXX, Peš, and Vg did not
read the word), while the word was, even for the Masoretes, a riddle, cf. the fact
that they used the *puncta extraordinaria* (GK §5n) here. W. Zimmerli, *Ezechiel:
2.Teilband, Ezechiel 25–48* (BKAT, XIII/2), Neukirchen-Vluyn 1969, 1181, suggested we consider this word as a wrongly inserted gloss in the text det. subst.
מִקְצֹעוֹת (V. 22Aa) ("Warscheinlicher ist hier aber das fälschlich nochmals als Glosse
in den Text geratene det. subst. מקצעות zu finden").

[222] E. Meier, *Die Israeliten und ihre Nachbarstämme: Alttestamentliche Untersuchungen*, Halle a.S. 1906, 441. Görg apparently missed this reference. Cf. also
Borée, *Die alten Ortsnamen Palästinas*, 100 (§30, #5), 101 (§31, #3), suggesting
(carefully, with question mark) we derive יְהוּד and יְהוּדָה from הוֹד.

[223] GB, 176, does already postulate the existence of the root *הוֹד. Cf. for הוֹד
furthermore: *HAL*, 231; *DBHE*, 171; D. Vetter, "הוֹד", *THAT*, Bd. I, 472–4; G.
Warmuth, "הוֹד", *ThWAT*, Bd. II, 375–9.

According to R. Samuel ben Meir (Raschbam) (see Jacob, *Das erste Buch*, 900);
Socin in GB, 176, הוֹד has to be derived from ידה, hiph.; but this is etymologically
very unlikely, cf. n. 248 below.

[224] Cf. Fowler, *TPN*, 85–6, on PNN with roots which are not attested elsewhere in
BHebr., but only in other Sem. languages, esp. Arab. Two other ע"ו-roots, whose

majesty";[225] אֲחִיהוּד "Brother is majesty";[226] עַמִּיהוּד, "Father's brother is majesty";[227] הוֹדִיָּה and הוֹדִיָּהוּ "majesty is YHWH";[228] and in EHebr. הודיה(ו).[229] Although in BHebr.*הוד is not attested as a verb, its existence as such is plausible and could be defended on the basis of a comparison with several other ע″ו-roots. The clearest example is the existence of the root טוב and its derivatives טוֹב and טוּב,[230] returning in the PNN אֲבִיטוּב, אֲחִיטוּב and טוֹבִיָּה(וּ).[231] These PNN have exactly the same construction as the PNN constructed with *הוד and therefore offer a solid basis for comparison. In the analysis of the names אֲבִיהוּד, אֲחִיהוּד and עַמִּיהוּד, most studies take the element הוד as a derivative from the noun הוֹד, mostly unvocalized and written as הוד.[232] The ana-

---

existence could be derived from a noun and from Arab. are *חוּץ > חוּץ (*HAL*, 286) and *קוֹל > קוֹל (*HAL*, 1012–5). Cf. also J. Barr, *Comparative Philology and the Text of the Old Testament*, Oxford 1968, 181–184.

[225] BDB, 4; *HAL*, 4–5; Ges[18], 5; *DCH*, vol. I, 104; G. Warmuth, "הוד", 379; Noth, *IPN*, 146; Oosterhoff, *Israëlietische persoonsnamen*, 36, 68; J.J. Stamm, "Hebräische Ersatznamen", in *Studies in Honor of Benno Landsberger on His Seventy-Fifth Birthday* (AS 16), Chicago, Ill. 1965, 413–424, 418 (= Stamm, *BHAN*, 69); Fowler, *TPN*, 81.

[226] *HAL*, 32; Ges[18], 37; *DCH*, vol. I, 189; Warmuth, "הוד", 379; Noth, *IPN*, 146; Oosterhoff, *Israëlietische persoonsnamen*, 36, 69; Stamm, "Hebräische Ersatznamen", 418 (= Stamm, *BHAN*, 69); Fowler, *TPN*, 81; BDB, 26: "brother of majesty".

[227] *HAL*, 799; Warmuth, "הוד", 379; Noth, *IPN*, 146; Oosterhoff, *Israëlietische persoonsnamen*, 36, 70; Stamm, "Hebräische Ersatznamen", 418 (= Stamm, *BHAN*, 69); Fowler, *TPN*, 81; König, *Wb*, 335: "mein Beschirmer ist Kraftfülle"; BDB, 770: "my kinsman is majesty".

Albright, "The Names 'Israel' and 'Judah'", 173, rejects the meaning "majesty" for the element הוד in עַמִּיהוּד and אֲבִיהוּד without giving any argument. He nevertheless proceeds with the re-vocalization עַמִּיְהוּד and אֲבִיְהוּד. Millard, "Meaning of the Name Judah", 217, seems to agree.

[228] König, *Wb*, 76; *HAL*, 231; Oosterhoff, *Israëlietische persoonsnamen*, 36, 70; Fowler, *TPN*, 81. Cf. furthermore also the shorted form הוֹד, הֹדִי (*HAL*, 229; Noth, *IPN*, 146; Fowler, *TPN*, 158), and probably also אֵהוּד (the etymology is uncertain: a shortened form of אֲחִי/אֲבִי + הוד "father/brother is majesty"? Cf. *HAL*, 18; Noth, *IPN*, 235; Fowler, *TPN*, 155). Or אֵי + הוד, "where is the majesty?", cf. the comparable אִיזֶבֶל, "where is his Highness?" (cf. *UF* 1, 188); אִיכָבוֹד, "where is the glory?" and probably also אִיעֶזֶר, "where is the help?" (?; cf. *HAL*, 41); see Stamm, "Hebräische Ersatznamen", 418 (= Stamm, *BHAN*, 69). Cf. also 'y'l, "where is El?", and Smith, *Early History of God*, 5, n. 29, 42, 65–6, n. 10.

[229] Fowler, *TPN*, 81; cf. also J. Tigay, *You Shall Have No Other Gods: Israelite Religion in the Light of Hebrew Inscriptions* (HSS, 31), Atlanta, Ga. 1986, 50.

[230] For the recurrence of ו- and וֹ-nouns of the same ע″ו-root, cf. אוֹר > אוֹר and אוּר (*HAL*, 23–25); דוֹר I > דוֹר I–III and דוּר (*HAL*, 208–9); רוֹם > רוֹם and רוּם (*HAL*, 1121–5); cf. also סוֹף > סוֹף and סוּפָה (*HAL*, 705–6); צוֹק I > צוֹק and צוּקָה (*HAL*, 951).

[231] Cf. also the PNN אִישְׁהוֹד and אִישׁ(־)טוֹב; *HAL*, 43.

[232] *HAL*, 4 (cf. also *op.cit.*, 32, 799, where reference is made to the entry הוֹד,

lysis of the names composed with the root טוב suggests we take הוֹד in
הוֹדִיָה and הוֹדִיָּה as a stative qal perf. similar to טוֹב in טוֹבִיָּה(וּ).[233] The
names אֲבִיהוּד and אֲחִיהוּד have likewise to be taken as nominal names
composed with the noun הוּד*, as is usual with the noun טוֹב.[234] Other
comparable derivations could be found in PN יְקוּתִיאֵל < קוּת* + אֵל, "El
nourishes";[235] LN יַבּוּס < בּוּס;[236] PN יְעוּשׁ from עוּשׁ(?);[237] PN יְכָנְיָה(וּ) <
כּוּן, "to set up; to establish" (hiph.).[238]

    These data make the argument for the existence of the root הוּד*
conclusive[239] and open up, at the same time, the opportunity to accept יְהוּדָה as a derivative of the impf. qal of הוּד*. However, the final ה-
appears to remain a stumbling block as it did for those scholars who
derived יְהוּדָה from the root ידה. The ending could best be considered
as the remnant of the theophoric element which was originally at the
end of the name.[240] This also seems to be suggested by the rendering
of the names in Aram. (yh(w)d) and Akk. (Ia-a-ḫu-du);[241] and this is

_____

op.cit., 231, which is explained as "הוּד* = הוֹד*"); DCH, vol. I, 104, 189–90; Warmuth, "הוֹד", 379; Noth, IPN, 146; Fowler, TPN, 81, 341–2. Contrast, however,
GB, 176, where the root הוד is given as a separate entry. Cf. also Ges[18], 5, 37.
Lexica are, however, not always uniform in their analysis of the PNN; cf. the fact
that Ges[18], 37, derives אֲחִיטוּב from אָח + טוֹב but אֲבִיטוּב is derived from אָב + טוֹב
(op.cit., 6).

[233]Fowler, TPN, 346.
[234]Fowler, TPN, 346.
[235]Also based on an Arab. root, e.g. qāta; cf. HAL, 411; Noth, IPN, 203, 35f.;
Barr, Comparative Philology, 182; Fowler, TPN, 86, 99, 359. Cf. also BDB, 429,
who derives the name from יק, "to preserve, be pious", but this proposal is less
attractive according to Fowler, op.cit., 99.
[236]HAL, 366.
[237]HAL, 401, 760; Barr, Comparative Philology, 182; Fowler, TPN, 168 (she does
not list this name in "Appendix 3: List of Ancient Hebrew Personal Names", 354).
[238]HAL, 391, 378–9; Noth, IPN, 202, n. 1; Fowler, TPN, 349.
[239]Cf. already GB, 176; furthermore Meier, Die Israeliten und ihre Nachbarstämme, 441; Görg, "Juda — Namensdeutung", 85–6.
[240]Cf. for the ה- as a remnant of theophoric elements, Noth, IPN, 38; Millard,
"Meaning of the Name Judah", 217, Fowler, TPN, 165–6; Zadok, Pre-Hellenistic
Israelite Antroponymy, 154–156 (§§220, 22111). Millard, art.cit., 217, gives several
examples of other abbreviated names ending at ה-. The best-known example (מִיכָה
< מִיכָאֵל/יְה(וּ), [< מִי + כְ + יְה(וּ) or אֵל; cf. HAL, 545; Noth, IPN, 144; Fowler, TPN,
152]) is problematic, however, because the כָה- at the end reflects the archaic
pronunciation of כְ < ka* (see BL, §82p; JM, §103b for this archaic form).
    Nevertheless, cf. also מַתַּתָּה with מַתִּתְיָה(וּ) (cf. HAL, 620; Noth, IPN, 170; Fowler,
TPN, 165); and probably also רְפָיָה with רְפָה, which both are names for the same
person (cf. also רְפָאֵל; see HAL, 1189–90, 1191). Further (not the same person,
but probably the same name): אֵלִיָּה(וּ) and אֵלָה (HAL, 50, 53); חֲשַׁבְנָה and חֲשַׁבְנְיָה
(HAL, 347); שְׁבַנְיָה(וּ) and שְׁבְנָה (= שְׁבְנָא; HAL, 1297–8); שְׁמַעְיָהוּ and שִׁמְעָה (HAL,
1457, 1459).
[241]Zadok, Pre-Hellenistic Israelite Antroponymy, 135 (§21369).

also confirmed by the occurence of the name יַעְקֹבָה (1 Chr. 4:36) next to the name יַעְקֹב, which are undoubtedly hypochoristic forms of the name יעקבאל*.[242] It has also been suggested we consider the ending as a ה-locale, which is sometimes found at the end of GNN.[243] However, since this ending has almost always[244] the *mil'el*-stress, whereas יְהוּדָה has the *milra'*-stress,[245] a shift in stress has to be assumed, when accepting this etymology. Finally, since we are dealing here with an imperfect, the ending might be explained as the very rare 3.p. of the cohortative (three occurrences),[246] which is also known from the Amarna tablets and found in Ugaritic.[247] However, since these occurrences have also the *mil'el*-stress, and are, furthermore, as rare as the non-contracted hiph. of ידה, this solution is not to be preferred.

In conclusion, the most preferable etymology for the name יְהוּדָה appears to be the derivation of the root הוד* impf. qal[248] while the ה– at the end is in all likelihood the result from the abbreviation of the final element אל or יה(ו), meaning "may N.N. be majesty, glorious" or the like.

---

[242] De Moor, *RoY*, 237, with n. 82.

[243] Cf. BL, §65n–x; Borée, *Die alten Ortsnamen Palästinas*, 101 (§31); Rainey, "The Toponymics of Eretz-Israel", 4.

[244] Cf. JM, §93c, for some three exceptions.

[245] Cf. JM, §15b. See also Rainey, "Toponymics of Eretz-Israel", 4.

[246] Cf. JM, §45a, n. 1; only three examples are listed: יָחִישָׁה (Isa. 5:19); תְּבוֹאָה (idem); תָּעֻפָה (Job 11:17).

[247] Cf. E. Verreet, *Modi Ugaritici: Eine morpho-syntaktische Abhandlung über das Modalsystem im Ugaritischen* (OLA, 27), Leuven 1988, 8–9, with n. 55; 126–8. For the Amarna tablets, see: A.F. Rainey, *Canaanite in the Amarna Tablets: A Linguistic Analysis of the Mixed Dialect used by Scribes from Canaan* (HdO 1.Abt., 25), Leiden 1996, Vol. 2, 254–63.

[248] Görg, "Judah — Namensdeutung", 85, suggested we relate the root הוד* with הדד (הד(ר) and the DN הדד. However, the connection with Arab. 'awada "be weighty" and *audat* "burden" (*HAL*, 231; Warmuth, "הוֹד", 375–9) is more likely, when compared to synonymous nouns of הוד (cf. Ps. 145:5a) such as כבוד, "weight, burden; splendour, honour, glory" (*HAL*, 436–7; cf. also PN יוֹכֶבֶד and De Moor, *RoY*, 150, n. 218; cf. also n. 228 above) and הָדָר, "splendour" (cf. *HAL*, 230, and Arab. *hadara* "effort made for nothing"); cf. Warmuth, *art.cit.*, 375–9, 375–6.
The connection between Hebr. roots with an initial ה and Arab. roots with initial *aleph* does occur several times, cf. Hebr. הֲ, הַ and הֶ and Arab. *'a* (*HAL*, 226); Hebr. הֶבֶל II and Arab. *'abāl* (*HAL*, 227); Hebr. הָה and Arab. *'āh* (*HAL*, 230); Hebr. הֵימָן and OSArab. *'ymn* (*HAL*, 235); Hebr. הַלֵּזֶה and OSArab. *'l ḏi* and Arab. *allaḏi* (*HAL*, 236); Hebr. הֵן and הִנֵּה and Arab. *'in* and *'inna* (*HAL*, 241–2); Hebr. הפך and Arab. *'afaka* (*HAL*, 243). If the connection of הוד* with Arab. *'awada* is correct, then the link between Hebr. הוד* and הד(ר) is very unlikely, for the latter word is connected with Arab. *hadda* (*HAL*, 228; Warmuth, *art.cit.*, 375; cf. also J.C. de Moor, H. de Vries, "Hebrew *hēdād* 'Thunder-storm'", *UF* 20 [1988] 173–7, 174).

2.4.1.2   The Meaning of שִׁילֹה in v. 10bA

2.4.1.2.1   The *Versiones*

From ancient times the saying concerning Judah in v. 10bA has posed a problem to exegetes, and no consensus is in sight.[249] The word שׁילה already troubled the ancient translators.[250] Notwithstanding the differences between the Vrs, they all point in one direction: the saying concerns a person who will come (יְבֹא), apparently the Messiah. This interpretation is found explicitly in TO and TN: עד [זמן] דייתי [מלכא] משׁיחא דדיליה היא מלכותא,[251] "until [the time King] Messiah comes, to whom belongs the Kingdom/ship".[252] This translation reflects the interpretation of the rabbis.[253] LXX interpreted our text in an almost similar way: ἕως ἂν ἔλθῃ τὰ ἀποκείμενα αὐτῷ, "until he comes for whom it was preserved". This rendering is undoubtedly based on the reading אֲשֶׁר לֹו = שֶׁלֹּה (praep. with suffix 3.p. msc.sg.);[254] a similar text is found with Aq. en Theod.[255] This interpretation is also found in TO and TN in the double translation דדיליה היא מלכות, and is also reflected in Peš.[256] Sam had the same text as MT: שׁילה,[257] but some manuscripts read שׁלה, as do some forty manuscripts of MT.[258] Finally, MT offered

---

[249]Cf. the remark of R. Martin-Achard, "A propos de la bénédiction de Juda en Genèse 49,8–12(10)", in: J. Doré (*et.al.* eds.), *De la Tôrah au Messie: Études ...H. Cazelles*, Paris 1981, 121–34, 126, after discussing the most recent solutions: "Mais le bilan n'est pas que négatif; un consensus semble s'établir entre les meilleurs des spécialistes pour éviter les exégèses saugrenues de Gn 49,10." Westermann, *Genesis 37–50*, 262–3, writes: "Es ist kein Ruhmesblatt der Exegese des AT, dass sich eine derartige Zahl von Untersuchungen mit diesem einen Wort beschäftigt hat", and "zu der gesamten Diskussion ist zu bemerken, dass sich in ihr ein Fortschritt zu *einem gewissen begrenzten Konsensus* nicht feststellen lässt" (emphasis, RdH).

[250]For a presentation of the different traditions, see Th.C. Vriezen, A.S. van der Woude, *De literatuur van Oud-Israël*, Wassenaar ⁴1973, 98–100.

[251]Between square brackets we noted the pluses of TN, which tallies *grosso modo* with TO. Yet, TN renders דדידיה instead of דדיליה, but obviously means the same.

[252]Translation by Grossfeld, *TOGen*, 158. The rendering of מלכותא is a matter of interpretation; cf. Dalman, *Hw*, 238.

[253]Cf. Skinner, *Genesis*, 521–3; M. Aberbach, B. Grossfeld, *Targum Onqelos on Genesis 49: Translation and Analytical Commentary* (SBL AS, 1), Missoula (MA) 1976, 14–6; A. Caquot, "La parole sur Juda dans le testament lyrique de Jacob (Genèse 49, 8–12)", *Sem* 26 (1976) 5–32, 20–1; Grossfeld, *TOGen*, 163, n. 25–6.

[254]M. Rösel, "Die Interpretation von Genesis 49 in der Septuagint", *BN* 79 (1995) 54–70, 63.

[255]Cf. Wevers, *Greek Text of Genesis*, 826, with n. 20.

[256]Caquot, "Parole sur Juda", 20.

[257]*Pace* Caquot, "Parole sur Juda", 20, who asserts that Sam read only שׁלה.

[258]W.L. Moran, "Gen 49,10 and its Use in Ez 21,32", *Bib* 39 (1958) 405–25; H.-P. Müller, "Zur Frage nach dem Ursprung der biblischen Eschatologie", *VT* 14 (1964) 276–93, 277; Caquot, "Parole sur Juda", 20.

as Q: שׁילו; this alternative reading is rather important, because it suggests that the Masoretes considered the י in שׁילה correct, and doubted only the final ה. This variant supports the consonantal text of MT, because it is only an orthographical "correction". This is proved in v. 11, where a similar Q-variant is offered for the ה ("archaic" 3.p. msc.sg.), into ו (3.p. msc.sg.).[259] In this respect it is interesting to refer to Ezek. 21:32, which could be understood as a reference to our text:[260]

A ruin, ruin, ruin I will make it; (32aA)	עַוָּה עַוָּה עַוָּה אֲשִׂימֶנָּה
This too will not be, (32bA)	גַּם־זֹאת לֹא הָיָה
until the arrival of whom the judgment is, and I shall give it. (32bB)	עַד־בֹּא אֲשֶׁר־לוֹ הַמִּשְׁפָּט וּנְתַתִּיו

If there exists a relationship between these two texts, and Ezek. 21:32 is later than Gen. 49:10,[261] it follows that already here שׁילה was interpreted as אֲשֶׁר לוֹ.

At first sight the Vrs seem to attest a uniform tradition, reading שֶׁלֹה (relative pronoun with praep. and suffix 3.p. msc.sg.) instead of שִׁילֹה. However, this uniformity is deceptive, because the translations had to add some extra explanatory words to the text. This is especially true of TO and TN: "messiah [king]" was added, without any direct indication in the text. The translations — including LXX — are therefore paraphrastic, and thus their value as witness is not very strong, since it seems to imply they had some trouble with the text. Furthermore, Aq and Theod are probably dependent on LXX;[262] while Peš may well be relying on Targumic traditions.[263] It may be

---

[259] The exact meaning of the vocalization and the Q-variant is difficult to establish. Nevertheless, this reading accentuates the differences with the Vrs, instead of offering a similar reading. S.R. Driver, "Genesis xlix.10: An Exegetical Study", *JPh* 14 (1885) 1–28, 7, refers to TPsJ, who added "messiah", as did TO. But שׁילה is explained as *his youngest son*, based on *שִׁלְיָה in Deut. 28:57. Later on, this interpretation would have been preferred over the interpretation of the Vrs, according to Driver, and is probably the source for the vocalization of MT. Driver's explanation explains also the Q-variant, which clearly read a suffix at the end of our word; see p. 127 below. Cf. also S.H. Levey, *The Messiah: An Aramaic Interpretation. The Messianic Exegesis of the Targum* (MHUC, 2), Cincinnati (OH) 1974, 9.

[260] Cf. also Mic. 4:8; 5:1, which might be references to Gen. 49:10 as well.

[261] Cf. below, Chapter Six.

[262] Cf. Würthwein, *Text des Alten Testaments*, 55–7.

[263] See on this possibility *e.g.* E. Tov, "Tekstgetuigen en tekstgeschiedenis van Het Oude en Nieuwe Testament: A. De tekst van het Oude Testament", *BijbH*, dl. 1, 217–62, 247; P.B. Dirksen, "The Old Testament Peshitta", in: M.J. Mulder, H. Sysling (eds.), *Mikra: Text, Translation, Reading and Interpretation of the Hebrew Bible in Ancient Judaism and Early Christianity*, Assen 1988, 255–97, 283–5; Tov,

concluded, therefore, that the ancient translations do not offer a solid basis for establishing the correct reading (and interpretation) of the text.[264] The reading שֶׁלֹה is only supported by some variants of MT and Sam; and the possible reference to our text in Ezek. 21:32 merely permits the conclusion that the author of that text read שֶׁלֹּה, but "this gives us no indication of the original reading in 49,10."[265] Finally we have to conclude, first, that the Vrs suggest the final ה– should be read as a suffix 3.masc.sg.; and secondly, with these four consonants שׁילה MT and Sam preserve the most difficult reading. We end this section therefore with the remark of Moran:

> Any view which begins with *šlh* as original has no explanation for the origin of *šylh*, a unique orthography, whatever the word or words it contains, in the entire Old Testament.[266]

2.4.1.2.2   Recent Solutions: שׁילה as a Ruler.

In modern research we can roughly distinguish three opinions,[267] of which the best known is that שׁילה somehow denotes a ruler. In this approach שׁילה is considered to be the subject of יָבֹא and denotes a ruler who will supersede the one described in v. 10a. Within this interpretation we can distinguish three sub-categories:

1. The text is suspected to be corrupt and emended into מֹשְׁלֹה "his ruler" (cf. 2 Sam. 23:3; Mic. 5:1),[268] שְׁאִילֹה "the one he asked for", שִׁילֹו "his newborn son" (on the basis of Rabbinic Hebr. שָׁלִיל "embryo");[269] or שָׁלֵו "der Geruhige".[270] All these solutions

---

Textual Criticism, 152; J.C. de Moor, F. Sepmeijer, "The Peshitta of Joshua", in: P.B. Dirksen, A. van der Kooij (eds.), *The Pehitta as a Translation: Papers read at the II Peshitta Symposium held at Leiden, 19–21 August 1993* (MPI, 8), Leiden 1995, 129–76; Würthwein, *Text des Alten Testaments*, 86–7, mentions a double relationship of Tg and later also LXX, but this point of view merits caution; cf. Tov, *op.cit.*, 152, with nn. 108–9.

[264]Jacob, *Das erste Buch*, 907, stated (quoted with approval by Moran, "Gen. 49,10", 415), "Die alten Übersetzungen (LXX, Targ) haben mit שׁילה nichts anzufangen gewusst und sich mit möglichster Anlehnung an den Konsonantenbestand nach Art der Haggada mit irgendeiner Paraphrase zu Helfen gesucht".

[265]Moran, "Gen 49,10", 417, n. 1.

[266]Moran, "Gen 49,10", 415.

[267]Cf. Müller, "Ursprung biblischen Eschatologie", 276–8.

[268]Procksch, *Genesis*, 269; Von Rad, *Erste Buch Mose*, 349; Westermann, *Genesis 37–50*, 247–8, 262–3.

[269]E. Sellin, "Die Schilohweissagung", in: *Theologische Studien: Th. Zahn . . .*, Leipzig 1908, 369–90. Skinner, *Genesis*, 520, lists these derivations (disapproving of them) next to the one mentioned in n. 259.

[270]Gunkel, *Genesis*, 482; Bruno, *Genesis – Exodus*, 320; J. Klausner, *The Mes-*

require either an emendation of the consonantal text, which is not supported by the Vrs, or are based on Rabbinic Hebrew[271] and are therefore unconvincing.

2. The word is connected with Akk. *šēlu/šīlu* "lord, ruler".[272] This etymology was based, however, on older glossaries, and Moran has shown on the basis of recent data that Akk. *šīlu* does not denote "lord, ruler".[273]

3. Finally, a number of modern scholars adopt the alternative reading of MT, Sam and the interpretation of TO, TN and LXX: שֶׁלֹּה, "(until comes) to whom it (*viz.* the sceptre, the ruler's staff [v. 10a]) belongs".[274] This construction was already rejected by Dillmann, who states that grammatically this is "kein Satz und

---

sianic Idea in Israel: From its Beginning to the Completion of the Mishnah, New York 1955, 29–31: שׁילה is to be derived from שׁלה, like שְׁלֹמֹה "Solomon" from שׁלם. Caquot, "Parole sur Juda", 26–7, reads שׁילה and considers it to be a PN in the sense of an "appellation caritative" of Solomon. Already G.Ch. Aalders, "De Silo-profetie (Gen. 49:10)", *GerThT* 15 (1914) 341–55; idem, "Nog iets over de Silo-profetie", *ibid.*, 430–1, considers שׁילה as a PN which he seeks to explain in a messianic way. The circumstance that we do not know the meaning of this name does not allow the conclusion that שׁילה is not a PN. According to Aalders, the most likely explanation has to take its departure from the root שׁלה "to live care-free, in happy rest".

[271]Skinner, *Genesis*, 520, says of these suggested etymologies of שׁליל and שׁליה that they are "obviously superficial and fallacious analogies".

[272]P. Riessler, "Zum 'Jakobsegen'", *ThQ* 90 (1908) 489–503, 494; G.R. Driver, "Some Hebrew Roots and Their Meanings", *JThS* 23 (1922) 69–73; F. Nötscher, "Gen. 49,10: שׁילה = akk. *šēlu*", *ZAW* 47 (1929) 323–325; E. Dhorme, *La Poésie biblique*, Paris 1931, 101, n. 3; Coppens, "Bénédiction de Jacob", 112–4; Von Nordheim, *Lehre der Alten*, Bd. II, 45. A similar solution was offered by H. Seebaß, "Die Stämmespruche Gen 49,3–27", *ZAW* 96 (1984) 333–50, 346, who tries to explain שׁילה by means of Eg. *śr*, "prince" (> *šiāra* [=Eg. "Lautstand" *śjr(w)*] > Hebr. "Lautstand" שׁילה). However, Hebr. already knows a word שַׂר "prince", to be linked to Eg. *śr* (*HAL*, 1259), which renders this suggestion unlikely.

[273]Moran, "Gen 49,10", 405–409; Barr, *Comparative Philology*, 120. Cf. also *AHw*, Bd. III, 1210–11; *CAD*, vol. Š, part. II, 274–6, 451–3.

[274]Driver, Genesis XLIX 10", 1–28; G. Beer, "Zur Geschichte und Beurteilung des Schöpfungsberichtes Gen 1,1–2,4a nebst einem Exkurs über Gen 49,8–12 und 22–26", in: K. Marti (Hrsg.), *Beiträge zur alttestamentlichen Wissenschaft: Fs K. Budde* (BZAW, 34), Giessen 1920, 20–30, 29; Böhl, *Genesis*, 49; Skinner, *Genesis*, 524; Müller, "Ursprung biblischer Eschatologie", 278, n. 2 (with literature; Gunkel, who was quoted by Müller, took in a later edition of his commentary a different point of view; cf. n. 270 above); Pehlke, *Genesis 49:1–28*, 170–4. Another interpretation of שׁלה was offered by W. Schröder, "Gen 49,10: Versuch einer Erklärung", *ZAW* 29 (1909) 186–198, who proposed to read שֵׁלָה, "Sela" the son of Judah. V. 10bA would have been an ironic expansion of the text, when Judah had lost his supremacy.

gar nicht zu verstehen".[275] Moran adds to this that as far as
he knows nobody has ever answered this objection by citing at
least one parallel for such a construction.[276] Therefore we agree
with Moran's harsh judgment, "we maintain that it is bad Hebrew, which, of course, we are more inclined to assign to exegetes
than to the author of Gen 49."[277]

2.4.1.2.3   שִׁילֹה Stands for the Village Shiloh

It is suggested — with reference to the vocalization of the word — to
regard שִׁילֹה as an *accusativus loci*: *viz* "Shiloh", as an alternative reading for the name of the village in the Ephraimite Hill Country.[278] The
saying would contain an appeal to a descendant of Judah (David?)
to come to Shiloh, the old cult centre, to assume dominion over the
other tribes.[279] This proposal, of which Lindblom was the most im-

---

[275]Dillmann, *Die Genesis*, 443; quoted with appreciation by Moran, "Gen 49,10",
409.

[276]Moran, "Gen 49,10", 410. This is also true for Pehlke, *Genesis 49:1-28*, 172,
although he mentions several examples of the use of the relative שׁ. However,
the presumed parallels he cites are unconvincing because they are by no means
comparable to the supposed construction. Apart from the grammatical aspect,
Pehlke tacitly emends the Hebr. text by omitting the י.

[277]Moran, "Gen 49,10", 410; he also points to the fact that all the Sem. Vrs
added an extra subject to this colon, which also demonstrates that the Hebr.
construction would have been grammatically incorrect. Furthermore he poses that
the construction is needlessly obscure in comparison with the rest of the poem and
that the parallelism with the following colon would be disturbed. His argument
(p. 410) that שׁ as a relative pronoun is a feature of the northern dialect, whereas
these verses arose in the south, has to be dismissed because this is an unproven
supposition.

[278]Khirbet Seilun nowadays (M.R. 177–162). There are several alternative
spellings in BHebr. for this name: שִׁלֹה (21×); שִׁלוֹ (8×); שִׁילוֹ (2×); cf. KBL, 973;
HAL, 1371.

[279]Von Herder, *Geist der Ebraeischen Poesie*, 77–8; Jacob, *Das erste Buch*, 907–
8; J. Lindblom, "The Political Background of the Shilo Oracle", in: *Congress
Volume, Copenhagen 1953* (SVT, 1), Leiden 1953, 78–87, 86; idem, *Prophecy in
Israel*, 77–8; O. Eissfeldt, "Silo und Jerusalem", in *Volume de Congres Strass-
bourgh 1956* (SVT, 4), Leiden 1957, 138–147; Zobel, *SuG*, 13; Emerton, "Some
Difficult Words", 83–88; H.-J. Zobel, "יִשְׂרָאֵל", *ThWAT*, Bd. III, 1000; Blum, *Die
Komposition der Vätergeschichten*, 262–3; D.G. Schley, *Shiloh: A Biblical City in
Tradition and History* (JSOTS, 63), Sheffield 1989, 161–163; A. Catastini, "Sul
Testo di *Genesi* 49:10", *Henoch* 16 (1994) 15–22.

A mixture of the first (subject of יָבֹא) and the second solution ("Shiloh") is
offered by M. Treves, "Shiloh (Genesis 49,10)", *JBL* 85 (1966) 353–356. He suspects v. 10bA to be an ironical expansion after the division of the Kingdom. In
view of the fact that Ahijah the Shilonite (1 Kgs. 11:29–39) had announced the
division, the phrase עַד כִּי יָבֹא אִישׁ שִׁילֹה, "until the man of Shiloh comes" would

portant advocate,[280] is based mainly on the amphictyonic hypothesis, in which it is suggested that in a central sanctuary (*in casu* Shiloh) the power of one tribe over the others was assumed. Shiloh was a kind of representative name of the northern tribes, a usage which is very common in the Hebrew Bible.[281]

Yet this interpretation is problematic too. First of all the spelling would be unique among the other thirty three occurences of the name in the Hebrew Bible, although not impossible. Emerton proposed we consider this reading as the most correct one because of the vocalization of the word. But exactly this vocalization has troubled exegetes throughout the ages which would never have been the case if "Shiloh" had been such an obvious choice. The vocalization שִׁילֹה may well have been a temporary solution on basis of the supposed *mater lectionis* ‎ʾ which apparently could be read only as ‎ʾ —.[282]

In addition it may be remarked that the Q-variant suggests that the vocalization is not meant for שִׁילֹה (K), but for שִׁילוֹ (Q). This would mean that the Masoretes were inclined to change the final ה into ו. This is remarkable because we do not find this Q-variant in the other twenty-one places where MT reads the defective שִׁלֹה, Apparently the Q-variant is not based on the orthography of the name "Shiloh". Because שִׁלֹה is the most common writing for this place name, it seems likely that the Masoretes would have retained שִׁלֹה, not the Q-variant שִׁילוֹ, if they had intended the place name. Invoking the vocalization of Q for understanding "Shiloh" is a dubious procedure because the vowels were not meant to convey that interpretation. The Q-variant with its vocalization has two parallels in v. 11, where the suffix ‎ה- has to be read as ‎ו-. This leads to the conclusion that vocalization of the final ה was meant to be a reading of a suffix 3.sg. masc. at the end of the word.[283]

Secondly, as Moran argues, there is no indication throughout the

---

have been added. In the later process of transmission of the text אִישׁ would have been omitted, causing all the problems with the interpretation.

[280] Eissfeldt, "Silo und Jerusalem", 141; Zobel, *SuG*, 13; both scholars defend a date in the period of the Judges.

[281] Cf. Zidon (Gen. 49:13), Zion, Joseph, Ephraim, Jezreel (Hos. 2:24); Lindblom, "Political Background", 86.

[282] Cf. Caquot, "Parole sur Juda", 23, n. 2. We are aware of the fact that the Masoretic vocalization preserves very ancient traditions; but this does not imply the correct vocalization in every case. We could refer to the interpretation in Ezek. 21:32 (E.T. 21:27) which took the word in a completely different sense; cf. Moran, "Gen 49,10", 416–8.

[283] The vocalization does not have to be correct; but the explanation of the final ה which has to be understood as a suffix, seems to be in line with the explanation of TPsJ, described in n. 259 above.

Hebrew Bible that one tribe gained ascendancy over the other tribes
in Shiloh, neither consistently, nor that it ever happened: "a tradition
of some sort would be necessary for Shiloh to become the symbol of
such an ascendancy".[284]

That Shiloh is less important than is assumed, is strengthened by
the fact that this town did not play an important role in Israel after
the division of the Kingdom.[285] When Jeroboam succeeded in break-
ing the Northern kingdom away from the Davidic-Solomonic empire,
it was important for him to appeal to older traditions, which could
function to strengthen his authority; he therefore made Shechem his
residence.[286] This seems to confirm the central role Shechem played in
the "premonarchical" period, when the first king in Israel also reigned
in this city (Judges 9).[287] Jeroboam choose Bethel and Dan as sanc-

---

[284]Moran, "Gen 49,10", 411. Cf. also already Skinner, *Genesis*, 522–3.

[285]The term "division of the Kingdom" is usual, but not proper: a better term
would probably be "the non-renewal of the personal union"; cf. H. Donner, "The
Separate States of Israel and Judah", in: J.H. Hayes, J.M. Miller (eds.), *Israelite
and Judaean History*, London 1977, 381–434, 385; for a description of the differences between North and South, cf. G.W. Ahlström, *The History of Ancient
Palestine from the Palaeolithic Period to Alexander's Conquest* (JSOTS, 146),
D. Edelman (ed.), Sheffield 1993, 543–9.

[286]Cf. the fact that — according to the DtrH — "all Israel" came to Shechem to
make Rehoboam king (1 Kgs. 12:1). See also J.M. Miller, J.H. Hayes, *A History
of Ancient Israel and Judah*, London 1986, 229–31; Ahlström, *History of Ancient
Palestine*, 543–51.

[287]On Shechem in the "premonarchical" period, cf. also below, Chapter Six, the
diachronical analysis of Gen. 47:27–49:33; esp. concerning Gen. 48:22; furthermore S. Tengström, *Die Hexateucherzählung: Eine literaturgeschichtliche Studie*
(CB OTS, 7), Lund 1976, 37ff.; Miller, Hayes, *History*, 230–1; W.T. Koopmans,
Joshua 24 as Poetic Narrative, Sheffield 1990, *passim*; Ahlström, *History of Ancient Palestine*, 548–9.

In the so-called "premonarchical" period power was much more dispersed than
the historical books would lead us to believe. On the one hand, we have the role
of the םיטפש, "judges", who acted in a similar way as the kings in Canaan; De
Moor, *RoY*, 199, n. 401; idem, "Ugarit and the Origin of Job", in: G.J. Brooke
et al. (eds.), *Ugarit and the Bible*, Münster 1994, 250-2. Incidentally, it may be
noted that the sons of certain judges rode on asses (Judg. 10:3–4; 12:13–4); see
N.P. Lemche, *Early Israel: Antropological and Historical Studies on the Israelite
Society before the Monarchy* (SVT, 37), Leiden 1985, 275; see also Gen. 49:11!
Riding asses was a privilege of kings as is confirmed by a magnificent example
from Mari, *ARMT*, tm. VI, 76:20–25:

> My Lord should not ride a horse;
> Let my Lord ride in a chariot or a mule,
> and he will thereby honour his royal head.

(quoted from: A. Malamat, *Mari and the Early Israelite Experience* (The Schweich
Lectures of the Britisch Academy; 1984), Oxford, 1989, 80).

tuaries for his cultic reform (1 Kgs. 12:16–18). This is remarkable, because he was very likely interested in a good and solid establishment of the cultic institutions. This seems to indicate that for some reason Bethel and Dan were more important than Shiloh, or at least more attractive; and that both cities were as good a choice as Shiloh. This implies that Shiloh was not as central and as important as usually assumed by scholars, and that it had at least several important competitors.[288] References to Shiloh in some later texts (Jer. 7:12–15; 26:6–9; Ps. 78:60–70) seem to imply that Shiloh was the central sanctuary in earlier days which would seem to strengthen the case for the importance of Shiloh. However, all three are late texts and seem to be influenced by the pro-Jerusalem (and pro-David and Solomon) ideology of 1 and 2 Samuel.

Finally, עַמִּים, "nations" (v. 10bB) — when used in the plural — is seldom used for the tribes of Israel alone, but mostly for *all* the nations (incl. or excl. Israel).[289] If this final colon is expressing a view concerning all the nations, this would not create a very comprehensible parallel with the coming to Shiloh in the preceding colon; just when we would expect some clarity for such an unclear saying. We therefore agree with Moran's remark, that "such symbolism seems much too sophisticated to be plausible".[290]

2.4.1.2.4   שִׁילֹה Is Made up of שַׁי לֹה

Finally there is a proposal by Moran to re-vocalize the text and to

---

On the other hand, typical features of the judges are attributed to king Saul in the narratives about his kingship. See 1 Sam. 11:1–11 and D. Edelman, *King Saul in the Historiography of Judah* (JSOTS, 121), Sheffield 1991, 59–60 ("a traditional *šōpēṭ*"); T.N.D. Mettinger, *King and Messiah: The Civil and Sacral Legitimation of the Israelite Kings* (CB OTS, 8), Lund 1976, 83–5.

[288]Donner, "Separate States", 286–8; Miller, Hayes, *History*, 242–4; Ahlström, *History of Ancient Palestine*, 551–4; cf. also M. Weippert, "Geschichte Israels am Scheideweg", *ThR* 58 (1993) 71–103, 96–8.

Jeroboam's choice to leave Shiloh aside may have been caused by the fact that the city was destroyed during Iron I. Archaeological research has shown that the site was occupied again during Iron II, which is also attested by biblical texts (1 Kgs. 11:29; 14:2, 4; Jer. 41:5; cf. also Schley, *Shiloh*, 165–7, 200); but the inhabitants were few, see: I. Finkelstein, *The Archaeology of the Israelite Settlement*, Jerusalem 1988, 228; idem, "Seilun, Khirbet", *ABD*, vol. 5, 1069–72; I. Finkelstein *et.al.* (eds.), *Shiloh: The Archaeology of a Biblical Site*, Tel Aviv 1993, 383–9.

[289]Exceptions are Gen. 28:3; 48:4 (cf. also 35:11, גּוֹיִם). GB, 596; *HAL*, 793; Von Rad, *Erste Buch Mose*, 349; Moran, "Gen 49,10", 411. See on the other hand Zobel, *SuG*, 13; Coppens, "Bénédiction de Jacob", 112, n. 2.

[290]Moran, "Gen 49,10", 411.

read: עַד כִּי־יָבָא שַׁי לֹה, "until tribute is brought to him".[291] According
to Moran, this translation alone retains and explains the MT שׁילה;
is grammatically correct; makes excellent sense and is concrete like
everything else in the poem; and finally is the only explanation that
really offers a parallel with the following colon.[292]

Jacob objects to this solution — which was found already in earlier sources — first, that in comparison with Isa. 18:7; Pss. 68:30;
76:12, one would expect the verb יבל instead of בוא, as was used in v.
10bA; while v. 10bB should have preceded our colon.[293] However, the
expectation of יבל is based on the appearance of this word in three
other texts. This is a very low frequency to justify the dismissal of
Moran's proposal which is grammatically correct. As Moran rightly
argues, it is questionable whether the use of שׁי was so fossilized that
no other verb could be applied.[294] On the other hand, יבל is used in
sacral as well as profane contexts which suggests that the verb יבל
did not have such a specific meaning that it was the only one applic-
able to שׁי.[295] Secondly, concerning the logical sequence of cola, there

---

[291]Moran, "Gen 49,10", 412–4. He was preceded by Ehrlich, *RG*, Bd. I, 246,
who, after referring to his earlier suggestion to read Sela (cf. also n. 274 above)
refers to Raši and Midrasch Rabba par. 98; cf. BerRab. 49:4: " *'Until Shilo comes'*.
This indicates that all the nations of the world will bring a gift to Messiah, the
son of David, as it says: 'In that time shall a present be brought (yubal shay)
unto the Lord of hosts' (Isa xviii 7). Transpose *'yubal shay'* and expound it, and
you find that it reads Shiloh"; quoted from Freedman, Simon, *Midrash Rabbah
translated into English*, 906–7; for another tradition, cf. 956. Hebr.: Theodor,
Albeck, *Bereschit Rabba*, 1219–20. Moran was followed by Speiser, *Genesis*, 362–4;
R. Criado, "Hasta que venga Silo (Gen. 49,10): Recientes explicaciones católicas",
EstB 24 (1965) 289–320; E. Testa, "La formazione letteraria della benedizione di
Giacobbe (Gen. 49,2–27)", *SBF LA* 23 (1973) 167–205, 193; Cross, Freedman,
Ancient Yahwistic Poetry, 83, n. 34; G.A. Anderson, *Sacrifices and Offerings
in Ancient Israel: Studies in their Social and Political Importance* (HSM, 41),
Atlanta (Ga) 1987, 34–6; Wenham, *Genesis 16–50*, 478; M.S. Smith, *The Ugaritic
Baal Cycle, volume I: Introduction with Text, Translation and Commentary of
KTU 1.1–1.2* (SVT, 55), Leiden 1994, 291; M. Baldacci, *La Scoperta di Ugarit:
La città-stato ai primordi della Bibbia*, Casale Monferrato 1996, 265, n. 291.

[292]Moran, "Gen 49,10", 412.

[293]Jacob, *Das erste Buch*, 907.

[294]According to J.C. de Moor, "Ugarit and Israelite Origins", in: J.A. Emerton
(ed.), *Congress Volume Paris 1992* (SVT, 61), Leiden 1995, 205–38, 220, n. 69,
the contracted Ugaritic form *ṯh* "his tribute" occurs twice with the verb *'ly* "to
come up" in KTU 2.33:25, 37. In line 29 of the same tablet the word is the object
of *šyt* "to put": "I am not going to put my wife (and) my boys as his (i.e. the
king's) tribute before the enemy". In a Hebrew inscription the word שׁי is the
object of the verb שׁקל "to weigh", cf. J. Naveh, "More Hebrew Inscriptions from
Meṣad Hashavyahu", *IEJ* 12 (1962) 27–32, 30-1.

[295]*HAL*, 366.

is no chronological order implied by the conjunction introducing the following colon.[296]

Although Moran gave a few arguments in favour of the reading שַׁי לֹה,[297] we believe his point can be strengthened by comparing other texts where שַׁי is used in order to establish the semantic field of the word. As this is only the case in three other biblical texts, it seems justified to include מִנְחָה which is a synonym as we shall see. There are several arguments to justify this choice:

1. The word שַׁי is used in three texts. Two points attract attention. To begin with, the verb used in connection with שַׁי is יבל. Secondly, שַׁי is always brought to God. In Ugarit the corresponding word $\underline{t}y$ is used, viz. in KTU 2.13:14; 2.30:13; 2.33:25, 37; 5.11:6 (?). In the first two texts $\underline{t}y$ is brought to a king; however, no verb is used to denote the bringing of the $\underline{t}y$, and ndr is used in an adjectival sense.[298] In KTU 2.33 the verbs 'ly "to come up" and $\check{s}yt$ "to put" are used[299] and $\underline{t}y$ denotes a gift of the king to his servant or to his enemies. In KAI No. 214:18 $\check{s}y$ is an alternative term for a sacrifice a king offers to the gods.[300]

2. The word שַׁי is usually rendered with "gift, tribute";[301] while מִנְחָה is mostly translated in a similar way, and, depending on the context, in addition with "(grain) offering";[302] the latter a more specific

---

[296]Moran, "Gen 49,10", 413.

[297]Moran, "Gen 49,10", 412–3.

[298]Cf. J.C. de Moor, "Frustula Ugaritica", *JNES* 24 (1965) 355–64, 358, n. 27; idem, "Review of F. Gröndahl, *Die Personennamen der Texte aus Ugarit* (Studia Pohl I), Roma 1967", *BiOr* 26 (1969) 105–8, 107–8; J. Hoftijzer, "Das sogenannte Feueropfer", in: *Hebräische Wortforschung: Fs ... W. Baumgartner* (SVT, 16), Leiden 1967, 114–34, 130–2; J.C. Greenfield, "Un rite religieux Araméen", *RB* 80 (1973) 47–52, 50–1; Dijkstra, De Moor, "Problematical passages in the Legend of Aqhâtu", 172 n. 14. For another interpretation of $tyndr$, viz. a toponym, see J.-L. Cunchillos, "Mes affaires sont terminees! Traduction et commentaire de KTU 2.13", *SEL* 5 (1989) 45–50, 47; M. Dietrich, O. Loretz, "Ugaritisch it, $tyndr$ und hebräisch '$\check{s}h$, $\check{s}y$ (KTU 1.14 IV 38; 2.13:14–15; 2.30:12–14a)", *UF* 26 (1994) 63–72; For epigrafical material: *DISO*, 296; *DNWSI*, part 2, 1125.

[299]See n. 294, above.

[300]Cf. J. Tropper, *Die Inschriften von Zincirli: Neue Edition und vergleichende Grammatik des phönizischen, sam'alischen und aramäischen Textkorpus* (ALASP 6), Münster 1993, 78–9.

[301]GB, 822; *HAL*, 1368; KBL, 964. For the Ug. material, see the literature above, in note 298; and furthermore M. Dietrich *et al.*, "Ein Brief des Königs an die Königin-Mutter (RS 11.872 = CTA 50): Zur Frage Ug. itt = Hebr. '$\check{s}h$?", *UF* 6 (1974) 460–2, 461; Pardee, UB, 453; J.L. Cunchillos-Ilarri, *Estudios de Epistolografía Ugarítica*. Valencia 1989, 133.

[302]Cf. *HAL*, 568–9; H.-J. Fabry, M. Weinfeld, "מִנְחָה", *ThWAT*, Bd. IV, 987–1001.

translation of the common meaning "gift".[303] In view of the parallels in usage (see below), it seems to us that מִנְחָה may be regarded as a synonym of שַׁי.

3. Like שַׁי, מִנְחָה could be used as an object of יבל hiph., for the bringing of tribute or offerings, see respectively Hos. 10:6; Zeph. 3:9–10; and in Ugarit: KTU 1.2:i.36–8; 1.3:v.33–4.[304] Furthermore מִנְחָה is used with בוא hiph. (frequently constructed with the preposition לְ), see Gen. 4:3; 43:26; Lev. 2:8 etc.; which would be the same in Gen. 49:10bA in combination with שַׁי. The verbs יבל hiph./hoph. and בוא hiph. are used in so-called AB.AB-parallelism in Ps. 45:15–6,[305] which justifies the conclusion that these verbs form a synonymous word-pair and are exchangeable. In view of the Ug. texts, it is important to mention the combination with Hebr. נדר and Ug. ndr. In two texts it is very clear how שַׁי and מִנְחָה belong to the same semantic level, first Isa. 19:21b:

| they will serve with sacrifice and burnt offering, | וְעָבְדוּ זֶבַח וּמִנְחָה |
| make vows to YHWH and perform them | וְנָדְרוּ־נֵדֶר לַיהוָה וְשִׁלֵּמוּ |

compared to Ps. 76:12:

Make vows and perform them to YHWH your God,	נִדְרוּ וְשַׁלְּמוּ לַיהוָה אֱלֹהֵיכֶם
all around bring gifts to the fearsome One	כָּל־סְבִיבָיו יֹבִילוּ שַׁי
	לַמּוֹרָא

From these two texts it becomes clear that both שַׁי and מִנְחָה could be used as parallels for נדרו וְשלמו ליהוה (נדר), "make vows and perform them for YHWH". Here KTU 1.2:i.36–8 is important as well:[306]

ʿbdk . bʿl . yymm .	Baʿlu is your slave, O Yammu,
ʿbdk . bʿl / nhrm .	Baʿlu is your slave, Naharu,
bn . dgn . ȧsrkm .	the son of Daganu is your prisoner!
hw . ybl . ȧrgmnk . kʾilm	He also must bring you tribute, like (other) gods,
[hw .] ybl . kbn . qdš .	[he][307] also must bring you gifts, like sons of
mnḥyk	Qudshu!"

---

[303] Fabry, "מִנְחָה", 990, remarked: "Da sie [mnḥh] häufig inhaltlich erklärt wird, scheint ihre inhaltliche Konkretisierung innerhalb eines bestimmten Rahmens variabel gewesen zu sein." Cf. also Smith, *Ugaritic Baal Cycle, vol. I*, 308–9, n. 164. Comparable (in KTU 1.2:1.37–8 parallel with mnḥy) is Ug. ȧrgmn and Hebr. אַרְגָּמָן, denoting "tribute" and "purple", depending on the context of the word; cf. *HAL*, 81–2; De Moor, *SPU*, 85, n. 2; *ARTU*, 159; Smith, *op.cit.*, 308, n. 163.

[304] *ARTU*, 18, 33.

[305] Cf. also Jer. 31:9. Further E. Zurro, *Procedimientos iterativos en la poesía ugarítica y hebrea*, Valencia, Rome 1987, 229.

[306] Baldacci, *La Scoperta di Ugarit*, 265, n. 91.

De Moor refers in connection with this text to Ps. 72:10 and KTU 1.3:v.33–4.[308] A comparison with Ps. 76:9–10 shows in addition that דִּין and שׁפט; Ug. ṯpṭ, "to judge" belongs to the king; cf. also Isa. 33:22; Ps. 95:3.

To the Ugaritic verb 'ly, used with ṯy as its object, corresponds Hebr. עלה and both the qal and hiph. of this verb are used frequently with the object מִנְחָה.

It can therefore be concluded that שַׁי and מִנְחָה are very close in meaning and apparently interchangeable. Both terms could be used for gifts or tribute for a king or a god.[309] Furthermore it was shown that יבל hiph./hoph. and בוא hiph. are parallel and that the use of בוא in our text does not constitute a serious objection to this interpretation.

In the preceding paragraphs we discussed the parallel use of שַׁי and מִנְחָה. Now we shall discuss the semantic fields of the two terms which might further corroborate Moran's interpretation.

2.4.1.2.5 The Semantic Field of שַׁי

First, the text of Gen. 49:10. The text clearly describes the power of a ruler, a prince (cf. v. 10a שֵׁבֶט, "scepter" and מְחֹקֵק, "ruler's staff") over other persons/tribes: "brothers, his father's sons" (vv. 8aB and 8bB) and "his enemies" (v. 8bA). They must bow down before him (שׁחה hithp.) and praise him (ידה hiph.). In v. 9 Judah is compared to a lion, "a *royal symbol* par excellence";[310] while v. 10a describes the duration of the lordship (לֹא יָסוּר, "shall not depart"), and parallel to our problematic verse, that other nations will obey (יִקְּהַת).[311]

---

[307] Restorations/additions according to *CARTU*, 14; cf. also *CML²*, 42; *TOML*, 132; *MLC*, 172. For a different reading (and addition) in line 38, see Smith, *Ugaritic Baal Cycle, vol. I*, 267–8. Translation according to *ARTU*, 33.

[308] *ARTU*, 33, n. 146.

[309] Cf. the conclusion of Greenfield, "Un rite religieux araméen", 51: "Il apparaît alors que *šay* et *minḥa* figurent dans des contextes analogues, mais que *minḥa*, en hébreu, est employé de façon plus large." See also Korpel, *RiC*, 492–4.

[310] I. Cornelius, "The Lion in the Art of the Ancient Near East", *JNSL* 15 (1989) 53–85, 59; Korpel, *RiC*, 538–41. J. Black, A. Green, *Gods, Demons and Symbols of Ancient Mesopotamia: An Illustrated Dictionary*, London 1992, 118–9: "In literature, the lion is a favourite metaphor for warlike kings and fierce deities".

[311] יִקְּהַת is the construct form of יְקָהָה, "obedience" (similarly in Prov. 30:17; cf. GB, 313–4; *HAL*, 411), a noun derived from the root *יקה/ו (< *yqy), "to obey", cognate with OSArab qht (root wqh; cf. Hebr. PN קְהָת); Arab. waqhat (root wqy/h); Akk. utaqqū (Dt-stem of wqi; cf. *GAG*, §§93.d, 106.o) and Ug. *w/yqy, "to obey" (see KTU 1.2:i.18, 34); cf. De Moor, "Review of Gröndahl", 106; Pehlke, *Genesis 49:1–28*, 178, with nn. 1–2, 179, with n. 1; B. Margalit, "Ugaritic Lexicography IV: The name Aqht", *RB* 95 (1988) 211–4, 212; *MLC*, 170, 172, 517; Moran, "Gen 49,10", 413, n. 6; M.S. Smith, "Mythology and Myth-

In Isa. 18:7 (the closing verse of the prophecy about Ethiopia) "a people tall and smooth" is bringing "gifts" (שַׁי) to YHWH on Mt. Zion. In 17:12–14 there is a description of "peoples" and "nations" who "despoil" and "plunder"; they are Ethiopia (18:1) and Egypt (19:1). Egypt too will worship and serve YHWH (19:21): וְעָבְדוּ זֶבַח וּמִנְחָה, "they will serve with sacrifice and offerings(?)". Important is the verb עבד, "to serve" which is used to denote the subordination of Egypt.[312] The reason for this change in Egypt is Gods salvation and deliverance from the oppressors (19:20).[313]

In Ps. 68:30 kings are bringing "gifts" (שַׁי) to YHWH, because of the temple in Jerusalem. According to v. 31–33 this happens after God has shown his power to the nations; then "bronze will be brought from Egypt" and "Ethiopia will stretch out her hands to God" (v. 32). The kingdoms have to sing praise to YHWH.

In Ps. 76:12 gifts (שַׁי) are brought to YHWH, the fearsome One, in Jerusalem/Zion (v. 2), the place of his dwelling. He is praised because "He uttered judgement from the heavens; saved all the oppressed of the earth" (vv. 9–10). The wrath of men shall praise (ידה hiph.) Him; He girds the residue of wrath upon Him (v. 11); He cuts off the spirit of princes, is terrible to the kings of the earth (v. 13). This psalm corresponds strongly with the afore-mentioned Ps. 68:26–36.

---

making in Ugaritic and Israelite Literatures", in: G.J. Brooke *et.al.* (eds.), *Ugarit and the Bible: Proceedings of the International Symposium on Ugarit and the Bible, Manchester, September 1992* (UBL, 11), Münster 1994, 293–341, 302, n. 42; Smith, *Ugaritic Baal Cycle, vol. I*, 290–1.

Pehlke, *op.cit.*, 179, n. 1, objected that Ug. *yqy* "protect" cannot be applied in this case, whereas Ug. *w/yqh* would not have been attested in Ugarit, but this is not correct. Since Hebr. ל"ה-verbs are originally ל"י- or ל"ו-verbs (and not *tertiae laryngalis* as Pehlke writes [p. 178]; cf. GK §75a–b; JM §79a–c), the basic root of קה' is very likely *yqy* (Smith, *op.cit.*, 290).

[312] Ug. *'bd* is used in Ugarit to denote the vassal of the Great King (KTU 2.23:3; 2.39:6), like the Akkadian word *ardu*, "slave" (PRU IV:49, line 12). The use of עבד in this text is the typically political language for vassalage (cf. also 2 Kings 16:7; 17:3; 24:1; Ezra 9:10; 2 Chron. 12:8) and forms a parallel to the bringing of tribute; cf. J.C. de Moor, "Contributions to the Ugaritic Lexicon", *UF* 11 (1979), 650–51; H. Ringgren *et.al.*, "עָבַד", *ThWAT*, Bd. V, 982–1012, 997. Smith, *Ugaritic Baal Cycle, vol. I*, 59, 308–9; and also the preceding note. The metaphor of "vassalage" is not recognized in the discussion of "servitude" in Korpel, *RiC*, 293–99, but "servitude" is taken rather literally.

[313] The parallel between Isa. 19:21 and Ps. 76:12 on the one hand and the parallel between Isa. 18:7 and 19:21 on the other (also שַׁי and מִנְחָה) once again justifies the equation of the two terms שַׁי and מִנְחָה. Cf. also Isa. 66:20, where מִנְחָה is used as "gift, offering" and more specifically as "cereal offering", which sufficiently illustrates the problem of a correct translation; on this text, cf. W.A.M. Beuken, *Jesaja, deel IIIb* (PredOT), Nijkerk 1989, 138–9.

There are some remarkable resemblances between these four texts:

- Praise and blessing of king or God are important components of all of them: "your brothers shall praise you (יוֹדוּךָ)" (Gen. 49:8); "Bless (בָּרְכוּ)[314] God in the great congregation"; "Sing (שִׁירוּ) to God, O kingdoms of the earth" (Ps. 68:33); "Blessed (בָּרוּךְ) be God" (Ps. 68:36); "Surely the wrath of men shall praise thee (תּוֹדֶךָ)" (Ps. 76:11).

- Power over enemies is a characteristic shared by God and king, "the hand on the neck of your enemies" (Gen. 49:8);[315] "Terrible is God ... he gives power and strength to his people" (Ps. 68:36); "the residue of wrath thou wilt gird gird upon thee" (Ps. 76:11); "who cuts off the spirit of princes, who is terrible to the kings of the earth" (Ps. 76:13); in connection with Isa. 18:7; cf. also 17:12–14; 19:10.

- Submission of and supremacy over other nations is also an important part of the semantic field: "him shall obey the peoples" (Gen. 49:10); "*kings* bear gifts to thee" (Ps. 68:30); "scatter the *people* who delight in war" (Ps. 68:31); "who is terrible to the kings of the world" (Ps. 76:13); "... a *people* tall and smooth, a people feared near and far, a nation, mighty and conquering" (Isa. 18:7) who will serve YHWH.

This summary demonstrates that the figurative language in Gen. 49:8, 10 corresponds to that of the other three texts in which שׁי was used. Universal rule, tremendous power, and the recognition by other nations. Although there are only a few other texts, the conclusion seems justified that the reading שׁי לה fits very well into the context of Gen. 49:8–12. However, we will offer a discussion of the semantic field of מִנְחָה as additional evidence.

2.4.1.2.6   The Semantic Field of מִנְחָה

The word מִנְחָה could be used as a designation for tribute to a foreign king,[316] for example in Judg. 3:15: וַיִּשְׁלְחוּ ... מִנְחָה לְעֶגְלוֹן מֶלֶךְ מוֹאָב,

---

[314] For the parallelism of ברך ‖ ידה, see Pss. 49:19; 100:4 (both imper.); in external parallelism Pss. 28:6–7; 67:6–7; 106:47–8 (= 1 Chron. 16:35–6).

[315] This expression is unique in the entire Hebr. Bible. See, however, Ps. 110:1, demonstrating that such phraseology was meant to illustrate the power of the person involved.

[316] מִנְחָה is not only used with the verbs בוא hiph. and יבל hiph./hoph., but also with נגש hiph., "to bring up"; נשא, "to lift, bring"; עבד, "to serve"; שׁוב hiph., "to bring back, carry"; and שׁלח, "to send".

"sent tribute to Eglon the king of Moab" (cf. also וַיַּעַבְדוּ ... אֶת עֶגְלוֹן,
"they served Eglon" in v. 14); further also 2 Kgs. 17:3 וַיָּשֶׁב לוֹ מִנְחָה,
"and he paid him tribute" (cf. ‖ עֶבֶד ... וַיְהִי לוֹ, "and he served him"
[RSV: "became his vassal"]); and finally Hos. 10:6 יוּבָל מִנְחָה, "brought
as tribute". It can denote, however, also the tribute of the nations to
an Israelite king, see for example 2 Sam. 8:2, 6 (1 Chron. 18:2, 6):
וַתְּהִי לְדָוִד לַעֲבָדִים נֹשְׂאֵי מִנְחָה, "and they became servants to David and
brought tribute"; 2 Chron. 17:11 מְבִיאִים מִנְחָה וְכֶסֶף מַשָּׂא, "they brought
presents and silver for tribute"[317] and also 2 Chron. 17:5 וַיִּתְּנוּ כָל יְהוּדָה
מִנְחָה, "and all Judah gave presents" (RSV: "brought tribute"). For the
latter example we find a parallel in Ps. 72:10:

May the kings of Tarshish and the isles bring tribute,	מַלְכֵי תַרְשִׁישׁ וְאִיִּים מִנְחָה יָשִׁיבוּ
kings of Sheba and Seba bring gifts.[318]	מַלְכֵי שְׁבָא וּסְבָא אֶשְׁכָּר יַקְרִיבוּ

מִנְחָה is also used for presents to honour a king, or to conciliate him;
see Gen. 43:26 וַיָּבִיאוּ לוֹ אֶת הַמִּנְחָה, "and they brought the present to
him".[319] Also 1 Kgs. 5:1 (E.T. 4:21) offers an example in connection
with king Solomon, ruler "over all the kingdoms from the Euphrates
to the land of the Philistines and to the border of Egypt: מַגִּשִׁים מִנְחָה

---

[317] מִנְחָה denotes in several texts "(cereal) offering" (Gen. 4:3; Lev. 2:8; 6:14, 21; Isa.
1:13; Jer. 17:26; 41:5) and these are therefore unsuitable for our purpose, because
the terminology is more cultic, though doubtlessly derived from the secular use.
The same is true for the combinations with the verbs שׁוב (Num. 18:9), נגשׁ (Am.
5:25; Mal. 2:12; 3:3–4), and עבד (Isa. 43:23). Although Isa. 19:21 belongs in fact
also to this group of texts, it offers some interesting parallels for our comparison.
In a number of texts the meaning of מִנְחָה lies between "gift" and more specifically "offering". In Mal. 1:12–14 impure offerings are denounced and this was
underscored by the statement "for I am a great King, says the Lord of hosts, and
my name is feared among the nations" (v. 14b). See also 2 Chron. 32:23: "And
many brought gifts (מִנְחָה) to the Lord to Jerusalem and precious things (מִגְדָּנוֹת)
to Hezekiah king of Judah". Cf. also Zeph. 3:10 and Isa. 66:20 (with regard to the
latter, see n. 313 above).

[317] מַשָּׂא, "burden, tribute"; HAL, 604.

[318] RSV rendered מִנְחָה with "gifts" (similar NBG; KBS); NEB with "tribute".
Although the text is "theological" in so far as the power of the kings is a gift of
God, at the same time it is clear that מִנְחָה denotes "tribute, taxation" here. For
an Ug. parallel, cf. KTU 1.15:i.3/7 and J.C. de Moor, K. Spronk, "Problematical
passages in the Legend of Kirtu, I–II", UF 14 (1982) 153–90, 173, with n. 5. It is
difficult to make a clear distinction between various possible translations of these
terms. Cf. for אֶשְׁכָּר also Ezek. 27:15, where "payment, merchandise" is meant. We
will return to Psalm 72 below.

[319] Cf. also the expression וַיִּשְׁתַּחֲווּ־לוֹ אָרְצָה, "and they bowed down before him to
the ground" in the same verse; also the fact that the brothers of Joseph called
their father עַבְדְּךָ, "your servant" (Gen. 43:28).

וְעֹבְדִים אֶת שְׁלֹמֹה כָּל יְמֵי חַיָּיו, "and they brought tribute and served Solomon all the days of his life". A similar phrase is found in 1 Kgs. 10:25 (2 Chron. 9:24): וְהֵמָּה מְבִאִים אִישׁ מִנְחָתוֹ ... דְּבַר שָׁנָה בְּשָׁנָ־ה, "Every one of them brought his present ... the thing year by year". The phrase "year by year" indicates that the present was more or less compulsory, in other words "tax, tribute". The bringing of such a "present" was also considered a sign of subordination to the king, as is testified by 1 Sam. 10:27: וְלֹא הֵבִיאוּ לוֹ מִנְחָה "and they brought no present/tribute to him". From the context it becomes clear that this "present" was usual, and when not offered might anger the king.

Next to the narrative texts, we also find the usage of מִנְחָה in the hymnic literature, not only intended as songs to God, but also to the king. In Ps. 45:13 other nations look for the favour of the king's bride with מִנְחָה; in 45:18 "the peoples will praise you" (עַמִּים יְהֹדוּךָ), namely the king;[320] and taken as a whole it is an exuberant exaltation of the king, with sayings like כִּסְאֲךָ אֱלֹהִים עוֹלָם וָעֶד, "your throne, O God, is for ever and ever" (v. 7); or עַל כֵּן מְשָׁחֲךָ אֱלֹהִים אֱלֹהֶיךָ, "therefore, O God, your God anointed you" (v. 8).[321] The strongest parallels with Gen. 49:8, 10 are to be found in Ps. 72, we offer here a synopsis of the relevant correspondences:

Genesis 49	Psalm 72
your brothers shall praise you (8)	May prayer be made for him (פלל)
	blessings be his all day long (ברך); (15)
	...call him blessed (אשר). (17)
your hand in the enemies' neck (8)	his enemies shall lick the dust (9)
your father's sons bow down before you (8)	wilderness-dwellers bow down before him (9)
	may all kings fall down before him, all nations serve him. (11)

---

[320] Cf. also Van der Merwe, "Judah in the Pentateuch", 38.

[321] The translation of אֱלֹהִים as a vocative cf. J. Ridderbos, *De Psalmen vertaald en verklaard, II: Psalm 42-106* (COT), Kampen 1958, 39. M. Dahood, *Psalms I, 1-50: Introduction, Translation and Notes* (AB, 16), Garden City, N.Y. 1966, 269-71, renders אֱלֹהִים as subject of the clause. A middle course is adopted by H.-J. Kraus, *Psalmen. 1. Teilband: Psalmen 1-59* (BKAT, XV/1), Neukirchen 1960, 330-1, who reads in v. 7 a vocative: "o Göttlicher" and in v. 8 adopts the Tg-variant "Jahwe, dein Gott". Cf. also Van Uchelen, *Psalmen deel II (41-80)* (PredOT), Nijkerk 1977, 34, 37, n. 13; *ARTU*, 212, n. 73. For a comprehensive discussion, including the religio-historical aspects, see Smith, "Mythology and Myth-making", 309-21 and especially 317-21.

the scepter shall not depart from Judah may his name endure for ever,
  nor ever[322] the ruler's staff (10)   his fame continue as long as the
                                                                  sun![323] (17)

they will bring him tribute (שַׁי) (10)   kings ... render him tribute (מִנְחָה),
                                              kings ... bring gifts (אֶשְׁכָּר). (10)

to him shall obey the people (10)   all nations serve him[324] (11).

Obviously it has to be granted that the texts quoted are not identical. The phrases in Gen. 49:8, 10 are unique in the Hebrew Bible.[325] The phrase "your father's sons will bow down before you" has a parallel which at the same time illustrates the impact of this saying, namely the question Jacob asked Joseph: "Shall I and your mother and your brothers indeed come to bow ourselves to the ground before you?" (Gen. 37:10).[326] The uniqueness of these phrases entailed that we had to make use of related sayings which are comparable and have the same tenor. However, the quantity of closely related idioms which is summarized in the following paragraph seems large enough to warrant the departure from MT.

2.4.1.2.7   Conclusion

We will summarize the preceding here. First, it was concluded that Hebr. שַׁי, Ug. *ty* could be brought to a god (Hebr.: YHWH) as well as to the king (Ug.);[327] while Hebr. מִנְחָה, Ug. *mnḥḥ*, as "present, tribute" could be brought to a god (Hebr.: YHWH; Ug.: Ba'al) and to the king (Hebr./Ug.). It was demonstrated that שַׁי and מִנְחָה were used identically and that a comparison of contexts was justified in order to establish the similarity of the context of the שַׁי-saying with other

---

[322] For the text, cf. section 2.4.1.3.3 below.

[323] Parallelism is based upon the everlasting "kingship" and "fame". For עַד ‖ עוֹלָם cf. the analysis of the poetic structure of the saying on Joseph.

[324] "To obey" and "to serve" are more or less parallels; cf. for a son, who "serves" his father, Mal. 3:17; or a son who does not "obey" his parents, Prov. 30:17. See esp. the fact that in Gen. 27:29 the people will serve him (49:10: "obey him"). "Serving" a king or God, parallel to the bringing of gifts, occurs frequently, cf. 1 Kgs. 5:1 (E.T. 4:21); and further nn. 311–312 above.

[325] Strictly spoken; for the phrase "your hand in the enemies' neck", cf. for example 2 Sam. 22:39–43 (‖ Ps. 18:39–43); Gen. 27:40; and also the afore-mentioned Ps. 110:1.

[326] Cf. also Gen. 42:6. Another important parallel to our text is Gen. 27:29 (and in addition 33:3). This theme of bowing down before brothers is unique in the Hebrew Bible.

[327] In Ug. it was also thought that a god could give *ty* to human beings; cf. the PNN *tydr* and *tyl* (De Moor, "Review of Gröndahl", 107–8).

passages concerning "tribute".

Secondly, מִנְחָה was used with the verb יבל (Hebr./Ug.) but also with בוא and other verbs. Concerning *ty* in Ug., we have no information on the use of verbs in connection with *ty* from the texts available at the moment; in Hebr. שַׁי is constructed three times with יבל. Based on the parallel of יבל ‖ בוא and the different verbs used for מִנְחָה, it may be concluded that the use of a certain verb is not decisive for the correctness of a possible reading of שַׁי in Gen. 49:10bA.[328]

Thirdly, it was shown that in our text unique expressions were used to denote the power that was privileged to "Judah". In the parallel colon v. 10bB a verb was used (קהת), which was used nowhere else in the Hebrew Bible. In our text a very rare expression was employed for a king/ruler from Judah.

Finally, it can be concluded that the saying about Judah as a whole is a magnification of a king/ruler from Judah, who will be honoured by his subjects and whose power will not end. Our text corresponds on many points with texts in the Psalms, praising the power of God or king (Pss. 45 and 72; in addition reference can be made to Pss. 2, 18, 21, 110).[329] These Psalms demonstrate clearly that in certain periods the king in Israel was seen as a god (Ps. 45:8).[330] These correspondences with the specific language of the Psalms, justify the conclusion that שׁילה was meant to be read as שַׁי לֹה "tribute to him".

2.4.1.3 Some Smaller Problems of Translation

2.4.1.3.1 Verse 9aB

The verb עָלִיתָ is rendered in this verse as "you grow up, may you grow up",[331] which is suggested by the reading of LXX: ἐκ βλαστοῦ, υἱέ μου, ἀνέβης "from being a shoot (i.e. a cub), my son, you have grown up".[332] This rendering of עלה is based on the use of the hiph. of עלה in Ezek. 19:3: וַתַּעַל אֶחָד מִגֻּרֶיהָ כְּפִיר הָיָה "and she brought up one of her whelps, a lion he became".[333] The verb is connected here

---

[328] *Pace* Jacob, *Das erste Buch*, 907.

[329] Cf. Smith, *Early History of God*, 55–60, 147–50; idem, "Mythology and Myth-making", 313–21. For Ps. 89 cf. also A. Caquot, "Observations sur le psaume 89", *Sem* 41–2 (1993) 133–58.

[330] Cf. Smith, "Mythology and Myth-making", 309–21.

[331] Cf. JPS; EÜ; FrB; Ges, *Thes*, 1023a ("*crescente*"); Ehrlich, *RG*, Bd. I, 245; Gunkel, *Genesis*, ³1910, 481; Speiser, *Genesis*, 365; Von Rad, *Erste Buch Mose*, 345; Scharbert, *Genesis 12–50*, 293; Sarna, *Genesis*, 336. On the optative rendering of the verb, cf. below the paragraph on the rendering of the verbal tenses.

[332] See Wevers, *Greek Text of Genesis*, 824–5.

[333] See *HAL*, 785: "hochbringen, das heist aufziehen"; H.A. Brongers, "Das Zeitwort 'ala und seine Derivate", in: M.S.H.G. Heerma van Voss *et al.* (eds.), *Travels*

too with prey: וַיְלַמֵּד לִטְרָף־טֶרֶף אָדָם אָכָל "and he learned to catch prey, he devoured men". Further in Isa. 53:2aA the verb is also used: וַיַּעַל כַּיּוֹנֵק לְפָנָיו "and he grew up like a plant before him", where the verb must mean "to grow up".[334] Next with this meaning is the nominal form עָלֶה, literary: "shoot up", meaning "leaves, foliage"[335] which is comparable to the verbal usage of Akk. *elû*, "to grow, come up".[336] In Akkadian this meaning is restricted to plants and clearly derived from the basic meaning of the verb "to go up, to ascend". However, since in Hebr. the causative of the qal can have the meaning "to bring up, raise" (Ezek. 19:3), whereas in Isa. 53:2 the qal is used for a human figure, this seems sufficient to justify the meaning in Hebrew for the qal "to grow, rise".[337] Speiser notes correctly that we are dealing here with a metaphorical rather than a physical sense; this might justify the unusual meaning for עלה in this verse, which seems to be connected with the growing importance of Judah.[338]

In this way it is explained why Judah could be called first a גּוּר and that later he will stoop down and crouch like a אַרְיֵה. The verb עלה is used also in another sense for lions, when they rise from their resting place.[339] However, the movement is in that case into a contrary direction than in our case, because in Genesis 49 the lion (whelp) would rise from the prey to lie down; whereas in the other cases he rises from his resting place to find his prey. For that reason it seems that this meaning of עלה is not as close to Genesis 49 than the hiph. of עלה in Ezek. 19:3.

2.4.1.3.2   Verse 10aB

Instead of MT רַגְלָיו "his feet", Sam reads דגליו, "his standards, banners".[340] Probably וּמְחֹקֵק "ruler's staff" was interpreted similar as

---

in the World of the Old Testament: Studies ... M.A. Beek (SSN, 16), Assen 1974, 30–40, 36. For another interpretation of Ezek. 19:3, see W. Zimmerli, *Ezechiel, 1.Teilband: Ezechiel 1–24* (BKAT, XIII/1), Neukirchen-Vluyn 1969, 418.

[334] J.L. Koole, *Jesaja II*, dl. 2: *Jesaja 49–55* (COT), Kampen 1990, 223; cf. also C. Westermann, *Das Buch Jesaja: Kapitel 40–66* (ATD, 19), Göttingen ⁴1981, 210.

[335] *HAL*, 785; Brongers, "Das Zeitwort *'ala*", 38. Cf. also Gen. 40:10; 41:22, for the verbal use in connection with plants.

[336] *CAD*, vol. E, 121. Cf. the following quotations: "starke Zedern, gewachsen auf den Höhen der Berge", and "ich liebe deine hochgewachsene Gestalt"; quoted after H.F. Fuhs, "עָלָה, *'ālāh*", *ThWAT*, Bd. VI, 84–105, 86. For Arabic, cf. J. Reider, "Etymological Studies in Biblical Hebrew", *VT* 2 (1952) 113–30, 115.

[337] *Pace* Alter, *Genesis*, 295.

[338] Speiser, *Genesis*, 365; Hecke, *Judah und Israel*, 187.

[339] Jer. 4:7; 49:19; 50:44; cf. also Isa. 35:9; Joel 1:6.

[340] See *e.g.* Num. 1:52; 2:2. Further *HAL*, 205.

מְחֹקְקִים, "who bear the leader's staff, commander",[341] which would result in a strange phrase when followed by רַגְלָיו, "his feet".[342] However,
MT is completely understandable and needs no alteration. Furthermore, rulers in the Ancient Near East are repeatedly pictured with a
ruler's staff or a scepter in the hand, but also with both objects.[343]

2.4.1.3.3   Verse 10a/b

According to the Masoretic accents v. 10bA starts with עַד כִּי, "until".[344] This reading does not fit very well in our context, because of
the proposed translation. Ehrlich proposed therefore to re-vocalize עד
as עֹד (עוֹד), "again, still", and in view of the ellipsis of לֹא (v. 10aA)
in our colon, to render with "no more, never".[345] The connection of
the verb סור and the particle עד is found at several places in the Hebr.
Bible;[346] while the particle עד (עוֹד) could be used at the end of a
clause.[347] Therefore, we prefer to follow the reading as proposed by
Ehrlich: וּמְחֹקֵק מִבֵּין רַגְלָיו עֹד, "nor ever the ruler's staff from between
his feet".

---

[341] For the former lemma, see Num. 21:18; Ps. 60:9 (E.T. 60:7); 108:9. For the
latter, cf. Judg. 5:14. For both, see *HAL*, 334.

[342] This is certainly the case when we consider the fact that in Deut. 28:57
רַגְלֶיהָ, denotes "womb". Undoubtedly this correspondence of almost similar words
between Gen. 49:10 and Deut. 28:57 has influenced later tradents like TO and
LXX; cf. above n. 259; further Rösel, "Die Interpretation von Genesis 49 in LXX",
63. See also M. Malul, "More on *Paḥad Yiṣḥāq* (Genesis XXXI 42, 53) and the
Oath by the Thigh", *VT* 35 (1985) 192–200, 195, n. 14, shows that "commander"
and "feet" would go very well, if "feet" is interpreted as an euphemism for the
privats parts (as happens in other texts), and then as a reference for "his posterity,
descendants".

[343] See *ANEP*, 129 (#371), 144 (#414). Further also O. Keel, *Die Welt der
altorientalischen Bildsymbolik und das Alte Testament am Beispiel der Psalmen*,
Zürich & Neukirchen-Vluyn 1972, 209 (#313), 301 (#433a); The scepter is often
a shepherd's club, see 208, 292 (#418). For the use of shepherd's terminology
to describe the king, see J.C. de Moor, "De goede herder: Oorsprong en vroege
geschiedenis van de herdersmetafoor", in: G. Heitink *et al.*, *Bewerken en bewaren:
Studies ... K. Runia*, Kampen 1982, 36–45. For a scepter in the hand of a king,
see the famous palette of king Nar-Mer in *ANEP*, 92–3 (##296–7); further: 133
(#379), 152 (#439), 153 (#442); see also the Assyrian king at 181 (#537). For
the staff, see: 134 (#383), 141 (#407), 152 (#441), 156 (#454), 159 (#463), 351
(#821), 353 (#837); in the hand of a deity: 165 (#477), 186 (#549), 191 (#572).

[344] Cf. Gen. 26:13; 2 Sam. 23:10.

[345] Ehrlich, *RG*, Bd. I, 246. Preceded by Von Herder, *Geist der Ebraeischen
Poesie*, 78, n. m; Vater, *Commentar über den Pentateuch*, Bd. I, 318–9, 322.

[346] See 1 Sam. 28:15; Ezek. 16:42; Hos. 2:19.

[347] C. Noldius, *Concordantiae particularum ebraeo-chaldaicarum*, ed. S.B. Tym-
pius, Jena 1734, 543–6. See also Gen. 49:26 — read by the Masoretes in a similar
way; but see BHS and below.

2.4.1.3.4 Verse 12

חַכְלִילִי is considered as the L-stam of חכל, "to be dark". This meaning is confirmed by the find of a wine-jar with the inscription יין כחל, "dark wine".[348] The translation of the inscription (assuming metathesis) was proposed by Demsky, on the basis of our text and Akk. *ekēlu*, "to be dark".[349] The prep. מִן is interpreted as a comparative ("than wine") rather than causal ("from"), fitting better the positive context.[350]

2.4.1.4 Rendering the Verbal Tenses

The first strophe (Gen. 49:8) refers mainly to the future. The first colon is a nominal clause which is in the present, followed by a verbal clause with a free *yiqtol* form, יוֹדוּךָ "(they) will praise you", referring to the future, similar to יִשְׁתַּחֲווּ "(they) shall bow" (49:8bB).[351] The nominal clause in verse 8bA is rendered here in future, which is close to an optative sense — being usual for nominal clauses in blessings and curses[352] — and is in accordance with the parallel free *yiqtol* forms in verses 8aB and 8bB.[353]

In the second strophe (49:9) the nominal clause in the first colon is interpreted as descriptive and therefore rendered again in the present: "a lion's whelp is Judah". The second colon contains a *qatal* form, עָלִיתָ refering mainly to the past: "you grew up"[354] (cf. already Gen. 49:4). But, next to this main temporal value the *qatal* has an optative nuance (which would contrast with 49:4): "may you grow up",[355] as is sometimes the case in poetry and elevated prose.[356] Moreover, within

---

[348]N. Avigad, "Two Hebrew Inscriptions on Wine-Jars", *IEJ* 22 (1972) 1–9.

[349]A. Demsky, " 'Dark Wine' from Judah", *IEJ* 22 (1972) 233–4. For Akk. *ekēlu*, cf. *AHw*, Bd. I, 193; *CAD*, vol. E, 64. Based on Akk. this translation was proposed already by A.S. Kapelrud, "Genesis xlix 12", *VT* 4 (1954) 426–8; KBL, 297; Speiser, *Genesis*, 366. Cf. also *HAL*, 300–1, where חַכְלִיל is etymologically related to כחל; further *DBHE*, 226; Pehlke, *Genesis 49:1–28*, 184–5.

[350]Cf. also C. Cohen, "The Meaning of צלמות 'Darkness': A Study in Philological Method", in: M.V. Fox *et al.* (eds.), *Texts, Temples and Traditions: A Tribute to Menahem Haran*, Winona Lake (IN) 1996, 287–309, 297, nn. 33–4; 299, n. 39.

[351]References to relevant passages in grammars are found on pp. 91–92 above.

[352]JM, §163b.

[353]Zobel, *SuG*, 10, defended the rendering of the tenses, by starting from the nominal clause in 49:8bA, which in his view apparently can be applied to the present alone. As a result, both *yiqtol* forms in vv. 8aB and 8bB are rendered as optative forms. In our opinion, the start from the verbal forms which are known (*i.c.* the *yiqtol* forms) is a better option, rather than starting from the unknown tense in a nominal clause. Moreover, Zobel does not take the context in consideration which interpret these sayings as predictions.

[354]For this interpretation of the verb עלה, cf. p. 139 above.

[355]Cf. Westermann, *Genesis 37–50*, 247: vom Raub ... steigt er hinauf".

[356]Cf. JM, §112k.

prophetic texts a future event can be expressed by the *qatal* as if the event has taken place already.[357] The two *qatal* forms in the following colon (49:9bA) might be interpreted in a similar way, which is especially suggested by the almost identical text in Num. 24:8–9 (one verb differs, but it still contains two *qatal* forms):

God brings him out of Egypt, (8aA)	אֵל מוֹצִיאוֹ מִמִּצְרַיִם
horns like of a wild ox are on him; (8aB)	כְּתוֹעֲפֹת רְאֵם לוֹ
He will eat the nations his adversaries, (8bA)	יֹאכַל גּוֹיִם צָרָיו
and shall break their bones in peaces, (8bB)	וְעַצְמֹתֵיהֶם יְגָרֵם
and pierce them through with his arrows. (8bC)	וְחִצָּיו יִמְחָץ
He stoopes down, lies like a lion, (9aA)	כָּרַע שָׁכַב כַּאֲרִי
like a "king's lion", who will raise him? (9aB)	וּכְלָבִיא מִי יְקִימֶנּוּ
Blessed is who blesses you, (9bA)	מְבָרֲכֶיךָ בָרוּךְ
and cursed is who curses you. (9bB)	וְאֹרְרֶיךָ אָרוּר

A similar unmistakable future use of a *qatal* is found in Num. 24:17bA, being followed by three *w-qataltí* forms, referring also to the future:[358]

I see him, but not now, (17aA)	אֶרְאֶנּוּ וְלֹא עַתָּה
I behold him, but not nigh; (17aB)	אֲשׁוּרֶנּוּ וְלֹא קָרוֹב
A star shall come forth out of Jacob (17bA)	דָּרַךְ כּוֹכָב מִיַּעֲקֹב
and a scepter shall rise out of Israel; (17bB)	וְקָם שֵׁבֶט מִיִּשְׂרָאֵל
It shall crush the forehead of Moab, (17cA)	וּמָחַץ פַּאֲתֵי מוֹאָב
and break down all the sons of Sheth (17cB)	וְקַרְקַר כָּל־בְּנֵי־שֵׁת

This use is remarkable because *qatal*, followed by *w-qataltí* for referring to the future is sometimes not even listed by grammars as a possiblity.[359] For that reason we prefer in this verse a future interpretation of the *qatal*, usually called the *perfectum propheticum*:[360] כָּרַע רָבַץ "he will stoop down, crouches".[361] The question in the following colon (49:9bB) confirms in each case the interpretation that the perspective of the saying is future: מִי יְקִימֶנּוּ "who will raise him?",[362]

---

[357] JM, §112h.

[358] Cf. also *e.g.* Joel 2:23a.

[359] Cf. *e.g.* JM, §119h.

[360] This was already suggested by C.F. Keil, *Biblischer Commentar über die Bücher Mose's*, Bd. 1: *Genesis und Exodus*, Leipzig 1878, 332; H.L. Strack, *Die Genesis übersetzt und ausgelegt*, München ²1905, 168.

[361] For a present rendering of these verbs see: NBG; NEB; EÜ; KBS; Cross, Freedman, *Ancient Yahwistic Poetry*, 73; Speiser, *Genesis*, 362; Sarna, *Genesis*, 56; Wenham, *Genesis 16–50*, 454, 476.

[362] יְקִימֶנּוּ is an energic form of the impf. hiph. 3.masc.sg. קוּם with a suff. 3.masc.sg. See Lett, §480; JM, §61f; Lett¹⁰, 49o. The energic force is merely phonetic not

symbolising the future immovable position of Judah. This is probably even better expressed when the clause is rendered as an asyndetic conditional clause:[363] "If he stoops down, crouches like a lion, a 'king's lion', who will raise him?" This immovable position is also indicated by the contents of the following strophe.

In the third, well-known strophe (49:10) Judah is being promised everlasting power among the nations, marked by the prohibitive formula לֹא + *yiqtol*, which is common for laws (Exod. 20:13–7):[364] לֹא־יָסוּר "(it) shall not depart". Here the *yiqtol* has a modal nuance "must", which is apparently more solemn than the jussive with אַל.[365] In the second colon ellipsis has taken place of this prohibitive formula, expressed in the translation by "nor ...". The third colon contains a free *yiqtol* form, referring again to the future, but the form may be a jussive form parallel to the following optative interpretation, expressing in this way emphatically the will of the patriarch.[366] The final colon is a nominal clause again and is therefore rendered as an optative clause "may (it) be".

The fourth strophe (49:11–2) has to be connected with the preceding strophe, because of the absence of the name of the subject, Judah. The strophe starts with a participle אֹסְרִי.[367] A participle used predicatively in Hebrew has become a temporal form: "it is like a substitute for the yiqtol".[368] However, the clause is principally a nominal clause and as such is also considered to have an optative value (see in the previous strophe the modal used *yiqtol*, and the possible jussive form), "may he bind".[369] As we argued before with regard to strophe

---

semantic, see JM, §61f.

[363] This would also be possible in Num. 24:9.

[364] Lett, §72i.4; JM, §113m; Lett¹⁰, §77l.

[365] JM, §113m.

[366] JM, §114h.

[367] The ' at the end of the participle is a so-called *'-compaginis*, which may be the remnant of an early case-ending (GK, §25k,l; BL, §65l; Lett¹⁰, §25h), although it is also found at the end of a st.abs. (BL, §65l). It is therefore more likely that it was placed to give the participle more dignity (GK, §90m; cf. also Lett, §25g) or for the sake of rhythm (JM, §93n). This is particularly reasonable because otherwise we have to consider either a transposition of words (BL, §65l) or a broken construct chain, which, as a grammatical feature is very unlikely (JM, §129a,u). W.L. Moran, "The Hebrew Language in its Northwest Semitic Background", in: G.E. Wright (ed.), *The Bible and the Ancient Near East: Essays ... W.F. Albright*, London 1961, 54–72, 60, 62, prefers to revocalize the word as an inf.abs. since participles with *hireq compaginis* are almost exclusively confined to appellatives. However, this is not "almost exclusively" confined to appellatives, many examples are found of other uses of this participle; cf. JM, §93n.

[368] JM, §121a.

[369] This optative rendering of 49:11–2 is rare, but cf. NBG with future.

I.B.i.2, the *qatal* (49:11b) can have an optative meaning too.[370] This becomes especially apparent in the final poetic verse of this strophe which is made up again of two nominal clauses but here rendered in the future, since it is not very likely that such clauses are optative.[371]

2.4.2 Analysis of the Poetic Structure

2.4.2.1 The Strophic Structure

Strophe I.B.i.1

Accents: [7]–10(!) | 5 ‖ [8]–2 | [8]–1.

Sep.↑: *setumah*; emphatic position יְהוּדָה;[372] אַתָּה; repetitive parallelism ךָ‑.

Sep.↓: repetitive parallelism ךָ‑ (4 times).

Int. ‖: **8a:** ךָ‑[374] ‑ךָ ‖ ךָ‑ ‖ אַתָּה ‖ יוֹדוּךָ[373] ‖ יְהוּדָה ‖ ‑ךָ‑. **8b:** אֹיְבֶיךָ ‖ בְּנֵי אָבִיךָ; ‑ךָ ... ‑ךָ ‖ ‑ךָ ...

Ext. ‖: יוֹדוּךָ (8aB) ‖ יָדְךָ (8bA) (assonance); אַחֶיךָ (8aB) ‖ בְּנֵי אָבִיךָ (8bB);[375] יוֹדוּךָ (8aB) ‖ יִשְׁתַּחֲווּ (8bB);[376]

Strophe I.B.i.2

Accents: [10]–5 | [8]–2 ‖ 12(!) | [8]–1.

Sep.↑: emphatic position מִטֶּרֶף; vocative בְּנִי;

Sep.↓: repetitive parallelism כְּ; מִי.[377]

Int. ‖: **9a:** גּוּר אַרְיֵה ‖ טֶרֶף;[378] **9b:** בְּנִי;[379] גּוּר אַרְיֵה ‖ כָּרַע רָבַץ ‖ יְקִימֶנּוּ;[380] וּכְלָבִיא ‖ כְּאַרְיֵה.[381]

---

[370] JM, §112k. Interestingly LXX reads here a future too; cf. Wevers, *Greek Text of Genesis*, 826.

[371] Cf. already RSV, although the preceding clauses were rendered in the present.

[372] See T. Muraoka, *Emphatic Words and Structures in Biblical Hebrew*, Jerusalem 1985, 97; Andersen, *Hebrew Verbless Clause*, 42: "title".

[373] Of course this parallelism is based on the folk etymology of the name יְהוּדָה. The birthstory in Gen. 29:35, where this etymology is given, is the only text where these words could be found as parallels.

[374] Formal parallelism; for אָב ‖ אִיב, cf. Mi. 7:6.

[375] See for this parallel Gen. 42:32 (also v. 13). Cf. for a comparable and much more frequent parallellism: Gen. 27:29: בְּנֵי אִמֶּךָ ‖ אַחֶיךָ; further also Gen. 43:29; Deut. 13:6; Pss. 50:20; 69:9; KTU 1.6:vi.10–11; 1.14:i.8–9. See also Avishur, *Stylistic Studies*, 435, with n. 3.

[376] See Ps. 138:2; cf. furthermore 2 Chron. 7:3; 29:30–1 (E.T. 29:29–30).

[377] Van der Lugt, *SSBHP*, 517.

[378] For טֶרֶף ‖ גּוּר see also Ezek. 19:3, 6; Nah. 2:13. For טֶרֶף ‖ אַרְיֵה, see Amos 3:4; cf. Isa. 31:4.

[379] Cf. *RSP*, vol. III, 42 (# 59).

[380] For קוּם ‖ כרע, see beside Num. 24:9, Ps. 20:9; Job 4:4. In prose texts: 1 Kings 8:54; Ezra 9:5. In juxtaposition: 2 Sam. 22:40 (Ps. 18:40); Ps. 17:13. For רבץ ‖ קוּם, see Prov. 24:15.

[381] See Num. 23:24; 24:9; Joël 1:6; Nah. 2:12. Cf. also Avishur, *Stylistic Studies*, 142; Van der Meer, *Oude woorden worden nieuw*, 44.

Ext.‖: גּוּר אַרְיֵה (9aA) ‖ אַרְיֵה(9bA) | וּכְלָבִיא (9bB); עָלִיתָ (9aB) ‖ יְקִימֶנּוּ
(9bB).³⁸² עָלִיתָ (9aB) ‖ רָבַץ (9bA);³⁸³ עָלִיתָ (9aB) ‖ כָּרַע (9bA).³⁸⁴

Strophe I.B.i.3

Accents: ⁽¹⁰⁾–5 | ⁽⁸⁾–⁽²?⁾–11(!) ‖ 5 | ⁽⁸⁾–1.

Sep.↑: prohibitive; עַד.³⁸⁵

Sep.↓: emph. particle כִּי;³⁸⁶ emphatic וְלוֹ.

Int. ‖: **10a**: שֵׁבֶט ‖ וּמְחֹקֵק ‖³⁸⁷ מֵ– ‖ מִבֵּין; מֵ– יָסוּר ‖ עַ(ה)ד;³⁸⁸ **10b**: שֵׁי יָבֹא ‖
יֶקְהַת;³⁸⁹ לֹה ‖ וְלוֹ;³⁹⁰

Ext.‖: יָסוּר (10aA) ‖ יָבֹא (10bA);³⁹¹ שֵׁבֶט (10aA) ‖ עַמִּים (10bB);³⁹² מִיהוּדָה
ו. ‖ – ה ‖ –ו ‖.

Strophe I.B.i.4

Accents: ⁽¹⁰⁾–5 | ⁽⁸⁾–2 ‖ ⁽¹⁰⁾–5 | ⁽⁸⁾–1 ‖ ⁽⁸⁾–2 | ⁽⁸⁾–1.

Sep.↑: Absent.

Sep.↓: *petuhah*.

Int. ‖: **11a**: עִירֹה ‖ בְּנִי אֲתֹנוֹ;³⁹³ **11b**: בַּיַּיִן ‖ וְלַשֹּׂרֵקָה.³⁹⁴ לַגֶּפֶן ‖ וּבְדַם עֲנָבִים;³⁹⁵

---

³⁸²For this parallel, cf. Pss. 24:3; 40:3; 74:23 (cf. also Jonah 1:2); Lam. 1:14. Further in parataxis: Jer. 6:4–5; 31:6; 49:28, 31.

³⁸³Cf. Ezek. 19:2, 4.

³⁸⁴Cf. 2 Kgs. 1:13 (although in prose); Ps. 78:31.

³⁸⁵Van der Lugt, *SSBHP*, 523, 587, n. 21.

³⁸⁶See Koopmans, *Joshua 24*, 210, n. 211; also Muraoka, *Emphatic Words and Structures*, 158–64.

³⁸⁷This word-pair is only found here; with another meaning and context it is found in Judg. 5:14.

³⁸⁸With regard to this parallel, see 1 Sam. 28:15; Ezek. 16:42; Hos. 2:19 (E.T. 2:15). In these texts the formula is reversed, in that the prohibitive לֹא is found in the second colon in connection with עַ(ה)ד.

³⁸⁹This parallel occurs only here. However, we could refer to the parallel of מִנְחָה ‖ עֶבֶד; see among others Judg. 3:14; 1 Kings 5:1 (E.T. 4:21); 2 Kings 17:3; Zeph. 3:9–10. See also KTU 1.2:i.36–8, where we find the chain *'bd* ‖ *'bd* ‖ *mnḥḥ* ‖ *'rgmn*; cf. M. Dahood, "Ugaritic-Hebrew Parallel Pairs", *RSP*, vol. III, 120. And cf. further also 2 Sam. 8:2, 6; Isa. 19:21.

³⁹⁰For the parallel לֹ ‖ לֹ, cf. Isa. 60:19; Job 29:15; Prov. 5:1; also: Dahood, Penar, "Ugaritic-Hebrew Parallel Pairs (I)", 242 (# 316).

³⁹¹See Isa. 31:2; Ezek. 11:18. In prose texts 2 Sam. 5:16; 2 Kings 4:10–1.

³⁹²Cf. Isa. 10:24; Mic. 7:14.

³⁹³For this parallel, see Zech. 9:9; cf. also Gen. 32:16; KTU 1.4:iv.4/7, 8/12 (note also the use of *gpn* here; cf. in this respect also KTU 1.19:ii.3–5). Further Vawter, "Canaanite Background", 2; Coppens, "Bénédiction de Jacob", 99; Dahood, Penar, "Ugaritic-Hebrew Parallel Pairs (I)", 303; Avishur, *Stylistic Studies*, 435.

³⁹⁴This pair occurs also in Jer. 2:21.

³⁹⁵The parallel of יַיִן ‖ דַם עֲנָבִים occurs furthermore only in the texts of Ugarit: KTU 1.4:iii.43–4; 1.4:iv.37–8; 1.5:iv.15–6; 1.17:vi.5–6. See also Vawter, "Canaanite Background", 2; Coppens, "Bénédiction de Jacob", 99; S. Gevirtz, "Asher in the Blessing of Jacob", *VT* 37 (1987) 154–163, 158; Dahood, Penar, "Ugaritic-Hebrew

.מֶחְלָב ‖ מִיֵּן 397 ‖ שֵׁנַיִם ‖ עֵינַיִם :12 .סוּתֹה ‖ לְבֻשׁוֹ 396‖ בְּ ‖ בְּ398.

Ext.‖: גֶּפֶן (11aA) ‖ יֵין (11bA)‖ יֵין (12A) (responsion);399 שֹׂרֵק (11aB)
‖ עֲנָבִים (11bB);400 ה — | וֹ— ‖ וֹ— | ה —.401

2.4.2.2   The Poetic Structure of Canticle I.B.i

Strophes I.B.i.1 and I.B.i.2

יְהוּדָה (8aA) ‖ יְהוּדָה (9aA); יִשְׁתַּחֲווּ (8bB) ‖ עָלִיתָ (9aB);402 יִשְׁתַּחֲווּ (8bB)
‖ כָּרַע רָבַץ (9bB);403 בְּנֵי (8bB) ‖ גּוּר (9aA);404 בְּנֵי (8bB) ‖ בְּנֵי (9aB);405
יִשְׁתַּחֲווּ (8bB) ‖ יְקִימֶנּוּ (9bB).406

Strophes I.B.i.1 and I.B.i.3

יוֹדוּךָ (8aA) ‖ עַמִּים (10bB);407 אַחֶיךָ (8aA) ‖ עַמִּים (10bB);408 יָדְךָ (8bA)
‖ שֵׁבֶט (10aA);409 יָדְךָ (8bA) ‖ רַגְלָיו (10aB);410 אֹיְבֶיךָ (8bA) ‖ עַמִּים
(10bB);411 אֹיְבֶיךָ (8bA) ‖ שֵׁבֶט (10aA);412 יִשְׁתַּחֲווּ (8bB) ‖ עַמִּים (10bB);413
לְךָ (8bB) ‖ לֹה | וְלוֹ (10b).

Parallel Pairs (I)", 208; Avishur, *Stylistic Studies*, 367; Zurro, *Procediemientos*, 203. Cf. Deut. 32:14; Sir. 39:26. For the parallel יֵין ‖ עֲנָבִים see Num. 6:3.

396 Dahood, Penar, "Ugaritic-Hebrew Parallel Pairs (I)", 134.

397 See Job 16:9; Prov. 10:26. Cf. Exod. 21:24; Lev. 24:20; Deut. 19:21; Cant. 7:5.

398 Ext. ‖ : Cant. 4:10–1; see Sir. 39:26 (instead of the word יֵין the expression עֵים דֹם is used). Cf. also Isa. 55:1; Cant. 5:1. See Avishur, *Stylistic Studies*, 119.

399 For the parallel, see Hos. 14:8.

400 See Isa. 5:2.

401 Zurro, *Procediemientos*, 204.

402 See Exod. 24:1; 1 Sam. 1:3; Zech. 14:16, 17; 2 Chron. 29:29; cf. also 1 Sam. 28:14; 1 Kings 17:36.

403 For the parallel of שׁחה, hitp. (see *HAL*, 284, 1351–2) with כרע, see Ps. 22:30; 2 Chron. 7:3; 29:29; and in juxtaposition in Ps. 95:6; Esther 3:2, 5.

404 This pair occurs also in ext. ‖ in Lam. 4:2–3.

405 Gen. 16:15; Hos. 2:2, 6 (E.T. 1:11; 2:4); Joel 4:6, 8 (E.T. 3:6, 8); Amos 2:11; Zech. 9:13; Pss. 62:10; 78:6; 132:12; Job 30:8; Prov. 10:1, 5. External ‖ : Isa. 51:18; Ezek. 23:23; Ps. 18:45–6; KTU 1.17:i.25–6 (cf. also 1.17:i.19–21). Cf. *RSP*, vol. I, 146 (# 112); Van der Meer, *Oude woorden worden nieuw*, 94, 95; Roersma, "First-Born of Abraham", *VANEP*, 234, 240.

406 For שׁחה hitp. ‖ קום see Gen. 37:7(!); Isa. 49:7; further: Gen. 19:1; 23:7; Exod. 33:10; 1 Sam. 20:41; 25:41; 2 Kings 2:19; Job 1:20.

407 These words are of course not found in parallelism as synonyms; they are however found frequently in the same context: Isa. 12:4; Pss. 35:18; 57:10; 105:1; 108:4. Further, they are found as subject and verb in Pss. 45:18; 67:4, 6; 79:13.

408 See Isa. 9:18; Jer. 29:16; cf. also Esth. 10:3.

409 יָד־ ‖ שֵׁבֶט is found in Amos 1:8; Ps. 125:3. Cf. also Isa. 10:5.

410 For this parallelism see Ezek. 25:6; Pss. 8:7; 31:9; 115:7; Prov. 26:6. Reversed in Ps. 36:12; and in syndetic parataxis in Ps. 22:17.

411 For this pair see Ezek. 39:27; Ps. 45:16; 74:18; and in antithetical parallelism in Jer. 21:7 (ext.par.); Nah. 3:13.

412 We find these words in Ps. 45:6–7.

413 These words are found as subject and verb in Jer. 13:10; Ezek. 46:3, 9.

Strophes I.B.i.1 and I.B.i.4

בְּנֵי (8aC) ‖ בְּנֵי (11aB).

Strophes I.B.i.2 and I.B.i.3

יָבֹא ‖ (9bB) יְקֻמֶּנּוּ ;[414](10bA) יָבֹא ‖ (9aB) עָלִיתָ ;(10aB)וּמִ- ‖ (9aB)מִ-
(10bA).[415]

Strophes I.B.i.2 and I.B.i.4

(9aB) בְּנֵי [416]; (11bB) וּבְדַם ‖ (9aB) מְטֻרָף ;(11aB) בְּנֵי אֲתֹנוֹ ‖ (9aA) גּוּר אַרְיֵה
‖ בְּנֵי (11aB).

Strophes I.B.i.3 and I.B.i.4

שֵׁבֶט (10aA) ‖ לְבֻשׁוֹ (11bA);[417] ־לְ| -לְ-(10b) ‖ -לְ| -לְ-(11a); ה – | -ֹו- (10b)
‖ ה – | -ֹו- (11a) ‖ -ֹו- | ה – (11b).

2.5   Zebulun (Gen. 49:13)

I.B.ii.1   פ

Zebulun – at the wide sea's beach he will dwell; (13aA)   זְבוּלֻן לְחוֹף יַמִּים יִשְׁכֹּן

May he be a beach for ships, (13bA)   וְהוּא לְחוֹף אֳנִיֹּת

and his spur facing Sidon. (13bB)   ס   וְיַרְכָתוֹ עַל־צִידֹן

2.5.1   Translation

The saying on Zebulun does not pose any major textual or philological problems.[418] The noun חוֹף is usually translated by "shore", but since it derives from a root חוף or חפף meaning "to enclose, embrace"[419] apparently an inward curving beach is meant. This is also suggested by the Ugaritic parallel *ḥp ym* in KTU 1.3:ii.7 because the scribe seems to have had the curving beach of Maʾḥadu/Minet el-Beida in mind.[420] So it appears that in our text the Gulf of Haifa (מִפְרָץ חֵיפָה)

---

[414] The parallelism בוא ‖ עלה is found in Isa. 37:24; Jer. 23:8 (cf. 23:7 ‖ 16:14); 27:22; Ezek. 11:24; 37:12; 38:9, 11, 18; 39:2; 40:6; Zech. 14:16, 18; Job. 5:26. Cf. further Avishur, *Stylistic Studies*, 653; Van der Meer, *Oude woorden worden nieuw*, 66; Kim, *Samson Cycle*, 286, n. 259.

[415] For the pair בוא ‖ קום see Num. 22:14; 2 Sam. 14:31; 1 Kgs. 17:10; Isa. 31:2; Jer. 23:5; 33:14; 49:14; Kim, *Samson Cycle*, 193, n. 89. Cf. also Isa. 2:19, 21. The pair is also found in ext. ‖ in Jonah 1:3, but was not listed in De Hoop, "Jonah 1:1–16", 160–1; it offers an additional argument for the poetic nature of the book.

[416] דָּם ‖ טֶרֶף is found in Ezek. 22:27; Nah. 3:1.

[417] These words are not paralleled elsewhere in the Hebrew Bible; cf. however Ps. 45:7, 14 where these two words also belong to the same context of royal ideology.

[418] TgO expands MT: והוא יכביש מחוזין בספינן וטוב ימא ייכול "and he will conquer provinces by ships; and the best of the sea he will consume". This paraphrasis does not presuppose a different text, but is inspired by Josh. 19:11 and Deut. 33:19; cf. Grossfeld, *TgOGen*, 166, nn. 34–5.

[419] GB, 249; HAL, 326; BDB, 342.

[420] Cf. De Moor, *SPU*, 94, n. 3.

was meant.[421]

Zobel renders the expression יִשְׁכֹּן לְ by "sich niederlassen in Richtung auf etwas hin" because "to live in, near" is expressed by either שכן with the prep. בְ or עַל.[422] Zobel refers to four passages where this combination would be found.[423] However, in two of these the rendering "to live in, at" is fully acceptable, namely in Ps. 7:6 and 120:6.[424] Therefore it is questionable whether Zobel's rendering is correct. The translation "lives at" is much more plausible, especially so since also the sayings about Issachar (49:14–15) and Dan (49:17) contain delineations of their territory.[425] יַמִּים is a *pluralis extensitatis*, the "wide sea", *i.e.* the Mediterranean.[426] The syntactical order is peculiar, Zebulun being in the dominant first position as a so-called *casus pendens*, as indicated by the Masoretes.

Several exegetes are suspicious of the repetition of the word לְחוֹף in verse 13bA. Such a repetition would be unusual in Hebrew poetry.[427] However, word-repetition in consecutive cola is a very common phe-

---

[421] Cf. also E. Taubler, *Biblische Studien: Die Epoche der Richter*, Hrsg. v. H.-J. Zobel, Tübingen 1958, 124. Remarkable is that a part of the coast south of Acco is called nowadays עֵמֶק זְבוּלוּן "Valley of Zebulun" (32°.52′ N.L.; 35°.05′ E.L. = GRID 157.255); cf. *Atlas of Israel: Cartography, Physical and Human Geography*, Tel Aviv, New York ³1985, map 2.

[422] Zobel, *SuG*, 15; similarly: Dillmann, *Die Genesis*, 444; Pehlke, *Genesis 49:1–28*, 186.

[423] Zobel, *SuG*, 15, n. 64: Pss. 37:27; 68:17; 120:6; and in Ps. 7:6 (Hi.).

[424] Ps. 7:6c reads: וְכִבוֹדִי לֶעָפָר יַשְׁכֵּן, "let my honour dwell in the dust"; and Ps. 120:6: רַבַּת שָׁכְנָה־לָּהּ נַפְשִׁי עִם שׂוֹנֵא שָׁלוֹם, "too long my soul had to live there, among those who hate peace". לְ is used twice in a temporal sense, *viz.* in Ps. 37:27 (cf. also v. 29); 68:17. In these texts לְ has to be translated "until", in an inclusive sense. On the verb, cf. GB, 827–8; *HAL*, 1387; *DBHE*, 73; A.R. Hulst, "שכן", *THAT*, Bd. II, 904–69; M. Görg, "שָׁכֵן; שָׁכַן", *ThWAT*, Bd. VII, 1337–48.

[425] Although earlier exegetes sometimes translated the prep. לְ like Zobel, they interpreted it in the sense of "unto"; cf. König, *Die Genesis*, 759 ("wird hin zum Gestade des Weltmeers wohnen"); Von Rad, *Erste Buch Mose*, 345, 350; Kittel, *Stammessprüche Israels*, 23–4. Cf. furthermore Gunkel, *Genesis*, ³1910, 483 ("wohnt am Gestade des Meeres"); Skinner, *Genesis*, 525 ("shall dwell by the shore of the sea"); Van Selms, *Genesis dl. II*, 277. The question whether לְ has to be translated by "in the direction of" or by "at, by" is left unanswered by Dillmann, *Die Genesis*, 445; Westermann, *Genesis 37–50*, 264–5.

[426] Cf. *inter alii*, Zobel, *SuG*, 15; H. Lamberty-Zielinski, *Das 'Schilfmeer': Herkunft, Bedeutung und Funktion eines alttestamentlichen Exodusbegriffs* (BBB, 78), Frankfurt a.M. 1993, 34–5, 122.

[427] Cf. the critical *apparatus* of BHS; Gunkel, *Genesis*, ³1910, 483; Skinner, *Genesis*, 525; Vawter, "Canaanite Background", 6; Kittel, *Stammessprüche Israels*, 23; Van Selms, *Genesis dl. II*, 277 (undecided); Cross, Freedman, *Ancient Yahwistic Poetry*, 74, 85, nn. 47–8, suggesting that Judg. 5:17 is older; Westermann, *Genesis 37–50*, 265; Hecke, *Juda und Israel*, 103, n. 7.

nomenon, not only in Hebrew, but also in ancient Oriental poetry in general.[428] There is no reason, therefore, to accept the conjectural emendations proposed by these scholars.[429]

Finally we have to consider the word יְרֵכָה. Its primary meaning is "backside" or rather "thigh",[430] but it is also a common metaphor for the "spur" of a mountain.[431] So the association with loftiness that is inherent in the root זבל has led to a semantic pun here.

2.5.1.1   Rendering the Verbal Tenses

In this saying the verbal tenses are rendered in the future. The verb in the first colon (49:13A) is a free *yiqtol* and is therefore rendered as a prediction of Zebulun's future dwelling: יִשְׁכֹּן "he will dwell".[432] The context of the following nominal clauses is future because of the preceding *yiqtol*. Therefore these clauses are interpreted as optative forms in the same vein as in verses 8, 10 and 12,[433] and therefore rendered in an optative sense.

2.5.2   Analysis of the Poetic Structure

Strophe I.iv.1
Accents: [6]–[8]–2 || [10]–5 | [8]–1.

---

[428]Cf. just Gen. 49:2 using twice the imperative וְשִׁמְעוּ "listen" (although some scholars are inclined to omit the first וְשִׁמְעוּ; see Cross, Freedman, *Ancient Yahwistic Poetry*, 72, 77, n. 1). Cf. further: Exod. 3:2 (see on this text P. Auffret, "A Prose Poem: The Burning Bush", *VANEP*, 2–3); Exod. 34:21 (M. Baldacci, "Old Prose — New Poetry", *VANEP*, 13–14); 1 Kgs. 19:15 (W.T.W. Cloete, "Distinguishing Prose and Verse in 2 Ki. 19:14–19", *VANEP*, 36–7 with n. 30); Is. 40:24a (J.C. de Moor, "The Integrity of Isaiah 40", in: M. Dietrich, O. Loretz (eds.), *Mesopotamica — Ugaritica — Biblica* (AOAT, 232). Kevelaer, Neukirchen-Vluyn 1993, 190); KTU 1.14:i.21–23; ii.9–10, 18–21; iii.2–3; etc. (*ARTU*, 192, 194, 196, etc.). For an Akk. example, see RS 17.155:1–4 (M. Dietrich, "Babylonian Literary Texts from Western Libraries", *VANEP*, 49–51); for Sumer, cf. ABZU PELAM, "The Defiled Apsu", in: M.E. Cohen, *The Canonical Lamentations of Ancient Mesopotamia*, vol. I, Potomac (MD) 1988, 47–61.

[429]With König, *Die Genesis*, 759. Cf. Dahood, Penar, "Ugaritic-Hebrew Parallel Pairs", 118 (# 53.e–g); Pehlke, *Genesis 49:1–28*, 187, n. 3. Dillmann, *Die Genesis*, 444–5; Zobel, *SuG*, 15–6; and Von Rad, *Erste Buch Mose*, 350, did even not consider the matter.

[430]*HAL*, 419; Ges[18], 498.

[431]See Korpel, *RiC*, 50 for the imagery.

[432]Lett, §72c; JM, §113b.
It might be considered we render the *yiqtol* here as a jussive, similar to Gen. 49:10bA. However, whereas the context of that saying is strongly influenced by the preceding prohibitive formula (10a), such emphasizing formulas are absent in the present saying. We render therefore the verbal tenses as normal future forms, though the jussive meaning cannot be ruled out completely.

[433]Cf. pp. 142–145 above.

Sep.↑: *petuḥah*; unicolon; זְבוּלֻן (*casus pendens*); emph. position of לְחוֹף
יַמִּים.

Sep.↓: *setumah*; emph. position of וְהוּא.

Int. ‖: **13a:** unicolon;[434] **13b:** הוּא ‖ וֹ־; עַל־צִידֹן ‖ לְחוֹף אֳנִיֹּת ‖ (harbour).

Ext.‖: זְבוּלֻן ‖ (13aA) וְהוּא ‖ (13bA); לְחוֹף יַמִּים ‖ (13aA) לְחוֹף אֳנִיֹּת ‖ (13bA);
עַל־צִידֹן ‖ (13aA) לְחוֹף יַמִּים (13bB).[435]

2.6 Issachar (Gen. 49:14–15)

I.B.iii.1   ס

Issachar is a strong ass, (14A)   יִשָּׂשכָר חֲמֹר גָּרֶם

that crouches between the donkey-packs. (14B)   רֹבֵץ בֵּין הַמִּשְׁפְּתָיִם

I.B.iii.2

And seeing the rest, that it is good, (15aA)   וַיַּרְא מְנֻחָה כִּי טוֹב

and the land, that it is pleasant; (15aB)   וְאֶת־הָאָרֶץ כִּי נָעֵמָה

He bends his shoulder to bear, (15bA)   וַיֵּט שִׁכְמוֹ לִסְבֹּל

and is a serving corvée worker. (15bB)   ס   וַיְהִי לְמַס־עֹבֵד

2.6.1 Translation

Issachar is described as an ass, which is גָּרֶם (pausal form of גֶּרֶם).
The Vrs did not transmit this text uniformly. LXX rendered the text
by τὸ καλὸν ἐπεθύμησεν "desired that which is good". This seems to be
an interpretation of חמד with an obscure object (גרס ?) instead of חמר
גרם.[436] Sam reads חמר גרים. גרים is an orthographical variant of MT,
"ass"[437] which is mostly interpreted as plur. of גֵּר: "(of) strangers".[438]

---

[434]One might perhaps consider the possibility that זְבוּלֻן is the first colon of a
bicolon. But the structure of the other sayings (vv. 3, 5, 8, 14, 16, 19, 21, 27)
favours our division.

[435]Cf. Isa. 23:2, 4; Jer. 25:22. Cf. also Vawter, "Canaanite Background", 6.

[436]S.I. Feigin, "*ḥamôr gārîm*, 'Castrated Ass'", *JNES* 5 (1946) 230.

[437]E. Tov, *Textual Criticism of the Hebrew Bible*, Minneapolis (MN), Assen 1992,
96–7.

[438]Feigin, "'Castrated Ass'", 232; A. Tal, "The Samaritan Targum of the Pentateuch", in: M.J. Mulder, H. Sysling (eds.), *Mikra: Text, Translation, Reading
and Interpretation of the Hebrew Bible in Ancient Judaism and Early Christianity*
(CRINT, II/1), Assen, Philadelphia (PA) 1988, 189–216, 210–1.

S. Gevirtz, "The Issachar Oracle in the Testament of Jacob", *ErIs* 12 (1975)
104*–112*, 105*, suspects in MT a part.act. of the root גור with an enclitic *mem*,
and refers to Sam גרים. According to Ges, *Thes*, 303a, the reading of Sam should
be related to Arab. *ǧarîm* "magno corpore praeditus"; similarly now H. Donner,
"The Blessing of Issachar (*Gen.* 49:14–15) as a Source for the Early History of
Israel", in: J.A. Soggin *et al.*, *Le Origini di Israele*, Rome 1987, 53–63, 54, n. 4,
"of strong constitution, of physical strength". The reading of Sam might well
represent גָּרֶם; cf. König, *Die Genesis*, 760, n. 4.

The consonants of Sam corroborate the גרם of MT against LXX. Peš
has *gbr' gnbr'* "strong man"; TgO עתיר בנכסין "rich in possessions";
TgN שבט תקיף "strong tribe"; TgPsJ חמד באריתא "desires the law";
Vg *asinus fortis* "strong donkey". Apparently most of the Vrs had
some trouble in accepting the comparison of Issachar with a donkey.
However, Sam confirms the reading of MT. Peš, TgN and Vg interpreted גרם as "strong", while Peš en TgN replaced חמר with a more
acceptable reading: resp. "man" and "tribe". TgO seems to interpret
חמר גרם as a symbol of richness,[439] and TgPsJ combined the reading
of TgN with LXX. It seems reasonable therefore, to conclude that all
the Vrs (including LXX[440]) had the same text as MT.[441]

In accordance with Peš, TgN and Vg, medieval scholars interpret
גֶּרֶם as "strong, sturdy"[442] and this is still the most common translation
for the lemma.[443] Several scholars have raised objections to this interpretation of גֶּרֶם because it has not been attested elsewhere.[444] However, the meaning of גרם "strong" is attested in Arab. with two similar expressions: *ḥimār ǧirmin* "strong ass" and *fars ǧirmin* "strong
horse".[445] The meaning "to be strong" for the root גרם is also attested

---

[439] For some references to Rabbinic literature, cf. Grossfeld, *TgOGen*, 166–7, nn.
37–38.

[440] Feigin, "'Castrated Ass'", 230, thinks LXX had an accidentally changed *Vorlage*. But since almost all translations had some trouble with חמר, LXX probably
had the same qualms and changed it intentionally.

[441] Feigin, "'Castrated Ass'", 231.

[442] Cf. Feigin, "'Castrated Ass'", 231, who refers to David ben Abraham al-Fāsī,
Rashi, Ibn-Ezra, Rashbam, Sforno.

[443] גֶּרֶם "bones", *e.g.* "bony", epexegetically for "strong"; cf. GB, 148; *HAL*, 195;
Ges[18], 229; *DBHE*, 145; Loewenstamm–Blau, *TLB*, vol. 3, 250. See RSV; furthermore Zobel, *SuG* 16; Pehlke, *Genesis 49:1–28*, 189–90; Donner, "The Blessing of
Issachar", 54; J.D. Heck, "Issachar: Slave or Freeman? (Gen 49:14–15)", *JETS*
29 (1986) 385–96. KBL, 194 offers only "bony ass", without the usual interpretation "strong". Similarly: NBG; Buber; LuthB; KBS; FrB. Also W. Herrmann,
"Issakar", *FuF* 37 (1963) 22; Hecke, *Juda und Israel*, 34–5.

[444] Feigin, "*ḥamôr gārîm*, 'Castrated Ass'", 232, who suggested that the meaning
of the word should be derived from Arab. and Syr. *grm* "to cut short, off, to
shear" and in this particular place "to castrate", although nowhere else attested.
Carmichael, "Some Sayings in Genesis 49", 437–8 with n. 8 seems to agree with
Feigin; cf. also NEB; J. Gray, "Israel in the Song of Deborah", in: L. Eslinger, G.
Taylor (eds.), *Ascribe to the Lord: Biblical and Other Studies in Memory of P.C.
Craigie* (JSOTS, 67), Sheffield 1988, 421–55, 444. Furthermore Cross, Freedman,
Ancient Yahwistic Poetry, 86 n. 50, agree with Feigin, although they suggest
an emendation of גֶּרֶם into גְּרִים "sinewy". However, there is no ground for this
emendation in the Vrs, nor in MT. Gevirtz, "The Issachar Oracle", 104*–112*,
offered another solution, deriving גרם from גור; cf. n. 438 above.

[445] Cf. R. Blachère *et al.*, *Dictionnaire Arabe–Français–Anglais* (Langue classique
et moderne), Tm. II, Paris 1970, 1461; GB, 148; *HAL*, 195; Ges[18], 229. See also

in the Aram. of the Targumim, see *e.g.* Prov. 5:19; 8:28; 18:10; TgN: Gen. 35:9.[446] Finally we can refer to Job 40:18 and Prov. 25:15, where the idea of "strong" is present.[447]

"A strong ass, that crouches between הַמִּשְׁפְּתָיִם, donkey-packs". The interpretation of the word הַמִּשְׁפְּתָיִם, which appears also in Judg. 5:16 and without the preformative *mem* in Ps. 68:14, is still a matter of debate. The main discussion can be reduced to one question: does הַמִּשְׁפְּתָיִם denote "saddlebags"[448] or "sheepfolds, converging walls".[449] In addition to these two translations Gevirtz, after rejecting these two (see also below), suggested that the word מִשְׁפְּתָיִם could be a *mqtl* formation of שׁפת which would be a variant of שׁפט "to judge, to provide".[450] Although none of the dictionaries renders the verb שׁפת as

---

Ges, *Thes*, and Donner, n. 438 above.

[446] Jastrow, *Dictionary*, 269; Dalman, *Hw*, 87; this interpretation is apparently accepted in J.F. Healey, *The Targum of Proverbs* (ArmB, 15), Edinburgh 1991, 20, 26. Gevirtz, "The Issachar Oracle", 104*, n. 1, stated that the evidence was inconclusive, referring to J. Levy, *Wörterbuch über die Talmudim und Midraschim*, Bd. I. Berlin 1924, 359–60. However, if he had consulted Levy's dictionary of the *Targumim* his judgement might have been more positive; cf. J. Levy, *Chaldäisches Wörterbuch über die Targumim*, Leipzig 1867, 154.

[447] Esp. Job 40:18 is important because of the parallel of גֶּרֶם ‖ עֶצֶם, both meaning "bones"; while the root עצם also has the meaning of "to be strong, mighty"; *HAL*, 822; Zobel, *SuG*, 16, n. 72; Pehlke, *Genesis 49:1–28*, 190; Heck, "Issachar: Slave or Freeman?", 388–90. These texts were rejected by Feigin, "'Castrated Ass'", 232, as conclusive arguments for this meaning of גֶּרֶם because there would have been a long time of linguistic development between the "Blessing of Jacob" and the late books of the O.T., such as Job and Proverbs.

[448] LuthB; KBS ("burden"); *HAL*, 616; *DBHE*, 443. Furthermore A. Saarisalo, *The Boundary Between Issachar and Naphtali: An Archaeological and Literary Study of Israel's Settlement in Canaan*, Helsinki 1927, 92; Skinner, *Genesis*, 526; J.E. Hogg, "The Meaning of hmšptym in Gen. 49:14 and Judg. 5:16", *AJSL* 43 (1926–27) 299–301; Speiser, *Genesis*, 367; Von Rad, *Erste Buch Mose*, 345, 350; J.C. de Moor, "Donkey-Packs and Geology", *UF* 13 (1981) 303–4; idem, "Ugaritic Smalltalk", *UF* 17 (1985) 221 (cf. also idem, "The Twelve Tribes in the Song of Deborah", *VT* 43 (1993) 491, n. 33); Hecke, *Judah und Israel*, 34f.; Heck, "Issachar: Slave or Freeman?", 390–1.

[449] NBG; RSV; NEB; FB; GB, 473; Cf. Feigin, "'Castrated Ass'", 232 with n. 15; O. Eissfeldt, "Gabelhürden im Ostjordanland", *FuF* 25 (1949) 8–10; idem, "Noch einmal: Gabelhürden im Ostjordanland", *FuF* 28 (1954) 54–6 (repr. in: idem, *KS*, Bd. III, 61–70). Kittel, *Stammessprüche Israels*, 24; Herrmann, "Issakar", 22; Zobel, *SuG*, 16, with n. 74; Seebaß, "Die Stämmesprüche Gen 49 3–27", 341, n. 28 (who, however, states that the meaning "Gabelhürden" for הַמִּשְׁפְּתָיִם is still not certain); Pehlke, *Genesis 49:1–28*, 191–6; Donner, "The Blessing of Issachar", 54, n. 5; Gray, "Israel in the Song of Deborah", 438, n. 57, 444; De Moor, *RoY*, 120, n. 96 (cf. also idem, "The Twelve Tribes", 491, n. 33).

[450] Gevirtz, "The Issachar Oracle", p. 106*–7*. The derivation of the word מִשְׁפְּתָיִם from שׁפת agrees with those scholars who render it "saddlebags"; cf. De Moor,

"to provide", Gevirtz assumed this meaning, referring to Isa. 51:5; Ps. 36:6; 67:4; 96:13, where in his opinion שׁפט has to be translated with "to provide for".[451] Furthermore, he added on the basis of the parallelism with נתן and פעל Isa. 49:4; Ezek. 7:3, 8; and Zech. 8:16 (the latter because of שׁפט סלום and the comparable שׁפת שׁלום in Isa. 26:12). However, in *none* of these texts is his reasoning compelling. Moreover, he suggested that מִשְׁפְּתָים, being a *mqtl* formation of שׁפט, could be rendered "province, territorial realm": "that is to say, the area over which jurisdiction was exercised. ... *byn hmšptym* ... the area between the frontier zones of city-states."[452] He refers to TgO, which translated the expression with בין תחומיא "between the boundaries" (cf. also Vg, Aq and Sym). However, TgO has ruled out the literal meaning of חֲמֹר in the preceding colon and consequently there was no room for "crouching" between "something", like an animal would do; furthermore, it is more likely that TgO associated מִשְׁפְּתָים with שׂפה "edge, limit", hence "border".[453] The proposal by Gevirtz is based on several changes in meaning of the text — גרם had to be derived from גור; רבץ means "squatter", an unusual meaning for this word in connection with animals — which were brought about by his search for strict synonymous parallelism. None of these proposals is really necessary in this verse and therefore we cannot adopt them.[454]

The definition of "sheepfold" is mostly derived from the meaning the word has in Judg. 5:16. This was strengthened by O. Eissfeldt's suggestion based on archaeological findings in Transjordan.[455] P.C. Craigie offered an Egyptian parallel *sbty*, meaning "enclosure".[456] However a real solution for the meaning of מִשְׁפְּתָים is not given along this line of interpretation, even though the meaning would fit in Judg. 5:16 and Ps. 68:14, because it is not clear from which root the word should be derived.[457]

"The Twelve Tribes", 491, n. 33.

[451] Gevirtz, "The Issachar Oracle", 106*, with n. 21; he followed a suggestion of H.L. Ginsberg, "A Strand in the Cord of Hebraic Hymnody", *ErIs* 9 (1969) 46–7.

[452] Gevirtz, "The Issachar Oracle", 106*.

[453] Cf. Grossfeld, *TgOGen*, 167, n. 38.

[454] We agree in this respect with Pehlke, *Genesis 49:1–28*, 192–3, although he is wrong in his denial that *gwr* could be used for animals; Gevirtz referred to Isa. 11:6a: וְגָר זְאֵב עִם־כֶּבֶשׂ "and a wolf shall dwell with a lamb".

[455] Eissfeldt, "Gabelhürden im Ostjordanland", 8–10; idem, "Noch einmal: Gabelhürden im Ostjordanland", 54–6 (= *KS*, Bd. III, 61–70).

[456] P.C. Craigie, "Three Ugaritic Notes to the Song of Deborah", *JSOT* 2 (1977) 33–49, 42.

[457] Gevirtz, "The Issachar Oracle", 105* disputed this meaning in Judg. 5:16 on basis of an emendation (עברים > עדרים) and that שׁרק would never have been used of "herds"; on this final point cf. J. Gray, *Joshua, Judges and Ruth* (NCB),

The rendering "saddlebags" or the like is mainly based on the interpretation of the word in Gen. 49:14. It has to be considered as a dual form of part. hiph. from the root שׁפת "to place, put".[458] The main question that we have to answer now, is whether the word מִשְׁפְּתָיִם could have had two different meanings, *e.g.* "saddlebags" and "sheepfolds", or does one meaning exclude the other? This discrepancy is caused by the fact that while "saddlebags" would fit best in Gen. 49:14; "sheepfolds" would fit better in Judg. 5:16 and Ps. 68:14. Understandably, Pehlke[459] and J.D. Heck[460] arrived at diametrically opposed views, the former starting with Judg. 5:16 and Ps. 68:14,[461] and finishing in "converging walls";[462] the latter starting from Gen. 49:14 and finishing in "saddlebacks".[463] However, although Pehlke knew the solution proposed by J.C. de Moor, he left it aside, apparently, because of a misunderstanding with De Moor's proposal.[464] De Moor gave the solution for this problem in several articles,[465] and in his study on the

London 1967, 287. Since Gevirtz needed an emendation to deny the usual, suitable meaning, his own argument is unconvincing.

[458] Cf. *HAL*, 616, 1511; De Moor, "Donkey-Packs and Geology", 304, nn. 11–3; for Ug. *ṯpd* cf. also J. Gray, *The Legacy of Canaan: The Ras Shamra Texts and Their Relevance to the Old Testament* (SVT, 5), Leiden ²1965, 70, n. 6. Cf. also Gevirtz, "The Issachar Oracle", 106*, who gave another meaning for *špt*. The poet would have depicted Issachar as an unwilling or recalcitrant donkey, one "who had strength enough, but preferred ease to exertion" (quoted by Gevirtz, from Skinner, *Genesis*, 526). According to Gevirtz v. 15b would contradict this emphatically: "it represents Issachar, the donkey, as docile and compliant in servitude, which is the very point of the poetic gibe" (Gevirtz, *art.cit.*, 106*). However, his peculiar translation of v. 15a is problematic (see below). In our view the contradiction is resolved by v. 15a: Issachar became a hard working slave, because of the rest and the land, which were כִּי טוֹב.

Another interpretation of שׁפת was presented by W. Robertson Smith, *Lectures on the Religion of the Semites*, London 1894, 377, n. 2; P. Haupt, "Der achtundsechzigste Psalm", *AJSL* 23 (1907) 236, n. 57; followed by W.F. Albright, "The Earliest Forms of Hebrew Verse", *JPOS* 2 (1922) 69–81, 78, n. 2; idem, "A Catalogue of early Hebrew Lyric Poems (Psalm 68)", *HUCA* 23 (1950–51) 1–39, 22; idem, *Yahweh and the Gods of Canaan*, Garden City (NY) 1968, 275, n. ee; Alter, *Genesis*, 296. It would denote "fireplace", based on 2 Kgs. 4:38, Ezek. 24:3, where the verb שׁפת is used for "putting a cooking pot on the fire". Cross, Freedman, *Ancient Yahwistic Poetry*, 86, n. 62, translated "rubbish heap", also related with שׁפת and esp. אֶשְׁפֹּת. However, שׁפת has the general meaning "to put, provide"; cf. Gevirtz, *art.cit.*, 105*–6*, with nn. 14, 23.

[459] Pehlke, *Genesis 49:1–28*, 191–6.
[460] Heck, "Issachar: Slave or Freeman?", 390–1.
[461] Pehlke, *Genesis 49:1–28*, 194.
[462] Pehlke, *Genesis 49:1–28*, 196.
[463] Heck, "Issachar: Slave or Freeman?", 391.
[464] Pehlke, *Genesis 49:1–28*, 191, n. 2; and more specifically 192 with n. 2.
[465] De Moor, "Donkey-Packs and Geology", 303–4; idem, "Ugaritic Smalltalk",

tribes in Judges 5 he wrote:

> It is certain that *mšptym* corresponds to Ugaritic *mtpdm* and primarily
> means 'donkey-pack'. ... However, because the V-shape of the sheep-
> fold resembled the shape of a donkey-pack, it was designated by the
> same word.[466]

Consequently, there is no contradiction between the meaning of the
word "sheepfolds" in Judg. 5:16,[467] or that in Ps. 68:14[468] on the one
hand; and "saddlebacks, donkey-packs" on the other hand.

The following bicolon, v. 15a, does not pose any serious problems
for the translator. Gevirtz, however, suggested a different translation
for this poetic verse for three reasons: 1. the parallel הָאָרֶץ ‖ מְנֻחָה is
not otherwise attested; 2. there would be a contradiction in saying
that Issachar "saw the rest is good" and that he became "a slave
at forced labour", for "rest" and "forced labour" are antithetic; 3.
"and most incriminating, the appearance of the *nota accusativi* in a
poem as early as this one undoubtedly is, is quite unexpected and
improbable".[469]

The argument from parallelism is not conclusive, because it happens very frequently in poetic texts that words from two cola, forming
together a bicolon, do not form a pair, simply because they are not
parallel.[470] Further, although these words do not form a strict pair
we find them — or the root of מְנֻחָה — in combination/association in
Deut. 3:20; 25:19; Josh. 1:13, 15 (cf. 22:4); Isa. 66:1; and esp. Deut.
12:9–10:[471]

221; idem, "The Twelve Tribes", 491, n. 33.

[466]De Moor, "The Twelve Tribes", 491, n. 33; idem, "Poetic Fragments in
Deuteronomy and the Deuteronomistic History", in: F. García Martínez *et.al.*
(eds.), *Studies in Deuteronomy: In Honour of C.J. Labuschagne* (SVT, 53), Leiden 1994, 183–96, 194, n. 49; idem, "Ugarit and Israelite Origins", Leiden 1995,
205–38, 210, n. 22.

[467]Although *DBHE*, 443, leaves this double meaning open, as indicated by a
question-mark. For Arab. parallels, cf. De Moor, "Donkey-Packs and Geology",
304, n. 13; idem, "Ugaritic Smalltalk", 221, n. 18.

[468]See also De Moor, *RoY*, 120, n. 96.

[469]Gevirtz, "The Issachar Oracle", 109*.

[470]We are referring to the phenomenon of enjambment, mostly known as the
so-called synthetic parallelism; cf. the examples given, but also the criticism on
the terminology of "synthetical" parallelism by S.A. Geller, *Parallelism in Early
Biblical Poetry* (HSM, 20), Missoula (MA) 1979, 375–85; W.G.E. Watson, *Classical Hebrew Poetry: A Guide to its Techniques* (JSOTS, 26), Sheffield ²1984,
332–5. Furthermore, we refer to the phenomenon of the unicolon; cf. De Moor,
"The Poetry of the Book of Ruth", 264, with n. 13; Watson, *op.cit.*, 12; 168–74.

[471]This text functioned at the background for the translation of TgO of our
text: וחזא חולקא ארי טב "On perceiving that his portion was good"; cf. Grossfeld,

For you have not come until now, to the rest (אֶל־הַמְּנוּחָה) and to the
inheritance (וְאֶל־הַנַּחֲלָה) which Yhwh your God gives you (9). And when
you go over the Jordan, and live in the land, (בָּאָרֶץ) which Yhwh your
God makes you inherit (מַנְחִיל אֶתְכֶם), and gives you rest (וְהֵנִיחַ לָכֶם) from
your enemies around and you live in safety (10) ....

Concerning Gevirtz's second argument — the antithesis between the
"rest" and "slave at forced labour" — we agree that these words
form an antithesis. However, they do not contradict each other; the
"good rest" and the "pleasant land" are vital conditions for Issachar
to accept an existence as a "slave at forced labour". Gevirtz's third
argument, the use of a *nota accusativi* in an ancient poem, is no reason
for a different translation. First of all it is possible that this *nota
accusativi* was inserted later on.[472] Or the text may have been not as
old as Gevirtz supposed; or the whole presupposition that the presence
of אֵת is impossible in older poetry was wrong.[473] Nevertheless, Gevirtz
suggests we render the text as follows:

> When he saw how advantageous was offering, (15aA)
>
>   and he found how expedient was tribute; (15aB)

מנחה in v. 15aA has to be taken as מִנְחָה "offering, present, tribute";
וְאֶת־הָאָרֶץ had to be split up again in ו<'>אתא רץ, that is to say:
ו<'>אתא 3.msc.sg. impf. with a *waw* conversive of אתה, "to find, to
come (upon)"[474] and רץ "gift, present, tribute".[475] However, Gevirtz's
argument makes a forced impression.[476] Nothing in the textual tradition suggests a major corruption and the text is understandable
as it stands. Finally, the saying becomes totally incomprehensible in
Gevirtz's translation: Issachar saw that offering was advantageous and
for that reason became a slave?[477]

TgOGen, 167, n. 39.

[472]Cf. D.N. Freedman, "Archaic Forms in Early Hebrew Poetry", *ZAW* 72 (1960)
101–7; Cross, Freedman, *Ancient Yahwistic Poetry*, 86, n. 55; Geller, *Parallelism*,
46 with n. 36; 66; Pehlke, *Genesis 49:1–28*, 197 with n. 1.

[473]Cf. J. Hoftijzer, "Remarks Concerning the Use of the Particle *'t* in Classical
Hebrew", כה: *1940–1965* (OTS, 14), Leiden 1965, 1–99, 50–88.

[474]אתה is normally translated by "to come" (cf. *HAL*, 98; Ges[18], 115: "to come");
in Deut. 33:21 and "very likely" in Job 37:22 the verb can be found parallel with
ראה. Cf. also Isa. 21:12; Job 3:25, in which a transitive meaning "to find" is more
appropriate, according to Gevirtz.

[475]רץ < רָצוֹן should be derived from רצה "to desire, accept" (cf. *HAL* 1195: רצה
II "pay, atone") or *הרץ "to bring". This meaning ("gift, present, tribute") is also
required in Isa. 56:7; 60:7; Mal. 2:13 (Gevirtz, "The Issachar Oracle", 109* with
nn. 44–5).

[476]Cf. the preceding footnotes and the lexica, *s.v.* for the suggested readings.

[477]We prefer the common translation for this text. Cross, Freedman, *Ancient*

The words סֵבֶל and מַס־עֹבֵד in the final poetic verse are discussed because it is important for our later discussion to establish their exact meaning. The meaning of סבל is not disputed, although Gevirtz would like to change the vocalization since a substantive might have been expected here, because of the parallelistic structure of the bicolon.[478] לִסְבֹּל should be read therefore as לְסֵבֶל.[479] The infinitive of סבל offers, however, a good text and does not need alteration.[480]

מַס־עֹבֵד in the following colon offers more problems for the interpreter, because the word מַס on its own is mostly used in the same way as מַס־עֹבֵד.[481] See e.g. Josh. 16:10bB: וַיְהִי לְמַס־עֹבֵד "they have become slaves to do forced labor" (RSV); and Judg. 1:30: וַיִּהְיוּ לָמַס "they became subject to forced labor" (RSV). It is argued that both texts express essentially the same thing,[482] and that עבד has to be considered a gloss or an apposition.[483] Donner in particular argues this on the basis of the use of massu in Akk. texts from Alalaḫ[484] and Amarna,[485] in which the word does not mean "corvée, forced labour" but "corvée or forced labourers, compulsory workers" in a collective

---

Yahwistic Poetry, 86, nn. 54, 56, (followed by Geller, *Parallelism*, 66), suggested we take the ה at the end of מנחה as a suff. 3.msc.sg. "his rest" and ארץ as אַרְצוֹ "his land" (cf. Peš). The text-critical evidence is not strong enough and there are no other obvious reasons to change the text. For the meaning of מְנֻחָה see A.R. Hulst, "De betekenis van het woord *m^enūḥā*", in: D.S. Attema *et al.*, *Schrift en Uitleg: Studies ... W.H. Gispen, Kampen 1970*, 69–75.

[478] Gevirtz, "The Issachar Oracle", 111*.

[479] Gevirtz, "The Issachar Oracle", 112*.

[480] Cf. T.N.D. Mettinger, *Solomonic State Officials: A Study of the Civil Government Officials of the Israelite Monarchy* (CB OTS, 5), Lund: Gleerup, 1971, 137–9; furthermore LXX: τὸ πονεῖν inf. of πονέω "toil, slave"; Peš: *lšw'bd'*.

[481] Except for our text, the expression מַס־עֹבֵד is found also in Josh. 16:10 and 1 Kgs. 9:21.

[482] Cf. Gevirtz, "The Issachar Oracle", 111*, with nn. 61–2; J.A. Soggin, "Compulsory Labor under David and Solomon", in: T. Ishida (ed.), *Studies in the Period of David and Solomon and Other Essays*, Winona Lake (IN) 1982, 259–67, 260–2; R. North, "מַס", *ThWAT*, Bd. IV, 1007–8; Donner, "The Blessing of Issachar", 59–61.

[483] A. Biram, "Mas 'obed", *Tarb* 23 (1951–52) 137–42; A.F. Rainey, "Compulsory Labour Gangs in Ancient Israel", *IEJ* 20 (1970) 191–202, 191; Soggin, "Compulsory Labor", 263, n. 20 (referring to A. Kahana, *Pêrûš madday* [Zitomir, 1904]; [Hebr.]); North, "מַס", 1007; Donner, "The Blessing of Issachar", 61.

[484] Cf. W.L. Moran, "The Hebrew Language in its Northwest Semitic Background", in: G.E. Wright (ed.), *The Bible and the Ancient Near East: Essays ... W.F. Albright*, London 1961, 57, 67, n. 16; A.F. Rainey, "Compulsory Labour Gangs", 192–3; see also *CAD*, vol. M/1, 327.

[485] A.F. Rainey, *El-Amarna Tablets 359–379* (AOAT, 8), Kevelaer, Neukirchen-Vluyn 1970, 24–7; idem, "Compulsory Labour Gangs", 194–5; see also *CAD*, vol. M/1, 327.

singular sense.[486] This meaning would fit very well in a text like 1 Kgs. 5:27 (E.T. 5:13):[487]

King Solomon raised corvée workers (מַס) out of all Israel; (27A)
and the corvée workers (הַמַּס) were thirty thousand men. (27B)

Furthermore this collective-personal meaning would fit in all other instances in the O.T.[488] Reference could also be made to the title given to the officers in the Davidic-Solomonic era who had the supervision of the corvée workers:[489] וַאֲדֹ(נִי)רָם עַל־הַמַּס "Ado(ni)ram was in charge over the corvée labourers" (2 Sam. 20:24; 1 Kgs. 4:6; 5:28).[490] This expression could be compared with וּבְנָיָה בֶּן־יְהוֹיָדָע עַל־הַכְּרֵי וְעַל־הַפְּלֵתִי "Benaiah, the son of Jehoiada was in charge over the Cherethites and the Pelethites" (2 Sam. 20:23[491]) or וַעֲזַרְיָהוּ בֶן־נָתָן עַל־הַנִּצָּבִים "Azariah was in charge over the officers" (1 Kgs. 4:5). The composition of מַס־עֹבֵד may be understood, according to Donner, as an apposition or a gloss in order to guarantee the personal meaning of מַס instead of the sometimes abstract meaning (cf. Esth. 10:1).[492] This function would correspond

---

[486]Donner, "The Blessing of Issachar", 59; cf. *AHw*, Bd. II, 619; *CAD*, vol. M/1, 327. The two lexica render *massu*, however, in a personal singular sense (Donner, *art.cit.*, 60, n. 21). Cf. already Mettinger, *Solomonic State Officials*, 131, nn. 18–9.

Heck, "Issachar: Slave or Freeman", 395, following KBL, 540, referring to A. Erman, H. Grapow, *Wörterbuch der Aegyptischen Sprache*, Bd. 2, Leipzig 1928, 135, argues that מַס has to be derived from Eg. *ms*, meaning "bearer". However, the Eg. verb *ms* means "to bring; present" persons or things, and with reflexive "betake" oneselve (cf. R.O. Faulkner, *A Concise Dictionary of Middle Egyptian*, Oxford 1976, 116); and the identical noun means "bringer" in designation of professions: of sacrifices and stones. The meaning of Eg. *ms* is thus only very distantly connected with "to bear". Moreover, Heck ignores the meaning of this word in the other Semitic languages and which makes very good sense here.

[487]I. Riesner, *Der Stamm 'BD im Alten Testament: Eine Wortuntersuchung unter Berücksichtigung neuerer sprachwissenschaftlicher Methoden* (BZAW, 149), Berlin 1979, 138; Donner, "The Blessing of Issachar", 60.

[488]Except for Esth. 10:1, where the meaning is clearly developed into an abstract sense like "tribute". Donner, "The Blessing of Issachar", 61, is not sure of Prov. 12:24; in our view this meaning would fit there too: "the slothful will become a corvee labourer". It may be clear, however, that sometimes מַס has to be taken as personal-singular.

[489]Donner, "The Blessing of Issachar", 60, n. 24.

[490]The same expression is found on a seal from the seventh century BCE: *lpl'yhw 'šr 'l hms* "(belonging) to Pela'yahu who is (in charge) over the corvée labourers"; cf. N. Avigad, "The Contribution of Hebrew Seals to an Understanding of Israelite Religion and Society", in: P.D. Miller *et al.* (eds.), *Ancient Israelite Religion: Essays ... F.M. Cross*, Philadelphia 1987, 195–208, 201, fig. 11; 204; *DNWSI*, part 2, 662.

[491]Cf. also 2 Sam. 8:18 and the critical *apparatus* of BHS.

[492]Donner, "The Blessing of Issachar", 61; cf. furthermore n. 483 above.

to that of the determinative *LÚ* in the Akk. expression from Alalaḫ and Amarna: $^{LÚ.MEŠ}massu$.

His suggestion for the interpretation of מַס in a collective-personal sense is very attractive, although it has to be used with some caution. Issachar is described in our text as one person and although he stands for the whole tribe, to translate מַס here in a collective sense is impossible and a personal-singular equivalent seems to be requested. However, the solution to consider עֹבֵד a gloss or an apposition[493] is unconvincing. The assumption of a gloss might have been acceptable in one place, but in three places it is very unlikely. We have to look for a different solution therefore. עֹבֵד was translated by Donner as a substantivated participle, "worker".[494] Because of the fact that the clause is verbal, and a substantive already precedes the participle, we could take עֹבֵד in an adjectival sense: "a serving corvée worker"[495] *viz.* one who has to work hard, without rest.[496]

In this respect we might feel inclined to follow the reasoning of Noth who, having discussed whether in 1 Kgs. 9:21 עֹבֵד has to be taken as an attributive or genitive of מַס,[497] decided in favour of an attributive meaning of עֹבֵד. He suggested that מַס could denote several grades of compulsory labour, and that עֹבֵד specified מַס as a very low form of compulsory labour. A person forced to do מַס־עֹבֵד was not a slave. Only for the period of his compulsory servitude he was comparable to a slave. However, the parallel use of מַס־עֹבֵד and מַס (cf. above) contradicts this kind of hypothetical classification. We agree with Soggin, therefore, that it is questionable whether מַס־עֹבֵד does denote the lowest form of statutory labour.[498] עֹבֵד just refers to the hard conditions of the מַס, not to any specific social class.[499]

With regard to the exact rendering of מַס we would prefer "corvee

---

[493]Cf. n. 483 above.

[494]Donner, "The Blessing of Issachar", 61. עֹבֵד being a part. act. G-st. of עבד; *HAL*, 730.

D. Künstlinger, "I. '*dy 'bd*. II. *lms 'bd*", *OLZ* 34 (1931) 609–612; Mettinger, *Solomonic State Officials*, 131, suggest to interpret עבד as "for always, eternally", etymologically related to אבד II. However, אבד II, seems to be disputed; cf. *HAL*, 3; Ges¹⁸, 3–4. Further, in *DBHE*, 14, and *DCH*, vol. I, 100 אבד II is even missing.

[495]So König, *Die Genesis*, 761; Dillmann, *Die Genesis*, 445 ("ein dienstbaren Fröhner").

[496]For the syntactical construction cf. 1 Kgs. 10:3 לֹא הָיָה דָּבָר נֶעְלָם מִן־הַמֶּלֶךְ "there was not a hidden thing from the king"; Deut. 4:24: כִּי יהוה אֱלֹהֶיךָ אֵשׁ אֹכְלָה הוּא "for YHWH, your God, he is a consuming fire"; furthermore see Waltke, O'Connor, *IBHS*, §37.1c; 37.4ab.

[497]M. Noth, *Könige* (BKAT, IX/1), Neukirchen-Vluyn 1968, 217.

[498]Soggin, "Compulsory Labor", 261.

[499]Cf. also Waltke, O'Connor, *IBHS*, §37.1ef.

worker", rather than "compulsory labourer". Although it might be a matter of nuance, the latter seems to indicate a forced element, whereas the former leaves open the possibility of a voluntary element of the worker. Because it is known that sometimes wages were paid to the corvée workers, they might also have been mercenaries.[500]

2.6.1.1   Rendering the Verbal Tenses

The correct rendering of the verbal tenses in this saying is rather difficult. The first colon contains a nominal clause, here rendered in the present in accordance with the other nominal clauses at the beginning of the sayings. In the second colon (49:14B) the participle רֹבֵץ is used as an attributive to חֲמֹר "an ass, that crouches ...",[501] whereas its temporal form is deduced from the preceding clause: the present.[502] It might be suggested we render the nominal clause here too in an optative sense, as we did before, hence "may he crouch ...". However, in the case of this saying it is not obvious if this "crouching between the donkey-packs" is restricted to the metaphor of the strong ass, or that it is meant as a future situation for the tribe of Issachar. Some scholars are inclined to interpret the "donkey-packs" as a description of the land of Issachar.[503] Although we cannot exclude this interpretation we prefer the safe rendering as a present metaphor for Issachar, only elaborated with regard to the future in the following strophe.

As a consequence of the rendering in the present of the preceding strophe, the following *wayyiqtol* forms in verse 15 cannot be considered narrative forms[504] but have to be regarded as present forms:[505] וַיַּרְא ... וַיֵּט ... וַיְהִי "and he sees ... he bends ... and is",[506] implying

---

[500] *CAD*, vol. M/1, 327; Rainey, "Compulsory Labour Gangs", 192–3.

[501] Cf. *e.g.* RSV; NBG; Buber; NEB; KBS; EÜ.

[502] The temporal form of an attributively used participle has to be derived from the context; cf. JM, §121i.

[503] This interpretation is found already in Genesis Rabba. For recent work, cf. Van Selms, *Genesis, dl. II*, 277; Westermann, *Genesis 37–50*, 266; Wenham, *Genesis 16–50*, 480.

[504] *Pace* already LXX, rendering aorist forms in verse 15b; further: RSV; Buber (verse 15b); NEB; Dillmann, *Die Genesis*, 466; Gunkel, *Genesis*, ³1910, 483; König, *Die Genesis*, 760, with n. 3 (already in verse 14); Skinner, *Genesis*, 525; Speiser, *Genesis*, 362; Westermann, *Genesis 37–50*, 247, 265; Sarna, *Genesis*, 339; Wenham, *Genesis 16–50*, 455; Alter, *Genesis*, 296.

[505] GK, §111u; JM, §§114j; 118o,r; compare also §115a,c.

[506] Cf. TO, rendering verse 15b with *yiqtol* forms, whereas verse 15a was regarded as past (*qatal*). See further NBG; KBS; EÜ. Cf. also NIV, rendering "he will bend ... and submit...". Similarly Pehlke, *Genesis 49:1–28*, 189, although rendering verse 15a into the past. Further: Jacob, *Das erste Buch*, 914 (although he renders the text in the past, he argues (referring to GK, §111u) that the verbal tenses are

succession to the first description and implying also a future force.[507]
When reading here a past for the *wayyiqtol*, the *wayyiqtol* is apparently interpreted as a free-standing *wayyiqtol*, independent from the
foregoing. In this way verse 15 is interpreted as a kind of *nachholende
Erzählung*: Issachar is called a crouching ass because he has bent his
shoulder and became a labourer. However, grammatically verse 15a
forms the logical continuation of verse 14, which best can be rendered
by "and when he sees . . .".[508] So he sees the rest (15aA) and the land
(15aB) at the moment he crouches between the donkey-packs and for
that reason he chooses to bend his shoulder. If our interpretation is
correct, a proposal to consider the "donkey-packs" as a geographical
designation for the territory of Issachar seems acceptable, since the
terms "rest" and "land" are in that case parallel terms for "between
the donkey-packs".[509]

The vocalization of the *wayyiqtol* (in general) is doubted by certain
scholars when referring to the present or the future.[510] Though, since
the *wayyiqtol* is used in many cases after a *perfectum propheticum*,[511]
and referring clearly to the future, it has to be asked if the interpretation of the *wayyiqtol* should not be brought into line with this fact
rather than suggesting in many cases a revocalization.[512]

"präsentisch"); Aalders, *Genesis*, dl. III, 189; Cross, Freedman, *Ancient Yahwistic Poetry*, 74, 86, n. 53 (omitting the *waw* at the beginning of the colon, with
reference to Vg); Heck, "Issachar: Slave or Freeman", 391–2 (although suggesting
to read *w^{e}yiqtol* for MT *wayyiqtol*).

[507] For the succession, see JM, §115a,c; for the future implication of present forms,
see JM, §112g; 118o,q. Cf. furthermore M.S. Smith, *The Origins and Development
of the Waw-Consecutive: Northwest Semitic Evidence from Ugarit to Qumran*
(HSS, 39), Atlanta (Ga) 1991, 12–5.

[508] For the necessity to add sometimes a word after "and" for the ו, cf. JM, §117d.

[509] This saying raises the same questions with regard to the definition of Genesis
49 as a "Blessing" in verse 28, as did the sayings on Reuben and on Simeon and
Levi. For these problems cf. above, section 1.4.4; and below section 2.12.1, and
further Chapter Three, the discussion on the genre of Genesis 49. On the problem if the saying on Issachar is negatively or positively, see temporarily Taubler,
Biblische Studien, 108–12; Heck, "Issachar: Slave or Free Man?", 385–96.

[510] F.R. Blake, *A Resurvey of Hebrew Tenses; with an appendix: Hebrew Influence
on Biblical Aramaic* (SPIB, 103), Roma 1951, 49, 75–6. In the case of Gen. 49:15,
see Cross, Freedman, *Ancient Yahwistic Poetry*, 74, 86, n. 53; Heck, "Issachar:
Slave or Freeman", 391–2. Cf. also JM, §118o, n. 2.

[511] The *perfectum propheticum* might be incorrect as a grammatical feature, but
it is, in each case, an existing and commonly recognized pattern, most likely a
rhetorical device (JM, §112h). However, the context expresses a future event for
the *qatal* (Mettinger, "Hebrew Verb System", 78), and that is, in case of the
wayyiqtol (being like a substitute for *qatal*; JM, §118a,o,s), the factor that gives
it a future interpretation.

[512] Cf. *e.g.* Isa. 9:17–9; Joel 2:23; Ps. 22:30; 109:28.

2.6.2 Analysis of the Poetic Structure

2.6.2.1 The Strophic Structure

Strophe I.B.iii.1

Accents: [8]–2 | [8]–1. ||

Sep.↑: *setumah*.

Int. ||: **14:** חֲמֹר || הַמִּשְׁפְּתָיִם;⁵¹³

Strophe I.B.iii.2

Accents: [10]–5 | [8]–2 || [10]–5 | [8]–1.

Sep.↑: כִּי and repetition כִּי.⁵¹⁴

Sep.↓: *setumah*; repetition of לְ; use of הָיָה.

Int. ||: **15a:** מְנֻחָה || וְאֶת־הָאָרֶץ;⁵¹⁵ כִּי טוֹב || כִּי נָעֵמָה;⁵¹⁶ **15b:** לִסְבֹּל || לְמַס־עֹבֵד.⁵¹⁷

Ext.||: absent.

2.6.2.2 The Poetic Structure of Canticle I.B.iii

Sep.↑: *setumah*.

Sep.↓: *setumah*.

Ext.||: יִשָּׂשכָר (14A) || לְמַס־עֹבֵד (15bB);⁵¹⁸ חֲמֹר (14A) || עֹבֵד (15bB);⁵¹⁹ הַמִּשְׁפְּתָיִם (14B) || מְנֻחָה (15aA);⁵²⁰ שְׁכְמוֹ (15bA); רֹבֵץ (14B) || גֶּרֶם (14A) || לִסְבֹּל (15bA).

2.7 Dan (Gen. 49:16–17/18)

II.A.i.1

	ס
Dan — his people will be strong, (16A)	דָּן יָדִין⁵²¹ עַמּוֹ
like one of the tribes of Israel; (16B)	כְּאַחַד שִׁבְטֵי יִשְׂרָאֵל

---

⁵¹³Based of course on the meaning of הַמִּשְׁפְּתָיִם "donkey-pack".

⁵¹⁴Cf. for this marker, De Moor, "The Poetry of the Book of Ruth, I", 277; idem, "Ruth, II", 29, 33; idem, "Micah 1: A Structural Approach", *SABCP*, 177; idem, "Isaiah 40", 198; Van der Meer, *Oude woorden worden nieuw*, 64, 104.

⁵¹⁵Although not strictly parallel, cf. Deut. 12:9–10 (p. 157 above); Isa. 66:1.

⁵¹⁶Cf. Pss. 135:3; 147:1; Job 36:11; Prov. 24:25; juxtaposed: Ps. 133:1; and in ext. || : Prov. 2:9–10. See Gevirtz, "The Issachar Oracle", 109*, n. 40; Dahood, Penar, "Ugaritic-Hebrew Parallel Pairs", 277 (# 385); Pehlke, *Genesis 49:1–28*, 196, n. 3. For the parallel כִּי || כִּי cf. a.o. Isa. 40:2; Joel 2:1, 11, 22; 4:13; Jon. 1:10, 12; Mi. 1:9, 12; Ruth 1:6, 13; 2:13; 3:11, 12; etc.

⁵¹⁷For סבל || עבד, cf. Exod. 6:5–6, where both words are synonymous. See also 2 Chr. 2:17. For סבל || מס, see Exod. 1:11; 5:28–29 (in the latter, they belong to the same semantic range).

⁵¹⁸For the parallelism of the roots שׂכר || עבד, cf. Gen. 29:15 (see also 31:41); Lev. 25:40 (ext.parallel in 25:6); Num. 18:31; 1 Kgs. 5:20 (E.T. 5:6); Job 7:2.

⁵¹⁹Cf. Gen. 12:16; 24:35; 30:43; 32:6; Exod. 20:17 Deut. 5:21; 1 Sam. 8:16.

⁵²⁰See Ps. 23:2!

⁵²¹Proposed reading: יָדֵן.

II.A.i.2

May Dan be a snake by the way, (17aA)   יְהִי־דָן נָחָשׁ עֲלֵי־דֶרֶךְ

  a viper by the path; (17aB)   שְׁפִיפֹן עֲלֵי־אֹרַח

that bites the horse's heels (17bA)   הַנֹּשֵׁךְ עִקְּבֵי־סוּס

  so that the rider falls backwards. (17bB)   וַיִּפֹּל רֹכְבוֹ אָחוֹר

[For your salvation I am waiting, YHWH!] (18)   וְלִישׁוּעָתְךָ קִוִּיתִי יהוה]

[ס]522

2.7.1 Translation

The translation of the saying on Dan has a long and uniform tradition. MT יָדִין is usually interpreted as an impf. 3.masc.sg. qal of the verb דִּין "to vindicate, judge".[523] Furthermore, the text uses a very common expression: דִּין עַם "to judge a people",[524] which seems to support the common interpretation. In most translations therefore the text is rendered:

> Dan will judge his people (16A)
>> like one of the tribes of Israel (16B)

However, the interpretation of this verse based on this rendering confronts the exegetes with some problems: Who are "his people" here? Some suggest that the people are Israel, in that the expression דִּין עַמּוֹ is also used for "God vindicating his people".[525] But this is unlikely because the following phrase "like one of the tribes of Israel"[526] would suggest that all tribes had judged / vindicated all Israel.[527] So it is most likely that עַמּוֹ refers to the tribe of Dan.[528] But, the next

---

[522]The *setumah* is placed between square brackets because Codex Leningradensis (see BHS) does not read a *setumah*. However, some codices (cf. BHK[1/2], Snaith) do read a *setumah* here (cf. also Maimonides, who might have used a tradition closely related to, or even identical with the Aleppo Codex [see Sanders, *Provenance of Deuteronomy 32*, 102–111, esp. 107]).

[523]Cf. already LXX; TN; and also the consonantal text of Sam. Further: RSV; NBG; EÜ; FrB. GB, 161; KBL, 208; *HAL*, 211; Ges[18], 248; *DBHE*, 156; *DCH*, vol. II, 434.

The last-named dictionary lists also 4QpGen[c] (= 4Q254) 5₃, but places דִּין יָדִין between square brackets, indicating that these words are not found in the manuscript.

[524]Cf. Deut. 32:36; Isa. 3:13; Pss. 7:9; 50:4; 72:2; 96:10; 135:14; Job 36:31; Ezra 7:25.

[525]Dillmann, *Die Genesis*, 467; Strack, *Genesis*, 169; Jacob, *Das erste Buch*, 915; Wenham, *Genesis 16–50*, 481.

[526]Wenham, *Genesis 16–50*, 481, has to denote v. 16B a "puzzling phrase".

[527]Aalders, *Genesis*, dl. III, 211. Cf. also Emerton, "Some Difficult Words", 89.

[528]Holzinger, *Genesis*, 259–60; Gunkel, *Genesis*, ³1910, 484; Skinner, *Genesis*, 527; König, *Die Genesis*, 761; Van Selms, *Genesis*, dl. II, 277; Von Rad, *Erste Buch Mose*, 351; Zobel, *SuG*, 19; Westermann, *Genesis 37–50*, 267; Scharbert,

problem is, who might "Dan" be in this connection? When he is the ancestor, what is his function here as "judge"? It is suggested by some that it is impossible that the ancestor is meant here, because we are dealing with a "tribal saying", which in its independent stage would have dealt with the tribe and not with its ancestor.[529] Yet this is a diachronical argument, which is not allowed in this stage of interpretation:[530] the context suggests that it was spoken to the ancestor.[531] This problem arises also with the interpretation that somehow we are here dealing with a Danite holder of the office in the amphictyony;[532] or that this is an ancient tradition which is connected with Dan.[533]

While the general form of the sayings in Genesis 49 is important, it offers no help to solve this problem. The sayings are constructed as nominal clauses (verses 3, 5, 14, 21, 22, 27) or as *casus pendens* constructions (verses 3, 8, 13, 19, 20). As there is a verb in this clause we might expect a *casus pendens* construction here:[534] "Dan — his people will judge", or "Dan — he will judge his people", but in both renderings the solution turns on the correct interpretation of 16B: "like one of the tribes of Israel".[535] Zobel refers to the fact that כְּאַחַד followed by מִן or a genitive construction is used when the preceding element is not a part of the following.[536] So verse 16B seems to suggest that what is said of Dan in verse 16A is usual for the other tribes of Israel, but in fact would not have been expected from Dan.[537] But in this respect the verb דִּין does not seem to fit in: עַמּוֹ is certainly the object here, but the question remains: "who" will judge/vindicate his people,[538] and, why "like one of Israel's tribes"?

Genesis 12–50, 294; H.M. Niemann, *Die Danieten: Studien zur Geschichte eines altisraelitischen Stammes* (FRLANT, 135), Göttingen 1985, 205, 206.

[529] Niemann, *Die Danieten*, 205. Cf. also Emerton, "Some Difficult Words", 88.

[530] For the diachronic analysis, cf. Chapter Six.

[531] Cf. Niemann, *Die Danieten*, 205.

[532] M. Noth, "Das Amt des 'Richters Israels'", in: W. Baumgartner *et.al.* (Hrsg.), *Festschrift Alfred Bertholet zum 80. Geburtstag*, Tübingen 1950, 404–15. The problem is, however, that עַמּוֹ must be identified with "Israel", which is unlikely (cf. above).

[533] Von Rad, *Erste Buch Mose*, 350–1.

[534] Emerton, "Some Difficult Words", 91.

[535] שֵׁבֶט in v. 16B could be considered a personification for "scepter" > "king", like in Num. 24:17 (cf. De Moor, *RoY*, 153; *HAL*, 1292). However, the problem remains the same: who will judge or vindicate, and what does "like one of the 'sceptres' of Israel" mean?

[536] Zobel, *SuG*, 19.

[537] Delitzsch, *Genesis und Exodus*, 342; Aalders, *Genesis*, dl. III, 213; Westermann, *Genesis 37–50*, 267.

[538] This question is sometimes answered with a reference to Samson (Judg. 13–16); cf. Dillmann, *Die Genesis*, 467; Aalders, *Genesis*, dl. III, 213; König, *Die*

Emerton writes in this connection:

> It is therefore difficult, even if not impossible, to find a meaning for the verse on the supposition that the verb means "to judge" or "to vindicate".[539]

and a little further:

> Perhaps the verb comes from a root different from that of the common verb "to judge". Although *radices hebraicae non multiplicandae sunt praeter necessitatem*, there is a case for postulating a new meaning here. A passage where a poet is seeking a play on words is the kind of place where a rare verb might be expected, and the presence of a different root from the one denoting judgement would make the play on words more subtle.[540]

C. Rabin suggests in view of the difficulties mentioned above, that the verb should not be derived from the root דין but from a root related to Arab. *dn(w)/dwn* "to be close".[541] Emerton however, raises some objections against this suggestion:[542] If the saying had to describe the northernmost part of the country, it is not very appropriately described as near; on the other hand the southern part — before the migration to the north (Judges 18) — is too obvious. Furthermore, Dan was a tribe too small for such a reference; also, a preposition might have been expected after the verb, as in Arabic. Emerton suggests, therefore, that we look for a different meaning of the root, from which the verb must have been derived. According to him, this could be the root דנן which should be pointed in our verse as יָדֹן "(unless a by-form דין is postulated)".[543] This root is comparable to Akk. *danānu* "to be strong",[544] which is also known in Ugaritic as *dn* in the D-stem.[545]

The meaning of the verse would be "despite its small size, Dan is a tribe to be reckoned with, and will maintain its position as a full tribe of Israel."[546] This interpretation makes good sense of the saying, and matches the following verse very well, where the comparison with a

---

Genesis, 762; Contrast Delitzsch, *Genesis und Exodus*, 342; Holzinger, *Genesis*, 259; Strack, *Genesis*, 173. Here also the problem remains, that the following clause does not make sense in this respect.

[539] Emerton, "Some difficult words", 89.

[540] Emerton, "Some Difficult Words", 90.

[541] C. Rabin, "Etymological Miscellanea", in: C. Rabin (ed.), *Studies in the Bible* (ScrHie, 8), Jerusalem 1961, 389.

[542] Emerton, "Some Difficult Words", 90.

[543] Emerton, "Some Difficult Words", 91.

[544] Cf. *AHw*, 159; *CAD*, vol. D, 81–6; for *dannu*, cf. *op.cit.*, 92–100.

[545] *CARTU*, 134; cf. Del Olmo Lete, Sanmartín, *DLU*, 134.

[546] Emerton, "Some Difficult Words", 91.

small snake suggests that Dan is rather small.[547] Although Emerton left the possibility open that v. 17 could originally have been independent,[548] we agree with him that the second verse, where Dan is compared to a deadly snake, is in line with the proposed meaning. Important to note is that דין in Ugaritic was written *dn*;[549] this early writing convention could have been the origin of the confusion about the change of ידן > דין and the insertion of the *yod* (cf. Ug. *dn* and Hebr. דן).[550]

The assumption of the existence of the root דנן would offer, in the birthstory of Dan, a good alternative interpretation for the problematic statement of Rachel, when Dan is born from Bilhah (Gen. 30:6): דְּנַנִּי אֱלֹהִים, usually rendered with "God has judged me" (RSV) or the like.[551] This contruction presents a grammatical problem if it were derived from דין with suffix נִי–, since it is not clear why the Masoretes would have placed a *dageš* in the second *nun*, a problem almost all Hebrew grammars mention.[552] Furthermore, commentators carefully avoid the problem and do not explain what lies behind the meaning of this "judgement".[553] דנן "to strengthen" would fit very well in this

---

[547]It is commonly acknowledged that Dan is here thought to be a rather small tribe (although this opinion is sometimes based on other descriptions of Dan, like Judg. 1:34; 17–18 [cf. also Judg. 13–16]); cf. e.g. Emerton, "Some Difficult Words", 90. The idea in connection with our text — that Dan is a rather small tribe — is favoured by the following scholars: Dillmann, *Die Genesis*, 467; Holzinger, *Genesis*, 260; Gunkel, *Genesis*, ³1910, 484; Skinner, *Genesis*, 527; Aalders, *Genesis*, dl. III, 213; Von Rad, *Erste Buch Mose*, Westermann, *Genesis 37–50*, 267; Scharbert, *Genesis 12–50*, 294; Pehlke, *Genesis 49:1–28*, 204; De Moor, *RoY*, 110 (who describes Dan — together with other tribes — as unsettled gangs, mostly engaged in warfare like the *'apiru*); Sarna, *Genesis*, 340; Wenham, *Genesis 16–50*, 481; Alter, *Genesis*, 297.

[548]Emerton, "Some Difficult Words", 90.

[549]Del Olmo Lete, Sanmartín, *DLU*, 134.

[550]Another possibility is that in an early stage of the transmission of the text, a *waw* was mistaken for a *yod*. But this was only possible in the Jewish-Aram. writing of the second century BCE. Although the Vrs apparently deny this possibility, they in fact only reflect the *interpretation* of the verb as ידין. It is more likely, however, that the confusion arose earlier, and later influenced the Vrs in their reading. It seems more probable, therefore, that a *yod* was inserted in an early stage of the transmission; because *waw* and *yod* had not much in common in old-Hebr. writing. Cf. J.C. de Moor, "Schriftsystemen en talen in de wereld van de bijbel, A: Schriftsystemen en niet-bijbelse talen", *BijbH*, dl. 1, 159; *ANEP*, 88 (# 286); *HAE*, Bd. II/1, 133, 149.

[551]NBG: "vindicated me" ("mij recht verschaft"); NEB: "has given judgement for me"; EÜ: "vindicated me" ("Gott hat mir Recht verschafft").

[552]Cf. BL, §56u″; GK, §§26g, 59f; Waltke, O'Connor, *IBHS*, 517, n. 64; JM, §62c.

[553]Cf. Skinner, *Genesis*, 387; Speiser, *Genesis*, 230; Van Selms, *Genesis dl. II*, 103; Von Rad, *Erste Buch Mose*, 237–8; Westermann, *Genesis 12–36*, 578.

context and could probably be paralleled with מרר "to strengthen" (in the sense of "to give offspring", used in Gen. 49:23 [cf. below] and in the Ug. texts). It seems, therefore, justified to read the words of Rachel in Gen. 30:6 as "God has strengthened me".[554]

Finally, we may refer to Gen. 6:3, the text Rabin started from: לֹא־יָדוֹן רוּחִי בָאָדָם לְעֹלָם "my spirit shall not יָדוֹן in man for ever". The meaning of the word is uncertain and already the Vrs had to guess at its meaning.[555] R.A. Rosenberg proposed to read יָדוֹן "remain strong", derived from the Akk. *danānu*.[556] His proposal is grammatically correct and in accordance with the vocalization of the text; furthermore the root may be present now in other texts as well (Gen. 30:6; 49:16). The support of these additional texts justifies the suggestion by Emerton that we introduce a new root in Hebrew: דנן "to be strong".[557]

2.7.1.1   Rendering the Verbal Tenses

The saying is rendered completely in the future. In verse 16A this is justified by the free *yiqtol* form יָדִן "to be strong".[558] Also the jussive יְהִי "may (he) be" in verse 17a does not cause any trouble.[559] The participle הַנֹּשֵׁךְ "that bites" (verse 17bA) is used as a predicate and may be considered to be a substitute for the *yiqtol*.[560] Since the nominal clause is in this case adjectival we render it with a present

---

The following scholars offer an explanation: Dillmann, *Die Genesis*, 324, reads that the matter is decided and conform to her wish ("ihren Wünschen gemäss"); Gunkel, *Genesis*, ³1910, 333, considers it — in fact in line with Dillmann — as normal in antiquity to regard a personal struggle as a lawsuit (referring to Ps. 43:1; 9:5). König, *Die Genesis*, 605, takes the struggle between Leah and Rachel as also a struggle against God: Rachel had to pray to God to end her suffering due to bareness. Similarly, although with some reservations, W.H. Gispen, *Genesis 25:12–36:43* (COT). Kampen 1983, 85. Aalders, *Genesis*, dl. II, 214, rejects Rachel's interpretation of these matters as only *her own* interpretation, since it would contradict 29:31; Rabin, "Etymological Miscellanea", 389, criticized the order of events in this text: it "puts the cause before the effect".

[554]דְּנָנִי should probably be re-vocalized as a pi'el דְּנֵנִי (cf. חִתַּתַנִי [Job 7:14]; לְבַבְתִּינִי [Cant. 4:9ab]); or as a po'el-form; cf. BL, §58xy, o'. It would however, offer a good explanation why the Masoretes still doubled the second *nun*.

[555]Peshiṭta Institute Communication XXII: P.B. Dirksen, "The Peshiṭta and Textual Criticism of the Old Testament", *VT* 42 (1992) 378.

[556]R.A. Rosenberg, "*Beshaggam* and *Shiloh*", *ZAW* 105 (1993) 258–61, 258.

[557]Emerton, "Some Difficult Words", 90–1; cf. now also *DCH*, vol. II, 455, 631; H. Seebaß, *Genesis I: Urgeschichte (1,1–11,26)*, Neukirchen-Vluyn 1996, 188.

[558]Lett, §72c; JM, §113b.

[559]Note, however, that Zobel, *SuG*, 18; Westermann, *Genesis 37–50*, 249, prefer to delete this word, because it would be added later to the saying, in order to join verse 17 with verse 16.

[560]JM, §121a.

meaning. The following clause is a consecutive clause,[561] in which a result is in many cases expressed by means of a *wayyiqtol* or *w-qataltí*.[562] As a consequence the following *wayyiqtol* is rendered in the sense of consecution: "so that falls ...".[563]

2.7.1.2 A Prayer (Verse 18)

The remarkable prayer is discussed here in the section on Dan, since the tradition of *setumah* and *petuḥah* took this short prayer as part of the Dan-saying. This verse is usually considered to be a gloss, added by a later writer, possibly with Samson the judge (יִדְ(י)ן derived from דין) in mind (cf. Judg. 13:5: יֵשַׁע). Within the analysis of the poetic structure of the text this prayer is indeed a *Fremdkörper*, probably confirming the view that this verse is a gloss.[564]

2.7.2 Analysis of the Poetic Structure

2.7.2.1 The Strophic Structure

Strophe II.A.i.1
Accents: [8]–2 | [8]–1.
Sep.↑: *setumah*; דָּן (*casus pendens*).[565]
Int. ||: **16:** דָּן || יִשְׂרָאֵל || עַמּוֹ ;שִׁבְטֵי;

Strophe II.A.i.2
Accents: [10]–5 | [8]–2 || [10]–5 | [8]–1.
Sep.↑: jussive יְהִי; repetition עֲלֵי.
Sep.↓: absent.
Int. ||: **17a:** נָחָשׁ || שְׁפִיפֹן; עֲלֵי־דֶרֶךְ || עֲלֵי־אֹרַח. **17b:** עִקְּבֵי || אָחוֹר; סוּס || רֹכְבוֹ.
Ext.||: נָחָשׁ (17aA) || הַנֹּשֵׁךְ (17bA); שְׁפִיפֹן || נָחָשׁ (17a) || סוּס (17bA).

2.7.2.2 The Poetic Structure of Canticle II.A.i

Sep.↑: *setumah*.
Sep.↓: absent.[566]
Ext.||: דָּן (16A) || דָּן (17aA).

---

[561] There is no clear distinction between "final clause" and "consecutive"; cf. JM, §168a.

[562] JM, §169c.

[563] JM, §118h.

[564] Cf. further the diachronical analysis in Chapter Six.

[565] De Moor, "Narrative Poetry in Canaan", 156, 159, 169; M.C.A. Korpel, "The Epilogue to the Holiness Code", *VANEP*, 123–50, 139; J.C. de Moor, "Syntax Peculiar to Ugaritic Poetry", *VANEP*, 191–205, 197.

[566] The *setumah* following verse 18, might be listed here. However, since this *setumah* is textual critically uncertain (see above, p. 164, n. 522), and follows on verse 18, which is not discussed within the analysis of the poetic structure, we do not list it here as an argument for our analysis.

2.8 Gad (Gen. 49:19)

II.A.ii.1   [ס][567]

Gad — when raiders will raid him, (19A)   גָּד גְּדוּד יְגוּדֶנּוּ

  he will raid their heel! (19B)   ס   [568]וְהוּא יָגֻד עָקֵב

2.8.1 Translation

In this saying a pun has been made on the name of גָּד by means of the
roots גדד II, "band together" and גוד, "attack".[569] This differs from
the pun in the birth story in Gen. 30:11 where a pun with the noun גַּד
"luck" seems to have been made.[570] In contrast to LXX, Peš and Vg
(and probably TO, TN, TPsJ) the final word in v. 19B is rendered
as a singular: עֲקֵבָם, "their heel", reading the *mem* before "Asher" in
verse 20A at the end of v. 19A. This practice can be considered a long
established concensus, and there is no need to elaborate on it.[571]

2.8.1.1 Rendering the Verbal Tenses

The verbal tenses are not problematic in this saying because we have
two free *yiqtol* forms which can be rendered as a future.[572] The text
is rendered as a conditional clause, which in Hebrew is sometimes
indicated by means of a simple *waw*.[573] The conditional character is
emphasized by the emphatic וְהוּא "and he ...".[574]

2.8.2 Analysis of the Poetic Structure

Strophe II.A.ii.1
Accents: [8]−2 | [8]−1.
Sep.↑: *setumah*; גָּד (*casus pendens*); repetition גדד.
Sep.↓: *setumah*.
Int. ||: גָּד || וְהוּא;[575] גָּד גְּדוּד יְגוּדֶנּוּ || יָגֻד עֲקֵבָם.

---

[567] Cf. for this *setumah* our discussion at p. 164, n. 522 above.

[568] Proposed reading: עֲקֵבָם.

[569] *HAL*, 170.

[570] Cf. LXX. Another tradition is reflected by TO, Peš and Q; see *HAL*, 169.

[571] Cf. NBG; RSV; Buber; LuthB; KBS; NEB; FrB. Furthermore: Dillmann, *Die Genesis*, 447; Gunkel, *Genesis*, ³1910, 484; König, *Die Genesis*, 763; Skinner, *Genesis*, 528, n. 19; Aalders, *Genesis*, dl. III, 190; Speiser, *Genesis*, 363; Zobel, *SuG*, 19; Van Selms, *Genesis dl. II*, 279; Von Rad, *Das Erste Buch*, 345; Cross, Freedman, *Ancient Yahwistic Poetry*, 75, 88–9, n. 68; Westermann, *Genesis 37–50*, 249; Pehlke, *Genesis 49:1–28*, 207; S. Gevirtz, "Asher in the Blessing of Jacob," *VT* 37 (1987) 154–63, 154; Wenham, *Genesis 16–50*, 458.

[572] Lett, §72c; JM, §113b; Lett¹⁰, §77c.

[573] JM, §167a,b.

[574] Zobel, *SuG*, 19.

[575] Formal parallelism.

2.9 Asher (Gen. 49:20)

II.A.iii.1   ס

Asher — may fatness be his food, (20A)   מֵאָשֵׁר[576] שְׁמֵנָה לַחְמוֹ

and he, let him bring forth royal delicacies. (20B)   וְהוּא יִתֵּן מַעֲדַנֵּי־מֶלֶךְ ס

2.9.1 Translation

With respect to the reading of אָשֵׁר (so LXX, Peš and Vg) instead of
מֵאָשֵׁר (MT, Sam, and TgO), see the preceding paragraph concerning
Gad. אָשֵׁר is considered to be a *casus pendens*, similar to vv. 8, 16,
18 and 19.[577] The difference in gender between שְׁמֵנָה (fem.) and לַחְמוֹ
(masc.)[578] does not pose a serious problem. The word שְׁמֵנָה was already
interpreted by Strack as a neuter,[579] while the feminine formative
could be used, among others, to form an abstract of an adjective.[580]
We therefore consider שְׁמֵנָה as a substantivated form of the adj. שָׁמֵן
"fat".[581] לֶחֶם is translated in a broad sense: "food".[582]

Gevirtz suggested we consider שְׁמֵנָה as a prefixed relative particle שׁ
with a perf. 3.masc.sg. D-st. of מני, in G-st. "to count" and in D-st. (in
our text): "to ration".[583] The saying on Asher would form a sarcastic
reference to the fact that a large part of the territory of Asher, twenty
cities, was given to the king of Tyre — the region of Cabul, 1 Kgs.
9:10–14 — while the remaining part would be rather small, since
the allotment of Asher compromised only twenty-two cities and their
villages (Josh. 19:30).[584] Asher had to apportion, to ration his bread,

---

[576] Proposed reading: אָשֵׁר; cf. the discussion below.

[577] König, *Die Genesis*, 763–4; Emerton, "Some Difficult Words", 91. Furthermore: Andersen, *The Verbless Clause*, 44.

[578] S. Gevirtz, "Asher in the Blessing of Jacob", *VT* 37 (1987) 154–63.

[579] H.L. Strack, *Die Genesis übersetzt und ausgelegt* (KK), München ²1905, 169;
König, *Die Genesis*, 764; Zobel, *SuG*, 19, with n. 93; 20, n. 94.

[580] Waltke, O'Connor, *IBHS*, 101–2, referring to E.A. Speiser, "Studies in
Semitic Formatives", *JAOS* 56 (1936) 22–46, esp. 37–46 (repr. in J.J. Finkel-
stein, M. Greenberg (eds.), *Oriental and Biblical Studies: Collected Writings of
E.A. Speiser*. Philadelphia (PA) 1967, 403–32, esp. 422–32).

[581] Cf. also Ug. *šmt* "fat" from *šmn*; and Gordon, *UT*, 492 (# 2439); Zobel, *SuG*,
20, n. 94; J.M. Sasson, "Flora, Fauna and Minerals", *RSP*, Vol. I, 448 (# 117).
Cf. furthermore בְּרִאָה in Hab. 1:16 and Rabin, "Etymological Miscellanea", 392;
A.S. van der Woude, *Habakuk, Zefanja* (PredOT), Nijkerk 1978, 30.

[582] *HAL*, 500; König, *Die Genesis*, 764; Zobel, *SuG*, 20; Pehlke, *Genesis 49:1–28*,
208. Rabin, "Etymological Miscellanea", 392, suggests we read לְחֻמוֹ instead of MT
לַחְמוֹ and translate "they of Asher eat fatness". Although the reading of לחמו as
a perf. 3.masc.plur. would be possible, Rabin's suggestion was motivated by the
mem before Asher in MT, which is better transposed to v. 19. Furthermore the
conjecture would result in a difference in number between vv. 20A and 20B.

[583] Gevirtz, "Asher", 158–9. The lexica give the verb as מנה, cf. *HAL*, 567.

[584] Gevirtz, "Asher", 155, with n. 2; 161.

"i.e. presumably, has difficulty in feeding itself, nevertheless provides the royal establishment, '(the) king', with 'delicacies'."[585] However, the D-st. of מנ implies an authoritative action by a powerful person (God or king), who rations something to somebody,[586] and it does not denote to ration oneself. Gevirtz's interpretation of the first colon is therefore not accepted, and the colon is translated in the more usual way: "Asher, fatness is his food".

The emphatic position of וְהוּא is remarkable, since it occurs also in vv. 13 and 19. Another problem is the exact translation of the expression מַעֲדַנֵּי־מֶלֶךְ, which is difficult to establish, because the function of this construct is not clear. The words used are both known, but the exact meaning of מֶלֶךְ is obscure. Does it mean "of a king" and is it meant in this manner as a general description of the delicacies: "delicacies fit for a king"? Another option is that מֶלֶךְ is specified: a specific king, meaning: "the delicacies of the king"; this is possible since the article in poetic texts is more often omitted. In the present context of this saying it seems appropriate to render the text in a more general way, since no king is known. However, since Genesis 49 is shaped in the form of a foretelling of the future, it is impossible to exclude the specified meaning, because the saying on Judah seems to contain also an allusion to a certain king. The expression is rendered more generally here, namely, "royal delicacies", because it offers the opportunity to include the specific meaning "the delicacies of the king".

2.9.1.1   Rendering the Verbal Tenses

This saying starts with a nominal clause which is very often rendered as a future form.[587] Since we interpreted several nominal clauses as an optative, in accordance with the jussive use in Gen. 49:17a, we read here, too, an optative: "may (it) be".[588] In accordance with this rendering, we interpreted the following *yiqtol* יִתֵּן as a jussive: "let him bring forth".[589]

2.9.2   Analysis of the Poetic Structure

Strophe II.A.iii.1

Accents: [8]–2 | [8]–1.

Sep.↑: *setumah*; *casus pendens*; emph. constructed nominal clause;

---

[585]Gevirtz, "Asher", 161.

[586]Cf. Job 7:3; Jonah 2:1; 4:6–8; Dan. 1:5, 10–1; also Ps. 16:5.

[587]Cf. *e.g.* RSV; NBG; JPS; NEB; NIV.

[588]JM, §163b.

[589]Cf. JM, §46, for the very special use of נתן in optative clauses, see *op.cit.*, §163d; On the word-order, cf. *op.cit.*, §155l.

וְהוּא (emph. position).

Sep.↓: *setumah*.

Int. ‖: **20:** אֲשֶׁר ‖ וְהוּא;590 שְׁמֵנָה ‖ מַעֲדַנֵּי־מֶלֶךְ; לַחְמוֹ ‖ מַעֲדַנֵּי־מֶלֶךְ.

2.10 Naphtali (Gen. 49:21)

II.B.i.1   ס

May Naphtali be a lambing ewe, (21A)   נַפְתָּלִי אַיָּלָה שְׁלֻחָה591

   that brings forth lovely lambs. (21B)   ס   הַנֹּתֵן אִמְרֵי־שָׁפֶר

2.10.1 Translation

The interpretation of the saying on Naphtali has a rather confusing tradition. The LXX rendered the saying as a plant metaphor: Νεφθαλὶ στέλεχος ἀνειμένον, ἐπιδιδοὺς ἐν τῷ γενήματι κάλλος "Naphtali is a stock set free, bestowing beauty by its produce".[592] It is likely that LXX interpreted Hebr. אילה as *אֵלָה "large tree, terebinth" instead of MT אַיָּלָה. Furthermore אמרי has to correspond apparently with γενήματι "fruits"; whereas שֶׁפֶר was translated into κάλλος "beauty".[593] LXX used the word γενήματι several times for Hebr. פְּרִי "fruit",[594] which would fit together with the verb נתן in the Hebr. expression נתן פְּרִי "give fruit".[595] However, except for Lev. 25:19, where the LXX renders פְּרִי with ἐκφόρια, the expression is translated (ἀπο)δίδωμι καρπός. Nowhere is the verb rendered with ἐπιδίδωμι as in our text; further, whereas in all these cases פְּרִי was rendered as a direct object, in Gen. 49:21B the direct object of נתן became a prepositional object ἐν τῷ γενήματι. It is likely, therefore, that LXX, as Wevers stated, "simply contextualized" the difficult text, because they "could make little sense of אמרי".[596]

TO paraphrased the saying, connecting the meaning with the land of Naphtali:[597] נפתלי בארע טבא יתרמי עדביה ואחסנתייה תהי מעבדא פירין יהון מודן ומברכין עליהון "Naphtali, his lot shall be cast on a good land,

---

[590] Formal parallelism.

[591] Proposed reading: אֵלָה שְׁלֻחָה; cf. the discussion below.

[592] Wevers, *Greek Text of Genesis*, 831.

[593] Grossfeld, *TOGen*, 169, n. 52, refers to Is. 17:10–1, for a probably source of inspiration for "this almost Midrashic rendering": "though you plant pleasant plants ... make them grow on the day that you plant them".

[594] According to Hatch-Redpath, 238–9, in Deut. 26:10; 28:4, 11, 18, 42, 51; 30:9; Isa. 3:10; 65:21; 7:20.

[595] Lev. 25:19; 26:4, 20; Jer. 17:10; Ezek. 34:27; Mic. 6:7; Zech. 8:12; Ps. 1:3; Prov. 31:31.

[596] Wevers, *Greek Text of Genesis*, 831.

[597] This connection with the land is reflected in the Midrashim; cf. Grossfeld, *TOGen*, 169, nn. 51–2.

and his inheritance shall be one producing fruit over which thanks and praises shall be recited".[598] Grossfeld refers to the Midrashim (Gen.Rab. 98:17; 99:12) to explain this enigmatic rendering. Especially the latter text is illuminating in this respect: "this alludes to the Valley of Gennesaret", which like a hind "is swift to ripen its fruit".[599] So Hebr. אַיָּלָה שְׁלֻחָה alludes to the fruitfulness of Naphtali's land and the speed of the ripening of the crops,[600] whereas שלחה influenced "to cast" in the Targum's "his lot shall be cast".[601] אָמְרֵי is here — as in TN and TPsJ — derived from אמר, meaning "saying, word", which, together with שֶׁפֶר ("lovely saying"), applies to prayers and religious maxims in Rabbinic theology.[602] So it appears that TO read the present consonantal text of MT, but replaced the metaphor with realistic terms,[603] referring to the fruitful land of Naphtali,[604] which is reminiscent to its translation of Gen. 49:15, 20, thus creating a coherent picture within its translation.[605] Although LXX also refers to "fruit" in this connection, this cannot be used to indicate a possible pre-Masoretic text, since LXX clearly had some trouble with the translation of this saying. It appears, therefore, a matter of coincidence in exegesis that both versions refer to "fruit", rather than a matter of textual variance.

Peš rendered the text as follows: *nptly 'yzgd' qlyl' yhb m'mr' špyr'* "Naphtali is a swift messenger, bringing pleasant words".[606] Finally,

---

[598]Translation according to Grossfeld, *TOGen*, 159.

[599]Quoted after Grossfeld, *TOGen*, 169, n. 51.

[600]Grossfeld, *TOGen*, 169, n. 51. TO's interpretation of the text (here as well as in other sayings; cf. *e.g.* Asher) as references to the land is in agreement with TO's preference for concrete statements to explain poetic metaphors; cf. Grossfeld, *op.cit.*, 169, nn. 49–50; and below.

[601]Grossfeld, *TOGen*, 169, n. 51.

[602]Grossfeld, *TOGen*, 169, n. 52. Cf. for a comparable rendering: TJon Josh. 10:12; 1 Sam. 22:1 (MT דבר; TJon שבח). Further, "thanks and praises" is at the same time a stock phrase in TO and TJon, which is added frequently; cf. Judg. 5:2, 9.

[603]This is typically translation technique of the Targums; cf. J.F. Stenning, *The Targum of Isaiah*, Oxford 1949, xiii; A. van der Kooij, *Die alten Textzeugen des Jesajabuches: Ein Beitrag zur Textgeschichte des Alten Testaments* (OBO, 35), Freiburg, Göttingen 1981, 175–181; W.F. Smelik, *The Targum to Judges* (OTS, 36), Leiden 1995, 98, 361.

[604]Grossfeld, *TOGen*, 169, n. 52.

[605]Smelik, *Targum of Judges*, 330, 364, 392, etc.

[606]Similarly TN: נפתלי אוגד קליל מבשר בשורן טבן "Naphtali is a swift runner, announcing good tidings," (McNamara, *TNGen*, 223). TPsJ added after runner (transl.: messenger), "like a hind"; cf. Maher, *TPsJGen*, 161. After this word-for-word translation, TN and TPsJ gave an expansion on the contents of this message: he had told Jacob at the beginning that Joseph was not dead!

MT itself interprets אילה as אַיָּלָה "hind", an interpretation which is also found in TPsJ, while Peš and TN seem to allude to this interpretation. Remarkable, however, is the fact that MT interprets אמרי as *אִמְרֵי "lambs (of)", an interpretation which is found nowhere else in the Vrs. Although the rendering of TPsJ (and implicitly of Peš and TN) sometimes occurs in modern translations,[607], namely a "hind", "giving beautiful words", this rendering is problematic too. The expression נתן אֹמֶר is possible of course (Ps. 68:12), but a "hind" that gives forth "beautiful words" is rather strange.[608] This was apparently felt by Peš and TN, who rendered it respectively "messenger" or "runner" instead of an animal name, which TPsJ added. The fact that these translations did not translate literally but interpreted the text by replacing the animal name with an assumed "meaning" indicates that the text was not clear to the translators themselves. Moreover, the metaphor in their translations is too broken to be likely.[609] Apparently TN, TPsJ and Peš also tried innovative ways to make some sense of the saying. A comparison of the Vrs with MT shows that they all presumably had the same consonantal text and that the differences can be explained as *interpretations*. The differences between MT and Vrs show that the interpretation of אילה (v. 21A) and אמרי (v. 21B) constituted the main difficulties and that the interpretation of the text is in fact completely dependant on the right interpretation of these two words.

If we compare several modern translations of the text, it could be concluded that the interpretation of אילה and אמרי is still disputed. For אילה we find: "hind"[610] or "terebinth".[611] When אילה is interpreted to be a plant, than אמרי is taken as connected with plants, like shoots, fruit or the like.[612] However, when אילה is rendered an animal, אמרי is

---

[607]Cf. n. 613 below.

[608]Note also the difference in number: the expression in Ps. 68:12 has the singular: אֹמֶר; whereas our text has the plural: אמרי "words".

[609]Cf. Dillmann, *Die Genesis*, 469; Gunkel, *Genesis*, ³1910, 485; Aalders, *Genesis*, dl. III, 214, has to confess his *nescio* ("wat de rest betreft, moeten wij, in verband met de onzekerheid van tekst en verklaring ons niet-weten belijden".) Speiser, *Genesis*, 367; Wenham, *Genesis 16–50*, 483. Cf. also the harsh judgement of Van Selms, *Genesis, dl. II*, 279, who calls this rendering "grotesque", and states that another rendering is preferred.

[610]RSV; NBG; Zobel, *SuG*, 20; Andersen, *The Verbless Clause*, 44; Westermann, *Genesis 37–50*, 247, 269; Sarna, *Genesis*, 342; Wenham, *Genesis 16–50*, 483; Pehlke, *Genesis 49:1–28*, 211.

[611]NEB; Cross, Freedman, *Ancient Yahwistic Poetry*, 89, n. 73; Van Selms, *Genesis, dl. II*, 279.

[612]Cross, Freedman, *Ancient Yahwistic Poetry*, 89, n. 73; Van Selms, *Genesis, dl. II*, 279.

interpreted as "words, message"[613] or "fawns, lambs".[614] The problems surrounding the translation of MT are discussed by Gevirtz.[615] First, he considers the lead of LXX in this situation too uncertain to follow, especially because of the unnecessary introduction of the botanical figure.[616] However, he also criticizes the normal rendering of אַיָלָה as "hind, doe", because אַיָלָה is mostly associated with high places (2 Sam. 22:34 = Ps. 18:34; Hab. 3:19). Secondly, because it is twice paired with *יַעֲלָה "mountain goat" (Job 39:1; Prov. 5:19);[617] and finally because אַיִל is difficult to distinguish from אַיִל "ram".[618] "Mountain sheep" seemed, therefore, "a more reasonable and appropriate denomination" to Gevirtz for אַיָלָה than "hind, doe". According to Gevirtz, this argument is strengthened by the fact that in the parallel colon אִמְרֵי־שָׁפֶר has to be considered הַנֹּתֵן by this אַיָלָה. In most translations — besides the rendering as "words"[619] — אִמְרֵי is translated as "fawns (of)".[620] However, *אֹמֶר has in Hebr., as in the other Semitic languages, the established meaning "sheep" or "lambs"; and the latter is not used to denote newborn deer/hinds. Furthermore, the young of this species is denoted by עֹפֶר (Cant. 2:9, 17; 8:14).[621] Therefore the most plausible interpretation for אילה in our verse is *אַיְלָה[622] (fem. of אַיִל I, "ram") "sheep, ewe".[623]

Gevirtz's arguments concerning our text are rather strong and convincing. Because of the consonantal similarity of *אַיְלָה "sheep, ewe" and אַיָלָה "hind", it is likely that a wrong vocalization led to the misinterpretation of the word. However, it is doubtful if he rightly questioned the identification of אַיָלָה as "hind, doe" in general.[624] In Ug. ảyl "doe" is attested in addition to ảl "fine sheep" and il "ram".[625] It

---

[613]NBG, Von Rad, *Erste Buch Mose*, 345, 351; Zobel, *SuG*, 20–1; Pehlke, *Genesis 49:1–28*, 212–4.

[614]RSV; Speiser, *Genesis*, 367; Westermann, *Genesis 37–50*, 247, 269; Sarna, *Genesis*, 342; Wenham, *Genesis 16–50*, 483.

[615]S. Gevirtz, "Naphtali in the 'Blessing of Jacob'", *JBL* 103 (1984) 513–21.

[616]Gevirtz, "Naphtali," 513, n. 1.

[617]*HAL*, 402: "'Steinbock' *Capra Nubiana* oder 'Felsenziege' *Capra Sinaitica*".

[618]Gevirtz, "Naphtali," 513–4.

[619]Cf. n. 613 above.

[620]Cf. n. 614 above.

[621]Gevirtz, "Naphtali," 515.

[622]For this vocalization cf. אַלָה < *אַיְלָה < *'ailat "terebinth", fem. of אַיִל II, which is vocalized similar to אַיִל I, "ram"; (*HAL*, 50). Cf. also the fact that LXX apparently read here אַיְלָה.

[623]As a fem.-form of אַיִל "ram", there is no need to render *אַיְלָה with "mountain-sheep, ewe"; *pace* Gevirtz, "Naphtali", 513–4.

[624]Gevirtz, "Naphtali," 513–4.

[625]For Ug. cf. J.C. de Moor, K. Spronk, "More on Demons in Ugarit (KTU

appears, therefore, that אַיָּלָה is correctly identified as a "hind, doe", but that in our text the Masoretic vocalization is wrong. Naphtali was described as a sheep, bringing forth (הנתן) "lambs".

In v. 21A שלחה is interpreted by the Masoretes as a part.pass. fem.sg. qal of שלח "to send, bestow",[626] mostly translated as "let loose" (cf. Job 39:5).[627] Gevirtz pointed to the fact that the verbs שלח and נתן are paralleled very frequently and stated that it is thus very likely that they are parallel here too.[628] הַנֹּתֵן is used in v. 21B in the meaning of "bringing forth" and neither the literal meaning of the passive of שלח "to be sent, be bestowed", nor the interpretation "let loose" seem to make sense in this context.[629] However, in another context אַיָּלוֹת "hinds"[630] is the subject of תְּשַׁלַּחְנָה (2.fem.plur. pi'el of שלח), namely in Job 39:1–3 (cf. also Job 21:10–11), with the meaning "to cast out, calve, give birth to". Gevirtz suggests, on the basis of a comparison of part.pass. of the qal with the pu'al of other verbs,[631] that שְׁלֻחָה as a part.pass. could be interpreted in a similar way as the pass. of the pi'el. In Gevirtz's opinion Naphtali would be the subject of this pass. verb, in the same way as the subject of the part.act. masc.sg. in v. 21B is the fem. אילה in v. 21A:[632]

Naphtali a mountain-ewe was born, (21A)
  who gives (birth to) lambs of the fold. (21B)

Although these changes in gender are possible in Hebrew poetry, there is reason to take another solution into consideration. In the other sayings the sons are named as subjects in a nominal clause or as casus pendens, and it is therefore very likely that this is also the case in the present saying. We have to look for something like "Naphtali — a ewe ..." or "Naphtali is a ... ewe", which would be more likely. The consonantal text leaves the possibility open for two other interpretations

---

1.82)," *UF* 16 (1984) 241; for Akk. cf. *CAD*, vol. A/1, 374: *alu* "fine sheep"; for Hebr. אַיִל and אֵיל (cs.) "ram", cf. *HAL*, 38–9.

[626] *HAL*, 1400.

[627] RSV; NBG.

[628] Gevirtz, "Naphtali," 517–8; cf. furthermore the structural analysis of this strophe below.

[629] Gevirtz, "Naphtali," 518. Of course the latter interpretation "let loose" was given in connection with the interpretation of אַיָּלָה as "hind, doe" and made in that context slightly better sense — although the diffuse tradition of the Vrs already testified to the problems of interpretation. However, since the parallel אמרי || אילה demands another rendering for אילה, so also שלחה must be considered anew.

[630] Or "mountain-ewes" according to Gevirtz, "Naphtali", 518

[631] Gevirtz, "Naphtali," 518; cf. also the similar meaning of שלח in qal and pi'el; see *HAL*, 1403.

[632] Gevirtz, "Naphtali," 520.

of the verb שלחה in line with the meaning "to give birth", namely a part.act. fem.sg. qal or a perf. 2.fem.sg. pi'el. The perf. 2.fem.sg. pi'el would not offer an interpretation much different from that given by Gevirtz, and the former suggestion of the part.act. fem.sg. qal should be considered, namely: שְׁלֵחָה. Since שלח qal and pi'el are very closely related it is not a problem to render the verb here with the meaning "to cast out, give birth to". The result would be: "Naphtali is a lambing ewe".

In the final colon we find the part.act. masc.sg. qal הַנֹּתֵן, which should be altered, according to some scholars, because of the fem. subject אַיָּלָה (or *אַיְלָה).[633] However, it is not absolutely necessary to consider *אַיְלָה as the subject of הַנֹּתֵן. Because Naphtali (masc.) is the subject of the preceding colon, it is possible to consider him here the antecedent of the final clause.

The final word of v. 21B, שֶׁפֶר, is usually translated with "good, lovely, beautiful, gracious".[634] Since the significance of שֶׁפֶר is not firmly established according to Gevirtz,[635] he suggests we relate the Hebr. אִמְרֵי־שָׁפֶר with Akk. *immir supūri* "sheep of the fold".[636] With this Akk. expression he offers an interesting parallel for our text, however, he slips too soon from the common rendering as "lovely, beautiful" to another possibility, without any discussion why this rendering is not acceptable. In his article he refers to Ps. 16:6, where שֶׁפֶר is used, omitting, however, to mention the fact that the word is used in parallel to נָעֵם in this text.[637] This parallel is important, because

---

[633] Cf. the critical *apparatus* of BHS; furthermore Skinner, *Genesis*, 528; Cross, Freedman, *Ancient Yahwistic Poetry*, 89, n. 73: *nātĕnâ*. Contrast, however, Dahood, *Psalms*, vol. III, 205.

[634] LXX: κάλλος; Vg: *pulchritudinis*; Peš: *špr'*; TN: טב. Furthermore RSV; StV; NBG; KBS; FrB; LuthB; Buber; GB, 859; *HAL*, 1509; *DBHE*, 761; Dillmann, *Die Genesis*, 469; Gunkel, *Genesis*, ³1910, 484; König, *Die Genesis*, 764; Speiser, *Genesis*, 363; Sarna, *Genesis*, 342; Wenham, *Genesis 16–50*, 483; Westermann, *Genesis 37–50*, 247, 249.

[635] Gevirtz, "Naphtali," 514–5, with n. 2. In n. 2 he writes, however, that the meaning of the verbal root שפר "to be beautiful, pleasing" is well attested in several dialects of Aramaic (cf. also *HAL*, 1509). Furthermore he refers also to Ps. 16:6 (|| נעם, RdH) and Job 26:13 (disputed).

[636] Gevirtz, "Naphtali," 516; Andersen, *The Hebrew Verbless Clause*, 44, 123. Cf. *CAD*, vol. I/J, 129.

[637] The parallel שֶׁפֶר || נָעֵם in Ps. 16:6 was used by M. Dahood to reconstruct KTU 1.23:1–2, with in line 2: *bn š[pr]*; cf. M. Dahood, "Ugaritic-Hebrew Parallel Pairs," *RSP*, vol. III, 114 (# 214) (Dahood seems to depart here from his suggested interpretation of Ps. 16:6 in Dahood, *Psalms*, vol. I, 89–90). Cf. however, C.M. Foley, "Are the 'Gracious Gods' *bn šrm*? A Suggested Restoration for KTU 1.23:1–2," *UF* 19 (1987) 61–74, esp. 63; cf. also the restoration in *MLC*, 440; *CARTU*, 51 (= *ARTU*, 118); and T.L. Hettema, "'That It Be Repeated': A Narrative Analysis

on the same page he also refers to Prov. 15:26, 16:24, where we find the expression אִמְרֵי־נֹעַם "pleasant words".[638] On the basis of this expression in Proverbs Gevirtz rejects the meaning "lovely, beautiful" for שֶׁפֶר, since the expression for "eloquence" is thus formed with נֹעַם. But, apart from the parallel of שֶׁפֶר ‖ נָעֵם, he does not discuss why שֶׁפֶר "lovely, beautiful" could not be used for אִמְרֵי "lambs". Because of the parallelism and the appearance of the similarly constructed expression אִמְרֵי־נֹעַם[639] we render the word שֶׁפֶר with "lovely, beautiful".[640]

The textual tradition had probably some trouble with this interpretation and wanted to avoid the comparison of the ancestor with a lambing ewe. Although this might be a reasonable argument against the suggested translation, this kind of "offending" metaphorical language is used also for God[641] and it appears, therefore, not to be a conclusive argument against the proposed rendering. Further, the comparison seems to refer to the (future) abundant "production" of lambs from Naphtali (a tribal or geographical region), that were probably "exported" to other regions (cf. the comparable use of the verb נתן in verses 20 and 21), and for that reason the present metaphor seems to fit very well. Finally, all possible interpretations have to handle the same problem, namely, that the ancestor is compared to something that in all cases has the feminine ending ה־, whereas in *all* the interpretations the masculine variant is present: *אֵיל "terebinth"; אַיָּל "fallow deer"; אַיִל "ram". It appears, therefore, that the emphatic masc. הַנֹּתֵן is there to correct this offending difference in gender.

2.10.1.1   Rendering the Verbal Tenses

The saying consists of two nominal clauses, of which the first is an animal metaphor similar to most of the other sayings. Although some of these sayings are rendered in the present tense,[642] we have rendered this clause with an optative meaning. This is suggested by the context (49:1aC, 28), identifying these sayings as blessings and as predictions of the future. Since the animal metaphor and the future action are closely related here we have chosen to render this saying in the optative sense. The second clause is adjectival, similar to Gen. 49:17bA. As such it is rendered as a present, but as an adjectival clause to the preceding clause it also has an optative sense.

---

of KTU 1.23," *JEOL* 31 (1989–90) 82, n. 19.

[638] Gevirtz, "Naphtali," 514.

[639] The Masoretes even placed a *maqqef* between both words in both cases.

[640] Cf. also M. Dahood, "Hebrew-Ugaritic Lexicography, XI," *Bib*, 54 (1973) 363.

[641] Cf. Korpel, *Rift in the Clouds*, 241–3; 246–52.

[642] *E.g.* Judah (49:9aA) and Joseph (49:22a).

2.10.2 Analysis of the Poetic Structure

Strophe II.B.i.1

Accents: [8]–2 | [8]–1.

Sep.↑: *setumah.*

Sep.↓: *setumah.*

Int. ‖: **21:** אֵילָה ‖ אִמְרֵי־שָׁפֶר; שְׁלֻחָה ‖ הַנֹּתֵן.[643]

2.11 Joseph (Gen. 49:22–26)

II.B.ii.1   ס

A young bullcalf is Joseph, (22aA)	בֵּן פֹּרָת[644] יוֹסֵף
a young bullcalf next to a well, (22aB)	בֵּן פֹּרָת[644] עֲלֵי־עָיִן
in the meadow he will stride towards the Bull, (22bA)	בָּנוֹת צָעֲדָה עֲלֵי־שׁוּר[645]
and he will make him strong so they will become numerous. (23aB)	וַיְמָרֲרֻהוּ[646] וָרֹבּוּ

II.B.ii.2

And if archers should harass him, (23bA)	וַיִּשְׂטְמֻהוּ[647] בַּעֲלֵי חִצִּים
his bow will remain stable, (24aB)	וַתֵּשֶׁב בְּאֵיתָן קַשְׁתּוֹ
and the arms of his hands become nimble, (24aC)	וַיָּפֹזּוּ זְרֹעֵי יָדָיו
by the hands of the Strong One of Jacob, (24bA)	מִידֵי אֲבִיר יַעֲקֹב
by the name of the Shepherd of Israel's stone (24bB)	מִשָּׁמרֹעֵה[648] אֶבֶן יִשְׂרָאֵל

II.B.ii.3

By El, your Father, who will help you, (25aA)	מֵאֵל אָבִיךָ וְיַעְזְרֶךָ
and by Shadday, who will bless you, (25aB)	וְאֵת שַׁדַּי וִיבָרְכֶךָּ
with blessings of the Heavens above, (25bA)	בִּרְכֹת שָׁמַיִם מֵעָל
blessings of the Flood, resting below, (25bB)	בִּרְכֹת תְּהוֹם רֹבֶצֶת תָּחַת
blessings of breasts and womb. (25bC)	בִּרְכֹת שָׁדַיִם וָרָחַם

---

[643] Gen. 38:16–7; Lev. 26:25; Deut. 24:1, 3; Joel 2:19; Mal. 2:2; Ps. 78:24–5; 106:15; 147:15–6; Job 2:4–5; 5:10; Qoh. 11:1–2; Lam. 1:13; KTU 1.17:vi.17–18, 26–28; 1.24:20–1; *KAI* 50:3–4. See also Gen. 25:6; 43:14; Jer. 29:17; 40:5; Ezek. 7:3; 17:15. U. Cassuto, "Parallel Words in Hebrew and Ugaritic", in: Cassuto, *BOS*, vol. 2, 60–8, 64; M. Held, "The Action-Result (Factive-Passive) Sequence of Identical Verbs in Biblical Hebrew and Ugaritic", *JBL* 84 (1965) 279, n. 32; Dahood, *Psalms*, vol. II, 241; idem, *Psalms*, vol. III, 348; Dahood, Penar, "Ugaritic-Hebrew Parallel Pairs", 219 (# 269); Avishur, *Stylistic Studies*, 542–3; Gevirtz, "Naphtali", 517–8; Van der Meer, *Oude woorden worden nieuw*, 78, n. 7; Korpel, "Epilogue to the Holiness Code", 133.

[644] Proposed reading: פֹּרָת; for all the proposed readings, cf. the discussion below.

[645] Proposed reading: בְּנוֹת צָעֲדָה עֲלֵי־שׁוֹר.

[646] Proposed reading: וַיְמָרֲרֻהוּ.

[647] Proposed reading: וַיִּשְׂטְמֻהוּ.

[648] Proposed reading: מִשָּׁם רֹעֶה.

II.B.ii.4

The blessings of your Father prevail (26aA)	בִּרְכֹת אָבִיךָ גָּבְרוּ
over the blessings of the eternal mountains, (26aB)	עַל־בִּרְכֹת הוֹרַי,[649] עַד
the longings of the everlasting hills. (26aC)	תַּאֲוַת גִּבְעֹת עוֹלָם
May they be on the head of Joseph, (26bA)	תִּהְיֶיןָ לְרֹאשׁ יוֹסֵף
and on the skull of one set apart of his brothers. (26bB) פ	וּלְקָדְקֹד נְזִיר אֶחָיו

2.11.1 Translation

In Gen. 49:22 we meet one of the more difficult verses to translate. Together with the following verses this saying presents the translator with some impenetrable problems.[650] This was already demonstrated in the introductory chapter where we gave mutually divergent translations of the same verse. When these renderings are compared with the translation offered above, the ambiguity of the Hebrew text is emphasized. However, the problems reflected in these translations are not restricted to our era, but are found already in the *Versiones*.

2.11.1.1 The *Versiones* on Verse 22

Although verse 22aA is translated rather uniformly by the Ancients, the renderings of verse 22bA differ widely. The vocalization of MT suggests that פֹרָת is understood as a part.act. qal fem. of פרה, "bear fruit, to be fruitful".[651] The first word, however, בֵּן, is vocalized as if it is a *status absolutus*,[652] while it may have been intended as a *constructus*,[653] preserving its usual stress because of the rhythm.[654]

---

[649]Proposed reading: הֲרֵי.

[650]Vawter, "Canaanite Background", 7; Speiser, *Genesis*, 367. Caquot, "Le parole sur Juda", 13, writes: "le verset 22 défie toute interprétation"; cf. also A. Caquot, "Ben Porat (Genèse 49,22)", *Sem* 39 (1980) 43–56, 43. According to Vater, *Commentar*, Bd. I, 326, פרת (v. 22) is judged to be the most difficult word of Genesis 49.

[651]*HAL*, 907.

[652]Jacob, *Das erste Buch*, 920; Caquot, "Ben Porat", 47–8.

[653]So it is suggested to re-vocalize בֵּן as בֶּן by Holzinger, *Genesis*, 261; Dillmann, *Die Genesis*, 469; Gunkel, *Genesis*, ³1910, 485. On the vocalization, cf. further p. 186 below.

[654]Skinner, *Genesis*, 529; Westermann, *Genesis 37–50*, 249; H.-D. Neef, *Ephraim: Studien zur Geschichte des Stammes Ephraim von der Landnahme bis zur frühen Königszeit* (BZAW, 238), Berlin 1995, 114. The rhythm in v. 22 is 3 + 3 + 3, whereas it would have been 2 + 2 + 3 if בֵּן had lost its stress and was connected by a *maqqeph* with the following word as is usual (but not always) in the construct state (I. Yeivin, *Introduction to the Tiberian Masorah* [MSt, 5], transl. and ed. by E.J. Revell, Missoula [Mt] 1980, §297). Compensation by leaving out the *maqqeph* after עֲלֵי was impossible, because this word, in combination with the following monosyllabic word, needs a *maqqeph* and a lightening of the stress in the first word in order to avoid two main stressed syllables one after the other (Yeivin, *op.cit.*,

LXX rendered verse 22aA, however, with υἱὸς ηὐξημένος Ιωσηφ, "a grown son is Joseph"; Peš rendered *br' dtrbyt' ywsp*, "a son who grows extraordinarily is Joseph"; TO: ברי דסני יוסף, "Joseph is my son, who shall be numerous"; finally Sam does not depart from the consonantal text of MT. The Masoretes and ancient translators apparently considered פרת as a derivative of the root פרה.[655] LXX, Peš, and TO remarkably depart from the usual interpretation of בֵּן as a *status constructus*. One might be inclined, therefore, to consider MT in the same vein and render the vocalized text with LXX: "a son who grows is Joseph". However, because פֹּרָת is fem., the adjectival sense is unlikely and the construct state the most probable.[656] Therefore, "a fruitful bough" or "a young fruit tree" seems the seems the most correct translation of MT בֵּן פֹּרָת.

In verse 22aB the Ancients start to diverge in their interpretation. Whereas the vocalized Hebr. text suggests the translation "a young fruit tree next to a well"; LXX translated υἱὸς ηὐξημένος ζηλωτός, "a grown son, living dignified"; Peš rendered *br' dtrbyt' sqy 'yn'*, "a son who grows extraordinarily, arise O fountain!"; and TO read: ברי דאתברך כגופן דנציב על עינא, "my son who shall be blessed like a vine that is planted near a spring of water". The rendering of LXX is significant but could have been derived from עֲלֵי עָיִן, "on who the eye is".[657] In TO this colon has probably been influenced by Isa. 32:12 (גֶּפֶן פֹּרִיָּה, "the fruitful vine"), but also associated with the tree planted by the water (cf. Ezek. 17:5, 8; 19:10–14; Ps. 1:3). Finally, Peš clearly interpreted עלי as an imper. of עלה, "go up, ascend".

The final colon is interpreted by the Masoretes as "daughters stride over the wall". The Hebr. text is rendered by LXX with υἱός μου νεώτατος πρός με ἀνάστρεφον, "my youngest son turn yourself to me"; Peš gave: *bnyn' smyk' dslq bšwr*, "a strong building, growing on a wall"; while TO produced: דמיא תרין שבטין יפקון מבנוהי יקבלון חולקא ואחסנתא, "two tribes shall emerge from his sons; they shall receive an inherited portion". Sam departs from MT in this colon: בני צעירי עלי שור, "my youngest son on the wall / for me a wall".[658] The latter tradition corresponds to LXX with regard to the first two words: "my youngest son",[659] but not with the final two words however:

§295). Moreover, even so the rhythm would have been irregular: 2 + 3 + 4.

[655] Neef, *Ephraim*, 113.

[656] On בֵּן as a construct state, cf. p. 186, with n. 677 below.

[657] Caquot, "Ben Porat", 46, n. 1.

[658] Caquot, "Ben Porat", 49.

[659] Wevers, *Greek Text of Genesis*, 831; M. Rösel, "Die Interpretation von Genesis 49 in der Septuaginta", *BN* 79 (1995) 54–70, 67.

"turn yourself to me" (LXX),[660] and "on the wall / for me a wall" (Sam).[661] Sam supports at least the final two words of MT עֲלֵי שׁוּר. However, the reading צעירי could be considered a misreading — or mis-interpretation of — צעדה. Peš also supports the final two words of MT, because *bšwr* corresponds with שׁור, whereas *dslq* points to the interpretation of עלי as a derivative of the root עלה.[662] The first word, *bnyn'*, seems to reflect an interpretation of בנות as a derivative of בנה — did they read בניה? — in addition they probably read for צעדה the slightly different סעדה, inf.cstr. fem. from סעד "to strengthen".[663] It is interesting to note here that LXX, Sam and Peš did not interpret צעדה as a finite verbal form but as a nominal form (LXX and Sam: צָעִיר; Peš: סְעָדָה); TO interpreted the verb as a future, using twice an impf., which might reflect an interpretation as a part. which normally can be rendered as a present. Finally TO seems to have understood בנות as "daughters", which apparently necessitated a midrashic exposition: the daughters were identified with the daughters of Zelophehad, who were granted an inheritance together with their male fellow tribesman (Num. 27:1–7).[664] However, this interpretation tends towards midrash and the meaning of the vocalized text still remains obscure. The usual solution that בָּנוֹת and בֵּן are parallel, and that בֵּן is indeed in *status constructus* with פֹּרָת seems the best interpretation of the *vocalized* text of verse 22:

A young fruit tree is Joseph,

  a young fruit tree next to the well,

    branches are running over the wall.

On the one hand, the fact that the *Versiones* differ so widely from each other, and, on the other hand, support the consonantal text of

---

[660]Instead of שׁור, it appears that LXX read שׁוב — the ב could have been confused with a ר; cf. Wevers, *Greek Text of Genesis*, 832; Rösel, "Die Interpretation von Genesis 49 in LXX", 67. The LXX might also have interpreted שׁור as סור, "to turn aside, off" (*HAL*, 706).

[661]Unless שׁור is considered an imper. of the root שׁור I, "gaze on, regard, see" (*HAL*, 1345). The syntax would be somewhat unusual, and nobody has suggested this reading for Sam. But, even then LXX and Sam would differ from each other in relation to MT.

[662]Aram. *slq* seems to be the most common rendering for the Hebr. עלה; cf. De Moor, *BCTP*, vol. I, 255–8; Smelik, *BCTP*, vol. II, 337–40, 516. Further, TgSam also renders עלי שׁור with סלק שׁור (Caquot, "Ben Porat", 49).

[663]Caquot, "Ben Porat", 49, n. 3. For the verb סעד see *HAL*, 719.

[664]Cf. Grossfeld, *TOGen*, 170, n. 55. The Hebr. עלי שׁור, which is left untranslated in TO, might be connected with the principle of *šûrat ha-ddîn*, because the daughters of Zelophehad had obtained their rights by a legal decision, according to Gen.Rab., 248.

MT at several places, obliges us to maintain the reading of MT's consonantal text. However, the fact that widely diverging solutions were sought in the final colon to translate this text, makes the assumption plausible that the common interpretation in the first colon (פרת < פרה) is corrupt.[665] This will be discussed later.

2.11.1.2 פרת — Derivative of פרה?

The previous section clearly demonstrates that the Ancients unanimously derived פרת from פרה. This interpretation has found its advocates up to the present day.[666] Although it is grammatically possible to understand פרת as a derivative of פרה, there are some serious objections against it:

1. בֵּן is never used for plants,[667] only human beings and animals are denoted with this word, for example "offspring of ..." or "young of ...". The translation "bough" (RSV) for בֵּן (masc.sg.) is also problematic, because in verse 22bA בָּנוֹת (fem.plur.) "boughs; branches" would have been used. For בָּנוֹת (or in sg. בַּת) the same rule applies, that it is used exclusively for human beings or animals, and never for plants. Moreover צָעֲדָה would here have been used uniquely with the meaning "to grow".[668]

2. In our chapter verse 22 would contain the sole plant metaphor, next to the animal metaphors for Judah, Issachar, Dan, Naphtali[669] and Benjamin.[670] Furthermore the continuation in verse

---

[665] Although Skinner, *Genesis*, 530, supposes that the text is corrupt; this is not necessarily so. It might be that the general interpretation is corrupt, because it avoids an offensive reading.

[666] Tuch, *Die Genesis*, 586–7; Procksch, *Die Genesis*, 273; König, *Die Genesis*, 765–6; Skinner, *Genesis*, 529; Aalders, *Genesis*, dl. III, 214; Von Rad, *Erste Buch Mose*, 345, 351; Caquot, "Ben Porat", 43–56; Westermann, *Genesis 37–50*, 247–9, 269–70; H. Seebaß, "Die Stammessprüche Gen. 49,3–27", *ZAW* 96 (1984) 333–50; Pehlke, *Genesis 49:1–28*, 214–9; Neef, *Ephraim*, 116–7; for an overview of the literature, cf. Caquot, *art.cit.*, 47, n. 2.

[667] *HAL*, 131–2; *DBHE*, 105 (refers with some restriction to Ps. 80:16b, cf. however RSV; NBG). Ges[18], 156, refers exclusively to our text; similarly J. Kühlewein, "בֵּן", *THAT*, Bd. I, 318; further H. Haag, "בֵּן", *ThWAT*, Bd. I, 672–4 — although he alludes to בן־שמן, "son of oil" for "fertile"; בן־שחר, "son of dawn" for Lucifer, the Day Star; בני־צשף, "sons of the glow" for "sparks"; for "arrows" the expressions בן־עשת "son of the bow" and בן־אשפתו, "son of the quiver" are mentioned (*art.cit.*, 674–5). For an exhaustive listing, cf. *DCH*, vol. II, 186, and further 207–8.

[668] This objection was made by Skinner, *Genesis*, 530; and referred to with approval by S. Gevirtz, "Of Patriarchs and Puns: Joseph at the Fountain, Jacob at the Ford", *HUCA* 46 (1975) 33–54, 37. Similarly Wenham, *Genesis 16–50*, 484–5.

[669] Not entirely certain; see however our discussion *ad loc.*

[670] Neef, *Ephraim*, 116, considers this argument methodically contestable, be-

23 would not very well fit in with this metaphor, if understood as a plant metaphor.[671]

3. Gen. 49:22bA would be a rather bleak elaboration of the metaphor, because the branches of a tree easily grow over a wall.[672]

Caquot[673] tries to overcome these criticisms by following the vocalization of the text seriously: he understands בֵּן not as a *constructus* but an *absolutus*; and he reads יוֹסֵף as a vocative:

A son (is) a fertile (plant), (O) Joseph,
  a son (is) a fertile (plant) next to a well,
    daughters (are) a climbing (plant) on a wall.[674]

His solution, however, is unconvincing. First, such a general saying concerning sons and daughters — hardly exclusive to Joseph — does not fit into the context of Genesis 49, where very specific sayings are made concerning the other sons/tribes. Secondly, the position of the vocative in this verse would be unusual. Thirdly, it is questionable whether בֵּן in this form cannot be read as a *status constructus*, as was stated by Caquot. Although Gen. 49:22 would almost be the sole occurrence of this phenomenon,[675] a comparison with שֵׁם I, "name",

---

cause it assumes the unity of form of Genesis 49, and ignores the acknowledged observation in research that the sayings were originally independent and could therefore be compared only conditionally. This argument itself is likewise contestable, however, because its point of departure is a fragmented text, which as a whole is really an ostensible unity. Therefore, it may be asked, as Neef himself does, "ob man so ohne weiteres von *der* Form des Stammesspruches überhaupt ausgehen kann" (Neef, *op.cit.*, 121).

[671] Almost every scholar, who rejects this translation, holds this opinion.

Pehlke, *Genesis 49:1–28*, 219, refers to the fact that the metaphor of a tree is used of the righteous person (Ps. 1:3; Jer. 17:8), and argues that, according to this comparison, "Joseph eminently qualifies as a righteous person who trusted in the Lord and avoided the company of the wicked. But this is what the wicked dislike so much; therefore, they attack him". Although this interpretation explains the relation between the verses 22 and 23, it seems too far-fetched to be likely.

[672] So *e.g.* Van Selms, *Genesis, dl. II*, 279.

Pehlke, *Genesis 49:1–28*, 218–9; Neef, *Ephraim*, 119, suggest we render "tendrils" ("Ranken"), which in that case would be a more positive elaboration of the metaphor. However, there is no reason in the text to render פֹּרָת here with "vine", and thus is the rendering with "tendrils" doubtful.

[673] Caquot, "Ben Porat", 54–6.
[674] Caquot, "Ben Porat", 56:

"Un fils (est) une (plante) féconde, (ô) Joseph,
  un fils (est) une (plante) féconde auprès d'une source,
    des filles (sont) une (plante) grimpant sur un mur."

[675] *HAL*, 131, lists Gen. 49:22 as the sole occurrence; contrast, however, Ges[18],

demonstrates that this lemma has always been vocalized as שֵׁם in the
construct form, when this word loses its stress.[676] But in the majority
of cases where the word has preserved its stress, it is vocalized שֵׁם,[677]
whereas even שֶׁם was vocalized in many cases שֵׁם and retained a
stress by means of the *meteg*.[678] A similar case is found for לֵב, which
in the construct form is vocalized לֵב: Exod. 7:13; 1 Sam. 17:32.[679]
Furthermore, the interpretation of יוֹסֵף as a vocative has no support
from the Vrs. Moreover, a comparison of verse 22aA with verse 9aA
demonstrates that both cola are accentuated identically, which might
suggest that the Masoretes did not consider יוֹסֵף a vocative form.[680]

Following an earlier proposal by Allegro,[681] Emerton suggested
that the form פורת for "Euphrates" in Qumran,[682] the spellings in
Christian Palestinian Aram. *pwrt*, in Josephus φοράς,[683] and Arab.
furât, might all reflect a pronunciation near to the original Akk. *pu-
rattu*. In his view it is therefore likely that פֹּרָת in Gen. 49:22 is a
way of spelling the name "Euphrates".[684] Again following Allegro,
he further proposed, on the basis of Aram. and Syr. בִּינָא "tamarisk",
and Akk. *bīnu* also meaning "tamarisk",[685] to understand בֵּן not as
"son" but as "ben-tree", a "tamarisk".[686] The expression בֵּן פֹּרָת has

---

156, listing 1 Sam. 22:20; Ezek. 18:10 as construct forms. However, only the latter can be considered a construct form, the former is an absolute form. Pehlke,
Genesis 49:1–28, 215, also refers to Gen. 30:19 בֶּן־שִׁשִּׁי, but this is not a genetive
construction, but שִׁשִּׁי is used here appositionally: "a sixth son".

[676] Gen. 16:15; 21:3; 1 Sam. 8:2; 1 Kgs. 16:24; Ezek. 39:16; Prov. 30:4. These cases
are all so-called context-forms; cf. Lett, §29g; 14m; whereas the cases referred to
in the next notes are not always in pause, although they have a pause-form.

[677] Tuch, *Die Genesis*, 586; cf. Gen. 4:26; 12:8; 13:4; 16:13; 21:33; 1 Sam. 8:2. *Pace*
Caquot, "Ben Porat", 47, n. 3, who doubts that בְּשֵׁם יהוה in Gen. 4:26; 12:8 has
to be translated with "au nom de YHWH". However, שֵׁם יהוה is always vocalized
this way; cf. Even-Shoshan, קוֹנְקוֹרְדַנְצִיָה, 1162c–63a. Further, שֵׁם in the construct
state is, except for the cases referred to in n. 676 above, always vocalized שֵׁם; cf.
Gen. 2:13, 14; 4:17, 19, 21; 10:25; 11:29; etc.; cf. further Even-Shoshan, *op.cit.*,
1161c–62b; and also Gevirtz, "Patriarchs and Puns", 38, n. 19; *HAL*, 1432. On
the pause-form, cf. n. 676 above.

[678] Cf. e.g. Gen. 26:20, 33 (for the latter, see BHK[1/2]; Snaith); see further Even-
Shoshan, קוֹנְקוֹרְדַנְצִיָה, 1162b–63a. On the pause-form, cf. n. 676 above.

[679] *HAL*, 488.

[680] Gevirtz, "Patriarchs and Puns", 40.

[681] J.M. Allegro, "A Possible Mesopotamian Background to the Joseph Blessing
of Gen. xlix", *ZAW* 64 (1952) 249–51.

[682] 1 QapGn21:12, 17, 28; 1QM2:11.

[683] *Ant.* I.i.3 (§39).

[684] Emerton, "Some Difficult Words", 92. Emerton slightly modifies Allegro's
suggestion to repoint פֹּרָת ("Possible Mesopotamian Background", 250).

[685] Cf. *CAD*, vol. B, 239–42.

[686] Emerton, "Some Difficult Words", 92–3. Allegro, "Possible Mesopotamian

therefore to be rendered by "a tamarisk of the Euphrates". Although the river Euphrates does not define the species, as was supposed by Allegro,[687] the poet might "have in mind a particular example of the species growing near the Euphrates".[688] The reason for the reference to the Euphrates would be that "the poet wishes to describe a flourishing tree growing near a river where it is well watered (cf. Num. 24:6; Jer. 17:8; Ps. 1:3), and here makes the water supply doubly assured by mentioning a spring."[689] However, the difficulty remains that בָּנוֹת (verse 22bA) is not used for plants and Emerton does not solve this main problem.[690] Although Emerton reduces the problem to just one colon (verse 22bA), it still is an obstacle which prevents us from applying a plant metaphor to Joseph.[691]

2.11.1.3   Joseph — A Young Bullcalf

The concensus solution to the problem is nowadays mostly found in considering the saying as an animal metaphor.[692] Ehrlich proposed

---

Background", 250, thinks that the "ben-tree" might be identified with the "poplar". This translation for בֵּין was suggested by Allegro for the *crux* in Isa. 44:4a on the basis of Akk., Arab., Aram. and Syr. parallels in: J.M. Allegro, "The Meaning of בין in Isaiah XLIV, 4", ZAW 63 (1951) 154–6. However, his solution is not widely accepted; cf. J.L. Koole, *Jesaja II vertaald en verklaard; deel I: Jesaja 40 tot en met 48* (COT), Kampen 1985, 265–6. The Akk. and Aram. cognates have clearly the meaning "tamarisk" for the word.

[687]Allegro, "Possible Mesopotamian Background", 250.

[688]Emerton, "Some Difficult Words", 93.

[689]Emerton, "Some Difficult Words", 93.

[690]Koole, *Jesaja II, dl. I*, 266, argues in connection with Allegro's solution to read בִּינָא in Isa. 44:4, that it is remarkable that TO as well as Peš, who had to know this word, did not recognize it in this particular context. The same argument is of course valid for our text.

[691]It might be that for verse 22bA Emerton followed the solution of Allegro, "Possible Mesopotamian Background", 250–1. He suggested that צעדה in 2 Sam. 5:24 in the top of the בכאים (sometimes suggested to be also the *Euphratean Poplar* [*op.cit.*, 250, n. 9], but the botanical identification is uncertain [cf. *HAL*, 124; Ges¹⁸, 148; *DCH*, vol. II, 169]) was "the name of the sound particularly associated with the poplar. This is readily understandable if we connect the word with the Arabic ṣuʿadāʾu 'deep sigh'." In Gen. 49:22bA this would result, with a slight repointing (because בנות should be taken as the singular noun written here with the original *nun*), in: בְּנוֹת צְעָדָה "daughter-of-sighing", "an apt and beautiful equivalent for בן פרת, '*Euphratean poplar*'." Further, שׁוּר might be identified with Sum. SAR/ŠAR, and the Akk. derivative *musarū*, meaning *inter alii* "plantation, garden". He therefore rendered verse 22bA as "a daughter-of-sighing in a garden". However, this solution is too far-fetched to be likely; cf. also Gevirtz, "Patriarchs and Puns", 37.

[692]The first to suggest it is Vater, *Commentar*, Bd. I, 326–7, who suggests we interpret פרת on the basis of Syr. *prʾ* and Arab. *frr* as "sheep", which would fit the meaning of the name of his mother רָחֵל. He was followed by Schumann,

to translate בנות צעדה in verse 22bA, being similar to Arab. *banāt ṣa'dat*, by "wild asses".[693] Based on the comparison of verse 22aAB with Deut. 33:17, he suggests we understand פרת to be an equivalent (if not a writing error) of פָּרָה, "cow".[694] However, Speiser was against changing species in the middle of a metaphor and suggests we read פרת, as a fem. of פֶּרֶא, "wild ass".[695] Gevirtz elaborates this proposal with etymological arguments, listing the different words derived from פר for "cow", "ass" and even "lamb".[696] According to Gevirtz this justifies the interpretation of פרת as "ass", stating that "the observation by Ehrlich is surely too precise to be merely fortuitous."[697] Nevertheless, verse 22bA still resists a suitable interpretation because עלי שור has been left unresolved. Speiser rendered "on a hillside", derived from שׁוּר, "wall, terrace" and referred to 2 Sam. 22:30; Ps. 18:30.[698]

Genesis, 756, who already proposed we vocalize פָּרָת "*vacca*"; further: Ehrlich, *RG*, Bd. 1, 250; Böhl, *Genesis*, 50, 144; E. Dhorme, *La poésie biblique* (La Vie Chrétienne), Paris 1931, 103; Vawter, "Canaanite Background", 7–9; Coppens, "La bénédiction de Jacob", 97–115; E. Taubler, *Biblische Studien: Die Epoche der Richter*, Hrsg. v. H.-J. Zobel, Tübingen 1958, 204–7 (although he still assumes the meaning "tree" in the second colon); Speiser, *Genesis*, 367; A.H.J. Gunneweg, "Über den Sitz im Leben der sog. Stammessprüche", *ZAW* 76 (1964) 245–255 (= idem, *Sola Scriptura. Beiträge zu Exegese und Hermeneutik des Alten Testaments*, Göttingen 1983, 25–35); V. Salo, "Joseph, Sohn der Färse", *BZ* 12 (1968) 94–5; Testa, "La benedizione di Giacobe", 167–205; Gevirtz, "Patriarchs and Puns", 33–54; J. Sanmartín, "Problemas de textologia en las 'bendiciones' de Moises (Dt 33) y de Jacob (Gn 49)", in: V. Collado, E. Zurro (eds.), *El misterio de la Palabra: Homenaja ... L. Alonso Schökel*, Madrid 1983, 75–96; Korpel, *RiC*, 532–43.

The wide range of solutions proposed by these scholars was the reason for Caquot, "Ben Porat", 44, to write "La constance des anciens sur ce point [פרת < פרה, RdH] contraste avec la diversité des conjectures modernes." However, the derivation of פרת from פרה is almost the only agreement between the Vrs.

[693]Ehrlich, *RG*, Bd. I, 250; he was already preceded by Vater, *Commentar*, Bd. I, 326–7; Schumann, *Genesis*, 756–7, who translates "*ferae*". Later Ehrlich was followed by Speiser, *Genesis*, 368; Gevirtz, "Patriarchs and Puns", 38–9; cf. J.B. Belot, *Vocabulaire Arabe-Français*, Beyrouth 1920, 410.

[694]Ehrlich, *RG*, Bd. I, 250. As noted before (n. 692 above), this rendering was already proposed by Schumann, *Genesis*, 756; J.P. Peters, "Jacob's Blessing", *JBL* 6 (1886) 99–116, 110–1. They were followed by Gunkel, *Genesis*, ²1902, 426, ("22 ist unübersetzbar"), the translation "junger Stier" is a possibility; ³1910, 485, ("22 ist teilweise unübersetzbar") "junger Stier" is the best translation; Böhl, *Genesis*, 50, 144; Dhorme, "La poésie biblique", 103; Bruno, *Genesis-Exodus*, 320–1; Vawter, "Canaanite Background", 7; Coppens, "La bénédiction de Jacob", 101, with n. 2; Taubler, *Biblische Studien*, 204–7; V. Salo, "Joseph, Sohn der Färse", *BZ* 12 (1968) 94–5. Testa, "La benedizione di Giacobe", 174–5; Sanmartín, "Problemas de textologia", 85–6; Korpel, *RiC*, 532, with n. 56.

[695]Speiser, *Genesis*, 367–8.

[696]Gevirtz, "Patriarchs and Puns", 38–9.

[697]Gevirtz, "Patriarchs and Puns", 38; similarly Speiser, *Genesis*, 368.

[698]Speiser, *Genesis*, 368.

However, because שׁוּר refers to a "man-made wall, enclosure, or forti-
fication, and not, as far as we are able to determine, to any feature of
the natural landscape",[699] this rendering is unlikely. For this reason
Gevirtz seeks to find the solution in the parallel of עַיִן and שׁוּר. The
latter is also a LN, and is found together with עַיִן in Gen. 16:7: Hagar
was found עַל הָעַיִן בְּדֶרֶךְ שׁוּר, "next to the spring on the way to Šur";
whereas Ishmael is called in this chapter פֶּרֶא אָדָם, "a wild ass of a
man" (Gen. 16:12).[700] Gevirtz considers these correspondences so remarkable that he develops a complete theory to prove the connection
of (the tribe of) Joseph with South Arabia. However, the function
of LN "Šur" in our text remains obscure and is not clarified by his
exposure. Furthermore, the suggestion of Ehrlich for understanding
בנות צעדה as "wild asses" is questionable because the correspondences
between the Arab. words and the Hebr. are far from secure.[701] Finally,
Speiser's and Gevirtz's suggestion to render פרת "ass" is also open to
criticism, because it is based on etymological grounds and not on the
context, nor on the Hebr. language itself.[702]

In her study on metaphors for the divine, M.C.A. Korpel also
discussed our passage and offered a very attractive solution.[703] She
regards, along with other scholars,[704] פרת as the primitive fem. form
of פַּר: פָּרֶת, "young cow, heifer" (Akk. b/purtu; Ug. prt).[705] בְּנוֹת in

---

[699]Gevirtz, "Patriarchs and Puns", 42.

[700]Gevirtz, "Patriarchs and Puns", 42–43. The connection with Šur was already
made by Ehrlich, RG, Bd. I, 250, although he did not reach the same conclusions.

[701]Cf. also Korpel, RiC, 532, n. 58.

[702]Cf. the previous note.

[703]Korpel, RiC, 532–4. She is followed by M. Baldacci, La Scoperta di Ugarit:
La città-stato ai primordi della Bibbia, Casale Monferrato 1996, 136.

[704]Cf. n. 694 above.

[705]Korpel, RiC, 532, n. 56, suggests we read *פֶּרֶת as a segolated fem. by-form
next to פָּרָה, like *בֹּמֶת next to בָּמָה (cf. HAL, 131; BL 597h; contrast, Ges[18], 155;
JM, §97Eb); which is supported by the Akk. spelling b/purtu. It may be objected,
however, that next to the form פָּרָה (Num. 19:2; Isa. 11:7; Hos. 4:16; HAL, 907),
the suffixed form פָּרָתוֹ is attested (Job 21:10; HAL, 907) as well as the construct
form פָּרוֹת הַבָּשָׁן (Am. 4:1; HAL, 907–8), which both suggest that the segolated form
did not exist, since the segolated absolute forms were derived from the segolated
construct forms (cf. JM, §89d). Since the archaic spelling recurs in the construct
state and in front of suffixes, and this spelling is the only one attested in Hebr.,
it seems more reasonable to regard פרת in our text as a primitive fem. form (JM,
ibid) of פַּר, viz. פָּרֶת, "young cow, heifer" (as was already proposed by Schumann,
Genesis, 756), next to the younger פָּרָה. The fact that we are dealing here with a
primitive spelling might be compared with the use of the "archaic" masc. suffixes
(ה-) in Gen. 49:10–11 next to the younger suffixes (ו-). The wrong vocalization
of this word in MT may be caused by the fact that this form was not regarded as
a fem. of פַּר any more — deliberately or not.

verse 22bA has to be vocalized בְּנָוֶה: prep. בְּ with the noun נָוֶה, "in the
meadow" (also with the primitive fem. sg. ending ה־), which offers
a very natural parallel to עֲלֵי עָיִן.[706] צָעֲדָה is, in its present form, a
perf. qal, 3.fem.sg. of צעד "to stride". The secure meaning given to
this verb does not justify a discussion and we will return to the exact
form of this verb below, after having discussed the other problems
in the text. The following עֲלֵי is generally considered as a prep. and
correctly so;[707] however, the object of this prep. was given a wrong
vocalization: שׁוּר, "wall", and has to be read as שׁוֹר, "bull", "because
the imagery of the preceding verse seems to be elaborated in this
verse, šwr can only be a parallel to prt."[708]

---

[706] This reading was suggested by Procksch, *Die Genesis*, 282; Böhl, *Genesis*, 50;
Coppens, "Bénédiction de Jacob", 101, n. 2; Testa, "Benedizione di Giacobbe",
175–6; cf. also the *apparatus* in BHS (although the plural בְּנוֹת, "in the meadows"
was suggested). Korpel, *RiC*, 532, n. 58, refers to the fact that נאות and water-
courses are linked more often (Isa. 35:7; Jer. 49:19; 50:44; Joel 1:20; Ps. 23:2).
For the view of Peters, "Jacob's Blessing", and Vawter, "Canaanite Background", cf. n. 708 below. Coppens, *art.cit.*, 101, suggested we modify the usual
punctuation, and read the first two words of v. 22b together with the preceding
עַיִן in one clause: "Une fontaine jaillit au milieu des prairies", and to interpret
this colon as a second form of simile applied to Joseph (for עלי cf. the following
footnote). However, this seems to us an unnecessary break with the preceding and
following metaphor; and in this case we prefer the classical punctuation.
Salo, "Joseph, Sohn der Färse", 94; Sanmartín, "Problemas de textologia", 86,
suggest we derive בנות from בנה, and render it with "creation"; whereas the latter even suggested we interpret צעדה as a noun with suff. 3.masc.sg. meaning
"footstep, pace", and figuratively "way of being". The latter interpretation is
incomprehensible in our opinion, whereas the former might be possible but superfluous in view of Korpel's solution for the complete text (but also because of the
parallelism between water and meadow, as indicated before).

[707] For another interpretation of עלי; cf. n. 708 below.

[708] Korpel, *RiC*, 532, n. 60. Reading here שׁוֹר "bull" was already proposed by
Peters, "Jacob's Blessing", 111; Gunkel, *Genesis*, ³1910, 485; Vawter, "Canaanite
Background", 8; Coppens, "Bénédiction de Jacob", 101; Salo, "Joseph, Sohn der
Färse", 94–5; Testa, "Benedizione di Giacobbe", 175; Sanmartín, "Problemas de
textologia", 86–7.
Peters, "Jacob's Blessing", 111–2, maintains the translation "daughters" for
בנות, which resulted in "daughters have marched in procession to a bull", in which
— according to Peters — we certainly find a reflection on Ephraim's religious
history.
Vawter, "Canaanite Background", 8, suggests we render the preceding עלי as
"offspring" (based on Ug. *'l*, "child") in a genitive construction with שׁוֹר; whereas
he followed the reading of Sam (and LXX) for the first two words of v. 22b: צעירי
בני with the following result for v. 22b: "the sons of my young man (i.e., son)
are offspring of a bull" (i.e., young bulls). Coppens, "Bénédiction de Jacob", 101,
suggests (v. 22aB.bA) reading "my son" (עול "suckling, infant" [*HAL*, 754] with
suff. 1.sg.), resulting in the rendering in v. 22b: "mon fils est un taureau". With
regard to v. 22b, Testa, "Benedizione di Giacobbe", 175, followed Vawter, reading

The most elucidatory part of Korpel's proposal was the suggestion to interpret וַיְמָרֲרֻהוּ in verse 23aB as the impf. D-stem (pi'el) 3.masc.*sg.* of the root מרר, "to strengthen"; based on Ugaritic, where this verb is attested in connection with blessing.[709] Ba'lu's request of Ilu in KTU 1.17:i.23–4 is in this connection very illustrative:[710]

ltbrknn ḷtr . il ảby	Please bless him, O Bull Ilu, my father,
tmrnn . lbny . bnwt	fortify him, O creator of creatures!

The archers in the following colon (verse 23bA) are commonly regarded as the subject of וַיְמָרֲרֻהוּ (cf. also the plur. vocalization of the verb); but Korpel's suggestion to consider שׁוֹר, "the Bull" in the preceding verse the subject, perfectly explains the preceding as well as the present colon.[711]

The next verb וָרֹבּוּ is, from a text-critical point of view, uncertain:[712] Sam (וירִיבהו) and LXX (ἐλοιδόρουν, impf. act. 3.plur. "curse") both suppose an imperfect instead of the perf. וָרֹבּוּ (< רבב) in MT; while the reading of Sam. is usually interpreted as וַיְרִיבֻהוּ "they strove with him" (more or less supported by LXX). However, if this imperfect form were correct,[713] Sam would also allow another reading here, namely*וַיֻּרְבֵּהוּ,[714] "and he made him great": impf. hiph. 3.masc.sg. of רבה, "make many, great"[715] with a suff. 3.masc.sg. However, if the

---

the two words as a gen. construction: "son of the bull", but as the subject of the preceding verb צָעֲד.

[709] Korpel, *RiC*, 533, n. 61. Similarly now: Baldacci, *La Scoperta di Ugarit*, 136. In case the verb would be interpreted as a *w^eyiqtol*, the vocalization of MT has to be changed into וִימָרֲרֻהוּ and in case of a *wayyiqtol*, into וַיְמָרֲרֻהוּ (cf. יְבָרֲכֵהוּ and יְבָרֲכוּךָ; see *HAL*, 153).

[710] Cf. also KTU 1.15:ii.15.

[711] Usually the verb is translated "bedrohen", "reizen" or "harry"; cf. Zobel, *SuG*, 5; Speiser, *Genesis*, 363; Westermann, *Genesis 37–50*, 248; Neef, *Ephraim*, 120. These renderings could all be considered paraphrases of מרר, "to be bitter". The proposal to translate מר(ר) in the Hebrew Bible also by "to strengthen" as well — although not for Gen. 49:23 — is already found in Gordon, *UT*, 438; cf. further O. Loretz, "Weitere ugaritisch–hebräische Parallelen", *BZ* 3 (1959) 293; S. & S. Rin, "Ugaritic – Old Testament Affinities, II", *BZ* 11 (1967) 89; D. Pardee, "The Semitic Root *mrr* and the Etymology of Ugaritic *mr(r)/brk*", *UF* 10 (1978) 249–288; W.A. Ward, "Egypto–Semitic *mr* 'Be Bitter, Strong'", *UF* 12 (1980) 357–360; *ARTU*, 227, n. 23; furthermore Pardee, *UB*, 421.

[712] Cf. Skinner, *Genesis*, 530.

[713] Also syntactically the perfect form between two imperfects of MT seems to be suspect; cf. Skinner, *Genesis*, 530.

[714] Cf. וַיֶּגֶל with וַיֶּרֶב; and of the suffixed forms: וַיַּגְלֶהָ and וַיַּגְלֵם with יַרְבְּךָ and אַרְבֵּהוּ (*HAL*, resp. 184 and 1098).

[715] Scholars are inclined to render the root רבב/ה sometimes with "to shoot (ar-

consonantal text is left unchanged, we cannot reach this meaning for
the verb (interpreting it as a pi‘el[716]) because it would require suffix
הו– at the end. Although the reading of a suffix is suggested by Sam,
TO, and probably LXX, interpreting the final ו as a suffix, we prefer
to maintain MT as the best reading.

The verb צָעֲדָה in verse 22bA has to be reconsidered in view of
the foregoing reinterpretation of the text. צָעֲדָה cannot be restricted
to the perf. qal, 3.fem.sg. of צעד, but may also be read as an ancient
perf. qal, 3.fem.*plur.* "they strode".[717] As was demonstrated above,
the latter solution is most likely for the vocalization of MT, in view of
the apparent subject בָּנוֹת "daughters". Korpel, implicitly changing the
vocalization of MT at several points,[718] suggests we take פרה "cow"
(49:22a) to be the subject of צָעֲדָה; although she does not exclude the
possibility that the following שׁוֹר "bull" is the subject and our text
represents an early readjustment of an original צָעַד עָלֶיהָ שׁוֹר, "the Bull
strode towards her".[719] However, since the vocalization of בנות and שׁוֹר
is incorrect,[720] because according to that vocalization בנות had to be
considered as the subject of צעדה, the vocalization of צעדה as a perfect
qal 3.fem.sg. and plur. is suspect also.[721] Further, it seems that פָּרָה
does not have such an important function in the text that it would
govern the verb. In the following colon (49:23aB) the object suffix

---

rows)", which they think would also fit in this context very well because of the
"archers" in verse 23bA; cf. KBL, 868–70; GB, 740–2; König, *Wb*, 428–9; *LVT*,
751–3; BDB, 914–6; *HAL*, 1094, 1096, 1099; Aalders, *Genesis dl. III*, 190, 214–5;
Zobel, *SuG*, 5; Van Selms, *Genesis dl. II*, 280: "archer" ("boogschutter"); Westermann, *Genesis 37–50*, 248–9 (although he hesitates about the correct reading
of *viz.* MT or LXX and Sam); Pehlke, *Genesis 49:1–28*, 220; Wenham, *Genesis
16–50*, 455, 485; Neef, *Ephraim*, 120; A. Guillaume, "Hebrew and Arabic Lexicography", *AbrN* 1 (1961) 14, compares Arab. *rmy* and Hebr. רבה; but he omitted
to mention the fact that there exists a Hebr. stem רמה, "to shoot", which seems to
make his comparison invalid. Speiser, *Genesis*, 368, calls רבב/ה " 'to shoot' a questionable stem". The meaning "to shoot (arrows)" for רבב/ה was already rejected
in Ges, *Thes*, 1253–4, because in all texts where scholars think this interpretation
is correct, the usual rendering "to be(come) many, great" does perfect justice to
the text. Korpel's interpretation of מרר "to make strong" in our text disposed of
one of the most important references for the meaning "to shoot (arrows)".

[716] According to *HAL*, 1097–8, the pi‘el and hiph. of רבה have identical meanings.

[717] Lett, §43d; GK, §44m; Berg, II, §4b; cf. also JM, §42f.

[718] Korpel, *RiC*, 532–3, nn. 58, 60 and 61.

[719] Korpel, *RiC*, 532, n. 59. The fact that next to this interpretation (פָּרָה as the
subject) she offers an additional solution (שׁוֹר as the subject), demonstrates that
her interpretation is not plausible in itself.

[720] Next to וימררהו in verse 23a.

[721] The interpretation of LXX, Sam and Peš (and TO?) argues against an in-
dicative sense as well since they did not render צעדה as a verbal but as a nominal
form (see the discussion above pp. 182–184).

seems to refer to the subject of the verb in verse 22bA, but the suffix is masculine and not feminine. Therefore, considering פְּרָת as the subject is unsatisfactory. Also Korpel's assumption of the mitigation does not help, because she has to assume a rather unusual syntax (although not an impossible one) with the subject placed after the object: צָעַד עָלֶיהָ שׁוֹר; whereas the objects would then change unexpectedly too: "the bull strode to *her* / and he strengthened *him* so they will become numerous".

Nevertheless, when the vocalization of the verb is disregarded for the moment, the verb not only can be considered as a *perfect* qal, 3.fem.sg. or plur. but also as an inf.cstr. with a feminine ending (slightly repointed *צַעֲדָה[722]) or as an inf.cstr. of צעד with (archaic) suffix 3.masc.sg.[723] (repointed *צַעֲדֹה[724]) "his striding" > "he strides".[725] The rendering of LXX, Sam and Peš (and probably TO) supports this interpretation of צעדה in so far that they considered the word a nominal form of the verb and not a finite form.[726] Both possibilities will now be discussed.

1. Whereas the use of the feminine form for a masculine subject might seem suspicious, this usage is attested in Ugarit in the legend of Kirtu,[727] where even a comparable syntax (the word-order differs) is found: *s't . bšdm . ḥtbh* "(you will) assault in the fields its wood-gatherers" (1.14:iii.7).[728] The feminine infinitive is used in this text as a future 2.masc.sg., because the subject is known from the verb in impf. 2.masc.sg. in line 5.[729] The use of the infinitive for the future as well as for the present and

---

[722] Cf. Lett, §50d; JM, §69a2; Lett[10], §51d. The vocalization צַעֲדָה could be considered in view of the vocalization of the inf.cstr. צְעָקָה (Jer. 49:21) and the same subst. (*HAL*, 976), comparable to the subst. צְעָדָה (*HAL*, 974). However, the inf.cstr. צְעָקָה in Jer. 49:21 is disputed (cf. *HAL*, 976), and for that reason too uncertain.

[723] For this suffix see already Gen. 49:10–11 and the discussion *ad loc.*

[724] Cf. Lett, §26e, §50d; JM, §94h, §69a2.

[725] The use of the infinitive of צעד is found also in בְּצַעְדְּךָ "in your striding" > "when you strode" (Judg. 5:4; Ps. 68:8).

[726] Cf. above pp. 182–184.

[727] J.C. de Moor, K. Spronk, "Problematic Passages in the Legend of Kirtu (I)", *UF* 14 (1982) 153–71, 167.

[728] Translation *ARTU*, 196; cf. also *MLC*, 295. Other interpretations: *CML*, 85; *TOML*, 521, n. 1.

[729] This feature is also known from El-Amarna, where the subject is even identified in a following clause; see A.F. Rainey, *Canaanite in the Amarna Tablets: A Linguistic Analysis of the Mixed Dialect Used by Scribes from Canaan*, vol. II: *Morphosyntactic Analysis of the Verbal System* (HdO, 25), Leiden 1995, 384, 386–8.

the past, as a substitute for finite verbal forms, is established in
Ugaritic texts[730] as well as in Amarna correspondence.[731] The
advantage of this solution is that it is rather close to the Masoretic vocalization of the text, although this cannot be considered
decisive.

2. The use of an archaic suffix ה– has already been attested next to
the younger ו– (49:10–11). A suffix added as the subject to the
inf.cstr. is found in several cases even where it might be considered superfluous.[732] The advantage of this solution is that
there is agreement in number and gender of subject and predicate, whereas the consonantal text remains unchanged. Furthermore, in this solution a parallel is found between verses 22bA
and 23aB by means of the suffixes, whereas otherwise it would
have been absent. When the text is rendered rather literal, the
result is:[733]

In the meadow his striding to the Bull,	בְּנוֹת צָעֲדָה עֲלֵי־שׁוּר
and He makes him strong and (him) numerous.	וַיְמָרֲרֻהוּ וָרֹבּוּ

It seems therefore justified to consider the verb *צָעֲדֹה as the inf.cstr.
of צעד with suffix 3.masc.sg. and to regard בֵּן פָּרָת in verse 22a as its
subject.

2.11.1.4   Other Translation Problems

2.11.1.4.1   Verse 24aB

In verse 24aB we follow MT וַתֵּשֶׁב;[734] LXX has συνετρίβη (aor. pass.
3.masc.sg. συντρίβω "to break, crush"), which seems to be a rendering

---

[730]Cf. J.C. de Moor, "Frustula Ugaritica", *JNES* 24 (1965) 355–64, 358–9; Dijkstra, De Moor, "Problematic Passages in the Legend of Aqhatu", 173–215, 191,
195, 199. Although the examples quoted from the Ug. texts in this article, are
often clauses with a clearly defined subject, indicating that the infinitive is used
as a finite verb, this is not necessarily normative. In the Amarna letters the
subject is sometimes known from the preceding or following text, not indicated in
the clause itself (Rainey, *Canaanite in the Amarna Tablets*, 384). In some other
examples from Ugarit, where the infinitive is used as a finite verb, the subject is
not mentioned explicitly; cf. in this respect KTU 1.17:vi.46 and Dijkstra, De Moor,
art.cit., 191.

[731]Rainey, *Canaanite in the Amarna Tablets*, 384–8.

[732]Gen. 2:17; 14:17; 29:19; 1 Ki. 21:3. See Lett, §73b; JM, §124s, n. 1; Lett[10],
§78b1.

[733]On the rendering of the verbal tenses, see the discussion below.

[734]Gen. 49:23b–24a is translated conditionally; cf. GK, §159b; Brockelmann,
Syntax, §164a.

of Hebr. וַתִּשָׁבֵר, "she was/you were broken down". Because an inter-change of ב and ר in the old Hebr. script is possible, and another ב follows after וַתֵּשֶׁב as the preposition affixed to the word בְּאֵיתָן, this assumption is possible. There are some objections to this reading how-ever. The most important objection is the fact that LXX translated the praep. ב in our text with μετα, which makes the "reading error" unlikely. Secondly, the suffix of קַשְׁתוֹ is rendered with a plural pos-sessive pronoun, similar to verse 24aC. Thirdly, in verse 24aC εζελυθη (aor. pass. 3.masc.sg. εχλυω) of LXX seems to be a rendering of Hebr. וַיָּפֹזּוּ (< פזר, "to scatter"), but the meaning "untie, weaken, tire" for εχλυω is dubious; especially as this error would have appeared for a second time in the same verse. It seems more likely, therefore, to con-sider LXX as reinterpretations of the Hebr. text, and, supported by Sam, to regard MT as the correct reading.[735]

2.11.1.4.2 אָבִיר: "Bull" or "Strong One"?

The translation "Bull of Jacob" for Hebr. אֲבִיר יַעֲקֹב is possible,[736] but not very likely.[737] The title is used in Isa. 1:24 (אֲבִיר יִשְׂרָאֵל in this

---

[735] Vawter, "Canaanite Background", 10; M. Dahood, "Is 'Eben Yiśrā'ēl' a Di-vine Title (Gn 49,24)?", *Bib* 40 (1959) 1002–1007; Van Selms, *Genesis dl. II*, 280, suggest other readings/translations; mainly founded on LXX (Vawter) or changes of the consonantal text (Dahood, Van Selms). MT offers, however, an intelligible text and emendation is therefore superfluous.

[736] The translation is favoured by Gunkel, *Genesis*, 485–6; Bruno, *Genesis*, 321; F. Løkkegaard, "A Plea for El, the Bull, and other Ugaritic Miscellanies", in: *Studia Orientalia Ioanni Pedersen Dedicata*, Copehagen 1953, 219–35, 222; E. Nielsen, "Ass and Ox in the Old Testament", *ibid.*, 263–74, 267; Vawter, "Canaan-ite Background", 11. Coppens, "Bénédiction de Jacob", 102; Dahood, "Divine Title?", 1006; Cross, *CMHE*, 4, n. 6; H. Motzki, "Ein Beitrag zum Problem des Stierkultus in der Religionsgeschichte Israels", *VT* 25 (1975) 470–485, 484; D.N. Freedman, "Divine Names and Titles in Early Hebrew Poetry", in: *Pottery, Po-etry and Prophecy: Collected Essays on Hebrew Poetry*, Winona Lake (IN) 1980, 77–129, 86–7; Testa, "Benedizione di Giacobbe", 177; A.H.W. Curtis, "Some Ob-servations on 'Bull' Terminology in the Ugaritic Texts and the Old Testament", in: A.S. van der Woude (ed.), *In Quest of the Past: Studies on Israelite Religion, Literature and Prophetism* (OTS, 26), Leiden 1990, 17–31, 27–8; S. Schroer, *In Israel gab es Bilder: Nachrichten von darstellender Kunst im Alten Testament* (OBO, 74), Freiburg & Göttingen, 1987, 96–7, n. 139; Korpel, *RiC*, 533–4; De Moor, *RoY*, 225, with n. 18; Smith, *Early History of God*, 16–19, 51; Baldacci, *La Scoperta di Ugarit*, 229; 320, n. 230; N. Wyatt, "Calf, עגל", *DDD*, 344–8, 345–6.

[737] Cf. *HAL*, 6; Ges[18], 7 (who even renders it "Lord" ["Herr"] in accordance with Hur. *ib/wr*, *eb/wr*; with a Ug. lexicographical list [Ug V, 232] where *e-wi-ri* is paralleled with *[b]e(?)-lu*; and further also in accordance with the use of some Ug. PNN, which are, however, not unequivocal; for a list of these names, see Aistleitner, *WUS*, 4–5 [# 34]); *DCH*, vol. I, 106. The translation was rejected by Procksch, *Die Genesis*, 275; Dillmann, *Die Genesis*, 470; H. Torczyner, "אביר kein

instance) but given the exilic/post-exilic texts Isa. 49:26; 60:16, the understanding of the title אֲבִיר as "Bull" is doubtful,[738] since in the exilic and post-exilic era theriomorphic descriptions of the divine were undoubtedly abandoned. It would be unlikely then, that terms which primarily denoted "bull" were still in use as an epithet for God. Furthermore, although theriomorphic descriptions and iconography were used for the divine in early Israel (pre-monarchic era and early monarchy),[739] not every possible expression has to be theriomorphic.[740]

Stierbild", *ZAW* 39 (1921) 296–300, translates also "Lord of Jacob"; König, *Die Genesis*, 767; Jacob, *Das erste Buch*, 922; Dhorme, *La poésie biblique*, 103; Speiser, *Genesis*, 369; Zobel, *SuG*, 22; Van Selms, *Genesis, dl. II*, 280; Von Rad, *Das erste Buch*, 346; C.E. L'Heureux, *Rank among the Canaanite Gods: El, Baʿal, and the Repha'im* (HSM, 21), Missoula (Ma) 1979, 50–51, with nn. 74, 82; A.S. Kapelrud, "אביר", *ThWAT*, Bd. I, 43–46; N.M. Sarna, "The Divine Title *'abhīr yaʿāqōbh*", in A.I. Katschie (ed.), *Dropsie College 70th Anniversary*, Philadelphia 1979, 389–96; Westermann, *Genesis 37–50*, 248; Sanmartín, "Problemas de textologia", 88–9; Pehlke, *Genesis 49:1–28*, 224, n. 1; Sarna, *Genesis*, 343; Wenham, *Genesis 16–50*, 486; M. Sæbø, "Divine Names and Epithets in Genesis 49:24b–25a: Some Methodological and Traditio-Historical remarks", in: A. Lemaire, B. Otzen (eds.), *History and Traditions of Early Israel: Studies Presented to E. Nielsen* (SVT, 50), Leiden 1993, 115–132, 125–6; M. Köckert, "Mighty One of Jacob", *DDD*, 1073–6; Neef, *Ephraim*, 122.

Further, with regard to the PNN containing the element אבי, see: Avigad, "Contribution of Hebrew Seals", 196; Fowler, *TPN*, 75, 87; *HAE*, Bd. I, 198, n. 2.

[738]Sæbø, "Divine names and Epithets", 126.

[739]Cf. G.W. Ahlström, "An Archaeological Picture of Iron Age Religions in Ancient Palestine", *StOr* 55 (1984) 117–145, 136–8; idem, *History of Ancient Palestine*, 554, n. 1; Schroer, *In Israel gab es Bilder*, 91–104 (cf. also 81–91); Korpel, *RiC*, 558–9, 621–8; De Moor, *RoY*, 179, n. 336, 225; idem, "Ugarit and Israelite Origins", *Congress Volume, Paris 1992* (SVT, 61), Leiden 1995, 205–38; Smith, *Early History of God*, 1–40, 145–50; O. Keel, "Conceptions religieuses dominantes en Palestine/Israël entre 1750 et 900", in: J.A. Emerton (ed.), *Congress Volume, Paris 1992* (SVT, 61), Leiden 1995, 119–44; Keel, Uehlinger, *GGG*, 146–8, 196–8, 317–21, 422–9.

[740]Cf. the remarks made by A. Alt, "Der Gott der Väter", *KS*, Bd. I, 1–78, 25; similarly Van Selms, *Genesis dl. II*, 280. (Curtis, "Some Observations on 'Bull' Terminology", 27–28, did not agree with Alt, cf. below).

It is stated that the Masoretes clearly heard the meaning "bull" in the word אָבִיר/אֲבִיר, and marked the differentiation by omitting the dageš in the six cases involved; cf. Kapelrud, "אביר", 44; Curtis, *art.cit.*, 27–28; Korpel, *RiC*, 533, n. 63. (Kapelrud, *art.cit.*, 44: "Aus der Art wie der Masoreten ihre Scheidung zwischen dagešierter und nicht-dagešierter Form an einem reinem Konsonantentext durchgeführt haben, kann man schließen, daß sie im Worte אביר deutlich den Begriff 'Stier' gehört haben.") However, this statement is hard to prove and other arguments could be given for the omission of the dageš. The most simple explanation is the fact that the dageš demands another pronunciation of the word, contrasting the name אָבִיר with the word אֲבִיר. By means of this differentiation every possible identification of the divine title with אֲבִיר, used for men, bulls and

As Kapelrud argues, it is very likely that the expression has been derived from a single background and developed in several directions; its basic meaning was "strength, force",[741] and as such it could be used in Akkadian for substantial buildings; in Akkadian, Aramaic[742] and Hebrew for people; in Ugaritic and Hebrew it could be used for strong animals like "bulls, (wild) oxen";[743] but also for "stallions" in Egypt as a Canaanite loan word[744] as well as in Hebrew (Jer. 8:16; 47:3; cf. also Judg. 5:22). It is also a remarkable fact that in Ugarit *ibr*, "bull" is nowhere used as an epithet for a deity,[745] as for example Ug.

---

stallions, was avoided. This omission, however, does not plead "for the original reading *'byr* 'Bull'" (Korpel, *op.cit.*, 533, n. 63). The only conclusion which could be safely drawn concerning the function of the dageš, is that it causes a different pronunciation of the word. As Van Selms, *Genesis dl. II*, 280, rightly observed, the meaning "stallion" is attested as often as "bull" but this does not lead to the rendering "Stallion of Jacob".

[741] *CAD*, vol. A/1, 38. Cf. the expression *dandannu qitrudu bēl abāri*, (Nergal) "almighty one, warrior, endowed with strength" and *šar tamḫāri be-el a-ba-ri u dunni*, (Nergal) "the king of the battle, lord of all strength"; cf. also Köckert, "Mighty One of Jacob", 1074.

An original meaning "bull' for אָבִיר is sometimes assumed; cf. Miller, "Animal Names", 180–1, with nn. 16–20; Cross, *CMHE*, 4–5, n. 6; Curtis, "Some Observations on 'Bull' Terminology", 27 (following Cross); De Moor, *RoY*, 225, n. 18; Korpel, *RiC*, 534, n. 65. The fact that אָבִיר is sometimes used as a designation for men (Ps. 22:13; 68:31), or strong people (1 Sam. 21:8; Isa. 10:13; Job 24:22; 34:20; Lam. 1:15) is compared with the Ug. *tr* "bull" and Hebr. שׁוֹר for noblemen in Isa. 23:8 (cf. M. Dahood, "*UT*, 128 IV 6–7, 17–18 and Isaiah 23:8–9", *Or* 44 (1975) 439–41; and our comments on 49:6 above). However, there is an important difference between the two words אָבִיר/אַבִּיר and שׁוֹר, and comparison is therefore hazardous: the former word is derived from the stem אבר I, with the basic meaning "to be strong" (GB, 4; *HAL*, 9; Köckert, "Mighty One of Jacob", 1074), which is still attested in Hebrew as a noun with the meaning "strength" (17 ×; contrast "bull", 5 × and "stallion", 4 ×); whereas שׁוֹר is a so called "primärnomen" and even an "altes Kultur- und Wanderwort" (*HAL*, 1346; H.J. Zobel "שׁוֹר", *ThWAT*, Bd. VII, 1199–1205, 1200). אָבִיר/אַבִּיר was thus used according to its original meaning for different, strong, and powerful animals, like bulls, oxen and stallions; for powerful men, and for a mighty (warrior-[?]) god. The word שׁוֹר, "bull", however, was a word for one specific animal, and as such it could be used as a metaphor of power (Zobel, *art.cit.*, 1203) for gods and kings. The development of the usage of these words was thus reversed, and the comparison of these two words is, therefore, a risky matter.

[742] See *DISO*, 3; *DNWSI*, 7; KAI, 214:15, 21 (with Bd. II, 215).

[743] See Aisleitner, *WUS*, 4–5; Kapelrud, "אביר", 43–4. See e.g. KTU 1.10:iii.21, 36; 1.12:ii.56.

[744] Miller, "Animal Names", 180, n. 16; Ges[18], 7, s.v. "אָבִיר".

[745] Cf. Köckert, "Mighty One of Jacob", 1073, who lists the available data for the use of *ibr* as an epithet in Ugarit. However, his rendering of the name *ibrd* with "Haddu is a bull" might be premature, since "in Hebrew, as in Akkadian, the original meaning of *'abbîr* must have been 'strong, powerful'" (*ibid.*), and

tr, Hebr. שׁוֹר, "Bull".[746] It seems preferable, therefore, — taking the development from "strength" to "bull, stallion" into consideration[747] — to translate אֲבִיר יַעֲקֹב/יִשְׂרָאֵל by "Mighty One of Jacob/Israel".

2.11.1.4.3   The Meaning of מִשָּׁם רֹעֶה אֶבֶן יִשְׂרָאֵל

In verse 24bB[748] we follow the common repointing of מִשֶּׁם as מִשָּׁם "by the name", with Peš and TO.[749] The following words, רֹעֶה אֶבֶן יִשְׂרָאֵל, are regarded by scholars as problematic because of the use of two unrelated epithets, of which the second, אֶבֶן יִשְׂרָאֵל is unique in the Hebrew Bible.[750] The former word, רֹעֶה "shepherd" is usually considered a reliable epithet, in accordance with other texts where God is called "Shepherd" (Pss. 23:1; 80:2). The word אֶבֶן, however, is mostly considered problematic.[751] Apparently TO considered this verse problematic, for the colon was rendered: דבמימריה זן אבהן ובנין זרעא דישראל "by Whose Memra he sustains fathers and children, the seed of Israel".[752] TO took אֶבֶן as an abbreviation for אָבוֹת וּבָנִים "fathers and

---

might be meant for *'br* in this name too. Secondly, the fact that Baʿlu sometimes took the shape of a bull (*ibr*, KTU 1.10:iii.35-7), does not provide the conclusive evidence that *ibr* meant "bull", when it was used as an epithet.

[746]Baldacci, *La Scoperta di Ugarit*, 253, n. 44, considers both terms to be synonymous, however, without any discussion of the problem on an etymological level. Of course Ug. *tr* and *ibr* could be used in parallel (KTU 1.12:i.32; ii.56), but this does not give any solution concerning the etymology of the word, nor concerning the meaning of the epithet.

[747]Kapelrud, "אביר", 44.

[748]Von Rad, *Das erste Buch*, 346, does not offer a translation of this verse at all.

[749]Cf. RSV; NEB; KBS; Gunkel, *Genesis*, 486; Skinner, *Genesis*, 531; Dhorme, *La poésie biblique*, 103, n. 6; Aalders, *Genesis*, dl. III, 190, n.**; Van Selms, *Genesis, dl. II*, 280-1; Testa, "Benedizione di Giacobbe", 177; Westermann, *Genesis 37-50*, 249; Sanmartín, "Problemas de textologia", 89; Pehlke, *Genesis 49:1-28*, 224-5; Wenham, *Genesis 16-50*, 458. Although Speiser, *Genesis*, 363, seems to prefer the reading of Peš, TO, he deletes it as "redundant". Cf. also below, p. 205.

Others prefer the *lectio difficilior* of MT, see NBG; Buber; EÜ; Tuch, *Die Genesis*, 588; Dillmann, *Die Genesis*, 471; König, *Die Genesis*, 767-8; Jacob, *Das erste Buch*, 922-3; Zobel, *SuG*, 23; Sarna, *Genesis*, 343; Sæbø, "Divine Names and Epithets", 120-1; Neef, *Ephraim*, 122.

[750]Dahood, "Divine Title?", 1002-7; Van Selms, *Genesis dl. II*, 280; Cross, Freedman, *Ancient Yahwistic Poetry*, 90, n. 77; Freedman, "Divine Names", 87.

[751]Dahood, "Divine Title", 1002-7, tries to solve the puzzle by a vertical transposition (when the text is written colometrically) and the omission of an *'ayin*. However, there is no textual support, whereas he does not offer reasonable arguments about how and why the text should have been mixed up.

[752]According to Sæbø, "Divine Names and Epithets", 119, v. 24bB of MT is missing except for the word "(the tribes of) Israel". He suspects, however, that v. 24bB TO contains an allusion to v. 25aA (*art.cit.*, 119, n. 13). This seems not to be correct, for every Hebr. word has a corresponding element in TO: MT מִשָּׁם

sons", [753] and this rendering recurs with some modifications in modern translations. Some scholars suggest we interpret אבן as a plural by-form of בֵּן "son" with a prosthetic *aleph*, [754] or to emend the text to בְּנֵי [755] (and re-point רֹעֶה as a construct form רֹעֵה [756]), resulting in the rendering: "the Shepherd of the sons of Israel". However, there is no evidence for בן with prosthetic *aleph* in classical Hebrew, nor is there any textual support for such a reading. [757]

Another alternative was proposed by Sanmartín, who, instead of אֶבֶן "stone", suggested we read the defective אָבִן (normally written as אָבִינוּ [758]) "our father", which somebody during the course of transmission piously has glossed. [759] This solution is unlikely, however, because of the assumption of the gloss whereas other solutions are possible. Further, "our father" — even if it would have been original in the text — can hardly have been spoken by a father himself; even though "Israel" and "Jacob", in the sense of "people" or "nation", are also used by the patriarch (Gen. 49:7). It may therefore be appropriate to consider the usual interpretation, suggested by the Masoretes: אֶבֶן: "stone".

Many scholars consider the word אֶבֶן to be an epithet: "Stone". This is based on the following arguments: *'bn* is the name of a deity known in Ugarit, [760] and it might also appear as an epithet in Amor.

ישׂראל MT > TO ;אבהן ובנין זרעא TO > אבן MT ;זן TO > רעה MT ;דבמימריה TO < ישׂראל. In this case אבן is supposed to be an abbreviation of אבות ובנים, "fathers and children", summarized in TO after the equivalents with זרעא; cf. Caquot, "Ben Porat", 55; Grossfeld, *TOGen*, 171, n. 59.

[753] Cf. the preceding note.

[754] Freedman, "Divine Names", 87; 122, n. 35. He refers to Isa. 14:19; Job 5:23, where a similar form could be found. Cf. further Van der Woude, in: H.A. Brongers, A.S. van der Woude, "Wat is de betekenis van *'ābnāyim* in Exodus 1:16?", *NedThT* 20 (1965/66) 241–254, 252; idem, "צוּר", *THAT*, Bd. II, 538–43, 541–2. See also FrB.

[755] Cross, Freedman, *Ancient Yahwistic Poetry*, 75, 90–1, n. 77; Van Selms, *Genesis, dl. II*, 280–1.

[756] This was also suggested by Dillmann, *Die Genesis*, 471; Skinner, *Genesis*, 531, without following the above described suggestions.

[757] The texts Freedman, "Divine names", 122, n. 35, referred to (cf. n. 754 above), do not need another interpretation for אבן, "stone".

[758] Gen. 19:31–4; 31:1, 14, 16; 42:13, 32; 43:28; 44:25, 31.

[759] Sanmartín, "Problemas de textologia", 89. This solution was offered in another context for a possible theophoric element *'bn* in Amor. and Ug. PNN; see Gröndahl, *Personennamen der Texte aus Ugarit* 87; Fowler, TPN, 204.

[760] Vawter, "Canaanite Background", 12; J.C. de Moor, "The Semitic Pantheon of Ugarit", *UF* 2 (1970) 187–228, 198; A. Cooper, "Divine Names and Epithets in the Ugaritic Texts", *RSP*, vol. III, 336; M.C.A. Korpel, "Stone", *DDD*, 1547–50. Contrast however: Gröndahl, *Personennamen der Texte aus Ugarit* 87; Fowler, *TPN*, 204.

PNN,[761] whereas the Hebr. LN אֶבֶן הָעֵזֶר "Ebenezer" (= "Stone-of-the-Help"; 1 Sam. 4:1; 5:1; 7:12.) suggests also the existence of such an epithet.[762] The interpretation of אֶבֶן as a divine epithet is especially strengthened by the argument that in the Hebrew Bible we also find the word צוּר יִשְׂרָאֵל "Rock of Israel" as an epithet for God.[763] Also the fact that the prophets criticize the worship of sacred stones and the gods of stone, suggests that there existed such a worship and thus in all likelihood also an epithet אֶבֶן.[764] It is considered justified, therefore, to interpret אֶבֶן as an epithet for God, which originally did not cause opposition, although later "it might have been on the fringe of what was considered theologically tolerable in Israel".[765] However, the aforementioned problem of two unrelated epithets, which are placed in apposition remains suspicious.

In order to solve the problems in this text, Sæbø points to the fact that the word רֹעֶה is usually taken to be a noun, but that in the closely related text Gen. 48:15b the same word is used *verbally* as a participle.[766] According to him it might be worth considering that רֹעֶה in our text was in its original setting a verbal form, and that verse 24bB "may be regarded as a sentence in its own right, in which the next two words (אֶבֶן יִשְׂרָאֵל, RdH) represent the subject, and רֹעֶה the predicate":[767] "from where the *Stone of Israel* is guarding (/protecting)".[768] He admits that the absolute use of a transitive verb is a major difficulty; but he asserts that the same could be said of the unrelated noun רֹעֶה here.[769] There are, however, some objections to his scheme. To begin with, the fact that derivatives of the same root are used in two closely related verses, cannot be considered as a reason to derive them both in the same way from that root (for example as

---

[761]Korpel, "Stone", 1548; cf. further also P. Xella, "L'Elemento *'bn* nell'ono-mastica Fenicio-Punica", *UF* 20 (1988) 387–392.

[762]Korpel, "Stone", 1549.

[763]2 Sam. 23:3; Isa. 30:29. For other texts, where צוּר is used for God, cf. *HAL*, 953. For this argument, cf. Schumann, *Genesis*, 761; Tuch, *Genesis*, 588; Gunkel, *Genesis*, 486; König, *Die Genesis*, 768; Skinner, *Genesis*, 531; Testa, "Benedizione di Giacobbe", 177; Caquot, "Ben Porat", 55; Sarna, *Genesis*, 344; Pehlke, *Genesis 49:1-28*, 226; Wenham, *Genesis 16–50*, 486; Korpel, "Stone", 1549.

[764]Kapelrud, "אֶבֶן", *ThWAT*, Bd. I, 50–3, 53; Sæbø, "Divine Names and Epithets", 127; Korpel, "Stone", 1549.

[765]Sæbø, "Divine Names and Epithets", 127.

[766]Sæbø, "Divine Names and Epithets", 126–7. Cf. Herder, *Geist der Ebräischen Poesie*, 85, who already mentioned this possibility.

[767]Sæbø, "Divine Names and Epithets", 126. See also Caquot, "Ben Porat", 55, who finds the verbal interpretation already in Peš and TO.

[768]Sæbø, "Divine Names and Epithets", 130.

[769]Sæbø, "Divine Names and Epithets", 127.

a noun, participle, or the like). The verbal use may be intended as a
kind of explanation of the epithet, or even as an aetiology. Secondly,
although the order (prepositional) Adjunct — Participle — Subject
(/Object) is not impossible (see Gen. 3:5), it is rather unusual.[770]
Thirdly, the clear parallel within verse 25 leads one to suspect that
the same may be found within verse 24bA:

Verse 24bA	יַעֲקֹב	אֲבִיר	יָד	מִן
Verse 24bB	יִשְׂרָאֵל	אֶבֶן	רֹעֵה	שֵׁם	מִן

Based on this parallel it may be expected that רֹעֶה is a noun and not
a verb.[771] Fourthly, as Sæbø admits,[772] the absolute use of a transitive
verb is a major difficulty, whereas it may be possible that רֹעֶה is not
unrelated as a noun here.[773] Finally, although another solution will
be offered below, it may be objected that it is usual in poetic texts to
place divine names and epithets in appositions to each other, not only
in the Hebrew Bible, but also in other texts from the ancient Near
East. Therefore, although scholars leave the possibility open that we
are dealing with an expanded text,[774] the apposition of these two
terms may be regarded as a usual description of the divine.

However, there is one solution which is left undiscussed, because
it is considered enigmatic: the word אֶבֶן might be translated in its original meaning "stone", leaving the connotation of an epithet aside.[775]
The term אֶבֶן "stone" is interchangeable with מַצֵּבָה "stele",[776] and

---

[770]Cf. JM, §154fc.

[771]Of course the noun רעה is a substantivated verb, or even a participle as Sæbø
suggests, but the point is if it is used verbally or not.

[772]Cf. p. 200 n. 769 above.

[773]Cf. the solution offered below.

[774]Cf. Gunkel, *Genesis*, ³1910, 485–6; Skinner, *Genesis*, 531; Westermann, *Genesis 37–50*, 272; Korpel, "Stone", 1149. Cf. also König, *Die Genesis*, 768, who
considers "Stone" to be an older expression than "Shepherd". Others, however,
consider אֶבֶן a later addition to the text; cf. NEB; Sanmartín, "Problemas de
textologia", 89 (reading אָבֶן "nuestro padre"); and for a short discussion, cf. *HAL*,
1176; K. van der Toorn, "Shepherd", *DDD*, 1457–9, 1459.

[775]See Dillmann, *Genesis*, 471; Procksch, *Die Genesis*, 274; Skinner, *Genesis*,
531; Dhorme, *La poésie biblique*, 103; Zobel, *SuG*, 23; Seebaß, "Die Stamme-
sprüche", 338; Neef, *Ephraim*, 122. These authors interpret the stone as a sacred
stone, either that of Bethel (Gen. 28:18–22; 35:14) (Dillmann, Skinner [?]; Zobel),
or that of Shechem (Gen. 33:20; Josh. 24:26–7) (Procksch, Skinner, Seebaß). See
also — with some critical remarks — Jacob, *Das erste Buch*, 923. Cross, Freedman, *Ancient Yahwistic Poetry*, 90, n. 77, could not make sense of it: "Israel-stone,
whatever that might mean", and they prefer an emendation.

[776]P. Welten, "Stele", *BRL²*, 321; Schroer, *In Israel gab es Bilder*, 357–9; J.C.
de Moor, "Standing Stones and Ancestor Worship", *UF* 27 (1995) 1–20.

it might be possible that אֶבֶן in our verse was meant in this way: "the stone (= stele) of Israel",[777] which might be strengthened by the fact that here we are dealing with a deathbed scene. Stelae were erected as a kind of memorial for deceased persons in or around a sanctuary and this might also be suggested by the usage of the word אֶבֶן in this context.[778] However, a combination with the preceding רֹעֶה "Shepherd" would result in a unique combination, whereas רֹעֶה in its present form is not related to another word. Of course the latter problem is easily solved by a slight repointing: רֵעֶה.[779] The first problem — that we are dealing here with a unique expression "the Shepherd of the stone of Israel" — might also be open to a solution. In the terminology in our verse a reminiscence may be found with the texts from Ugarit. In a recent study on standing stones and ancestor worship, De Moor discusses the well known text KTU 1.17:i.25–28:[780]

wykn . bnh . bbt	Let him have a son in his house,
šrš . bqrb | hklh .	a root within his palace,
nṣb . skn . ilibh .	someone to set up the stelae of his father-gods,
bqdš | ztr . ʿmh .	in the sanctuary the solar disk of his clan,
lârṣ . mššû . qtrh |	to make his smoke come out from the earth,
lʿpr . ḏmr . âṯrh .	from the dust the Protectors[781] of his holy place.

---

[777] Although scholars mostly consider אֶבֶן to be an epithet, they still connect it with the events narrated in Gen. 28:18–22; 35:14; cf. Gunkel, *Genesis*, 486 (considering it an old cult-name in Bethel); Jacob, *Das erste Buch*, 923; Pehlke, *Genesis 49:1–28*, 226, n. 1; Sarna, *Genesis*, 344; Wenham, *Genesis 16–50*, 486; Neef, *Ephraim*, 122; De Moor, "Standing Stones", 18–9.

[778] Cf. also W. Zwickel, *Der Tempelkult in Kanaan und Israel: Studien zur Kultgeschichte Palästinas von der Mittelbronzezeit bis zum Untergang Judas* (FAT, 10), Tübingen 1994, 72. However, these stelae cannot be linked with the graves of the ancestors; cf. *op.cit.*, 65–7.

[779] Dillmann, *Genesis*, 471; Skinner, *Genesis*, 531; Jacob, *Das erste Buch*, 923. This repointing is also appropriated by others, who interpreted אֶבֶן as "sons"; cf. p. 199, nn. 754–755 above.

[780] De Moor, "Standing Stones", 7–10.

[781] Interpreting the word as a participle of the verb ḏmr, cf. M. Dijkstra, J.C. de Moor, "Problematical Passages in the Legend of Aqhâtu", *UF* 7 (1975) 171–215, 175–6, with n. 44; B. Margalit, *The Ugaritic Poem of Aqhat: Text — Translation — Commentary* (BZAW, 182), Berlin 1989, 273; O. Loretz, "Nekromantie und Totenevokation in Mesopotamien, Ugarit und Israel", in: B. Janowski *et.al.* (Hrsg.), *Religionsgeschichtliche Beziehungen zwischen Kleinasien, Nordsyrien und dem Alten Testament: Internationales Symposion Hamburg, 17.–21. März 1990* (OBO, 129), Freiburg, Göttingen 1993, 285–318, 288–9; M.J. Boda, "Ideal Sonship in Ugarit", *UF* 25 (1993) 9–24, 16 (discussing other suggestions). The reading "guardian of his abode" is found already in U. Cassuto, "Daniel and his Son in Tablet II D of Ras Shamra", *BOS*, vol. 2, 200–2, albeit he interprets it as the duty of the son. Another rendering for ḏmr, was proposed by *TO*, tm. I, 422; *MLC*,

The final colon is very interesting in this connection. Ug. *ḏmr* "to guard", goes back to the same ancient Sem. root as Hebr. שָׁמַר "to tend, guard",[782] which could be used for tending the flock like a shepherd.[783] Reference may be made to the fact that Ug. *rʿy* "shepherd" and *ḏmr* "guard" are both applied to Baʿlu in Ug. onomastics: *ḏmrhd*, *ḏmrd* and *ḏmrbʿl* "Haddu/Baʿlu is Protection" next to the LN *hdrʿy* "Haddu is Shepherd",[784] while Ug. *rʿy* is also an epithet of Baʿlu.[785] In the Hebrew Bible the corresponding Hebrew roots are connected with God: Hebr. רֹעֶה "Shepherd" is a well known epithet, although it is not used as such very often: "the Shepherd of Israel",[786] whereas שֹׁמֵר "guardian" is also used for God: "The Guardian of Israel";[787] while the latter verb also returns in Hebr. names: שְׁמַרְיָה(וּ), שִׁמְרִי.[788] These data may be considered sufficient reason to equate the titles Ug. *ḏmr* and Hebr. רֹעֶה as semantic parallels,[789] functioning in the same way

---

369; K. van der Toorn, "Funerary Rituals and Beatific Afterlife", *BiOr* 48 (1991) 45–6: interpreting it verbally, as a perfect tense: "... and from the dust protect his place".

[782]De Moor, *RoY*, 248.

[783]Gen. 30:31; 1 Sam. 17:20; Hos. 12:13. Cf. esp. Jer. 31:10: ושמרו כרעה עדרו "and tend them like a shepherd his flock". In Ugarit *ḏmr* "protection" was connected with Baʿlu the Saviour, *rpủ* (KTU 1.108.20–25), "the god who is judging in Hadduraʿiyu (= Hadad is shepherd)" (KTU 1.108.3). In an almost identical ritual (K. Spronk, *Beatific Afterlife in Ancient Israel and in the Ancient Near East* [AOAT, 219], Kevelaer, Neukirchen-Vluyn 1986, 177), described in KTU 1.20–22, Baʿlu the Saviour (KTU 1.22:i.8) is called explicitly "Shepherd" (KTU 1.21:ii.6). For the spirits, invoked by Daniʾilu, the title *rpủ(m)* "Saviour(s)" also prevails in these texts. If the restoration in *CARTU*, 120 (= *ARTU*, 271) is correct, one of their functions appears to be *ḏmr* "to protect" (KTU 1.22:i.2). In the restoration and translation in M. Dijkstra, "The Legend of Danel and the Rephaim", *UF* 20 (1988) 35–51,40–2, an unknown deity is called the *rʿy* of the *rpim*, which is repeated in his restored lines 13–4.

[784]Cf. J.C. de Moor, "De goede herder: Oorsprong en vroege geschiedenis van de herdersmetafoor", in: G. Heitink *et al.*, *Bewerken en bewaren: Studies ... K. Runia*, Kampen 1982, 36–45, 44; idem, *RoY*, 247. Cf. also the preceding n. 783.

[785]KTU 1.21:ii.6; *ARTU*, 266, with n. 269.

[786]Ps. 80:2; see also Ps. 23:1; Qoh. 12:11 (?). Cf. also Isa. 40:11; Ps. 78:52–5, 70–2. Further: G. Wallis, "רָעָה;רֹעֶה", *ThWAT*, Bd. VII, 566–76, 572–3; J.W. Vancil, "Sheep, Shepherd", *ABD*, vol. 5, 1187–90, 1189; Sæbø, "Divine Names and Epithets", 126, nn. 34–5; Van der Toorn, "Shepherd", 1457–9.

[787]Ps. 121:4 (cf. the complete Psalm, where שמר is used to describe God's care); further Gen. 28:15, 20; Num. 6:24; Jer. 31:10 (together with רעה!); Ps. 12:8; 16:1; 17:8; 25:20 etc.

[788]*HAL*, 1467–8; Fowler, *TPN*, 104, 363; De Moor, *RoY*, 248. רעה in Hebr. PN is absent, although רְעוּאֵל might contain the element רעה I, "to tend, shepherd"; Fowler, *TPN*, 123–4; 194; 360.

[789]It is remarkable that BHS here suggests we read מִשָּׁמֵר אבן instead of MT; similarly Böttcher, according to Dillmann, *Die Genesis*, 455; Procksch, *Die Ge-*

in the context of ancestral cult.

Despite the obvious difference in meaning between אֶבֶן and *aṯr*, the Ugaritic and Hebrew passages could refer to a similar concept and the object of *ḏmr* in KTU 1.17:i.28, *aṯrh* "his holy place", could be compared in certain respects with the אֶבֶן יִשְׂרָאֵל "stone of Israel".[790] It is even possible that אֶבֶן may not solely mean "stone" here. In accordance with the use of Hitt. *ḫuwaši*, denoting a single stele, but also an area with standing stones[791] and similarly according to the plural *sikkānātu* in Emar,[792] the word could be used to denote the area where the אֲבָנִים have been assembled.[793] If this were correct, the

---

nesis, 274. Further it may be noted that Peters, "Jacob's Blessing", 112, renders "the protection of Israel's Rock (?)"; although he does not comment upon this rendering.

[790] According to K. van der Toorn, "Ilib and the 'God of the Father'", *UF* 25 (1993) 379–87, 383, n. 32, the exact meaning of *aṯr* "holy place", cannot be established, but he does not substantiate this statement, and it seems an exaggeration in view of the Akk. material (cf. the reference to *AHw*, below; on Van der Toorn's translation of the text, cf. De Moor, "Standing Stones", 7–9). For *aṯr*, one might think of "a special cultic room in private houses"; Spronk, *Beatific Afterlife* 146, n. 5; in the same vein: J.C. de Moor, "The Ancestral Cult in KTU 1.17:I.26–28", *UF* 17 (1985) 407–9, 409 (cf. the translation of *aṯr* in KTU 1.20:ii.1–2; 1.21:ii.3–4 etc. in *ARTU*, resp. 268, 266; and in addition *ibid*, 266, n. 265). See also Dijkstra, De Moor, "Problematical Passages", 175–6; Boda, "Ideal Sonship in Ugarit", 16. However, the Akk. *aširtu(m)* might denote just a sanctuary, not directly connected with a private house, whereas *ešertu(m)* is a "chapel, sanctuary", and an "inner room in a temple" (*AHw*, Bd. I, 80, 253–4). So, although in the context of the Aqhat-legend the proposed interpretation of *aṯr* as a "special cultic room" might fit very well (cf. once more KTU 1.20–22; De Moor, "Standing Stones", 12–3), a more general translation like "chapel" for *aṯr* may nevertheless be called for. This is also suggested by the parallel with the preceding *qdš* "sanctuary" in 1.17:i.26. Since in the sanctuary the *skn* "stelae" of the *ilib* are set up, the semantic relation is considered to be sufficient reason to equate both words Ug. *aṯr* and Hebr. אֶבֶן, even though their meanings are different (cf. however, the following footnote).

[791] T.N.D. Mettinger, *No Graven Image? Israelite Aniconism in Its Ancient Near Eastern Context* (CB OTS, 42), Stockholm 1995, 129–30; De Moor, "Standing Stones", 13.

[792] Cf. Mettinger, *No Graven Image?*, 130; De Moor, "Standing Stones", 14, with n. 84.

[793] Mettinger, *No Graven Image?*, 130–2; De Moor, "Standing Stones", 19. In this case it is interesting that Mettinger, *op.cit.*, 131–2, refers to the fact that "the designation of the stele as *sikkānum* has resulted in a theophoric element, namely *sakkō/ūn*, known for instance from 'Sanchuniathon' (*sknytn*)". On pp. 131–2, n. 110, he refers to the occurrence of DNN with the element *'bn*, and for this element in Phoenician-Punic names to a study of Xella (see n. 761 above). The many similarities between these two words are certainly no coincidence. For the discussion of the element *'bn* in PNN, cf. the literature mentioned in n. 760 above.

word אָבֶן in the construct state (to be repointed as אָבֶן[794]) would be written defective here, as is common in ancient Semitic texts. Finally, returning to the first word of this colon (מִשָּׁם), it is remarkable that in the context of the ancestral cult, described in KTU 1.22, it is *šm il* "the name of Ilu" which has power to revive the dead (KTU 1.22:i.6–7). This strengthens the proposed emendation of the vocalization, because "the name" here apparently has power to strengthen somebody.[795] In conclusion, this translation and interpretation of the text, which leaves the consonantal text unscathed, but repoints slightly two words (מִשָּׁם < מִשָּׁם; רֹעֶה < רֹעֶה), and reinterprets the proper noun "Stone" as a regular noun "stone, stele", might provide the solution to all the problems encountered in this colon.

2.11.1.4.4 Verse 25aA

In verse 25 fewer problems are found and renderings of the texts are mainly uniform. The exact translation of אֵל אָבִיךָ causes some difficulty, because it has to be asked if the relationship of אֵל and אָבִיךָ is a genitive construction: "God of your father"[796] or appositional: "God, your father".[797] The latter interpretation is favoured nowadays,

---

[794]See *HAL*, 7.

[795]Cf. also the fact that it is even the "blessing" of the name of Ilu which has such power (KTU 1.22:i.7), whereas in Gen. 49:25aB also the "blessings" give strength to a son. For שֵׁם as a substitution for a deity, cf. B. Becking, "Shem", *DDD*, 1443–5.

[796]This rendering is found in many translations: NBG; KBS; FrB; RSV; NEB; Buber; EÜ; and in many other studies (note that most studies offer *no* discussion on this rendering): Vater, *Commentar*, Bd. I, 326; Peters, "Jacob's Blessing", 112; Procksch, *Die Genesis*, 274; Dhorme, *La poésie biblique*, 103; Bruno, *Genesis-Exodus*, 192; Kittel, *Stammessprüche Israels*, 33; Speiser, *Genesis*, 363; Zobel, *SuG*, 6; Testa, "Benedizione di Giacobbe", 178; Cross, Freedman, *Ancient Yahwistic Poetry*, 75, 91, n. 98; Westermann, *Genesis 37–50*, 248, 272–3.
Some scholars consider אֵל as the DN "El", rendering "El of your father": Seebaß, "Stämmesprüche", 338; De Moor, *RoY*, 234; Wenham, *Genesis 16–50*, 486. Although such a construction of a proper noun in the construct state seems to be problematical, cf. Cross, *CMHE*, 49; it is evidently not impossible, see J.A. Emerton, "New Light on Israelite Religion: The Implications of the Inscriptions from Kuntillit 'Ajrud", *ZAW* 94 (1982) 2–20, 3–9. However, it is questionable if the DN El needed such a determinative, and in our opinion the classical interpretation "god of the father(s)" should be maintained *when a genitive construction is read*.

[797]Vawter, "Canaanite Background", 12; Coppens, Bénédiction de Jacob", 102; Van Selms, *Genesis, dl. II*, 281 (suggesting that it might be the required rendering); N. Wyatt, "The problem of the 'God of the Fathers'", *ZAW* 90 (1978) 101–4; Freedman, "Divine Names and Titles", 86, 112; idem, "'Who Is Like Thee'", 327; Korpel, *RiC*, 533; Smith, *Early History of God*, 16–7; Baldacci, *La Scoperta di Ugarit*, 237; De Moor, "Standing Stones", 19.

mainly on the basis of the Ugaritic evidence. The Bull Ilu (*ṯr il*) is
also called "father": *ṯr ảbh* "the Bull, his (Kirtu's) father";[798] *ṯr ảbk
il* "the Bull, your father Ilu";[799] *lṯr il ảby* "O Bull Ilu, my father".[800]
The comparison of our text with the Ugaritic material is justified
by the fact that, similar to our text, the Bull Ilu strengthens (*mrr*)
and blesses (*brk*) in the Ugaritic texts.[801] Another argument is found
in the Ug. expression *ilib* "the god/El who is father", "the divine
ancestor, deified father".[802] This name denotes the deified ancestors,
who after their death are united with El/Ilu. The latter also bears
the name *ilib* as the god, who is father of all other deities.[803] These
deities, connected with the stelae, are expected to protect and bless
the son and the family.[804] Protection and blessing are functions that
are both found in Gen. 49:24–5. Although the Ug. *ilib* is sometimes
used in a plural form,[805] we take the expression אֵל אָבִיךָ to be singular,
because of the parallels רֹעֶה (verse 24bB), and שַׁדַּי (verse 25aB), both
singular, and in accordance with the two singular verbal forms in verse
25a (וִיבָרְכֶךָּ; וְיַעְזְרֶךָּ). אָבִיךָ is therefore rendered as an apposition in the
absolute state: "El, your father".

2.11.1.4.5   וְאֵת שַׁדַּי: Textual Criticism and Etymology

As in some Hebr. manuscripts[806] and supported by LXX, Peš and
TN, scholars almost universally read in verse 25aB וְאֵל[807] instead of

---

[798]KTU 1.14:i.41–2; ii.6; *ARTU*, 193.

[799]KTU 1.14:ii.23; *ARTU*, 194.

[800]KTU 1.17:i.23–4; *ARTU*, 227.

[801]KTU 1.15:ii.15; 1.17:i.23–4.

[802]For the rendering of this word, cf. Van der Toorn, "Ilib and the 'God of the Father'", 382; De Moor, *RoY*, 232–4; idem, "Standing Stones", 7–8; J.F. Healey, "Ilib", *DDD*, 836–40.

[803]De Moor, "Standing Stones", 8; cf. also idem, "El the Creator", in: G. Rendsburg *et.al.* (eds.), *The Bible World: Essays ... C.H. Gordon*, New York 1980, 171–187, 185; idem, *RoY*, 242.

[804]De Moor, "Standing Stones", 12; see KTU 1.108:22–6.

[805]KTU 1.17:i.26.

[806]Aalders, *Genesis*, dl. III, 190, n.***; cf. also Sæbø, Divine Names and Epithets", 121, with n. 19; de Rossi, *Variae Lectiones*, 46. Schumann, *Genesis*, 762, lists the following manuscripts: K84, 150; R766, 807; pr. 903, 988, 1031. Cf. also the Q-reading.

[807]GB, 77; KBL, 100; *HAL*, 97, 1320; Ges[18], 115; KBS; FrB; RSV; NEB; EÜ; Vater, *Commentar*, Bd. I 328–9; Schumann, *Genesis*, 764; Tuch, *Die Genesis*, 588; Gunkel, *Genesis*, ³1910, 486; Procksch, *Die Genesis*, 274; Skinner, *Genesis*, 531; Aalders, *Genesis*, dl. III, 190, n.***; Bruno, *Genesis-Exodus*, 192, 321; Zobel, *SuG*, 24, n. 122; Van Selms, *Genesis, dl. II*, 281; Von Rad, *Das erste Buch*, 346; Cross, *CMHE*, 9, n. 23; Freedman, "Divine Names and Titles", 86; Westermann, *Genesis 37–50*, 249; Pehlke, *Genesis 49:1–28*, 228–9; Korpel, *RiC*, 533; Sæbø,

with MT (with TO and Vg) וְאֵת, mostly taken as אֵת II, "with, by".[808] However, the prevalence of the reading of LXX, Peš, TN is questionable because a reading error of ת for a ל is unlikely in the old Hebrew script,[809] whereas a misreading of אֵל שַׁדָּי would be unique.[810] We have to assume therefore a correction of the text; but a correction of אֵת for אֵל must be rejected, for it is no improvement; whereas the reading אֵל for אֵת is likely in the book of Genesis, where all other occurrences of שַׁדַּי are preceded by אֵל.[811] So the reading of LXX, Peš and TN, has to be considered as the *lectio facilior*, and for that reason the reading of MT is preferred, interpreting אֵת in our verse similar to אֵת in Gen. 4:1:[812] "by means of".[813] With this reading we arrive at the same interpretation as those who consider the prep. מִן in the preceding colon as a prep. with "double duty",[814] resulting in the same rendering.[815]

"Divine Names and Epithets", 116–21, 128–9; E.A. Knauf, "Shadday", *DDD*, 1416–23, 1417; Baldacci, *La Scoperta di Ugarit*, 136, n. 8; 237.

[808]For this lemma: GB, 77; KBL, 100; *HAL*, 97–8; Ges[18], 114–5; *DBHE*, 81; *DCH*, vol. I, 448–53. However, the last mentioned dictionary does not consider אֵת in Gen. 49:25aB to be אֵת II, but regards it as אֵת I, the "object marker" (*ibid.*, 439–48), and esp. as a "resumptive or emphatic particle" (*ibid.*, 447).

[809]Cf. the table of alphabets in *ANEP*, 88, # 286; further: *HAE*, Bd. II/1, 164–7, 207–8.

[810]In all verses where the words אֵל and שַׁדַּי occur together, these readings are certain and the textual witnesses do not differ from each other: Gen. 17:1; 28:3; 35:11; 43:14; 48:3; Exod. 6:3; Ezek. 10:5; Job 8:3, 5; 13:3; 15:25; 22:17; 23:16; 27:2, 11, 13; 33:4; 34:10, 12; 35:13. The same applies to אֱלוֹהַּ and שַׁדַּי: Job 5:17; 6:4; 22:26; 27:10; 31:2; 40:2. The sole exception which could be found is in Job 11:7, where according to BHS one manuscript reads שָׁמַיִם for שַׁדַּי. These data do not exclude the possibility that the DNN in the Bible sometimes cause some trouble in the area of textual criticism, even though special attention seems to be given with regard to the correct transmission of the names; cf. Tov, *Textual Criticism*, 200, with n. 13; 256–7; and further Smelik, *Targum to Judges*, 318–21.

[811]Gen. 17:1; 28:3; 35:11; 43:14; 48:3.

[812]Cf. König, *Die Genesis*, 768–9; for Gen. 4:1 see *DCH*, vol. I, 452.

[813]Cf. also Mi. 3:8; Job 26:4; 1 Chr. 2:18. Cf. further: M. Dahood, "Northwest Semitic Notes on Genesis", *Bib* 55 (1974) 76–82, 77; H.-P. Müller, "Einige alttestamentliche Probleme zur aramäischen Inschrift von Dēr 'Allā", *ZDPV* 94 (1978) 56–67, 66, n. 64; R. Althann, "Does *'et* (*'æt*) sometimes signify 'from' in the Hebrew Bible?", *ZAW* 103 (1991) 121–4, 122; Neef, *Ephraim*, 122–3. Pehlke, *Genesis 49:1–28*, 229, considers this interpretation possible although he seems to prefer the reading of LXX, Peš and TN.

[814]See Jacob, *Das erste Buch*, 923; Wenham, *Genesis 16–50*, 486. König, *Genesis*, 768–9, considers this unlikely in this case.

[815]Cf. also H. Niehr, G. Steins, "שַׁדַּי", *ThWAT*, Bd. VII, 1078–1104, 1084. MT is followed by NBG; Buber; Dillmann, *Die Genesis*, 471 (although not quite certain); König, *Die Genesis*, 768–9; Jacob, *Das erste Buch*, 923; Speiser, *Genesis*, 363; Wyatt, "The Problem of the 'God of the Fathers'", 101–2; Smith, *Early History of God*, 17; Wenham, *Genesis 16–50*, 486; A. Caquot, "Une contribution ougaritique

The following שַׁדַּי is rendered with "Shaddai", in agreement with
the vocalization of MT. It is remarkable that in this context the epithets אֵל אָבִיךָ, רֹעֶה and שַׁדַּי are used in parallelism, suggesting that
these terms relate to the same deity. In the Ugaritic text KTU 1.108.12
šd[816] is a deity. The word is used in the context of the ancestral cult,
together with mlk "Maliku" and the rpʾum "Saviours" (the ilib?). Our
text, Gen. 49:24 also contains several reminiscences to the ancestor
cult, so an evaluation of the data concerning שַׁדַּי and šd is called for.

1.   שַׁדַּי in the Hebrew Bible is an epithet of El, and is used in apposition to as well as in parallelism with the name אֵל.[817] It further
also occurs in parallelism with the name "YHWH".[818] However, it
functions also as a kind of exclusive name of God, because it is used
independently of any other name in Ezek. 1:24; Ps. 68:15.

2.   The vocalization of the plural שֵׁדִים (Deut. 32:17; Ps. 106:37) suggests an important difference in meaning between שַׁדַּי (= God) and
שֵׁדִים (= no gods).[819] The plural also seems to occur in Job 19:29,
where the consonantal text reads שדין. This lemma nevertheless seems
to refer to God, or at least to think positively concerning the שׁדים\ן
contrary to the שֵׁדִים of Deut. 32:17 and Ps. 106:37.[820] Usually שֵׁדִים is
translated by "demons", but Vorländer has shown that they must be
considered as deities.[821] Although Deut. 32:17aA rejects their divinity, in verse 17aB they are paralleled to אֱלֹהִים "gods". In other texts

---

à la préhistoire du titre divin Shadday", in: J.A. Emerton (ed.), *Congress Volume:
Paris 1992* (SVT, 61), Leiden 1995, 1–12, 11.

[816]Or šdy: the exact delimitation cannot be established, because the final eight
characters of KTU 1.108.12, šdyṣdmlk, are not separated by a word-divider; cf.
D. Pardee, *Ras Shamra-Ougarit IV: Les textes para-mythologiques de la 24e cam-
pagne (1961)* (Mémoire, 77), Paris 1988, 77, fig. 8c and a; *pace CARTU*, 77;
Spronk, *Beatific Afterlife*, 178. However, the correctness of the word division by
Pardee ("šdy ṣd mlk"), may be doubted (Pardee, *op.cit.*, 110; followed in KTU²,
125; contrast however *UF* 12 [1980] 174, 177, 421). A new text found during the
excavations of 1992 at Ras Shamra (RS 92.2016 = KTU 9.432) also contains the
DN šd (cf. Caquot, "Préhistoire du titre divin Shadday", 4–12); together with the
occurrence of šd in KTU 1.166.12, this argues in favour of the reading šd in KTU
1.108.12.

[817]For the occurrences, cf. n. 810 above.

[818]Cf. Isa. 13:6; Joel 1:15; Ruth 1:21. See also Ps. 91:1–2.

[819]On these texts, cf. Sanders, *Provenance of Deuteronomy 32*, 182–3.

[820]Cf. J.C. de Moor, "Ugaritic and the Origin of Job", in: G.J. Brooke *et alii*
(eds.), *Ugarit and the Bible* (UBL, 11), Münster 1994, 225–57, 236, with n. 68
(bibliography).

[821]H. Vorländer, *Mein Gott: Die Vorstellungen vom persönlichen Gott im Alten
Orient und im Alten Testament* (AOAT, 23), Kevelaer, Neukirchen-Vluyn 1975,
218. He is followed by Sanders, *Provenance of Deuteronomy 32*, 183, with n. 455.

the divinity of אֱלֹהִים "gods" is denied in a similar way.[822]

3. In the plaster texts of Deir ʿAllā the *šdyn* and the *'lhn* are more or less synonymous.[823] The *šdyn* have to be considered as gods, or even more likely as a race of "gods".[824] *šdyn* seems to be the plural of *šdy* and it is commonly assumed that this corresponds to the Hebr. שַׁדַּי, for the *y* in *šdyn* is not a *mater lectionis*.[825]

4. Another occurrence of *šdy* is attested in a Thamudic inscription: *'lšdy*,[826] adding however nothing to our knowledge of the name.[827] In Palmyra one inscription is found, where several gods are put together: *bwl'str wšdy' 'lyh' ṭby'* "Bel, Astar and Shaddai,[828] good gods". Further, there is a Palmyrene deity called *šdrp'* "Shadrapa", whose name means "*šd* is healer",[829] probably to be equated with Baʿlu "the

---

[822]See 2 Kgs. 19:18; Isa. 37:19; Jer. 2:11; 5:7; 16:20; Hos. 8:6; 2 Chr. 13:9.

[823]J.A. Hackett, *The Balaam Text from Deir ʿAllā* (HSM, 31), Chico (Ca) 1980, 85–89; H. & M. Weippert, "Die 'Bileam'-Inschrift von *Tell Deir ʿAllā*", *ZDPV* 98 (1982) 77–103, 92; M. Delcor, "Des inscriptions de Deir ʿAlla aux traditions bibliques, à propos des *šdyn*, des *šedim* et de *šadday*", in: M. Görg (Hrsg.), *Die Väter Israels: Beiträge zur Theologie der Patriarchenüberlieferungen im Alten Testament*. Stuttgart 1989, 33–40, 36; De Moor, *RoY*, 125, n. 116; Niehr, Steins, "שַׁדַּי", 1082; Caquot, "Préhistoire du titre divin Shadday", 8–9; M. Dijkstra, "Is Balaam also among the Prophets?", *JBL* 114 (1995) 43–64, 61.

[824]Dijkstra, "Is Balaam also among the Prophets?", 61.

[825]The first to propose this correspondence was J. Hoftijzer, "Interpretation and Grammar", in: J. Hoftijzer, G. van der Kooij (eds.), *Aramaic Texts from Deir ʿAlla* (DMOA, 19), Leiden 1976, 173–324, 275–6. Cf. Num. 24:4, 16; and further Delcor, "Deir ʿAlla", 39–40; Smith, *Early History*, 23; Caquot, "Préhistoire du titre divin Shadday", 8; cf. also Sanders, *Provenance of Deuteronomy 32*, 183, with n. 456.

[826]Niehr, Steins, "שַׁדַּי", 1082–3; Knauf, "Shaddai", 1416.

[827]Cf. *HAL*, 1320.

[828]There is some debate whether *šdy'* is plural or singular. It was usually assumed that it was an emphatic plural; cf. DISO, 292; H.-P. Müller, "Gott und die Götter in den Anfängen der biblischen Religion: Zur Vorgeschichte des Monotheismus", in: O. Keel (Hrsg.), *Monotheismus im Alten Israel und seiner Umwelt* (BB, 14), Fribourg 1980, 99–142, 130–1. However, because of the *šdyn* of the plaster texts in Deir ʿAllā, scholars are nowadays inclined to read *šdy'* as a singular; cf. Hoftijzer, "Interpretation and Grammar", 276, n. 15 (but contrast *DNWSI*, part 2, 1111); Niehr, Steins, "שַׁדַּי", 1083.

[829]H. Gese, *Die Religionen Altsyriens*, Stuttgart 1970, 198–201; J. Teixidor, *The Pantheon of Palmyra* (EPRO, 79), Leiden 1979, 101–6; J.C. de Moor, "Demons in Canaan", *JEOL* 27 (1981–2) 106–19, 119; Pardee, *Textes para-mythologique*, 110, with n. 180; A. Lemaire, "Déesses et dieux de Syrie-Palestine d'après les inscriptions (c. 1000–500 av.n.è.)", in: W. Dietrich, M. Klopfenstein (Hrsg.), *Ein Gott allein? JHWH-Verehrung und biblischer Monotheismus im Kontext der israelitischen und altorientalischen Religionsgeschichte* (OBO, 139), Freiburg, Göttingen 1994, 127–58, 131; Caquot, "Préhistoire du titre divin Shadday", 7: "*šd*

Healer".[830] Like Phoenician demons *šdrp'* is associated with scorpions.[831] This might be remarkable because the iconographical material from Palestine shows that the god with the scorpions occurs here too.[832] In this iconography Egyptian material is used which was applied originally to the god Horus, the saviour god.[833]

5. "Ugaritic evidence suggests that in West Semitic the word was already used from an early time onward as a designation for deities".[834] *šd* and *rp'u* balance each other in KTU 1.166.13–4. In 1.108.11–2 *šd* might form a parallelism with a demon, while the word is sometimes vocalized as *šēdu*.[835] The text runs as follows:[836]

wyšt . il [ ]	and let the god [ ]
il gnt . 'gl il [*'tk*]	the god who sucked out the bullcalf of Ilu, ['Atiku]
[*yšt . yd*]*d . il . šd*	[who ... the belov]ed of Ilu, Shedu.

Whereas other scholars are inclined to relate *šd* with Hebr. שָׂדַי and Ug. *šd* "field",[837] it is at least worth considering another vocalization for *šd*:

wyšt . il [ ]	and let the god [ ]
il gnt . 'gl il [*'tk*]	the god who sucked out the bull calf of Ilu, ['Atiku]
[*yšt . yd*]*d . il . šd*	[who ... the belov]ed of Il(u), Shad(d)u.

Although it is logical to expect that *šd* parallels *'tk*, it is possible that the name *il* had an apposition, resulting in the parallelism: "the bull-calf of Ilu, ['Atiku] ‖ the beloved of Ilu Shad(d)u", or interpreting

---

guérisseur".

[830]De Moor, "Demons in Canaan", 119.

[831]Teixidor, *Pantheon of Palmyra*, 106; De Moor, "Demons in Canaan", 119.

[832]Knauf, "Shaddai", 1420.

[833]Gese, *Religionen Altsyriens*, 200–1; Keel, Uehlinger, *GGG*, 130–2; Caquot, "Préhistoire du titre divin Shadday", 6.

[834]Sanders, *Provenance of Deuteronomy 32*, 182–3, with n. 454, referring to De Moor, "Demons in Canaan", 119; Caquot, "Préhistoire du titre divin Shaddai", 4–12.

[835]De Moor, "Demons in Canaan", 119, with nn. 55–6.

[836]Text and restoration according to *CARTU*, 77; cf. also De Moor, "Demons in Canaan", 119, n. 56. The delimitation of the cola differs between several scholars, but since the central words are read the same, this is of minor importance; cf. p. 208, n. 816 above.

[837]M. Dietrich, O. Loretz, "Baal *rpu* in KTU 1.108; 1.113 und nach 1.17 vi 25–33", *UF* 12 (1980) 171–82, 174, 177; O. Loretz, "Die kanaanäische Ursprung des biblischen Gottesnamens El *Šaddaj*", *UF* 12 (1980) 420–1; cf. also Pardee, *Textes para-mythologiques*, 110.

the word *il* here as a noun: "the god Shad(d)u". In view of the (reconstructed) text, however, the most likely interpretation is the first one of those three: "the belov]ed of Il(u), Shad(d)u". It is important to note that this text (KTU 1.108) is an incantation in which the spirits of the death are invoked: here *šd* is connected with *rpu̇ mlk ʿlm* "Raphium, king of eternity" (KTU 1.108.1, 20–1).[838] This connection suggests a link with the title *rʿh* of this Rephaim (the *ilib*), who are listed here at the end of the text.[839]

It may also be noted that in RS 92.2016/KTU 9.432 (the text Caquot referred to) *kbkb* "star" is used as a determinative (comparable to Akk. DINGER) to *šd*.[840] Stars are part of the Ugaritic belief, where it was thought that the spirits of kings and heroes became stars.[841] This makes the linking of *šd* with the ancestral cult even stronger, and the suggestion that we are dealing here with deified figures plausible.[842]

The etymology of the DN שַׁדַּי is not definitely established;[843] although there is a very strong tendency to connect the word with Akk. *šadu* "mountain",[844] and more specifically with Akk. *šaddûʾa, šaddāʾu*

---

[838] De Moor, "Standing Stones", 11, with n. 61; cf. also Pardee, *Textes paramythologiques*, 110; Niehr, Steins, "שַׁדַּי", 1080–1.

[839] Spronk, *Beatific Afterlife* 147–9. Cf. the parallel in Gen. 49:25 of אל אביך and שַׁדַּי; and further p. 203, with nn. 783–785 above.

[840] Caquot, "Préhistoire du titre divin Shaddai", 5; this view is approved by P. Bordreuil, "Les tablettes alphabétiques de Ras Shamra et de Ras Ibn Hani (1986–1992)", in: M. Dietrich, O. Loretz (hrsg.), *Ugarit: Ein ostmediterranes Kulturzentrum im Alten Orient: Ergebnisse und Perspectiven der Forschung*; Bd. I: *Ugarit und seine altorientalische Umwelt* (ALASP, 7), Münster 1995, 1–5, 2.

[841] De Moor, "Standing Stones", 11, with n. 62. This view was not restricted to the Ugaritic world but was shared by the Israelites and even left its traces in Ancient Judaism, cf. W.F. Smelik, "On Mystical Transformation of the Righteous into Light in Judaism", *JSJ* 26 (1995) 122–44; cf. in addition: idem, *Targum of Judges*, 482–5. Further *ARTU*, 262, n. 241–2.

[842] Hackett, *Balaam Text from Deir ʿAllā*, 88-9, points to the fact that in Ps. 106, where the שֵׁדִים occurs, an explicit linking with the cult of the death is made (Ps. 106:28), next to the offering to the שֵׁדִים. Sanders, *Provenance of Deuteronomy 32*, 183, n. 454, also refers to the fact that in Ps. 106:37 שֵׁדִים is a designation for the Canaanite gods. On Ps. 106:28, cf. also Spronk, *Beatific Afterlife*, 231–2, 249. Cf. in this respect PN עַמִּישַׁדַּי and K. van der Toorn, "Ancestors and Anthroponyms: Kinship Terms as Theophoric Elements in Hebrew Names", *ZAW* 108 (1996) 1–11, 7.

[843] Cf. Vorländer, *Mein Gott*, 216–9; M. Weippert, "שַׁדַּי", *THAT*, Bd. II, 873–81, 875–80; *HAL*, 1319–21; Niehr, Steins, "שַׁדַּי", 1080–3.

[844] *CAD*, vol. Š/I, 49–59, this noun is sometimes used as an epithet, cf. *op.cit.*, 57–8. Cf. further: Cross, *CMHE*, 52–6; Weippert, "שַׁדַּי", 879–80; *HAL*, 1320–1.
Sometimes the word is linked with Hebr. שָׂדֶה "field"; cf. W. Wifall, "El Shaddai or El of the Fields", *ZAW* 92 (1980) 24–32; Loretz, "Kanaanäische Ursprung *El*

"Mountain-dweller".[845] Concerning Ug. *šd*, however, the meanings
seem to differ between an etymological connection with Akk. *šedu*
"demon"[846] or Hebr. שָׂדַי and Aram. *šdyn*.[847] In view of the data listed
above an etymological connection between Ug. *šd* and Hebr. שָׂדַי is to
be preferred.[848] There are two options:

1. Ug. *šd* goes back to old Sem. **šad(d)ay*. In Ugaritic the final
weak vowel dropped out in nouns, as in Ug. *šd* < **šaday* > Hebr.
שָׂדֶה ("archaic"[849]: שָׂדַי), "field".[850] So if Ug. *šd* is to be derived from
*šad(d)ay, a connection between Hebr. שָׂדַי and Ug. *šd* is possible,
together with the equation of other occurences of *šdy(n)* in the
plastertext of Deir 'Allā, the Thamudic inscription, and those of
Palmyra. Furthermore, it is interesting that Ug. *šd* is also linked
with the שֵׁדִים (Deut. 32:17; Ps. 106:37; cf. also Job 19:29),[851] which
undoubtedly are to be linked with the *šdyn* of Deir 'Allā.[852]

Šadday", 420–1; Knauf, "Shaddai", 1416–7, 1420–1. The word שָׂדֶה can probably
be linked with Akk. *šadu*; see W.H. Propp, "On Hebrew *śāde(h)*, 'Highland' ",
VT 37 (1987) 230–6; De Moor, "The Twelve Tribes", 492, with n. 39; Knauf,
"Shaddai", 1416. Cf. also *CAD*, vol. Š/I, 58–9. Contrast, however, Cross, *CMHE*,
44–5, n. 42.

[845] *CAD*, vol. A/1, 43; De Moor, *RoY*, 125, n. 116. Cf. also Cross, *CMHE*, 52–6;
Weippert, "שָׂדַי", 879–80.

[846] De Moor, "Demons in Canaan", 119; Pardee, *Textes para-mythologiques*, 110;
Caquot, "Préhistoire du titre divin Shadday", 6, 10–2.

[847] Loretz, "Kanaanäische Ursprung *El Šadday*", 420–1; similar Knauf, "Shaddai", 1420–1.

Cross, *CMHE*, 52–5 (followed by Weippert, "שָׂדַי", 879–80) suggests on the basis
of PN *śa-di-'-m-i / śadê-'mmî* in Eg. syllabic orthography (cf. Hebr. עַמִּישַׁדָּי and
שְׁדֵיאוּר [*HAL*, resp. 799 and 1321]) and on the equation of Eg. *ś* with Sem. *t̠* or
ś, whereas Hebr. *š* requires a Sem. *t̠* or *š*, that for the etymology a *t̠* is required,
which would result in an equation with Ug. *t̠d*, "breast" (*op.cit.*, 55). However, the
transcription of the sibilants of Sem. words and names is not uniform although a
certain regularity can be discerned. Eg. *ś* is sometimes used for Sem. *š* and thus
also for Ug. *š* (whereas Hebr. is spelled sometimes with *ś*!): cf. J.E. Hoch, *Semitic
Words in Egyptian Texts of the New Kingdom and Third Intermediate Period*,
Princeton (NJ) 1994, 255 (# 384, Hebr. *ś*), 256 (# 359, Hebr. *ś*), 258 (# 365),
260 (# 369, Hebr. *ś*[?]), 263 (# 372 [cf. Ug. *yśr*]; # 373), 270 (# 384); further
409–10, and especially 417–8 (cf. also the tables, pp. 431–7).

[848] Pardee, *Textes para-mythologiques*, 110, n. 180; Caquot, "Préhistoire du titre
divin Shaddai", 5–12.

[849] Lett, §33g; JM, §§89b; 90c; 96Bf; cf. also Sanders, *Provenance of Deuteronomy 32*, 169.

[850] This is comparable to the disappearance of the *w* and *y* as second consonant
by contraction in Ugaritic, and which (re)occur in later Hebrew (Lett, §32m, with
n. 1); cf. Ug. *mt = motu* < **mawtu* > מָוֶת "death"; *bt = bētu* < **baytu* > בַּיִת "house".

[851] De Moor, "Demons in Canaan", 119.

[852] Sanders, *Provenance of Deuteronomy 32*, 183.

In this connection it is important to note that in Palmyra *šdrp'* was vocalized as *Šadrap'a*,[853] which is an important parallel to Hebr. שַׁדַּי; whereas on the other hand *šdrp'* is "perhaps even to be equated with Ba'lu/Ba'al 'the Healer, Saviour' (Ugaritic *rp'u b'l*, Phoenician *b'l mrp'*)".[854] Furthermore, the *šdy'* in the Palmyrene inscription quoted above,[855] has, together with the other deities, been given an additional qualification: "the good gods".[856]

The fact that Ug. *šd* and Phoen. *šdy* could be linked with Ba'lu/Ba'al, but also with 'El in Israel and probably in Ugarit, might require circumstantial evidence. De Moor has suggested in another context that El "displaced Ba'al and became the Almighty to whom all other divine beings were subjected",[857] and that he even replaced Ba'al as the owner of Mt. Zaphon.[858] In this view it could be remarkable that the two deities are both named with the epithet *šd(y)*, "Shaddai", "the Mountain-dweller". This confirms their connection with mountains in Ug. and Hebr. literature and makes therefore the proposed etymology plausible. Moreover, it is interesting that in the book of Job, where a reflection of El's usurpation of Mt. Zaphon can be found,[859] and in Psalm 68, which describes how El took possession of Bashan,[860] the name שַׁדַּי is used as an independent epithet for El.[861]

2. The second solution was already offered by Nöldeke: שַׁדַּי was given a wrong vocalization; it contains the DN שֵׁד with a pronominal suffix: "my *šed*".[862] The form would be comparable with the

---

[853]The vocalization is known from the Greek transcriptions of the name; cf. Teixidor, *Pantheon of Palmyra*, 101–6, esp. 104; cf. also Caquot, "Préhistoire du titre divin Shaddai", 7–8.

[854]De Moor, "Demons in Canaan", 119.

[855]Cf. p. 209 (# 4) above.

[856]De Moor, "Demons in Canaan", 119, suggests on the basis of the linking of *šd* and *rp'* that the Palmyrene god *šdrp'* was a good genius; this is confirmed by the attribute *'lh' ṭb'* "good god" to *šdrp'* in another Palmyrene inscription ; cf. Teixidor, *Pantheon of Palmyra*, 101.

[857]De Moor, "Ugarit and the Origin of Job", 241; cf. also idem, *RoY*, 103–8; idem, "Ugarit and Israelite Origins", 217–22.

[858]De Moor, "Ugarit and Israelite Origins", 217–22; idem, "Ugarit and the Origin of Job", 241–2.

[859]See De Moor, "Ugarit and the Origin of Job", 242. Cf. Job 26:7; 37:22.

[860]De Moor, *RoY*, 118–28; idem, "Ugarit and Israelite Origins", 224–33.

[861]Cf. Ps. 68:15; Job 5:17; 40:2 (next to twenty-nine other occurences in the book of Job); further, De Moor, "Ugarit and the Origin of Job", 236.

[862]Th. Nöldeke, "Besprechung von: Fr. Delitzsch, *Prolegomena eines neuen hebräisch-aramäischen Wörterbuchs zum Alten Testament*", *ZDMG* 40 (1886) 718–43, esp. 735–6. Similarly: G. Hoffmann, *Über einige phönikische Inschriften*,

title אֲדֹנָי[863] whereas the meaning of the designation שֵׁד would be unknown, as is the case with אֵל.[864] If this suggestion is correct, then a shift in vocalization from *šedu* to *šadu* had taken place, whereas a deliberate shift of the vocalization in Hebrew, to differentiate between שַׁדַּי and שֵׁדִים, is not impossible.[865] In Akk. texts the *šedu* could have a pronominal suffix, similar to Hebr. DNN,[866] as was suggested for שַׁדַּי by Nöldeke. Compare the following quotation: "the people *in šedia idmiqa in lamassija immira*, prospered under my *šedu*, were happy under my *lamassu* spirit".[867] This suggests that the Akk. *šedu* were so-called personal gods,[868] who protected and blessed their protégées, probably comparable to Gen. 49:24–5.[869] In this text the protective and blessing function of שַׁדַּי is stressed, which undoubtedly returns in the other texts in Genesis,[870] whereas it is remarkable that in the LXX שַׁדַּי is translated with θεος and a possessive pronoun.[871]

Although the latter option (2) cannot be excluded especially on account of the "theological" aspects of protection and blessing, it is less likely because it has to be assumed that the vocalization of an important epithet was changed during the course of transmission from שֵׁדִי into שַׁדַּי; whereas the latter vocalization is attested in extra-biblical

---

Göttingen 1889, 53–5; D.B. Duhm, *Das Buch Hiob* (KHC), Tübingen 1897, 34; Vorländer, *Mein Gott*, 218–9; Caquot, "Préhistoire du titre divin Shaddai", 10–1.

[863] The suffix is frozen in pause; cf. *HAL*, 12.

[864] Cf. Caquot, "Préhistoire du titre divin Shaddai", 11.

[865] Cf. Vorländer, *Mein Gott*, 216.

[866] Cf. Emerton, "New Light on Israelite Religion", 3–9.

[867] *CAD*, vol. Š/II, 257 (# b'). Cf. also Vorländer, *Mein Gott*, 47–8; 218.

[868] Weippert, "שַׁדַּי", 876, denies that Akk. *šedu* is used for the great gods. However, as Vorländer, *Mein Gott*, 47–8, has shown, the *šedu* and *lamassu* are used many times as parallels to the great gods, and *lamassu* is sometimes even used to denote Marduk.

[869] Cf. Vorländer, *Mein Gott*, 47–8, where the following quotation concerning the identical *lamassu* is found: "[i]l-ka la-ma-as-sà-ka ù [. . . š]a i-ka-ra-ba-ak-kum, 'Dein Gott, dein lamassu und [. . .], der dich segnet'". Cf. *CAD*, vol. Š/II, 257–8.

[870] Cf. Vorländer, *Mein Gott*, 219–21. This aspect of a personal and protective deity is also emphasized in the book of Job, where we find a discussion with Job's personal god, very often called שַׁדַּי. This might be comparable to Mesopotamian texts where discussions with the personal gods are found, and in which connection the *šedu* also are mentioned; cf. *op.cit.*, 221–3; W.G. Lambert, *Babylonian Wisdom Literature*, Oxford 1960, 32, lines 43–6.

[871] Vorländer, *Mein Gott*, 220; S. Olofsson, *God Is My Rock: A Study of Translation Technique and Theological Exegesis in the Septuagint* (CB.OTS, 31), Stockholm 1990, 111–6; M. Rösel, "Die Übersetzung der Gottesnamen in der Genesis-Septuaginta", in: D.R. Daniels *et.al.* (Hrsg.), *Ernten, was man sät: Fs K. Koch*, Neukirchen-Vluyn 1991, 357–77, 373–4.

texts for the element *šd* (cf. the name *Šadrapa*, mentioned above). It appears therefore more appropriate to follow the first option and derive Ug. *šd* and Hebr. שַׁדַּי and other attestations of *šdy(n)* from the same root. In all likelyhood the word means "Mountain-dweller", like the Akk. *šaddā'u / šaddû'a*.[872] However, for the moment it is more important to show that the DN *šd(y)* is attested throughout West Semitic cultures as a deity, which might be linked with personal belief and probably with the ancestral cult (KTU 1.108).

Further, the Hebrew Bible (Deut. 32:17, Ps. 106:37) as well as the texts of Deir 'Allā show that the name was also used as a general designation for "gods". The difference in vocalization between שֵׁדִים and שַׁדַּי suggests that we are dealing here with two different words, and that the suggested relations are only ostensible. However, it is conceivable that שֵׁדִים in Deut. 32:17, Ps. 106:37 originally had a vocalization similar to שַׁדַּי but during the course of transmission this word was "reinterpreted" in line with Akk. *šedu* "demons", to avoid the impression that אֵל שַׁדַּי had the same name as the לֹא אֱלֹהַ (Deut. 32:17).[873] This later differentiation is comparable to the artificial differentiation between אָבִיר and אַבִּיר.

Summarizing, we may conclude that these data make the connection between the several usages of *šd(y)* acceptable and thus also the linking of Ug. *šd* and Hebr. שַׁדַּי. The parallels found until now are in favour of linking Hebr. שַׁדַּי with the other Semitic occurences. Because *šd(y)* seems to denote a (personal) protective deity in the texts of the Umwelt, sometimes even in connection with the ancestral cult (KTU 1.108), it supports the present rendering and interpretation of Gen. 49:22–6 as a text with strong reminiscences of the personal (and ancestral) cult in Canaan.

2.11.1.4.6 Verse 26

In verse 26a there remains a rather difficult textual problem. The LXX and Sam read in addition to MT אָבִיךָ: καὶ μητρός σου / ואמך "and (of) your mother", whereas TO, TN and Peš follow MT. The text of MT is considered the original one, since it is conceivable that this word was added to remove the idea that אָבִיךָ would refer to God, whereas an omission is unlikely. The same decision to relate אָבִיךָ with Jacob as blessing father seems to have taken place in the reading of MT, TO, TN and Peš, in the final word of the following colon: הוֹרַי, part. plural qal of הרה "to conceive, be pregnant" with suff. 1.sg. "those

---

[872]De Moor, *RoY*, 125, n. 116.
[873]Cf. Vorländer, *Mein Gott*, 216, although he suggested it the other way round.

who have conceived me", which would result in the translation "the blessings of your father increase the blessings of my progenitors".[874] That such a (re-)interpretation took place, is assumed because of the reading of LXX and Sam for MT הוֹרַי: ὀρέων μονίμων/הרי עד "eternal mountains". This reading agrees very well with the parallel in verse 26aC: תַּאֲוַת גִּבְעֹת עוֹלָם "the wishes of the everlasting hills",[875] returns also in the saying on Joseph in Deut. 33:15, and therefore the reading of Sam (supported by LXX) of the consonantal text is accepted.[876]

However, the fact that MT reads הוֹרַי may have its history. This can be discovered following the proposal of Freedman to read in verse 26aA not MT גָּבְרוּ עַל "are mightier than" but a differently separated גִּבֹּר וְעַל "Warrior and Exalted One".[877] In his translation both words are taken to be nouns, but they may also be appositions: "mighty and exalted". Usually reference is made to the preceding colon, where two epithets of the goddess 'Anatu are used and thus this rendering of verse 26aA is considered legitimate.[878] In addition to this rendering it would be interesting to read also the following colon:

Blessings of your father, mighty and exalted; (26aA)	בִּרְכֹת אָבִיךָ גִּבֹּר וְעַל
blessings of my progenitors of old (26aB)	בִּרְכֹת הוֹרַי עַד

This too would be in accordance with the meaning of the preceding verses, where we found several reminiscences of the ancestral cult. The root גבר, sometimes used as a nomen "hero", is indeed a word

---

[874] גבר is interpreted in the sense TO did, comparable with the meaning גבר has in Gen. 7:19, 24; cf. Grossfeld, *TOGen*, 172, n. 64.

[875] Cf. p. 223, n. 916 below.

[876] Cf. the fact that the modern lexica do not discuss this lemma *s.v.* הרה, but directly *s.v.* הַר: Ges[18], 285–6. Cf. also *HAL*, 244–5. In *DCH*, vol. II, 506, the word is listed under a separate lemma: [הוֹר] "mountain" (based on G.J. Thierry, "Remarks on Various Passages of the Psalms", P.A.H. de Boer, *Studies on Psalms* [OTS, 13], Leiden 1963, 77–97, 79–82; and an unpublished manuscript of D.W. Thomas; see *op.cit.*, 637), as well as *s.v.* הרה ("those who conceived me"), see *op.cit.*, 591–2. *DBHE*, 188–90, does not discuss this text. Cf. also Neef, *Ephraim*, 123–4, with n. 599.

[877] Freedman, "Divine Names", 87; idem, " 'Who Is Like Thee?' ", 325. Cf. also M. O'Connor, *Hebrew Verse Structure*, Winona Lake 1980, 178; Smith, *Early History of God*, 16–7, 35 n. 80.

According to Vawter, "Canaanite Background", 16, the text is corrupt and originally named a male and female deity here; he hesitates to mention their names however. Speiser, *Genesis*, 370, instead of MT reads ברכת אביב ונבל "blessings of grain-stalk and blossom"; almost similar to I. Sonne, "Genesis 49.25–26", *JBL* 65 (1946) 303–306, 304, who reads בעל "ear and bloom". Since the consonantal text makes good sense, these versions are disregarded.

[878] Freedman, "Divine Names", 87; idem, " 'Who Is Like Thee?' ", 325; Smith, *Early History of God*, 16–7, 35 n. 80.

that might be connected with the ancestral cult.[879] However, this rendering is out of place here because of its present context, and especially because of the following colon. We will nevertheless return to this rendering in connection with the diachronic analysis.

נְזִיר (st.cstr. of נָזִיר) (26bB) is derived from the root נזר, which occurs in all Semitic languages and has a basic meaning "withdraw from normal usage, single out".[880] Originally the noun נָזִיר had this basic meaning,[881] whereas it receives a special connotation from the context (cf. Num. 6:1–21) or by means of a genitive construction: נְזִיר אֱלֹהִים (Judg. 13:5, 7; 16:17) and נְזִיר אֶחָיו (Gen. 49:26). It is very likely that on the basis of its usage in Numbers 6 where someone vows him- or herself to God, the genitive construction in Judg. 13:5, 7; 16:17 is usually considered to be a *genitivus objectivus*, "put aside/dedicate *to* God", whereas the story suggests however a *genitivus subjectivus*: "put aside *by* God", since he is a נָזִיר "from birth".[882] The unique formula in Gen. 49:26 may be explained by the Joseph-story, where Joseph is put aside *by* his brothers, who tried to get rid of him (Gen. 37:18–28). So we do not follow the suggestions to render נָזִיר here with "prince" or "leader" as is sometimes suggested on the basis of the meaning נֵזֶר "crown".[883] נֵזֶר "crown" and נָזִיר with the assumed meaning "prince", is in all cases connected with the fact that the person involved is an annointed one.[884] The connotation of a special task may, however, be preserved[885] since this act of the brothers receives a theological explanation at the end of the story, for there it is God who changed this for the good (לְטֹבָה; Gen. 50:20).

2.11.1.5 Rendering the Verbal Tenses

With respect to the verbal tenses the Joseph saying is the most difficult text of Genesis 49. Throughout this chapter we have tried to

---

[879]Cf. Ezek. 32:21, 27; 39:18, 20; further Spronk, *Beatific Afterlife*, 229–30; P.W. Coxon, "Gibborim", *DDD*, 654–5. Compare also the fact that גִּבּוֹר is used to denote angels, Joel 4:11; Ps. 103:20; and cf. H. Kosmala, "גָּבַר", *ThWAT*, Bd. I, 901–19, 911–2.

[880]KBL, 605; *HAL*, 646; J. Kühlewein, "נָזִיר, nāzīr, Geweihter", *THAT*, Bd. II, 50–3, 50; G. Mayer, "נזר", *ThWAT*, Bd. V, 329–34, 329.

[881]Kühlewein, "נָזִיר, nāzīr, Geweihter", 50.

[882]Cf. also K.F.D. Römheld, "Von den Quellen der Kraft", *ZAW* 104 (1992) 28–52, 48–9.

[883]Cf. *HAL*, 645; Van Selms, *Genesis dl. II*, 281; Sarna, *Genesis*, 344–5; Wenham, *Genesis 16–50*, 487.

[884]Cf. Lam. 4:7, 21; and also our discussion below in section 4.4.4.5.

[885]Westermann, *Genesis 37–50*, 275: "... der zu einer besonderen Tat 'unter seinen Brüdern' Geweihte". Speiser, *Genesis*, 370: "... one who is distinguished from his fellows and consecrated to a specific task". See also Neef, *Ephraim*, 124.

render the verbal tenses according to the context (Gen. 49:1–2, 28), where the sayings are qualified as predictions of the tribes' future. However, because צעדה in verse 22bA is vocalized in the Masoretic tradition as a *qatal*, followed immediately by a *wayyiqtol* and a *w-qatalti*, and next by three *wayyiqtol* forms, it is common usage to render verse 22b–24a in the past tense. But, on the other hand there are also some verbal forms which can be regarded as future forms, like the *yiqtol* forms in verse 25a or the jussive in verse 26b. The question now is, whether these tenses within the saying are generally rendered correctly and if the tenses must all be the same. These questions arise from two problems.

1. The vocalization of the verbal forms צעדה (49:22bA) and וימררהו (49:23aB) raises questions. The former has before been interpreted as an inf.cstr., whereas — following Korpel's proposal to read the latter verb as an impf. D-stem 3.masc.sg. of the root מרר[886] — it may be asked whether the vocalization of the latter as a *wayyiqtol* is still correct. It is possible that here we are dealing with a *wᵉyiqtol* and that the present *wayyiqtol* is due to the Masoretic interpretation.[887] The same applies to the following *wayyiqtol* in verse 23b, וַיִּשְׂטְמֻהוּ, which likewise may be regarded as a *wᵉyiqtol*, וְיִשְׂטְמֻהוּ, since the preceding verbs were misinterpreted.[888]

---

[886] Cf. p. 191, with n. 709 above.

[887] It is not solely the Masoretic interpretation, that misunderstood the text, but as might be clear from the foregoing discussion of the textual witnesses (see above pp. 182–184), the text was generally misunderstood. For that reason it is doubtful if we have to consider the tradition of LXX and TO (cf. also TN and TPsJ) reliable when they render the verbal tenses respectively as aorist forms and as *qatal* forms with a *waw copulativum* (for the latter tradition this is the usual form to render Hebr. *wayyiqtol*, cf. Smelik, *Targum of Judges*, 615, n. 1728). It is remarkable for example that in verse 22b LXX has an imperative for a Hebr. noun (שׁור), whereas TO has (although paraphrasing) *yiqtol* forms; and in verse 25a (see already Gen. 49:15) LXX has aorist forms, referring to the past for Hebr. *wᵉyiqtol* whereas TO has *yiqtol* forms, referring to the future. For that reason the Versiones cannot be considered to be absolutely reliable concerning the verbal tenses in this saying.

[888] Note that Korpel, *RiC*, 533, also renders Gen. 49:23b–24a as a conditional clause by adding "if" between brackets: "And (if) archers harrased him ...". It appears that she suggests implicitly to interpret the first verbal form as a *wᵉyiqtol*, since the *wayyiqtol* at the beginning of a protasis is rare and only occurs in a strictly narrative context (1 Sam. 2:16; 17:35; but this usage seems to be improper, see JM, §118n), and is certainly not continued by a future tense (cf. below). Except for these two examples the *wayyiqtol* does not occur at the beginning of the protasis, but only when preceded by a *qatal*, whereas it can occur at the

2. In verse 25a two energic forms are used that have unmistakably to be rendered as references to future acts.[889] However, these verbal forms are part of the list of epitheta describing the presence of the deity by whom the bow of Joseph *remained* or *will remain* stable. In fact verse 24b and 25a are parallels:

By the hands of the Strong One of Jacob,	מִידֵי אֲבִיר יַעֲקֹב
by the name of the Shepherd of Israel's stone;	מִשָּׁם רֹעֶה אֶבֶן יִשְׂרָאֵל
By El, your Father, who will help you,	מֵאֵל אָבִיךָ וְיַעְזְרֶךָ
and by Shadday, who will bless you,	וְאֵת שַׁדַּי וִיבָרְכֶךָּ

In our view the rendering of the verbal tenses in verse 25a has to be in accordance with the way verse 23b–24a is rendered and *vice versa*.[890]

In view of the foregoing it might be considered logical to interpret the verbal tenses as future forms, at least not as past tenses. As in the case of an inf.cstr. the tense is mainly derived from the context,[891] we will first discuss those parts of the saying where the infinitive is not used.

According to the Masoretic tradition in Gen. 49:23b a *wayyiqtol* (וַיִּשְׂטְמֻהוּ) has to be read, suggesting a past tense. However, such an interpretation of the verb can be doubted as we noted above,[892] since the preceding verbs were misunderstood. We have, therefore, to verify if we are dealing here with a narrative form (= past; *wayyiqtol*), or at least a *waw* expressing a slight idea of succession,[893] or a future with a *waw copulativum* (*weyiqtol*). In order to establish this we shall list the relevant syntactical elements together with the rendering of RSV as an illustration of the problems involved:[894]

---

beginning of the apodosis. See esp. J.C.L. Gibson, *Davidson's Introductory Hebrew Grammar — Syntax*, Edinburgh 1994, §§120–2; cf. further E. König, *Historisch-Kritisches Lehrgebäude der Hebräischen Sprache*, Bd. II/2: *Syntax*, Leipzig 1897, §390; C. Brockelmann, *Hebräische Syntax*, Neukirchen 1956, §§164–72; Lett, §80g; Waltke, O'Connor, *IBHS*, §§31.6.1; 32.1.2; 32.2.1; 33.3.1e; 38.2; JM, §§167b; 176b; Lett[10], §85g–l; A. Niccacci, *The Syntax of the Verb in Classical Hebrew Prose* (JSOTS, 86), Sheffield 1990, §§95–7; 107; 111.

[889]The energic *nun*, is usually assimilated with suffix 2.masc.sg. (cf. JM, §79k; for some exceptions: BL, §48s; JM, §61g). However, this *nun* has no semantic value, but only phonetic, see JM, §61f; Lett[10], §49o.

[890]Cf. also NIV, leaving the possibility of a future open in the footnotes.

[891]Cf. JM, §124s.

[892]See above, pp. 182–184.

[893]JM, §115c.

[894]The relation between Gen. 49:23b–24a and 49:24b–26 is denied by Westermann at a diachronic level, because he considers Gen. 23–24a to be an independent

The archers ... harassed him, (23bA)	וַיִּשְׂטְמֻהוּ בַּעֲלֵי חִצִּים
(his bow) remained (24aB)	וַתֵּשֶׁב
(his arms) were made agile (24aC)	וַיָּפֹזּוּ
by El ..., who will help you, (25aA)	מֵאֵל ... וְיַעְזְרֶךָ
who will bless you, (25aB)	וִיבָרְכֶךָּ

As can be seen here the rendering of the verbal forms is not congruent, as they should be. The two last mentioned verbal forms listed here are clearly $w^e yiqtol$ forms[895] and thus very likely in the future tense,[896] which is in accordance with the following jussive תְּהְיֶיןָ (49:26bA). It is therefore rather unlikely that the preceding tenses are in the past: "archers harassed him, but his bow remained stable ... by El, ... who will help you". A future rendering (with a conditional interpretation as Korpel has suggested[897]) is in our view much more likely: "and if archers harass him, his bow will remain stable ... by El, ... who will help you". However, if this conclusion is correct the Masoretic vocalization of the verb וַיִּשְׂטְמֻהוּ as a *wayyiqtol* should be corrected into a $w^e yiqtol$: וְיִשְׂטְמֻהוּ.[898]

Returning to the first strophe (Gen. 49:22–23a), we have to deal with the rendering of *צָעֲדָה (49:22bA) and וְרֹבּוּ וַיְמָרֲרֻהוּ (49:23aB). The inf.cstr. which is atemporal, can be used as a substitute for a finite verb with a past, present or future tense, that has to be derived from the context.[899] However, we are dealing here principally with a nominal clause and the tense is thus primarily the present.[900] In the context the preceding clauses (49:22aAB) are also both nominal and generally rendered in the present. The following strophe (49:23b–25), however, is rendered in the future, resulting in a present and a future context for this infinitive, but certainly not a past. Since in our text we are dealing with a blessing it might be considered possible that the

---

tribal saying, whereas vv. 24b–25a are in his view a transition which is created by a redactor (*Genesis 37–50*, 271–2). However, he himself refers to the fact that earlier and modern exegetes consider verse 24b a continuation of verse 24a. But, as was stated at the beginning of this chapter, in our translation the text is approached synchronically, disregarding for the moment such diachronic considerations. Moreover, even a supposed editor might have shaped these verses in such a way that they should continue vv. 23–24a.

[895] The energic form is mainly preserved in pausal forms, Lett, §480; Lett¹⁰, §490.

[896] There is to our knowledge no translation of this text, rendering here a past tense. Modern translations, commentaries, etc., all render these two verbs in the future. On the differences between the Versiones, cf. p. 218, n. 887 above.

[897] Korpel, *RiC*, 533; see p. 218, n. 888 above.

[898] Cf. above, p. 218, n. 888.

[899] JM, §124s. Cf. also the evidence from Ugarit and the Amarna letters referred to above, pp. 192–194.

[900] JM, §112a; cf. the participle, *op.cit.*, §121c.

inf.cstr. in this connection, implies a future meaning as an extension of its use as a present.[901] The following verbal form, וימררהו, is vocalized as a *wayyiqtol*. Since a *yiqtol* form with *waw* continuing an inf.constr. is almost always a *wayyiqtol*,[902] this is the most plausible form here too, hence וַיְמָרֲרֻהוּ. Although the *wayyiqtol* normally does not imply of succession when continuing a non-finite form,[903] the idea of succession might be implied here, comparable with such a usage after a participle and a nominal clause.[904] Interpreted in this way the first part of the saying on Joseph already functions as a blessing, in contrast with the classical interpretation as a narrative:[905] "… in the meadow he strides towards the Bull, and He will strengthen him and make him numerous". This interpretation matches our proposed rendering of the following strophe, where it was suggested we read "and if archers harass him" (49:23bA); which might be the continuation of a present or a future tense.

2.11.2   Analysis of the Poetic Structure

2.11.2.1   The Strophic Structure

Strophe II.B.ii.1

Accents: [10]–5 | [8]–2 || [6]–[8]–1(?) | [8]–2(?).

Sep.↑: *setumah*; emphatic position בֶּן פָּרָת; repetition of בֶּן פָּרָת.

Sep.↓: emphatic position בְּנָות.

Int. ||: **22a:** בֵּן פָּרָת || בֵּן פָּרָת. **22b/23a:** ־ה || הו־.

Ext.||: פָּרָת (22aA, aB) || שׁוֹר (22bA);[906] עֲלֵי עָיִן (22aB) || בְּנָות (22bA);[907] עֲלֵי (22aB) || עֲלֵי (22bA);[908] יוֹסֵף (22aA) || ורבו (23aB).[909]

---

[901] Cf. in this respect the use of the participle, JM, §121c–e.

[902] JM, §§118l; 124q.

[903] JM, §118m; cf. however also *op.cit.*, §124q, with reference to Isa. 38:9.

[904] JM, §118r.

[905] The classical interpretation of verse 23 in the Joseph saying as a narrative is best demonstrated by the rendering of TO interpreting the "archers" as his opponents, mighty men, referring in this way to Gen. 37. See Grossfeld, *TgOGen*, 170, n. 60. But also LXX with its rendering of verse 23a (εἰς ὃν διαβουλευόμενοι ἐλοιδόρουν "conferred against him and insulted him") seems to suggest a conspiracy, which could be interpreted as a reference to Genesis 37; cf. Rösel, "Die Interpretation von Genesis 49 in LXX", 67–8.

[906] פָּרָת and שׁוֹר are used as parallels in Job 21:10; פַּר and שׁוֹר are parallels in Ps. 69:32.

[907] Cf. Korpel, *RiC*, 532, n. 58.

[908] Cf. Gen. 16:7 (at a fountain); Ps. 2:2; 18:11; 24:2; 27:3; Job 2:1; 6:5; Further Dahood, Penar, "Ugaritic-Hebrew Parallel Pairs, I", 292–3 (## 418–20); Korpel, "Epilogue to the Holiness Code", 144; Roersma, "First-Born of Abraham", 227, n. 46.

[909] In this text there is probably a pun on the meaning of the name Joseph,

Strophe II.B.ii.2

Accents: $^{[8]}$–1$^{(?)}$ | $^{[10]}$–5 | $^{[8]}$–2 || $^{[10]}$–5 | $^{[8]}$–1.

Sep.↑: tricolon; change of subject.

Sep.↓: repetition מִן.

Int. ||: **23b/24a:** חִצִּים||קַשְׁתּוֹ; וַתֵּשֶׁב בְּאֵיתָן || וַיָּפֹזּוּ. **24b:** מִידֵי || מִשָּׁם; אֲבִיר
רֹעֶה אֶבֶן יִשְׂרָאֵל || יַעֲקֹב.^{910}

Ext.||: זְרֹעֵי יָדָיו (24aC) || מִידֵי(24bA).^{911}

Strophe II.B.ii.3

Accents: $^{[13]}$–7 | $^{[10]}$–5 || $^{[10]}$–5 | $^{[8]}$–2 | $^{[8]}$–1.

Sep.↑: emphatic position מֵאֵל אָבִיךָ; repetition אֵל (also suffix ־ךָ).

Sep.↓: tricolon; repetition בִּרְכֹת (3 ×).

Int. ||: בִּרְכֹת || בִּרְכֹת **25b:** ^{912}וִיבָרְכֶךָּ || וְיַעְזְרֶךָ || וְאֵת שַׁדַּי || מֵאֵל אָבִיךָ **25a:** ||
תְּהוֹם רֹבֶצֶת תָּחַת || שָׁמַיִם מֵעָל; בִּרְכֹת.^{913}

Ext.||: וִיבָרְכֶךָּ (25aB) || בִּרְכֹת (25bABC); שַׁדַּי (25aB) || שָׁדַיִם (25bC).^{914}

Strophe II.B.ii.4

Accents: $^{[7]}$–10$^{(?)915}$ | $^{[5]}$–– | $^{[8]}$–2 || $^{[10]}$–5 | $^{[8]}$–1.

Sep.↑: tricolon; emphatic position בִּרְכֹת אָבִיךָ; repetition בִּרְכֹת.

Sep.↓: תִּהְיֶין (jussive); repetition praep. לְ; *petuḥah*.

"may He add" or "He adds"; very likely a hypocoristic form of a theophoric name like אֶלְיָסָף, "Eliasaph" (Num. 1:14) or יוֹסִפְיָה, "Josiphiah" (Ezra 8:10); cf. Fowler, *TPN*, 166, 347; Oosterhoff, *Israëlitische persoonsnamen*, 45, 55, 63. Because the name יוֹסֵף is formed with the impf. hiph. of the stem יסף, it is comparable with a name like *יַעֲקֹבְאֵל, "Jacob-El", cf. De Moor, *RoY*, 237. יסף || רבב occurs in Qoh. 11:18; יסף || רבה in Prov. 9:11; cf. also Deut. 17:16; Job 34:37: Qoh. 1:16.

^{910}Syntactic parallelism; the epitheta אֲבִיר and רֹעֶה are clearly parallels here, but exclusively in our text. For the names יַעֲקֹב || יִשְׂרָאֵל cf. Koopmans, *Joshua 24*, 194, n. 109.

^{911}For the parallel יָד || יָד see Gen. 16:12; Ps. 106:10; 123:2. Further Dahood, Penar, "Ugaritic-Hebrew Parallel Pairs, I", 195 (# 217); Roersma, "First-Born of Abraham", 228, n. 60, 229, 241.

^{912}Formal parallelism; the grammatical form of the verb as well as the use of the suffix justify this parallelism; whereas the meaning of both verbs also corresponds.

^{913}For תְּהוֹם || שָׁמַיִם cf. Gen. 7:11; Deut. 33:13; Ps. 107:26; Prov. 8:27; further in Ug. texts: KTU 1.3:iii.21v.; iv.60v.; see also 1.100:1. Cf. Avishur, *Stylistic Studies*, 407; U. Cassuto, "The Israelite Epic", in: Cassuto, *BOS*, vol. II, 79–80; Dahood, Penar, "Ugaritic-Hebrew Parallel Pairs, I", 358; J.S. Kselman, "A Note on Gen. 7:11", *CBQ* 35 (1973) 491–3.

^{914}This parallelism is based on the etymology of the name אֵל שַׁדַּי, "El the Mountain dweller" (De Moor, *RoY*, 125, n. 116). But even if this etymology should prove to be incorrect, the parallelism by assonance remains.

^{915}The Masoretic accentuation suggests we read vv. 26aAB as one colon, (*viz.* $^{[7]}$–$^{[10]}$–$^{[5]}$), which would almost fit in with the offered translation. However, as was indicated above, the text is problematic and the colometry offered above fits well with both interpretations.

Int. ||: **26a:** בְּרֹכֹת || בְּרֹכֹת || תַּאֲוַת; הָרֵי עַד || גִּבְעֹת עוֹלָם.916 **26b:** לְרֹאשׁ ||
נְזִיר אֶחָיו || יוֹסֵף ;917וּלְקָדְקֹד.

Ext.||: אָבִיךָ (26aA) || אֶחָיו (26bB); הָרֵי (26aB) || לְרֹאשׁ (26bB).918

2.11.2.2 The Poetic Structure of Canticle II.B.ii

Sep. ↑: *setumah.*
Sep. ↓: *petuḥah.*

Ext. parallelism of strophes II.B.ii.1 and II.B.ii.2

יוֹסֵף (22aA) || יַעֲקֹב (24bA) | יִשְׂרָאֵל (24bB);919 עַיִן (22aB) || אֶבֶן (24bB);
ה- | -הוּ (23aB) || הוּ- (23bA) | ־וֹ (24aB) | יְ- (24aC).

Strophes II.B.ii.1 and II.B.ii.3

עַיִן (22aB) || תְּהוֹם (25bB);920 בְּנוֹת (22bA) || שַׁדַּי (25aB);921 וַיְמָרֲרֻהוּ (23aB)
|| בִּרְכֹת (25bA) | בִּרְכֹת (25bB) | בִּרְכֹת (25bC).922

Strophes II.B.ii.1 and II.B.ii.4

בְּנוֹת (22bA) || יוֹסֵף (26bA); בֵּן (22aA) | בֵּן (22aB) || אֶחָיו (26bA);923 יוֹסֵף
| גִּבְעֹת (26aC);924 וַיְמָרֲרֻהוּ (23aB) || בִּרְכֹת (26aA) | הָרֵי (26aB) || (22bA)
בִּרְכֹת (26aB).925

---

916 See for this parallellism especially Hab. 3:6; also Deut. 33:15 (עַד is replaced here by קֶדֶם) and Avishur, *Stylistic Studies*, 698. For גִּבְעָה || הַר Isa. 2:2, 4; 10:32; 30:17, 25; 31:4; 40:12; 41:15; 54:10; 65:7. Cf. in Ug. the word-pair ǵr || gbʿ in KTU 1.3:iii.27ff; 1.6:ii.15v. See further S. Gevirtz, "The Ugaritic Parallel to Jer 8:23", *JNES* 20 (1961) 46, with nn. 13–4; P.B. Yoder, "A-B Pairs and Oral Composition in Hebrew Poetry", *VT* 21 (1971) 480; W.G.E. Watson, "Fixed Pairs in Ugaritic ans Isaiah", *VT* 22 (1972) 463–4. עַד || עוֹלָם are found in Isa. 26:4; Ps. 89:29–30 (ext. ||); 145:21 (syndetic); cf. further Avishur, *op.cit.*, 163, 698. See also Ps. 138:8 and Dahood, *Psalms III*, 282.

917 Cf. Deut. 33:16; Pss. 7:17; 68:22. For bibliographical references, cf. Dahood, Penar, "Ugaritic-Hebrew parallel Pairs", 335 (# 511).

918 רֹאשׁ could be used for the upper part of a mountain: 2 Sam. 15:32; furthermore could both words be used for comparison with the other word, cf. Ps. 133:2–3; Lam. 5:16, 18.

919 For יוֹסֵף || יַעֲקֹב, see Obad. 1:18; Ps. 77:16. יוֹסֵף || יִשְׂרָאֵל is found in Pss. 80:2; 81:5, 6.

920 See for this parallelism Prov. 8:24; in syndetic parataxis Deut. 8:7; construct: Gen. 7:11; 8:2; Prov. 8:28. Cf. Dahood, Penar, "Ugaritic-Hebrew Parallel Pairs", 300, # 436; Avishur, *Stylistic Studies*, 165.

921 This parallelism is based on the etymology of שַׁדַּי "mountain-dweller" (cf. above). If this etymology is also connected with שָׂדֶה/שְׂדֵי "field", then a reference could be made to Joel 1:19–20, where שָׂדֶה || נָאוֹת is found. Further, נָוֶה "meadow" is also paralleled with "mountains" and "hills"; cf. n. 924 below.

922 See KTU 1.15:ii.15; 1.17:i.23–24; iv.32–33. See Avishur, *Stylistic Studies*, 325.
923 Cf. our discussion of strophe I.iii.1 (Gen. 49:8) above.

924 For the pair בְּנוֹת (22bA) || הָרֵי (26aB), see Jer. 9:9; 31:23; 50:19; Ezek. 34:14 (twice). For בְּנוֹת (22bA) || גִּבְעֹת (26aC), cf. Ps. 65:13.
925 See n. 922 above.

Strophes II.B.ii.2 and II.B.ii.3

אָבִיר (25aA); סמן ‖ (24bB) מִן | (24bA) מִן ‖ (25aA); מֵאֵל ‖ (23bA) בַּעֲלֵי
יַעֲקֹב ((24bA) | רֹעֶה אֶבֶן יִשְׂרָאֵל ‖ (24bB) מֵאֵל אָבִיךָ | (25aA) שַׁדַּי (25aB).⁹²⁶

Strophes II.B.ii.2 and II.B.ii.4

יַעֲקֹב (24bA) | יִשְׂרָאֵל ‖ (24bB) יוֹסֵף (26bA).⁹²⁷

Strophes II.B.ii.3 and II.B.ii.4

אָבִיךָ (25aA) ‖ אָבִיךָ (26aA); שַׁדַּי (25aB) ‖ הֲרִי (26aB) | גִּבְעֹת (26aC);⁹²⁸
בִּרְכֹת (25bA) | בִּרְכֹת (25bB) | בִּרְכֹת (25bC) ‖ בִּרְכֹת (26aA) | בִּרְכֹת (26aB);
שָׁמַיִם (25bA) ‖ הֲרִי (26aB);⁹²⁹ מֵעַל (25bA) ‖ עַל (26aB).

2.12   Benjamin and Conclusion (Gen. 49:27–28)

II.B.iii.1   פ

Benjamin is a wolf, who will tear apart, (27A)	בִּנְיָמִין זְאֵב יִטְרָף
in the morning he will devour the prey (27B)	בַּבֹּקֶר יֹאכַל עַד
and in the evening he will divide the spoil (27C)	וְלָעֶרֶב יְחַלֵּק שָׁלָל

II.B.iii.2

All these are the twelve tribes of Israel, (28aA)	כָּל־אֵלֶּה שִׁבְטֵי יִשְׂרָאֵל שְׁנֵים עָשָׂר
And this is what their father said to them, when he blessed them, (28bA)	וְזֹאת אֲשֶׁר־דִּבֶּר לָהֶם אֲבִיהֶם וַיְבָרֶךְ אוֹתָם
each according to his blessing he blessed them. (28bB)	אִישׁ אֲשֶׁר כְּבִרְכָתוֹ בֵּרַךְ אֹתָם

2.12.1   Translation

The first strophe does not contain any translational problems. A short
remark seems appropriate concerning the etymology of the name Benjamin. In Gen. 35:16–21 Benjamin was first named בֶּן־אוֹנִי "Son of my
sorrow", but Jacob renamed him as בִּנְיָמִין "Son of the right hand" or
more likely "Son of the South". Here in Genesis 49 another pun on
the name seems to be made, although with the help of Aramaic: the
morning and the evening might refer to יְמִין "days",⁹³⁰ suggesting that
the name means "between the days".⁹³¹

---

⁹²⁶Formal parallelism.

⁹²⁷See p. 223, n. 919 above.

⁹²⁸This parallelism is also based on the etymology of the name שַׁדַּי "mountain-
dweller". If the link with שָׂדֶה/שָׂדַי is justified (cf. above) this parallel is made even
stronger; for the triplet see Isa. 55:12; cf. for the pair שַׁדַּי ‖ הֲרִי 2 Sam. 1:21; Obad.
1:19. שָׂדֶה is found in asyndetic parataxis with גִּבְעוֹת in Jer. 13:27.

⁹²⁹Cf. Isa. 14:13; 49:13 (see also 44:23); 63:9; Pss. 144:5; 147:8.

⁹³⁰Cf. Dan. 12:13.

⁹³¹Cf. also the expression בֵּין הָעַרְבַּיִם; *HAL*, 831.

The root ברך in verse 28 is translated in its most usual sense: "to bless";[932] although not every single "blessing" is a word with a good wish or approval as one would expect in the case of ברך but sometimes even with a curse (אָרוּר "cursed", verse 7aA; cf. also verses 3–4). Of course we could assume that the writer used the word ברך here in addition to its usual meaning "to bless" in its euphemistic sense for "to curse";[933] or interpret ברך in this verse in the ordinary Hebr. usage: "to greet, say goodbye".[934] However, in this way the merit of ברך is restricted to a word and its possible sentimental value, whereas the contents of the wish has no significance. In his study on charismatic leadership, K. van der Toorn has suggested that the patriarchs as bearers of the בְּרָכָה are endowed with spiritual powers, in many respects resembling those of the later prophets.[935] Next to their gift of intercession there is their power to confer good or evil by pronouncing a benediction or a curse.

> The blessing is not merely the expression of a wish; it actually provokes and initiates what it announces, similar in this to the prophetic oracle ... The patriarchs are both *kāhin* and *sayyid*, or, according to the Hebrew idiom, *nābî'* as well as *nāśî* (Gen 23,6). Their *berākâ* is a supernatural force, not unlike the *baraka* which until recently Berber seers were creditied with in Morocco.[936]

Understood in this way Genesis 49 could be interpreted as a kind of prophecy, provoking what it pronounces.

2.12.1.1 Rendering the Verbal Tenses

In the saying on Benjamin the verbal tenses do not cause much trouble. The saying starts with a nominal compound sentence of which the relative clause is verbal.[937] The nominal clause is rendered in the

---

[932] *HAL*, 153–4; Ges[18], 178–9; *DBHE*, 118–9; *DCH*, vol. II, 267–71; C.A. Keller, G. Wehmeier, "ברך", *THAT*, 353–76; J. Scharbert, "ברך, בְּרָכָה", *ThWAT*, Bd. I, 808–41.

[933] See 1 Kgs. 21:10, 13; Ps. 10:3; Job 1:5, 11; 2:5, 9; cf. *HAL*, 153; Ges[18], 179; *DBHE*, 119; *DCH*, vol. II, 268; Keller, Wehmeier, "ברך", 358; Scharbert, "ברך, בְּרָכָה", 827–8; Speiser, *Genesis*, 375.

[934] Keller, Wehmeier, "ברך", 359: "In der Sprache des isr. Alltags heißt *brk* pi. (Subj.: Menschen; Obj.: Menschen) zunächst ganz einfach 'grüßen' ... bzw. 'sich verabschieden'". Cf. also *HAL*, 153; Ges[18], 179; Scharbert, "ברך, בְּרָכָה", 835–6; Speiser, *Genesis*, 375.

[935] K. van der Toorn, "From Patriarchs to Prophets: A Reappraisal of Charismatic Leadership in Ancient Israel", *JNSL* 13 (1987) 191–218, 198–201.

[936] Van der Toorn, "From Patriarchs to Prophets", 200–1. For the Berber seers in Morocco he referred to the study of Lindblom, *Prophecy in Ancient Israel*, 85.

[937] JM, §158a.

present, but the verbal clause is a *yiqtol*, יִטְרָף and thus most likely future:[938] "he will tear apart". The saying continues with two *yiqtol* forms, also rendered in the future.[939]

The second strophe is a resumption of the contents of the blessing and each colon is a nominal clause. The first clause (49:28aA) is a simple nominative clause with a subject and a predicate and rendered as a present. The second clause (49:28bA) is a double compound nominal clause with a relative clause followed by a circumstantial clause. The main clause is rendered in the present ("and this is"), whereas the relative clause, introduced with אֲשֶׁר, has a *qatal* form and is thus in the past. The following circumstantial clause starts with a *way-yiqtol* וַיְבָרֶךְ which is consequently also rendered in the past.[940] The rendering of the final colon, containing a *qatal* can go without further discussion.

2.12.2   Analysis of the Poetic Structure
2.12.2.1   The Strophic Structure

The delimitation of strophes in this text is problematic because the first strophe is formed of one poetic verse, making a delimitation upwards or downwards questionable. The delimitation upwards (from the Joseph-saying) is formed by the *petuḥah*, after v. 26, while the delimitation of the strophes of the Joseph-saying are fixed. This justifies the delimitation of the Benjamin-saying as a strophe separated from the Joseph-saying.

The delimitation downwards is justified by the fact that v. 28 forms the framework of the so-called Blessing, and also because this conclusion is an independent strophe with a unicolon and a bicolon according to the Masoretic accentuation (also confirmed by the contents of the two poetic verses, 28a and 28b). Furthermore there is a clear difference in style, since most cola in the "Blessing" are relatively short, the final strophe, v. 28, however, contains three cola of successively five, six and again five stresses. These arguments justify the delimitation of these two strophes as independent unities.[941]

---

[938] JM, §113b. Here a repeated action cannot be excluded; *ibid.*, §113c.1.

[939] Contrast RSV; NBG.

[940] JM, §159.

[941] The delimitation of framework and testament does not necessarily result in independent unities; cf. the fact that the framework of the "Testament of David" (1 Kgs. 2:1–10) is an integral part of the poem, and that vv. 1–2 *and* 9–10 both together form a strophe containing the introduction to the direct speech, as well as the direct speech itself. Cf. on this matter R. de Hoop, "The Testament of David: A Response to W.T. Koopmans", *VT* 45 (1995) 270–9.

Strophe II.B.iii.1

Accents: [10]–5 | [8]–2 | [8]–1.

Sep.↑: *petuḥah*; tricolon; emphatic position בִּנְיָמִין.

Int. ‖: יִטְרָף ‖ יֹאכַל ‖ יְחַלֵּק; יִטְרָף ‖ עַד ‖ שָׁלָל; בַּבֹּקֶר ‖ וְלָעֶרֶב.[942]

Strophe II.B.iii.2

Accents: [12]–[8]–2 ‖ [17]–[10]–5 | [12]–[8]–1.

Sep.↑: unicolon; אֵלֶּה.[943]

Sep.↓: וְזֹאת;[944] repetition אֲשֶׁר,[945] ברך (root) and אֹתָם.

Int. ‖: **28a:** unicolon. **28b:** אֲשֶׁר ‖ אֲשֶׁר;[946] וַיְבָרֶךְ אוֹתָם ‖ בֵּרַךְ כִּבְרְכָתוֹ אֹתָם.[947]

Ext.‖: אֲבִיהֶם (28aA) ‖ שִׁבְטֵי יִשְׂרָאֵל (28aA);[948] וְזֹאת (28bA) ‖ כָּל אֵלֶּה (28aA) (28bA).[949]

Because of the change of style between these two strophes, it can be doubted if the final strophe is indeed poetry. Undoubtedly the final strophe does not contain the same kind of poetry as the sayings, but this may be due to the occurrence of a so-called unicolon (verse 28aA) as well as to the different kind of poetry involved: next to the lyric poetry of the sayings we find in this strophe so called "narrative poetry".[950] One important feature of this kind of poetry is that next to the so-called *parallelismus membrorum* a much more important element is external parallelism: parallelism crossing the boundaries of poetic verses and strophes and sometimes comprises the whole poem. The parallelism within the strophe is rather strong, but the same is true for the external parallelism of this strophe with the first strophe of the canto (verses 1–2); cf. the following:

וַיִּקְרָא (1aA) | וַיֹּאמֶר (1aB) ‖ דִּבֶּר (28bA); בָּנָיו (1aA) ‖ אֲבִיהֶם (28bA); לְכֶם (1aB) ‖ לָהֶם (28bA); אֶתְכֶם (1aC) ‖ אוֹתָם (28bA) | אֹתָם (28bB); אֲשֶׁר

---

[942] This pair is found in parallel in Isa. 17:14; Ezek. 24:18; Zeph. 3:3(!); Pss. 30:6; 90:6; Qoh. 11:6; and in syndetic parataxis in Pss. 55:17; 65:9; Job 4:20.

[943] For אֵלֶּה as a marker of separation, cf. Van der Lugt, *SSBHP*, 512; idem, *Poetry of the Book of Job*, 489; Koopmans, *Joshua 24*, 220; Korpel, "Epilogue to the Holiness Code", 137–8.

[944] Van der Lugt, *Poetry of the Book of Job*, 493; Korpel, "Epilogue to the Holiness Code", 137–8; 140.

[945] Cf. for אֲשֶׁר as a so-called "prose-particle" Koopmans, *Joshua 24*, 169–71.

[946] For the parallelism of אֲשֶׁר ‖ אֲשֶׁר, see Van der Meer, *Oude woorden worden nieuw*, 80, 92; Koopmans, *Joshua 24*, 171 n. 34, 208–9 with n. 202; Kim, *Samson Cycle*, 199 with n. 120; Korpel, "Epilogue to the Holiness Code", 135, 139.

[947] For ברך ‖ ברך, see Dahood, Penar, "Ugaritic-Hebrew Parallel Pairs", 149.

[948] For this pair, cf. Kim, *Samson Cycle*, 211 with n. 179 (with literature).

[949] Formal parallelism because the "sons" are here considered to be the tribes of Israel, blessed by their "father". Further, the father is named "Israel".

[950] Cf. section 2.2.2, for the same discussion concerning the introductory strophe.

(1aC) ‖ אֲשֶׁר (28bA) | אֲשֶׁר (28bB); אֶתְכֶם (1aC) יִשְׂרָאֵל (2aB) ‖ יִשְׂרָאֵל
(28aA); בְּנֵי יַעֲקֹב (2aA) ‖ אֲבִיהֶם (28bA); אֲבִיכֶם (2aB) ‖ אֲבִיהֶם (28bA).

Next to this external parallelism, reference has to be made to the very strong inclusion at the level of sub-canto II of כְּאַחַד שִׁבְטֵי יִשְׂרָאֵל "like one of the tribes of Israel" (16aB) ‖ כָּל־אֵלֶּה שִׁבְטֵי יִשְׂרָאֵל שְׁנֵים עָשָׂר "all these are the twelve tribes of Israel" (28aA). Based on the internal and external parallelisms it appears that the introductory strophe (I.i.1) as well as the closing strophe (II.vi.2) are written in verse and together form the poetic framework of Genesis 49.

2.12.2.2 The Poetic Structure of Canticle II.B.iii

Sep.↑: *petuḥah.*
Sep.↓: absent.
Ext.‖: בִּנְיָמִין (27A) ‖ יִשְׂרָאֵל (28aA).

2.13 The Macrostructure of Genesis 49

In the preceding paragraphs the poetic structure of Genesis 49 was defined colometrically in strophes and canticles. Each poetic unit appears to be built up carefully and contains many forms of parallelism between the different parts. The parallelisms between strophes I.A.i.1 and II.B.iii.2 noted above, for example are remarkable,whereas these parts are mostly considered to be written in prose. Such composition techniques seem to suggest a carefully composed work of art. A closer look at the macrostructure seems to confirm this. We will present now first the text of Genesis 49, structured colometrically in strophes, canticles and sub-cantos, and then continue with a discussion of the macrostructure.

2.13.1 The Structured Text of Genesis 49[951]

ס

I.A.i.1

And Jacob called to his sons (1A)	וַיִּקְרָא יַעֲקֹב אֶל־בָּנָיו
and said: "Gather that I may tell you (1B)	וַיֹּאמֶר הֵאָסְפוּ וְאַגִּידָה לָכֶם
what will happen to you in days hereafter. (1C)	אֵת אֲשֶׁר־יִקְרָא אֶתְכֶם בְּאַחֲרִית הַיָּמִים
Assemble and listen, sons of Jacob, (2A)	הִקָּבְצוּ וְשִׁמְעוּ בְּנֵי יַעֲקֹב
and listen to Israel your father. (2B)	וְשִׁמְעוּ אֶל־יִשְׂרָאֵל אֲבִיכֶם

---

[951] The Hebrew text presented below, which diverges in some cases from MT [marked with (!), or with square brackets], has been defended above in the present chapter.

I.A.i.2

Reuben, my firstborn are you, (3A)　　　　　רְאוּבֵן בְּכֹרִי אַתָּה

　my might and the firstling of my strength, (3B)　כֹּחִי וְרֵאשִׁית אוֹנִי

　　superior in tallness, and superior in power; (3C)　יֶתֶר שְׂאֵת וְיֶתֶר עָז

deceptive like water — you shall have no　　פַּחַז כַּמַּיִם אַל־תּוֹתַר
　　　　　　　　　　　　　　superiority, (4A)

　for you went up to your father's bed, (4B)　כִּי עָלִיתָ מִשְׁכְּבֵי אָבִיךָ

　　then you defiled the concubine's couch. (4C)　אָז חִלַּלְתָּ יְצוּעִי עָלָה

. . . . פ

I.A.ii.1

Simeon and Levi are brothers, (5A)　　　　שִׁמְעוֹן וְלֵוִי אַחִים

　weapons of violence are their knives. (5B)　כְּלֵי חָמָס מְכֵרֹתֵיהֶם(!)

My soul shall not enter in their company, (6aA)　בְּסֹדָם אַל־תָּבֹא נַפְשִׁי

　my glory shall not rejoice in their gathering; (6aB)　בִּקְהָלָם אַל־תֵּחַד כְּבֹדִי

I.A.ii.2

For in their anger they slew a man, (6bA)　　כִּי בְאַפָּם הָרְגוּ אִישׁ

　in their wantonness they hamstrung a bull; (6bB)　וּבִרְצֹנָם עִקְּרוּ־שׁוֹר

cursed be their anger, for it is fierce, (7aA)　אָרוּר אַפָּם כִּי עָז

　and their wrath, for it is cruel, (7aB)　　וְעֶבְרָתָם כִּי קָשָׁתָה

　　I will divide them in Jacob, scatter them in　אֲחַלְּקֵם בְּיַעֲקֹב וַאֲפִיצֵם
　　　　　　　　　　　　　　Israel (7aC)　בְּיִשְׂרָאֵל

─────────────────────────────────────── ס

I.B.i.1

Judah are you, (8aA)　　　　　　　　יְהוּדָה אַתָּה

　your brothers shall praise you, (8aB)　　יוֹדוּךָ אַחֶיךָ

Your hand shall be on your enemies' neck, (8bA)　יָדְךָ בְּעֹרֶף אֹיְבֶיךָ

　your father's sons shall bow to you. (8bB)　יִשְׁתַּחֲווּ לְךָ בְּנֵי אָבִיךָ

I.B.i.2

A lion's whelp is Judah, (9aA)　　　　גּוּר אַרְיֵה יְהוּדָה

　may you grow up, my son, from the prey; (9aB)　מִטֶּרֶף בְּנִי עָלִיתָ

If he stoops down, couches as a lion, (9bA)　כָּרַע רָבַץ כְּאַרְיֵה

　a "king's lion": "who will raise him?" (9bB)　וּכְלָבִיא מִי יְקִימֶנּוּ

I.B.i.3

The sceptre shall not depart from Judah, (10aA)　לֹא־יָסוּר שֵׁבֶט מִיהוּדָה

　nor the ruler's staff ever from between his feet, (10aB)　וּמְחֹקֵק מִבֵּין רַגְלָיו עַד(!)

For certain, let tribute come to him, (10bA)　כִּי־יָבֹא שַׁי לֹה(!)

　and may the obedience of the peoples be to him. (10bB)　וְלוֹ יִקְּהַת עַמִּים

I.B.i.4

May he bind his foal to the vine, (11aA)	אֹסְרִי לַגֶּפֶן עִירֹה
and his ass's colt to the choice vine; (11aB)	וְלַשֹּׂרֵקָה בְּנִי אֲתֹנוֹ
May he wash his garments in wine, (11bA)	כִּבֵּס בַּיַּיִן לְבֻשׁוֹ
and his vesture in the blood of grapes; (11bB)	וּבְדַם־עֲנָבִים סוּתֹה
His eyes shall be darker than wine, (12A)	חַכְלִילִי עֵינַיִם מִיָּיִן
his teeth whiter than milk. (12B)	וּלְבֶן־שִׁנַּיִם מֵחָלָב

. . . . ף

I.B.ii.1

Zebulun – at the wide sea's beach he will dwell; (13aA)	זְבוּלֻן לְחוֹף יַמִּים יִשְׁכֹּן
May he be a beach for ships, (13bA)	וְהוּא לְחוֹף אֳנִיֹּת
and his spur facing Sidon. (13bB)	וְיַרְכָתוֹ עַל־צִידֹן

. . . . ס

I.B.iii.1

Issachar is a strong ass, (14A)	יִשָּׂשכָר חֲמֹר גָּרֶם
that couches between the donkey-packs; (14B)	רֹבֵץ בֵּין הַמִּשְׁפְּתָיִם

I.B.iii.2

And he sees the rest, that it is good, (15aA)	וַיַּרְא מְנֻחָה כִּי טוֹב
and the land, that it is pleasant; (15aB)	וְאֶת־הָאָרֶץ כִּי נָעֵמָה
He bends his shoulder to bear, (15bA)	וַיֵּט שִׁכְמוֹ לִסְבֹּל
and is a serving corvée worker. (15bB)	וַיְהִי לְמַס־עֹבֵד

══ ס

II.A.i.1

Dan — his people will be strong, (16A)	דָּן יָדֹ[וּ](!) עַמּוֹ
like one of the tribes of Israel; (16B)	כְּאַחַד שִׁבְטֵי יִשְׂרָאֵל

II.A.i.2

May Dan be a snake by the way, (17aA)	יְהִי־דָן נָחָשׁ עֲלֵי־דֶרֶךְ
a viper by the path; (17aB)	שְׁפִיפֹן עֲלֵי־אֹרַח
that bites the horse's heels (17bA)	הַנֹּשֵׁךְ עִקְּבֵי־סוּס
so that the rider falls backwards. (17bB)	וַיִּפֹּל רֹכְבוֹ אָחוֹר

[For your salvation I am waiting, YHWH!] (18)	[לִישׁוּעָתְךָ קִוִּיתִי יהוה]

. . . . [ס]

II.A.ii.1

Gad — when raiders will raid him, (19A)	גָּד גְּדוּד יְגוּדֶנּוּ
he will raid their heels! (19B)	וְהוּא יָגֻד עֲקֵבָם(!)

. . . . ס

II.A.iii.1

Asher — may fatness be his food, (20A)   אָשֵׁר(!) שְׁמֵנָה לַחְמוֹ

  and let he bring forth royal delicacies. (20B)   וְהוּא יִתֵּן מַעֲדַנֵּי־מֶלֶךְ

                                 ס

II.B.i.1

May Naphtali be a lambing ewe, (21A)   נַפְתָּלִי אִילָה(!) שְׁלֻחָה(!)

  that brings forth lovely lambs. (21B)   הַנֹּתֵן אִמְרֵי־שָׁפֶר

. . . . ס

II.B.ii.1

A young bullcalf is Joseph, (22aA)   בֵּן פֹּרָת(!) יוֹסֵף

  a bullcalf next to a well, (22aB)   בֵּן פֹּרָת(!) עֲלֵי־עָיִן

in the meadow he will stride towards the Bull, (22bA)   בָּנוֹת צָעֲדָה עֲלֵי־שׁוֹר(!!)

  and he will make him strong so they will become
                  numerous. (23aB)   וַיְמָרֲרֻהוּ(!) וָרֹבּוּ

II.B.ii.2

And (if) archers will harass him, (23bA)   וַיִּשְׂטְמֻהוּ(!) בַּעֲלֵי חִצִּים

  his bow will remain stable, (24aB)   וַתֵּשֶׁב בְּאֵיתָן קַשְׁתּוֹ

    and the arms of his hands become nimble, (24aC)   וַיָּפֹזּוּ זְרֹעֵי יָדָיו

by the hands of the Strong One of Jacob, (24bA)   מִידֵי אֲבִיר יַעֲקֹב

  by the name of the Shepherd of Israel's stone (24bB)   מִשָּׁם(!) רֹעֶה אֶבֶן יִשְׂרָאֵל

II.B.ii.3

By El, your Father, who will help you, (25aA)   מֵאֵל אָבִיךָ וְיַעְזְרֶךָּ

  and by Shadday, who will bless you, (25aB)   וְאֵת שַׁדַּי וִיבָרְכֶךָּ

with blessings of the Heavens above, (25bA)   בִּרְכֹת שָׁמַיִם מֵעָל

  blessings of the Flood, resting below, (25bB)   בִּרְכֹת תְּהוֹם רֹבֶצֶת תָּחַת

  blessings of breasts and womb. (25bC)   בִּרְכֹת שָׁדַיִם וָרָחַם

II.B.ii.4

The blessings of your Father prevail (26aA)   בִּרְכֹת אָבִיךָ גָּבְרוּ

  over the blessings of the eternal mountains, (26aB)   עַל־בִּרְכֹת הָרַי(!) עַד

    the longings of the everlasting hills. (26aC)   תַּאֲוַת גִּבְעֹת עוֹלָם

May they be on the head of Joseph, (26bA)   תִּהְיֶין לְרֹאשׁ יוֹסֵף

  and on the skull of one set apart of his brothers. (26bB)   וּלְקָדְקֹד נְזִיר אֶחָיו

. . . . פ

II.B.iii.1

Benjamin is a wolf, who will tear apart, (27A)   בִּנְיָמִין זְאֵב יִטְרָף

  in the morning he will devour the prey, (27B)   בַּבֹּקֶר יֹאכַל עַד

    and in the evening he will divide the spoil." (27C)   וְלָעֶרֶב יְחַלֵּק שָׁלָל

II.B.iii.2

All these are the twelve tribes of Israel, (28aA)	כָּל־אֵלֶּה שִׁבְטֵי יִשְׂרָאֵל שְׁנֵים עָשָׂר
And this is what their father said to them, when he blessed them, (28bA)	וְזֹאת אֲשֶׁר־דִּבֶּר לָהֶם אֲבִיהֶם וַיְבָרֶךְ אוֹתָם
each according his blessing he blessed them. (28bB)	אִישׁ אֲשֶׁר כְּבִרְכָתוֹ בֵּרַךְ אֹתָם

2.13.2 The Formal Structure of the "Blessing"

The preceding text shows next to the strophic delimitation, defended in the preceding sections of this chapter, a division into canticles, sub-cantos and cantos.[952] The delimitation of the canticles has in fact already affected the preceding sections, because in each section we discussed one canticle, which coincides with a saying on a tribe. This division was defended with reference to the *setumah* and *petuhah* and does not need further elaboration here.

The next step is to set out the delimitation of the (sub-)cantos. It is possible to make a division of the text based mainly on the contents, namely, between the sons of Leah (six) and the other sons (also six). Such a division might function as the main structuring pattern of the text providing two cantos of similar length, namely eleven strophes (see below). In this connection we might also recall the fact that Sarna emphasizes the chiastic structuring of the tribes according to their mothers:[953]

LEAH — Bilhah–Zilpah ‖ Zilpah–Bilhah — RACHEL

Although this division does not tally completely with our analysis of the macrostructure, Sarna's observation clearly demonstrates that this listing has been built up very carefully.

An additional sub-division is possible next to this one, namely the one occuring in several other listings of the twelve tribes: the tribes grouped by threes.[954] This is especially evident in the case of the first three tribes, who are all cursed, in contrast to the first tribe of the following triad: Judah. As additional structuring elements the following might be mentioned:[955]

---

[952] For the definition of these terms, cf. section 2.1.2, above.

[953] Sarna, *Genesis*, 331; similarly: Wenham, *Genesis 16–50*, 469; Jagersma, *Genesis 25–50*, 256–7.

[954] Cf. esp. Num. 2:3–31; 10:14–28. Cf. also J.C. de Moor, "The Twelve Tribes in the Song of Deborah", *VT* 43 (1993) 483–94, 492–4.

[955] Here we only list some significant features. Additional parallelisms and extra

1. Sub-canto I.A is joined together by the inclusion of יַעֲקֹב "Jacob" (1aA; 7aC), but also the responsion[956] of the pair יַעֲקֹב and יִשְׂרָאֵל "Jacob and Israel" (2a; 7aC). Also important is the antithetic parallelism הָאָסְפוּ "gather" (1aB) with אֲחַלְּקֵם and וַאֲפִיצֵם (7aC). Also worth noting is the identical order of syntactical elements mentioned before in the section on the verbal tenses.

2. Sub-canto I.B is held together by the parallels between יִשְׁתַּחֲוּוּ "shall bow" (8bB), יִקְּהַת "obedience" (10bB) || עֹבֵד "serving" (15bB); רָבַץ (9bA) || רֹבֵץ (14B).[957]

3. Sub-canto II.A is formed by means of the repetitive parallelism of עִקְּבֵי (17bA) || עֲקֵבָם (19B), and וְהוּא (19B) || וְהוּא (20B).

4. Sub-canto II.B is held together by the use of animal metaphors (the two preceding strophes had no animal metaphor); moreover the parallelism of אַיָּלָה (21A) || פָּרָת (22aA) is quite strong.[958] Finally the second and third canticle are linked by the recurrent use of the root ברך.

The following tables provide a survey of the statistics from the analysis presented in the foregoing sections. These tables will be followed by a more thorough presentation of the poetic structure and a discussion of the results.

Canto	Sub-canto	Canticle	Strophe	Verses
I	A	i	1	2 (3+2)
			2	2 (3+3)
		ii	1	2 (2+2)
			2	2 (2+3)
I	B	i	1	2 (2+2)
			2	2 (2+2)
			3	2 (2+2)
			4	3 (2+2+2)
		ii	1	2 (1+2)
		iii	1	1 (2)
			2	2 (2+2)

arguments for parallelism etc. will be discussed below, in the sections "The Poetic Structure of ...".

[956] The term "responsion" is used to describe the phenomenon that parallel words, suffixes, etc. in a poetic text have corresponding positions in different strophes, canticles, etc.

[957] In Num. 2:3–8, these tribes are also grouped together.

[958] Cf. the discussion below.

Canto	Sub-canto	Canticle	Strophe	Verses
II	A	i	1	1 (2)
			2	2* (2+2[+1])
		ii	1	1 (2)
		iii	1	1 (2)
II	B	i	1	1 (2)
		ii	1	2 (2+2)
			2	2 (3+2)
			3	2 (2+3)
			4	2 (3+2)
		iii	1	1 (3)
			2	2 (1+2)

These data can be summarized as follows:

Canto I		Canto II	
Sub-canto A	Sub-canto B	Sub-canto A	Sub-canto B
Canticles: 2	Canticles: 3	Canticles: 3	Canticles: 3
Strophes: 4	Strophes: 7	Strophes: 4	Strophes: 7
Verses: 8	Verses: 14	Verses: 5	Verses: 13

Canto	Subtotals			
I	2 subcantos	5 canticles	11 strophes	22 verses
II	2 subcantos	6 canticles	11 strophes	18 verses
Totals:	4 subcantos	11 canticles	22 strophes	40 verses

The second table shows that there is a strong correspondence between canto I and canto II. The regularity of the number of canticles is disturbed by the joint saying for Simeon and Levi, which also results in an odd number of canticles. However, the identical number of strophes in the corresponding sub-cantos (I.A and II.A both contain four strophes; I.B and II.B both seven strophes) is remarkable, whereas the identical number of strophes within a sub-canto (eleven) and the number of canticles in the whole canto (eleven) is also significant. However, next to such formal features of this blessing, is the poetic structure, based on parallelism, which is of fundamental importance for our understanding of the structure of the text. For this reason these features will be discussed below.

2.13.3   The Poetic Structure of Canto I

2.13.3.1   Sub-canto I.A

Parallelism of Canticle I.A.i and I.A.ii

הֵאָסְפוּ (1aB) ;(7aC) יִשְׂרָאֵל ‖ (2aB) יִשְׂרָאֵל ;(7aC) יַעֲקֹב ‖ (7aC); יַעֲקֹב (1aA; 2aA) יַעֲקֹב
‖ בְּקֹהֲלָם (6aB); הִקָּבְצוּ (2aA) ‖ בִּקְהָלָם (6aB);[959] עֹז (3aC) ‖ עֹז (7aA);[960]
אֵל (4aA) ‖ אֵל (6aA) ‖ אֵל (6aB) ‖ כִּי (4aB) ‖ כִּי (6bA) ‖ כִּי (7aA) ‖ כִּי
(7aB); הֵאָסְפוּ (1aB) ‖ וַאֲפִיצֵם ... אֲחַלְּקֵם (7aC)

2.13.3.2   Sub-canto I.B

Canticle I.B.i and I.B.ii

רָבַץ (9bA) ‖ יִשְׁכֹּן (13aA).[961]

Canticle I.B.i and I.B.iii

בְּעָרְפְּ (8bA) ‖ שְׁכֶם (15bA);[962] רָבַץ (9bA) ‖ רֹבֵץ (14B);[963] יְקָהַת (10bB)
‖ עֹבֵד (15bB);[964] עִירֹה (11aA) ‖ אֲתֹנוֹ (11aB) ‖ חֲמֹר (14A).[965]

Canticle I.B.ii and I.B.iii

יָמִים (13aA) ‖ הָאָרֶץ (15aB);[966] יִשְׁכֹּן (13aA) ‖ רֹבֵץ (14B); וְהוּא לְ– (13bA)
‖ וַיְהִי לְ– (15bB).

2.13.3.3   Parallelism of Sub-canto I.A and Sub-canto I.B

Canticle I.A.i and I.B.i

יַעֲקֹב (2aA) ‖ יִשְׂרָאֵל (2aB) ‖ יְהוּדָה (8aA);[967] בְּנֵי (1aA) ‖ בְּנֵי (2aA) ‖
(8bB) ‖ בְּנֵי (11aB); אֲבִיכֶם (2aB) ‖ אָבִיךְ (4aB) ‖ אָבִיךְ (8bB); אַתָּה (3aA)
‖ מִשְׁכְּבֵי (4aB) ‖ עָלִיתָ (9aB); עָלִיתָ (4aB) ‖ לֹא (10aA); אֵל (4aA) ‖ אַתָּה
(8aA); עָלִיתָ (4aB) ‖ רָבַץ (9bA).[968]

Canticle I.A.i and I.B.ii

כַּמַּיִם (4aA) ‖ יָמִים (13aA);[969] מִשְׁכְּבֵי (4aB) ‖ יִשְׁכֹּן (13aA);[970] יְצוּעִי (4aC)

---

[959] For אֹסֶף ‖ קָבַץ ‖ קָהָל see Joel 2:16; for קבץ with object קָהָל see Ezra 10:1.
[960] Cf. Ps. 68:29, 35.
[961] For the external parallelism of these verbs, see Isa. 13:20–21 (twice).
[962] Although these two words do not occur in parallelism, they alternate with one another in the expression הִפְנָה שְׁכֶם/עֹרֶף "they turned their backs" (resp. 1 Sam. 10:9 and Jer. 32:33; 48:39; cf. *HAL*, 1385.
[963] For this parallelism cf. Isa. 11:6–7; 13:20–21; Ezek. 34:14–15; Zeph. 2:14–15.
[964] These words are more or less synonymous; cf. p. 134, with nn. 311–312 and p. 138, n. 324.
[965] This triplet is found in Zech. 9:9. For חֲמוֹר ‖ אָתוֹן see Gen. 12:16; 45:23 (prose).
[966] See Dahood, Penar, "Ugaritic-Hebrew Parallel Pairs", 122–123 (# 64).
[967] For this triplet, cf. *e.g.* Isa. 48:1; Mic. 1:5. For the parallelism of יְהוּדָה ‖ יִשְׂרָאֵל see e.g. Isa. 5:7; 11:12; Jer. 3:8; 5:11; Hos. 4:15; Pss. 76:2; 114:2.
[968] Cf. Job 11:18–19.
[969] See Isa. 17:12; 43:16; 57:20; Ezek. 27:26, 34; Nah. 3:8; Hab. 3:15; Pss. 77:20; 78:13; 93:4; 107:23; Prov. 8:29.
[970] Cf. the fact that in Gen. 35:22, where the misbehaviour of Reuben is narrated,

‖ יִשְׁכֹּן (13aA).[971]

Canticle I.A.i and I.B.iii

כִּי (4aB) ‖[973] גֶּרֶם ‖ (14A) עָז (3aC) ;[972] וַיֵּרֶא ‖ (15aA) וְשָׁמְעוּ (2aA)
מִנְחָה ‖ (4aB) מִשְׁכְּבֵי [974];(14B) רֹבֵץ ‖ (4aB) עָלִיתָ (4aB); כִּי ‖ (7aB) | כִּי (7aA)
(15aA);[975] מִשְׁכְּבֵי (4aB) ‖ רֹבֵץ (14B).

Canticle I.A.ii and I.B.i

תָּבֹא (6aA) אָחִים (5aA) ‖ אַחֶיךָ (8aB); אֶל (6aA) | אֶל (6aB) ‖ לֹא (10aA);
יָבֹא ‖ (10bA); כַּבְדִּי (6aB) ‖ יִשְׁתַּחֲווּ (8bB);[976] אָרוּר (7aA) ‖ יוֹדוּךָ (8aB);[977]
יִשְׂרָאֵל ... יַעֲקֹב (7aC) ‖ יְהוּדָה (8aA).[978]

Canticle I.A.ii and I.B.ii

תָּבֹא (6aA) ‖ יִשְׁכֹּן (13aA);[979] יִשְׂרָאֵל (7aC) ‖ צִידֹן (13bB).

Canticle I.A.ii and I.B.iii

כִּי (6bA) | כִּי (7aA) | כִּי (7aB) ‖ כִּי (15aA) | כִּי (15aB); שׁוֹר (6bB) ‖ חֲמֹר
(14A);[980] עָז (7aA) ‖ גֶּרֶם (14A).

2.13.4   The Poetic Structure of Canto II

2.13.4.1   Sub-canto II.A

Parallelism of Canticle II.A.i and II.A.ii

עִקְבֵי (17bA) ‖ עֲקֵבָם (19B).

Canticle II.A.ii and II.A.iii

וְהוּא (19B) ‖ וְהוּא (20B); יָגֻד (19B) ‖ יִתֵּן (20B).[981]

2.13.4.2   Sub-canto II.B

Canticle II.B.i and II.B.ii

אַיָּלָה (21A) ‖ פֹּרָת (22aA; aB).[982]

---

the root of מִשְׁכְּבֵי, viz. שׁכב "to lie down" is used next to שׁכן "to dwell".

[971] Cf. Ps. 139:8–9, where יצע is found in ext. parallelism with שׁכן.

[972] For שׁמע ‖ ראה, see Roersma, "The First-Born of Abraham", 237.

[973] This parallelism is based on the meaning of both words here, namely, "strong".

[974] See Gen. 49:9!

[975] See Isa. 57:2 where the root נחה is used with the prepositional object מִשְׁכְּבוֹתָם.

[976] For this parallelism (or probably better: semantically related words), cf. Dahood, Penar, "Ugaritic-Hebrew Parallel Pairs", 175 (# 174); cf. also J.C. de Moor, P. van der Lugt, "The Spectre of Pan-Ugaritism", *BiOr* 31 (1974) 3–26, 13.

[977] Antithetical parallelism; cf. Jer. 20:13–14, where a similar antithetic parallelism is found with הלל. ארר is used mostly in antithetic parallelism with ברך.

[978] Cf. n. 967 above.

[979] For the parallel usage, mostly in a synthetic parallelism, see Mic. 4:10; Zech. 2:14; 8:8; Job 24:3.

[980] Cf. e.g. Isa. 1:3; 32:20 (syndetic parataxis); Job 24:3.

[981] Grammatical parallelism.

[982] This parallelism is based on the proposed interpretation of אַיָּלָה; cf. for this pair the male forms פַּר ‖ אַיִל, which are many times counted in sevenfold, see

Canticle II.B.ii and II.B.iii

כְּבִרְכָתוֹ (28bA) | וִיבָרְכֶךָ (25aB) | בִּרְכַּת (25bA; bB; bC; 26aA; aB) || וַיְבָרֶךְ (28bA) | בֵּרַךְ (28bB); אָבִיךָ (25aA) | אָבִיךָ (26aA) || אֲבִיהֶם (28bA).

2.13.4.3 Parallelism of Sub-canto II.A and Sub-canto II.B

Canticle II.A.i and II.B.ii

יָדָן (16A) || וַיְמָרֲרֻהוּ (23aB);[983] יְהִי (17aA) || תִּהְיֶין (26bA); עֲלֵי (17aA) | עֲלֵי (17aB) || עֲלֵי (22aB) | עֲלֵי (22bA).

Canticle II.A.i and II.B.iii

כָּל־אֵלֶּה שִׁבְטֵי יִשְׂרָאֵל שְׁנֵים עָשָׂר (16B) || כְּאַחַד שִׁבְטֵי יִשְׂרָאֵל (28aA).

Canticle II.A.iii and II.B.ii

וְהוּא יִתֵּן (20B) || הַנֹּתֵן (21B).

2.13.5 Parallelism in the Blessing

In addition to the parallelism between strophes I.A.i.1 and II.B.iii.2, listed above in section 2.12.2.1, the following parallelisms are found between the two cantos:[984]

2.13.5.1 Canto I with Canto II

Canticle I.A.i

בָּנָיו (1aA) || בֶּן (22aA, aB); הַיָּמִים (1aC) || בְּנִימִן (27A) | בַּבֹּקֶר (27B) | וְלָעֶרֶב (27C);[985] יַעֲקֹב (2aA) | יִשְׂרָאֵל (2aB) || יַעֲקֹב (24bA) | יִשְׂרָאֵל (24bB); יִשְׂרָאֵל (2aB) || יִשְׂרָאֵל (16B); אֲבִיכֶם (2aB) | אָבִיךָ (4aB) || אָבִיךָ (25aA; 26aA) | אֲבִיהֶם (28bA); וְרֵאשִׁית (3aB) || לְרֹאשׁ (26bA).[986]

Canticle I.A.ii

אַחִים (5aA) || אֶחָיו (26bB); שׁוֹר (6bB) || שׁוֹר (22bA); אָרוּר (7aA) || בֵרַךְ (root: 25aB, bA, bB, bC; 26aA, aB);[987] יַעֲקֹב (7aC) || יַעֲקֹב ... יִשְׂרָאֵל ... יִשְׂרָאֵל (24bA) | יִשְׂרָאֵל (24bB); יִשְׂרָאֵל (7aC) || יִשְׂרָאֵל (16B).

Num. 23:1, 29; Ezek. 45:23; Job 42:8.

[983] Parallelism is based on the emended text; cf. our discussion *ad.loc.*

[984] The parallelisms are listed from each canticle of canto I with canto II, and *visa versa.*

[985] This parallelism is partly based on the suggested pun with the name Benjamin (cf. section 2.12.1 above), in the sense of "between the days". The parallelism with בַּבֹּקֶר and וְלָעֶרֶב remains nevertheless unaffected when this pun would not be present. For the triplet יוֹם || בֹּקֶר || עֶרֶב, see Dan. 8:26 (although in prose). For the pair יוֹם || בֹּקֶר cf. Isa. 17:11; 28:19; 38:13; Amos 4:4; 5:8; Pss. 73:14; 90:14. The pair יוֹם || עֶרֶב is found in Jer. 6:4; and for יוֹמָם || עֶרֶב in Ezek. 12:4, 7.

[986] Because רֵאשִׁית is derived from רֹאשׁ (cf. *HAL*, 1091), this parallelism is justified; cf. Prov. 8:22–23, and probably also Amos 6:6–7.

[987] Antithetical parallelism.

Canticle I.B.i

מְטֹרָף (8aB) ‖ אֶחָיו (26bB); גּוּר אַרְיֵה (9aA) ‖ בֶּן פֹּרָת (22aA, aB); אָחִיךְ
(9aB) ‖ יִטְרָף (27A); בְּנִי (9aB) ‖ בֵּן (22aA, aB); שֵׁבֶט (10aA) ‖ שִׁבְטֵי
(16B); עַמִּים (10bB) ‖ עַמּוֹ (16A); בְּנִי אֲתֹנוֹ (11aB) ‖ בֶּן פֹּרָת (22aA, aB);
עֵינַיִם (12A) ‖ עֵין (22aB).

Canticle I.B.ii

וְהוּא (13bA) ‖ וְהוּא (19B; 20B).

Canticle I.B.iii

וַיְהִי (15bB) ‖ יְהִי (17aA) | תִּהְיֶין (26bA).

2.13.5.2   Canto II with Canto I

Canticle II.A.i

יִשְׂרָאֵל (16B) ‖ יִשְׂרָאֵל (16B) ‖ שֵׁבֶט (10aA); שִׁבְטֵי (16B) ‖ עַמִּים (10bB); עַמּוֹ (16A) ‖ יִשְׂרָאֵל
(2aB; 7aC); יְהִי (17aA) ‖ וַיְהִי (15bB).

Canticle II.A.ii

וְהוּא (19B) ‖ וְהוּא (13bA).

Canticle II.A.iii

וְהוּא (20B) ‖ וְהוּא (13bA).

Canticle II.B.ii

גּוּר אַרְיֵה (22aA, aB) ‖ בָּנָיו (1aA) | בְּנִי (9aB); בֶּן פֹּרָת (22aA, aB) ‖ בֵּן
(9aA) | בְּנִי אֲתֹנוֹ (11aB); עֵין (22aB) ‖ עֵינַיִם (12A); שׁוֹר (22bA) ‖ שׁוֹר
(6bB); יַעֲקֹב (24bA) | יִשְׂרָאֵל (24bB) ‖ יַעֲקֹב (2aA; 7aC) | יִשְׂרָאֵל (2aB;
7aC); אָבִיךְ (25aA; 26aA) ‖ אֲבִיכֶם (2aB) | אָבִיךָ (4aB); ברך (root: 25aB,
bA, bB, bC; 26aA, aB) ‖ אָרוּר (7aA); תִּהְיֶין (26bA) ‖ וַיְהִי (15bB); לְרֹאשׁ
(26bA) ‖ וְרֵאשִׁית (3aB); אָחִיו (26bB) ‖ אַחִים (5aA) | אָחִיךְ (8aB).

Canticle II.B.iii

בִּנְיָמִין (27A) | בַּבֹּקֶר (27B) | וְלָעֶרֶב (27C) ‖ הַיָּמִים (1aC); יִטְרָף (27A) ‖
מְטֹרָף (9aB).

2.13.6   Observations on the Macrostructure

The analysis of the poetic structure as listed above gives some remarkable results, which will now be discussed. It is usually assumed that the Blessing was made up of several independent sayings, gathered and inserted here in the deathbed episode by a certain "editor" (J, P, R^P) provided with a framework (verses 1–2 and 28). The poetic analysis does not confirm this assumption, it even might contradict this assertion in certain respects, though not conclusive. We will recapitulate the facts here.

The framework, written as narrative poetry, proves to form a strong frame around the factual Blessing (verses 3–27) as was shown already in section 2.12.2.1. However, the parallelism of the framework is not only confined to the framework itself, other relationships are also present. Strophe I.A.i.1 contains the pair יִשְׂרָאֵל ‖ יַעֲקֹב, returning in verses 7 and 24. Furthermore, the family relationship is emphasized in the framework (בָּנָיו v. 1aA; בְּנֵי v. 2aA; אֲבִיכֶם v. 2aB; אֲבִיהֶם v. 28bA) as well as in the sayings (בְּכֹרִי v. 3aA; אָבִיךְ v. 4aB; בְּנֵי אָבִיךְ v. 8bB;[988] cf. also the use of אַחִים v. 5aA; אָחִיו v. 8aB; אֶחָיו v. 26bB), while other word-pairs could be mentioned too. The final strophe II.B.iii.2 is not only linked to the first strophe (I.A.i.1), but, as was stated before, has a strong parallel with strophe II.A.i.1: כָּל־אֵלֶּה (16B) ‖ כְּאַחַד שִׁבְטֵי יִשְׂרָאֵל שִׁבְטֵי יִשְׂרָאֵל שְׁנֵים עָשָׂר (28aA); whereas the root ברך is used frequently in strophes II.B.ii.3–4 and furthermore only in strophe II.B.iii.2. It appears, therefore, that the framework was not just composed as a loose introduction to the Blessing, but that the framework and Blessing are strongly interrelated.

Another aspect the analysis shows, is that there are many verbal parallels between the first three sayings mutually and with the other sayings, especially in the Dan and Joseph sayings. The fact that the first three sayings (Reuben, Simeon & Levi and Judah) together with the saying on Joseph are related, has already been observed by Eissfeldt.[989] When we take a look at the relationship between canto II and canto I, the number of parallels between canticle II.B.ii and canto I, and especially canticle I.A.i–ii and I.B.i, is at least remarkable and seems to confirm Eissfeldt's observations.

The parallelisms of the Joseph-saying are all the more remarkable because parallelisms with the other sayings in canto II are almost absent. The only relationship that is found is with canticle II.A.i, the Dan-saying (יְהִי ‖ תִּהְיֶן; יָדֻן ‖ וַיְמָרֲרֻהוּ; עֲלֵי | עֲלֵי ‖ עֲלֵי | עֲלֵי), and with strophe II.B.iii.2 (the final framework strophe). The relation of the Joseph-saying with strophes II.A.i.1 and II.B.iii.2 is noteworthy again, because the most important verbal repetitions from canto I in canto II are found next to the Joseph-saying in the Dan-saying and in the final strophe (which itself is also strongly related to the Dan-saying). The exceptional position of the Joseph-saying might also be seen from the way each saying starts with the name of Jacob's sons. Each saying begins first with the name of the son, in a *casus pendens*

---

[988] In vv. 25aA and 26aA there is also a reference made to אָבִיךְ, but it seems to refer to a deity, or a deified ancestor. So, although it offers parallels for the structural analysis, it is not listed here.

[989] Cf. section 1.3.6 above.

construction or as the subject of the clause. The only exception is found in the saying on Joseph which starts with בֵּן פֹּרָת יוֹסֵף "a young bullcalf is Joseph" (v. 22aA). This syntax is further only used in the *second* strophe on Judah, where we read: גּוּר אַרְיֵה יְהוּדָה "a lion's whelp is Judah" (v. 9aA), whereas the first strophe (v. 8) applies the common pattern of the other sayings. This significant difference in syntax with the other sayings might be an indication of the different character of the Joseph-saying. In each case, it appears that canticle II.B.ii with the Joseph-saying is placed rather loosely within canto II, related only to canto I and to strophes II.A.i.1 and II.B.iii.2.

The canticle containing the Dan-saying is in fact rather important within the whole composition. The canticle not only has some parallels with the larger canticles (I.A.i–ii; I.B.i; II.B.ii; II.B.iii), but also with the smaller canticles. It forms a link in the chain of parallels which these smaller canticles form together:

I.B.ii:	וְהוּא לְ–				
I.B.iii:	וַיְהִי לְ–	וַיְהִי			
II.A.i:		יְהִי	עֲקֵבִי		
II.A.ii:			עֲקֵבָם	וְהוּא	
II.A.iii:				וְהוּא	וְהוּא יִתֵּן
II.B.i:					הַנֹּתֵן

This linking of the different canticles is striking, and is strengthened by the use of "responsions"[990] of these repetitions (except for היה in vv. 15bB and 17aA). This parallelism of the smaller canticles is not just coincidence, the verbal repetitions are found also on other levels,[991] because other word-pairs are used throughout the Blessing and the strong regularity in the composition point in the direction of a carefully composed work of art. It appears, therefore, that the Blessing together with its framework, has been composed with considerable skill and attention to detail. The idea of originally independent sayings brought together and inserted here, with the framework added to it, is difficult to maintain in the light of these observations.

On the other hand there are some important differences, not shown directly by the listing of the many parallels present in the text. It was already indicated above that the references to the family relationship occurred in the framework and the Blessing. An important parallelism was the one caused by the noun אָב "father". However, we mentioned

---

[990] For this term, cf. above, p. 233, n. 956.

[991] Cf. the repetitions of רבץ (9bA, 14B); וְהוּא (13bA, 19B; 20B); טרף (9aB; 27A).

already the difference in the use of this noun in the framework and the sayings of Reuben and Judah on one side, and in that of Joseph on the other.[992] In the Joseph-saying the word אָב is used as an epithet, or at least as a designation for a deified ancestor, whereas in the other sayings the noun is used in its normal human meaning "father". At several points these differences in meaning are present: בֵּן is found in v. 22aAB, but contrary to the use of this noun in verses 1aA and 9aB, the noun does not express a family relationship, but was used in a metaphor: בֵּן פָּרָת "young bullcalf" and the phrase of verse 22aA is in fact only parallel to verse 9aA: גּוּר אַרְיֵה יְהוּדָה "a lion's whelp is Judah"; while a similar genitive construction with בֵּן is found in verse 11aB: בְּנִי אֲתֹנוֹ "his ass's colt". In verses 6bB and 22bA(emendation) the noun שׁוֹר "bull" is used, but whereas the metaphor in verse 6 is at the human level ("prince"), in verse 22 it is a designation for a deity, thus comparable to the different use of אָב. In verse 26bB the word אֶחָיו "his brothers" is used, which is in fact comparable to the use of אַחֶיךָ in verse 8aB. Finally, the word-pair יִשְׂרָאֵל ‖ יַעֲקֹב "Jacob ‖ Israel" is also found in verse 2a and 7aC, whereas יִשְׂרָאֵל "Israel" is also used in verses 16B and 28aA. There is a remarkable difference in use of the name "Israel" here, because the framework suggests in verse 28 that "Israel" is a people, which had "Israel" as its ancestor (verse 2aB). The idea of the "people" Israel returns in verse 7aC once more, but is absent in verse 24b where "Israel" is used for the dying patriarch. When these data are combined with the observations given above on the parallels between the Joseph-saying and the other parts of canto II, it is remarkable that this saying is connected rather loosely with the rest of the Blessing. Furthermore, the relatively large number of epithets in verses 24–26, which have no parallels in the rest of the Blessing, marks off the saying of Joseph from the other sayings as a different kind.

Summarizing, it can be concluded that on the basis of the analysis of the poetic structure Genesis 49 forms a much more coherent unity than is commonly credited to it. Verbal repetitions and word-pairs are present throughout the Blessing and suggest the hand of a very skilled composer. This composer (editor or author) knew how to relate framework and Blessing in a very artful way. On the other hand, although many parallels occur, the Joseph-saying is a kind of *Fremdkörper* within the Blessing, since its parallels with other parts of canto II are rather weak, whereas other parallels are partly based on words with other meanings.

---

[992]Cf. above, p. 239, n 988.

2.14   Rendering the Verbal Tenses: Summary

At the end of this chapter a short overview of the rendering of the verbal tenses seems to be a requisite. In section 2.2.1.1 it was suggested that Gen. 49:1b is the interpretatival context for the whole "blessing": the patriarch will tell his sons what will happen to them in later days. When we take a look at the modern Bible translations we discover that this line is followed *grosso modo*. However, when we look at the rendering of the tenses in the commentaries it is remarkable that some scholars render the *yiqtol* form in most cases as a present tense and not as a future form — though from verse 8 on.[993] The results of our own rendering can be found in the table at the end of this chapter. In this table we have listed the following elements:

1. the type of the main clause: nominal (49:3A), verbal (49:4A) or neither of them (49:16B);

2. the verbal form, when present: *qatal* (49:4B), *yiqtol* (49:7c) (jussive; 49:4A), *w^e yiqtol* (49:25aA), *wayyiqtol* (49:15aA), participle (49:7A), infinitive (49:22bA), or that ellipsis has taken place (49:7B);

3. the tense (or form) in which it was rendered: past (49:4B), present (49:3A), future (49:4A) (alternatively optative [49:7A]);

4. the evidence for this rendering: is this rendering grammatically certain (+) (49:3A), are other interpretations possible which might be sometimes even more obvious (±) (49:9aB), or is the evidence derived from the context (cont.) (49:8bA);

5. finally the scope of a strophe is listed: is it future, present or past? This scope is not the sum of all the verbal tenses in a strophe, but an indication for the intention of the speaker: had he in mind to say something concerning the future, present or past? To this interpretation a short sigla is added to indicate if this interpretation is obvious (+) or that other interpretations are equally possible (±).

These findings can be summarized as follows. In most strophes (fifteen out of twenty) the scope is obviously the future even though references to the present and/or past are found (for example 49:3–4). In three

---

[993] Cf. *e.g.* Gunkel, *Genesis*, 480–7; Zobel, *SuG*, 4–6; Westermann, *Genesis 37–50*, 247–8.

strophes the scope is in our view also the future, but other interpretations cannot be excluded. Finally, in two strophes (one saying: Issachar) a present rendering was defended because this seems the most likely one, although we assume with some other scholars a future force in the second strophe. The interpretation of the complete text results in our view in a "blessing", which has indeed the future situation of the tribes in mind. Even if one would be inclined to render some of the verbs in another way than we did (see 49:9, 22bA–23aB), the scope of the *complete* sayings is still the future. In view of the synchronic reading of the text this conclussion is important because it fits in with the short remark by the patriarch that he will announce his sons the future (49:1b). The bold remark by Holzinger, quoted above,[994] that we are not dealing here with predictions, is refuted therefore at a synchronic level. However, some sayings are poly-interpretable and might be rendered in another way when separated from their context. This possibility can certainly not be excluded, but this holds true for only a small number of sayings, or parts of them (49:9, 14–15, 21, 22bA–23aB). So it appears that at a diachronic level Holzinger's statement may be right in only a small number of cases. However, this matter will be discussed more thoroughly in Chapters Three and Six on the genre and on the diachronic analysis.

2.15 Recapitulation

1. In the first saying Reuben is rebuked for having laid with his father's concubine. As the oldest son he turned out to be unreliable in his father's estimation and is therefore called פַּחַז כַּמַּיִם "deceptive like water" (4aA), because he defiled יְצוּעִי עָלָה "the concubine's couch" (4aC). The word עָלָה is interpreted with the help of Arabic, where the word *'lh* means "concubine".

2. The second saying contains the rebuke directed to Simeon and Levi because they slaughtered Shechem. Shechem, the prince of the city is named in the rebuke שׁוֹר "bull", which is a common epithet for princes in ancient Near Eastern culture. מְכֵרֹתֵיהֶם (5aB) denotes "their knives", if this word is derived from the root כרת "to cut", with the preformative מ, indicating an instrument for cutting, *viz.* "knife".

3. In the saying on Judah a pun is made on his name by means of the root ידי hiph. "to praise". It might be incorrect to use

---

[994]See above, p. 92, n. 66.

this pun for etymological purposes, since there remain some grammatical problems; a more likely etymology is to derive the word from the root הוד "to be majesty".

4. The well-known enigma in verse 10bA שִׁילה is puzzling because of an incorrect vocalization of the word, while the word also proves to be built up of two independent words: שַׁי לה meaning "tribute to him". This interpretation matches the context well, because Judah receives the most important position among the brothers, where the three elder brothers receive rebukes. The description of Judah in this blessing in fact fits a king, since the text contains many reminiscences of the kingship of Solomon.

5. Contrary to the usual rendering of the Dan saying, deriving the verb in the first colon (16A) from דין "to judge", the verb is emended to יָדִן and derived from the root דנן "to be strong". This verb matches the context of the saying better, and also the birth-story of Dan (Gen. 30:6). In this way the saying expresses that, despite its small size, Dan will be strong like one of the tribes of Israel.

6. Naphtali is compared to a "ewe", אַיָּלה, the female form of אַיִל I, "ram" (vocalization according to LXX, who interpreted the word however as "terebinth"), bringing forth beautiful lambs.

7. The saying on Joseph contains the most problems for the translation of the text. Following the majority of scholars, the first strophe is interpreted as an animal metaphor. Decisive for the correct interpretation is, however, to read verse 23a as part of the first strophe. The verb מרר (v. 23aB) is interpreted as the D-stem of the root, meaning "to strengthen", comparable to Ugaritic usage. Understood in this way the saying compares Joseph to a young bull (פֶּר, 49:22) who is blessed and strengthened by the Bull (interpreting the consonants שׁור as שׁוּר, cf. Ug. ṯr), very probably the epithet of El.

8. The difficult phrase מִשָּׁם רֹעֶה אֶבֶן יִשְׂרָאֵל (24bB) is interpreted as a reference to the ancestor cult. אֶבֶן is not regarded as an epithet as is usual, but just as "stone", and more specifically "stele", set up for the deceased ancestor. In that sense רֹעֶה "Shepherd" is the protector of the stele of Israel.

9. It is suggested we link the DN שַׁדַּי with šd(y), known from the Umwelt (Phoenicia, Ugarit, Deir 'Alla). This deity is known as

a protective spirit, which in Ugarit appears to have some links with the ancestor cult but might also be connected there with Ba'lu, the "saviour god".

10. The analysis of the poetic structure of the Blessing suggests that both framework and Blessing form one well integrated unity. The framework is written in so-called "narrative poetry", which is different in style from the sayings, but is nevertheless poetry. The framework is connected with the sayings on Reuben, Simeon & Levi, Judah, Dan and Joseph by means of verbal repetitions.

11. The saying on Dan has a kind of key function being connected with the framework and the larger sayings as well as with the smaller sayings like a link in a chain.

12. The use of verbal repetition throughout the blessing is very noticeable. It is, however, most remarkable in the way the sayings from Zebulun, Issachar, Dan, Gad, Asher and Naphtali are linked together in a kind of chain.

13. Although the Joseph-saying has many parallels with the larger sayings, the loose place it has in its own canto, and the contents of the saying, do not suggest a firm interrelationship with the rest of the Blessing.

Name	Strophe	Verse	Clause	Verb	Tense	Evid.	Scope
Reuben	I.A.i.2	3A	nom.	—	pres.	+	
		3B	nom.	—	pres.	+	
		3C	nom.	—	pres.	+	
		4A	verb.	juss.	fut.	+	
		4B	verb.	*qat.*	past	+	
		4C	verb.	*qat.*	past	+	fut.$^+$
Simeon & Levi	I.A.ii.1	5A	nom.	—	pres.	+	
		5B	nom.	—	pres.	+	
		6aA	verb.	juss.	fut.	+	
		6aB	verb.	juss.	fut.	+	fut.$^+$
	I.A.ii.2	6bA	verb.	*qat.*	past	+	
		6bB	verb.	*qat.*	past	+	
		7A	nom.	part.	opt.	+	
		7B	nom.	ell.	opt.	+	
		7C	verb.	*yiqt.*	fut.	+	fut.$^+$
Judah	I.B.i.1	8aA	nom.	—	pres.	+	
		8aB	verb.	*yiqt.*	fut.	+	
		8bA	nom.	—	fut.	cont.	
		8bB	verb.	*yiqt.*	fut.	+	fut.$^+$
	I.B.i.2	9aA	nom.	—	pres.	+	
		9aB	verb.	*qat.*	opt.	±	
		9bA	verb.	*qat.*	fut.	±	
		9bB	verb.	*yiqt.*	fut.	+	fut.$^\pm$
	I.B.i.3	10aA	verb.	*yiqt.*	fut.	+	
		10aB	verb.	ell.	fut.	cont.	
		10bA	verb.	*yiqt.*	fut.	+	
		10bB	nom.	—	opt.	cont.	fut.$^+$
	I.B.i.4	11a	nom.	part.	opt.	cont.	
		11a	nom.	ell.	opt.	cont.	
		11b	verb.	*qat.*	opt.	cont.	
		11b	verb.	ell.	opt.	cont.	
		12	nom.	—	opt.	cont.	
		12	nom.	—	opt.	cont.	fut.$^+$
Zebulun	I.B.ii.1	13a	verb.	*yiqt.*	fut.	+	
		13b	nom.	—	opt.	cont.	
		13b	nom.	—	opt.	cont.	fut.$^+$
Issachar	I.B.iii.1	14A	nom.	—	pres.	+	
		14B	nom.	part.	pres.	+	pres$^+$
	I.B.iii.2	15aA	verb.	*way.*	pres.	cont.	
		15aB	verb.	ell.	pres.	cont.	
		15bA	verb.	*way.*	pres.	cont.	
		15bB	verb.	*way.*	pres.	cont.	pres.$^+$

Name	Strophe	Verse	Clause	Verb	Tense	Evid.	Scope
Dan	II.A.i.1	16A	verb.	*yiqt.*	fut.	+	
		16B	—	—	fut.	cont.	fut.$^+$
	II.A.i.2	17aA	verb.	juss.	opt.	+	
		17aB	verb.	ell.	opt.	cont.	
		17bA	nom.	part.	pres.	+	
		17bB	verb.	*way.*	pres.	+	fut.$^+$
Gad	II.A.ii.1	19A	verb.	*yiqt.*	fut.	+	
		19B	verb.	*yiqt.*	fut.	+	fut.$^+$
Asher	II.A.iii.1	20A	nom.	—	opt.	cont.	
		20B	verb.	*yiqt.*	fut.	+	fut.$^+$
Naphtali	II.B.i.1	21A	nom.	—	opt.	cont.	
		21B	nom.	part.	pres.	+	fut.$^\pm$
Joseph	II.B.ii.1	22a	nom.	—	pres.	+	
		22a	nom.	ell.	pres.	+	
		22bA	nom.	inf.	fut.	±	
		23aB	verb.	*way.*	fut.	±	fut.$^\pm$
	II.B.ii.2	23bA	verb.	$w^ey.$	fut.	±	
		24aB	verb.	*way.*	fut.	±	
		24aC	verb.	*way.*	fut.	±	
		24bA	—	—	—	cont.	
		24bB	—	—	—	cont.	fut.$^+$
	II.B.ii.3	25aA	verb.	$w^ey.$	fut.	+	
		25aB	verb.	$w^ey.$	fut.	+	
		25bA	—	—	—	+	
		25bB	—	—	—	+	
		25bC	—	—	—	+	fut.$^+$
	II.B.ii.4	26aA	verb.	*qat.*	pres.	+	
		26aB	—	—	pres.	+	
		26aC	—	—	pres.	+	
		26bA	verb.	juss.	opt.	+	
		26bB	verb.	ell.	opt.	+	fut.$^+$
Benjamin	II.B.iii.1	27A	verb.	*yiqt.*	fut.	+/±	
		27B	verb.	*yiqt.*	fut.	+/±	
		27C	verb.	*yiqt.*	fut.	+/±	fut.$^+$

TABLE: SURVEY OF VERBAL TENSES[995]

---

[995] Used abbreviations and sigla: nom. = nominal clause; verb. = verbal clause; *qat.* = *qatal*; *yiqt.* = *yiqtol*; $w^ey.$ = $w^eyiqtol$; *way.* = *wayyiqtol*; juss. = jussive; part. = participle; ell. = ellipsis; inf. = infinitive constructus; pres. = present; fut. = future; opt. = optative; evid. = evidence; cont. = contextual; + = certain, most obvious; ± = other interpretations are possible, and might be more obvious.

Chapter 3

Genesis 49: The Genre

3.1 Introduction

In Chapter One we concluded that a further discussion of the genre of Genesis 49 was necessary because the assumption that this text is a collection of so-called "tribal sayings" is questionable for several reasons. First of all some exegetes doubt that the sayings in Genesis 49 originated and circulated independently before they were included in our text. Secondly, as a consequence we must ask if the *Sitz im Leben* — a collective military operation or religious event — is defined correctly in earlier scholarly literature. Finally, the development from oral into written tradition (and the supposed differences between these two stages) is uncertain. It might, therefore, be asked if the supposed genre of the "tribal saying" exists, and if this definition is correct for Genesis 49.

The definition of the genre "tribal saying" is based mainly on some specific parts of the Hebrew Bible and on theoretical reconstructions of the development of Israel's literature. Unequivocal evidence from Israel's *Umwelt* for the existence of such a genre is virtually lacking in scholarly literature. As far as we are aware, H.-J. Zobel is the only one who refers to an extra-biblical text -an Arabic satire- as an example for the existence of tribal sayings.[1] For Zobel this reference is based on the supposition that there exists a certain degree of corresponding cultures between both nations, allowing us to make such a comparison.[2] However, the use of data derived from Arabian culture should be used cautiously, because Arabic literature is by no means representative of the world of ancient Israel,[3] and also there are important differences between the cultures of ancient Israel and the Arabian

---

[1]Zobel, *SuG*, 54, n. 6. He refers to B.R. Sanguinetti, "Satire contre les principales tribus Arabes: Extrait du *Raîhân al-Albâb*, Manuscrit Arabe de Leyde, n° 415, fol. 156 v°, i 58 v°", *JA* 5 (1853) 548–72.

[2]Zobel, *SuG*, 54: argues that in most sayings reference is made to events which are important to the tribe involved: the tribe and its experience are the main interest. This means, according to Zobel, that there is still a strong tribal consciousness, which is confirmed by a look at "similar occurrences of Arabic poetry", because there too the aim is the glorification of one's own tribe or the ridicule of the other. It is acknowledged here that "wir in den Stammessprüchen ein echtes Erbe aus der nomadischen Vergangenheit der israelitischen Stämme vor uns haben, wie es nach ihrem Überwechseln ins Kulturland noch geraume Zeit weiterlebte, ...".

[3]We have to reckon with a distance of at least a thousand years, cf. De Moor, *Mondelinge overlevering*, 4, 40, n. 10.

world.[4] For that reason we should look for the existence of this genre in the ancient Near East itself. If this genre did exist, it is likely that we will find some traces of it in Israel's *Umwelt*.

In order to find evidence of these traces, the literature of the Umwelt has been scanned comprehensible but not exhaustively. Legal texts were excluded, because these appear to be a genre in which tribal sayings are absent. Emphasis was placed on royal texts in which battles against other nations were reported, but also other literary texts such as myths, legends, etc. were scanned in order to find traces of this genre. However, the scan is necessarily a selective sample survey because of the enormous amount of literature which cannot be covered in the present study. For our survey we examined, apart from the common textbooks,[5] texts from Sumer,[6] ancient Mesopotamia in general,[7]

---

[4]Cf. C.H.J. de Geus, *The Tribes of Israel: An Investigation Into Some of the Presuppositions of Martin Noth's Amphictyony Hypothesis* (SSN, 12), Assen 1976, 150–156; N.P. Lemche, *Early Israel: Anthropological and Historical Studies on the Israelite Society before the Monarchy* (SVT, 37), Leiden 1985, 95–136.

[5]*ANET*; W. Beyerlin, *Religionsgeschichtliches Textbuch zum Alten Testament* (ATD.Erg, Bd. 1), Göttingen 1975; K. Galling (Hrsg.), *Textbuch zur Geschichte Israels*, Tübingen ³1979; *TUAT*, Bd. I–III; W.W. Hallo, K.L. Younger (eds.), *The Context of Scripture*, vol. I: *Canonical Compositions from the Biblical World*, Leiden 1997.

[6]J. van Dijk, *LUGAL UD ME-LÁM-bi NIR-ĜÁL: Le récit épique*, Leiden 1983; E.I. Gordon, *Sumerian Proverbs: Glimpses of Everyday Life in Ancient Mesopotamia*, New York 1968; Å.W. Sjöberg, E. Bergman, *The Collection of the Sumerian Temple Hymns* (TCS, III), New York 1969.

The general references considered were: W. Heimpel, *Tierbilder in der Sumerischen Literatur* (StP, 2), Roma 1968; S.N. Kramer, "Sumerian Similes: A Panoramic View of Some of Man's Oldest Literary Images", *JAOS* 89 (1969) 1–10.

[7]R. Borger, *Die Inschriften Asarhaddons, Königs von Assyrien* (AfO.B, 9), Graz 1956; J.S. Cooper, *Sumerian and Akkadian Royal Inscriptions, I: Presargonic Inscriptions* (AOS.TS, vol. I), New Haven (CT) 1986; A.K. Grayson, *Assyrian Royal Inscriptions, vol. I: From the Beginning to Ashur-resha-ishi I*; vol. II: *From Tiglath-pileser to Ashur-nasir-apli II* (RANE), Wiesbaden 1972; 1976; idem, *Assyrian and Babylonian Chronicles* (TCS, V), New York 1975; idem, *Assyrian Rulers of the Third and Second Millennia BC (to 1115 BC)* (RIM.AP, 1), Toronto 1987; W.G. Lambert, *Babylonian Wisdom Literature*, Oxford 1960; S. Parpola, K. Watanabe, *Neo-Assyyrian Treaties and Loyalty Oaths* (SAA, II), Helsinki 1988; A.C. Piepkorn, *Historical Prism Inscriptions of Ashurbanipal* (AS, 5), Chicago (IL) 1933; E. Sollberger, J.-R. Kupper, *Inscriptions Royales Sumeriennes et Akkadiennes* (LAPO), Paris 1971; D.J. Wiseman, *Chronicles of Chaldaean Kings (625–556 B.C.) in the British Museum*, London 1956; J.S. Cooper, *The Curse of Agade*, Baltimore (MD) 1983.

General: G. Buccellati, "Towards a Formal Typology of Akkadian Similes", in B.L. Eichler et al. (eds.), *Kramer Anniversary Volume: Cuneiform Studies in Honor of S.N. Kramer* (AOAT, 25), Keverlaer, Neukirchen 1976, 59–70; D.

Mari,[8] ancient Syria/Palestine,[9] Ugarit,[10] and Egypt.[11] Though the material from the Arabian world has to be used with some caution as as noted above, we examined the more recent Arabic texts in order to establish the existence of this genre in the Arabian world.[12]

The aim of the present chapter is to establish whether the definition of a collection of tribal sayings is correct for Genesis 49. For that

---

Marcus, "Animal Similes in Assyrian Royal Inscriptions", *Or* 46 (1977) 86–106.

[8] *Les Archives Royales de Mari*, Tm. I–XXVI, Paris 1950–1988; A. Marzal, *Gleanings from the Wisdom of Mari* (StP, 11), Rome 1976.

General: A. Malamat, *Mari and the Early Israelite Experience* (Schweich Lectures 1984), Oxford 1989; E. Noort, *Untersuchungen zum Gottesbescheid in Mari: Die "Mariprophetie" in der alttestamentlichen Forschung* (AOAT, 202), Kevelaer, Neukirchen-Vluyn 1977.

[9] T.G. Crawford, *Blessing and Curse in Syro-Palestinian Inscriptions of the Iron Age* (AUS 7: TR, 120), Bern 1992; E. Lipiński, *Studies in Aramaic Inscriptions and Onomastics* (OLA, 1), Leuven 1975; J.T. Milik, *Recherches d'épigraphie Proche-Orientale, I: Dédicaces faites par des Dieux (Palmyre, Hatra, Tyr) et des thiases sémitiques à l'époque romaine*, Paris 1972.

General: I. Browning, *Palmyra*, London 1979; J. Hoftijzer, *Religio Aramaica: Godsdienstige verschijnselen in Aramese teksten* (MVEOL, 16), Leiden 1968; J. Teixidor, *The Pantheon of Palmyra* (EPROER, 79), Leiden 1979.

[10] M. Dietrich *et alii*, *The Cuneiform Alphabetic Texts from Ugarit, Rash Ibn Hani and Other Places (KTU: second edition)* (ALASP, 8), Münster 1995.

General: P.D. Miller, "Animal Names as Designations in Ugaritic and Hebrew", *UF* 2 (1970) 169–187; J.C. de Moor, P. Sanders, "An Ugaritic Expiation Ritual and Its Old Testament Parallels", *UF* 23 (1991) 283–300.

[11] M. Lichtheim, *Ancient Egyptian Literature*. Vol. I: *The Old and Middle Kingdoms*; Vol. II: *The New Kingdom*, Berkeley 1973, 1976.

General: A. Loprieno, *Topos und Mimesis: Zum Ausländer in der Ägyptischen Literatur* (ÄA, 48), Wiesbaden 1988; H. Grapow, *Die bildlichen Ausdrücke des Aegyptischen: Von Denken und Dichten einer altorientalischen Sprache*, Leipzig 1924.

[12] T. Nöldeke, *Beiträge zur Kenntnis der Poesie der alten Araber*, Hannover 1864 (repr. Hildesheim 1967); A. Saarisalo, "Songs of the Druzes", *StOr* 4.1 (1932) 1–144; L. Haefeli, *Spruchweisheit und Volksleben in Palaestina*, Luzern 1939; R. Klinke-Rosenberger, *Das Götzenbuch: Kitâb al-Aṣnâm des Ibn al-Kalbî: Übersetzung mit Einleitung und Kommentar* (SOA, 8), Leipzig 1941; H.A.R. Gibb, *The Travels of Ibn Baṭṭūṭa* A.D.: Translated with revisions and notes from the Arabic text edited by C. Dedrémery and B.R. Sanguinetti, Vol. I–III, Cambridge 1958–71; A.J. Arberry, *Arabic Poetry: A Primer for Students*, Cambridge 1965; W. Caskel, *Gamharat an-Nasab: Das genealogische Werk des Hišām ibn Muḥammad al-Kalbī*, Bd. 1, Leiden 1966; Ibn Khaldûn, *The Muqaddimah: An Introduction to History* (Bollingen Series, 43), Translated by F. Rosenthal, New York [2]1967; R.A. Nicholson, *A Literary History of the Arabs*, Cambridge 1969; F.J. Abela, *Proverbes populaires du Liban sud: Saïda et ses environs*; Préface de G.C. Anawati (Les litteratures populaires de toutes les nations, Tm. 28; Tm. 32), Paris 1981, 1985; T. Seidensticker, *Die Gedichte des Šamardal ibn Šarik: Neuedition, Übersetzung, Kommentar*, Wiesbaden 1983; C. Bailey, *Bedouin Poetry from Sinai and the Negev: Mirror of a Culture*, with a Foreword by W. Thesiger, Oxford 1991.

reason our search will be in two fronts:

1. a search for possible tribal sayings.

2. a search for sayings comparable to Genesis 49;

The form search is meant to find sayings which are beyond all doubt "tribal sayings". In order to identify what a tribal saying, we will give a definition below on the basis of unequivocal examples of tribal sayings. The latter search is performed in order to find parallels for the different "sayings" of Genesis 49, even when such examples would not be selected for the former search. This possibility must be left open because the genre of Genesis 49 is under discussion. Theoretically it is possible that we could find examples of other genres which are parallel to the "sayings" of Genesis 49, but not to the tribal sayings. After presenting and discussing the material we have found, we will look at the hebrew material. First we will discuss some problems involved with form criticism such as the definition of a genre and the possibility of establishing certain stages of the tradition with the help of form criticism. Then, after a short discussion of Deuteronomy 33 and Judges 5, we will discuss the definition of the genre of the different "sayings" in Genesis 49 more extensively in order to draw some conclusions with regard to our investigation.

3.2 A Definition of Forms

Before presenting our findings, it is necessary to give a more precise definition of the genre "tribal saying". Such a definition must distinguish between genre, form and motif in connection with the "tribal saying", as was recently emphasized by S. Beyerle in his study on Deuteronomy 33.[13]

A genre is a coined word field with a certain form (grammatical, syntactic) and content,[14] being constitutive for the genre. In a genre different motifs may be applied, which are not restricted to one genre, for example theophany, metaphor, or comparison. However, as we have seen before,[15] a too narrow definition as given by Gunkel and others may exclude certain sayings in Genesis 49 itself. For that

---

[13]S. Beyerle, *Der Mosesegen im Deuteronomium: Eine text-, kompositions- und formkritische Studie zu Deuteronomium 33* (BZAW, 250), Berlin 1997, 96–9; cf. also J. Barton, "Form Criticism: Old Testament", *ABD*, vol. 2, 838–41, 839–40; K. Koch, *Was ist Formgeschichte?: Methoden der Bibelexegese*, Neukirchen ⁴1981, 20.

[14]Content must be included; see: Barton, "Form Criticism (O.T.)", 840; Beyerle, *Mosesegen im Deuteronomium*, 96–9; cf. also Koch, *Was ist Formgeschichte?* 20.

[15]Cf. above, section 1.4.2.

reason we have to define the genre and describe its form based on criteria, which are not based on a western perception of Semitic literature but only on data found in that literature itself. We will start therefore with the definition of the genre on the basis of unequivocal "tribal sayings": the sayings in the Arabic satire, Zobel referred to.[16] Although they are found in Arabic literature and not in the *ancient* Near East itself, these sayings are the only examples which are described in the literature itself as "tribal sayings" and are therefore our only reliable source to describe what a "tribal saying" is.

3.2.1 Tribal Sayings

The text to which Zobel referred (which has been translated rendered by Sanguinetti) is a satire, containing sayings on Arabian tribes in a kind of repetitive narrative framework as follows: a man speaks a negative saying on the tribe that accommodates him, a woman of the tribe asks him of which tribe he is, and he answers the question. Then she asks him if he knows the saying, that says ..., and she quotes a negative saying on the man's own tribe. Hearing the saying, the man denies that he belongs to that tribe. Thereupon the woman asks again to which tribe he belongs and he gives another name; then she asks again if he knows the saying, that says ..., and she recites a negative saying concerning the last mentioned tribe etc. By means of this framework fortyfive "tribal sayings" are recited, mocking other tribes — sometimes even in a very obscene way.[17]

The aim of the satire is expressed at the end. After the man is rebuked by the fortyfive sayings, the woman reproves the man for reciting a negative saying on his hosts. And at the end she says: "Do not meddle yourself looking for vices of others; because all peoples have their faults and their good qualities, except for the envoys of God and those whom he has chosen among his worshippers, and whom he has protected against their enemies."[18] In other words: stop reciting these sayings which can only convey negative ideas about each other. This is the context in which the sayings are found.

We will now offer several notable sayings from this text which can function as the framework for the description of the "tribal saying".

---

[16]Sanguinetti, "Satire" (n. 1 above).

[17]Cf. just the apologies Sanguinetti, "Satire", 549, makes before offering the text and translation: "Je regrette beaucoup que ce texte contienne quelques vers obscènes, et quelquefois même orduriers."

[18]Sanguinetti, "Satire", 572: "Ne te mêle pas de rechercher les vices des autres; car chaque peuple a des défauts et de bonnes qualités, à l'exclusion des envoyés de Dieu et de ceux qu'il a élus parmi ses adorateurs, et qu'il a protégés contre leur ennemi."

Each saying will be followed with a short classification, where we will describe form (length; clause; tense) and contents, but also the motifs being applied. We will start with the saying on the Bénou Tamîm:[19]

> The Tamîmites are better conductors on the roads of disgrace,
>> than are the birds called sandgrouse (to the water);
>>> but when they venture onto the streets of generosity, they go astray.
> I see the night chased away by the day;
>> but I never see the greatest outrages turn away from Tamîm.
>
> If a flea climbs on the back of a louse,
>> attack the two troops of the Tamîm (men and women),
>>> confident of their complete withdrawal.
> We have slaughtered animals pronouncing the name of God,
>> and our work was finished with that;
>>> but a Tamîm never slaughtered invoking the Eternal.

Length: four poetic verses.[20]
Clause:[21] nominal.
Tense: past, present.
Content: disapproval of another tribe; self-approbation.
Motifs:[22] comparison, generalization / contrast / comparison / disapproval in contrast with self-approval.

Of the tribe of the Thakîf it is said:[23]

> The genealogists have lost the trace of the Thakîfs ancestor;
>> and they do not have another ancestor than the error.

---

[19]Sanguinetti, "Satire", 562. I am endebted to dr. F. Sepmeijer, Kampen, who checked the English translation of the quoted sayings against the original Arabic text. In several cases he suggested a different translation from Sanguinetti's, who sometimes offered a quite free translation. The original French translation runs: "Les Tamîmites sont meilleurs conducteurs dans les chemins de la honte, / que ne sont les oiseaux appelés *katha* (vers l'eau); / mais s'ils s'engagent dans les voies des actions généreuses, ils s'égarent. // Je vois la nuit qui est dissipée par le jour; / mais je ne vois jamais les plus grandes ignominies se détourner de Tamîm. /// Si une puce montée sur le dos d'un pou / faisait une attaque sur les deux troupes de Tamîm (hommes et femmes), / certes qu'ils reculeraient tous. // Nous avons égorgé des animaux en prononçant le nom de Dieu, / et notre action en cela a été complète; / mais Tamîm n'a jamais rien égorgé en invoquant l'Éternel."

[20]We will use here the terminology which is derived from the description of Hebrew poetry in order to obtain a more uniform picture.

[21]Here we will describe the first clause in which the tribe's name is mentioned.

[22]The motifs which are used will be listed by poetic verse: When the same motif is used in a new poetic verse it will be listed again.

[23]Sanguinetti, "Satire", 564: "Les généalogistes ont perdu la trace du père des Thakîf; / et ils n'ont pas d'autre père que l'égarement.// (*continued next page*)

To cite the Thakîfs origin as far as they bring themselves in connection with
one,
and that, in fact, is an impossible matter.
They are the pork of the dung pit, kill them though;
for their blood is allowed to you.

Length: three poetic verses.
Clause: verbal; tribe's name used in genitive in object.
Tense: present, cohortative.
Content: disapproval of another tribe; self-approbation.
Motifs: genealogy, mockery / idem / metaphor, summons to kill.

In this saying we find a metaphor, describing the members of the
tribe as "pork of the dung pit". However, the metaphor is not worked
out to characterize the tribe and the behaviour of its members, but
it alone justifies a certain negative behaviour towards this tribe by
the members of the tribe who pronounced it. The character of the
"metaphor" is in our view much more that of calling names. Next we
have the saying on Lakîth:[24]

The Lakîth is the worst of those who mount a riding animal;
and the vilest of those who crawl on the surface of the earth.
Verily! May God curse the Benou Lakîth,
remnant of kinship to the people of Loth (i.e. Sodomites).

Length: two poetic verses.
Clause: nominal; tribe subject.
Tense: present.
Content: disapproval.
Motifs: generalization, disapproval / wish (of curse), metaphor.[25]

There are also short sayings, consisting of only one verse-line, like the
saying on Khath'am:[26]

When you whistle one time at the Benou Khath'am,
they fly away in the countries, accompanied by grasshoppers.

Citer l'origine des Thakîfites, ou qu'eux mêmes ils se rattachent à quelqu'un, /
c'est là, en effet, une chose impossible. // Ils sont les porcs des latrines, tuez-les
donc; / car leur sang est pour vous une chose permise."

[24]Sanguinetti, "Satire", 566: "Lakîth est le plus mauvais de tous ceux qui mon-
tent les bêtes de somme; / et le plus vil de tous ceux qui marchent sur la surface
de la terre. // Hé! que Dieu maudisse les Bénou Lakîth, / restes d'une lignée du
peuple de Loth (c'est-à-dire sodomites)."

[25]The metaphor is used again at the level of calling names and is clearly gen-
eralizing. The relation with reality seems farfetched.

[26]Sanguinetti, "Satire", 566: "Si tu siffles une seule fois les Bénou Khath'am, /
ils volent dans la contrée, en compagnie des sauterelles."

Length: one poetic verse.
Clause: verbal (conditional); tribe object.
Tense: present.
Content: disapproval.
Motifs: generalisation, comparison(?).

The next example from this text is the saying on the Chaybânites, which runs as follows:[27]

> The Chaybânites are numerous,
>   all of them are detestable, vile;
> Among them there is not an illustrious man, nor a person of honour,
>   nor a noble man, nor a generous person.

Length: two poetic verses.
Clause: verbal (?); tribe subject.
Tense: present.
Content: disapproval.
Motifs: generalisation.

Remarkable is the fact that specific events or behaviour are not mentioned, which gives these sayings a rather general character. This general character enables someone to pronounce an almost similar saying on different tribes with only a slight alteration. Compare for example the following three sayings; first on the 'Abs:[28]

> Since a woman of the Bénou 'Abs gives birth to a boy,
>   announce her the blame she has acquired.

The next on the Ghany:[29]

> Since a woman of the Benou Ghany gives birth to a boy,
>   announce her a proficient tailor (having been born).

Finally the third on the Azdite:[30]

> Since an Azdite woman gives birth to a boy,
>   announce her a proficient sailor (having been born).

---

[27]Sanguinetti, "Satire", 569: "Les Chaybânites sont nombreux; / mais ils sont tous de basse extraction, vils. // Il n'y a parmi eux ni un homme illustre, / ni un personnage honoré, ni un individu noble, ni un généreux."

[28]Sanguinetti, "Satire", 564: "Lorsqu'une femme des Bénou 'Abs met au monde un garçon, / félicite-la de la honte qu'elle s'est acquise."

[29]Sanguinetti, "Satire", 564: "Lorsqu'une femme des Bénou Ghany a enfanté un garçon, / donne-lui la bonne nouvelle d'un tailleur habile."

[30]Sanguinetti, "Satire", 565: The final saying: "Lorsqu'une femme Azdite accouche d'un garçon, / félicite-la d'un fameux matelot." This saying has to be connected with the fact that in Oman many men of the Azdites are sailors according to Sanguinetti, art.cit., 565, n. 1.

Length: one poetic verse.
Clause: verbal (causal); tribal name genitive.
Tense: past, present.
Content: generalising mockery.
Motifs: generalisation.

The satire from which these sayings are quoted, is unique in the
Umwelt as far as we know, because it gives the impression that independent sayings are collected here and reshaped into a narrative. This
is suggested most strongly by the introductory formula of each saying "Do you know the one that says:".[31] Though it may be doubted
whether these sayings once functioned independently, the need for
such a satire testifies to the existence of such a habit among the
Arabian tribes.[32] So even if the sayings quoted above were not originally independent, they do reflect a reality where this kind of saying
functions. Therefore we may draw some conclusions from this Arabic
example concerning the character of the sayings and their content:

1. the sayings are in verse;

2. they all have a different length, varying between one and four
   poetic verses;

3. the life setting of such negative sayings is a different tribe, regarding itself as superior to the other;

4. the sayings are rather generalising and stereotypical;[33] characterizations are absent, abuse is used; the main content is disapproval and this is also the aim.

3.2.2   Genesis 49

With regard to Genesis 49 it is necessary to describe its form precisely
in order to have an exact definition of what we are looking for. It is
appropriate to give a definition of the sayings in such a manner that

---

[31]Sanguinetti, "Satire", 562–71: "Connais-tu celui qui a dit".

[32]This might also be derived from the fact that we are dealing here with a
satire. A satire is "an artistic form, chiefly literary and dramatic, in which human
or individual vices, follies, abuses, or shortcomings are held up to censure by
means of ridicule, derision, burlesque, irony, or other methods, sometimes with
an intent to bring about improvement" (*The New Encyclopædia Britannica*, vol.
10, Chicago [15]1974, 467).

[33]This characterization is also given by Zobel, *SuG*, 54, n. 6, who describes them
as given mostly in the form of statements ("...überwiegend in die Aussageform
gehalten").

every form found in Genesis 49 can be included (both short and long, with and without metaphor or pun, etc.). In this description we will use the same categories as we did in the previous section. As a parallel to the sayings of Genesis 49 we therefore include a text,

1. which is rather short, although sometimes consisting of several strophes (Simeon and Levi, Judah, Joseph);

2. which contains the name of a tribe or an eponym as the object of the saying (all sayings), though the name may be used grammatically as *casus pendens*, or as subject;

3. which characterizes the tribe or ancestor in a nominal clause (Reuben; Simeon & Levi; Issachar; Naphtali; Joseph), although a verbal clause could also be used (Zebulun; Dan);

4. which applies the following motifs to characterize the tribe:

    (a) a reference to certain events or conditions, including leadership or subordination (Reuben; Simeon and Levi; Judah[?]; Issachar [?]; Joseph[?]);

    (b) a simile or metaphor (Reuben; Judah; Issachar; Dan; Naphtali; Joseph; Benjamin);

    (c) a pun (Reuben[?]; Judah; Issachar; Dan; Gad);

    (d) reference to professional activity (Issachar; Asher[?]; Naphtali[?]);

    (e) reference to the territory (Zebulun; Issachar[?]; Asher[?]; antithetical: Simeon and Levi);

    (f) reference to prosperity (Judah; Asher; Joseph);

    (g) description of the appearance (Judah);

5. which expresses praise or rebuke, or even blessing or curse (Reuben; Simeon and Levi; Judah; Joseph) together with the reason for rebuke or curse (Reuben, Simeon and Levi);

6. which could obviously have functioned independently from a literary context.[34]

---

[34]This final element is a matter of dispute with regard to Genesis 49, for some scholars deny the possibility that the sayings of Genesis 49 have functioned independently (see above, section 1.4.1). However, in order to establish a possible existence of the genre this criterion seems requisite.

For possible parallels between this Hebrew form-definition and the one presented in the previous section see the material in the next sections where each saying will be followed by a short characterization as was given in the section on the tribal sayings, but in addition we will define the genre of each example.

3.2.3 Tribal Sayings in Israel's *Umwelt*

3.2.3.1 Arabian

The existence of independent sayings and proverbs on other tribes or people as the tribal sayings described above, is confirmed by the fact that short sayings naming and mocking other people still exist in Palestine:[35]

> The Arab has a good heart,
>   the European a good tongue.

Length: one poetic verse.
Clause: verbal; other people subject (only in the second part).
Tense: present.
Content: self-approbation and disapproval.
Motifs: generalisation, contrast.
Genre: nationalistic proverb.

The well-known animosity of the Palestinians against the Jews is expressed with the following saying:[36]

> Palestine is our country,
>   and the Jews are our dogs.

Length: one poetic verse.
Clause: nominal; other people subject (only in the second part).
Tense: present.
Content: disapproval.
Motifs: generalisation, "metaphor".
Genre: nationalistic proverb.

Remarkable in the latter saying is the fact that the metaphor is used to abuse, not to characterize the other group. The former saying has a characterization of the Europeans, functioning to contrast one's own group positively. In this sense they are comparable to the tribal

---

[35]L. Haefeli, *Spruchweisheit und Volksleben in Palaestina*, Luzern 1939, 165: "Der Araber hat ein gutes Herz, / der Europäer eine gute Zunge."

[36]Haefeli, *Spruchweisheit und Volksleben in Palaestina*, 166: "Palästina ist unser Land, / und die Juden sind unsere Hunde."

sayings described above.

Other "sayings" are found scattered in Arabic poetry, but they are always part of a larger literary context. In a love poem of 'Umar ibn Abī Rabī'a, the first-person narrator, who is in love with a woman asks her a question, the answer in the second part is relevant to us:[37]

> I said: "Who are you?" She answered:
>   "I am one emaciated by passion, worn out by sorrow.
>
> We are the people of al-Khaif, of the people of Minā;
>   for any slain by us there is no retaliation."

Length: one poetic verse (part of larger context).
Clause: nominal; own tribe subject.
Tense: present.
Content: self-approbation.
Motifs: generalisation, boasting.
Genre: self-presentation.

A similar form of self-presentation is found in a genealogical poem:[38]

> I am Abu Zabyān. Telling lies is not in my line;
>   Verily I am Abu l-'Uffa. From my mother's side my uncle is al-Lahabah.
> As noblest known by descent, be it from Dibyān or Bakrr ibn Ta'alabah.
>   We resist the band of robbers at the day of Aḥsabah

Length: two poetic verses.
Clause: nominal; own tribe subject (in the second part).
Tense: future (boasting).
Content: self-approbation.
Motifs: genealogy, boasting.
Genre: genealogical poem.

The text is in so-called raǧaz-verse; it does not contain any metaphor or pun; a short characterization is given in the final poetic verse. The main goal of the poem seems to be offering genealogical information.

Another example is found in a lament of the poetess Alchansâ' for the death of her murdered brothers Mu'âwiya and Ṣachr. After the

---

[37]The poem is found in: A.J. Arberry, *Arabic Poetry: A Primer for Students*, Cambridge 1965, 40–43.

[38]W. Caskel, *Gamharat an-Nasab: Das genealogische Werk des Hišām ibn Muḥammad al-Kalbī*, Bd. 1, Leiden 1966, 45: "Ich bin Abu Zabyān. Zu lügen liegt mir hier nicht nah; / Fürwahr ich bin Abu l-'Uffa. Von Mutters Seite ist mein Ohm al-Lahabah // Als edelster bekannt von Abkunft, sei's von Dibyān oder Bakrr ibn Ta'alabah / Wir sind der Raubschar Gegner an dem Tag von Aḥsabah."

death of one of the murderers by someone of another tribe — instead
of the revenge by her own tribe — she writes:[39]

> I swear that I will never end to sing a song to the Qais,
>   the companions of Amrâr, in every gathering.
> May Sulaim give up their flint and their gravel for you,
>   may you all have your noses and ears split!

Length: two poetic verses.
Clause: verbal; other tribe and own tribe object.
Tense: present and future (promise and wish).
Content: approbation and curse.
Motifs: —
Genre: oath and curse.

This text is set in the context of a lament, in which the clarification
of the contents of the quoted strophes is found, and which is certainly
connected with a specific event. This is an important difference between this text and the definition, where the explanation has to be
found in the saying itself because it could obviously have functioned
independently from a literary context.

   In bedouin poetry we find a poem by a smuggler who was ill-
treated by the men of his own clan and was left by his wives when he
was in prison:[40]

> My clan's like hyenas at small stinking pools,
>   Crouched to the ground like hyenas drinking.
>
> As life must end, so women are lesser than men,
>   And the poor take heart when calamities come.
>
> And I, once a wolf that preys inside camps,
>   Who charged upon non-bearing mares like Jidea,
>
> Am now but a walker with shattered bones
>   Stumbling and fumbling midst boulders and stones.

Length: four poetic verses.
Clause: nominal; own clan subject.

---

[39]The poems are found in T. Nöldeke, *Beiträge zur Kenntnis der Poesie der
alten Araber*, Hannover 1864 (repr. Hildesheim 1967), 157–82; the quotation is
from p. 162: "Ich schwöre dass ich niemals aufhören werde, dem Qais, / dem
Genossen der Amrâr, in jeder Versammlung ein Lied darzubringen! // Möge Su-
laim, ihr Kiesel und ihr Kies, für dich hingeben, / mögen ihnen alle Nase und Ohr
gespalten werden!

[40]C. Bailey, *Bedouin Poetry from Sinai and the Negev: Mirror of a Culture*,
with a foreword by W. Thesiger. Oxford 1991, 24–28, 26–7.

Tense: present.
Content: disapproval, lament.
Motifs: description, metaphors.
Genre: poem of nostalgia.[41]

Another saying is found in a poem which has to restore the honour of a chief of a neighbouring tribe, the Tiyāhā:[42]

> The Tiyāhā tribe are stallions — battle stallions shod with shoes,
>   Stallions who, although held back, the bloody fray would choose.

Length: one poetic verse.
Clause: nominal; other clan subject.
Tense: present.
Content: approbation.
Motifs: description, metaphor.
Genre: hymnic description.

In yet another poem, a plea for mercy, the king is described:[43]

> He's a hawk who's higher than _shāhīn_ hawks[44] in flight,
>   And he scatters feathers whenever he bites.

Length: one poetic verse.
Clause: nominal, subject not mentioned by name.
Tense: present.
Content: approbation.
Motifs: description, metaphor.
Genre: hymnic description.

These three examples are quotations from poems written recently by bedouin poets. With their metaphorical language they suit the definition as given above, although they are unmistakably part of a larger poem. In the following a short eulogia on a tribe is given:[45]

> The glory did not fall short of you, you sons of Ḥasan,
>   and it did not pass you, O clan of Masʿud.

---

[41] Bailey, _Bedouin Poetry_, 24, calls this poem this way; "lament" or the like might be correct too.

[42] Bailey, _Bedouin Poetry_, 91–7, 94.

[43] Bailey, _Bedouin Poetry_, 104–9, 106.

[44] Bailey, _Bedouin Poetry_, 106, n. 10: "The _shāhīn_ hawk cited in the Arabic text is the long-winged _Falco tinnunculus_ variety, native to the Arabian peninsula. The image is used in bedouin poetry to allude to a person's martial prowess".

[45] T. Seidensticker, _Die Gedichte des Šamardal ibn Šarik: Neuedition, Übersetzung, Kommentar_, Wiesbaden 1983, 52: "Der Ruhm ist nicht hinter euch zurückgeblieben, ihr Söhne Ḥasans, / und er ist nicht an euch vorübergegangen, Sippe Masʿuds. // (continued on the next page)

He will settle down where you have settled down,
  and he will never forsake you,
    as long as fate alternates between white people and dark.
When you are present, there are blessings with you for the friend;
  but when you are far away, there are no benefactions.

Length: three poetic verses.
Clause: verbal; clan's name nominative.
Tense: past, present, future.
Content: praise.
Motifs: description (almost theophanic).
Genre: hymne.

These relatively young texts function very well as examples of how
people assess each other in a tribal society. Sometimes language and
description are even very close to that of the sayings in the Hebrew
Bible. This may be illustrated by one song of the Druzes, where we
find a praise of the power of the leader (named "Ali") comparable to
Gen. 49:8–12 for Judah:[46]

Ali, the people praise you,
  O the regret of Amr, for you he died and was angry,
O Ali, he who is followed by the tribe of God and who commands,
  On your sword is written the victory from above (God).

O Ali, you own the necks of your enemies,
  And hold the saddled horses in the battle,
Happy are you in your refusal, O possessor, O lion,
  He is your friend on the day when the lances are drawn against you.

Length: two poetic verses (twice).
Clause: verbal; leader's name in nominative.
Tense: present.
Content: approbation.
Motifs: description.
Genre: hymnic description.

To these strophes we may add one more, taken from a different song:[47]

Er wird sich niederlassen, wo ihr euch niedergelassen habt, / und er wird euch
nicht verlassen, / solange das Schicksal zwischen weißhäutigen und dunklen ab-
wechselt. // Wenn ihr anwesend seid, gibt es für den Freund Wohltaten bei euch,
/ seid ihr fern, so gibt es keine Wohltaten."

[46]A. Saarisalo, "Songs of the Druzes", *StOr* 4.1 (1932) 1–144, 28–31; quoted
are strophe 1 and 4.

[47]Saarisalo, "Songs of the Druzes", 50.

You are Antar, you are Jafar, you are a falcon,
  You are a hawk, you are a free man, you are a falcon,
You are a pepper in the nostrils of the enemies,
  Your claws are always upon the necks of the enemies.

Length: two poetic verses.
Clause: nominal, leader subject.
Tense: present.
Content: approbation.
Motifs: description, metaphors.
Genre: hymnic description.

These strophes, using metaphorical language to praise the leader of the tribe, are part of a larger literary unity and do not function independently. Further, in the text no indication is found that certain strophes functioned independently at an earlier stage and were incorporated in the present poem.

On the basis of this material from Arabic literature we have to assume now that there were both: independent sayings, which might indeed be called "tribal sayings", *and* pronouncements on tribes (or peoples and leaders) in the context of larger literary units. This coincides with the critique of Muilenburg on form criticism, and with the view of Gunkel himself,[48] that certain forms are also applied by authors to serve their purpose. Similar, apparently, to the fact that certain motifs could be applied in different genres, genres could be applied in different contexts. Another important feature is the fact that the length of the sayings does not always match the "original" shortness of the "tribal sayings" usually assumed by scholars.[49] The tense is generally the present, but can be the future in the context of a (theophanic) description. Concerning the contents it is remarkable that positive sayings are pronounced on the tribe itself, on its leader, or on allied tribes. Negative sayings were generally meant for other tribes or on obvious enemies. Finally, sayings on several tribes are not found in one poem or the like, or it is a complete literary framework, which also explains why these different tribes are mentioned in this context.[50]

We will now continue with the data found in the literature of the ancient Near East. Not much data has been found in Sumerian,

---

[48] Cf. above, section 1.4.3.

[49] Cf. *e.g.* Kittel, *Stammessprüche Israels*, 66–79; Westermann, *Genesis 37-50*, 250-1.

[50] Cf. the satire, discussed above; and also the lament by Alchansâ (above, p. 260).

Akkadian or Egyptian literature.

3.2.3.2   Sumerian

In the Sumerian temple hymns with their elevated speech some examples have been found of hymnic descriptions of a deity. Of course they are not parallel to the *"tribal* sayings"; however, because they use similar forms and motifs as in Genesis 49 they are worth noting. The first example refers to the deity Asarluḫi:[51]

> Your prince is the highly esteemed prince, Asarluḫi, the highly esteemed one,
>> The hero, born to? (be) a prince, a leopard, who seizes prey,
> He is like an onrushing storm, he gores the rebellious land,
>> As long as it is not obedient, he pours out poisonous foam upon it.

Length: two poetic verses.
Clause: nominal, deity subject.
Tense: present.
Content: approbation.
Motifs: description, metaphors.
Genre: hymnic description.

The following quotation describes the temple of Ningublam in Kiabrig (gá-bur-ra)[52] and the deity Ningublam:[53]

> Gaburra, holy cattle-pen which ... the cows (fed with) *musur*-plants,
> Your prince (is) a great wild ox, an elephant? who rejoices at his strength,
>> A wild bull with horns, who rejoices at his ...

Length: two poetic verses.
Clause: nominal, deity subject.
Tense: present.
Content: approbation.
Motifs: description, metaphors.
Genre: hymnic description.

The final quotation describes the deity Numušda:[54]

---

[51]Å.W. Sjöberg, E. Bergman, *The Collection of the Sumerian Temple Hymns* (TCS, III), New York 1969, 25; r. 140–3; for a similar "saying", cf. 42, rr. 432–5. Some incomplete "sayings" are found on 21, r. 73 (lion); 22, rr. 90–2 (lion, mountain); cf. also 30, r. 216; 44, rr. 458–9; 47, r. 508.

[52]Sjöberg, Bergman, *Sumerian Temple Hymns*, 81.

[53]Sjöberg, Bergman, *Sumerian Temple Hymns*, 26, r. 150–2.

[54]Sjöberg, Bergman, *Sumerian Temple Hymns*, 40, rr. 398–402; for the restoration of the text, cf. p. 125.

[Your] prince (is) the seed of a (the) steer, engendered by a wild ox in ...,
  A great [bison] with speckled eyes, a lord with teeth of a lion,
Who snatches the calf with (his) claws,
  Who catches [a man in his net],
    [The strong one] who snatches [the bull],

Length: two poetic verses.
Clause: nominal, deity subject.
Tense: present.
Content: approbation.
Motifs: description, metaphors.
Genre: hymnic description.

Unfortunately the examples are rather fragmentary, but what may
be clear from these examples is that they have been derived from
Sumerian temple hymns and, as such, are part of a larger literary
context. There is no reason to assume that they once existed independently. Also important to note is the fact that the motifs applied
in the sayings were apparently not restricted to tribes, nations, or
their eponymic ancestors, but could be applied to deities too. The
parallels we note with Genesis 49 are especially found in the sayings
on Judah and on Joseph. Next to syntactical parallels, the metaphors
are remarkably close to those found in the Judah and Joseph saying: the highly esteemed prince (cf. 49:8); a leopard, who seizes prey
(49:9); a great wild ox / a wild bull (49:22); seed of a (the) steer,
engendered by a wild ox (49:22).

3.2.3.3   Akkadian

In Akkadian only one example was found of a text giving a characterization of a certain people. This example occurs in the *Curse of
Agade*, where the Gutium are described:[55]

  Not classed among people, not reckoned as part of the land,
    Gutium, a people who know no inhibitions,
      With human instincts, but canine intelligence, and monkey's features —

Length: one poetic verse.
Clause: verbal, delaying of subject.
Tense: present.
Content: "disapproval".
Motifs: comparison.
Genre: description.

---

[55] J.S. Cooper, *The Curse of Agade*, Baltimore (Md) 1983, 56–9.

The characterizations of the Gutium became stereotypes for describing them as barbarians and even bestial mountaineers,[56] but there is no indication that the description quoted here ever functioned as an independent saying; the description is part of a larger literary composition. The deity Enlil is looking for the possibility to take revenge and then he sees the Gutium who could destroy others for him. That this description of the Gutium cannot be separated from its literary context is clear from the fact that the literary feature of the delaying of devices is used:[57] a description is given, before one is aware of whom it is said. This might be shown by quoting the wider context of this description:

> Enlil, because his beloved Ekur was destroyed, what should he destroy for it?
>> He looked toward the Gubin mountains,
>>> He scoured all of the broad mountain ranges —
> Not classed among people, not reckoned as part of the land,
>> The Gutium are a people who know no inhibitions,
>>> With human instincts, but canine intelligence, and monkey's features
>>> Enlil brought them out of the mountains.

3.2.3.4   Egyptian

In the *Instruction to Merikare* the following description of the Asiatics is given:[58]

> The Asiatic is a crocodile on its shore,
>> It snatches from a lonely road,
>>> It cannot seize from a populous town.

Length: one poetic verse.
Clause: nominal, people subject.
Tense: present.
Content: disapproval.
Motifs: metaphoric description.
Genre: assessment.

This short section is in fact the closest parallel to the sayings found in Genesis 49 in the Ancient Near East. Remarkable is the rather short

---

[56]W.W. Hallo, "Gutium", *RdA*, Bd. 3, 708–20, 709.

[57]For this feature, cf. Sanders, *The Provenance of Deuteronomy 32*, 159, n. 300 (bibliography); cf. furthermore J.C. de Moor, "Syntax Peculiar to Ugaritic Poetry", *VANEP*, 191–205, esp. 197–205.

[58]M. Lichtheim, *Ancient Egyptian Literature: A Book of Readings*, Vol. I: *The Old and Middle Kingdoms*, Berkeley (CA) 1973, 104; similar in A. Loprieno, *Topos und Mimesis: Zum Ausländer in der Ägyptischen Literatur* (ÄA 48), Wiesbaden 1988, 24. Cf. also D.B. Redford, *Egypt, Canaan, and Israel in Ancient Times*, Princeton (NJ) 1992, 66–8.

and powerful characterization expressing that there is no reason to fear the Asiatics. They have no power to enter the cities and are apparently only able to make some attacks at the fringes, which is certainly no threat to the Egyptians in the cities. The "saying" is found in an instruction of a king[59] to his son Merikare, who is instructed not to concern himself with the Asiatic. The saying fits very well in the context. Because of its short and powerful expression it could have functioned independently,[60] but it must be stressed that there is no indication in the text that it did function as such, nor is there any indication that it did so in later times.

Another example of metaphorical description of foreigners is found in the *Prophecies of Neferti*, although absolutely of a different kind than the preceding one:[61]

A strange bird will breed in the Delta marsh,
  Having made its nest beside the people,
    The people having let it approach by default.
Then perish those delightful things,
  The fishponds full of fish-eaters,
    Teeming with fish and fowl.
All happiness has vanished,
  The land is bowed down in distress,
    Owing to these feeders, Asiatics who roam the land.
Foes have risen in the East,
  Asiatics have come down to Egypt.

Length: four poetic verses.
Clause: verbal; name of people is found in third poetic verse; in fact the land is subject.
Tense: future.
Content: disapproval; in fact: disaster.
Motifs: metaphor.
Genre: oracle of disaster.

---

[59]The king is probably Khety, which is indicated by some traces at the fragmentary beginning of the text. However, which Khety of the kings with that name preceding Merikare is not certain. Lichtheim, *Ancient Egyptian Literature*, vol. I, 97, refers to a study of J. von Beckerat, *ZÄS* 93 (1966) 13–20, who suggests that it could be the king with the pre-nomen Nebkaure.

[60]The foreigners were a literary topos in Egyptian literature. This happened in several ways like the one above quoted; but also in just ordinary descriptions, which were embedded in literary contexts. Cf. Loprieno, *Topos and Mimesis*, 22–30.

[61]Quoted from Lichtheim, *Ancient Egyptian Literature*, vol. I, 141; cf. also Loprieno, *Topos and Mimesis*, 27; Redford, *Egypt, Canaan, Israel*, 66–9.

This example is rather long, and although a metaphor is used as a characterization — the Asiatic is the bird in the first six lines[62] — and a disapproval is apparent too, it certainly cannot be paralleled to Genesis 49. In Genesis 49, as also in the Arabic tribal sayings, the name of the tribe is given at the beginning usually as the subject in a nominal clause, but never in such a way with a metaphor. Further, the oracle uses the metaphor to describe the condition of the land rather than to give a description of the Asiatic.

3.2.3.5 Summary

Just one unequivocal parallel with a motif comparable to the sayings of Genesis 49 was found in the literature of the ancient Near East: the Egyptian "saying" on the Asiatics from the *Instruction to Merikare*. However, this parallel fits very well in its literary context, a so-called royal testament.[63] Other "sayings" were hard to find and the examples found all function in a literary context in which they are firmly embedded. Moreover, some of the examples are not concerned with tribes or people but with deities and are part of hymns. This suggests that the metaphorical language found in Genesis 49 is not restricted to "sayings" but can be part of a wider spectrum of literary genres. It also suggests that the form which is applied in Genesis 49 is not restricted to sayings on tribes but could also be used for hymnic descriptions of the divine. Finally, no independent functioning is attested, nor can it be deduced from the material we have presented.

These conclusions differ slightly from the results drawn from Arabic literature: we found clear indications for the existence of independent sayings on tribes; though on the other hand we also found "sayings" — comparable to the Sumerian hymnic descriptions — which are evidentialy part of a larger poetic text. Moreover, the texts found were not restricted to tribes or clans but were also about leaders, comparable with the saying on Judah (Gen. 49:8–12).

It may be concluded now, that a genre "tribal saying" did exist in the Arabian world; in the ancient Near East this might have been possible too, though no unequivocal indications are found for this assumption. Moreover, in the case of positive sayings the only form found is hymnic and literary motifs are used to serve this aim; this is especially clear from the fact that the examples are partly derived from temple hymns or from eulogia on a tribal leader. So in this case it may be doubted whether the designation "tribal saying" is correct and

---

[62] Lichtheim, *Ancient Egyptian Literature*, vol. I, 141, with 144, n. 4.

[63] On the *Instruction to Merikare* as a royal testament; cf. p. 310, with n. 224 below.

other genres are suggested therefore. In the case of negative sayings, which might indeed be called "tribal sayings", metaphors are mostly applied to abuse, not to characterize the tribe involved.

In view of these conclusions it would be challenging to discuss the genre of the classical *dicta probantia* of the genre "tribal saying", namely Deuteronomy 33, Judges 5 and of course Genesis 49. However, as noted in Chapter One there are several methodological problems with regard to form criticism and to the conclusions reached on the basis of form critical arguments. For our study of Genesis 49, the questions concerning the original length and form of the sayings and the authenticity on basis of form criticism are the most relevant. For that reason we will now start with a discussion of some texts from the Hebrew Bible which are in some way closely related to the genres found in Genesis 49. Several texts deal with other nations and although these texts are generally not defined as "sayings" but as "oracles", they offer a good opportunity to discuss some relevant elements for our form critical discussion. Moreover, a comparison with prophetic oracles has already been suggested by others who compare the sayings on Reuben, and Simeon and Levi with a prophetic lawsuit,[64] or the saying on Judah with messianic oracles.[65]

3.2.3.6 The Hebrew Bible

3.2.3.6.1 Oracles against Other Nations

In the Hebrew Bible, especially in the prophetic books, we find oracles against foreign nations (Amos 1:1–2:3; Isa. 13–23; Jer. 46–51; Ezek. 25–31). These oracles have been studied in scholarly literature with regard to (*inter alii*) the literary- and form-critical problems involved.[66] Based on texts like Num. 21:27–30; 22–24, 1 Sam. 15:2–3, 1 Kgs. 20:26–30, Isa. 7:5–7, it has been argued that oracles against the nations had their context in warfare and especially in the tradition of Holy War,[67] comparable with the use of oracles and curses against the enemy during military campaigns in other ancient Near Eastern

---

[64]Kittel, *Stammessprüche Israels*, 93, n. 1; Westermann, *Genesis 37–50*, 253–5.

[65]C. Westermann, "Micha 5, 1–3", in: G. Eichholz (Hrsg.), *Herr, tue meine Lippen auf: Eine Predigthilfe*, Bd. 5: *Die alttestamentlichen Perikopen*, Wuppertal-Barmen ²1961, 54–9; idem, *Genesis 37–50*, 262.

[66]G. Fohrer, "Remarks on Modern Interpretation of the Prophets", *JBL* 80 (1961) 309–19; J.H. Hayes, "The Usage of Oracles against Foreign Nations in Ancient Israel", *JBL* 87 (1968) 81–92; J. Barton, *Amos's Oracles against the Nations* (MSSOTS, 6), London 1980.

[67]Gottwald, *All the Kingdoms of the Earth*, New York 1964, 48; Hayes, "Oracles against Foreign Nations", 81–3.

cultures, like Sumer, Mari, Hittite,[68] and to the Egyptian execration texts.[69] This warfare context always supposes a kind of cultic context[70] which might also be discerned more or less independently from the foregoing: the cultic ceremonies of lamentation (see Psalms 20, 21, 60; Lam. 4:21–2; 2 Kgs. 18:13–19:37).[71] Though it may be doubted whether the general definition of the *Sitz im Leben* of these oracles is correct in all cases,[72] the material offers some interesting features concerning the supposed genre of the "tribal sayings".

As we have seen in Chapter One both the cultic background (defended especially by Gunneweg) and the warfare (for example, Westermann) played a role in the description of the *Sitz im Leben* of Genesis 49. However, a comparison of form critical problems in connection with these prophetic oracles with those relating to Genesis 49 has not been made.[73] This is not because the tribes are not *foreign* nations, since this point is sometimes ignored (deliberately) by the prophets themselves (compare Amos 1:3–2:16). More important is the fact that only the first two sayings in Genesis 49 have the characteristic features of a prophetic oracle, but in this case we are dealing with an oracle against an individual and not against a nation. Nevertheless a short discussion of some of these texts might be relevant for our study of the genre of the tribal saying. Our discussion will concern Num. 21:27–30; 24:15–25; Amos 1:3–2:16; Mic. 4:8; 5:1.

3.2.3.6.2   Numbers 24:15–25

In Num. 24:18–9, 20b, 21b–22, 23b–24 some sayings (מְשָׁלִים) on other nations are given. The first to quote is the one on Amalek (Num. 24:20b):

The first of nations is Amalek, (20bA)	רֵאשִׁית גּוֹיִם עֲמָלֵק
but his last shall be unto destruction. (20bB)	וְאַחֲרִיתוֹ עֲדֵי אֹבֵד

---

[68] Hayes, "Oracles against Foreign Nations", 84–7.

[69] A. Bentzen, "The Ritual Background of Amos i 2–ii 16", in: P.A.H. de Boer (ed.), *Oudtestamentische Studiën*, dl. 8, Leiden 1950, 85–99.

[70] Bentzen, "Ritual Background of Amos i 2–ii 16", 85–99; cf. also J.C. de Moor, P. Sanders, "An Ugaritic Expiation Ritual and its Old Testament Parallels", *UF* 23 (1991) 283–300, 296–7.

[71] Hayes, "Oracles against Foreign Nations", 87–9; De Moor, Sanders, "An Ugaritic Expiation Ritual", 296–7.

[72] Barton, *Amos's Oracles*, 8–15.

[73] Sometimes we find a comparison on the basis of the listing of tribes and nations; but details are not worked out, however; cf. *e.g.* J. Lindblom, "The Political Background of the Shiloh Oracle", in: *Congress Volume, Copenhagen 1953* (SVT, 1), Leiden 1953, 78–87; idem, *Prophecy in Ancient Israel*, Oxford 1962, 239–40.

On the Kenite (Num. 24:21b–22):

Enduring is your dwelling place, (21bA)	אֵיתָן מוֹשָׁבֶךָ
and your nest is set in the rock; (21bB)	וְשִׂים בַּסֶּלַע קִנֶּךָ
Yet Cain will be destroyed (22aA)	כִּי אִם־יִהְיֶה לְבָעֵר קָיִן
How long shall Asshur take you away captive? (22aB)	עַד־מָה אַשּׁוּר תִּשְׁבֶּךָ

And finally on the Kittim(?) (Num. 24:23b–24):[74]

Woe, who will be safe from the North? (23b)	אוֹי מִי יִחְיֶה מִשְּׂמֹאול(!)
let him get out from the hand of the Kittim! (24aA)	וְצִים[??] מִיַּד כִּתִּים
They oppressed Asshur and Eber, (24aB)	וְעִנּוּ אַשּׁוּר וְעִנּוּ־עֵבֶר
and he also shall come to destruction. (24aC)	וְגַם־הוּא עֲדֵי אֹבֵד

Next to these sayings, which are rather short (only one or two poetic verses) and immediately concerned with the nations involved, there is also a longer one, Num. 24:10–14:

The oracle of Balaam the son of Beor, (15bA)	נְאֻם בִּלְעָם בְּנוֹ בְעֹר
the oracle of the man whose eye is opened (15bB)	וּנְאֻם הַגֶּבֶר שְׁתֻם הָעָיִן
The oracle of him who hears the words of God (16aA)	נְאֻם שֹׁמֵעַ אִמְרֵי־אֵל
and knows the knowledge of the Most High (16aB)	וְיֹדֵעַ דַּעַת עֶלְיוֹן
Who sees the vision of the Almighty (16bA)	מַחֲזֵה שַׁדַּי יֶחֱזֶה
falling down, but having his eyes uncovered. (16bB)	נֹפֵל וּגְלוּי עֵינָיִם

I see him, but not now, (17aA)	אֶרְאֶנּוּ וְלֹא עַתָּה
I behold him, but not nigh; (17aB)	אֲשׁוּרֶנּוּ וְלֹא קָרוֹב
A star shall come forth out of Jacob (17bA)	דָּרַךְ כּוֹכָב מִיַּעֲקֹב
and a scepter shall rise out of Israel; (17bB)	וְקָם שֵׁבֶט מִיִּשְׂרָאֵל
It shall crush the forehead of Moab, (17cA)	וּמָחַץ פַּאֲתֵי מוֹאָב
and break down all the sons of Seth (17cB)	וְקַרְקַר כָּל־בְּנֵי־שֵׁת

Edom shall be dispossessed, (18aA)	וְהָיָה אֱדוֹם יְרֵשָׁה
and Seir, his enemies, shall be dispossessed, (18aB)	וְהָיָה יְרֵשָׁה שֵׂעִיר אֹיְבָיו
while Israel will do valiantly. (18aC)	וְיִשְׂרָאֵל עֹשֶׂה חָיִל
By Jacob shall dominion be exercised, (19aA)	וְיֵרְדְּ מִיַּעֲקֹב
but the survivors of cities will be destroyed. (19aB)	וְהֶאֱבִיד שָׂרִיד מֵעִיר

This text is generally considered to be a unity,[75] whereas the following

---

[74]Cf. De Moor, *RoY*, 154, who is followed here. For another reading of משמאול as "because of Sumu'el" (= "Assyrian" form of ישמעאל), cf. M. Dijkstra, "The Geography of the Story of Balaam: Synchronic Reading as a Help to Date a Biblical Text", in: J.C. de Moor (ed.), *Synchronic or Diachronic? A Debate on Method in Old Testament Exegesis* (OTS, 34), Leiden 1995, 72–97, 84, n. 49.

[75]Cf. *e.g.* H. Rouillard, *La péricope de Balaam (Nombres 22–24): La prose et les oracles* (ÉtB, n.s. 4), Paris 1985, 415–69.

sayings (24:20b, 21b–22, 23b–24) are considered to be later additions to the present text,[76] or, together with verses 18–19, a later addition to the Balaam Story.[77] Important in this connection is that all these sayings are called מָשָׁל "saying" (24:15, 20, 21, 23), yet there is a clear difference in length and form. So a מָשָׁל does not have a uniform shape nor a uniform length, making the definition of the form of a מָשָׁל a hazardous undertaking.

In scholarly literature there is no consensus on the origin of these sayings. The two positions that are defended illustrate significantly the problem of our research in Genesis 49. The sayings — or at least some of them — are considered old and as such adopted in a relatively younger Balaam Story.[78] Or, on the other hand, the final three sayings are, together with the section on Edom (including the framework, hence verses 18–25), considered to be a later addition to an older Balaam Story.[79] In the discussion on the history of the story it becomes apparent that the form of the sayings is of no importance with regard to the possible history of the text. Some of the sayings are interpreted as later additions to the text by the editor or even by a later, second editor. In this connection it is recognized by scholars that the editors of the text could insert a saying they imitated from existing forms, as has already been suggested by Gunkel with regard to the history of Israelite literature. The arguments for a definite time of origin of the sayings are in fact all derived from their contents and from their function in the text. For the moment it is important to conclude that the definition of such a saying as a מָשָׁל does not enable us to differentiate between older and younger (expanding) sayings. And secondly, the form and length of the מָשָׁל could differ considerably in the opinion of the ancients:

1. The saying could start with the introduction of the prophet (Num. 24:3–4, 15b–16), or it could be left out (Num. 24:20b, 21b–22, 23b–24).

2. The saying could start by mentioning the name of the nation involved in the first poetic verse (24:20b, 23b–24a), or later in the second poetic verse (24:22), or even after the introduction and after the praise of another nation (24:17c, 18a).

---

[76] Rouillard, *La péricope de Balaam*, 448–50.

[77] G.B. Gray, *A Critical and Exegetical Commentary on Numbers* (ICC), Edinburgh 1903, 371–3; Dijkstra, "Geography of the Story of Balaam", 95–6.

[78] Cf. *e.g.* De Moor, *RoY*, 151–5 (with bibliography).

[79] Cf. *e.g.* Dijkstra, "Geography of the Story of Balaam", 95 (cf. p. 73, n. 6 for other opinions and bibliography).

3. The saying could consist of one (24:20b) or two poetic verses (24:21b–22, 23b–24), and even of three strophes (24:15b–19).

The problems involved with the form critical study of Genesis 49 are also illustrated abundantly by means of the problems raised by the so-called "song of Heshbon" (Num. 21:27b–30).

3.2.3.6.3 A Taunt Song

The song of Heshbon is announced in Numbers as a song which was sung by the ballad singers (הַמֹּשְׁלִים):

Come to Heshbon, (27bA)	בֹּאוּ חֶשְׁבּוֹן
let the city of Sihon be built and restored. (27bB)	תִּבָּנֶה וְתִכּוֹנֵן עִיר סִיחוֹן

For fire went out from Heshbon, (28aA)	כִּי־אֵשׁ יָצְאָה מֵחֶשְׁבּוֹן
flame from the city of Sihon. (28aB)	לֶהָבָה מִקִּרְיַת סִיחֹן
It devoured Ar of Moab, (28bA)	אָכְלָה עָר מוֹאָב
the lords of the heights of the Arnon. (28bB)	בַּעֲלֵי בָּמוֹת אַרְנֹן

Woe to you, Moab; (29aA)	אוֹי־לְךָ מוֹאָב
you are destroyed, people of Chemosh; (29aB)	אָבַדְתָּ עַם־כְּמוֹשׁ
He gave his sons as fugitives, (29bA)	נָתַן בָּנָיו פְּלֵיטִם
his daughters as captives to ... Sihon. (29bB)	וּבְנֹתָיו בַּשְּׁבִית לְ...סִיחוֹן[80]

We shot at them, Heshbon is destroyed to Dibon, (30aA)	וַנִּירָם אָבַד חֶשְׁבּוֹן עַד־דִּיבוֹן
and we laid waste until Nophash, which is to Medeba. (30aB)	וַנַּשִּׁים עַד־נֹפַח אֲשֶׁר עַד־מֵידְבָא

Usually this song is considered an old song inserted by the writer of Numbers. Nevertheless, whereas the writer of Num. 21:27a suggests that the whole text of Num. 21:27b–30 is sung by the singers, modern research assumes some redactional expansions especially in verses 27b and 30.[81] But this version of the song is not the only one, in Jer. 48:45–6 another one is found:

For fire went out from Heshbon, (45bA)	כִּי־אֵשׁ יָצָא מֵחֶשְׁבּוֹן
and a flame from the midst of Sihon; (45bB)	וְלֶהָבָה מִבֵּין סִיחוֹן

---

[80] Usually לְמֶלֶךְ אֱמֹרִי סִיחוֹן "to Sihon, the king of the Amorites" in verse 29 is considered to be a gloss since it breaks up the poetry (cf. P.J. Budd, *Numbers* [WBC, 5], Waco [TX] 1984, 242, 245). By leaving out the words מֶלֶךְ אֱמֹרִי (indicated by the dots in the text) the rhythm is restored.

[81] This assumption seems to be confirmed by our strophic delimitation, because verse 27b and 30a can be distinguished from verses 28–9, whereas the last mentioned verses together form two strophes.

It consumed the skull of Moab, (45cA)

וַתֹּאכַל פְּאַת מוֹאָב

the crown of the sons of tumult. (45cB)

וְקָדְקֹד בְּנֵי שָׁאוֹן

Woe to you, O Moab, (46aA)

אוֹי־לְךָ מוֹאָב

the people of Chemosh are destroyed; (46aB)

אָבַד עַם־כְּמוֹשׁ

For your sons have been taken captive, (46bA)

כִּי־לֻקְּחוּ בָנֶיךָ בַּשֶּׁבִי

and your daughters into captivity. (46bB)

וּבְנֹתֶיךָ בַּשִּׁבְיָה

The relationship of these two versions is part of a more wide-ranging discussion on the inter-relationship of Num. 21:21–35, Deut. 2:24–3:11 and Judg. 11:19–26. Whereas the chronological prevalence of the version in Numbers is the classical assumption finding its defenders until today,[82] others prefer the prevalence of the Deuteronomistic version together with Jeremiah's version of the song.[83] However, for our argument the chronological order is irrelevant.[84] Our point is that these two versions could *both* be considered to be independent of each other: if the version in Numbers had been unknown to us, we would not suggest that Jeremiah could have used another version (like the one found in Numbers). This statement might be supported by the fact that some scholars suggest that Jeremiah's version records the original one. On the other hand, if we had only the version of Numbers it would be difficult to defend a late origin for this song.

With regard to these two versions of the song it is important to note that it is suggested by the ancients that the ballad singers had

---

[82] J.R. Bartlett, "The Conquest of Sihon's Kingdom: A Literary Re-examination", *JBL* 97 (1978) 347–51; U. Köppel, *Das deuteronomistische Geschichtswerk und seine Quellen: Die Absicht der deuteronomistischen Geschichtsdarstellung aufgrund des Vergleichs zwischen Num 21, 21–35 und Dtn 2, 26–3, 3* (EHS.T, 122), Bern 1979.

[83] J. Van Seters, "The Conquest of Sihon's Kingdom: A Literary Examination", *JBL* 91 (1972) 182–97; idem, "Once Again—The Conquest of Sihon's Kingdom", *JBL* 99 (1980) 117–24; K.A.D. Smelik, " 'Een vuur gaat uit van Chesbon'. Een onderzoek naar Numeri 20:14–21; 21:10–35 en parallelplaatsen", *ACEBT* 5 (1984) 61–109. Further bibliographical references and description of previous research are found with Budd, *Numbers*, 241–6.

[84] In the view of the present author the prevalence of the version in Numbers is to be preferred. The adaptation of the phrase נָתַן בָּנָיו פְּלֵיטִם "he (= Chemosh, Num. 21:29aB) gave his sons as fugitives" (Num. 21:29b) — suggesting the power of other gods — to the phrase כִּי־לֻקְּחוּ בָנֶיךָ בַּשֶּׁבִי "for your sons have been taken captive" (Jer. 48:46bA) is more likely than the other way round. Further, LXX of Jer. 48 omits these verses, whereas it is evident that the present text of Jer. 48 has adopted several passages from other biblical books, and these facts also argue against an original reading in Jeremiah. For Jeremiah cf. B.J. Oosterhoff, *Jeremia*, dl. I (COT), Kampen 1990, 60–1; W. McKane, *Jeremiah*, vol. II (ICC), Edinburgh 1996, 1155–1202.

songs that were longer than one or two poetic verses,[85] having at least two strophes. Assuming now for the moment the priority of the version in Numbers, we might conclude, with regard to our research, the following:

1. The text in Numbers suggests by its reference to the ballad singers that taunt songs on other cities and nations existed and were sung.[86] In this sense the song offers a good parallel to the so-called "tribal saying", where other tribes are the subject of the saying.

2. The version in Numbers demonstrates that old songs could be reworked and expanded in a way the editor thought opportune.

3. The version in Jeremiah demonstrates the possibility that old texts were adopted and reworked in such a way that they would be no longer recognized as such if we did not have an earlier version.

Next to oracles against other nations and taunt songs being more or less negative texts, messianic prophecies are also found in the prophetic books, paralleled sometimes with Genesis 49 and Deuteronomy 33.

3.2.3.6.4 Amos 1–2

The Book of Amos opens with a list of oracles against foreign nations ending however with two oracles against Judah (2:4–5) and Israel (2:6–16[?]). It is probable that here we are dealing with one of the earliest examples of this kind of oracle.[87] Two characteristic oracles may be quoted here, the first one is against Damascus (Amos 1:3–5):

Thus says Y<small>HWH</small>: (3aA)	כֹּה אָמַר יהוה
For three transgressions of Damascus, (3aB)	עַל־שְׁלֹשָׁה פִּשְׁעֵי דַמֶּשֶׂק
and for four, I will not make return, (3aC)	וְעַל־אַרְבָּעָה לֹא אֲשִׁיבֶנּוּ
For they threshed Gilead with iron threshers. (3bA)	עַל־דּוּשָׁם בַּחֲרֻצוֹת הַבַּרְזֶל אֶת־הַגִּלְעָד
I will send a fire upon the house of Hazael, (4bA)	וְשִׁלַּחְתִּי אֵשׁ בְּבֵית חֲזָאֵל
it will devour the fortresses of Ben-Hadad; (4bB)	וְאָכְלָה אַרְמְנוֹת בֶּן־הֲדָד

---

[85] Contrast Gunkel's assumption that they could only remember one or two poetic verses!

[86] The use of the root משל "make up a saying, proverb, mocking verse", related to the noun מָשָׁל (*HAL*, 611–2) is remarkable.

[87] Barton, *Amos's Oracles*, 3, 15.

I will break the bar of Damascus, (5aA)	וְשָׁבַרְתִּי בְּרִיחַ דַּמֶּשֶׂק
cut off the inhabitants from the valley of Aven; (5aB)	וְהִכְרַתִּי יוֹשֵׁב מִבִּקְעַת־אָוֶן
and him that holds the scepter of Beth-Eden, (5bA)	וְתוֹמֵךְ שֵׁבֶט מִבֵּית עֶדֶן
and the people of Aram shall be exiled to Kir," says YHWH. (5bB)	וְגָלוּ עַם־אֲרָם קִירָה אָמַר יהוה

The second oracle is the one against Judah (2:4–5):[88]

Thus says YHWH: (4aA)	כֹּה אָמַר יהוה
For three transgressions of Judah, (4aB)	עַל־שְׁלֹשָׁה פִּשְׁעֵי יְהוּדָה
and for four, I will not make return, (4aC)	וְעַל־אַרְבָּעָה לֹא אֲשִׁיבֶנּוּ
For they rejected the law of YHWH, (4bA)	עַל־מָאֳסָם אֶת־תּוֹרַת יהוה
and have not kept his statutes; (4bB)	וְחֻקָּיו לֹא שָׁמָרוּ
But their lies have led them astray (4cA)	וַיַּתְעוּם כִּזְבֵיהֶם
after which their fathers walked. (4cB)	אֲשֶׁר־הָלְכוּ אֲבוֹתָם אַחֲרֵיהֶם

I will send a fire upon Judah, (5aA)	וְשִׁלַּחְתִּי אֵשׁ בִּיהוּדָה
it will devour the fortresses of Jerusalem. (5aB)	וְאָכְלָה אַרְמְנוֹת יְרוּשָׁלָ͏ִם

For the study of Genesis 49 it is interesting that scholars are inclined to regard three oracles, the ones against Tyre, Edom and Judah, as later additions to the list on the basis of their form. In his commentary on Amos, H.W. Wolff discusses the form of these oracles extensively and argued in favour of the later addition of the aforementioned three oracles.[89] Wolff lists five elements which are characteristic for four oracles out of the eight (Damascus, Gaza, Ammon and Moab): 1. introductory messenger formula (*Botenformel*); 2. the general announcement of irrevocability; 3. the specific reason with disclosure of guilt; 4. the specific execution of the threat of punishment; 5. the closing messenger formula.[90] In his view the first, second and fifth element contain, except for the names, an identical phrasing, the syntax and size of the third and fourth element are identical, in the phrasing the first bicolon of the fourth element is comparable.[91] From these rigidly identically structured oracles three oracles distinguish themselves on the basis of formal criteria: Tyre, Edom and Judah. Only the first and the second element are the same in these oracles; in the third element, although starting with עַל and an infinitive, the infinitive clause

---

[88]The authenticity of the oracle against Judah is doubted by several scholars together with the ones against Tyre and Edom. We will return to that problem below.

[89]H.W. Wolff, *Dodekapropheton 2: Joel, Amos* (BKAT, XIV/2), Neukirchen-Vluyn 1969, 164–75.

[90]Wolff, *Dodekapropheton 2*, 164–5.

[91]Wolff, *Dodekapropheton 2*, 165.

is shortened and elaborated with verbal clauses; the fourth element is shortened and is only a third of the other threat of punishment; the fifth element is completely absent. Next to these formal arguments he lists some superficial language historical (*sprachgeschichtliche*) arguments,[92] meant to strengthen the form critical arguments, in order to regard 1:9–12 and 2:4–5 as later additions.

With regard to the form critical arguments some remarks are in order here. Statistically the exclusion of *three* oracles out of eight on the basis of the form of just *four* other oracles out of these eight is untenable, especially if one (the remaining eighth) oracle differs considerably from all the foregoing (see especially the fourth and fifth element) but is still considered to be original. Moreover, whereas Amos apparently adopted parts of the form of his oracles from a wisdom genre (graded numerical saying[93] and shaped them into the present form, external evidence for the authentic form of the oracles is lacking. It seems therefore methodologically incorrect to use one half of the text as a criterion for authenticity of the other half of the text. Furthermore, the argument for the expansion of the disclosure of guilt, and the contraction of the threat of punishment is indefensible as an argument against the authenticity of these oracles in view of ancient Near Eastern language, in which certain forms, like messenger formulas, could be expanded and contracted at the writer's pleasure.[94]

---

[92]Our judgment that his arguments are superficial, can be justified by the following observations. Wolff, *Dodekapropheton*, 170, states that the oracle against Tyre includes almost literally the oracle against Gaza (1:6b), whereas the Edom oracle in essence remembers the oracles against Damascus and Ammon, but that the Edom oracle generalizes the original wording. With regard to Judah it is a fact that the accusation is only restricted to the relationship with God, whereas also the reference to YHWH in the third person (2:4b) does not tally with the messenger formula (2:4aA) and first person in the end. Wolff ignores however the many reminiscences between the different oracles, which makes an argument of the reminiscences of the Tyre and Edom with other oracles untenable; see *e.g.* "I will cut off the inhabitants from ..." (5aB; 8aA; cf. also 2:3aA); "him that holds the scepter from ..." (5bA; 8aB); next to the many frequently used words throughout this chapter. Also the change in person is an argument he cannot use consistently; cf. for example 2:13, which is original in his view, whereas 2:10–12 should be secondary (*op.cit.*, 172). Finally, the form critical and literary critical arguments contradict each other: identical form is an argument for authenticity; almost identical wordings an argument for later expansion, whereas the identical wording of the first and second element, and the beginning of the fourth element are excluded. In view of these arguments Wolff's literary critical arguments are void and consequently his argument for the later addition based on these arguments is also void.

[93]J.L. Mays, *Amos: A Commentary* (OTL), London 1969, 23.

[94]See especially J.C. de Moor, "The Art of Versification in Ugarit and Israel, I:

Finally, in his commentary on Amos C. van Leeuwen has questioned the correctness of the form critical arguments in favour of a later addition of the three oracles:[95]

> Moreover, with regard to the form critical arguments by which the authenticity of the aforementioned prophecies are challenged, it may be asked if the form critical approach of the text does not exceed its competence, when it forces a prophetic oracle into the mould of the form. In other words: is it possible that a prophet, who has chosen a certain outline as general framework, allows himself certain departures from that outline when considering it to be opportune for his message?[96]

Summarizing it can be concluded that the form critical arguments against the authenticity of some of these oracles are insufficient to prove their later addition to the original. It might even be doubted if such arguments are valid to prove such an addition because a later editor would imitate the original rigidly to make the text fit in better. However, with regard to our investigation of the genre of the "tribal saying" it is important to note that

1. Form criticism is in fact unable to demonstrate an original independence of a certain genre within the text. On the basis of the form one cannot argue against the authenticity of a text because the author — but also a singer or a prophet during the oral tradition — was always able to expand or to contract a certain form and to allow himself certain departures from the original form.

2. The demonstration of a certain genre in a *literary* text does not prove its independence from its context, rather the opposite. The oracles against the other nations are grouped together

---

The Rhythmical Structure", in: Y. Avishur, J. Blau (eds.), *Studies in Bible and the Ancient Near East Presented to S.E. Loewenstamm*, Jerusalem 1978, 119–139; idem, "The Art of Versification, II: The Formal Structure", *UF* 10 (1978) 187–217, esp. 189–90 (example no. 43); idem, "The Art of Versification, III: Further Illustrations of the Principle of Expansion", *UF* 12 (1980) 311–315; idem, "The Poetry of the Book of Ruth, (part I)", *Or* 53 (1984) 262–283, esp. 262–71.

[95] C. van Leeuwen, *Amos* (PredOT), Nijkerk 1985, 51–2.

[96] Van Leeuwen, *Amos*, 51: "Bovenal echter is ten aanzien van de vormkritische argumenten waarmee men de echtheid van de genoemde profetieën bestrijdt, de vraag te stellen of de vormkritische benadering van een tekst haar competentie niet overschrijdt, als zij een profetisch woord qua vorm in een keurslijf perst; met andere woorden: zou een profeet die een bepaald schema als algemeen kader kiest, zich op bepaalde punten geen afwijkingen van dat schema mogen veroorloven, indien hij dat voor zijn boodschap dienstig acht?" Cf. also W. Rudolph, *Joel — Amos — Obadja — Jona* (KAT, XIII/2), Gütersloh 1971, 119–20.

by Amos (at least those against Damascus, Gaza, Ammon and Moab), together with a differing oracle, the one against Israel. Moreover it is likely that these oracles are part of a larger unit which starts with an introductory saying (1:2) and ends with 3:1–8. So a genre could even be adopted in a larger context.

3.2.3.6.5 Micah 4:8 and 5:1

In Micah 4:8 we read the following:

And [to] you, O Migdal-Eder (8aA)	וְאַתָּה מִגְדַּל־עֵדֶר
O Hill of the daughter of Zion, to you shall come, (8aB)	עֹפֶל בַּת־צִיּוֹן עָדֶיךָ תֵּאתֶה
The former dominion shall enter, (8bA)	וּבָאָה הַמֶּמְשָׁלָה הָרִאשֹׁנָה
the kingdom to the daughter of Jerusalem. (8bB)	מַמְלֶכֶת לְבַת־יְרוּשָׁלָ͏ִם

Micah 5:1 (E.T. 5:2) reads:

And [from] you, O Bethlehem Ephrathah (1aA)	וְאַתָּה בֵּית־לֶחֶם אֶפְרָתָה
who is little to be among the clans of Judah, (1aB)	צָעִיר לִהְיוֹת בְּאַלְפֵי יְהוּדָה
From you shall come forth for me (1bA)	מִמְּךָ לִי יֵצֵא
one who is to be ruler in Israel, (1bB)	לִהְיוֹת מוֹשֵׁל בְּיִשְׂרָאֵל
whose origin is from of old, from ancient days. (1bC)	וּמוֹצָאֹתָיו מִקֶּדֶם מִימֵי עוֹלָם

In these two passages the reference to tribes has changed for cities or villages. Westermann[97] compared these texts with the tribal sayings of Genesis 49 and Deuteronomy 33, which in his view "unmistakably introduced a form of tradition of benedictions (to be found in *e.g.* Numbers 22–24)."[98] Interestingly Westermann considers Mic. 5:2 to be a later addition, so that verse 3 originally continued verse 1.[99] So apparently the similarity of form to the "tribal sayings" is no reason to assume a short text of one or two poetic verses, as he does later in his commentary on Genesis.[100] With regard to Gen. 49:8–12, 22–26 for example, he assumes later expansions because the complete sayings are too long for the assumed standard form.[101]

---

[97] See above, p. 269, n. 65.

[98] Westermann, "Micha 5, 1–3", 54: "... die offenbar eine Traditionsform von Heilssprüchen einleiteten (z. B. in Nm 22–24 zu erkennen)."

[99] Westermann, "Micha 5, 1–3", 55–6.

[100] Westermann, *Genesis 37–50*, 250.

[101] Westermann, *Genesis 37–50*, 250. Westermann was recently criticized for his view on these two texts of Genesis 49 by J.A. Wagenaar, *Oordeel en heil: Een onderzoek naar samenhang tussen de heils- en onheilsprofetieën in Micha 2–5*, Utrecht 1995, 251–3, stating that the original form of the saying is no criterion for later literary wording and that accordingly no verdict can be made on their

The analysis of the redactional activity on Mic. 4:8 has not reached an assured consensus and scholars differ over its relationship to the context: was it added later in the redactional process and shaped after the form of Mic. 5:1, 3;[102] or is it part of Mic. 4:6–8,[103] or Mic. 4:1–9?[104] The discussion of the problems involved would go beyond the scope of the present study, and in this respect the discussion on Mic. 5:1–3 (E.T. 5:2–4) is less complicated. Though some scholars consider verse 2 to be a later expansion,[105] others are inclined to read these three verses as an original unity:[106]

And [from] you, O Bethlehem Ephrathah (1aA)	וְאַתָּה בֵּית־לֶחֶם אֶפְרָתָה
who are little to be among the clans of Judah, (1aB)	צָעִיר לִהְיוֹת בְּאַלְפֵי יְהוּדָה
From you shall come forth for me (1bA)	מִמְּךָ לִי יֵצֵא
one who is to be ruler in Israel, (1bB)	לִהְיוֹת מוֹשֵׁל בְּיִשְׂרָאֵל
whose origin is from of old, from ancient days. (1bC)	וּמוֹצָאֹתָיו מִקֶּדֶם מִימֵי עוֹלָם

Therefore He shall give them up until the time the one to bear will bear (2aA)	לָכֵן יִתְּנֵם עַד־עֵת יוֹלֵדָה יָלָדָה
then the rest of his brothers will return to the sons of Israel (2aB)	וְיֶתֶר אֶחָיו יְשׁוּבוּן עַל־בְּנֵי יִשְׂרָאֵל
He will stand and shepherd in YHWH's strength, (3aA)	וְעָמַד וְרָעָה בְּעֹז יהוה
in the majesty of the name of YHWH his god, (3aB)	בִּגְאוֹן שֵׁם יהוה אֱלֹהָיו
they shall dwell because now he shall be great to the end of the earth. (3aC)	וְיָשָׁבוּ כִּי־עַתָּה יִגְדַּל עַד־אַפְסֵי־אָרֶץ

As we noted before with regard to Westermann, it is remarkable that the saying in verse 1 is commonly viewed as continued in a following verse, 2 or 3, and that the form as a tribal saying is no reason to

---

size beforehand. However, the independence of Mic. 4:8 from the foregoing verses 6–7 is based by Wagenaar himself on the form, derived from the tribal saying (op.cit., 252, n. 240), which seems somehow inconsistent with his earlier criticism.

[102] H.W. Wolff, Dodekapropheton 4: Micah (BKAT, XIV/4), Neukirchen-Vluyn 1982, 86–7, 90; cf. also J.L. Mays, Micah: A Commentary (OTL), London 1976, 102–4; Wagenaar, Oordeel en heil, 252–3.

[103] J. Ridderbos, De Kleine Profeten opnieuw uit de grondtekst vertaald en verklaard (KV), Kampen 1930, 84–6; W. Rudolph, Micha — Nahum — Habakuk — Zephanja (KAT, XIII/3), Gütersloh 1975, 82–5; L.C. Allen, The Books of Joel, Obadiah, Jonah and Micah (NICOT), Grand Rapids (MI) 1976, 328–31; R.L. Smith, Micah–Maleachi (WBC, 32), Waco (TX) 1984, 38–9.

[104] A.S. van der Woude, Micha (PredOT), Nijkerk 1976, 127–52.

[105] Westermann, "Micha 5, 1–3", 55–6; Wolff, Micha, 106–7, 117–8; Mays, Micah, 133–4.

[106] Rudolph, Micha, 98, with n. 28; Van der Woude, Micha, 169–71; Allen, The Books, 344, with n. 30; Wagenaar, Oordeel en heil, 252–3.

consider verse 1 to be independent. Considerations concerning the original size of the saying have to be taken on the basis of the contents and not on the original shape of a literary genre. So, if Westermann is right with regard to the definition of Mic. 5:1 as a kind of "tribal saying", we may conclude that the length of such a saying could differ and sometimes might contain more than one or two poetic verses. Moreover, prophets, writers or editors, were apparently able to adapt certain genres and transform them into the shape they needed.[107]

3.2.3.6.6 Summary

Though examples like the "taunt song" seem to confirm the idea that songs and sayings on (other) cities, peoples, or tribes did exist, this evidence is of little value for the theory of tribal sayings in Genesis 49. The problem is that — though it is probable that such songs did exist — the genre was not bound to a certain *Sitz im Leben* but could be adopted and the form could even be adapted in other contexts, even literary contexts. The point that genres could be adopted and adapted in other contexts can be demonstrated in the case of the oracles against the nations by Amos, who adapted parts of a wisdom genre (graded numerical saying) into a prophetic oracle. Further, it is clear from the oracles of Balaam and of Micah that a prophet could change the form of his oracles considerably, and that he was not bound to just one outline or to one length of his sayings. Also regularly recurring elements in a text, like vocative or a messenger formula are no indication that the text is build up of independent occurrences of these genres. The form might be chosen deliberately to have a kind of refrain or to build up to a certain climax. It appears that the use of form critical arguments in a literary critical debate is rather unstable and, in fact, as was stated by Muilenburg en Van Leeuwen, beyond the competence of form criticism.

3.2.4 Conclusions

With regard to the existence of tribal sayings in the Semitic literature and the Hebrew Bible's use of oracles against other nations the following conclusions can be drawn.

1. The existence of "tribal sayings" is confirmed in the later Arabian world. In the ancient Near East, however, no absolute evidence has been found. Occurrences of different versions of a song like the song of Heshbon and also the comment in Num. 21:27a

---

[107]Mays, *Micah*, 113.

suggest that taunt songs (and thus sayings too?) on other cities and nations existed.

2. The examples of hymnic sayings however do not suggest the existence of a genre of positive "tribal sayings". The examples given from Arabian as well as Sumerian literature are both derived from odes (Arabian) and hymns (Sumerian) and this latter designation (hymns) might therefore be a better definition. Negative sayings apply metaphors and other literary features rather as stereotypes.

3. Many sayings use nominal clauses or comparable syntax to describe the tribe involved, but in longer sayings after the nominal clauses verbal clauses are also used. Most sayings are concerned with the present; the past and the future are almost absent or only there to serve the sayings concerning the present.

4. It is impossible to define one uniform length for a genre like the "tribal saying" or "oracle": prophets, singers, writers could adapt the length of sayings as much as they wanted and considered opportune.

5. Next to the independent occurrence and origin of such sayings we have to conclude that comparable texts occur firmly embedded in the literary context in which they also originated. Hence, the coherence of a supposed "tribal saying" with the present literary context might be original.

6. In order to establish the existence of the genre "tribal saying" in Genesis 49 and the relation of these sayings to their literary context, a discussion of the genre of the sayings of Genesis 49 is required.

The necessity formulated in the final conclusion will be elaborated in the section below. In this section we will try to establish the genre of the different sayings as precisely as possible.

3.3   The Genre of the Sayings in Genesis 49

3.3.1   Introduction

As has been demonstrated in Chapter One, the definition of the sayings' genre in Genesis 49 is dominated by the study of Greßmann, who defined these sayings as "tribal sayings". This becomes especially clear in the work of Kittel and Zobel, where this definition is not questioned. Even if in certain cases parallels with prophetic oracles could be demonstrated, such as Reubens, the definition of "tribal saying" was still maintained. However, these definitions proved to be based on several pre-suppositions of which one of the most important was the gradual development of Israel's literature from a simple to a more complex form. But in fact the most important pre-supposition was the idea itself that here we were dealing with independent sayings referring to the individual tribes in a pre-literary stage of Israel's history.

The supposition that in Deuteronomy 33 we are dealing with tribal sayings was recently tested by Beyerle in his study on that chapter.[108] He concluded however, that the genre "tribal saying" did not exist in Deuteronomy 33, because sufficient distinctive features could not be defined.[109] His rather differing genre-definitions have in his view a compositional critical value, because the hymnic elements from the framework-psalm may be considered to be an enhancement in comparison to the sayings. It moves from several wish-forms, describing the divine care more or less as possibilities, to is-forms in the descriptions, ending in a hymn for the described situation.[110] In this situation where it is not possible to describe the *Sitz im Leben* of the sayings,[111] a scholar is forced to direct his attention to the *Sitz in der Literatur* of the sayings and the collection.

If Beyerle is correct, the existence of "tribal sayings" in the Hebrew Bible is doubtful. With regard to Judges 5 it is generally acknowledged that this song is problematic and does not contain "tribal sayings" in the same manner as Genesis 49 and Deuteronomy 33, and that in it we are only dealing either with related forms functioning together,[112] or with a preliminary stage of the tribal sayings,[113] or with only a few

---

[108] Beyerle, *Mosesegen im Deuteronomium* (p. 251, n. 13 above).

[109] Beyerle, *Mosesegen im Deuteronomium*, 274. He defined the saying on Reuben as a wish (pp. 105–6); on Judah as a prayer (pp. 112–3); on Levi as a description ending in a prayer (pp. 135–6); on Benjamin in the context of the psalm as a historical allusion, and in the present form as a description (pp. 150–1); on Joseph as a blessing (pp. 188–9); on Zebulun and Issachar as a mixture of thanksgiving psalm and hymn (pp. 207–8); on Gad more or less as a blessing (pp. 232–3); on Dan, depending on the rendering as a wish or as a description (pp. 243–4); on Naphtali as an address (253–4); and finally on Asher as a blessing (268–9).

[110] Beyerle, *Mosesegen im Deuteronomium*, 274–5.

[111] Beyerle, *Mosesegen im Deuteronomium*, 274.

[112] Cf. Kittel, *Stammessprüche Israels*, 71. J.C. de Moor, "The Twelve Tribes in the Song of Deborah", *VT* 43 (1993) 483–93, defended a reconstructed pre-Davidic version of Judg. 5:13–18, built up as a carefully composed poem, suggesting a prelimenary stage of the song rather than an independently functioning part.

[113] Westermann, *Genesis 37–50*, 251.

real tribal sayings.[114] The only text thus remaining is Genesis 49: to which genre do the different sayings belong? This is the main question in the following sections.

3.3.2   Reuben

In the introduction the fact was mentioned that the saying on Reuben was compared with prophetic oracles. Kittel for example paralleled the saying on Reuben — together with the sayings on Simeon & Levi, on Judah and on Meroz (Judg. 5:23) — with the prophetic oracle.[115] He maintains for these sayings his general definition of "tribal saying". It may be asked, however, on what ground this can be maintained when a text has all the features of another genre?

A prophetic oracle against a people has the twofold structure of argument and announcement. The first element consists of accusation and its display; the other element of God's intervention and its consequences.[116] This genre has, however, been developed from the lawsuit against the individual,[117] consisting of accusation and the announcement of judgement.[118] In the saying on Reuben we find the following structure:[119]

address	Reuben, my firstborn are you, (3A)
	my might and the first of my strength, (3B)
	superior in tallness, and superior in power; (3C)
announcement	deceptive like water, you shall have no superiority, (4A)
accusation	for you went up to your father's bed, (4B)
	then you defiled the concubine's couch. (4C)

The address is formulated in nominal clauses, describing in this way a certain situation. Then, in the announcement, which contains in fact a second address to the "real" Reuben: "deceptive like water", the judgement is announced by means of a negative optative clause (jussive with אַל): "you shall have no superiority". The announcement is followed by the accusation in a כִּי-phrase and *qatal*-forms describ-

---

[114]Zobel, *SuG*, 44–52.

[115]Kittel, *Stammessprüche Israels*, 91–5; already Greßmann, *Anfänge Israels*, 94. Cf. also C. Westermann, *Grundformen prophetischer Rede* (BEvTh, 31), München ⁵1978, 141, n. 18, who thinks that the saying on Reuben was originally a curse, which is not recognisable any more.

[116]Westermann, *Grundformen prophetischer Rede*, 122. In the same way: Kittel, *Stammessprüche Israels*, 92.

[117]Westermann, *Grundformen prophetischer Rede*, 120–2.

[118]Westermann, *Grundformen prophetischer Rede*, 94–5.

[119]See Westermann, *Genesis 37–50*, 253. Kittel, *Stammessprüche Israels*, 8, considers verse 3C as the anacrusis for verse 4A, containing already the accusation, with in verse 4A the curse.

ing Reuben's sin in the past: "for you went up...you defiled ...". It appears that here we have indeed a *lawsuit against an individual*, although not a prophetic one. But a lawsuit is not restricted to prophets; rather, the prophetic lawsuit is derived from the courtroom, and this genre could be applied every time when someone has to judge someone's behaviour. The definition partly suits the framework[120] where the father gathers his sons to announce their future, which results in the present saying denying his oldest son's right to the superior position (in the future) because of his past sin. Since there is absolutely no indication that we are here dealing with a tribe called "Reuben", but evidently with an individual, we may conclude with regard to the genre that Gen. 49:3-4 is not a "tribal saying".

3.3.3 Simeon & Levi

In Chapter Two we pointed out that the form of the saying on Simeon and Levi has an almost identical structure to the one on Reuben. As a consequence, following Kittel and Westermann, it may be considered that here too we are dealing with a lawsuit against individuals.[121] Zobel, however, challenges this similarity because there is no curse in the Reuben saying, the collective meaning of Simeon and Levi is clearly present, and the statement on Simeon and Levi is given in the third person, in contrast to the second person of the Reuben saying.[122] On the argument of the absence of the curse in the Reuben saying we will return below, the two other arguments will be discussed here.[123] The collectivity argument cannot be directed against the similarity, because this collectivity is found in the final part of the curse (49:7C), and this part is referring to the future, meaning the future of the tribes. Since in verse 1 the patriarch announced that he wants to predict the future of his sons, the curse suits the context where it is referring to this future of the sons, *viz.* the tribes.

---

[120]Westermann, *Genesis 37-50*, 253.

[121]Kittel, *Stammessprüche Israels*, 93-4; Westermann, *Genesis 37-50*, 253-5. Westermann, however, considers the saying an exact imitation of the prophetic lawsuit, which presupposes the shift from the individual to the people. As we wrote before, it appears that the lawsuit is not derived from prophetic speech, but from court.

[122]Zobel, *SuG*, 8.

[123]In fact we are here dealing with literary-critical and not with form-critical arguments, so in fact they have to be discussed in Chapter Six: the diachronic analysis. But because some of these arguments could be used to prevent us from considering the genre of a complete saying as a unity we shall deal with them here. The final verdict on the question of unity or diachronic different layers has, however, to be given in Chapter Six.

The argument from the difference in person (second and third) is more complicated and also more important because the same argument is used with regard to the different parts of the Judah saying.[124] The argument from the difference in person is used very frequently in scholarly literature to discern different layers in a text. The validity of this argument is questionable, however, in the light of the literary compositions in Israel's *Umwelt*, like, for example, Ugaritic literature. It appears that in ancient Semitic literature the change of person is a rather common feature. In this connection the opening scene of the Ugaritic legend of Kirtu (KTU 1.14–16) is illustrative. In this scene, Kirtu is lying on his bed, mourning because of the wives he has lost and the absence of offspring (1.14:i.1–35), when the god Ilu descends to him in a dream and says (1.14:i.36–43):[125]

*mảt	krt . kybky*	What is the matter with Kirtu, that he weeps
*ydmʿ . nʿmn . ǵlm	il*	that he sheds tears, the gracious lad of Ilu?
mlk [.] *trảbh	yảrš*	Does he request the kingship of the Bull, his Father,
hm . drk[*t*]	*kảb . ảdm*	or dominion like the father of man?

Ilu's address of Kirtu starts in the third person. However, after Kirtu has answered Ilu, revealing what he really wants, namely a wife and children, Ilu speaks a second time to him (1.14:ii.9–11):

t[*r*]*ths . wtảdm*	Wash and scrub yourself,
rhs [. *y*]*dk . ảmt*	wash your hands and forearms,
ủṣb[*ʿtk*] *ʿd* [.] *tkm*	your fingers, up to the shoulder.

Here the third person is changed into the second, but after Ilu has given the instructions for a sacrifice, the direct speech continues without any introductory formula or change in scene in the third person, ending with a shift again to the second person (1.14:ii.27–30):

*wyrd	krt . lggt*	Then Kirtu has to descend from the roof;
*ʿdb	ảkl . lqryt*	let him set out food for the town,
htt . lbt . hbr	wheat for the daughter Khuburu.
yip . lhm . dhmš	Let him bake bread of the fifth,
mǵd [.] *tdt . yrhm*	provisions of the sixth month.
ʿdn [.] *ngb . wyṣi*	Let an army be provisioned and let it go out,
ṣbủ . ṣbi . ngb	let a mighty host be provisioned,
wyṣi . ʿdn . mʿ	yes, let a strong army go out!

---

[124]Cf. the following section where the arguments will be given.
[125]Text according to *CARTU*, 79; translation according *ARTU*, 193.

ṣbůk . ůl . mảd	Let your host be a numerous force,
tlt . mảt . rbt	three hundred myriads,
ḫpṯ . dbl . spr	innumerable conscripts,
ṯnn . dbl . hg	countless troopers.

Whereas such examples could be multiplied, from this example it can be concluded that a change in person is a rather common literary feature. For that reason we are inclined to consider the argument against a possible common background of both sayings — because of the difference in person — untenable. The change in person has to be regarded in our text (Genesis 49 as a whole; but also in the separate sayings) as a literary feature and as such it cannot be used against its unity. The structure of the saying on Simeon & Levi is as follows:

address	Simeon and Levi are brothers, (5A)
	weapons of violence are their knives. (5B)
announcement	My soul shall not enter their company, (6aA)
	my glory shall not rejoice in their gathering; (6aB)
accusation	For in their anger they slew a man, (6bA)
	in their wantonness they hamstrung a bull; (6bB)
curse + reason	Cursed be their anger, for it is fierce, (7A)
	and their wrath, for it is cruel, (7B)
realisation	I will divide them in Jacob, scatter them in Israel (7C)

The address is here too formulated in nominal clauses. Though Kittel considers the second colon (49:5B) to contain the accusation and its display,[126] we might — similar to verse 4A — find here an address in which the negative character of the two brothers is revealed. Only after the address follows the announcement: "My soul shall not enter ..., my glory shall not rejoice ...". Though scholars tend to leave verse 6a out as a later insertion because of the language, which seems to be related to the Psalms and to Wisdom circles,[127] and because this verse would mitigate against the rest of the saying,[128] it appears to us to be the announcement of judgement, in which the dying patriarch refuses his sons his future presence in their gatherings.[129] Another vestige is already found in the address, where Simeon and Levi are called אַחִים "brothers", a term which seems to be connected

---

[126] Kittel, *Stammessprüche Israels*, 93; similarly Westermann, *Genesis 37–50*, 256.

[127] Westermann, *Genesis 37–50*, 256; cf. also: idem, *Grundformen prophetischer Rede*, 141.

[128] Kittel, *Stammessprüche Israels*, 13.

[129] In section 2.3.1, we already referred to this interpretation. See esp. J.C. de Moor, "Standing Stones and Ancestor Worship", *UF* 27 (1995) 1–20, 15–6.

with the cult of the dead and which can probably already be found in Gen. 31:54.[130] This interpretation as an announcement of judgement is confirmed by the identical syntactic form as in verse 4A, following the address: a negative optative clause (jussive with אל). The announcement is followed by the accusation, introduced with כי with verbal forms in the *qatal*, referring to the past.[131] The accusation is followed by a curse together with the reason why, again introduced by כי. The curse is worked out in the final colon where an announcement of judgement is found again: "I will divide them in Jacob, scatter them in Israel". According to Westermann we have here a compulsion of the form (*Formzwang*) in that the divine speech is given in the 1.p.sg. corresponding to the form of the lawsuit.[132] However, when verse 6a is considered an announcement by the patriarch, using already the 1.p.sg., it is unnecessary to regard the forms here as divine speech. In fact we find here an elaboration of the announcement of judgement in verse 6a: their gatherings and company will be divided and scattered throughout Israel.[133] So, just as in Gen. 49:3–4, we find here a *lawsuit against the (two) individual(s)*, directed against them because of their behaviour.

Finally, Kittel denies a relation with the framework (49:1–2, 28) and considers the saying (without verse 6a) an independent saying, but the proposed interpretation relates the present saying strongly to the framework,[134] identical to the relation of Gen. 49:3–4 and 8–12 with this context.[135] The absence of the curse in Gen. 49:3–4 has already been mentioned above as an argument against the identical form of the saying on Reuben and on Simeon & Levi. The remaining identical elements of both sayings argues already against the relevance of this argument; and, moreover, the discussion above of the oracles against foreign nations in Amos demonstrates that a total identity of form cannot be expected.

---

[130]De Moor, "Standing Stones", 15–6.

[131]Westermann, *Genesis 37–50*, 256, denies that כי refers to verse 6a but considers it to refer to verse 5. However, in the case of verse 4, the identical כי-phrase refers back to the announcement. The main problem appears to be the interpretation of verse 6a as a statement comparable to, for instance, Ps. 1:1, or in contrast, as a reference to the cult of the dead, where the father refuses his future presence in the gatherings of his sons.

[132]Westermann, *Genesis 37–50*, 255; cf. also Kittel, *Stammessprüche Israels*, 13.

[133]Blum, *Komposition der Vätergeschichte*, 216, n. 26, noted the relationship, though interpreting these verses as divine speech. Cf. also U. Schorn, *Ruben und das System der Zwölf Stämme Israels: Redaktionsgeschichtliche Untersuchungen zur Bedeutung des Erstgeborenen Jakobs* (BZAW, 248), Berlin 1997, 248–55.

[134]De Moor, "Standing Stones", 16.

[135]Kittel, *Stammessprüche Israels*, 13.

3.3.4 Judah

The definition of the genre of Gen. 49:8–12 is problematic because it is confused by all kinds of literary critical arguments, like the change in person between verse 8 and 9, the threefold occurrence of the name of Judah, and a difference in contents.[136] However, the arguments appear to be unconvincing when they are carefully tested. The argument of the change of person between verses 8 and 9 appears to be void as was demonstrated in the section above, but, moreover: in verse 9 we find again the change of person between verses 9aA, 9aB and 9b, which would also argue against the unity of verse 9.[137] The argument of the repetition of the name of Judah is similarly untenable, because the emphatic use of the name in such a context could be deliberate,[138] like the threefold expression for a lion, which Kittel considers to be an emphatic reference to Judah's power.[139] Moreover there is a clear difference in the use of the name "Judah", because the first is found in an address, the second in a comparison, and the third is used as a kind of prepositional object. Besides, in prophetic literature we frequently find the repetition of names in oracles which might suggest that the repetition of certain names was not as problematic as it is apparently to us.[140] Finally the difference in contents is also questionable. Though it is clear that in verse 9 we have the start of a description of Judah as a lion (not found in the foregoing nor in the following strophe), as a metaphor for a ruler it suits the context very well. Compare the strophe we quoted before from the Sumerian temple hymns:

> Your prince is the highly esteemed prince, Asarluḫi, the highly esteemed one,
> The hero, born to? (be) a prince, a leopard, who seizes prey,
> He is like an onrushing storm, he gores the rebellious land,
> As long as it is not obedient, he pours out poisonous foam upon it.

---

[136]Kittel, *Stammessprüche Israels*, 15; Zobel, *SuG*, 10–5, 55, 58, 59, 72–6, 79–80; Westermann, *Genesis 37–50*, 258–9.

[137]Kittel, *Stammessprüche Israels*, 14–5, emended the text in order to maintain the differentiation between three parts (Die "Dreiteilung des Textes läßt sich nur mit Hilfe der bei Köhler vorgeschlagenen Konjektur für Vers 9 exakt durchführen" [*op.cit.*, 15]). Cf. also Zobel, *SuG*, 10–1; Westermann, *Genesis 37–50*, 259.

[138]Cf. the examples given above from the songs of the Druzes (pp. 262–262), where the name "Ali" occurs in both strophes. The complete song contains eight strophes, in seven out of them the name Ali is used in the first line; cf. Saarisalo, "Songs of the Druzes", 28–31. Cf. also song VI (p. 14); song XV (p. 34–7). Yet, even in Hebr. poetry this argument is not very strong; cf. *e.g.* Num. 6:24–6.

[139]Kittel, *Stammessprüche Israels*, 17.

[140]Cf. *e.g.* the oracle against Moab, Isa. 15–6; Ezek. 25:8–11; or against Edom in Ezek. 25:12–4, where in three strophes the name of Edom occurs also in the first poetic verse of each strophe (see W.T. Koopmans, "Poetic Reciprocation: The Oracles against Edom and Philistia in Ezek. 25:12–17", *VANEP*, 113–22).

Apparently a person described in a hymnic description could also be compared with a leopard, applying the motif of a metaphor in the context of a hymn. In fact we find the same phenomenon in Balaam's oracles; compare the second oracle in Num. 23:18b–24:[141]

"Rise, Balak, and hear; (18bA)	קוּם בָּלָק וּשֲׁמָע
listen to me, O son of Zippor: (18bB)	הַאֲזִינָה עָדַי בְּנוֹ צִפֹּר
God is not a man, that He should lie, (19aA)	לֹא אִישׁ אֵל וִיכַזֵּב
or a son of man, that He should repent. (19aB)	וּבֶן־אָדָם וְיִתְנֶחָם
Has He said, and will He not do it? (19bA)	הַהוּא אָמַר וְלֹא יַעֲשֶׂה
or has He spoken, and will not fulfill it? (19bB)	וְדִבֶּר וְלֹא יְקִימֶנָּה
Behold, a command to bless I received: (20aA)	הִנֵּה בָרֵךְ לָקָחְתִּי
He has blessed, and I cannot revoke it. (20aB)	וּבֵרֵךְ וְלֹא אֲשִׁיבֶנָּה
He has not beheld misfortune in Jacob; (21aA)	לֹא־הִבִּיט אָוֶן בְּיַעֲקֹב
nor has He seen trouble in Israel. (21aB)	וְלֹא־רָאָה עָמָל בְּיִשְׂרָאֵל
YHWH their God is with them, (21bA)	יהוה אֱלֹהָיו עִמּוֹ
and the shout of a king among them. (21bB)	וּתְרוּעַת מֶלֶךְ בּוֹ
God brings them out of Egypt; (22aA)	אֵל מוֹצִיאָם מִמִּצְרָיִם
he is like the horns of a wild ox to him. (22aB)	כְּתוֹעֲפֹת רְאֵם לוֹ
For there is no enchantment against Jacob, (23aA)	כִּי לֹא־נַחַשׁ בְּיַעֲקֹב
no divination against Israel; (23aB)	וְלֹא־קֶסֶם בְּיִשְׂרָאֵל
Now it shall be said of Jacob and Israel, (23bA)	כָּעֵת יֵאָמֵר לְיַעֲקֹב וּלְיִשְׂרָאֵל
'What has God wrought!' (23bB)	מַה־פָּעַל אֵל
Behold a people! As a lioness it rises up, (24aA)	הֶן־עָם כְּלָבִיא יָקוּם
and as a lion it lifts itself; (24aB)	וְכַאֲרִי יִתְנַשָּׂא
it does not lie down, till it devours the prey, (24bA)	לֹא יִשְׁכַּב עַד־יֹאכַל טֶרֶף
and drinks the blood of the slain." (24bB)	וְדַם־חֲלָלִים יִשְׁתֶּה

This phenomenon is also found in the third oracle, Num. 24:3b–9:[142]

---

[141] This text has to be considered a unity; cf. A. Tosato, "The literary Structure of the First Two Poems of Balaam", *VT* 29 (1979) 98–107; Rouillard, *La péricope de Balaam*, 273–320.

[142] According to Rouillard, *La péricope de Balaam*, 345–88, this oracle is not a unity but the work of two authors. The first author created the introduction (vv. 3b–4) and the paradisiacal oracle (vv. 5–6), whereas the second created the second part with the help of catchwords (v. 7) and quotations (vv. 8–9). Though the present author is not convinced by this solution, it does not contradict our argument since the second author apparently considered the metaphor of the lion suitable to the context.

The oracle of Balaam the son of Beor, (3bA)   נְאֻם בִּלְעָם בְּנוֹ בְעֹר

the oracle of the man whose eye is opened, (3bB)   וּנְאֻם הַגֶּבֶר שְׁתֻם הָעָיִן

The oracle of him who hears the words of God; (4aA)   נְאֻם שֹׁמֵעַ אִמְרֵי־אֵל

who sees the vision of the Almighty, (4aB)   אֲשֶׁר מַחֲזֵה שַׁדַּי יֶחֱזֶה

falling down, but having his eyes uncovered: (4aC)   נֹפֵל וּגְלוּי עֵינָיִם

How fair are your tents, O Jacob, (5aA)   מַה־טֹּבוּ אֹהָלֶיךָ יַעֲקֹב

your encampments, O Israel! (5aB)   מִשְׁכְּנֹתֶיךָ יִשְׂרָאֵל

Like valleys stretching far, gardens next to a river, (6aA)   כִּנְחָלִים נִטָּיוּ כְּגַנֹּת עֲלֵי נָהָר

like aloes that YHWH has planted, (6bA)   כַּאֲהָלִים נָטַע יהוה

like cedars beside the waters. (6bB)   כַּאֲרָזִים עֲלֵי־מָיִם

Water shall flow from his buckets, (7aA)   יִזַּל־מַיִם מִדָּלְיָו

and his seed shall be in many waters. (7aB)   וְזַרְעוֹ בְּמַיִם רַבִּים

His king shall be higher than Agag, (7bA)   וְיָרֹם מֵאֲגַג מַלְכּוֹ

and his kingdom shall be exalted. (7bB)   וְתִנַּשֵּׂא מַלְכֻתוֹ

God brings him out of Egypt; (8aA)   אֵל מוֹצִיאוֹ מִמִּצְרַיִם

He is like the horns of a wild ox to him. (8aB)   כְּתוֹעֲפֹת רְאֵם לוֹ

He shall eat up the nations his adversaries, (8bA)   יֹאכַל גּוֹיִם צָרָיו

crumble their bones, pierce with his arrows. (8bB)   וְעַצְמֹתֵיהֶם יְגָרֵם וְחִצָּיו יִמְחָץ

He couches, lies down, like a lion, (9aA)   כָּרַע שָׁכַב כַּאֲרִי

a lioness; who will rouse him? (9aB)   וּכְלָבִיא מִי יְקִימֶנּוּ

Blessed is who blesses you, (9bA)   מְבָרֲכֶיךָ בָרוּךְ

and cursed who curses you. (9bB)   וְאֹרְרֶיךָ אָרוּר

Both examples demonstrate that the metaphor of a lion could be considered part of a blessing.[143] Therefore it appears to us that the second strophe with the lion metaphor on Judah could be a part of a larger unity.[144]

Westermann rejects the unity of Gen. 49:8–12 on the basis of the arguments given above and divides the text in the three afore-mentioned parts. In his view the first two parts (v. 8 and v. 9) are both tribal sayings, whereas the third part (vv. 10–12) is a promise

---

[143] C. Westermann, *Prophetische Heilsworte im Alten Testament* (FRLANT, 145), Göttingen 1987, 23, describes the seer's oracle as a powerful word, strongly related to a blessing. It is remarkable that Gen. 49:10–12 and Num. 24:5–7 are in his view comparable as visions of the fruitful land; therefore it is in our view even more remarkable that both sayings have in their context the description of the powerful king, who is like a lion.

[144] Cf. already Greßmann, *Anfänge Israels*, 176–7; further Wenham, *Genesis 16– 50*, 476.

of blessing (*Segensverheißung*).[145] The first "tribal saying" (v. 8) is in his view a description of Judah in the present tense, which suits especially the context of Judges 5, where a tribe is praised because of its bravery. In each case this saying does not mean that Judah was to receive the leadership (not to mention the kingship) among the tribes as is thought by other scholars.[146] However, Westermann apparently overlooked the very close parallel of this verse with Gen. 27:29, which in his view is a leadership's-blessing (*Herrschaftssegen*):[147]

Let peoples serve you (29aA)	יַעַבְדוּךָ עַמִּים
and nations bow down to you; (29aB)	וְיִשְׁתַּחֲוּוּ לְךָ לְאֻמִּים
Be lord over your brothers, (29bA)	הֱוֵה גְבִיר לְאַחֶיךָ
and may your mother's sons bow down to you; (29bB)	וְיִשְׁתַּחֲוּוּ לְךָ בְּנֵי אִמֶּךָ
Cursed is who curses you, (29cA)	אֹרְרֶיךָ אָרוּר
and blessed is who blesses you. (29cB)	וּמְבָרֲכֶיךָ בָּרוּךְ

In his commentary he only states that verse 29bA contains a reminiscence of the tribal sayings Gen. 49:8; Deut. 33:16.[148] However, whereas Gen. 27:29 can be considered a blessing, it might be asked why Gen. 49:8 could not be a blessing, especially because the tenses of verse 8 appear to relate this text to the future.[149] Judah is assigned power over his brothers and over the nations in the same way as his father by his deceit of Isaac; nevertheless, in this sense verse 8 is related very strongly to the preceding sayings and to the framework.[150] An exact definition is hard to give however, but in view of the parallel with Gen. 27:29 and of the concluding definition in verse 28, it might be appropriate to characterize the text as a *blessing* in which the leadership in Israel is unreservedly assigned to Judah. Whereas in verse 8 Judah's supremacy is promised, we find in verse 9 a description of Judah's power and sovereignty,[151] while verse 10–12 contains an assignment of the everlasting power followed by the blessed situation of the land.[152] In contrast, however, to the preceding sayings on Reuben

---

[145]Westermann, *Genesis 37–50*, 257. A similar delimitation (though the chronology may differ) is found in Zobel, *SuG*, 72–80; Hecke, *Juda und Israel*, 185–8.

[146]Westermann, *Genesis 37–50*, 258; contrast however his, "ידה hi., preisen", *THAT*, Bd. I, 674–82, 674, where he suggests that the verb ידה is used because of the rise of the tribe.

[147]Westermann, *Genesis 12–36*, 537–8.

[148]Westermann, *Genesis 12–36*, 538.

[149]Cf. above, section 2.4.1.4. With regard to vv. 8aB and 8bB, see also Zobel, *SuG*, 10. For the *yiqtol* as an appropriate verbal form for the genre "blessing", see *op.cit.*, 24, with n. 121.

[150]Cf. Kittel, *Stammessprüche Israels*, 17; 98–100.

[151]Kittel, *Stammessprüche Israels*, 17–8.

[152]Westermann, *Prophetische Heilsworte*, 23.

and Simeon & Levi, this blessing has no structure corresponding to a certain genre.

The different character of both preceding sayings (vv. 3–4, 5–7), in contrast to the others, is recognized by all scholars and as texts related to the context they are generally separated from the following (vv. 8–27).[153] With regard to the verses concerning Judah, it has been suggested that the first two verses (vv. 8, 9) are both tribal sayings.[154] It has to be asked now, if our definition of the complete saying on Judah as a kind of messianic blessing or oracle contradicts or even excludes the definition of these verses as "tribal sayings". We are again partly dealing with literary critical questions, but these cannot be ruled out here, principally because it is possible that a certain genre is adopted and even adapted in another genre, as has happened with, for example, the lament, being used in Amos 5:1–3 as an announcement of the irrevocable judgement against Israel.[155] Similarly it is possible that in the present context a tribal saying has been adopted because it would suit the intention of the writer.

With regard to the first strophe (v. 8) it is very questionable for several reasons if we are really dealing with a tribal saying. First of all the text has been written as a prediction of the future, applying several *yiqtol* forms, which have to be regarded as descriptions of future events.[156] This feature is unknown in the Arabic tribal sayings and does not suit the general understanding of tribal sayings as descriptions of, or reactions to, the present situation of a tribe. Secondly, the different motifs used in this strophe, as well as the syntax suggest a genre comparable to the genre of Gen. 27:29, namely a "blessing" in which the leadership is assigned to the-one-to-be-blessed.[157] Finally, a "tribal saying" defenition to apply to this text, the contents of the text will have to be taken into account. This will have to explain what the supposed meaning is of such a prediction and what the supposed

---

[153]Cf. Westermann, *Genesis 37–50*, 253. In his, *Grundformen prophetischer Rede*, 141, he suggests an earlier form for both "tribal sayings" (Reuben, and Simeon & Levi), which does not recur in his commentary again, however.

[154]Westermann, *Genesis 37–50*, 257.

[155]Cf. further Westermann, *Grundformen prophetischer Rede*, 145–6; more generally pp. 143–7.

[156]*Pace* Westermann, *Genesis 37–50*, 259.

[157]The suggested *Sitz im Leben* for both texts is the deathbed of the father, which would only strengthen this definition. Although the factual *Sitz im Leben* of a genre does not necessarily suit the described *Sitz im Leben* in a literary context, it does not seem to be problematic to consider here the deathbed of a father as the *Sitz im Leben* of these "leadership-blessings". In this respect Zobel's remark is illuminating: "Es liegt nahe, sich Jakob als Redenden vorzustellen" (Zobel, *SuG*, 10; cf. furthermore *op.cit.*, 79; see also Kittel, *Stammessprüche Israels*, 17).

Sitz im Leben is for this kind of sayings. However, as far as we are aware such an explanation has not been offered[158] which seems to be the best counter-argument. So in conclusion, Gen. 49:8 has to be considered as a "leadership-blessing" but not as a "tribal saying".

With regard to the second strophe (v. 9) the situation is somewhat different. The definition of this verse as an independent saying is partly based on a rather one-sided view of ancient Semitic literature, excluding the change of person (2. or 3.p.sg.) and similarly the possibility of change in the motifs applied (like metaphors), as we have discussed before. The parallels from the *Umwelt* suggest however, that the present context of this verse as a blessing, with a kind of hymnic description of the time to come, could be original. For that reason the described genre for the present strophe as a tribal saying is by no means compelling. On the other hand, when interpreting the use of *qatal* forms in this verse as past tenses describing certain conditions, the possibility that we are dealing here with a kind of tribal saying cannot be excluded. But that is the most that can be said with regard to the genre of this strophe, because as part of a larger text it does fit in its present position.

Excursus: What is a Blessing?

The use of the term "blessing" in connection with Genesis 49 is somewhat confusing and usually disputed because the sayings on Reuben and Simeon & Levi are more like a lawsuit, a condemnation or a curse, so that the definition of these sayings as blessings in Gen. 49:28b is inappropriate. In Chapter Two it was stated that in the word בְּרָכָה we are dealing with a powerful word, provoking what it pronounces. With regard to the saying on Judah we have argued that the use of the term בְּרָכָה "blessing" in Gen. 49:28b is correct.[159] A short description of what can be considered a blessing as genre might be appropriate in order to give a correct definition of the following sayings.

Usually a blessing is considered "a magical self-fulfilling thought, a power loaded saying, working out what it says".[160] Although this

---

[158]Unless the text is interpreted as a reference to the present, see Westermann, *Genesis 37–50*, 259, who excludes a reference to the leadership of Judah, which does not appear to be completely in line with the meaning of the text.

[159]In this respect we can refer also to Westermann, who — though strongly favouring the tribal-saying-theory — also uses terms like "blessing-wishes for the tribes" (*Segenswünsche für Stämme*) for the sayings (*Genesis 37–50*, 277), or even with regard to verse 28b states: "Zu diesem Satz paßt die nachträgliche Einfügung des Jakobsegens gut" (*op.cit.*, 223).

[160]W. Schottroff, *Der altisraelitische Fluchspruch* (WMANT, 30), Neukirchen-Vluyn 1969, 164: "ein magisch-selbstwirksam gedachtes, machtgeladenes Wort,

magical meaning cannot be assumed in all blessings in the Hebrew
Text, we still find a certain reminiscence of this meaning in the Hebrew Text. Its shortest form (and therefore the original one[161]), is the
short formula בָּרוּךְ אַתָּה, being considered the basic form of the blessing that could be expanded with some more specific pronouncements,
unfolding the intended blessing. An important feature with regard
to a blessing is the fact that the blessing formula is not necessarily
part of the blessing itself, but that the unfolding pronouncements are
the blessing.[162] These pronouncements give the contents of the blessing without using the formula (בָּרוּךְ). Blessings use imperative forms,
jussive forms,[163] as well as the normal *yiqtol*.[164] Zobel lists two additional characteristics, which might argue for the definition of a saying
as a blessing: the address-form (use of 2.p.sg. or plur.) and the closed
composition.[165] As was argued, however, with regard to the saying on
Simeon & Levi, the form of address in the 2.person cannot be considered a constitutive element because the 3.person is sometimes used
as a form of address in ancient Near Eastern literature, even in blessings. Compare KTU 1.19:iv.32–40, where Pughatu, the daughter of
the king Dani'ilu is speaking because she wants to revenge the death
of her brother Aqhatu:

ltbrkn . ảlk . brktm |	"Please bless me, (that) I may go blessed,
tmrn . ảlk . nmrrt |	fortify me, (that) I may go fortified!
imḫṣ . mḫṣ . ảḫy .	I want to slay the slayer of my brother,
ảklm | *kly .* [ ]*l . ủmty .*	I want to destroy the destroyer of my kin!"

---

das selbst schafft, was es zuspricht". Cf. also G. Wehmeier, *Der Segen im Al-
ten Testament: Eine semasiologische Untersuchung der Wurzel* brk (ThD, 6),
Basel 1970, 198; C. Westermann, "Segen", *BHH*, Bd. III, 1757–8; W.J. Harrelson,
"Blessings and Cursings", *IDB*, vol. I, 446–8, 446; K. van der Toorn, "From Pat-
riarchs to Prophets: A Reappraisal of Charismatic Leadership in Ancient Israel",
JNES 13 (1987) 191–218, 198–201; W.J. Urbrock, "Blessings and Curses", *ABD*,
vol. 1, 755–61. Contrast C.W. Mitchell, *The Meaning of BRK "To Bless" in the
Old Testament* (SBL.DS, 95), Atlanta 1987.

[161] The consideration that the shortest form is the most original one, is of course
based on the theory concerning the development of ancient Israelite literature
from short and simple to long and complicated. This opinion has been criticized
before in Chapter One. For a concise description of the blessing this generalisation
will however do.

[162] Schottroff, *Der altisraelitische Fluchspruch*, 174; Wehmeier, *Der Segen im
Alten Testament*, 222.

[163] Schottroff, *Der altisraelitische Fluchspruch*, 174–5.

[164] Zobel, *SuG*, 24, with n. 121, refering to the blessings in Gen. 12:2–3; 22:17;
27:28–9, 39–40; 48:20.

[165] Zobel, *SuG*, 24. For the former argument, cf. also Schottroff, *Der altisraelitische Fluchspruch*, 164–5.

wyʿn . dnil . mt . rpi .	And Dani'ilu, the Saviour's man, answered:
npš . tḥ[.] *pǵ*[*t*]	*ṯkmt .*	"(By) my soul, may Pughatu, who carries water on
mym .	her shoulder, live!
ḥspt . lš'r	*ṭl .*	She who scoops up dew from the wool,
ydʿt[.] *hlk . kbkbm*	*ảrḥ .*	who knows the course of the stars, travel
hy . mḫ .	smoothly!
tmḫs . mḫs [. *ảḫh*]		may she slay the slayer of her brother,
tkl . mkly . 'l . ủmt[*h*]		may she destroy the destroyer of [her] kin!"

It appears therefore that the argument from the form of address must
be modified, if only to take into consideration the fact that the third
person might be used for the blessing of an absent person.[166] Finally,
as Beyerle has emphasized, form and contents belong together and
this can certainly be regarded as a constitutive element of the blessing.[167] The prophesied future has somehow to do with a blessed situation, usually described in terms of fertility, progeny, power etc.;[168]
and might be compared even to the prophetic oracle describing the
future in terms as having already been accomplished.[169]

The text from Ugarit, quoted above, is also interesting regarding
the question if a blessing could contain negative aspects. In answer
to the request of his daughter Pugathu, Dani'ilu blesses his daughter.
However, the characteristic introductory formula "and he blessed" is
missing here, and the introduction is restricted to *wyʿn* "and he answered". This remarkable transition offers a rather interesting parallel
to a text of which the blessing-character is also disputed, namely Gen.
27:39 (quoted in its context):[170]

Esau said to his father, (38A)	וַיֹּאמֶר עֵשָׂו אֶל־אָבִיו
"Have you but one blessing, my father? (38B)	הַבְרָכָה אַחַת הִוא־לְךָ אָבִי
Bless me, me also, my father" (38C)	בָּרֲכֵנִי גַם־אָנִי אָבִי
And Esay lifted up his voice and wept. (38D)	וַיִּשָּׂא עֵשָׂו קֹלוֹ וַיֵּבְךְּ
And Isaac, his father answered and said him: (39A)	וַיַּעַן יִצְחָק אָבִיו וַיֹּאמֶר אֵלָיו

Behold, away from the fatness of the earth is your	הִנֵּה מִשְׁמַנֵּי הָאָרֶץ יִהְיֶה
dwelling (39B)	מוֹשָׁבֶךָ
and away from the dew of heaven on high. (39C)	וּמִטַּל הַשָּׁמַיִם מֵעָל
By your sword you shall live, (40aA)	וְעַל־חַרְבְּךָ תִחְיֶה
and you shall serve your brother; (40aB)	וְאֶת־אָחִיךָ תַּעֲבֹד

---

[166]Schottroff, *Der altisraelitische Fluchspruch*, 165. Cf. also KTU 1.17:i.37–53.

[167]Beyerle, *Mosesegen im Deuteronomium*, 189.

[168]Schottroff, *Der altisraelitische Fluchspruch*, 174.

[169]Wehmeier, *Der Segen im Alten Testament*, 222.

[170]The text is presented here colometrically for the sake of clarity, without the
suggestion that the framework of the "blessing" would have been written in verse.

but when you break loose (40bA)　　　　וְהָיָה כַּאֲשֶׁר תָּרִיד

　you shall break his yoke from your neck (40bB)　　וּפָרַקְתָּ עֻלּוֹ מֵעַל צַוָּארֶךָ

And Esau hated Jacob (41aA)　　　　וַיִּשְׂטֹם עֵשָׂו אֶת־יַעֲקֹב

because of the blessing his father blessed him　　עַל־הַבְּרָכָה אֲשֶׁר בֵּרֲכוֹ אָבִיו
　　　　　　　　　　　with. (41aB)

This text is literary critically very complex,[171] but it should be clear in itself that the pronouncement on Esau can hardly be called a blessing in the positive sense we are used to.[172] However, the identical structure of the request for blessing and the following answer in this text and the Ugaritic example, suggests that we may read the pronouncement on Esau as a בְּרָכָה "blessing" too. Unfortunately the following phrase (v. 41aB) is open to several interpretations,[173] but one of the possible readings is that Esau hated Jacob because of the blessing he (Esau) received. Since another interpretation is possible (the blessing he [Jacob] received) we cannot put too much weight on this. Nevertheless, the way the text is structured suggests the interpretation that the pronouncement on Esau can be considered a blessing. It might be compared in this respect to the saying on Zebulun, who also received a dwelling place, and on Issachar whose share is hard work for a (in this case) good land. Apparently the Hebrew writers had less trouble considering such sayings, like the one on Esau, but also the one on Reuben and on Simeon & Levi, a בְּרָכָה. In this case, however, the rendering "blessing" is not very appropriate because of the meaning we attach to it.[174]

　　The use of the term בְּרָכָה in Genesis may point into another direc-

---

[171] The pericope is generally ascribed to J and E, taking the final verse (v. 41) belonging to J. The foregoing verses should belong to E, except for v. 40b, being a later addition. Cf. Gunkel, *Genesis*, ³1910, 314; Skinner, *Genesis*, 373–4; Westermann, *Genesis 12–36*, 540.

[172] Gunkel, *Genesis*, ³1910, 314, considers the pronouncement a curse, in contrast to the blessing on Jacob. However, he refers here to the contents, without saying anything concerning the genre. Similarly Skinner, *Genesis*, 373; Schottroff, *Der altisraelitische Fluchspruch*, 161.

[173] It is remarkable that of the many commentaries on this passage of Genesis, there is no one that discusses the exact meaning of this clause and especially of the suffix in בֵּרֲכוֹ.

[174] Cf. also Wenham, *Genesis 16–50*, 212, who states that "Whether Isaac's eventual response should be described as a blessing is moot." Westermann, *Genesis 12–36*, 539, defends the description "blessing", by stating that there is still something positive in it (תִחְיֶה "you shall live"). Cf. also the remark by J. Scharbert, "בְּרָכָה, ברך", *ThWAT*, Bd. I, 808–41, 835: "...finden wir das, was wir als Segen bezeichnen, nur in der Wurzel ברך, die sich aber semantisch nicht mit "segnen" deckt, sondern Gruß, Glückwunsch, Dank, Lobpreis miteinschließt."

tion. In Genesis 27 it is Jacob who לָקַח בִּרְכָה "has stolen the blessing" of his brother Esau (Gen. 27:35, 36). In Gen. 33:11, when Jacob meets Esau, we find the same idiom: קַח־נָא אֶת־בִּרְכָתִי, but in this case the word בְּרָכָה is usually rendered in another way: "accept, I pray you, my gift".[175] The meaning "gift, present" occurs several times, even in those cases were the element of "blessing" is absent;[176] it appears therefore that בְּרָכָה is something with which someone can be "gifted, bestowed". This meaning is found especially in Genesis 27, where the בְּרָכָה Jacob took away (27:35, 36) has clearly material implications,[177] comparable to Gen. 33:11 and 1 Sam. 30:26, where the character of the בְּרָכָה is even more tangible.[178] Since in Genesis the "blessing" is apparently closely related to the inheritance of the promise (of the land), בְּרָכָה might need a more descriptive rendering in this case, like "testamental saying". However, since the term "testament" has in fact the same problems covering the meaning of the Hebr. בְּרָכָה we will maintain the usage of the term "blessing", be it *faute de mieux*.

3.3.5 Zebulun

In his commentary Greßmann defines the sayings on Reuben and Judah as oracles because they refer to the future.[179] Though we might differ somewhat with regard to the exact definition, here we agree with him that these sayings could be considered some kind of oracle

---

[175]RSV; cf. also NBG; KBS; NEB; JPS; BDB, 139; *DBHE*, 120; *DCH*, vol. II, 272–3; C.A. Keller, G. Wehmeier, "ברך", *THAT*, 353–76, 365–6; Driver, *Genesis*, 299; Skinner, *Genesis*, 413; Von Rad, *Erste Buch Mose*, 265–6; Westermann, *Genesis 12–36*, 636, 641; Sarna, *Genesis*, 230.
Some prefer nevertheless to keep the element of greating or blessing in it: EÜ (*Begrüßungsgeschenk*); FB; Gunkel, *Genesis*, ²1902, 325; ³1910, 367 (*Begrüßungsgeschenk*); König, *Die Genesis*, 633 (*Bewillkommungsgabe*); Jacob, *Das erste Buch*, 646–7 (*Segensgabe*); Aalders, *Genesis*, dl. 3, 34, 38 (*begroetingsgave*). Others consider it to be a present accompanied by a בְּרָכָה "blessing"; cf. KBL, 155; *HAL*, 154; GB, 118; Ges¹⁸, 180; Scharbert, "ברך, בְּרָכָה", 831–2; Dillmann, *Die Genesis*, 366. Contrast: Alter, *Genesis*, 186, who prefers "blessing" because of the identical idiom in Gen. 27:35, 36. Similarly: Wenham, *Genesis 16–50*, 299; Jagersma, *Genesis 25:12–50:26*, 120.

[176]Cf. Josh. 15:19; Judg. 1:15; 1 Sam. 30:26; 2 Kgs. 5:15. See also 1 Sam. 25:27; Ps. 21:4.

[177]Scharbert, "ברך, בְּרָכָה", 831–2, considers the effect of the blessing only a secondarily element. However, what is bestowed on Jacob could apparently not be given to Esau (compare the gift of the dew of heaven, and the fatness of the earth). For that reason the material impact of this blessing appears to be more important than is assumed by Scharbert.

[178]Cf. for the close relationship between "words" and "things", the Hebr. דָּבָר "word, matter, thing" (*HAL*, 202–3).

[179]Greßmann, *Anfänge Israels*, 180.

because they refer to the future. However, beside these two sayings we also mentioned the saying on Simeon & Levi as a lawsuit concerning the future of both tribes. In the saying on Zebulun a reference to the future is given: "he will dwell" (Gen. 49:13), whereas in the second poetic verse the nominal clause is rendered in accordance with the future interpretation as an optative. The use of nominal clauses is found in blessings and curses,[180] and mostly rendered in the optative sense. In this way the saying would suit the definition of verse 28, that we are dealing with a blessing. Syntactically this saying is more or less comparable to the first strophe in the saying on Judah, which was similarly defined as a blessing. However, another possibility is that the nominal clause is rendered as a strict parallel to its preceding clause, disregarding the context, which would result in "and he will be a beach for ships...". In this way a definition as a prediction or an oracle would be more to the point. In both cases the first clause, verse 13A, is the key phrase for our understanding of the saying on Zebulun as a reference to the tribe's future. Since the suggested rendering for verse 13bA "may he be ..." is parallel to the syntax of verse 8, and suits the definition in the framework (v. 28), this rendering is still to be preferred together with the definition of this saying as a *blessing*.

Westermann's defence for the saying on Zebulun has already been described in Chapter One.[181] His discussion of this matter demonstrates in fact the problematic character of the general definition of these sayings as "tribal sayings". If it has to be assumed that we are dealing here with a tribal saying, the meaning of this saying proves to be rather obscure, as his discussion demonstrates.[182] Interpreting the saying as a בְּרָכָה "blessing", in which apparently a certain region is ascribed to Zebulun,[183] accompanied by the wish that it may be a harbour for ships, would offer fewer problems and seems therefore to be the most probable interpretation.

3.3.6 Issachar

The definition of the genre of the saying on Issachar is complicated. In its present context we suggested rendering the saying with a kind of future connotation, thus ending with the idea of "he will bend ... he will be ...". Understood in this way the saying may be considered

---

[180] JM, §163b.

[181] See above, sections 1.3.7; 1.4.2.

[182] Westermann, *Genesis 37–50*, 264–5.

[183] Note that Westermann, *Genesis 37–50*, 247 (*inter alii*) rendered the *yiqtol* as a present tense; whereas in the pronouncement on Esau the *yiqtol* forms were rendered as future tenses (idem, *Genesis 12–36*, 528).

a prediction of Issachar's future, after comparing him with a strong
donkey. However, since the content of this saying is usually assumed
to be negative it is used against the definition of Genesis 49 as a
blessing (v. 28). As was suggested in our Excursus, the Hebrew word
בְּרָכָה might have suited such a saying, even when it is not clearly
positive. In this way we might also suggest considering the saying
on Issachar to be a "blessing", though in the sense of "testamentary
saying". However, before we deal with the possibility that the saying
on Issachar belongs to another genre, it has to be asked if such a
negative interpretation of the saying on Issachar as mentioned before
is indeed correct.

It is usually assumed that the saying contains a mocking element,
because Issachar is compared to a strong ass[184] and will become a
"serving labourer".[185] However, E. Taubler has argued that the comparison in verse 14A is clearly not negative because a Palestinian ass
is clearly something different from its European cousin, being commonly regarded as a symbol of stupidity. The Palestinian ass is a
very beautiful animal and even considered to be more valuable than
a horse.[186] Neither is the use of the root רבץ negative, because it is
used in the same way for the lion, that couches (Gen. 49:9bA), giving
a majestic impression of such an animal.[187] For that reason Taubler
argues that the first poetic verse where Issachar is compared to the
ass is certainly not negative. However, the following lines are usually
understood as negative, also in Taubler's interpretation, because the
expression מַס־עֹבֵד is generally interpreted as a negative one. Still, as
was argued in Chapter Two, it must be doubted if the word מַס has to
be considered a contemptuous expression for a *compulsory* labourer,
or that it might be considered a more neutral expression for a corvée
worker.[188] Moreover, the fact that the land of Issachar is described

---

[184]Cf. *e.g.* Speiser, *Genesis*, 367: "It is apparent that this pronouncement is
caustic rather than complimentary".

[185]Cf. *e.g.* Wenham, *Genesis 16–50*, 480: "Here Jacob rather more rudely states
that Issachar is not a hired man but a slave".

[186]E. Taubler, *Biblische Studien: Die Epoche der Richter*, Tübingen 1958, 108–
12, esp. 109–10. Cf. also Aalders, *Genesis*, dl. 3, 212; Zobel, *SuG*, 16; Van Selms,
Genesis, dl. II, 277; J.D. Heck, "Issachar: Slave or Freeman? (Gen. 49:14–15)",
JETS 29 (1986) 385–96, 387.

[187]Heck, "Issachar: Slave or Freeman", 389, emphasizes that the word is certainly
not used to denote laziness.

[188]The *Concise Oxford* gives for *corvée* as the first historical meaning: "a day's
work of unpaid labour due to a lord from a vassal"; however, for that reason the
word "corvée" would even be incorrect, since it could be done freely, and was even
rewarded with wages; cf. for this final element, *CAD*, vol. M/1, 327; A.F. Rainey,
"Compulsory Labour Gangs in Ancient Israel", *IEJ* 20 (1970) 191–202, 192–3.

as טוֹב (cf. Gen. 1:4, 10) suggests a positive appreciation of the land where Issachar lives. So, it can be doubted if the saying on Issachar is absolutely negative. It may be that the position of a labourer (מַס) is not one of the upper class (cf. Prov. 12:24; Lam. 1:1), but then neither is of the lowest class. The fact that Issachar chooses freely for this work — as it is at least suggested by the saying — makes it a kind of work that is not absolutely negative. It appears that this price of hard working is paid by Issachar because the land and rest are worth it. If our interpretation is correct, Gen. 49:14–15 appears to be less negative than is usually assumed, and might even contain a kind of appreciation for Issachar.

If the saying is regarded as independent of its literary context, the tenses of the verbs require a different interpretation, but that does not change very much because the *wayyiqtol* forms cannot be rendered here as past tenses, as we argued above in section 2.6.1.1. Nevertheless, if understood as a description in the present tense *and* with a more or less negative connotation, this text represents one of the most likely examples of a tribal saying, mocking the tribe of Is-sachar.[189] But in this case much depends on the interpretation of the saying because if the meaning is positive then one of the most characteristic elements of a tribal saying (as we found them in the Arabic sayings) would be absent. But even if our suggested interpretation of the expression מַס־עֹבֵד should prove to be incorrect, we would still have our doubts if the negative connotation of this expression would be strong enough to neutralize the rather positive remarks concerning Issachar in the first two poetic verses (vv. 14–15a), thus giving the saying in that way a general negative meaning. The longer examples of tribal sayings are generally negative, not just at the end. We can conclude therefore that although it cannot be proved that the saying on Issachar is not a tribal saying, it is very likely that it is not.

3.3.7 Dan

The two verses on Dan are said to consist of two originally independent sayings (v. 16 and v. 17).[190] The arguments for this division are the

---

[189]The presupposition that this tribal saying was originally short and not longer than one or two lines (Westermann, *Genesis 37–50*, 250), is false, because this saying consists of three poetic verses, whereas no scholar has suggested that we emend the text in order to establish the "original length", which in fact happens in other cases (as for instance the Dan-saying), while the Issachar-saying is accepted without any problem as a tribal saying (*op.cit.*, 265–6).

[190]Gunkel, *Genesis*, ³1910, 484; Kittel, *Stammessprüche Israels*, 27; C.A. Simpson, *The Early Traditions of Israel: A Critical Analysis of the Pre-deuteronomic Narrative of the Hexateuch*, Oxford 1948, 155 (considering v. 16 an independent

double use of Dan's name in association with a pun (v. 16) and an animal comparison (v. 17). These two points are apparently considered to be decisive to divide the text into two originally independent sayings. Because of the phrase "like one of the tribes of Israel" (v. 16B) Wenham regards the first part as indicating a possible weakness in Dan, which is also hinted at in the second part.[191] In his opinion the phrase "like one of the tribes of Israel" is a puzzling phrase which might be a hint that Dan was not as strong as the other tribes. This interpretation is apparently confirmed by means of the wish (using the jussive), that he may be a snake, a viper, "small but potent".[192] Wenham's interpretation is supported by some scholars who suggest we delete יְהִי (v. 17aA) as a linking addition,[193] which seems to suggest that the text as it stands is a unity. The interpretation of the text as a unity is strengthened in our view by the proposed emendation, reading יָדִן instead of יָרִין, since in that case the prediction of being strong and the wish of being like a small but deadly snake supplement each other rather well.[194]

With regard to the genre of this text, it appears that יְהִי is rather crucial for the interpretation. Since it gives the saying the dimension of a wish or a future meaning, it apparently does not suit the genre of the "tribal saying":

> The יהי at the beginning of 17a is either a jussive with an indicative meaning or a redactional attachment linking the second with the first Dan-saying. On no account can it label the saying as a wish or as a future, because that does not suit the text of the saying, being a pure depiction of Dan doings, like verse 9.[195]

It thus appears that the text as it stands contradicts the definition of this saying as a tribal saying, as was unwillingly admitted by Wester-

---

addition); Zobel, *SuG*, 17–9; Westermann, *Genesis 37–50*, 267.

[191] Wenham, *Genesis 16–50*, 481.

[192] Wenham, *Genesis 16–50*, 481.

[193] Simpson, *Early Traditions of Israel*, 155, 366, n. 435; Zobel, *SuG*, 18; Westermann, *Genesis 37–50*, 249.

[194] Emerton, "Some Difficult Words", 90–1.

[195] Westermann, *Genesis 37–50*, 267: "Das יהי am Anfang von 17a ist entweder eine Jussivform mit indikativer Bedeutung oder eine redaktionelle Verbindung des zweiten mit dem ersten Dan-spruch, keinesfalls kann es den Spruch als einen Wunsch bestimmen oder als futurisch, das paßt nicht zum Text des Spruches, der eine reine Schilderung dessen ist, was Dan tut, wie V. 9." (References to literature by Westermann were left out in this quotation). Cf. also the difference in the rendering of the verbal tenses in this saying with the pronouncement on Jacob and Esau by Westermann, as described above, p. 299, n. 183.

mann by means of the suggested emendation. We therefore deem it unnecessary to discuss even the possibility of the existence of a tribal saying in these two verses. The text suggests a future situation for Dan in which he will be strong like the other tribes of Israel and will be like a deadly viper beside the road, ready to bite a horse. So, here we are at the level of a prediction, a good wish, or even better: at the level of a בְּרָכָה "blessing", announcing the future of the descendants of Dan.

3.3.8 Gad

The saying on Gad is in its form comparable to the saying on Zebulun (v. 13) and Dan (v. 16).[196] By means of the use of the *yiqtol*-forms the saying is built as a prediction comparable to the other sayings. It is obvious that this saying is also considered a בְּרָכָה "blessing" in which the future of Gad is depicted.

3.3.9 Asher

The saying starts with a nominal clause, which would normally be rendered as a present, having in that way a descriptive character. However, because of the following verbal clause, containing a *yiqtol*, we suggested reading in verse 20A an optative and interpret the *yiqtol* as a jussive. In this way the saying will match the description given to the foregoing sayings very well: a בְּרָכָה "blessing". This rendering of the tenses is however the maximal interpretation of the saying in its context. Another possibility is to interpret verse 20B as a future: "and he will bring forth ... ", which would lead to the rendering of verse 20A as "fatness will be ...". However, even with this rendering we are dealing with future forms, which would still suit the definition of these sayings as a "blessing". It would appear that the argument that a future tense and the wish do not fit the form of a tribal saying[197] can be used here too, which makes it possible to exclude that genre for the saying on Asher also.

3.3.10 Naphtali

The rendering of the tense of this saying is based strictly on the context, because it does not contain finite verbal forms. For that reason the definition of this saying as a blessing is circumstantial, based on the verbal forms used in the other sayings, on the definition of the other sayings as בְּרָכֹת "blessings", and on the framework where this

---

[196] Zobel, *SuG*, 19.

[197] This was suggested in Westermann, *Genesis 37–50*, 267, with regard to the saying on Dan.

definition is also given (vv. 1aC, 28).

Disregarding for the moment the context, it is possible to render this saying in a descriptive manner in the present tense: "Naphtali is ... bringing forth ...". In this way we would have a strictly descriptive text as is usually assumed for the tribal sayings. Although this formal criterion suits the genre, it does not correspond with the findings of the *Umwelt* in which tribal sayings were contemptuous. So in this respect the saying cannot be considered a "tribal saying". But even when following the description of Zobel and Westermann that a saying may also contain praise, it must be asked what the praise in this saying is which would also suit the defined *Sitz im Leben*. Much depends in this case on the interpretation of the Hebrew text,[198] but even if the text is rendered differently, it appears unlikely to the present author that this saying is an independent saying used to characterize the tribe of Naphtali. However, a definitive verdict on the genre of this saying cannot be given and much depends on the interpretation of the text.

3.3.11 Joseph

In the saying on Joseph we are confronted with almost the same problems as in, for example, the saying on Judah and on Dan. By the defenders of the tribal-sayings-theory the text is divided into three parts, namely verse 22, 23–24a and 24b–26.[199] Zobel considers the second part (vv. 23–24a) to be a later expansion of verse 22, continuing by means of the *wayyiqtol*-forms the preceding statement in verse 22.[200] This interpretation suggests that the connection between verses 22 and 23–24a is rather strong, whereas verses 23–24a can hardly be considered a tribal saying. Westermann has also some problems defending the original form of the second part as a tribal saying. For him the *wayyiqtol*-forms in verse 23 continuing verse 22 are precarious too, whereas the absence of the name at the beginning of the supposed saying in verse 23 appears to be problematic because it is a requisite to describe the saying as an independent tribal saying. Moreover, verse 23–24a contains neither a comparison with an animal, nor a pun, which also argues against the definition. This compels him to suggest that the editor, who joined these two sayings, left out the be-

---

[198] Zobel, *SuG*, 20–1, suggests we read, "Naphtali ist eine freischweifende Hinde; er verkündet Worte der Siegensbotschaft". Westermann, *Genesis 37–50*, 269, renders "Naphtali — eine flüchtige Hindin, die liebliche Lämmer bringt". For the discussion of the correct rendering, cf. above, section 2.10.

[199] Zobel, *SuG*, 21–25; Westermann, *Genesis 37–50*, 269–75.

[200] Zobel, *SuG*, 22.

ginning of the second saying in order to create a better transition.[201]
Of course it might also be asked why the editor did not leave out
the names in the other instances where they were used twice (Judah,
Dan).[202] However, in our view it is a precarious argument to assume
the existence of omitted data, because such an argument cannot be
falsified, whereas everything can be proved by it. Moreover, it is a
conjecture which is only permissible if the text as it stands is absolutely unintelligible; but even then we have to be cautious. It appears
that Zobel's as well as Westermann's problems with the text as it
stands, demonstrate that the theory of tribal sayings has reached its
limits in this text. Even the suggested interpretation of this saying[203]
would not change much for their interpretation of the text as tribal
sayings. For that reason we will now try to establish the genre of the
text on the basis of the available data.

It is commonly acknowledged that in verses 25–26 we are dealing
with a blessing, not with tribal sayings,[204] therefore we do not have
to argue this case. It has been suggested that in verses 24b–25a we
find the transition to these blessings, in which the help of the divine is
assured.[205] As we have demonstrated above,[206] the verbs in verse 25a
are a continuation of the preceding verbs in verse 23b–24a, whereas
the verses 24b and 25a are parallels.[207] It appears therefore that verses
24b–25a indeed form the transition from the foregoing to the following
and thus bind the commonly recognized blessing with the preceding
passages. However, even in the preceding passage (vv. 23b–24a) we
find a promise for the future, formulated in a conditional clause: "and

---

[201] Westermann, *Genesis 37–50*, 270–1.

[202] For the unity of Gen. 49:22–6 see also H.-D. Neef, *Ephraim: Studien zur
Geschichte des Stammes Ephraim von der landnahme bis zur frühen Königszeit*
(BZAW, 238), Berlin 1995, 126; Beyerle, *Mosesegen im Deuteronomium*, 186–7,
n. 300.

[203] Cf. above, section 2.11.

[204] Cf. *e.g.* Zobel, *SuG*, 24; Westermann, *Genesis 37–50*, 271.

[205] Westermann, *Genesis 37–50*, 271–2. However, according to Westermann this
transition is also created by the editor in order to connect this blessing with the
tribal saying of vv. 23–24a. An important argument to distinguish vv. 24b–25a
from the foregoing "tribal saying" is that the transition contains references to the
divine, which is in his view impossible for a tribal saying, being solely secular.

[206] Cf. section 2.11.1.5.

[207] Zobel, *SuG*, 24, does not agree whith this because he considers v. 25a tied
only very loosely to the preceding v. 24b by means of מִן which is, in his view, a
later addition. In his view a completely different theme is introduced in verse 25,
justifying this distinction. However, in our view v. 25a is a logical continuation
of v. 24b, together forming a kind of transition, whereas v. 25aB contains the
binding element linking v. 25a with v. 25b, namely וִיבָרְכֶךָ, followed by the בִּרְכֹת
in vv. 25b–26a.

if ... his bow will ...". The animal comparison, with the following promise of strength and multitude,[208] is in a similar way filled with blessing — the verb מרר D-st. is even in parallel with ברך — and therefore might be described as part of the blessing. Although in the first strophe we find an animal-metaphor, there are some obstacles to consider this part a tribal saying. In this saying there is no disdaining element, which is so characteristic for the Arabian sayings. Secondly, the description that is given of Joseph is of an individual and not a collective, because the metaphor of the Bull, who blesses him is normally applied to a king. But also the idea behind it is individual and not collective. It seems therefore very unlikely that we are dealing here with a "tribal saying". For that reason the whole saying on Joseph is defined as a בְּרָכָה "blessing".

3.3.12 Benjamin

The comparison with a wolf is generally meant to depict a fearful person in a negative way in the Hebrew Bible,[209] corresponding to the comparison with a lion.[210] However, the comparison with a lion demonstrates at the same time that the fearful element is not necessarily a negative essential of the comparison, because in the oracles of Balaam the comparison with the lion is evidently positive,[211] similar to that in the blessing of Judah (Gen. 49:9). The fact that the lion and the wolf are used several times as a parallel pair,[212] suggests in our saying a similar positive meaning for this comparison.[213] Because of the use of *yiqtol*-forms and because of the content, it seems justified to consider this saying a בְּרָכָה "blessing" too, in the same way as the saying on Judah.

3.3.13 Summary

The foregoing discussion on the genre of the different sayings in Gen-

---

[208] In section 2.11.1.5 we have defended an interpretation of this text as a promise, and rendered the verbal forms in a future sense. However, even if one cannot agree with this rendering of verse 22b–23a preferring the narrative forms, this passage (vv. 22–23a) would still match the complete saying on Joseph as in Deut. 33:13–17; cf. Beyerle, *Mosesegen im Deuteronomium*, 189.

[209] Cf. Ezek. 22:27; Zeph. 3:3; see also for the wolf as an awesome animal, Isa. 11:6; 65:25; Jer. 5:6; Hab. 1:8. See also Zobel, *SuG*, 25.

[210] Cf. Ezek. 22:25; Zeph. 3:3.

[211] Num. 23:24; 24:9.

[212] Isa. 11:6; 65:25; Jer. 5:6; Ezek. 22:25, 27; Zeph. 3:3. Cf. also the similar phrases regarding the lion in Num. 23:24 (and Isa. 11:6; 65:25) with the one regarding the wolf in Gen. 49:27.

[213] Cf. also Zobel, *SuG*, 25, who refers to Arabic literature, where the metaphor of the wolf is used to describe a brave king.

esis 49 has resulted into the following situation. The first two sayings on Reuben and Simeon & Levi, both have the character of a lawsuit against an individual, a genre which is not necessarily restricted to prophets, but originated at the court, and could be applied in many contexts. In the present context it fits the framework where a father gives an oracle or prediction of his sons future (49:1aC), comparable to the saying on Judah, which is also an oracle of a father on his son. The use of the term בְּרָכָה "blessing" in Genesis as "gift" (33:11) and as "testamentary saying" (27:35–41) make it even possible to consider the sayings on Reuben and Simeon & Levi as בְּרָכֹת "blessings". In fact, as was stated, the term "blessing" for the rendering of בְּרָכָה is inappropriate here, and "testamentary saying" would probably be better, though open to misunderstanding too. It is commonly acknowledged that the first three sayings of this pericope serve to justify the hegemony of Judah over the other tribes. In that sense the definition for the first two sayings as "blessings (= testamentary sayings)" would serve rather well.

The following nine sayings (vv. 8–27) were all shown to fit into their immediate contexts, so that they too may be regarded as predictions of the future of these tribes (49:1aC), and as such as בְּרֹכֹת "blessings" (49:28b),[214] as in the above mentioned sense of "testamentary saying". It was further argued that the longer form of some of the sayings is by no means an indication of redactional activity or expansion of these sayings in a different way. Rather, on the contrary, it was argued that sometimes differing contents may well have originally belonged together as is the case in other genres.

It was further argued that in many cases the definition "tribal saying" for these texts is not appropriate. The characteristic mocking element in the tribal sayings in the *Umwelt* is missing in almost all cases. Furthermore, these tribal sayings from the *Umwelt* are mostly related to the present in contrast to the sayings in Genesis 49, being aimed at the future. Only in three cases was the possibility not absolutely excluded that we could be dealing with originally tribal sayings, namely those for Judah (v. 9), Issachar (vv. 14–15) and Naphtali (v. 21). However, it was argued for all three that their form suits the present context but that it could not be established beyond doubt

---

[214]Cf. also Pehlke, *Genesis 49:1–28*, 58–62, although the meaning of the word בְּרָכָה has to be modified much more than Pehlke does. Nevertheless, we may quote here, as Pehlke already did (*op.cit.*, 58, n. 1) Wehmeier, *Der Segen im Alten Testament*, 98, who states that "In den Rahmungen der Stammessprüche klingt *bᵉrākā* fast wie die Bezeichnung einer literarischen Gattung ... Die einzelnen Stammessprüche bekommen dadurch den Charakter von Segensworten."

that they were originally independent sayings.

It may be concluded now that these sayings all fit into the framework as powerful predictions with the general character of what we would call a "blessing". As such all the sayings relate to the present framework as the deathbed-"blessing" of the patriarch in which he expressed his final will to his sons. If we now have to define the genre for Genesis 49, we would prefer to describe the sayings as "testamentary sayings" in the sense of "sayings announcing the last will".

3.4 Mid-Term Review

The definition in the previous section of these sayings as "testamentary sayings", brings us close to the definition of others, who have defined the genre of the whole pericope, as a so-called large-scale genre (*Großgattung*), as a testament.[215] However, as was argued in Chapter One, the definition of a testament as given by Von Nordheim might be too narrow, because whereas he suggests this genre to be part of a wisdom tradition, the genre "testament" is derived from the juridical realm and transferred from there into the literary realm. A testament — original or pseudepigraphic — is intended to regularize certain affairs legally after the death of the testator; although in the case of pseudepigraphy "legitimize" would be a better term. A "testament" is regarded as a *document in which a testator identifies his (material and/or spiritual) estate, and his last will concerning this estate in the event of his death.* Such a "testament" as a *literary* product has its life setting (a.) *in the period after the death of the intended speaker (sometimes after a considerable amount of time),* (b.) *in the social context where the testator has some authority,* and (c.) *in a situation being explained, confirmed or criticized by the testament and which is apparently in need of such a document.*[216]

What might be asked now is if Genesis 49 has indeed such a function: the reference to the hegemony of Judah over his elder brothers, for instance, must it indeed be justified? A careful analysis of Genesis 49 in its literary context has to answer such questions. But in order to solve these questions we have first to establish the *Sitz im Leben* of this genre more precisely. Where did this genre originate? What was the exact purpose of these documents? Who might have been interested in them? To define the possible *Sitz im Leben* of such a testament more clearly we will give a short description of examples

---

[215] Cf. above, section 1.3.8.1.

[216] Cf. J. Bergman, "Gedanken zum Thema 'Lehre — Testament — Grab — Name'", in: E. Hornung, O. Keel (Hrsg.), *Studien zu altägyptischen Lebenslehren* (OBO, 28), Freiburg, Göttingen 1979, 73–104, 76–85.

of testaments in the ancient Near East.

3.5 The Testament in the Ancient Near East

In the texts of the Ancient Near East many testaments have been found that can be considered "legal" documents, regularizing affairs concerning the estate of the testator. In Chapter One we already referred to the existence of this kind of document in Egypt, the so-called Imet-per (*jmjt-pr*).[217] These documents were in use from the Old until the New Kingdom in Egypt, and all using the same formulas. The introduction of the document by date, title and name is followed by a "regarding"-phrase and an execution-part. The conclusion of the document is formed by a list of witnesses, to give the document a legal status.[218]

Similar documents have been found in Emar where they have a style comparable to the Egyptian documents, starting with the name of the testator and concluding with a list of witnesses.[219] Here we also find several documents concerning the succession of the deceased, although it might be assumed that the eldest son received a preferential share.[220] The regulation of succession is also found in Assyrian documents, the so-called "succession treaties" of Sennacherib and Esarhaddon. These treaties were made by a ruler in favour of one of his sons — sometimes even without regard to the elder ones![221] The existence of

---

[217]K.B. Gödecken, "Imet-per", *LdÄ*, Bd. III, 141–5. See also W. Pestman, "The Law of Succession in Ancient Egypt", in: J. Brugman *et al.*, *Essays on Oriental Laws of Succession* (SDIO, 9), Leiden 1969, 58–77, 62–3.

[218]Gödecken, "Imet-per", 142.

[219]See D. Arnaud, *Recherches au Pays d'Aštata. Emar VI: Textes sumériens et accadiens*, Tm. 3: Texte (ERC.S, 18), Paris 1986, 11–3, 23–4, 41–7, 49–52, 55, 77–9, 117–9, 136–9, 188–208, 214–5. A discussion of the general features is found with G. Beckman, "Family Values on the Middle Euphrates in the Thirteenth Century B.C.E.", in: M.W. Chavalas (ed.), *Emar: The History, Religion, and Culture of a Syrian Town in the Late Bronze Age*, Bethesda (Md) 1996, 57–75, esp. 69–75. For Mesopotamia in general see F.R. Kraus, "Von altmesopotamischen Erbrecht, ein Vortrag", in: J. Brugman *et al.*, *Essays on Oriental Laws of Succession* (SDIO, 9), Leiden 1969, 1–17; M. David, "Ein Beitrag zum mittelassyrischen Erbrecht", *ibid.*, 78–81.

[220]Beckman, "Family Values on the Middle Euphrates", 73. These documents have been published in: Arnaud, *Recherches au Pays d'Aštata. Emar VI.3*, 101–3, 105–6, 205–6.

[221]S. Parpola, K. Watanabe, *Neo-Assyrian Treaties and Loyalty Oaths* (SAA, II), Helsinki 1988, xxviii–xxxi; 18; 28–58; E. Reiner, "Akkadian Treaties from Syria and Assyria", *ANET*, 531–41, 534–41); cf. also *op.cit.*, 62–64; R. Borger, "Die Vasallenverträge Asarhaddons mit medischen Fürsten", *TUAT*, Bd. I/2, 160–76. For Essarhaddon's account of the succession of Senacherib, cf. R. Borger, *Die Inschriften Asarhaddons, Königs von Assyrien* (AfO.B, 9), Graz 1956, 39–

such documents, though not explicitly called a "testament",[222] clearly demonstrates the existence of this practice, but what is even more: the need for them.

Next to the original, "legal" testaments, made in the presence of witnesses, there are the other "testaments" to which we have referred to before. In Chapter One we referred to Bergman, who shows that the term "testament" not merely applies to the "legal" documents but also to the sapiential documents, the so-called "Instructions".[223] The most significant example is the *Instruction for Merikare*, which may be regarded as a wisdom text, but on the other hand has to be considered a pseudepigraphic royal testament to legitimate the reign of King Merikare.[224] Similarly the *Instruction of Amunemhet* might be mentioned, which is also pseudepigraphic and belongs to the propagandistic literature of Egypt.[225] It appears, however, that pseudepigraphy was practised frequently in Egypt[226] and functions *inter alii* in Egyptian royal ideology,[227] to legitimize the reign of the new king as the legitimate successor. This function of legitimizing the *status quo* also occurs in *Papyrus Harris I*, which was written by Ramses IV on behalf of his father Ramses III.[228] It may be concluded therefore that propaganda in Egypt did not hesitate to use the authority of deceased authoritative persons to establish the power of the king.[229]

Also, in Mesopotamia, literature was used in the service of propaganda, even though the use of pseudepigraphic testaments for this purpose has not been demonstrated.[230] A special feature of the pro-

---

45; A.L. Oppenheim, "Babylonian and Assyrian Historical Texts", *ANET*, 265–317, 289–90; H.W.F. Saggs, *The Might that was Assyria*, London 1984, 104–6; cf. furthermore K.R. Veenhof, "De geschiedenis van het oude Nabije Oosten tot de Tijd van Alexander de Grote", *BijbH*, dl. I, 278–441, 416–20.

[222]See also Kraus, "Von altmesopotamischen Erbrecht", 4–5.

[223]See section 1.4.4.

[224]Lichtheim, *Ancient Egyptian Literature*, vol. I, 97; G. Posener, "Lehre für Merikare", *LdÄ*, Bd. III, 986–9; L.G. Perdue, "The Testament of David and Egyptian Royal Instructions", in: W.W. Hallo *et al.* (eds.), *Scripture in Context*, vol. II, Winona Lake (In) 1983, 79–96, esp. 85–7; Von Nordheim, *Lehre der Alten II*, 133.

[225]Lichtheim, *Ancient Egyptian Literature*, vol. I, 135–6; Perdue, "Testament of David and Royal Egyptian Instructions", 87–9; Von Nordheim, *Lehre der Alten II*, 134–9.

[226]Also the *Instruction of Ptahhotep* (*ANET*, 412–4) is pseudepigraphic; cf. Bergman, "Gedanken", 89.

[227]See E. Blumental, "Königsideologie", *LdÄ*, Bd. III, 526–31.

[228]Cf. P. Grandet, *Le Papyrus Harris I (BM 9999)*, tome I, Paris 1994, 103–7.

[229]Cf. also R.J. Williams, "Literature as a Medium of Political Propaganda in Ancient Egypt", in: W.S. McCullough (ed.), *The Seed of Wisdom: Essays ... T.J. Meek*, Toronto 1964, 00–00.

[230]For propaganda in Mesopotamia in general, see M. Liverani, "The Ideology

pagandistic literature is the so-called "apology", known from Hittite culture,[231] and Syria (Idrimi of Alalach),[232] but also applied in Mesopotamia by Esarhaddon, Ashurbanipal and Shamsi-Adad V.[233] Of particular importance is Esarhaddon's account of his accession to the throne by official appointment of his father, which was in fact a novelty in Assyria.[234] The whole description of this event is an apology for the fact that he was not the eldest son but nevertheless became king.[235] It has been shown that this account is interesting for the light it throws on certain texts in the Hebrew Bible, and especially the "Succession Narrative" (2 Samuel 9–20; 1 Kings 1–2).[236] It appears that the latter narrative has a structure and function comparable to Esarhaddon's account, though differences cannot be brushed aside.[237]

This comparable structure and function is the more striking since the "Testament of David" (1 Kgs. 2:1–10) as a part of the Succession

---

of the Assyrian Empire", in: M.T. Larsen (ed.), *Power and Propaganda: A Symposium on Ancient Empires* (Mes[C], 7), Copenhagen 1979, 297–317; J. Reude, "Ideology and Propaganda in Assyrian Art", in: *ibid.*, 329–43. Cf. also E. Cancik-Kirschbaum, "Konzeption und Legitimation von Herrschaft in neuassyrischer Zeit: Mythos und Ritual in VS 24,92", *WdO* 26 (1995) 5–20.

[231] H.A. Hoffner, "Propaganda and Political Justification in Hittite Historiography", in: H. Goedicke, J.J.M. Roberts (eds.), *Unity and Diversity: Essays in the History, Literature, and Religion of the Ancient Near East*, Baltimore 1975, 49–62; H. Tadmor, "Autobiographical Apology in the Royal Assyrian Literature", in: H. Tadmor, M. Weinfeld, *History, Historiography and Interpretation: Studies in Biblical and Cuneiform Literatures*, Jerusalem 1983, 36–57, 54–5.

[232] Tadmor, "Autobiographical Apology", 54–5.

[233] Cf. Tadmor, "Autobiographical Apology", 36–57; T. Ishida, "The Succession Narrative and Esarhaddon's Apology: A Comparison", in: M. Cogan, I. Eph'al (eds.), *Ah, Assyria... : Studies in Assyrian History and Ancient Near Eastern Historiography Presented to H. Tadmor* (ScrH, 33), Jerusalem 1991, 166–73.

[234] Tadmor, "Autobiographical Apology", 38. The historical reliability of the events described is attested by means of a succession treaty of Sennacherib in which he appointed his youngest son as his heir. Cf. *op.cit.*, 38, with n. 9; further: S. Parpola, "Neo-Assyrian Treaties from the Royal Archives of Nineveh", *JCS* 39 (1987) 161–89, 163–4, 178–80; S. Parpola, K. Watanabe, *Neo-Assyrian Treaties and Loyalty Oaths* (SAA, II), Helsinki 1988, 18.

[235] On the different versions of Esarhaddon's inscription and the ideological significance, cf. M. Liverani, "Critique of Variants and the Titulary of Sennacherib", in: F.M. Fales, *Assyrian Royal Inscriptions: New Horizons in Literary, Ideological, and Historical Analysis* (OAC, 17), Roma 1981, 225–57. See also L.D. Levine, "Preliminary Remarks on the Historical Inscriptions of Sennacherib" in: H. Tadmor, M. Weinfeld, *History, Historiography and Interpretation: Studies in Biblical and Cuneiform Literatures*, Jerusalem 1983, 58–75; M. Cogan, "Omens and Ideology in the Babylonian Inscription of Esarhaddon", in: *ibid.*, 76–87.

[236] See Tadmor, "Autobiographical Apology", 56; Ishida, "Succession Narrative and Esarhaddon's Apology", 166–73.

[237] Ishida, "Succession Narrative and Esarhaddon's Apology", 173.

Narrative, has been compared to Egyptian propagandistic literature, namely, the royal "testaments" for Merikare and Amunemhet.[238] It has been emphasized by several scholars that the Succession Narrative has a propagandistic bias, whether it is original[239] or added later.[240] These observations imply that the aforementioned texts in the Hebrew Bible, were written in historical situations needing ideology, apology and propaganda.[241] It cannot be excluded therefore that texts in the Hebrew Bible, which are somehow related to political situations, may reflect propagandistic features.

Summarizing, we may conclude that a "testament", as a literary product, functioned very appropriately at the royal court. It functioned as legitimation or as apology for the reign of the king, and for that reason he and the circles around him were more interested in the existence of such a document. In case of pseudepigraphy it might therefore be supposed that these circles were responsible for it.

3.6   Genesis 49 as a Testament?

In section 3.4 above, we stated that our definition of the sayings in Genesis 49 as "testamentary sayings" came closest to the definition

---

[238] Perdue, "Testament of David and Egyptian Royal Inscriptions", 79–96.

[239] J. Blenkinsopp, "Theme and Motif in the Succession History (2 Sam. xi 2ff) and the Yahwist Corpus", in: *Volume de Congrès: Genève 1965* (SVT 15), Leiden 1966, 44–57; J.J. Jackson, "David's Throne: Patterns in the Succession Story", *CanJTh* 11 (1965) 183–195; J.S. Rogers, "Narrative Stock and Deuteronomistic Elaboration in 1 Kings 2," *CBQ* 50 (1988) 398–413; J.S. Ackerman, "Knowing Good and Evil: A Literary Analysis of the Court History in 2 Samuel 9–20 and 1 Kings 1–2", *JBL* 109 (1990) 41–64; M.A. Sweeney, "The Critique of Solomon in the Josianic Edition of the Deuteronomistic History", *JBL* 114 (1995) 607–622; R. de Hoop, "The Testament of David: A Response to W.T. Koopmans", *VT* 45 (1995) 270–9.

[240] L. Delekat, "Tendenz und Theologie der David-Salomo-Erzählung", in: F. Maass (Hrsg.), *Das ferne und nahe Wort: Fs L. Rost* (BZAW 105), Berlin 1967, 26–36; J. Conrad, "Zum geschichtlichen Hintergrund der Darstellung von Davids Aufstieg", *ThLZ* 97 (1972) 321–332; idem, "Der Gegenstand und die Intention der Geschichte von der Thronfolge Davids," *ThLZ* 108 (1983) 161–176; J.W. Flanagan, "Court History or Succession Document? A Study of 2 Samuel 9–20 and 1 Kings 1–2", *JBL* 91 (1972) 172–81; J. Van Seters, "Problems in the Literary Analysis of the Court History of David", *JSOT* 1 (1976) 22–29; F. Langlamet, "Pour ou contre Salomon? La rédaction prosalomonienne de I Rois, I–II", *RB* 83 (1976) 321–379, 481–528.

[241] Cf. for some general observations on this topic P.D. Miller, "Faith and Ideology in the Old Testament", in: F.M. Cross *et al.* (eds.), *Magnalia Dei, The Mighty Acts of God: Essays on the Bible and Archaeology in Memory of G.E. Wright*, Garden City 1976, 464–79. Cf. also T.C. Römer, "Transformations in Deuteronomistic and Biblical Historiography: On 'Book-Finding' and Other Literary Strategies", *ZAW* 109 (1997) 1–11.

of others who described this text as a testament. In section 3.5 the testament was described as a kind of political document, meant as legitimation or apology for the *status quo*. In the Hebrew Bible several testaments are found[242] and some of them might indeed have functioned as a kind of legitimation. In fact Genesis 49 could contain such propagandistic features as well, because here we are dealing with a text where one of the twelve brothers, Judah, is appointed as the successor of his father and as the leader of his brothers, receiving a blessing comparable to the one his father received (Gen. 49:8; compare 27:28–9).[243] Because Judah is not the eldest as is suggested by the genealogies found in Genesis, it appears that Genesis 49 functions as part of an apology for the position Judah occupies.[244]

If Genesis 49 is defined as a testament, then it is simultaneously placed in its literary context: the Deathbed Episode. As a testament it would fit the present context, although this was usually denied to this pericope on the basis of its supposed genre and provenance. If now Genesis 49 is described as a part of its literary context, other problems arise. As was noted in Chapter One scholars ruled out the possibility that Genesis 49 was a part of one of the classical documents J, E or P. However, the Deathbed Episode is generally considered to be a part of the Jacob and/or Joseph Story and composed out of these documents, or it is considered a later addition to these stories. Even the Deathbed Episode is problematic, because scholars are not unanimous regarding its provenance, and many solutions have been put forward to explain the context. In other words: the relation between the problematic Genesis 49 and the problematic Deathbed Episode is still problematic.

---

[242] Cf. the already mentioned Genesis 27; and also with some restrictions Gen. 9:18–27. Further, Deuteronomy 31–4 (Von Nordheim, *Lehre der Alten II*, 52–64. Cf. Koopmans, *Joshua 24*, 398); Joshua 23–4 (Von Nordheim, *op.cit.*, 65–72; Koopmans, *op.cit.*, 398); 1 Kings 2:1–10 (Von Nordheim, *op.cit.*, 18–28; W.T. Koopmans, "The Testament of David in 1 Kings II 1–10", *VT* 41 [1991] 429–49; cf. also De Hoop, "Testament of David", 270–9, esp. 275–6).

[243] See on this matter: B.J. van der Merwe, "Joseph as Successor of Jacob", in: *Studia Biblica et Semitica: Th.C. Vriezen ... dedicata*, Wageningen 1966, 221–32; idem, "Judah in the Pentateuch", *ThEv(SA)* 1 (1968) 37–52.

[244] Cf. here the introductory remarks by Tadmor, "Autobiographical Apology", 36–7, concerning the occurrence of apologies in the ancient Near East: "Literary compositions by kings who assumed their office in an irregular fashion are not uncommon in the literature of the ancient Near East ... they are usually of an apologetic nature, explaining the irregular circumstances under which their royal authors, not being first in the line of succession, reached their thrones. ... The term 'apology' ... may be applied also to other similar autobiographical compositions, even when the apologetic section is only part of a longer royal inscription."

In order to overcome this impasse we have to analyse the text anew. First we will present a *synchronic* reading of the complete Deathbed Episode, trying to describe the meaning of the text and its interrelationships.[245] By means of this analysis we shall establish if the supposed apologetic element, which has been suggested by some, is indeed present and if so, how this element came to be embedded in the whole Episode. Further, it must also become clear if our definition of the genre of the sayings as "testamentary sayings", and the definition of Genesis 49 as a "testament", do indeed correspond. But, probably more important is the need to establish if the classical separation of Genesis 49 from its context is justified, and thus if the possible legalizing or apologetic element of Genesis 49 is not found in the context.[246] Or, as an alternative possibility, does Genesis 49 have indeed relations with its context and can the purpose of Genesis 49 be found there too? Besides, even if it is possible that the purpose of legalisation can somehow be found, it is, on the other hand, contradicted by other elements in the Deathbed Episode, resulting in certain tensions in the final text.[247] If the problems such as described do occur, they will be dealt with in the part on the *diachronic* reading of the text, which follows the *synchronic* reading. There we will try to define the possible layers in the text and look for a coherent theory to explain the diachronic processes which have resulted in this final product.

3.7 Recapitulation[248]

1. There is insufficient evidence to uphold the idea that Genesis 49 is a collection of "tribal sayings". The essential mocking element is absent in most of the sayings. Further, most of them are orientated toward the future in contrast to the real "tribal sayings", which are concerned with the present. Since the existence of "tribal sayings" in Deuteronomy 33 has been recently contested, it would appear that the use of this genre in the Hebrew Bible may have to be abandoned.

---

[245] On the priority of the synchronic analysis, compare E. Talstra, *Solomon's Prayer: Synchrony and Diachrony in the Composition of I Kings 8, 14–61* (CBET, 3), Kampen 1992, 84 with n. 4. See already I. Willi-Plein, "Historiographische Aspekte der Josefgeschichte", *Henoch* 1 (1979) 305–31, 305.

[246] Van der Merwe, "Joseph as Successor of Jacob", 229–30, refers to "a clashing of traditions" between the context and "blessing".

[247] Willi-Plein, "Historiographische Aspekte", 308.

[248] The first part of this chapter was recapitulated in section 3.2.4, p. 281 above.

2. The sayings on Reuben and on Simeon & Levi can be considered as a lawsuit against an individual. The lawsuit is, however, not a prophetic genre but a genre originated in the juridical realm and transferred from there into other realms like the prophetic and/or the domestic scene.

3. The third saying in Genesis 49 is a blessing in the sense that the leadership is assigned to Judah. It is comparable to the blessing on Jacob, which he had stolen from his father Isaac and brother Esau. By means of this blessing Judah was appointed to succeed his father.

4. The Hebr. בְּרָכָה is semantically not completely covered by the word "blessing", which has in our understanding the meaning of a "good wish". It also can be used as "gift" and as a "testamentary saying", which is not restricted to something positive. Understood in this way the word בְּרָכָה can also be used in a negative saying in which the succession is denied to the eldest sons (Esau, Reuben, and Simeon & Levi).

5. In this way the sayings in Genesis 49 could be considered "testamentary sayings" in which the patriarch announces his final will concerning his estate. As such Genesis 49 could also be described as the "testament" of Jacob, suiting the present context: the Deathbed Episode. In this way form critical observations cannot be used any longer as literary critical arguments against the unity of the Deathbed Episode and thus against the position of Genesis 49 in its present context.

6. A "testament" as a literary product functioned at the court as a legitimizing or an apologetic document in which the reign of the current king was justified. The apology was mostly applied in those cases where the king assumed his office in an irregular fashion, being not the first in the line of succession. It appears that Genesis 49 has an identical function, legitimizing the position of Judah over his elder brothers.

7. Although Genesis 49 suits as a testament in its present context rather well, its context — the Deathbed Episode — is a similarly problematic text, of which the provenance is also disputed. It seems justified therefore to analyse the complete Deathbed Episode at a *synchronic* and *diachronic* level in order to establish the possible process which gave rise to its present form.

Chapter 4

The Deathbed Episode (Genesis 47:29–49:33)

A Synchronic Reading

4.1 Introduction

In Chapter One we argued that Genesis 49 cannot be separated in advance from its literary context when performing a diachronic analysis. In fact such a separation (if present) has to be the result of the analysis instead of its presupposition. Now starting with a *synchronic* reading we have even more to take into consideration the apparent context of Genesis 49. This was also suggested in the discussion on the genre of Genesis 49, where we found that our text is a "testament", which fits its present context, the Deathbed Episode quite well.

The Deathbed Episode in Genesis 47:29–49:33 forms the end of the Jacob Tradition and that of the Joseph Story simultaneously: elements of both narratives converge here.[1] Moreover, occasionally we even find references to the Abraham and Isaac traditions, relating this very episode to the whole of Genesis. In this section on the synchronic reading of the Deathbed Episode we will pay attention to the following aspects: 1. The relation of this episode to the whole of Genesis. 2. The meaning of the text (Gen. 47:29–49:33). 3. The function and purpose of this episode in its context. With the description of these aspects we will try to establish if Genesis 49 or even the complete Deathbed Episode can be considered a "testament" and if the apologetic aspect favouring Judah is indeed as important as was suggested in the foregoing chapter. Secondly, the aim will be to establish the coherence of the Deathbed Episode: is the style and purpose of this narrative consistent, is there a unity of thought? Or are there certain discrepancies in the text which disturb the unity of thought; are there different accents in the text which might exclude each other?

4.2 The Surface Structure of the Deathbed Episode

The Deathbed Episode (Gen. 47:29–49:33) consists of four scenes[2] which can each be considered to be the continuation of the preceding scene, whereas the first scene is a logical succession to the preceding sections where Israel/Jacob is mentioned. It appears that the composition of the Deathbed Episode is chiastic in structure:

---

[1] Wenham, *Genesis 16–50*, 459.
[2] Skinner, *Genesis*, 502.

> A   47:29–31: instructions for the funeral
> B   48:1–22: adoption and blessing
> B' 49:1–28: blessing
> A' 49:29–33: instructions for the funeral

The scenes AB and B'A' mirror each other. Remarkable is the fact that both AB and B'A' begin with a formula, which also reflects the differences between both parts:

47:29aB   וַיִּקְרָא לִבְנוֹ לְיוֹסֵף וַיֹּאמֶר לוֹ

49:1aA   וַיִּקְרָא יַעֲקֹב אֶל־בָּנָיו וַיֹּאמֶר

The first part (47:29–48:22) is concerned with Joseph; the second part (49:1–33) deals with the twelve sons. In this way the Deathbed Episode is divided over two parts,[3] falling apart into two scenes each. The first part (47:29–48:22) is described by Seebaß at the synchronic level as a relatively coherent unity, in which the beginning (47:[28,] 29–31) balances the end (48:21–22).[4] This arrangement would result in a threefold division of the first part instead of our twofold division. However, although Seebaß assumes correctly that there are some interrelations between 47:29–31 and 48:21–22, the transition in 48:1 — marking a new scene[5] — is stronger than the transition found in 48:21. Moreover, in the second part of the episode (49:1–33) this balance appears to be absent. Though the final verse in the fourth scene (49:33) with the phrase וַיְכַל יַעֲקֹב לְצַוֹּת אֶת־בָּנָיו "and Jacob finished charging his sons", might mirror 49:1, where Jacob calls his sons, וַיִּקְרָא יַעֲקֹב אֶל־בָּנָיו וַיֹּאמֶר, this phrase rather balances the opening phrase of the fourth scene, וַיְצַו אוֹתָם וַיֹּאמֶר אֲלֵהֶם (49:29). In addition the final verse of the Deathbed Episode balances other phrases too: compare for example וַיֶּאֱסֹף רַגְלָיו אֶל־הַמִּטָּה (48:2b) with וַיִּתְחַזֵּק יִשְׂרָאֵל וַיֵּשֶׁב עַל־הַמִּטָּה (49:33B), and אֲנִי נֶאֱסָף אֶל־עַמִּי (49:29aB) with וַיִּגְוַע וַיֵּאָסֶף אֶל־עַמָּיו (49:33C). Finally, each scene is clearly marked by an opening phrase, dividing the whole Episode into these four scenes (47:29; 48:1; 49:1, 29). Therefore in our view Seebaß' analysis is inadequate because he did not involve the whole Deathbed Episode in his synchronic analysis, but restricted himself to the first part only (47:29–48:22).

---

[3] According to Skinner, *Genesis*, 502, the first two scenes "may be conveniently treated together".

[4] H. Seebaß, "The Joseph Story, Genesis 48 and the Canonical Process", *JSOT* 35 (1986) 29–43, esp. 29–30.

[5] G.W. Coats, "Redactional Unity in Genesis 37–50", *JBL* 93 (1974) 15–21, esp. 18; E. Blum, *Die Komposition der Vätergeschichte* (WMANT, 57), Neukirchen-Vluyn 1984, 250.

Although each scene is marked by an opening phrase, not every scene has a closing phrase. The first one ends with Israel's bowing on his bed (47:31), although this can also be considered as the beginning of further action (see 1 Kgs. 1:47).[6] The third ends with a kind of resumé (49:28), whereas the fourth scene is the apparent final clause for the whole episode, ending with the death of the patriarch (49:33). The second scene, but in fact the first as well, is open-ended and the transition is only given by the opening phrase of the next scene.

4.3 The Literary Context

The context of the Deathbed Episode is described by scholars in different ways although there is much in common in all these characterizations. As we noted in the introduction to this chapter, in the Deathbed Episode two traditions or narrative strands seem to converge: the Jacob and the Joseph Story. Because of this coalescing of traditions Wenham considers these two traditions in their present form to be two parts of one large story: the biography of Jacob (Gen. 25:19–50:26), starting with "the family history of Isaac" (25:19–35:29), followed by "the family history of Jacob" (37:2–50:26).[7] Although the linking of these two stories can certainly be argued, we have to be careful to isolate these two "family histories" (תּוֹלְדֹת) from the other family histories in Genesis because there are cross-references to the other "family histories" as well.[8] The "biography of Jacob" cannot be isolated from its context, namely the traditions of the patriarchs (Gen. 12–50), or — widening the circle a little more — even the book of Genesis.[9] The

---

[6]Seebaß, "The Joseph Story", 29.

[7]Wenham, *Genesis 16–50*, xxvi, 345; cf. Coats, "Redactional Unity in Genesis 37–50", 15–21.

[8]Houtman, *Der Pentateuch*, 423–32. Compare also J.J. Scullion, "Genesis, The Narrative of", *ABD*, vol. II, 941–62, 949, who divides the story of the patriarchs into two parts, the Abraham cycle and the Jacob-Esau cycle, noting that "the figure of Isaac joins the two parts; he is the channel through which the promises made to Abraham (26:3, 5, 24; 28:3–4) pass on to Jacob. This division is not arbitrary, as each part begins with the *tôlĕdôt* formula ...".

[9]It would be possible to go even further and describe the (Jacob- and) Joseph Story as part of the Pentateuch. This tradition then functions to bridge the gap between Canaan as the promised land and the people in Egypt (Noth). This element is also present in the Deathbed Episode (*e.g.* 48:21) and has certainly to be taken into consideration. However, it appears that the cross-references between the different traditions in Genesis are considerably stronger than those with the rest of the Pentateuch. The end of Genesis and the beginning of Exodus might be regarded as a kind of watershed: in Genesis we are still dealing with the eponyms of Israel and the twelve tribes as individuals, although the idea of the tribes becomes gradually apparent (Genesis 49), whereas in Exodus there is an allusion

following description will position the Deathbed Episode in its literary context, which is formed by the book of Genesis, the patriarchal
traditions, the biography of Jacob, and the Joseph Story.

The book of Genesis has been constructed as a genealogical document in which genealogies function at a redactional and a conceptual
level.[10] The various sections of Genesis are all prefaced with the phrase
"these are the generations of ..." and in this way the book is organ-
ized as a genealogical document from the generations of heaven and
earth (Gen. 2:4a) to the genealogical descent of Israel's ancestors (see
the table on page 321).[11] Yet, beside the redactional functioning the
genealogies have a conceptual function as well:

> The linear genealogy from Adam to Jacob serves to define Israel's rela-
> tionship to its neighbours and other foreign nations (the descendants of
> Noah, Gen 9:25–27 and Genesis 10; Moab and Ammon, Gen 19:30–38;
> Ishmael, Genesis 16; Edom, Gen 25:25–34). The segmented lineage of
> Jacob's sons serves to define the internal relationships of Israel, clari-
> fying the relationships among the tribes and affirming the genealogical
> unity that binds them together as a nation. The idiom of kinship re-
> lationships, whether real or ascribed, is a key organization principle
> in the type of society called a segmentary lineage system.... Derived
> from this social base, the genealogical structure of the Genesis nar-
> ratives served to define Israelite identity as a function of the kinship
> relationships of their ancestors.[12]

The genealogical element thus forms the framework for the composition of Genesis, providing at the same moment a chronological framework.[13] As a recurrent motif throughout the book there is one aspect

---

to the idea of the individual eponyms of the tribes (*e.g.* Exod. 1:1–8), but from
the beginning of the book of Exodus we are dealing with the tribes of the *people*
Israel. For that reason it seems justified to restrict our description to the book of
Genesis.

[10]R.S. Hendel, "Genesis, Book of", *ABD*, vol. II, 933–41, esp. 935.

[11]Hendel, "Genesis, Book of", 935; Houtman, *Der Pentateuch*, 424–5. J. Blenkinsopp, *The Pentateuch: An Introduction to the First Five Books of the Bible*
(ABRL), New York 1992, 58–9; 99–100; 108–9 defends a structure of two fivefold
arrangements of the *toledot* series, forming a framework for the whole of Genesis.

[12]Hendel, "Genesis, Book of", 935; cf. also J.P. Fokkelman, *Narrative Art in
Genesis: Specimens of Stylistic and Structural Analysis* (SSN, 17; 2nd edition:
BibS, 12), Assen 1975, Sheffield ²1991, 238–40; T.D. Alexander, "From Adam to
Judah: The Significance of the Family Tree in Genesis", *EvQ* 61 (1989) 5–19;
Blenkinsopp, *The Pentateuch*, 109.

[13]Cf. on this matter, Blenkinsopp, *The Pentateuch*, 47–50, 108–9. For a more
complete review with extensive bibliography, see M. Cogan, "Chronology: Hebrew
Bible", *ABD*, vol. I, 1002–11.

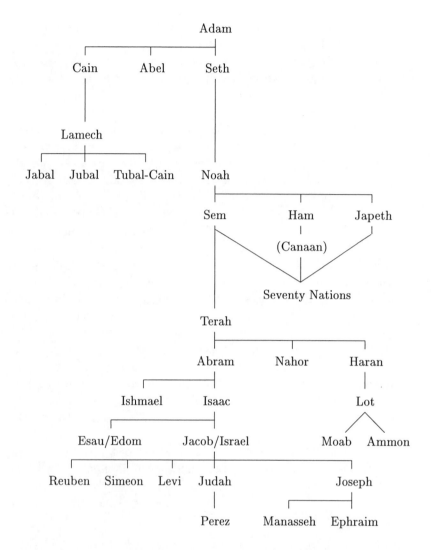

TABLE: THE GENEALOGICAL FRAMEWORK OF GENESIS

that is strongly connected to this genealogical theme: it is the strife between brothers in which the youngest generally has the supremacy.[14]
The motif of strife between brothers can be found earlier in the narrative of Cain and Abel (Gen. 4:1–7),[15] but occurs in the patriarchal

---

[14]Cf. R. Syrén, *The Forsaken First-Born: A Study of a Recurrent Motif in the
Patriarchal Narratives* (JSOTS, 133), Sheffield 1993; G.W. Coats, "Joseph, Son
of Jacob", *ABD*, vol. III, 976–81, 977; Blenkinsopp, *The Pentateuch*, 109.

[15]B.T. Dahlberg, "The Unity of Genesis", in: K.R.R. Gros Louis (ed.), *Literary*

traditions and the Joseph Story time and again as a kind of fate connected to the genealogy of Israel.

The motif of the struggle between the elder and younger brother for their birthright is strongly connected to the problem of progeny (Ishmael and Isaac), which is one of the main themes in the patriarchal traditions: Sarah, Rebekah and Rachel are barren and only because God opens their wombs[16] the continuation of the generations is secured.[17] This theme of offspring is one of the three themes that frequently occur in the promises given to the patriarchs, namely sons, land and blessing (Gen. 12:1–3; 22:17–18; 26:3–5; 28:13–15).[18] However, it appears that the main theme that supports all the others is the theme of "blessing". Progeny, protection, property, land etc. are all received because of God's blessing.[19] But this blessing appears to become the subject of strife for the primogeniture between the brothers: Ishmael has to depart without being blessed; Esau hates his brother because of the blessing he received; and finally in the "blessing" of Genesis 49 the successor of Jacob (and thus the inheritor of the patriarchal blessing) is named. In the Abraham cycle the promise of Gen. 12:1–3 is not fulfilled and at the end of Genesis it still waits for its final achievement: the promise of the land is explicitly postponed (Gen. 15:13–16), the promise of a great nation cannot be fulfilled within one generation.[20] In this way the promise to Abraham is not restricted to the person of Abraham, but by means of the open ending the future generations (the readers) are involved in the narrative.

If we take a closer look at the Jacob Traditions, the theme of the struggle between the brothers Esau and Jacob dominates the whole story. As an announcement of the plot the divine oracle to Rebekah (Gen. 25:23) is placed at the beginning, hinting at how the story will develop and end:[21]

Interpretations of Biblical Narratives, Vol. II, Nashville (TN) 1982, 126–33, esp. 130–1; Syrén, *The Forsaken First-Born*, 37.

[16] Cf. the note that God opened also Leah's womb (Gen. 29:31), although it is not stated that she was barren.

[17] Fokkelman, *Narrative Art in Genesis*, 239.

[18] L.A. Turner, *Announcements of Plot in Genesis* (JSOTS, 96), Sheffield 1990, 51–114; T.D. Alexander, "Abraham Re-Assessed Theologically", in: R.S. Hess *et al.* (eds.), *He Swore an Oath: Biblical Themes from Genesis 12–50*, Carlisle ²1994, 7–28, esp. 9–11; Fokkelman, *Narrative Art in Genesis*, 241. Cf. Scullion, "Genesis, The Narrative of", 953–4, who discerns six promises.

[19] Fokkelman, *Narrative Art in Genesis*, 240.

[20] Cf. Blenkinsopp, *The Pentateuch*, 110–1.

[21] Turner, *Announcement of Plot*, 114; Scullion, "Genesis, The Narrative of", 950–1.

Two nations are in your womb (23aB)   שְׁנֵי גיים בְּבִטְנֵךְ

  and two peoples, born of you, shall be divided; (23aC)   וּשְׁנֵי לְאֻמִּים מִמֵּעַיִךְ יִפָּרֵדוּ

  and one people shall be stronger than the other, (23bA)   וּלְאֹם מִלְאֹם יֶאֱמָץ

  the elder shall serve the younger. (23bB)   וְרַב יַעֲבֹד צָעִיר

At the end of the story it is obvious that the two have indeed been
divided and that the youngest has obtained the blessing of his father.
He acquired great wealth in such a manner that he is even able to
share from the (stolen) blessing with his brother (Gen. 33:11);[22] but
as Turner has rightly pointed out, in Genesis Esau does not serve his
younger brother, nor is the younger stronger than the elder.[23] So, in
this sense the plot of the Jacob Story has not reached its fulfilment
and has an open ending.

    The Joseph Story starting at Genesis 37 takes up the thread of the
preceding Jacob Story. The family conditions are those as described
in Genesis 29–30, where the different mothers are mentioned and the
strife between the mothers seems to continue in the relationship of
the sons.[24] The theme of the Story can be described in a twofold
sense: divine providence[25] and the (family) struggle for power.[26] The
aspect of divine providence is usually connected with the idea that
the promise to the patriarchs could be passed on: Joseph was sold to
Egypt where he rose to power, so he could preserve a whole nation
alive. Hence the theme of divine providence has to be connected with
the theme of the blessing promised to Abraham. By means of this

---

[22]Scullion, "Genesis, The Narrative of", 952.

[23]Turner, *Announcement of Plot*, 132–5.

[24]Coats, "Joseph, Son of Jacob", 977.

[25]The theme of divine providence is especially emphasized (although not exclusively) by those who consider the Joseph Story to be a product of Wisdom circles; cf. for the discussion of this point *inter alii* R.N. Whybray, "The Joseph Story and Pentateuchal Criticism", *VT* 18 (1968) 522–8; G.W. Coats, "The Joseph Story and Ancient Wisdom: A Reappraisal", *CBQ* 35 (1973) 285–97. According to R.E. Longacre, the story is completely one of divine providence: R.E. Longacre, "Who Sold Joseph into Egypt?" in: R.L. Harris *et al.* (eds.), *Interpretation and History: Essays ... A.A. MacRae*, Singapore 1986, 75–91, 79; idem, *Joseph, A Study in Divine Providence: A Text Theoretical and Textlinguistic Analysis of Genesis 37 and 39–48*, Winona Lake (IN) 1989; see also J.A. Soggin, "Notes on the Joseph Story", in: G.A. Auld (ed.), *Understanding Poets and Prophets: Essays ... G.W. Anderson* (JSOTS, 152), Sheffield 1993, 336–49. For an opposite view, see below, n. 27.

[26]F. Crüsemann, *Der Widerstand gegen das Königtum: Die antiköniglichen Texte des Alten Testamentes und der Kampf um den frühen israelitischen Staat* (WMANT, 49), Neukirchen-Vluyn 1978, 143–55; Blum, *Die Komposition der Vätergeschichte*, 240; W. Dietrich, *Die Josephserzählung als Novelle und Geschichtsschreibung; Zugleich ein Beitrag zur Pentateuchfrage* (BThSt, 14), 13–5; Coats, "Joseph, Son of Jacob", 977.

motif, which has been developed very skilfully as is generally acknowledged, Joseph has become an instrument in God's hand (Gen. 45:5–
8; 50:20).[27] This aspect of divine providence gives the power struggle
between the brothers a different character. The question found in 37:8,
10 — if Joseph were to reign over his brothers — is significant in this
connection because it deals with this problem and calls the leadership
of Joseph into question. The development of the plot, however, gives
the answer to the question: Joseph will reign and his brothers will bow
down before him. But it is fulfilled in a different way from what the
brothers and Jacob apparently assumed. Joseph receives his power in
order to preserve life, that is the purpose and his power is completely
restricted to this aspect. This is demonstrated by the fact that at the
end, when Jacob blesses his sons, not Joseph but Judah is bestowed
with the leadership's blessing. Joseph's power is thus restricted to the
events described in the present narrative and the plot seems to have
reached its end.[28]

However, by means of the blessing on Judah (Gen. 49:8–12) the
development of the plot takes an unexpected turn. At first sight it
appears that the plot has reached the end in the Joseph Story: the
brothers have prostrated themselves indeed before Joseph. But un-
foreseen the promise of the everlasting leadership among the brothers is given to Judah. This corresponds to the other elements in the
Joseph Story where Judah has a leading role and surpasses his elder
brother Reuben. However, the announcement of Gen. 49:8–12 coin-

---

[27]Turner, *Announcement of Plot*, 165–9, argues vigorously against the idea
that in these texts we are dealing with a sort of "predestinarian theologoumena"
(*op.cit.*, 169). In his view these texts only confirm the point found in the other preceding ancestral stories, "that attempts to thwart God's purpose merely speed its
triumph". However, in our view his argumentation does not exclude the idea of divine providence but only denies a specific kind of predestination, which excludes
human activity. In this respect the characterization by Dietrich is instructive:
"Freilich, die beteiligten Menschen sind durch Gottes Walten nicht entmündigt,
sind nicht wie Marionetten benutzt worden, sondern haben als freie Subjekte
gehandelt, so, daß sich auf geheimnisvolle Weise der Plan Gottes erfüllte." (*Die
Josephserzählung*, 14).

[28]Turner, *Announcement of Plot*, 165, denies that the plot has been fulfilled.
The plot is given in two dreams, and in one of them Joseph's father and mother
have to bow down before him. Since this is not fulfilled in the Joseph Story, Turner
argues that the plot did not reach its end. However, there is one text in which it is
said that the patriarch prostrates himself (Gen. 47:31) albeit without mentioning
before whom, or with what purpose he bowed down. As far as we are aware this
text is not discussed by Turner, and although the text is certainly very difficult
to interpret this is to be regretted because in this way he did not weigh all the
arguments before reaching his conclusions. For this problem, see our discussion
below in section 4.4.2.2.

cides with other announcements (of plot) in Genesis because it does
not reach its end, and we are left with an open ending again. The
inheritance of the land is postponed, Esau did not serve his brother
and the younger was not stronger, the brothers do not bow down to
Judah nor is tribute brought to him. Apparently the plot of Genesis
is waiting to be fulfilled in the future, beyond the borders of the Book
of Genesis itself, because within the narrative framework of Genesis
it did not reach its final accomplishment.[29] The question is now: what
is the meaning of the Deathbed Episode in Genesis, what motifs are
applied here, and what function do they have within their literary
context?

4.4 The Deathbed Episode

4.4.1 The Prelude: Genesis 47:27-28

In Gen. 47:27-28 the story of Jacob[30] coming to Egypt is resumed
from Gen. 47:11-2. Here, in verse 27, we are told that Israel settled in
the land of Goshen and — with a stock-phrase in Genesis[31] — that
וַיִּפְרוּ וַיִּרְבּוּ מְאֹד "they were fruitful and multiplied exceedingly". The
phrase used here to state that Israel settled in Egypt is identical to
the phrase that stated that Jacob settled in Canaan:

37:1   וַיֵּשֶׁב יַעֲקֹב בְּאֶרֶץ מְגוּרֵי אָבִיו בְּאֶרֶץ כְּנָעַן
47:27   וַיֵּשֶׁב יִשְׂרָאֵל בְּאֶרֶץ מִצְרַיִם בְּאֶרֶץ גֹּשֶׁן

The use of the different names "Jacob" and "Israel" seems to have
been done deliberately. The name "Israel" mostly refers to the patriarch throughout the story and at first sight this seems to have happened here too because וַיֵּשֶׁב is singular. But in the following clause
(47:27B) the verbal forms, which appear to have "Israel" as their subject, refer apparently to the people "Israel", for the verbal forms are
in the plural. "Israel" is thus at the same time the patriarch himself
but also his descendants, the "sons of Israel".[32]

Verses 27-28 form a remarkable transition from the preceding

---

[29]The observations at the end of the study by Fokkelman, *Narrative Art in
Genesis*, 238, are very instructive at this point.

[30]In the following we will use the name "Jacob" when this is the case in the text
we are discussing or as a general reference to this patriarch; the name "Israel"
will be used when this is deemed necessary.

[31]For the syndetic construction of רבה and פרה, see beside our text: Gen. 1:22,
28; 8:17; 9:1, 7; 17:20; 28:3; 35:11; 48:4. For the combination of רבה and/or פרה
with מְאֹד, see Gen. 7:18; 15:1; 17:2, 6, 20; 34:12; 41:19, 49. The phrase is also used
in the introduction to Exodus; cf. Exod. 1:7.

[32]See *inter alii* Sarna, *Genesis*, 323; Hamilton, *Book of Genesis*, 621, n. 1.

scenes to the following. Here we are told that Israel settles and gains possessions in the land (וַיֵּאָחֲזוּ). The noun אֲחֻזָּה which is derived from this verb is used also in 47:11 and is almost an ironical inclusion of the report of Joseph's land policy, where the Egyptians have to sell their land to Joseph (47:13–26).[33] On the other hand the expression "were fruitful and multiplied exceedingly" seems to anticipate the introduction to Exodus.[34]

In verse 28 the age of Jacob is given, a topic which is frequently dealt with in the book of Genesis in connection with the genealogies but also in the context of narratives like here or in 47:8–9.[35] Again an allusion is found to the beginning of the Joseph Story: Jacob lived seventeen years in Egypt, whereas the note that Jacob settled in Canaan is followed by a statement concerning Joseph's age: seventeen years (37:2).[36] The same order of וַיֵּשֶׁב (47:27) and וַיְחִי (47:28) is found in the note on Joseph's death (50:22).[37] By means of idiom and theme this small section connects the following episode firmly to the framework of Genesis and might therefore be labelled as the prelude to the Deathbed Episode.

4.4.2   Part I: Genesis 47:29–31

4.4.2.1   "Do Not Bury Me in Egypt"

The beginning of the Deathbed Episode is remarkable. There are two important parallels to this text. The first one is in the episode of Isaac's deathbed (Gen. 27:1–4), where Esau is called to his father in order that Isaac could bless him. Apparently it was usual that the

---

[33] K.A. Deurloo, "Vrij in het land der slavernij", in: K.A. Deurloo, W. Veen (red.), *De gezegende temidden van zijn broeders: Jozef en Judah in Genesis 37–50*, Baarn 1995, 136–44, 142–4. Jagersma, *Genesis 25–50*, 246.

[34] Jagersma, *Genesis 25–50*, 246.

[35] L. Ruppert, *Die Josephserzählung der Genesis: Ein Beitrag zur Theologie der Pentateuchquellen* (StANT, 11), München 1965, 178–9, with n. 40 offers very interesting computations (referring to others), showing that the age of the patriarchs can be factorized as follows:

Age of Abraham   175 years = 5 × 5 × 7 years   (Gen. 25:7)
Age of Isaac   180 years = 6 × 6 × 5 years   (Gen. 35:28)
Age of Jacob   147 years = 7 × 7 × 3 years   (Gen. 47:28)

Now the sum of the factors, as Ruppert demonstrated, is seventeen, which is identical to the number of years that Joseph lived together with his father in Canaan (37:2) and in Egypt (47:28), relating in this way Joseph to the patriarchs. Sarna, *Genesis*, 324, notes that a similar pattern occurs in Abraham's lifetime, leving as many years in his father's house (12:4), as in the lifetime of Isaac (21:5; 25:7).

[36] Wenham, *Genesis 16–50*, 450.

[37] Wenham, *Genesis 16–50*, 450.

eldest son, or in each case the son to be assigned as the successor, was called to his father *alone*. In the second parallel we find a similar situation, in 1 Kgs. 2:1 David calls his successor when his death is near. The episode starts with almost identical phrases as in Gen. 47:29:

The days of David to die drew near, (1A)	וַיִּקְרְבוּ יְמֵי־דָוִד לָמוּת
and he charged Solomon his son, saying: (1B)	וַיְצַו אֶת־שְׁלֹמֹה בְנוֹ לֵאמֹר

B.J. van der Merwe considers this similarity as an indication that Joseph was appointed as the successor of the Patriarch.[38] This identical feature is remarkable indeed and therefore his suggestion is worth considering, certainly with a view to other elements in the Deathbed Episode that seem to suggest Joseph's prominent position.[39] It appears that Joseph is the new *paterfamilias*, who is responsible for the funeral of his father and on the other hand for the בֵּית־אָב "father's house".[40]

However, in the context of the Joseph Story this feature might be explained — as usually happens[41] — as being due to the fact that Joseph has an important position in Egypt and as such was the one who could arrange the funeral. This idea is certainly emphasized by the preceding passage in which Joseph's land policies are narrated (47:13–26). Remarkable is for example the fact that the patriarch addresses his son almost as the Egyptians did: נִמְצָא־חֵן בְּעֵינֵי אֲדֹנִי "let us find favour in the eyes of my lord" (47:25) and אִם־נָא מָצָאתִי חֵן בְּעֵינֶיךָ "if I have found favour in your eyes" (47:29).[42] Thus, by means of the context the manner of asking Joseph this favour is directed into the direction of this interpretation. However, in this scene there is no explicit reference found to Joseph's position in Egypt nor — as it seems — to his position as possible successor of the patriarch. Important to note, however, is the fact that part of the idiom applied here to describe the approaching death, is mostly used for people of

---

[38] B.J. van der Merwe, "Joseph as Successor of Jacob", in: *Studia Biblica et Semitica: Th.C. Vriezen ... dedicata*, Wageningen 1966, 221–32, 225.

[39] Cf. Van der Merwe, "Joseph as Successor of Jacob", 225–6; see also below the discussion on *e.g.* 48:21–2 and 49:22–6.

[40] With regard to the role of the *paterfamilias*, cf. K. van der Toorn, *Family Religion in Babylonia, Syria and Israel: Continuity and Change in the Forms of Religious Life* (SHCANE, 7), Leiden 1996, 20–6; 154–5; 192; 198–9.

[41] Westermann, *Genesis 37–50*, 205.

[42] Cf. on the importance of the position of the passage in 47:13–26 before the Deathbed Episode: E.M. McGuire, "The Joseph Story: A Tale of Son and Father", in: B.O. Long (ed.), *Images of Man and God: Old Testament Short Stories in Literary Focus*, Sheffield 1981, 9–25, esp. 17–8.

noble standing. The expression is "to lie with the fathers" and, beside the use for Moses and Israel, it is used for the death of kings.[43] It seems to suggest a certain important position for the patriarch comparable to that of a ruler,[44] which is confirmed by the archaeological data that the possession of special graves, like caves, was a priveledge of the elite.[45] The suggestion that the patriarch is depicted as a ruler here, who will be succeeded by his son Joseph is very likely in view of the final phrase in 47:31.

4.4.2.2   And Israel Bowed Himself . . . (47:31)

The interpretation of the phrase וַיִּשְׁתַּחוּ יִשְׂרָאֵל עַל־רֹאשׁ הַמִּטָּה "and Israel bowed himself at the head of his bed" (31aC) is problematic. Westermann states with regard to this phrase: "The exact meaning of the expression עַל־רֹאשׁ הַמִּטָּה is not recognizable any more".[46] Wenham writes rather soberly in his commentary:

> "Jacob bent over." The narrative does not explain exactly why he did. Is it just the weakness of the approaching death or a gesture of gratitude or prayer? By its ambiguity, it leaves open all these interpretations.[47]

Some scholars expect to read here a reference to God for whom the patriarch bows himself in gratitude.[48] This reading is usually compared with the deathbed episode in 1 Kings 1–2, where David bowed himself down before God on his bed (1:47). It might be expected that this unambiguous reading of 1 Kgs. 1:47 influenced the interpretation of our text.[49] Yet, we might ask could the patriarch only have bowed himself down before God or could he have bowed himself for a

---

[43]Van der Merwe, "Joseph as Successor of Jacob", 221–2.

[44]Van der Merwe, "Joseph as Successor of Jacob", 221–2; cf. also our discussion of Gen. 49:3–4. Yet, the term "ruler" might suggest too much; in all probability we have to think here of the head of a clan or tribe, not of a "king" or the like. For the role of leaders of extended families and clans, cf. Van der Toorn, *Family Religion in Babilonia, Syria and Israel*, 190–4.

[45]Cf. C.H.J. de Geus, "Funeral Monuments and Tomb-Markings in Biblical Israel?" *AcAL* 32 (1993) 107–19, 109.

[46]Westermann, *Genesis 37–50*, 206: "Was die Wendung עַל־רֹאשׁ הַמִּטָּה genau bedeuten soll, ist nicht mehr erkennbar". Cf. also Speiser, *Genesis*, 356–7.

[47]Wenham, *Genesis 16–50*, 450. Similarly, Sarna, *Genesis*, 324.

[48]Cf. Gunkel, *Genesis*, ³1910, 470; Skinner, *Genesis*, 503; Aalders, *Genesis*, dl. III, 179–80; Van Selms, *Genesis, dl. II*, 265–6; Westermann, *Genesis 37–50*, 206; Scharbert, *Genesis 12–50*, 286. It is suggested by Holzinger, *Genesis*, 252; Greßmann, "Ursprung und Entwicklung der Joseph-Sage", 6, that a teraphim was placed at the head of the bed (with reference to 1 Sam. 19:13, 16). This was disputed by König, *Die Genesis*, 743.

[49]Cf. *e.g.* De Fraine, *Genesis*, 318.

human being instead, *i.c.* Joseph?[50] The possibility of this interpretation is generally not considered, although it is possible because שחה hithp. "to bow down"[51] is used rather frequently with regard to human beings, even without mentioning the object explicitly by means of a preposition and suffix, noun or name, because the object could be known from the context.[52] Since in this limited context Israel and Joseph are the only persons present it might be expected that Jacob bowed down before Joseph, without mentioning this explicitly.

This interpretation is in fact implied by the patriarch's very polite way of speaking, and especially by the use of the phrase אִם־נָא מָצָאתִי חֵן בְּעֵינֶיךָ "if now I have found favour in your eyes" (29bA). This could be illustrated with a comparison of this scene with, for example, 2 Sam. 16:4b:[53]

And Ziba said: "I bow myself down,	וַיֹּאמֶר צִיבָא הִשְׁתַּחֲוֵיתִי
let me find favour in your eyes, my lord the king."	אֶמְצָא־חֵן בְּעֵינֶיךָ אֲדֹנִי הַמֶּלֶךְ

Such a comparison makes it likely that the patriarch bowed himself before the very same person as he addressed with this phrase. In this way the dream of 37:9–10, and especially the plot which was announced in 37:10, is fulfilled.[54]

However, the usual rendering of the clause in 47:31aC is not as obvious as is commonly assumed. The combination of שחה hithp. with

---

[50]Böhl, *Genesis*, 135; Seebaß, "The Joseph Story", 29, 33. The possibility was left open by De Fraine, *Genesis*, 318. This interpretation is rejected by König, *Die Genesis*, 743; Scharbert, *Genesis 12–50*, 286. J.S. Ackerman, "Joseph, Judah, and Jacob", in: K.R.R. Gros Louis (ed.), *Literary Interpretations of Biblical Narratives*, Vol. II, Nashville (TN) 1982, 85–113, 108–9, considers the text leaves this matter ambiguous on purpose, the patriarch bowing down "in gratitude to the son, but, more important, acknowledging and accepting the mysterious arrangements of providence".

[51]We follow the classical etymology for this verbal form; cf. J.A. Emerton, "The Etymology of *hištaḥᵃwah*", in: H.A. Brongers *et al.*, *Instruction and Interpretation: Studies in Hebrew Language, Palestinian Archaeology and Biblical Exegesis* (OTS, 20), Leiden 1977, 41–55; J.C. de Moor, K. Spronk, "More on Demons in Ugarit (KTU 1.82)", *UF* 16 (1984) 237–50, esp. 242. For another etymology, cf. the literature in *HAL*, 1351–2.

[52]Examples of texts where the object (human and divine) of שחה hithp. is not mentioned are found in 1 Sam. 20:41; 24:9 (E.T. 24:8); 25:41; 28:14; 2 Sam. 16:4; 1 Kgs. 1:47. Somewhat ambiguous texts, where the object might be indicated by means of the so-called double duty suffix, are found in Gen. 18:2; 19:1; 22:5; 33:3, 6, 7; 43:28; 48:12(!); Exod. 4:31; 12:27; 18:7; 24:1; 33:10; 34:8 etc.

[53]The combination of שחה hithp. together with the expression מָצָא חֵן בְּעֵינֵי is found rather frequently; see 2 Sam. 14:22; Ruth 2:10; cf. also Gen. 18:2–3; 33:7–8; Exod. 34:8–9. This confirms the interpretation defended above.

[54]*Pace* Turner, *Announcement of Plot*, 165.

prep. עַל is usually interpreted in the Hebrew Bible as "to bow down on/at ...".[55] Yet another meaning is found in Lev. 26:1, לְהִשְׁתַּחֲוֺת עָלֶיהָ "to bow down to them", which suggests that the prep. עַל does not solely meant "on" but also "to" in combination with שחה hithp.[56] A second problem in this clause arises from the fact that the textual witnesses are not unanimous in their readings. LXX and Peš differ from MT מִטָּה "bed" in that LXX reads τῆς ῥάβδου αὐτοῦ and Peš ḥwṭrh, both meaning "his staff", supposing Hebr. מַטֶּה or better מַטֵּהוּ.[57] The reading of LXX and Peš is generally not adopted because it does not offer a better reading than MT.[58] Nevertheless, there is some good reason to consider these readings anew. The Hebr. expression רֹאשׁ הַמִּטָּה occurs in the three other cases — though in plural — attaching a different vocalisation to the latter word: רָאשֵׁי הַמַּטּוֹת "the heads of the tribes" (Num. 30:2; 1 Kgs. 8:1; 2 Chr. 5:2).[59] רֹאשׁ הַמַּטֶּה "head of the tribe" appears to be thus a current idiom and the meaning of Hebr. מַטֶּה "staff, tribe" in Gen. 47:31 corresponds in this way remarkably to the reading of the LXX and Peš.[60] The rendering of this phrase would be "and Israel bowed himself for the head of the tribe", indicating that Joseph indeed has succeeded the patriarch and became the head of the tribe[61] as Van der Merwe suggested. The interpretation

---

[55]Cf. 1 Kgs. 1:47; Ezek. 46:2; Zeph. 1:5. See also 2 Sam. 14:33; 1 Kgs. 1:23.

[56]See also Isa. 60:14, where in comparison with Lev. 26:1 a rendering "before, to, at" for Hebr. עַל is the most likely. Cf. also Westermann, *Genesis 37–50*, 200, 206, who renders our text "zu Häupten des Bettes".

[57]NIV follows LXX in this reading. The interpretation is found also in Hebr. 11:21. LXX and Peš presuppose a suffix after מטה and no article in front of it like in MT and Sam. In our view this difference might be explained as an interpretative addition, because they could not make sense of it that the patriarch would bow "upon/at/before the top of the staff" and for that reason added a possesive pronoun or suffix: "upon/at/before the top of *his* staff". For the general character of the LXX of Genesis, which might explain such additions, see: J.W. Wevers, "An Apologia for Septuagint Studies", *BIOSCS* 18 (1985) 16–38, esp. 28–38; idem, *Notes on the Greek Text of Genesis* (SCSt, 35), Atlanta (GA) 1993, xii–xv; M. Rösel, *Übersetzung als Vollendung der Auslegung* (BZAW, 223), Berlin 1994, 16–20. See also J. Schreiner, *Septuaginta-Massora des Buches der Richter: Eine textkritische Studie* (AnBib, 7), Rome 1957, 7–10; E. Tov, *The Text-Critical Use of the Septuagint in Biblical Research* (JBSt, 3), Jerusalem 1981, 217–28.

[58]Speiser, *Genesis*, 356–7. J. Barr, "Vocalization and the Analysis of Hebrew", in: *Hebräische Wortforschung: Fs ... Walter Baumgartner* (SVT, 16), Leiden 1967, 1–11, 3 assumes influence of ῥάβδος in Gen. 30:32, 38 and says of the LXX's rendering: "His rendering is no evidence of the contemporary vocalization."

[59]See *HAL*, 543. Cf. also the expression רָאשֵׁי שִׁבְטֵ (Deut. 1:15; 5:23; 29:9 (E.T., 29:10); 1 Sam. 15:17. On the tirle רֹאשׁ in the Hebrew Bible, see also J.R. Bartlett, "The Use of the Word רֹאשׁ as a Title in the Old Testament", *VT* 19 (1969) 1–10.

[60]On the use of the Vrs for this meaning, cf. below.

[61]If this interpretation is correct, the "house of Israel" and "sons of Israel" are

suits the context rather well, because the patriarch addresses Joseph very politely as if he were a high placed person. Nevertheless, it is obvious that LXX and Peš do not support this interpretation, because Hebr. רֹאשׁ "leader" is mostly rendered with an obvious equivalent, like ἄρχοντος (Num. 30:2; 2 Chr. 5:2),[62] whereas LXX applies the prep. ἐπί (in combination with the verb προσκυνέω) to render the locative ה (*i.c.* אַרְצָה > ἐπὶ τὴν γῆν; Gen. 18:2; 24:52 etc.) or the prep. עַל in the sense of "on, at" (1 Kgs. 1:47; Zeph. 1:5). We can only conclude with regard to the reading of the LXX and Peš that they have pointed in the direction of this interpretation. Problematic is the question whether this interpretation could be read at a synchronic level and thus as a part of the *Letztgestallt* (although not any longer recognized by the Masoretes and the Vrs), or, that it is a part of a diachronic reading, probably belonging to an earlier pre-editorial text. That this interpretation was not recognized (or was rejected) seems apparent, because the idea that Joseph was called "the head of the tribe" is improbable in view of the whole context, especially the blessing on Judah (49:8–12), whereas the paronomasia[63] with מִטָּה (48:2; 49:33) has certainly contributed to the reading of MT. In this way the other interpretation of MT and Vrs could be explained, but it has to be asked if this reading was still intended in the final edition of the consonantal text. It might be supposed since LXX and Peš apparently still knew this tradition. However, we are inclined to consider that the proposed interpretation does not fit the present context of the whole Deathbed Episode (including Genesis 49). For that reason we would suggest maintaining the reading of MT at the synchronic level, and reconsider the proposed reading later on in the section on the diachronic reading.

With regard to the interpretation of MT we would like to return to our remarks made above in the first paragraphs of this section. Although scholars are generally inclined to take the bowing of the patriarch as an indication of his gratitude towards God, this interpretation must be rejected. The patriarch is together with Joseph on the scene and it is more probable (also in view of his words to Joseph) that he bows himself before Joseph. As was said before, the (human) object of שׁחה hithp. is not always mentioned explicitly if it is already

---

designated here with the word "tribe". We will return on this matter below.

[62] MT of 1 Kgs. 8:1 has a plus in comparison with the reading of LXX, and the latter did apparently not read רֹאשׁ הַמַּטֹּה. Only Origines rendered the expression here: πασας κεφαλας των ραβδων.

[63] On paronomasia cf. I. Kalimi, "Paronomasie im Buch der Chronik", *BZ* 41 (1997) 78–88 (with additional literature).

known from the context.[64] Therefore, we consider the prostration of
the patriarch to be directed to Joseph.

4.4.3   Part II: Genesis 48:1–22

4.4.3.1   Introduction

In his study of Genesis 48, Seebaß presented a synchronic reading of
this chapter and defended for this chapter the following division:[65]

Exposition (vv. 1f.)

(a)   arrangement by Israel that Ephraim and Manasseh should not
      inherit as grandsons, but as sons (vv. 3–6, [7])
(b)   introduction of the sons in person (vv. 8–12)
(c)   blessings for Joseph and his sons (vv. 13–20a)

Conclusion (v. 20b)

Seebaß' analysis is influenced by the fact that Genesis 49 is excluded
in advance from the analysis of the Deathbed Episode. In his analysis
this results in the suggestion that verses 21–22 reflects the introductory section in 47:29–31.[66] However, in our view[67] the final two verses
(48:21–22) do not reflect 47:29–31[68] and should be considered, therefore, as part of the second scene. These two verses are described by
Seebaß as the aim of the whole chapter (including 47:29–31), describing Israel's provisions for Joseph to have priority over his brothers.[69]
Yet, it could be questioned whether these verses should be considered
as the aim of this scene or that they are just a part of it and, in some
respect, unrelated to the other parts. If 48:20b is just the resuming
phrase of 48:13–20, then 48:21–22 would conclude this scene:

Exposition (vv. 1f.)

(a)   arrangement by Israel that Ephraim and Manasseh should not
      inherit as grandsons, but as sons (vv. 3–6, [7])
(b)   introduction of the sons in person (vv. 8–12)
(c)   blessings for Joseph and his sons (vv. 13–20)

Conclusion: Joseph receives an extra heritage (v. 21–22)

---

[64]Cf. above, p. 329, with n. 52.

[65]Seebaß, "The Joseph Story", 30.

[66]Seebaß, "The Joseph Story", 29, 31–2.

[67]See p. 318.

[68]Seebaß, "The Joseph Story", 32 rightly points out that both scenes are "Israel-
Joseph scenes" in which Joseph's sons are of no importance and which enclose in
this way 48:1–20, but the transition from verse 20 to verses 21–22 (made in verse
20b according to Seebaß) is not a change of scene as is found in 48:1.

[69]Seebaß, "The Joseph Story", 30, 32.

4.4.3.2   And it Was Told to Joseph ... (48:1–2)

This passage forms the introduction to the following passage in which
the patriarch adopts and blesses Joseph's sons. Here the persons on
the scene are introduced too, we do not have the patriarch alone
together with his son Joseph, but Joseph takes his two sons with him.
Mentioning their names, as happens here, presupposes that they are
known already: Manasseh and Ephraim. The order of the names indicates who is the oldest as is narrated in their birth story (cf. 41:50–52),
which has the features of other birth stories in Genesis. Apparently
the function of this scene is to give Joseph the opportunity to bring in
his sons,[70] because if this element were absent this transition would
not have any function in the development of the story.

The passage starts with a transitional phrase, apparently intended
to round off the preceding passage because that passage had an open
ending.[71] וַיְהִי אַחֲרֵי הַדְּבָרִים הָאֵלֶּה marks in each case a new scene in the
narrative. Remarkable in this case is that again it was told to Joseph
alone, his other brothers are not informed about their father's illness.
A second remarkable point is the fact that together with the change of
scene the name of the patriarch changes into "Jacob" (48:2a) and then
back into "Israel" (48:2b). The change in names of the patriarch is
based on the tradition that Jacob received a new name (Gen. 28:32;
35:10), but the function of changing the names, thus using the old
name time and again, is unclear.

4.4.3.3   "Ephraim and Manasseh Will Be Mine" (48:3–7)

The speech of the patriarch (Jacob) might be described as the adoption of Ephraim and Manasseh. This adoption is put between two
references to events in the land of Canaan, both related to Jacob's
progeny:

> God appeared and blessed him,
> promise of progeny and land. (vv. 3–4)
>> Adoption of Ephraim and Manasseh,
>> later sons of Joseph will be called by their name. (vv. 5–6)
> Rachel's death and burial,
> (implied: no possibility of progeny; v. 7)

The patriarch refers in his words to his journey through the land
of Canaan, which is described in Gen. 35:1–15, and the idiom he

---

[70]Seebaß, "The Joseph Story" 31.

[71]As Seebaß, "The Joseph Story", 29 has indicated already, the phrase seems
to suggest further action. A comparable transition is found in Exod. 4:31–5:1.

applies is identical to Gen. 35:6, 9–12. However, the words of the
promises he quotes resemble more closely the words found in Gen.
28:3, using the words of the blessing of Isaac.[72] By means of this
echoing of other blessings, the blessing Jacob received is placed in line
with the blessings of his fathers Abraham and Isaac.[73] This reference
to the appearance of God and his promise functions as a kind of
legitimation for the adoption in the following verses, which is indicated
by the וְעַתָּה "and now" (48:5).[74]

The reference to Rachel's death is a puzzling line in the whole
of the Deathbed Episode: why does the patriarch refer to Rachel's
death here? Many scholars have tried to solve this puzzle by means of
diachronic solutions. But even so the verse appears to be a stumbling
block, because it was not accepted as part of the same layer as the
preceding verses (P) and therefore considered a gloss, or a part of E,
assuming in that case that some text has been omitted during the
compilation of the sources.[75] Speiser ascribes this embarrassment to
a reading at first glance. In his view the verse has to be connected to
the preceding passage. Jacob is robbed of Rachel, and hence "Jacob
feels justified in substituting two of Rachel's grandsons for such other
sons as fate may have prevented her from bearing."[76] This solution
is reasonable, because the reference to Rachel's death reminds the
reader of the cause of her death, namely the birth of the youngest son:
Benjamin. In our view, Blum is correct in assuming here in verses 3–7
an intentional unit, even if this section consists largely of quotations
from other texts.[77] The reference to Ephrat, however, is in this context

---

[72]Wenham, *Genesis 16–50*, 463.

[73]Wenham, *Genesis 16–50*, 463.

[74]See especially: H.A. Brongers, "Bemerkungen zum Gebrauch des adverbialen
w^e '*attāh* im Alten Testament (Ein lexikologischer Beitrag)", *VT* 15 (1965) 289–99.
Cf. also Gunkel, *Genesis*, ³1910, 496; Skinner, *Genesis*, 504; Westermann, *Genesis 37–50*, 207–8; Blum, *Die Komposition der Vätergeschichte*, 251–2; Scharbert,
Genesis 12–50, 286–7.

[75]Cf. *e.g.* Holzinger, *Genesis*, 252–4; Gunkel, *Genesis*, ³1910, 470–1; Skinner,
Genesis, 504–5; Westermann, *Genesis 37–50*, 208–9; Scharbert, *Genesis 12–50*,
287.

[76]Speiser, *Genesis*, 359. He was followed by Redford, *Biblical Story of Joseph*,
22; Blum, *Die Komposition der Vätergeschichte*, 252; Syrén, *The Forsaken First-
Born*, 136–7; Hamilton, *Book of Genesis*, 630.

[77]Blum, *Die Komposition der Vätergeschichte*, 252.
L. Schmidt, *Literarische Studien zur Josephsgeschichte* (BZAW, 167), Berlin
1986, 254, does not agree with Blum because the relation between v. 7 and vv.
3–6 does not have any basis in the text in his view. Jacob is only interested in his
grandsons to let them share in the promise which is described in vv. 3–4, and not
as a supplement to the fulfilment of the promise. However, it is remarkable that
first we find a reference to the possibility that Joseph could beget more children

remarkable because there might exist a connection between the names Ephrat(ah) and Ephraim. Yet, with this connection we are coming close to questions of a diachronic character, which cannot be answered here.[78]

The adoption of Ephraim and Manasseh is a well-known text. With the words לִי־הֵם "they are mine" the patriarch adopts Joseph's two sons; the idiom expresses an absolute state of full ownership.[79] With these words Ephraim and Manasseh are unmistakably adopted by the patriarch as can also be derived from parallels in the *Umwelt*.[80] The following clause (48:5b) is ambiguous, although usually not recognized as such. אֶפְרַיִם וּמְנַשֶּׁה כִּרְאוּבֵן וְשִׁמְעוֹן יִהְיוּ־לִי can be rendered in two ways. The first is the most common: "Ephraim and Manasseh, like Reuben and Simeon, they shall be mine".[81] Rendering the text in this way the clause emphasizes that these two sons of Joseph will be true sons of Jacob in the same way as (for example) Reuben and

---

after his two adopted sons, and then the remark וַאֲנִי "but I ..." together with the account of Rachel's death. This does not exclude, however, Schmidt's suggestion that this reference was given because otherwise we would only have a reference to Rebekah's funeral in the Deathbed Episode (Schmidt, *op.cit.*, 255). However, this might also be due to the narrator or editor and not necessarily to a glossator.

[78]Cf. K.-D. Schunck, "Ophra, Ephron und Ephraim", *VT* 11 (1961) 188–200; J. Heller, "Noch zu Ophra, Ephron und Ephraim", *VT* 12 (1962) 339–41.

[79]A comparable clause is found in Cant. 2:16 (cf. also 6:3): דּוֹדִי לִי וַאֲנִי לוֹ "my beloved is mine and I am his". See also Exod. 6:7; 1 Sam. 1:2; Isa. 43:1; 44:5; Amos 9:7; and W. Vogels, "Invitation à revenir à l'alliance et universalisme en Amos ix 7", *VT* 22 (1972) 223–39, esp. 230–2.

[80]I. Mendelsohn, "A Ugaritic Parallel to the Adoption of Ephraim and Manasseh", *IEJ* 9 (1959) 180–3, esp. 180.

H. Donner, "Adoption oder Legitimation? Erwägungen zur Adoption im Alten Testament auf dem Hintergrund der altorientalischen Rechte", *OrAn* 8 (1969) 87–119, argues against the use of this terminology because the children are not adopted in the official legal manner in the sense that they become part of Jacob's household and, as such, are not subjected to his authority. Moreover, in his view adoption is unknown in Israel because we do not find any trace of it in Israel's laws. However, H.J. Boecker, "Anmerkungen zur Adoption im Alten Testament", *ZAW* 86 (1974) 86–9, has argued against Donner because Ps. 2:7; 2 Sam. 7:14 must be considered as adoption formulae. See also S.M. Paul, "Adoption Formulae: A Study of Cuneiform and Biblical Legal Clauses", *Maarav* 2 (1979–80) 173–85, esp. 173–5. Since there is a clear correspondence between Ps. 2:7; 2 Sam. 7:14 and our text (compare also 48:16, and Mendelsohn, *art.cit.*, 180–1), we prefer the term "adoption" for the act described in Gen. 48:5.

[81]KJ; StV; RSV; Driver, *Genesis*, 376; König, *Die Genesis*, 744; Jacob, *Das erste Buch*, 865; Westermann, *Genesis 37–50*, 201; Wenham, *Genesis 16–50*, 453.

Speiser, *Genesis*, 354, renders "Ephraim and Manasseh shall be mine, no less so than Reuben or Simeon" (see also JPS). The words "no less than" are a paraphrase of Hebr. כְּ "like" and give the impression of a "double translation" leaving other interpretations open.

Simeon are. This rendering seems to be confirmed by the following clause in verse 6a: וּמוֹלַדְתְּךָ אֲשֶׁר־הוֹלַדְתָּ לְךָ יִהְיוּ אַחֲרֵיהֶם "But the offspring you bring forth after them, yours they will be". However, it might be asked if this clause is meant to contrast verse 5b or verse 5a, since verse 6a applies a similar terminology in verse 5a.[82]

Yet another rendering would be possible, as can be derived in any case from TO. In this version we read אפרים ומנשה כראובן ושמעון יהון קדמי "Ephraim and Manasseh, like Reuben and Simeon they shall be before me".[83] The interpretation of TO is nowhere referred to, as far as we are aware.[84] Nevertheless, this rendering is found also in recent translations and commentaries: "Ephraim and Manasseh like Reuben and Simeon they shall be to me".[85] This interpretation might be defended with reference to other texts where we find the idiom הָיָה לְ כְּ, as in, for example, Jer. 23:14:[86]

All of them became like Sodom to me (14bA)	הָיוּ־לִי כֻלָּם כִּסְדֹם
and its inhabitants like Gomorrah. (14bB)	וְיֹשְׁבֶיהָ כַּעֲמֹרָה

Another example, coming even closer to our text, can be found in 2 Sam. 12:3, where the prophet Nathan says concerning the ewe lamb of the poor man: וַתְּהִי־לוֹ כְּבַת "and it was to him like a daughter".[87] Although there are some examples of a possessive meaning for this idiom,[88] it appears to us that the interpretation of TO is solid. In the previous paragraph we referred to verse 6a; now when this text is taken into consideration as well, it seems that a word-play with the prep. לְ has been made.

---

[82]We will return to this matter below.

[83]LXX and Peš have a reading which is as ambiguous as MT. LXX reads Εφραιμ καὶ Μανασση ὡς Ρουβην καὶ Συμεων ἔσονταί μοι, in which μοι can be interpreted as a *dativus possessivus* ("will be mine") or as a *dativus commodi* ("will be to me"). Peš reads *'prym wmnš' dyly nhwwn 'yk rwbyl w'yk šm'wn nhwwn ly* "Ephraim and Manasseh are mine, like Reuben and Simeon they will be to me/mine". In the second clause Peš left out the possessive particle *dy*, which gives an ambiguous reading comparable to MT and LXX, and which is very close to TO. According to T. Muraoka, *Emphatic Words and Structures in Biblical Hebrew*, Jerusalem, Leiden 1985, 17, n. 39, Peš shows a conflation of the two interpretations.

[84]The only exception is the note in Muraoka, *Emphatic Words and Structures*, 17, n. 39, suggesting that TO offers another interpretation than MT. As will be argued below this is very doubtful.

[85]NBG; EÜ; Gunkel, *Genesis*, ³1910, 496; Procksch, *Genesis*, 560; Böhl, *Genesis*, 47; Aalders, *Genesis*, dl. III, 180; Jagersma, *Genesis 25–50*, 250.

[86]See also Exod. 22:24; Lev. 19:34; Isa. 29:2, 11; 30:13; Jer. 12:8; 15:18; 23:12; Hos. 11:4; 13:7; 14:5.

[87]LXX and Peš render this text with a similar idiom as in Gen. 48:5.

[88]Cf. Lev. 5:13; Num. 18:18.

your two sons born *to you*	שְׁנֵי־בָנֶיךָ הַנּוֹלָדִים לְךָ
... they are *mine*	... לִי־הֵם
like Reuben and Simeon they will be *to me*	כִּרְאוּבֵן וְשִׁמְעוֹן יִהְיוּ־לִי
your offspring ... will be *yours*	וּמוֹלַדְתְּךָ ... לְךָ יִהְיוּ

In addition, this interpretation can be strengthened on the basis of the syntactic construction of the clause: כִּרְאוּבֵן וְשִׁמְעוֹן are positioned emphatically in comparison with the other examples of this idiom.[89] This seems to indicate that the comparison with Reuben and Simeon is rather important, but this is unlikely because they are sons *of* Jacob, rather it is probably because of what they are *to* Jacob. However, what do we gain by this comparison?

It appears that in 1 Chr. 5:1 we find one of the first interpretations of this text, which is comparable to the interpretation of TO as described above. Here we read that נִתְּנָה בְּכֹרָתוֹ לִבְנֵי יוֹסֵף בֶּן־יִשְׂרָאֵל "his [Reuben's] birthright was given to the sons of Joseph, the son of Israel".[90] Although it is sometimes mentioned that Reuben and Simeon are the eldest sons of Jacob,[91] the fact that Ephraim and Manasseh are equalled to Reuben and Simeon is not worked out by scholars as being important. The conclusion which is mostly drawn from these words is that Joseph's sons are put on a par with Jacob's sons and that Reuben and Simeon are just mentioned as examples of two sons[92] König denies the interpretation that Ephraim and Manasseh became the first-born sons of Jacob,[93] and the fact that this matter is generally not discussed in scholarly literature might reflect a general assent to this denial.[94] Sometimes a reference is found in scholarly literature to the fact that the descendants of Joseph receive in this way a double share in Israel, which might in the view of these scholars be interpreted that Joseph has received the double share of

---

[89] In most examples listed above in n. 86, the order is הָיָה לְ' כִּ'; in Hos. 14:6 the order of the final two particles is reversed: אֶהְיֶה כַטַּל לְיִשְׂרָאֵל. The order כִּ' הָיָה לְ' (Gen. 48:5) is found nowhere else.

[90] This interpretation is found in Procksch, *Genesis*, 562; I. Willi-Plein, "Historiographische Aspekte der Josefsgeschichte", *Henoch* 1 (1979) 305–31, 324; Ackerman, "Joseph, Judah, and Jacob", 109; Syrén, *The Forsaken First-Born*, 136–7.

[91] *E.g.* Speiser, *Genesis*, 357; Sarna, *Genesis*, 326; Hamilton, *Genesis*, 629.

[92] Cf. Skinner, *Genesis*, 504; Aalders, *Genesis*, dl. III, 184; Speiser, *Genesis*, 357; Westermann, *Genesis 37–50*, 208; Schmidt, *Literarische Studien*, 254; Wenham, *Genesis 16–50*, 463.

[93] König, *Die Genesis*, 744, n. 3.

[94] J. Van Seters, *Abraham in History and Tradition*, New Haven (CT) 1975, 88, n. 76, is the only one from recent scholars who explicitly denies this possibility: "It is hard to see how this verse can mean that Ephraim and Manasseh were substituted for Reuben and Simeon, the first and second born, or given their preferential shares, although 1 Chron. 5:1–2 seems to interpret it this way".

the oldest son,[95] but this is not based on verse 5b though it can be derived from verse 5a and 6a. The emphatic position of Reuben and Simeon is not explained by all this.

Commonly the adoption of Ephraim and Manasseh is interpreted as a positive event for Joseph but this point of view must be seriously questioned. First of all Joseph's sons are no longer his sons, but the patriarch's (לִי־הֶם) which in view of the great value attached to the having of sons in the (ancient) Near East is a very encroaching event.[96] The consequence of Jacob's action is that now Joseph has no sons any more, and unless he would beget one later he would be childless. His name is wiped out completely because it will be the patriarch's name which will be called in them (וְיִקָּרֵא בָהֶם שְׁמִי, 48:16b).[97] In view of what we know concerning the tradition of Joseph it is clear that this is indeed very constricting because the tradition does not make any mention of sons born to Joseph, and it appears that he himself needed to adopt his great-grandchildren (50:23).[98] Secondly, the equation with Reuben and Simeon contains, from a strictly synchronic point of view, a very clear message. If the sayings concerning these two tribes in Genesis 49 are considered regarding the position of Ephraim and Manasseh the message is obvious: "you shall have no superiority". The equation to Reuben and Simeon cannot be considered positive, it has to be regarded as a denial of a possible leading position of Joseph or his sons. In fact this equation to Reuben and Simeon is in line with the question put by Jacob at the beginning of the Joseph Story: "Should I, and your mother and your brothers come to bow

---

[95]Van der Merwe, "Joseph as Successor of Jacob", 226; Van Selms, *Genesis. dl. II*, 266.

[96]Scharbert, *Genesis 12–50*, 287, is the only one, who notes that this is a very radical event, but he attributes it to the fact that sons which were not born in Canaan could not claim any inheritance in the eyes of P (the generally assumed writer of vv. 3–6[7]).

[97]The invocation of his name and the names of his fathers might refer to the ancestor cult in which the spirits were invoked (Ug. *qrá*; Hebr. קָרֶא) by their name; cf. De Moor, *RoY²*, 356. It appears that in this respect Joseph's name is wiped out indeed, because the patriarch declaired that the names of the sons born later to Joseph will be called by the name of their brothers, so their name will not invoced upon (if reading this expression as a reference to the ancestor cult), or their name will not be mentioned anymore, but only the names of the patriarch's sons.

[98]It has to be noted that being childless is generally considered a curse in the ancient Near East; cf. Gen. 15:1–3; 20:18; 30:1–2; Lev. 20:20–1; 1 Sam. 1:5–7; 15:33; 2 Sam. 6:23; Isa. 47:9; Jer. 15:7; 22:30; Hos. 9:12, 14; KTU 1.14–16; 1.17–19. See also: O.J. Baab, "Child", *IDB*, vol. A–D, 508; J.A. Grassi, "Child, Children", *ABD*, vol. I, 904–7, esp. 904–5; Van der Toorn, *Family Religion in Babylonia, Syria and Israel*, 130.

ourselves to the ground before you?" (37:10b). The Joseph Story has answered this question positively, but it is clear that this is only because of Joseph's position in Egypt, not because of a general leading position among the brothers. Again with reference to Genesis 49, this position will be given to Judah: "your father's sons shall bow down to you" (49:8bB).[99]

Finally, the reference to Ephraim and Manasseh in verse 5b is not given in the order of their birth (Gen. 41:50–52), that order is followed by the narrator in verse 1, telling that Joseph took Manasseh and Ephraim. Here the patriarch, obviously familiar with the names of Joseph's two sons, places the name of Ephraim before Manasseh. It is an implicit announcement of what will happen in verse 14, where the patriarch will put Ephraim before Manasseh.[100] The order is by no means incidental, but in view of the fact that the patriarch uses here this order against the order the narrator applies in verse 1, it has to be considered as a purposeful anticipation.

4.4.3.4   And Israel Saw the Sons of Joseph (48:8–12)

The following section (vv. 8–12) closely resembles the other Deathbed Episode in Genesis, namely the deathbed of Isaac. The most significant resemblance is of course the fact that the patriarch's eyes are כָּבְדוּ מִזֹּקֶן "heavy because of age" (48:10a), which is also told of Isaac (27:1).[101] But there are more correspondences to be found, as H. Jagersma has shown.[102] The question Israel asks in the beginning, מִי־אֵלֶּה "who are these", reflects Isaacs question to Jacob and Esau: מִי אַתָּה "who are you" (27:18bB, 32aA). Also the purpose to bless them, (וַאֲבָרְכֵם) might be related to the blessing of Isaac's son: תְּבָרֶכְךָ נַפְשִׁי (27:4b, 25aB). Finally, when Joseph's sons are brought to the patriarch, he kisses them and embraces them וַיִּשַּׁק לָהֶם וַיְחַבֵּק לָהֶם (48:10b), reminding us of Isaac's blessing of Jacob, when the latter kisses his father. However, the pair of "to kiss" and "to embrace" recurs also at other moments in Genesis, when first Laban and later Esau meet Jacob (respectively in 29:13; 33:4).[103] When we now return to Israel's

---

[99] Van der Merwe, "Joseph as Successor of Jacob", 231.

[100] Cf. Sarna, *Genesis*, 326; Wenham, *Genesis 16–50*, 463; Jagersma, *Genesis 25–50*, 250.

[101] De Fraine, *Genesis*, 320; Wenham, *Genesis 16–50*, 464; V.P. Hamilton, *Book of Genesis: Chapters 18–50* (NICOT), Grand Rapids (MI) 1995, 634; Jagersma, *Genesis 25–50*, 251. In view of Blum, *Die Komposition der Vätergeschichte*, 253, Genesis 48 is "als Entsprechung und 'Gegenstück' zu der in Gen 27 gestaltet".

[102] Jagersma, *Genesis 25–50*, 251–2.

[103] The order of the words is reversed, but this happens also in the Ugaritic texts where this word-pair is found too; cf. KTU 1.17:i.40–1; 1.19:ii.15; 1.23:51, 56;

question to Joseph מִי־אֵלֶּה "who are these?" it has to be noted that
this question is also found in the episode describing the meeting of
Esau and Jacob (Gen. 33:1–17). Esau asks מִי־אֵלֶּה לָּךְ "who are those
with you?"[104] The answer of Jacob is comparable to the one Joseph
gives to him later: הַיְלָדִים אֲשֶׁר־חָנַן אֱלֹהִים אֶת־עַבְדֶּךָ "the children God
gave graciously to your servant".

The text has, however, some remarkable features. Whereas the
references to the ages of the patriarch and Joseph etc. suggest that
Joseph's sons are about twenty years old,[105] the scene suggests that
we are dealing here with small children. The patriarch's demand to
Joseph קָחֶם־נָא אֵלַי "bring them to me" (48:9b) as well as the phrases
וַיַּגֵּשׁ אֹתָם אֵלָיו "brought them to him" (48:10bA)[106] and וַיּוֹצֵא יוֹסֵף אֹתָם
מֵעִם בִּרְכָּיו "and Joseph made them go away from[107] his knees" (48:12a)
does not suggest that we are dealing with independent adults, but
with children who are strongly dependent on their parents.[108] Some
scholars, however, emphasize that because the text does not say that
the sons were *on* his knees they do not have to be necessarily young
children but that young men could also stand at the knees of the
patriarch.[109] Also Israel's question "who are these?" (48:8) is to be
explained in the context of the whole episode. Sarna explains several
aspects of this episode, like this question, as a continuation of the preceding adoption (vv. 3–7),[110] whereas others consider the possibility

---

see Dahood, Penar, "Ugaritic-Hebrew Parallel Pairs", 174 (# 172), 282 (# 395);
Avishur, *Stylistic Studies*, 356; Hamilton, *Book of Genesis*, 634, n. 26.

[104] Note that in 48:8 Sam and LXX read in addition to MT לָּךְ "with you", which
might be derived from the reading of MT in 33:5.

[105] Cf. Gen. 41:50; 45:6, 11; 47:28.

[106] Cf. this phrase with for example 1 Sam. 1:25b: וַיָּבִיאוּ אֶת־הַנַּעַר אֶל־עֵלִי "and they
brought the boy to Eli".

[107] It is almost generally acknowledged nowadays that the sons are taken מֵעִם
"away from" his knees (*e.g.* Westermann, *Genesis 37–50*, 210), not suggesting that
the patriarch had them *on* his knees as can be found in the older commentaries
(*e.g.* Gunkel, *Genesis*, ³1910, 472; but compare still NEB; Davidson, *Genesis
12–50*, 294; Blum, *Die Komposition der Vätergeschichte*, 251, n. 44; Jagersma,
Genesis 25–50, 252) but that they were standing *at, near* his knees.

[108] This is recognized by many scholars; see *e.g.* Westermann, *Genesis 37–50*,
209; Scharbert, *Genesis 12–50*, 287; Jagersma, *Genesis 25–50*, 251–2. Note that
Hamilton, *Book of Genesis*, 634, considers the possibility that (as an alternative
to other solutions) this episode might originally have been positioned shortly after
Jacob's arrival in Egypt, somewhere around 46:30. As will be referred to in the
diachronic analysis other scholars consider the possibility that this event took
place shortly after Jacob's arrival in Egypt.

[109] Jacob, *Das erste Buch*, 876; Aalders, *Genesis*, dl. III, 185–6; Hamilton, *Book of
Genesis*, 635. Van Selms, *Genesis dl. II*, 267, ignores the whole matter and simply
states that the patriarch asks "who the two men are" ("wie de twee mannen zijn").

[110] Sarna, *Genesis*, 327; this suggestion was appreciated by Wenham, *Genesis*

that it is a formal prelude to the blessing.[111] Another reaon for the question is that the patriarch simply wants to identify the sons, which he can only see very vaguely (this explanation is sometimes combined with his deceit of his own father at his blessing in Genesis 27).[112]

Verse 12 seems to form a kind of interlude between the introduction of the two sons and their blessing. After the patriarch has kissed and embraced them and has spoken some words to Joseph, Joseph sends his sons away from his father and bows before him to the ground — following MT.[113] This resembles of course the end of the first scene where the patriarch has bowed himself before his son. Apparently this episode causes scholars fewer difficulties than the preceding one, where the patriarch bows himself down, since it is generally considered that Joseph bows himself before his father in a grateful gesture,[114] although some scholars prefer to combine the gesture towards the patriarch with a thankful bowing before God, which is however without any basis in the text.[115]

4.4.3.5 And He Put Ephraim before Manasseh (48:13–20)

The scene which describes how Jacob places Ephraim before Manasseh is well known. The text and translation offer few problems to the translator although attention might be paid to a problem which is of some importance to the consistency of the text. This problem was briefly discussed by E. Talstra in his inaugural lecture:[116] it is found in verse 17, where Joseph sees that his father יָשִׁית his right hand on the head of Ephraim. Has the *yiqtol* form of the verb to be rendered as a past tense as usually happens or is the verb indeed to be rendered as an imperfect? Thus, do we have to render the text by "Joseph saw that his father laid his right hand on the head of Ephraim",[117] or by

---

16–50, 464. Cf. already Ehrlich, *RG*, Bd. I, 239, although he wants to rearrange the text, placing vv. 8–9 before verse 3.

[111] De Fraine, *Genesis*, 320; Hamilton, *Book of Genesis*, 634.

[112] Van Selms, *Genesis dl. II*, 267; cf. Wenham, *Genesis 16–50*, 464.

[113] Sam, LXX, Peš and TN read a plural here: "they bowed themselves", which seems to fit better in the text, suggesting that they all, or the two sons bowed to the ground. However, the reading of MT might be considered as the *lectio dificilior*, since the bowing of Joseph certainly interrupts the flow of the story.

[114] E.g. Aalders, *Genesis*, dl. III, 186; Van Selms, *Genesis dl. II*, 268; Wenham, *Genesis 16–50*, 464; Hamilton, *Book of Genesis*, 635.

[115] Jacob, *Das erste Buch*, 876; Westermann, *Genesis 37–50*, 211.

[116] E. Talstra, *Schermen met Schrift: De kombinatie van bijbelwetenschappen en computer geïllustreerd aan de tekst van Genesis 48*, Amsterdam 1992, 16–21.

[117] See StV; NBG; KJ; RSV; EÜ; Gunkel, *Genesis*, ³1910, 474; Aalders, *Genesis*, dl. III, 181, 187–8; De Fraine, *Genesis*, 321; Speiser, *Genesis*, 356; Westermann, *Genesis 37–50*, 201, 214–5; Wenham, *Genesis 16–50*, 454, 465.

"Joseph saw that his father would lay (or was to lay) his right hand on the head of Ephraim".[118] Since the *yiqtol* demands an "imperfect" or "future" rendering, Talstra questioned the usual way of rendering which, in his view, tries to gloss over the text, doing away with a syntactic problem.[119]

A comparison with comparable syntactic constructions[120] demonstrates that the *yiqtol* should be rendered as indicating what is or was going to happen.[121] In our case this would argue for the latter rendering of our text. It is sometimes argued that according to verse 14 Jacob had already laid his hands crosswise on the heads of the two sons and that Joseph's reaction was too late.[122] Only by considering 48:15–16 as a later addition would this problem be solved since verses 17–19 would follow rather well after verse 14.[123] However, it might be objected that by means of this grammatical feature in verse 17 which does not narrate a consecutive line of events but rather by employing the *yiqtol* it becomes apparent that Jacob still did not lay his hands on the heads of the boys and did not pronounce the blessing. In this way verses 17–19 function as a kind of parenthesis,[124] or as a *nachholende Erzählung*,[125] telling what Joseph did before Jacob pronounced the blessing on the two boys. As N. Lohfink suggested with regard to the use of the *nachholende Erzählung* in the book of Jonah, this literary device could be used because at the position where we want to read our text (*i.c.* vv. 17–19 after v. 14) it was not appropriate for the narrator.[126] In this way it appears that Joseph's protest does not come too late as is usually argued against the unity of the text, because the protest which had to follow (in fact after verse 14) would have disturbed the blessing for both. By placing Joseph's reaction here in verse 17, the blessing could be pronounced after placing the hands on their heads which might have seemed to be a more appropriate order of events. Talstra argues here, however, that the grammatical feature is a signal for the diachronic development of the text,[127] but in our

---

[118] JPS; NEB; NIV; König, *Die Genesis*, 747; Hamilton, *Book of Genesis*, 639.

[119] Talstra, *Schermen met Schrift*, 19.

[120] Perfect or imperfect consecutive of ראה or ידע, followed by a clause with an imperfect which is introduced by the particle כי.

[121] Talstra, *Schermen met Schrift*, 20.

[122] See Wenham, *Genesis 16–50*, 465–6.

[123] *E.g.* Westermann, *Genesis 37–50*, 212.

[124] Hamilton, *Book of Genesis*, 639, n. 1; 641.

[125] N. Lohfink, "Und Jona ging zur Stadt hinaus (Jona 4:5)", *BZ* 5 (1961) 185–203; A.S. van der Woude, *Jona, Nahum* (PredOT), Nijkerk 1978, 51–2.

[126] Jacob, *Das erste Buch*, 880–1. Talstra, *Schermen met Schrift*, 21, agrees at the level of the synchronic reading.

[127] Talstra, *Schermen met Schrift*, 21; cf. in this way also Kebekus, *Die Josefer-*

view the grammatical element argues in this case *against* a diachronic development and might be considered as a suitable or required artistic feature in the text.[128]

The whole course of events described in this section develops rather smoothly, but there is in fact one problematic line, which causes some difficulty in the transition from verse 14 to verses 17–19. It is the brief line וַיְבָרֶךְ אֶת־יוֹסֵף "and he blessed Joseph" (48:15aA). This line was already problematic for the ancient translators, because in place of MT, Sam, TO, Peš "Joseph", the LXX has the reading αὐτούς "them", which is preferred by some modern commentators.[129] Other commentators object, however, that Joseph is being blessed here in his sons and that the reading of MT should be followed,[130] which seems very probable in the light of the Semitic concept of corporate personality — the identification of the individual and the collective. However, notwithstanding this interpretation, which might be correct, the interpretation is factually incorrect because these two are not Joseph's sons any more.[131] So, in the line of the narrative, following the adoption described in verses 5–6, and the remark that the name of the patriarch (and not Joseph's) may be called in them (48:16), the reference to Joseph is not appropriate and the rendering of LXX seems to be more in line with the blessing.[132] However, in the LXX we are undoubtedly dealing with a harmonization, which might be considered as the *lectio facilior* and which is therefore not to be followed.[133]

The motif[134] presented here in this section is strongly connected

---

zählung, 200.

[128] This argumentation does not exclude the possibility that the text did have a diachronic development, but this has to be argued on the basis of other considerations. In our view the text was indeed edited, but this will be argued in the section on the diachronic analysis. Here it is important to note that the narrator or editor applied a literary device which is not uncommon.

[129] Procksch, *Genesis*, 421, 424; Speiser, *Genesis*, 355, n. *g*; B. Vawter, *On Genesis: A New Reading*, London 1977, 454; Hamilton, *Book of Genesis*, 633, n. 19.

[130] Gunkel, *Genesis*, ³1910, 473; König, *Die Genesis*, 746–7; Aalders, *Genesis*, dl. III, 186, n. 1; De Fraine, *Genesis*, 321; Van Selms, *Genesis, dl. II*, 268; Wenham, *Genesis 16–50*, 465.

[131] Schmidt, *Literarische Studien zur Josephsgeschichte*, 266.

[132] Schmidt, *Literarische Studien zur Josephsgeschichte*, 266.

[133] Westermann, *Genesis 37–50*, 212; Schmidt, *Literarische Studien zur Josephsgeschichte*, 266; Kebekus, *Die Joseferzählung*, 200, n. 25.

[134] We use the term "motif" to designate here the recurrent pattern in the stories of Genesis, following Syrén, *The Forsaken First-Born*, 11–3. In contrast to Syrén, we prefer the definition "a distinctive feature or element of a design or composition" (*The Shorter Oxford Dictionary*), because the motif of the 'forsaken first-born' is a "distinctive" feature of the *literary composition* of Genesis as a

with the rest of the book of Genesis. Here the youngest son also
gains precedence over the eldest, as we have already seen with Cain,
Ishmael, Esau, Zerah, and will also see with Reuben.[135] Next to this
motif, references to the patriarchs are abundantly present and link in
that respect this section also to the whole of Genesis. This effect is
even reinforced by the theme of the blessing, which is connected with
the gift of a multitude of descendants.

4.4.3.6 "And I Give to You ..." (48:21–22)

After the patriarch has pronounced his blessings upon Ephraim and
Manasseh he addresses Joseph again. He knows that he is going to
die and that he will not return to Canaan alive. However, he is sure
that God will make his son and the brothers return to the "land of
the fathers". שׁוּב אֶל־אֶרֶץ אֲבֹתֵיכֶם "return to the land of your fathers"
has already been found at the other occasion that the patriarch was
in exile — though singular there — (Gen. 31:3). In the context of the
Pentateuch we have to take this idiom as a reference to the Exodus,
although in that context the verb שׁוּב (hiph.) is not used but עלה
(hiph.) and יצא (hiph.),[136] a difference which might already be found
in the comparable passage in 50:24: וְהֶעֱלָה אֶתְכֶם מִן־הָאָרֶץ הַזֹּאת "and
He will bring you up out of this land". Although in some studies
we find the remark that our verse (v. 21) is not connected with the
following one (v. 22),[137] this must be questioned. The present verse
(21) should be considered a prelude to the following in which the
patriarch bestows on his son a special part of the land. The gift in
verse 22 can only have meaning if Joseph and his brothers will "return
to the land of the fathers".[138]

Verse 22 contains an enigmatic saying by the patriarch and a convincing solution is difficult to find. First we have to deal with the
object the patriarch gives away: שְׁכֶם (followed by the numeral אַחַד)

---

whole. It *is* a leading theme in Genesis, in the sense that recognizing it is decisive
for grasping the idea behind the composition of the book (*pace*, Syrén, *op.cit.*,
11).

[135] De Fraine, *Genesis*, 321; Vawter, *On Genesis*, 455; Hamilton, *Book of Genesis*,
636–7; Jagersma, *Genesis 25–50*, 252.

[136] The use of יצא (hiph.) with regard to the Exodus is found in Exodus many
times: see 6:13, 26; 7:4; 12:17, 42, 51; 16:3, 6, 32; 20:2; 29:46; 32:11 and is thus
not used only since Deut. 1:27 for the "older" הֶעֱלָה as is suggested by *HAL*, 407b.

[137] Schmitt, *Die nichtpriesterliche Josephsgeschichte*, 71–2, n. 302; Kebekus, *Die
Joseferzählung*, 201–2.

[138] Aalders, *Genesis*, 189; Van Selms, *Genesis, dl. II*, 270; Vawter, *On Genesis*, 456; Schmitt, *Die nichtpriesterliche Josephsgeschichte*, 71–2, n. 302; Schmidt,
Literarische Studien zur Josephsgeschichte, 269; Wenham, *Genesis 16–50*, 466.

which is rendered in several ways. Secondly, the words אֶחָד עַל־אַחֶיךָ have to be considered because these too have led to rather different renderings. Finally there remains the problem we have to deal with in the diachronic analysis: who was the patriarch who has conquered שְׁכֶם with his sword and with his bow? This is a tradition which is unknown to us, so what are we to make of it?

With regard to the word שְׁכֶם several solutions have been suggested. שְׁכֶם followed by אַחַד (construct form of אֶחָד) might suggest that אַחַד modifies שְׁכֶם, suggesting that the word can be modified, thus "(one) shoulder", with the following words it could denote (literally taken) "one shoulder above his brothers" (cf. 1 Sam. 10:23),[139] but such a solution seems rather far-fetched,[140] and in combination with נתן un-likely. It is sometimes interpreted as a part of the inheritance divided by the patriarch sitting at a banquet and, as such, it is rendered as "one portion",[141] but "portion" is without any philological sup-port.[142] However, if we still take אַחַד as a modification for שְׁכֶם — as MT seems to suggest[143] — then we should consider the possibility that שְׁכֶם "shoulder, neck"[144] is used here in a metaphorical sense for "mountain-slope" like its synonym כָּתֵף "shoulder".[145] But the modi-fication by אַחַד remains problematic, especially in view of the problem that שְׁכֶם is at the same time LN "Shechem", a connection which was already felt in LXX, TN, TPsJ, and probably in Sam,[146] and later

---

[139]Procksch, *Genesis*, 422.

[140]König, *Die Genesis*, 748.

[141]See Peš and TO, which have "portion"; similarly: KJ; JPS; NIV (as a possib-ility in a note); Gunkel, *Genesis*, ³1910, 474 (suggesting a deliberately openness to several interpretations). See also De Fraine, *Genesis*, 322; Van Selms, *Genesis*, dl. II, 270 (with reference to 1 Sam. 9:23–4).

[142]Sarna, *Genesis*, 330.

[143]The Masoretic accents give a conjunctive accent after שְׁכֶם, although the word אַחַד is vocalized as in the *status constructus*, suggesting a connection with the following words. The latter argument has to used with some caution because this might be due to rhythm, cf. GK, §130g.

[144]*HAL*, 1384.

[145]StV ("ridge of land"); RSV; NBG; NEB; NIV (the final two "ridge of land"); Skinner, *Genesis*, 507; König, *Die Genesis*, 748; Aalders, *Genesis*, dl. III, 189–90; De Fraine, *Genesis*, 322; Westermann, *Genesis 37–50*, 217; Hamilton, *Book of Genesis*, 640, 642–4; Jagersma, *Genesis 25–50*, 254.

[146]Some manuscripts of Sam read the fem. form אחת which seems to indicate that שכם was interpreted as a fem. form, which would fit for a city (Lett, §23d1), whereas שְׁכֶם "shoulder" is masc. as might be derived from Zeph. 3:9, where אֶחָד (masc.) is used as the modification for שְׁכֶם "shoulder". So, apparently, Sam had a LN in mind; cf. König, *Die Genesis*, 748; E. Nielsen, *Shechem: A Traditio-Historical Investigation*, Copenhagen 1955, 83.

Alter, *Genesis*, 291, suggests on the basis of Zeph. 3:9 to render שְׁכֶם אַחַד in Gen.

by many commentators.[147] However, in this case אֶחָד is problematic
and can hardly be related to "Shechem" (note the incongruence in
gender), although this has always been the dominant interpretation
for this verse. If we would abandon the interpretation, which relates
אֶחָד to the preceding word, the rendering would be rather easy in
verse 22aA: "and I give to you Shechem" — though some historical
problems might be felt.[148] The problem we have to deal with in that
case is the meaning of the following words אַחַד עַל־אַחֶיךָ, literally "one
above your brothers".

As we noted before, אֶחָד is usually related to שְׁכֶם, whereas the following עַל־אַחֶיךָ "above your brothers" is taken in a comparative sense,
thus to Joseph is given one "portion/ridge of land/mountain-slope"
more than his brothers.[149] Yet, the text (including the vocalisation)
allows another interpretation, suggested by Speiser, who connected
אֶחָד with the following words (עַל־אַחֶיךָ), but considered it as a reference to Joseph: "the one who is above/unique among" his brothers.[150]
Speiser rendered verse 22a: "As for me, I give you, as the one above
your brothers, Shechem".[151] The rendering by Speiser has not found
many adherents, but it ought to be considered very carefully. In Hebrew there are no absolute parallels to this construction which would
require a similar rendering.[152] In the texts of Ugarit a more obvious

---

48:22 in the same way, namely as "with single intent". However, in Zeph. 3:9 the
adverbial use of this idiom refers back to a plural subject (כֻּלָּם in v. 9bA), and the
clause could literally be rendered by "to serve Him with one shoulder", meaning
something like "serving shoulder to shoulder" (*HAL*, 1384), whereas in Gen. 48:22
the subject is obviously singular, and a literal rendering would be rather odd: "I
give to you with one shoulder". It appears therefore that the similarity between
the two verses is only superficial. A similar suggestion has been found already
with Jacob, *Das erste Buch*, 887–8, who interpreted it, however, paraphrastically
as a reference to the common part of the land of Ephraim and Manasseh, where
the grave of Joseph would be.

[147]Holzinger, *Genesis*, 255; Gunkel, *Genesis*, ³1910, 474–5; Skinner, *Genesis*,
507; Procksch, *Genesis*, 422; Böhl, *Genesis*, 138; König, *Die Genesis*, 748; Jacob,
Das erste Buch, 884–9; Aalders, *Genesis*, dl. III, 189–90; Nielsen, *Shechem*, 283–6;
De Fraine, *Genesis*, 322; Speiser, *Genesis*, 356, 358; Vawter, *On Genesis*, 456–7;
Scharbert, *Genesis 12–50*, 290; Sarna, *Genesis*, 330; Wenham, *Genesis 16–50*,
466; Hamilton, *Book of Genesis*, 642–3; Jagersma, *Genesis 25–50*, 254.

[148]See Nielsen, *Shechem*, 284–6.

[149]This interpretation is followed by most of the exegetes listed above in n. 147.

[150]Speiser, *Genesis*, 358. This rendering is followed in NAB; and appreciated by
Vawter, *On Genesis*, 456.

[151]Speiser, *Genesis*, 356.

[152]There are some texts in which a strong combination of אֶחָד with the prep. עַל
is found. In view of the proposed interpretation, 2 Kgs. 25:19 ‖ Jer. 52:25 is interesting. Further, by means of ellipsis Zech. 4:3 offers a comparable construction:
וְאֶחָד [זַיִת] עַל־שְׂמֹאלָהּ "and one [olive tree] on its left" (cf. also 1 Kgs. 7:38, where a

parallel is found, which supports Speiser's rendering, namely KTU
1.4.vii.49–52:[153]

aḥdy . dym|lk . ʿl . ilm	I alone am the one who can be king over the gods,
lymrủ | ilm . wnšm .	who can fatten gods and men,
dyšb| ʿ . hmlt . ảrṣ .	who can satisfy the multitudes of the earth!

This parallel indicates that the numeral could be applied to indicate
one position over (*ʿl*) others. A definitive rendering for our clause is
difficult to establish, because several renderings are possible for the
numeral אֶחָד. However, it seems that if the numeral is separated from
the preceding word, a substantivated form is beyond doubt, whereas it
appears that although the numeral is rendered as a *cardinal* numeral
("one"), the meaning is very close to — if not equal to — an ordinal
meaning: "the first",[154] which is comparable to the use of רִאשׁוֹן (< רֹאשׁ
"head"; see Gen. 47:31; 49:26[155]). Yet, instead of taking אַחַד עַל־אַחֶיךָ
as an adverbial clause to the suffix in לְךָ in verse 22aA, as Speiser
did, we might read it as a kind of vocative and propose the following
rendering for Gen. 48:22:

And I, I give Shechem to you (22aA)	וַאֲנִי נָתַתִּי לְךָ שְׁכֶם
— O One above your brothers — (22aB)	אַחַד עַל־אַחֶיךָ
which I took from the hand of the Amorites (22bA)	אֲשֶׁר לָקַחְתִּי מִיַּד הָאֱמֹרִי
with my sword and my bow. (22bB)	בְּחַרְבִּי וּבְקַשְׁתִּי

Here again it could be asked whether this reading is still "synchronic",
or if this interpretation is going beyond the intention of the so-called
Letztgestallt of the text. It is quite diffcult to decide this matter, because the implication of this reading in connection with the proposed
reading of Gen. 47:31 is far-reaching. Since the interpretation of 47:31
should not to be read at the level of the synchronic reading, it might
be asked if the interpretation of Gen. 48:22a could still be read at the
synchronic level. In our view this reading is in line with the crucial

---

"complete" construction is found). However, we must admit that these examples
are certainly not decisive in favour of our rendering; they only make it possible.

[153] For the use of *aḥd*, meaning "(I) alone" as subject in a clause, see KTU
1.2.i.25–6; cf. also Del Olmo Lete, Sanmartín, *DLU*, 16; O. Loretz, *Des gottes
Einzigkeit: Ein altorientalisches Argumentationsmodell zum "Schma Jisrael"*,
Darmstadt 1997, 57, n. 249. Compare these texts also with texts applying Ug. *in*,
Hebr. אַיִן "there is not": KTU 1.3:v.32–4 ǁ 1.4:iv.43–6; Ps. 95:3. For the use of
מֶלֶךְ עַל , see Gen. 37:8, and as another example Judg. 9:8–15.

[154] See 1 Sam. 1:2. Cf. *HAL*, 30.

[155] Nielsen, *Shechem*, 284, refers in connection with 48:22 to 49:26, but only
because the gift of Shechem indicates a position of Joseph as *king*. The proposed
rendering of 48:22aB firmly underlines Nielsen's suggestion.

question in Gen. 37:8, where the brothers ask Joseph הֲמָלֹךְ תִּמְלֹךְ עָלֵינוּ "are you indeed to be king over us?" The verse might thus be related to the contents of the Joseph Story, in which Joseph was placed above his brothers, and consequently could be called "One above your brothers". Yet it is obvious that this interpretation corresponds quite well with the proposed reading of 47:31 and might have far-reaching implications at the diachronic level.

The final clause (48:22b) offers in fact no problems for the translator, unless one felt some hesitation regarding the patriarch as a warrior who conquered Shechem by his sword and bow. Apparently some of the Targumists had problems with that idea, because in TN we find a double denial of this interpretation: "not with my sword and my bow, but by my merits and by my good works, which are better for me than my sword and my bow. ...by my merits and my good works, which are better for me than my sword and my bow".[156] Nielsen considers the possibility that the expression לָקַח מִיַּד might be rendered by "to receive from one's hand", almost "to buy" (2 Kgs. 5:20; cf. Prov. 31:16), whereas the prep. בְּ might be interpreted as a בְּ-*pretii*, suggesting that the patriarch received the part he handed over "from the hand of the Amorites, by placing in return my military capacity at his disposal".[157] However, he himself seems not to be convinced and admits "that the traditionist of Josh. 24:12 interpreted Gen. 48:22 as a boast of military exploits".[158]

If our interpretation of verse 22 is correct, it is understandable why the verse has met such divergent explanations in the Versiones and in the Tiberian Masoretic tradition. The primary meaning was not in line with the main theme of Genesis, which favours Judah as the successor of the patriarch. In this connection Van der Merwe points to a "clashing of traditions": in one tradition Judah is appointed as Jacob's first-born and successor, and in the other Joseph was the first-born and successor, traces of which have been found.[159] It appears that the latter tradition is indeed found here in verse 22, where Joseph is addressed as "one above your brothers". The former tradition is found also in the present scene, when the patriarch announces that Joseph's sons are no longer Joseph's but his, but that they will be *to him* as Reuben and Simeon. The comparison with these two sons is elucidated by Jacob's blessing in the following scene: Gen. 49:1–28.

---

[156] Translation quoted from McNamara, *TgNGen*, 214.
[157] Nielsen, *Shechem*, 285.
[158] Nielsen, *Shechem*, 285; cf. also Koopmans, *Joshua 24*, 352–3.
[159] Van der Merwe, "Joseph as Successor of Jacob", 229.

4.4.4 Part III: Genesis 49:1–28

4.4.4.1 Introduction

In Chapter Two we have pointed out at several places that Genesis 49 was embedded in its context by means of several cross-references.[160] This happens in several sayings with regard to the specific object of the saying, for instance Reuben. However, next to such specific elements which connect the different sayings to their context, certain elements are found throughout the Blessing, or belong to the general outline of Genesis 49. Before we start with the description of some of the sayings, we will describe the more general features of the Blessing.

As the most decisive feature we have to mention the need of a context for this blessing. The blessing alone (49:1–28), without its present context (47:29–48:22; 49:29–33) would be detached and isolated, because in the text itself (49:1–28) no reason is given why the patriarch would call his sons and "bless" them. Thus, although the blessing has been given a framework, the framework itself is in need of the wider context, and especially 47:29–48:1, where it is told that Jacob is about to die. The whole blessing is thus placed in the context of the deathbed as the words of the dying patriarch who gives his sons a final blessing.

In the framework of the blessing (vv. 1–2, 28) two expressions are used, that have to be mentioned here. It concerns the expression בְּאַחֲרִית הַיָּמִים "in the days hereafter" in verse 1, and the fact that the sons are specified with כָּל־אֵלֶּה שִׁבְטֵי יִשְׂרָאֵל שְׁנֵים עָשָׂר "all these are the twelve tribes of Israel". The first expression, "in the days hereafter", betrays the focus of the text, it is not concerned with the past but with the days that will follow after the narrated events. The expression functions thus as a signal for the reader[161] that the following text is concerned with future times, and possibly with the time at which the text is read. Also the second expression, specifying the sons as "tribes", functions in this way because it becomes apparent that, what is said of the "sons", concerns in fact the "tribes". As

---

[160] Of course, all this is valid only if we follow the flow of the narrative in Genesis and subject ourselves to its chronology of events. Diachrony in the modern sense, like the obvious question of what came first, the sayings of Genesis 49 or their explanation in the wider context, is not at issue now.

[161] The present author is aware of the fact that the term "hearer" might be a more appropriate expression in view of some of the present "readers", because we are dealing here with narratives which might have been narrated in front of an audience, *viz.* the "hearers". However, because the present study is written in the twentieth century, in a western country and in the context of the scientific discourse, in which narratives are "read" and not "narrated", we prefer the term "reader".

J. Fokkelman has pointed out in his study on Genesis, beyond the events narrated in the text, there is the historical reality in which these events are narrated.[162] By means of the framework the focus of the whole blessing is directed towards the future, at which the text is aimed. In that future the blessing will apparently have some relevance, predicting and in that way explaining, and probably even legitimating future states of affairs.

The presentation of the twelve tribes as the "sons of Jacob", and of the patriarch as "Israel, your father" (49:2) connects our chapter to the birth-story of the twelve and to the different genealogical listings in the previous story (Gen. 29:31–30:24; 35:23–26; 46:8–27). In this way the principal unity of the twelve sons (tribes) is emphasized as a group with one common ancestor: Israel (= Jacob). Throughout the blessing elements are used which connect the text with its context. The parallelism of Jacob ‖ Israel (49:2, 7, 24) presupposes Gen. 32:22–32, where it is narrated that Jacob receives his second name: Israel (see also 35:10). Thus the story of renaming is requisite to understand the juxtaposition of these two names as the name of *one* eponymic father. Also the use of the different terms for family relationship is in this respect important: בְּנֵי יַעֲקֹב "sons of Jacob"; יִשְׂרָאֵל אֲבִיכֶם "Is-rael your father" (v. 2); בְּכֹרִי "my firstborn" (v. 3); אָבִיךָ "your father" (v. 4); אַחִים "brothers" (v. 5);[163] אַחֶיךָ "your brothers"; בְּנֵי אָבִיךָ "sons of your father" (v. 8); אֶחָיו "his brothers" (v. 26). Finally, it may be noted that in Genesis 49 only five sons, who all played a key role in the preceding Jacob and Joseph Stories (Gen. 29:31–48:22) have an important and/or large saying (Reuben, Simeon and Levi, Judah, and Joseph). This is especially remarkable because in this list the chronological order of the birth of the sons as was described in Gen. 29:31–30:24 is only followed with regard to the aforementioned sons (and Benjamin, finally).[164] Also the fact that the sons are grouped in a chiastic pattern,[165] in which the Leah group balances the Rachel-group, is significant. All this emphasizes the relationship of the bless-ing with its context. We will now discuss several of these sayings in more detail.

---

[162] Fokkelman, *Narrative Art in Genesis*, 238–41.

[163] Even more important is Jacob's denial of his presence in their gatherings: his return in the seances of his progeny. Cf. above, section 2.3.1; and J.C. de Moor, "Standing Stones and Ancestor Worship", *UF* 27 (1995) 1–20, esp. 16.

[164] Note that the order of the first four sons is always the same in the other genealogical lists in Genesis, whereas the order of Issachar and Zebulun is reversed (Gen. 49:13–15), or that the position of the Rachel tribes is shifted to that before the Bilhah and Zilpah tribes (Gen. 35:23–6).

[165] Cf. Sarna, *Genesis*, 331; see also above, section 2.13.2.

4.4.4.2 Reuben

In the first saying on Reuben we are confronted with a part of the recurring motif in Genesis, the first-born and his endangered position. Reuben is according to Gen. 29:32 the first-born of the patriarch and as such he might be considered the future heir. However, it is told that Reuben defiled his father's bed, *viz.* he tried to usurp power from his father in that he tried to seize his father's "harem" (Gen. 35:22).[166] He had thus forfeited his rights as the first-born already. However, the short report of it has an open ending. There is no mention of the patriarch's reaction. Apparently this reaction had to wait for his final words on his deathbed. Yet Reuben played his part after this event. In all other instances where he is on the scene his intentions fail and he is overshadowed by his younger brother Judah.[167] In this way Reuben's dismissal as first-born is not only justified by his misbehaviour, but also by his failing to act effectively as the oldest brother.

4.4.4.3 Simeon and Levi

The second saying is concerned with the two brothers who took revenge for the rape of their sister Dinah in a massacre of the city of Shechem, described in Genesis 34. The relation of this saying with Genesis 34 is sometimes felt to be problematic, mainly because of the rendering of verse 5b but especially verse 6bB: "they hamstrung a bull", because no such event is reported in Genesis 34. However, the fact that שׁור "bull" could be used as a designation for a prince,[168] re-

---

[166] Cf. 2 Sam. 3:6–8; 12:8; 16:21–2; 1 Kgs. 2:17, 20–2. See also: A. van Selms, "Die oorname van 'n harem deur 'n nuwe koning", *HTS* 8 (1949) 25–41, esp. 36–7; idem, *Genesis, dl. II*, 164–5; M. Tsevat, "Marriage and Monarchical Legitimacy in Ugarit and Israel", *JSS* 3 (1958) 237–43; Van der Merwe, "Joseph as Successor of Jacob", 221, with nn. 2–3; R. Gordis, "Edom, Israel and Amos — An Unrecognized Source for Edomite History", in: A.I. Katsh, L. Nemoy (eds.), *Essays on the Occasion of the Seventieth Anniversary of the Dropsie University (1909–1979)*, Philadelphia (PA) 1979, 109–32, 111, n 3; T. Ishida, *The Royal Dynasties in Ancient Israel: A Study on the Formation and Development of Royal-Dynastic Ideology* (BZAW, 142), Berlin 1977, 74; idem, "Solomon's Succession to the Throne of David — A Political Analysis", in: T. Ishida (ed.), *Studies in the Period of David and Solomon and Other Essays*, Winona Lake (IN) 1982, 175–87, 186, n. 27; P.K. McCarter, *II Samuel: A New Translation with Introduction, Notes and Commentary* (AB, 9), Garden City (NY) 1984, 112–3; 300; 384–5. For a Ugaritic parallel, see *ARTU*, 210. See also EA, no. 196.

[167] In literary critical studies of the Joseph Story a differentiation is made between the Judah- and Reuben-layer, closely related to the sources J and E. Since we are dealing with a *synchronic* approach here, we may ignore these problems for the moment. In the evaluation of the arguments in favour of such a distinction (below, section 5.23.3), we will deal with this matter more fully.

[168] Cf. above, section 2.3.1.

moves an important stumbling block. The testament of the patriarch recalls in this saying the events described in Genesis 34. But not only that text is recalled here, indirectly we are linked with the birth-story in Gen. 29:31–30:24, where it is reported that Dinah is a sister of the first degree (30:21). The cruel revenge was rejected by the patriarch, and as such he denies them his presence in their future gatherings.[169] This denial is — like the preceding saying — the rounding up of an unconcluded narrative, because in Gen. 34:31 the final word is given to the sons and not to the patriarch. His final words on this case are postponed until the moment of his death.

4.4.4.4 Judah

As was argued before in Chapter Three and also at the end of section 4.1.3 above, the blessing of Judah contains the promise of an everlasting leadership, which is strongly connected to the blessing his father received (27:27–29). In the first and third strophes the everlasting future dominion over his brothers is given to Judah (49:8aB, bB) in the same way as happened to his father. Similarly the dominion over his enemies is given to him (v. 8bA), and also the servitude of other people (v. 10bB). The blessing Judah receives is in every respect more elevated, and in its language it clearly surpasses the blessing his father received. His pre-eminence becomes clear from several aspects. The number of descriptions of Judah's future power in clear terms is larger than the one given to Jacob (four poetic verses, against three for Jacob), whereas in a metaphorical strophe Judah's power is described in more glowing terms (49:9). Also the promised fertility surpasses the blessing his father received: Isaac wishes his son "plenty of grain and wine" (27:28C). To Judah an abundance is promised, so that he can bind his foal to the vine and wash his garments in wine (49:11). By means of this blessing Judah is made Jacob's major heir, who inherits the blessing of the patriarchs.

Although 1 Chr. 5:1 suggests that Judah only received the leadership, whereas the right of the first-born was given to Joseph, it is obvious from the comparison of these two blessings that Judah received the blessing of the first-born. In Gen. 27:27–29 Jacob received the blessing which was intended for the first-born (Esau), Judah receives a similar blessing after his elder brothers were denied their rights as the "first-born". This is also confirmed by the context of the Joseph Story, where Judah implicitly takes the lead.[170] This fits in with the announcement of the plot at the beginning of the Joseph

---

[169] For the interpretation of this denial, see above, section 2.3.1.

[170] Cf. Blum, *Die Komposition der Vätergeschichte*, 261; Sarna, *Genesis*, 335.

Story, as we noted before.[171] The announcement of the plot is found in the question put to Joseph if he was to reign over his father and his brothers as a king (Gen. 37:8, 10).[172] This plot has in fact a twofold development. First, Joseph receives a position in Egypt which results in the fulfilment of the dreams. But, as we noted before, the fulfilment is entirely different from what his father and brothers assumed, because they expected that the dream referred to a kingship of Joseph over their own group (הֲמָלֹךְ תִּמְלֹךְ עָלֵינוּ "are you indeed to be king over us?" v. 8). The leading position among the brothers is now explicitly given to Judah in Genesis 49. At the same time the saying on Judah demonstrates that Jacob's question was not intended to exclude the kingship of one of the brothers, but that it was unlikely in his eyes for *Joseph* to receive the kingship among the brothers. This is in fact the second development, an unexpected turn in the plot of the narrative, although this plot will not reach its fulfilment in Genesis itself. However, in this way it suits even better the context of Genesis in which the plots of the Abraham and Jacob stories are not fulfilled either. Apparently this fulfilment is a distant prospect, waiting for what will come בְּאַחֲרִית הַיָּמִים "in days to come" (49:1C).

4.4.4.5 Joseph

Almost at the end of the list we find the blessing of Joseph, which is in length comparable to Judah's. Also the use of the language applied in this blessing has some features that seem to point in a similar direction. In section 2.11.1.3 we defended a rendering for the saying on Joseph, which in its language is very close to the mythological language of Ugarit.[173] The description of Joseph as a young bull depicts him as a young and powerful animal, which in itself is not very peculiar. It is even an almost romantic picture: a young bull, standing next to a well.[174] However, the following line mentions a Bull (שׁוֹר), who

---

[171]See above, section 4.1.3.

[172]Turner, *Announcement of Plot*, 143–73.

[173]Cf. especially Korpel, *RiC*, 532–4, on this matter.

[174]It might be coincidence, but Shechem, the town Joseph received from his father (48:22), was in an area with an abundant supply of water. According to L.E. Toombs, "Shechem (Place)", *ABD*, vol. 5, 1174–86, esp. 1175, Shechem had a guaranteed water supply: "In the village of Balâṭah, approximately where the S[outhern] wall of the ancient city [Shechem] would have been, there is a copious spring. It is the best of many such springs in the plain of ʿAskar, and provides water not only for the village of Balâṭah but also for neighboring communities in times of drought when their own springs have dried up." As far as we are aware, it was only G.R.H. Wright, "An Egyptian God at Shechem", *ZDPV* 99 (1983) 95–109, 101, who referred to the possible geographical implication of the well in the saying on Joseph (49:22aB). Cf. also G.E. Wright, "Shechem, 'The

will strengthen him (מרר D-st.) and make him numerous (רבה pi'el). This language corresponds to the two legends from Ugarit on kings, who were desperate because of the lack of progeny (KTU 1.14–16; 1.17–19). In both legends Ilu is called a "Bull" (*tr*), who can bless (*brk*) and strengthen (*mrr*) the kings. The fact that the Bull is also called "Ilu, my Father" in these contexts (KTU 1.15:ii.24; 1.17:i.23) a term which returns in 49:25 (אֵל אָבִיךָ), is remarkable and points to an elevated position for Joseph: kings were regarded as the sons of deities.[175] Moreover, the blessing in verse 25bC of "breasts and womb" Joseph receives, might be paralleled to the blessing Yassubu, the (promised) first-born of Kirtu received (KTU 1.15.ii.25–28):

tld . yṣb [.] *ǵlm*	She will bear the lad Yassubu,
ynq . ḥlb . aṯrt	who will imbibe the milk of Athiratu,
mṣṣ . ṯd [.] *btlt* [. *'nt*]	who will suck the breast of the Virgin 'Anatu,
mšnq[*t*]	the wet-nurs[es of . . .]

Such metaphors are intended to describe the elevated position of the king[176] and it might be that this blessing in Gen. 49:25bC has a similar meaning. In any case, Ug. *ṯd* "breast" and Ug. *rḥm* "womb" are both epithets of 'Anatu and may be hidden here behind these terms.[177]

With regard to the saying of Joseph it is important to note that next to the (possibly coincidental) relationship[178] of the present saying with the previous scene (part II), where Joseph received Shechem, there are some other points worth mentioning. First, it is remarkable that Shechem was conquered by "the sword and the bow", whereas

---

Uncrowned Queen of Palestine", in: idem, *Shechem: The Biography of a Biblical City*, New York 1964, 9–22, esp. 11–3; R.J. Bull, "Water Sources in the Vicinity", in: Wright, *Shechem*, 214–28; G.E. Wright, "Shechem", *EAEHL*, vol. IV, 1083–94, 1086; E.F. Campbell, "Shechem", *NEAEHL*, vol. IV, 1345–54, 1346. More general: A. Zertal, "The Water Factor during the Israelite Settlement Process in Canaan", in: M. Heltzer, E. Lipiński (eds.), *Society and Economy in the Eastern Mediterranean (c. 1500–1000 B.C.)* (OLA, 23), Leuven 1988, 341–52.

[175] See 2 Sam. 7:13; Ps. 2:7; 89:27–8; KTU 1.14:i.41.

[176] Cf. J. Gray, *The KRT Text in the Literature of Ras Shamra: A Social Myth of Ancient Canaan*, Leiden ²1964, 59; M. Weippert, "Die Bildsprache der neuassyrischen Prophetie", in: H. Weippert *et al.*, *Beiträge zur Prophetischen Bildsprache in Israel und Assyrien* (OBO, 64), Freiburg, Göttingen 1985, 55–93, esp. 61–4, 71–8; De Moor, *ARTU*, 206, n. 51. Sucking the breasts of the goddess is also described for the "gracious gods": KTU 1.23.24; and for Marduk, see E.A. Speiser, "Akkadian Myths and Epics", in: *ANET*, 60–119, 64.

[177] For these epitheta see KTU 1.6:ii.5, 27; 1.13:19–22; 1.15:ii.6; 1.23:13, 16; cf. also Korpel, *RiC*, 124. For iconographic material see A. Caquot, M. Sznycer, *Ugaritic Religion* (IoR, XV.8), Leiden 1980, plates 28a; 29b; *ANEP*, 829.

[178] See above, n. 174.

Joseph is assured of help from above against the "archers", who might attack him (49:23bA) and that "his bow" (v. 24aB) will remain stable.[179] In this way the saying seems to refer back to the inheritance Joseph received and which apparently still has to be defended. Secondly, Joseph is the only one to receive "blessings" *expressis verbis* (49:25–26) and which is in view of the blessing of "Joseph" in 48:15a noteworthy. Apparently Joseph received many blessings in contrast with his brothers, even in contrast to Judah. This final point has to be noted because it still seems to suggest his favourable position.

Finally, we might refer to the last poetic verse, where Joseph is called the "one set apart of his brothers" (49:26bB).[180] This title fits very well in the present context of the Joseph Story, where Joseph is set apart as a kind of "Nazirite" to save his family from death. Some scholars prefer to render "prince" here, which would fit rather well with the proposed interpretation of Gen. 47:31 and 48:22.[181] Yet, as we noted before, we assume there is not enough warrant for the defence of this interpretation of the word. In those cases a Nazirite ("one set apart") has to fulfill a special office, the title "Nazirite" is not related to the fact that he might be of high rank,[182] but to the fact that he is chosen for that office and which is often linked with an anointment.[183] In our view we have to consider Joseph's title in 49:26bB as a reference to the function he fulfilled for his family,[184] comparable to, for example, the role of Samson who had to deliver his people (Judg. 13:5).

4.4.4.6 The Remaining Brothers

The sayings on the other brothers are all very loosely embedded in

---

[179]To this possible relationship was referred by N.K. Gottwald, *The Tribes of Yahweh: A Sociology of the Religion of Liberated Israel 1250–1050 B.C.E.*, London 1979, 541–2, 552.

[180]For this rendering, see above, section 2.11.1.4.6.

[181]Vawter, *On Genesis*, 468.

[182]*Pace* J. Milgrom, *Leviticus 1–16: A New Translation with Introduction, Notes and Commentary* (AB, 3), New York 1991, 512–3; J. Renkema, *Klaagliederen vertaald en verklaard* (COT), Kampen 1993, 367; Hamilton, *Book of Genesis*, 683, n. 21.

[183]Cf. for the combination of the root נזר "to set apart" and משׁח "to anoint" the following texts: Num. 8:9, 12; 2 Sam. 1:10, 14; 2 Kgs. 11:12; Pss. 89:39–40 (ET, 89:38–9); 132:17–8. In Lam. 4:7 the rendering "princes" is usually defended, but here too it is striking that in v. 20 reference is made to the "anointed". This does not necessarily lead to another rendering for "princes", but a rendering like "consecrated ones" (namely for a special office) might have been more appropriate; cf. A. van Selms, *Jeremia deel III en Klaagliederen* (PredOT), Nijkerk 1974, 140.

[184]Wenham, *Genesis 16–50*, 487; Jagersma, *Genesis 25–50*, 263.

their context, as they do not refer to any events in the context, except
that some of them seem to allude to the birth-stories (Gen. 29:31–
30:24; 35:16–18). The first relation that might be considered is the
fact that the number of brothers is in accordance with the birth-
stories. The whole list functions as a survey of the twelve tribes of
Israel (49:28) and in that sense the number twelve seems to be rather
important here. The fact that the order of sayings in Genesis 49 has
the chiastic pattern of the names of the mothers,[185] presupposes knowledge derived from the birth-stories and suggests a link with these
narratives (29:31–30:24; 35:16–18). This also seems to be indicated
by the fact that several of these sayings seem to refer to the same etymology of the names as has happened in the birth-stories. However,
at the same time most of these sayings seem to have been created as
a kind of proclamation of the tribes' future, rather than as a general
characterization, and in this manner the etymology functions in the
same pattern of past–future as was found in the sayings of Reuben
and Simeon & Levi.

The birth-story of Zebulun (30:19–20) contains apparently two
etymologies of the name Zebulun. The first is with the verb זבד "to
make a gift", which seems to be a kind of pun rather than an etymology, in the sense of serious analysis of root meanings.[186] The second
etymology seems more to the point and is based on the root זבל "to
raise (up)", which as a verb occurs only here.[187] Leah says here הַפַּעַם
יִזְבְּלֵנִי אִישִׁי which could be rendered by "at last my man will raise
me/exalt me/honour me".[188] The word יַרְכָה "spur (of a mountain)"

---

[185]See above, section 2.13.2. Note that in the birth-story a different chiastic
pattern is applied; cf. Sarna, *Genesis*, 245.

[186]See J. Barr, "Etymology and the Old Testament", in: J. Barr *et al.*, *Language
and Meaning: Studies in Hebrew Language and Biblical Exegesis* (OTS, 19), Leiden 1974, 1–28, 26.

[187]The meaning of זבל "to raise (up)" is now generally accepted on the basis of
Ug. *zbl* (J.C. de Moor, "Studies in the New Alphabetic Texts from Ras Shamra,
I", *UF* 1 [1969] 168–88, 188; M. Held, "The Root *zbl/sbl* in Akkadian, Ugaritic
and Biblical Hebrew", *JAOS* 88 [1968] 90–6, esp. 91–2); Arab. *zabala* (Lane, I/3,
1212); Akk. *zabalu* (*CAD*, vol. Z, 1–5). See: Sarna, *Genesis*, 210; Hamilton, *Book
of Genesis*, 276, with nn. 12–4 (with literature!); Jagersma, *Genesis 25–50*, 78–9.
Cf. also Wenham, *Genesis 16–50*, 248.
זְבֻל is sometimes rendered by "exalted dwelling" (*HAL*, 252; Ges[18], 293), it may
be noted, however, that on the basis of Hab. 3:11; and 1 Kgs. 8:13; 2 Chr. 6:2, the
emphasis is to be placed on "exalted", rather than on "dwelling", which might
also be suggested in Isa. 63:15. This is of course not to deny that Ps. 49:15 is
notoriously difficult and hard to interpret.

[188]RSV; JPS; NIV. Some scholars suggest we revocalize the verb as pi'el, see:
Held, "The Root *zbl/sbl*", 91; Westermann, *Genesis 12–36*, 581; (J. Hempel, "Ein
Vorschlag zu Gen 30 20", *ZAW* 64 [1952] 286, gave his permission: "Wer will, mag

in 49:13bB might be a semantic pun on the meaning of זבל, suggesting that the loftiness which is inherent in the root זבל will be relevant in the future. The saying predicts the future inheritance of Zebulun at the coast, presumably at the Gulf of Haifa.[189] The reference to the loftiness might include even (a part of) the Carmel, which looks out over the Gulf of Haifa.[190] In this way the past (birth, name-giving) and the future (inheritance) are connected in the blessing.

The same seems to apply to the saying on Issachar, where we find a clear reference to the folk-etymology of the name יִשָּׂשׂכָר "Issachar" < אִישׁ "man" + שָׂכָר "(of) wages",[191] or יֵשׁ "there is" + שָׂכָר "wages".[192] In Gen. 30:17–18 we find this etymology again, where Leah expects to receive a reward (שָׂכָר) because she gave her maid to her husband.[193] In Genesis 49 this name is connected with Issachar's future because he seems bound to become a serving corvée worker (*nomen est omen*).[194]

The saying on Dan similarly refers to past and future, since it applies the same etymology as is used in the birth-story (30:6).[195] Dan's

---

יְזָבְלֵנִי oder יְזְבְּלֵנִי punktieren"). Since the verb was already enigmatic for Vrs (cf. Wevers, *Greek Text of Genesis*, 483; Grossfeld, *TgOGen*, 108–9, n. 7), it might be that the vocalisation is just a guess. However, because the piʻel is sometimes close in meaning to the qal (JM, §52d; Lett, §41i), the qal of זבל might also be correct. The root זבל means "to raise (up), lift" and could denote something like "my man will raise me (from my inferior position)"; cf. J. Gamberoni, "זְבֻל", *ThWAT*, Bd. II, 531–4, esp. 533–4.

[189] See above, section 2.5.1.

[190] Cf. also Deut. 33:19, which seems to connect "mountain" and "sea".

[191] Cf. *HAL*, 422–3. Although the א is missing in the name's first element and the שׂ differs (שׂ instead of אִישׁ), this might be of minor importance for the correctness of the etymology, because in Semitic languages sometimes the initial *aleph* and *yod* interchange. See C.D. Isbell, "Initial 'Aleph-Yod Interchange and Selected Biblical Passages", *JNES* 37 (1978) 227–36.

[192] Cf. *HAL*, 422–3. This phrase is found in Jer. 31:16; 2 Chr. 15:7; see also Isbell, "Initial 'Aleph-Yod Interchange", 229; Sarna, *Genesis*, 210.

Sarna, *loc.cit.*, suggests we derive the consonantal spelling from an archaic causative verbal form *yašaskir*, "May He (God) grant favour/reward", which seems a probable suggestion if we are indeed dealing here with a personal name. Cf. also Wenham, *Genesis 16–50*, 247, who refers to an Amorite name attested at Mari: *yaskur-il* "May El be gracious".

[193] For the idea that children might be a reward, see Ps. 127:3 (Hamilton, *Book of Genesis*, 275).

[194] Sarna, *Genesis*, 210, suggests that Gen. 49:14–5 contains another etymology ("man of wages"), departing from the one found in 30:18 ("there are wages/is reward", differing also from the one in 30:16 "I hired you"). However, it is questionable if the etymology in 30:18 is so obvious in meaning that we could be sure that it differs from the one in Gen. 49:14–5. In both texts it is possible that a pun is made on the root שׂכר, without claiming that one of these is correct.

[195] In Chapter Two a different rendering than the usual one was proposed for דָּנַנִּי (30:6) and יָדִין (49:16), deriving the verb from the root דנן "to be strong"

birth and his name are connected with דנן "to be strong", because
God would have strengthened Rachel (30:6). In 49:16 the root דנן occurs again as the "fate" of Dan. He will be strong like the other tribes
of Israel and as such he will be like a small, but deadly animal, who
will attack his much stronger enemies with a decisive stroke.

The sayings on Gad, Asher and Naphtali cannot be connected
with the birth-stories like their predecessors. In the birth-story of Gad
(30:9–11) the name גָּד "Gad" has been connected with גַּד "fortune" by
Leah's exclamation בְּגָד, which, according to TO, TPsJ and Q might
be interpreted as "fortune has come" (< בָּא גָד),[196] or, if following K,
LXX, as "what luck!".[197] However, in Gen. 49:19 the name is related
to the root גדד II, "band together" and גוד "attack" and cannot be
related to the birth-story. Similarly the name of Asher is not related
to the birth-story, because there the name is connected with אַשְׁרִי
"fortunate, blessed".[198] In Gen. 49:20 an etymology of the name, or
a pun on it, is apparently absent. Finally, the saying on Naphtali is
likewise not related to the birth-story by means of the etymology of
the name. In the birth-story the name נַפְתָּלִי "Naphtali" is related to
the root פתל "twist, wrestle".[199] In Gen. 49:21 the name is linked with
נפל in the sense of "be born",[200] but we might be dealing here with a
pun, as in the birth-story of Zebulun.

Finally, there is the saying on Benjamin, whose name did not receive an explanation in the birth-story, although a certain meaning
seems to be suggested by the contrast with the name Ben-Oni (35:18).
The meaning of both names is disputed; for Ben-Oni the most likely
one is still the classical one which derives בֶּן־אוֹנִי "Ben-Oni" from
בֶּן "son (of)" + *אוֹנִי "mourning" (< אנה "to mourn").[201] The name
בִּנְיָמִין is thought to be composed from בֶּן "son (of)" + יָמִין "the right
hand",[202] or "the south" (< "right hand").[203] In this case יָמִין "right

---

(section 2.7.1). However, even if the reader is not convinced by our suggestion,
the following remarks will not lose their value, because it is generally accepted that
in Gen. 30:6 and 49:16 we find the same etymology, which is generally supposed
to be found in the root דין "to judge".

[196] Hamilton, *Book of Genesis*, 272, n. 2.

[197] Sarna, *Genesis*, 208. See also Wenham, *Genesis*, 246.

[198] Sarna, *Genesis*, 209; Wenham, *Genesis 16–50*, 246; Hamilton, *Book of Genesis*, 273. The last named scholar (following TO and Sym) reads בְּאָשְׁרִי similarly
as בְּגָד in the preceding verse as בָּא אֹשֶׁר "my blessedness has come".

[199] Sarna, *Genesis*, 208; Wenham, *Genesis 16–50*, 245–6; Hamilton, *Genesis*, 271–2.

[200] See Isa. 26:18.

[201] HAL, 22; Wenham, *Genesis 16–50*, 326–7; Hamilton, *Genesis*, 383, n. 8; 384–5.

[202] HAL, 396; Ges[18], 467–8.

[203] HAL, 396–7; Ges[18], 468. "South" is probably the correct etymology; describing Benjamin(ites) as "son of the south", like in Mari; cf. Sarna, *Genesis*, 243;

hand" stands for the "right side", as the good side for luck and happiness.[204] In contrast with Ben-Oni the element יָמִין has also been read as יָמִים "days" (see already Sam), which could indicate the wish that Benjamin would be given many days, *i.e.* would become very old,[205] or that he was the "son of my old age" (Jacob's).[206] This interpretation ties in with the pun we noted in Chapter Two, that "morning" and "evening" in the saying might refer to יָמִין "days", suggesting that the name means "between the days".[207] If the last-mentioned interpretation of 35:18 were correct, there would indeed be a relationship between birth-story and blessing. However, there are too many uncertain factors in this interpretation to draw any firm conclusions.

In conclusion, it appears that the sayings concerning the other seven brothers are only loosely connected with the previous context. These sayings are in this sense more important as predictions of the tribes' future, than as sayings which have to relate the tribes' past to the future. This could be an indication that the contents of the sayings are only meant to refer to the future, which is predicted in them. But their main function might be to complete the number of the twelve tribes in the Blessing of the patriarch.

4.4.4.7 Conclusion

The function of Genesis 49 seems obvious, although some tension can be felt. First, the important sayings in the blessing are all related to the sons who have played a certain role in the context. The first two sayings are directed against sons who did not act according to their father's will, and even went against it. As a result all three sons are passed over by their father with regard to the birthright, which is finally given to Judah. In this way not only the leading position of Judah is legitimated, but also the leading position of a younger brother over the older. Judah is made the tribe which has received the leading position among "his brothers", he has inherited the promise of the patriarchs and from him the scepter will not depart. On the other hand we have the saying on Joseph which has clearly royal features and is comparable in length with Judah's saying. However, whereas Joseph received such abundant blessings, at the end it is revealed why: he has been the "one set apart" from his brothers. The tensions which

---

Wenham, *Genesis 16–50*, 327; Hamilton, *Book of Genesis*, 385–6.

[204] *HAL*, 396; Ges[18], 468. Wenham, *Genesis 16–50*, 327; See also Hamilton, *Book of Genesis*, 385.

[205] This interpretation is noted by Hamilton, *Book of Genesis*, 385, with n. 18.

[206] Offered already by Rashbam, noted in Sarna, *Genesis*, 243.

[207] See above, section 2.12.1.

might be felt between the saying on Judah and the one on Joseph is eliminated: Judah's blessings are for the future and his future office; Joseph's blessing is for his former office. Moreover, it might be asked what function the blessing on Joseph will have in the future because in fact he has been made childless (Gen. 48:5), and he will not have an heir any more! By means of the final verse (v. 28) Jacob's speech is summarized as a blessing, indicating that we are dealing here with the final will of the patriarch concerning his descendants. The fact that all twelve sons are addressed by their own names makes the idea of a mistakenly given blessing (Genesis 27) impossible.

4.4.5   Part IV: Genesis 49:29–33

In this final scene the patriarch recalls the past after having focused on the future of the tribes.[208] Here he recalls the events described in the previous sections of Genesis, not only in the Jacob stories but even in the Abraham narrative. He charges[209] his sons to bury him in Canaan in the grave his grandfather bought from the Hittites.[210] Jacob's retrospection concerns thus the whole preceding generation, beginning with Abraham and Sarah, his grandparents, followed by Isaac and Rebekah, his parents, and finally by his first wife, Leah.[211]

---

[208] Hamilton, *Book of Genesis*, 688, notes this contrast and for that reason he considers it unfortunate that Gen. 49:1–28 is commonly isolated from the following verses (whether justified or not).

[209] "Charged", the rendering for Hebr. צוה pi'el, is sometimes considered, on the basis of Arab. *wṣy* (form II and IV), to have the meaning of "to make a last testament, to give parting charges", as in, for example, 1 Kgs. 2:1; 2 Kgs. 20:1 (cf. *e.g. HAL*, 947; J. Gray, *I & II Kings* [OTL], London 1964, 97). Van der Merwe, "Joseph as Successor of Jacob", 225, n. 3, admits that the absence of the root צוה could be used as a counter-argument against the idea that we already find in 47:29–48:22 a part of Jacob's testament (an argument which could similarly be used against our genre-definition of Genesis 49 in Chapter Three). Van der Merwe (*loc.cit.*) objected, however, that in 1 Chr. 28:20 the root אמר was used (instead of צוה in 1 Kgs. 2:1), which, in our view, justifies the use of אמר in Gen. 47:29; 48:3, 49:1. Secondly, it has to be stressed that the root צוה is too general in meaning to deny the definition "testament" to texts on the basis of the argument that this root would be absent. On the other hand we have to admit that this use of the root צוה gave rise to *postbiblical* Hebr. צַוָּאָה "last will and testament" (Dalman, *Hw*, 360; Sarna, *Genesis*, 346).

[210] A curious retrojection of the present into the past seems to take place in Hamilton, *Book of Genesis*, 688, when he states that "a Hittite foreigner of two generations ago" is mentioned by Jacob. Abraham, however, said to the Hittites when he wanted to buy the cave (23:4): "I am a stranger and a sojourner among you".

[211] His (chronologically) second wife, Rachel, was mentioned already in 48:7, because he did not bury her in the family grave, but on the road to Ephrat. Note that the burials of the two matriarchs were not previously mentioned in Genesis.

In this section the demand directed to Joseph is repeated here and elaborated by the reference to the family grave and the explicit mentioning of the names of the patriarchs and matriarchs, whereas in 47:30 it was just asked to let him lie with his fathers. This explicit reference to the purchase of the field and cave of Machpelah is in line with the tradition that the land of Canaan is the land of sojourning and that the people of Israel are not indigenous in Canaan.[212]

Finally the patriarch dies. In this description we find the unique phrase וַיֶּאֱסֹף רַגְלָיו אֶל־הַמִּטָּה "and he drew his feet on the bed", which seems to follow 48:2. Sarna doubts if we have to take this phrase literally as if Jacob were sitting with his feet over the side of the bed because this posture would be unlikely "for one about to breath his last". He considers whether this phrase might be a figurative expression for dying, especially because the usual threefold formula וַיִּגְוַע וַיָּמָת וַיֵּאָסֶף אֶל־עַמָּיו "he breathed his last and he died and he was gathered to his people" (Gen. 25:8, 17; 35:29) is incomplete and the missing וַיָּמָת "and he died" could thus have been replaced by this phrase.[213] Sarna's observation concerning the threefold formula seems incorrect, because the position within the formula is not identical. In addition, Sarna argues that the first וַיֶּאֱסֹף "and he gathered ..." goes together with the final וַיֵּאָסֶף "and he was gathered". However, this argument could also be used to explain why the threefold formula was broken in order to fit the whole Deathbed Episode. There it was first narrated that "Israel summoned his strength and sat on the bed" (48:2) and it seems only logical, to regard the phrase in 49:33 as the counterpart of 48:2. It might indeed be strange to have such a clear change of scene between these two phrases, like the one in 49:1, where the patriarch calls his sons, while he seems to have remained in the same position as he was in the preceding scene. But since the two phrases reflect each other so clearly, there seems no reason to take one of them literally and the other one figuratively.

4.5 The Deathbed Episode: Ideological Features

In the previous pages we have tried to describe the Deathbed Episode (Gen. 47:29–49:33) from a synchronic perspective. During our synchronic analysis we have shown that the transmitted version of the text implies more than a story about deceased people. In several passages the focus is the future and not the past, and the sons are not just "sons", but they represent the "tribes" as well. The reference to

---

[212]Westermann, *Genesis 37–50*, 223–4.
[213]Sarna, *Genesis*, 347.

the "days hereafter" (49:1), together with the contents of the following text (49:3–27), might disclose something of the historical reality in which the text originated or was intended to function. This seems the more obvious as in this text the power is bestowed on one person beyond whom we know lies a complete tribe, as was disclosed by the text itself:[214] namely Judah. This fact suggests that we are dealing here with an apologetic element in the Deathbed Episode that functions to legitimate, for one reason or another, the position of Judah *vis-à-vis* the other brothers/tribes.

In Chapter Three we asked if the legalizing or apologetic element of Genesis 49 as a testament could be found in the context as well, or that the classical separation of the Blessing from its context was justified.[215] As was demonstrated, Judah plays a crucial role in the wider context of the Joseph Story.[216] However, except for 49:8–12, Judah is absent in the Deathbed Episode and nothing is said of him. If we want to find any apologetic aspect of Genesis 49 in the encompassing Deathbed Episode, we have to look at the role and function of the persons who are present there. Next to the dying patriarch, who is of importance here because he bestows the power upon the one he prefers, the other main character at the scene is Joseph. It might be interesting now to describe the role of Joseph and try to analyse what ideological elements could be hidden behind that description.

From the beginning of the Joseph Story (37:3–4) to the end in the Deathbed Episode, it is obvious that Joseph was his father's favourite. Nevertheless, it is simultaneously clear from the beginning that even in his father's view it is rather unlikely that he will have a leading position among his brothers (37:10). However, the plot, as announced at the beginning of the Joseph Story (37:8, 10), develops in a different direction than his father and brothers expected. At the end of the Story they have all bowed down before Joseph in Egypt, where he has become the ruler and the plot is fulfilled. As was shown above, this development of plot in the Joseph Story is in contrast with the development of other plots in Genesis.[217] In the case of the other stories in Genesis it was concluded that their plot was not fulfilled within the narrative framework of Genesis itself, but that it was still to be fulfilled in the future. However, as we have tried to show with regard to the Joseph Story, we find two different developments of plot there, a fulfilled one and an unfulfilled one. The question put

---

[214] כָּל־אֵלֶּה שִׁבְטֵי יִשְׂרָאֵל שְׁנֵים עָשָׂר "all these are the twelve tribes of Israel" (49:28).
[215] See above, section 3.6.
[216] For Judah's role, cf. also below, section 5.23.3.
[217] Cf. above, section 4.3.

at the beginning of the Joseph Story, whether the brothers would bow down before Joseph (37:8, 10), is at the end negatively answered with regard to the future, for then the brothers will bow down before Judah (49:8). In this way the different plots in Genesis, still waiting to be fulfilled, are finally brought together in the blessing of Judah. The fulfilment of this plot is foreseen by the patriarch בְּאַחֲרִית הַיָּמִים "in days hereafter". The answer at the end (49:8) concerns the tribes, which seems to suggest that the question at the beginning similarly concerns the tribe of Joseph, not only the patriarch. The fact now that the question concerning leadership among the brothers (tribes?) appears to involve Joseph, suggests that Judah not only had to strive with his older brothers, but that somehow Joseph might have been a threat as well.

In the case of the Joseph Story it is remarkable that Judah functions as a kind of antipole to Joseph, which is probably best illustrated by the scene containing Judah's speech (44:18–34). But what might be even more important is that both Judah and Joseph are depicted in the Joseph Story as instruments or means by which many people are saved: Judah as the one, who suggested the sale of Joseph to Egypt; Joseph as a victim and later as a ruler in Egypt. While the suggestion to sell Joseph was evil in intent; God meant it for good (45:5; 50:20). In this way Judah is assigned a crucial role in the whole Joseph Story, next to Joseph. However, the end of the Story is very obvious: it is Judah, who surpasses his brother Joseph in that he receives the future power among his brothers while Joseph's dominion is restricted to the power he received in Egypt. In the "days hereafter" he will have to bow down before Judah as well (49:8). The position of Judah on the one hand, is described by means of events in the past, where he himself proved to be the true leader and an instrument in God's hand. On the other hand, his position is described by means of the blessing in Genesis 49 as a future dominion over the brothers (tribes).

In the Deathbed Episode there are several elements in Joseph's role which can partly be described as the opposite of Judah's role. Joseph's position is considerably weakened in the Deathbed Episode. At first sight it appears that he is still his father's favourite when he is called to his father alone (Gen. 47:29–31). Yet, the patriarch's adoption of Joseph's sons (48:5) eliminates Joseph's position in the future considerably. In addition, the two adopted sons are equated with Reuben and Simeon, who are put aside by Jacob (49:3–4, 5–7) in favour of Judah (49:8–12). Although Ephraim and Manasseh receive fertility blessings from Jacob (48:15–20), on the basis of this equation with Reuben and Simeon a future leading position in Israel is denied

to them.[218] On the other hand, there are other features in the whole
episode which seem to contradict the preceding somewhat and point
in another direction. Joseph's role at the deathbed suggests that he
is called as the oldest son and Israel's heir. One of the enigmas of the
present text is the fact that the consonantal text suggests that Joseph
is called the ראש המטה "head of the tribe" (47:31), which would fit very
well with the title in 48:22: אַחַד עַל־אַחֶיךָ "one above your brothers", but
which is hardly in line with the trend of the whole story. Moreover, the
fact that the patriarch bestowed Shechem on Joseph (48:22), a crucial
town in Canaan throughout history, suggests again an important role
for Joseph. Finally, the blessing which Joseph receives in Gen. 49:22–
26 has some characteristics that could be compared with motifs from
the legends of Ugaritic kings and are likewise in line with the features
described above.

On the basis of these elements in Joseph's description, his role
can best be qualified as a "double role". The Deathbed Episode contains positive and negative elements regarding Joseph's future. Ideolo-
gically, the negative elements for Joseph correspond with the favoured
position of Judah in Genesis 49 and strengthen the latter's position
considerably. After the Deathbed Episode and its epilogue Joseph will
have played his role and Judah will take the lead. It might be concluded therefore that Genesis 49 is not a *Fremdkörper*, but that it is
in line with some of the elements that are found in the wider context (the Joseph Story), and that the smaller context (the Deathbed
Episode) functions to provide a firm foundation for the future position
of Judah as described in Genesis 49.

On the other hand, the positive features in Joseph's role raise
some serious questions with regard to this episode. Why do we find
in this episode these dark lines about Joseph, which are certainly not
in line with Judah's favoured position? Do these contradictory elements betray something of the history of the text? Who were the
parties interested in these ideological features? These questions demand another analysis of this episode, namely one from a diachronic
perspective. In our diachronic analysis in Chapter Six we will try to
detect if the ideological or apologetic elements described in the present
chapter are due to a diachronic development of the text. However, before performing this analysis, we will first describe previous research
into the Deathbed Episode and the different solutions that have been

---

[218] For the discussion of this equation with Reuben and Simeon, cf. our discussion
above, pp. 335–339. Note that the verbal form used to announce this equation is
a *yiqtol*: יִהְיוּ "they will be" (48:5). In this way the equation is thus clearly focused
on the future.

offered to solve the problems found there.

4.6 Recapitulation

1. The Deathbed Episode (Gen. 47:29–49:33) is built up of four scenes, which are arranged chiastically.

2. The Joseph Story (Genesis 37–50) has one plot — the question whether Joseph will be king over his brothers (37:8, 10) — with two focal points. The first is within the narrative framework and is fulfilled in favour of Joseph. The second is beyond the borders of the narrative and awaits the future, where it will be fulfilled in favour of Judah (49:8).

3. The consonantal text of Gen. 47:31 and of 48:22 has been obscured during the course of transmission. The reading it seems to hide and which is partly supported by LXX and Peš points in the direction of an important position for Joseph, which is not in line with a synchronic reading of the Deathbed Episode.

4. The adoption of Ephraim and Manasseh by the patriarch cannot be considered positive for Joseph, because not his name is continued in them, but his father's (48:16). Moreover, the fact that they are equated with Reuben and Simeon has to be regarded as an act of putting them aside, comparable to the way these two sons will be excluded (49:3–4, 5–7).

5. The Deathbed Episode and the Blessing in Genesis 49 cannot be regarded as independent entities. Both function to give a strong foundation to Judah's future position. The Deathbed Episode in its present form weakens Joseph's position, whereas in the Joseph Story his importance is brought back as the instrument by which the nation would be saved. Judah's leadership is proved in the Joseph Story and is confirmed by the patriarch in the Blessing.

6. Joseph and Judah are apparently rivals. Some elements, in the texts, point in the direction of Joseph's leadership among the brothers. Other elements deny this and ascribe the future leadership among the brothers (tribes) to Judah. These diverging lines seem to contradict each other and might reflect different historical situations. This has to be investigated in the diachronic analysis.

Chapter 5

Intermezzo: Previous Research on the Joseph Story

With an Emphasis on the Deathbed Episode

5.1 Introduction

In the previous chapter we concluded that a diachronic analysis has to be performed in order to explain some of the contradicting elements in the text. As was noted, in the Deathbed Episode we find some ideological tensions in the description of Joseph. On the one hand, his position is apparently described as the eldest son, who is responsible for the funeral of his father. On the other hand, his importance is restricted to the Joseph Story, which functions in the past, while his future position is minimized and Judah is favoured. The favourite position of Joseph as eldest son, which is partly based on a different reading of the Hebr. consonantal text, is not always recognized. Nevertheless, many times scholars have demonstrated that the text of the Joseph Story, and especially the Deathbed Episode is composite. In the present chapter we will describe former solutions to the problems felt. In addition we will deal with the problem of the dating of the text, which is relevant for the diachronic analysis, and, on the other hand, important to the historiography of Early Israel.

5.2 The Eighteenth and Nineteenth Century

As already noted in Chapter One, the French doctor Jean Astruc was the first to separate Genesis 49 from the Joseph Story on the basis of different Divine names used in the Testament as well as in its context.[1] Whereas in the Joseph Story the name אֱלֹהִים prevails, in Genesis 49 the name יהוה is used (49:18). Together with chapters 38 and 39, where also the name יהוה is used, Astruc assigned these chapters to a different document than the remaining chapters of the Joseph Story (Genesis 37; 40–48; 49:28–33; 50). The Joseph story is in this connection considered to be an organic part of one document, comprising the narrative material from Genesis 1 to Exodus 1–2.[2]

Almost the same results were found by J.G. Eichhorn in his intro-

---

[1]J. Astruc, *Conjectures sur les mémoires originaux dont il paraît que Moyse s'est servi pour composer le Livre de la Genèse: Avec des remarques qui appuient ou qui éclaircissent ces conjectures*, Bruxelles [Paris] 1753, 263–7.

[2]For an overview of Astruc's assignment of the several documents, see Houtman, *Der Pentateuch*, 63–70, and esp. 66.

duction,[3] as well as by J.S. Vater in his commentary on the Pentateuch,[4] who were both inclined to read the Joseph Story as a basic-
ally coherent narrative, which was transmitted as a single document.[5]
With regard to Gen. 47:29–50:14, Vater was not convinced of its unity
and assumed the presence of the work of another author here. Gen.
49:29–33 could be by another author than the one who wrote 47:29–
31, whereas 50:12–13 which refers back to 49:29–33, could also have
been inserted; "allein es ist möglich, nicht notwendig".[6]

However, a few years before Vater, C.D. Ilgen[7] in his study on
Genesis, distinguished two sources in the Joseph Story, Sopher Eliel
harischon and Sopher Eliel haschscheni.[8] According to him the deathbed scene is also composed out of these two sources: Gen. 47:28; 48:3–
7; 49:29–33; 50:12–13 belong to the first Sopher Eliel, while 47:29–
48:2, 9–22; 50:2–11, 14 belong to the second Sopher Eliel. Ilgen was
cautiously followed in his suggestion by W.M.L. de Wette,[9] who lists

---

[3] J.G. Eichhorn, *Einleitung in das Alte Testament*, Tl. 2, Leipzig ²1787, 292:
"fast ganz".

[4] J.S. Vater, *Commentar über den Pentateuch, mit Einleitungen zu den einzelnen Abschnitten der eingeschalteten Übersetzung von Dr. Alexander Geddes'
merkwürdigen critischen und exegetischen Anmerkungen, und einer Abhandlung
über Mose und die Verfasser des Pentateuchs*, Halle 1802-5.

[5] There are some important differences between Eichhorn and Vater with regard to the origin of the book of Genesis: Eichhorn held the view that Genesis
contained mainly parts of two mutually independent historical works, with in addition several independent documents (Gen. 2:4–3:24; 14; 33:18–34:31; 36:1–43;
49:1–27); cf. Houtman, *Der Pentateuch*, 72–6. Vater, on the other hand, was inclined to view the Pentateuch as a compilation of "fragments" "von denen man,
wenn man wolle, sagen könne, daß sie zwei parallele Reihen darstellen, von denen
eine aus Kreisen stamme, in denen man Gott mit Elohim bezeichne, und die andere aus Kreisen, in denen man Gott Jehova nenne" (Houtman, *op.cit.*, 82). With
respect to Genesis 49 and the Joseph Story, they were in close agreement.

[6] Vater, *Commentar*, Bd. I, 330. Vater adds this restriction because 50:14 does
not follow seamless at 50:11.

[7] Vater, knew the work of Ilgen and he discussed it in several places in his
commentary. However, he did not agree with him concerning the Joseph Story.

[8] C.D. Ilgen, *Die Urkunden des Jerusalemischen Tempelarchivs in ihren Urge-
stalt als Beytrag zur Berichtigung der Geschichte der Religion und Politik aus den
Hebräischen mit kritischen und erklärenden Anmerkungen, auch mancherley dazu
gehörigen Abhandelungen Theil I: Die Urkunden des ersten Buchs von Moses*,
Halle 1798. On Ilgen, cf. Houtman, *Der Pentateuch*, 79–80; B. Seidel, *Karl David
Ilgen und die Pentateuchforschung im Umkreis der sogenannten älteren Urkun-
denhypothese* (BZAW, 213), Berlin 1993. For Ilgen's view on the Joseph Story we
had to use secondary literature: Vater, *Commentar*, Bd. III, 713; G.A. Schumann,
*Genesis Hebraica et Graece: Recognovit et digessit varias lectiones notasque criti-
cas subiunxit argumentis historico-criticis illustravit et cum annotatione perpetua;
Volumen I: Genesin complectens*, Lipsiae 1829, lxv.

[9] W.M.L. de Wette, *Beiträge zur Einleitung in das Alte Testament*, II. *Kri-*

extensively Ilgen's arguments for the distinction of these layers in
the Joseph Story.[10] In this comprehensive list the foundations were
laid for the literary criticism of the Joseph Story in later times. The
literary-critical arguments, which will be given below, show that in
almost all cases Ilgen and De Wette were the first to introduce these
arguments. This might be demonstrated by the work of L. Schmidt
on the Joseph Story in 1986, who in many respects agrees with the
arguments of Ilgen and de Wette.[11]

Pentateuchal studies crystallized in the work of J. Wellhausen,[12]
who mainly followed the arguments of Ilgen and De Wette concerning
the composite character of the Joseph Story. In his era the documentary hypothesis took shape on the basis of the work of Graf and
Kuenen.[13] Four layers or documents were now distinguished in the
Pentateuch, which came into being in the order J, E, D, and P.[14]
While Ilgen and De Wette distinguished two layers in the Joseph
Story, Wellhausen was convinced that, in addition to these two, labelled J and E, there were some traces of P[15] as well. Concerning J
and E it was crucial for Wellhausen to identify these two sources in
the Joseph Story:

For this final part of Genesis the main source is also JE. It could be

---

tik der Israelitischen Geschichte. Erster Teil: Kritik der mosaischen Geschichte,
Halle 1807 (repr. Darmstadt 1971), 142–68. On De Wette, see J.W. Rogerson,
*W.M.L. de Wette, Founder of Modern Biblical Criticism: An Intellectual Bio-
graphy* (JSOTS, 126), Sheffield 1992; concerning De Wette's *Beiträge*, cf. pp.
49–56; further Houtman, *Der Pentateuch*, 84–7.

[10]De Wette, *Beiträge*, Bd. II, 142–68, 157, n. *, writes: "Es wird mir nicht zum
Vorwurf gemacht werden, daß ich Ilgen abgeschrieben; wo etwas schon getan ist,
kann man nichts mehr tun, ich mußte aber die wichtigste Punkte herausheben,
um des Zusammenhangs willen, und weil nicht jeder Ilgens Buch sogleich bei der
Hand hat."

[11]L. Schmidt, *Literarische Studien zur Josephsgeschichte* (BZAW, 167), Berlin
1986; idem, "Josephsnovelle", *TRE*, Bd. 17, 255–8.

[12]We will not mention here other scholars, who also followed the arguments
of Ilgen and De Wette and distinguished several layers in the Joseph Story, or
who contradict these results. Cf. Dillmann, *Die Genesis*, 391; Holzinger, *Genesis
erklärt*, 252–5.

[13]Houtman, *Der Pentateuch*, 98–107.

[14]Ilgen discerned three layers in Genesis, a theory later defended anew by
H. Hupfeld, *Die Quellen der Genesis und die Art ihrer Zusammensetzung von
neuem untersucht*, Berlin 1853. This study might be considered to be the basis of
the newer documentary hypothesis; cf. Houtman, *Der Pentateuch*, 95. However,
mainly through the work of Ilgen it was already possible to reach the same results
as Wellhausen did.

[15]Wellhausen denoted P with Q (=*Quatuor*, "Vierbundesbuch"), because this
source narrates four covenants; cf. J. Wellhausen, *Die Composition des Hexateuchs
und der historischen Bücher des Alten Testaments*, Berlin ³1899, 1–2.

anticipated that this work would be compiled, as usual of J and E; our earlier results imply such an assumption and would be undermined if it could not be proven. I consider beginning "to cut up this fluent story of Joseph into several documents" not amiss, but to be as necessary as the decomposition of Genesis on the whole. Cf. de Wette, Beiträge II, 146ff.[16]

So, when these two recensions were proven to be just one layer, the theory of two continuing historical works J and E could be dismissed.[17] However, as Schmidt argued, the reference to De Wette demonstrated that the arguments brought forward by Wellhausen, were not solely based on the wish to prove his theory, but based on doublets and contradictions found in the text itself.[18] According to Wellhausen there was scarcely another passage within Genesis where the stratification of the documents was so obvious as in the final part of chapter 47 and the beginning of the next.[19] He distinguished in the Deathbed Episode Gen. 48:3–7, 49:29–33 and 50:12–13 as belonging to P, while it was uncertain to which source 49:28 belonged: P, or together with 49:1–27 to JE.[20] Concerning the origin of 49:1–27 he was unsure. In his judgment it belonged to JE, whereas it certainly could not belong to E. The coherence of J does not support the origin of 49:1–27 from J, although there are some connections (Gen. 34; 35:22 with 49:3–7). But this coherence must not be overemphasized, because it is possible that the narrator did not compose this poem himself but found it

---

[16]Wellhausen, *Composition*, 52: "Die Hauptquelle ist auch für diesen letzten Abschnitt der Genesis JE. Es ist zu vermuten, daß dies Werk hier wie sonst aus J und E zusammengesetzt sei; unsere früheren Ergebnisse drängen auf diese Annahme und würden erschüttert werden, wären sie nicht erweisbar. Ich halte das Beginnen, 'diese fliessende Erzählung von Joseph nach Quellen zerstückeln zu wollen', nicht für verfehlt, sondern für so notwendig, wie überhaupt die Dekomposition der Genesis. Vgl. de Wette Beiträge II 146ss."

[17]For that reason this statement of Wellhausen is often used to demonstrate that Wellhausen only challenges the unity in order to hold on to the newer documentary hypothesis; see *e.g.* W. Rudolph, "Die Josefsgeschichte", in: P. Volz, W. Rudolph, *Der Elohist als Erzähler: Ein Irrweg der Pentateuchkritik?* (BZAW, 63), Berlin 1933, 143–83, 146; H. Donner, *Die literarische Gestalt der alttestamentlichen Josephsgeschichte* (SHAW.PH, 1976.2), Heidelberg 1976, 7–8; F. Crüsemann, *Der Widerstand gegen das Königtum: Die antiköniglichen Texte des Alten Testaments und der Kampf um den frühen israelitischen Staat* (WMANT, 49), Neukirchen-Vluyn 1978, 143, n. 11; Westermann, *Genesis 37–50*, 8.

[18]Schmidt, *Literarische Studien zur Josephsgeschichte*, 131.

[19]Wellhausen, *Composition*, 59: "Es gibt kaum eine Stelle der Genesis, wo die Schichtung der Quellen handgreiflicher wahrzunehmen ist, als der Schluss des 47. und der Beginn des 48. Kapitels...".

[20]Wellhausen, *Composition*, 52.

in extenso in its present form.[21] Further Gen. 47:29–31 belongs to J, while Gen. 48:1–2, 8–22 contains the work of E. The latter is derived from the use of אֱלֹהִים, the frequent usage of אֵת instead of the verbal suffix, נשק and חבק with ל, and וַיִּשְׁתַּחוּ לְאַפָּיו אָרְצָה (verse 12) instead of אַפַּיִם אָרְצָה.[22]

In the following section the main problems of the Joseph Story will be noted. These problems necessitated a literary critical analysis and remained the basis of all literary critical studies during the following century.

5.3   Literary Problems in the Joseph Story

The following problems in the Joseph Story were observed:

1. In the episode on Joseph's sale to Egypt (37:18–36) the report on Judah's words is inconsistent with that on Reuben's. According to the former, the brothers throw Joseph into the pit with the intention of letting him die. On Judah's advice they sell him to a passing caravan of Ishmaelites, who sell him into slavery in Egypt. According to the latter, the brothers throw Joseph into the pit because of Reuben, who wants to save his life. But passing Midianite traders take/steal him away from the pit and sell him to Egypt (cf. 40:15).[23]

2. There is some tension in respect to whom Joseph is sold, and where Joseph is brought when he is put into custody. It seems that Joseph's first lord as well as the keeper of the prison are both captain of the guard (Gen. 39:1, 22; 40:4). Further, it seems strange that the "eunuch" ("Verschnittene", סָרִיס) of Pharaoh should have had a wife. Two layers can be discerned: According to one source Joseph is sold to Potiphar, the captain of the guard, who had the superintendence of the state prison. Joseph, as his slave, is put there in charge of the other prisoners. According to the second, he is sold to an Egyptian (without a name),[24] who placed him at the head of his household. After the incident with the man's wife Joseph is taken to the prison, where the eunuch of Pharaoh (without a wife!), being captain

---

[21]Wellhausen, *Composition*, 60.

[22]Wellhausen, *Composition*, 60.

[23]De Wette, *Beiträge*, Bd. II, 142–4; Wellhausen, *Composition*, 52–3.

[24]Cf. 39:1, which is overburdened; therefore the words "Potiphar, an officer of Pharaoh, the captain of the guard" are considered a later addition, which results in "an Egyptian bought him from the Ishmaelites"; De Wette, *Beiträge*, Bd. II, 148; Wellhausen, *Composition*, 52.

of the guard, is the superintendent, and whose favour is won by Joseph.[25]

3. A similar difference is found in the episode of the brother's first return from Egypt (Gen. 42:29–43:15). Simeon has to remain in Egypt as a hostage in order to make the brothers return with Benjamin, their youngest brother. When the brothers return to Canaan and report everything to their father (Jacob), he forbids them to take Benjamin back with them to Egypt because he believes he has lost two sons already (Joseph and Simeon). Even when Reuben offers his two sons as hostages he abides by his decision. However, in the next episode when the famine grows worse it is Judah who knows how to convince his father (Israel) to let them go. Here the points at issue are the famine and Benjamin, who might be killed; Simeon is not mentioned here at all.[26]

4. The way the returned money is found in the previous section might also contain some doublets (Gen. 42:25–28, 35–36). Although they had provisions for their journey (42:25), one of them strangely opens his sack at the lodging place to feed his ass (42:27) and finds his money there. He tells his brothers who are shocked and say to each other: "What is this that God has done to us?" In 42:35 it is told that after they came home they empty their sacks and find the money, which scares them all, including their father. It might be expected that when one of the brothers has found his money the others would also have opened their sacks to look if the same thing has happened to them.[27]

5. Gen. 45:9 tells us how Joseph invites his father and brothers, with their families, to come to Egypt, where they can live in the land of Goshen (45:10). On the other hand, when Pharaoh hears that Joseph's brothers have come, he orders Joseph to let them return to fetch their father and families, in order to let them have "the best of the land of Egypt" and eat "the fat of the land" (45:18). This seems to contradict 46:31, where Joseph says to his brothers that he will go and tell Pharaoh that they have come. He instructs them to ask Pharaoh to allow them to

---

[25] De Wette, *Beiträge*, Bd. II, 146–9; Wellhausen, *Composition*, 52.
[26] De Wette, *Beiträge*, Bd. II, 149–51; Wellhausen, *Composition*, 55–6.
[27] De Wette, *Beiträge*, Bd. II, 152; Wellhausen, *Composition*, 56–8.

sojourn (לָגוּר) in the land of Goshen for a short time, till the
famine was over.[28]

6. When Joseph is told that his father is ill (48:1) he takes his two
sons with him and goes to his father. Jacob adopts them: "your
two sons ... are mine" (48:5). In verse 8 Jacob sees Joseph's
two sons and asks: "Who are these?" It is remarkable that he
asks this question when he had adopted them only a short time
before.[29]

5.4   The Twentieth Century; B.D. Eerdmans

The conclusions of Wellhausen did not go unchallenged,[30] although his
analysis of the Joseph Story was accepted *grosso modo* within critical
scholarship. However, in his discussion of the Documentary Hypothesis, the Dutch scholar B.D. Eerdmans criticized also some results
of the analysis of the Joseph story.[31] On the basis of his *religionsgeschichtliche* approach, in which he principally considered the name
אֱלֹהִים to be a polytheistic denotation of the divine, which only later
could be applied solely to YHWH,[32] he denied the possibility of discerning the different documents in the Pentateuch on the basis of
the use of the Divine names אֱלֹהִים and יהוה.[33] Thus he principally
denied the existence of the documents J and E, but also indirectly
questioned the validity of P.[34] Concerning the Joseph Story he was
certain that the present text is composite and contains two different presentations besides some later additions. In order to distinguish
the different layers he used as a criterion the different names of the
patriarch Jacob and Israel, of which the former was in his view the
oldest.[35] The Deathbed Episode, especially Gen. 48:8–22 failed in his
view to support the Documentary Hypothesis because of the tight
unity of this passage.[36] According to him the following stratification

---

[28]De Wette, *Beiträge*, Bd. II, 152–6; Wellhausen, *Composition*, 58–9.

[29]De Wette, *Beiträge*, Bd. II, 156; Wellhausen, *Composition*, 59–60.

[30]Cf. Kraus, *Geschichte*, 374–7; Houtman, *Der Pentateuch*, 114–5.

[31]B.D. Eerdmans, *Alttestamentliche Studien*, Bd. I: *Die Komposition der Genesis*, Gießen 1908, 65–71.

[32]Eerdmans, *Komposition der Genesis*, iv, 1–2, 35–36.

[33]For a more substantial description of his approach, cf. Houtman, *Der Pentateuch*, 173–8.

[34]Eerdmans, *Komposition der Genesis*, 2–33, questions the existence of P in
which he found older (polytheistic) as well as younger (monotheistic) material.

[35]Eerdmans, *Komposition der Genesis*, 65–6, 87.

[36]Eerdmans, *Komposition der Genesis*, 69.

of the different layers (which did not differ substantially from Well-hausen's analysis) fits the text best: the Jacob-layer is preserved in Gen. 47:28; 49:1a, 29–33; 50:12–13; the Israel-layer: 47:29–31; 48:1, 2b, 8–22; 50:1–11, 14–26; later additions are 48:2a, 3–6. Finally Gen. 49:1b–28 is inserted by the redactor who used both layers, because in verse 2 he used Jacob and Israel together.[37]

5.5 H. Gunkel

In his commentary on Genesis, H. Gunkel presents a literary critical analysis of the Joseph Story, comparable to that of Wellhausen.[38] But, in his commentary as well as in a later article on the Joseph Story he adds form-critical considerations to this literary critical approach, based on his principal interest in the pre-literary stage of the biblical narratives.[39] In his view the Joseph Story is a "novella", originating from a "cycle of sagas" ("Sagenkranz"), in which several legends of Joseph were woven into one coherent narrative.[40] In this new composition — according to his general description of the origin of a novella — the narrator made some appropriate changes, inserted a few repetitions, and emphasized some aspects, in order to mould the story into a new artistic work.[41] The basis of such a novella, however, was one coherent narrative, built up from several single stories, which are not based each on an independent tradition, but which are from the beginning parts of a larger composition.[42] This composition is a

---

[37]Eerdmans, *Komposition der Genesis*, 70–1.

[38]H. Gunkel, *Genesis übersetzt und erklärt* (HK, I/1), Göttingen ²1902, ³1910, 401–97. In his view E is especially prominent, since it is from this source that the fundamental idea has been preserved (*op.cit.*, 396).

[39]On Gunkel's view on the pre-literary stage, cf. above, section 1.3.2.

[40]Gunkel, *Genesis*, ³1910, 396–7; idem, "Die Komposition der Joseph-Geschich-ten", *ZDMG* 76 (1922) 55–71, 66–8.

[41]Gunkel, "Komposition der Joseph-Geschichten", 59. On the origin of a novella he writes: "... es kann eine ursprüngliche Einzelerzählung in einer Zeit tie-ferer seelischer und künstlicher Entwicklung ins Breite geführt werden. Mit-tel solcher Erweiterung sind etwa, daß dieselbe Szene um ihrer Schönheit oder ihres Gedankens wegen mehrere Male, natürlich mit gewissen, wohlabgestimmten Änderungen, wiedergegeben, oder daß man das Vorgefallene in langen Reden noch einmal berichtet und eigentümlich beleuchtet." But it is also conceivable "... daß der Erzähler, in dem Wunsche, seine Geschichte recht bunt und mannigfaltig zu gestalten, überlieferte Sagen andersartiger Herkunft in sie einsetzt und nach seinen Zwecken umformt."

[42]Gunkel, "Komposition der Joseph-Geschichten", 66–7. According to Gunkel (*art.cit.*, 61, 66) this original form contains: 1. Joseph's abduction to Egypt; 2. The first encounter of the brothers with Joseph in Egypt; 3. The second encounter; 4. Joseph reveals himself to his brothers; 5. Jacob travels to Egypt and stays in Goshen; 6. Jacob's final will; 7. Jacob's funeral and Joseph's death.

tale — like many other stories in Genesis — and is in that form a pure
family narrative without any historical relation, and without the name
Joseph.[43] According to Gunkel this view of the story is not in conflict
with the literary analysis of the text, because in the Joseph Story the
different sources correspond with each other.[44] On the other hand, in
his view, all future research on the documents of this narrative will
have to take into account the described investigations of the text, in
order not to tear apart a substantially coherent work.[45]

The analysis of the Deathbed Episode in his commentary — perhaps somewhat differing from the view found in his article on the
Joseph Stories[46] — divides the text into J, E and P. An important
difference with Wellhausen is the fact that in Gen. 48:8–22 where
Wellhausen only finds E, he discerns — here following Budde and
A. Dillmann[47] — both J and E, mainly based on the doublets and
tensions in the text. In 48:1 a complete new section begins, doubling
47:29–31. Joseph is called to his father in 47:29–31, while in 48:1 he
comes freely after having heard that his father is ill. According to
48:10a Jacob cannot see, but in verses 8a, 11 he sees Joseph and his
sons. Joseph brings his sons to his father twice (48:10b, 13). 48:17–
19 is the continuation of verses 13–14, whereas verses 15–16 disturb
the course of events. The preference of Ephraim before Manasseh is
expressed in 48:13–14 by means of an action, on the other hand in
48:20 it is expressed by means of a word.[48] This results in the following stratification of the different documents:[49] J is preserved in
Gen. 47:29–31; 48:2b, 9b–10a, 13–14, 18–19; 49:33aB; 50:1; document
E is found in 48:1–2a, 7–9a, 10b–12, 15–17, 20–21 (22?); while 47:28;
48:3–6; 49:1a, 28bB–33aA, 33b contains P. Finally Gen. 49:1b–28abA
is inserted by J[b].[50]

---

[43]Gunkel, "Komposition der Joseph-Geschichten", 68.

[44]Gunkel, "Komposition der Joseph-Geschichten", 60–1.

[45]Gunkel, "Komposition der Joseph-Geschichten", 61.

[46]Gunkel, "Komposition der Joseph-Geschichten", 57, announced a fifth edition
of his commentary on Genesis in which his view on the Joseph Story would have
been incorporated; however, this revised edition did never appear.

[47]Gunkel, *Genesis*, ²1902, 414; ³1910, 470. K. Budde, "Genesis 48,7 und die
benachbarten Abschnitte", *ZAW* 3 (1883) 56–86, 61; Dillmann, *Die Genesis*,
445–7.

[48]Gunkel, *Genesis*, ²1902, 413; ³1910, 469.

[49]For the analysis of 47:29–48:22; 49:33aB, 50:1, see Gunkel, *Genesis*, ²1902,
413; ³1910, 469; for the analysis of the parts belonging to P, see *op.cit.*, ²1902,
436; ³1910, 496.

[50]Gunkel, *Genesis*, ²1902, 421; ³1910, 478. A simmilar stratification for Genesis
49 is found already in Wellhausen, *Composition*, 52, as a suggestion.

5.6 H. Greßmann

Similar to Gunkel's approach is that of H. Greßmann, who considers the Joseph Story as an originally non-Israelite king's tale ("Königs-märchen").[51] It was probably narrated in this tale that Joseph was the king of Egypt, but in later times this aspect was suppressed because it was unlikely that Joseph became a king in Egypt, and for that reason he was made a minister.[52] Only in the course of transmission did the Joseph Story acquire the character of a family tale. Greßmann in his article is more interested in the form-critical analysis of the narrative, than in the literary-critical analysis because these results are not always reliable.[53] However, as with Gunkel, this does not lead to an abandoning of the results of the literary analysis; on the contrary, where appropriate, he refers to these results.[54]

The Deathbed Episode is analysed in a form-critical way. Greß-mann distinguishes two motives in this episode: the final will of Jacob concerning his funeral and the blessing of Ephraim and Manasseh.[55] The former motive, found in 47:29–31 is indispensable for the Joseph Story; the second, however, is independent from the preceding and has an aetiological character in that it seeks to explain why Ephraim has the prevalence over Manasseh. The story had its own history, partly through mutilating previous versions, since two and probably three versions are recognizable in this passage.[56] Tribal historical considera-tions — following E. Meyer[57] — permit Greßmann to suggest that when Jacob gives Shechem to Joseph (48:22), he could not possibly

---

[51] H. Greßmann, "Ursprung und Entwicklung der Joseph-Sage", in: H. Schmidt (Hrsg.), ΕΥΧΑΡΙΣΤΗΡΙΟΝ: *Studien zur Religion und Literatur des Alten und Neuen Testaments; Fs H. Gunkel*, Göttingen 1923, 1–55; cf. esp. 18–21, 34–5; 51–2.

[52] Greßmann, "Ursprung und Entwicklung", 52–3.

[53] Cf. Greßmann, "Ursprung und Entwicklung", 2: "Da indessen Jahwist und Elohist nicht überall mit Sicherheit zu unterscheiden sind, so kommt die Quel-lenkritik vielfach zu abweichenden Ergebnissen. Überdies bleiben auch dann noch Unebenheiten, Risse und Brüche in der Darstellung, die sich durch Quellenkritik gar nicht beseitigen lassen, *weil sie jenseits der Quellen im Stoffe selbst liegen und uns in die Vorgeschichte der mündlichen Überlieferung führen*" (emphasis RdH).

[54] Cf. *e.g.* Greßmann, "Ursprung und Entwickelung", 22, where the problems in Gen. 37:36; 39:1–23 are explained with the help of the Documentary Hypothesis.

[55] Greßmann, "Ursprung und Entwickelung", 5–6.

[56] Greßmann, "Ursprung und Entwickelung", 6–8. The two versions are recog-nized in this way: the first one describes how Jacob blessed them with his hands crossed; while in the second one he placed Ephraim in the blessing before Ma-nasseh (48:14 and 20 respectively). Here the two documents J and E are clearly present; cf. Gunkel (p. 374, with n. 48 above).

[57] Greßmann, "Ursprung und Entwickelung", 8; E. Meyer, *Die Israeliten und ihre Nachbarstämme: Alttestamentliche Untersuchungen*, Halle 1906, 227, 414–5.

have been in Egypt because he could not have possessed Shechem while he lived in Egypt. Therefore this passage does not presuppose the emigration of Jacob to Egypt, but when the tradition of Joseph's stay in Egypt was already known, it implicates Joseph's temporary return to his dying father in Canaan.[58] But even when the foregoing narration suggests that Joseph receives Shechem, it is more likely that originally Ephraim got the city, because he actually possessed the city in later times. When we abandon the connection with the foregoing narrative, it may be assumed that besides Joseph and his sons (now adopted by Jacob), Benjamin is also present, and hence all Rachel's sons are present. This would explain the mysterious verse 7, because the reference to Rachel's death is closely connected with Benjamin's birth.[59] It is unlikely that this passage belonged to the Joseph story, as it contradicts it on two decisive points: according to the Joseph Story Jacob dies in Egypt, but here he dies in Canaan. Secondly, according to the Joseph Story Ephraim and Manasseh are Joseph's sons, but here they are viewed next to (Joseph and) Benjamin as Jacob's (and Rachel's) sons, although the adoption compensates for this difference to some extent. However, in Greßmann's view it is likely that this passage was not a part of the Joseph Story but originally belonged to the Jacob Saga and was only secondarily inserted into the Joseph Story.[60]

5.7   O. Eissfeldt

Within a modified form of Wellhausen's theory, it is usual to discern several layers (for example J^1, J^2, J^3) within the different documents in a way closely related to the supplementary hypothesis.[61] This resulted, however, in a fragmentation of the documents, which undermined the reliability of the theory.[62] R. Smend reacted to this and

---

[58]Greßmann, "Ursprung und Entwickelung", 7–8.

[59]Greßmann, "Ursprung und Entwickelung", 7.

[60]Greßmann, "Ursprung und Entwickelung", 8.

[61]Cf. Wellhausen, *Composition der Hexateuch*, 207–8. On this development see Houtman, *Der Pentateuch*, 139–44 (the description of Wellhausen is found on pp. 140–1).

[62]Houtman, *Der Pentateuch*, 143. Cf. also the remark of O. Eissfeldt, *Hexateuch-Synopse: Die Erzählung der fünf Bücher Mose und des Buches Josua mit dem Anfange des Richterbuches in ihre vier Quellen zerlegt und in deutscher Übersetzung dargeboten samt einer in Einleitung und Anmerkungen gegebenen Begründung*, Leipzig 1922, 3: "So ist die neuere Urkunden-Hypothese, die mit ihrer Annahme von drei hexateuchischen Erzählungs-Quellen, von J, E und P eine so glatte Lösung des Hexateuch-Problems zu bieten schien, erweicht worden. Die Größe J ist von der Forschung in fortschreitendem Maße als eine Addition

developed a five-document theory on the origin of the Pentateuch in which he differentiated between J^1 and J^2 (two independent, parallel existing documents), plus the usual E, D and P.[63]

This theory was welcomed with some enthusiasm by O. Eissfeldt, who changed the names of the two J-documents to L (= "Laien-quelle") and J.[64] L is in this case a *Yahwistic* document, but, in comparison to the others, the most profane one, which still reflects the nomadic lifestyle and in which the narratives are connected rather loosely and contain archaic characteristics.[65] In his view L is the oldest document, originating in the period of David and Solomon,[66] while J must have come from around 850 BCE, and E between 800–750 BCE.[67] L contains poetical, legendary-novelistic phrasing of tribal-historical events, like Reuben's misbehaviour (Gen. 35:21–22a) and that of Simeon and Levi (Gen. 34), as well as the scolding curses (Gen. 49:3–7), and including the Judah-Tamar story (Gen. 38).[68] These might be contrasted with narratives like the Joseph Story, which is clearly much more individualistic and in which the tribal-historical aspect has disappeared completely.[69] In this respect Eissfeldt follows the Wellhausian analysis of the Joseph Story, discerning three documents — J, E, and P.[70] Within the Deathbed Episode Eissfeldt discerns the layers in accordance with the analysis of Gunkel, only differing with him about the problematic Gen. 48:7, which Eissfeldt considers to be a later addition.[71]

Interesting in this respect is Eissfeldt's assignment of Gen. 49:3–7 to L, together with Gen. 34,[72] 35:21–22a; 38. Whereas it is usual to

---

zweier Unterfäden und mehrerer Einzelstücke erkannt worden, und ... E und P stellen sich nun als ein durch Überarbeitung und Ergänzung alteriertes Gebilde dar. Aber ein deutliches, allgemein überzeugendes, Bild vom Werden der einzelnen Quellenwerke und des gesamten Hexateuch ist nicht entworfen worden."

[63] Eissfeldt, *Hexateuch-Synopse*, 4; Houtman, *Der Pentateuch*, 144.

[64] Cf. Eissfeldt, *Hexateuch-Synopse*, ix–x; for some criticism on Smend's study, see *op.cit.*, 4. On L, see further, idem, *Die Genesis der Genesis*, Tübingen 1958, 10–2; idem, *Einleitung in das Alte Testament*, Tübingen 1976, 224, 258–64.

[65] Houtman, *Der Pentateuch*, 145.

[66] Eissfeldt, *Genesis der Genesis*, 28–30.

[67] Eissfeldt, *Genesis der Genesis*, 30–2.

[68] Eissfeldt, *Genesis der Genesis*, 28.

[69] Eissfeldt, *Genesis der Genesis*, 28–9.

[70] Cf. Eissfeldt, *Hexateuch-Synopse*, 22–30 (esp. 23), 76*–106*; idem, *Genesis der Genesis*, 22–7.

[71] Eissfeldt, *Hexateuch-Synopse*, 268.

[72] Eissfeldt, *Hexateuch-Synopse*, 69*–71*, divided this story into two layers: L and E, according to Gunkel's analysis of this narrative in J and E. In his later studies, (*Genesis der Genesis*, 8–9, 22, 28–9; *Einleitung*, 258–62) Eissfeldt ascribed the Shechem story in its entirety to L.

separate Genesis 49 from its direct context (Gen. 37–50), as well as
from the rest of Genesis, Eissfeldt maintained its direct connection
on a documentary level. In his view Gen. 38 has to be taken into
consideration as well: the present saying on Judah (Gen. 49:8–12)
could be a later interpolation for an originally negative saying in the
style of Deut. 33:7, referring to the Tamar incident. Also the saying
on Joseph — in which he gained the right of primogeniture — was
in this period replaced by the present, more neutral one (vv. 22–26).
The other sayings are not connected with the context of Genesis and
are inserted later, when a complete composition with sayings on all
the twelve tribes was required. Only the sayings concerning Reuben,
Simeon, Levi (Judah and Joseph) are in accordance with the context,
and the others sayings — especially the saying on Joseph (vv. 22–
26), apparently contradicting the J and E story of the blessing of
Ephraim and Manasseh — disturb this context to some extent. This
collection (Gen. 49:8–27) cannot be ascribed to one of the two parallel
narrative strands (J and E) therefore it is assumed that we are dealing
with independent (non-source-dependent) separate units, inserted in
the appropriate place.[73] Although Eissfeldt does not mention an exact
date for this redaction, it may be assumed that in his view it must
have taken place in the time that P was combined with the other three
sources, L, J and E, and the sayings already occupied their present
position in the P-framework (49:1a, 28b),[74] as Gen. 49:1b–28a would
otherwise form a torso.[75] However, another possibility could be the
loss of certain phrases, originally forming more appropriate transitions
from one scene to another.

5.8 W. Rudolph

In reaction to the continuing fragmentation of the four-source documentary theory W. Staerk, P. Volz and W. Rudolph (among others)
criticized the existence of E.[76] In a joint publication with Volz, Rudolph studied the Joseph Story, questioning the source-analysis in
which two main layers were discerned (J and E).[77] Rudolph declared
that he neither denied the right of source-criticism, nor the existence
of J to be the oldest, nor that of P to be the youngest source; but
that his main problem was the fragmentation of verses over several

---

[73]Eissfeldt, *Hexateuch-Synopse*, 268*; idem, *Genesis der Genesis*, 9–10, 16–7
(n. 1), 43–4; idem, *Einführung*, 304–5.

[74]Cf. Eissfeldt, *Genesis der Genesis*, 67–8.

[75]Cf. Eissfeldt, *Hexateuch-Synopse*, 102*–3*.

[76]Houtman, *Der Pentateuch*, 149–53.

[77]Rudolph, "Die Josefsgeschichte", (see n. 17 above), 143–83.

documents. As this fragmentation is especially related to E, this E is suspect. Hence he proposed the following solution:

> ... in Genesis there is no E in the way of a continuing document, i.e. as a coherent presentation of legendary or historical events in the sense of the Jahwist.[78]

According to Rudolph, Wellhausen's argument for the source-criticism of the Joseph Story[79] demonstrates that the analysis was not challenged by the Joseph Story itself but solely by the preceding sections in Genesis, where such an analysis seems appropriate.[80] Referring to the work of Gunkel, Greßmann and Holzinger, who all question the relevance of the source-criticism of the Joseph Story, he questions the need for such an analysis.[81] For that reason the arguments for the source-analysis of the story, like different names of God, the names of the third patriarch (Jacob or Israel), or the so-called *Sprachbeweis* are discussed by him, but validity is denied to them all.[82]

The argument based on the different names of God is a very delicate one for source-criticism within the Joseph Story, and Rudolph emphasizes this point, declaring that the argument argues *against* the analysis itself.[83] In his view the names are used according to a certain plan: יהוה is used only when the narrator himself is speaking (chap. 39); but when the acting persons are talking יהוה is never used, instead אֵל שַׁדַּי is used in Palestine (43:14), and אֱלֹהִים in Egypt;[84] although אֱלֹהִים is once used by the narrator (46:2), but this can be seen as a later addition (46:1aB–5a).[85] The use of the names of the

---

[78] Rudolph, "Die Josefsgeschichte", 145: "... es gibt in der Genesis keinen E als durchlaufender Quelle d.h. als eine zusammenhängende Darstellung von sagenhaften oder geschichtlichen Begebenheiten im Sinne der Jahwisten". Cf. also P. Volz, "Grundsätzliches zur elohistischen Frage: Untersuchung von Genesis 15–36", in: P. Volz, W. Rudolph, *Der Elohist als Erzähler: Ein Irrweg der Pentateuchkritik?* (BZAW, 63), Berlin 1933, 1–142, 24–5.

[79] Cf. p. 369 above.

[80] Rudolph, "Die Josefsgeschichte", 146.

[81] Rudolph, "Die Josefsgeschichte", 146. For Gunkel and Greßmann, cf. pp. 373–375 above.

[82] Rudolph, "Die Josefsgeschichte", 146–51.

[83] Rudolph, "Die Josefsgeschichte", 148.

[84] Rudolph, "Die Josefsgeschichte", 148.

[85] Rudolph, "Die Josefsgeschichte", 149. Gen. 46:1aB–5a is an alien element within the rest of the Joseph Story. Whereas God is everywhere the invisible governor of human fate, here in this text he unexpectedly acts personally ("God spoke to Israel"). Further, the story of Jacob and his sons is here linked suddenly with the earlier Isaac — similar to 48:15–16. Finally, this text, as well as 48:15–16, contradicts other parts of the story (e.g. 46:3 and 45:28; 48:15–16 and 48:20); cf.

third patriarch — J uses Israel; E Jacob — is unreliable, because
of the problematic use of these names in chapter 48, where in both
cases some exceptions have to be considered.[86] The argument of the
"Sprachbeweis" is dismissed in the same way, because it is used arbit-
rarily.[87] After having reviewed these arguments, Rudolph, following
the text, discusses in greater detail the alleged doublets, repetitions
and contradictions.[88]

Rudolph's discussion of the Joseph Story confirms his introductory statement that he does not deny the right of, nor the need for,
literary-criticism.[89] In his commentary on the text it becomes obvious that, in addition to the documents J and P, he is obliged to consider later additions in the story, perhaps connected with E, yet not
as an independent narrative layer.[90] In his analysis of the Deathbed
Episode[91] he agrees with the attribution of Gen. 47:27b–28; 48:3–6;[92]
49:28bB–33aA, 33b; 50:12–13 to P. However, in the remaining verses
of this episode Rudolph has to assume some layers in the text too.
First, Gen. 48:1–2 looks like a new start, not connected directly to the
preceding chapter. But, according to Rudolph there is no indication
here of the beginning of a new *document*.[93] Here the narrator only
seems to make use of another tradition, not incorporated into the
Joseph Story before.[94] Such irregular transitions from one tradition

---

art.cit., 149, 165, 171–2.

[86]Rudolph, "Die Josefsgeschichte", 149–50. These exceptions are clearly laid
out in Eissfeldt, *Hexateuch-Synopse*, 100*–1* (vv. 11 and 21).

[87]Rudolph, "Die Josefsgeschichte", 151, referring to the argument that J uses
אֲמֶחְתְּ׳, and E שֹׁק. This argument is invalid in 42:27 (J) and can only be sustained
with the help of the LXX.

[88]Rudolph, "Die Josefsgeschichte", 152–77.

[89]Rudolph, "Die Josefsgeschichte", 145.

[90]The same applies to Volz, cf. Houtman, *Der Pentateuch*, 151–2.

[91]Rudolph, "Die Josefsgeschichte", 168–75.

[92]The problematic 48:7 is considered to be part of J, and was originally found
after verse 11, where the emotions of seeing Joseph and his children made Jacob
remember the death of his beloved wife. We have to consider nevertheless some
emendations in this text (וַאֲנִי should be removed, or replaced with בְּנִי, and has to
be followed by an additional וְגַם, or even וְגַם אַתָּה אֲבַדְתְּ ו, "and you too were lost and
…"). The transposition of v. 7 from its original context to its present place was
caused by a retrospective view on Gen. 35, where the revelation in Luz (35:5), to
which 48:3–6 seems to refer, is directly followed by the report of Rachel's death.
See Rudolph, "Die Josefsgeschichte", 168–70. However, the three final words of v.
7 might be considered glosses, if not v. 7b in its entirety (*art.cit.*, 170, n. 1).

[93]Such a distinction would cause an unbridgeable gap between 47:31 and 48:2b
in his view; Rudolph, "Die Josefsgeschichte", 170.

[94]With the assumption of the use of different traditions by J, Rudolph is clearly
influenced by the work of Gunkel and Greßmann; cf. in this connection the remark
of Greßmann, p. 375, n. 53 above.

to another are not unusual in J, and these transitions form all the (mistaken) evidence for the differentiation between J¹ and J².⁹⁵

Secondly, Gen. 48:15–16 seems to interrupt the course of the narrative from verse 14 to verses 17–18. Rudolph agrees with this observation, because Joseph's attempt to correct his father's interchange of the blessings on his sons would be too late, when it only follows in verse 17. Further, verses 15–16 seem to anticipate the blessing in verse 20; and finally they are the only reference in the Joseph Story, except for P and Gen. 46:1aB–5a, which refer back to the earlier Patriarchs.⁹⁶ Since Gen. 46:1aB–5a also forms a later addition to the narrative,⁹⁷ it may be assumed that here the same hand has inserted Gen. 48:15–16.

Rudolph's opinion was not approved of at first, because the literary critical analysis of Wellhausen and Gunkel of this narrative had dominated the discussion for a long time. In later years Rudolph's plea for the principal unity of the narrative was advocated more successfully by G. von Rad,⁹⁸ whereas other scholars refer with approval to Rudolph's challenge of the source criticism of this story.⁹⁹

Rudolph's differentiation between the several traditions used by the narrator (J),¹⁰⁰ also caused some confusion. Rudolph dismisses the idea that the Elohist is an independent document, and prefers a tradition-historical approach explaining the irregular transitions within a narrative by means of differing traditions. Whereas de Vaux follows him in rejecting the combination of a Jahwistic and Elohistic *document* and accepts solely the combination of several traditions

---

⁹⁵Rudolph, "Die Josefsgeschichte", 170. Cf. also *art. cit.*, 172, where Gen. 48:21–22 is considered to be brought in from another tradition.

⁹⁶Rudolph, "Die Josefsgeschichte", 171–2.

⁹⁷Cf. p. 380, with n. 85 above.

⁹⁸Schmidt, *Literarische Studien zur Josephsgeschichte*, 128–9.

⁹⁹A. Jepsen, "Zur Überlieferungsgeschichte der Vätergestalten", *Fs. A. Alt*, Leipzig 1954, 139–55 (= *WZ(L).GS* 3 [1953/54] 265–81); S. Mowinckel, *Erwägungen zur Pentateuch Quellenfrage*, Oslo 1964, 61–3; R.N. Whybray, "The Joseph Story and Pentateuchal Criticism", *VT* 18 (1968) 522–8, 528 with n. 1; T.N.D. Mettinger, *Solomonic State Officials: A Study of the Civil Government Officials of the Israelite Monarchy* (CB OTS, 5), Lund 1971, 152–5, esp. 153; R. de Vaux, *Histoire ancienne d'Israël*, Tm. I: *Des origines à l'installation en Canaan*, Paris 1971, 278–81, 294–6 (E.T. = *Early History of Israel: To the Exodus and Covenant of Sinai*, London 1978, 292–5, 311–3); Donner, *Literarische Gestalt der Josephsgeschichte*, 24–35 (although with some modifications); F. Crüsemann, *Der Widerstand gegen das Königtum: Die antiköniglichen Texte des Alten Testamentes und der Kampf um den frühen israelitischen Staat* (WMANT, 49), Neukirchen-Vluyn 1978, 143–5.

¹⁰⁰Cf. p. 380, with n. 94f. above.

by one author,[101] he calls one tradition Elohistic and the other Jahwistic,[102] which opens the back door to the discarded independent
Elohist.[103]

5.9 M. Noth

In his study of the history of Pentateuchal traditions M. Noth also
discussed the Joseph Story.[104] In his opinion the Joseph Story is
rather young compared to the other Patriarchal and Exodus traditions, which can both be found in the "historical creed" (Josh. 24:2b–
13).[105] The Joseph Story, which includes all kinds of universal narrative motives (Gunkel and Greßmann), found its origin in the question:
"Jacob and his sons went to Egypt (Josh. 24:4), how did it come to
pass?",[106] a conclusion, also to be reached from its connecting function between the Patriarchal and Exodus narratives.[107] This narrative
originated in the circle of the "House of Joseph", which might be concluded from the fact that Joseph is the principal character in the
story. The narrative does not contain many local traditions; whereas
the reference to Dothan (Gen. 37:17) might be original, Hebron (Gen.
37:14) is probably a later redactional expansion, similar to the secondary reference to Beer-sheba (46:1b–5a).[108]

Although the story is apparently a northern tradition, it is found
in all three Genesis documents: J, E and P.[109] In many respects Noth
follows the classical analysis of the different documents, taking also
into account criteria like the names of Judah and Reuben, Jacob and
Israel.[110] In his view Gen. 47:29–31 is a part of J, but the remaining

---

[101] De Vaux, *Histoire ancienne d'Israël*, 279–80 (E.T., 295).

[102] De Vaux, *Histoire ancienne d'Israël*, 294 (E.T., 311).

[103] Cf. also Crüsemann, *Widerstand gegen das Königtum*, 144, with n. 18.

[104] M. Noth, *Überlieferungsgeschichte des Pentateuch*, Stuttgart 1948 (repr. Darmstadt 1960), 226–32.

[105] With the reference to the "historical creed" (Noth, *Überlieferungsgeschichte des Pentateuch*, 226), he follows von Rad's study on the form-critical problem of the Pentateuch: G. von Rad, *Das formgeschichtliche Problem des Hexateuch* (BWANT, 26), Stuttgart 1938, 1–11, esp. 6 (= idem, *Gesammelte Studien zum Alten Testament* [TB 8], München 1965, 9–86, esp. 14).

[106] Noth, *Überlieferungsgeschichte des Pentateuch*, 228.

[107] Noth, *Überlieferungsgeschichte des Pentateuch*, 226–7: "Sie stellt vielmehr die breite und kunstvolle erzählerische Entfaltung einer Themenverbindung dar" (227). Westermann, *Genesis 12–50* (EdF, 48), Darmstadt 1975, 62, pointed out that a similar theory is found with B. Luther, "Die Persönlichkeit des Jahwisten", in: E. Meyer, *Die Israeliten und ihre Nachbarstämme*, Halle 1906, 105–73, 146.

[108] Noth, *Überlieferungsgeschichte des Pentateuch*, 230.

[109] Cf. Noth, *Überlieferungsgeschichte des Pentateuch*, 7–40.

[110] Cf. Noth, *Überlieferungsgeschichte des Pentateuch*, 31, n. 100 — where he

Deathbed Episode (except for Gen. 48:3–6, P) in Genesis 48 is solely
E. Although a clear proof of unity in the remaining episode has not
been found,[111] a division over the different documents would not solve
the problems in the text either. Noth holds that this chapter, however,
did not belong to the original, independent functioning Joseph Story
but originated as a later addition to the Jacob tradition.[112]

5.10 G. von Rad

Emphasis is laid on the literary character of the Joseph Story by
G. von Rad, who is certainly influenced by the work of Gunkel.[113]
Von Rad has devoted several influential studies to the Joseph Story
in which a strong tension between the unity of the narrative and
the diversity of different documents and/or traditions exists. It is
sometimes emphasized that he departs from Gunkel, because von Rad
denies the Joseph story to be a "cycle of sagas" ("Sagenkranz"[114]), but
considers it to be a coherent narrative from the beginning to the end
of which no single part has existed independently before.[115] However,
although von Rad disagrees in this respect with the analysis of the
Joseph Story by Gunkel, it cannot be overlooked that von Rad's view
on the Joseph Story yet corresponds in many respects to Gunkel's.

Von Rad accepts the analysis of this story as derived from two
documents, J and E (next to the obvious P-layer).[116] In his description
of how these two documents were composed into one literary work,
his words are very much like Gunkel's description of the origin of a
novella:

> The text of this chapter is ... a highly artistic composition from the

---

has to assume an original reading "Judah" for "Reuben" —, 38, n. 136 — where
"Israel" in 48:2b is considered an addition.

[111] Even on the contrary: Gen. 48:15–16 has to be considered an expansion, while
in his view there is a gap between vv. 7 and 8, and v. 2b is a later addition; see
Noth, *Überlieferungsgeschichte des Pentateuch*, 38, n. 136.

[112] Noth, *Überlieferungsgeschichte des Pentateuch*, 227, n. 564.

[113] G. von Rad, "Josephsgeschichte und ältere Chokma", in: *Congress Volume:
Copenhagen 1953* (SVT, 1), Leiden 1953, 120–7, 120 (= idem, *GSAT*, 272–80,
272); idem, *Die Josephsgeschichte* (BSt, 8), Neukirchen-Vluyn 1954 (= idem,
Gottes Wirken in Israel, Neukirchen-Vluyn 1974, 22–41); idem, *Erste Buch Mose*,
283–4; 356–62. On the dependency of von Rad on Gunkel in general, cf. Houtman,
Der Pentateuch, 188–95, esp. 188.

[114] Gunkel, "Komposition der Joseph-Geschichten", 66–8.

[115] G. von Rad, "Josephsgeschichte und ältere Chokma", in: *Congress Volume:
Copenhagen 1953* (SVT, 1), Leiden 1953, 120–7, 120 (= idem, *GSAT*, 272–80,
272); idem, *Erste Buch Mose*, 283, 356.

[116] Von Rad, *Erste Buch Mose*, 284.

documents J and E. .... The redactor has combined them in such a way, that he inserted in the Jahwistic Joseph Story substantial parts from the Elohistic parallel version and created an even richer narrative. In any case, the benefit of this combination of documents is considerably greater than its disadvantage.[117]

This is also stressed by the remark in his article on the Joseph Story and ancient wisdom that "the Joseph Story is a novel through and through".[118] But, as R.N. Whybray puts it,[119] in this article von Rad "does not deal with problems of source criticism, and the reader is likely to receive the impression that he is here speaking of a single writer of genius who, in an age of exceptional cultural achievement created an entirely original novel...." Von Rad finds in it a consistently high level of literary skill, not confined to purely literary traits; the Joseph Story exhibits from beginning to end one distinct view. "In short it is an outstanding example of wisdom literature and a product of that cultural enlightenment, which was characteristic of court circles in Israel in the reign of Solomon and which was due to foreign, especially Egyptian, influence."[120] According to von Rad, J and E had both contained the characteristics of wisdom literature which is typical for the period of the "enlightenment", which made both versions interchangeable.[121]

According to von Rad the Joseph Story was composed from the three documents J, E and P; and in this respect he does not differ from other scholars.[122] The text on which J and E based their stories is however difficult to reconstruct, although the form found in J and E is probably not the original one.[123] In its present form the story is a novella in which the tribal historical aspects have disappeared, the brothers all became real persons in whom the tribes are no longer conceivable: it would otherwise be incomprehensible why only Reuben

---

[117]Von Rad, *Erste Buch Mose*, 284: "Der Text dieser Kapitel ist ... eine kunstvolle Komposition aus den Darstellungen der Quellen J und E. ... Der Redaktor hat sie nun derart miteinander verbunden, daß er in die jahwistische Josephsgeschichte umfangreiche Teile der elohistischen Parallelfassung eingelegt und so eine noch reichere Erzählung geschaffen hat. Jedenfalls ist der Gewinn dieser Quellenmischung ein unvergleichlich größerer als ihr Nachteil." Cf. also his *Die Josephsgeschichte*, 5 (= *Gottes Wirken*, 22). For Gunkel's description of the origin of the novella, cf. p. 373, with esp. n. 41 above.

[118]Von Rad, "Josephsgeschichte und Chokma", 120 (*GSAT*, 272).

[119]Whybray, "The Joseph Story", 524.

[120]Whybray, "The Joseph Story", 523–4.

[121]Cf. also Whybray, "The Joseph Story", 527, n. 1.

[122]Whybray, "The Joseph Story", 524, 527.

[123]Von Rad, *Erste Buch Mose*, 356.

and Judah are the spokesmen in this narrative.[124]

The only aspect with a possible historical significance is that the theme comes from central Palestine and somehow reflects the prominency of Joseph over his brothers.[125] This tribal historical aspect occurs definitely in Genesis 48, because the position of Ephraim and Manasseh, described in this chapter, clearly reflects the interrelationship of these two tribes.[126] Therefore, this chapter certainly could not have belonged to the original Joseph Story, although J and E did found it already a part of the Joseph novella.[127] Von Rad's description of the layers in this episode is by and large the same as Gunkel's, although some differences in detail do appear.[128]

5.11 R.N. Whybray

Von Rad's thesis that the Joseph Story is the product of wisdom circles at the Davidic-Solomonic court, and his assumption on the other hand that the story in its present form is composed from the documents J and E, is criticized by Whybray.[129] In his article on the Joseph Story he clearly appreciates von Rad's thesis concerning the wisdom origin,[130] but thinks this contradicts the source-criticism of the narrative. In his view there are two main objections:

1. The fact that we have to view this literary masterpiece as a conflation of two separate earlier novels is highly dubious. The characteristics von Rad ascribes to the Joseph Story (delicacy and subtlety; careful construction) could be found in a work of one single author, but not in a conflated document. "The removal by a third person of sections of one such work and their

---

[124] Von Rad, *Erste Buch Mose*, 357.

[125] Von Rad, *Erste Buch Mose*, 357.

[126] Von Rad, *Erste Buch Mose*, 339.

[127] Von Rad, *Erste Buch Mose*, 344; cf. also his remark on p. 357: "Die Erzählung 1.Mose 48 war ... ein selbständiger Erzählungsstoff; er fällt durch die Direktheit seines Hinweises auf Stammesgeschichtliches aus dem Tenor der Josephsgeschichte heraus."

[128] Von Rad, *Erste Buch Mose*, 339.

[129] Whybray, "The Joseph Story", 522–8; cf. also R.N. Whybray, *The Making of the Pentateuch: A Methodological Study* (JSOTS, 53), Sheffield 1987, 54–5.

[130] Whybray, "The Joseph Story", 528. Later on Whybray was to question the evidence for dating the wisdom literature in the period of David and Solomon; see R.N. Whybray, "Wisdom Literature in the Reigns of David and Solomon", in: T. Ishida (ed.), *Studies in the Period of David and Solomon and Other Essays*, Winona Lake (IN) 1982, 13–26; cf. also R.P. Gordon, "A House Divided: Wisdom in Old Testament Narrative Traditions", in: J. Day *et al.* (eds.), *Wisdom in Ancient Israel: Essays in Honour of J.A. Emerton*, Cambridge 1995, 95–105; A. Lemaire, "Wisdom in Solomonic Historiography", *ibid.*, 106–18.

replacement with excerpts from another by a different author, however similar the two might be, could only have the effect of spoiling both."[131] So it has to be a complete literary unity, both in conception and execution; or it is a conflation and von Rad's estimate is illusory.[132]

2. Von Rad's appraisal of the Joseph Story as a product of wisdom literature from the Solomonic age of enlightenment is also questionable. When both versions J and E contain these elements, they have to go back to a common source[133] which already itself possessed these characteristics.[134] Because the *Jahwist* is a contemporary of the author of the Succession Narrative, and member of the Judean court during Solomon's reign or somewhat later, that common source must be written — if not rewritten in the same generation by the Jahwist — a generation earlier. However, the story does not reflect an earlier period,[135] but clearly the age of the "enlightenment" of the early monarchy. Whybray's conclusion is: "in other words, there was not enough time for the earlier stages of its composition to have taken place".[136]

Whybray admits that these objections could be refuted if it is just assumed that the E-version was essentially different in character from the one found in J:

> It would then be possible to suppose that the J version was an original composition, hardly if at all dependent on any earlier source, while E was based on a different, pre-Solomonic tradition about Joseph which J had not used; and that the redactor combined these two very different versions of the history of Joseph.[137]

However, because J and E are essentially identical and interchangeable in von Rad's view, his theory on the literary character is inconsistent with his view on its composition.[138] Whybray is convinced by von

---

[131]Whybray, "The Joseph Story", 525.

[132]Whybray, "The Joseph Story", 525.

[133]This is necessary because E is not a simple reworking of J but a complete independent parallel version; cf. von Rad, *Formgeschichtliche Problem*, 16 (*GSAT*, 26–7); Noth, *Überlieferungsgeschichte des Pentateuch*, 40–1.

[134]Whybray, "The Joseph Story", 526.

[135]Cf. the fact that von Rad considers the tribal historical aspect completely absent within the Joseph Story (cf. p. 385 above).

[136]Whybray, "The Joseph Story", 526.

[137]Whybray, "The Joseph Story", 527.

[138]Whybray, "The Joseph Story", 527.

Rad's appreciation of the literary quality of the Joseph Story and
the role of the early monarchy involved, and therefore considers the
documentary hypothesis in need of re-examination, at least for this
part of Genesis. In his view these chapters demonstrate clearly the
need for a solution concerning its origin, but show on the other hand
also the shortcomings of the classical documentary hypothesis: "It
may be that we shall end by concluding with Volz and Rudolph that,
in these chapters at least, the idea of 'Der Elohist als Erzähler' is
indeed 'ein Irrweg der Pentateuchkritik'."[139]

5.12 H. Donner

Also H. Donner criticizes the tension between unity and diversity in
von Rad's work on the Joseph Story:[140]

> Everything known of the character and the presentation of the old
> Pentateuchal documents is a summons to draw a conclusion from the
> form-critical definition by G. von Rad and a new interpretation which
> he himself has not drawn. One cannot have it both ways: the Joseph
> Story as a novella *and* as a part of the Pentateuchal documents J
> and E. Either it is a cycle of sagas along the lines of the Abraham
> traditions, or even better those of Jacob, which is conceivable and to
> be expected in a Jahwistic and Elohistic version. Or it is actually a
> novella in G. von Rad's sense, in which case it belongs neither to J nor
> to E, and should be considered a literary entity in its own right.[141]

Donner is rather critical about the attempts to discern the different
documents within the Joseph Story, because of the fact that from

---

[139] Whybray, "The Joseph Story", 528. The re-examination of the documentary
hypothesis led him to regard the origin of the books of Genesis to Numbers as
the creation of one single author, using material of earlier but also quite recent
date (in some respects a "new version of the Fragment Hypothesis"), in order to
create a kind of "prologue" to the Deuteronomistic History; cf. Whybray, *Making
of the Pentateuch*, 221–42 (quote from p. 222).

[140] Donner, *Literarische Gestalt der Josephsgeschichte*, 12–4.

[141] Donner, *Literarische Gestalt der Josephsgeschichte*, 14: "Alles, was über den
Charakter und die Darstellungsweise der alten Pentateuchquellen bekannt ist,
fordert dazu heraus, aus G. v. Rads formgeschichtlicher Bestimmung und Neuin-
terpretation eine Konsequenz zu ziehen, die er selber nicht gezogen hat. Man kann
nicht beides haben: die Josephsgeschichte als Novelle *und* als Bestandteil der Pentateuchquellen J und E. Entweder ist sie doch ein Sagenkranz nach der Art der
Abraham-, mehr noch der Jakobüberlieferungen, dann ist sie in einer jahwistischen und elohistischen Fassung denkbar und zu erwarten. Oder sie ist in der Tat
eine Novelle im Sinne G. v. Rads, dann gehört sie weder zu J noch zu E, sondern
ist als eine literarische Größe für sich anzusehen."

all criteria for the literary criticism[142] only the criterion of formal
literary indications could be used (which on its own is not sufficient
to justify the source-analysis), supplemented in single cases with the
very uncertain criterion of differing conceptions.[143] The criterion of
idiom is dismissed on the basis of an evaluation of several examples,
which demonstrates that this criterion is insecure and quite subjective; no further external criteria are used, while the key-chapter is
only Genesis 37.[144] Furthermore, the results of the source-analysis
do not correspond with the insight on the Jehovistic editor based on
the whole Pentateuch: this editor used J as his primary document
("Grundschrift") and inserted E only complementary. In the Joseph
Story he has frequently worked in a different way, connecting the
complete versions of J and E into totally new unities (like in Gen. 37),
or he inserted fragments of J into the version of E (Gen. 41–42).[145]
Finally, the connection with the documentary layers before and after
the Joseph Story are unconvincing: the final Yahwistic part before
Gen. 37 is Gen. 35:21–22, where Reuben sleeps with the concubine of
his father, Israel. This scene ends very abruptly, without any transition to a following scene; whereas Reuben in the Joseph Story is
ascribed to E.[146] After an exemplifying discussion of the analysis of
Gen. 45 in which he argues that tensions, doublets, etc. could all be
considered literary features utilized by the narrator, he concludes:

> The transmitted text of the Joseph Story cannot be divided with cer-
> tainty between the narrative complexes J and E with the required reli-
> ability, which is otherwise also accessible in the Pentateuch. The criteria
> of the Pentateuchal source-criticism fail at Gen. 37–50.[147]

This negative result takes us back to the thesis of the character of the
Joseph Story as a novella, by von Rad, although not without difficulties of its own. If this story is an independent literary entity, having
originated at the Solomonic court, the question arises who inserted

---

[142]Donner, *Literarische Gestalt der Josephsgeschichte*, 15: Divine names; idiomatic usage; theological and political concepts; formal literary indications (doublets, tensions, seams); connection with different documentary layers before and
following; careful consideration of the procedure of the Pentateuchal editors.

[143]Donner, *Literarische Gestalt der Josephsgeschichte*, 16.

[144]Donner, *Literarische Gestalt der Josephsgeschichte*, 17–9.

[145]Donner, *Literarische Gestalt der Josephsgeschichte*, 19.

[146]Donner, *Literarische Gestalt der Josephsgeschichte*, 20.

[147]Donner, *Literarische Gestalt der Josephsgeschichte*, 24: "Der überlieferte
Textbestand der Josephsgeschichte kann nicht mit der nötigen, anderwärts im
Pentateuch auch erreichbaren Sicherheit auf die Erzählwerke des Jahwisten und
des Elohisten verteilt werden. Die Kriterien der Pentateuchquellenscheidung ver-
sagen an Gen. 37–50."

the present version of the story here. If the Yahwist did not do it —
or he was narrator and editor both — it must have been inserted by
the Jehovistic editor (R^{JE}) in the pre-Exilic period. But J and E both
need to account for the transition of Jacob and his sons from Canaan
to Egypt, in order to link the patriarchal narratives with the Exodus.
It has to be assumed therefore that R^{JE} replaced the Jahwistic and
Elohistic versions of this transition from Canaan to Egypt by the
Joseph Story, convinced that the Joseph novella told the very same,
but "more elaborated, accurate, impressive".[148] It is even possible
that J only contained a rather poor note on the transition, and R^{JE}
at this time did not add any parts of E in his primary document (J),
but inserted the Joseph Story.

Donner is convinced that the fundamentals of this thesis could
be proven, because within the present Joseph Story there are four
parts that do not easily fit in because they correspond clearly with
the patriarchal narratives: Gen. 41:50–52; 46:1aβ–5a; 48; 50:23–25. In
these four parts the arguments of literary criticism make sense, which
they do not in the other parts of the Joseph Story.[149]

In his view Genesis 48 is clearly a tribal historical aetiology, which
makes it distinct from the Joseph Story: it describes the elevation of
two tribes of the "house of Joseph" to real "son-tribes" (*Sohnesstäm-
men*), making both sons function as eponyms for their tribes. Several
times the scene refers to events outside the Joseph Story, whereas
it also contains an isolated aetiological note on Shechem. Further, it
may be added that Genesis 48–49 interrupts the account of Jacob's
death. According to Donner, the final illness of the patriarch starts
in 47:29 and in 47:31 it is said, " 'then Israel bowed himself upon the
head of the bed', that is he began to die".[150] The report of his death is
found in 49:33, which together with the preceding verses (Gen. 49:29–
33) belongs to P, except for the phrase "he drew up his feet into the
bed", which immediately follows 47:31.[151] Genesis 48 is distinct from
chapter 49 because in the former the criteria of source-analysis can be
applied to the text, mainly as Gunkel has done: verses 3–6 are clearly
P and the remaining verses could be divided over J and E, "and in
fact with solid evidence".[152]

According to Donner one correction of Gunkel's analysis might be

---

[148] Donner, *Literarische Gestalt der Josephsgeschichte*, 25–6.

[149] Donner, *Literarische Gestalt der Josephsgeschichte*, 26–7.

[150] Donner, *Literarische Gestalt der Josephsgeschichte*, 31.

[151] Donner, *Literarische Gestalt der Josephsgeschichte*, 31.

[152] Donner, *Literarische Gestalt der Josephsgeschichte*, 31: "... und zwar mit
schöner Evidenz."

appropriate. Although J and E contain blessings (J: vv. 13–14, 17–19; E: 15–16, 20), these are missing in P. Since P is fond of blessings this seems strange, especially considering that E apparently contains two blessings. Sound arguments to assign these verses to E are difficult to find; on the other hand the sole tripartite blessing is found in Num. 6:24–26 (P), so it might be considered that verses 15–16 belong to P and should follow directly after verses 3–6.[153] Several arguments are in favour of this proposal: the relation of לִפְנֵי הִתְהַלֵּךְ in verse 15 with Gen. 17:1 (P; although 24:40 is J); the mostly Exilic and post-Exilic hymnic predicates of God (גֹּאֵל,[154] רֹעֶה); finally the connection between עַל שֵׁם אֲחֵיהֶם יִקָּרְאוּ בְּנַחֲלָתָם in verse 6 and וַיִּקָּרֵא בָהֶם שְׁמִי in verse 16 are not to be ignored.[155] Genesis 48 is later added by R[JE] and not by R[P], this might also be concluded from the short note in Gen. 48:2b: "then Israel summoned his strength, and sat up in bed", which refers back to 47:31 and forward to 49:33, both parts of the Joseph Story on Jacob's death. This note employs the idiom of J, which is usually the basic document of the Jehovistic work.[156]

The completion of the Deathbed Episode according to the Joseph Story is found solely in the note in Gen. 49:33*, followed by the description of the mourning for his death in Gen. 50:1ff. The remaining verses, 49:29–33 belong to P. So the editor (R[P]) removed the account of Jacob's death from the original Joseph Story to replace it by the priestly version.[157] Finally, for several problematic passages Donner has, like Rudolph, to consider the existence of a later editor who expanded or glossed the text in the cases involved, as in the episode with the Ishmaelites and Midianites (Gen. 37:25–28).[158]

Summarizing, according to Donner we have to assume the existence of an independent Joseph Story, which had no links with the patriarchal narratives. This version — instead of the usual E — was added by R[JE] to J, while only at four places do we find the J and E version together because these parts were essential for the Pentateuchal theme. Genesis 48 is such an essential episode, which not only preserved J and E, but also a large segment of P. Finally, no single version is preserved completely: in the Deathbed Episode 49:33* we find the remnants of the original Joseph Story, whereas the J- and

---

[153]Donner, *Literarische Gestalt der Josephsgeschichte*, 32–3. In this case אֶת־יוֹסֵף in v. 15 has to be read according to LXX: αὐτούς = אוֹתָם (cf. *loc.cit.*, nn. 56–7).

[154]Donner, *Literarische Gestalt der Josephsgeschichte*, 33, n. 58: "Die dunkle Stelle Gen. 49,24 bleibt außer Betracht."

[155]Donner, *Literarische Gestalt der Josephsgeschichte*, 33–4.

[156]Donner, *Literarische Gestalt der Josephsgeschichte*, 34.

[157]Donner, *Literarische Gestalt der Josephsgeschichte*, 34–5, with n. 61.

[158]Donner, *Literarische Gestalt der Josephsgeschichte*, 44–5.

E-versions of the patriarch's death are completely lacking, as is the beginning of the Deathbed scene from P. These missing parts are left out for the sake of a better, clearer text found in the other versions; although in certain cases the editor not only inserted two or three versions but also added his own editorial remarks (Gen. 48:2b).

5.13 G.W. Coats; C. Westermann

The results of the work of Gunkel, Greßmann, Noth and von Rad are found with some minor revisions in the studies of G.W. Coats[159] and C. Westermann.[160] According to Coats, Genesis 39–41 probably formed the kernel of an originally independent "political legend", which could be connected with wisdom circles found at the Solomonic court.[161] The Joseph Story as a whole (Genesis 37 and 39–47:27a) is a novella, which has as a theme a familial strife, comparable to the themes of the Abraham and Jacob sagas.[162] It is difficult to define the *Sitz im Leben* of this complete story: wisdom elements do appear, but also theological as well as political ones, and so the cultural atmosphere is wide ranging.[163] Genesis 38 and 47:28–50:14 are kind of "parasites" in the Joseph Story, that "function to incorporate the Joseph Story into the larger narration".[164] In his view repetition might be explained as a narrative technique, whereas doublets like that of the Midianites and Ishmaelites could be explained as glosses. The complete story seems to be a unit, perhaps composed, but at least taken up by the Yahwist to bridge the gap between Canaan and Egypt.[165]

Westermann, who was initially inclined to regard the Joseph Story as derived from J and E,[166] later in his commentary prefers a com-

---

[159]G.W. Coats, "The Joseph Story and Ancient Wisdom: A Reappraisal", *CBQ* 35 (1973) 285–97; idem, "Redactional Unity of Genesis 37–50", *JBL* 93 (1974) 15–21; idem, *From Canaan to Egypt: Structural and Theological Context for the Joseph Story* (CBQ MS, 4), Washington (DC) 1976; idem, *Genesis, With an Introduction to Narrative Literature* (FOTL, vol. I), Grand Rapids (MI) 1983, 259–315; idem, "Joseph, Son of Jacob", *ABD*, vol. 3, 976–81.

[160]Westermann, *Genesis 37–50*, 8–12, 16.

[161]Coats, "Joseph Story and Ancient Wisdom", 288–92; idem, "Joseph, Son of Jacob", 977. He even suggests the possibility of a pre-Solomonic, Egyptian origin, because the kernel does not contain any specific Israelite features.

[162]Coats, "Joseph, Son of Jacob", 977.

[163]Coats, *From Canaan to Egypt*, 86–9.

[164]Coats, "Redactional Unity of Genesis 37–50", 15; cf. also his *From Canaan to Egypt*, 51, 72. Gen. 46:1b–4 also is secondary, cf. *op.cit.*, 49, 67.

[165]Coats, *From Canaan to Egypt*, 79; idem, "Joseph, Son of Jacob", 979, 981.

[166]C. Westermann, "Die Joseph-Erzählung (1.Buch Mose)", *CPH* 5 (1966) 11–118, 11–25.

bination of a literary-critical and traditio-historical approach. In his view an original Joseph Story is preserved in parts of Genesis 37 and 46–50, and also in 39–45; whereas the conclusion of the Jacob Story is preserved in Genesis 37 and 46–50.[167] This could also be concluded from the occurence of P in Genesis 37–50: P only occurs in Genesis 37 and 46–50, and is here similarly fitted in as in Genesis 12–36. All P-references concern Jacob and thus P confirms that Genesis 46–50, without the texts of the Joseph Story, belongs to the Jacob Story.[168] Contrary to Noth, who considers the Joseph Story the explanatory story describing how Jacob came to Egypt, Westermann assumes that the Joseph Story presupposes the Jacob Story.[169] The two different layers found in Genesis 37 might be explained by the combination of the Jacob and Joseph Story, and not by the dependence on two different documents. Finally, the later inserted texts, Genesis 38 and 49, are in this way no longer additions to the Joseph Story, but both belong to the end of the Jacob Story.[170] The Joseph Story is clearly a unity, found by the Yahwist — he is certainly not the author — and has been fitted into the Jacob Story by intertwining it into chapters 37 and 46–7.[171]

His analysis of the text shows that the intertwining of Jacob and Joseph Story also took place in the Deathbed Episode,[172] where not only the original ending of both stories is found, but also a mass of editorial expansions. The conclusion to the Jacob Story is formed by the classical P layer: 48:3–6, 49:1a, 28b, 29–33; 50:12–13.[173] The final part of the (original) Joseph Story is formed by Gen. 47:29–31; 48:1–2, 8–12; 49:29*–33* (apparently lost by doubling because the present version belongs to P); 50:1–11, 14–21.[174] Not every tension in

---

[167]Westermann, *Genesis 37–50*, 8; he refers especially to Gen. 46:1–7 as a strong indication that a different tradition is taken up here, because this text differs clearly from the previous sections, similar to Genesis 48.

[168]Westermann, *Genesis 37–50*, 8–9.

[169]Westermann, *Genesis 37–50*, 9–10.

[170]Westermann, *Genesis 37–50*, 9.

[171]Westermann, *Genesis 37–50*, 16. On the composite character of Genesis 37, cf. *op.cit.*, 24, 34–5, where he argues that vv. 1–2 belong to P, whereas the remaining part belongs to the Joseph Story, although this part clearly shows a composite character and especially in verses 18–30. In this episode the references to Reuben and Judah are clearly doublets (vv. 25b–27, 28b are doublets, cf. *op.cit.*, 33–4), which according to Westermann emphasizes the fact that the Joseph Story as a whole deals with the questions of supremacy and authority between family and state (*op.cit.*, 34–5).

[172]Cf. Westerman, *Genesis 37–50*, 239–42.

[173]Westerman, *Genesis 37–50*, 240.

[174]Westerman, *Genesis 37–50*, 239–40.

the text is removed by his analysis,[175] because he sometimes explains problematical passages (like 48:15–16 between verses 13–14 and 17–20) as additions by the editor, closely connected with elements from the Patriarchal narratives.[176] In this way the apparent relations or similarities with the Patriarchal narratives are explained, without the need of a continuing document J or E; and thus, following the current trend, he considers the Joseph Story an independent unit.

5.14 Ad Fontes! Back from the Unity to the "Sources"

Although von Rad's work created a strong emphasis on the unity of the Joseph Story in scholarly literature,[177] his own work, as well as the work of the others just mentioned, testifies to the composite character of the text of the Joseph Story. This dilemma is clearly demonstrated by H.J. Boecker, who writes:

> H. Donner's alternative "One cannot have it both ways: the Joseph Story as a novella *and* as part of the Pentateuchal documents J and E" is certainly impressive and seems logically irrefutable, but finally it does no justice to the literary data. There we have indeed both: on the one hand, and foremost, the intellectual and stylistic unity of the narrative, for which the generic term "novella" might be the most appropriate description; and on the other hand, a series of undeniable tensions within the narrative.[178]

Undoubtedly, these "undeniable tensions" stimulated the beginning of a renewed interest in the literary composition of the text, which

---

[175]Cf. the transition from 49:29–31 to 48:1–2a/b, which is usually considered to be borderline between J and E.

[176]Westermann, *Genesis 37–50*, 241–2.

[177]In addition to works already cited, the following should be referred to: E. Otto, "Die 'synthetische Lebensauffassung' in der frühköniglichen Novellistik Israels", *ZThK* 74 (1977) 371–400; I. Willi-Plein, "Historiographische Aspekte der Josefsgeschichte", *Henoch* 1 (1979) 305–31; J.A. Soggin, "Notes on the Joseph Story", in: A.G. Auld (ed.), *Understanding Poets and Prophets: Essays ... G.W. Anderson* (JSOTS, 152), Sheffield 1993, 336–49.

[178]H.J. Boecker, "Überlegungen zur Josephsgeschichte", in: J. Hausmann, H.-J. Zobel (Hrsg.), *Alttestamentlicher Glaube und biblische Theologie: Fs H.D. Preuß*, Stuttgart 1992, 35–45: "H. Donners Alternative 'Man kann nicht beides haben: die Josephsgeschichte als Novelle *und* als Bestandteil der Pentateuchquellen J und E' ist zwar beeindruckend und scheint logisch unanfechtbar zu sein, wird aber letztlich eben doch nicht dem literarischen Befund gerecht. Da haben wir nämlich beides: auf der einen Seite und vor allem die gedankliche und stilistische Geschlossenheit der Erzählung, wofür der Gattungsbegriff Novelle wohl doch der angemessenste ist, auf der anderen Seite aber eben auch eine Reihe von unübersehbaren Spannungen innerhalb der Erzählung".

was marked by the publication of D.B. Redford's monograph on the Joseph Story,[179] although he was preceded in 1965 by L. Ruppert.[180] Since the appearance of Redford's study, however, six other monographs have been published, all studying the genesis of the Joseph Story,[181] and in the same period many articles appeared on the same topic.[182] Because the literary analysis of the Joseph Story by L. Ruppert is to a large extend comparable with that of Gunkel,[183] we will start the review of recent literary criticism of the Joseph Story with the study of Redford.

5.15 D.B. Redford; W. Dietrich; N. Kebekus

D.B. Redford suggests an approach which differed largely from the classical Documentary Hypothesis concerning the Joseph Story.[184] He rejects in principle the common Pentateuchal Documentary Hypo-

---

[179]D.B. Redford, *A Study of the Biblical Story of Joseph (Genesis 37–50)* (SVT, 20), Leiden 1970.

[180]L. Ruppert, *Die Josephserzählung der Genesis: Ein Beitrag zur Theologie der Pentateuchquellen* (StANT, 11), München 1965; L. Ruppert, "Die Aporie der gegenwärtigen Pentateuchdiskussion und die Josepherzählung der Genesis", *BZ* 29 (1985) 31–48, 36, considers Redford the turning point with respect to previous research; similarly H.-C. Schmitt, *Die nichtpriesterliche Josephsgeschichte: Ein Beitrag zur neuesten Pentateuchkritik* (BZAW, 154), Berlin 1980, 13–5.

[181]H. Seebaß, *Geschichtliche Zeit und theonome Tradition in der Joseph-Erzählung*, Gütersloh 1978; Schmitt, *Die nichtpriesterliche Josephsgeschichte* (previous footnote); L. Schmidt, *Literarische Studien zur Josephsgeschichte* (BZAW, 167), Berlin 1986; W. Dietrich, *Die Josepherzählung als Novelle und Geschichtsschreibung: Zugleich ein Beitrag zur Pentateuchfrage* (BThSt, 14), Neukirchen-Vluyn 1989; N. Kebekus, *Die Joseferzählung: Literarkritische und redaktionsgeschichtliche Untersuchungen zu Genesis 37–50*, Münster 1990; H. Schweizer, *Die Josefsgeschichte: Konstituierung des Textes*, Tl. I–II (TTHLLI, Bd. 4), Tübingen 1991 (cf. also his, *Joseph: Urfassung der alttestamentlichen Erzählung (Genesis 37–50)*, Tübingen 1993).

[182]K.R. Melchin, "Literary Sources in the Joseph Story", *ScEs* 31 (1979) 93–101; Ruppert, "Die Aporie der gegenwärtigen Pentateuchdiskussion", 31–48; H.-C. Schmitt, "Die Hintergründe der 'neuesten Pentateuchkritik' und der literarische Befund der Josephsgeschichte Gen 37-50", *ZAW* 97 (1985) 161–79; H. Seebaß, "The Joseph Story, Genesis 48 and the Canonical Process", *JSOT* 35 (1986) 29–43; J. Scharbert, "Josef als Sklave", *BN* 37 (1987) 104–28; L. Ruppert, "Zur neueren Diskussion um die Josephsgeschichte der Genesis", *BZ* 33 (1989) 92–5; Boecker, "Überlegungen zur Josephsgeschichte".

[183]Cf. Ruppert, "Zur Diskussion um die Josefsgeschichte", 93. In his more recent articles on the Joseph Story, Ruppert takes into account the possibility of later additions by a redactor alongside the existence of different documents within the narrative; cf. *art.cit.*, 95–7; and already his, "Die Aporie der gegenwärtigen Pentateuchdiskussion", 38–48, esp. 46.

[184]Redford, *Biblical Story of Joseph*, 106–86, and esp. 178–86; cf. also D.B. Redford, *Egypt, Canaan, and Israel in Ancient Times*, Princeton (NJ) 1992, 422–9.

thesis as his starting-point, preferring instead to start with an "empirical examination". Such an examination has to concern itself with discrepancies of an objective nature, first of all contradictions, but also other detracting phenomena (similar to the Documentary Hypothesis) within onomasticon, plot details, and style.[185]

According to Redford the Joseph Story is a "Märchen-Novelle",[186] which had a basic form, and was several times expanded and placed in its present position by the editor of Genesis. To discern the basic narrative he uses the same criteria as classical Pentateuchal criticism. The most important of these is the use of the names of the father Jacob and Israel, and those of the good brothers Reuben and Judah,[187] resulting in the usual Jacob-Reuben- and Israel-Judah-combinations. He does not ground these layers in the two different documents J and E, but considers the Israel-Judah-layer a later expansion of the Jacob-Reuben-layer.[188] The expansions by the Genesis-editor (very close to P, or even identical[189]) are mainly found in passages which show clear connections with other texts outside the Joseph Story, such as Gen. 37:1-2; 38; 46:1-4, 5-7, 8-27; 48; 49; 50:7-14, 22-26.[190] The original Joseph Story included large parts of 37, 40-45, and also 47:12. The Judah-expansion contains parts, usually considered as doublets and thus as parts of another document, and furthermore those parts which expand the Story at the end including the death and burial of the patriarch (Israel) (Gen. 47:29-31; 50:1-6).[191]

An important departure from previous research is Redford's dating of the story and its expansions. He studied the vocabulary of the Joseph Story and compared it with "late Hebrew"[192] and Aramaic,

---

[185]Redford, *Biblical Story of Joseph*, 107.

[186]Redford, *Biblical Story of Joseph*, 66-8.

[187]Redford, *Biblical Story of Joseph*, 131-5. He discussed the use of names in the context of "onomasticon", where he discussed the use of Divine names as criterion, and also the name of the first master of Joseph.

[188]Westermann, *Genesis 12-50*, 64, comments: "Bei *Redford* kommen die drei Schichten der Ruben-Version, der Juda-Erweiterung und der des Genesis-Herausgebers den klassischen drei Quellen so nahe (wie er es auch selber sieht [cf. Redford, *Biblical Story of Joseph*, 252-3; RdH]), daß man eher von einer traditionsgeschichtlichen Korrektur der Quellentheorie sprechen könnte." And apart from the dating of the basic narrative and its additions "kann man die drei langen Kapitel, in denen er die Quellenanalyse behandelt und abweist, in wesentlichen Punkten als eine Bestätigung der Kriterien für die Quellenscheidung ansehen, obwohl er zu anderen Schlüssen kommt".

[189]Redford, *Biblical Story of Joseph*, 23, with n. 1; 253.

[190]Redford, *Biblical Story of Joseph*, 3-27, 182-6.

[191]Cf. Redford, *Biblical Story of Joseph*, 182-6.

[192]In order to define what is "late", he lists as "late books" those written "within

he reaches the tentative conclusion that "the cumulative weight of the examples cited ... suggests rather strongly that a close approximation exists between the idiom of the Joseph Story and the Hebrew usage current during and after the Exile."[193] By studying the Egyptian colouring of the Joseph Story[194] he reaches the conclusion that the probable genuine Egyptian elements in the Joseph Story cannot be dated before the seventh century BCE. In his view the comparison of the Joseph Story with Biblical and extra-Biblical data favours a date for its composition between the mid-seventh and mid-fifth century,[195] and the expansions have to be dated even later.

Redford's literary analysis was accepted by W. Dietrich in his booklet on the Joseph Story,[196] although his dating of the several layers is unacceptable to Dietrich. In Dietrich's view the original Reuben-layer has to be dated in the period shortly after the partition of the United Kingdom (926 BCE), because it reflects many features of that period.[197] In the same manner the later adaptation of the novella, with the Judah-expansion, could be dated much earlier: shortly after the collapse of the Northern Kingdom the Joseph Story appeared at the court of the Southern Kingdom, where scribes ("Hezekiah's men", Prov. 25:1?) adapted the Joseph Story, with many reminiscences of the Davidic history, to the political situation of that time.[198]

A similar analysis can be found in the work of N. Kebekus, in whose view the present Joseph Story consists of an original Joseph Story, which was expanded by two additional redactional layers.[199] The original form of the story was a Reuben-account (preserved in Gen. 37:5–45:8*)[200] which was first expanded by the so-called "Reuben

---

approximately one-half century of the Exile, during the Exile, or in post-Exilic times. Such a definition covers the following books and parts of books in the O.T.: Leviticus, Deuteronomy, those portions of the Pentateuch indisputably assigned to P, the Deuteronomistic framework of the Historical Books, Ruth, Chronicles, Ezra, Nehemiah, Esther, Job, Psalms, Proverbs, Jeremiah, Lamentations, Ezekiel, Daniel, Jonah, Nahum, Habakkuk, Zephaniah, Haggai, Zechariah, Malachi"; Redford, *Biblical Story of Joseph*, 54. He admits that the list he offers is not new, although much enlarged compared with the works of F. Giesebrecht and A. Kuenen in the nineteenth century (*op.cit.*, 54–5, with n. 6).

[193] Redford, *Biblical Story of Joseph*, 65.

[194] Redford, *Biblical Story of Joseph*, 187–243.

[195] Redford, *Biblical Story of Joseph*, 252–3.

[196] Dietrich, *Die Josephserzählung* (p. 394, n. 181 above), 67, n. 200.

[197] Dietrich, *Die Josephserzählung*, 59–66, esp. 64.

[198] Dietrich, *Die Josephserzählung*, 71–8, esp. 76.

[199] N. Kebekus, *Die Joseferzählung: Literarkritische und redaktionsgeschichtliche Untersuchungen zu Genesis 37–50*, Münster 1990; for a summary of the different layers in Gen. 37–50, see pp. 344–5.

[200] Kebekus, *Die Joseferzählung*, 233–57.

Expansion", which might be connected with the work of R^{JE} who inserted the expansion into the Jacob Story (the story was expanded to Gen. 37:3–50:26*).[201] A final expansion is the work of the redactor of the Pentateuch (R^{P}), who inserted the Judah-layer, and who is also responsible for the insertion of several independent traditions, like Gen. 38*, 39*, 49:1b–28b* and further the insertion of the Priestly layer within the Story.[202] Kebekus assumes a Judah-expansion instead of an independent Judah-document because the Judah-layer presupposes the Reuben-tradition, and because of the fact that without the assumption of the loss of text no continuous parallel narrative tradition can be reconstructed.[203] The basic story has to be dated in the eighth century, in the period of Hezekiah, where it was shaped in order to sketch the ideal government of the officials, and at the same time to show how necessary they were.[204] The final expansion with its mainly theological interest took place in the post-Exilic era, where the reminiscences of the ideal Davidic king reflect the eschatological hope for the coming of the Messiah.[205]

With regard to Genesis 48 we only have to reckon with two layers within the Deathbed Episode. However, Kebekus considers R^{P} as the redactor who also inserted several parts of P into the narrative (*e.g.* Gen. 48:3–6) which in fact brings us back to the three well-known layers, albeit with slightly different names. Gen. 48:3–6 is considered to be part of P, whereas the other layers belong to R^{JE} and R^{P}. However, the transition from 47:31 to 48:1 is not regarded as a shift in layer, as is usual, but apparently a shift between two scenes.[206] His further analysis does not differ considerably from others and reference might be made to the table on page 425 below.

5.16 H. Seebaß

H. Seebaß has, on several occasions, contributed to the debate on the final chapters of Genesis.[207] In his book *Geschichtliche Zeit* he approaches these chapters in a literary critical way, in that he assumes the text to be made up of J, E and P. In addition to these layers

---

[201] Kebekus, *Die Joseferzählung*, 258–90.

[202] Kebekus, *Die Joseferzählung*, 291–335.

[203] Kebekus, *Die Joseferzählung*, 23, n. 82.

[204] Kebekus, *Die Joseferzählung*, 251–3.

[205] Kebekus, *Die Joseferzählung*, 310–35.

[206] Cf. Kebekus, *Die Joseferzählung*, 204–5.

[207] H. Seebaß, *Geschichtliche Zeit und theonome Tradition in der Joseph-Erzählung*, Gütersloh 1978; idem, "Die Stammessprüche Gen. 49,3–27", *ZAW* 96 (1984) 333–50; idem, "The Joseph Story, Genesis 48 and the Canonical Process, *JSOT* 35 (1986) 29–43.

he reckons with a substantial important post-Exilic redaction of the
story, mainly found in Genesis 41* and 47:13–26, and rather fragmentary in Gen. 45:6–7, 8bBC, 9aB, 11aB, 26aB. Here an Egyptian
motive of a seven-year famine was adopted into the narrative and
Joseph was made the second man of Egypt.[208] It is not unlikely that
in order to achieve this goal the later redaction replaced a note of P
on Joseph's rise to power, with a note ascribing a lower position to
him.[209]

However, after removing the assumed later additions, together
with the P-layer, the remainder becomes a well-rounded narrative
with a clear structure, in which the Deathbed Episode in Gen. 47:29–
48:2, 8–22; 49:2–28bA; 50:1–7a, 8–11, 14 is described as the climax of
the Joseph Story.[210] The Deathbed Episode is analysed in an almost
identical fashion as is common, although there are some characteristic
features, such as 48:1–2 is ascribed entirely to E, whereas verse 2b is
generally ascribed to J. Further 49:3–28bA is attributed completely
to J,[211] where Judah has the most important share (49:8–12) surpass-
ing Joseph (49:22–26).[212] In addition he argues that R[JE] rearranged
the text at two places: 48:20aBC was originally situated in J after
47:29–31; and 48:15–16 came in E after verses 21–22.[213]

5.17 H.-C. Schmitt

The theory of redactional expansions of a basic document (Redford) is
modified by H.-C. Schmitt. He developed the theory of gradual expansion of the Joseph Story based to a large extent on the observations of
the classical Documentary Hypothesis. In his analysis he discerns five
layers in total: the original Joseph Story (Judah-Israel-layer),[214] a first
Elohistic redaction (Reuben-Jacob-layer), a late Yahwistic redaction

---

[208]Seebaß, *Geschichtliche Zeit*, 18–63. Cf. also his "The Joseph Story", 35–8.
The Egyptian text with the famine motive is found in *ANET*, 31: "The Tradition
of Seven Lean Years in Egypt".

[209]Seebaß, *Geschichtliche Zeit*, 61–2.

[210]Seebaß, *Geschichtliche Zeit*, 62; idem, "The Joseph Story", 35–8.

[211]Cf. also Seebaß, "Die Stammessprüche", 348–50, where he considers 49:3–7a,
8a, 10–17, 19–27 as the original song in which Joseph had the central position,
but which was found and modified by J reflecting the political situation of his
time.

[212]Seebaß, *Geschichtliche Zeit*, 69–70.

[213]Seebaß, "The Joseph Story", 33–5.

[214]This layer might in certain respects be equated with J; but Schmitt prefers
to use different names for the other layers for fear of being identified with the
classical source-analysis. He therefore uses the names "Judah-Israel-layer" for
J and "Reuben-Jacob-layer" for E; see Schmitt, *Die nichtpriesterliche Josephsgeschichte*, 5, n. 3.

of the "Elohistic History", the Priestly redaction[215] and several loose additions.[216] According to Schmitt it must be questioned whether the chronological order for the 'Reuben' and 'Judah'-layers, suggested by Redford, is correct.[217] The Reuben-layer presupposes the Judah-layer because Reuben is always pictured as the better brother in contrast to Judah.[218] In the Reuben-layer the previous version was reworked in order to provide the narrative with a historical-theological base, and to add an ideal example for the "sons of Israel".[219]

The original narrative, according to Schmitt, was considerably longer than those in the studies of, for example, Redford and Westermann, where parts of the original story are even found in Genesis 47–50. This is due to the fact that the original Joseph Story belongs to the Judah-layer (or J), which preserved parts of practically every episode in the Book of Genesis. With regard to Gen. 47:28–49:33 his conclusions coincide to a large extent with the results obtained by Gunkel.[220] The most important difference between his study and Gunkel's is his view on the different layers. According to Schmitt J has to be considered the basic story, E has added to this story several parts according to his own theology, while a late J-redaction again elaborated on this version. In post-Exilic times the story received its final redaction by P. Another interesting difference with Gunkel's analysis is Schmitt's identification of Gen. 48:17–20aA as belonging to the Judah-layer, whereas Gunkel attributes it to E.[221] Schmitt argues that the time of J, the Davidic-Solomonic era, was the most plausible date for the origin of this part.[222]

5.18 E. Blum

In his study on the composition of the Patriarchal History according to the "traditio-historical" (*überlieferungsgeschichtliche*) method developed by R. Rendtorff,[223] E. Blum offers an analysis of Gen-

---

[215] Although the Priestly layer within the Joseph Story has the character of a redactional expansion, Schmitt still prefers to consider P as a document instead of a redactor; cf. Schmitt, "Hintergründe der 'neuesten Pentateuchkritik'", 177–9.

[216] Schmitt, *Die nichtpriesterliche Josephsgeschichte*, 5–20 *et passim*; idem, "Die Hintergründe der 'neuesten Pentateuchkritik'", 171–7.

[217] Schmitt, *Die nichtpriesterliche Josephsgeschichte*, 16–20.

[218] Schmitt, *Die nichtpriesterliche Josephsgeschichte*, 19–20.

[219] Schmitt, *Die nichtpriesterliche Josephsgeschichte*, 20.

[220] See also the table on p. 425 below.

[221] Schmitt, *Die nichtpriesterliche Josephsgeschichte*, 68; Gunkel, *Genesis*, 469.

[222] Schmitt, *Die nichtpriesterliche Josephsgeschichte*, 152–6; cf. however 156, n. 338, where he admits that a later time of origin is also possible.

[223] E. Blum, *Die Komposition der Vätergeschichte* (WMANT, 57), Neukirchen-

esis 37–50 in which he also discusses the Deathbed Episode found in Gen. 47:29–49:33.[224] According to Blum a northern tradition from the time of the reign of Jeroboam I, called the Jacob narrative (found in Gen. 25:19–34; *27–33), forms the basic composition in Genesis. This composition originally contained several independent legends[225] in which the importance of the fathers as ancestors is already assumed.[226] This northern Jacob tradition was soon elaborated with some aetiological notes,[227] and then interwoven in a later stage with a Judah orientated tradition-layer on several sons (= tribes) of Jacob (Gen. 34; 35:21–22a; 38; 49:1–27).[228]

The Joseph Story is studied in this connection as part of the Patriarchal History and therefore the traditio-historical questions concerning the text, namely the diachronic unity, meaning(s) and historical context, as well as diachronic demarcation are discussed.[229] According to Blum the Joseph Story is an independent, non-composite text, which originated in the period of the northern kingdom,[230] and therefore the traditional source criticism is irrelevant.[231] However, this does not exclude the possibility that several passages in the Joseph Story were inserted later, especially those connecting the Joseph Story with the patriarchal traditions, like Gen. 38,[232] 41:50–52; 46:1–5a, 8–27; 48;

Vluyn 1984, 1–2. For Rendtorff's work, cf. principally R. Rendtorff, *Das überlieferungsgeschichtliche Problem des Pentateuch* (BZAW, 147), Berlin 1976; further also idem, "Der 'Jahwist' als Theologe? Zum Dilemma der Pentateuchkritik", in *Congress Volume, Edinburgh 1974* (SVT, 28), Leiden 1975, 158–66 (= idem, "The 'Yahwist' as Theologian? The Dilemma of Pentateuchal Criticism", *JSOT* 3 [1977] 2–9); idem, "Pentateuchal Studies on the Move", *JSOT* 3 (1977) 43–5. The last named article was in answer to the responses by R.N. Whybray, J. Van Seters, N.E. Wagner, and G.W. Coats in the same issue of *JSOT*, pp. 11–32, to his first mentioned article. For a description, cf. Houtman, *Der Pentateuch*, 236–8.

[224]Blum, *Die Komposition der Vätergeschichte*, 204–70; for Gen. 49, cf. *op.cit.*, 228–9; for Gen. 48, see pp. 250–4.

[225]Blum, *Die Komposition der Vätergeschichte*, 66–203; cf. esp. p. 202, where he mentions the episodes on the conflict between Jacob and Esau (Gen. 25:29–34; 27) the sanctuary legend of Bethel (28:11–13); and the account of the treaty between Jacob and Laban (31:45–54).

[226]Blum, *Die Komposition der Vätergeschichte*, 202–3.

[227]Blum, *Die Komposition der Vätergeschichte*, 204–9. Blum calls this version the *"erweiterte Jakoberzählung"*; the aetiological notes are preserved in Gen. 33:18*, 20; 35:6–7*, 8, *16–20 (*op.cit.*, 209).

[228]Blum, *Die Komposition der Vätergeschichte*, 209–29.

[229]Blum, *Die Komposition der Vätergeschichte*, 229–30.

[230]Cf. on this dating the final section of this chapter.

[231]Blum, *Die Komposition der Vätergeschichte*, 230–1; in this matter Blum especially criticizes the work of Seebass, but also that of Donner, which in his view is still too strongly influenced by the Documentary Hypothesis.

[232]Blum, *Die Komposition der Vätergeschichte*, 244–6. Although Blum had dis-

49:(28)29–33; 50:12–13, 22–26, all belonging to the so-called Judaic Text Group (*judäische Textgruppe*).[233]

This list, with the later added passages, shows that in Blum's view the deathbed Episode (Gen. 47:29–49:33) is composite. He considers 48:1 a new introduction, duplicating the scene in 47:29–31, where Jacob's passing away is introduced (47:31b),[234] and immediately continued in scene and contents by 50:1–11.[235] Genesis 48 is undoubtedly composite, but scholars were too much inclined to find doublets, literary tensions, and suchlike within the text. However, 48:3–7 belongs to a younger tradition layer since it contains many references to, and quotations from, Gen. 35:9–15, 16–20,[236] as well as connections with the so-called "El-Shadday-layer".[237] We should note 48:3–7 alongside 47:27b, where the same keywords of the fertility blessing in 35:11; 48:4 (פרה and רבה) occur, and where also the shift from a personal to a collective use of "Israel" is manifest.[238]

The problematic verses in 48:15–16 are also considered to be inserted later because first, from the fact that verse 17 is composed as the sequel to verse 14, the tense of the כי-clause suggests simultaneity. Secondly, Joseph's protest came too late after the blessing. And thirdly, the blessing for Ephraim and Manasseh follows in verse

---

cussed this text before in connection with the Judah orientated tradition-layer, he had to discuss it here once more, because of its positioning within the Joseph Story. Because of the identical phrasing in Gen. 37:32–33 and 38:25–26, he suggested that the Joseph Story had been known to the responsible editor of the Judah orientated texts, who changed the text in 37:32–33 in accordance with 38:25–26.

[233] Blum, *Die Komposition der Vätergeschichte*, 244–57.
[234] Blum, *Die Komposition der Vätergeschichte*, 250. The view that 47:31b describes somehow the death of Jacob and is followed by 50:1 is also found in O.H. Steck, *Die Paradieserzählung: Eine Auslegung von Genesis 2,4b–3,24* (BiSt, 60), Neukirchen-Vluyn 1970, 120 (repr. in: idem, *Wahrnehmungen Gottes im Alten Testament: Gesammelte Studien* [ThB, 70], München 1982, 9–116. 108); Donner, *Literarische Gestalt der Josephsgeschichte*, 30–1; T.L. Thompson, *The Origin Tradition of Ancient Israel, I: The Literary Formation of Genesis and Exodus 1–23* (JSOTS, 55), Sheffield 1987, 129–30. Cf. also Schweizer, *Die Josefsgeschichte* (cf. below), 354.
[235] Blum, *Die Komposition der Vätergeschichte*, 250, the explicit note on Jacob's death is preserved in the younger layer of 49:29–33 (cf. on its traditio-historical classification below), whereas the original note on his death in the older layer had to retreat. It is unlikely in his view that the note of 49:33aB וַיֶּאֱסֹף רַגְלָיו אֶל־הַמִּטָּה "and he drew his feet at the bed" would belong to this ancient layer, because it presupposes at least 48:2.
[236] Blum, *Die Komposition der Vätergeschichte*, 251–2.
[237] Blum, *Die Komposition der Vätergeschichte*, 251: "El-Šaddaj-Gruppe". Cf. also *op.cit.*, 263–70.
[238] Blum, *Die Komposition der Vätergeschichte*, 252, n. 56.

20 (with the names and reference to verses 14 and 17–19). However, Blum does not find any indications for a traditio-historical classification of 48:15–16, and suggests that a general blessing with some modifications was inserted here.[239]

The final verse of this pericope (48:22) is considered to be part of the reconstructed Episode,[240] which is a "tribal historical aetiology", presupposing the expanded Jacob narrative as well as the Joseph Story. The reference to Shechem emphasizes the exceptional status of Joseph once again, closely following the exceptional status of Joseph's sons.[241] Verse 21, nevertheless, is a later addition, possibly to be connected with the D-revision, which can also be found at the end of Genesis in 50:22–26.[242] Gen. 48:21 is structurally parallel to 50:24, notwithstanding some changes in expressions. Furthermore, 48:21 stands out from its context because Jacob speaks of the Israelites and their return in the 2nd person plural, whereas further on in chapter 48 he talks to Joseph or only to his sons. Finally, the combination of the promise that God will be with them, together with that of their future return is also found in another D-revision: Gen. 28:15 (with הֲשִׁיב).[243] Genesis 48, but not the later additions in verses 3–7, 15–16 and 21, proves in this connection to be a coherent, but also a dependent entity, not comprehensible without its context, namely the Joseph and the Jacob Stories.[244]

Finally, in Gen. 49:(28)29–33 Jacob's wish to be buried in Canaan is narrated for a second time, but in this case the wish is uttered in the presence of all his sons. With the reference to Machpelah and Mamre and the note on Jacob's death in a typical phrasing, this scene has its parallel with the death scenes of the other patriarchs. Similarly the account of the funeral in 50:12–13 is shaped in the same form and in this way includes 49:29–33, but at the same time it replaces the original account of the funeral.[245] Apart from these later additions, Gen. 50:1–11, 14–21 forms the literary homogeneous conclusion to the Joseph Story.[246]

---

[239]Blum, *Die Komposition der Vätergeschichte*, 253, with n. 60 for the tradition historical classification.

[240]Gen. 48:1–22, without vv. 3–7, 15–16; cf. Blum, *Die Komposition der Vätergeschichte*, 253.

[241]Blum, *Die Komposition der Vätergeschichte*, 253–4.

[242]Blum, *Die Komposition der Vätergeschichte*, 255–6.

[243]Blum, *Die Komposition der Vätergeschichte*, 257.

[244]Blum, *Die Komposition der Vätergeschichte*, 253.

[245]Blum, *Die Komposition der Vätergeschichte*, 254–5.

[246]Blum, *Die Komposition der Vätergeschichte*, 255.

5.19 L. Schmidt

The traditional Documentary Hypothesis is defended by L. Schmidt as the appropriate tool to analyse the Joseph Story.[247] Schmidt argues that the tensions within the text cannot be solved by means of a Supplementary Hypothesis (Redford, Schmitt). In order to strengthen his argument, he gives five examples of problems that are best solved by the Documentary Hypothesis:

1. The use of the different names for the father (Jacob/Israel).

2. Simeon is left as a hostage in Egypt (Gen. 42:18–24, 33–34), but is sometimes not mentioned in the discussion on returning to Egypt for the second time (43:1–10).

3. The doublet of the money found in the bags (Gen. 42:27–28 / Gen. 42:35).

4. The doublets in the revealing scene (Gen. 45:1–15).

5. The doublet of the Ishmaelites and Midianites together with the names of Reuben and Judah (Gen. 37:25–30).[248]

In his view the tensions in the story are solved satisfactorily by discerning the documents J, E and P. The similarities and differences between J and E are not explained in the way Noth did by assuming a basic document (*Grundschrift*), but solely on the assumption that E knew J.[249]

Although Schmidt's analysis in general does not depart very much from the analysis of Gunkel,[250] the differences within 48:1–22 are remarkable. Verses 8a and 11 are usually assigned to E, but the name of the father is here Israel, whereas E always uses Jacob. In his view this argues against an assignment to E, and because it is closely related to the Joseph Story as a whole it has therefore to be assigned to J.[251]

Verse 19 cannot be assigned to any of the three documents because of the usage of מְלֹא הַגּוֹיִם "multitude of nations". The plural of גּוֹי for the tribes of Israel is typical in P,[252] and thus every tribe could be

---

[247]L. Schmidt, *Literarische Studien zur Josephsgeschichte*.

[248]Schmidt, *Literarische Studien zur Josephsgeschichte*, 133–8.

[249]Schmidt, *Literarische Studien zur Josephsgeschichte*, 140–1; 281–7.

[250]Ruppert, "Zur Diskussion um die Josefsgeschichte", 94–5, lists the differences between Gunkel and Schmidt.

[251]Schmidt, *Literarische Studien zur Josephsgeschichte*, 257–8.

[252]Gen. 17:5, 16; 35:11; cf. also 48:4, where עַם, which is for P identical with גּוֹי, is used in plural.

considered a גּוֹי or an עַם, but not — as in 48:19 — a מְלֹא הַגּוֹיִם. Because J and E consider Israel to be a גּוֹי (singular), there is no proof that the plural גּוֹיִם was used before the Exile for Israel. The consequence is that at least 48:19 has to be considered a later addition, probably even later than P.[253] Because 48:19 cannot be separated from the scene where the Patriarch blesses Ephraim and Manasseh (48:13–14, 17–20), while P already places Ephraim before Manasseh in 48:5, this part does certainly not belong to P. Since verse 13b is a resumption of verse 10b, we have to consider this part to be an even later expansion of the basic narrative, added in order to emphasize that Ephraim was placed before Manasseh.[254] Because of the absence of E in other parts and because of the proposed Exilic or post-Exilic date by others (Ruppert, Donner, Westermann), 48:15–16 is also considered to be a later addition, though not of the same hand as these verses, but written by an earlier editor because of the interruption of 48:13–14, 17–20.[255]

The transitional 48:1–2a is commonly ascribed to E; but because E is not present any more in chapter 48 according to Schmidt's analysis, this is unlikely and another hypothesis is proposed.[256] Because the phrase וַיְהִי אַחֲרֵי הַדְּבָרִים הָאֵלֶּה "and it happened after these things" occurs twice in J (39:7; 40:1), marking the transition from one scene to another, a transition might also be intended here by J. Nevertheless, 48:1aB.2a do not belong to J (father's name is Jacob; and it is the second account of his illness) and therefore it has to be considered whether 48:1aB–2a contains a partial introduction of P to verses 3–6.[257] Verse 1b certainly does not belong to P, because Manasseh is mentioned here before Ephraim and therefore this verse is ascribed to J. The editor, who inserted P into the text, left out a phrase of J between verses 1aA and 1b in favour of P.[258]

The concluding verses, 48:21–22, are a unity and a late expansion of the whole episode. The tradition that Joseph was buried in Shechem (Josh. 24:32) is presumed here and so he was buried on his own property. However, the tradition that Jacob/Israel conquered Shechem

---

[253]Schmidt, *Literarische Studien zur Josephsgeschichte*, 258–9.

[254]Schmidt, *Literarische Studien zur Josephsgeschichte*, 259–60. Because Gen. 48:9b–10a is in fact a preparation for verse 13b, this passage also belongs to the expansion in 48:13–14, 17–20.

[255]Schmidt, *Literarische Studien zur Josephsgeschichte*, 266–7.

[256]Schmidt, *Literarische Studien zur Josephsgeschichte*, 266: "Diese Überlegungen zu v. 1–2a bleiben notwendig hypothetisch. Es sollte aber deutlich werden, daß die Zuweisung an E keineswegs gesichert ist".

[257]Schmidt, *Literarische Studien zur Josephsgeschichte*, 264–5.

[258]Schmidt, *Literarische Studien zur Josephsgeschichte*, 265.

is unique in the Hebrew Bible, because in Genesis 34 Shechem is slaughtered, but did not become Israel's property. How the author of these verses got this idea cannot be ascertained any more. He probably combined the tradition of the acquisition of the land by Jacob (33:19) with the tradition of the slaughter of Shechem.[259] Further, Joseph's burial in Shechem has also tribal-historical relevance because the father had assigned the city to Joseph and so Shechem belongs to Joseph's heirs.[260]

Concerning Genesis 49, Schmidt's analysis is in accordance with the scholarly opinion that 49:1a, 28bA–33aA.b belongs to P, and that 49:2–27 is inserted into P by means of the connecting verses 1b and 28a.bA; whereas 49:33aB belongs to J.[261]

5.20 H. Schweizer

In 1991 H. Schweizer published the first two volumes of a planned three-volume study on the Joseph Story.[262] In these first two volumes Schweizer presents a literary analysis of the Joseph Story according to his method developed and described in another study.[263] In the planned third volume the interpretation of the text will be presented. In fact this final volume might be considered to be the goal of the whole project Schweizer is working on. The question was whether, with careful literary analysis, it was possible to recover the original version of the Joseph Story in order to — when the project was successful — "subject this version to a text linguistic description within the meaning of a comprehensive *synchronic* analysis".[264] In this way a *diachronic* approach is set aside for the moment (without denying its legitimacy)[265] in favour of a description of the text, which should facilitate a return to the text in a hermeneutical sense.[266]

---

[259]Schmidt, *Literarische Studien zur Josephsgeschichte*, 269–71.

[260]Schmidt, *Literarische Studien zur Josephsgeschichte*, 271.

[261]Schmidt, *Literarische Studien zur Josephsgeschichte*, 127, 277.

[262]H. Schweizer, *Die Josefsgeschichte: Konstituierung des Textes*, Tl. I–II (TTHLLI, Bd. 4), Tübingen 1991, Bd. I, 5, n. 18.

[263]H. Schweizer, *Biblische Texte verstehen: Arbeitsbuch zur Hermeneutik und Methodik der Bibelinterpretation*, Stuttgart 1986; cf. also his, "Literarkritik", *ThQ* 168 (1988) 23–43.

[264]Schweizer, *Die Josefsgeschichte*, Bd. I, 5: "... diese Version einer textwissenschaftlichen Deskription zu unterziehen im Sinn einer ausführlichen *synchronen* Analyse".

[265]Schweizer, *Die Josefsgeschichte*, Bd. I, 5, n. 20, announces that diachronic questions will be treated after the interpretation.

[266]Schweizer, *Die Josefsgeschichte*, Bd. I, 5–6. His book, *Joseph: Urfassung der alttestamentlichen Erzählung (Genesis 37–50)*, Tübingen 1993, might in this respect be considered an attempt to enable this return (*op.cit.*, 6).

There is however yet another reason why Schweizer publishes his "interpretation" separately from his literary criticism. In previous research he distinguishes two deficiencies. First, former reconstructions of the original text did not present a text, "free from communicative impertinences, gaps, immense contradictions, remarks between parentheses about all the information that is lost".[267] Secondly, following on from the former remark, as a rule the reconstruction of previous text stages is confounded with "text interpretation", because literary critical exegesis did not develop text linguistic instruments for such an interpretation.[268] In order to avoid former pitfalls and to reach the goal of recovering the original Joseph Story, a strict distinction between the different stages of the method has to be made. Literary criticism is in this respect part of the first step, the constitution of the text, so that the order "textual criticism — translation — literary criticism" will lead to the second part, where this constituted text can then be interpreted by: "syntax — semantics — pragmatics".[269] Because Schweizer's project is not yet complete and the volume on interpretation has not yet been published, in which the diachronic questions will be discussed,[270] we can only present his textual remarks, translation and literary-critical arguments concerning the Joseph Story.

His treatment of the Deathbed Episode can be divided into two parts: Gen. 48:1–22 is treated as part of the Joseph Story, although the conclusions of the literary observations will lead to a different point of view. Yet, Gen. 49:1–33 has been set apart beforehand from the Joseph Story together with Genesis 38 and is studied only after the discussion of Genesis 37; 39–48; 50.[271] However, the rather difficult section of Gen. 49:3–27 is not discussed at all, neither at a textual level, nor a literary critical level.[272] Such a discussion is superfluous because it is obvious that this passage does not belong to the Joseph

---

[267]Schweizer, *Die Josefsgeschichte*, Bd. I, 3: "... der frei ist von kommunikativen Zumutungen, Löchern, immensen Widersprüchen, Klammerbemerkungen über das, was wohl alles an Informationen ausgefallen sei".

[268]Schweizer, *Die Josefsgeschichte*, Bd. I, 4.

[269]Schweizer, *Die Josefsgeschichte*, Bd. I, 5.

[270]Cf. p. 405, n. 265 above.

[271]Schweizer, *Die Josefsgeschichte*, Bd. I, 325–41; this section was prepared by N. Rabe. In this connection Seebass is blamed for having related Genesis 38 to the Joseph Story, and esp. to Genesis 44. In the opinion of Schweizer/Rabe, Genesis 38 provides Judah with salient features at the level of the final redaction of Genesis 37–50, but they are "völlig belanglos" to Genesis 44. Seebass' view reveals, therefore, according to Schweizer/Rabe, a disdain of literary critical observations and the manyfold insights contained in scholarly literature (*op.cit.*, 325–6).

[272]For the former, cf. Schweizer, *Die Josefsgeschichte*, Bd. I, 332, n. 373; for the latter, cf. below.

Story.[273] In addition, the shift from sons to tribes is not easy to understand, even when parts are clearly anticipating future situations, because it is neither introduced nor reflected upon in the other parts of Genesis 49.[274]

On the basis of literary criticism Gen. 48:1–22 is considered to be a later addition to the text, which is concluded from the shift between 47:31 and 48:1. The phrase at the end of Gen. 47:31, that Israel וַיִּשְׁתַּחוּ עַל־רֹאשׁ הַמִּטָּה "bowed at the head of the bed" has to be interpreted as describing Israel's death. If 47:31 does not describe the death of the father, then 48:2b would form a very neat connection with 47:31; but it seems more appropriate to interpret it in the sense of his demise because the whole tendency of 47:29–31 seems to point in this direction.[275] Because of this tension it would be premature to consider the reminiscence between these two verses (47:31, 48:2b) as an indication that they could belong to the same layer. To consider the expression in 47:31 as a description of Israel's thanks to God for Joseph's oath, as is suggested by some scholars, is not justified because "thanks" and "God" do not occur in this verse. The reader expects Israel to die here (47:29a), and therefore one may suspect that such a solution is to prevent Israel from dying, because he is still needed in Genesis 48 to continue the different documents.[276] The text of Genesis 48 apparently confronted Schweizer and his method with insurmountable problems:

Especially in Genesis 48 the search for coherence is obviously much more difficult. The previous work has already shown that in this chapter the unscrupulous addition of heterogeneous texts was practised par-

---

[273]Schweizer, *Die Josefsgeschichte*, Bd. I, 332, n. 373: "Massiv treten textkritische Schwierigkeiten in den VV. 3–27 auf, die jedoch augenfällig nicht zur Disposition der Josefsgeschichte gehören und daher aus arbeitsökonomischen Gründen nicht einer textkritischen Durchleuchtung unterzogen werden sollen".

[274]Schweizer, *Die Josefsgeschichte*, Bd. I, 333, 336.

[275]Schweizer, *Die Josefsgeschichte*, Bd. I, 290.

[276]Schweizer, *Die Josefsgeschichte*, Bd. I, 290, n. 299: "Wegen dieser Spannung dürfte es sich als voreilig erweisen, die bestehenden Wortanklänge als Indiz für Zugehörigkeit zu *einer* Schicht zu werten". According to H.-C. Schmitt "bedeute das 'neigen' nicht 'sterben' sondern — aus Altersschwäche — danke Israel 'auf dem Bette' (Gunkel) Gott für den von Josef abgelegten Schwur. Dagegen: (a) Von 'Dank' und 'Gott' ist nicht die Rede. (b) Literarisch (ab V. 29a) steht der Leser in der Erwartung des Todes Israels. Daher — (c) — besteht die hohe Wahrscheinlichkeit, daß die Deutung Gunkels mühsam verhindern soll, daß Israel schon in Gen 47 stirbt; die vorausgesetzte Quellentheorie braucht ihn als Lebenden noch in Gen. 48. — Welch eine Anstrengung, den Text gegen den Strich zu bürsten! Quellentheorie als künstliche Beatmung eines klinisch bereits Toten...?"

ticularly vehemently.[277]

According to his analysis the text of Genesis 48 is a mixture of four "layers"[278] and some fragments:

1. The Israel-layer[279] consists of the texts found in 48:1aA,[280] 2b, 8–9, 10b–11, 21(?).[281]

2. The Jacob-layer[282] contains 48:1aB–2a, 3–4aA,[283] 4b–5a.[284]

3. The E=M-layer[285] is found in 48:5b–6, 13–14, 17–19a, 20a.[286]

4. The E>M-layer[287] exists of 48:19b*,[288] 20c.[289]

5. Several parts could not be classified, these are "fragments": 48:1aA,[290] 4aB, 7abA, 7bB, 10a, 12, 15, 16, 19b,[291] 20b, 22.[292]

---

[277] Schweizer, *Die Josefsgeschichte*, Bd. I, 301: "Die Suche nach Zusammenhängen ist offenbar in Gen 48 besonders erschwert. Schon die bisherige Arbeit zeigte, daß in diesem Kap. die bedenkenlose Addition heterogener Texte besonders heftig betrieben wurde."

[278] "Layer" (*Schicht*) is used here in the sense of a continuously readable text where the component parts follow each other in an acceptable order. However, this does not say that these layers form independent texts. Cf. Schweizer, *Die Josefsgeschichte*, Bd. I, 303.

[279] Not to be confused with the Judah-Israel-layers and Jacob-Reuben-layers of other scholars, which are alternative names for the J- and E-documents. In this context the Israel-layer is found only in Genesis 48, where the different layers are connected on the basis of a common subject or a common theme; *e.g.* Ephraim and Manasseh treated equally (E=M-layer) or Ephraim put before Manasseh (E>M-layer); cf. Schweizer, *Die Josefsgeschichte*, Bd. I, 303, with nn. 318–20, 322.

[280] On this verse, see below, n. 292.

[281] Here we use the common annotation for the Hebrew verses used throughout the present study. The Israel-layer according to Schweizer's verse-annotation is: Gen. 48:1a, 2e–f, 8a–9f, 10c–11d, 21a–e (Schweizer, *Die Josefsgeschichte*, Bd. I, 301–3; idem, Bd. II, 191–2).

[282] Cf. n. 279 above.

[283] Read to the first *zaqeph qaton*, [5].

[284] Schweizer, *Die Josefsgeschichte*, Bd. I, 301–3; idem, Bd. II, 192–3: Gen. 48:1b–2d, 3a–4d, 4f–5c.

[285] Cf. n. 279 above.

[286] Schweizer, *Die Josefsgeschichte*, Bd. I, 301–3; idem, Bd. II, 193–4: Gen. 48:5d–6d, 13a–14f, 17a–19g, 20a.

[287] Cf. n. 279 above.

[288] On this verse, see below, n. 292.

[289] Schweizer, *Die Josefsgeschichte*, Bd. I, 301–3; idem, Bd. II, 194: Gen. 48:19h–i, 20d.

[290] On this verse, see below, n. 292.

[291] On this verse, see below, n. 292.

[292] Schweizer, *Die Josefsgeschichte*, Bd. I, 301–3; idem, Bd. II, 144–9: Gen. 48:1a,

Striking is the fact that the number of fragments in Schweizer's analysis is rather high and only the E=M-layer is larger here than the sum of all the fragments together.[293] Further it is remarkable that Gen. 48:3–6(7), which is usually considered to be a unity belonging to P, here consists of two layers and a fragment. 48:4aB does not belong to the context (48:3–4aA, 4b–5a) because Jacob in 4aB is an indirect addressee and in 4aA a direct one, while in 4aB the same is told as in 4aA, only using other words.[294] On the other hand, the contents of the promise in 4aB is not any more the foundation of the declaration in verse 4b,[295] and although "your descendants" (4bA) may mean *factually* the same as "company of peoples" (4aB), *lingually* it appears a regress. Further, there is a tension in contents: אֶרֶץ is determined finitely, meaning an individual country, and therefore it can be asked what then is the relation between the "company of peoples" and this "individual land"?[296] The two layers which have to be discerned (on the one hand 48:3–4aA, 4b–5a, and on the other 48:5b–6) are differentiated because of the tension between 48:5a and 5b. Although verse 5b appears to be an explanation of 5a, both declarations do not match completely: verse 5a is "possessive", and 5b is comparative and thus more distant.[297] Furthermore there is a difference between 4b and 6a, because the terminology for descendants (זֶרַע and מוֹלֶדֶת) differs.[298] With these two arguments the separation is founded well, according to Schweizer.[299] With this description we have presented one of the most remarkable differences between the work of Schweizer and other literary critical scholars.

5.21   The Joseph Story in Historical Perspective

The study of the historical background of biblical texts is governed by the principle aptly put by J. Wellhausen in his well-known dictum:

4e, 7a–c, 7d, 10a–b, 12a–b, 15a–f, 16a–c, 19h–i, 20b–c, 22a–b. It was clearly difficult to classify 48:1aA, 19h–i correctly, both are considered to be fragments as well as parts of a layer; cf. *op.cit.*, Bd. I, 302–3.

[293]Schweizer presented the text in "utterance units" (*Äußerungseinheiten*), which can be found in his *Die Josefsgeschichte*, Bd. II, 144–9. In this presentation Genesis 48 contains 98 units, which can be divided over the different layers as follows (in the order presented above): 24 : 19 : 30 : 3 : 25. Thus the number of units considered as fragments is 25, whereas the E=M-layer contains 30.

[294]Schweizer, *Die Josefsgeschichte*, Bd. I, 291, 297.

[295]Schweizer, *Die Josefsgeschichte*, Bd. I, 291.

[296]Schweizer, *Die Josefsgeschichte*, Bd. I, 297.

[297]Schweizer, *Die Josefsgeschichte*, Bd. I, 291.

[298]Schweizer, *Die Josefsgeschichte*, Bd. I, 291.

[299]Schweizer, *Die Josefsgeschichte*, Bd. I, 297.

> The materials here [in the Patriarchal narratives] are not mythical but national, and therefore more transparent, and in a certain sense more historical. It is true, we attain to no historical knowledge of the patriarchs, but only of the time when the stories about them arose in the Israelite people; this later age is here unconsciously projected, in its inner and outward features, into hoar antiquity, and is reflected there like a glorified mirage.[300]

This approach to the biblical text — based largely on literary criticism — received an important impetus from the form critical method, modifying the historical contexts of traditions and redactions, supporting the supposition that the traditions originated in events.[301] This principle also governs the research into the historical background and date of origin of the Joseph Story. In this paragraph the different opinions which determine the scholarly discussion nowadays will be presented, proceeding from a maximalist to a minimalist approach to the biblical texts — and even beyond.

Some scholars assume that the account preserved in the Joseph Story is based on an old national epic which preserved the events leading to the sojourn of the Israelites in Egypt.[302] But the extent

---

[300] J. Wellhausen, *Prolegomena zur Geschichte Israels*, Berlin ²1883, 336 (⁶1905, 316): "Der Stoff ist hier nicht mythisch, sondern national; darum durchsichtiger und in gewissem Sinne historischer. Freilich über die Patriarchen ist hier kein historisches Wissen zu gewinnen, sondern nur über die Zeit, in welcher die Erzählungen über sie im israelitischen Volke entstanden; diese spätere Zeit wird hier nach ihren inneren und äußeren Grundzügen, absichtslos ins graue Altertum projicirt und spiegelt sich darin als ein verklärtes Luftbild ab." English translation according to J. Wellhausen, *Prolegomena to the History of Israel*, Edinburgh 1885, 318–9.

Illustrative of the fact that this principle still governs historical studies is the remark of G.W. Ahlström, *The History of Ancient Palestine from the Palaeolithic Period to Alexander's Conquest* (JSOTS, 146), D. Edelman (ed.), Sheffield 1993, 30, that if some of the exiled people had learned about Ur after they had been taken to Babylonia, "that could lead to the conclusion that the whole Abraham story is not a piece of history but rather a literary product aimed at a religious and political situation of a much later time than its supposed Bronze Age setting." Cf. in this respect also his excursus on Abraham, pp. 180–7. See further also K.A.D. Smelik, *Converting the Past: Studies in Ancient Israelite and Moabite Historiography* (OTS, 28), Leiden 1992, 5; T.L. Thompson, "Text, Context and Referent in Israelite Historiography", in: D. Edelman (ed.), *The Fabric of History: Text, Artifact and Israel's Past* (JSOTS, 127), Sheffield 1991, 65–92, 67–8; and further p. 420, with n. 356, below.

[301] Cf. Thompson, "Text, Context and Referent", 65–92, 65–7; idem, "Israelite Historiography", *ABD*, vol. 3, 206–12.

[302] Cf. W.F. Albright, *From the Stone Age to Christianity*, Baltimore (MD) ²1946, 183–5; G.E. Wright, *Biblical Archaeology*, Philadelphia 1957, 53.

to which these events have been preserved is estimated differently. K.A. Kitchen for example considers even the price of Joseph's sale — twenty shekels of silver, Gen. 37:28 — as exact information concerning its time of origin, because during the eighteenth century BCE this was the price of slaves, whereas in earlier times they were cheaper and later dearer.[303] Close to this period is the relation with the period of the Hyksos in Egypt in the seventeenth and sixteenth century BCE,[304] a period when the power of Semites in Egypt is historically testified.[305] Others prefer, however, a more general date during the eighteenth dynasty of Egypt (mid-sixteenth till end fourteenth century BCE).[306] More specifically the Joseph Story is related to the Amarna period in the fourteenth century BCE, considering Joseph even to be the chief minister of Akhenaten.[307] On the other hand, on the basis of similar data from Egypt D.B. Redford proposes a date during the

---

[303] Cf. K.A. Kitchen, *Ancient Orient and Old Testament*, London 1966, 52–3. With regard to prices of slaves in Mesopotamia, this might be correct; cf. now M.A. Dandamayev, "Slavery (Ancient Near East)", *ABD*, vol. 6, 58–62, 60. However, according to an official contract from Ugarit (RS 16.191 + 16.272; KTU 3.4) at the end of LB seven people could be bought free as slaves for a hundred (shekels) silver, which is an average price of fourteen shekels for a slave. See R. Yaron, "A Document of Redemption from Ugarit", *VT* 10 (1960) 83–90; J.C. de Moor, "De vrijkoop van slaven in het Oude Nabije Oosten", *VoxTh* 34 (1964) 73–9, 75–6; B. Kienast, "Rechtsurkunden in ugaritischer Sprache", *UF* 11 (1979) 431–52, 448–50.

[304] Date according to E. Hornung, *Grundzüge der ägyptischen Geschichte*, Darmstadt ²1972, 67–71.

[305] W.F. Albright, *JBL* 37 (1918); G.E. Wright, *Biblical Archaeology*, 53–58; R.K. Harrison, *Old Testament Times*, London 1970, 94–7, 123–4; R. De Vaux, *Histoire ancienne d'Israël*, Tm. I, Paris 1971, 297–303, esp. 301–2 with n. 112 (E.T., 313–320, 318–9); J. Bright, *A History of Israel*, London ²1972, 85; M. Sarna, "Israel in Egypt", in: H. Shanks (ed.), *Ancient Israel: A Short History from Abraham to the Roman Destruction of the Temple*, Washington (DC) 1988, 31–52, 37–8; B. Halpern, "The Exodus of Egypt", in: H. Shanks *et al.*, *The Rise of Ancient Israel*, Washington 1992, 86–113, 91–9.

[306] See J. Vergote, *Joseph en Égypte: Genèse Chap. 37–50 à la lumière des études égyptologiques récentes* (OBL, 3), Louvain 1959.

[307] H.H. Rowley, *From Joseph to Joshua: Biblical Traditions in the Light of Archaeology* (The Schweich Lectures 1948), London 1950, 116–20 (esp. 118). Cf. also T.J. Meek, *Hebrew Origins*, New York ²1950, 29, who also considers this date possible. Recently N. Shupak, "סיפור יוסף — בין אגדה להיסטוריה", in: M.V. Fox *et al.* (eds.), *Texts, Temples, and Traditions: A Tribute to Menahem Haran*, Winona Lake (IN) 1996, 125*–33*, defended the theory that the narrative was based on the autobiography of an Egyptian official of possible Semitic origin, who had a prominent position at the Egyptian court of the Eighteenth Dynasty pharaohs, even probably during the Amarna Period. Later, with the rise of the Northern Kingdom this story was reworked in its present form, in order to legitimize the emergence of a king from the House of Joseph.

Saitic dynasty, the seventh and sixth century BCE,[308] which would invalidate the historicity of the narrative.

The departure from the historical approach, which sought for the exact period when Joseph rose to power, was mainly caused by the recognition of Gunkel, Greßmann, von Rad and others, that the Joseph Story is a *literary* composition, a novella.[309] Von Rad even stated that the Joseph Story

> has no historical-political concern whatsoever, also a cult-aetiologic tendency is lacking, and we even miss a salvation-historical and theological orientation. ... the Joseph Story with its clearly didactic tendency belongs to the ancient wisdom school.[310]

Although this approach may betray a non-historical attitude, history is still found in its argumentation. This is especially evident in von Rad's view on the historical origin of the Joseph Story. History is the soil in which this narrative originated, namely the age of enlightenment during David's and Solomon's reign.[311] Several characteristics, like narrative and psychological skill, foreign customs, Joseph as the embodiment of the scribal ideal, and a particular view of God's activity in human affairs,[312] occur in the Joseph Story and are of fundamental importance for our understanding of this story as a narrative from the age of enlightenment. Although the narrative is denied a historical concern, this understanding of the Joseph Story is historical to the core, since it still understands the narrative as a product of a certain place and period leaving its traces throughout the narrative, discernable for a critical reader. Whereas scholars were inclined to consider the Joseph Story a document with historical information, von Rad approaches the document as a literary document marked by the time in which it originated.

M. Noth came close to defend the aetiological character for the Joseph Story, which has the function of bridging the gap between the

---

[308] Redford, *Biblical Story of Joseph*, 187–243; idem, *Egypt, Canaan, and Israel in Ancient Times*, Princeton (NJ) 1992, 422–9.

[309] Cf. in this respect also p. 419, with n. 350, below.

[310] G. von Rad, "Josephgeschichte und ältere Chokma", in: *Congress Volume, Copenhagen 1953* (SVT, 1), Leiden 1953, 120–7, 126 (= idem, *GSAT*, 279): "... hat keinerlei historisch-politische Anliegen, ebenso fehlt ihr eine kultätiologische Tendenz, endlich vermissen wir eine spezifisch heilsgeschichtlich-theologische Ausrichtung. ... Die Josephsgeschichte mit ihrer deutlichen didaktischen Tendenz gehört der älteren Weisheitslehre zu."

[311] Cf. von Rad, "Josephsgeschichte und Chokma", 120 (= idem, *GSAT*, 272).

[312] On this matter cf. R.N. Whybray, "The Joseph Story and Pentateuchal Criticism", *VT* 18 (1968) 522–8, 527 with n. 1.

Patriarchal and Exodus narratives.[313] In his view, the Joseph Story is younger than the other traditions, having originated in the circles of the House of Joseph, but already found in the documents J, E, and P. Genesis 48 belongs entirely to E, and is only a later addition to the Jacob traditions, whereas Gen. 47:29–31 belongs to J and was originally part of the Joseph Story.

However, as there are no clear data, making historical reconstructions reliable,[314] and taking into account the literary character of the Joseph Story, scholars are inclined to put the value of the Joseph Story as a historical document into perspective.[315] The Joseph Story is approached as a "tribal historical" document: all kinds of elements in the narrative reflect historical situations.[316] According to this approach, which was defended by O. Kaiser and in certain respect also by I. Willi-Plein,[317] the story is based on the historical memory of the sojourn in Egypt of the tribe of Joseph. The animosity of the brothers against Joseph would reflect the tensions between the "younger", recently immigrated "Josephites" or "Israelites" and the "older" tribes settled in the land.[318] The historical background of the narrative is reflected partly in Judah's preferential treatment, reflecting the Davidic-

---

[313]M. Noth, *Überlieferungsgeschichte des Pentateuch*, Stuttgart 1948 (repr. Darmstadt 1960), 226–7. Cf. also p. 382, n. 107 above.

[314]Cf. De Vaux, *Histoire ancienne d'Israël*, 301–3 (E.T., 318–20). See also p. 418, with n. 346 below.

[315]In fact this is comparable to the use of historical documents from the ancient Near East, of which the most well-known might be the references to the legendary hero Gilgamesh; cf. on this matter *e.g.* J.C. de Moor, "Egypt, Ugarit and Exodus", in: N. Wyatt *et al.* (eds.), *Ugarit, Religion and Culture: Essays ... J.C.L. Gibson* (UBL, 12), München 1996, 213–247, 214. For a more elaborate treatment of the problem of historiography in Hebrew and other ancient Near Eastern texts, see Smelik, *Converting the Past*, 1–34.

[316]Cf. for a short qualification L. Ruppert, *Die Josephserzählung*, 17–8; C. Westermann, *Genesis 12–50* (EdF, 48), Darmstadt 1975, 57.

[317]See O. Kaiser, "Stammesgeschichtliche Hintergründe der Josephsgeschichte: Erwägungen zur Vor- und Frühgeschichte Israels", *VT* 10 (1960) 1–15; I. Willi-Plein, "Historiographische Aspekte der Josefsgeschichte", *Henoch* 1 (1979) 305–331.
They were preceded by O. Eissfeldt, who strongly emphasized the national historical (*volksgeschichtlichen*) element over the novelistic and personal. Cf. further A. Jepsen, "Zur Überlieferungsgeschichte der Vätergestalten" *Festschrift A. Alt*, Leipzig 1953/4 (= *WZ Leipzig* 3 [1953/4]), 139–155; E. Täubler, *Biblische Studien: Die Epoche der Richter*, Tübingen 1958, 176–203. Concerning the approach of the early history of the tribe of Joseph, Taubler was in many respects followed by C.H.J. de Geus, *The Tribes of Israel: An Investigation Into Some of the Presuppositions Martin Noth's Amphictyony Hypothesis* (SSN, 12), Assen 1976, 70–96.

[318]Kaiser, "Stammesgeschichtliche Hintergründe", 14.

Solomonic era, and the Judaic origin of J; the positive approach to Reuben betrays the hand of E;[319] on the other hand the place of origin of the Joseph Story within Josephite circles emerges from the names of the places in Genesis 37: Shechem and Dothan.[320] In each case,

> the migration because of a shortage of pasture, the settlement in Goshen, the, also in the Exodus tradition supposed, fate as slaves, are materials which the narrator, in order to breach the gap between the Patriarchal and the Exodus tradition, borrowed from historical memory in order to use them both in a general Israelite and novelistic individual manner.[321]

Others see especially in Genesis 48 tribal historical elements, reflecting a struggle between Ephraim and Manasseh.[322] Willi-Plein concludes in her study that the Joseph Story was originally independent from the Patriarchal narratives, and that only Joseph was alone with his father at the moment of his death: he received the blessing with his two sons (Genesis 48).[323] Joseph's role here betrays the hegemony of Joseph over the other tribes, which is also demonstrated in the gift of Shechem, the later capital. She closes her description of the Joseph Story with the statement that this story,

> in its narrative form of the personal fate of its hero, is at the same time historiography in the sense that in the personal act the potential history of the groups, which can be led back to these persons, is emerging. As an historical work it answers both questions: a) How did the sons of Israel come in Egypt? and b) How do the entities Joseph-Ephraim-Manasseh-Israel relate to each other?[324]

---

[319]Kaiser, "Stammesgeschichtliche Hintergründe", 4.

[320]Kaiser, "Stammesgeschichtliche Hintergründe", 5.

[321]Kaiser, "Stammesgeschichtliche Hintergründe", 14–5: "Die Abwanderung infolge einer Weidenot, die Ansiedlung in Gosen, das auch in der Exodustradition vorausgesetzte Sklavenlos sind Materialien, die der Erzähler, bei seiner Aufgabe, eine Brücke zwischen der Väter- und der Auszugstradition zu schlagen, geschichtlicher Erinnerung entnahm, um sie gesamtisraelitisch und zugleich novellistisch-individuell auszuwerten".

[322]Ruppert, *Die Josephserzählung*, 17–8; E.C. Kingsbury, "He Set Ephraim for Manasseh", *HUCA* 38 (1967) 129–136; Westermann, *Genesis 12–50*, 58. Cf. also von Rad, *Erste Buch Mose*, 263; Donner, *Literarische Gestalt der Josephsgeschichte*, 31.

[323]Willi-Plein, "Historiographische Aspekte", 308–10; 321. Cf. for this point of view already B.J. van der Merwe, "Joseph as Successor of Jacob", in: *Studia Biblica et Semitica: Th.C. Vriezen ... dedicata*, Wageningen 1966, 221–232.

[324]Willi-Plein, "Historiographische Aspekte", 322: "... in der das persönliche Schicksal ihrer Hauptfigur darstellenden Erzählungsform zugleich in dem Sinne Geschichtsschreibung ist, daß durch die persönliche Handlung die potentielle

The Story, with its slight criticism of Judah, does not reflect the Solomonic court, but more likely the Northern Kingdom during the reign of Jeroboam I, in the time shortly after the ending of the "personal union" between North and South.[325] In the view of B.J. van der Merwe[326] we are indeed dealing with a text in which Joseph is the favourite, but which was edited and expanded at the Davidic-Solomonic court by another tradition in which Judah was the favourite (Genesis 49).[327]

The approaches of Noth and von Rad have proved to be the most enduring, as in most studies the problem of the historical background of the Joseph Story is confined to the question of the place and time of origin, as already noted in Willi-Plein's article. In fact the dating and historical background of the Joseph Story are now mainly restricted to the political situations of the Northern and Southern kingdoms, and the story is seen as a reflection on these historical developments. In this connection the interpretation of the entire Joseph Story and more specifically the role of the different persons is of crucial importance for the historical classifications of the story and its different layers. The following datings have been advocated:

1. Whenever the role of Judah in the Joseph Story is considered to be more or less positive, reflecting Judah's hegemony, the Story — or the Judah-layer (sometimes J) — is dated in the Davidic-Solomonic era. In this connection the reflection of the governmental organization is of some importance, since it must reflect a well-organized royal court.[328]

2. If the leading position of Joseph is interpreted as the most important element of the narrative, then the period of the North-

---

Geschichte der sich auf diese Personen zurückführenden Gruppen hindurchschimmert. Als Geschichtswerk gibt sie Antwort auf die beide Fragen a) Wie kamen die Söhne Israels nach Ägypten? und b) Wie verhalten sich die Grössen Josef-Ephraim-Manasse-Israel zueinander?" Cf. in this connection Noth's description of the origin of the Joseph Story, and note that Kaiser also referred to the question "How did Israel come into Egypt?" (cf. above).

[325] Willi-Plein, "Historiographische Aspekte", 323.

[326] Cf. n. 323 above.

[327] Van der Merwe, "Joseph as Successor of Jacob", 229–30; idem, "Judah in the Pentateuch", *ThEv(SA)* 1 (1968) 37–52.

[328] F. Crüsemann, *Der Widerstand gegen das Königtum: Die antiköniglichen Texte des Alten Testamentes und der Kampf um den frühen israelitischen Staat* (WMANT, 49), Neukirchen-Vluyn 1978, 143–55; Donner, *Literarische Gestalt der Josephsgeschichte*, 24; Schmitt, *Die nichtpriesterliche Josephsgeschichte*, 150–63; Schmidt, *Literarische Studien zur Josephsgeschichte*, 273. Cf. already von Rad and Kaiser, above.

ern kingdom after the break up of the United Monarchy is regarded as the most appropriate time of origin. Here the reflection of the governmental organization is also of importance, as it might reflect the Northern court, shortly after the end of the United Monarchy,[329] or even in the eighth century.[330] The Judah-layer is sometimes classified as an expansion of the Reuben-layer, at the time when Judah became important again following the fall of the Northern Kingdom.[331]

3. The identification of Joseph with Solomon is considered to be an indication of its place of origin in the Southern Kingdom, whereas the Reuben-basic-layer might be a Judaic adaptation and rearrangement of an originally Northern tradition.[332] This is confirmed by the fact that Joseph is not depicted as a king, but only as a royal officer, which seems to reflect the time when there was no longer a Northern Kingdom, namely the end of the eighth century (under Hezekiah),[333] whereas the Judah-expansion took

---

[329]Dietrich, *Die Josephserzählung*, 64–66; Shupak, "סיפור יוסף", (p. 411, n. 307 above), 125*–33*. Cf. also Willi-Plein above.

[330]Blum, *Die Komposition der Vätergeschichte*, 234–44.

[331]Blum, *Die Komposition der Vätergeschichte*, 258–63; Dietrich, *Die Josephserzählung*, 71–8.

In some respects T.L. Thompson, *The Origin Tradition of Ancient Israel, I: The literary Formation of Genesis and Exodus 1–23* (JSOTS, 55), Sheffield 1987, 192–3, could be mentioned here too, since he dates the Pentateuchal historiographical tradition in its united form (from Abraham's calling in Mesopotamia until the wilderness wanderings) as a product of the late seventh or early sixth centuries, when the Passover festival is observed for the first time, because of the reforms associated with the reign of Josiah. The Joseph Story in its present form presupposes the Patriarchal and Exodus traditions in some form, which both might have existed earlier. Such an earlier existence of the Joseph Story is not denied, but in any case, "the specific nature and form of this pre-existence can neither be assumed nor determined". The correctness of his own dating has been questioned in his "Text, Context and Referent", 74, with n. 4; idem, *Early History of the Israelite People: From the Written and Archaeological Sources* (SHANE, 4), Leiden 1992, 387, with n. 59 (although he assumes there that he defended an Exilic or early post-Exilic date, which he did not! Cf. his *Origin Tradition*, 194: "It might be tempting ... to find a home for this ideology in the exile itself, or ... even later, in the post-Exilic period. ... This, however, I do not think should be done. We lack evidence for it."). Compare especially his harsh judgment on his own dating: "our understanding of the Josianic reform and of the prophetic and covenantal ideologies that presumably supported it is essentially based on a historicistic and naïve reading of 2 Kings, which is, after all, a product of the same spectra of traditions that use 2 Kings for their referential context" (Thompson, "Text, Context and Referent", 91–2; idem, *Early History of the Israelite People*, 399).

[332]Kebekus, *Die Joseferzählung*, 250–7.

[333]Kebekus, *Die Joseferzählung*, 255.

place in the post-Exilic era.[334]

4. An Exilic dating is proposed by A. Meinhold, who regards the Joseph Story as a "Diaspora novella", having the Israelite-Judaic Diaspora existence as subject.[335] In his view four points are significant: first, the election of YHWH does not fail; secondly, the importance of the diaspora for the exiles, as well as for the foreign nations; thirdly, the attestation of YHWH's uniqueness; finally the motivation for activity in exile.[336]

5. A post-Exilic date is preferred by N.P. Lemche — although earlier dates are not absolutely excluded.[337] In his view, 1. the pronounced monotheistic range of thoughts in even the oldest layers of the Pentateuch does not tally with the Solomonic era,[338] whereas the existence of a Solomonic court has to be doubted;[339] 2. the idea of immigrating strangers (Abraham, Jacob) does not fit the population of Judah and Jerusalem during the reign of Josiah, which was mostly autochthonous for over almost a thousand years;[340] 3. the use of prose narratives first became popular in Greece and spread in the classical and Hellenistic era, which makes an Exilic dating also unlikely.[341]

---

[334]Kebekus, *Die Joseferzählung*, 333–4.

[335] A. Meinhold, "Die Gattung der Josephsgeschichte und des Estherbuches: Diasporanovelle I", *ZAW* 87 (1975) 306–24; idem, "Die Gattung der Josephsgeschichte und des Estherbuches: Diasporanovelle II", *ZAW* 88 (1976) 72–93. J.A. Soggin, *An Introduction to the History of Israel and Judah*, London ²1993, 94, agrees with the classification of "Diaspora novella", even though his dating differs; cf. below n. 337.

The comparison of the Joseph Story and the Book of Esther had previously been made by L.A. Rosenthal, "Die Josephsgeschichte mit den Büchern Ester und Daniel verglichen", *ZAW* 15 (1895) 278–84; idem, "Nochmals der Vergleich Ester, Joseph — Daniel", *ZAW* 17 (1897) 125–8. Cf. also K. Butting, "The Book of Esther: A Reinterpretation of the Story of Josef [*sic*]: Innerbiblical Critique as a Guide for Feminist Hermeneutics", *ACEBT* 13 (1994) 81–7.

[336]Meinhold, "Die Gattung der Josephsgeschichte, I", 323.

[337]N.P. Lemche, *Die Vorgeschichte Israels: Von den Anfängen bis zum Ausgang des 13. Jahrhunderts v. Chr.* (BE, Bd. 1), Stuttgart 1996, 212–8. The post-Exilic date is also preferred by J.A. Soggin, "Notes on the Joseph Story", in: A.G. Auld (ed.), *Understanding Poets and Prophets: Essays ... G.W. Anderson* (JSOTS, 152), Sheffield 1993, 336–49, 344.

[338]Lemche, *Die Vorgeschichte Israels*, 214–5 (cf. 210).

[339]Lemche, *Die Vorgeschichte Israels*, 215, referring to two recent studies concerning this period: D.W. Jamieson-Drake, *Scribes and Schools: A Socio-Archaeological Approach* (JSOTS, 109; SWBAS, 9), Sheffield 1991; H.M. Niemann, *Herrschaft, Königtum und Staat* (FAT, 6), Tübingen 1993.

[340]Lemche, *Die Vorgeschichte Israels*, 215–6.

[341]Lemche, *Die Vorgeschichte Israels*, 216–7.

5.22   The Biblical Text and Historiography

While many of the scholars referred to, considered the Joseph Story
more or less historically important, as going back to ancient traditions, the story is dismissed as irrelevant to historical purposes in a
study by T.L. Thompson and D. Irvin on the Joseph and Moses narratives,[342] and more recently in N.P. Lemche's study on the prehistory
of Israel.[343] Although a historical core is not denied *per se*,[344] in their
view these narratives are irrelevant to the historian of Israel's origins
on the basis of the facts that[345]

1. Scholars are unable to identify any element of these narratives
   with a historically established occurrence or situation in the
   second millennium.[346]

2. The place of identifiable historiographical intent in the earliest
   and primary elements of the tradition[347] is almost consistently

---

The extent to which these stories reflect ancient traditions in Lemche's view
is unclear. In his view the narrator was acquainted with old narratives and legends, but he did not revise them, following exact analytical methods. "Das ist
eine Feststellung, die eigentlich nicht mit einem genauen geschichtlichen Nach-
weis erhärtet werden muß" (*op.cit.*, 68–9). However, the text has been revised
and adapted, especially for its insertion in the larger context where it has the
function of an interlude. "Nichtsdestoweniger muß betont werden, daß alle diese
Bearbeitungen und Revisionen zu keiner Änderung der Intention der Erzählung
oder ihrer Handlung geführt — und der Erzählung auch keine wesentlichen neuen
Elemente beigefügt haben" (*op.cit.*, 48).

[342]T.L. Thompson, D. Irvin, "The Joseph and Moses Narratives", in: J.H. Hayes,
J.M. Miller (eds.), *Israelite and Judaean History*, London, Philadelphia 1977, 149–
212. Cf. in this connection also T.L. Thompson, *The Historicity of the Patriarchal
Narratives* (BZAW, 133), Berlin 1974; idem, "The Background of the Patriarchs:
A Reply to William Dever and Malcolm Clark", *JSOT* 9 (1978) 2–43; idem, "Text,
Context and Referent in Israelite Historiography", 65–92; idem, *Early History
of the Israelite People, passim*. See furthermore his, "History and Tradition: A
Response to J.B. Geyer", *JSOT* 15 (1980) 57–61, which was a response to J.B.
Geyer, "The Joseph and Moses Narratives: Folk-Tale and History", *JSOT* 15
(1980) 51–6.

[343]Lemche, *Die Vorgeschichte Israels*, 47–51, 68–73. Cf. further N.P. Lemche,
The Canaanites and Their Land: The Tradition of the Canaanites (JSOTS, 110),
Sheffield 1991, 156–73; idem, "The Old Testament — A Hellenistic Book?" *SJOT*
7 (1993) 163–93. The same approach is found in Ahlström, *History of Ancient
Palestine*, 180–7, where Abraham functions as a *pars pro toto* for the patriarchs.

[344]Lemche, *Die Vorgeschichte Israels*, 51.

[345]The following list is adopted from Thompson, "History and Tradition", 58;
bibliographical notes are partly from this article (p. 5, nn. 5–7).

[346]Cf. Thompson, Irvin, "The Joseph and Moses Narratives", 149–66; Lemche,
Die Vorgeschichte Israels, 49–50.

[347]Cf. Thompson, Irvin, "The Joseph and Moses Narratives", 177; Lemche, *Die*

ignored by almost a generation of literary critics.[348]

3. The ability of historians and archaeologists to write a history of
   Israel's origins largely independent of biblical interpretation is
   increasing.[349]

It is stressed, that such a denial is methodologically correct since in
these texts we are dealing with literature created for other purposes
than for offering real history.[350] Thompson demonstrates this point in
the context of his discussion concerning the *bytdwd*-inscription found
at Tel Dan,[351] by comparing biblical literature with the Mesha stele
from Moab. The literary nature of the Mesha stele is in his view
comparable to 1–2 Kings, the use of theological metaphors, "clearly
betrays the language of story, in a genre not distant from that of
the sources of I–II Kings".[352] This use of metaphors throughout the
inscription emboldens Thompson to state that

Vorgeschichte Israels, 212–8.

[348]Thompson, "Text, Context and Referent", 67.

[349]Thompson, "Background of the Patriarchs", 37; idem, *Origin Tradition of
Israel*, 27; idem, *Early History of the Israelite People*, 398–412; idem, "Gösta
Ahlström's History of Palestine", in: S.W. Holloway, L.K. Handy (eds.), *The
Pitcher is Broken: Memorial Essays for Gösta Ahlström* (JSOTS, 190), Sheffield
1995, 420–34, esp. 427–34; N.P. Lemche, "Is it Still Possible to Write a History of
Ancient Israel?" *SJOT* 8 (1994) 165–90; idem, *Die Vorgeschichte Israels*, 68–73,
74–6, 109–150.

[350]Thompson, Irvin, "The Joseph and Moses Narratives", 178–80, 210–2;
Thompson, *Origin Tradition of Ancient Israel*, 194–8; idem, *Early History of the
Israelite People*, 353–66; Lemche, *Die Vorgeschichte Israels*, 68–9.

[351]T.L. Thompson, "'House of David': An Eponymic Referent to Yahweh as
Godfather", *SJOT* 9 (1995) 59–74. This *bytdwd* inscription is published in: A.
Biran, J. Naveh, "An Aramaic Stele Fragment from Tel Dan", *IEJ* 43 (1993)
81–98; idem, "The Tel Dan Inscription: A New fragment", *IEJ* 45 (1995) 1–18.
From the vast amount of literature concerning this important inscription, we refer
to M. Dijkstra, "An Epigraphic and Historical Note on the Stela of Tel Dan",
BN 74 (1994) 10–4; F.H. Cryer, "On the Recently-Discovered 'House of David'
Inscription", *SJOT* 8 (1994) 3–19; idem, "A 'Betdawd' Miscellany: Dwd, Dwd'
or Dwdh?" *SJOT* 9 (1995) 52–8; idem, "Of Epistemology, Northwest-Semitic
Epigraphy and Irony: The 'bytdwd/House of David' Inscription Revisited", *JSOT*
69 (1996) 3–17; A. Lemaire, "Epigraphie Palestinienne: Nouvaux Documents, I.
Fragment de Stele Arameenne de Tell Dan (IXe s. av. J.-C.)", *Henoch* 16 (1994)
87–93; B. Becking, "Het 'Huis van David' in een pre-exilische inscriptie uit Tel
Dan", *NThT* 49 (1995) 108–23; A. Demsky, "On Reading Ancient Inscriptions:
The Monumental Aramaic Stele Fragment from Tel Dan", *JANES* 23 (1995) 29–
35; C.H.J. de Geus, "Een belangrijke stele uit Tel Dan, Israël", *Phoenix* 41.3
(1995) 119–30; K.A.D. Smelik, "Nieuwe ontwikkelingen rond de inscriptie uit Tel
Dan", *ACEBT* 14 (1995) 131–41.

[352]Thompson, "House of David", 64.

the literary nature of this text needs to be taken very seriously; so much so that it is quite doubtful that we are talking of a person Omri at all, even in the phrase "Omri, king of Israel".[353]

Having pointed out that in this inscription and in 2 Kings 3 we are dealing with a similar story with the same plot motif, whereas only the names have changed with the story's variants, he writes:

> The centrality of this metaphorical language does not permit us to put II Kings 3 against the Mesha stele in a contest of historicity, whereby we might assert a date for the stele or the biblical tradition as of an event. Nor does it allow us to assert historicity for any of the kings involved in these stories. What we have are two variations of what is clearly a single, literarily conceived, story and not historical texts at all.[354]

A positive appraisal of the truly historical in biblical traditions "can only begin when we have a detailed historical understanding *which is independent of the tradition in question*".[355] However, historically we must not expect too much from such affirmations:

> To the extent that a traditional narrative can be recognised as "historical", it can disclose meaning *which has been brought to the past or associated with the past by tradition, and only accidentally and rarely meaning which that past itself might be given in an historical account.*[356]

When we finally take into account the fact that the continuity in historical records and historical knowledge in ancient Palestine has been broken repeatedly, it might be clear that the historical referent only goes back as early as our sources allow us: to the Hellenistic period.[357]

In conclusion, it is the question for evidence, principally falsifiable, that forms historical probability.[358] This evidence is not found in narratives like the Joseph Story.[359] It may be obvious, however, that in

---

[353] Thompson, "House of David", 64.

[354] Thompson, "House of David", 65. For another approach, taking both biblical text and inscription serious as equal texts containing historical information, see Smelik, *Converting the Past*, 59–92, esp. 80–92.

[355] Thompson, "History and Tradition", 59 (emphasis, Thompson). Cf. also his "Text, Context and Referent", 92.

[356] Thompson, "History and Tradition", 60 (emphasis, Thompson).

[357] Thompson, "House of David", 74.

[358] N.P. Lemche, T.L. Thompson, "Did Biran Kill David? The Bible in the Light of Archaeology", *JSOT* 64 (1994) 3–22, 3, with n. 2.

[359] Cf. Lemche, *Die Vorgeschichte Israels*, 33.

addition to this method which seems to strive to be the very counterpart of the classical fundamentalistic approach to the Bible and Israel's history,[360] more moderate attitudes are found.[361] It might be appropriate to present at this point a more balanced approach in order to present a clear picture of the methodological *status quaestionis* concerning the historiography of Israel and Judah.

The problem of historiography is put in a broader context by K.A.D. Smelik in a study on ancient Israelite and Moabite historiography.[362] In his methodological considerations he suggests an approach in three successive stages. First, the relevant biblical texts are analysed from a historical point of view. Secondly, the general situation in the period concerned is established on the basis of extra-biblical sources. Finally, the results of the preceding two stages are combined to reach a historical reconstruction.[363] In the first two stages the search for ideological tendencies in the texts involve looking for "hidden messages", and with regard to the biblical text the linking of this tendency with a given period of ancient Israel's history.[364]

Closely related is E.A. Knauf's approach, which he himself calls a minimalist approach.[365] History has to be written on the basis of primary sources such as archaeology and contemporary documents. The books of the Hebrew Bible are only a *primary* source for the

---

[360]Cf. Thompson's remarks against a "fundamentalistic bible", in his "House of David", 72–4; further Lemche, *Die Vorgeschichte Israels*, 218–24, on "Was suchen wir in der Bibel?", a paragraph which looks very strange at the end of a historical study and which has much more the character of an apology than of a methodological consideration, which usually is found at the beginning of a book.

[361]Cf. *e.g.* G.W. Ahlström, "The Role of Archaeological and Literary Remains in Reconstructing Israel's History", in: D.V. Edelman (ed.), *The Fabric of History: Text, Artifact and Israel's Past* (JSOTS, 127), Sheffield 1991, 116–41; E.A. Knauf, "From History to Interpretation", *ibid.*, 26–64; J.M. Miller, "Is it Possible to Write a History of Israel without Relying on the Hebrew Bible?" *ibid.*, 93–102; A.D.H. Mayes, "The Place of the Old Testament in Understanding Israelite History and Religion", in: A.G. Auld (ed.), *Understanding Poets and Prophets: Essays ... G.W. Anderson* (JSOTS, 152), Sheffield 1993, 242–57.

[362]Smelik, *Converting the Past* (p. 410, n. 300 above), 1–35.

[363]Smelik, *Converting the Past*, 22.

[364]Smelik, *Converting the Past*, 23–4; Ahlström, "The Role of Archaeological and Literary Remains", 133, with n. 2.

[365]Cf. E.A. Knauf, "King Solomon's Copper Supply", in: E. Lipiński (ed.), *Studia Phoenicia, XI: Phoenicia and the Bible* (OLA, 44), Leuven 1991, 167–86, 171–3. Although at first sight Knauf's study appears to be out of order here since it deals with king Solomon, it is relevant because the period of Solomon's reign is of crucial importance for the dating of the Joseph Story as well as in the historiography of Israel. Cf. also Knauf, "From History to Interpretation", 51–3; Ahlström, "The Role of Archaeological and Literary Remains", 116–41.

period of their final redaction, in this sense 1 Kings 1–11 is only a
secondary source for the tenth century BCE as far as the text contains contemporary documents from that period.[366] If material from
these chapters should demonstrably pre-date the final redaction, then
the lowest possible date is the most likely one, given that memories,
traditions and books evaporate in the course of history. "The question cannot be: 'Is it possible that event E mentioned in source S
did happen?'" but rather: "What can we responsibly assume to have
happened in the area A, at the time T, on the basis of the complete
primary documentation that is available concerning A and T?"[367]
1 Kings 1–11 is certainly not based on annals, as archaeology provides sufficient evidence to conclude that Jerusalem did not become
the centre of a state prior to the end of the eighth century BCE.[368] The
production of annals began under Jeroboam or Rehoboam, whereas
the "chronicle of Solomon" (1 Kgs. 11:41), which provided the material for 1 Kings 3–11, was probably composed during the reign of
Josiah, depicting "Solomon as the king Josiah intended to be",[369] although scattered pieces of poetry and notes on his activities may have
been preserved.[370]

5.23 Recapitulation

1. The Joseph Story (Genesis 37–50) is almost generally viewed as
   a text with different literary layers and therefore with a complex
   literary history. This view is even stronger with respect to the
   Deathbed Episode (Gen. 47:29–49:33), because sometimes the
   Joseph Story is thought to be (or approached as) a literary
   unity, but then only confined to Genesis 37, 39–47, *50, whereas
   Genesis 48 — not to mention chapter 49 — is viewed as a later
   addition (Coats, Westermann).

2. The basic assumption concerning the Joseph Story, and more
   specifically the Deathbed Episode, seems to be the stratification
   of this text according to the classic Documentary Hypothesis:
   the text is compiled from two documents: J and E by a redactor,
   R^{JE}, while in later times the P-document was added to the text
   (*e.g.* Gunkel, Noth, von Rad, Seebaß, Schmidt).

---

[366] Knauf, "From History to Interpretation", 51–3. Cf. also Ahlström, "The Role
of Archaeological and Literary Remains", 117.
[367] Knauf, "King Solomon's Copper Supply", 171–2.
[368] Reference is made to the work of Jamieson-Drake, *Scribes and Schools*.
[369] Knauf, "King Solomon's Copper Supply", 174.
[370] Knauf, "King Solomon's Copper Supply", 179, with nn. 47–50.

3. Other methodological approaches to the Joseph Story are the so-called Supplementary Hypothesis (a), and the Traditio-Historical Approach (b):

   (a) The first approach assumes a basic document, later expanded by editor(s). The different layers are for the most part closely related to the traditional documents J, E and P (Schmitt, Kebekus).

   (b) The other approach discerns an originally independent Joseph Story, later expanded with several passages, in this way connecting the Joseph Story with the patriarchal traditions (Blum).

4. Despite the view that the Joseph Story is composite, there is a strong emphasis on the literary quality of the Story, connected with wisdom circles at a royal court (von Rad). Because of the tension between these two points of view, a solution is sought either in the denial of the validity of the Documentary Hypothesis (Whybray; cf. already Rudolph) or in a marginalization of the reworked parts to some obviously composite passages (Donner, Coats, Westermann).

5. Since the stratification of the Joseph Story is impossible if based solely on the use of Divine names, other criteria are decisive and reflected in the names of the different layers: the Judah-(Israel-) and Reuben-(Jacob-)layer. In addition to the supposed different names of the older brothers, Judah and Reuben, and the names of the patriarch, Jacob and Israel, the difference between Ishmaelites and Midianites is also an important criterion for the identification of the different layers.

6. Genesis 49 is commonly accepted as derived from a tradition, independent from the classical documents J, E, or P.

7. The stratification of the P-layer in the Deathbed Episode is almost generally regarded as an established fact. Gen. 47:28, 48:3–6, 49:1a, 28bB–33aA.b are ascribed to P, and many scholars who initiated a completely new investigation (Schmitt, Kebekus; cf. also Blum, who considers 48:3–7 to be a later addition) take the stratification of P for granted, together with the view on Genesis 49.

8. Gen. 48:7 and 15–16 are problematic passages and the classification differs sharply, while the attribution of 48:21–22 is

also difficult. Verse 7 is successively considered to belong to E (Gunkel), to P (Seebaß, Schmitt), to a later addition (Schmidt), or an addition by R^P (Kebekus). Verses 15–16 are thought to be part of E (Gunkel, Seebaß, Schmitt), of P (Donner), or a later addition (Schmidt).

9. The stratification of the Deathbed Episode according to the Documentary Hypothesis did not lead to a consensus concerning the classification of the different layers within the documents J and E. However, Gen. 47:29–31 is in this analysis generally ascribed to J / Judah-(Israel-)layer and therefore within the literary-critical analysis of the Joseph Story it is looked upon as one of the most certain classifications. Concerning the remaining text (Genesis 48) analyses differ between, on the one hand, a general attribution to E (Wellhausen, Noth) and on the other hand, a denial of the occurrence of E-material within Genesis 48, and distinguishing the layers between J and a later addition (Schmidt).

10. Scholars presenting a new investigation, and opposing (partly or completely) the classical stratification of the Deathbed Episode, have in addition to some of the classical layers to reckon with possible later additions (Rudolph, Seebaß, Schmitt, Schmidt, Kebekus) which might result even in a sum of eight different layers within the Deathbed Episode (Schweizer). On the other hand scholars take into account the possible loss of some passages (Donner, Seebaß) and the rearrangement of the text (Seebaß).

11. The Joseph Story is related to many periods of Israel's history, from the eighteenth century BCE until the Hellenistic period. The former suggestion, together with other attempts to relate the Joseph Story with historical events, has almost been abandoned now. Predominantly the Story is considered a kind of political metaphor, reflecting the political situation of the United Monarchy and the later Northern and Southern kingdom.

12. The use of the Joseph Story, and also the biblical text in general, for historiographical purposes is a hotly disputed topic nowadays. However, only a few scholars are inclined to dismiss the biblical text as irrelevant to the early history of Israel. A moderate approach is preferred by most scholars, fluctuating, however, between a minimalist and maximalist approach.

Text	H.G.	H.S.	H.-C.S.	L.S.	N.K.	H.Schw.
47:28	P	P	P	P	P	Fr
47:29–31	J	J	G	J	Je*	JG
48:1aA	E	E	E	E(?)	Je	I*
48:1aB–2a	E	E	E	E*	Je	Jc
48:2b	J	E	G	J	Je	I
48:3–5a	P	P	P	P	P	Jc*
48:5b–6	P	P	P	P	P	Ep=M
48:7	E	P	P(?)	Z	R^P	Fr*
48:8a	E	E	G	J	Je	I
48:8b	E	E	E	J	Je	I
48:9a	E	E	E	J	Je	I
48:9b	J	J	G	Z	Je	I
48:10a	J	J	G	Z	Je	Fr
48:10b	E	E	E	J	R^P	I
48:11	E	E	E(?)	J	R^P	I
48:12	E	E	E	J	R^P	Fr
48:13–4	J	J	G*	Z	Je	Ep=M
48:15	E	E	E(?)	Z*	R^P	Fr
48:16	E	E	E(?)	Z*	R^P	Fr
48:17	J	J	G	Z	Je	Ep=M
48:18	J	J	G	Z	Je	Ep=M
48:19a	J	J	G	Z	Je	Ep=M
48:19b	J	J	G	Z	Je	Ep>M*
48:20a	(?) E	J	Z	Z	Je	Ep=M
48:20b	E	J	Z	Z	Je	Fr
48:20c	E	J	Z	Z	Je	Ep>M
48:21	E	E	E(?)	Z	Je	I(?)
48:22	E(?)	E	E/Z(?)	Z	R^P	Fr
49:1a	P	J	P	P	P	Add^I
49:1b–2	J^b	J	P/Z(?)	Z	X	Add^I
49:3–28abA	J^b	J	P/Z(?)	Z	X	Add^{II}
49:28bB–32	P	P	P	P	P	Add^I
49:33aA	P	P	P	P	P	Add^I
49:33aB	J	P	G/P(?)	J	Je	Add^I
49:33b	P	P	P	P	P	Add^I

TABLE: SUMMARY OF LITERARY-CRITICAL RESEARCH
GEN. 47:28-49:33[371]

[371]In this table the following abbreviations were used for the authors. H.G. =

5.24   Evaluation of the Previous Research

5.24.1   Introduction

The literary analysis of the Joseph Story has still not found its final solution, as may be reasonably concluded on the basis of the recapitulation and table presented at the end of the previous section. The widely diverging results obtained by scholars would seem to indicate a lack of reliable methods to investigate the problems. It will be useful here to point out where, according to our view, no satisfactory answer has yet been put forward which has met the general approval of scholars.

Before doing so, however, there is one caveat to point out. Concerning Gen. 49:1–28 there is a general concensus among scholars to exclude this passage from the literary analysis of the Joseph Story. This exclusion is based on the results of previous scholarly research of Genesis 49, defining the sayings as "tribal sayings" and ascribing the framework to P, and which is now generally taken for granted.[372] This is remarkable because several scholars have attempted an entirely new investigation because the results of previous research are not convincing. However, by excluding Genesis 49 in advance from literary criticism they place their own research almost inevitably in line with previous research of which the results were rejected by them before. So if the genesis of the Joseph Story has to be investigated anew, this can only start from the existing connection between Story and Blessing. In view of so many failed "solutions" a new investigation, starting with the literary structure as a unity is legitimate.

H. Gunkel; H.S. = H. Seebaß; H.-C.S. = H.-C. Schmitt; L.S. = L. Schmidt; N.K. = N. Kebekus; H.Schw. = H. Schweizer.

For the stratification of the text the following sigla were used. * = classification not complete; the reader is referred to the preceding discussion; Add = addition-layer E = Elohist; Ep=M = Ephraim and Manasseh equally treated-layer; Ep>M = Ephraim put before Manasseh-layer; Fr = fragment; G = *Grundschrift*, basic document; I = Israel-layer; J = Yahwist; Jc = Jacob-layer; Je = Yehowist, R^{JE}; P = Priestly layer; R = *Redaktor*, editor; X = independent tradition; Z = *Zusatz*, addition.

[372]This not only happened to Genesis 49 but also, though less unanimously, to Genesis 38 and later, as we shall see, to the assumption of a Priestly layer within the narrative. See, however, recently: K.A. Deurloo, "Eerstelingschap en Koningschap: Genesis 38 als integrerend onderdeel van de Jozefcyclus", *ACEBT* 14 (1995) 62–73; idem, "Genesis 37,2–11 als thematischer Auftakt zum Josef-Juda-Zyklus", in: E. Talstra (ed.), *Narrative and Comment: Contributions to Discourse Grammar and Biblical Hebrew presented to W. Schneider*, Amsterdam 1995, 71–81; J.P. Fokkelman, "Genesis 37 and 38 at the Interface of Structural Analysis and Hermeneutics", in: L.J. de Regt *et al.* (eds.), *Literary Structure and Rhetorical Strategies in the Hebrew Bible*, Assen, Winona Lake (IN) 1996, 152–87.

Admittedly, however, this will raise many questions but these will have to be investigated in their own right. But first, points that have not been satisfactorily concluded in previous studies will be reviewed next.

5.24.2 Jacob and Israel

The names "Jacob" and "Israel" in the Joseph Story, and especially in the Deathbed Episode (Gen. 47:29–49:33), have not been used in a consistent manner. This fact has induced scholars to assume that the alternation of these names is due to the combination of several different sources into one narrative.[373] But this criterion of different names was criticized by Rudolph and others because of the fact that it could not be applied consistently. In places where one would expect to find the name "Jacob" (for example 48:8a, 11 and 21) the name "Israel" is found.[374] However, despite the objections against this criterion a definitive solution has not yet been found,[375] and scholars still consider this inconsistent use of the names "Jacob" and "Israel" as one of the most significant indications for the assumed stratification of the text.

Rudolph's arguments against the use of these names as identification marks of a document according to the Documentary Hypothesis are still relevant. When "Israel" belongs to the Yahwist and "Jacob" to the Elohist, "Israel" cannot be applied in parts belonging to E.[376] In order to solve this problem the defenders of the Documentary Hypothesis have to assume exceptions or later expansions,[377] or they have to develop a completely new analysis.[378] But, in order to do this, they have to take into consideration extra layers within the

---

[373]Cf. e.g. Coats, "Redactional Unity of Genesis 37–50", 18; Schmidt, *Literarische Studien zur Josephsgeschichte*, 133–5.

[374]See Rudolph, "Die Josephsgeschichte", (p. 369, n. 17 above), 149–51; and Donner, *Literarische Gestalt der Josephsgeschichte* (p. 369, n. 17 above), 39; see also Westermann, *Genesis 12–36*, 668–9; Schmitt, *Die nichtpriesterliche Josephsgeschichte* (p. 394, n. 180 above), 68–9; and E. Talstra, *Schermen met Schrift: De kombinatie van bijbelwetenschappen en computer geïllustreerd aan de tekst van Genesis 48*, Amsterdam 1992, 12, with nn. 20–1. In fact we are dealing here with the classical objection against the criteria of the Documentary Hypothesis, since similar objections are raised against the use of Elohim and Yhwh; cf. Houtman, *Der Pentateuch*, 377–83.

[375]Cf. Talstra, *Schermen met Schrift*, 11–2.

[376]Rudolph, "Die Josephsgeschichte", 149–50.

[377]Cf. for example Ruppert, *Die Josepherzählung* (p. 394, n. 180 above), 163–4.

[378]See Schmidt, *Literarische Studien zur Josephsgeschichte*, 253–71, who follows in many respects Gunkel's analysis, but who considers E to be absent in chapter 48.

text.[379] However, the assumption of yet another layer only complicates the theory and in this way contradicts a principle for literary criticism (and theory in general) as formulated by W.H. Schmidt that the most simple hypothesis is preferable.[380] The fact that the criterion of the names seems to complicate rather than solve the problems in the text makes this criterion unreliable as a norm to distinguish between the different documents.

The problems literary critics have to face because of these names, especially within the Deathbed Episode, force us to look for a different solution. It has sometimes been suggested that the inexplicable occurrence of a name (for example "Israel" within E) is due to the work of an editor (R^P or E^2).[381] Other approaches, suggesting a gradual expansion of the basic document, hold on to the basic idea of the Documentary Hypothesis that each name has to be linked with *one* layer. It is exactly this assumption that proves to be false: when an editor is reworking a basic document in which for example the name "Jacob" is used and he wants to stress *inter alii* by his reworking that this "Jacob" is in fact the same person as "Israel", he will use the name "Israel" several times in the text he inserts in order to create the intended effect. However, this does not exclude him from using the name "Jacob" in his insertions. Rather, he is able to use both names because in his conception they stand for the same person. Expressed in a table, this accounts for the following possibilities:

Basic Document	Editorial Layer
Jacob	Israel (sometimes Jacob)
Israel	Jacob (sometimes Israel)

The first consequence of this observation is that if one name is held to belong to the basic document (*e.g.* "Jacob"), it is no longer a reliable criterion for the definition of that document because the editor could have used either name. In fact the problem is even more complex because Hebrew syntax does not necessarily have to mention the subject by means of a personal pronoun, name or noun, it is possible that an

---

[379]Cf. also Houtman, *Der Pentateuch*, 417.

[380]W.H. Schmidt, "Plädoyer für die Quellenscheidung", *BZ* 32 (1988) 1–14, 3: "Dabei verdient die Hypothese den Vorzug, die mit möglichst wenigen Annahmen möglichst viele Anstöße und Auffälligkeiten des Textes verständlich zu machen weiß, insofern viele Argumente unterschiedlicher Art aufgreift, zusammenfaßt und zu deuten unternimmt."

[381]Cf. *e.g.* Gunkel, *Genesis*, ³1910, 469–70, regarding "Israel" in vv. 8, 11, 21: "falsches Explicitum".

editor inserted only the editorial name (*e.g.* "Israel") in a clause of
the basic document (where no subject was mentioned), thus deceiv-
ing the literary critic into believing that the whole clause is editorial,
whereas only the subject is. From this it follows that the use of the
names "Jacob" and "Israel" as a criterion to distinguish between the
different layers within the text is ambiguous and can only be used as
an additional argument and not as of a principal one.

Finally, it might be suggested that both names were used in the
basic document. This suggestion is based on Gen. 32:22–32, which
seems to contain an archaic tradition.[382] This could be confirmed by
the fact that the names "Jacob" and "Israel" are paired in assumed
archaic texts like Gen. 49:7, 24; Deut. 33:4–5, 10, 28.[383] In other words,
the use of both names might be due to the "author" of the basic document, who already knew this ancient tradition of renaming. However,
the tradition of renaming in Gen. 32:22–32 is in itself improbable,
because it is based on false (folk) etymologies. First, "Jacob" is a
(hypocoristic) theophoric name (< יעקבאל*) meaning "may El/Ilu follow (him) closely".[384] The narrative of renaming is, however, based
on the negative etymology of the name Jacob, deriving the name of

---

[382]Cf. De Moor, *RoY*, 232, 255–6 [see also 90–1]); Korpel, *Rift in the Clouds*,
510, with n. 572.

[383]For Deut. 33:28 it has been argued that in this text the original form of the
name "Jacob", namely יעקבאל* is preserved; see D.N. Freedman, "The Original
Name of Jacob", *IEJ* 13 (1963) 125–6. This suggestion is based on the argument that the construction אֶל־אָרֶץ "to, toward the land" "makes no sense in the
context" (*art.cit.*, 126). However, the preposition אֶל does not solely mean "to,
toward", but also "in, at"; cf. 1 Sam. 17:3; 1 Kgs. 8:30; and in combination with
the verb ישב 1 Kgs. 13:20; Jer. 29:16 ("on"); 35:15. Furthermore, it is commonly
known that אֶל and עַל are interchangeable (cf. e.g. *HAL*, 49; R.J. Tournay, "Le
Psaume et les Bénédictions de Moïse", *RB* 103 [1996] 196–212, 210; S. Beyerle,
*Der Mosesegen im Deuteronomium: Eine text-, kompositions- und formkritische
Studie zu Deuteronomium 33* [BZAW, 250], Berlin 1997, 39) whereas these two
prepositions cause some differences between the textual witnesses, as is the case
in Deut. 33:28, where Sam reads עַל. Interpreting אֶל here as "in" offers a good
reading:

Israel dwells in safety (28aA)	וַיִּשְׁכֹּן יִשְׂרָאֵל בֶּטַח
Jacob dwells alone (28aB)	בָּדָד עֵין יַעֲקֹב
in a land of grain and must (28bA)	אֶל־אֶרֶץ דָּגָן וְתִירוֹשׁ
yes, his skies drip with dew. (28bB)	אַף־שָׁמָיו יַעַרְפוּ־טָל

The almost common emendation for עֵין > עֵן as a verbal form of the root עון "to
dwell" is followed here; cf. Freedman, *art.cit.*, 126; E. Nielsen, *Deuteronomium*
(HAT, I/6), Tübingen 1995, 298, 307 (referring to Num. 23:9, where we find לְבָדָד
יִשְׁכֹּן); Tournay, *art.cit.*, 209–10. In view of the above mentioned interchangeability
of אֶל and עַל the reading of Sam is not followed and the "restoration" of יעקבאל*
rejected.

[384]See De Moor, *RoY*, 237, n. 82.

the root עקב considering Jacob to be the subject of the verb in a negative sense (see Gen. 27:36). Secondly, the narrative is based on the incorrect etymology of the name "Israel" ("he strove with El"; see Gen. 32:29).[385] Since both names "Jacob-El" and "Israel" have a comparable meaning ("may El/Ilu follow [him] closely" and "may El/Ilu fight [for him]"[386] respectively), it appears that such a renaming was superfluous.[387] For that reason it is at the same time unlikely that this renaming reflects a historical "renaming" of any kind,[388] but rather a merging of two persons/groups into one. The fact that the renaming is narrated in a story where we find a threefold aetiology (Peni'el, not eating the sinew of the hip, and why sons of Jacob are called "Israel"), which is a typical literary characteristic of the book of Genesis, makes this tradition highly suspect. The reference in this connection to Gen. 49:7, 24; Deut. 33:4–5, 10, 28 is in the context of the present study disputable, because the archaic nature of Gen. 49:7, 24 has to be tested, which in fact is also true for the texts in Deuteronomy 33. It might be recalled here that both names are used inconsistently within the Deathbed Episode, suggesting some sort of stratification of the text. For that reason the inconsistent use of these two names will be deemed a mark of the text's stratification, but used only as an additional argument for the delimitation of the different layers.

5.24.3   Reuben and Judah

The two brothers Reuben and Judah are frequently mentioned in the discussion on the stratification of the text. These two brothers are usu-

---

[385] For the correct etymology, cf. the following footnote.

[386] De Moor, *RoY*, 238, n. 86.

[387] F. Zimmermann, "Folk Etymology of Biblical Names", in: *Volume du Congrès, Genève 1965* (SVT, 15), Leiden 1966, 311–26, 320–1.

[388] *Pace* Korpel, *Rift in the Clouds*, 510, with n. 572, who states that the story of Gen. 32:22–32 "has such a close parallel in the Ugaritic literature that the tradition contained in the place name Penuel and in the explanatory vv. 28, 30 deserves our full confidence." However, the fact that a tradition has a parallel in Ugaritic literature does not make it more reliable than other traditions.

O. Eissfeldt, "Renaming in the Old Testament", in: P.R. Ackroyd, B. Lindars (eds.), *Words and Meanings: Essays ... D.W. Thomas*, London 1968, 69–79, 76–7, suggests that at the basis of this story there is an event in history where the tribe of Jacob, belonging to the Syrian-Arabian desert or to Mesopotamia, transferred its allegiance to the El who resided at one of its semi-nomadic stopping-places. This tribe reshaped its own neutral name "Jacob" into one which would witness to the majesty of El, *yśr'l*, something like "El is Lord." Since the name "Jacob" appears to be a hypocoristic "Elohistic" name (cf. above), his theory is refuted. On the supposed contrast between the two types of society and the related religion, see De Moor, *RoY*, 236–7.

ally connected with the layers related to the two patriarchal names discussed above, which are sometimes called the Jacob-Reuben-layer ($\approx$ E) and the Israel-Judah-layer ($\approx$ J). With regard to Genesis 37, where the Midianites and Ishmaelites clearly form a literary problem in verse 28, scholars make, on the one hand, a connection between those parts where Reuben is mentioned and those mentioning the Midianites, and, on the other hand between the texts mentioning Judah and the Ishmaelites. However, contrary to the argument of the two names "Jacob" and "Israel" (one person, acting identically within a given text), and the argument of "Midianite" and "Ishmaelite" merchants in chapter 37, "Reuben" and "Judah" are two different persons, who act also differently. So it remains to be seen whether these two brothers really represent two different traditions or if they belong to the layer that is dependent on one and the same person (author or editor).[389] The argument of the two brothers is mainly based on the text found in Genesis 37 and 42, so at first sight it may seem unimportant to the present study. However, since Reuben is mentioned in Gen. 48:5, and — probably more importantly — both Reuben and Judah are mentioned in Gen. 49:3–4, 8–12, this literary problem is as important as the others.[390]

In order to get a clear picture of the problems found in the text, Kebekus' argumentation is presented here.[391] The order of events in Gen. 37:18–24 suggests that the brothers were persuaded not to kill

---

[389]Kebekus, *Die Joseferzählung*, 7, n. 4, argues that, since narrator as well as editor could have used certain literary techniques, and a text is apparently created accordingly, this does not prove its literary unity when formal and objective arguments contest this unity. Although this might be correct, the application of such a literary technique argues against the composite character of the text, or at least against the tensions which could be explained by the literary technique.

[390]R.E. Longacre, "Who Sold Joseph into Egypt?" in: R.L. Harris *et al.* (eds.), *Interpretation and History: Essays ... A.A. MacRae*, Singapore 1986, 75–91, 79–80, considers Genesis 49 as "crucial and culminative", where we find the material for deducing the broader macrostructure.

[391]Kebekus, *Die Joseferzählung*, 7–8. Cf. also Seebaß, *Geschichtliche Zeit* (cf. p. 394, n. 181 above), 73–8; Schmitt, *Die nichtpriesterliche Josephsgeschichte*, 23–32; Schmidt, *Literarische Studien zur Josephsgeschichte*, 146–8; Dietrich, *Die Josepherzählung* (cf. p. 394, n. 181 above), 19–26. See also Kaiser, "Stammesgeschichtliche Hintergründe", 4–5 K.R. Melchin, "Literary Sources in the Joseph Story", *ScEs* 31 (1979) 93–101; J. Scharbert, "Josef als Sklave", *BN* 37 (1987) 104–28; S.E. Loewenstamm, "Reuben and Judah in the Cycle of Joseph Stories", in: idem, *From Babylon to Canaan: Studies in the Bible and its Oriental Background*, Jerusalem 1992, 35–41 (orig. in: *Fourth World Congress of Jewish Studies*, Jerusalem 1969, 69–70); J.A. Soggin, "Notes on the Joseph Story", in: A.G. Auld (ed.), *Understanding Poets and Prophets: Essays ... G.W. Anderson* (JSOTS, 152), Sheffield 1993, 336–49.

Joseph but to throw him into a pit (37:20) because of Reuben's intervention (37:21–22) since in verse 24 he is thrown into the pit alive.
However, this appears to be contradicted by Judah's speech (37:26–
27) which presumes the brothers' intent to kill Joseph. It is also difficult to reconcile that on the one hand the brothers see a caravan
of Ishmaelites coming (37:25) and sell Joseph to them on Judah's
advice (37:27); but on the other hand, that Midianites pull Joseph
out of the pit and sell him to the Ishmaelites (37:28a) without being
noticed by the brothers (cf. 37:29). Moreover there is a clear tension
between verse 25aA ("then they sat down to eat") and verses 29–30:
from verses 24–25aA it could be derived that the brothers sat down
near to the pit (a going away is not reported) whereas according to
verses 29–30 they had clearly left the site. Finally, arguing from another angle, in the present form of the narrative the function of the
Midianites is hardly understandable, they only function as a kind of
"intermediary", who only do what the brothers have decided to do,
namely to sell Joseph to the Ishmaelites. It is therefore questionable
if this "ineffectiveness" of the Midianites can be explained plausibly
with the help of literary techniques. So far the tensions in the text as
Kebekus observed them.

A few remarks are in order here. First of all, it cannot be denied
that the role of the Midianites in the text is difficult to understand
and might reflect a certain stratification of the text.[392] However, the
description of the tensions in the text is not accurate in every instance.
Within the order of events in the narrative it might be concluded
with Gunkel that the Midianites were counted as Ishmaelites at the
final redactional level (cf. Judg. 8:24) and that *the brothers* were the
subject of the verb וַיִּמְשְׁכוּ.[393] This might be deduced from the fact that
in verse 28bB it is said that *they* (= Ishmaelites, v. 28aC) brought
Joseph to Egypt, while in verse 36 it is said that the *Midianites* sold
him into Egypt (and see 39:1, where it says again the Ishmaelites).

---

[392] A certain stratification in Gen. 37:28 is defended by many scholars, even by
those who contest the classical stratifications of the Joseph story; cf. *e.g.* Donner,
Literarische Gestalt der Josephsgeschichte, 44–5; G.W. Coats, *From Canaan to
Egypt: Structural and Theological Context for the Joseph Story* (CBQ MS, 4),
Washington (DC) 1976, 17.

[393] Gunkel, *Genesis*, ³1910, 409; H.C. White, "Reuben and Judah: Duplicates
or Complements?" in: J.T. Butler *et al.* (eds.), *Understanding the Word: Essays
...B.W. Anderson* (JSOTS, 37), Sheffield 1985, 73–97, 78.

Contrast, however, E.A. Knauf, "Midianites and Ishmaelites", in: J.F.A.
Sawyer, D.J.A. Clines (eds.), *Midian, Moab and Edom: The History and Archae-
ology of Late Bronze and Iron Age Jordan and North-West Arabia* (JSOTS, 24),
Sheffield 1983, 147–62, 147, who thinks that both texts contradict each other.

Besides, the decision not to regard the brothers as the subject of וַיִּמְשְׁכוּ (v. 28aB), not reading a change of subject between verse 28aA and 28aB, is a matter of interpretation, in contrast to the acceptance of the change of subject between verse 28aC and 28aD, which is not even discussed.[394] However, if a change in subject is not found (though not explicitly asserted), as is the case in verses 28aA and 28aB, a continuation of the subject may be just as probable in verses 28aC and 28aD, concluding that the Midianites "sold Joseph to the Ismaelites and (they = *the Midianites*) brought him to Egypt". Compare the combination of subject and verb in Gen. 37:27–28:

come, let sell him to the Ishmaelites ...	... לְכוּ וְנִמְכְּרֶנּוּ לַיִּשְׁמְעֵאלִים
and his brothers listened	וַיִּשְׁמְעוּ אֶחָיו
and Midianite traders passed by	וַיַּעַבְרוּ אֲנָשִׁים מִדְיָנִים סֹחֲרִים
and (they) drew up and lifted up Joseph ...	... וַיִּמְשְׁכוּ וַיַּעֲלוּ אֶת־יוֹסֵף
and (they) sold ... to the Ishmaelites ...	... וַיִּמְכְּרוּ ... לַיִּשְׁמְעֵאלִים
and (they) brought Joseph to Egypt	וַיָּבִיאוּ אֶת־יוֹסֵף מִצְרָיְמָה

Of course the most obvious interpretation here is that the Ishmaelites (28aC) brought Joseph to Egypt (28aD); but similarly the most likely interpretation of verse 28aB is that the brothers drew Joseph out of the pit and sold him to the Midianites/Ishmaelites (37:28aC),[395] which is already suggested by the phrase וַיִּשְׁמְעוּ אֶחָיו "and his brothers listened" (37:27).[396] It is not disputed that the text is complex on a diachronical level and the designations "Ishmaelites" and "Midianites" might indeed belong to two different layers.[397] But on a synchronic level the reading is not as complicated as is suggested by Ke-

---

[394] Although the problems in the text are felt by many scholars, the decision to consider the Midianites as the subject here *at a synchronic level* is not made by many scholars. But cf. also I. Willi-Plein, "Historiographische Aspekte der Josefsgeschichte", *Henoch* 1 (1979) 305–331, 313; E.A. Knauf, *Midian: Untersuchungen zur Geschichte Palästinas und Nordarabiens am Ende des 2. Jahrtausends v. Chr.* (ADPV), Wiesbaden 1988, 27. However, such a reading is not restricted to "critical" scholars, but has even been found with medieval scholars and with modern ones who are inclined to consider the Joseph Story a unity; cf. B. Jacob, *Das erste Buch*, 706, with reference to Rabbi Samuel ben Meir (Raschbam); Aalders, *Genesis*, dl. 3, 86–7; E. Lowenthal, *The Joseph Narrative in Genesis: An Interpretation*, New York (NY) 1973, 27; J.S. Ackerman, "Joseph, Judah, and Jacob", in: K.R.R. Gros Louis (ed.), *Literary Interpretations of Biblical Narratives*, Vol. II, Nashville 1982, 85–113, 99–100; Sarna, *Genesis*, 261.

[395] Longacre, "Who Sold Joseph into Egypt?" 75–91. Fokkelman, "Genesis 37 and 38", 164, n. 20, points out that vv. 28a and 28d form an inclusion, with the traders the subject of the first and the last verb forms, whereas the brothers are the subject of the second and third verb forms.

[396] Fokkelman, "Genesis 37 and 38", 161, with n. 16.

[397] Houtman, *Der Pentateuch*, 417.

bekus: the Midianites do not function as "intermediaries" who sold
Joseph to the Ishmaelites, but are seen as Ishmaelites themselves.[398]

The argument that Judah's speech contradicts the brothers' resig-
nation to kill Joseph because of Reuben is void. Judah's speech indeed
suggests that the brothers did not renounce the idea that Joseph had
to die; but contrary to Kebekus' suggestion, this is not suggested by
the preceding text. The preceding text suggests that Reuben gave the
brothers the idea that they kill Joseph indirectly by throwing him into
the pit, but that they did not shed blood (37:22). Judah's speech in
fact criticizes the idea that they do not shed blood this way, although
his words do not suggest that he cares: "What profit is it, if we slay
our brother?" (37:26). As suggested above there is not necessarily any
friction between the episode of the Midianites and Judah's speech: the
brothers sold Joseph to the Midianites/Ishmaelites. So in verse 29 the
brothers know that Joseph is gone and when Reuben comes to them,
saying that "the lad is gone" he does not tell them anything new.

Kebekus suggests that in verse 29 there exists a tension with verse
25, because there is a difference in scene. In his view the fact that no
mention is made of going away from the pit, suggests that they are
still there, and sat down there to eat (37:26). However, it appears
that Kebekus is overcharging the narrative's information here. When
reading the story in this way, the problem is even more complicated
than Kebekus assumes, because the circumstance that the brothers
went to the pit is not told either. Thus, how they came to the pit to
throw Joseph into it (37:24) is a puzzle. Or, could it be that the reader
is supposed to fill in such changes in the scene himself when they are
not mentioned explicitly? Such abrupt changes are quite common
in Ancient Near Eastern literature in, for example, direct speech.[399]

---

[398]In Judg. 8:24 a similar problem is found, because there the Midianites are
identified as Ishmaelites. Usually the reference in verse 24b is considered a later
interpolation or a gloss. But one way or another, at a certain moment in the history
of the text the Midianites are considered to be Ishmaelites. Cf. Knauf, "Midianites
and Ishmaelites", 152; idem, *Ismael: Untersuchungen zur Geschichte Palästinas
und Nordarabiens im 1. Jahrtausend v.Chr.* (ADPV), Wiesbaden ²1989, 14, who
holds this view only concerning Judg. 8:24. See also Houtman, *Der Pentateuch,*
416–7.

[399]Cf. W.G.E. Watson, "Abrupt Speech in Ugaritic Narrative Verse", *UF* 22
(1990) 414–20 (with lit.) (= idem, *Traditional Techniques,* 425–30). In the Hebrew
Bible the phenomenon of abrupt speech is found in e.g. Mic. 4; see A.S. van der
Woude, "Micah in Dispute with the Pseudo-Prophets", *VT* 19 (1969) 244–60;
idem, "Micah IV 1–5: An Instance of the Pseudo-Prophets Quoting Isaiah", in
Symbolae biblicae et mesopotamicae F.M.Th. Liagre Böhl dedicatae, Leiden 1973,
396–402; cf. also S.A. Meier, *Speaking of Speaking: Marking Direct Discourse in
the Hebrew Bible* (SVT, 46), Leiden 1992, esp. 23–42.

The same applies to change of scenes. This might be demonstrated by means of a discussion of a few passages in the legend of Aqhatu (KTU 1.17–19). In the beginning of this legend an abrupt change of scene is made, which, according to the criteria of doublets and abrupt change, might mark a seam in the text. The Ugaritic king Dani'ilu is mourning and brings offerings to the gods because he has no son. After seven days Ba'lu comes to him and asks (KTU 1.17:i.17–21):[400]

ảbynm | dnil . mt . rpi .	Is Dani'ilu, the Saviour's man, miserable,
ảnḫ . g̣zr | mt . hrnmy .	Is the hero, the Harnamite man, sighing?
din . bn . lh | km . ảḫh .	Because he has no son like his brothers,
w . šrš . km . ảryh |	nor root like his kinsmen?
bl . iṯ . bn . lh . k(!)mảḫh .	He has no son like his brothers,
wšrš | km . ảryh .	nor root like his kinsmen!

Clearly there is a seam in the text, but this seam has to be considered at a synchronic level: the scene has changed and the speaker of the first two lines (Ba'lu), speaking to Dani'ilu, is also the speaker of the third line, but now directing his speech to Ilu, apparently at Ilu's abode. A similar abrupt change of the scene is found in KTU 1.19:i.19, where directly following the speech of the goddess 'Anatu after the murder of Aqhat, the scene is changed to the gate of the town where king Dani'ilu is judging. A few lines further Dani'ilu is riding through the fields with his daughter (KTU 1.19:ii.1–25), when they see Aqhat's two servants coming. These servants, who left with Aqhat, know of the death of Aqhat. It is remarkable, however, that according to KTU 1.18:ii.14–15 they were not present at the scene when he was killed since they were left in the encampment.[401] Without any reference to how they could have known that Aqhat is dead, we are told in KTU 1.19:i.11–13 that they are mourning, saying "how bitter, how bitter". Furthermore there is no account of these two servants departing from the encampment or from the scene of death and going to Dani'ilu.[402] But subsequently we read in KTU 1.19:ii.25–29 that they bring the

---

[400]See *ARTU*, 226–7; *MLC*, 334, 368. For a different interpretation cf. *TOML*, 420–1; B. Margalit, *The Ugaritic Poem of AQHT: Text, Translation, Commentary* (BZAW, 182), Berlin 1989, 266–7.

[401]The interpretation of De Moor, *ARTU*, 245, is followed; though other interpretations of this text are suggested; cf. *TOML*, 438; *MLC*, 384; Margalit, *The Ugaritic Poem of AQHT*, 155, 334–5. The point remains, however, that there is no account that his two servants were present at the banquet and have witnessed his death. It has to be concluded by the reader.

[402]A similar abrupt transition was suggested by Kebekus to betray a seam in the account: it was not mentioned that the brothers left the pit in which Joseph was thrown. Cf. also KTU 1.3:iii.25–30, where a similar device is found.

news of Aqhat's death, being apparently very well informed concerning the cause of his death, since they refer to 'Anatu's words and the way he was murdered (KTU 1.19:ii.29–30, 38*–39):[403]

hlm . tnm | [*q*]*dqd .*	Twice they struck the skull
tltid . 'l . ùd[*n*] |	three times above the ear.
. . .	
[*ảt*]*r'ntyql .*	Under (the feet of) 'Anatu he fell,
l . tš'ly . hwt .	she could not make him rise.
[*š*]*sảtkrh . npšhm*	She made his soul depart like wind,
kitl . brltkm [. *qtr . bảph*]	(his) life like spittle, like smoke from his nose!

Obviously there was no problem for the author of this Ugaritic legend to omit certain phases of the "events" in order to keep the story going, supposing the hearers/readers to fill in the gaps themselves. So, when such literary devices are applied in other ancient Near Eastern texts, we may assume that such devices were also at the disposal of the Hebrew writer. Therefore, when abrupt changes are found in the text they do not necessarily mark a (diachronical) seam in the text, but might easily be explained as a literary technique to keep the story going.

In fact such a literary device is found in the transition from verse 28 to 29. Whereas it appears that in the preceding verses all the brothers are involved, in verse 29 Reuben apparently does not know of the sale of Joseph to Egypt. Hence, a tension could be created between these two episodes. However, the conclusion that the account of Reuben is thus part of a different layer, in which the brothers did not sell Joseph, is in fact a *diachronic* solution for what might also be concluded *synchronically*: Reuben was apparently not at the scene when Joseph was sold.[404] This is what the narrative suggests, although without mentioning it explicitly, but applying a common literary device.

Furthermore, when considering the arguments to divide Reuben and Judah over two different documents or layers, it appears that in fact Judah and Reuben presuppose each other and are thus indispensable for the continuation of the story.[405] If Joseph had not been

---

[403] For the events they refer to, cf. respectively KTU 1.18:iv.23–4; 1.17:vi.44–5; 1.18:iv.40–1; 1.18:iv.24–6, 36–7. Further *ARTU*, 253–55, with nn. 198, 207–9. For the marginal text of KTU 1.19:ii.38*, see M. Dijkstra, J.C. de Moor, "Problematic Passages in the Legend of Aqhatu", *UF* 7 (1975) 173–215, 208, nn. 297–8; *CARTU*, 113; *ARTU*, 254, n. 207; *KTU²*, 58.

[404] Cf. also Fokkelman, "Genesis 37 and 38", 163–4.

[405] Cf. the fact that *Reuben's* cry of despair הַיֶּלֶד אֵינֶנּוּ "the boy is not with us"

sold by his brothers to Egypt, but stolen by the Midianites according to the Reuben-layer, it would be rather odd that the brothers
subsequently suggest to their father that Joseph was devoured by
a wild animal — without knowing whether he might be alive and
brought back to his father.[406] So their action is illogical within the
course of events and therefore unacceptable as a reconstruction of the
original narrative.[407] The acts of the brothers make sense only when
they are a continuation of the preceding sale of Joseph to the Midian-
ites/Ishmaelites. On the other hand, Judah's suggestion to sell Joseph
to Egypt presupposes that Joseph had already been thrown into the
pit. But it was Reuben who suggested to throw him into the pit alive
(verse 22) and without this suggestion and its execution, Judah's proposal is uncomprehensible.[408] The only way to solve this problem is
to suggest that an original document (J) read "Judah" in verse 22
instead of "Reuben", but that the Redactor who merged the different
documents changed this "Judah" into "Reuben" in order to create
a smoother narrative.[409] However, no evidence for this suggestion is
provided,[410] whereas Judah's speech in verse 22 would form a doublet
with verse 26, where he suggests again not to kill Joseph, but this

---

(37:30) returns as a kind of keyword in the following story, in the speech of the
brothers: הָאֶחָד אֵינֶנּוּ "the one is not with us" (42:13, 32), and later in *Judah's*
speech for Benjamin: הַנַּעַר אֵינֶנּוּ "the lad is not with us" (44:30, 34, cf. 31); see:
Willi-Plein, "Historiographische Aspekte des Josefsgeschichte", 313.

[406]Cf. Seebaß, *Geschichtliche Zeit*, 74. However, Seebaß comes forward with this
suggestion in order to find an indispensable continuation of the story. After reconstructing the different documents he concludes, that the E-layer had no account
of the theft by the Midianites (only of their passing by [37:28aA] and of their sale
of Joseph to Egypt [v. 36a]), nor that the brothers sold him; but in his reconstruction the brothers try to deceive their father without having any information
whether Joseph had been saved or sold into Egypt.

[407]Kebekus, *Die Joseferzählung*, suggests that Gen. 37:31–34 is mainly dependent on a first expansion (Reuben-expansion / Je), so it does not belong to the
original narrative. But as these verses are part of the Reuben-expansion, still
without mentioning Judah, the criticism is also valid for this analysis.

[408]Coats, *From Canaan to Egypt*, 17; White, "Reuben and Judah", 81.

[409]Wellhausen, *Composition*, 54; Noth, *Überlieferungsgeschichte des Pentateuch*,
31, n. 100; Schmidt, *Literarische Studien zur Josephsgeschichte*, 146–7. Against
this solution it has been objected by Redford, *Biblical Story of Joseph*, 142; Donner, *Literarische Gestalt der Josephsgeschichte*, 38, n. 74, that this change in name
is not attested by any manuscript and thus a *quellenkritische Verlegenheitslösung*
(Donner). However, although it might indeed be a stop-gap solution, the argument is a textual critical argument in a literary-critical discussion and therefore
void (Schmidt, *op.cit.*, 147).

[410]Cf. the previous section, where it was showed that a similar change of names
of Jacob and Israel is necessary in order to enable the assignment of certain parts
of the text to the supposed documents.

time to sell him to the Ishmaelites.[411]

Finally, we might consider an argument of Schmitt, who also finds a tension between the two brothers, but who considers the Reuben-layer to be a later criticism of the Judah account, because Reuben is always pictured as a better brother than Judah.[412] In our view this observation is not correct. Judah's suggestion to sell Joseph to Egypt, which in itself was an evil gesture, is explained at the end of the Joseph Story as God's will (Gen. 50:20; see also 45:5–8): "As for you, you meant evil against me; but God meant it for good, to bring it about that many people should be kept alive, as they are today".[413] In this way Judah appears to be the instrument by which God brought Joseph to Egypt, whereas Reuben's plan was only to bring Joseph back to his father.[414] In Genesis 42 and 43 both brothers argue with their father that he should let Benjamin go to Egypt and Judah knows how to win the plea by putting himself as a surety for Benjamin.[415] The prominent role of Judah is also confirmed henceforth by Judah's speech before Joseph (45:18–34), which is a sequel to his former speech (Genesis 42); and further in that the patriarch sent Judah ahead to Joseph (Gen. 46:28), suggesting that Judah's prominent position was recognized already by his father. So, within the Joseph Story it appears that Reuben and Judah are no aliases but competitors, both striving for power. The sole tension within the narrative is found in the scene of Joseph's sale to the Midianites/Ishmaelites and Reuben's reaction to it. But this is not so much a tension with regard to the episodes where Judah is mentioned, and might easily be caused by the diachronical complicated Midianite/Ishmaelite-episode.

In conclusion, the solutions proposed for the literary problems in

---

[411]Redford, *Biblical Story of Joseph*, 142.

[412]Cf. Schmitt, *Die nichtpriesterliche Josephsgeschichte*, 19–20.

[413]This conclusion of the Joseph Story has lead Longacre to describe the Joseph Story as a story of "divine providence"; cf. Longacre, "Who Sold Joseph to Egypt?" 79; idem, *Joseph*, 43. Similar: Willi-Plein, "Historiographische Aspekte der Josefsgeschichte", 322; Soggin, "Notes on the Joseph Story", 344.

[414]Cf. Ackerman, "Jacob, Joseph and Judah", 99–100.

[415]Schmitt, *Die nichtpriesterliche Josephsgeschichte*, 19, n. 64, suggests that Reuben's offer of his two sons is more than Judah's suggestion. However, Reuben's offer to kill his sons as a surety is not effective in this situation, where his father is mourning for two sons already (Joseph and Simeon) and fears the death of the third one (Benjamin). Therefore Judah's surety is more moderate, whereas the fact that Judah puts *himself* as a surety might also appear more trustworthy.

Strictly on a synchronic level, it might be suggested that Jacob deems Reuben not trustworthy, since he has deceived his father (Gen. 35:22; cf. also our rendering of Gen. 49:4 in section 2.2 below); see: Ackerman, "Jacob, Joseph and Judah", 100; Fokkelman, "Genesis 37 and 38", 164, n. 21.

the Joseph Story, that is, dividing Reuben and Judah over two layers, are not conclusive. On the one hand, Reuben's actions are ineffective, first to save Joseph (Genesis 37) and afterwards to return to Egypt with Benjamin (Genesis 42). Thus the plausibility of an independent document (E) or the priority of the Reuben layer before the Judah-redaction has to be excluded. On the other hand, Judah's actions presuppose Reuben's (Gen. 37:26–27). If different layers for both brothers are assumed, this can only be explained on the assumption that certain parts of the original Judah-layer are lost or that the original name "Judah" was changed into "Reuben" (Gen. 37:21–22). In our view we have to assume that both brothers belong to the same layer, and when a redactional process has taken place in the Joseph Story, Reuben and Judah both belong either to the original narrative, and can therefore return also in the editorial layer, or they are part of the editorial layer and did not occur in the original Joseph Story.[416] In a table, it gives the following picture:

Basic Document	Editorial Layer
Reuben and Judah	Reuben and Judah
—	Reuben and Judah

From the preceding discussion it may be concluded that the arguments in favour of the Documentary Hypothesis and the posibility of two independent documents, J and E, in Genesis 37 are not compelling.[417] Reuben and Judah cannot be devided over two different documents without assuming that certain passages have been left out or changed. Since an incomplete or fragmentary layer does not suggest an independent document, but rather a redactional layer, our findings point in the direction of a kind of Redaction Hypothesis. This is in line with the recent tendency of scholars to look for redactional or supplementary layers within the Pentateuch, rather than for different documents.[418] This might be demonstrated by the following section on the Priestly *document* or Priestly *editor*.

5.24.4 The Priestly What?

Although two scholars, H.-C. Schmitt and N. Kebekus express themselves in moderately critical terms on the issue of the classical solution

---

[416] Of course it is also possible that both belong to one original document J or E; or both belonged to both documents; or finally: both are the work of R^JE.

[417] Cf. also Houtman, *Der Pentateuch*, 418.

[418] Cf. *e.g.* Houtman, *Der Pentateuch*, 422–3, who suggests a combination of the Fragment-, Supplement- and Traditio-Historical (*Kristallisations*) Hypothesis.

of source-analysis, they both use, like L. Schmidt, source P without
any restraint. Gen. 47:28 and 48:3-6(7) are assigned then, in accordance with Gunkel's analysis, to P. Other parts, however, are with-
drawn from this assignment for several reasons, of which the most
cogent one is repetition. This criterion, usually referred to as "doublets" in the narrative, is one of the crucial arguments in assigning a
certain text to a different source.

With regard to our story it is important to ask why the scene,
described in 48:13-20 does not belong to P, since in this scene the
preference of Ephraim over Manasseh is also the central theme.[419]
This problem was seen by L. Schmidt, who concluded that 48:19 in
particular could not belong to P, because P mentions Ephraim before
Manasseh in 48:5.[420] Moreover, Schmidt points to another argument,
namely the use of גּוֹיִם in 48:19, which in his view is impossible for
P. According to P each tribe would be one גּוֹי (35:11, contrast 48:4).
Ephraim, however, would be a מְלֹא־הַגּוֹיִם.[421] In our view Schmidt is
magnifying a minor difference which forces him to assume a large secondary expansion because the use of גּוֹיִם had to be later than P. Such
minor differences in vocabulary can never be reliable indications of
a different source. This becomes especially clear when we take into
consideration that the use of מְלֹא־הַגּוֹיִם in relation to Ephraim may
have been used to indicate that he would surpass the tribe of Manasseh which would be only an עַם. It is not unreasonable, therefore,
to take the plural גּוֹיִם in our verse as a *pluralis intensivus*.[422] If this
understanding of the plural of גּוֹי in 48:19 is correct, and consequently
removes the reason for not ascribing this verse to P, we may note the
perceptive remark of J.A. Emerton: "We must not expect rigid uniformity in P, and minor variations in wording are not to be regarded
as proof of diversity of authorship."[423]

The problem concerning P arises not only in 48:13–20 but also
in 48:1–2a. According to Schmidt this part can not be assigned to
P because Manasseh is mentioned here before Ephraim because in
verse 5 Ephraim was called before Manasseh.[424] Yet, Schmidt ignores
verse 5 where it is Joseph's father who changes the order of names,

---

[419]Recently Talstra, *Schermen met Schrift*, 10–1, referred to this point.

[420]Schmidt, *Literarische Studien zur Josephsgeschichte*, 259.

[421]Schmidt, *Literarische Studien zur Josephsgeschichte*, 258–9.

[422]Cf. already Ehrlich, *Randglossen*, Bd. I, 240; Speiser, *Genesis*, 358.

[423]J.A. Emerton, "The Priestly Writer in Genesis", *JThS* 39 (1988) 381–400,
385. We are aware of the fact that Emerton uses this argument against the theory
of Rendtorff and others in defence of the unity of the commonly accepted P-texts.
However, his statement applies to the present case just as well.

[424]Schmidt, *Literarische Studien zur Josephsgeschichte*, 265–6.

whereas in verse 1 it is the narrator who tells us — using the order of birth (41:50–52) — that Manasseh and Ephraim are brought to Joseph's father.[425] With this remark the narrator prepares the scene for Manasseh and Ephraim to be brought to Joseph's father for the patriarch to switch the order of their names. This again indicates that there exists more cohesiveness among the several parts in which Ephraim and Manasseh are mentioned than scholars have conceded thus far.[426] This coherence argues against the division of the text over JE on the one hand, and P on the other; and argues even in favour of the assignement to one and the same layer, *viz.* JE or P.

The existence of P as an independent source has now been discussed for several decades and has still not found an established consensus.[427] With regard to the Joseph-story it is rather difficult to establish a consecutive narrative using P-material on its own and it had to be assumed by several scholars who regard P as an independent source that several parts of P were left out in favour of the JE layer.[428] Such assumptions however, make the theory of an independent source P even less likely than before.

Any discussion of P tends to run into complications given that any revision of P will have knock-on effects regarding the need to revise the JE layer to accommodate it. The extent of the sources, especially the extent of P, that once found an almost unanimous consensus, has now become a subject of hot debate. The defenders of the redactorial P minimize the extent of P as much as they can. His contribution

---

[425]Cf. Jacob, *Das erste Buch* 866–8; E. Lowenthal, *The Joseph Narrative in Genesis: An Interpretation*, New York (NY) 1973, 136.

[426]It should also be noted here that a change in the order of paired names is a common feature in Semitic literature: cf. the common order of "Moses and Aaron", next to "Aaron and Moses" (Exod. 6:20, 27; Num. 3:1). Furthermore the paired names of deities in Ugarit also change order frequently without the need to introduce sources into the text; cf. *e.g.* 'Anatu and 'Athtartu in KTU 1.2:i.40; 1.114:23–4, and 'Athtartu and 'Anatu in KTU 1.114:9–11, 26–7.

[427]We mention only some recent works on this point here: Cross, *CMHE*, 293–325; R. Rendtorff, *Das überlieferungsgeschichtliche Problem des Pentateuch* (BZAW, 147), Berlin 1977; B.S. Childs, *Introduction to the Old Testament as Scripture*, London 1979, 147; S. Tengström, *Die Toledotformel und die literarische Struktur der priesterlichen Erweiterungsschicht im Pentateuch* (CB OTS, 17), Lund 1982; for a different point of view, cf. K. Koch, "P — Kein Redaktor! Erinnerung an zwei Eckdaten der Quellenscheidung", *VT* 37 (1987) 446–67; Emerton, "The Priestly Writer in Genesis" 381–400.

[428]Cf. Schmidt, *Literarische Studien zur Josephsgeschichte*, 265–6, 287–9; Seebaß, *Geschichtliche Zeit*, 18–9, 61–2; Emerton, "The Priestly Writer in Genesis", 393–5. Emerton even assumes that P left parts out in his original work, because he already knew JE and took knowledge of this material for granted among his readers.

would have consisted in small formulas here and there, like the *toledot*-formula, meant to modify JE according to the views of the priestly writers. The opponents of this view, however, try to maximize the P-strand as much as possible to create a consecutive P-narrative.

5.24.5   The Provenance of the Deathbed Episode

The attempts to date the Joseph Story and Genesis 49 did not lead to a consensus. As was demonstrated before, the discussion on these texts is burdened with the heritage of previous literary criticism and the paradigms settled by it. This point may be demonstrated with the help of the usual allocation of the two documents J and E to the Southern kingdom (J) in the tenth or ninth century BCE, and the Northern Kingdom (E) in the eighth or seventh century BCE. The allocation to North and South reminds one of Procrustus' bed because all attempts to date the Joseph Story are measured against the events connected with the supposed origin of J and E, and the work of R^{JE}. However, next to this supposed order of documents, the possibility ought to be considered that E came before J,[429] and thus antedated a possible Yahwistic era.[430] In the case of the Joseph Story it is usually assumed that references to Joseph as a leader are understandable only as references to Solomonic kingship,[431] or to the leaders of the Northern kingdom after the breakup of the United Monarchy. This view is based mainly on the description of the rise of the monarchy in Israel as found in the Books of Samuel, suggesting that kingship arose during Early Iron I, whereas in the days of the Judges there was no

---

[429]This suggestion is found already in the nineteenth century with the adherents of the Supplement Hypothesis, like H.G.A. Ewald, F. Bleek and J.C.F. Tuch. For this theory and its arguments, cf. Houtman, *Der Pentateuch*, 91–5. See for this suggestion also König, *Die Genesis*, 61–6. The suggestion is still worthwhile considering, given that in the development of Israel's religion it is obvious that 'El(ohim) came before YHWH. If the name YHWH is "younger" than 'El(ohim), as is commonly accepted, it seems only logical that Israel's oldest traditions belong rather to an Elohistic-tradition than to a Yahwistic-tradition. Cf. on this religious historical development De Moor, *RoY*; M.S. Smith, *The Early History of God: Yahweh and the Other Deities in Ancient Israel*, San Francisco 1990; R.K. Gnuse, *No Other Gods: Emergent Monotheism in Israel* (JSOTS, 241), Sheffield 1997.

[430]Of course there have been other proposals for dating the Yahwist, such as the post-exilic era by *e.g.* M. Rose, *Deuteronomist und Jahwist: Untersuchungen zu den Berührungspunkten beider Literaturwerke* (AThANT, 67), Zürich 1981; J. Van Seters, *Der Jahwist als Historiker* (ThSt, 134), Zürich 1987; idem, *Prologue to History: The Yahwist as Historian in Genesis*, Louisville (KY) 1992. Obviously, these proposals will be considered in the present study, but these earlier dates are relevant because of a possible change in order of J and E, which is usually not considered when J is dated in the tenth or ninth century.

[431]Crüsemann, *Der Widerstand gegen das Königtum*, 143–55.

king in Israel.[432] But this approach does not take into account that tradition itself suggests that the North was a relatively independent realm before David became king.[433] This is at least suggested by the rather difficult, but partly ancient, tradition in Judges 9, that Abimelech, the son of Jerubba'al,[434] a Manassite from Ophra,[435] became king in Shechem.[436] In this connection it is important to note that the descriptions of the judges sometimes betray "royal" features, whereas on the other hand, the description of king Saul is comparable with the description of a judge.[437] In addition, it has to be noted that the title "king" might have been applied for very different types of leaders, varying from local sheikhs to the Pharao in Egypt.[438] It might, therefore, be possible that references to a leadership of Joseph not only reflect the kingship in the Northern kingdom after the United Monarchy, but might also reflect the political situation in the North in pre-Davidic times. Such a situation would fit in with the possibility that during the Solomonic era a certain Joseph narrative was edited in a pro-Judahite way (mostly with reference to the Jahwist).

---

[432]Cf. the fact that this description of history still governs the view — or at least the terminology — of historians: N.P. Lemche, *Early Israel: Anthropological and Historical Studies on the Israelite Society before the Monarchy* (SVT, 37), Leiden 1985; J. Strange, "The Transition from the Bronze Age to the Iron Age in the Eastern Mediterranean and the Emergence of the Israelite State", *SJOT* 1 (1987) 1–19; I. Finkelstein, "The Emergence of the Monarchy in Israel: The Environmental and Socio-Economic Aspects", *JSOT* 44 (1989) 43–74; R. Neu, *Von der Anarchie zum Staat. Entwicklungsgeschichte Israels vom Nomadentum zur Monarchie im Spiegel der Ethnosoziologie*, Neukirchen 1992; E.–M. Laperrousaz (ed.), *La protohistoire d'Israel: de l'exode a la monarchie*, Paris 1991.

[433]Cf. 2 Sam. 2–3.

[434]Note the Ba'alistic name, which received a reinterpretation in Judg. 6:32, "Let Ba'al contend (against him)", but which undoubtedly must be interpreted as an authentic Ba'alistic name, meaning "Let Ba'al contend (for him)" or "Let Ba'al be great" (*HAL*, 414), as is suggested by the corruption of this name in 2 Sam. 11:21, which is comparable to other Ba'alistic names from the North, like Eshba'al/Ish-bosheth (1 Chron. 8:33/2 Sam. 2:8) and Meribba'al/Mephi-bosheth (1 Chron. 8:34/2 Sam. 4:4).

[435]H. Donner, "Ophra in Manasse: Der Heimort des Richters Gideon und des Königs Abimelech", in: E. Blum *et al.* (Hrsg.), *Die hebräische Bibel und ihre zweifache Nachgeschichte: Fs R. Rendtorff*, Neukirchen 1990, 193–206.

[436]Cf. on this text the discussion in Fritz, *Die Entstehung Israels*, 43–5; also — rather shortly — Lemche, *Early Israel*, 274, with n. 84.

[437]On this matter, see section 2.4.1.2.3, n. 285, above. Cf. furthermore E.A. Knauf, "King Solomon's Copper Supply", in: E. Lipiński (ed.), *Studia Phoenicia, XI: Phoenicia and the Bible* (OLA, 44), Leuven 1991, 167–86, 181, n. 55.

[438]Cf. N. Na'aman, "The Contribution of the Amarna Letters to the Debate on Jerusalem's Political Position in the Tenth Century B.C.E.", *BASOR* 304 (1996) 17–27, esp. 20–1.

Such an assumption with regard to the Joseph Story — and without historicizing the whole story at the same time — has, as far as the present author is aware, been suggested only in recent times by Van der Merwe in his studies, but was never further elaborated.[439] Of course literary critics take into consideration that ancient traditions were used in the Joseph Story, but it is usually thought that the different Documents represent these traditions, not that they are revisions of these traditions — at least not extensively. However, on the other hand, it is generally assumed that not only ancient traditions, like Judges 5; 9:7–14; Habakkuk 3; and Psalm 68 have been adapted in the Old Testament, but even Genesis 49. So, if it has already been assumed that an ancient tradition was adapted in these places then why not in the Joseph Story itself? The possibility that such an adaption, including a thorough revision, took place in the case of the Joseph Story cannot be excluded *a priori*. This suggestion is theoretically possible and should be considered alongside other suggestions which date the Joseph Story much later. In order to break free from the classical paradigms produced by literary and historical criticism *all* possibilities must be left open until the diachronic analysis has been performed.

5.24.6   The Discussion on Historiography

According to some, the possibility of a pre-Davidic Solomic tradition must be ruled out categorically because of the assumed impossibility of literary activity of any kind at the Davidic-Solomonic court at the beginning of Early Iron II,[440] not to mention the period before! The

---

[439] Van der Merwe, "Joseph as Successor of Jacob", 221–32; idem, "Judah in the Pentateuch", 37–52.

[440] Cf. D.W. Jamieson-Drake, *Scribes and Schools: A Socio-Archaeological Approach* (JSOTS, 109; SWBAS, 9), Sheffield 1991; H.M. Niemann, *Herrschaft, Königtum und Staat* (FAT, 6), Tübingen 1993, 110, 267; E.A. Knauf, "King Solomon's Copper Supply", in: E. Lipiński (ed.), *Studia Phoenicia, XI: Phoenicia and the Bible* (OLA, 44), Leuven 1991, 167–86, 172; H. Niehr, "The Rise of YHWH in Judahite and Israelite Religion: Methodological and Religio-Historical aspects", in: D.V. Edelman (ed.), *The Triumph of Elohim: From Yahwisms to Judaisms* (CBET, 13), Kampen 1995, 45–72, 53; Lemche, *Die Vorgeschichte Israels*, 215.
    Niemann, *op.cit.*, 110, with n. 494; 267, with n. 98, refers to the work of other scholars for his assumption that the period of script and writing in Judah only starts in the eighth century BCE. In this connection he refers *inter alii* to the work of A.R. Millard, "An Assessment of the Evidence for Writing in Ancient Israel", J. Amitai (ed.), *Biblical Archaeology Today: Proceedings of the International Congress on Biblical Archaeology, Jerusalem April 1984*, Jerusalem 1985, 301–12; K.A.D. Smelik, *Writings from Ancient Israel: A Handbook of Historical*

evidence produced for this assumption, based to a large extent on the analysis of the archaeological data of Judah in Early Iron II by D.W. Jamieson-Drake, is shaky. Jamieson-Drake refers to the scarcity of data, which should have warned scholars against following his conclusions too quickly.[441] However, although he is also non-dogmatic in leaving open other possible interpretations,[442] others have interpreted his results as definitively established facts. But arguments based on the absence of certain features in Jerusalem or other areas can only form an *argumentum e silentio* and such arguments are mischievous in the historical debate.[443] Moreover, next to possible

---

and Religious Documents, Edinburgh 1991 (Niemann refers to the German edition, just to be clear). However, Niemann's reference to Millard and Smelik is rather selective. As Smelik points out in his study schools existed in 10th century Judah, which might be derived from the Gezer calendar and the 'Izbet Ṣarṭah ostracon (Smelik, *op.cit.*, 18–28). However, in that period not the (later developed) paleo-Hebrew script was used, but the Phoenician, similar to the 'Izbet Ṣarṭah ostracon. The use of this Phoenician alphabet seems to indicate foreign influence at the level of writing in the tenth century. This seems to be confirmed by biblical data, where reference is found to Sheva, David's secretary (2 Sam. 20:25), who might have been a foreigner (Smelik, *op.cit.*, 20). Millard, on the other hand, refers to attestations of epigraphy during the early monarchic period, but also gives a sufficient explanation why the finds from that period are rather rare (Millard, *art.cit.*, 305). A similar scarce attestation of writing is found in the major Assyrian sites of Assur, Kalah and Nineveh from the ninth century BCE, the time of the powerful kings Ashurnasirpal II and Shalmaneser III. This phenomenon is explained by "the general archaeological truth that only the last phase of a building's occupation and the remains of the last decades of a prosperous town yield many finds. Objects and texts dating from more than three generations before a destruction are comparatively unusual." It appears therefore that Niemann's conclusions (and references to these conclusions, cf. Lemche, *op.cit.*, 215, n. 6) based on this assumption are not solid and demand a revision. See on this subject also A.R. Millard, "The Knowledge of Writing in Iron Age Palestine", *TynB* 46 (1995) 207–17.

[441] Jamieson-Drake, *Scribes and Schools*, 15, 46, 87–92.

[442] Resulting in the remarkable situation that scholars, who argue opposite points of view regarding the rise of a state during David's lifetime, refer to his study; see F. Willesen "Om fantomet David", *DTT* 56 (1993) 249–65. Cf. in addition W. Zwickel, "Wirtschaftliche Grundlagen in Zentraljuda gegen das Ende des 8. Jh.s aus archäologischer Sicht: Mit einem Ausblick auf die wirtschaftliche Situation im 7. Jh.", *UF* 26 (1994) 557–92, (referring at p. 557, n. 4, rather harshly to Jamieson-Drake); N. Na'aman, "The Contribution of the Amarna Letters", 21–2 (clearly distinguishing between the work of Jamieson-Drake and his "followers").

[443] Cf. the fact that neither the presence of a temple, nor that of a palace in Jerusalem has been demonstrated (Thompson, *Early History of the Israelite People*, 333, n. 74). As these two buildings were probably situated on the Ophel, it is doubtful whether the existence of a kingdom, or that of a cult will ever show up (on this matter cf. more elaborately, Na'aman, "The Contribution of the Amarna Letters", 18–9). However, this problem also remains for the eighth and

archaeological data there is textual data which cannot simply be ignored, as G.W. Ahlström remarks:

> We cannot completely disregard the biblical information about the Davidic-Solomonic kingdom, even if it is not contemporary with the artifacts that can be dated to this period. States have always needed propaganda to rule their territory by divine command, and this propaganda may have been kept alive through generations, especially in such a case as that of David, the usurper. It should be self-evident that the textual depiction of the era of the "United Monarchy" is by nature biased and at times fictional.[444]

So it appears that differences between textual and archaeological remains are to be expected, because the exaggeration of events is a well known pattern in ancient Near Eastern texts.[445]

With this final reference to biblical and other ancient Near Eastern texts, we move on to another problem, namely the approach defended so vehemently by T.L. Thompson. His approach of these texts as pure "literary" texts, only traceable to a religious community in the Hellenistic period,[446] or even as "holy books"[447] and "holy writ",[448] has to be considered a biased approach, which even influences the treatment of other near Eastern texts,[449] and does not reckon with the possibility that biblical texts had their own awareness of history.[450] This is demonstrated by Thompson's treatment of the Mesha stele,

---

seventh century. But, as the size of the city increased so quickly in comparison with other settlements; evidence of trade of luxury goods is found; there has been a development of elite and state structures; this might suggest the existence of such a temple! (Cf. Thompson, *ibid.*) But, in both cases it is arguing on the basis of absence of certain data, and the conclusions reached are therefore dubious.

[444] Ahlström, "Role of Archaeological and Literary Remains", 137–8.

[445] J.M. Miller, "Old Testament History and Archaeology", *BA* 50 (1987) 55–63; idem, "Solomon: International Potentate or Local King", *PEQ* 123 (1991) 28–31; contrast however: A.R. Millard, "Does the Bible Exaggerate King Solomon's Golden Wealth?" *BAR* 15 (1989) 20–29, 31, 34; idem, "Texts and Archaeology: Weighing the Evidence. The Case for King Solomon", *PEQ* 123 (1991) 19–27; idem, "Solomon: Text and Archaeology", *PEQ* 123 (1991) 117–8.

[446] Lemche, "The Old Testament — A Hellenistic Book?" 163–93; Thompson, "House of David", 74.

[447] B.O. Long, "On Finding the Hidden Premises", *JSOT* 39 (1987) 10–4, 12.

[448] Ahlström, "Role of Archaeological and Literary Remains", 129.

[449] Thompson, "House of David", 63–5.

[450] Approaching the different books as only understandable from the same (Hellenistic) era, Genesis and Joshua; Joshua and Judges, is an unhistorical approach in itself and as such an incomprehensible argument in a historical debate; *pace* Lemche, "The Old Testament — A Hellenistic Book?" 163–93; Thompson, "House of David", 74.

where king Omri disappears into thin air as an eponymic referent of
the dynasty for the sake of literacy. Whereas king Mesha, in this inscription, refers to a king who has occupied the land during the reign
of his father about twenty or thirty years before,[451] it appears that
this king did not exist, he is only an eponym. What is even more
extraordinary is Thompson's assertion that no historicity of any of
the kings involved in these stories can be asserted.[452] The implication of Thompson's approach is that even king Mesha, the king who
erected this stele and who is a main character in this story, cannot be attributed historicity on the basis of this stele! The logic of
Thompson's argumentation is that this stele, which is a monumental
inscription and thus a well established genre, must have been erected
in later times[453] by an apparently unknown person who used Mesha's name as a pseudepigraph. This is absolutely contrary to all we
know of ancient Near Eastern monumental inscriptions, where kings
always boast of their "mighty acts".[454] Thompson's "argumentation
is complicated" and absolutely *not* clear.[455] Given Thompson's approach even primary sources for the history of Palestine would be
excluded from a reconstruction of the past. Such a conclusion raises
serious doubts about the methodology itself which could lead to these
results.

In ancient Near Eastern texts we are undoubtedly dealing with
ideological and theological concepts. The same applies to in the official
documents. We must take these factors into account. But, instead of
considering the biblical documents on a different level (as Thompson
suggests we do), because Judaism and Christianity considered them
their holy books,[456] it seems more appropriate to regard these books
as the documents they originally were, namely ancient Near Eastern

---

[451]Smelik, *Converting the Past*, 80–3.

[452]Thompson, "House of David", 65 (cf. p. 420, with n. 354 above).

[453]According to Thompson, "House of David", 65, "there is no compelling reason
to date either the story or the inscription as early as is customary."

[454]Cf. M. Liverani, "Memorandum on the Approach to Historiographic Texts",
Or 42 (1973) 178–94; H. Tadmor, "History and Ideology in the Assyrian Royal
Inscriptions", in: F.M. Fales (ed.), *Assyrian Royal Inscriptions: New Horizons
in Literary, Ideological, and Historical Analysis* (OAC, 17), Roma 1981, 13–33;
A. Laato, "Assyrian Propaganda and the Falsification of History in the Royal
Inscriptions of Sennacherib", *VT* 45 (1995) 198–226.

[455]Contrary to what Thompson, "House of David", 63, himself thinks: "The
argumentation is complicated but I think clear."

[456]Cf. R.P. Gordon, "Who Made the Kingmaker? Reflections on Samuel and
the Institution of the Monarchy", in: A.R. Millard *et al.* (eds.), *Faith, Tradition
& History: Old Testament Historiography in Its Near Eastern Context*, Winona
Lake (IN) 1994, 255–69, 256.

texts, and, as such, open to historical research and criticism. In this respect the different books of the Hebrew Bible can and should be tested separately on the information they contain, analysing ideological — theological *and* political — concepts, which will undoubtedly result in a different assessment for Genesis from that for 1–2 Kings. Only afterwards this information can be compared with other sources of information, such as archaeology and other ancient Near Eastern texts, which have been tested in a similar way.[457]

Finally J.M. Miller seriously questions the possibility of writing a history without making use of the Hebrew Bible.[458] Apart from the observation that such a history would be rather thin, he argues that every archaeologist, historian or sociologist from Palestine has made use of biblical data and will keep doing so.[459] The Hebrew Bible has in fact offered a kind of intellectual matrix and we are relying on the data offered by this book. Miller rightly says: "The appropriate question is not *whether* we should use the Hebrew Bible in historical research, but *how* we should do it".[460] We must use the historical documents we have, even if Israelite, or probably more accurately: Judahite civilization has created its own form of history.[461] First we have to accept that the writers wrote history[462] — being aware of the fact that it it is rather ideological historiography than empirical history[463] — then this may be followed by a critical evaluation in which we analyse the

---

[457] Cf. Smelik, *Converting the Past*, 22.

[458] Miller, "Is It Possible to Write a History of Israel without Relying on the Hebrew Bible?" in: D. Edelman (ed.), *The Fabric of History: Text, Artifact and Israel's Past* (JSOTS, 127), Sheffield 1991, 93–102; similarly Ahlström, "Role of Archaeological and Literary Remains", 116–8. See also H. Seebaß, "Dialog über Israels Anfänge: Zum Evolutionsmodell von N.P. Lemche, Early Israel, VTS 37, Leiden (1985)", in: J. Hausmann, H.-J. Zobel (Hrsg.), *Alttestamentlicher Glaube und biblische Theologie: Fs H.D. Preuß*, Stuttgart 1992, 11–19, 14–5.

[459] Referred to with approval by A.D.H. Mayes, "The Place of the Old Testament in Understanding Israelite History and Religion", in: A.G. Auld (ed.), *Understanding Poets and Prophets: Essays … G.W. Anderson* (JSOTS, 152), Sheffield 1993, 242–57, 256, n. 11.

[460] Miller, "History of Israel without Hebrew Bible?" 100–1.

[461] Free rendering after J. Huizinga, quoted by Ahlström, "Role of Archaeological and Literary Remains", 134, with n. 6.

[462] Cf. J.C. de Moor, "Egypt, Ugarit and Exodus", in: N. Wyatt *et al.* (eds.), *Ugarit, Religion and Culture: Essays … J.C.L. Gibson* (UBL, 12), München 1996, 213–247, 214.

[463] On this differentiation, see Ahlström, *History of Ancient Palestine*, 44. We prefer the term "ideological" rather than Ahlström's "religious" historiography, because the latter is too much restricted to one sphere, whereas "ideological" includes religious as well as political interests (although the Ancients would not have differentiated between these spheres).

audience, the aims of the author, the organisation of material, literary style, use of legendary traits, and then, finally a critical evaluation of the significance of the text itself.[464]

5.24.7 Recapitulation[465]

1. The use of the names "Jacob" and "Israel" cannot be used as a principal argument for discerning different layers within the Joseph Story. Since its use is not consistent it might, on some occasions, betray a certain stratification of the text. Because of this possibility it can only be considered as a supporting argument for the delimitation of different layers.

2. It is extremely doubtful whether the two brothers, Reuben and Judah, belong to two different layers within the text. They are each other's competitors in the narrative, a pattern which continues up to and including Genesis 49.

3. The existence of the Priestly Document cannot be ascertained since a continuing narrative string is missing. Also the classical delimitation of P in the Deathbed Episode is open to debate, since there are some verses which are usually considered to be part of other layers, but which could also be assigned to P, or *vice versa*.

4. The search for the historicity of the Joseph Story and of the Deathbed Episode is concentrated mostly on a "tribal historical" interpretation. The attempts to date these narratives are marked by classical paradigms, which have strongly influenced the results of present research. In order to break free from these paradigms we have to leave open *all* possibilities (including the very early ones) for dating these texts until a diachronic analysis has been completed.

5. The possibility of an early date (pre-eighth century BCE) for biblical texts is excluded in advance by some scholars on the basis that a national state in Palestine, showing advance stages in administration and literature, only arose during the eighth century. However, this assumption is questionable and must be

---

[464] Ahlström, "Role of Archaeological and Literary Remains", 133, n. 2. Cf. also Miller, "History of Israel without Hebrew Bible?" 101; Smelik, *Converting the Past*, 22–3.

[465] The recapitulation of previous research is found above, p. 422.

disputed since archaeological and textual data may point in a
different — and also more differentiated — direction.

6. The discussion on kingship in early Israel is strongly influenced
   by the biblical picture of Judges and 1–2 Samuel. There is, however, reason to suppose a more differentiated picture of the existence of "kings" during Israel's history before the "rise of the
   monarchy".

Chapter 6

The Deathbed Episode Once More:

Diachronic Reading and Historical Considerations

6.1 Introduction

In the previous chapter we pointed out that the study of the Joseph
Story, and in particular the Deathbed Episode (Gen. 47:29–49:33), has
still not lead to a consensus with regard to its origin. In Chapter Three
we discussed the genre of Genesis 49 and argued that it should be considered a testament rather than a collection of tribal sayings. Then, in
Chapter Four, we showed that the Deathbed Episode forms a coherent
narrative in which the "testament" functions very well, though it appears that the episode contains two traditions which seem to exclude
each other. One tradition favours Joseph as the most important son,
whereas the other seems to favour Judah and thus weakens Joseph's
position.

In the present chapter we will read the whole episode from a diachronic point of view. This reading will be performed on the basis
of the results reached in the previous chapters, namely, the coherent perspective of the Blessing (Genesis 49) in its present form and
context, and the two different perspectives on the true heir of the
patriarch, Judah or Joseph. An attempt will be made to establish if
these different results are due to a diachronic development of the text.
If so, we will try to establish if this diachronic development can shed
some light on the historical context in which the text and possible
redaction(s) have originated.

6.2 Some Methodological Considerations

With regard to the methodology applied in this chapter some remarks
may be in order. In the common diachronic studies of the Deathbed
Episode many arguments are used to seperate one layer from another.
It appears that almost every kind of criterion has been used: linguistic, literary-critical, form-critical, redaction-critical, traditio-historical etcetera. However, in the previous chapter we have shown that
many questions still remain regarding the diachronic reading. For that
reason we offer here some considerations with regard to our reading.

In Chapter One it has been argued that the linguistic features in
Genesis 49 are too ambiguous to reach any conclusions concerning the
date of origin of the text. Similarly, the historical arguments advanced

in previous research are sometimes rather one-sided and preoccupied with a pre-monarchic period as the time of origin, instead of taking other periods from history into consideration as well. In the translation of the sayings in Chapter Two, we have demonstrated that most of these sayings have been formulated as predictions of the tribe's future,[1] whereas the remaining sayings could be explained in a similar manner.[2] This feature of the sayings suits their present literary context, which purports to give them as a kind of prophecies by the patriarch on his deathbed. The analysis of the poetic structure of Genesis 49 has shown that the Blessing in its present form (including the framework) is a much more coherent unity than is commonly credited to it. This is confirmed by the form criticism of the text, which has shown that the sayings in Genesis 49 have to be regarded as "blessings (= testamentary sayings)", fitting in this sense the literary context. With regard to the classical definition of the sayings as "tribal sayings" we concluded that only in three sayings could this definition not be ruled out completely, but that in most of the cases this definition is not adequate.

Now, if these results are correct and related to each other, it would appear that Genesis 49 is much more a part of its literary context than is usually assumed. This conclusion is confirmed by the synchronic reading of the text. There we found that in Genesis 49 Judah is favoured as the true heir of his father, whereas Joseph's position appears to be comparable, though restricted to the past. However, in view of the literary context — the remaining parts of the Deathbed Episode (Gen. 47:29–48:22; 49:29–32) — Joseph's position is weakened with regard to the future, which finally supports Judah's position in the Blessing. In this sense it appears that the Deathbed Episode is much more a coherent episode than is usually assumed. On the other hand, it was shown that several aspects in the text sustain a different interpretation, in which Joseph is favoured as the oldest (or at least as the most important) son, who might be considered his father's heir.

Methodologically we have arrived at a stalemate. It has been shown that the results of form criticism could by no means be used to define the origin of Genesis 49. First of all, the general definition of the sayings as tribal sayings has been shown to be inadequate in most of the cases. Secondly, even if that definition were correct this would not add anything to our knowledge of the origin of the text,

---

[1] This has been demonstrated for the following sayings: Reuben, Simeon & Levi, Judah (in the vv. 8, 10, 11–2), Zebulun, Dan, Gad, Asher, Joseph, and Benjamin. On this matter, cf. above, section 2.14.

[2] This concerns Judah (v. 9), Issachar, Naphtali.

because theoretically it is possible that a writer or editor could have imitated the form of the tribal saying, which brings us back to the question of literary criticism. Finally, the results of form criticism also bring us back to the question of literary criticism, for it has been demonstrated that Genesis 49 as a "testament", is well embedded in its literary context and, as such, there is no reason to assume that the testament originated independently from this context. For that reason the question of the origin of Genesis 49 is thrown back to the question of the origin of its context, a problem usually tackled along the lines of literary criticism.

Unfortunately, with regard to the literary criticism of the Deathbed Episode we end up with yet another stalemate. In the previous chapter we evaluated several criteria applied in literary-critical studies to discern the layers from each other and concluded that they were unreliable. This has been demonstrated for the use of the two names of the patriarch, "Jacob" and "Israel", and we argued that this criterion can only be used as an additional argument, not as a principal one. As for the assumed different layers connected with the two brothers Reuben and Judah, we have tried to demonstrate that they functioned within the Joseph Story as competitors and not as equivalents, and that their occurrence cannot be used as a hallmark of one certain document. Finally, with regard to the Priestly document we also found that the criteria for delimitating this document were not compelling and that other divisions of the text over different documents were possible. All this argues against the results of the literary critical approach and even against the method itself, because, as we have shown, the same method has lead to considerably different results. All this pleads for a very cautious use of the literary-critical arguments in the debate concerning the genesis of the text.

Several arguments stemming from within literary criticism might be mentioned in order to elucidate the problems facing us. In the previous chapter we have argued that several arguments, like an unexpected change of scene, or a change in person (*e.g.* from 2.p. to 3.p.), are literary devices which occur in other Semitic literary compositions without raising doubts concerning the unity of such texts. Also the argument of vocabulary, as used to separate P from other layers, is sometimes a dubious argument. J.A. Emerton — though arguing in favour of P — has stated that we must not expect a rigid uniformity in wording.[3] However, the problem is even more complicated because the study by J. Tigay of the different recensions of the

---

[3] J.A. Emerton, "The Priestly Writer in Genesis", *JThS* 39 (1988) 381–400, esp. 385.

Gilgamesh Epic has demonstrated that the redactional activity of an editor was sometimes very extensive.[4] The result of his study is, in short, that the epic is composed of several separate tales (comparable to Gunkel's view of Genesis[5]) which have been joined together by (an) editor(s).[6] As an important feature it is demonstrated that the wording of the text of the epic changed considerably during the course of transmission.[7] Tigay explains part of these differences as follows:

> A few of the changes in wording seem to be chronologically conditioned, with the late version adopting language which is especially prevalent in late sources. However, the number of late variants using demonstrably late language does not seem extensive, and many of the late variants seem to employ language not less ancient than the language they replace. The changes may therefore be based largely on the subjective artistic judgment or taste of the later editors, not new linguistic developments.[8]

In case the evolution of the Gilgamesh Epic might be considered representative of the genesis of literary compositions in the ancient Near East, it should be noted that the implications are quite wide-ranging. Probably the most important implication is that the exact wording of an ancient version which has been revised once during the course of transmission cannot be established beyond doubt any more. An editor was apparently free to change the existing text not only by adding completely new episodes[9] but also by changing the wording

---

[4]J. Tigay, *The Evolution of the Gilgamesh Epic*, Philadelphia (PA) 1982, 241–50; idem, "The Evolution of the Pentateuchal Narratives in the Light of the Evolution of the *Gilgamesh Epic*", in: J. Tigay (ed.), *Empirical Models for Biblical Criticism*, Philadelphia (PA) 1985, 21–52.

[5]Tigay, "Evolution of the Pentateuchal Narratives", 32.

[6]Tigay, "Evolution of the Pentateuchal Narratives", 35–41.

[7]Tigay, "Evolution of the Pentateuchal Narratives", 40, lists as the less extensive changings the following types: "(1) different grammatical and lexical forms of the same word; (2) synonyms or words functioning similarly; (3) added words or phrases; (4) different formulas, such as those introducing direct speech; (5) expansion by the addition of new lines which are synonymous or parallel to older ones; (6) contraction of parallel or synonymous lines into fewer lines; (7) reformulation of lines with negligible, partial or complete change of meaning; and (8) textual corruption." As the more extensive changes in the epic he lists (*art.cit*, 41): "(1) the restructuring of sections; (2) the assimilation to each other of related passages; and (3) changes in the roles of characters."

[8]Tigay, "Evolution of the Pentateuchal Narratives", 40–1, with n. 83, referring to Tigay, *The Evolution of the Gilgamesh Epic*, 55–72; A. Rofé, "Joshua 20: Historico-Literary Criticism Illustrated", in: J. Tigay (ed.), *Empirical Models for Biblical Criticism*, Philadelphia (PA) 1985, 131–147, 146, n. 83.

[9]Tigay, "Evolution of the Pentateuchal Narratives", 31, 41.

and even the roles of the characters.[10] Consequently, when an ancient text has undergone a redactional process, the diachronic reading has to restrict itself mainly to the *Endgestallt* of the text, because that is the only available evidence. In this sense it appears that the main purpose of the diachronic reading will be redaction criticism. However, it depends strongly on the character of the text and the possibility of uncovering the redactional process to reach a previous stage of tradition, to know what conclusions can be drawn from this process. Since we have found several enigmatic passages in the text which do not seem to correspond with the general tendency of Genesis to favour Judah as the true heir of his father, this might point in the direction of a possible previous stage of tradition. Consequently, it leaves the possibility open of discerning a previous stage of tradition with its own possible form and contents.

Concerning the sayings in Genesis 49 some additional criteria will be taken into consideration, because in the Blessing we are dealing with a text that has been classified many times as archaic and composed of independent sayings, reflecting the early history of Israel. These matters will need to be discussed here. In our discussion of the Blessing we will give due attention to these arguments, weighing once again the problems of scope, origin, context etcetera. In fact this will constitute the final part of our discussion on Genesis 49 and the question of its provenance. In that section it must finally be established to what extent the theory concerning the independent origin of the supposed tribal sayings is an absolute desideratum to explain their origin, or, alternatively, that the origin of these sayings can be sufficiently explained from their position within the present literary context and the diachronic process that took place.

In the following diachronic reading the literary critical arguments will be used quite reticently. The emphasis of our reading will be put on the results of the synchronic reading of the Deathbed Episode. In that reading we established that in Genesis there is a thread which leads to the leadership of Judah culminating in the blessing in Genesis 49. Yet, in some difficult passages (like 47:31; 48:22) it appeared that readings other than those commonly read are possible. These readings strongly favour Joseph's position as the most important son of the patriarch. We described the tension between these two tendencies as ideological differences, due to a shift of the *status quo* in favour of Judah. As a working hypothesis we postulate therefore:

In an ancient version of the Deathbed Episode Joseph's father said

---

[10]Cf. above, n. 7.

farewell to Joseph as his most important son. In a later stage of history this version was revised to legitimize the leading position of (the tribe of) Judah, who rose to power and for one reason or another had to defend his position. This revision resulted in a deathbed account which still reflects both historical situations.

In our reading we will consider the following elements decisive for the stratification of the different layers in the Deathbed Episode.

1. In the following analysis the main argument will consist of the different tendencies that were found in Chapter Four. If a text favours Joseph as the heir of his father it will be considered as belonging to one layer, which for the moment we will call the "pro-Joseph layer". If the tendency of the text tends to diminish Joseph's position somewhat, or clearly functions to strengthen Judah's position it will *for the moment* be regarded as a part of the "pro-Judah layer".[11]

2. A second argument will be found in those elements of the text that function within the overall structure of Genesis. We may consider such elements to be the references to genealogies, to recurring motifs like the strife between the younger and older brothers, to the inheritance of the blessing of the patriarchs, etcetera. All these elements will *for the moment* be considered to be part of the "pro-Judah" layer, because the main thread of Genesis tends strongly to support the position of Judah.[12]

3. As additional arguments the observations from other literary-critical analyses will be considered without accepting, however, the classification of the documents presented in those studies. The most obvious stratification will be the general assumption of the P-layer within the Deathbed Episode. It will be verified, nevertheless, whether such an argument corresponds with the two preceding arguments, which are considered the main arguments in our diachronic reading.

At the end of our analysis the results will be evaluated. It will be noted if there is a certain consistency in the layers we have isolated

---

[11] We emphasize the tentative character of the classification "pro-Judah layer", because we may have to allow for more editorial layers than one. For the moment we will work, however, with a minimum of layers, for — as W.H. Schmidt has argued — the simplest hypothesis which explains the most should be preferred. Cf. W.H. Schmidt, "Plädoyer für die Quellenscheidung", *BZ* 32 (1988) 1–14, 3.

[12] Cf. the preceding note.

and if the stratification explains the tensions found in the Deathbed Episode. Then, if the results are sound, we will investigate for the possibility of dating the text and the historical state of affairs that might have produced the different layers within the text.

6.3 The Deathbed Episode, I: Genesis 47:29–48:22

6.3.1 The Prelude: Genesis 47:27–28

In the diachronic analyses of the prelude, 47:27a is ascribed to J because it seems to continue 47:12, which is also ascribed to J.[13] The note that Israel — here used in the singular for the patriarch — settled in Egypt is an important part of the Joseph Story as a whole. It has been suggested by Noth and others that the Joseph Story was composed as a kind of "bridge" to close the gap between, on the one hand, the patriarchs in the land of Canaan and, on the other hand, the Exodus of Israel out of Egypt.[14] It cannot be denied that at its present position the Story functions in this way now.[15] Yet, it does not exclude the possibility that a once independent tradition about Joseph in Egypt may have been adapted here to bridge that gap.[16] The fact that the scene is in Egypt, plays a role in some parts of the Deathbed Episode and the question is, to which strand in the nar-

---

[13] Gunkel, *Genesis*, ³1910, 465; Westermann, *Genesis 37–50*, 191.

[14] M. Noth, *Überlieferungsgeschichte des Pentateuch*, Stuttgart 1948 (Darmstadt ²1960), 226–7. Cf. already B. Luther, "Die Persöhnlichkeit des Jahwisten", in: E. Meyer, *Die Israeliten und ihre Nachbarstämme*, Halle 1906, 105–73, 146.

[15] Houtman, *Der Pentateuch*, 427, "... [allerdings muß] hervorgehoben werden, daß die Genesis an sich, wie abgerundet sie auch ist, einen Torso bildet. Das Buch verlangt angesichts dessen, was über die den Patriarchen gegebenen Verheißungen berichtet wird ... einer Fortsetzung, wobei man sich des Eindrucks nicht erwehren kann, daß die gesamte Etzählung über Joseph und seine Laufbahn in Ägypten darauf abzielt, die Patriarchen-Erzählungen über Israel in Ägypten in Exodus anschließen zu lassen. Auch der Beginn von Ex. 1 ist offensichtlich mit dieser Intention geschrieben."

[16] Cf. O. Kaiser, "Stammesgeschichtliche Hintergründe der Josephsgeschichte: Erwägungen zur Vor- und Frühgeschichte Israels", *VT* 10 (1960) 1–15; I. Willi-Plein, "Historiographische Aspekte der Josefsgeschichte", *Henoch* 1 (1979) 305–31. In fact this question is the counterpart of the questions concerning the traditions of Moses and the Exodus. These narratives might also go back to independent traditions about how rebellious people had to flee from Egypt, and which were adapted in a later phase to the present version of "whole Israel" coming out of Egypt; cf. on this matter De Moor, *RoY*, 136–51; *RoY*², 208–33; idem, "Egypt, Ugarit and Exodus", in: N. Wyatt *et al.* (eds.), *Ugarit, Religion and Culture: Proceedings of the International Colloquium ... Edinburgh, July 1994; Essays ... J.C.L. Gibson* (UBL, 12), Münster 1996, 213–47. In this sense the "Joseph Story" and the "Exodus Story" might have been two completely independent traditions, dealing with two different groups of people in two completely different periods.

rative does it belong: the "pro-Joseph" or "pro-Judah" layer? Since in 47:29–31 the scene is obviously in Egypt, our classification might be partly dependent on the setting of that section. However, the relation of this verse to the rest of the "prelude" will also be of some importance.

In verse 27a we are confronted with the use of a certain idiom as a hallmark of the different layers. In our verse the phraseology used to describe the settlement of Israel in Egypt, וַיֵּשֶׁב יִשְׂרָאֵל בְּאֶרֶץ מִצְרַיִם בְּאֶרֶץ גֹּשֶׁן "and Israel dwelt in the land of Egypt, in the land of Goshen" (47:27a) is very close to וַיֵּשֶׁב יַעֲקֹב בְּאֶרֶץ מְגוּרֵי אָבִיו בְּאֶרֶץ כְּנָעַן "and Jacob dwelt in the land of the sojournings of his father, in the land of Canaan" (37:1).[17] Despite the "almost literal correspondence", 47:27a is ascribed to J, whereas 37:1 is ascribed to P.[18] Syntactically and idiomatically these phrases are identical with only one minor difference, namely the name of the patriarch: "Jacob" (37:1) and "Israel" (47:27a). To establish the exact relationship between these two phrases is quite difficult, but it is doubtful if they belong to the same layer. As we noted above, it depends on whether 47:27a belongs to the "pro-Joseph" or the "pro-Judah" layer. 37:1 is completely in line with one of the motifs in Genesis, namely that the land of Canaan is the land of the promise, where the patriarchs were originally "sojourners" (גֵרִים). In our view, therefore, we can consider 37:1 to be closely related to those parts of Genesis that form the framework of the book, namely the "pro-Judah"-layer. Concerning 47:27a we have to postpone our judgement until the remaining text of the prelude has been analysed.

After 47:27a a change in number occurs. The subject apparently remains the same, namely "Israel", but the singular verbal form has changed into plural forms indicating that "Israel" is not solely the patriarch but proleptically considered to be the people "Israel". It seems therefore that those who noted a difference in layer between 47:27a and 27b may be right in detecting a seam in the text here. In this way the narrative is placed in the perspective of the future when Israel will become a people. For a similar pattern, we may refer to the closing formula in 49:28, where ancestors and tribes are suddenly merged. However, the change in number in 47:27b does not necessarily indicate that we are dealing with a layer different from the one in the preceding verse. It may have been done deliberately, in order to emphasize that the patriarch "Israel" is indeed the ancestor of the people "Israel". For that reason we have to postpone our judgement

---

[17]Westermann, *Genesis 37–50*, 25.

[18]Westermann, *Genesis 37–50*, 26: "fast wörtliche Entsprechung".

concerning verse 27a, until we have analysed the rest of the "prelude".

Concerning the prelude, verses 27b–28 are usually ascribed to the Priestly document.[19] With that classification the relationship of these verses with other parts of Genesis is emphasized very clearly, a relationship which we are inclined to underline. As has been demonstrated in Chapter Four, these verses resemble in their wording other verses in Genesis, occurring throughout the book as a kind of thread, forming the framework on which Genesis has been built. The expressions to describe the fertility and growth (פרה ורבה) recur several times and might be considered to be one of those stock-phrases which form the building blocks of Genesis.[20]

The reference in 47:27b to the land of Egypt (47:27a) by means of בָּהּ "in it" follows very smoothly after verse 27a (except of course for the change in number). Because verse 27b is usually ascribed to P, it is supposed to have originally followed after 47:11b, where it would follow just as smoothly after a reference to the land "Egypt". The idea that these two verses (v. 11b* and v. 27b*) would indeed continue the line of the narrative is in favour of the supposition that one document (P in this case) was merged with another one, which is assumed to end in 47:27a (J). However, it might be asked why the editor, who merged both documents, separated 47:27b from 47:11b, because the narrative would have developed even more smoothly if the text had been split up *after* 47:27b. Moreover, the need to split up the original *before* 47:27b is not evident.[21] In our view this argues against the idea that two *documents* have been merged. If we have to assume an editorial layer here, one could imagine that the editor, in order to adapt the document to his own ideas, inserted here a remark concerning the fertility and growth of the people. Admittedly, the idea of two documents cannot be excluded completely, even though we have to allow for the "clumsy redactor" in that case.[22] Finally, in 47:28 we find a reference to the age of the patriarch which might be considered one of the characteristic features of Genesis. Therefore this verse should be assigned to the strand that binds the whole of

---

[19]Cf. *e.g.* Gunkel, *Genesis*, ³1910, 495–6; Speiser, *Genesis*, 354, 358–9; Westermann, *Genesis 37–50*, 192.

[20]Note that these are generally considered to be part of P and the priestly tradition. That classification and ours is based on the same observation, namely that these phrases occur several times in a similar context.

[21]Cf. the reconstructed text in Westermann, *Genesis 37–50*, 183–4, where it is possible to compare the different options. In our view it is incomprehensible why the editor would have placed the phrase with plural subjects (corresponding with the plurals in 47:11b) after verse 27a, causing an incongruence in number.

[22]Barr, *Comparative Philology*, 68.

traditions in Genesis into a unity, the "pro-Judah" layer.[23]

When we return to 47:27a, the problem remains that for the moment we are not able to establish conclusively to which layer this verse belongs to. It appears that after verse 27a a seam in the text is found, whereas the following verses 27b–28 belong to a layer which supports the framework of Genesis, the "pro-Judah" layer. This seam might argue in favour of a different layer for verse 27a, if verse 27a were clearly part of the "pro-Joseph" layer. However, as we have argued, it is possible that the writer or editor, who was responsible for verse 27b (Israel plural), was also responsible for verse 27a (Israel singular), comparable to how in 49:28 ancestors and tribes are merged. Moreover, the matter is complicated by the fact that verses 27b–28 form the transition to the Deathbed Episode. But in fact 47:27a, together with 47:12 seems to form the rounding off of the narrative in 46:28–47:12 and it forms in this way the stepping stone from which 47:27b–28 can move on to the Deathbed Episode. Should 47:27b–28 be considered part of an additional layer, 47:27a might indeed form a closing remark after the tradition found in 47:12.[24] 47:27a is a kind of resumption of a preceding narrative and most likely does not belong to the Deathbed Episode itself but to the preceding narrative. Since the patriarch is here named "Israel" we prefer to ascribe this verse to a layer similar to that found in 47:29–31, but, as was indicated in the previous chapter, this argument is certainly not decisive in this case.

6.3.2   Genesis 47:29–31

This section in which Israel, the patriarch, asks Joseph to bury him in Canaan and not in Egypt, is commonly regarded as a coherent text belonging to only one document (mostly J).[25] Indeed there is no

---

[23]Cf. Gen. 37:2; 41:6a; 47:5–11, to confine ourselves to the Joseph Story.

[24]Cf. a similar function in Gen. 37:1, which seems to continue 36:29 (which is again comparable to 25:7–11, 19–20).

[25]Cf. Gunkel, *Genesis*, ³1910, 469; Speiser, *Genesis*, 359; H.-C. Schmitt, *Die nichtpriesterliche Josephsgeschichte: Ein Beitrag zur neuesten Pentateuchkritik* (BZAW, 154), Berlin 1980, 66; Westermann, *Genesis 37–50*, 203–4; L. Schmidt, *Literarische Studien zur Josephsgeschichte* (BZAW, 167), Berlin 1986, 201–2. As far as we are aware only the following author discerns an additional layer in this passage: N. Kebekus, *Die Joseferzählung: Literarkritische und redaktionsgeschichtliche Untersuchungen zu Genesis 37–50*, Münster 1990, 188–9, considering verse 30a as a later addition, because the remark "and when I lie down with my fathers" (30aA), would come too late after the request not to bury him in Egypt (29bB), the remark "carry me out of Egypt" would be a duplication of the similar request in 29bB. Further, the remark "bury me in their burying place" (30aC) seems to contradict the remark in 50:5, where the patriarch should have said that he has hewn his own tomb. However, first, in view of the Semitic way

reason to assume that this scene is composite. Nevertheless, in the synchronic reading we have discussed one specific problem in the text which might reflect a tradition departing from the outlines of Genesis favouring Judah. It concerns the textually difficult verse in 47:31, where the consonantal text reads וישתחו ישראל על־ראש המטה, usually rendered according to MT: "and Israel bowed himself at the head of his bed". In Chapter Four we argued that the patriarch bowed himself down before Joseph, which seems to be implied already in the words of the patriarch "if I have found favour in your eyes" (47:29), which is an expression that is usually associated with prostration before the person adressed.[26] Moreover, the textual witnesses, as well as modern scholars seem to have trouble with the expression. Modern scholars are generally puzzled why the patriarch bowed down at or to the *head* of the bed. It is suggested that there a terephim or the like was placed, or that the patriarch actually bends down dying on the head of the bed,[27] adding in this way a completely new meaning to the verb השתחוה. Yet, we argued that the most likely reading of this text was *partly* reflected by LXX and Peš, who read respectively τῆς

---

of speaking, verse 30a appears to be an emphasizing request, which specifies the preceding request and for that reason the additional character is not conlusive. Further the contradiction with 50:5 is superfluous, because the one does not exclude the other. One could have hewn his own tomb in a family grave and so 47:30a does not contradict 50:5. On family-graves and cave-tombs, cf. R. Gonen, *Burial Patterns & Cultural Diversity in Late Bronze Age Canaan* (ASOR.DS, 7), Winona Lake (IN) 1992, 9–15; C.H.J. de Geus, "Funeral Monuments and Tomb-Markings in Biblical Israel?" *AcAL* 32 (1993) 107–19, 109–10; idem, "Graven en sociale verhoudingen tijdens de Israëlitische monarchie", *Phoenix* 42,1 (1996) 23–34. On the burial practices (among others in the tombs of the ancestors) and their importance, cf. K. Spronk, *Beatific Afterlife in Ancient Israel and in the Ancient Near East* (AOAT, 219), Kevelaer, Neukirchen-Vluyn 1986, 238–44; E. Bloch-Smith, *Judahite Burial Practices and Beliefs about the Dead* (JSOTS, 123), Sheffield 1992, 110–6; see also J.C. de Moor, "Standing Stones and Ancestor Worship", *UF* 27 (1995) 1–20, esp. 13–7; idem, *RoY*², 352–59.

[26]See 2 Sam. 14:22; Ruth 2:10; cf. also Gen. 18:2–3; 33:7–8; Exod. 34:8–9.

[27]Cf. most vehemently H. Schweizer, *Die Josefsgeschichte: Konstituierung des Textes*, Tl. I–II (TTHLLI, Bd. 4), Tübingen 1991, Tl. I, 290, n. 299 (quoted on p. 407, n. 276 above); and further, H. Donner, *Die literarische Gestalt der alttestamentlichen Josephsgeschichte* (SHAW.PH, 1976.2), Heidelberg 1976, 30–1; O.H. Steck, *Die Paradieserzählung: Eine Auslegung von Genesis 2,4b–3,24* (BiSt, 60), Neukirchen-Vluyn 1970, 120 (repr. in: idem, *Wahrnehmungen Gottes im Alten Testament: Gesammelte Studien* [ThB, 70], München 1982, 9–116. 108); E. Blum, *Die Komposition der Vätergeschichte* (WMANT, 57), Neukirchen-Vluyn 1984, 250; T.L. Thompson, *The Origin Tradition of Ancient Israel, I: The Literary Formation of Genesis and Exodus 1–23* (JSOTS, 55), Sheffield 1987, 129–30. J.W. Wevers, *Notes on the Greek Text of Genesis* (SCSt, 35), Atlanta (GA) 1993, 806. See also, Speiser, *Genesis*, 357.

ῥάβδου αὐτοῦ and ḥwṭrh, both meaning "his staff", reflecting Hebr.
מַטֵּה,[28] "staff" instead of MT מִטָּה "bed". The expression רֹאשׁ הַמִּטָּה
seems to be a current idiom, occuring three more times (in plural)
in MT, vocalized in that case as רָאשֵׁי הַמַּטּוֹת, meaning "heads of the
tribes".[29] The reading in our text is obviously singular and therefore
may be read as וַיִּשְׁתַּחוּ יִשְׂרָאֵל עַל־רֹאשׁ הַמַּטֶּה "and Israel bowed himself
for[30] the head of the tribe".[31] At the *synchronic* level, this reading
was rejected by us — though we had some doubts — because this
reading does not fit the context in which Judah is appointed as the
successor of the patriarch (49:8–12). Reading the text now from a
diachronic point of view the problem occurs again, but in this case
we are willing to follow the proposed reading.

The deferential way in which the patriarch addresses his son has
been noted by scholars[32] and this polite manner of speaking might
be due to Joseph's high rank in Egypt.[33] The development of the
narrative according to MT supports this interpretation, even that
Israel bowed himself for Joseph — though he did it *at the head of his
bed,* (without mentioning the object). In the context of the diachronic
reading, the interpretation "head of the tribe" might even be the more
appropriate reading, designating Joseph in this way as the successor
of his father,[34] the new *paterfamilias.* If our reading is correct then
this would seem to be the most obvious indication of different layers
in the text of the Deathbed Episode. With regard to our passage,
this episode certainly belongs to the "pro-Joseph" tradition, which,
according to Van der Merwe clashes with the "pro-Judah" tradition.[35]

Remarkable here is the use of מַטֶּה "tribe" for the descendants of
Israel. This is unique. The word is used for the tribes named after the
twelve sons of the patriarch,[36] but it is never used for the descendants

---

[28]In fact LXX and Peš reflect Hebr. מַטֵּהוּ, with a suffix and without article,
a difference that occurs more often between MT and LXX. In addition, cf. our
remarks in section 4.4.2.2.

[29]For a more extensive discussion, cf. above, section 4.4.2.2.

[30]הִשְׁתַּחֲוָה עַל is mostly rendered by "to bow down on/at ... "; see 1 Kgs. 1:47;
Ezek. 46:2; Zeph. 1:5. Yet, Lev. 26:1; Isa. 60:14, support the meaning "to bow
down to/before ... "; cf. furthermore the discussion in section 4.4.2.2.

[31]On the title רֹאשׁ; cf. J.R. Bartlett, "The Use of the Word רֹאשׁ as a Title in
the Old Testament", *VT* 19 (1969) 1–10.

[32]Westermann, *Genesis 37–50*, 204–5; Wenham, *Genesis 16–50*, 450.

[33]Procksch, *Genesis*, 268; Gunkel, *Genesis*, ³1910, 470.

[34]The view that Joseph was in fact the successor of his father was defended by
B.J. van der Merwe, "Joseph as Successor of Jacob", in: *Studia Biblica et Semitica:
Th.C. Vriezen ... dedicata*, Wageningen 1966, 221–32.

[35]Van der Merwe, "Joseph as Successor of Jacob", 229.

[36]Cf. *e.g.* Exod. 35:30; Num. 1:49.

of Israel as a whole.[37] This naming defines Israel at the same level as happens with the other "tribes of Israel". מַטֶּה is found many times in texts which are ascribed to P, but this does not indicate that it is exclusively P-language, nor that it would have been initiated by P.[38] Moreover, the use in texts considered to belong to P all refer to one of the tribes of Israel by מַטֶּה never to Israel itself, which is mostly called עַם "people".[39] We might even add, that מַטֶּה "tribe" does not define "Israel" as we know it from the Hebrew Bible, where already in the period of the Judges Israel is called a "people" existing of several "tribes". Although aware of reasoning on an *argumentum e silentio* basis, it seems very likely that this terminology for Israel was abandoned at a rather early stage because it could not be applied to an entity supposed to be composed of several "tribes". The exact sociological meaning of the word מַטֶּה is hard to establish here. In our text it might have been closely related to the בֵּית אָב "father's house" (= "extended family"), from the fact that, in the context of the Deathbed Episode, the family of the patriarch is mostly referred to as the בֵּית־אָב,[40] even though the expression רָאשֵׁי בֵית־אֲבֹתָם "heads of their fathers' houses" also occurs.[41] Important to note here is the fact that if the descendants of Israel as a whole are called מַטֶּה "tribe", then this seems to imply that *Joseph* is not regarded as the ancestor of a "tribe" in this layer of the narrative,[42] but much more as the new *paterfamilias* after his father "Israel". The role he has in 47:29–31, as

---

[37] As was noted by N.P. Lemche, *Early Israel: Anthropological and Historical Studies on the Israelite Society Before the Monarchy* (SVT, 37), Leiden 1985, 430.

[38] H. Simian-Yofre, "מַטֶּה, *maṭṭæh*", *ThWAT*, Bd. IV, 818–26, 822. Simian-Yofre (following M. Noth) considers it a rather common exilic and post-exilic idiom. However, the dating on the basis of occurrences in late texts still is an *argumentum e silentio*. The word *mt* "staff" occurs in Ugaritic texts, consequently the meaning "tribe" might have been known there already. To date a work on the basis of specific word occurrences in specific texts is hazardous.

[39] Cf. Josh. 8:33; 2 Sam. 18:7; 19:41; 1 Kgs. 16:21; Ezra 2:2; 9:1; Neh. 7:7.

[40] Cf. for example Gen. 47:12; 50:8, 22.

[41] Exod. 6:14; Num. 7:2. For the discussion of the different terms and their sociological meaning, cf. C.H.J. de Geus, *The Tribes of Israel: An Investigation into Some of the Presuppositions of Martin Noth's Amphictyony Hypothesis* (SSN, 12), Assen 1976, 133–56; Lemche, *Early Israel*, 245–90; K. van der Toorn, *Family Religion in Babylonia, Syria and Israel: Continuity and Change in the Forms of Religious Life* (SHCANE, 7), Leiden 1996, 183–205 (cf. also pp. 20–6); S. Bendor, *The Social Structure of Ancient Israel: The Institution of the Family* (Beit 'Ab) *from the Settlement to the End of the Monarchy* (JBSt, 7), Jerusalem 1996.

[42] This interpretation does not imply that the character of Joseph is not functioning as a eponym in this narrative, but only that he does not function as the ancestor of a "tribe" called "Joseph".

the one being responsible for the funeral of his father, is clearly that
of the new head of the family.[43]

In our text we are confronted once again with an idiom which
is regarded as the hallmark of a certain document. Here it concerns
the expression שִׂים־נָא יָדְךָ תַּחַת יְרֵכִי "put your hand under my thigh"
(47:29). E. Speiser, for example, considers our passage to be clearly
from J, not only because of the name "Israel" for the patriarch, but
also because of this expression, "which is known elsewhere from only
one passage (xxiv 2) in a celebrated account by J".[44] Statistically,
this argument is untenable. Just because the expression occurs once
in a certain document (J), does not make it "J-language". Because
the assumed document J alone has one example of the expression, and
E and P do not have it, does not imply that they did not know the
expression.[45] Moreover, it might be possible that our text "borrowed"
this expression from Gen. 24:2 at an editorial level, or *vice versa*;
or that both are used in different traditions, adopted here by the
editor. The fact that this practice has also been found in Akk. texts,[46]
suggests that it was a common accompaniment at oaths in the Semitic
world and cannot be restricted to only one document. For that reason
the classification of the text on the basis of this expression is rejected.

From the passage under discussion we note the following characteristics. The support is clearly pro-Joseph, in the sense that Joseph
is considered the most important son of his father, who has to arrange
the funeral and who is called the "head of the tribe". The patriarch
is called at the beginning of this scene by his name "Israel" only once
and the other name "Jacob" does not occur in this passage. This might
be an indication — albeit very tentative for the moment — that the
name "Israel" for the patriarch is connected with the "pro-Joseph"
layer. Finally, the scene is obviously in Egypt, which is the main concern of the whole passage: they are in Egypt and Israel wants to be
buried in Canaan. Finally, the scene has no ending where it might
just as well have continued.

---

[43]Cf. in this connection also the duties of the son, described in KTU 1.17:i.26–7;
and Van der Toorn, *Family Religion*, 154–5; idem, "Worshipping Stones: Of the
Deification of Cult Symbols", *JNSL* 23 (1997) 1–14, esp. 9.

[44]Speiser, *Genesis*, 359. Similarly Gunkel, *Genesis*, ³1910, 469.

[45]Cf. (in a different context) E. Ullendorff, "Is Biblical Hebrew a Language?"
BSOAS 34 (1971) 241–55, 243: "The fact that words for 'blessing' or 'whoring'
are frequent merely determines the genre of literature collected in the OT, while
the apparent absence of words denoting 'spoon' or 'niece' does not imply that the
Hebrews ate their food with their fingers and indulged in nepoticide practices.".

[46]M. Malul, "Touching the Sexual Organs as an Oath Ceremony in an Akkadian
Letter", *VT* 37 (1987) 491–2.

6.3.3 Genesis 48:1-2

This passage, which forms the introduction to the second scene,[47] proves to be a difficult one in many diachronic studies. As can be concluded from the table set out in Chapter Five, the different parts of this passage have been ascribed to several documents. In studies putting forward the classical documentary hypothesis, vv. 1–2a are ascribed to E, and v. 2b is ascribed to J.[48] However, some recent studies have found this division problematic and offer different analyses. Speiser suggests we delete "Israel" in verse 2b, because the whole passage should belong to E, and the occurrence of the name "Israel" was probably been caused by merging the two traditions.[49] On the other hand, L. Schmidt in his analysis of the whole scene ascribed several E-passages to J, doubting for that reason the further existence of E in the other assumed E-passages, amongst them our verses (vv. 1–2a). He considered the possibility that our passage contains a remnant of a P-introduction to vv. 3–6, namely in vv. 1aB–2a. But vv. 1aA, 1b together with v. 2b belong to J and needed a transition to the following scene.[50] These differences demonstrate that much depends on how the rest of this scene is read and analysed.

Questioning the passage from an ideological perspective we are left with similar problems. Much will depend on how we read the following passages. In verse 1 we first note the beginning of the new scene, which is rather abrupt after the preceding one.[51] Of course the phrase וַיְהִי אַחֲרֵי הַדְּבָרִים הָאֵלֶּה "and it happened after these things" (48:1aA) is a well-known transitional phrase, marking the changeover from one scene to another. As such 48:1aA could indeed have functioned after 47:31, making a new transition from the preceding passage to the present one.[52] The phrase וַיְהִי אַחֲרֵי הַדְּבָרִים הָאֵלֶּה is used five more times in Genesis. In these five other instances the phrase marks either the transition from a preceding completed narrative to a new

---

[47] Cf. above, section 4.2, for the division into four scenes.

[48] Cf. Gunkel, *Genesis*, ³1910, 469. See also Schmitt, *Die nichtpriesterliche Josephsgeschichte*, 66–73.

[49] Speiser, *Genesis*, 354, 375, 359. Similarly: Vawter, *On Genesis*, 451.

[50] Schmidt, *Literarische Studien zur Josephsgeschichte*, 264–7.

[51] Cf. the fact that some scholars are inclined to consider Chapter 48 a tradition completely separate from 47:29–31. See *e.g.* Donner, *Literarische Gestalt der Josephsgeschichte*, 31; Blum, *Die Komposition der Vätergeschichte*, 250–1. See also Wenham, *Genesis 16–50*, 449, who considers 48:1 also a significant new departure in the narrative, and for that reason reads 47:27–31 as part of the preceding passage, taking 48:1ff. as a completely new pericope.

[52] This is defended by Schmidt, *Literarische Studien zur Josephsgeschichte* 265, ascribing 48:1aA to J. Cf. also Kebekus, *Die Joseferzählung*, 204–5.

one,[53] or the transition within a narrative from one passage to the next.[54] In our case, however, the preceding scene (47:29–31) is not completed,[55] nor does our passage presuppose the preceding passage and therefore the phrase וַיְהִי אַחֲרֵי הַדְּבָרִים הָאֵלֶּה cannot mask the abrupt transition here.

The phrase in verse 1aA has been attributed to J- as well as to E-documents[56] and as such it cannot be firmly classified in source criticism, and sometimes even proves to be a real "stumbling block".[57] Moreover, because it is a clear transitional phrase it could be applied in the course of a narrative after, for example, the introductory passage (see 39:7) or in any place where it seems essential for the flow of the narrative. Thus it is likely that a narrator could have used it wherever he preferred. This was argued by Schmidt, who classified this phrase as belonging to J[58] and thus to the same layer as the preceding passage (47:29–31) and verse 2b, which is in his view also part of J.[59] On the other hand, it could be used after a completed narrative to introduce a new episode, which might have been taken from another tradition than the preceding narrative, and in that case it could be an editorial phrase as well.[60] In sum, the phrase cannot be classified on formal criteria, neither as editorial, nor as original, and

---

[53]Gen. 22:1, 20.

[54]Gen. 39:7, 40:1. Cf. also 15:1, which follows a completed narrative (14:1–24), but which might also presuppose 14:21–24, where Abraham refuses a reward from any man, so that no one could say that he made Abraham rich. Yet in 15:1, God promises a reward to Abraham, which will be very great. As such the phrase also presupposes "these things before".

[55]Cf. in this respect H. Seebaß, "The Joseph Story, Genesis 48 and the Canonical Process", *JSOT* 35 (1986) 29–43, esp. 29, 33.

[56]Cf. Gen. 15:1 (J); 22:1 (E), 20 (J); 39:7 (J); 40:1 (E).

[57]The attribution of the different verses in the previous note, is based on Gunkel, *Genesis*, ³1910, respectively on pp. 177, 236, 243, 421, 427. His argumentation is, however, quite unbalanced because concerning 22:20 (J), he writes (*op.cit.*, 243): "die Phrase וַיְהִי אַחֲרֵי הַדְּבָרִים הָאֵלֶּה beweist nicht für E, sondern findet sich auch in J 39:7". Regarding 39:7 he argues (*op.cit*, 421): "Die Formel וַיְהִי אַחֲרֵי הַדְּבָרִים הָאֵלֶּה bei E gewöhnlich, findet sich auch 22₂₀ bei J". Finally, with regard to 40:1 he states (*op.cit*, 427): "Sprachlich beweisen für E: וַיְהִי אַחֲרֵי הַדְּבָרִים הָאֵלֶּה [48:]1, eine besonders in E häufige Phrase". However, the phrase occurs in J three times (15:1; 22:20; 39:7) and three times in E (22:1; 40:1; 48:1), according to his analysis. Consequently, the phrase is no proof at all for any of these documents. Moreover, the phrase occurs in obviously late texts too: Esth. 2:1; 3:1; Ezra 7:1; cf. also the probable Deuteronomistic passages Josh. 24:29; 1 Kgs. 17:17; 21:1.

[58]Schmidt, *Literarische Studien zur Josephsgeschichte*, 265. He considers 39:7 and 40:1 as well as belonging to J (in contrast to Wellhausen and Gunkel, who regard 40:1 as E).

[59]Schmidt, *Literarische Studien zur Josephsgeschichte*, 265.

[60]Cf. *e.g.* Gen. 15:1; 22:1, 20; 40:1, where this *could be* the case.

it depends on the rest of our analysis how it should be classified.

As has been noted in Chapter Four, verse 1, after the transitional phrase (v. 1aA), seems to serve to let Joseph bring in both his sons, Manasseh and Ephraim.[61] The announcement to Joseph that his father is ill (v. 1aBC) does not add anything new to the narrative until then. The new element is clearly the phrase in verse 1b: וַיִּקַּח אֶת־שְׁנֵי בָנָיו עִמּוֹ אֶת־מְנַשֶּׁה וְאֶת־אֶפְרָיִם "and he took his two sons with him, Manasseh and Ephraim". The reference to the two sons of Joseph in the order of their birth is in line with their birth story (41:50–52), which has the same characteristics as the other birth stories in Genesis. In fact the birth story in which the order of their birth is given is a prerequisite for the present scene (48:1–22) where they will change places.[62] So, the present passage, using the sequence Manasseh and Ephraim, could be related to their birth story, apparently based on the scheme of birth stories in Genesis: birth — naming (— etymology).[63] For that reason the birth story in 41:50–52 might be considered part of the framework of Genesis.[64] Our verse (48:1), following the order of the birth of both sons, seems to form a bridge between the birth story, on the one hand, and the passage where their order is reversed, on the other hand. As such verse 1 is again a prerequisite for the passage where their order is reversed by the patriarch (48:14–20). Thus 48:14–20 needs 48:1; and for its part, 48:1 needs 41:50–52.

In the following verse (2a) the occurrence of the name "Jacob", followed in the next verse (2b) by the name "Israel" is remarkable. Verse 2a still seems to be part of the transitional character of the preceding verse (48:1). This verse presupposes that Joseph has left his father: Joseph is told that his father is ill and he takes both his sons to go to his father. Then, for the development of the narrative it is apparently necessary that the patriarch is informed of Joseph's coming, so that he may gather his strength and sit up on the bed. The change in names is notable, because in verse 3a the name changes back again to "Jacob". These changes of name might support the idea of a certain stratification of the text. In this respect we note that "Jacob" is connected to the part in which a new scene is created and where Joseph brings in his two sons, Manasseh and Ephraim. This is especially clear in the following passage, starting in verse 3a with the

---

[61] Vawter, *On Genesis*, 452; Seebaß, "The Joseph Story", 31.

[62] Cf. Gunkel, *Genesis*, ³1910, 433; Kebekus, *Die Joseferzählung*, 79–80.

[63] See Gen. 4:1, 25; 19:36–8; 21:1–7; 25:21–6; 29:31–30:24; 35:16–8; 38:29–30; 41:50–2. The stress on the birth of children might also be reflected in the structuring תּוֹלְדֹת-formula; on this formula, cf. Houtman, *Der Pentateuch*, 424–5.

[64] Cf. also Kebekus, *Die Joseferzählung*, 79–80.

name "Jacob" and where Joseph's two sons are adopted.

Verse 2b is usually thought to be connected with the preceding scene, where Israel bowed down at the head of the bed (47:31). 48:2b seems a reasonable continuation of this verse: וַיִּתְחַזֵּק יִשְׂרָאֵל וַיֵּשֶׁב עַל־הַמִּטָּה "and Israel gathered his strength and sat on the bed". However, the proposed interpretation of 47:31, in which we read that Israel bowed himself for "the head of the tribe", seems to disturb this continuation. Yet, this is superficial, because after the prostration of the patriarch we may still expect that he had to "gather his strength" to sit on the bed. Moreover, it has to be noted that the usually assumed position of the patriarch, bowing at his bed, has no basis any more. For that reason it seems more logical that he prostrated himself on the ground in front of Joseph.[65] The statement that "he gathered his strength and sat on the bed" (48:2b) forms in that case a logical continuation and as such, the frequently offered stratification of the text, connecting 47:31 with 48:2b, might still be correct. Yet, the transitional phrase in 48:1aA might have formed the transition from 47:31 to 48:2b: "And it happened after these things, ... that Israel summoned his strength and sat on the bed". As we argued, the phrase is used in the midst of narratives, to mark the transition from one passage to another, and in this sense it would fit in here very well, without the abrupt transition it marks between 47:31 and 48:1.

Summarizing the preceding observations, we note that the phrase וַיְהִי אַחֲרֵי הַדְּבָרִים הָאֵלֶּה (1aA) is hard to classify. It could be part of the "pro-Joseph" as much as of the "pro-Judah" layer. The classification of this phrase depended on the results of the rest of the analysis. Verse 1 (except for v. 1aA) is a passage whose function is to introduce Joseph's sons, Manasseh and Ephraim, to the scene. Since this little passage is connected to the birth story (41:50–52) as well as to the adoption and the reversal of their order (48:3–6, 14–20), it seems likely that this passage is part of the same layer. The same applies to verse 2a where the name "Jacob" is found, and which is part of the same layer as the preceding verse. Finally verse 2b might form a continuation from the "pro-Joseph" tradition found in 47:29–31.

6.3.4 Genesis 48:3–7

The coherence of 48:3–6 is seldom doubted, though their connection with the context is questionable. It is doubted by several scholars

---

[65]In several studies it is noted that it would have been more normal that the patriarch would have bowed himself on the ground, rather than on his bed if he were not dying. Cf. Gunkel, *Genesis*, ³1910, 471; De Vaux, *La Genèse*, 208; Vawter, *On Genesis*, 451.

whether verse 7 belongs to the same layer as verses 3–6, and even that
verse 7 should belong to the same layer as the context of this passage
(48:1–2, 8–22: JE). Usually 48:3–6(7) is assigned to P, because 48:8
is considered to follow seamlessly after verse 2.[66] The whole passage
seems to refer back to Gen. 35:6, 9–12, where identical phrases and
idioms are found, and which itself seems to be related to Gen. 17:1–8;
28:3.[67] The relationship between these passages is obvious and further
discussion of their connection is superfluous.[68] Yet, the reference of
our passage goes beyond the borders of the Joseph Story and relates
our passage, in this respect, to the rest of the book of Genesis. For
that reason we may safely assume that at least 48:3–4 is part of the
layer that creates the whole of the Jacob- and Joseph-narratives. We
may note here that in both passages (35:6, 9–12; 48:3) the name of
the patriarch is "Jacob".

In the second part of our passage the patriarch adopts Joseph's
two sons. As we have argued in Chapter Four,[69] this act of the patriarch must be considered to have negative consequences for Joseph.
He is made childless, which in the ancient Near East is thought to
be a curse,[70] and Joseph is apparently forced to adopt his great-
grandchildren in later times (50:23).[71] In our view this act of adoption
might therefore be considered part of the "pro-Judah" layer, because
it weakens Joseph's position. In this verse the order of Manasseh and
Ephraim is reversed by the patriarch as a prelude to the reversal
in 48:14–20.[72] Usually these verses (vv. 5–6) are considered to be a

---

[66] Cf. e.g. Speiser, Genesis, 354–5, 358–9; Westermann, Genesis 37–50, 207.
These considerations are also found with those who do not adhere to the classical
documentary hypothesis; cf. e.g. Blum, Die Komposition der Vätergeschichte,
250–2; Kebekus, Die Joseferzählung, 196–7.

[67] Sarna, Genesis, 242; Wenham, Genesis 16–50, 463.

[68] Beside the fact that the patriarch's reference to this event is obvious, we may
refer to the following recurring idiom: לוּזָה אֲשֶׁר בְּאֶרֶץ כְּנָעַן (35:6; cf. 48:3aB); וַיֵּרָא
אֱלֹהִים אֶל־ ... וַיְבָרֶךְ אֹתוֹ (35:9; cf. 17:1; 48:3aBb); אֲנִי אֵל שַׁדַּי (35:11; cf. 17:1; 48:3aB);
גּוֹי וּקְהַל גּוֹיִם יִהְיֶה מִמֶּךָּ (35:11aC; 17:4, 5, 6; פְּרֵה וּרְבֵה (35:11aB; cf. 17:2, 6; 48:4aB);
48:4aC); וְאֶת־הָאָרֶץ ... לְךָ אֶתְּנֶנָּה וּלְזַרְעֲךָ אַחֲרֶיךָ אֶתֵּן (35:12; cf. 17:8; 48:4b). Compare
finally also אֲחֻזַּת עוֹלָם (17:8; 48:4).

[69] Cf. above, section 4.4.3.2.

[70] Cf. the following texts: Lev. 20:20–1; 1 Sam 15:33; 2 Sam. 6:23; Jer. 15:7;
22:30(!); Hos. 9:12, 14. See also KTU 1.14–16; 1.17–19, where the gift of children
as well as the loss of them is ascribed to the gods.

[71] Note that the adoption ("born on the knees") occurs in those cases where one
was to remain childless; cf. Gen. 30:3; Ruth 4:16–7.

[72] The preference of Ephraim in this context is remarkable. Beside the fact that
Joseph's oldest son is moved back, it might be that there existed some relationship
between Judah and Ephraim, though obscured by the tradition. This possibility
is supported by the following facts: the gentilicum אֶפְרָתִי denotes an "Ephrathite"

tradition independent of 48:14–20, because the latter would repeat this reversal. However, though the names are reversed proleptically in 48:5, Ephraim does not receive here the most important share as the oldest son. So, these passages cannot be regarded as duplicates of each other and may therefore be regarded as supplements.[73]

One of the concerns of our passage is that Ephraim and Manasseh are put on a par with Reuben and Simeon (48:5b), which in view of the sayings in Gen. 49:3–7 is quite negative.[74] Yet, this was argued in Chapter Four from a synchronic point of view, which might be invalid in view of diachronic considerations. For that reason we have to review these matters here again. In several diachronic studies of the Deathbed Episode, Gen. 49:1–28 is considered to be inserted here by an editor, who inserted the P-elements (49:1–2, 28) and the supposed tribal sayings (49:3–27) in their present position. As a consequence, it appears that in the Deathbed Episode, both the adoption and equation of Ephraim and Manasseh with Reuben and Simeon, on the one hand, and the negative sayings about Reuben and Simeon, on the other, are due to *one* editor (R[P]).[75] The editor must have been aware of the fact that by means of the insertion of these texts, he

---

from Bethlehem (1 Sam. 17:12; Ruth 1:2) as well as an "Ephraimite" (Judg. 12:5 [contrast Willesen, below]; 1 Sam. 1:1 [cf. however, Haran, below]; 1 Kgs. 11:26). The gentilicum "Ephrathite" is derived from אֶפְרָת/תָה "Ephrat(ah)", which is (near) Bethlehem, see Gen. 35:19; 48:7 (or are these two references glosses?); Mic. 5:1; Ruth 4:11; and might denote a region, which included Bethlehem (cf. Sarna, below). Yet, the narrative in Judg. 19 (see 19:1, but compare also v. 16) suggests a close relationship between Bethlehem and Ephraim (cf. also Judg. 17:7–8). Finally, close to Jerusalem there was a territory or village, which was called "Ephraim" (2 Sam. 13:23; cf. 1 Mac. 11:34; John 11:54). For the possible relationship of Judah and אֶפְרָתִי see M. Haran, "*Zebaḥ hayyamîm*", *VT* 19 (1969) 11–22, esp. 15–7; F. Willesen, "The אפרתי of the Shibboleth Incident", *VT* 8 (1958) 97–8. All this is not to deny the enormous problems of identification of toponyms in the biblical tradition; with regard to Ephrat(ah) and Ephraim, cf. *inter alii* K.D. Schunck, "Ophra, Ephron und Ephraim", *VT* 11 (1961) 188–200; Vawter, *On Genesis*, 364; Sarna, *Genesis*, 407–8 (excursus 27); H.O. Thompson, "Ephraim (Place)", *ABD*, vol. 2, 556; idem, "Ephraim, Forest of", *ibid.*, 557; L.M. Luker, "Ephrathah (Place)", *ibid.*, 557–8; H.-D. Neef, *Ephraim: Studien zur Geschichte des Stammes Ephraim von der Landname bis zur frühen Königszeit* (BZAW, 238), Berlin 1995.

[73] A certain connection of 48:3–6 with the following verses was suggested already by Donner, *Literarische Gestalt der Josephsgeschichte*, 32–4, who suggested we connect 48:3–6 with vv. 15–16. However, this suggestion has not found many adherents.

[74] Cf. once again above, section 4.4.3.3.

[75] Cf. Schmitt, *Die nichtpriesterliche Josephsgeschichte*, 66–7, n. 274; 73, n. 305; Schmidt, *Literarische Studien zur Josephsgeschichte*, 207–8. Cf. also Kebekus, *Die Joseferzählung*, 207–8, 214, who regards these texts as having been inserted by the Judah-Redaktion (more or less comparable to R[P]).

would create this negative implication for Ephraim and Manasseh. This consideration suits the general view on the date of P, which is placed near the Exile, when the Northern Kingdom had already been destroyed.[76] Other analyses, like that of Seebaß, ascribe 49:1-2, 28aA to J and assume the insertion of the supposed tribal sayings also to be by J.[77] Yet, in that case too, we may suppose similar knowledge from the side of the editor (R[P]) concerning the negative tenor the equation of Ephraim and Manasseh with Reuben and Simeon in 48:3–6 would have. For that reason it may be concluded that the suggested relation between 48:3–6 and 49:3–7 is also presupposed in other diachronic studies, even though they do not reach the same conclusion as we did. As a consequence we may suppose that the editor, when he inserted 48:3–6 simultaneously with 49:3–27 or later, had some reason to add this equation of Ephraim and Manasseh with Reuben and Simeon to the existing tradition.[78] In our view the editor was well aware of the implication of this equation and his purpose was to diminish the authority of Joseph, which would pave the way for Judah's leading position in 49:8–12.

Finally, 48:7 is rather difficult to classify. Scholars do not agree whether it belongs to the same layer as verses 3–6 (P) or whether it is a later gloss, or the remnant of another document (E). In the chapter on the synchronic reading we argued that the relationship of verse 7 with the preceding verses might be stronger than is usually assumed. Verses 3–6 refer back to Gen. 35:6, 9–12 and in this respect the reference of verse 7 to the events following after 35:1–15 seems

---

[76]Cf. Houtman, *Der Pentateuch*, 375–6. Of course other (earlier) datings for P have been suggested, as Houtman points out, cf. *op.cit.*, 375, n. 55; see recently J. Milgrom, "Priestly ('P') Source", *ABD*, vol. 5, 454–61. Yet, the general view on P as exilic or post-exilic is shared by the scholars referred to in the preceding note, and that is our point.

[77]Cf. H. Seebaß, *Geschichtliche Zeit und theonome Tradition in der Joseph-Erzählung*, Gütersloh 1978, 69–70; idem, "Die Stammessprüche Gen. 49,3–27", *ZAW* 96 (1984) 333–50, 348–50; idem, "The Joseph Story, Genesis 48 and the Canonical Process", *JSOT* 35 (1986) 29–43, 35–8. For comparable positions, see Gunkel, *Genesis*, ³1910, 478; Speiser, *Genesis*, 371. Though Blum in his study comes to different results in terms of the different traditions and the names they have, the order of events with regard to 48:3–7 and 49:1–28 is described in such a manner that it is comparable to the order as suggested by Seebaß and others; see his *Die Komposition der Vätergeschichte*, 228–9, 250–3.

[78]Even if we have to assume that the editor had this passage already in front of him in the P-document, we have to conclude that he agreed with it, otherwise he would have left it out. This is obvious here, because the supposed R[P] (according to the analyses) left out other passages too, as for example, the introduction to the present scene, and even the moment of death of the patriarch (49:33), which — as is assumed — has been preserved in only one version.

obvious. As Blum has argued the reference to Rachel's death implies that Jacob is unable to beget any children (cf. the emphatic וַאֲנִי "but I") in contrast to Joseph (48:6).[79] For that reason we are inclined to consider this verse to belong to the same layer as the preceding verses. The implication is that verse 7, together with the preceding verses is part of the pro-Judah layer. The fact that verse 7 refers back to Gen. 35:16–20 makes it indeed plausible that this verse belongs to the layer which covers large parts of Genesis and connects them intimately. In other words it is also part of the tradition which forms the framework of Genesis and thus the "pro-Judah" layer. Yet, the small explanatory remark הִוא בֵּית לָחֶם "that is Bethlehem" (7bB; similar as in 35:19) might be considered to be a gloss, which seeks to combine several traditions concerning the grave of Rachel and the geographical reference אֶפְרָת "Ephrat".[80]

6.3.5   Genesis 48:8–20

In diachronic studies of the Deathbed Episode, Gen. 48:8–20 appears to cause scholars several problems. The main problems involved are the following. First of all, the statement that the patriarch's eyes became heavy with age and he could not see (48:10a) is thought to contradict the remark of the patriarch that he saw not only Joseph's face but also Joseph's children (48:11).[81] Moreover, the fact that Joseph took his sons twice to the patriarch is considered problematic because the patriarch asked in 48:9 to bring them that he could bless them, whereas only after they are brought to him for the second time does he bless them.[82] For that reason 48:9b–10a is, in several studies, considered to be part of a different layer which had to pave the way for the passage with the changeover of Israel's hands (vv.13–

---

[79] Blum, *Die Komposition der Vätergeschichten*, 252.

[80] Kebekus, *Die Joseferzählung*, 197, n. 9.

[81] Cf. Schmidt, *Literarische Studien zur Josephsgeschichte*, 260.

[82] Schmitt, *Die nichtpriesterliche Josephsgeschichte*, 68; Schmidt, *Literarische Studien zur Josephsgeschichte*, 260; Kebekus, *Die Joseferzählung*, 198–9. Yet, the first- and last named scholars are not convinced by the argument that the patriarch would be blind. In their view it could simply denote a bad-seeing, which disabled him to see clearly (Schmitt, *op.cit.*, 68: "Überinterpretation"; Kebekus, *op.cit.*, 199, n. 17).
Blum, *Die Komposition der Vätergeschichte*, 251, n. 44, suggested that the first time Joseph placed his sons on his father's lap was to let him caress them. The second time it was in order that he could bless them. Yet, it might still be asked why this had to happen twice; was it impossible for the patriarch to bless them after he had caressed them? Moreover, why did Joseph have to prostrate himself on the ground when he took them away the first time? These questions are still unsolved, despite Blum's suggestion. See also Schmidt, *op.cit.*, 257.

20).[83] Secondly, as was indicated in the synchronic analysis,[84] verses 15–16 seem to interrupt the coherence of verses 14–17,[85] but also the note that וַיְבָרֶךְ אֶת־יוֹסֵף "he blessed Joseph" (48:15aA) is problematic, for the LXX reads αὐτούς "them", instead of "Joseph". Many scholars find the disturbance of the coherence of vv. 14–17 in the fact that Joseph's reaction comes too late. However, in line with E. Talstra's observations on Genesis 48,[86] it was argued that Joseph's reaction might be considered a kind of *nachholende Erzählung* which is a purely literary device.[87] In our view, the problem is found in the fact that the patriarch blesses Joseph (48:15aA), but according to the contents of the blessing this is a blessing for the boys (v. 16aB) and not for Joseph himself. This indicates the idea of a corporate personality, suggesting that Joseph is blessed in his sons. Yet, as was argued in Chapter Four, this is factually not in the line of the narrative, because the two boys were not Joseph's any more but became Jacob's sons (48:5–6; cf. also v. 16, וְיִקָּרֵא בָהֶם שְׁמִי "let my name be called in them"). So, the mentioning of Joseph here is not appropriate and the rendering of the LXX seems more reasonable, though we consider it the *lectio facilior*, which is not to be accepted.

The solutions offered for the problems in this passage are in our view unconvincing. Schmidt's study suggests that there might be more coherence in the text than is usually assumed, for he suggests that 48:8–12 might be part of J, with only vv. 9b–10a as a later addition, similar to vv. 13–20, of which vv. 15–16 is also an independent later addition. Blum suggests, however, that 48:8–20 is a coherent narrative, with only vv. 15–16 as a later addition. However, both scholars are unable to classify the later addition and to offer an explanation for its presence. Other solutions, based on the Documentary Hypothesis, offer a quite fragmented text divided principally over the two remaining layers J and E. As an example we may offer Seebaß's solution, who suggests verse 15–16 should follow verse 12, both as part of E (together with 48:1–2, 8–9a, 10b–11, 21–22).[88] To this sugges-

---

[83]Schmitt, *Die nichtpriesterliche Josephsgeschichte*, 68; Schmidt, *Literarische Studien zur Josephsgeschichte*, 260; Kebekus, *Die Joseferzählung*, 198–9.

[84]Section 4.4.3.5, above.

[85]Cf. Schmidt, *Literarische Studien zur Josephsgeschichte*, 256, 266–7. Cf. also W. Rudolph, "Die Josefsgeschichte", in: P. Volz, W. Rudolph, *Der Elohist als Erzähler: Ein Irrweg der Pentateuchkritik?* (BZAW, 63), Berlin 1933, 143–83, 171–2.

[86]E. Talstra, *Schermen met Schrift: De kombinatie van bijbelwetenschappen en computer geïllustreerd aan de tekst van Genesis 48*, Amsterdam 1992, 16–21.

[87]See our discussion above, section 4.4.3.5.

[88]Seebaß, *Geschichtliche Zeit*, 67–8.

tion he adds that Joseph is here blessed in his sons.[89] Moreover, J in his reconstruction is, according to his own judgment, with approval quoting here M. Noth, "quite broken and scarcely still in its original shape".[90] The result of his study is that in several cases he has to assume that some parts of the text have been lost, which he thereupon tries to restore again.[91] However, in those cases we are dealing with conjectures that have no basis in the text and serve only to defend the beleagured literary-critical analysis. For that reason we will try to offer another solution for the present passage using the arguments offered at the beginning of our chapter, such as looking for elements in favour of Joseph and elements which are not, or which support those that do not favour him.

6.3.5.1 Genesis 48:8–12

If the passage under discussion (48:8–12) is treated separately from the following passage (48:13–20), fewer problems will be left. Not simply because the problems in vv. 13–20 are left out, but, taken on its own, our passage appears to be a much more coherent text.[92] Moreover, there is an argument favouring a separate discussion of these two passages. Coming directly to the point, we refer here to the fact that in verse 12 the sons of Joseph are depicted as only little boys, whereas according to the whole Joseph Story his two sons are nearly twenty years old. Yet, the rest of the Deathbed Episode could correspond well with the latter idea, but verse 12 does not (neither does the reference in vv. 9b and 10b).[93] So, there might be some tension between this description of events and the supposed age of Manasseh and Ephraim. Furthermore, it is remarkable that in our passage two elements are completely absent: the names of Joseph's sons and their number.[94] The description of the scene is apparently rather simple and the appearance of the sons has been kept quite

---

[89] Seebaß, *Geschichtliche Zeit*, 67–8, with n. 14.

[90] Seebaß, *Geschichtliche Zeit*, 69: "sehr brüchig und kaum noch in seinem ursprünglichen Zustand".

[91] Seebaß, *Geschichtliche Zeit*, 69, n. 21; 70, n. 23.

[92] See Blum, *Die Komposition der Vätergeschichte*, 251, who states that, although the whole chapter is undoubtedly composite, most of the analyses of this chapter are "m.E. allzusehr auf das aufspüren von Dubletten, literarkritischen Spannungen usw. aus." With approval he refers, however, to the work of Wellhausen, Rudolph and Noth, who all three considered 48:8–14 at least to be part of one literary layer (*op.cit.*, 251, nn. 45–47).

[93] Cf. Hamilton, *Book of Genesis*, 635.

[94] *Pace* Van Selms, *Genesis, dl. 2*, 267, who stated twice that our text knows these two sons. Though indeed suggested in 48:1, our text offers no evidence for his statement.

sober. We are, however, confronted with some problems in the text that have to be discussed. In the preceding section we already referred to the note that the patriarch could not see (v. 10a). How does this relate to texts like verse 8 and 11, where it is said that he did see? Secondly, in the present passage we do not find a "blessing" of the boys, though the patriarch intended to do this (v. 9). Finally, the main problem is still the classification of our passage as belonging to the "pro-Joseph" or the "pro-Judah" layer.

The problem of the patriarch's ability to "see" has often inclined scholars to consider our passage composite. In 48:8 we read וַיַּרְא יִשְׂרָאֵל אֶת־בְּנֵי יוֹסֵף "And Israel saw the sons of Joseph". In 48:11 Israel says to Joseph: רְאֹה פָנֶיךָ לֹא פִלָּלְתִּי וְהִנֵּה הֶרְאָה אֹתִי אֱלֹהִים גַּם אֶת־זַרְעֶךָ "to see your face I did not expect, but look! God made even me see your offspring". Now in verse 10a it says וְעֵינֵי יִשְׂרָאֵל כָּבְדוּ מִזֹּקֶן לֹא יוּכַל לִרְאוֹת "and the eyes of Israel were heavy with age, he was unable to see". The last quotation seems to contradict the preceding ones, "unable to see" seems to exclude "to see".[95] However, in recent times scholars are more and more inclined to regard the remark of Israel being unable to see, as a moderate way of "not seeing", namely in the sense that he was not able to discern the faces of the boys clearly.[96] In fact the idiom suggested does not imply that he is blind. The construction of לֹא יָכֹל "not being able" followed by the inf.constr. לִרְאוֹת "to see" is used to express that someone is not able to see something clearly or to discern something, or even is not allowed to see.[97] Finally, the question in 48:8 מִי־אֵלֶּה "who are these?" after the statement וַיַּרְא יִשְׂרָאֵל

---

[95] Gunkel, *Genesis*, ³1910, 472; Procksch, *Genesis*, 269; Skinner, *Genesis*, 505.

[96] Van Selms, *Genesis*, dl. 2, 267; Schmitt, *Die nichtpriesterliche Josephs-geschichte*, 68; Westermann, *Genesis 37–50*, 210; Kebekus, *Die Joseferzählung*, 199, n. 17; Wenham, *Genesis 16–50*, 464; Hamilton, *Book of Genesis*, 633–4. Yet, this interpretation had already been defended in earlier times by scholars who disputed the documentary hypothesis: cf. Keil, *Genesis*, 322; Rudolph, "Die Josefsgeschichte", 171; Jacob, *Das erste Buch*, 874–5; Aalders, *Genesis*, dl. 3, 183.

In the following we rule out any suggestion of medical terminology in the Hebrew idiom here, for in our view the Hebrew idiom applies a descriptive way of characterizing the problems one could have with seeing. However, the expression וְעֵינֵי יִשְׂרָאֵל כָּבְדוּ מִזֹּקֶן לֹא יוּכַל לִרְאוֹת "and the eyes of Israel were heavy with age, he was unable to see" might suggest that the patriarch had a typical geriatric complaint with his eyes, namely something like cataract. In such cases people are near-sighted and they are simply "unable to see" anything too far away from them. See: Th. Struys, *Ziekte en genezing in het Oude Testament*, Kampen 1968, 187, with reference to W. Ebstein, *Die Medizin im Alten Testament*, Stuttgart 1901, 158. Yet, in addition to cataract other forms of eye disorders are possible, without implying complete blindness; cf. also R.K. Harrison, "Blindness", *IDB*, vol. A–D, 448–9; M. Sussman, "Sickness and Disease", *ABD*, vol. 6, 6–15, esp. 12.

[97] Cf. Gen. 44:26; Exod. 10:5; 33:20; 2 Sam. 17:17; Ps. 40:13. See also Esth. 8:6.

אֶת־בְּנֵי יוֹסֵף "and Israel saw the sons of Joseph", might already imply that the patriarch was not able to see,[98] and only when Joseph's sons are brought near could he see them (48:11). For that reason the more common interpretation nowadays, that Israel could not discern clearly, is, in the context of the narrative, the most likely and therefore to be followed.

Nevertheless, despite this interpretation verse 10a (together with verse 9b) is ascribed to a layer different from the surrounding verses (vv. 9a, 10b). Even Schmidt, who considers the remaining passage (48:8–9a, 10b–12) to be a unity, still regards vv. 9b–10a as a later addition.[99] The main argument for his delimitation appears to be that verses 9b–10a have no function in the text other than a preparation for the scene in verse 13–20. Schmidt, in fact, excludes other arguments, for even the patriarch's name does not allow him to distinguish v. 10a from the other verses like vv. 8 and 12. Yet, because vv. 9b–10a, 13–14 and 17–20 are considered a later addition, it is no problem that in both layers the name "Israel" is used. It is generally recognized that 48:10a is presupposed in the following passage where the patriarch crosses his hands,[100] and Schmidt is undoubtedly right there.[101] Yet, this is no argument why 48:10a should belong to the same layer as 48:13–14, 17–20, because a later addition has somehow to correspond with the elements present in the text in order to fit in, and that could be the case in our text just as well.

The answer to the problem if 48:9b–10a is added, is, however, dependent on the question whether verse 10a has indeed no function in its present position and secondly, if the reference to Israel's weak eye-sight is dependent on Isaac's deathbed account as is assumed by Schmidt.[102] In the previous paragraph we already referred to the fact that in verse 8 Israel's question, "Who are these?" suggests a certain near-sightedness of Israel, which in our view argues against Schmidt's assumption that verse 10a has no function in the passage 48:8–12. Moreover, Schmidt himself argues that the verb ראה "to see" had the function of a motto (*Leitwort*) in the layer to which he attributed

---

[98]Cf. *e.g.* Keil, *Genesis*, 322; Rudolph, "Die Josefsgeschichte", 170–1; Van Selms, *Genesis, dl. 2*, 267; Wenham, *Genesis 16–50*, 464; Hamilton, *Book of Genesis*, 633–4.

[99]Schmidt, *Literarische Studien zur Josephsgeschichte*, 260. A comparable analysis is found in Westermann, *Genesis 37–50*, 203–4, 209–11.

[100]Blum, *Die Komposition der Vätergeschichte*, 251, n. 44; Sarna, *Genesis*, 327; Kebekus, *Die Joseferzählung*, 198–9; Wenham, *Genesis 16–50*, 464.

[101]Similarly Westermann, *Genesis 37–50*, 210.

[102]Schmidt, *Literarische Studien zur Josephsgeschichte*, 260–1. Similarly Blum, *Die Komposition der Vätergeschichte*, 253.

48:8–9a, 10b–12 (J).[103] The texts to which he refers (45:28; 46:1, 28–30) have indeed strong resemblances with our text, such as that the patriarch is prepared to die now that he has seen Joseph's face again. The reference to Israel's heavy eyes, and disabled seeing (clearly) would alsofit in this layer, because we find a reference here to Israel's old age in combination with seeing (48:10a).

Regarding the dependency of our passage on Genesis 27 it appears that Schmidt's argumentation is problematic. Genesis 27 is to be attributed to J,[104] whereas Schmidt attributes 48:8–9a, 10b–12 also to J, but regards verses 9b–10a, 13–14, 17–20 as a later addition which used and adapted Genesis 27.[105] Of course, this is possible: the J-passages could be identified on the basis of their comparable style, whereas the additional passages could be identified on the basis of their comparable style and on the fact that the plot was adapted. However, here it should be asked, first of all, why the other J-passages (48:8–9a, 10b–12) could not have been part of the additional layer that adapted Genesis 27. Secondly, why would J himself not have been able to adapt the plot of Genesis 27 in the way the assumed editor of the additional layer did? These questions are pertinent especially if we consider the parallel J-passages in 48:8–12 and Genesis 27. The parallels are not just restricted to 48:10a, 13–20 alone. In fact, parallels occur throughout 48:8–12,[106] and these corresponding elements might suggest a certain relationship between these two texts. However, at first sight there is no reason to exclude vv. 9b–10a from 48:8–12 as a later addition on the basis of these correspondences, for in none of the verses of our passage is there a hint of the plot of Genesis 27.

Yet, one problem still remains in 48:8–12 possibly indicating a cer-

---

[103]Schmidt, *Literarische Studien zur Josephsgeschichte*, 261: "Hier [in v. 11; RdH] steht der Begriff 'sehen', dem bei J in 45,28; 46,1aα.28–30 geradezu die Funktion eines Leitwortes zukam."

[104]Speiser, *Genesis*, 205, 210–11. See esp. Westermann, *Genesis 12–36*, 530–1, with a short reference to the history of research.

[105]Schmidt, *Literarische Studien zur Josephsgeschichte*, 260–1.

[106]The parallels to be found are — next to the obvious problem with the eyes (27:1; 48:10a) — the following: Israel's question מִי־אֵלֶּה "who are these?" (48:8), and Isaac's question מִי אַתָּה בְּנִי "who are you, my son?" (27:18). Secondly, the note that Joseph brought his sons close to him (וַיַּגֵּשׁ, 48:10b) and Isaac's request to Jacob to come near (גְּשָׁה־נָּא, 27:21, cf. v. 25), Thirdly, the blessing by Israel, וַאֲבָרֲכֵם "and I will/ that I may bless them" (48:9b), and by Isaac: לְמַעַן תְּבָרֶכְךָ נַפְשִׁי "that my soul may bless you" (27:25). Finally, Joseph's sons are kissed: וַיִּשַּׁק אֹתָם אֵלָיו וַיִּשַּׁק לָהֶם "and he (Joseph) brought them near and he (Israel) kissed them", and Isaac is kissed (other way round): וַיִּגַּשׁ וַיִּשַּׁק־לוֹ "and he (Jacob) came near and kissed him (Isaac)" (27:27, cf. v. 26). Cf. Wenham, *Genesis 16–50*, 464; Jagersma, *Genesis 25–50*, 251.

tain relationship and a common motif. It is the short remark of the
patriarch, after he asked Joseph to take his sons to him: וַאֲבָרֲכֵם, "and
I will/ that I may bless them". It is in fact this word that causes the
problems in reading our passage because the patriarch does not bless
them when they are brought to him, only after the somewhat remarkable transition of verses 12–13, are they blessed. In this way, the patriarch's wish to bless them, points to the following passage (48:13–
20), where by means of the blessing the preferential status will be
given to Ephraim. This might suggest that in our text the word וַאֲבָרֲכֵם
is added as the preparation for the following passage.[107] This suggestion is confirmed by the fact that the statement that Israel's eyes are
"heavy with age" (v. 10a) following Israel's wish to bless Joseph's
sons, is quite abrupt, because these two elements are in fact not related to each other: both elements are preparatory for the following
passage, where Joseph supposes a mistake because of his father's disabled seeing, and where Israel will bless them. However, in itself the remark that Israel could not see is not related to Israel's wish to bless the
boys.[108] Yet, his request to take the boys to him, followed by the explanatory statement that his eyes were heavy with age, might offer a
more intelligible text, suggesting that he wanted them close to him in
order to see them. In that case Israel's wish וַאֲבָרֲכֵם "that I may bless
them" would be a later addition, relating this passage to the following
one. If this is correct, the text might be represented as follows:

And Israel saw the sons of Joseph (8A)	וַיַּרְא יִשְׂרָאֵל אֶת־בְּנֵי יוֹסֵף
and he said, "Who are these?" (8B)	וַיֹּאמֶר מִי־אֵלֶּה
And Joseph said to his father, (9aA)	וַיֹּאמֶר יוֹסֵף אֶל־אָבִיו
"They are my sons, whom God gave me here." (9aB)	בָּנַי הֵם אֲשֶׁר־נָתַן־לִי אֱלֹהִים בָּזֶה
And he said, "Bring them to me, please", (9b*)	וַיֹּאמֶר קָחֶם־נָא אֵלַי
[that I may bless them]	[וַאֲבָרֲכֵם]
for the eyes of Israel were heavy with age, (10aA)	וְעֵינֵי יִשְׂרָאֵל כָּבְדוּ מִזֹּקֶן
he was unable to see. (10aB)	לֹא יוּכַל לִרְאוֹת

---

[107] Relating וַאֲבָרֲכֵם to 48:13–20 would be in agreement with many literary critical
studies, though, in contrast to these studies, we would prefer to attribute only this
word of 48:9b–10a to the same layer as (parts of) 48:13–20. Yet, it still has to be
shown that we find in that passage a different layer than the one found in 48:8–12.
For the literary-critical studies, cf. Seebaß, *Geschichtliche Zeit*, 69–70; idem, "The
Joseph Story", 33; Schmitt, *Die nichtpriesterliche Josephsgeschichte*, 68; Schmidt,
Literarische Studien zur Josephsgeschichte, 260–1; Kebekus, *Die Joseferzählung*,
198–9.

[108] In this respect we disagree with those scholars who ascribe 48:9b–10a to one
layer (see the previous footnote). In our view the abrupt transition from "that I
may bless them" to "for the eyes of Israel were heavy with age" does not allow
for a common layer.

And he brought them near to him, (10bA)   וַיַּגֵּשׁ אֹתָם אֵלָיו

and he kissed them and embraced them. (10bB)   וַיִּשַּׁק לָהֶם וַיְחַבֵּק לָהֶם

And Israel said to Joseph, (11A)   וַיֹּאמֶר יִשְׂרָאֵל אֶל־יוֹסֵף

"To see your face, I had not thought, (11B)   רְאֹה פָנֶיךָ לֹא פִלָּלְתִּי

and look! God made me even see your seed". (11C)   וְהִנֵּה הֶרְאָה אֹתִי אֱלֹהִים גַּם אֶת־זַרְעֶךָ

And Joseph removed them from his knees, (12A)   וַיּוֹצֵא יוֹסֵף אֹתָם מֵעִם בִּרְכָּיו

and bowed himself with his face to the earth. (12B)   וַיִּשְׁתַּחוּ לְאַפָּיו אָרְצָה

The final question that has to be answered now is, to which layer our passage should belong. In our passage it is hard to establish if the tendency is in the line of the pro-Joseph or the pro-Judah layer. As might be clear from the discussion of the possible addition of וַאֲבָרֲכֵם "that I may bless them", the arguments that can be given for the allocation of the text to a specific layer are closely dependent on the discussion of 48:13–20. Therefore we will discuss this passage first, before treating the assignment of the text to the different layers.

6.3.5.2   Genesis 48:13–20

In this well-known passage, where the patriarch attempts to give Ephraim the preferential status with his spectacular act of placing his hands crosswise on the heads of his grandsons, disturbing in this way Joseph's careful arrangement, there is only one part of the text considered problematic, namely verses 15–16. The transition from verse 14 to verse 17 is thought by some to be disturbed by verses 15–16, because after verse 16 Joseph's reaction to the patriarch's action would be too late. However, as we have written before, the syntactic structure of 48:17 suggests by means of the use of the imperfect for the patriarch's placing his hand: וַיַּרְא יוֹסֵף כִּי־יָשִׁית אָבִיו יַד־יְמִינוֹ עַל־רֹאשׁ אֶפְרַיִם, a rendering like "and Joseph saw that his father would lay (or: was to lay) his right hand on the head of Ephraim". In this way verses 17–19 seem to function as a parenthesis or *nachholende Erzählung*.[109]

However, although this interpretation might remove the major obstacle to the unity of the passage under discussion (vv. 13–20), one problem in the text — to which the LXX already testified — still remains. In 48:15aA (MT[110]), it is related that the patriarch blesses *Joseph*, which seems to be contradicted by 48:16, because in this verse his sons are blessed (הַנְּעָרִים, "the boys"),[111] with a reference to the

---

[109]Cf. above, sections 4.4.3.5; 6.3.5, for a more elaborate discussion and the appropriate bibliographic references.

[110]Similarly in Sam, TO, Peš.

[111]L. Ruppert, *Die Josephserzählung der Genesis: Ein Beitrag zur Theologie der Pentateuchquellen* (StANT, 11), München 1965, 164.

adoption ("may my name be proclaimed in them").[112] As Schmidt already pointed out, 48:15aA cannot imply that Joseph is blessed in his sons here because Joseph's sons had already been adopted in 48:5.[113] LXX reads here αὐτούς "them", harmonizing the text in that way,[114] indicating that "Joseph" is out of place here and that in fact the two sons are being blessed. This harmonization is in line with an earlier one, namely in 48:12, where MT reads וַיִּשְׁתַּחוּ לְאַפָּיו אָרְצָה "he (= Joseph) bowed himself down with his face to the earth", where Sam, LXX, TN suggest the following reading: וַיִּשְׁתַּחֲווּ לְאַפָּיו אָרְצָה "they bowed themselves down before him to the earth". Finally, a comparable harmonization recurs in 48:20, the text of the blessing:

By you Israel will bless, saying, (20bA) בְּךָ יְבָרֵךְ יִשְׂרָאֵל לֵאמֹר

God make you as Ephraim and as Manasseh (20bB) יְשִׂמְךָ אֱלֹהִים כְּאֶפְרַיִם וְכִמְנַשֶּׁה

Here too the LXX tries to adjust the singular and plural, reading in 48:20bA ἐν ὑμῖν "by you (pl.)" instead of בְּךָ "by you (sg.)",[115] though the singular concerns in this case the boys and not Joseph.[116] In 48:12, 15aA Joseph's role is considered problematic and for that reason the text is adjusted in line with the course of events in the Deathbed Episode, ascribing more importance to Ephraim and Manasseh. However, the link between 48:12 and 15a might indicate some of the diachronic relations of the text. In verse 12 (MT) it is Joseph who prostrates himself before Israel, in verse 15 (MT) it is Joseph who is blessed. In both cases this seems to have been problematic for the Ancients because the whole chapter suggests that the sons of Joseph are to be blessed. This suggestion is created in fact in 48:9b: "that I may bless them", the phrase we considered as a possible later addition.[117] If this consideration is correct, it would make both phrases in 48:12 and 15a even more remarkable, because these two verses are usually ascribed to the same layer (verse 15 generally in its entirety,

---

[112]Cf. Hamilton, *Book of Genesis*, 638, with n. 39, referring to a comparable expression in Akkadian; but also to Ezra 2:61 (|| Neh. 7:63). See also Van der Merwe, "Joseph as a Successor of Jacob", 226.

[113]Schmidt, *Literarische Studien zur Josephsgeschichte*, 266.

[114]J.W. Wevers, *Notes on the Greek Text of Genesis* (SCS, 35), Atlanta (GA) 1993, 815.

[115]Wevers, *Greek Text of Genesis*, 818.

[116]According to E.C. Kingsbury, "He Set Ephraim before Manasseh", *HUCA* 38 (1967) 129–36, 131–2, the reading of the LXX is inadvisable, because, first, cultic blessing formula (he considers the blessing to be "cultic") are in the singular (*e.g.* Num. 6:23–26, where the antecedent of the blessing is plural); and second, the singular has to be understood as distributive.

[117]Cf. above, pp. 478–479.

together with v. 16).[118] In his study of the Joseph Story, L. Ruppert has defended the connection between 48:12 and 15a, excluding, however, 48:15b–16 because of its "solemn style"[119] and because the verses (vv. 15b–16) cannot continue verse 15a because the objects of the blessing differ (Joseph in v. 15a; the boys in v. 16).[120] He suggests therefore that the blessing in verse 20b might originally have been a continuation of 48:15a, attributing these verses to E, whereas the later addition of 48:15b–16 would belong to E^2. Yet, with his assignment of verse 15a and 20b to the same layer we are confronted with the same problem as in verse 15, as H.-C. Schmitt rightly noted, because in verse 20 Ephraim and Manasseh are also the focus of the blessing, and "Israel" is used here as a designation of the later people.[121] For that reason Ruppert's analysis of 48:15a.20b as part of the same layer cannot be regarded as conclusive. Nevertheless his analysis in which he attributed 48:12.15a to the same layer and verses 15b–16 to a later one, might be worth considering. This might be argued in part on the basis of H. Donner's observations about our passage.[122]

In his discussion of the text Donner notes the fact that most analyses of Genesis 48 attribute the blessings to J and E, but not to P, whereas P is the one most fond of blessings.[123] As E seems to have two (48:15–16, 20) blessings, of which the former is hard to assign to E with any certainty, he suggests we consider the possibility that 48:15–16 belongs to P, following after 48:3–6.[124] In order to let the narrative

---

[118]Gunkel, *Genesis*, ³1910, 469; Ruppert, *Die Josephserzählung der Genesis*, 164; Seebaß, *Geschichtliche Zeit*, 67–69; idem, "The Joseph Story", 33–4 (though suggesting we transpose vv. 21–2 before vv. 15–6); Kebekus, *Die Joseferzählung*, 200–1.

[119]Ruppert, *Die Josephserzählung der Genesis*, 164: "das Stück 48,15b.16 wirkt schon durch seinen feierlichen Stil wie ein Fremdkörper im JE-Zusammenhang."

[120]R. Syrén, *The Forsaken First-Born: A Study of a Recurrent Motif in the Patriarchal Narratives* (JSOTS, 133), Sheffield 1993, 137, suggests that the phrase "he blessed Joseph" is anticipating in fact Genesis 49. Westermann, *Genesis 37–50*, 212, suggests that in an older version of the narrative, after the introduction of the blessing (48:15aA), originally a blessing of Joseph was found, before the blessing of the boys.

[121]Schmitt, *Die nichtpriesterliche Josephsgeschichte*, 69–70. Schmitt states that the reference to Israel as a people in 48:20 is totally unexpected, and occurs only here in the Joseph Story and further in Genesis only in 34:7. He apparently overlooked the reference to Israel as a plural in 47:27b.

[122]H. Donner, *Die literarische Gestalt der alttestamentlichen Josephsgeschichte* (SHAW.PH, 1976.2), Heidelberg 1976, esp. 30–4.

[123]Donner, *Literarische Gestalt der Josephsgeschichte*, 32. For a more extensive description of Donner's analysis, cf. above, section 5.12.

[124]Donner, *Literarische Gestalt der Josephsgeschichte*, 33. However, he suggests we follow the reading of LXX in 48:15a αὐτούς = אֹתָם (*op.cit.*, 33, n. 57).

continue uninterrupted he is, however, forced to suggest we follow the reading of LXX in 48:15a αὐτούς = אֹתָם "them".[125] Now, his remarks upon the rest of the blessing are of some interest for the problems facing us, even though Donner primarily seems to be interested to prove its late provenance and in this way the possible Priestly origin of this section. First, in 48:15 the expression הִתְהַלֵּךְ לִפְנֵי is found also in the other patriarchal narratives, Gen. 17:1 (P; "admittedly also in 24:40, J").[126] Secondly, the hymnic descriptions of God found in 48:15–16 are, according to Donner, Exilic or post-Exilic (רעה, גאל). Finally, the relationship between עַל שֵׁם אֲחֵיהֶם יִקָּרְאוּ בְּנַחֲלָתָם (48:6) and וְיִקָּרֵא בָהֶם שְׁמִי in verse 16 is not to be ignored.[127] All this might support the idea that 48:15–16 is not to be attributed to E but to P.[128] Yet, it might be asked if Donner's chronological classification is completely correct and if his attribution to one document is evident. First, his classification of the hymnic predicates as Exilic and post-Exilic might be false in view of the "dark passage Gen. 49:24", which he did not consider, but where רֹעֶה is used as a description for a personal god.[129] In view of Ugaritic material it is now clear that the epithet of a deity as a shepherd is not late, but quite early.[130] The attribution of the expression הִתְהַלֵּךְ לִפְנֵי is not evidently P, as he himself admits (24:4, J), but also occurs in completely different contexts, which makes its attribution to P problematic.[131] Nevertheless, Donner's observation that the text of the blessing is closely related to other texts in Genesis is worth considering. The fact that the expression הִתְהַלֵּךְ לִפְנֵי occurs also in Gen. 17:1 (P) and 24:40 (J) is remarkable, especially in view of the fact, that the latter text mentions the מַלְאָךְ "angel", which is also found in 48:16. Donner did not mention this text, while he admits that מַלְאָךְ was not specific to P.[132] However, these correspondences

---

[125] Donner, *Literarische Gestalt der Josephsgeschichte*, 33, n. 57, although this is the *lectio facilior*, which he is cautious to accept in other cases (*op.cit*, 34, n. 59).

[126] Donner, *Literarische Gestalt der Josephsgeschichte*, 33; see also Kebekus, *Die Joseferzählung*, 328.

[127] Donner, *Literarische Gestalt der Josephsgeschichte*, 34.

[128] Donner, *Literarische Gestalt der Josephsgeschichte*, 33.

[129] Donner, *Literarische Gestalt der Josephsgeschichte*, 33, n. 58: "Die dunkle Stelle Gen. 49,24 bleibt außer Betracht".

[130] Cf. J.C. de Moor, "De goede herder: Oorsprong en vroege geschiedenis van de herdersmetafoor", in: G. Heitink *et al.*, *Bewerken en bewaren: Studies ... K. Runia*, Kampen 1982, 36–45, 44; idem, *RoY*, 247; *RoY²*, 336; Korpel, *RiC*, 448–52. Compare also above, pp. 203–4.

[131] Cf. 1 Sam. 2:30, 35; 12:2; 2 Kgs. 20:3; Isa. 38:3; Pss. 56:14; 116:9; Esth. 2:11. Moreover the expression has close parallels in Ugarit and Babylonia, (*ARTU*, 177, n. 13).

[132] Donner, *Literarische Gestalt der Josephsgeschichte*, 34.

between 48:16 and 24:40 (J) would argue in favour of the assignment
of 48:16 to J. This is strengthened by the fact that in Gen. 17:1, commonly attributed to P, the name יהוה "Yhwh" is used,[133] arguing in
fact for an assignment to J.[134] So, if we are to apply the literary critical arguments here, it appears that the relationship between these
texts might be stronger than is suggested by the assignment to the
different documents.[135] In view of the fact that in Gen. 48:3–6(7) we
found also other expressions in common with Genesis 17, it is just
possible that several parts of the Deathbed Episode may be dependent on the same redaction or tradition that lies behind Genesis 17.
Our text refers back to these traditions, where God appears to Abraham and where several epithets are used for God, which Jacob uses in
Genesis 48 as well. The fact that this blessing refers back to the other
patriarchs and their traditions on the one hand, and on the other,
that it concerns a blessing for the adopted sons of the patriarch —
the former sons of Joseph — all this might suggest that we are dealing
here with a part of the "pro-Judah" layer, which also formed large
parts of the framework of Genesis. Yet, although this might be true
for the contents of the blessing in 48:15b–16, this still does not apply
to verse 15a. As we suggested, its apparent continuation of verse 12,
does at least suggest a common layer for these two verses. However,
it will be dependent on the rest of our analysis how verses 12 and 15a
should be classified.

Analysing our passage (vv. 13–20) from an ideological point of
view, we have to consider the following: In 48:13–14 we find the
anacrusis of this famous passage, Joseph making a careful arrangement so his father could bless the two boys properly, Manasseh, the
eldest opposite the right hand, and Ephraim, the youngest opposite
the left (v. 13).[136] Yet, the patriarch stretches out his right hand and
lays it on the head of Ephraim, whereas the left hand is placed upon
Manasseh's head. So it appears that the recurrent motif of the "forsaken firstborn" is applied here, which in itself might suggest a com-

---

[133] Houtman, *Der Pentateuch*, 383, already pointed out that such texts like Gen.
17:1 are problematic with regard to the use of the different Divine names.

[134] Westermann, *Genesis 12–36*, 308–9, tries to overcome this problem by assuming that P in Gen. 17:1–3a offers an existing tradition, while 17:3b–21 interpret
and expand that tradition.

[135] Note that in Gen. 17:1 a reference to the age of Abraham is made, which is
regarded as one of the hallmarks of P. Yet, this criterion was also found in 47:28,
which we considered to be part of the overall structure of Genesis, labelled as
the "pro-Judah" layer. This too might argue in favour of the assignment of 17:1;
24:40; 48:16 to the "pro-Judah" layer.

[136] Syrén, *The Forsaken First-Born*, 138.

mon background for our passage and those other passages adopting this motif.[137] Yet, there is more to say on that. By granting Ephraim the preferential position over Manasseh, the patriarch passed over Joseph's eldest son. The implication of this element in the context of the whole scene may be clear. First, Joseph's sons are adopted; secondly, they are put on a par with Reuben and Simeon (negatively; cf. 49:3–7); thirdly, Joseph's family structure, according to the narrative, is turned upside down, the youngest is put before the eldest.

This account is generally considered to be an aetiology, explaining why Ephraim in later times became more important than the tribe of Manasseh.[138] At the moment we are not concerned with the question which situation this aetiology tries to explain.[139] Our concern here is to point out that Manasseh has apparently no supremacy in the idea of the writer, which does not have to be defined in terms of power, or the like.[140] At any rate, the scope of the whole passage seems to be in line with the tendency to weaken Joseph's position by means of this death-bed account,[141] and here it is achieved by passing over Joseph's oldest son. Therefore we consider 48:13–14 to be part of the "pro-Judah" layer, supporting in the end Judah's superior position in Israel.

Important to note here is the fact that the patriarch is called "Israel", both in verses 13 and 14, whereas in other cases we found that the name "Israel" was used in the "pro-Joseph" tradition. As we have shown in Chapter Five, the occurrence of the name that is originally in the "basic document" cannot function as an indication for that "basic document", because an editor could have also used that name.[142] In fact this phenomenon might also occur here, because

---

[137]See esp. Syrén, *The Forsaken First-Born*, 137–9. In addition, cf. De Fraine, *Genesis*, 321; Vawter, *On Genesis*, 455; Hamilton, *Book of Genesis*, 636–7; Jagersma, *Genesis 25–50*, 252.

[138]This seems to be expressed the most clearly by Kingsbury, "He Set Ephraim before Manasseh", 129: "No one doubts that the aetiology contained in Gen. 48 is some sort of explanation of the reversal of status between Manasseh and Ephraim in which the latter, at one time the lesser, rose above the former."

[139]For a short description of the possible situations, see Kingsbury, "He Set Ephraim before Manasseh", 129; Schmitt, *Die nichtpriesterliche Josephsgeschichte*, 153–6.

[140]We will return to this subject later in this section, because the contents of the supremacy might be defined in the text itself.

[141]Cf. Schmitt, *Die nichtpriesterliche Josephsgeschichte*, 153–6, who considers 48:13–4, 17–9 to be part of the "Judah-layer", which favours Judah, and which in this connection criticizes the apparent close relationship between Joseph and Manasseh (cf. *op.cit.*, 152, n. 321). Yet, Schmitt considers this favourite position of Ephraim an indication for the geographical provenance of the Joseph Story according to the "Judah-layer".

[142]Cf. above, section 5.23.2.

"Israel" is used for the patriarch in texts that we assigned to the "pro-Joseph" layer (47:29–31, 48:2b), whereas this name occurs also in the "pro-Judah" layer (48:13–14). Nevertheless, one part of this text could still be part of the "pro-Joseph" layer, the short phrase in which it is said that Israel stretched out his right hand (48:14aA): וַיִּשְׁלַח יִשְׂרָאֵל אֶת־יְמִינוֹ. This phrase does not mention the object of the blessing but only forms the beginning of one, for which we have parallels from Ugarit, although in one case Ilu, the god who is about to bless, takes a cup in his hand, KTU 1.17:i.34–6:[143]

[ks .]yiḫd . il{.} bdh .	Ilu took the cup in his hand, (34)
ybrk	[dnì]l . mt . rpi .	he blessed Dani'ilu, the Saviour's man, (34/5)
ymr . ġzr	[mt . ḫ]rnmy	fortified the hero, the Harnamite man. (35/6)

In fact, this Ugaritic text is a good example of how the hand might be raised at the act of blessing and subsequently is followed by the blessing, which might be the case in 48:14*–15* as well. In that way, it would appear that a part of what we assigned to the "pro-Judah" layer, may originally have been part of the "pro-Joseph" layer, revealing a Deathbed Episode in which Joseph was blessed by his father. Now somewhat anticipating the discussion on 48:8–12, it has been suggested above, that verse 15aA might originally have continued verse 12. If verse 14aA is part of that same layer, it might even offer a smoother course of narrated events, as can be seen below:

And Joseph removed them from his knees, (12A)	וַיּוֹצֵא יוֹסֵף אֹתָם מֵעִם בִּרְכָּיו
and bowed himself with his face to the earth. (12B) …	וַיִּשְׁתַּחוּ לְאַפָּיו אָרְצָה
Then Israel stretched out his right hand (14aA) …	וַיִּשְׁלַח יִשְׂרָאֵל אֶת־יְמִינוֹ
and blessed Joseph. (15aA)	וַיְבָרֶךְ אֶת־יוֹסֵף

---

[143] A more elaborated version is found in KTU 1.15:ii.17–21, where it is said that he Ilu took the beaker in his right hand. The Ugaritic text quoted above, is from *CARTU*, 103; the translation from *ARTU*, 229. For the argumentation to restore the text, cf. M. Dijkstra, J.C. de Moor, "Problematic Passages in the Legend of Aqhâtu", *UF* 7 (1975) 171–215, 177.

"Taking the cup in his (right) hand" is based on the *literary* testimony. In this connection the *iconic* material from Ugarit is very illustrative. The cup is sometimes in the *left* hand, and the right hand raised for blessing; see: A. Caquot, M. Sznycer, *Ugaritic Religion* (IoR, XV.8), Leiden 1980, plate 8 (= *ANEP*, 352, # 826). Yet, it also occurs that the left hand is raised and the right hand holds the cup; however, in that case it is not clear if we are dealing with a blessing scene; cf. *op.cit.*, plate 7, and p. 23 (= *ANEP*, 168, # 493). For additional iconic material from *inter alii* Hazor and Megiddo, cf. the bibliography in J.C. de Moor, "Ugarit and Israelite Origins", in: J.A. Emerton (ed.), *Congress Volume, Paris 1992* (SVT, 61), Leiden 1995, 205–38, 215–6, nn. 45–8; idem, *RoY*², 128–9, nn. 118–21.

With regard to 48:15aB–16 it has already been considered that the text of the blessing is closely related to the "pro-Judah" layer, because it contains many references to the patriarchs,[144] a reference to the adoption, and the promise of progeny, all of which strengthens this supposition. The text is in verse, although Westermann denies this, against, for example BHS, because it would not be rhythmic.[145] Yet, rhythm (or metre) in its strict sense as Westermann seems to want it, is certainly not a criterion for poetry,[146] but writing the text colometrically would result in two well-balanced strophes:

The God before whom (15bA)[147]	הָאֱלֹהִים אֲשֶׁר
my fathers walked, Abraham and Isaac; (15bB)	הִתְהַלְּכוּ אֲבֹתַי לְפָנָיו אַבְרָהָם וְיִצְחָק
The God who shepherded me (15cA)	הָאֱלֹהִים הָרֹעֶה אֹתִי
from my past to this day; (15cB)	מֵעוֹדִי עַד־הַיּוֹם הַזֶּה

The angel who redeemed me from all evil (16aA)	הַמַּלְאָךְ הַגֹּאֵל אֹתִי מִכָּל־רָע
may he bless the boys; (16aB)	יְבָרֵךְ אֶת־הַנְּעָרִים
And let my name be called in them, (16bA)	וְיִקָּרֵא בָהֶם שְׁמִי
and my fathers' name, Abraham and Isaac, (16bB)	וְשֵׁם אֲבֹתַי אַבְרָהָם וְיִצְחָק
and let them be numerous in the midst of the land. (16bC)	וְיִדְגּוּ לָרֹב בְּקֶרֶב הָאָרֶץ

A very clear reference to the geographical position of both tribes is found in the final colon, where the patriarch wishes that they will be

---

[144] Cf. *e.g.* Westermann, *Genesis 37–50*, 213–4.

[145] Westermann, *Genesis 37–50*, 213. Similarly Van Selms, *Genesis, dl. 2*, 268, had some trouble with the metre.

[146] J.C. de Moor, "The Art of Versification in Ugarit and Israel, I: The Rhythmical Structure", in: Y. Avishur, J. Blau (eds.), *Studies in Bible and the Ancient Near East Presented to S.E. Loewenstamm*, Jerusalem 1978, 119–39; idem, "The Art of Versification, II: The Formal Structure", *UF* 10 (1978) 187–217; idem, "The Art of Versification, III: Further Illustrations of the Principle of Expansion", *UF* 12 (1980) 311–5. For a recent review, cf. P. Sanders, *The Provenance of Deuteronomy 32* (OTS, 37), Leiden 1996, 134–5 (with literature).

[147] The first poetic verse (48:15b) is undoubtedly the most difficult to delimit. In this case we have followed one of the possible delimitations of Ps. 1:1, which is an obvious example of enjambement, and syntactically more or less comparable to 48:15b:

Blessed is the man,	אַשְׁרֵי־הָאִישׁ
who does not walk in the counsel of the wicked.	אֲשֶׁר לֹא הָלַךְ בַּעֲצַת רְשָׁעִים

For this delimitation cf. RSV; NIV; NEB; Buber; J. Ridderbos, *De Psalmen vertaald en verklaard, I: Psalm 1–41* (COT), Kampen 1955, 9; N.A. van Uchelen, *Psalmen, deel I (1–40)* (PredOT), Nijkerk 1971, 9; a different lay-out is found in NBG; JPS; H.J. Kraus, *Psalmen, 1.Teilband* (BKAT, XV/1), Neukirchen-Vluyn 1960, 1; M. Dahood, *Psalms I: 1–50* (AB, 16), Garden City (NY) 1966, 1.

numerous בְּקֶרֶב הָאָרֶץ "*in the midst of the land*".[148] Moreover, in this blessing it is already said in which way Ephraim was to come before Manasseh, namely in becoming more numerous than his brother. This is suggested by the answer the patriarch gives to Joseph, when the latter protests: "I know my son, I know; he also shall become a people, and he also shall be great; nevertheless his younger brother shall be greater than he, and his descendants shall become a multitude of peoples" (48:19). This implies that the aetiology that is given here is not *per se* concerned with the political development after the end of the United Monarchy, but that it concerns the population growth of both tribes.[149]

It might be asked now once more if 48:15b–16 is contemporary with 48:13–14, 17–19, or not. As was argued before, the syntactic construction of 48:17, with Joseph's late reaction to the crosswise hands, might support a contemporaneous origin, yet, some still deny it. Though we are convinced that this interpretation of the text explains the late reaction of Joseph sufficiently, it cannot be denied that the narrative does not develop smoothly. But, are the alternative solutions for this problem convincing? There are three models put forward to solve the problem in our passage:

1. The solution of the documentary hypothesis, two different documents contradicting each other: 48:13–14, 17–19 belongs to J, 48:10b–12, 15–16 belongs to E.[150]

2. The expansion theory, supposing a basic document, that was expanded several times. So, a basic Judah-, or Reuben-layer is

---

[148] *HAL*, 1060. This rendering is found in Seebaß, *Geschichtliche Zeit*, 71, with n. 28; idem, "The Joseph Story", 34; S. Beyerle, *Der Mosesegen im Deuteronomium: Eine text-, kompositions- und formkritische Studie zu Deuteronomium 33* (BZAW, 250), Berlin 1997, 188. Note that in most translations אֶרֶץ is rendered as "earth" (*e.g.* RSV; NIV) and that קֶרֶב is interpreted prepositionally as "in", excluding "midst" (*e.g.* NBG; NIV), whereas in the context of the blessing it is most likely that the expression refers to the "midst of the land" where they will live, because God will bring them back to the land (v. 21). Moreover, in other texts the expression is rendered mainly by "in the midst of", while the rendering of אֶרֶץ is determined by the context, "earth" or "land", but in several cases RSV renders "earth", where the possibility of "land" cannot be excluded; cf. Exod. 8:18 (ET 8:22); Isa. 5:8; 6:12; 10:23; 19:24; 24:13; Ps. 74:12. In the following texts we find the rendering "in the land" (RSV): Deut. 4:5; 15:11; 19:10; Isa. 7:22.

[149] Cf. Schmitt, *Die nichtpriesterliche Josephsgeschichte*, 153–6.

[150] Cf. Gunkel, *Genesis*, ³1910, 469; Skinner, *Genesis*, 502–3, 506; Seebaß, *Geschichtliche Zeit*, 67–9. Though Schmidt, *Literarische Studien zur Josephsgeschichte*, closely follows the documentary hypothesis, his analysis of 48:13–22 differs considerably because he assumes a later addition here, though 48:15–6 is independent from the rest.

supposed, which was later revised by respectively the Reuben-
or Judah-layer, and probably some other. In that case 48:13–14,
17–19 are the earliest parts in the text and 48:15–16 was added
later.[151]

3. Originally Joseph was blessed here, followed by a blessing for
the two boys. The blessing for Joseph however is lost, and only
the blessing for the boys has remained.[152]

In our view, the first solution should be dismissed because of the fact
that some of the problems would remain in one of the documents,
mostly E, for it would be narrated that the patriarch blessed Joseph,
while his words were directed to the boys. Westermann has argued
correctly in this respect that part of the blessing ceremony was the
identification, in order that the correct party would receive the blessing. In the context of the patriarchal traditions it is unlikely, in his
view, that it would have been narrated in this way.[153] However, with
regard to the second solution the same objection might be raised,
for it is questionable if a later editor or glossator, who inserted the
verses 15–16, would have prefaced these verses by "and he blessed
Joseph" (15aA), whereas he knew that the boys were blessed. Moreover, he would have known that the text could not develop smoothly
any more and might have anticipated that his insertion would disturb
the course of events. Finally, regarding Westermann's solution that
Joseph was originally blessed here but that the text of that blessing
is lost, we have to object that this is only a supposition. There are no
arguments for the text having been left out, it is not clear what kind
of text it would have been, and we are unable to falsify the argument.

Nevertheless, it is possible that a solution can be found in the
combination of the second and third proposal. Ruppert suggested that
48:15b–16 is a later addition to 48:15a, which was originally followed
by 48:20. Though this solution would correspond with Westermann's
supposition that Joseph was originally blessed here, the final part
of Ruppert's suggestion (48:20 after v. 15a) was demonstrated to be
unlikely, because it would result in the same problems as in the text of
48:15–16. To solve the problem, we might ask why the editor created
this text in which the patriarch blessed *Joseph*, but in his words he
blessed *the boys*? If he is responsible for 48:15aA, it might be expected
that he would have written that the patriarch blessed the boys.

---

[151]Schmitt, *Die nichtpriesterliche Josephsgeschichte*, 69–71; Kebekus, *Die Joseferzählung*, 199–201.

[152]Westermann, *Genesis 37–50*, 212.

[153]Westermann, *Genesis 37–50*, 212.

A solution to this problem might be indeed Ruppert's thesis that 48:15b–16 was added later to verse 15a, whereas also Westermann's supposition that Joseph was blessed here is true, though it has to be asked if the "narrated" blessing (48:15a) has to be followed by a "spoken" blessing (like e.g. 48:15b–16). But, if it were true that the original narrative contained Joseph's blessing here, why did the editor disturb the text in this way, creating a narrative which does not develop smoothly? Apparently he was forced to accept the text of the original narrative and had to gloss over the fact that Joseph had this prominent position. By inserting the blessing of the boys here, it seemed that Joseph was a collective for the two boys. Thus, supposing that "and he blessed Joseph" (v. 15a) had not been followed by the blessing of the boys (vv. 15b–16), but directly by verse 17, the suggestion would still have been that Joseph himself was blessed. By adding the event of the hands laid crosswise on the heads (vv. 13–14), and then the statement that Joseph was blessed (v. 15aA), followed by the blessing of the boys (vv. 15b–16), the editor revised the narrative in such a way that the "pro-Joseph" evidence was lost.[154] In conclusion, we would prefer to assign 48:15aB–16 to the same layer as 48:13–14, additions that had to polish away that it was Joseph himself who is blessed. Yet, even if one cannot agree on the allocation of both passages to the same "pro-Judah" layer, we are still in line with most analyses, which consider at least vv. 15aB–16 to be a later addition to an earlier version.

Finally, we can be brief in discussing the last part of our passage (vv. 17–20). It is a continuation of the preceding text, where the patriarch had put his hands crosswise on the heads of Ephraim and Manasseh. Here Joseph's protest does not help, the youngest is put before the oldest. This is mainly found in 48:17–19, in almost all diachronic studies ascribed to the same layer as vv. 13–14.[155] Moreover, we would like to emphasize here that Israel's answer to Joseph (48:19) refers to his blessing in 48:15b–16, where he blessed the boys with the wish of multiplying, doing this with his right hand on Ephraim's head, i.e. Ephraim received the strongest blessing.[156] Thus the argument by some scholars that the blessing does not concern the priority

---

[154]It might also be considered that the real blessing of Joseph had to be postponed, to enable a blessing of Joseph in the midst of the twelve (Gen. 49:22–26), otherwise Joseph would have received two blessings, or he would have received one apart from his brothers.

[155]Cf. above p. 425, the table summarizing the literary critical research on Gen. 47:28–49:33.

[156]Gunkel, Genesis, ³1910, 472; Skinner, Genesis, 525–6; H.-J. Fabry, J.A. Soggin, "יָמִין, jāmîn", ThWAT, Bd. III, 658–663, 660; Jagersma, Genesis 25–50, 252.

of Ephraim,[157] can only be correct if the blessing is read apart from the crossing of the hands by the patriarch. If the blessing is read as part of this passage, however, it is clear that the contents are meant to be more for Ephraim and less for Manasseh. Concerning verse 20 the scholarly literature is not uniform, although it can be concluded that it is generally considered to be a verse which supports Ephraim's preferential status. In that way it is regarded as following 48:15–16,[158] or as part of the same layer as 48:13–14, 17–19,[159] or a later addition to the whole passage.[160] In our view the general consensus that this verse supports the priority of Ephraim is to be followed and as such we may assign it to the "pro-Judah" layer, which we also found in the preceding verses.[161]

Summarizing, we conclude that Gen. 48:13–20 is a product of the "pro-Judah" editor, who revised the original "pro-Joseph" story. In this passage verses 13, 16–20 are completely from this editor and verses 14 and 15 were revised by means of additions (in combination with the afore-mentioned verses). The original "pro-Joseph" layer in these two verses consisted of two clauses, namely in 48:14: וַיִּשְׁלַח יִשְׂרָאֵל אֶת־יְמִינוֹ "Then Israel stretched out his right hand"; and in 48:15: וַיְבָרֶךְ אֶת־יוֹסֵף "and (he) blessed Joseph".

6.3.5.3   Genesis 48:8–12 Once More

Now, we would like to return to the preceding passage, 48:8–12, the analysis of which we considered to be dependent on the following passage (48:13–20). If our analysis of that passage is correct, that in 48:14a.15aA a part of the "pro-Joseph" layer is found, which would be a smooth continuation of verse 12, while the remaining verses would be part of the "pro-Judah" layer, then this would be helpful in the assignment of 48:8–12. In this passage there was only one element, as was argued before, supporting the idea developed in the next passage

---

[157]Kebekus, *Die Joseferzählung*, 200, n. 26.

[158]Gunkel, *Genesis*, ³1910, 469–70.

[159]Schmidt, *Literarische Studien zur Josephsgeschichte*, 259–60; Kebekus, *Die Joseferzählung*, 200.

[160]Schmitt, *Die nichtpriesterliche Josephsgeschichte*, 69–70.

[161]Schmitt, *Die nichtpriesterliche Josephsgeschichte*, 69–70, states that the blessing is a later added expansion, being originally a saying in Israel, which here elaborates on Ephraim's priority. In his view it is still visible that the saying is added, because of the fact that is connected "quite clumsily" ("ziemlich plump") to the preceding וַיְבָרֲכֵם בַּיּוֹם הַהוּא by means of לֵאמוֹר (48:20a). Yet, if the final argument concerning the use of לֵאמוֹר following after this clause is a correct observation, the same would have to be considered in 48:20bA, where we can read: בְּךָ יְבָרֵךְ יִשְׂרָאֵל לֵאמֹר. Further, we might have to assume the same "clumsy editor" in Gen. 1:22; Deut. 29:18; 1 Kgs. 1:47; 8:55; Isa. 19:25, because we find the same syntax there.

(vv. 13–20) that Ephraim and Manasseh are to be blessed, in contrast to the statement that the patriarch blessed Joseph (48:15aA). This concerns the short wish of the patriarch in verse 9b, וַאֲבָרְכֵם "that I may bless them". If this word is to be considered a later addition, preparing the blessing of the boys instead of Joseph, it appears that a very clear pattern emerges from the analysis. The text in its present form supports the idea that, although Joseph had a special position in Israel's heart, he was not the most important person. He does not receive a blessing, but the new sons of Israel do: Ephraim and Manasseh. Also the tribe that seems to be the closest to Joseph, Manasseh, is passed over and Ephraim is given priority. Yet, if we remove these elements a different story occurs: Israel meets Joseph's sons (no names, no number), kisses them and embraces them. Then he expresses his happiness to Joseph. Joseph bows down before his father and is blessed by him. Summarizing, we may conclude that in contrast to the following passage (48:13–20), the editorial adaptation of our passage has been very subtle. By adding only one word (וַאֲבָרְכֵם), the effect of the whole scene changed, preparing in this way the blessing of Ephraim and Manasseh, instead of the blessing of Joseph (vv. 13–20). We consider 48:8–12 as part of the "pro-Joseph" layer, except for the additional וַאֲבָרְכֵם "that I may bless them" in verse 9b. However, if the "pro-Joseph" layer had ended (for the moment) with 48:15aA, וַיְבָרֶךְ אֶת־יוֹסֵף "and he blessed Joseph", then it might be asked if a blessing will follow in which Joseph is to be blessed. The answer to that question will be found in part in the next section.

6.3.6 Genesis 48:21–22

The final passage of Chapter 48 has been the subject of many different interpretations. Some scholars assign these two verses to one of the layers they isolated in the previous passages, for example E[162] or a large additional layer.[163] Others consider these verses as independent late additions,[164] or only one verse of it.[165] Further, some scholars are inclined to read in 48:21 as a reference to the Exodus, as described in the book of Exodus, and thus as a literary dependent on that tradition,[166] although some scholars emphasize the fact that the Exodus

---

[162]Gunkel, *Genesis*, ³1910, 474; Seebaß, *Geschichtliche Zeit*, 70–1.

[163]Schmidt, *Literarische Studien zur Josephsgeschichte*, 268–9.

[164]Schmitt, *Die nichtpriesterliche Josephsgeschichte*, 71–2, n. 302; Westermann, *Genesis 37–50*, 216–7. See also Blum, *Die Komposition der Vätergeschichte*, 253–4, 257.

[165]Kebekus, *Die Joseferzählung*, 203.

[166]Gunkel, *Genesis*, ³1910, 474, who suggests that this verse is placed here to create a bridge between the Joseph Story and the Exodus.

is here described as a return home, comparable to Gen. 31:3.[167] On the other hand, in 48:22 an early, independent tradition is thought to be present, describing the patriarch as a warrior, who conquered with his sword and his bow a "mountain-ridge" or "Shechem".[168] In our review we will especially consider two aspects of this discussion; first, if these two verses are interrelated, or independent of each other. Secondly, their function in the narrative and their relation to the wider context (Exodus), with the question in mind whether these two verses support one of the two layers in particular: the "pro-Joseph" or the "pro-Judah" layer.

As was noted above, some scholars deny the coherence between 48:21 and 22, considering the latter added to the former. In Chapter Four we argued that verse 22 presupposes in its present context verse 21, because they are in Egypt, and have to return to Canaan before the gift of Shechem would be relevant. Yet, it may be asked if this supposition is relevant at a diachronic level. Gunkel, for example, supposes that verse 22 has been part of another tradition in which the patriarch divided the inheritance between his sons, and finally gives Joseph "one part over his brothers" (אַחַד עַל־אַחֶיךָ).[169] In his view, this also supposes that the patriarch is not in Egypt, but has to be in Canaan, otherwise he would not be able to divide the land between his sons.[170] Beside the comparable structure of 48:21 with 50:24, and some correspondence to 28:15, Blum finds a sharp distinction between 48:21 and the rest of the chapter, because 48:21 refers to "the Israelites and their return in the 2.p.plur." but in the other parts only directs Joseph or his sons,[171] whereas he seems to assume that verse 22 is independent of 48:8–20.[172] Kebekus considers 48:21

---

[167]Kebekus, *Die Joseferzählung*, 201–2, with n. 30.

[168]Skinner, *Genesis*, 507; Vawter, *On Genesis*, 359, 456–7; Sarna, *Genesis*, 330, see also *op.cit.*, 405–7 (excursus 26); Hamilton, *Book of Genesis*, 643.

[169]On the interpretation of the Hebrew, cf. above section 4.4.3.6; and below.

[170]Gunkel, *Genesis*, ³1910, 474, referring to E. Meyer, *Die Israeliten und ihre Nachbarstämme: Alttestamentliche Untersuchungen*, Halle 1906, 414–5. Cf. also Skinner, *Genesis*, 507; Noth, *Überlieferungsgeschichte des Pentateuch*, 91–2; Ruppert, *Die Josephserzählung der Genesis*, 177; H. Seebaß, *Der Erzvater Israel und die Einführung der Jahweverehrung in Kanaan* (BZAW, 98), Berlin 1966, 28; idem, *Geschichtliche Zeit*, 70–1, n. 27; Schmitt, *Die nichtpriesterliche Josephsgeschichte*, 71–2, n. 302; Westermann, *Genesis 37–50*, 217; Kebekus, *Die Joseferzählung*, 201–2.

[171]Blum, *Die Komposition der Vätergeschichte*, 254: "48,21 hebt sich zudem dadurch von seinem Kontext ab, daß Jakob hier von den Israeliten und ihrer Rückführung in der 2. Pers.Pl. redet, während er in Kap. 48 ansonsten allein Joseph oder dessen Söhne anspricht."

[172]Blum, *Die Komposition der Vätergeschichte*, 254, 257.

to refer to the Exodus as a home coming, whereas verse 22 seems to refer to a more warlike conquest of the land, emphasizing in this way different aspects.[173] Apparently much depends on how 48:22 is interpreted, and to a lesser degree on the reading of 48:21.

However, we might start with Blum's suggestion that 48:21 should be set apart from 48:8–20 because the patriarch here applies the 2.p.plur. to the Israelites. First, as far as we are aware, there is no reference to the בְּנֵי יִשְׂרָאֵל in this text, neither in the sense of "sons of Israel", nor as "Israelites". Moreover, it would be possible to understand this 2.p.plur. "you" just as a reference to Joseph and his sons, who are in Blum's view the object in the preceding verses. Yet, even if we were to relate this 2.p.plur. to Joseph and his brothers, it would still be possible, because the patriarch makes a distinction between himself, who will die in Egypt, and the others, who will return to Canaan. The plural might anticipate thus the reference to Joseph's "brothers" in 48:22, which does not contradict *per se* the preceding scene, where Joseph was called to his father alone. If Joseph indeed had a preferential status among the brothers, his presence alone with Israel would be possible. In this respect 48:21 is thus connected to the preceding passage, because it supposes the scene to be in Egypt,[174] whereas it is re-lated to the following verse (48:22), referring to the return of Joseph and his brothers. Yet, does this reference to the return of the others imply the Exodus from Egypt, as is supposed by some scholars? It appears to us, that this is not conclusive. The return to the land of their fathers is described as a homecoming, comparable with 31:3 indeed.[175] As such there is thus an important difference in the description of the event of the Exodus, which is generally described in terms like יצא hiph., "make ... come/go out" and עלה hiph. "bring up, lead up" (50:24, etc.). Yet, in that context the land is considered to be a promised land, and a gift of God, previously occupied by others; not the land of the fathers, but promised to them.[176] In this respect it is important to refer to the fact that some scholars consider the original setting of the Deathbed Episode shortly after the patriarch arrived in Egypt, and not — as 47:28 suggests — seventeen years after his arrival in Egypt.[177] Their suggestion corresponds to our analysis

---

[173]Kebekus, *Die Joseferzählung*, 201–2, with n. 30.

[174]Cf. Schmitt, *Die nichtpriesterliche Josephsgeschichte*, 71–2, n. 302.

[175]Kebekus, *Die Joseferzählung*, 201–2, n. 30.

[176]Cf. Gen. 50:24; Exod. 3:8, 17; 33:1; Lev. 25:38.

[177]This is mainly argued with regard to verses 8–9, where the patriarch asks who the boys with Joseph are. Cf. Gunkel, *Genesis*, ³1910, 472; von Rad, *Erste Buch Mose*, 340; Westermann, *Genesis 37–50*, 209; Hamilton, *Book of Genesis*, 634. Cf. also Seebaß, "The Joseph Story", 35–6. Contrast, however, Schmidt, *Literarische*

of 47:28, which we considered to be part of the overall structure of
Genesis, as such the duration of Israel's sojourn in Egypt is unknown
in the "pro-Joseph" layer.[178] If this analysis is correct, the words of
the patriarch might suggest that Joseph will return to Canaan in the
near future, after the famine is over. In that case, the allotment of
Shechem to Joseph would also be reasonable, otherwise the objections
by some scholars, that it seems unlikely that the patriarch would allot
the inheritance of the land while in Egypt would be justified.[179] Now
the narrative simply suggests that the patriarch left Shechem and
took refuge in Egypt during the famine, where he bestows the city to
his favourite son. Finally, the words of 48:21 clearly reflect 47:29–31
and for that reason might belong to the same layer.[180]

The final verse of this chapter, 48:22, contains the allotment of
Shechem to Joseph. Scholars often had trouble classifying this verse
as part of one of the layers they identified in our chapter. Many of
them acknowledge the fact that the allotment of Shechem to Joseph is
an indication of his preferential status.[181] Certainly, this is influenced
by the note in verse 22aB אֶחָד עַל־אַחֶיךָ "one above your brothers".
This phrase is often interpreted as an attributive to the preceding שְׁכֶם
"Shechem", as an extra allotment to Joseph. Yet, in Chapter Four we
argued that this was grammatically unlikely and that, modifying a
suggestion of Speiser,[182] it is more likely we consider אַחַד עַל־אַחֶיךָ a
vocative for Joseph, resulting in the following rendering:

And I, I give Shechem to you (22aA)	וַאֲנִי נָתַתִּי לְךָ שְׁכֶם
O One above your brothers; (22aB)	אַחַד עַל־אַחֶיךָ
which I took from the hand of the Amorites (22bA)	אֲשֶׁר לָקַחְתִּי מִיַּד הָאֱמֹרִי
with my sword and my bow. (22bB)	בְּחַרְבִּי וּבְקַשְׁתִּי

Studien zur Josephsgeschichte, 263.

[178] This might be related to Joseph's reference to the Exodus in 50:22–26, which,
because of the giving of Joseph's age and the clear idiom of the Exodus, might be
part of the overall structure of Genesis, which tries to create a bridge here between
the Joseph Story and the Exodus. (Free after Noth, *Überlieferungsgeschichte des
Pentateuchs*, 226–8, who suggests that the Joseph Story is the bridge between
Patriarchal traditions and the Exodus.)

[179] Cf. above, p. 492, with n. 170.

[180] Kebekus, *Die Joseferzählung*, 204–5.

[181] Seebaß, *Geschichtliche Zeit*, 70, "Nicht nur wird Joseph durch [48:]22 zum
Haupterbe gemacht, ... "; Schmitt, *Die nichtpriesterliche Josephsgeschichte*, 71–
2, n. 302, "einer alten Tradition vom Tod Jakobs in Palästina ... [der] die Vor-
rangstellung Josephs betonen will"; Blum, *Die Komposition der Vätergeschichte*,
254, "Sonderstellung Josephs"; Kebekus, *Die Joseferzählung*, 203: "Bevorzugung
Josephs"; Hamilton, *Book of Genesis*, 644, "... the concluding note is one about
Joseph's preferential status over his brothers".

[182] Speiser, *Genesis*, 358.

In this way the usual interpretation of this verse, referred to above,[183] appears to be correct, insofar as this verse indeed implies Joseph's preferential status. It is even pronounced *expressis verbis* by the patriarch, who assigns to Joseph the role of "head of the tribe".[184] Consequently this verse might be assigned to the "pro-Joseph" layer. Yet, this verse has some reminiscences to other texts all concerning the region of Shechem. For that reason we have to discuss the possible relationship with these verses first, before attributing this verse to a certain layer.

A part of Joshua's speech in Joshua 24 might echo the note in our verse that the patriarch conquered Shechem "by his sword and his bow" from the Amorites:[185]

And I sent before you the panic, (12aA)	וָאֶשְׁלַח לִפְנֵיכֶם אֶת־הַצִּרְעָה
and I drove them out before you, (12aB)	וַתְּגָרֶשׁ אוֹתָם מִפְּנֵיכֶם
the two kings of the Amorites (12aC)	שְׁנֵי מַלְכֵי הָאֱמֹרִי
not with your sword and with your bow. (12aD)	לֹא בְחַרְבְּךָ וְלֹא בְקַשְׁתֶּךָ

Moreover, in the Jacob traditions we find several references to Shechem which should also be considered. First, is the purchase of a piece of land near Shechem (33:19; Josh. 24:32), and secondly, the raid of Simeon and Levi against Shechem (Gen. 34; 49:5–7). The question is now, how are these texts to be related, if this is possible at all?

First of all, it appears that Josh. 24:12 is a kind of theological correction to Gen. 48:22 which seems to be a boast of Israel on his military power.[186] In this respect Josh. 24:12 emphasizes the idea of the gift of the land, against Gen. 48:22, which considers at least a

---

[183] See above, n. 181.

[184] For this interpretation, cf. already Seebaß, *Der Erzvater Israel*, 39, "Chef des Hauses" (see also his n. 140). Seebaß's interpretation is now confirmed by our rendering of וישתחו ישראל על־ראש המטה in 47:31, with "and Israel bowed himself before the head of the tribe" (cf. above, p. 461).

[185] For the sake of clarity we present MT here as it stands, referring the reader for the discussion of the difficulties in Josh. 24:11–2 and a possible solution to W.T. Koopmans, *Joshua 24 as Poetic Narrative* (JSOTS, 93), Sheffield 1990, 183–4, 201–3. Yet, compare also D. Edelman, "Book Review of: W.T. Koopmans, *Joshua 24 as Poetic Narrative* (JSOTS, 93), Sheffield 1990", *JNES* 52 (1993) 308–10, 309, concerning the "two kings of the Amorites". The possibility of a relationship of Gen. 48:22 to Josh. 24:12 is even not considered in V. Fritz, *Das Buch Josua* (HAT, 1/7), Tübingen 1995, 249.

[186] Cf. E. Nielsen, *Shechem: A Traditio-Historical Investigation*, Copenhagen 1955, 90, 284–5; Koopmans, *Joshua 24*, 121.

Ruppert, *Die Josephserzählung der Genesis*, 177, considers the possibility that Gen. 48:22 could be a later correction to Josh. 24:12 (see also Nielsen, *Shechem*, 285), because the supposed editor of this text, E², saw in the allotment to Joseph not a property *in* Shechem, but the city of Shechem itself, being Jacob's spoils of

part of the land to be conquered by weapons.[187] Yet, although some scholars consider 48:22 as an allusion to the settlement in Canaan (*i.e.* after the Exodus),[188] it is more likely that we are dealing here with an ancient tradition.[189] Yet, although it might be correct that in Josh. 24:32 both texts are combined into one tradition, namely, that Joseph inherited the piece of land near Shechem,[190] the question has to be asked, which tradition is the oldest? There are three possibilities:

1. Both traditions (Gen. 33:19 and 48:22) are independent of each other and concern different persons ("Jacob" and "Israel") and also completely different events. In that case it is impossible to establish which tradition is the oldest. Yet, although this possibility cannot be ruled out completely, we think it to be very unlikely. If "Jacob" and "Israel" are originally not referring to the same person or figure, then it still seems unlikely that we are dealing with references to different events.[191]

---

war. He appreciates Gunkel's suggestion therefore (*Genesis*, ³1910, 373, 474), that 48:22 might be an allusion to the events described in Judges 9, where Abimelech, a man from Joseph, captures Shechem. Ruppert dates this supposed editor, E², in the period of the exile of the house of Joseph in Assyria (Ruppert, *op.cit.*, 176), who might have hoped for a return of "Joseph" and the restoration of Shechem as the capital of a unified Israel (*op.cit.*, 178). Yet, although Ruppert first dismissed the interpretation of נָתַתִּי לְךָ "I give to you" as a kind of prophecy of the future inheritance still to be conquered (*e.g.* Tuch, Delitzsch, Strack), he brings this interpretation in by the back door as a future hope for the exiles, based on the possible event in Judges 9. In our view, this interpretation is too complicated to be likely, whereas the "simple" interpretation as an aetiology, explaining how Israel and/or Joseph came to inherit Shechem is the more likely.

[187] Cf. also A. Rofé, "The Family-Saga as a Source for the History of the Settlement", *ErIs* 24 (1993) 187–91 (Hebr.).

[188] Koopmans, *Joshua 24*, 352; Kebekus, *Die Joseferzählung*, 201–2, with n. 32.

[189] This tradition is in scholarly literature labelled as a "pre-Mosaic tradition", or a tradition concerning a "pre-Mosaic" raid. Cf. G.E. Wright, *Shechem: The Biography of a Biblical City*, New York 1965, 132; Sarna, *Genesis*, 330; Hamilton, *Book of Genesis*, 643. It may be obvious, however, that such a classification is impossible nowadays because of the shift of paradigms for Israel's early history. Even if a Moses-figure had existed, we still have to allow for the possibility that the Exodus concerned only a small number of people and that so-called "proto-Israelites" or even "Israelites" dwelt already a long time in Canaan. In other words, we have to reckon with the possibility that there was much more continuity than discontinuity. Cf. De Moor, *RoY*, 136–51; idem, "Egypt, Ugarit and Exodus", in: N. Wyatt *et al.* [eds.], *Ugarit, Religion and Culture: Essays ... J.C.L. Gibson* [UBL, 12], München 1996, 213–247.

[190] Ruppert, *Die Josephserzählung der Genesis*, 177.

[191] Cf. *e.g.* Gunkel, *Genesis*, ³1910, 474–5, who denies that we are dealing with the same events in these texts. This interpretation seems to be based on the idea that these traditions refer to historical events. In that case his observation

2. It might be considered that 48:22 is a kind of correction or criticism of 33:19, where the patriarch buys a piece of land near Shechem.[192] The argument in favour is that it would emphasize that there is a distinct character of the patriarchs in contradistinction to the original inhabitants of the land.[193] Yet, it appears that 33:19 makes also a clear distinction between the patriarchs and the inhabitants, because the purchase of the land was in the case of the cave of Machpela apparently sufficient warrant to make a distinction between the patriarch and the inhabitants. In the case of the patriarchal grave we would expect an even greater distinction; yet, this is absent.[194]

3. The tradition in 48:22 is the original one. Yet, this tradition supposes first of all that the land was (partly) conquered by the patriarchs, and secondly, that Joseph received Shechem as his inheritance. As Josh. 24:32 demonstrates, Genesis in its present shape suggests that Joseph received a piece of land near Shechem, not the town itself.[195] In this sense, Gen. 33:19 and chapter 34 might be considered a correction to 48:22. The patriarch bought a small piece of land of the sons of Hamor, yet, his sons were aggressive towards Shechem (the son of Hamor).[196]

---

might be correct. Yet, in our view we have to allow for the literary aspect in these traditions, which only refer very vaguely to a certain event. It might be, for example, that one tradition is original, while the other is not, but just a *literary* reaction and correction of the former.

[192]Ruppert, *Die Josephserzählung der Genesis*, 177; Nielsen, *Shechem*, 285 (though with some doubts).

[193]Nielsen, *Shechem*, 285.

[194]Ruppert, *Die Josephserzählung der Genesis*, 178, suggests that in 48:21-2 a theological shift took place, in which Joseph became passive, Israel took over his position and became the instrument by whom God bestows gifts to Joseph. In our view we are dealing here with an *Überinterpretation* of the text and the narrative. Even if Ruppert's literary-critical analysis should prove to be correct, we might still ask if such conclusions can be derived on the basis of such a small amount of textual data.

[195]Note also the introduction to the Joseph Story in 37:1, suggesting that the land of Canaan is the land of the "sojournings" of the patriarchs. This verse seems to exclude military exploits by the patriarch, but even more suggests that the patriarch sojourned himself also in the land of Canaan, and had no base camp of his own in the land. He settled in the surroundings of Hebron, not near Shechem (35:27; 37:1, 14).

[196]It might even be that in the name חֲמוֹר "Hamor" we are dealing with a pun on אֱמֹרִי "Amorite"; cf. J.A. Soggin, "Genesis Kapitel 34. Eros und Thanatos", in: A. Lemaire, B. Otzen (eds.), *History and Traditions of early Israel: Studies Presented to Eduard Nielsen* (SVT, 50), Leiden 1993, 133-5, 134 (note that Shechem became a personal name in this story, comparable to Hamor). The idea of a pun

This aggressive behaviour of Simeon and Levi is judged to be wrong (34:30; 49:5–7),[197] and in this sense the patriarch's statement that he took Shechem by his sword and by his bow, seems to be converted into an ironical or even disapproving allusion to the massacre by his sons. Understood in this sense Josh. 24:12 is not so much a *criticism* of Gen. 48:22, but in fact a plain formulation of what the patriarch should have said in the present form of Genesis.[198] Yet, seen from a diachronic perspective the saying in 48:22 suggests indeed that the patriarch took Shechem with his sword and his bow, and this was a kind of boast of his military exploits.

If this interpretation is correct, there is sufficient reason in this text to assign 48:21–22 to the "pro-Joseph" layer. In that layer the patriarch bestowed Shechem upon his son, the city he captured from the Amorites[199] with his sword and his bow. As Seebaß already suggested Joseph was treated there as the head of the tribe, who received the capital as his property. It suggests that Joseph was the chief man indeed. Yet, the whole of the book of Genesis, forming as it were an interpretative framework for the text, suggests that the capture of Shechem was cursed by the patriarch (49:5–7). In this way the gift Joseph receives is neutralized as the piece of land the patriarch bought from the "hand of the sons of Hamor" (33:19).

---

is emphasized by the fact that in 48:22 Israel took Shechem מִיַּד הָאֱמֹרִי "from the hand of the Amorites" and in 33:19 he bought the land מִיַּד בְּנֵי־חֲמוֹר "from the hand of the sons of Hamor". The use of a pun cannot be excluded in this case, because another very likely pun is found in the fact that the patriarch says he did it with his sword and "his bow", בְקַשְׁתִּי; in 33:19 Jacob bought the land for a hundred קְשִׂיטָה "pieces", a rare word for money, which occurs next to Job 42:11, only in Josh. 24:32 (*HAL*, 1073). It is possible that by means of the puns the probably unwanted interpretation of 48:22 was neutralized.

[197] Jacob emphasizes here that his number is small and that he would not be able to make a stand against the inhabitants of the land. This remark does not fit someone, who on another occasion, will bestow the city he would have conquered.

[198] It might be noted that in Genesis 34 as well as in 33:18–20, the patriarch is named "Jacob"; in 48:21–2 his name is "Israel". It is remarkable that until now in our analysis the name "Israel" appeared in the so-called pro-Joseph layer and in the pro-Judah layer, whereas "Jacob" only occurred in those texts which were regarded as later additions. This too might suggest that we are dealing here with different traditions.

[199] On the problems involved with the Amorites in biblical texts, like Gen. 48:22; cf. J.C. de Moor, "Ugarit and Israelite Origins", in: J.A. Emerton (ed.), *Congress Volume, Paris 1992* (SVT, 61), Leiden 1995, 205–38, esp. 233–8, with *inter alii* n. 136 for bibliographical references. For an opposite point of view, cf. J. Van Seters, "The Terms 'Amorite' and 'Hittite' in the Old Testament", *VT* 22 (1972) 64–81.

6.4   Mid-Term Review

In section 6.2 we postulated the following working hypothesis:

> In an ancient version of the Deathbed Episode Joseph's father said farewell to Joseph as his most important son. In a later stage of history this version was revised to legitimize the leading position of (the tribe of) Judah, who rose to power and for one reason or another had to defend his position. This revision resulted in a deathbed account which still reflects both historical situations.

After analysing Gen. 47:29–48:22 we may evaluate the results of our analysis in the light of this working hypothesis. Summarizing the results of the preceding analysis, it appears that the working hypothesis accounts for the data found in Gen. 47:29–48:22 quite well.[200] The "pro-Joseph" layer begins in 47:29–31, the text that favours Joseph clearly as the most important son, who has to take care of his father's funeral. At the end of this scene the patriarch bows down before his son, "the head of the tribe" (47:31). The transitional phrase "and it happened after these things" (48:1aA) marks in the present context a quite abrupt transition from one scene to the other. Yet the phrase is also used for the transition from one passage to another within ongoing narratives. In this way it may have been used in the "pro-Joseph" layer, marking the transition from the foregoing passage to 48:2b. In fact 48:1aA, 2b forms the beginning of the next passage, which continues largely in 48:8–12, the passage where the patriarch meets Joseph's sons (whose names nor number are given) After their meeting Joseph takes his sons away from his father's knees, bows down before his father and is blessed (48:12, 14aA, 15aA). Yet, the words of the blessing do not follow immediately after the phrase "and he blessed Joseph". The words the patriarch spoke to Joseph are found in 48:21–2. Here the patriarch assures Joseph that he will return to the land of his fathers, and he bestows Shechem on his son. Vawter already has labelled these two verses as a sort of blessing[201] which might be a sort of testament, similar to what we found in Chapter Three concerning the genre of Genesis 49. Yet, the Deathbed Episode does not come until the end of it and it is dependent on the result of the subsequent analysis of Genesis 49, whether the blessing of Joseph

---

[200] The text of Gen. 47:29–48:22 is presented in a synopsis below (pp. 582–593), in order to offer the reader a quick overview of the text and of the results of the analysis.

[201] Vawter, *On Genesis*, 456, "And there is, finally, a blessing for Joseph himself, or a bequest, or something similar for which we have no specific term, ..."

and the Deathbed Episode itself, will end up here with these words,
or if there is a sequel to it.

The possible redactional layer was labelled the "pro-Judah" layer
because the content of that layer supports Judah's preferential status
(found in Genesis 49) in such a way that Joseph's position is weakened. It starts with the introduction of Manasseh and Ephraim into
the scene in 48:1aB–2a being a prerequisite for the following scene,
dealing in several aspects with these two sons. After the introduction
of Joseph's two sons into the scene (48:1aB–2a), Jacob adopts them
as his own in a sort of addition to the sons he received already (48:5–
6). The legitimation appears to be found in God's promise of many
descendants to the patriarch, to which Jacob referred in the preceding verses (48:3–4). In the following passage, mainly belonging to the
"pro-Joseph" layer (48:8–12), the trend is altered by means of an in-
genious insertion in verse 9, וַאֲבָרְכֵם "that I may bless them".[202] By
means of this single word the trend of the whole scene is changed, and
even when it is said in 48:15 וַיְבָרֶךְ אֶת־יוֹסֵף "and he blessed Joseph",
this is generally read in the light of the foregoing statement of the patriarch that he wanted to bless the boys. In fact Joseph's prostration
before his father (v. 12) has become a useless act of which the exact
meaning has been lost. This is reinforced by the next passage, 48:13–
20, in which the patriarch's words of blessing are directed to Joseph's
two sons, not to Joseph. The content of the passage is characterized
by the change of the blessing generally bestowed on the first-born son
but now on the youngest and by means of references to the other patriarchal narratives. By giving Ephraim a blessing greater (by means
of the right hand) than the one to Manasseh, the oldest son of Joseph
is passed over, not only by the patriarch but in fact by God, who will
fulfil the blessing proclaimed on these two sons. Both themes, "patriarchs" and "forsaken first-born", create a strong connection with the
rest of Genesis and as such might be due to the editor who created the
framework of Genesis, labelled as the "pro-Judah" layer.[203] Finally,
this passage (48:13–20) functions as a kind of wedge, driven in between the introduction of Joseph's blessing (48:15a) and the contents
of that blessing (48:21–2). This adaptation of the original narrative,
removing the fact that Joseph was blessed alone by his father there,
opens the way for the following scene (49:1–28), where all the sons of
the patriarch (including Joseph) are named and blessed. Yet, in that
case Judah finally receives the preferential status and the blessing of
Joseph (49:22–26) seems to be pushed to the background.

---

[202]Cf. above, pp. 478–479.
[203]Cf. above, p. 456.

If our reconstruction of the "pro-Joseph" and "pro-Judah" layer is correct, there are a few elements in both layers that may be of some importance for the further discussion.

1. The name of the patriarch is an important element in many studies of the Deathbed Episode. In the "pro-Joseph" layer the name "Israel" is consequently used for Joseph's father. The additional "pro-Judah" layer contains the names "Jacob" and "Israel", which is in accordance with our suggestion that in a redactional layer both names could be applied. This result contrasts with the usual assumption that the name "Israel" is to be connected with the supposed "Judah-layer"[204] or "J". Our analysis demonstrates that the "pro-Joseph" layer must be connected with the name "Israel" for the patriarch, and that the "pro-Judah" layer tries to combine both names "Jacob" and "Israel" as being the names of one person.

If indeed this merging of the names of the patriarch is part of the "pro-Judah" layer, this might be connected to the fact that the tradition concerning the renaming ("Jacob" > "Israel") of the patriarch is not part of the Joseph Story (Genesis 37–50), but that it is positioned outside it, in the Jacob Story (Gen. 32:22–32; 35:9–10). Secondly, as a part of the "pro-Judah" layer we found that the Deathbed Episode was related to the whole of Genesis by means of the addition of the name "Jacob" and of the references to the other two patriarchs, Abraham and Isaac. To this aspect we may add, that the triplet "Abraham, Isaac and Jacob" is the most frequent,[205] while the triplet "Abraham, Isaac and Israel" occurs only four times,[206] of which none are in Genesis, and at least two in clearly late (post-exilic) texts. This might also argue for an independent origin of (a) tradition(s) concerning "Israel", while the traditions concerning Jacob might

---

[204]It should be noted that our "pro-Judah layer" and the "Judah-layer" in other literary-critical studies are principally different entities because of the usual distinction of the latter from a "Reuben-layer", a distinction which is not followed in our analysis (cf. above, section 5.23.3). Of course it cannot be ruled out that there will be several correspondences between the "pro-Judah layer" and the "Judah-layer", however, we have to allow for them both, correspondences and differences, and the result will depend on the analysis.

[205]For the triplet, see Gen. 50:24; Exod. 2:24; 3;6, 15, 16; 4:5; 6:3, 8; 33:1; Lev. 26:42; Num. 32:11; Deut. 1:8; 6:10; 9:5, 27; 29:12; 30:20; 34:4; 2 Kgs. 13:23; Jer. 33:26. Cf. also Gen. 31:53; 32:10; 35:27, where these names occur within one verse.

[206]Exod. 32:13; 1 Kgs. 18:36; 1 Chr. 29:18; 2 Chr. 30:6. Cf. also 1 Chr. 1:34.

have been connected from the beginning with the other two patriarchs, Abraham and Isaac.

2. The classical distinction based on the names יהוה and אֱלֹהִים is impossible to maintain in the hitherto analysed passage. In the "pro-Joseph" layer we find references to God by means of the general name or assignment אֱלֹהִים "God, god(s)". Yet, the "pro-Judah" layer has an almost similar use of references to God,[207] which makes a distinction on the basis of the Divine names impossible.[208]

3. The Deathbed Episode, as preserved in the "pro-Joseph" layer, took place in Egypt. This might be inferred from several elements in the text: the request of Israel to be buried in Canaan instead of in Egypt (47:29–31), the remark by the patriarch that he was glad to see Joseph again and even his sons (48:11), and the assurance by the patriarch that God will make them return to the land of their fathers (48:21). In the analysed passages we did not find a clear shift of the import of their sojourn in Egypt. However, a certain shift was sensed, brought about by the addition of the duration of the sojourn (47:28, being related to Joseph's age, 37:2) and of the ages of the persons involved (47:28, cf. also 50:22–26), which are regarded as parts of the overall structure of Genesis. Though Israel assured Joseph that, in contrast to himself, Joseph would be brought back to Canaan alive (48:21), elements of the overall structure seem to tell us the opposite: Joseph died in Egypt (50:26). In this case the "pro-Joseph" layer is revised by the addition of "pro-Judah" elements, probably to create a bridge between the story of Joseph's sojourn in Egypt and the Exodus.

4. In the original "pro-Joseph" layer, as noted above, Joseph was blessed and granted with Shechem by the patriarch. Yet, by means of the adoption and blessing of Ephraim and Manasseh a twofold goal is achieved. First, Joseph is deprived of his sons and the continuation of his name has been removed in favour of the

---

[207]In the "pro-Judah" layer Jacob also refers to אֵל שַׁדָּי "El Shaddai", which is usually attributed to P, who also is assumed to use אֱלֹהִים. Even if we deem the definition of P questionable, this difference in Divine names cannot be considered a discriminating criterion.

[208]Only the clear references to the revelation of God to the patriarchs in certain contexts might enable such a distinction, as in 48:3–4. However, such a distinction is not based on the use of the Divine names but much more on the content of the text.

continuity of the name of Jacob (48:6, 16). Secondly, the exclusive position of Joseph as the only one having being blessed[209] has been erased, which makes the blessing of the twelve sons more comprehensible in this context.

These elements might be of some help in the following discussion of Genesis 49, the principal subject of our study.

6.5 The Deathbed Episode, II: Genesis 49:1–33

6.5.1 The "Testament of Jacob": Genesis 49:1–28

6.5.1.1 Introduction

In previous chapters we referred several times to the fact that Genesis 49 is generally thought to be a collection of (partly) independent sayings. However, the findings of our study of those chapters differ considerably from the general view on this issue.

1. First of all, the analysis of the poetic structure of the "Testament" showed that the text was composed in a regular fashion, integrating the framework (as "narrative poetry") and "blessings" to form a unity.[210] By means of many verbal repetitions the different blessings are interrelated very carefully and, as such, the text reveals the hand of a skilled composer.[211] On the other hand we pointed out that, although the Joseph-saying has many parallels with the larger sayings (Reuben, Simeon & Levi, Judah), it is related quite loosely to its own canto (49:16–28). Moreover, the contents of the Joseph-saying do not suggest a firm interrelationship with the rest of the Blessing, neither the sayings in the first canto, nor the one in its own canto.[212]

2. Our suggested genre definition of Genesis 49 differs from the most common solution that Genesis 49 should be considered a collection of "tribal sayings". First of all, it was concluded on the basis of extra-biblical and biblical texts that a genre definition cannot be used as a literary-critical argument to separate a saying from its literary context as an insertion. Secondly, it was argued that the sayings in Genesis 49 do not correspond with the examples of tribal sayings in the *Umwelt*. Moreover,

---

[209] Cf. also Genesis 27, where the oldest son (Esau) is called alone to his father (Isaac) in order to be blessed.

[210] Cf. above, pp. 238–9.

[211] Cf. above, pp. 238–9, 240.

[212] Cf. above, pp. 239–40, 241.

the latter sayings are concerned with the present, but most of the sayings in Genesis 49 are concerned with the future. Based on the contents of the sayings and on the discussion of the use of the term בְּרָכָה — generally rendered as "blessing" — it was suggested that we consider the sayings of Genesis 49 as "testamentary sayings", which do not necessarily have to be positive. In these sayings the patriarch announced his last will concerning his estate and, as such, Genesis 49 may be described as a "testament", fitting its present literary context — the Deathbed Episode — very well.

3. In the synchronic reading we first of all showed that Genesis 49 is well embedded in its present context (Gen. 47:29–49:33), because the framework itself (49:1–2, 28) presupposes the Deathbed Episode as the context in which the patriarch announces the Blessing.[213] Furthermore, the Blessing as a whole also suggests the wider context of the Book of Genesis because it presupposes the birth-story of the twelve ancestors of the tribes (including their mothers),[214] it suggests family-relationships throughout the blessing, and on several occasions it refers to events told in the narratives outside the Joseph Story. Finally, the blessing in its present form cannot be separated from its context as a completely independent entity. Genesis 48 (adoption and blessing of Ephraim and Manasseh; their equation to Reuben and Simeon) and Genesis 49 (the Testament of Jacob), both function to give Judah's future position firm ground. In the Testament this can be concluded from the curses pronounced on Reuben and Simeon & Levi, and the blessing given to Judah, which clearly resembles the blessing Jacob received from Isaac (Gen. 27:27–29). On the other hand, the blessing of Joseph is, though positioned at the end, comparable to the blessing of Judah, and suggests by its language Joseph's important position which is hardly conceivable as meant for just a favourite son.

These results are of fundamental importance to the further analysis of Genesis 49, because it means that we must look for a different solution for the problems facing us. In this respect the preceding diachronic analysis of Gen. 47:29–48:22 might offer us the right context in which to read the Testament of Jacob from a diachronic perspective.

---

[213] Section 4.4.4.1.
[214] Cf. above, section 4.4.4.1, esp. p. 350.

As noted above, in the synchronic reading we pointed out that Gen. 49:1–28 as a testament is firmly embedded in its literary context — the Deathbed Episode. The Testament presupposes the whole deathbed scene, for if we were to isolate Genesis 49 from its context it would be like a suspended torso, leaving the question why and when the patriarch pronounced these blessings as an enigma. Yet, in the present form of the Deathbed Episode, it is clear that they were meant as predictions foretelling the future of the later tribes of Israel (49:28) and pronounced by the patriarch on his deathbed.

In the foregoing analysis of the first part of the Deathbed Episode (47:29–48:22) several characteristics were isolated which are of importance to our analysis. To begin with, the two preceding scenes (47:29–31; 48:1–22) contain clear elements of the "pro-Joseph" and the "pro-Judah" layers, which confirms our working hypothesis that an original deathbed narrative ("pro-Joseph") was revised in order to explain and legitimize political changes in favour of Judah, and to weaken Joseph's position ("pro-Judah"). Secondly, it was found that the "pro-Judah" layer apparently attempted to merge two traditions concerning "Israel" and "Jacob". Of these two traditions, the former concerning "Israel" belongs to the "pro-Joseph" layer and was part of the original narrative. Yet, the equation of the two is due to the editor who was responsible for the "pro-Judah" layer, and who might have used *both* names, "Jacob" as well as "Israel". These elements will now be taken into consideration in our analysis of Genesis 49.

6.5.1.2   The Framework of the Testament (49:1–2, 28)

Our analysis of the Testament will start with some observations on the framework (49:1–2, 28). Generally literary critics make a distinction in the framework between elements of P (49:1A, 28bB) belonging to the narrative strand of P, and editorial expansions connecting the sayings with P (49:1BC, 28a.bA) and they also separate off the supposed introduction to the collection of sayings, interpreting these sayings as the words of a father to his sons (49:2).[215] In this analysis P would thus narrate that the patriarch called his sons, וַיִּקְרָא יַעֲקֹב אֶל־בָּנָיו "then Jacob called his sons" (49:1A) and blessed them, וַיְבָרֶךְ אוֹתָם אִישׁ אֲשֶׁר כְּבִרְכָתוֹ בֵּרַךְ אֹתָם "and he blessed them, each according to his blessing he blessed them" (49:28bB).[216] Important to note in this connection is

---

[215]Speiser, *Genesis*, 370, 375, 377; Schmitt, *Die nichtpriesterliche Josephsgeschichte*, 73, with n. 305; Westermann, *Genesis 37–50*, 223, 252; Schmidt, *Literarische Studien zur Josephsgeschichte*, 127–8, 207; Kebekus, *Die Joseferzählung*, 209. Cf. also Ruppert, *Die Josephserählung der Genesis*, 162.

[216]Cf. *e.g.* Westermann, *Genesis 37–50*, 252.

that P, who, according to the general view, is partial to blessings, here misses the contents of the blessing again, as in Genesis 48.[217] Further, it is remarkable that some scholars assume that Gen. 49:2–27 (though sometimes without including the first three sayings) already existed independently and was inserted by the Priestly or post-Priestly editor. In this case we apparently have to assume that these sayings already existed in a collection, independently of any literary context.[218]

Yet, these analyses are unconvincing. First of all, it is a weakness in those analyses that, although P has a certain fondness for blessings, in chapter 48 as here, the contents of the blessing are missing. In connection with the Deathbed Episode this certainly does not argue in favour of the Documentary Hypothesis. Secondly, the assumption that Gen. 49:2–27 existed independently of any literary context is very unlikely. The assumed introductory verse,

| Assemble and listen, O sons of Jacob, (2A) | הִקָּבְצוּ וְשִׁמְעוּ בְּנֵי יַעֲקֹב |
| and listen to Israel your father. (2B) | וְשִׁמְעוּ אֶל־יִשְׂרָאֵל אֲבִיכֶם |

is, in itself, too obscure to function properly as an introduction to this collection of sayings. Westermann is certainly right in his observation that this verse interprets the following sayings as words of a father to his sons,[219] yet, it might be asked whether this verse itself is not in need of a proper introduction. In our view the assumed collection (49:2–27) is a torso, of which we can only guess what the rest of it lookes like. The same applies to the first sayings of the collection, because the harsh judgement on Reuben and Simeon & Levi is enigmatic. Such a judgement is understandable in response to a certain event, yet as part of an independent poem without any context (but apparently intended to be recited in this form more often) this judgement is unclear. Moreover, most of the other sayings are predictions[220] and as such they are incomprehensible if the father announced these words to them without a suitable introduction. In fact the meaning of these words is explained by the words of verse 1BC:

---

[217] Cf. Donner, *Literarische Gestalt der Josephsgeschichte*, 32–4.

[218] Westermann, *Genesis 37–50*, 252; Schmidt, *Literarische Studien zur Josephsgeschichte*, 207; Kebekus, *Die Joseferzählung*, 209.

An insertion in the Jahwist corpus is preferred by M. Noth, *Das System der zwölf Stämme Israels* (BWANT, 4/1), Stuttgart 1930 (Darmstadt ²1966), 7–8; Seebaß, *Geschichtliche Zeit*, 69–70, 78. M. Noth later preferred the assignment to the P-corpus: M. Noth, *Überlieferungsgeschichte der Pentateuch*, Stuttgart 1948 (Darmstadt ²1966), 18, with n. 54.

[219] Westermann, *Genesis 37–50*, 252.

[220] Gen. 49:8, 10, 11–12[?], 13, 16–7, 19, 20, 27; cf. also 49:23b–24, 25, 26. On this matter, cf. our discussion in Chapter Two of the verbal tenses, and especially the summary on pp. 242–3, with the table on pp. 246–7.

"Gather that I may tell you (1B)   הֵאָסְפוּ וְאַגִּידָה לָכֶם

  what will happen to you in days hereafter" (1C) אֵת אֲשֶׁר־יִקְרָא אֶתְכֶם שְׂאֵת אַחֲרִית

הַיָּמִים

which interpret the following sayings as predictions of the days that will follow.[221] For that reason verse 1BC cannot be separated from the following summons in verse 2, nor can the collection be read and understood properly without this complete summons. In this sense the verses 1BC–2 are a suitable introduction to the present collection of which most sayings are a prediction of the tribes' future days.[222] For that reason we are not convinced by those analyses which assign 49:1BC and 2 to two different traditions, and on the other hand assign 49:1A.28b to P.

Nevertheless, the framework is in our discussion quite important because it seems to suggest the "pro-Judah" layer. The most significant element in the first two verses is the parallelism of "Jacob" and "Israel" as the father of the sons mentioned in the Testament. As we argued in the mid-term review above,[223] the equation of these two names is part of the "pro-Judah" layer, because neither the parallelism of these two, nor the name "Jacob" alone was found in the "pro-Joseph" layer. For that reason we might consider this to be an indication that in this text the parallelism Jacob ‖ Israel is at least the work of the same hand as in the preceding verses, namely the one responsible for the "pro-Judah" layer. However, this observation does not automatically imply that Gen. 49:1–2 is entirely dependent on that layer. It might be possible, for example, that in verse 1A "Jacob" has been added, and also in verse 2A, or even that the whole phrase is an addition. Thus, in that case the transition from the blessing of Joseph (48:14aA, 15aA, 21–22) to the blessing of the others might have been adapted to later developments.

Considering this possibility, we will now make an attempt to re-

---

[221] *Pace*, Westermann, *Genesis 37–50*, 252–3 (among others), who renders the words אַחֲרִית הַיָּמִים "at the end of days" and who understands it in this sense as an eschatological announcement, which is only suitable for the eschatological ruler announced in 49:8–10. However, the expression has to be rendered as "days hereafter" as was argued before (see pp. 86–7), and in this sense it suits most of the sayings in Genesis 49.

[222] Here we refer to our analysis of the poetic structure of 49:1–2, in which we argued that the whole verse is a coherent composition in which many word-pairs are found (cf. above, pp. 92–97; see also Sarna, *Genesis*, 332). For that reason every literary-critical analysis of these verses, discerning different layers in this text, has to be based on very solid arguments, otherwise it tears apart what appears to be a unity.

[223] Cf. above, pp. 501–502.

construct a version of the text of 49:1–2 that does not contain any
elements of the supposed "pro-Judah" layer and which might have
been part of the "pro-Joseph" layer. First of all, it is quite possible
possible that in verse 1A "Jacob" was added to an original clause
without an explicit subject. In that case this clause might have run
as follows: וַיִּקְרָא אֶל־בָּנָיו וַיֹּאמֶר (49:1A*) in which it would have to be
rendered: "Then he called his sons and said", presuming the subject
to be known from the previous passages. However, the following text
— the direct speech — has to fit in as well. Yet, it is at this point
that problems arise. First, the summons by the patriarch, which is
found in verse 1,

"Gather that I may tell you (1B)   הֵאָסְפוּ וְאַגִּידָה לָכֶם

  what will happen to you in days hereafter" (1C) אֵת אֲשֶׁר־יִקְרָא אֶתְכֶם שֵׁאת אַחֲרִית
                                                    הַיָּמִים

suggests that what follows is related to the future. Yet, it can be
inferred from the contents of the Testament that the import of the
future affairs is mainly found in the first three sayings, resulting in
the leadership of Judah. The other sayings, beginning with the one on
Zebulun (49:13), are also related to the future,[224] but it seems unlikely
that — if we were to exclude the first three sayings as being clearly
part of the "pro-Judah" layer — the introduction in verse 1 would fit
the other sayings (49:13–27), for they seem hardly important enough
to be pronounced in this way as predictions of the future. In that
case we might assume that the saying on Joseph (being the largest
in this case) would form the culmination of what would happen in
future days. However, such a climax is absent in the Joseph-saying,
which has much more an optative sense than a pronouncing sense as
is announced in verse 1BC. Consequently we have to take the first
part of the summons (49:1) as a part of the "pro-Judah" layer, characterizing the following sayings, and especially the three first sayings,
as predictions of the future. As such verse 1BC cannot be considered
to be part of the "pro-Joseph" layer, and the verse has to be left out
of the attempted reconstruction.[225]

  Because of the parallelism found in verse 2, it seems odd to regard
the whole of verse 2A as an addition, inserted before verse 2B. This

---

[224] Cf. in this respect our discussion of the verbal tenses in these sayings in
Chapter Two, cf. especially the summary on pp. 242–3.

[225] We are aware of the fact that we have argued that verse 1BC can hardly
be separated from verse 2. However, in our attempt to delimit a "pro-Judah"
layer and to reconstruct a possible "pro-Joseph" layer, we have to consider the
possibility.

impression is strengthened when we take verse 2B to be the continuation of verse 1A*.[226] Consequently, if we consider the possibility of an adaptation of the text here, we have to assume that, just as in verse 1A, "Jacob" was added, and that in our verse בְּנֵי "sons of" has to be revocalized as בָּנַי "my sons". Yet, as we argued already concerning Westermann's analysis, it seems to us that the remaining summons still would not fit the remaining sayings because directly following the summons the blessings would have been pronounced. This version only contains a summons to listen, without any argument why these sayings are pronounced. Compare the following reconstruction, which would be the result of the foregoing considerations:

Then he called to his sons and said, (1A*)	וַיִּקְרָא אֶל־בָּנָיו וַיֹּאמֶר
Assemble and listen, my sons, (2A*)	הִקָּבְצוּ וְשִׁמְעוּ בָּנַי
and listen to Israel, your father. (2B)	וְשִׁמְעוּ אֶל־יִשְׂרָאֵל אֲבִיכֶם

In our view, this attempted reconstruction clearly demonstrates the *improbability* of this solution, because the final clause, mentioning the name of the patriarch ("Israel") demands for a counterpart in the preceding clause: "Jacob", which we left out as being added — or we have to assume the addition of "Israel" in the final colon as well. Moreover, it is very unlikely that this reconstruction would precede some (or all) of the blessings. For that reason it appears to us that the whole introduction to the Testament is a coherent unity, which from the beginning had both names of the patriarch in it, and which was placed here in order to introduce the other sons into the scene and simultaneously to create the impression that the patriarch "Jacob/Israel" pronounced these sayings on his deathbed, finally appointing Judah as his successor. Consequently this introduction in its entirety has to be assigned to the "pro-Judah" layer.

Concerning the concluding verse of the Testament (49:28) a similar assignment must be considered. First of all the strophe presupposes the presence of the twelve sons as in the birth-story. This presupposes, in fact, the presence of the first three sayings on the first four sons, which might undoubtedly be regarded as the "pro-Judah" elements at the beginning of the Testament. Secondly, this final verse also seems to presuppose that the sayings were predictions because the sons to whom their father spoke have become "tribes". In this way the narrator abandons for the moment the level of narrated events and becomes a commentator. As a commentator he interprets what has happened in the preceding scene, namely, that what is spoken here by the patriarch are actually words directed to the tribes and not just words

---

[226] As reconstructed above, on the previous page.

to his sons in the past.[227] Thirdly, the assignment of these sayings as
בְּרָכֹת "blessings" is also strongly related to the first three sayings in
which the successor of the patriarch is appointed.[228] For that reason
we consider this verse also to be a part of the "pro-Judah" layer, characterizing these sayings (49:3–27) as the last will of the patriarch.

This assignment has, however, far-reaching consequences. An obvious conclusion is that, if the framework is indeed part of the "pro-
Judah" layer, the rest of the Testament in its present shape cannot
be part of the "pro-Joseph" layer, because an appropriate transition
from the preceding scene (48:1–22) to the following one is missing.
In this sense we may conclude, on the basis of the analysis of the
framework alone, that the Testament in its present form is part of the
"pro-Judah" layer. Of course the sayings have to be discussed separately in order to establish (if possible) if such a saying is the product
of the "pro-Judah" editor, or that he used older material (in the sense
of "tribal sayings").

Disregarding some minor differences, this result might appear very
similar to the results of the literary-critical analyses as described
above, which suggest that the Testament is a later addition to the
Deathbed Episode. Though at first sight this seems possible, there
are some important differences which should not be ignored. The most
important difference that should be emphasized here is the fact that
the framework is, in our analysis, assigned to the same editor who
revised the preceding narrative. Secondly, in those analyses no motif
nor any convincing explanation is offered why a possible editor would
have inserted these sayings here and put them in Jacob's mouth.[229]

---

[227] Here we might refer once again to the remarks by J. Fokkelman, *Narrative Art in Genesis: Specimens of Stylistic and Structural Analysis* (SSN, 17; 2nd edition: BibS, 12), Assen 1975, Sheffield ²1991, 238–40, who directed attention to the historical context in which the narratives were related.

[228] Schmitt, *Die nichtpriesterliche Josephsgeschichte*, 73, n. 305, argued *contra* Noth, *Überlieferungsgeschichte der Pentateuch*, 18, that the final words, in which Genesis 49 is called a "blessing", do not belong to the same layer as the preceding words, and certainly not to the same layer as 49:1BC, because the assignment "blessing" is not in line with the "prediction of the future". However, as we argued, the "telling of the future" is not just a "telling", but an announcement of the last will. This corresponds to the meaning of בְּרָכָה as we defined it in the excursus in Chapter 3 (following section 3.3.4) for this context, namely "blessing", in the sense of a "testamentary saying".

[229] Westermann, *Genesis 37–50*, 252, suggests that the editor did this in order to grant these sayings validity and dignity ("um ihnen Geltung und Würde zu verleihen"). But Westermann does not explain why the editor wanted to preserve these sayings, nor why it was necesary that these words gained more validity and dignity. Yet, in this way it appears that the editor was not interested in

Our analysis emphasizes the apparent "pro-Judah" purport of the Testament and leads us to the view that the editor intended to grant Judah the favourite position, thus pushing Joseph more or less into the background. In the following sections we will discuss the sayings seperately, considering the possibility that the editor could either have used older traditions in this text or that he wrote it himself.

6.5.1.3 Reuben (49:3–4)

According to our synchronic reading the saying on Reuben clearly contains elements which support the "pro-Judah" tendency of the Testament. As such it corresponds to our analysis of the framework (49:1–2, 28). In its wording the saying clearly reveals the father condemning his son, the words בְּכֹרִי "my first-born" (49:3A), and אָבִיךָ "your father" (v. 4B) are in this respect very plain. These words clearly suppose the family circle in which the saying is pronounced and as such the saying fits in quite well into its literary context.

These observations argue at the same time against the supposition of some scholars that the saying itself, or Gen. 49:2–28*, existed independently, and was later inserted into its present position. Actually, the Reuben-saying would be incomprehensible if it were separated from that context, comparable to the shorter sayings like the one on Asher.[230] Moreover, concerning the genre, we already argued that there is no reason to regard this saying as a "tribal saying", but that it has more the character of a lawsuit, in this case by a father against his son.[231] Concerning Reuben's offence there is no indication of a tribal-historical context, which might be an explanation for the described event or for what is said in the saying concerning this action. Also the fact that he is called the "first-born" is difficult to explain. Zobel suggested in this connection that this must be related to the number of men (warriors) in that tribe, analogous to the fact that Benjamin is the youngest and the smallest.[232] In that case it might even suggest

---

the contents and purpose of these sayings in their present form. The patriarch's mouth is just used to preserve a collection of sayings, but actually the editor did not have the intention to make the patriarch say something specific. He was only concerned in preserving these sayings.

[230] Cf. in this respect Wenham's remark, quoted above, p. 53, with n. 255.

[231] Cf. above, section 3.3.2. Westermann, *Genesis 37–50*, 255, still considers the possibility that there was an older and completely different ("ganz anderer") tribal saying in which Reuben was praised. This older, real tribal saying was adapted, corresponding to the later non-existence of the tribe, according to the tradition found in Gen. 35:22 into its present form. In our view this is a conjecture, for which the evidence is lacking and which is not even demanded by the text.

[232] Zobel, *SuG*, 63, n. 3.

that Reuben would have been the most important tribe in a possible confederation of tribes.[233] However, no such indications are found in the traditions concerning Reuben;[234] neither is there any indication that the tribe of Reuben would ever have tried to seize power in Israel, except from the event described in Gen. 35:22.[235] We are forced to admit that very little is known of the tribe and that our knowledge is virtually restricted to some geographical descriptions.[236] For that reason each suggestion concerning a *tribal*-historical background for this account will have the character of a conjecture.[237]

Scholars sometimes take the patriarch's rebuke as an indication that the tribe did not exist anymore, or has been reduced considerably at the moment this saying originated.[238] The interpretation suggested by the Testament itself (see 49:28) is that the Reuben-saying — and thus also his offence (?) — should be considered at a tribal-historical level. However, Reuben's offence and the consequence it had for him, are described in a strictly individual sense, which might argue against a *tribal-historical* interpretation.

In Chapter Four we argued that Reuben's action might be construed as an attempt to seize power by seizing his father's "harem".[239] Texts supporting this interpretation are found in 2 Sam. 3:6–8; 12:8 and 1 Kgs. 2:17, 20–22, and especially in 2 Sam. 16:20–23. The last passage is part of the account of Absalom's revolution against his father. Absalom is advised that he should go and take his father's concubines: בּוֹא אֶל־פִּלַגְשֵׁי אָבִיךְ "go in to the concubines of your father"

---

[233] Cf. Speiser, *Genesis*, 274; F.M. Cross, "Reuben, First-Born of Jacob", *ZAW* 100 Suppl. (1988) 46–65, 46–7, and *passim*.

[234] J.B. Curtis, "Some Suggestions Concerning the History of the Tribe of Reuben", *JBR* 33 (1965) 247–49, 249.

[235] Sarna, *Genesis*, 245, suggests that the involvement in the rebellion against Moses (Num. 16) is in some way related to the tribe's loss of status. However, the descent of Dathan and Abiram from Reuben hardly seems to be important in this connection, because Korah, a son of Levi, was also rebellious without any consequences for the tribe of Levi. Only their personal family clans were wiped out completely. Moreover, their rebellion cannot be considered a usurpation of power, but only a questioning of the existing power. For that reason Sarna's suggestion seems improbable to us.

[236] These geographical references appear to be ambigious, because many of the cities assigned to Reuben were also assigned to Gad, or appear to be part of Moab (according to the Mesha stele); cf. Curtis, "History of the Tribe of Reuben", 247, with n. 1; 248, n. 8.

[237] Cf. Zobel, *SuG*, 63–4.

[238] Zobel, *SuG*, 63; Van Selms, *Genesis, dl. II*, 274; Westermann, *Genesis 37–50*, 255. See also Sarna, *Genesis*, 332; Wenham, *Genesis 16–50*, 472–3.

[239] Cf. above, section 4.4.4.2, with n. 160 for bibliographic references. In addition, see Sarna, *Genesis*, 244–5; Hamilton, *Book of Genesis*, 387

(16:21),[240] resulting in וְשָׁמַע כָּל־יִשְׂרָאֵל "and all Israel will hear". In Gen. 35:22 a similar expression is applied to Reuben's action when he slept with Bilhah, his father's concubine: וַיֵּלֶךְ רְאוּבֵן וַיִּשְׁכַּב אֶת־בִּלְהָה פִּילֶגֶשׁ אָבִיו "and Reuben went and lay with Bilhah his father's concubine", resulting in וַיִּשְׁמַע יִשְׂרָאֵל "and Israel heard [of it]". The similarity of idiom confirms the idea that Reuben's action should be considered as a revolt, and is consequently condemned by his father. The open ending after the narration of this event is in this sense significant and the "sentence" given in the Testament appears to be the logical response to Reuben's offence. In a certain respect the sentence on Reuben's offence would fit Absalom's as well. Even the way Reuben is called פַּחַז כַּמַּיִם "deceptive like water", would suit Absalom also very well, because he deceived his father twice (2 Sam. 13:23–27; 15:7–12).[241] So, it appears that in these two texts (Gen. 35:22; 49:3–4) a strictly individual element is merged with a tribal-historical element, in that the sentence on Reuben is considered to have consequences for the descendants of Reuben (49:28).

In Deut. 33:6 it appears that Reuben's existence is threatened, which suggests that Reuben's importance has declined considerably. In the Song of Deborah (Judg. 5:15–6) Reuben is also described in rather negative tones, as one who stayed behind when the other tribes went out to battle. However, if we take a further look at the possible history of Reuben it becomes apparent that the tribe disappeared from the historical scene at a certain moment. In Judg. 3:15–30 it is told that Moab conquered the territory between the Arnon and Heshbon.[242] In the census of David (2 Sam. 24:5–6) and in the list of districts under Solomon (1 Kgs. 4:19) mention is made of Gad (Gilead in the latter text) in Transjordan, but not of Reuben.[243] For that reason we may assume that in the period of the United Monarchy the tribe of Reuben has disappeared, or at least has lost its significance.[244] For

---

[240] Absalom's action is described in the same way: וַיָּבֹא אַבְשָׁלוֹם אֶל־פִּלַגְשֵׁי אָבִיו "and Absalom went in to his father's concubines" (2 Sam. 16:22).

[241] Cf. also the remark by Curtis, "History of the Tribe of Reuben", 249: "The incest attributed to Reuben then becomes meaningful as a reading back into the ancient times of the sexual laxness of the house of David (II Sam. 11; 13; 16:22); in fact, *the crime of Absalom is precisely the one inputed to Reuben.*" [italics, RdH].

[242] Note also the fact that Mesha mentions Gad occupying Moab's territory, but no mention is made of Reuben: "but the men of Gad dwelt in the land of Ataroth from time immemorial".

[243] As Curtis, "History of the Tribe of Reuben", 248, rightly notes, this is no indication that the tribe did not exist. However, combined with the fact that other texts also point in the direction of Reuben's disappearance, this might be considered an additional indication of its absence.

[244] For a more elaborate discussion, see Curtis, "History of the Tribe of Reuben",

the period before the monarchy we have some narratives concerning
the settlement of the tribe of Reuben, but as indicated before, the description of the allotment of Reuben does not correspond with data
from other sources, describing the territory of Gad or Moab.[245] In
our view these considerations suggest that Reuben disappeared quite
early from the historical scene, comparable probably to the demise of
the tribe of Simeon.[246]

Finally, the saying on Reuben corresponds very well to the literary motif in Genesis, namely the device of the "forsaken first-born".
However, if we are dealing here with an obvious literary pattern, and
if that literary pattern fits its literary context so clearly, it might be
asked whether the historical background of these texts (35:22; 49:3–4)
should not be found in the time that this literary work originated. A
literary text is usually more related to the time in which it is first
narrated, than to the time of which it is narrating.[247] In this way
the account of Reuben's misbehaviour might actually correspond to
a completely different era. Yet, such questions can only be answered
after we have analysed the complete Deathbed Episode and evaluated
the results of that analysis. With regard to our analysis, we can conclude that the text of the saying on Reuben, composed as a kind of
lawsuit of a father against his son because of the latter's misbehaviour,
fits its literary context very well. As such there is no reason to assume
that the editor adapted some older material concerning Reuben for
its present context. For that reason we consider the saying on Reuben
to be part of the pro-Judah layer, which originated in the time when
that layer was added to the original narrative.

6.5.1.4 Simeon & Levi (49:5–7)

What has been said of Reuben applies in certain respects also to the
saying on Simeon and Levi. This saying has, in its present position, the
function of supporting the "pro-Judah" tendency of the Testament.[248]

247–49; Cross, "Reuben, First-Born of Jacob", 46–65.

[245] Curtis, "History of the Tribe of Reuben", 247.

[246] In this connection Curtis' observations are quite interesting, suggesting that
the tribe of Reuben might have been "absorbed by the quite heterogeneous group
that came to be known as Judah" ("History of the Tribe of Reuben", 247, and
passim). Because Simeon also seems to have been absorbed by Judah, and even
the group of Levi appears to have had its basis in the later territory of Judah,
this suggestion is certainly worthwhile considering.

[247] Cf. in this context the remark by Curtis, quoted above (p. 513, n. 241), and,
of course, the famous dictum of Wellhausen, quoted above, p. 410, with n. 300.

[248] E. Nielsen, *Shechem: A Traditio-Historical Investigation*, Copenhagen 1955,
281; Blum, *Komposition der Vätergeschichte*, 228.

The implication is that this saying, and the account to which it refers, are to be considered part of that layer; the saying supports Judah's preferential status, and the account in Genesis 34 forms the explanatory background for this saying.[249] In this section the problem to be discussed is, whether we are dealing here with some older material, which has been adapted to its present context, or not? However, the first problem we have to deal with is once again the question whether Gen. 49:5–7 does indeed refer back to Genesis 34.

In the previous chapters we argued that Genesis 34, together with 33:19, might form a correction to 48:22.[250] In the final text the patriarch is depicted as a warrior who conquered Shechem with his own sword and bow. In Genesis 34 the patriarch is depicted very differently, namely, as one who does not fight for the honour of his daughter and seeks for peaceful arrangements rather than use violent and aggressive actions. Yet, if we are dealing here with a correction, the question is whether the story is a literary composition (and functioning as an aetiology) rather than an ancient (and historical) tradition which has been handed down.[251]

The account of the rape of Dinah and its aftermath has in recent research almost generally led to the conviction that the text is composite. This composite character is found in some doublets or tensions in the text, such as the fact that Shechem negotiates unexpectedly at the scene (34:11), because initially his father Hamor was the only one here (vv. 6, 8–10); this doublet is reflected in a double answer in the text (vv. 14 and 15–18). Accordingly, the execution of the request is thought to be repeated (vv. 19 and 20–24) and finally the plundering of the city is thought to have been narrated also in a double account (vv. 25*–26, 30–1 and 27–29).[252] The suggested solutions reckon with the fact that the classical Documentary Hypothesis fails at this text[253] and the solutions offered are just variations on the

---

[249]Blum, *Komposition der Vätergeschichte*, 219, with n. 39; 228.

[250]See section 6.3.6 above, esp. p. 497.

[251]Cf. also Blum, *Komposition der Vätergeschichte*, 219, n. 39. Blum supposes that Genesis 34 goes back to an ancient tradition, which is also reflected in 48:22. Yet, Genesis 34 is an aetiology, very likely using this tradition in which Simeon & Levi were originally not the main actors.

[252]For a more detailed discussion, cf. S. Lehming, "Zur Überlieferungsgeschichte von Gen 34", *ZAW* 70 (1958) 228–50; A. de Pury, "Genèse xxxiv et l'histoire", *RB* 76 (1969) 5–49; E. Otto, *Jakob in Sichem: Überlieferungsgeschichtliche, archäologische und territorialgeschichtlichen Studien zur Entstehungsgeschichte Israels* (BWANT, 110), Stuttgart 1979, 170–75; P. Kevers, "Étude littéraire de Genèse, xxxiv", *RB* 87 (1980) 38–86, esp. 40–7; Westermann, *Genesis 12–36*, 651–4; Blum, *Komposition der Vätergeschichte*, 210–6.

[253]Wellhausen's analysis of this text is classical in this respect; he found, however,

Supplementary Hypothesis, even when the terminology has in several cases still been derived from the Documentary Hypothesis.[254] Even though it might be that the end of the account is adapted,[255] there are still scholars who consider the narrative to a large extent to be the original account.[256]

Most of the literary-critical analyses referred to above assume that somehow the mention of Simeon and Levi in this account is original. This assumption considerably interferes with the question of a relationship between Genesis 34 and 49, because it is generally assumed that Gen. 49:5–7 does not exactly refer to the events of Genesis 34 and that the relation between these two is ostensible.[257] Yet, if both traditions appear to be old, it is difficult to maintain that these texts are not related to each other.[258] Even though the originality of Simeon & Levi's position in this account has been questioned by S. Lehming and A. de Pury, who considered the possibility of Simeon and Levi being added later in this account as a kind of explanatory expansion,[259] Blum has convincingly argued that Gen. 34:25–26 and 27–29 do not exclude, but presuppose each other.[260] Consequently Simeon

---

only a *fragmentary* preserved J-version (with Shechem and Simeon & Levi) beside an E-version (with Hamor and sons of Jacob). The compound of these two was revised by a layer closely related to P; see his *Composition der Hexateuchs und der historischen Bücher des Alten Testaments*, Berlin ³1899, 45–7, 314–6.

[254] Cf. *e.g.* Gunkel, *Genesis*, ³1910, 369–71; Skinner, *Genesis*, 417–8; Noth, *Überlieferungsgeschichte der Pentateuch*, 31, n. 99; Westermann, *Genesis*, 651–4; Blum, *Komposition der Vätergeschichte*, 214–6; N. Wyatt, "The Story of Dinah and Shechem", *UF* 22 (1990) 433–58.

[255] This adaptation might be found in Gen. 34:30–1 and very likely in 35:1–4; in that case 35:5 would form the original ending of this story. Cf. the literature in the preceding footnote.

[256] B.D. Eerdmans, *Alttestamentliche Studien, I: Die Komposition der Genesis*, Gießen 1908, 62–4; E. Nielsen, *Shechem: A Traditio-Historical Investigation*, Copenhagen 1955, 241–83; F.C. Fensham, "Gen. xxxiv and Mari", *JNSL* 4 (1975) 87–90.

[257] For this matter, cf. our discussion in Chapter Two.

[258] Cf. Lehming, "Zur Überlieferungsgeschichte von Gen 34", 228–33.

[259] Lehming, "Zur Überlieferungsgeschichte von Gen 34", 244–6; de Pury, "Genèse xxxiv et l'histoire", 16–26. An indication of this assumption is seen in the fact that Simeon and Levi occur quite late in the scene.

[260] Blum, *Komposition der Vätergeschichte*, 219, n. 39 (cf. also 215, n. 22). Blum argues that the acts of Simeon & Levi and those of the other "sons of Jacob" are completely different, one narrates the killing of the Shechemites, while the other narrates the plundering of the slain. Note especially the very clear וַיֵּצְאוּ "and they went away" (34:26) and the emphatic position of the new subject (inversion), both of which exclude the possibility that both actions would have been due to the same group, namely the "sons of Jacob". Moreover Lehming ("Zur Überlieferungsgeschichte von Gen 34", 242, n. 70) needs an additional emendation

& Levi must be considered to be original in this account, which might have been created as a kind of aetiology for the background of 48:22, 49:5–7, and probably of other texts as well.

Some additional arguments may be listed in order to defend the thesis that Genesis 34 is a literary composition,[261] which was created as a kind of literary background for Gen. 49:5–7, comparable to Gen. 35:22 and 49:3–4. First of all, the narrative itself has been built up of contrasting figures: Shechem in contrast to Simeon & Levi;[262] Hamor in contrast to the sons of Jacob.[263] The main goal of the narrator in this context seems to be to contrast Shechem's righteous behaviour with Simeon & Levi's unjustified excessive revenge.[264] Secondly, as J.A. Soggin emphasizes, the names of Shechem and Hamor are neither of them personal names, but both derived from other names, a place-name (Shechem) and a pun on the name of a people (Amorites).[265] Such elements emphasize the literary character of the text, arousing the reader's attention. Thirdly, the account of Genesis 34 is linked to the other narratives of Genesis by means of recurring motifs, some-times even a quotation (let all your males be circumcised; cf. 17:10), or presupposed narratives (birth-story of Dinah; 30:21).[266] In our view these observations strengthen the idea that in Genesis 34 we are deal-ing with a narrative that is part of the "pro-Judah" layer. Fourthly, it offers a narrative background for the saying on Simeon & Levi, and as such it also serves the motif of the "forsaken first-born", where in

---

of the text in order to make his case acceptable. See also Wenham, *Genesis 16–50*, 315–6.

[261] For the other arguments, offered before, cf. 6.3.6 above, esp. p. 497.

[262] Blum, *Komposition der Vätergeschichte*, 211–2, refers in this respect to the law-texts dealing with such events (Exod. 22:15–6; Deut. 22:28–9), and he points out that Shechem acts here righteously according to the law. Simeon and Levi by contrast act violently, and certainly not in accordance with the law. A certain expression occurs three times in the narrative at crucial places, interrelating the antithesis of the four main figures in the narrative, of which the first and the final even form a chiastic pattern (Sarna, *Genesis*, 238; Hamilton, *Book of Genesis*, 370), וַיִּקַּח אֹתָהּ ... וַתֵּצֵא דִינָה "and Dinah went out ... and he (Shechem) took her" (34:2); וְלָקַחְנוּ אֶת־בִּתֵּנוּ "and we take our daughter" (34:17); וַיִּקְחוּ אֶת־דִּינָה ... וַיֵּצֵאוּ "and they took Dinah ... and they went out" (34:26).

[263] Note how Hamor's arguing in favour of the circumcision (v. 23) is clearly reversed in the revenge by the sons of Jacob (v. 27). See: Blum, *Komposition der Vätergeschichte*, 210–1; Sarna, *Genesis*, 238.

[264] Blum, *Komposition der Vätergeschichte*, 213.

[265] J.A. Soggin, "Genesis Kapitel 34. Eros und Thanatos", in: A. Lemaire, B. Otzen (eds.), *History and Traditions of early Israel: Studies Presented to Eduard Nielsen* (SVT, 50), Leiden 1993, 133–5, 134.

[266] Cf. Wenham, *Genesis 16–50*, 307–10. See also Fokkelman, *Narrative Art in Genesis*, 238–9.

the end a younger brother will receive the preferential status.[267] In our view, these observations support the thesis that Genesis 34 was created in order to "correct" the possible impression of 48:22, that the patriarch conquered Shechem.

Because of the saying on Simeon & Levi — normally thought to be a "tribal saying" — the account in Genesis 34 is generally thought to have a tribal-historical background. Yet, as in the preceding section, a comparison with a narrated event (concerning *individuals*) forces itself upon us. It is the account of the rape of Tamar by Amnon in 2 Sam. 13, which has certain striking resemblances:[268]

Gen. 34:7   כִּי־נְבָלָה עָשָׂה בְיִשְׂרָאֵל ... וְכֵן לֹא יֵעָשֶׂה

2 Sam. 13:12   כִּי לֹא־יֵעָשֶׂה כֵן בְּיִשְׂרָאֵל אַל־תַּעֲשֵׂה אֶת־הַנְּבָלָה הַזֹּאת

More similarities between these two stories occur, though in some cases we have to say dissimilarities or, more precisely, antitheses. Both, Shechem and Amnon, love the girls: Shechem afterwards, and Amnon before the rape. Amnon's reaction is, in this respect, antithetical, because after he raped Tamar, he hates her, "the hatred with which he hated her was greater than the love with which he had loved her" (2 Sam. 13:15). Shechem himself asks for the girl to be his wife; Tamar suggests it before she is raped, but Amnon does not listen, afterwards he sends her away (13:13, 16–17); in contrast again, Shechem even appears to have kept Dinah in his house (34:17, 26). The comparison with Tamar demonstrates that this is not to be understood as if Dinah was held as a hostage,[269] but that his inten-

---

[267]This conclusion excludes in our view the possibility that we consider the account in Genesis 34 as having a positive attitude towards Simeon & Levi. Some scholars suggested this, describing Simeon & Levi as "true Israelites"; *e.g.* Nielsen, *Shechem*, 282. Comparable: M. Sternberg, *The Poetics of Biblical Narrative*, Bloomington (IN) 1985, 445–75; idem, "Biblical Poetics and Sexual Politics: From Reading to Counterreading", *JBL* 111 (1992) 463–88; Wenham, *Genesis 16–50*, 315–7; Alter, *Genesis*, 193–4. However, such a judgement depends strongly on what might be considered to be righteous in this case. Blum, *Komposition der Vätergeschichte*, 212, has argued this on the basis of comparison with biblical laws (Exod. 22:15–6; Deut. 22:28–9), and in comparison with the account of the rape of Tamar (2 Samuel 13). This comparison is very important because it shows that the consequences for Dinah after the revenge are even worse than before; cf. below, and further: D.N. Fewell, D.M. Gunn, "Tipping the Balance: Sternberg's Reader and the Rape of Dinah", *JBL* 110 (1991) 193–211, esp. 210. These observations do not ignore the fact that Jacob is quite passive. However, his silence in this matter, and his disapproval of Simeon & Levi's revenge, seem to imply that he preferred the marriage of Dinah (Fewell, Gunn, *art.cit.*, 210–1).

[268]See also Blum, *Komposition der Vätergeschichte*, 212.

[269]This was suggested by Sternberg, *Poetics of Biblical Narrative*, 468; he was followed by Wenham, *Genesis 16–50*, 315; Alter, *Genesis*, 193. In this case it is

tions were genuine. Dinah's fate is, in this case, thus much better than Tamar's, who says when being sent away: "No, my brother, for this wrong in sending me away is greater than the other which you did to me".[270] Actually, the revenge by Simeon & Levi created the same effect for Dinah as for Tamar after being sent away, and Tamar's words apply in this way to their action: their wrong in "taking her away" is greater than the other of "taking her".[271] Further, both fathers, Jacob and David, hear of it, yet, in both cases their reactions are disappointing. David becomes very angry but does nothing (13:21); Jacob holds his peace until his sons come home, but then he does not do anything, until his sons have killed Shechem (34:30-1). The revenge of the rape is performed by the brothers of the girl (Simeon & Levi; Absalom), and it is emphasized that they are the woman's brothers. The revenge is based on deceit: a complex of lies is created in order to kill the perpetrator. These elements might suggest a certain relationship between these two stories, although how this dependency is to be regarded is a matter of dispute. For the moment it is important to note that Shechem, the non-Israelite, is the more righteous; Simeon & Levi, Amnon and Absalom are untrustworthy. Yet, the similarity of Absalom and Simeon & Levi is striking, because in this case the saying on Simeon & Levi (49:5-7) could be applied to Absalom also, comparable to the saying on Reuben. The individual element once again appears to have been merged with tribal-historical elements, because the verdict by the patriarch will finally be applied to the descendants of Simeon & Levi.

Returning now to the saying on Simeon & Levi (49:5-7), two questions remain. One: does our saying refer indeed to the episode in Genesis 34; and, two: is our saying adopted in the "pro-Judah" layer, and probably adapted and expanded to fit its present position, or is the

---

argued that at the final moment it is revealed that Dinah is in Shechem's house and that he has taken her captive. Yet, this is clearly a misreading of the text, because in 34:17 the "sons of Jacob" said already that if the Shechemites will not do as asked, they "will take Dinah and will leave". This already presupposes that Dinah is with Shechem and this threat does not necessarily imply violence.

[270] Fewell, Gunn, "Tipping the Balance", 210, with n. 38. They suggest — and very likely correctly — that Tamar's "fate is not unlike that of David's concubines, 'defiled' by Absalom, and hence condemned to be shut up to the day of their death, living as widows in the king's house (2 Sam. 20:3)."

[271] Sternberg, "Biblical Poetics and Sexual Poilitics", 482, tries to counter Fewell and Gunn's argument, with reference to Deut. 22:28-9 (quoted by the latter), because that text would forbid contact with Canaanites, which would legitimize Simeon & Levi's action. However, as Blum, *Komposition der Vätergeschichte*, 212-3 argues, in the words of the sons "Shechem did a folly in Israel" (34:7), which places the whole account within Israelite law.

text a unity? With regard to the first question, we have already argued in Chapter Two that the saying could refer to Genesis 34 quite
well. In Genesis 34 it is explicitly stated that, beside the other men
of Shechem, Simeon & Levi killed Hamor and his son Shechem ("the
prince of the land", 34:2). In our view this is reflected in the words of
the patriarch (49:6),

For in their anger they slew a man, (6bA)	כִּי בְאַפָּם הָרְגוּ אִישׁ
in their wantonness they hamstrung a bull; (6bB)	וּבִרְצֹנָם עִקְּרוּ־שׁוֹר

Generally it is ignored that both "man" and "bull" are singular.[272]
Interestingly, the singular would correspond in this respect to the
text of Genesis 34, where Hamor and Shechem are mentioned separately.[273] Also the reference to their anger (אַף; 49:6b, 7a) corresponds
to the anger of the brothers (חרה; 34:7).[274] Further, the address which
calls Simeon & Levi "brothers", whose "knives" (מְכֵרֹתֵיהֶם < כרת) are
weapons of violence, is to be regarded as a reference to this account:
"Simeon and Levi, Dinah's *brothers*, took their *swords* . . ." (34:25).[275]
Because Genesis 34 ends with the rhetorical question, without further
reaction on the part of the patriarch, it is, when looked at from the account in Genesis 34, clear that 49:5–7 is the response to the offence of
the brothers, comparable to the saying on Reuben in answer to 35:22.
But, is this conclusion also logical when looked at from Gen. 49:5–7?
In Chapter Three it has been argued that the saying on Reuben and
the one concerning Simeon and Levi have identical structures with
an analogous import, which argues in favour of a same genre definition, namely a lawsuit.[276] Yet, it might still be asked if in this case
it was originally a *prophetic* lawsuit (and thus directed against the
tribes), or one of a father against his sons. Furthermore it must be
considered whether an ancient saying has been adopted and adapted
here to make the saying fit into its present context. In fact that is the

---

[272] Cf. RSV; NBG; NEB; NAB; NIV; JPS; EÜ.

[273] For the question whether שׁוֹר "bull" fits the context, we refer to our discussion
in Chapter Two (esp. pp. 98–101). It might suffice here to refer to the fact that
"bull" (*tr*) is in Ugaritic used as a metaphor for a "prince". Further the term עקר
might be a pun on circumcision (note that כרת "to cut" is used for circumcision
as well as for castration).

[274] Cf. the fact that חָרָה אַפּוֹ is a current idiom used quite frequently (*HAL*,
74, 337). Furthermore the meaning "anger" for אַף is generally considered to be
derived from חָרָה אַפּוֹ (*HAL*, 74).

[275] Note that the sword (חֶרֶב) is an instrument to "cut off" (כרת); see 1 Sam.
17:51; Nah. 3:15; cf. also Ezek. 14:17; 21:8, 9; 25:13; 29:8 and eventually Jer. 48:12;
50:16; Ezek. 14:21). This also might argue in favour of the proposed rendering of
מְכֵרֹתֵיהֶם "their knives" as derived from כרת.

[276] Cf. above, pp. 285–8, esp. 287–8.

second question mentioned above.

With regard to the second question we would argue that the text as a whole has the character of a lawsuit by a father, even if the terms "father" and "son" are absent here. Following De Moor's interpretation of the text, Gen. 49:6a, 7C should be considered the curse of a father who denies his future "entering" in his sons' gatherings (סוֹד; קָהָל), and as such he will scatter them.[277] In this sense the saying on Simeon and Levi is a reaction to Genesis 34[278] and, in view of the following curse, their action described there is condemned by their father. There is no indication that the text is composite,[279] for that reason it appears to us that there is no reason to assume an older layer here in the text in the form of a saying or the like, that would have been adopted and adapted. Together with the narrative of Genesis 34 the saying is considered to be the product of the "pro-Judah" layer, which was created to give Judah the final preferential status over Simeon and Levi. The events that were narrated as the cause of this curse can hardly be considered historical. It appears that both, narrative and saying, seek to explain certain conditions which seem to escape our categories. The only thing with regard to history that can be concluded from the saying in Genesis 49 is that it seems to suppose that neither the tribe of Simeon nor Levi lived together anymore, but that both were scattered over Israel.[280]

---

[277] J.C. de Moor, "Standing Stones and Ancestor Worship", *UF* 27 (1995) 1–20, esp. 15–6; and cf. further above, pp. 288–9.

It is argued by scholars that 49:7C is hardly a word by a patriarch, but has to be a word of God spoken by a prophet; cf. Nielsen, *Shechem*, 279; Zobel, *SuG*, 8–9; Westermann, *Genesis 37–50*, 257; cf. also Hamilton, *Book of Genesis*, 652. However, by means of their scattering they will not have any סוֹד or קָהָל and as such we may consider this final verse to be the consequence of verse 6a (cf. Blum, *Komposition der Vätergeschichte*, 216, n. 26), and thus also the word of the patriarch. Moreover, by interpreting this verse as referring to the ancestral cult it supposes indeed a kind of "divine" action that will scatter them.

[278] Of course one could argue that another interpretation of Hebr. מְכֵרֹתֵיהֶם is possible here. Since most of the suggestions prefer to interpret the word as a kind of weapon, these interpretations do not make any difference for the argumentation above. Yet, if one would prefer the rendering "trade" as suggested by Speiser, Caquot and De Moor (cf. p. 107 above), even it might be considered to fit in the context, if interpreted in the sense of "dealing". Thus even in that case the saying might fit its context, yet, this interpretation of מכר is unknown to us.

[279] See also Zobel, *SuG*, 8.

[280] In this we agree with De Geus, *The Tribes of Israel*, 102, that "it is impossible to conclude the existence of a secular tribe of Levi on the basis of *this* passage [Genesis 34]", and the similar conclusion with regard to Gen. 49:5–7 (*op.cit.*, 103). On the other hand, considering other comparable narratives (Exod. 32:25–29), it might be considered whether an aetiology was needed, explaining why a group like the Levites became a priestly tribe. Secular and priestly do not exclude each

6.5.1.5   Judah (49:8–12)

It might be obvious that the saying on Judah in its present form supports Judah's preferential status and as such is to be assigned to the "pro-Judah" layer.[281] Moreover, in Chapter Three it has been argued that there is no reason to consider this text to be composite, even if we find a change in person and of motif in this text. The most that we could say concerning the possibility of ancient material embedded in the saying, is that it is possible that verse 9 originally functioned independently. But the text of verse 9 functions very well in its present position and for that reason we consider the complete text of the saying on Judah to be the product of a "pro-Judah" poet. Yet, this formulation is chosen deliberately, because we cannot assign this text automatically to the "pro-Judah" layer, it must be considered whether our text was adopted in its present form in the Testament. It cannot be excluded of course that before the "pro-Judah" layer took shape already certain "pro-Judah" texts existed.[282] In the case of the saying on Judah this should be considered carefully, because the text contains hymnic motifs that correspond with hymns found in the *Umwelt*.[283] Such hymns occur without any literary context and as such it cannot be excluded that the Judah-saying functioned in a similar way and was included only later in its present context because the editor thought it suitable. However, in that case the parallel to Gen. 27:29 should be explained in terms of Gen. 27:29 being an adaptation of the blessing of Judah in 49:8–12 (editorially spoken) instead of the other way round. Moreover, we have to assume that the text of 49:8, 10 was adapted to its context, because most of the verbal forms of this saying are *yiqtol* forms, implying that the saying is a prediction. The assumption of such an adaptation is a conjecture, because it is by no means required by the text, this makes the consideration improbable, though not impossible. Yet, in fact we are not able to solve this problem here, because we still do not know enough of the "pro-Judah" layer. For that reason we must postpone our judgement concerning this saying (as being included or as an integral part of the "pro-Judah" layer) to a later stage of our analysis.

---

other necessarily, cf. in this respect De Moor, *RoY*, 166–7; *RoY*², 260–1.

[281] Cf. on this matter sections 3.3.4 and 4.4.4.4 above.

[282] Because the date of the "pro-Judah" layer has not yet been established by us, we have for the moment to allow for a period of several centuries in which that layer could have originated. Such a layer could have been created quite late, but it is theoretically possible that such a hymn or blessing was composed in an earlier period.

[283] Here we refer especially to a song of the Druzes, of which two strophes were quoted. See pp. 262–3 above.

Yet, with regard to the saying on Judah a pressing question arises, namely, to what period does this saying refer? It is generally acknowledged by scholars that this saying refers to the period in which Judah occupies a leading position, starting with the rise of the kingship of David. It is especially this period (and that of Solomon) which is described in 2 Samuel and 1 Kings 1–11 as the most glorious time for the tribe of Judah among his brothers. Consequently this text, or a part of it, is considered to refer to the period of David (or Solomon).[284] However, there are diverging views looking in completely opposite directions, one preferring an earlier date for some parts of the saying, and the other one choosing a much later date. The attempts to find an earlier date for parts of this saying are mainly influenced by the idea that in Genesis 49 we are dealing with tribal sayings. It was Zobel in particular who defended an early date, suggesting that verse 9 could contain a reference to Judah's settlement in the south as reflected also in Genesis 38.[285] In his view the saying is governed by fear,[286] because in the first line Judah is called a גּוּר אַרְיֵה "a lion's whelp", not (normally) an animal that hunts independently. According to verse 9 this גּוּר went out for prey (טֶרֶף), which is only done by young lions (כְּפִיר) and the lion or lioness, but not by a whelp.[287] According to Zobel this is also reflected in the second part of this strophe (49:9b), where the גּוּר "whelp" — and not Judah! — stoops down, crouches (כָּרַע רָבַץ) like (כְּ) a lion, a "kings lion". These verbs are never used for a גּוּר and for that reason Zobel considers that Judah is described as living in a dangerous situation without the protection a whelp would need.[288]

---

[284] Skinner, *Genesis*, 524; Zobel, *SuG*, 79 (49:8; vv. 9–12 date from the early monarchy, *op.cit.*, 73–9); Vawter, *On Genesis*, 461–2; Westermann, *Genesis 37–50*, 264 (only 49:10–2 — "Aber notwendig ist das nicht; es kann durchaus aus der Richterzeit ... sein."); Hecke, *Juda und Israel*, 185–8; Sarna, *Genesis*, 335 ("the Testament of Jacob can only have in mind this period"); Wenham, *Genesis 16–50*, 478; Hamilton *Book of Genesis*, 658 (?); Alter, *Genesis*, 294 ("distinctly Davidic coloration"); Jagersma, *Genesis 25–50*, 259 ("not impossible"); J.A. Soggin, *Das Buch Genesis: Kommentar*, Darmstadt 1997, 543.

[285] Zobel, *SuG*, 73–5.

[286] Zobel, *SuG*, 12.

[287] Zobel, *SuG*, 12.

[288] Zobel, *SuG*, 12. He suggests we read the final two words of v. 9, מִי יְקִימֶנּוּ, as a wish formulated as a question: "Wenn ihn doch jemand auscheuchte!". In his view this reflects the dangerous situation in which Judah is (*op.cit.*, 73). However, we regret that we are unable to follow Zobel's reasoning here. Because, if Zobel's rendering is correct, one would rather expect that the wish was formulated as a prohibition. But why would anyone wish to frighten the lion away? Or does Zobel mean that Judah must not settle down and assimilate in this case with the Canaanites, as in Genesis 38 (*op.cit.*, 74)? Yet, in our verse assimilation is not a topic and for that reason it seems unlikely to us. Anyway, this interpretation is

However, in our view Zobel's arguments are not completely conclusive, because nowhere is it mention+ed that the גּוּר went alone for prey, nor that he caught it himself.[289] Furthermore, the second part (49:9b) is certainly to be interpreted as a positive description, which, as Zobel admits himself,[290] is already transparent for Judah and refers in a *positive* sense to the lion's whelp[291] comparable to the other strophes which are all three formulated in a positive sense.[292] Consequently, the tribal-historical background for this saying, describing the earliest period of Judah's settlement as a dangerous situation must be dismissed. The identical metaphor for Israel in Num. 24:9 identifies our comparison as a positive description and applying here the strongest and most dangerous animal for Judah, it describes Judah as the strongest and most fearful tribe.[293] The saying that Judah is a lion's whelp, who "rose from the prey"[294] and now crouches as a lion, sug-

---

too far fetched to be reasonable and we prefer the classical interpretation of these words, "who will raise him?"

[289] Cf. also Nah. 2:12–13, where the lion catches prey for his whelps. See also Hecke, *Juda und Israel*, 197, with n. 4.

[290] Zobel, *SuG*, 12.

[291] A reference to a lion's whelp or a young lion is in itself too obscure to allow us a positive or negative interpretation of verse 9a. The comparison with a young lion, devouring prey could be applied to God in a positive and in a negative sense depending on the context; cf. Isa. 31:4 (positive) and Hos. 5:14 (negative). The same applies to kings and people, Mic. 5:8 (positive regarding the people of Israel); Ps. 17:12 (negative); and applied as a metaphor for young kings it is used more or less neutral (Ezek. 19:5; Nah. 2:11), whereas the mentioning of the fact that such an animal could devour men is regarded as a negative aspect (Ezek. 19:3, 6). In this sense, the comparison of Judah with a lion's whelp (49:9a) needs a context to give the text its proper interpretation, and without it, it would be too obscure. Because, the direct context is formed by the positive description of Judah as the leader of his brothers (v. 8) and the comparison of this young lion with the grown up lions (v. 9b) it has to be interpreted as a positive saying regarding Judah.

[292] The final strophe is formulated in a positive sense, describing the excessive abundance of the land, suggesting that one did not have to be careful with vines (49:11a), and could use wine as water (49:11b). Wine was accepted as a positive element in the land, and drunkeness was even not condemned as such (except for the cult, see 1 Sam. 1:12–4). Cf. Gen. 9:20–9, where no negative attitude is found; similarly Judg. 9:13, describing wine as cheering gods and men. Cf. on this matter also P. Sanders, *The Provenance of Deuteronomy 32* (OTS, 37), Leiden 1996, 176–7, with n. 410; 226–7. Contrast, however, De Moor, *RoY²*, 285–6.

[293] Westermann, *Genesis 37–50*, 260.

[294] In Chapter Two (pp. 139–40) we defended the rendering "grow up" for עלה, based on *inter alii* Ezek. 19:3. Moreover, we defended an optative rendering for the *qatal* form of this verb. With regard to the former interpretation, we will not stress this matter here, because we are aware that it is a matter of interpretation. For the final interpretation of this poetic verse (v. 9a) it might be of some minor importance: did the whelp rise (= climb up) to lay down on a higher place, or

gests that Judah is quite young at the historical scene, but nevertheless an entity someone has to reckon with very seriously.[295] In our view
such a description implies a situation where Judah has taken his leading position among the "brothers" and for that reason the *terminus
post quem* should be set after the rise of the Davidic kingship.[296]

Blum, on the other hand, though he does not suggest that our
text originated in that period, suggested that the saying on Judah
gained topicality in the time of Josiah.[297] In this context he considers the possibility that Gen. 49:10bA (MT) עַד כִּי־יָבֹא שִׁילֹה should
be considered a revision, phrased with regard to Josiah. In his view
we have to read here "Shiloh" following the Masoretic text. According to Blum this village was cultically and politically neutral and
not discredited like other Northern cities (Bethel, Shechem, Gilgal,
Samaria), and as such it was not considered to be in competition
with Jerusalem.[298] Therefore this village was the most appropriate
symbol for the tradition of "whole Israel", namely the twelve-tribes-
system. Yet, as we have argued already in Chapter Two with regard to
this interpretation of the consonantal text, the Masoretic vocalisation
does not offer this interpretation when we consider the *Qere*-reading.
Secondly, there is no indication in Israel's traditions that a coming to
Shiloh would form a certain ascendency of one tribe over the others.
Thirdly, and even more decisive in our view, Shiloh did not have a positive connotation in the Deuteronomistic tradition, which can be derived from Ps. 78:60,[299] where Shiloh is forsaken in favour of Jerusa-

---

did he grow up, and become like a lion, who stoops down, crouches? With regard
to the *qatal* form having an optative nuance, this interpretation is based on the
context of the saying. Further, we have to admit that even if the author intended
this verbal form in the sense we have interpreted it, it must still be considered a
vaticinium ex eventu, and as such the historical background to which this verbal
form refers will be the past. For that reason we do not bring this matter into the
discussion.

[295] Hecke, *Judah und Israel*, 187; S. Beyerle, *Der Mosesegen im Deuteronomium:
Eine text-, kompositions- und formkritische Studie zu Deuteronomium 33* (BZAW,
250), Berlin 1997, 238.

[296] Hecke, *Judah und Israel*, 188.

[297] Blum, *Komposition der Vätergeschichte*, 261–3.

[298] Blum, *Komposition der Vätergeschichte*, 262.

[299] The dating of Psalm 78 has not been established, but a pre-Exilic date, though
after the fall of Samaria seems the most acceptable; cf. R.J. Clifford, "In Zion
and David a New Beginning", in: B. Halpern, J.D. Levenson (eds.), *Traditions
in Transformation: Essays ... F.M. Cross*, Winona Lake (IN) 1981, 121–3; J.C.
de Moor, M.C.A. Korpel, "Fundamentals of Ugaritic and Hebrew Poetry", *UF*
18 (1986) 173–212, 208, n. 71 (= *SABCP*, 1–61, 55, n. 72); P. Sanders, *The
Provenance of Deuteronomy 32* (OTS, 37), Leiden 1996, 309, with nn. 77–80 (for
bibliographic references).

lem.[300] Finally, as we have argued, the best reading for this *crux* is to take the consonantal text as containing two words: שַׁי לֹה "tribute to him", which semantically fits best into its direct context. For that reason Blum's assumption that this verse might be a new revised version from the period of Josiah must be abandoned when based on his interpretation of שִׁילֹה .

Of course, it might be asked if it is possible that the saying on Judah still refers to this period. In our view, this question cannot be answered on the basis of this text alone, because the text itself does not contain sufficient indications for such an assumption. These indications must be derived from the whole of our analysis and the character of the redaction and the ideology we may find in it. Nevertheless, it is in our view hard to deny the possibility that the saying on Judah may have received special attention during the time of king Josiah. The hope expressed in the saying will undoubtedly also have inspired the ideology behind Josiah's politics.[301] But, in our view there is little or no evidence in the description of Josiah's reign in the book of Kings, suggesting that this saying (Gen. 49:8–12) might have been adapted during that period. However, shortly afterwards the prophet Ezekiel (Ezek. 19:1–9; 21:32) referred to two elements in the saying on Judah, which gives us in each case a solid — be it a quite rough — *terminus ante quem*, namely the Exile from 587/6

---

[300]Blum, *Komposition der Vätergeschichte*, 263, with n. 30, refers also to Jer. 7:12 as an indication of the important position of Shiloh. Yet, though he admits in passing that the references in Jeremiah 7 are quite critical, he ignores the ideological meaning of Shiloh that is found in the fact that is has been destroyed and that the house of the Lord (בֵּית יהוה) was removed from it (Ps. 78:60, "He forsook his dwelling at Shiloh"). The role of Shiloh (and the *tent of meeting*) in the Deuteronomistic History (in a positive, or even better, not a negative but just a describing sense, only in Josh. 18:1, 8, 9, 10; 19:51; 21:2; 22:9, 12), can be explained as a uniformizing tradition, which reckons with possible earlier traditions that there was a *house of the Lord* in Shiloh. H.-C. Schmitt, "Die Josephsgeschichte und das Deuteronomistische Geschichtswerk: Genesis 38 und 48–50", in: M. Vervenne, J. Lust (eds.), *Deuteronomy and Deuteronomic Literature: Fs C.H.W. Brekelmans* (BEThL, 133), Leuven 1997, 391–405, 398, although prefering a post-exilic date.

[301]This might also be deduced from the fact that the saying on Judah, was taken up rather critically by Ezekiel some time after the death of Josiah, see Ezek. 19:1–9; 21:32. It is generally accepted that these texts are based on Gen. 49:9, 10; cf. G.Ch. Aalders, *Ezechiël, I; Hfdst. 1–24* (COT), Kampen 1955, 307–8, 347–8; W. Zimmerli, *Ezechiel, 1.Teilband: Ezechiel 1–24* (BKAT, XIII/1), Neukirchen-Vluyn 1969, 424, 494–6; A. Laato, *Josiah and David Redivivus* (CB OTS, 33), Lund 1992, 176; P.C. Beentjes, "What a Lioness Was Your Mother: Reflections on Ezekiel 19", in: B. Becking, M. Dijkstra (eds.), *On Reading Prophetic Texts: Gender-Specific and related Studies in Memory of F. van Dijk-Hemmes* (BIS, 18), Leiden 1996, 21–35, 26–9.

BCE.[302] If we consider the predictions of the patriarch יוֹדוּךָ אַחֶיךָ "your brothers shall praise you" (48:8aB) and יִשְׁתַּחֲווּ לְךָ בְּנֵי אָבִיךָ "your father's sons shall bow to you" (48:8bB) to refer to historical events in the sense of *vaticinium ex eventu*, the *terminus ante quem* moves considerably in the direction of the date *post quem*. The period that Judah's brothers (had to) praise(d) him, and bow(ed) down to him ended with the break up of the United Monarchy, after Solomon's death. Undoubtedly, other kings (like Josiah) might have had such aspirations but no information is preserved that anyone was able to fulfil this "prediction" of the patriarch. If another king had been the "fulfilment" of Jacob's Testament the documents would have reported it. For that reason, we consider the period of the United Monarchy — in each case at the level of the final redaction of DtrH — as the period to which the saying on Judah should be applied.[303]

A date for the saying on Judah after the rise of the Davidic king-ship is also supported by the consideration that the first and third strophe (49:8, 10) contain expressions which are all closely related to the royal psalms, magnifying the position of the king.[304] The Psalms we are refering to are especially Pss. 2; 18; 21; 45; 72; 110; most of which can be related to the Davidic dynasty, even though an exact dating of these Psalms is impossible.[305] However, with regard to the

---

[302]The date of the Exile is generally accepted, though scholars do not agree on the exact year; see: J.A. Soggin, *An Introduction to the History of Israel and Judah*, London ²1993, 264–5. A strong case for the date in 586 BCE has been made by L. McFall, "A Translation Guide to the Chronological Data in Kings and Chronicles", *BS* 148 (1991) 3–45, esp. 10. For the dating of the first twenty-four chapters of Ezekiel in the period before the Exile, cf. Aalders, *Ezechiël, I*, 9–20; Zimmerli, *Ezechiel, 1.Teilband*, 1*–4*.

[303]It might be obvious that the description of the United Monarchy, and espe-cially of Solomon, cannot be adopted without critical reflection. For the problems involved, and the most recent discussion on these matters, cf. G.N. Knoppers, "The Vanishing Solomon: The Disappearance of the United Monarchy from Re-cent Histories of Ancient Israel", *JBL* 116 (1997) 19–44; D. Edelman, "Foreword", in: L.K. Handy (ed.), *The Age of Solomon: Scholarship at the Turn of the Millen-nium* (SHCANE, 11), Leiden 1997, xv–xx; J.M. Miller, "Separating the Solomon of History from the Solomon of Legend", *ibid.*, 1–24; A. Millard, "King Solomon in His Ancient Context", *ibid.*, 30–53; N. Na'aman, "Sources and Composition in the History of Solomon", *ibid.*, 57–80; E.A. Knauf, "Le Roi Est Mort, Vive le Roi! A Biblical Argument for the Historicity of Solomon", *ibid.*, 81–95; W.G. Dever, "Archaeology and the 'Age of Solomon': A Case Study in Archaeology and His-toriography", *ibid.*, 217–51. Furthermore, cf. our discussion below, pp. 604–617.

[304]Cf. above, pp. 129–39.

[305]For Ps. 2, cf. J. Ridderbos, *De Psalmen vertaald en verklaard, I: Psalm 1–41* (COT), Kampen 1955, 20–2 (Davidic era); J.P.M. van der Ploeg, *Psalmen uit de grondtekst vertaald en uitgelegd* (BOT, VIIb), Roermond 1973, 40 (circle of Judaic kings); T.N.D. Mettinger, *King and Messiah: The civil and sacral Legitimation*

second strophe (49:9) the problem arises whether the expressions in
this text are original or if they are dependent on other texts. This
problem crops up in a twofold sense, first the comparison with a גּוּר
אַרְיֵה "lion's whelp" is also applied to Dan in the Blessing of Moses
(Deut. 33:22). Secondly, the comparison with a lion that crouches is
found also in Moses' Blessing, כְּלָבִיא שָׁכֵן (Gad, 33:20) as well as in
the oracles of Balaam (Num. 24:9a), where we even find an almost
identical bicolon.[306] Usually the different sayings are all considered to
be original and independent of other texts,[307] although the sayings of
the same ancestor are mostly compared.[308] However, S. Gevirtz at-

---

of the Israelite Kings (CB OTS, 8), Lund 1976, 258–9 (Solomonic era); H.-J.
Kraus, *Psalmen, 1.Teilband: Psalmen 1–59,* (BKAT, XV/1), Neukirchen ⁵1978,
146 (Judean/Jerusalemite circles); P.C. Craigie, *Psalms 1–50* (WBC, 19), Waco
(TX) 1983, 64–5 (coronation of a Davidic king).

For Ps. 18, cf. Ridderbos, *op.cit.*, 145–6; Van der Ploeg, *op.cit.*, 119–21 (one
of the oldest Psalms, yet not demonstrable to be Davidic, has resemblances with
texts from the late monarchy); Kraus, *op.cit.*, 285–7 (period of David or Solomon,
with later adjustments); Craigie, *op.cit.*, 171–2 (the Davidic era).

For Ps. 21, cf. Ridderbos, *op.cit.*, 176–7 (לדוד: Davidic); Van der Ploeg,
op.cit., 147 (pre-Exilic period); Kraus, *op.cit.*, 316 (judaic monarchy); O. Loretz,
*Die Königspsalmen: Die altorientalisch-kanaanäische Königstradition in jüdischer
Sicht. Teil 1, Ps. 20, 21, 72, 101, 144* (UBL, 6), Münster 1988, 90–3 (pre-Exilic,
with post-Exilic adaptations); Craigie, *op.cit.*, 190 (Davidic tradition).

For Ps. 45, cf. Ridderbos, *De Psalmen vertaald en verklaard, II: Psalm 42–106*
(COT), Kampen 1958, 34 (post-Solomonic); J.S.M. Mulder, *Studies on Psalm 45,*
Oss 1972 (seventh century); Van der Ploeg, *op.cit.*, 227 (8th century or later, but
pre-Exilic); Kraus, *op.cit.*, 488–9 (probably monarchy in Judah; cf. the parallels
to 2 Samuel 7); Craigie, *op.cit.*, 338 (some point in the history of the Hebrew
monarchy).

For Ps. 72, cf. Ridderbos, *op.cit.*, 229–30 (Solomonic era); Van der Ploeg,
op.cit., 427–8 (late monarchy); H.-J. Kraus, *Psalmen, 2.Teilband: Psalmen 60–
150* (BKAT, XV/2), Neukirchen ⁵1978, 656–7 (early monarchy); Loretz, *op.cit.*,
127–9 (pre-Exilic, with post-Exilic adaptations).

For Ps. 110, cf. J.P.M. van der Ploeg, *Psalmen deel II: Psalm 76 t/m 150* (BOT,
VIIb), Roermond 1975, 247–51 (pre-Exilic; hard to be more specific); Mettinger,
op.cit., 258–9 (Solomonic era); Kraus, *op.cit.*, 930 (early monarchy); Th. Booij,
"Psalm cx: Rule in the Midst of Your Foes", *VT* 41 (1991) 396–407, esp. 406
(early monarchy); L.C. Allen, *Psalms 101–150* (WBC, 21), Waco (TX) 1983,
83–85 (Davidic era).

[306] The only difference is that there is a different verb for lying down. Gen. 49:9bA
reads כָּרַע רָבַץ כְּאַרְיֵה and Num. 24:9aA has כָּרַע שָׁכַב כַּאֲרִי. In our view this is a
difference of minor importance.

[307] Cf. in this respect the very thorough study of Beyerle, *Der Mosesegen im
Deuteronomium*, 218–20, 237–8, who refers in his discussion on the saying on Gad
and Dan in Deuteronomy 33 to the saying in Gen. 49:9, but who does not consider
the possible dependency of one text on the other, although he did consider this
possibility in the case of the Joseph-saying (*op.cit.*, 185–8).

[308] Most notably, of course, Zobel, *SuG*, 62–126. See also, for example, Beyerle

tempted to prove that Judah was related to Dan's history, on the basis of, on the one hand, the inclusion of the "hand" and "feet" in the first strophe,[309] and "eyes" and "teeth" in the final strophe, in his view reflecting the phraseology of the *ius talionis*; the metaphors applied in these verses were in fact legal metaphors and might thus be an allusion to the name "Dan", meaning "to judge".[310] On the other hand, the lion metaphor also refers to Dan, and as such Gevirtz supposed the poet "would appear to acknowledge Judean supremacy and dominion over properties that had formerly been Danite".[311] Yet his attempt is generally considered to have failed because of the the emendation and the highly speculative way of arguing which he needed in order to prove his case.[312] Regarding the relationship with Deuteronomy 33 there is probably no discussion of this matter with regard to Gen. 49:9 because a relationship cannot be established. The only apparent correspondence between the sayings is that a "lion's whelp" is used as a metaphor, or the comparison "crouches like a lion" is applied, but that does not prove any relationship. However, if a certain development from the Testament of Jacob to the Blessing of Moses can be found,[313] this might suggest a literary dependency, especially when it is clear that the saying on Judah has been "emptied" completely in Deuteronomy 33. In this case the correspondences are, however, almost too insignificant to allow any conclusions, but one could imagine that Deuteronomy 33 "borrowed" these expressions from Genesis 49. The correspondence with the Balaam-saying is, however, more significant and one might wish that a clear relationship could be estab-

---

(previous footnote); M. Sæbø, "Divine Names and Epithets in Genesis 49:24b–25a: Some Methodological and Traditio-Historical Remarks", in: A. Lemaire, B. Otzen (eds.), *History and Traditions of Early Israel: Studies Presented to Eduard Nielsen* (SVT, 50), Leiden 1993, 115–32, 123–4.

[309] S. Gevirtz, "Adumbrations of Dan in Jacob's Blessing on Judah", *ZAW* 93 (1981) 21–37. Gevirtz had to add a complete colon to the present text (parallel to 49:8bA on the basis of a parallel found in 1QM 12:10, reading in that case (*art.cit.*, 23–6),

Your hand on the neck of your enemies	יָדְךָ בְּעֹרֶף אֹיְבֶיךָ
and your foot on the backs of (the) slain,	וְרַגְלְךָ עַל בָּמֳתֵי חָלָל

However, this reading is not found, nor even hinted at in any of the textual wittnesses. Moreover, it disturbs even the poetic composition of the strophe — despite its parallelism — because this addition has to be inserted in the middle of the text, resulting in a division of these two cola over the first and second poetic verse. In our view this reading is thus very unlikely and therefore not followed.

[310] Gevirtz, "Adumbrations of Dan", 29.

[311] Gevirtz, "Adumbrations of Dan", 37.

[312] Cf., for example, Hecke, *Israel und Juda*, 186, n. 4.

[313] Cf. Sæbø, "Divine Names and Epithets", 123–4.

lished. Yet, in this case a literary dependency one way or the other is hard to prove. Both texts have — if our dating for Gen. 49:8–12 is correct — the rise of the Davidic kingship as the *terminus post quem*.[314] The *terminus ante quem* for the Balaam Story is the second half of the ninth century BCE,[315] whereas the saying on Judah has the Exile as an absolute *ante quem*, and most likely the end of the "United Monarchy".[316] Consequently, both texts came into being in almost the same time span, and besides a certain dependency of one text on the other, one could even assume that both texts are part of the same tradition.[317] In the context of the present study it should be stressed that a possible relationship between our text and other texts does not change the established dates for them. After all, comparisons with lions belong to the standard stock phrases of ancient oriental writers.[318]

6.5.1.6   Joseph (49:22–26)

It is indisputable that the saying on Joseph favours him as a very important person. The characterization as a young bull-calf, being blessed and strengthened by the Bull (שׁוֹר) seems to imply Joseph's importance. We have argued this already in Chapter Four, where we showed that the language applied here to Joseph betrays the elevated position of a king as, for instance, in Ugarit.[319] This corresponds with the picture of Joseph as it was given in the previous parts of the Deathbed Episode describing Joseph as the successor of his father Israel. Furthermore, we referred to the fact that there are several relations between this blessing of Joseph and the first part of the Deathbed Episode (47:29–48:22), like "Shechem" (48:22) and the

---

[314] For the Balaam Story, cf. M. Dijkstra, "The Geography of the Story of Balaam: Synchronic Reading as a Help to Date a Biblical Text", in: J.C. de Moor (ed.), *Synchronic or Diachronic? A Debate on Method in Old Testament Exegesis* (OTS, 34), Leiden 1995, 72–97, 94–6. But see Korpel, *RiC*, 534–5; De Moor, *RoY*, 151–5; *RoY*², 245–9.

[315] Dijkstra, "The Geography of the Story of Balaam", 94.

[316] Cf. M. Weinfeld, "The Davidic Empire — Realization of the Promise to the Patriarchs", *ErIs* 24 (1993) 87–92 (Hebr.).

[317] Even if one has to assume an early date for the sayings of Balaam, this would not exclude our suggestion. Cf. *e.g.* Korpel, *RiC*, 535, who considers Gen. 49:9 to be derived from Num. 24:9. However, because she assumes a reinterpretation in Num. 24:8–9 (similarly De Moor, *RoY*, 152; *RoY*², 246) which in her view was originally applied to God and only later to the people, it might well be that the "reinterpretation" of Num. 24:8–9 and the adoption in Genesis 49 occurred in the same period.

[318] See *e.g. CAD*, vol. L, 24–25; idem, vol. N, 195.

[319] Cf. above, pp. 353–4.

abundant water supply by a "well" (49:22);[320] the conquest by "sword and bow" (48:22) and the "archers", harassing Joseph (49:23b); the blessing of Joseph (48:15a) and the blessing he received *expressis verbis* (49:25b–26a).[321] In our view these features argue in favour of the assignment of the saying on Joseph as a part of the "pro-Joseph" layer. Moreover, whereas the other sayings needed the framework (49:1–2) to introduce the other sons on the scene, this is not necessary for Joseph and the saying might thus be a continuation of the "pro-Joseph" layer in 48:22. After Joseph received Shechem as his inheritance (addressed in 2.p.sing.), he is blessed by the patriarch (in the 3.p.sing. as happens more often in blessings[322]) with progeny (22b–23a), divine protection (23b–24) and abundant blessings (25–26).

However, this does not imply that the whole saying is part of one layer or that no adaptation by the "pro-Judah" layer could have taken place. On the basis of the form-critical argument of the "tribal sayings" some scholars considered our text to be composite, 49:22 being the original saying, 49:23–24 and 49:25–26 being later additions.[323] However, in the previous chapters we have seen that the text of the saying on Joseph forms a coherent unity, in the sense that verbal forms continue the preceding forms very well, and that the text as a whole could easily be understood as a blessing. It seems to us, therefore, that the assumption of whole strophes being added here is hard to defend any more.[324] Nevertheless, in Chapter Two (on the text and translation) we indicated some diachronic tensions in 49:26a. Moreover, in Chapter Four we argued that the title נְזִיר fits best in the present context of the Joseph Story, characterizing Joseph as having a special function saving his family. It might be that such a title reflects much more the "pro-Judah" layer, making Joseph only important for what he did in the past, than for what he might be among his brothers. These kind of considerations will now be discussed below.

---

[320] Cf. above, p. 353, with n. 174.

[321] Cf. above, pp. 354–5.

[322] Cf. in this respect the Ugaritic evidence, which demonstrates that this was not uncommon in ancient Semitic literature; see KTU 1.17:i.37–53; 1.19:iv.36–40 (cf. also 1.22:iii.1–14). Blessings in the 2.p. are also found: KTU 1.15:ii.21–iii.19; 1.17:v.37–9.

[323] Cf. Zobel, *SuG*, 21–5, 115–20,123–6; De Geus, *Tribes of Israel*, 90–2; J. Van Seters, "The Religion of the Patriarchs", *Bib* 61 (1980) 220–33, 226. Cf. also Westermann, *Genesis 37–50*, 271–2.

[324] H. Seebaß, "Die Stämmesprüche Gen 49 3–27", *ZAW* 96 (1984) 333–50, 334–9; Sæbø, "Divine Names and Epithets", 122–4, 129–32; H.D. Neef, *Ephraim: Studien zur Geschichte des Stammes Ephraim von der Landnahme bis zur frühen Königszeit* (BZAW, 238), Berlin 1995, 124–6; Beyerle, *Der Mosesegen im Deuteronomium*, 186–7, n. 300.

The first indication we encounter in this text that might suggest an adaptation of the text is the fact that in 49:24b we find the names "Jacob" and "Israel" used in parallelism:

by the hands of the Strong One of Jacob, (24bA)   מִידֵי אֲבִיר יַעֲקֹב

    by the name of the Shepherd of Israel's stone (24bB)   מִשֵּׁם(!) רֹעֵה(!) אֶבֶן יִשְׂרָאֵל

The occurrence of both names, and especially the name "Jacob" was considered to be part of the "pro-Judah" layer, and that might be the case here as well. Yet, in the context of the saying, which might be regarded as largely to be part of the "pro-Joseph" layer, it might be expected that the name "Israel" originally belonged to the "pro-Joseph"-saying. This argument seems to be substantiated by the fact that in contrast to the first epithet, אֲבִיר יַעֲקֹב (24bA), the next three epithets, רֹעֵה אֶבֶן יִשְׂרָאֵל (24bB), אֵל אָבִיךָ (25aA), שַׁדַּי (25aB), seem somehow to be related to the ancestor cult, which was abandoned in later times.[325] This might argue in favour of the assignment of the first epithet containing the name "Jacob" to the "pro-Judah" layer, and the final three (24bB–25aB) to the "pro-Joseph" layer. These three cola might have formed together a tricolon:

by the name of the Shepherd of Israel's stone, (24bA*)   מִשֵּׁם(!) רֹעֵה(!) אֶבֶן יִשְׂרָאֵל

    by El, your Father, who will help you, (25aB*)   מֵאֵל אָבִיךָ וְיַעְזְרֶךָ

      and by Shadday, who will bless you, (25aC*)   וְאֵת שַׁדַּי וִיבָרְכֶךָ

It is inherent in each reconstruction that — despite the arguments — it has a certain amount of uncertainty. Yet, one small element in this reconstruction is even more uncertain than the rest; it concerns the element מִשֵּׁם "by the name" at the beginning of verse 24bB. In Chapter Two we pointed out that "the name" was already in Ugarit a powerful designation for the divine,[326] so for that reason we did not change the consonantal text of this colon. Yet, in the previous colon (49:24bA) the help of the divine was designated by means of מִידֵי "by the hands of", which corresponds perfectly with the "hands" in the previous verse (49:24aC). It might be considered for that reason that the text in the "pro-Joseph" layer was the following מִידֵי ... רֹעֵה אֶבֶן יִשְׂרָאֵל "by the hands of ... the Shepherd of Israel's stone"; and that the words אֲבִיר יַעֲקֹב מִשֵּׁם "... the Strong One of Jacob, by the name of ..." were added. In contrast to the analysis in Chapter Two, where

---

[325] Cf. above, pp. 198–205, esp. 201–5 on רֹעֵה אֶבֶן יִשְׂרָאֵל; pp. 205–6 on אֵל אָבִיךָ; and pp. 206–15, esp. 210–1, on שַׁדַּי. Even if our interpretation of these epithets as being related to the ancestor cult might be false in all three cases, it is still a fact that these three epithets are found in, or have evident parallels in the religious literature of Ugarit in contrast to the first one.

[326] Cf. above, p. 205.

the promise of divine protection continued in the next strophe, the result would be that the reconstructed tricolon (24bA*–25aC*) forms one strophe together with 49:23b–24aC, confining the promise to this strophe:

And (if) archers will harass him, (23bA)	וַיִשְׂטְמֻהוּ(!) בַּעֲלֵי חִצִּים
his bow will remain stable, (24aB)	וַתֵּשֶׁב בְּאֵיתָן קַשְׁתּוֹ
and the arms of his hands become nimble, (24aC)	וַיָּפֹזּוּ זְרֹעֵי יָדָיו
by the hands of { } the Shepherd of Israel's stone, (24bA*)	מִידֵי { } רֹעֶה אֶבֶן יִשְׂרָאֵל
by El, your Father, who will help you, (25aB*)	מֵאֵל אָבִיךָ וְיַעְזְרֶךָ
and by Shadday, who will bless you, (25aC*)	וְאֵת שַׁדַּי וִיבָרְכֶךָ

In this way the physical similarity between the hands of Joseph and the hands of El is preserved. This similarity reflects the ancient near eastern royal ideology, depicting the king as the son of the deity, and as such the proposed reading might reflect even better the "pro-Joseph" layer in which Joseph is regarded as Israel's successor.

The second indication that an adaptation of the text has taken place was found in 49:25b, as already described in Chapter Two.[327] There we suggested the following reading of 49:26a,

Blessings of your father, mighty and exalted, (26aA)	בִּרְכֹת אָבִיךָ גָּבַר וְעָל(!!)
blessings of my progenitors of old,(26aB)	בִּרְכֹת הוֹרַי עַד[328]

Because of the parallelism with the following colon (49:26aC), we considered this rendering incorrect at the level of the *synchronic* reading. Now reading this text from a diachronic perspective there might be some reason to follow the interpretation offered above. First of all, the suggested reading is philologically correct[329] whereas the reading הוֹרַי (MT) is the *lectio difficilior* and as such it has a priority over LXX and Sam.[330] Because Joseph is granted here the blessings of his

---

[327] Cf. above, pp. 215–7; we will not repeat the arguments here.

[328] Most likely the expression הוֹרַי עַד has to be considered as a "broken construct", in which the suffix is placed between the first and the second noun. For similar constructions, see: Lev. 26:42, אֶת־בְּרִיתִי יַעֲקוֹב, literally: "my covenant of Jacob" (JM, §129A, n. 4: יַעֲקוֹב "is virtually in the genitive"; two other examples in Lev. 26:42; cf. also Jer. 33:20); Hab. 3:8, מַרְכְּבֹתֶיךָ יְשׁוּעָה "Your chariots of victory"; other examples are found in Lev. 6:3; 2 Sam. 22:33; Ezek. 16:27; Ps. 71:7. Cf. E. König, *Lehrgebäude der hebräischen Sprache: Syntax*, Leipzig 1897, §277a–b; JM, §129A, with n. 4; Waltke, O'Connor, *IBHS*, §9.3d. Another solution is proposed in J.C.L. Gibson, *Davidson's Introductory Hebrew Grammar — Syntax*, Edinburgh ⁴1994, §39, rem. 1, who suggests that the second noun may be used " 'adverbially' (*in respect of*)".

[329] Cf. previous footnote.

[330] The adjustment of הוֹרַי to הַרְרֵי by LXX and Sam is much better to understand in view of the parallelism with גִּבְעֹת "hills", than a reverse adjustment by the Masoretes.

(deified) father and of his ancestors, this interpretation supports the reading of the Deathbed Episode as being partly "pro-Joseph", for this blessing might have been given to the most important son, generally the eldest. Further, the reading corresponds very well with our interpretation of the preceding verses as being affiliated with the ancestor cult,[331] because in this reading the ancestors of the patriarch are considered to have the power to bless.[332]

As a consequence, however, the following colon of this poetic verse, תַּאֲוַת גִּבְעֹת עוֹלָם "the longings of the everlasting hills" (26aC) is not parallel any more to the preceding bicolon. In the preceding colon (49:26aB) the construct בִּרְכֹת הוֹרַי עַד (MT) or, if one would prefer the reading of LXX and Sam, בִּרְכֹת הַרְרֵי עַד still could be interpreted as a genitive *subjectivus*, parallel to the blessing power of Heavens and Flood (49:25b). Yet, while "mountains" and "hills" might have been powers in the ancient Near East which were able to "bless", comparable to "Heavens" and "Flood", in 49:26aC this power is not attributed to the hills, for the word תַּאֲוָה "longing, desire" turns the hills into object, instead of subject and in this way the listing of "blessings" is disturbed. Therefore this colon (49:26aC) does not correspond with the preceding verses and might be regarded as a later addition to the text. As such an addition it created a reinterpretation of the text in which the ancestor cult and Joseph's preferential status seems to be out of place and the colon is thus assigned to the "pro-Judah" layer.

In this respect the differences between our text and Deut. 33:13–16a are significant, the latter runs:

Blessed by YHWH be his land (13bA)	מְבֹרֶכֶת יהוה אַרְצוֹ
with the choicest gifts of heaven above, (13bB)	מִמֶּגֶד שָׁמַיִם מִטָּל
and of the flood, crouching below; (13bC)	וּמִתְּהוֹם רֹבֶצֶת תָּחַת
and with the choicest fruits of the sun, (14aA)	וּמִמֶּגֶד תְּבוּאֹת שָׁמֶשׁ
and with the choicest yields of the months; (14aB)	וּמִמֶּגֶד גֶּרֶשׁ יְרָחִים
and with the best of the ancient mountains (15aA)	וּמֵרֹאשׁ הַרְרֵי־קֶדֶם
and the abundance of the everlasting hills; (15aB)	וּמִמֶּגֶד גִּבְעוֹת עוֹלָם
with the choicest gifts of the earth and its fullness; (16aA)	וּמִמֶּגֶד אֶרֶץ וּמְלֹאָהּ
and the favour of him that dwelt in thornbush. (16aB)	וּרְצוֹן שֹׁכְנִי סְנֶה

The most important difference is, in our view, the fact that in Deut.

---

[331] Cf. already De Moor, "Standing Stones", 19; idem, *RoY*², 360.

[332] Cf. above 216–7, with n. 878. On the deified ancestors, cf. De Moor, *RoY*, 229–52; *RoY*², 317–61; idem, "Standing Stones", 1–20; K. van der Toorn, *Family Religion in Babylonia, Syria and Israel: Continuity and Change in the Forms of Religious Life* (SHCANE, 7), Leiden 1996, 55–8, 125–6, 153–77, 218–25, 231–5.

33:15 the reference to "the blessings of your father, גבר ועל/גברו על"
is missing, whereas the word בִּרְכֹת "blessings of" (49:26a) is absent
in Deut. 33:15, which reads וּמֵראֹשׁ "the best".[333] In addition the text-
critically uncertain הֹורַי "my progenitors" (MT) is in Deut. 33:15 a
certain reading הַרְרֵי "mountains of", in which only the orthography
might differ (Sam: הרי). In our view the text of Deut. 33:13–16 leaves
no room for misunderstanding as does the text of Gen. 49:25b–26a,
and it appears to us that the former might be a reinterpretation of
the latter.[334] This is suggested first by the occurrence of the "blessing
by YHWH" at the beginning, emphasizing that YHWH is the principal
provider of the blessing, which is specified in the following list.[335] Secondly, the "blessings" are "interpreted" as the "fruit, production" of
the land; but in Genesis 49:25–26 it occurs that the genitive construction might be a genitive *subjectivus*, suggesting even that "Heavens",
"Flood" and "Breast and Womb" are powers who provide blessings.[336]
This is not directly obvious from the text as it was rendered and presented in its strophic structure in Chapter Two,[337] because 49:25b
seems to be the accusative of the verb in the preceding colon, וְאֵת
שַׁדַּי וִיבָרְכֶךָ "by Shadday, who will bless you" (49:25aC). However, if
our diachronic analysis is correct and 49:23bA–25aC* forms indeed a

---

[333]Cf. Zobel, *SuG*, 37; J. Van Seters, "The Religion of the Patriarchs", *Bib* 61
(1980) 220–33, 226. They suggest that 49:25–26 was borrowed from Deut. 33:13–7
with a few changes in order to make Genesis 49 more like a blessing. However, the
editor apparently also added the word "blessings" here, because it was missing in
the "original" blessing of Moses. On the other hand, the editor apparently also
omitted the "blessing by YHWH" (33:13a), which seems very improbable if he
wanted to make this text (Gen. 49) more like a blessing as these scholars suggest.

[334]With regard to other parts of the blessing, Korpel, *RiC*, 534, 535, suggests
also a revision of Gen. 49:22–6 in Deut. 33:13–7. Cf. also Sæbø, "Divine Names
and Epithets", 123–4, 132. *Pace* Zobel, *SuG*, 37; De Geus, *Tribes of Israel*, 90–1;
Van Seters, "The Religion of the Patriarchs", 226. They consider Gen. 49:25–6
to be dependent on Deut. 33:13–7 with a few changes. In this we differ also with
Beyerle, *Der Mosesegen im Deuteronomium*, 187, who concluded that no literary
dependency existed in any direction between Deut. 33:13–7 and Gen. 49:22–6.
In our view these scholars overlooked the obvious theological differences, which
are undoubtedly due to a Deuteronomistic editor. This is especially clear from
the fact that the elements of the ancestor cult in Gen. 49:22–6 have completely
disappeared in the version of Deuteronomy 33.

[335]Cf. also Sæbø, "Divine Names", 132.

[336]Cf. C. Houtman, *Der Himmel im Alten Testament: Israels Weltbild und
Weltanschauung* (OTS, 30), Leiden 1993, 58–9, who reads in our text (together
with Deut. 33:13; Isa. 45:8) a more personal representation of שָׁמַיִם. The blessings
are commonly interpreted as "rain and dew", see *ibid.*, 184, 188. On "Heaven"
and "Flood" as a divine powers in the ancient Near East, cf. M. Hutter, M. de
Jonge, "Heaven", *DDD*, 736–42; B. Alster, "Tiamat", *ibid.*, 1634–9.

[337]Pp. 180–1 above.

strophe as presented above,[338] then 49:25b is not so much the continuation of verse 25aC, but the beginning of a new strophe:[339]

The blessings of the Heavens above, (25bA)	בִּרְכֹת שָׁמַיִם מֵעָל
the blessings of the Flood, resting below, (25bB)	בִּרְכֹת תְּהוֹם רֹבֶצֶת תָּחַת
the blessings of Breasts and Womb, (25bC)	בִּרְכֹת שָׁדַיִם וָרָחַם
the blessings of your father, mighty and exalted (26aA)	בִּרְכֹת אָבִיךָ גָּבַר וְעָל(!!!)
the blessings of my progenitors of old, { } (26aB)	[340]{ } בִּרְכֹת הוֹרַי עַד
may (they) be on the head of Joseph, (26bA)	תִּהְיֶין לְרֹאשׁ יוֹסֵף
and on the crown of one set apart of his brothers. (26bB)	וּלְקָדְקֹד נְזִיר אֶחָיו

In this way "the blessings of . . ." are the subject of the verb תִּהְיֶין "may (they) be" in 49:26bA.[341] It appears to us that, understood in this way, the different designations for the divine are not monotheistic, or a "witness to the 'unity' of the patriarchal God",[342] but still reflect the polytheistic background of Israel's religion.

The repetition of בִּרְכֹת "blessings of" in 49:26a forms a contra-indication against our strophic delimitation of 49:25b–26, even though this might be neutralized by the parallelism in the strophe itself.[343] Yet this indication might also be a signal that the text in its present

---

[338] Cf. above, p. 533.

[339] For strophes of seven cola, cf. Korpel, De Moor, "Fundamentals", 188, 197 (= *SABCP*, 1–61, 25, 37); J.C. de Moor, "Syntax Peculiar to Ugaritic Poetry", *VANEP*, 191–205, 198 (two strophes of seven cola in a canticle of four). Strictly the repetition of בִּרְכֹת in the second poetic verse might form a contra-indication against the strophic delimitation. However, because of the strong parallelism with the preceding verse, and because of the fact that this list of blessings forms the subject of the verb in the final verse (cf. below), this contra-indication might be neutralized. Cf. for example, Korpel, De Moor, *art. cit.*, 198 (KTU 1.6:vi.16–20), (= *SABCP*, 38). Identical strophic structures with enumerations causing "repetitive parallelism" in the midst of a strophe are found in J.C. de Moor, "Narrative Poetry in Canaan", *UF* 20 (1988) 149–171, 154 (str. VI.1), 161 (str. II.2). Yet, this contra-indication might indicate that the text was also adapted here by means of a later expansion; cf. the following discussion in the main text.

[340] The text would have run as follows,

The blessings of your father, mighty and exalted (26aA)	בִּרְכֹת אָבִיךָ גָּבַר וְעָל(!!!)
the blessings of my progenitors of old, (26aB)	בִּרְכֹת הוֹרַי עַד
the longings of the everlasting hills. (26aC)	תַּאֲוַת גִּבְעֹת עוֹלָם

[341] The possibility of interpreting the syntactical function of this list of blessings in the sense of the accusative and of subject was noted by Gunkel, *Genesis*, ³1910, 486.

[342] Sæbø, "Divine Names and Epithets", 132. It has to be noted, however, that Sæbø and other scholars (cf. below) argued the monotheistic character of the text on the basis of *Letztgestalt* of the text, whereas our suggestion is based on an assumed *Vorlage*. Cf. also Korpel, *RiC*, 570; De Moor, *RoY*, 225; *RoY*², 312–3.

[343] Cf. above, p. 536, n. 339.

form is composite. In the final colon the title נְזִיר is used for Joseph, concerning which we argued that it might fit the present context of the Joseph Story rather well. It might be that this title is given to Joseph with regard to his function to save his family and that it was not part of the "pro-Joseph" layer. In this respect the use of the word רֹאשׁ "head" in 49:26aA is also remarkable, because in 47:31 it was used as the title of Joseph: רֹאשׁ הַמַּטֶּה(!) "head/leader of the tribe". It could be that a comparable title is used here also, but that it was obscured by a later expansion of the text. It is possible, for example, that יוֹסֵף "of Joseph" (26bA) and וּלְקָדְקֹד נְזִיר "on the crown of the one set apart" (26bB) were added, and that the original text ran: תִּהְיֶין לְרֹאשׁ אֶחָיו "may they be for[344] the head/leader of his brothers".[345] As we said before, in this form the text reflects the title found in 47:31, but not only that one, but also the one in 48:22, אַחַד עַל־אַחֶיךָ "one above your brothers".[346] Yet, this matter cannot be established beyond question and for that reason we prefer to present the text as follows, leaving both options open,

The blessings of the Heavens above, (25bA)	בִּרְכֹת שָׁמַיִם מֵעָל
the blessings of the Flood, resting below, (25bB)	בִּרְכֹת תְּהוֹם רֹבֶצֶת תָּחַת
the blessings of Breasts and Womb, (25bC)	בִּרְכֹת שָׁדַיִם וָרָחַם
the blessings of your father, mighty and exalted (26aA)	בִּרְכֹת אָבִיךָ גָּבֹר וְעַל
the blessings of my progenitors of old { }, (26aB)	בִּרְכֹת הוֹרַי עַד { }
may (they) be on the leader of {Joseph,}	תִּהְיֶין לְרֹאשׁ {יוֹסֵף}
{on the crown of the *n^ezir* of} his brothers. (26b*)	{וּלְקָדְקֹד נְזִיר} אֶחָיו

In conclusion we may say that the text in its present form supports a pro-Joseph import. However, it might be that the text contains several later additions, which bring in the idea of the parallelism of "Jacob" and "Israel" (49:24b); removing carefully the idea of the "progenitors of old" (26aA); and, finally, probably giving Joseph the title נְזִיר instead of רֹאשׁ. Yet, it appears to us that the redaction was not so much concerned with theological items, like the removing of the "progenitors of old",[347] as with the political consequence this blessing implied

---

[344] For היה לְ with this meaning, cf. *HAL*, 234.

[345] Even though the expression רֹאשׁ אֶחָיו "head/leader of his brothers" is not found in this form in the Hebrew Bible, it might have existed; cf. Neh. 12:7, רָאשֵׁי כֹּהֲנִים וַאֲחֵיהֶם "the heads of the priests and their brothers" (see also 1 Chr. 12:33 [E.T. 12:32]).

[346] Vawter, *On Genesis*, 468, found this reflection of 48:22 already in MT, on the basis of the title of נְזִיר for Joseph. In his view "there is no doubt that Joseph represents supremacy in Israel" in this saying.

[347] Note that the references to the ancestor cult also occur in 49:5–7, which was assigned to the "pro-Judah" layer. This implies that the adaptation of the text

for Joseph, namely that he was regarded as the oldest son. In our view
that is the reason why the adaptation of the text "removed" the "progenitors", by adding תַּאֲוַת גִּבְעֹת עוֹלָם "the longings of the eternal hills"
(49:26aC).

If these diachronic observations on the blessing of Joseph are correct, this suggests that the complete text of the blessing in the "pro-
Joseph" layer would have been as presented here below. The effect of
our analysis is in each case that the blessing is found in three strophes
whose contents present each a unity of thought, although they continue the thought of the previous strophe:

A young bullcalf is Joseph, (22aA)	בֵּן פֹּרָת יוֹסֵף
a young bullcalf next to a well, (22aB)	בֵּן פֹּרָת עֲלֵי־עָיִן
in the meadow he will stride towards the Bull, (22bA)	בָּנוֹת צָעֲדָה עֲלֵי־שׁוּר
and he will make him strong so they will become numerous. (23aB)	וַיְמָרֲרֻהוּ וָרֹבּוּ

And (if) archers will harass him, (23bA)	וְיִשְׂטְמֻהוּ(!) בַּעֲלֵי חִצִּים
his bow will remain stable, (24aB)	וַתֵּשֶׁב בְּאֵיתָן קַשְׁתּוֹ
and the arms of his hands become nimble, (24aC)	וַיָּפֹזּוּ זְרֹעֵי יָדָיו
by the hands of { } the Shepherd of Israel's stone, (24bA*)	מִידֵי { } רֹעֶה אֶבֶן יִשְׂרָאֵל
by El, your Father, who will help you, (25aB*)	מֵאֵל אָבִיךָ וְיַעְזְרֶךָּ
and by Shadday, who will bless you, (25aC*)	וְאֵת שַׁדַּי וִיבָרְכֶךָּ

The blessings of the Heavens above, (25bA)	בִּרְכֹת שָׁמַיִם מֵעָל
the blessings of the Flood, resting below, (25bB)	בִּרְכֹת תְּהוֹם רֹבֶצֶת תָּחַת
the blessings of Breasts and Womb, (25bC)	בִּרְכֹת שָׁדַיִם וָרָחַם
the blessings of your father, mighty and exalted (26aA)	בִּרְכֹת אָבִיךָ גָּבַר וְעַל
the blessings of my progenitors of old { }, (26aB)	בִּרְכֹת הוֹרַי עַד { }
may (they) be on the head of {Joseph,}	תִּהְיֶין לְרֹאשׁ {יוֹסֵף}
{on the crown of the n^{e}zir of} his brothers. (26b*)	{וּלְקָדְקֹד נְזִיר} אֶחָיו}

6.5.1.7 The Remaining Brothers
6.5.1.7.1 The Listing of the Names

Starting with the remaining brothers it might be appropriate to discuss briefly the order of the list here. The order of the different lists
has been debated ever since M. Noth discussed them in his famous
Das System der zwölf Stämme Israels.[348] In this study Noth distin-

---

was primarily directed against the political implications of the text and not so
much against the theological import.

[348] M. Noth, *Das System der zwölf Stämme Israels* (BWANT, 4/1), Stuttgart
1930 (Darmstadt ²1966), 3–28. Cf. also his *Geschichte Israels*, Göttingen ²1954,
83–104. The following studies are examplary for the discussion of the the-
ories of Noth: J. Hoftijzer, "Enige opmerkingen rond het Israëlitische 12-

guishes two types of lists, one is system "A" which contains Levi and Joseph; the second, system "B", where Ephraim and Manasseh replace Joseph and lacks Levi. The latter system, "B", is a geographical system, summing up the geographic position of the tribes in the land: there are two versions of this system.[349] The chronology of these lists is a very complex problem: was system "A" prior to system "B" or *vice versa*? Noth himself suggested that system "A" was prior to system "B" and that the latter was created in order to meet the changed conditions. However, in this construction the question of the existence of a secular tribe of Levi, and also the ancientness of the occurrence of Joseph in these lists is crucial, because should the early existence of one of them be denied Noth's thesis would collapse.[350] Yet, for the moment it will have to suffice to note that our list follows the genealogical order (system "A") as was suggested by Noth,[351] even though the order is chronologically not in accordance with the birth-story (Gen. 29:31–30:24). As we have seen before, the first four brothers in this list are the oldest and they are generally placed in the order of their birth dates. The following two, Zebulun and Issachar, are also Leah-"sons" and as such it is understandable that they appear here, though their order is reversed. The Leah-group is immediately followed by the "concubine-sons" (Bilhah and Zilpah) and finally by the youngest two, the Rachel-"sons". The listing of the so-called concubine-sons betrays no geographical order and therefore the chiastic ordering of the whole list firmly establishes our list as a genealogical list. Yet, the question of the chronological order, which is quite often connected with the observations on the genealogical and geographical system, cannot be answered in the context of the present study.

6.5.1.7.2   Zebulun (49:13)

The saying on Zebulun gives a description of the future dwelling place

---

stammensysteem", *NedThT* 14 (1959/60) 241–63; H. Weippert, "Das geographische system der Stämme Israels", *VT* 23 (1973) 76–89; De Geus, *The Tribes of Israel, passim*; K. Namiki, "Reconsideration of the Twelve-Tribe System of Israel", *AJBI* 2 (1976) 29–59; B. Halpern, *The Emergence of Israel in Canaan* (SBL.MS, 29), Chico (CA) 1983, 109–33.

[349] Weippert, "Das geographische System", 76–89; De Geus, *The Tribes of Israel*, 70–2, 111–9.

[350] Cf. De Geus, *The Tribes of Israel*, 69–119, where these matters are discussed extensively. Next to the two points mentioned, other elements are important as well (also listed and discussed by De Geus), as, for instance, the origin of Judah, and the uses of "Gad" and "Gilead".

[351] Noth, *Das System*, 7–8.

of Zebulun, namely close to the Gulf of Haifa. However, the geographical description of the allotment of Zebulun (Josh. 19:10–16) does
not correspond with our text because the territory of Zebulun is cut
off from the sea by Asher and Manasseh (Josh. 17:7–10; 19:24–31).
Other geographical references to Zebulun are practically absent:[352] in
Judges we find an obscure reference to Aijalon (Judg. 12:11–12); in
Deut. 33:18–19 reference is made to the mountain, which Zebulun has
in common with Issachar (generally identified as Mount Tabor), but
reference is made to the sea and the sand once more. What is there to
say of the geographical element in Gen. 49:13 — a description which
is mostly absent in the discussion of Zebulun's territory — in relation
to the stated geographical references?

In Judg. 12:11–12 the judge אֱ(י)לוֹן "Elon" is buried בְּאַיָלוֹן, "in
Aijalon" in the land of Zebulun. This geographical designation has
not been finally settled yet, because the only Aijalon known from the
Hebrew Bible is in the (southern) district of Dan;[353] it is unknown in
the district of Zebulun.[354] It might, however, be that the vocalisation
of this geographical designation is not completely correct, because it
is remarkable that the consonants of the GN (אילון) are identical to
those of the PN אֱ(י)לון, which might be an indication that the name
of the judge is related to the place where he was buried.[355] It might
also be possible that the name does not denote a place name but the
name of a region, namely the *Geba'ot 'Allonim*.[356] The implication
would be that these hills are indeed part of the territory of Zebulun
as Z. Gal described it on the basis of Josh. 19:10–16.[357]

---

[352] In the Book of Chronicles the descendants from Zebulun are missing, which
is to be regretted because these lists very often contain geographical names.

[353] Josh. 10:12; 19:42 (V. 43: Elon); 21:24. According to 2 Chr. 11:10 it is found
in Judah.

[354] J. Simons, *The Geographical and Topographical Texts of the Old Testament: A
Concise Commentary in 32 Chapters*, Leiden 1959, 300; Z. Kallai, *Historical Geography of the Bible: The Tribal Territories of Israel*, Jerusalem, Leiden 1986, 189.

[355] R.G. Boling, *Judges: A New Translation with Introduction and Commentary*
(AB, 6A), Garden City (NY) 1975, 216. Cf. also the fact that the name "Elon"
is a "typical" Zebulunite name (Gen. 46:14). See: Simons, *The Geographical and
Topographical Texts*, 300; Boling, *ibid.*

[356] For the geographical description, see Z. Gal, *Lower Galilee during the Iron
Age* (ASOR.DS, 8), Winona Lake (IN) 1992, 2.

[357] Gal, *Lower Galilee*, 98–102; cf. also his, "Cabul, Jiphtah-El and the Boundary between Asher and Zebulun in the Light of Archaeological Evidence", *ZDPV*
101 (1985) 114–27; idem, "Regional Survey Projects: Revealing the Settlement
Map of Ancient Israel", in: A. Biran, J. Aviram (eds.), *Biblical Archaeology Today, 1990: Proceedings of the Second International Congress on Biblical Archaeology, Jerusalem, June–July 1990*, Jerusalem 1993, 453–8, 455–6. There have been
attempts to identify the place name with Khirbet el-Lun near Ḥannathon in the

The descriptions of the territory of Zebulun in Josh. 19:10–16, together with the allotments of Asher, Issachar and Manasseh seem to exclude the possibility that Zebulun's territory reached the sea, because in Josh. 17:10 it is said that Manasseh reached Asher in the north. Even though Gal argued that the Allonim hills are part of the territory of Zebulun, this would still imply that the territory was separated from the sea by the plain of Acco, which belongs to the territory of Asher according to Joshua's lists.[358] In this connection the list of Solomon's districts (1 Kgs. 4:7–19) is also discussed because the names Asher, Naphtali and Issachar are here given to a district, yet Zebulun is not mentioned in this text. In an attempt to find Zebulon in this list scholars have referred to the ninth district in 1 Kgs. 4:16, which is described as בְּאָשֵׁר וּבְעָלוֹת generally rendered with "in Asher and Be'aloth/in Aloth". Though there has been a suggestion to emend the latter word into Zebulun,[359] it appears that MT offers the best reading here, even though it does not correspond with the general tribal inheritances as we know it. W. Zwickel suggested we interpret the enigmatic בְעָלוֹת in 1 Kgs. 4:16 as a reference to the "heights", which might be a reference to the Geba'ot 'Allonim.[360] In Zwickel's view this provides the only possibility of identifying the territory of Zebulun again, because he excluded the other higher area near Asher, the Carmel, as belonging to the district of Dor, the fourth district (1 Kgs. 4:11). However, the district of Dor has no further specification and might therefore be restricted to the coastal area and the northern part of the Sharon-plain up to the Carmel.[361] If that were correct,

---

territory of Zebulun; cf. Kallai, *Historical Geography*, 189, with n. 186; Gal, *op.cit.*, 102. However, the survey of the site revealed only remnants from Iron Age II and later periods, Gal, *op.cit.*, 25.

[358] Gal, *Lower Galilee*, 100–2; idem, "Cabul, Jiphthah-El and the Boundary between Asher and Zebulun", 124–7. For the description of the Allonim hills, cf. *op.cit.*, 2.

[359] For this emendation and its refution, cf. G.W. Ahlström, "A Note on a Textual Problem in 1 Kgs 4:16", *BASOR* 235 (1979) 79–80; idem, *The History of Ancient Palestine from the Palaeolithic Period to Alexander's Conquest* (JSOTS, 146), D. Edelman (ed.), Sheffield 1993, 512–3.

[360] W. Zwickel, "Der vermisste Stamm Sebulon in 1 Könige iv 7–19", *VT* 47 (1997) 387–9. In reading here a reference to the "heights", Zwickel follows a suggestion of Ahlström, "A Note on a Textual Problem in 1 Kgs 4:16", 79–80; idem, *History of Ancient Palestine*, 512–3. The latter objected, however, also against a combination of this text with the tribal allotments, which he considered to be an anachronism (cf. Ahlström, *op.cit.*, 513, n. 2, 514). Gal, *Lower Galilee*, 106, already suggested assigning the Allonim hills to the ninth district.

[361] Ahlström, *History of Ancient Palestine*, 511; V. Fritz, "Die Verwaltungsgebiete Salomos nach 1Kön. 4,7–19", in: M. Weippert, S. Timm (Hrsg.), *Meilenstein: Fs H. Donner* (ÄAT, 30), Wiesbaden 1995, 19–26, 22. Contrast, however, Kallai,

it would imply that the Carmel was part of the ninth district and in that case בְעָלוֹת might have been a reference to Mount Carmel. This seems to be confirmed by the fact that Jokneam (לְכַּרְמֶל "at Carmel"; Josh. 12:22) is excluded from the fifth district (1 Kgs. 4:12), indicating that it belonged to the district north of the fifth, most likely the ninth district. According to Josh. 21:34 this city is part of the Zebulunite allotment,[362] indicating that the territory ascribed to Zebulun in Joshua's lists was in the system of Solomon's districts part of the ninth district together with Asher.

With respect to the text of 1 Kgs. 4:16 N. Na'aman has argued that if Asher and Zebulun lived here together[363] this might "explain the extremely problematic allusion to Zebulun in Jacob's blessing".[364] If Na'aman is right, this might also explain why in Judg. 5:17b it could be said that *Asher* "dwelled at the wide sea's beach", applying here also חוֹף "curving beach", similar to that in the saying on Zebulun (49:13).[365] It would imply that both tribes (or districts) reached the present Gulf of Haifa, probably Zebulun in the southern part including the Carmel,[366] which was in later times considered to be the

---

Historical Geography, 60–1.

[362] Kallai, *Historical Geography*, 181–3. Against this interpretation Gal, *Lower Galilee*, 99, with n. 5, objected that the value of the list of Levitical cities is limited because there are important differences between the list in Joshua 21 and 2 Chronicles 6. However, this argument does not contradict Kallai's arguments of which the most important one is that Jokneam is nowhere considered to be part of Manasseh, but in Joshua 21 it is part of Zebulun.

[363] N. Na'aman, *Borders and Districts in Biblical Historiography* (JBSt, 4), Jerusalem 1986, 192–3, prefers the emendation of בעלות into זבולון (see p. 541, with n. 359 above), because no better solution had been offered until then. However, it is possible to consider the territory described as being partly the territory of Zebulun, without accepting the emendation; cf. Zwickel, "Der vermisste Stamm Sebulon", 387–9, and our discussion above. Moreover, it should be emphasized that the system of Solomon's districts was not so much concerned with the tribal system, as with provisioning the court (cf. below).

[364] Na'aman, *Borders and Districts*, 192–4 (see also his map on p. 189).

[365] For the interpretation of חוֹף as "curved beach", cf. above, pp. 148–50.

[366] The inclusion of the Carmel in the territory of Zebulun does not imply that that region would have been settled extensively, which was in all likelihood not the case; cf. Fritz, "Die Verwaltungsgebiete Salomos", 26. However, this does not imply that the Carmel was not important, cf. H.O. Thompson, "Carmel, Mount", *ABD*, vol. 1, 874–5; and the discussion below. In this connection the discussion of the territorial political system of the city-states in Late Bronze Palestine is very interesting. In that era the plain of Acco was divided between two city-states (Acco and Achshaph), and the southern part of it belonged together with the Carmel and the south-western part of the later territory of Zebulun to the realm of Achshaph. See most recently I. Finkelstein, "The Territorial-Political System of Canaan in the Late Bronze Age", *UF* 28 (1996) 221–55, esp. 238–9, 254 (map 1).

boundary of Asher and Manasseh (Josh. 17:10–11, 19:26). Finally, the interpretation of בְּעָלוֹת as a reference to (part of) Zebulun, might contain a pun on the name Zebulun, when derived from זבל "to raise (up)". Na'aman has suggested that these texts (1 Kgs. 4:16; Gen. 49:13) demonstrate that the tribal geography was flexible,[367] "which was quite different from the boundary system as recorded in Josh. 13–19".[368] In any case, it appears that there are important differences in function and dimensions between the system of Solomon's twelve districts and the tribal allotments.[369] The twelve districts of Solomon as described in 1 Kgs. 4:7–16 were to supply the court with food for a month,[370] but Judah is not included in this list. On the other hand, the tribal inheritances might have been partly based on ancient border descriptions, but they were intended to divide the land among the twelve tribes, included Judah.[371] Na'aman has demonstrated that the lists in Joshua 13–19 partly depart from the reality and have to be considered literary creations and not an actual administrative division.[372]

---

[367] In fact there is a quite dynamic aspect in the existence of the tribes themselves; cf. Zobel, SuG, 127–8; De Geus, The Tribes of Israel, 112.

[368] Na'aman, Borders and Districts, 194. The flexibility might also be deduced from the fact that in later times the district near the sea of Chinnereth, where Capernaum is found, is called the land of Zebulun and Naphtali (Mat. 4:13 < Isa. 8:23 [ET, 9:1]).

[369] Despite Kallai's statement (Historical Geography, 313), that there is agreement between both systems as far as the overall geographic-political picture is concerned, he also lists very important differences between both systems which might be due to the different purposes they serve.

[370] Na'aman, Borders and Districts, 167–180; Ahlström, History of Ancient Palestine, 514; V. Fritz, Das erste Buch der Könige (ZBK.AT, 10.1), Zürich 1996, 51.

[371] Na'aman, Borders and Districts, 84–95; V. Fritz, Das Buch Josua (HAT, 1/7), Tübingen 1995, 7–8.

[372] Na'aman, Borders and Districts, 76–95. Cf. also H. Donner, Geschichte des Volkes Israel und seiner Nachbarn in Grundzügen, Tl. 1: Von den Anfängen bis zur Staatenbildungszeit (ATD.Erg, 4/1), Göttingen 1984, 129; N.P. Lemche, Early Israel: Anthropological and Historical Studies on the Israelite Society before the Monarchy (SVT, 37), Leiden 1985, 285; Fritz, "Die Verwaltungsgebiete Salomos", 26, n. 39. That the boundary system was as old as the United Monarchy was defended inter alii by Kallai, Historical Geography, 279–93; Na'aman, Borders and Districts, 92–4; Gal, Lower Galilee, 96–8. These scholars considered these lists in Joshua to be from the same period as the districts of Solomon, because the same data would have been applied in these lists as in the lists of Solomon's districts. The two lastmentioned scholars based their argument also on archaeological data, namely that Lower Galilee was not occupied during a later era. However, it can be objected that the creation of these lists does not necessarily have to be dependent on occupied geographical sites; and secondly that it is possible that these lists applied data from an earlier period, but moulded in the shape of later political or theological ideas; cf. De Geus, Tribes of Israel, 73–5; Fritz, Das Buch Josua, 7–8.

As a consequence the tribal boundaries as we know them have to be considered carefully, taking into account other geographical information as well and even giving prevalence to them over the information deduced from the lists in Joshua. However, because these lists contain the most detailed information, as literary creations they are certainly not *per se* based on fiction. For that reason they may function as the basis to which the other information is added, albeit as a correction.

This complicated problem of the geographical descriptions found in the Hebrew Bible and now especially concerning Zebulun might be elaborated on by the following observations, anticipating slightly the discussion of Issachar in the following section. First, this anticipation might be justified by the fact that in Deut. 33:18–19 Zebulun and Issachar are named in one saying, although the introduction says that the saying is directed to Zebulun: וְלִזְבוּלֻן אָמַר "and of (or "to") Zebulun he said" (33:18aA). This might betray some common background for these two tribes which is rather obscured by the tradition. Secondly, the boundary description of Zebulun and Issachar seems to suggest that both bordered on Manasseh. Yet, the boundary description of Manasseh suggests that Manasseh only bordered on Asher and Issachar (Josh. 17:10–11). Mentioning the cities Manasseh had בְּיִשָּׂשׂכָר "at Issachar"[373] we find several cities that are probably even closer to Zebulun than to Issachar. However, Zebulun is not mentioned here, but Issachar is, suggesting that the border of Issachar went on quite far.[374] However, the reference to Asher and Issachar might also imply an inclusive thinking, just meaning Manasseh's border from Issachar to Asher.[375] Nevertheless, the combination of the

---

[373] The preposition בְּ is commonly rendered with "in", however, Kallai, *Historical Geography*, 173, has objected against this rendering that it "presents fundamental problems and and is inadmissible. For in the system of boundary descriptions the Land was divided into allotments adjoining one another, and not inside one another." Reference was made to GK, §119h, k. This suggestion was followed by Z. Gal, "The Settlement of Issachar: Some New Observations", *TA* 9 (1982) 79–87. According to Judg. 1:27–8, these were cities belonging to the Manassite district, and therefore we follow Kallai's suggested rendering.

[374] This has led several scholars to the conclusion — though mostly based on the rendering of "in Issachar" in Josh. 17:11 —that the territory of Issachar reached even up to the Carmel, cf. M. Noth, "Studien zu den historisch-Geographischen Dokumenten des Josua-Buches", *ZDPV* 58 (1958) 185–255, 207–8 (= idem, *Aufsätze zur biblischen Landes- und Altertumskunde*, Bd. I: *Archäologische, exegetische und topographische Untersuchungen zur Geschichte Israels*, Neukirchen-Vluyn 1971, 229–280, 246). However, Simon, *The Geographical and Topographical Texts*, 186, already had his doubts, though he also considered the cities in the plain of Jezreel to be theoretical parts of Issachar.

[375] Simons, *The Geographical and Topographical Texts*, 168–9, n. 149.

text of Deut. 33:18–19 and Josh. 17:11 might suggest that there has
been a period in history when those two territories were combined.
The reference to the mountain in their territory might be allusive to
the territory in this context. Generally it is thought that the reference
to the mountain where they "shall offer right sacrifices" is a reference
to mount Tabor, which is located at their common boundary,[376] but
the assumption that there was a cult on Tabor rests only indirectly on
Hosea 5:1,[377] where it is said that the priests have been a "net spread
upon Tabor". However, in the context of the saying (Deut. 33:18–19)
a reference to the Carmel might be more appropriate, because in the
next verse reference is made to the Mediterranean Sea,[378] which in
combination with a mountain would argue in favour of the Carmel.
This also seems appropriate because it is known that this mountain
has served cultic purposes in many times.[379] In this connection it is
interesting to refer to the fact that some scholars have considered the
tenth province of Issachar (1 Kgs. 4:17), to be combined with (a part
of) Zebulun, because the territory of Issachar would be too poor to
supply the court with food.[380] Furthermore, we may also refer in this
context to the fact that large parts of Issachar and Zebulun, together
with the other Galilean tribes were combined into one district under
the Assyrian occupation as the province Megiddo,[381] which seems to
argue in favour of a geographical argument to connect these territories. Nevertheless, these considerations do not provide us with the

---

[376]Cf. BHS; R. Frankel, "Tabor, Mount", *ABD*, vol. 6, 304–5; Beyerle, *Der Mosesegen im Deuteronomium*, 197, with n. 339.

[377]Beyerle, *Der Mosesegen im Deuteronomium*, 197–8.

[378]Beyerle, *Der Mosesegen im Deuteronomium*, 201, with n. 354.

[379]Thompson, "Carmel, Mount", 875. Important might also be the fact that the contest between Elijah and the priests of Ba'al was at the Carmel, which in the whole of DtrH might be considered as a contest for the most זִבְחֵי־צֶדֶק "right sacrifice" (Deut. 33:19).

[380]A. Saarisalo, *The Boundary between Issachar and Naphtali: An Archaeological and Literary Study of Israel's Settlement in Canaan*, Helsinki 1927, 95; Kallai, *Historical Geography*, 68–9; Gal, *Lower Galilee*, 106. *Pace* Fritz, "Die Verwal-tungsgebiete Salomos", 24. It is remarkable that Josephus described the territory of Issachar as containing "Mount Itabyrion (= Tabor) and Mount Carmel and all of lower Galilee as far as the river Jordan", whereas he described the province of Asher as "the coast about Ake (= 'Acco)"; F. Josephus, *Jewish Antiquities*, Book VIII, 36–7 (quoted after the Loeb Classical Library edition).

[381]Cf. Saarisalo, *The Boundary between Issachar and Naphtali*, 95; Noth, "Historisch-geographischen Dokumente", 208, n. 41. See also Isa. 8:23 (ET, 9:1), where the land of Zebulun and of Naphtali might be called "Galilee of the na-tions", and which seems to refer to the Assyrian occupation of the north; cf. H. Wildberger, *Jesaja, 1.Teilband: Jesaja 1–12* (BKAT, X/1), Neukirchen-Vluyn 1972, 372–3.

absolute proof that Zebulun once lived at the sea, yet, they demonstrate that it is certainly not impossible.

With regard to a possible historical situation to which the saying on Zebulun referred we have to conclude that there is no historical basis to date the saying. It is possible that it was the period of the United Monarchy because in that period the territory of the state also included the coast along the present Gulf of Haifa, the northern part of which was lost in later days.[382] From the earlier period we do not have sufficient information to allow us to draw any conclusions. Archaeological evidence shows in any case that settlement in the territory of Zebulun increased in Iron I;[383] yet, with regard to the area under consideration here (the coastal area), the question remains whether certain sites are part of Asher, Manasseh or Zebulun.[384]

6.5.1.7.3 Issachar (49:14–15)

In Chapter One we briefly described how the saying of Issachar played a role in the historical debate concerning Israel's early history. We mentioned Alt's suggestion that the *ḫapiru*, serving the king of Megiddo near Shunem (EA 250, 365), should be identified with the Issacharites,[385] which would imply a settlement of the Issacharites in the fourteenth century BCE. This identification seems to be supported by the fact that in our saying the word מַס is used, which is also applied to these corvee workers (Akk. *massu*).[386] Yet, in the evaluation we argued that the usual identification of the Issacharites with the *ḫapiru* in the region of Shunem is by no means compelling and that another

---

[382] Cf. *inter alii* Fritz, "Die Verwaltungsgebiete Salomos", 24, with n. 28.

[383] Gal, *Lower Galilee*, 84–93, 94–6. Cf. also I. Finkelstein, *The Archaeology of the Israelite Settlement*, Jerusalem 1988, 94–7.

[384] This discussion especially deals with the problem if Manasseh in Josh. 17:10–1 indeed reaches Asher, or that it only touched upon Carmel, comparable to the fourth district of Solomon, Dor (1 Kgs. 4:11), which is here assigned to Manasseh (cf. n. 361 above). This is especially important in view of the fact that at the north-eastern foot of Carmel a small, but very important harbour village was found: Tell Abu Hawam, biblical Shichor-Libnath (Josh. 19:26). On this site, cf. E. Anati, "Abu Hawam, Tell", *EAEHL*, vol. 1, 9–12; J. Balensi *et al.*, "Abu Hawam, Tell", *NEAEHL*, vol. 1, 7–14. This village was not part of Asher's territory, yet the *Hinterland* of the village was certainly not Manasseh, because the contact would be seriously hampered by the Carmel. For that reason it might be considered that it was Zebulun, which — as the patriarch announced — "would live at the beach of the sea" (Gen. 49:13) and reached the sea here on a small strip of land.

[385] Cf. above, pp. 58–9.

[386] Cf. H. Donner, "The Blessing of Issachar (*Gen.* 49:14–15) as a Source for the Early History of Israel", in: J.A. Soggin *et al.*, *Le Origini di Israele*, Rome 1987, 53–63.

dating is possible.[387] In the period of Solomon for example there were still Israelites levied to corvée work (1 Kgs. 5:27–28 [E.T., 5:13–14])[388] and so the saying could be a pun from that period on the name of the group in the territory of Issachar — a name, which in itself might have been an old nickname.

The identification of the Issacharites with the *massu*-people in the surroundings of Shunem has been criticized by S. Herrmann.[389] The fact that in this area *massu*-people worked, does not necessarily lead to the conclusion that these were the same people as those who are related in another tradition to corvée work and would live later in this area. Corvée workers were not *per se* bound to a fixed area of living and, as such, the people of the fourteenth century BCE are not necessarily Issacharites, because this group might easily have moved from that area. This point has been substantiated on the basis of archaeological information by Z. Gal.[390] The archaeological survey of the territory of Issachar has demonstrated that the settlement in the territory of Issachar can only be traced from the tenth century BCE on.[391] This settlement occurs in almost the same period as the change in population in the plain of Jezreel, where the cities became Israelite,[392] after having been Canaanite until the eleventh century.[393] Because of this absence in continuity, the identification in the classical[394] interpretation of these early *massu*-people with the people that settled in the same area only since the tenth century is problematic. On the other hand, the name "Issachar" might have been a nickname applied to any group of "mercenaries" or "corvée workers",

---

[387]Cf. above, pp. 77–8.

[388]Contrast 1 Kgs. 9:21–2, where it is said that Solomon raised corvée work from non-Israelites, but not from the Israelites. We will return to this problem below.

[389]S. Herrmann, *Geschichte Israels in alttestamentlicher Zeit*, München ²1980, 127–9. See also Hecke, *Juda und Israel*, 102–3; Ahlström, *History of Palestine*, 513, n. 2.

[390]Gal, "The Settlement of Issachar", 79–86.

[391]Gal, "The Settlement of Issachar", 80–1; idem, "Iron I in Lower Galilee and the Margins of the Jezreel Valley", in: I. Finkelstein, N. Na'aman, *From Nomadism to Monarchy: Archaeological and Historical Aspects of Early Israel*, Jerusalem 1993, 35–46, esp. 45; Finkelstein, *Archaeology of the Israelite Settlement*, 94–7.

[392]Gal, "Settlement of Issachar", 80–1; Finkelstein, *Archaeology of the Israelite Settlement*, 92–3; idem, "Ethnicity and Origin of the Iron I Settlers in the Highlands of Canaan: Can the Real Israel Stand Up?" *BA* 59 (1996) 198–212, 201.

[393]Cf. D.L. Esse, "The Collared Pithos at Megiddo: Ceramic Distribution and Ethnicity", *JNES* 51 (1992) 81–103, esp. 88–95, 101–2.

[394]This interpretation is found in almost every commentary and study of the text. Cf. in addition to the literature mentioned in Chapter One; *e.g.* Zobel, *SuG*, 85–7; Westermann, *Genesis 37–50*, 266; Sarna, *Genesis*, 338–40; Hamilton, *Book of Genesis*, 666–7.

rather than a name connected to only one group (= tribe). Moreover, it is possible that the name Issachar was somehow related to the area where those early "corvée workers" had been at work according to the El Amarna letters. Finally, it should be emphasized that the saying of Issachar in itself reflects conditions that already existed in the Amarna period, so it cannot be excluded that the saying of Issachar originated in that period.[395] So, in this sense, the classical interpretation cannot be ruled out completely.

With regard to our saying it is important to note that Issachar settled for the sake of the "land" and the "rest", and was willing to pay the price of being a מַס עֹבֵד "serving corvée worker". Some scholars consider the description "who rests between the donkey packs", and the terms "good" and "rest" as a reference to the territory in which Issachar settled.[396] In view of the direct idiomatic parallel of this expression with the description of the forced labour Solomon raised (1 Kgs. 9:21)[397] it is striking that the settlement in the territory of Issachar began in the era of the United Monarchy. Yet, of course the reference in 1 Kgs. 9:21–22 seems to contradict the relationship between Gen. 49:15–16 and the events during the reign of Solomon, because it denies that any of the Israelites were made to עֶבֶד "slave". However, 1 Kgs. 9:21–22 also contradicts 1 Kgs. 5:27–28 (E.T. 5:13–14) where it is said that Solomon raised corvée work (מַס) out of all Israel.[398] Some scholars have tried to remove the contradiction between 1 Kgs. 9:21–22 and 5:27–28 (E.T. 5:13–14) by suggesting that there is a difference between simple מַס and מַס עֹבֵד, the latter meaning a permanent slavery or corvée work.[399] However, as has been argued in Chapter Two,[400] the identical use of מַס and מַס עֹבֵד argues against

---

[395] This raises the question whether the interpretation of the saying as refering to the territory of Issachar (cf. the following main text) might be wrong.

[396] Van Selms, *Genesis, dl. II*, 277; Westermann, *Genesis 37–50*, 266; Sarna, *Genesis*, 339; Wenham, *Genesis 16–50*, 480.

[397] Cf. also 1 Kgs. 4:6; 5:27–8 (ET, 5:13–4); 9:15; 12:18. It is true, of course, that in later times there was also "forced labour"; cf. N. Avigad, "The Chief of the Corvée", *IEJ* 30 (1980) 170–3; idem, "The Contribution of Hebrew Seals to an Understanding of Israelite Religion and Society", in: P.D. Miller *et al.* (eds.), *Ancient Israelite Religion: Essays ... F.M. Cross*, Philadelphia (PA) 195–208, 203–4. Yet, our main interest is now the combination of "corvee work" and "settlement", a combination that is not found in later times as far as we are aware.

[398] J. Gray, *I & II Kings* (OTL), London 1964, 148, 233–4; H.A. Brongers, *I Koningen* (PredOT), Nijkerk 1967, 107–8.

[399] M. Haran, "The Gibeonites, the Nethinim and the Sons of Solomon's Servants", *VT* 11 (1961) 159–69, 162–4; Mettinger, *Solomonic State Officials*, 128–39.

[400] Pp. 158–61.

this classification. Some observations tend to support the interpretation that Solomon did force Israel (*i.e.* the North) to corvée work, comparable to the description of Issachar in Gen. 49:14–15:

1. In 1 Kgs. 5:28 we find the note that Adoniram[401] was עַל־הַמַּס "in charge of the corvée". In 1 Kgs. 12:4 Rehoboam is asked to lighten the hard service (עבד) of his father, but when he refused, Israel rebelled against him, and they stoned to death Adoram, the taskmaster over מַס "corvée work". In our view the course of events demonstrates that the Israelites (*i.e.* North Israel) were forced to do hard corvée work under Solomon.[402]

2. In Gen. 49:15 it is said that Issachar will bend his shoulder לִסְבֹּל "to bear", which is used parallel to the expression מַס עֹבֵד (49:15bB). The root סבל in Exod. 1:11 is juxtaposed alongside מס suggesting that these words are related.[403] In 1 Kgs. 5:29 (E.T. 5:15) it is related that Israelites also functioned as "burden-bearers" (נֹשֵׂא סַבָּל), while in 1 Kgs. 11:28 it is said that Jeroboam

---

[401] The name אֲדֹנִירָם "Adoniram" is probably a later, theological correction of the Baʻalistic name אֲדֹרָם "Adoram"; cf. 2 Sam. 20:24; 1 Kgs. 4:6; 5:28; 12:18. For this interpretation, see 1 Chr. 10:18: הֲדֹרָם "Hadoram" which contains the theophoric element הדד/אדד "Hadad". Because in the list of officials, where this correction seems to have taken place, an identical correction has taken place (אֲלִיחֹרֶף > אליחרף; 1 Kgs. 4:3 [cf. Mettinger, *Solomonic State Officials*, 29–30]), and as known more often in the Deuteronomistic History, whereas the Chronicler preceived mostly the original form, this interpretation of the name "Adoniram" is the most likely. See Mettinger, *op.cit.*, 133.

[402] The text in 1 Kgs. 9:21–22 might be considered as a later (Deuteronomistic) elaboration of the text (cf. the expression "to this day"), see I. Mendelsohn, "On Corvée Labor in Ancient Canaan and Israel", *BASOR* 167 (1962) 31–6, 33, with n. 15; Gray, *I & II Kings*, 234; Brongers, *I Koningen*, 107–8; G.W. Ahlström, *Royal Administration and National Religion in Ancient Palestine* (SHANE, 1), Leiden 1982, 36, n. 61. Contrast, however, Mettinger, *Solomonic State Officials*, 134–5; M.J. Mulder, *Koningen vertaald en verklaard, deel I: I Koningen 1–7* (COT), Kampen 1987, 185. This text can be related to Deut. 20:10–8, dealing with the besieged cities. In 20:16–7 we find the listing of the people of the land who should be put to death, the Hittites, Amorites, Canaanites, Perizzites, Hivites and Jebusites, which corresponds to the list of people Solomon let do corvée work, the Amorites, Hittites, Perizzites, Hivites and Jebusites. In our view the relationship between these two texts is comparable to the relationship between 1 Kgs. 10:14–11:8 and Deut. 17:14–20. On the relation between Israelites and Canaanites in biblical literature, cf. C. Houtman, "Zwei Sichtweisen von Israel als Minderheit inmitten der Bewohner Kanaans: Ein Diskussionsbeitrag zum Verhältnis von J und Dtr(G)", in: M. Vervenne, J. Lust (eds.), *Deuteronomy and Deuteronomic Literature: Fs C.H.W. Brekelmans* (BEThL, 133), Leuven 1997, 213–31.

[403] Cf. also Mettinger, *Solomonic State Officials*, 138.

was set לְכָל־סֵבֶל of the house of Joseph.[404] This too suggests that during Solomon's reign the Israelites had to do corvée work in the same sense as Issachar in Gen. 49:14–15.

3. Although it is denied in 1 Kgs. 9:22 that any of the Israelites were was made to slave (עֶבֶד), it is obvious from 1 Kgs. 12:4 that the service of the Israelites should be considered as slavery. The terms applied here for their service, עֲבֹדַת אָבִיךָ הַקָּשָׁה, is the same as applied to the "hard service" of the Israelites in Egypt: עֲבֹדָה קָשָׁה (Exod. 1:14). In our view it is therefore unmistakable that Solomon's reign in the North was based on exploitation of the human resources for the benefit of his own power and glory.

4. It has been argued that it is inconceivable that "thousands of Israelites should have been reduced to outright slavery — for no crime or indebtedness — without this giving rise to immediate and violent repercussions".[405] Generally it has been considered to be problematic and an injustice that Solomon would have forced the Israelites to do corvée work and for that reason the restriction in 1 Kgs. 9:21–22 is accepted as somehow a reliable source of information concerning the corvée work during Solomon's reign.[406] However, these considerations are mainly based on the presuppositions that (1), Israel is not indigenous in the land (cf. 1 Kgs. 9:21–22); (2) all Israel is principally a unity, and Judah and Israel are one. Yet, the former supposition has to be doubted very seriously, because it is almost commonly acknowledged that archaeological and textual data suggest that the early Israelites may be regarded as autochtonous in Canaan (within its biblical borders).[407] The second point is contradicted

---

[404] It is not clear, whether בֵּית יוֹסֵף "house of Joseph" refers only to the tribes Ephraim and Manasseh, or to the North in general; Mettinger, *Solomonic State Officials*, 134.

[405] Haran, "The Gibeonites", 163–4.

[406] Cf. Haran, "The Gibeonites", 162–4; Mettinger, *Solomonic State Officials*, 134–7; Mulder, *I Koningen 1–7*, 184–5.

[407] Cf. on this matter the following works, which might reflect the present state of research and the diverging scholarly views: A. Kempinski, "How Profoundly Canaanized Were the Early Israelites", *ZDPV* 108 (1992) 1–7; W.G. Dever, *Recent Archaeological Discoveries and Biblical Research*, Seattle (WA) 1990, 39–84; idem, "Archaeological Data on the Israelite Settlement: A Review of Two Recent Works", *BASOR* 284 (1991) 77–90; idem, "'Will the Real Israel Please Stand Up?' Archaeology and Israelite Historiography: Part I", *BASOR* 297 (1995) 61–80; idem, "'Will the Real Israel Please Stand Up?' Part II: Archaeology and the Religions of Ancient Israel", *BASOR* 298 (1995) 37–58; V. Fritz, "Die Landnahme der israelitischen Stämme in Kanaan", *ZDPV* 106 (1990) 63–77; Finkelstein, *The*

by the text of 1 Kings itself, reflecting the dichotomy of Judah
and Israel by distinguishing between these two entities.[408] For
that reason it has to be doubted whether Solomon would have
had any scruple to force the Israelites to do corvée work.[409]

In our view these data argue in favour of the assumption that Solomon
subdued Israel to corvée work and that consequently Issachar was also
forced to do this work. As a consequence the saying of Issachar could
be related to the era of David and Solomon, because the features described in that saying fit this era quite well. However, the description

---

Archaeology of the Israelite Settlement, passim; idem, "Ethnicity and Origin of
the Iron I Settlers in the Highlands of Canaan: Can the Real Israel Stand Up?"
BiAr 59 (1996) 198–212; idem, "The Great Transformation: The 'Conquest' of the
Highlands Frontiers and the Rise of the Territorial States", in: T.E. Levy (ed.),
The Archaeology of Society in the Holy Land, London 1995, 349–65; O. Loretz,
Ugarit und die Bibel: Kanaanäische Götter und Religion im Alten Testament,
Darmstadt 1990; De Moor, *RoY*[(2)], *passim*; idem, "Ugarit and Israelite Origins",
in: J.A. Emerton, *Congress Volume: Paris 1992* (SVT, 40), Leiden 1995, 205–
38; Korpel, *RiC, passim*; M.S. Smith, *The Early History of God: Yahweh and the
Other Deities in Ancient Israel*, San Francisco 1990; H.M. Barstad, "Nye bidrag til
spørsmålet om det gamle Israels religion", *NTT* 92 (1991) 217–26; C.H.J. de Geus,
"Nieuwe gegevens over het oude Israël", *Phoenix* 37 (1991) 32–41; R. Gnuse, "Is-
raelite Settlement of Canaan: A Peaceful Internal Process", *BTB* 21 (1991) 56–
66, 109–17; H. Ringgren, "Early Israel", in: *Storia e Tradizioni di Israele: Scritti
... J.A. Soggin*, Brescia 1991, 217–20; A.J. Frendo, "Five Recent Books on the
Emergence of Ancient Israel: Review Article", *PEQ* 124 (1992) 144–51; N. van
der Westhuizen, H. Olivier, "Die oorsprong van Israel volgens resente navorsing",
In die Skriflig 26 (1992) 221–46; N.K. Gottwald, "Recent Studies of the Social
World of Premonarchic Israel", *CR:BS* 1 (1993) 163–89; R.S. Hess, "Early Israel
in Canaan: A Survey of Recent Evidence and Interpretations", *PEQ* 125 (1993)
125–42; P. Kaswalder, "L'archeologia e le origine di Israele", *RivBib* 41 (1993)
171–88; K. van der Toorn, *Family Religion in Babylonia, Syria and Israel: Continuity and Change in the Forms of Religious Life* (SHCANE, 7), Leiden 1996,
183–205.

[408]Cf. 1 Kgs. 2:32; 4:7(!), 19(!), 20; 5:5 (E.T. 4:25). This distinction is recognized
also in the studies on this period, especially in connection with the corvée work
and the division of the North into twelve districts, excluding Judah (apparently)
from the duty to provide the court with food; cf. A. Alt, "Die Staatenbildung
der Israeliten in Palästina", in: *KS*, Bd. II, 1–65, 43–4; idem, "Israels Gaue unter
Salomo", *ibid.*, 76–89, 89; Mulder, *I Koningen 1–7*, 185. For a partly different
meaning, cf. Mettinger, *Solomonic State Officials*, 121–124; cf. further pp. 136–
9. With regard to the twelve districts, contrast Na'aman, *Borders and Districts*,
167–201.

[409]It was quite common for a king to make use of the resources of his land,
including the people who were living in it. This is known, for example, from
Ugarit where the use of the labour of men and beast was the right of the king; cf.
J. Gray, *The Legacy of Canaan: The Ras Shamra Texts and their Relevance to the
Old Testament* (SVT, 5), Leiden 1957, 163; idem, *I & II Kings* (OTL), London
1964, 129–30, 131–2, 233.

of Issachar is, as noted above, mostly related to the *ḫapiru* from the Amarna period; is such a relatively late dating conceivable then? It has recently been argued by W. Zwickel,[410] that during Iron-I there were still groups in Palestine comparable to these *ḫapiru*, even though the name *ḫapiru* itself is absent in documents from the period after the Late Bronze. The best example which Zwickel gives, is the anti-Saulite gang of David (1 Sam. 22:2), which was closely connected to the establishment of David's reign. But even at the end of Solomon's reign it appears that such gangs were wandering around.[411] So, if the *ḫapiru* are not mentioned anymore in texts after the end of the Late Bronze, it does not imply such groups disappeared. Even in Solomon's era Issachar might have been a group of mercenaries who were rewarded with land, comparable to the reward of the *ḫapiru* by Labayu.[412] This indeed corresponds to the data of the survey performed by Gal, demonstrating that the territory of Issachar was only settled from the tenth century BCE on.[413]

In conclusion it has to be said that the identification of the Issacharites, as described in the saying of Issachar (Gen. 49:14–5), with the *massu*-people from the Amarna letters is by no means the only solution for the understanding of this saying. It has been shown that according to 1 Kings 1–11, during Solomon's reign Israelites had to do corvée work, a phenomenon that even lasted until the seventh century (Jer. 22:13). Because gangs, comparable to the early *ḫapiru*, occured even in Solomon's era, whereas settlement in the territory of Issachar began during the same era, a dating of this saying during Solomon's reign is to be preferred over the earlier one (also in view of the discussion of the preceding sayings).

6.5.1.7.4 Dan (49:16–17) and the Prayer (49:18)

The saying on Dan is hard to date and to relate to any tradition. Although some scholars preferred to split the saying into two distinct sayings,[414] we argued that there is no reason to separate the text of the

---

[410] W. Zwickel, "Der Beitrag der *Ḫabiru* zur Entstehung des Königtums", *UF* 28 (1996) 751–66.

[411] Zwickel, "Der Beitrag der *Ḫabiru*", 765, n. 46, referring *inter alii* to 1 Kgs. 11:24, which corresponds to his conclusion that the existence of such groups ended in the tenth century BCE.

[412] Zwickel, "Der Beitrag der *Ḫabiru*", 752–3, with n. 13, referring to EA 287:31; 289:21–4.

[413] Gal, "The Settlement of Issachar", 80–1.

[414] Cf. *e.g.* Zobel, *SuG*, 17–8, 55–61, 88–92, 96–7; H.M. Niemann, *Die Daniten: Studien zur Geschichte eines altisraelitischen Stammes* (FRLANT, 135), Göttingen 1985, 195–6.

saying over two different traditions, because the final part (49:17) is in fact an illustration of, and an elaboration on the first part (49:16).[415] The saying opens with the wish that Dan may be strong,[416] like one of the tribes of Israel, followed by the wish ("may he be", jussive) that he may be like a small but deadly animal.

In the comparison of Dan with the שְׁפִיפֹן "viper" scholars recognized the species of the Cerastes.[417] In Zobel's view this species might be regarded as an indication for the territory in which Dan lived, and if one had to choose between the northern and the southern region, the latter has to be preferred.[418] The reference to the "horse" and the "rider"[419] are explained by him as references to the Egyptian armies, or to the local Canaanite kings who might have owned these chariots. In his view, this would result in a dating for our saying between 1550 and 1225 BCE.[420]

Yet, H.M. Niemann has convincingly demonstrated that Zobel's geographical conclusion is by no means compelling because, first, the species is not decisively defined; secondly, the difference in soil- and vegetation-conditions between the northern and southern territory of Dan is not as different as Zobel presumed; thirdly, the assumed species occurs also in the northern part of Israel.[421] Niemann himself prefers the northern territory where the city of Dan is found. In his view, the image of a small animal that attacks a much bigger animal attracts the attention, not the animal itself, so Dan is not meant as an aggressive people but just as a small people albeit one that is able to defend itself.[422] The image of the horse and its rider might suggest the threat of a powerful and dangerous assailant; yet the snake that

---

[415]Cf. in this respect already J.A. Emerton, "Some Difficult Words in Genesis 49", in: P.R. Ackroyd, B. Lindars (eds.), *Words and Meanings: Essays ... D.W. Thomas*, London 1968, 81–93, 90, although he did not exclude the possibility that the saying originally consisted of two independent sayings.

[416]On this rendering, cf. above, pp. 165–8.

[417]Zobel, *SuG*, 18. For additional bibliographical references and other interpretations of the species, cf. Niemann, *Die Daniten*, 197, with nn. 13–15.

[418]Zobel, *SuG*, 88.

[419]Zobel, *SuG*, 18–9, relates the "rider" exclusively to the riding of a chariot. However, the root רכב is to ambiguous to render it exclusively to the riding of a chariot alone, or, on the other hand, to a rider who sits on the horseback; cf. for the latter opinion S. Mowinckel, "Drive and/or Ride in O.T.", *VT* 12 (1962) 278–99, 288. This question is in fact irrelavant to the dating of the text, for horse riding occured already in quite early times, cf. A.R. Schulman, "Egyptian Representations of Horsemen and Riding in the New Kingdom", *JNES* 16 (1957) 263–71; W. Decker, "Sattel", *LdÄ*, Bd. V, 494.

[420]Zobel, *SuG*, 88–9.

[421]Niemann, *Die Daniten*, 197–8, with n. 18.

[422]Niemann, *Die Daniten*, 199–200.

is willing to attack such an assailant suggests the comparison with a people that refuses to retreat. This would imply that we are here dealing with a people with a territory to defend, rather than with nomadic people who would give ground more easily and move to less dangerous areas[423] — which seemed to have been the case in the southern district, where they came from, according to the biblical tradition.[424] Finally, in his view the image of the "horse" and its "rider" are, if the northern district is thought of, best interpreted as the Arameans who lived to the north and north-east of Dan. This political power is in its magnitude the most suited candidate for this image, especially because the territory of the Arameans, namely Syria is connected with horses and horse breeding.[425]

In our view both positions represented above attach too much weight to the image of the "horse" and "its rider" (49:17b). The image is primarily meant to make a contrast to the much smaller "viper", and was not necessarily meant to describe an enemy who possessed horses (and probably chariots), although it might have been in view. Yet, with regard to the possible powers who might have formed the threat for Dan (Egypt or Aram) both observations seem to be possible, whereas other identifications cannot be excluded. The identification of these enemies might partly depend on the supposed territory Dan lived in. In our view Niemann's observation — that the image of the snake suggests a small people who refuses to retreat — is to the point here. So, as argued in the previous paragraph, this implies that Dan had a territory to defend, which would suggest Dan's to the territory in the North.[426] In addition it might be noted that Dan's position in the North is of strategic importance and for that reason too their function "to be strong like one of the tribes of Israel" is best related to the northern territory.[427] Although Egypt controlled for a

---

[423] Cf. on this subject also E.J. van der Steen, "The Central East Jordan Valley in the Late Bronze and Early Iron Ages", *BASOR* 302 (1996) 51–74, 66.

[424] Niemann, *Die Daniten*, 200–1.

[425] Niemann, *Die Daniten*, 201–2. Cf. with regard to the horses and horse breeding and their origin H. Weippert, "Pferd und Streitwagen", *BRL*, 250–5; L. Störk, "Pferd", *LdÄ*, Bd. IV, 1009–13.

[426] The fact that Dan is described as attacking "the heels" might imply a kind of guerrilla war (De Moor, *RoY*, 110; *RoY*², 117). Yet, this provides no solution with regard to the dating of our saying or the conditions Dan lived in, because the description of Dan as a small and comparatively vulnerable entity would also fit Dan in a period when it was settled and lived in a city. The wish that he would be like a viper, small but deadly, defending itself against invading enemies is also conceivable with regard to the city of Dan located at the most remote borders.

[427] It goes without saying that the northern territory is more or less identical to the city. The people of middle Bronze Age II-C and Late Bronze, "as well as those

long time during the Late Bronze Age the territory of Palestine and might be meant therefore in this saying as well, it seems more plausible that if the northern territory is meant, enemies invading from the north are thought of, which most likely refers to the Arameans.

With regard to the possible period to which this saying can be related, the time Dan was found at this strategic position within the boundaries of Israel might be considered to be the most relevant period. Considering the period that the Arameans became a threat to the northern part of Israel, the *terminus post quem* is generally placed after 1100 BCE,[428] but in light of recent studies this date might be set toward the end of the thirteenth century BCE.[429] This dating corresponds with the period that a new settlement started at Tel Dan at the beginning of Iron Age I, when the city was occupied by a new group of settlers. The *terminus ante quem* is of course the end of Iron IIB, when the territory was incorporated in the Assyrian province of Megiddo and no longer part of the Israelite territory.[430]

On the other hand, the Israelite territory was restricted to central Palestine and part of Transjordan until the reign of David.[431] If we take the beginning of this period, Iron Age I, this time raises some

---

of the Iron Age I, lived within the enclosure and safety of the earthen ramparts. Neither did the tribe of Dan venture outside these ramparts" (A. Biran, "Dan, Tel", *EAEHL*, vol. I, 313–21, 321).

[428] Niemann, *Die Daniten*, 202–3. Cf. also B. Mazar, "The Aramean Empire and Its Relations with Israel", *BA* 25 (1962) 97–120, 101–2 (= idem, *The Early Biblical Period: Historical Essays*, Jerusalem 1986, 151–72, 154–5); A. Malamat, "The Aramaeans", in: D.J. Wiseman (ed.), *Peoples of Old testament Times*, Oxford 1973, 134–55, 134–5.

[429] K.R. Veenhof, "De geschiedenis van het oude Nabije Oosten tot de tijd van Alexander de Grote", *BijbH*, dl. 1, 278–441, 343 (after the thirteenth century); J.C. de Moor, "Ugarit and the Origin of Job", in: G.J. Brooke *et al.* (eds.), *Ugarit and the Bible: Proceedings of the International Symposium on Ugarit and the Bible, Manchester, September 1992* (UBL, 11), Münster 1994, 225–57, 229; idem, "Ugarit and Israelite Origins", 235 (with bibliography in nn. 131–4); idem, *RoY²*, 135–6.

[430] Cf. for the archaeological description of Dan: A. Biran, "Dan (Place)", *ABD*, vol. 2, 12–7; "Dan", *NEAEHL*, vol. 1, 323–32; idem, *Biblical Dan*, Jerusalem 1994, 125–273.

[431] Cf. the map in *e.g.* W. Dietrich, *Die frühe Königszeit in Israel: 10. Jahrhundert v. Chr.* (BE, 3), Stuttgart 1997, 158, Abb. 12 (= Ahlström, *History of Ancient Palestine*, map 13 [between pp. 542-3]). See also A.D.H. Mayes, "The Period of the Judges and the Rise of the monarchy", in: J.H. Hayes, J.M. Miller (eds.), *Israelite and Judaean History*, London 1977, 285–331, 329; H. Jagersma, *De geschiedenis van Israël in het oudtestamentische tijdvak*, Kampen ²1984, 131–2; Mulder, "Geschiedenis van Israël", 72. Contrast Y. Aharoni, M. Avi-Yonah, *The Macmillan Bible Atlas*, New York, London 1968, 61 (map 90), taking the "Ashurites" from 2 Sam. 2:9 as a designation for the whole Galilean region.

problems. Although we know for sure from the Mernephtah stele that there existed a people called "Israel" at the end of Late Bronze/Early Iron I, and that, on the other hand, from that period several ancient texts using the name "Israel" were preserved in the Hebrew Bible[432] yet, this does not imply that Dan was already a part of Israel in that era. In our view we do not have any decisive clues which would allow us to come to that conclusion.

Yet, with regard to our diachronic analysis we may refer to one specific feature in the text, that clearly marks our text as distinct from the "pro-Joseph" layer. The wish is pronounced that Dan may be strong "like one of the tribes of Israel" (שִׁבְטֵי יִשְׂרָאֵל), which implies that Israel consists of several "tribes" (שְׁבָטִים). Our proposed reading of Gen. 47:31, however, seems to suggest that Israel itself was regarded as a "tribe" (מַטֶּה).[433] This difference betrays a different perception of the entity "Israel" and as such it reveals the different layers of the text. The idea of Israel being a "tribe" is found in the "pro-Joseph"

---

[432] Cf. esp. Psalm 68. For the interpretation and dating of this Psalm, cf. De Moor, *RoY*, 118–28; *RoY*², 171–98; idem, "Ugarit and Israelite Origins", 205–38.

Of course one might like to refer to Judges 5, where several tribes are listed, *inter alii* Dan (Judg. 5:17aB), yet this reference is not without problems, because the listing of the tribes is suspect. Note for example that several entities are praised for partaking in the battle, using a designation which is more or less geographical; Judg. 5:14 seems to give *in nuce* a description of Israel as known later under Saul's reign (cf. above, with previous footnote [note for example the threefold מִן "from" in this verse]). On the other hand some are only questioned why they did not partake; but Meroz, an unknown city(?) is cursed (5:23). This makes the references to the other tribes suspect and it might well be that these were added later on, comparable to Ps. 68:26–36 (cf. De Moor, *ibid.*), whereas the partaking groups or regions were only described in 5:14 (Ephraim is generally considered to be a GN; Benjamin might contain a reference to the south; Zebulun to the Carmel[?; cf. our discussion above]; Machir a reference to the Bashan region). Cf. for the problems and other solutions, H.-P. Müller, "Der Aufbau des Deboraliedes", *VT* 16 (1966) 446–59; N. Na'aman, "Literary and Topographical Notes on the Battle of Kishon (Judges iv–v)", *VT* 40 (1990) 423–36; H. Schulte "Richter 5: Das Debora-Lied, Versuch einer Deutung", in: E. Blum *et al.* (Hrsg.), *Die hebraeische Bibel und ihre zweifache Nachgeschichte: Fs R. Rendtorff*, Neukirchen-Vluyn 1990, 177–91; J.C. de Moor, "The Twelve Tribes in the Song of Deborah", *VT* 43 (1993) 483–94; H.-D. Neef, "Deboraerzählung und Deboralied: Beobachtungen zum Verhähltnis von Jdc. iv und v", *VT* 44 (1994) 47–59; D. Vieweger, "Überlegungen zur Landnahme israelitischer Stämme unter besonderer Berücksichtigung der galiläischen Berglandgebiete", *ZDPV* 109 (1993) 20–36, 23–4.

[433] Cf. above, pp. 462–464. The fact that a different word is used for "tribe", *viz.* מַטֶּה and שֵׁבֶט, is unimportant. Both words have an identical etymology (basic meaning is "rod, staff, etc."), whose meaning was apparently synonymous, see Isa. 9:3; 10:5, 15, 24; 14:5; 28:27; Ezek. 19:11, 14. Furthermore, Num. 18:2 (cf. also 36:3) and Josh. 13:29 clearly demonstrates that both words in the sense of "tribe" were synonyms.

layer; yet, the idea of Israel consisting of several tribes belongs to the "pro-Judah" tradition.

Coming to the end of our text we are confronted with a remarkable interjection (49:18), almost generally considered to be a gloss. In our view there is no evidence in the Testament itself, or in the context that this line must have belonged to the patriarch's speech. On the contrary, the analysis of the poetic structure of the Testament showed a regular structure at the macro level, but only if verse 18 is considered a later expansion. The insertion of this line might betray an early liturgical setting of our text,[434] where the prediction of Dan attacking his enemies is followed by the prayer for God's salvation, derived from the Psalms.[435] This gloss might betray at the same time an early interpretation of the text as a reference to Samson, probably reflecting Samson's final prayer in the temple of Dagon (Judg. 16:28).[436] However, as a gloss the line belongs neither to the "pro-Joseph", nor to the "pro-Judah" layer.   .

6.5.1.7.5   Gad (49:19)

The saying on Gad is a skilful play with words; yet, it does not contain any historical information which might be valuable to our study.[437] The tribe is depicted as living in an area where the danger of being raided is great. However, the tribe will be able to defend itself.[438] Historically the tribe can be traced to at least the beginning of Iron Age II, which is made clear by the Mesha inscription, line 10, stating that Gad lived there "from old",[439] which might agree with the date

---

[434] D.N. Freedman, "The Poetic Structure of Deuteronomy 33", in: G.A. Rendsburg *et al.* (ed.), *The Bible World: Essays ... C.H. Gordon*, New York 1980, 25–46, 34.

[435] Ps. 119:166; cf. also Pss. 38:16; 39:8 55:24b. See: Van Selms, *Genesis, dl. II*, 278; Westermann, *Genesis 37–50*, 268; Sarna, *Genesis*, 341; Wenham, *Genesis 16–50*, 481–2; Hamilton, *Book of Genesis*, 670–2.

[436] On later interpretations, cf. TN; TPsJ; and Genesis Rabba, 98:14; 99:11. See also R. Syrén, *The Blessings in the Targums: A Study on the Targumic Interpretations of Genesis 49 and Deuteronomy 33* (AAA.H, 64/1), Åbo 1986, 113–5.

[437] Zobel, *SuG*, 99, 100–1; Sarna, *Genesis*, 341; Hamilton, *Book of Genesis*, 672–3.

[438] As noted with Dan, the attacking of the heels might betray a kind of guerrilla war (cf. p. 554, n. 426 above). In connection with Gad this might suggest that Gad is still a kind of raiding band itself. Yet, this does not help with regard to the date of this saying or the conditions Gad lived in, because people who lived in a city could also raid (פשט, 1 Sam. 27:8; גְדוּד, 2 Sam. 3:22), and attack the enemy from behind at the heels, cf. 1 Sam. 30. Finally, as we have argued with regard to Issachar, raiding groups (גְּדוּד) existed a long time in Palestine, so this might apply to Gad also.

[439] Cf. De Geus, *The Tribes of Israel*, 110. According to De Geus " 'of old' must be understood in the sense of 'as far as memory reaches', *i.e.* about three genera-

of 1 Sam. 13:7, where Gad and Gilead are mentioned side by side.[440] The territory of Gad is firmly established as being located in Transjordan, which corresponds with the fact that they lived in an area that is easily attacked by invading groups. However, this seems to be the most that can be said on the historical background of this saying, because the territory suffered frequently from raids by other people. With regard to the territory of this tribe we have to be careful because there seems to be a kind of interrelationship of this tribe "Gad" with an entity called "Gilead". The latter, however, seems to be a mainly *geographical* designation,[441] whereas the former is mainly a *tribal* designation. The observations on the historical background based on archaeological research is seriously hampered by the fact that in the same period (*viz.* the Iron Age) other groups settled in that area as well (Ammon, Moab, Edom).[442] Unfortunately the historical data do not supply sufficient information to permit any conclusions concerning the territory of Gad. At the end of Late Bronze and the beginning of Iron I there has been an enormous increase of settlements in the area,[443] which may be connected partly to the settlement of Gad in that region. Yet, there is too little information to allow us to draw any firm conclusions.

6.5.1.7.6   Asher (49:20)

It might be derived from the text that Asher lives in a very fertile

---

tions."

[440]De Geus, *The Tribes of Israel*, 110.

On the basis of the plusses to 1 Sam. 11, found in 4QSamᵃ, F.M. Cross suggested that in 1 Sam. 11 not Gad alone, but originally Reuben and Gad were found; cf. his, "The Ammonite Oppression of the Tribes of Gad and Reuben: Missing Verses from 1 Samuel 11 Found in 4QSamuelᵃ", in: H. Tadmor, M. Weinfeld (eds.), *History, Historiography and Interpretation: Studies in Biblical and Cuneiform Literatures*, Jerusalem, Leiden 1983, 148–58. Yet, in our view it is more likely that we are dealing with a later addition, adding in this way the tribe of Reuben (who also lived in that territory according to Num. 32; Josh. 13) to the text, rather than that a whole passage mentioning Reuben would have been omitted because of haplography.

[441]Cf. in this respect De Geus, *The Tribes of Israel*, 108–11. Although he assumes that in Judg. 5:17 "Gilead" is used as a tribal name (De Geus, *op.cit.*, 110), it might be interpreted as a collective designation for the people who lived in Gilead; compare a similar use for Meroz in verse 23. So, in our view it might be interpreted as a geographical designation as well.

[442]Finkelstein, *Archaeology of the Israelite Settlement*, 113.

[443]J.A. Sauer, "Transjordan in the Bronze and Iron Ages: A Critique of Glueck's Synthesis", *BASOR* 263 (1986) 1–26; Finkelstein, *Archaeology of the Israelite Settlement*, 112–7; Van der Steen, "The Central East Jordan Valley", 62–3 (and *passim*).

land. This is generally associated with the coast west of the Galilean hill country, covering the plain of Acco up to Tyre.[444] This territory was particularly suited for olive orchards and vineyards,[445] and this seems to be expressed in our saying as well.[446] The territory is known by this name in Egyptian documents, dating from the beginning of the thirteenth century.[447] The description that Asher will bring forth royal delicacies is sometimes interpreted — with reference to Judg. 1:31–32 — as a description of Asher's settlement among the Canaanite city-states or its obeisance to the Phoenician court, to which it had to deliver food.[448] However, the text is not negative (note the wishful imperfect יִתֵּן "will bring forth" or even "let him bring forth"[449]) and it might therefore reflect the responsibility to provide the Solomonic court with food from its own abundance (1 Kgs. 4:7).[450] or even to its own king in "pre-monarchic" times.[451] However, the saying is absolutely too general to relate it to a specific period and it might fit into another period just as well, even, for example, into the period of the Judges, in which the implication of the saying might also have been "delicacies fit for a king". Yet, because the territory of Asher became part of the Israelite state only during the reign of David,[452] it seems quite unlikely that the saying would have originated in "pre-monarchic" times.[453] On the other hand it has been argued that the

---

[444] Cf. *e.g.* Westermann, *Genesis 37–50*, 268.

[445] Cf. also Deut. 33:24.

[446] D.V. Edelman, "Asher", *ABD*, vol. 1, 482–3.

[447] G.W. Ahlström, *Who Were the Israelites?* Winona Lake (IN) 1986, 63; Edelman, "Asher", 482. For the discussion of the location of the territory, cf. H.-W. Fischer-Elfert, *Die satirische Streitschrift des Papyrus Anastasi I: Übersetzung und Kommentar* (ÄA, 44), Wiesbaden 1986, 192; De Moor, *RoY²*, 178.

[448] Kittel, *Stammessprüche Israels*, 31–2; Zobel, *SuG*, 101–2; Westermann, *Genesis 37–50*, 269; Sarna, *Genesis*, 341–2; Hamilton, *Book of Genesis*, 674.

[449] Cf. above, p. 172. *Pace* Kittel, *Die Stammessprüche Israels*, 31–2; Westermann, *Genesis 37–50*, 269; Hecke, *Judah und Israel*, 104, with n. 2; who all found a rebuke in this saying.

[450] Von Rad, *Erste Buch Mose*, 351; Hamilton, *Book of Genesis*, 674.

[451] De Moor, *RoY²*, 178, with reference to Papyrus Anastasi I.139 (565–7).

[452] Ahlström, *Who Were the Israelites?* 63–5; Edelman, "Asher", 482. With regard to the Galilean tribes, 1 Chr. 12:40 is remarkable and seems to imply, as Ahlström, *op.cit.*, 91–2, rightly argues, that Saul did not reign in the Galilean area.

[453] This does not exclude the possibility that certain tribes (or people of certain regions) had contact with each other and made a coalition against common enemies, as reflected in, for instance, Judges 4 and 5. In that case it appears that such contacts could surmount even "unoccupied" (*viz.* Canaanite) territory. Note that people from the North and Transjordan (Zebulun, Machir), as well as from the South (Ephraim, Benjamin) were involved in the battle in the plain of Jezreel (Judg. 5:14). Cf. also p. 556, n. 432, above.

saying can hardly have been circulating independently during the reign of Solomon.[454] However, this objection is based exclusively on the form-critical argument of the "tribal saying"; nevertheless, as part of its literary context[455] there seems to be no objection against a date during the monarchy.

6.5.1.7.7   Naphtali (49:21)

The interpretation of the saying on Naphtali is, of course, strongly dependent on the interpretation of the Hebrew text. Our rendering, which represents Naphtali as a "lambing ewe, that brings forth lovely lambs" cannot be interpreted as pejorative.[456] In our view the verse is rather positive concerning Naphtali, yet, this is in fact the most that can be said of Naphtali on the basis of this verse. The tribe's territory is found in Upper Galilee,[457] in which more extensive settlement[458] began at the end of the twelfth and beginning of the eleventh century BCE.[459] However, a relation between the historical background of the tribe and this saying seems completely absent.

6.5.1.7.8   Benjamin (49:27)

In this saying Benjamin is compared with a wolf. The wolf, like the lion,[460] is one of the most dangerous and threating animals in the Hebrew Bible. The wolf hunts especially in the evening and at night[461] and this characteristic feature of the animal is also found in our saying. It

---

[454]Kittel, *Die Stammessprüche Israels*, 31.

[455]Cf. once again Wenham's objection against the assumption that the saying on Asher would have been a tribal saying; Wenham, *Genesis 16–50*, 469–70 (cf. above, p. 53, with n. 255).

[456]In this respect we do not agree with those who interpret the saying in a negative sense, like S. Gevirtz, "Naphtali in the 'Blessing of Jacob'", *JBL* 103 (1984) 513–21; or leave the possibility of a pejorative meaning open, like Sarna, *Genesis*, 342; S.P. Jeansonne, "Naphtali", *ABD*, vol. 4, 1021–2, 1021; Wenham, *Genesis 16–50*, 483; Hamilton, *Book of Genesis*, 677.

[457]R. Frankel, "Galilee (Prehellenistic)", *ABD*, vol. 2, 879–95, 889.

[458]Breeding sheep is not restricted to a nomadic or settled society, cf. Gen. 30:40 (Jacob, nomadic); 1 Sam. 16:11; 17:15 (David, settled in Bethlehem). Moreover, the image of the shepherd is frequently used in settled societies for gods and kings, which implies that breeding sheep was an obvious part of that society. On the imagery, cf. J.C. de Moor, "De goede herder: Oorsprong en vroege geschiedenis van de herdersmetafoor", in: G. Heitink *et al.*, *Bewerken en bewaren: Studies ... K. Runia*, Kampen 1982, 36–45; J.W. Vancil, "Sheep, Shepherd", *ABD*, vol. 5, 1187–90.

[459]Finkelstein, *Archaeology of the Israelite Settlement*, 97–110.

[460]Cf. the fact that in Ezek. 22:25, 27 the lion and the wolf are used in an identical fashion; in Zeph. 3:3 as parallels.

[461]Hab. 1:8; Zeph. 3:3.

is significant that this animal, together with the lion (אֲרִי), is used to depict kings and princes, albeit generally because of their dangerous character.[462] In our view the saying contains, because of this, an allusion to the fact that there has been a king from Benjamin.[463] The use of the metaphor of the wolf for the kings of Judah as dangerous and fearful rulers might be of some importance for the diachronic analysis, again similar to that of the use of the lion for Judah.[464] Compare especially the occurrence of this metaphor in Zeph. 3:3 which resembles this saying and might betray knowledge of our saying:[465]

Her judges are wolves of the evening, (3bA)	שֹׁפְטֶיהָ זְאֵבֵי עֶרֶב
they have no strength[466] in the morning. (3bB)	לֹא גָרְמוּ לַבֹּקֶר

In Ezek. 22:27 we find a similar comparison applied to Israel's princes (שָׂרֶיהָ), which might partly be dependent on Zeph. 3:3b,[467] but which in view of the other allusions to Genesis 49 in the first part of Ezekiel might also reflect knowledge of our text. Compare especially the use in the first part of Ezekiel of several elements of Genesis 49 which seems to give a clear *terminus ante quem*, and in that respect the Exile might be considered the era before which our text originated.

6.5.1.8 Additional Comments and Summary

Summarizing now the results of the diachronic reading of the Testa-

---

[462]Ezek. 22:27; Zeph. 3:3. Cf. also A.S. van der Woude, *Habakuk, Zefanja* (PredOT), Nijkerk 1978, 126, also referring to the seal of Shema‘ (ANEP, # 276).

[463]In this respect we do not agree with Zobel, *SuG*, 107–8; Wenham, *Genesis 16–50*, 487, that the saying has to be old, because it does not reflect a leadership from Benjamin, not to say the kingship of Saul. Yet, we have to admit that it is just an allusion to this kingship and that the metaphor of wolves could be used for raiding troops of the Chaldeans as well (Hab. 1:8).

[464]Cf. above, p. 526.

[465]For this difficult verse, and the problems of interpretation, see: Van der Woude, *Habakuk, Zefanja*, 126–7; B. Jongeling, "Jeux de mots en Sophonie iii 1 et 3?" *VT* 21 (1971) 541–7; idem, "Inzake Zefanja 3:3b", in: F. García Martínez *et al.* (red.), *Profeten en profetische geschriften*, Kampen, Nijkerk s.a. [1987], 117–8; E. Ben Zvi, *A Historical-Critical Study of the Book of Zephaniah* (BZAW, 198), Berlin 1991, 190–5; J. Vlaardingenbroek, *Sefanja vertaald en verklaard* (COT), Kampen 1993, 172–3; A. Berlin, *Zephaniah: A New Translation with Introduction and Commentary* (AB, 25A), New York 1994, 128–9.

[466]This interpretation is found in I.J. Ball, *A Rhetorical Study of Zephaniah*, Berkeley (CA) 1988, 157–9; Ben Zvi, *Book of Zephaniah*, 913–4, on the basis of the meaning of the noun גֶּרֶם "bone", and especially in Gen. 49:14 with the meaning "strong". In other translations we find renderings like "to gnaw off" for the verb גרם, cf. *HAL*, 195; or "who do not restrain, slow down their step", Van der Woude, *Habakuk, Zefanja*, 126 (with reference to LXX).

[467]Vlaardingenbroek, *Sefanja*, 168–9; Berlin, *Zephaniah*, 138.

ment of Jacob, we have reached the following conclusions. The framework of the Testament (49:1–2, 28) must be taken as part of the "pro-Judah" layer, being created to introduce the other sons of the patriarch into the scene.[468] As the patriarch's final words on the future of his sons it functions as the interpretative introduction to what follows . Simultaneously, this framework functions as the key to the classification of all the other sayings. Gen. 49:1–2 introduces the other sons into the scene, which is necessary for the course of the events, in order to allow Jacob to utter his sayings. Therefore it is inevitable to assign the sayings on the other brothers to a different layer than the one of the framework.

The sayings on Reuben and on Simeon & Levi can be considered to be part of the "pro-Judah" layer, because they function within the Testament as the legitimation of Judah's preferential status, although he is the younger brother. These sayings are not regarded as ancient sayings adopted in the text.[469] In the Testament Judah is given the first place among his brothers and as such these sayings seems to reflect a period when Judah had the leading position among his brothers. We did not find any indications that older material was used in the saying on Judah, and if so, we have to assume the adaptation of the text in certain cases. Yet, no such indications were found. The Joseph-saying favours Joseph as very important and as such it might be assigned to the "pro-Joseph" layer. Yet, several lines in the text might have been added in order to adapt the text. In our view 49:24bA, 26aC and a part of 26b were added whereas these additions did not concern theological but political issues.

With regard to the assignment to the "pro-Judah" or the "pro-Joseph" layer of the sayings on the remaining brothers (Zebulun, Is-

---

[468] As mentioned before, the fact that Joseph would be alone on the scene with his father corresponds to Isaac's blessing of Jacob (though intended for the eldest son Esau; Genesis 27). Especially remarkable is the fact that Isaac intends to bless his oldest son with the lordship over his brothers, without their presence (27:29; note the plural [also in 27:37 "all his brothers"], whereas we know only of one brother, *viz.* Esau; cf. also p. 570, n. 497 below). So, in our view it cannot be a problem that in our analysis Joseph is called "the first one among his brothers" (48:22), whereas these brothers are not at the scene at that moment, nor any later. Cf. also below, where we will deal with the addition of the other brothers to the text.

[469] Cf. recently U. Schorn, *Ruben und das System der Zwölf Stämme Israels: Redaktionsgeschichtliche Untersuchungen zur Bedeutung des Erstgeborenen Jakobs* (BZAW, 248), Berlin 1997, 248–55, who summarizes her analysis of Gen. 49:3–12 "Im Zusammenhang mit den bereits aufgewiesenen inhaltlichen und formalen Übereinstimmungen dürften die hier genannten sprachlichen Beobachtungen deutlich machen, daß die untersuchten Verse einer hand zuzuweisen sind."

sachar, Dan, Gad, Asher, Naphtali and Benjamin), we have to conclude that there is virtually no basis for such an assignment, except for their being introduced by the "pro-Judah" framework. In the saying on Dan we found only one small indication that might form a contrast with the "pro-Joseph" layer, namely the reference to the "tribes of Israel", contrasted with Israel as a tribe (47:31) and which might therefore be regarded as being part of the "pro-Judah" layer.[470] Regarding the other sayings we did not find any indication which would allow an assignment to either of these two layers. Possibilities for a chronological classification of the text on the basis of textual and archaeological data appeared to be limited. With regard to Zebulun we concluded that an origin in the era of the United Monarchy is likely, whereas an earlier date during Iron I cannot be excluded. For Issachar it appeared that an origin during the tenth century was the most likely. For the saying on Dan we found — next to the "pro-Judah" element — an origin after 1100 BCE and before the end of Iron II. Concerning Gad and Naphtali we were unable to infer any conclusions, whereas we dated the saying on Asher somewhere during the monarchy. Finally in the saying on Benjamin it is possible that there was a reference to the kingship of Saul although only as an allusion. Because the metaphor found in the saying on Benjamin in Zeph. 3:3 and Ezek. 22:27 seems to be applied in a negative sense to the rulers of Judah, we can assume that the Exile forms the *terminus ante quem*.

As a consequence we have to assign the bulk of Genesis 49:1–28 to the "pro-Judah" layer. The framework (49:1–2, 28), which was assigned to the "pro-Judah" layer, and the first three sayings (49:3–12), are in fact the key to this assignment, forcing us to assign the sayings, except the one of Joseph (49:22–26), to this layer. This conclusion corresponds with the fact that the analysis of the poetic structure showed a regular composition, which suggests that the poem in its present form is the work of a skilled composer. If we would permit the possibility of a few smaller additions to the text, the regular structure would be disturbed. In our view, only the assumption of a very thorough editing, in which the other sayings were added to the blessing of Joseph found in the "pro-Joseph" layer, satisfactorily explains the present regular structure and a possible earlier version mentioning Joseph as the only one being blessed. Other assumptions have to allow for the disturbance of that structure. This is especially important with regard to the relationship between the saying on Judah and

---

[470]Cf. above, p. 556.

the one on Joseph in the Testament. As has been argued the present structure of the Testament is also shaped by the genealogical information found in Genesis, of which the most important one is the role of the different mothers.

Now there is one important element throughout the Testament that is of eminent importance, that is the leadership among the brothers. As is obvious in the present form it is Judah who has gained this position, but only because his older brothers were passed over. However, is it possible that Judah, for instance, originally did not have this position within the Testament because his saying was added later on, or expanded very thoroughly? And could it consequently be possible that the deathbed episode in the "pro-Joseph" layer would already have comprised the rest of the Testament with the sayings on eleven or twelve brothers (ex- or including Judah), or even only the northern tribes (excluding Reuben, Simeon & Levi and Judah) with Joseph, in that case, as the most important one? In our view these questions can only be answered negatively for the following reasons,

1. As already stated in every other scheme the regular structure of the poem would be disturbed. In our view this would argue against all the other possibilities that have been suggested. Moreover, we have to ignore for the moment the assignment of the framework to the "pro-Judah" layer, which is, in our view, indispensable for any collection of sayings on the brothers.

2. If we were to consider the possibility of the presence of only the northern tribes in the Testament, the order of sayings would be rather peculiar since Joseph, the penultimate son, would be the most important one. Further, the order of the sons would have lost its (genealogical) significance, making this suggestion very unlikely.

3. If we were to consider the possibility that the Judah-saying was added only later, the order of the sayings would be rather odd. First we would have the denial to the first three sons of their position as possible firstborn sons, which would in fact imply that Zebulun would be the next in line. However, it is only Joseph who has the important saying; but, this importance is quite implicit, whereas the denial to the first three sons is formulated very explicitly. Such a situation would demand a much more explicit assignment of the leadership to the one who was designated to receive it.

4. The same expectation would apply in fact to the possibility that the Judah-saying was rather small and unimportant, compared to, for example, Zebulun or Asher. In both cases the position of Joseph as the penultimate son, gaining the leadership (although only implicitly) would contradict the practice of assigning the leadership to the son first in line as expressed by the sayings on Reuben and Simeon & Levi.

In our view all these arguments argue in favour of the assignment of the bulk of the Testament of Jacob (excluding the saying on Joseph) to the "pro-Judah" layer. The "pro-Joseph" layer of the Deathbed Episode consisted in that case only of the blessing of Joseph (49:22–26), except for some later additions. In this case the number twelve apparently belongs to the "pro-Judah" layer, which is confirmed by the fact that the number twelve occurs often more in Genesis outside the Joseph Story (Gen. 22:20–24; 25:13–15; 36:10–14).[471] So it may have been the practice of the composer of the "pro-Judah" layer to organize genealogies by means of, among other criteria, the number twelve.

6.5.2 The Decease of the Patriarch (Genesis 49:29–33)

The final scene contains Jacob's instructions concerning his decease and burial in the family grave. It has been noted that this passage mirrors Jacob's request to his son Joseph to be buried in Canaan (47:29–31).[472] In literary-critical studies the main part of the passage (49:29–33aA.b) is generally assigned to P.[473] Only the note of the patriarch drewing his feet into the bed (49:33aB) is considered to be part of one of the layers found in 47:29–48:22, generally the same as in 47:31 and 48:2 (because of the several references to the מִטָּה "bed" in these texts).[474]

In our analysis we do not differ considerably from previous studies with regard to the delineation of the different layers in the text. This applies especially to 49:29–33aA, which is in our view part of the layer we labelled "pro-Judah". This might be obvious from the

---

[471] Mulder, "Geschiedenis van Israël", 22.

[472] Cf. above, Chapter Four; see also Westermann, *Genesis 37–50*, 222; Schmidt, *Literarische Studien zur Josephsgeschichte*, 263–4.

[473] Cf. Gunkel, *Genesis*, ³1910, 469, 496–7; Skinner, *Genesis*, 536; Ruppert, *Die Josephserzählung der Genesis*, 163; Schmitt, *Die nichtpriesterliche Josephs-geschichte*, 73, nn. 305–6; Schmidt, *Literarische Studien zur Josephsgeschichte*, 207–8, 263.

[474] Cf. next to the studies listed in the previous footnote, Kebekus, *Die Josef-erzählung*, 209–10, who also isolated 49:33aB from its context.

fact that the charge of the sons to bury him in his fathers' grave (49:29) presupposes the preceding passage (49:1–28) and especially 49:1–2, where the other sons were introduced into the scene. In fact this introductory passage (49:1–2) is a prerequisite for the present passage (49:29–33aA) and therefore the latter text might be assigned to the same layer as the former, namely the "pro-Judah" layer. In addition it should be noted that our passage relates the whole Deathbed Episode again with the preceding patriarchal narratives by means of the reference to the cave in the field of Machpelah (Genesis 23),[475] and the mention of the ancestors who should be buried there. It is in this respect significant that the cave of Machpela is in the territory of Judah and that the grave of the patriarch is positioned in Judah in contrast to some traditions who wanted to have the patriarch buried in the surroundings of Shechem (Acts 7:16).[476] The patriarchal tradition, including now the tradition concerning Joseph's father Israel, is related to Judah and there, in Judah, the patriarch is buried according to this tradition. In our view the assignment of this tradition to the "pro-Judah" layer is therefore obvious.

With regard to the clause וַיֶּאֱסֹף רַגְלָיו אֶל־הַמִּטָּה rendered, "Then he drew his feet up (into) the bed" (49:33aB), we agree with those scholars who relate this verse to the same layer as 48:2b,[477] in our analysis the "pro-Joseph" layer. The close relationship between these two verses is almost generally acknowledged and further argumentation is superfluous.[478] The final clause, וַיִּגְוַע וַיֵּאָסֶף אֶל־עַמָּיו "he breathed his last and was gathered to his people" (49:33b) is commonly regarded as the end of the P-account. Yet this classification of the final clause is problematic because we have to assume that parts of another document were left out for the sake of the version of P.[479] The absence

---

[475] I. Willi-Plein, "Historiographische Aspekte der Josepfsgeschichte", *Henoch* 1 (1979) 305–31, 309.

[476] Cf. Van Selms, *Genesis, dl. II*, 288. See also Nielsen, *Shechem*, 21–2; H. Seebaß, *Der Erzvater Israel: und die Einführung der Jahweverehrung in Kanaan* (BZAW, 98), Berlin 1966, 47.

[477] Cf. Kebekus, *Die Joseferzählung*, 209, n. 3.

[478] The fact that the subject is not explicitly mentioned anymore in this clause, when 49:33b is isolated from the preceding clause (49:33aA), is nowhere regarded as problematic, Yet, if it is taken as a continuation from the "pro-Joseph" layer, the subject is mentioned in 48:21, where Israel is mentioned in the introduction to the direct speech, וַיֹּאמֶר יִשְׂרָאֵל אֶל־יוֹסֵף "and Israel said to Joseph" (48:21aA).

[479] Schmitt, *Die nichtpriesterliche Josephsgeschichte*, 73, n. 306; Schmidt, *Literarische Studien zur Josephsgeschichte*, 208; Seebaß, *Geschichtliche Zeit*, 18, 62; Emerton, "The Priestly Writer in Genesis", 393–5; Blum, *Komposition der Vätergeschichte*, 250; Kebekus, *Die Joseferzählung*, 212; D.M. Carr, *Reading the Fractures of Genesis: Historical and Literary Approaches*, Louisvill (KY) 1996,

of a doublet of this crucial moment in this account argues forcefully against the theory of the merging of two comparable traditions and in favour of a kind of editorial layer.[480] I. Willi-Plein attempted to escape this problem by assigning וַיִּגְוַע "and breathed his last" with the previous clause (49:33aB) to the same layer, and the final וַיֵּאָסֶף אֶל־עַמָּיו to P.[481] N. Kebekus objected to the suggestion that the expression וַיִּגְוַע does not belong to the same layer as 48:2b (his "Reuben-layer"), because that layer would apply the verb מות "to die" (47:29, 48:21).[482] However, Kebekus has pointed out that גוע and מות are used in juxtaposition (Gen. 25:8, 17; 35:29) and hence that both verbs may belong to the same tradition,[483] while it also might be objected that the verb גוע would not have been the appropriate term in those verses where מות was used. Regarding Willi-Plein's suggestion it can be objected that she has to break up an expression which occurs several times (even in combination with the verb מות[484]) and this separation seems rather unlikely to us. For that reason we prefer to consider 49:33aB.b as part of the "pro-Joseph" layer, which was later supplemented by the "pro-Judah" layer, making use of the already present account of the patriarch's death.[485]

6.5.3   The Aftermath: "... And He Wept" (50:1)

Formally the Deathbed Episode might be considered to have come to an end here. Yet the aftermath of the death of the patriarch is interesting with regard to our analysis of the Deathbed Episode. We have argued that once there existed a narrative about Joseph (the "pro-Joseph" layer) which was adapted in accordance to changing political situations by means of the addition of a "pro-Judah" layer. In the defended "pro-Joseph" layer Joseph was in fact the only son of Israel on the scene (47:29–48:22; 49:22–26, 33aB.b), whereas the occurrence of the other sons is due to the "pro-Judah" layer. As has been pointed out already by Willi-Plein, the account in 50:1 would suggest once again that Joseph is the only son present at the scene:[486]

114–20.

[480]Cf. *inter alii* Cross, *CMHE*, 307, with n. 45; 321.

[481]Willi-Plein, "Historiographische Aspekte", 309.

[482]Kebekus, *Die Joseferzählung*, 210, n. 6.

[483]Kebekus, *Die Joseferzählung*, 213.

[484]Kebekus, *Die Joseferzählung*, 212, with n. 12.

[485]W. Dietrich, *Die Josephserzählung als Novelle und Geschichtsschreibung: Zugleich ein Beitrag zur Pentateuchfrage* (BThSt, 14), Neukirchen-Vluyn 1989, 68, n. 203, prefers also to read 49:33aB.b together, independent from the preceding verses (49:28–33aA).

[486]Willi-Plein, "Historiographische Aspekte", 309. Cf. also Blum, *Komposition*

And Joseph fell on his father's face, (1aA)   וַיִּפֹּל יוֹסֵף עַל־פְּנֵי אָבִיו

   and he wept over him, and kissed him. (1aB)   וַיֵּבְךְּ עָלָיו וַיִּשַּׁק־לוֹ

This passage clearly resembles the emotional reunion of father and son
in 46:29–30,[487] and can be considered the continuation of the "pro-
Joseph" layer because it only mentions Joseph mourning for his father.
This exclusive position of Joseph towards his father is also reflected in
50:7–8, where — disregarding the abundant Egyptian ceremonial[488]
— the description concerning the family is:

And Joseph went up to bury his father, ... (7aA)   וַיַּעַל יוֹסֵף לִקְבֹּר אֶת־אָבִיו

and all the house of Joseph, (8aA)   וְכֹל בֵּית יוֹסֵף

and his brothers and his father's house. (8aB)   וְאֶחָיו וּבֵית אָבִיו

In our view these texts still betray Joseph's leading position among
his brothers, not as the Egyptian ruler, but Joseph as the patriarch's
successor.[489] These texts substantiate our thesis that Joseph was originally the most important son in the narrative, but was pushed to
the background by means of a very thorough revision of the original
narrative.

6.6   Character of the Redaction

6.6.1   Introduction

At the beginning of this chapter we described the basis on which our
diachronic analysis of the Deathbed Episode was to be performed.
This basis is formed by the results reached in the previous chapters,
namely the coherent perspective of the Blessing in its present form
and context, and, on the other hand, the two different perspectives on
the true heir of the patriarch, Judah or Joseph. This tension between
the two perspectives was caused by ideological differences, due to a

---

der Vätergeschichte, 250

[487] In fact Gen. 46:29–30 can be characterized as preluding the Deathbed Episode;
note the idiom reoccurring in the Deathbed Episode.

[488] Cf. in this respect Seebaß, *Geschichtliche Zeit,* 61, who suggests that this
tradition concerning Joseph as the second man in Egypt is a later tradition.

[489] According to Blum, *Komposition des Vätergeschichte,* 250, Gen. 50:1ff. is
the original continuation of 47:29–31, while the original death-report was replaced by the present one in 49:33. His observation that 50:1ff. follows in content as well as scenically after 47:29–31 supports our analysis that both texts
belong to the same layer. Furthermore, these passages are generally ascribed to
J (or its equivalents) and, as such, also assigned to the same layer. Cf. Ruppert,
Die Josephserzählung der Genesis, 163 (who even discussed 50:1 as a part of
the Deathbed Episode); Donner, *Literarische Gestalt der Josephsgeschichte,* 30–
4; Schmitt, *Die nichtpriesterliche Josephsgeschichte,* 73–4; Schmidt, *Literarische
Studien zur Josephsgeschichte,* 207–8.

shift in the *status quo*. We postulated as a working hypothesis:[490]

> In an ancient version of the Deathbed Episode Joseph's father said
> farewell to Joseph as his most important son. In a later stage of
> history this version was revised to legitimize the leading position
> of (the tribe of) Judah, who rose to power and for one reason
> or another had to defend his position. This revision resulted in a
> deathbed account which still reflects both historical situations.

Several elements in the text were considered to be decisive for the
stratification of the different layers.[491] The mid-term review revealed
already that the working hypothesis functions quite well in explaining
the tensions found in the first part of the Deathbed Episode (47:29–
48:22).[492] It will now be evaluated whether this analysis did explain
all the tensions in the text and if so, the results will then be described
against the background of other literary-critical analyses.

6.6.2 The "Pro-Joseph" Layer

In the working hypothesis it has been postulated that an ancient version reflecting the "pro-Joseph" tendency has been adapted by a later
editor. It appears that this assumption can be maintained at the end
of our analysis. It is clearly Judah who is favoured as the true heir of
his father and whose position is supported by the final version of Genesis. Joseph's position in the final version is certainly not unimportant
but limited by his role as the ruler in Egypt. The promise of the future
dominion over the brothers is given to Judah. Yet, the "pro-Joseph"
layer contains several elements suggesting Joseph's important position. This is described best by B.J. van der Merwe as "Joseph as
successor of Israel".[493] These elements were especially found in:

1. Gen. 47:29–31, where Joseph is called alone to his father's deathbed; where he is the only one being responsible for Israel's funeral, and where Israel bows himself before Joseph.[494]

2. Gen. 48:14aA, 15aA, 21–22, where Joseph is blessed by his
   father; where he receives Shechem, the northern capital after

---

[490]Cf. above, pp. 455–456.

[491]Cf. above, p. 456, for the argumentation.

[492]Cf. above, p. 499, section 6.4.

[493]With only a slight correction of the patriarch's name by us: B.J. van der
Merwe, "Joseph as Successor of Jacob", in: *Studia Biblica et Semitica: Th.C.
Vriezen ... dedicata*, Wageningen 1966, 221–32. Apparently Van der Merwe over-
looked the element of the patriarch's name in the text.

[494]Even if one is not willing to accept our proposed reading of 47:31 רֹאשׁ הַמַּטֶּה
"head of the tribe", it still has to be considered that Israel bowed himself "at the
head of the bed" *before Joseph*. Cf. our argumentation above on p. 328–332.

the end of the United Monarchy; and where he is called "One above your brothers".[495] This scene anticipates the following part, where Joseph is blessed and it excludes at the same time the presence and blessing of other brothers.

3. Gen. 49:22–26, where Joseph is described as a bullcalf, comparable to Ugaritic metaphors for kings and their offspring; where he is blessed *expressis verbis* in contrast to his other brothers.

4. Gen. 49:33aB–50:1 where Joseph appears to be alone at the scene with his father.[496]

The persons involved in the "pro-Joseph" layer are Israel the patriarch and Joseph his son. Others present at the scene are Joseph's sons, whose names are not mentioned. It is suggested that Joseph has brothers (48:22), yet, neither their number is given nor their names mentioned in this episode. Apparently these data (number and names of Joseph's brothers and sons) were at the moment of origin of this version either unimportant or unknown (*i.e.* there was no such tradition at that moment),[497] suggesting that at the moment of the origin of this account Joseph was the only important son. The background of this tradition may be that at the time of origin Joseph was not yet considered the ancestor of a tribe, comparable to (later?) entities like Zebulun, Benjamin, or Ephraim, but only as a leader of Israel, ruling in Shechem. Furthermore, it is important that the scene is situated in Egypt: the patriarch asked his son to bring him up from Egypt

---

[495] Even if one is not willing to accept this interpretation of 48:22aB. it has to be admitted that Joseph is placed above his brothers in that he receives Shechem, "one above your brothers".

[496] Unless the other brothers are conisidered to be very cold-hearted, lacking any expression of emotion when their father dies in contrast to Joseph who wept and kissed his father, it is significant that only Joseph is mentioned here.

[497] The same idea is found in Genesis 27:29, 37, where it is said that Jacob had brothers (plural), although they are unknown (see also Gen. 31:37, 46). According to Westermann, *Genesis 12–36*, 537, "your brothers" and "your mother's sons" does *offenkundig* not refer to real brothers. Usually this reference is considered a poetic diction, rather than a factual reference. According to Blum, *Die Komposition der Vätergeschichte*, 193, with n. 15, this text clearly refers to the period of the Davidic-Solomonic era, when Israel not only reigned over Edom but also over other "related" nations (Moab, Ammon, Aram, Ishmael). Cf. also Van Selms, *Genesis dl. II*, 80; Davidson, *Genesis 12–50*, 140; Sarna, *Genesis*, 193; Wenham, *Genesis 16–50*, 210; Hamilton, *Book of Genesis*, 222; Jagersma, *Genesis 25–50*, 41. Nevertheless, "real brothers" or not, the interpretation we required in Gen. 27:29, 37; 31:37, 46, might also be applied to Gen. 48:22.

and to bury him in Canaan.[498] In fact, we may conclude that the "pro-Joseph" layer as we found it, was a quite simple tradition which did not reflect an idea of a great Israel in the episode concerned, but reckoned much more with an entity "Israel" at a tribal level.[499] In our view this sober narration of the Deathbed Episode offers a balanced report in which Joseph is indeed the most important son and the possible others (48:22) are just unimportant passers-by.

Two specific points might be mentioned here especially. First, as we said in the previous paragraph Israel the patriarch was with Joseph on the scene. The name "Israel" as the name of the patriarch was found in the Deathbed Episode to be characteristic of the "pro-Joseph" layer. However, as we argued already in Chapter Five, the name belonging to the oldest (adapted) layer, may occur in the younger, redactional (added) layer as well, because the editor had the opportunity to use both names.[500] For that reason the use of the characteristic name of the oldest layer could not be used as an absolute criterion to distinguish between the different layers. On the other hand, the use of both names as a word-pair, and the use of the other name (*i.e.* "Jacob") could be considered as an indicator for the hand of the editor. So, it is not remarkable that "Israel" was used in the "pro-Judah" layer as well (Gen. 48:20; 49:2, 7) and on the other hand that "Jacob" was added in the midst of the blessing in the "pro-Joseph" layer (49:24bA). In our view the analysis could sufficiently explain the occurences of both names and is in line with our working hypothesis.

Secondly, we noted in our analysis that the adaptation of the text was not caused by religious, but rather by political motifs. With regard to the "pro-Joseph" layer a few points might be noted. First of all, the use of the Divine name is restricted to אֱלֹהִים "Elohim" (48:9, 11, 21) and אֵל "El" (49:25), and שַׁדַּי "Shadday" (49:25; not *El* Shadday!), but the name יהוה "YHWH" is absent.[501] Secondly, it

---

[498] Of course, the staging of this Episode in Egypt presupposes that Joseph has come to Egypt and most probably before his father (cf. 48:11). Our analysis is restricted, however, to Gen. 47:29–50:1, so we cannot describe the capture of Joseph and his deportation to Egypt according to the "pro-Joseph" layer (if present). Yet, as we have noted before (cf. pp. 432–434 above), Gen. 37:25–8 might be composite and betray an adaptation of the text here as well. Note for example the prominent position of Judah in the pericope, proposing the providential solution (45:5, 7; 50:20), which might suggest that the hand of the "pro-Judah" editor has been at work here.

[499] Cf. Gen. 47:31 in our translation, pp. 461–464 above.

[500] Cf. pp. 427–430 above.

[501] The absence of the *Tetragrammaton* is, however, also found in the "pro-

appears that the religion was in its appearance very close to the religious language and perception of Ugarit. This is found especially in the "Blessing of Joseph", where the "Bull" strengthens (49:22), and where blessings are provided by Heavens, Flood, and Breast & Womb (49:25), but also by the (deified?) ancestors (49:26). The latter aspect reflects the possibility of an ancestor cult, vestiges of which were also found in 49:24bB, reflecting the whole scene as a Deathbed Episode quite well.

6.6.3 The "Pro-Judah" Layer

The "pro-Judah" layer might be described best by means of the elements that were added to the older "pro-Joseph" layer.

1. The name "Jacob" was added to the older layer as the former name of the patriarch "Israel". Use was made of a tradition from outside the Joseph Story (Gen. 32:22–32; 35:9), being part of the overall structure of Genesis (*i.e.* renaming of a person).[502]

2. "Manasseh" and "Ephraim" were added to the Episode as the sons of Joseph, who were at the scene in the older layer, yet without their names being mentioned. The use of their names and the reference to their order of birth presumes their birth-story (Gen. 41:50–52), which is also part of the overall structure of Genesis (*i.e.* using the folk etymology of the names; the theme of the forsaken first-born).[503]

3. The adoption and blessing of "Manasseh" and "Ephraim" as sons of Jacob reflects one of the main themes of Genesis, namely the struggle for progeny against barrenness. By means of this adoption Joseph is, however, left "childless" and forced to adopt later on one of his great-grandchildren. Yet, the blessing of the two sons obscures the fact that originally only Joseph was blessed in the older layer (48:15aA), paving the way for the blessing of the other brothers (49:1–28).

4. The pronouncement of the Testament here in the Deathbed Episode is made possible by the adaption of the preceding scene, where Joseph's sons were blessed (48:15aB–20) instead of Joseph himself (48:15aA). The framework (49:1–2, 28) makes use of the

---

Judah" layer, whereas the name was found only once in a gloss (49:18).

[502] An element in the text that functions within the overall structure of Genesis, was named as a possible argument to classify a text as being part of the "pro-Judah" layer. Cf. above, p. 456, no. 2.

[503] Cf. above, p. 467, with nn. 63–64.

pair "Jacob ‖ Israel" and as such it is part of the "pro-Judah" layer, whereas the interpretation of the following words as "predictions of later days" is especially important for Judah. The fact that the Testament in its present form is a poem with a quite regular structure argues in favour of reading the Testament as a coherent text.

5. With the addition of the other eleven sons, the family of the patriarch is made to consist of twelve sons, a number that occurs more often in Genesis in connection with families (and peoples). With the addition of these brothers who are identified by their names, the tribes represented by these names became close relatives and, from a political point of view, form one nation.[504] This technique of explaining the (later political) relationships between several groups by means of family-relations is applied very often in Genesis[505] and as such could also be considered part of the overall structure of Genesis.

6. It is most significant that the later dominion over the brothers is given to Judah. He receives more or less the same blessing as his father received (Gen. 27:27–29). The promise to Abraham and to Jacob of becoming a multitude of nations seems now to be fulfilled in Jacob (cf. 48:3–5), so, this blessing is not passed on any longer.

7. The addition of the command to bury the patriarch in the grave of his fathers (49:29–32) links our episode once again to the other stories *outside* the Joseph Story. By means of this reference to the grave of Abraham and Sarah, Isaac and Rebekah, and Leah, the Deathbed Episode has now clearly become part of the patriarchal narratives of Abraham, Isaac and *Jacob*. Yet, the grave of the patriarch — and thus of *Israel* — is now set in the territory of Judah,[506] whereas it is possible that there

---

[504] This does not exclude the possibility that certain tribes in this list were related already in earlier times, like *e.g.* Zebulun, Ephraim, Benjamin, who, as we argued before (p. 556, n. 432), were found in the song of Deborah. Yet, there their names seem much more to represent a geographical entity.

[505] Cf. *e.g.* Gen. 10:1–32; but especially interesting from a political point of view are: 16:1–16; 21:8–21; 25:12–8 (Abraham > Ishmael); 19:30–8 (Lot > Moab and Ammon); 25:19–26; 36:1–42 (Isaac > Esau = Edom).

[506] Note that this happened also with the grave-tradition of Rachel, who was apparently buried in the North, but later her grave was located in the South near Bethlehem (48:7).

existed such a grave of *Israel* in the northern territory in the surroundings of Shechem.[507]

Summarizing it can be concluded that the "pro-Judah" layer forms a very extensive revision of the older "pro-Joseph" layer. The adaptation of the text might be characterized as a political revision, reflecting in all probability the political changes that took place up until the time of the revision and in a wider sense the political scene at that moment. Religiously there is no shift found between the "pro-Joseph" and "pro-Judah" layer. Indeed, on the contrary, possible references to the ancestor cult were found in the "pro-Joseph" layer (49:24–26), but without any restriction also in the "pro-Judah" layer (49:6a). Only one smaller change might be observed here, that is the addition of the divine element אֵל "El" before the name/epithet "Shaddai", making it in that way a compound name "El Shaddai" (48:3). The true reason behind this change is hard to establish, but it might reflect a monolatristic tendency, whereas the former use of שַׁדַּי "Shaddai" might reflect a more polytheistic tendency in which the name represents a separate deity.[508] Yet, the fact that in relatively late texts the name "Shaddai" is used still independently (*e.g.* Isa. 13:6; Ezek. 1:24), calls for prudence in this respect.

In our view the working hypothesis and the criteria for the diachronic analysis, formulated at the beginning of this chapter provided us with the appropriate arguments to analyse the Deathbed Episode in a consistent manner. It might be obvious, however, that the results of our analysis departs from other studies of the Joseph Story and of Genesis 49; but, to a large extent also of certain paradigmas in pentateuchal research, like the existence of P (whether as a document or as a redactional layer). For that reason the results of our analysis will now be compared with other studies of the Joseph Story.

---

[507] Cf. Acts 7:15–6, although the value of this reference is not very high, because the knowledge of the scriptures seems to be somewhat confused in this speech; so this tradition might have been mixed up also.

[508] A far-reaching suggestion in that direction was recently proposed by H. Lutzky, "Shadday as a Goddess Epithet", *VT* 48 (1998) 15–36. She considers the etymology of שַׁדַּי < I שַׁד (Proto-Sem. *ṯd*) "breast" as an indication that we are dealing here with an epithet of Asherah (comparable to the epithet *rḥm* "womb"). Even though we do not exclude the possibility that goddesses have been part of the pantheon of the Israelite ancestors (cf. our discussion of Gen. 49:25bC), and consider Lutzky's suggestion worthwhile, yet, her discussion of the etymology and religious-historical aspects are not convincing. Especially the fact that she does not sufficiently discuss the Ugaritic evidence which suggests at least a different etymology for *šd* "daemon" (related to "Shaddai", *art.cit.*, 28–9) and *ṯd* "breast" is a considerable weakness in her argumentation.

6.6.4   Previous Research and Present Analysis

Previous research on the Joseph Story has been discussed in Chapter Five[509] and without exaggeration one can say that the results of previous research differ widely. Nevertheless the results of previous research can be classified under different approaches:[510]

1. The analysis of the text according to the classical Documentary Hypothesis, discerning *grosso modo* between J, E, R[JE] and P.

2. The analysis according to the Supplementary (or Redactional –) Hypothesis and according to the Traditio-Historical Approach.

3. The Literary Approach, emphasizing the literary qualities and also the unity of the Story.

We can now compare the results of our analysis from previous research, and can start with two observations. First of all, our analysis differs strongly from previous research in that it *included* (parts of) Genesis 49 as an integral part of the different layers found in the Deathbed Episode. Secondly, the results of our analysis of the Deathbed Episode differ strongly from the classical Documentary Hypothesis (the Deathbed Episode does *not* consist of originally different independent documents), but they are affiliated in certain respects with the Supplementary Hypothesis, and to some extent with the Literary Approach.

With regard to the first observation, it might be obvious that our analysis of the Blessing differs sharply from most of the other studies on the Joseph Story and on Genesis 49 itself. As has been stated in Chapter One, Genesis 49 was separated from its context already by J. Astruc in his *Conjectures* and this situation has survived up to the present day. Yet, our analysis has demonstrated that first of all Genesis 49 in its present form has an important function within the Joseph Story with regard to the question of the true heir of the patriarch Jacob/Israel (cf. Gen. 37:10 and 49:8). Secondly, it has been demonstrated that a part of Genesis 49 (vv. 22–26) functioned in an earlier version of the Deathbed Episode, in which Joseph was favoured

---

[509]The recapitulation of previous research can be found on pp. 422–424; the recapitulation of the discussion is presented on pp. 449–450. For another review of previous research of the *whole* Joseph Story, cf. now C. Paap, *Die Josephsgeschichte, Genesis 37–50: Bestimmungen ihrer literarischen Gattung in der zweiten Hälfte des 20. Jahrhunderts* (EHS.T, 534), Frankfurt aM 1995.

[510]A slightly different classification is found in Paap, *Die Josephsgeschichte*, *passim*. Yet, despite the differences in the framework of our studies, the pattern remains the same.

as the patriarch's (Israel's) successor, an element that could already be found in the previous passages of the Deathbed Episode (*inter alii* Gen. 47:29–31). For that reason it must be concluded that the Joseph Story — or at least the Deathbed Episode — cannot be read and studied without accepting the presence of the Testament in it.

Probably most significant are the differences of our analysis with the Documentary Hypothesis, which supposes that our text (as a part of Genesis) is a compilation from the documents J, E, and P. In Chapter Five we ventured some criticism against the almost dogmatic assumption of the existence of P in Pentateuchal studies. In our analysis we interpreted those elements showing some relationship with the overall structure of Genesis as being part of the "pro-Judah" layer. Our argument for this was that the main thread of Genesis finally tends to support Judah's position and as a consequence many of the texts in the Deathbed Episode which are usually assigned to P are, in our analysis, assigned to the "pro-Judah" layer. In our view the advantage of this classification is that it does justice to the clear thread throughout Genesis, which is generally assigned to P;[511] on the other hand it can explain the sometimes clear correspondences between the assumed different documents.[512] Moreover, the most important aspect is that this classification explains the differences between the different layers in the Deathbed Episode from a *political* point of view, rather than from a *religious* point of view, which is characteristic for the classification in J, E, and P,[513] or on the basis of specific vocabulary, which is hard to discern.

A second point of departure is found in the number of layers in the Deathbed Episode and the character of these layers. First of all, the number of layers is reduced to only two, which is in comparison to the other solutions a rather small number. The most significant difference is found of course in the fact that we have sought to explain the origin and occurence of Genesis 49 in the context of the Deathbed Episode and even more widely in that of the Joseph Story. The relationship between Testament and context was found to center in the sayings

---

[511] In this respect our analysis corresponds with those who consider P to be a redactional layer, because P does not form a self-contained unit.

[512] Cf. for example the discussion of Gen. 48:15–6 by H. Donner, *Literarische Gestalt der Josephsgeschichte*, 32–3 (cf. above, p. 390, with n. 153).

[513] Of course a certain recognition of political aspects is found in the differentiation between J (South) and E (North). Yet, the present analysis places emphasis on the political differences, rather than on the religious differences, which were hard to find in this Episode. On the problem of the classification of the different documents on the basis of the different religious concepts, cf. Houtman, *Der Pentateuch*, 396–403.

concerning Judah and Joseph, in which the former had of course a clear "pro-Judah" tendency,[514] while the latter could be related to the "pro-Joseph" layer in the rest of the Deathbed Episode.[515] This data, combined with the fact that Gen. 49:1–28 is viewed as a poetic composition, forms a well-balanced, regular structure; and the fact that the text as a whole has to be regarded as a testament, which is supported by the most important parts (vv. 3–4, 5–7, 8–12) or at least not contradicted (vv. 22–26), argues in favour of an approach which integrates Genesis 49 in the same layers as those found in its context.[516] Our study resulted in an assignment of the different parts of the whole Deathbed Episode to just two different layers (and one later gloss, 49:18), which differs sharply from the Documentary Hypothesis which distinguishes here four layers (oral tradition of Genesis 49; further J,E, and P), to five or six (the work of R^{JE} and/or R^P) and the obvious gloss (49:18). Yet, the most important difference between our analysis and the Documentary Hypothesis is found in the general character of the different layers and in their chronological order in comparison to the two documents J and E. First of all, the character of the two different layers is certainly not that of two comparable traditions, later merged by an editor, but that of one independent tradition that was adapted by an editor into a different narrative which had a completely different purport. Secondly, the chronological order of the different layers is very different from the Documentary Hypothesis, which has the order J–E. A comparison of the assumed geographical context of the two documents — J in the South, E in the North — with the most likely geographical background of the "pro-Joseph" and "pro-Judah" layers[517] suggests a chronological or-

---

[514] Cf. Gen. 37:8, 10, with 49:8; and see our discussion above, pp. 352, 361–3.

[515] Cf. Gen. 47:29–31; 48:22 with 49:22–24; cf. above, pp. 353–5; 363–4.

[516] This result does not argue, of course, against the possbility of "inset hymns" in Hebrew narrative; yet, it argues for a more cautious approach of these matters in which principally the possibility is considered that the hymn was an integral part of the narrative framework. On these matters, cf. esp. J.W. Watts, *Psalm and Story: Inset Hymns in Hebrew Narrative* (JSOTS, 139), Sheffield 1992; idem, " 'This Song': Conspicuous Poetry in Hebrew Prose", *VANEP*, 345–58. Cf. Watts' statement, that "Ironically, these poems [in narrative] likely have the ... effect on many modern readers of the Hebrew Bible who, unacquainted with the songs' music, are tempted by the rare vocabulary, archaic grammatical constructions, and obscure allusions in many of these songs to skip to the next prose story" (*art.cit.*, 346, n. 3). His statement raises the question whether this explanation could also apply to the present state of research on the Deathbed Episode.

[517] It goes without saying that the layer that favours Joseph as the true successor of his father in Shechem originated in the territory of his dominion, *viz.* the North; while the "pro-Judah" layer will have had its origin in the South.

der that differs from the Documentary Hypothesis. The northern, "pro-Joseph" layer (being revised by the addition of the "pro-Judah" layer) must be considered the oldest document and thus the first one in order. The southern, additional layer is consequently the youngest and last one in order.[518]

With these final remarks we tie on to a comparison with those studies favouring the supplementary or redactional-critical approach. In general these studies are still strongly influenced by the paradigms of the literary critical approach and especially the Documentary Hypothesis.[519] This is found especially in the work of H.-C. Schmitt, who followed in many respects the observations of the Documentary Hypothesis but applied a different terminology for the classical documents J and E.[520] Another solution is found by Redford, Dietrich and Kebekus,[521] who suggest that the Reuben layer ($\approx$ E) is earlier and has been adapted by the Judah layer. However, the latter stud-

---

[518] In this respect our analysis seems to support the idea of recent scholars (e.g. D.B. Redford, W. Dietrich, N. Kebekus) who considered the northern version of the Joseph Story (mostly called the Reuben-[Jacob-]version) to be the oldest and the southern version (Judah-[Israel-]version) the youngest; for a comparison with these analyses cf. our following discussion in the main text. Yet, concerning J and E, there is some correspondence with the ideas of earlier scholars who preferred the revised order of the documents, namely first E and later J, such as, for instance A. Dillmann and E. König; cf. Houtman, Der Pentateuch, 115–6, nn. 33, 35. More clearly, however, the general characteristics of our results seem to correspond with the theory of those scholars of the first half of the nineteenth century, who favoured a Supplementary Hypothesis in which an elohistic work was edited by an jehovistic editor, such as, for instance, J.J. Stähelin, H.G.A. Ewald, J.C.F. Tuch, F. Bleek etc.; cf. Houtman, op.cit., 91–5. Yet, the question which might be raised in this connection, whether we are dealing in our case with a "basic document" (Grundschrift) comprising the whole patriarchal story or even everything from the creation to the Exodus which has been adapted by an editor, cannot be answered here because we are only dealing with one episode of the book of Genesis. So in this respect we cannot decide in favour of a "Fragmentary Hypothesis" (though including the revision by the hand of the "compiler"), or a "Supplementary, or rather Redactional Hypothesis" (with a "basic document"). Moreover, it might be appropriate here to emphasize, that the terms "elohistic" and "yahwistic" do not function in the context of our analysis because the DN YHWH is absent in this episode (except for Gen. 49:18). Moreover, in case of an editorial adaptation of the text we have to account for the fact that the editor was able to use both DNN El(ohim) and YHWH; cf. our remarks with regard to Jacob and Israel, and Reuben and Judah in the previous chapter (sections 5.23.2–3).

[519] Cf. in this respect the comments in C. Westermann, Genesis 12–50 (EdF, 48), Darmstadt 1975, 64, on the method applied by Redford (quoted above, p. 395, n. 188).

[520] Cf. H.-C. Schmitt, Die nichtpriesterliche Josephsgeschichte: Ein Beitrag zur neuesten Pentateuchkritik (BZAW, 154), Berlin 1980, 5, n. 3.

[521] Cf. above, pp. 394–7.

ies, as well as the former by Schmitt, are based on the supposition that Reuben and Judah are more or less doublets and as such have to be divided over two different layers, a supposition which is highly questionable.[522] One of the most significant differences between the results of our analysis and former studies is found in the identification of the most important son of the patriarch in the different layers. In our study we have argued that the true struggle between the brothers *at the level of different layers* is found between Joseph and Judah, not between Reuben and Judah. In our view the latter contrast functions in only one layer to demonstrate Judah's supremacy among the brothers and somehow seems to function as a legitimation for the dominion of a younger brother (= tribe?) over the older ones. The contrast between Joseph and Judah as we have found it seems to be glossed over somehow, but this contrast can be related without any problem to the historical conflict between North (Joseph) and South (Judah). In this sense our analysis corresponds to those studies who have found the prevelance of the northern tradition over the southern.

A second point of importance, especially relevant for the historical background of these texts, is the fact that the name "Israel" is not related with the (later) southern layer (usually: Judah-Israel layer) but with the northern one. In former studies a tribal historical background of the Joseph Story (the sons as representatives of the tribes) was still found in all the identified layers. Yet, as far as our study of this part of the Joseph Story reached, it appears that this tribal historical background is absent in the earliest version ("pro-Joseph") because the "brothers" of Joseph are treated there anonymously (48:22; 49:26b) and are incorporated only in the editorial "pro-Judah" layer by their names in the narrative.

Thirdly, the redaction of the original version has been rather extensive and — as far as we are able to establish — added several new aspects to the Joseph Story, which caused a shift in the intention of the Story. In fact this redaction might have created a whole new story. In this respect our analysis differs from the other supplementary or redactional-critical approaches because they assigned the later redactional expansions to different traditions or layers. In this way the shift of the intention of the original narrative to the final version has been caused by several different persons/schools. Our analysis seems to support much more the idea of a coherent adaptation and revision of the text by only one editor who had a very specific goal in mind, namely legitimizing the supremacy of Judah in Israel. This extensive

---

[522]Cf. our discussion above, pp. 430–9.

revision of the original "pro-Joseph" version resulted in a new "Joseph Story"[523] which justifies the literary approaches of the Joseph Story finding much more coherence in the Story than is usually assumed by literary critics.

With the conclusion that the redaction created a whole new story we have reached the final point of comparison with other approaches. The approaches of the Joseph Story as more or less a literary unity do not exclude the possibility that some redactional activity took place or that the story was preserved in the documents J, E and P, but they minimize the adaptation of the text or the differences between the documents as much as possible in order to preserve the literary quality of the Story.[524] The tension between this final approach and the previously discussed approaches is found especially in the work of R.N. Whybray and H. Donner, who criticized von Rad's assumption that we were dealing here with a novella and with a conflation of the Pentateuchal documents. However, if our analysis is correct that the original story has been revised extensively creating a whole new story, this would agree with von Rad's statement that "the Joseph Story is a novel through and through".[525] In this sense Donner's remark "one cannot have it both ways: the Joseph Story as a novella *and* as a part of the Pentateuchal documents J and E"[526] might be correct with regard to the Documentary Hypothesis, it nevertheless has to be reconsidered in the sense that the Joseph Story in its present form might be a literary masterpiece *and* the product of a rather extensive adaptation of an ancient tradition in order to enable its adoption

---

[523]It has to be noted, however, that the terminology "Joseph Story" seems to suppose an independent narrative, with a beginning and end on its own. Yet, in fact are we dealing here with a continuous story, of which the Joseph Story is "part Four" (after the three patriarchal stories), or even "part Five" (after the primeval and patriachal stories).

[524]Cf. the discussion of G. von Rad; R.N. Whybray; H. Donner; G.W. Coats; C. Westermann in Chapter Five, above. See also the section on E. Blum, who in general considered the Joseph Story to be originally a unity, which only had a few redactional expansions in order to relate the narrative to the other traditions of Genesis (cf. Paap, *Die Josephsgeschichte*, 119–22).

[525]G. von Rad, "Josephsgeschichte und ältere Chokma", in: *Congress Volume: Copenhagen 1953* (SVT, 1), Leiden 1953, 120–7, 120 (= idem, *GSAT*, 272–80, 272).

[526]Donner, *Literarische Gestalt der Josephsgeschichte*, 14. Cf. also R.N. Whybray, "The Joseph Story and Pentateuchal Criticism", *VT* 18 (1958) 522–8, 525, who states "If the Joseph Story as we now have it is a literary masterpiece *in* von Rad's *sense*, it must be a complete literary unity both in conception and execution; if it is a conflation of two sources, then von Rad's estimate of its high qualities *as a novel* must be largely illusory."

in the whole of Genesis.[527] Yet, this statement also reflects the main difference between our analysis and former studies. Those studies consider the Joseph Story as a literary work on its own which has been incorporated into the book of Genesis with some small adaptations to make it fit in. Our analysis suggests that the original version needed a very extensive expansion and revision in order to create the present literary work of art, which at the same time would make it fit into its new literary context and to the changed political conditions.

In conclusion, our diachronic analysis of the Deathbed Episode differs in many respects from previous studies. The most significant difference is found in the fact that according to our analysis Genesis 49 belongs to the same traditions as those found in Genesis 47:29–48:22 and 49:29–33. Secondly, we have found only two different traditions: a basic story (the "pro-Joseph" tradition) and an extensive, editorial layer (the "pro-Judah" tradition). Thirdly, the basic document we found, the "pro-Joseph" layer, did not reflect the traditions concerning "great Israel", consisting of twelve (or a smaller number of) tribes, but this tradition reflected a quite modest view on a small (tribal) group that lived in central Palestine in the vicinity of Shechem. Finally, the main reason for the expansion and adaptation of the older tradition was (as far as it concerns the Deathbed Episode) not a shift in religious thinking but a shift in political conditions and the need for a legitimation of these changes.

6.6.5 The Reconstructed Text: A Synopsis

6.6.5.1 Introductory Remark

On the following pages the complete text of the Deathbed Episode, as it was analysed by us, will be printed out according to the classification "pro-Joseph" or "pro-Judah" layer. To allow the reader a quick overview the text will be printed out on the left page in Hebrew and on the right page in "translation". The word "translation" is not completely correct because the English on these pages reflects the Hebrew sometimes rather literally, ignoring correct English syntax and style.

6.6.5.2 The Text

See the following pages.

---

[527] As was shown in Chapter Five, Donner does not deny the final point, he even explicitly discerns certain redactional expansions in the present form of the Joseph Story (cf. above, pp. 388–90). Yet, as we said above, the possible expansions are restricted to only the most problematic parts of the Joseph Story.

Pro-Judah layer	Pro-Joseph layer	
	וַיִּקְרְבוּ יְמֵי־יִשְׂרָאֵל לָמוּת	47:29
	וַיִּקְרָא לִבְנוֹ לְיוֹסֵף	
	וַיֹּאמֶר לוֹ	
	אִם־נָא מָצָאתִי חֵן בְּעֵינֶיךָ	
	שִׂים־נָא יָדְךָ תַּחַת יְרֵכִי	
	וְעָשִׂיתָ עִמָּדִי חֶסֶד וֶאֱמֶת	
	אַל־נָא תִקְבְּרֵנִי בְּמִצְרָיִם	
	וְשָׁכַבְתִּי עִם־אֲבֹתַי	47:30
	וּנְשָׂאתַנִי מִמִּצְרַיִם	
	וּקְבַרְתַּנִי בִּקְבֻרָתָם	
	וַיֹּאמַר אָנֹכִי אֶעֱשֶׂה כִדְבָרֶךָ	
	וַיֹּאמֶר הִשָּׁבְעָה לִי	47:31
	וַיִּשָּׁבַע לוֹ	
	וַיִּשְׁתַּחוּ יִשְׂרָאֵל עַל־רֹאשׁ הַמִּטָּה פ	
	וַיְהִי אַחֲרֵי הַדְּבָרִים הָאֵלֶּה	48:1
וַיֹּאמֶר לְיוֹסֵף		
הִנֵּה אָבִיךָ חֹלֶה		
וַיִּקַּח אֶת־שְׁנֵי בָנָיו עִמּוֹ		
אֶת־מְנַשֶּׁה וְאֶת־אֶפְרָיִם		
וַיַּגֵּד לְיַעֲקֹב וַיֹּאמֶר		48:2
הִנֵּה בִּנְךָ יוֹסֵף בָּא אֵלֶיךָ		
	וַיִּתְחַזֵּק יִשְׂרָאֵל	
	וַיֵּשֶׁב עַל־הַמִּטָּה	
וַיֹּאמֶר יַעֲקֹב אֶל־יוֹסֵף		48:3
אֵל שַׁדַּי נִרְאָה־אֵלַי בְּלוּז בְּאֶרֶץ כְּנָעַן		
וַיְבָרֶךְ אֹתִי		
וַיֹּאמֶר אֵלַי		48:4
הִנְנִי מַפְרְךָ וְהִרְבִּיתִךָ		
וּנְתַתִּיךָ לִקְהַל עַמִּים		
וְנָתַתִּי אֶת־הָאָרֶץ הַזֹּאת		
לְזַרְעֲךָ אַחֲרֶיךָ אֲחֻזַּת עוֹלָם		
וְעַתָּה שְׁנֵי־בָנֶיךָ הַנּוֹלָדִים לְךָ בְּאֶרֶץ מִצְרַיִם		48:5
עַד־בֹּאִי אֵלֶיךָ מִצְרַיְמָה לִי־הֵם		
אֶפְרַיִם וּמְנַשֶּׁה		
כִּרְאוּבֵן וְשִׁמְעוֹן יִהְיוּ־לִי		
וּמוֹלַדְתְּךָ אֲשֶׁר־הוֹלַדְתָּ אַחֲרֵיהֶם לְךָ יִהְיוּ		48:6
עַל שֵׁם אֲחֵיהֶם יִקָּרְאוּ בְּנַחֲלָתָם		

	Pro-Joseph layer	Pro-Judah layer
47:29	And the days came for Israel to die he called his son Joseph and said to him "If I have found favour in your eyes, put your hand under my thigh, and act loyally and truly to me. Do not bury me in Egypt,	
47:30	But let me lie with my fathers; carry me up from Egypt, and bury me in their burying place." And he said, "I will do as you said."	
47:31	He said, "Swear to me"; and he swore to him. And Israel bowed down for the head of the tribe.	
48:1	And it was after these things, that	
		it was said to Joseph, "Look, your father is ill", and he took his two sons with him, Manasseh and Ephraim.
48:2		And it was told to Jacob and said, your son Joseph came to you; [then]
	Israel summoned his strength and he sat on the bed.	
48:3		And Jacob said to Joseph, "El Shaddai appeared to me at Luz in the land Canaan and He blessed me.
48:4		And He said to me, 'Lo, I'll make you fertile and numerous and I'll make you a company of peoples, and I will give this land to your seed after you, for an eternal possession.'
48:5		And now, your two sons, born to you in the land of Egypt before I came to you in Egypt, they are mine: Ephraim and Manasseh, like Reuben and Simeon they are to me.
48:6		Your offspring born after them is yours, they shall be called by the name of their brothers in their inheritance.

Pro-Judah layer	Pro-Joseph layer	
וַאֲנִי בְּבֹאִי מִפַּדָּן		48:7
מֵתָה עָלַי רָחֵל בְּאֶרֶץ כְּנַעַן בַּדֶּרֶךְ		
בְּעוֹד כִּבְרַת־אֶרֶץ לָבֹא אֶפְרָתָה		
וָאֶקְבְּרֶהָ שָּׁם בְּדֶרֶךְ אֶפְרָת		
הִוא בֵּית לָחֶם		
	וַיַּרְא יִשְׂרָאֵל אֶת־בְּנֵי יוֹסֵף	48:8
	וַיֹּאמֶר מִי־אֵלֶּה	
	וַיֹּאמֶר יוֹסֵף אֶל־אָבִיו	48:9
	בָּנַי הֵם אֲשֶׁר־נָתַן־לִי אֱלֹהִים בָּזֶה	
	וַיֹּאמַר קָחֶם־נָא אֵלַי	
וַאֲבָרֲכֵם	וְעֵינֵי יִשְׂרָאֵל כָּבְדוּ מִזֹּקֶן	48:10
	לֹא יוּכַל לִרְאוֹת	
	וַיַּגֵּשׁ אֹתָם אֵלָיו	
	וַיִּשַּׁק לָהֶם וַיְחַבֵּק לָהֶם	
	וַיֹּאמֶר יִשְׂרָאֵל אֶל־יוֹסֵף	48:11
	רְאֹה פָנֶיךָ לֹא פִלָּלְתִּי	
	וְהִנֵּה הֶרְאָה אֹתִי אֱלֹהִים גַּם אֶת־זַרְעֶךָ	
	וַיּוֹצֵא יוֹסֵף אֹתָם מֵעִם בִּרְכָּיו	48:12
	וַיִּשְׁתַּחוּ לְאַפָּיו אָרְצָה	
וַיִּקַּח יוֹסֵף אֶת־שְׁנֵיהֶם		48:13
אֶת־אֶפְרַיִם בִּימִינוֹ מִשְּׂמֹאל יִשְׂרָאֵל		
וְאֶת־מְנַשֶּׁה בִשְׂמֹאלוֹ מִימִין יִשְׂרָאֵל		
וַיַּגֵּשׁ אֵלָיו		
	וַיִּשְׁלַח יִשְׂרָאֵל אֶת־יְמִינוֹ	48:14
וַיָּשֶׁת עַל־רֹאשׁ אֶפְרַיִם וְהוּא הַצָּעִיר		
וְאֶת־שְׂמֹאלוֹ עַל־רֹאשׁ מְנַשֶּׁה		
שִׂכֵּל אֶת־יָדָיו		
כִּי מְנַשֶּׁה הַבְּכוֹר		
וַיֹּאמַר	וַיְבָרֶךְ אֶת־יוֹסֵף	48:15
הָאֱלֹהִים אֲשֶׁר		
הִתְהַלְּכוּ אֲבֹתַי לְפָנָיו אַבְרָהָם וְיִצְחָק		
הָאֱלֹהִים הָרֹעֶה אֹתִי		
מֵעוֹדִי עַד־הַיּוֹם הַזֶּה		
הַמַּלְאָךְ הַגֹּאֵל אֹתִי מִכָּל־רָע		48:16
יְבָרֵךְ אֶת־הַנְּעָרִים		
וְיִקָּרֵא בָהֶם שְׁמִי		
וְשֵׁם אֲבֹתַי אַבְרָהָם וְיִצְחָק		
וְיִדְגּוּ לָרֹב בְּקֶרֶב הָאָרֶץ		

Pro-Joseph layer	Pro-Judah layer
	48:7 But I, when I came from Padan, Rachel died to my sorrow in the land of Canaan on the way when there was still some distance to go to Ephrath; and I buried her there on the way to Ephrath" (that is, Bethlehem).
48:8 Then Israel saw the sons of Joseph and he said, "who are these?"	
48:9 And Joseph said to his father, "They are my sons, God gave me here." And he said, "Bring them to me, please"	that I may bless them."
48:10 for the eyes of Israel were dim with age, and he was not able to see (well); so he brought them to him, and he kissed and embraced them.	
48:11 And Israel said to Joseph, "To see your face, I had not expected, and lo, God showed me your seed too."	
48:12 Joseph removed them from his knees and bowed down, his face to the earth.	
48:13	And Joseph took them both, Ephraim in his right to Israel's left, and Manasseh in his left to Israel's right and he brought them near.
48:14 And Israel streched out his right hand,	and laid it upon the head of Ephraim, though the youngest, and his left upon the head of Manasseh, crossing his hands, for Manasseh was the first-born.
48:15 And he blessed Joseph	and said, "The God before whom my fathers went, Abraham and Isaac; The God who shepherded me from my past to this day;
48:16	The angel, redeeming me from all evil may he bless the boys; And let my name be called in them, and my fathers', Abraham and Isaac, and let them be numerous in the midst of the land."

Pro-Judah layer	Pro-Joseph layer	
וַיַּרְא יוֹסֵף כִּי־יָשִׁית אָבִיו יַד־יְמִינוֹ		48:17
עַל־רֹאשׁ אֶפְרַיִם וַיֵּרַע בְּעֵינָיו		
וַיִּתְמֹךְ יַד־אָבִיו לְהָסִיר אֹתָהּ		
מֵעַל רֹאשׁ־אֶפְרַיִם עַל־רֹאשׁ מְנַשֶּׁה		
וַיֹּאמֶר יוֹסֵף אֶל־אָבִיו		48:18
לֹא־כֵן אָבִי		
כִּי־זֶה הַבְּכֹר		
שִׂים יְמִינְךָ עַל־רֹאשׁוֹ		
וַיְמָאֵן אָבִיו וַיֹּאמֶר		48:19
יָדַעְתִּי בְנִי יָדַעְתִּי		
גַּם־הוּא יִהְיֶה־לְּעָם וְגַם־הוּא יִגְדָּל		
וְאוּלָם אָחִיו הַקָּטֹן יִגְדַּל מִמֶּנּוּ		
וְזַרְעוֹ יִהְיֶה מְלֹא־הַגּוֹיִם		
וַיְבָרֲכֵם בַּיּוֹם הַהוּא לֵאמוֹר		48:20
בְּךָ יְבָרֵךְ יִשְׂרָאֵל לֵאמֹר		
יְשִׂמְךָ אֱלֹהִים כְּאֶפְרַיִם וְכִמְנַשֶּׁה		
וַיָּשֶׂם אֶת־אֶפְרַיִם לִפְנֵי מְנַשֶּׁה		
	וַיֹּאמֶר יִשְׂרָאֵל אֶל־יוֹסֵף	48:21
	הִנֵּה אָנֹכִי מֵת	
	וְהָיָה אֱלֹהִים עִמָּכֶם	
	וְהֵשִׁיב אֶתְכֶם אֶל־אֶרֶץ אֲבֹתֵיכֶם	
	וַאֲנִי נָתַתִּי לְךָ שְׁכֶם	48:22
	אַחַד עַל־אַחֶיךָ	
	אֲשֶׁר לָקַחְתִּי מִיַּד הָאֱמֹרִי	
	בְּחַרְבִּי וּבְקַשְׁתִּי פ	
וַיִּקְרָא יַעֲקֹב אֶל־בָּנָיו		49:1
וַיֹּאמֶר הֵאָסְפוּ וְאַגִּידָה לָכֶם		
אֵת אֲשֶׁר־יִקְרָא אֶתְכֶם בְּאַחֲרִית הַיָּמִים		
הִקָּבְצוּ וְשִׁמְעוּ בְּנֵי יַעֲקֹב		49:2
וְשִׁמְעוּ אֶל־יִשְׂרָאֵל אֲבִיכֶם		
רְאוּבֵן בְּכֹרִי אַתָּה		49:3
כֹּחִי וְרֵאשִׁית אוֹנִי		
יֶתֶר שְׂאֵת וְיֶתֶר עָז		
פַּחַז כַּמַּיִם אַל־תּוֹתַר		49:4
כִּי עָלִיתָ מִשְׁכְּבֵי אָבִיךָ		
אָז חִלַּלְתָּ יְצוּעִי עָלָה		

	Pro-Joseph layer	Pro-Judah layer
48:17		Joseph saw his father was to lay his right hand on Ephraim's head, it was bad in his eyes; he took his father's hand to move it from Ephraim's on Manasseh's head.
48:18		And Joseph said to his father, "Not so, father, for this one is the first-born, put your right hand on his head."
48:19		But his father refused, and said, "I know, my son, I know, he also shall be a people, also be great; yet, his younger brother shall be greater than he, his seed will be a multitude of peoples."
48:20		So he blessed them on that day, saying, "By you Israel will bless, saying, May God make you as Ephraim and as Manasseh"; and so he placed Ephraim for Manasseh.
48:21	And Israel said to Joseph, "Look, I am about to die, but God will be with you, return you to the land of your fathers.	
48:22	And I give Shechem to you, O One above your brothers; which I took from the hand of Amorites with my sword and my bow."	
49:1		And Jacob called to his sons and said: "Gather that I may tell you what will happen to you in days hereafter.
49:2		Assemble and listen, sons of Jacob and listen to Israel your father.
49:3		Reuben, my firstborn are you, my might and firstling of my strength, superior in tallness and in power;
49:4		deceptive like water — no superiority, for you went up to your father's bed, then defiled the concubine's couch.

Pro-Judah layer	Pro-Joseph layer	
שִׁמְעוֹן וְלֵוִי אַחִים		49:
כְּלֵי חָמָס מְכֵרֹתֵיהֶם(!)		
בְּסֹדָם אַל־תָּבֹא נַפְשִׁי		49:
בִּקְהָלָם אַל־תֵּחַד כְּבֹדִי		
כִּי בְאַפָּם הָרְגוּ אִישׁ		
וּבִרְצֹנָם עִקְּרוּ־שׁוֹר		
אָרוּר אַפָּם כִּי עָז		49:
וְעֶבְרָתָם כִּי קָשָׁתָה		
אֲחַלְּקֵם בְּיַעֲקֹב וַאֲפִיצֵם בְּיִשְׂרָאֵל		
יְהוּדָה אַתָּה		49:
יוֹדוּךָ אַחֶיךָ		
יָדְךָ בְּעֹרֶף אֹיְבֶיךָ		
יִשְׁתַּחֲווּ לְךָ בְּנֵי אָבִיךָ		
גּוּר אַרְיֵה יְהוּדָה		49:
מִטֶּרֶף בְּנִי עָלִיתָ		
כָּרַע רָבַץ כְּאַרְיֵה		
וּכְלָבִיא מִי יְקִימֶנּוּ		
לֹא־יָסוּר שֵׁבֶט מִיהוּדָה		49:
וּמְחֹקֵק מִבֵּין רַגְלָיו עַד(!)		
כִּי־יָבֹא שַׁי לֹה(!)		
וְלוֹ יִקְּהַת עַמִּים		
אֹסְרִי לַגֶּפֶן עִירֹה		49:
וְלַשֹּׂרֵקָה בְּנִי אֲתֹנוֹ		
כִּבֵּס בַּיַּיִן לְבֻשׁוֹ		
וּבְדַם־עֲנָבִים סוּתֹה		
חַכְלִילִי עֵינַיִם מִיָּיִן		49:
וּלְבֶן־שִׁנַּיִם מֵחָלָב		
זְבוּלֻן לְחוֹף יַמִּים יִשְׁכֹּן		49:
וְהוּא לְחוֹף אֳנִיּוֹת		
וְיַרְכָתוֹ עַל־צִידֹן		
יִשָּׂשכָר חֲמֹר גָּרֶם		49:
רֹבֵץ בֵּין הַמִּשְׁפְּתָיִם		49:
וַיַּרְא מְנֻחָה כִּי טוֹב		
וְאֶת־הָאָרֶץ כִּי נָעֵמָה		
וַיֵּט שִׁכְמוֹ לִסְבֹּל		
וַיְהִי לְמַס־עֹבֵד		

	Pro-Joseph layer	Pro-Judah layer
49:5		Simeon and Levi are brothers, weapons of violence are their knives.
49:6		My soul enter not in their company, my glory rejoice not in their gathering; For in their anger they slew a man, in their wantonness hamstrung a bull;
49:7		cursed be their anger, for it is fierce, and their wrath, for it is cruel, I will divide them in Jacob, scatter them in Israel
49:8		Judah are you, your brothers shall praise you, Your hand on your enemies' neck your father's sons shall bow to you.
49:9		A lion's whelp is Judah, may you grow up, my son, from prey; If he stoops down, couches as a lion, a "king's lion": "who will raise him?"
49:10		The sceptre shall not depart from Judah nor the ruler's staff ever from between his feet, For certain, let tribute come to him, and may the peoples obey him.
49:11		May he bind his foal to the vine, and his ass's colt to the choice vine; May he wash his garments in wine, and his vesture in the blood of grapes;
49:12		His eyes shall be darker than wine, his teeth whiter than milk.
49:13		Zebulun — at the wide sea's beach he will dwell; May he be a beach for ships, and his spur facing Sidon.
49:14		Issachar is a strong ass, couching between the donkey-packs;
49:15		And he sees the rest, that it is good, and the land, that it is pleasant; He bends his shoulder to bear, and is a serving corvée worker.

Pro-Judah layer	Pro-Joseph layer	
דָּן יָדִֹן(!) עַמֹּו כְּאַחַד שִׁבְטֵי יִשְׂרָאֵל		49:16
יְהִי־דָן נָחָשׁ עֲלֵי־דֶרֶךְ שְׁפִיפֹן עֲלֵי־אֹרַח הַנֹּשֵׁךְ עִקְּבֵי־סוּס וַיִּפֹּל רֹכְבֹו אָחֹור		49:17
[לִישׁוּעָתְךָ קִוִּיתִי יְהוָה]		49:18
גָּד גְּדוּד יְגוּדֶנּוּ וְהוּא יָגֻד עֲקֵבָם(!)		49:19
אָשֵׁר(!) שְׁמֵנָה לַחְמֹו וְהוּא יִתֵּן מַעֲדַנֵּי־מֶלֶךְ		49:20
נַפְתָּלִי אַיָּלָה(!) שְׁלֻחָה(!) הַנֹּתֵן אִמְרֵי־שָׁפֶר		49:21
	בֵּן פֹּרָת(!) יֹוסֵף בֵּן פֹּרָת(!) עֲלֵי־עָיִן בָּנֹות צָעֲדָה עֲלֵי־שׁוּר(!!)	49:22
	וַיְמָרְרֻהוּ(!) וָרֹבּוּ	49:23
	וְיִשְׂטְמֻהוּ(!) בַּעֲלֵי חִצִּים וַתֵּשֶׁב בְּאֵיתָן קַשְׁתֹּו וַיָּפֹזּוּ זְרֹעֵי יָדָיו מִידֵי ...	49:24
אֲבִיר יַעֲקֹב מִשָּׁם(!)	... רֹעֶה אֶבֶן יִשְׂרָאֵל	
	מֵאֵל אָבִיךָ וְיַעְזְרֶךָּ וְאֵת שַׁדַּי וִיבָרְכֶךָּ בִּרְכֹת שָׁמַיִם מֵעָל בִּרְכֹת תְּהֹום רֹבֶצֶת תָּחַת בִּרְכֹת שָׁדַיִם וָרָחַם	49:25
	בִּרְכֹת אָבִיךָ גָּבְרוּ וְעַל(!!) בִּרְכֹת הֹורַי עַד	49:26
תַּאֲוַת גִּבְעֹת עֹולָם ... יֹוסֵף וּלְקָדְקֹד נְזִיר ... (??)	תִּהְיֶיןָ לְרֹאשׁ ... ... אֶחָיו	
בִּנְיָמִין זְאֵב יִטְרָף בַּבֹּקֶר יֹאכַל עַד וְלָעֶרֶב יְחַלֵּק שָׁלָל		49:27

Pro-Joseph layer	Pro-Judah layer
	49:16 Dan — his people will be strong, like one of the tribes of Israel;

	49:17 May Dan be a snake by the way,
	  a viper by the path;
	that bites the horse's heels
	  so that the rider falls backwards.

	49:18 [For your salvation I'm waiting, YHWH!]
	49:19 Gad — when raiders will raid him, he will raid their heels!
	49:20 Asher — may fatness be his food, and let he bring forth royal delicacies.
	49:21 May Naphtali be a lambing ewe, that brings forth lovely lambs.

49:22 A bullcalf is Joseph
  a bullcalf next to a well,
in the meadow he will stride towards
 the Bull,
49:23 and he will make him strong so they
 will become numerous.
And (if) archers will harass him,
49:24 his bow will remain stable,
  the arms of his hands be nimble,
by the hands of ...
  ...the Shepherd of Israel's stone,
49:25 by El, your Father, who will help you,
  and by Shadday, who will bless you,
The blessings of the Heavens above,
  blessings of the Flood, resting below,
  blessings of breasts and womb,
49:26 blessings of your father, mighty, exalted
blessings of my progenitors of old,
 	
  may they be on the head of ...
    ... (of) his brothers.
	the Strong One of Jacob, by the name of
	
	the longings of the everlasting hills.
	Joseph, on the crown of the $n^e zir$ of (?)

	49:27 Benjamin is a wolf, who will tear apart,
	  in the morning he'll devour the prey,
	  and in the evening divide the spoil."

Pro-Judah layer	Pro-Joseph layer	
כָּל־אֵלֶּה שִׁבְטֵי יִשְׂרָאֵל שְׁנֵים עָשָׂר		49:28
וְזֹאת אֲשֶׁר־דִּבֶּר לָהֶם אֲבִיהֶם וַיְבָרֶךְ אוֹתָם		
אִישׁ אֲשֶׁר כְּבִרְכָתוֹ בֵּרַךְ אֹתָם		
וַיְצַו אוֹתָם וַיֹּאמֶר אֲלֵהֶם		49:29
אֲנִי נֶאֱסָף אֶל־עַמִּי		
קִבְרוּ אֹתִי אֶל־אֲבֹתָי		
אֶל־הַמְּעָרָה אֲשֶׁר בִּשְׂדֵה עֶפְרוֹן הַחִתִּי		
בַּמְּעָרָה אֲשֶׁר בִּשְׂדֵה הַמַּכְפֵּלָה		49:30
אֲשֶׁר עַל־פְּנֵי־מַמְרֵא בְּאֶרֶץ כְּנָעַן		
אֲשֶׁר קָנָה אַבְרָהָם אֶת־הַשָּׂדֶה		
מֵאֵת עֶפְרֹן הַחִתִּי לַאֲחֻזַּת־קָבֶר		
שָׁמָּה קָבְרוּ אֶת־אַבְרָהָם		49:31
וְאֵת שָׂרָה אִשְׁתּוֹ		
שָׁמָּה קָבְרוּ אֶת־יִצְחָק		
וְאֵת רִבְקָה אִשְׁתּוֹ		
וְשָׁמָּה קָבַרְתִּי אֶת־לֵאָה		
מִקְנֵה הַשָּׂדֶה וְהַמְּעָרָה		49:32
אֲשֶׁר־בּוֹ מֵאֵת בְּנֵי־חֵת		
וַיְכַל יַעֲקֹב לְצַוֹּת אֶת־בָּנָיו		49:33
	וַיֶּאֱסֹף רַגְלָיו אֶל־הַמִּטָּה	
	וַיִּגְוַע וַיֵּאָסֶף אֶל־עַמָּיו	
	וַיִּפֹּל יוֹסֵף עַל־פְּנֵי אָבִיו	50:1
	וַיֵּבְךְּ עָלָיו וַיִּשַּׁק־לוֹ	

	Pro-Joseph layer	Pro-Judah layer
49:28		All these are the twelve tribes of Israel,
		And this is what their father said to
		them, when he blessed them,
		each according his blessing he blessed
		them.
49:29		Then he charged them and said them,
		I am to be gathered to my people,
		bury me with my fathers
		in the cave in the field of Ephron
		the Hittite,
49:30		in the cave in the field of Machpelah,
		facing Mamre in the land Canaan
		which Abraham bought with the field
		from Ephron the Hittite as a cemetry.
49:31		There they buried Abraham
		and Sarah his wife,
		there they buried Isaac
		and Rebekah his wife,
		and there I buried Leah;
49:32		the buy of the field and the cave
		which is in it, was from the Hittites.
49:33		When Jacob finished charging his sons,
	(Then) he gathered his feet into the bed	
	breathed his last and was gathered to	
	his people.	
50:1	And Joseph fell on his father's face	
	and he wept over him and kissed him.	

6.7   Historical Considerations

6.7.1   Introduction: The Problem

Previous research on Genesis 49 and on the Joseph Story generally sketched two different pictures with regard to the historical background of these final chapters of Genesis. With regard to Genesis 49 the scholarly view is that the sayings in this chapter reflect the situation among the tribes in the so-called pre-monarchic period. However, with respect to the Joseph Story the scholarly opinions differ considerably, because the origin of the narrative as a unity or as a product of different traditions is decisive for the analysis of the historical background of the narrative. Yet, putting aside these differences for the moment, a description of the historical background of the Joseph Story could be set at the beginning at the eighteenth century BCE, followed by the Hyksos period, the Amarna period, the pre-monarchic period, the United Monarchy, the Northern kingdom directly after the end of the United Monarchy, the time of Hezekiah, or Josiah, and finally the Exilic and post-Exilic period.[528] In these datings we have to differentiate between two main approaches, one is a more or less historistic approach, considering the narrative as a report of historical events with regard to Joseph, and on the other hand an approach which takes the Story as a kind of historical narrative,[529] reflecting a historical background in which the main figures of the narrative might represent historical entities (sometimes "tribes", and sometimes just "Israel") in a later time than the narrated one. In addition a kind of middle course is found sometimes with those who consider part of the narrated events as historical events although the narrative might have been revised considerably in a later period, reflecting in that way the period of revision.

   The present study reached a different conclusion concerning the origin of the two literary entities, Genesis 49 and the remaining part of the Deathbed Episode (Gen. 47:29–48:22; 49:29–33), namely that the whole Deathbed Episode has to be regarded as a unity, both in its final version ("pro-Judah" version) as well as in the pre-revised version ("pro-Joseph" version). This conclusion forces us to look for a historical background of these versions, in which one might expect that an editor was interested to revise a "pro-Joseph" text in a "pro-Judahite" manner and, on the other hand, an earlier period in which

---

[528] For a description of the different proposals, cf. above, pp. 409–14, 442–4.

[529] Cf. H.M. Barstad, "History and the Hebrew Bible", in: L.L. Grabbe (ed.), *Can a 'History of Israel' Be Written?* (JSOTS, 245; ESHM, 1), Sheffield 1997, 37–64.

a "pro-Joseph" text could have originated. In our analysis it has been shown that the "pro-Judah" layer reflected a period in which somehow the prominent position of Judah over the other brothers is to be expected. The fact that this position is justified in the Deathbed Episode and is simultaneously in some tension with the "pro-Joseph" tendency, suggests that Judah's position was in need of legitimation, while there was also some need of a minimization of Joseph's position as apparently the oldest (or, at least the most important) son (*viz.* tribe). In our diachronic reading of the Deathbed Episode we suggested that the saying of Judah (Gen. 49:8–12) reflects the period of David and Solomon when the house of Judah reigned over "all Israel", while the first two sayings on Reuben and Simeon & Levi have to be dated in the same period because they are composed in order to support Judah's position within the Testament. Concerning the other sayings in Gen. 49:13–21, 27, the possibility of an exact dating seems virtually impossible, but they were assigned to the same layer as the saying on Judah[530] and as such they might reflect the time of the United Monarchy as well. If this assignment is correct, it might imply that the construction of the system of the twelve tribes originated during the same period, while in that sense the birthstory of the twelve and the Testament create the historical basis for that system.

Yet, whereas almost a decade ago such a thesis could be advanced without too much objection,[531] we are nowadays confronted with serious objections from different directions. For that reason we will discuss the findings of our diachronic analysis in relation to other dating proposals. In order to achieve this, we will consider first the different era which have been proposed for the Joseph Story and the Testament, varying from the post-Exilic era to the pre-monarchic period. Secondly, we will discuss the possibility of a dating during the reign of David and Solomon in relation to the different objections that might be advanced against this dating.

6.7.2   The Exilic and Post-Exilic Era

A post-Exilic dating has been suggested by N.P. Lemche,[532] although

---

[530]Cf. above, pp. 561–565.

[531]W.G. Dever, "Archaeology and the 'Age of Solomon': A Case Study in Archaeology and Historiography", in: L.K. Handy (ed.), *The Age of Solomon: Scholarship at the Turn of the Millennium* (SHCANE, 11), Leiden 1997, 217–51, 217; G.N. Knoppers, "The Vanishing Solomon: The Disappearance of the United Monarchy from Recent Histories of Ancient Israel", *JBL* 116 (1997) 19–44, 27–33.

[532]N.P. Lemche, *Die Vorgeschichte Israels: Von den Anfängen bis zum Ausgang des 13. Jahrhunderts v. Chr.* (BE, Bd. 1), Stuttgart 1996, 212–8. Cf. also

in his study he is in general concerned with the origin of Genesis as a "historical" writing. As we noted already in Chapter Five,[533] in his view the pronounced monotheistic outlook, the idea of immigrating strangers and the late date of origin of prose narratives argue in favour of a post-Exilic date. Nevertheless, Lemche does not exclude the possibility that the Pentateuch contained older material and has only been expanded in the post-Exilic era.[534] In addition we might refer to the arguments of H.-C. Schmitt and J.A. Soggin, of whom the latter's arguments are rather comparable to those of A. Meinhold, defending an Exilic date.[535] In Soggin's view the vision of Joseph as a blessing for Israel and for the foreign nation (Egypt) is intended to reassure to the readers that "it is the God of Israel who grants wisdom to the faithful and who directs human acts, even wicked ones, in order that good should finally come out of them as a result."[536] In the post-Exilic era things were not going well for Judah, political independence seemed for ever lost; the re-establishment of the Davidic dynasty has been put off to the end of time; the rule of the priests must at times have been hard to endure, considering the readiness of so many priests to compromise with the occupying powers."[537] Schmitt, finally, is strongly concerned with the final chapters of Genesis and argues on the basis of the contents of Gen. 49:1–12 for a post-Exilic date for at least Genesis 49.[538] In Schmitt's view the "twelve-eponymes-system" fails in the Joseph Story (at least in his "Judah-Israel layer"), and Gen. 49:8–12 establishes why Judah, the fourth in line, becomes the leader of his brothers.[539] The saying has to be interpreted in his view in an "eschatological-messianic" way, which is confirmed by the introduc-

---

J.A. Soggin, "Notes on the Joseph Story", in: A.G. Auld (ed.), *Understanding Poets and Prophets: Essays ... G.W. Anderson* (JSOTS, 152), Sheffield 1993, 336–49, 344; H.-C. Schmitt, "Die Josephsgechichte und das Deuteronomistische Geschichtswerk: Genesis 38 und 48–50", in: M. Vervenne, J. Lust (eds.), *Deuteronomy and Deuteronomic Literature: Fs C.H.W. Brekelmans* (BEThL, 133), Leuven 1997, 391–405.

[533] Cf. above, p. 417.

[534] Lemche, *Die Vorgeschichte Israels*, 218: "Mit solchen Erwägungen soll nicht ausgeschlossen sein, daß der Pentateuch sehr wohl wenigstens teilweise älter und in der nachexilischen Zeit nur mit Zusätzen erweitert worden sein kann".

[535] A. Meinhold, "Die Gattung der Josephsgeschichte und des Estherbuches: Diasporanovelle I", *ZAW* 87 (1975) 306–24; idem, "Die Gattung der Josephsgeschichte und des Estherbuches: Diasporanovelle II", *ZAW* 88 (1976) 72–93. See also J. Van Seters, *Prologue to History: The Yahwist as Historian in Genesis*, Louisville (KY) 1992, 332.

[536] Soggin, "Notes on the Joseph Story", 344.

[537] Soggin, "Notes on the Joseph Story", 344.

[538] Schmitt, "Josephsgeschichte und Deuteronomische Geschichtswerk", 396–9.

[539] Schmitt, "Josephsgeschichte und Deuteronomische Geschichtswerk", 398.

tion of the Blessing, where the contents of the Blessing are related to the "end of days" (49:1C).[540]

However, in our view there are some problems with the assumption of this date and the arguments put forward to support it. Starting with Lemche's arguments, it might first be asked if the book of Genesis has indeed a pronounced monotheistic outlook as he assumes. We have argued with regard to Genesis 49 that we find here the remnants of an ancestor cult, which implies a polytheistic outlook.[541] Lemche considers certain passages in Genesis (*e.g.* Gen. 31:19, 30, 32, 34–5) as traces of an earlier religion-historical stage which have survived. Yet, these passages are examples of the un-monotheistic outlook of Genesis, which might be corrected later on by the addition of other texts (Gen. 35:2–4).[542] Lemche adduces some examples for the monotheistic believe of the patriarchs, such as the election of Abraham by God or His revelation to Abraham and Jacob.[543] But, as far as we are aware, the idea of the personal God who reveals himself to one of his protégées is found already in the Ugaritic legend of king Kirtu (KTU 1.15–17).[544] Moreover, monotheistic religion is attested already at the end of the Late Bronze in Egypt, and its influence is also found in Canaan, so it might be a too easy argument for a late date of Genesis.[545] Therefore, his argument for the clear monotheistic thought in

---

[540]Schmitt, "Josephsgeschichte und Deuteronomische Geschichtswerk", 398: "Näherliegend scheint mir eine eschatologisch-messianische Interpretation des Judaspruches zu sein, wofür auch die Einleitung des Jakobsegens in Gen 49,1b mit ihrer Feststellung spricht, daß der Segen Jakobs sich auf das bezieht, was 'am Ende der Tage' geschieht."

[541]Cf. above, pp. 110–1; see also p. 532, with n. 325.

[542]Cf. Lemche, *Die Vorgeschichte Iraels*, 210, 214–5.

[543]Lemche, *Die Vorgechichte Israels*, 210.

[544]On the subject of revelation in Ugarit in comparison with the Hebrew Bible, see A. Jeffers, "Divination by Dreams in Ugaritic Literature and in the Old Testament", *IBS* 12 (1990) 167–83. On Kirtu, cf. J.C. de Moor, "The Crisis of Polytheism in Late Bronze Ugarit", in: *Crisis and Perspectives: Studies in Ancient Near Eastern Polytheism, Biblical Theology, Palestinian Archaeology and Intertestamental Literature* (OTS, 24), Leiden 1986, 1–20, 12–4; idem, *RoY*, 89–93; *RoY*², 91–5. On the "pre-priestly" material in the patriarchal narratives in Genesis and the question if we are dealing here with monotheistic or monolatristic tendency, cf. V. Fritz, "Die Bedeutung der vorpriesterschriftlichen Vätererzählungen für die Religionsgeschichte der Königszeit", in: W. Dietrich, M.A. Klopfenstein (Hrsg.), *Ein Gott allein? JHWH-Verehrung und biblischer Monotheismus im Kontext der israelitischen und altorientalischen Religionsgeschichte* (OBO, 139), Freiburg, Göttingen 1994, 403–11. See also Houtman, *Der Pentateuch*, 228.

[545]Lemche, *Die Vorgeschichte Israels*, 211, doubts if we are dealing with a *monotheistischer Umbruch* in Akhenaten's reform, and he suggests that this reform was rather politically than religiously inspired. Even if this is true, it still remains a fact that the contents of Akhenaten's reform was monotheistic. On the

these episodes cannot bear the burden of proof for a post-Exilic date for these texts.

The idea of the immigrating strangers was used against a dating during the reign of king Josiah, because this would not fit in easily with a settled people. In this context the argument seems unlikely because such an origin tradition does not correspond with the *present* situation of a people, even though it might reflect a *recent past*. Yet, origin traditions making reference to a nomadic past or the like were preserved sometimes during long periods, as for example, the Amorite dynasties in Mesopotamia.[546] In addition it might be argued that Deutero-Isaiah presupposes the narratives of Genesis. Apparently these narratives had such a form in which history moved from creation, along the patriarchs to the Exodus. Even (*Ur-*)Deuteronomy must have been known by him and it therefore appears that the dating of the origin of these narratives in or after the Exile is quite hazardous.[547]

The assumption that prose narratives originated late is a very insecure argument. First of all, an exact definition (and consequently a clear cut division) of poetry and prose in the Hebrew Bible is hard to provide and several passages in the book of Genesis have been identified as poetry.[548] However, independently of the question how

---

religion of the New Kingdom and its impact on Canaan, cf. De Moor, *RoY*, 42–68, 101–3; *RoY*², 41–71, 103–5 (with ample bibliography); T.N.D. Mettinger, "Aniconism — A West Semitic Context for the Israelite Phenomenon", in: Dietrich, Klopfenstein (Hrsg.), *Ein Gott allein?* 159–78; idem, *No Graven Image? Israelite Aniconism in Its Ancient Near Eastern Context* (CB OTS, 42), Stockholm 1995, 49–54.

[546] Cf. K.R. Veenhof, "Geschiedenis van het oude Nabije Oosten tot de tijd van Alexander de Grote", *BijbH*, dl. I, 278–441, 322–3. Cf. also K. Whitelam, "Israel's Traditions of Origin: Reclaiming the Land", *JSOT* 44 (1989) 19–42, 21–7, presenting material from different cultures and contexts in which *settled* people developed origin traditions that do not correspond with their present situation. As Whitelam demonstrates, the most important question with regard to those traditions (Israel's and those from different cultures) is the question, who was interested in the development of such origin traditions?

[547] Cf. in this respect B.J. van der Merwe, *Pentateuchtradisies in die prediking van Deuterojesaja*, Groningen 1955, 90–144.

[548] On the problem in general, cf. W.G.E. Watson, *Classical Hebrew Poetry: A Guide to its Techniques* (JSOTS, 26), Sheffield ²1986, 44–62; J.C. de Moor, W.G.E. Watson, "General Introduction", *VANEP*, ix–xviii; Regarding specific texts in Genesis, see: J.S. Kselman, "A Note on Gen. 7:11", *CBQ* 35 (1973) 491–3; idem, "The Recovery from Poetic Fragments from the Pentateuchal Priestly Source", *JBL* 97 (1978) 161–73; B. Porten, U. Rappaport, "Poetic Structure in Genesis IX 7", *VT* 21 (1971) 363–9; M.H. Lichtenstein, "Idiom, Rhetoric and the Text of Genesis 41:16", *JANES* 19 (1989) 85–94; L. Roersma, "The First-Born of Abraham: An Analysis of the Poetic Stucture of Genesis 16", *VANEP*, 219–42;

Gen. 49:1–2 should be regarded — as poetry or prose — reference can be made to a structurally comparable passage in the *Umwelt*, which is evidently from the eighth century BCE, namely the plaster text from Deir 'Alla.[549] In this text the following passage is found (combination I.4–6):[550]

wy'mr. lhm	And he said to them:
šbw. 'hwkm. mh. šd[yn]w	"Return! I shall tell you what the *shaddayin* are ...
lkw. r'w. p'lt. 'lhn	Go on, consider the doings of the gods.
'l[h]n. 'tyhdw	The gods have gathered together,
wnṣbw. šdyn. mw'd	and the shaddayin have met in assembly."

In our view this text is in its structure comparable to the introduction of the Testament in Gen. 49:1–2:[551]

And Jacob called to his sons (1A)	וַיִּקְרָא יַעֲקֹב אֶל־בָּנָיו
and said: "Gather that I may tell you (1B)	וַיֹּאמֶר הֵאָסְפוּ וְאַגִּידָה לָכֶם
what will happen to you in days hereafter. (1C)	אֵת אֲשֶׁר־יִקְרָא אֶתְכֶם
	בְּאַחֲרִית הַיָּמִים
Assemble and listen, sons of Jacob, (2A)	הִקָּבְצוּ וְשִׁמְעוּ בְּנֵי יַעֲקֹב
and listen to Israel your father." (2B)	וְשִׁמְעוּ אֶל־יִשְׂרָאֵל אֲבִיכֶם

Even though this text is not an exact parallel, it might be an indication that the literature in Genesis is in its form comparable to clearly pre-Exilic, extra-biblical texts.[552] In addition it has to be em-

---

H.-F. Richter, "Das Liedgut am Anfang der 'jahwistischen Urgeschichte'", *WdO* 25 (1994) 78–108. Cf. also our analysis of the framework of Genesis 49.

[549] For the dating of the text, cf. G. van der Kooij, "Book and Script at Deir 'Alla", in: J. Hoftijzer, G. van der Kooij (eds.), *The Balaam Text from Deir 'Alla Re-evaluated*, Leiden 1991, 239–62, 257 (between 800 and 720 BCE); M. Dijkstra, "Response to Lectures of Prof. E Puech and Dr. G. van der Kooij", in: *ibid.*, 263–70, 267 ("a date around or even before 800 confirmed by C¹⁴ datings, becomes almost inevitable.").

[550] Quoted after A. Wolters, "Aspects of the Literary Structure of Combination I", in: Hoftijzer, van der Kooij (eds.), *The Balaam Text from Deir 'Alla Re-evaluated*, 294–304, 295. Another interpretation of the text is found in M. Weippert, "The Balaam Text from Deir 'Allā and the Study of the Old Testament", *ibid.*, 151–84, 154–6.

[551] Next to this text, which is the most relevant for our research, reference could be made to Gen. 28:10–7 which, despite other differences, also shows comparable literary features.

[552] Cf. in this respect also the examples adduced in R.S. Hendel, *The Epic of the Patriarch: The Jacob Cycle and the Narrative Traditions of Canaan and Israel* (HSM, 42), Atlanta (GA) 1987, *e.g.* 61–2. Furthermore, on these problems C. Conroy, "Hebrew Epic: Historical Notes and Critical Reflections", *Bib* 61 (1980) 1–30; W.G.E. Watson, *Classical Hebrew Poetry: A Guide to its Techniques* (JSOTS, 26), Sheffield ²1986, 83–6.

phasized that the text of the Hebrew Bible is in the view of many scholars extensively adapted to a quite uniform text according to a standarized form of (biblical) Hebrew. For that reason the argument of a late origin of prose naratives cannot be considered to be decisive, for it cannot be excluded that the revision of the text also included an addition of typically prose-style elements.

Finally, as a principal argument against a date for the origin of the Deathbed Episode during or after the Exile it should be noted that this date raises insurmountable problems with regard to the intepretation of the text. First of all some of the aetiologies found in the text, like the priority of Ephraim over Manasseh (Gen. 48:13–20) are superfluous and even incomprehensible if the Northern kingdom would had terminated some centuries before.[553] In case these narratives reflect indeed the situation in which they originated, as the famous dictum of Wellhausen states,[554] a date of origin after the end of the Northern kingdom seems illusionary. This becomes especially clear when considering the legitimizing function of the Deathbed Episode in favour of Judah and diminishing Joseph's position. During and after the Exile there was no need anymore to defend Judah's position over Joseph and the other brothers because they were lost.[555] In our view Schmitt's argument that Judah's position had to be established as a younger brother over the others is in this respect unnecessary. Such a position might have been defended at the time it was questioned, but not at the moment when nobody could question it anymore.[556] Furthermore, whereas Soggin states that the things were not going well for Judah,[557] it should be pointed out that the Deathbed Episode and the whole Joseph Story suggest that Judah's star is rising. Fur-

---

[553]Cf. in this respect also L. Ruppert, "Zur neueren Diskussion um die Josefsgeschichte der Genesis", *BZ* 33 (1989) 92–7, esp. 97.

[554]This dictum is quoted above, p. 410. Cf. also our reference to K. Whitelam on p. 601, n. 563, below.

[555]Cf. also n. 553, above.

[556]Concerning Schmitt's interpretation of בְּאַחֲרִית הַיָּמִים as an eschatological reference to the "end of days", see our discussion of this expression above, pp. 86–7, with n. 26. The expression means literally "in the afterwards of days" (= "in days hereafter"; cf. Seebaß, below), the *interpretation* "in the end of days" can only be defended in a small number of texts, namely in Dan. 2:28; 10:14; and possibly in Isa. 2:2 = Mi. 4:1; Ezek. 38:16; Hos. 3:5. Cf. H. Seebaß, "אַחֲרִית", *ThWAT*, Bd. I, 224–8, esp. 227–8. Yet, even for these texts a rendering "in days hereafter" would be possible, because even though a new era might brake through (a "kingdom to come"), time apparently will continue and thus the "end of days" is not predicted. Schmitt's interpretation of the expression is therefore biased and consequently his argument for dating in the post-Exilic era is weakened.

[557]Soggin, "Notes on the Joseph Story", 344.

thermore, the attempt to minimize Joseph's position in the subtle manner we find in Genesis 48 and by the contrast between Gen. 37:10 and 49:8, can only imply that there existed a tension between the two entities represented by these two brothers Judah and Joseph. For that reason the date during or after the exile is in our view unlikely and we would prefer therefore much more the option left open by Lemche,[558] namely that Genesis originated before the Exile whereas only some expansions might have been added.

The arguments adduced above apply in our view also to the Exilic era, the period to which other scholars prefer to date the Joseph Story.[559] In addition to these arguments it might be objected that the Exile is hardly a period in which Israel would have been able to invent its (prologue to) history. Lamentations and Second-Isaiah — to the latter Van Seters also refers[560] — clearly testify of the great distress in which the Jewish community was living during the Exile.[561] It is remarkable that the narratives in Genesis do not reflect in this respect the situation of the Exile, neither simply with regard to the country, nor regarding the crisis in which the Jewish community was. Yet, this does not exclude the possibility that the people of the Exile found new hope, a kind of programme in these narratives of the Pentateuch.[562] But, it seems unlikely that the body of these stories originated during the Exile without leaving any clear traces of this period in these narratives.[563]

---

[558] Lemche, *Die Vorgeschichte Israels*, 218.

[559] Meinhold, "Die Gattung der Josephsgeschichte, I", 306–24; Van Seters, *Prologue to History*, 332.

[560] Van Seters, *Prologue to History*, 332.

[561] Cf. B. Albrektson, *Studies in the Text and the Theology of the Book of Lamentations*, Lund 1963, 214–39; J. Renkema, *Misschien is er hoop: De theologische vooronderstellingen van het boek Klaagliederen*, Franeker 1983, 130–9, 238–9, 267–323, 325–31; J.C. de Moor, "The Integrity of Isaiah 40", in: M. Dietrich, O. Loretz (Hrsg.), *Mesopotamica — Ugaritica — Biblica: Fs K. Bergerhof* (AOAT, 232), Kevelaer, Neukirchen 1993, 181–216, esp. 208–11.

[562] Cf. Lemche, *Die Vorgeschichte Israels*, 216.

[563] It is interesting to refer in this respect to some of the remarks in K. Whitelam, "Between History and Literature: The Social Production of Israel's Traditions of Origin", *SJOT* 5.2 (1991) 60–74. Although he himself prefers to read many of the traditions concerning the occupation of the land as a late tradition (see also his "Israel's Traditions of Origin", 19–42; idem, *The Invention of Ancient Israel: The Silencing of Palestinian History*, London 1996), he draws attention to the use of the past in the present. After referring to other studies, he states, "it is noteworthy that many stories of migration or external conquest present political or economic ties or provide justifications for occupying a particular territory". Yet, in our view the justification of post-Exilic affairs is missing in texts like, for instance, Genesis. On the other hand, this does not exclude the fact that after

6.7.3   The Pre-Exilic Era: The Two States

In this section we will discuss the possibility of a date after the end of
the United Monarchy under David and Solomon for the different layers
in the Deathbed Episode. As described in Chapter Five[564] several
arguments are put forward to defend a date during that period, yet,
in most of these cases we are dealing with studies which are concerned
with the Joseph Story *without* the Testament of Jacob. It is, however,
interesting to observe that most of these proposals are based on the
observation that the Joseph Story had principally a positive attitude
towards Joseph and that the Story was adapted later in a more pro-
Judahite fashion. The positive attitude toward Joseph is considered
to be an indication that the narrative originated in Josephite circles,
viz. the Northern Kingdom. The question of Joseph's kingship (Gen.
37:8) is, in the view of these scholars, answered positively: Joseph has
to be regarded as the king of his brothers. This narrative is regarded
as a product of the court of Jeroboam in Shechem after the ending
of the United Monarchy,[565] but when Joseph's measures are taken
into consideration then they are considered as reflecting the eighth
century Northern Kingdom and its policy.[566] Then, after the decline
of the Northern Kingdom the tradition is adopted in the South and
adapted to the situation of that time; an adaption, which might have
taken place during the reign of Hezekiah[567] or Josiah.[568]

This picture of an initial "Josephite" tradition in which Joseph
is regarded as the leader of his brothers, which is corrected later in
the South corresponds very well with the results of our analysis. In
Blum's analysis the function of Genesis 49 is taken into consideration
and as such — even if we differ widely in our analysis at other points

---

the Exile the narratives in Genesis could be used to justify certain situations,
even though they were not written with an eye to that era. But, with regard to
pre-Exilic affairs, we might refer to the "absence" of Jerusalem in Genesis (cf.
Genesis 14) and the positive attitude towards the cities Shechem and Bethel, and
the open-minded approach to the fact that the patriarchs sacrificed at these sites.

[564] Cf. above, pp. 415–7.

[565] I. Willi-Plein, "Historiographische Aspekte der Josefsgeschichte", *Henoch* 1
(1979) 305–331, 308; W. Dietrich, *Die Josepherzählung als Novelle und Geschichtsschreibung: zugleich ein Beitrag zur Pentateuchfrage* (BThSt, 14), Neukirchen 1989, 59–66; N. Shupak, "סיפור יוסף — בין אגדה להיסטוריה", in: M.V. Fox *et
al.* (eds.), *Texts, Temples, and Traditions: A Tribute to Menahem Haran*, Winona
Lake (IN) 1996, 125*–33*.

[566] Blum, *Die Komposition der Vätergeschichte*, 260–3.

[567] Dietrich, *Die Josepherzählung*, 71–8, esp. 76; N. Kebekus, *Die Joseferzählung:
Literarkritische und redaktionsgeschichtliche Untersuchungen zu Genesis 37–50*,
Münster 1990, 250–7.

[568] Blum, *Die Komposition der Vätergeschichte* 260–3.

— the recognition of the pro-Joseph and pro-Judahite tendencies in the Joseph Story is significant.[569] However, in our view there is an important obstacle to date a "pro-Judahite" redaction after the fall of Samaria. It is the question of the legitimizing and/or aetiological function of the narratives in Genesis, or how the past — to say it in the words of Whitelam — "is used to address questions of the present".[570] In case the Joseph Story of Genesis and the Deathbed Episode in particular are considered as explanations of "a present" it is hard to envisage how this Deathbed Episode explains the political structure of power during the reign of Hezekiah and Josiah. As we argued already above (section 6.5.1.5[571]) there are no data available to suggest that Judah had a leading position among his other "brothers" during the reign of Hezekiah, nor that he had such during Josiah's reign. Also the blessing of the patriarch of Ephraim and Manasseh (part of the "pro-Judah" layer) in which Ephraim's strength over Manasseh is predicted (Gen. 48:19), seems to be out of date, when the land is laid waste by the Assyrians. Nothing in these stories, however, reflects the Assyrian campaigns in the North, nor the deportation of the people, nor the fall of its capital Samaria. It might be objected of course that this part of the narrative was part of the "pro-Joseph" layer and that it originated as such in an earlier period. Yet, even in that case, the problem remains that the other obvious "pro-Judah" elements are unlikely a product of the era after the fall of Samaria. For that reason these elements ought to be dated in an earlier period in which they might have been originated.

The suggestion by some scholars that the original Joseph Story (including the Deathbed Episode, but without the Testament in Genesis 49) originated during the reign of Jeroboam has also to be rejected. According to Willi-Plein the Joseph Story contains a slight criticism of Judah[572] reflecting a Northern attitude. However, it has been argued several times that Judah is favoured as the true heir of his father and that Joseph was, in fact denied that position. This problem is solved explicitly in Genesis 49 (vv. 8–12), and, on the other hand, by the subtle manner of depriving Joseph of his power (Genesis 48). There-

---

[569] Cf. Blum's statement (*Die Komposition der Vätergeschichte*, 260): "Wie m.E. noch zu erkennen ist, wurden diese [*viz.* "ausgeprägt israelitischen Überlieferungen", RdH] auch nicht durch Eingriffe in die Textsubstanz transformiert, sondern durch die behutsame Einarbeitung einer judäischen Gegenposition, welche (besonders in dem neugebildeten Höhepunkt Gen 49*) nun Juda die Stelle Josephs einnehmen läßt, 'korrigiert'."

[570] Whitelam, "Between History and Literature", 66–7.

[571] Esp. pp. 525–526.

[572] Willi-Plein, "Historiographische Aspekte", 323 (cf. above, pp. 414–5).

fore, a dating of large parts of the Deathbed Episode during the reign of Jeroboam has to be denied.

6.7.4   The Pre-Monarchic Period

Considering Israel's earliest traditions, it has generally been thought that the sources J and E used ancient oral traditions of Israel's origin. For that reason it might be asked whether the Deathbed Episode, and more specificly Genesis 49, has been part of a pre-monarchic tradition. This question arises especially with regard to the question whether the "pro-Judah" layer within the Deathbed Episode could have existed already in the pre-monarchic era.

This question is in fact hypothetical, for, as far as we are aware, there is no scholar nowadays who has defended such a theory, and the question can be answered rather shortly in the negative. We have no indications at all that during the pre-monarchic era Judah had a leading position in Israel.[573] The literary testimony of the Hebrew Bible to that era is unmistakable[574] in the sense that Judah only rose to power because of David's reign.[575] For that reason there seems no reason to consider this question any further.

6.7.5   The Davidic and Solomonic Era

With the last conclusion in the preceding paragraph concerning the rise of Judah during David's reign we have reached the final part of our historical considerations. Is it historically probable that the Deathbed Episode in its present form came into being during the reign of David or Solomon? We will try to give an answer to this question by approaching the problem from two different directions,

---

[573]In fact, scholars sometimes even asume that Judah only became part of Israel at the moment David established his power over "all Israel" and united in that way both political entities. Cf. *e.g.* Ahlström, *History of Ancient Palestine*, 460–7; W. Dietrich, *Die frühe Königszeitin Israel: 10. Jahrhundert v. Chr.* (BE, 3), Stuttgart 1997, 160–3 (cf. also *op.cit.*, 263–8). This assumption is based mainly on the report of the rise of David's kingship in 2 Samuel 2–4, but also on texts in Judges where traditions concerning judges from Judah are lacking (Dietrich, *op.cit.*, 160, with n. 9) and the tribe of Judah is apparently absent in the Song of Deborah (but contrast J.C. de Moor, "The Twelve Tribes in the Song of Deborah", *VT* 43 [1993] 483–93; yet, also in his reconstruction of the list of tribes, De Moor assumes that Judah gained power under David, not before [*art.cit.*, 490–1]).

[574]This has even to be said with respect to Judg. 1:2, which does not imply Judah's leadership even though it reflects an unmistakable positive attitude toward Judah. However, this might be compared to the identical pattern in Genesis 37–47, where Judah also has an important function without being the explicit leader.

[575]Cf. the short overview in Sarna, *Genesis*, 335.

namely from a historical point of view and from an ideological point of view. To begin with, is it historically probable that in the era of David and Solomon such a literary activity as the "pro-Judahite" revision was performed? Secondly, why should such a redaction of the Deathbed Episode have been performed and who might have been interested in this revision?

6.7.5.1   The Historical Probability

A review of the state of the question concerning the Davidic and Solomonic Era has been offered sufficiently by G.N. Knoppers in his paper on the vanishing Solomon,[576] whereas the recent collection of papers on *the Age of Solomon* magnificently represents the *status quaestionis*.[577] However, the different problems with regard to the era under discussion may be listed here for the sake of clarity and will be briefly discussed further on:

1. The information concerning David and Solomon in the Hebrew Bible is an integral part of the Deuteronomistic History being composed at least three hundred years after the death of Solomon. For that reason these stories are considered to be at least inaccurate[578] or even to be of legendary character.[579]

---

[576] Knoppers, "The Vanishing Solomon", 19–44 (cf. above, p. 595, n. 531).

[577] L.K. Handy (ed.), *The Age of Solomon: Scholarship at the Turn of the Millennium* (SHCANE, 11), Leiden 1997.

[578] The attitude towards the portrayal of these two kings differs strongly in this respect; yet, despite the differences, there is a strong tendency to consider the picture of their era as being (partly) a product of the Deuteronomistic historian. From recent publications, cf. *e.g.* Ahlström, *History of Ancient Palestine*, 455–542, see esp. 501; Dietrich, *Die frühe Königszeit*, 18–33; G. Auld, "Re-Reading Samuel (historically): 'Etwas mehr Nichtwissen'", in: V. Fritz, P.R. Davies (eds.), *The Origins of the Ancient Israelite States* (JSOTS, 228), Sheffield 1996, 160–9; N. Na'aman, "Sources and Composition in the History of David", in: *ibid.*, 170–86; idem, "Sources and Composition in the History of Solomon", in: Handy (ed.), *The Age of Solomon*, 57–80; J.M. Miller, "Separating the Solomon of History from the Solomon of Legend", in: *ibid.*, 1–24; E.A. Knauf, "Le roi est mort, vive le roi! A Biblical Argument for the Historicity of Solomon", in: *ibid.*, 81–95.

[579] T.L. Thompson, *Early History of the Israelite People: From the Written and Archaeological Sources* (SHANE, 4), Leiden 1992, 306–7 (regarding the existence of a "United Monarchy"); idem, "'House of David': An Eponymic Referent to Yahweh as Godfather", *SJOT* 9 (1995) 59–74, esp. 63–5; N.P. Lemche, T.L. Thompson, "Did Biran Kill David: The Bible in the Light of Archaeology", *JSOT* 64 (1994) 3–22, esp. 16–21; M.M. Gelinas, "United Monarchy—Divided Monarchy: Fact or Fiction?", in: S.W. Holloway, L.K. Handy (eds.), *The Pitcher is Broken: Memorial Essays for G.W. Ahlström* (JSOTS, 190), Sheffield 1995, 227–37; H.M. Niemann, "The Socio-Political Shadow Cast by the Biblical Solomon", in: L.K. Handy (ed.), *The Age of Solomon: Scholarship at the Turn of the Millennium*

2. The archaeological picture of tenth century Palestine has become a matter of dispute in a twofold manner:

    (a) As referred to already in Chapter Five, it is argued on the
        basis of the "socio-archaeological" study of D.W. Jamie-
        son-Drake[580] that archaeology provides sufficient evidence
        to conclude that Jerusalem did not become the centre of a
        state in tenth century Palestine.[581]

    (b) The archaeology of the "age of Solomon" has been criti-
        cized several times, suggesting that "Solomonic buildings"
        are in fact the products of later periods.[582] Partly based on
        this discussion it has recently been proposed that the main
        strata of the early Iron II should be dated in the ninth cen-
        tury BCE and not — as has been common — in the tenth
        century.[583]

Did the archaeological picture of tenth century Palestine provide sufficient evidence to conclude that Jerusalem cannot have been the centre
of a state? Of course this depends partly on one's definition of a
"state" and in addition of "chiefdom", which is usually used as an
alternative term for the kingship of David and Solomon, implying
that their magnitude has to be put in perspective. Concerning the
situation of tenth-century Palestine we adhere to the conclussion of

---

(SHCANE, 11), Leiden 1997, 252–95, esp. 272.

[580]D.W. Jamieson-Drake, *Scribes and Schools: A Socio-Archaeological Approach*
(JSOTS, 109; SWBAS, 9), Sheffield 1991. Cf. also H.M. Niemann, *Herrschaft,
Königtum und Staat: Skizzen zur soziokulturellen Entwicklung im monarchischen
Israel* (FAT, 6), Tübingen 1993; idem, "The Socio-Political Shadow", 252–95.

[581]Cf. *inter alii* E.A. Knauf, "King Solomon's Copper Supply", in: E. Lipiński
(ed.), *Studia Phoenicia, XI: Phoenicia and the Bible* (OLA, 44), Leuven 1991,
167–86, 171–3; idem, "Le roi est mort, vive le roi!" 81–2; P.R. Davies, *In Search
of 'Ancient Israel'* (JSOTS, 148), Sheffield 1992, 67–70; N.P. Lemche, "Is it Still
Possible to Write a History of Ancient Israel?" *SJOT* 8 (1994) 165–90, 185; H.
Niehr, "The Rise of YHWH in Judahite and Israelite Religion: Methodological
and Religio-Historical aspects", in: D.V. Edelman (ed.), *The Triumph of Elohim:
From Yahwisms to Judaisms* (CBET, 13), Kampen 1995, 45–72, 53; idem, "Some
Aspects of Working with the Textual Sources", in: L.L. Grabbe (ed.), *Can a
'History of Israel' Be Written?* (JSOTS, 245; ESHM, 1), Sheffield 1997, 156–65,
159.

[582]G.J. Wightman, "The Myth of Solomon", *BASOR* 277/278 (1990) 5–22; D.
Ussishkin, "Notes on Megiddo, Gezer, Ashdod, and Tel Batash in the Tenth to
Ninth Centuries B.C.", *ibid.*, 71–91; I. Finkelstein, "On Archaeological Methods
and Historical Considerations: Iron Age II Gezer and Samaria", *ibid.*, 109–19

[583]I. Finkelstein, "The Date of the Settlement of the Philistines in Canaan", *TA*
22 (1995) 213–39; idem, "The Archaeology of the United Monarchy: An Alternative View", *Levant* 28 (1996) 177–87.

C. Schäfer-Lichtenberger that "the notion of chiefdom ... is not able to sufficiently describe the formation of political associations in tenth-century Palestine".[584] It has to be emphasized, however, that we are in that case dealing with an "early state", which partly might be on the level of the transitional state.[585]

Yet provided that Jamieson-Drake followed similar criteria as Niemann and Schäfer-Lichtenberger when he named tenth-century Judah a chiefdom, the question arises whether the archaeological data does lead up to that conclusion indeed. Recently one of his followers,[586] N.P. Lemche wrote on this book

> At a seminar in Copenhagen ... it became evident that Jamieson-Drake's book is not a major piece of work. Not so much because of its methodology , which is faultless, but because of the material on which he based his theories. Seemingly, Jamieson-Drake is dependent on material of low scholarly value, dated archaeological reasoning, wrong or simply bad archaeology, misleading conclusions, and so on.[587]

For example, Jamieson-Drake applied statistical techniques for his study in which he took into consideration luxury items, but also public buildings in ancient Judah. Yet, this technique is in this case rather dangerous, because even if Jamieson-Drake reckons with the fact that not every site might have provided its information,[588] the information from Jerusalem causes an enormous miscalculation. There has been

---

[584]C. Schäfer-Lichtenberger, "Sociological and Biblical Views of the Early State", in: V. Fritz, P.R. Davies (eds.), *The Origins of the Ancient Israelite States* (JSOTS, 228), Sheffield 1996, 78–105. Cf. also J. Portugali, "Theoretical Speculations on the transition from Nomadism to Monarchy", in: I. Finkelstein, N. Na'aman, *From Nomadism to Monarchy: Archaeological and Historical Aspects of Early Israel*, Jerusalem 1994, 202–17. It is to be regreted that H.M. Niemann, without giving any argument rejects her conclusions; see his "The Socio-Political Shadow", 260, n. 19. In our view the description of David's and Solomons' court in the Deuteronomistic History contains sufficient material to conclude that Judah has passed the stage of chiefdom in that era; certainly if we follow Niemann's criteria to distinguish between chiefdom and state (*art.cit.*, 283–4, n. 87; idem, *Herrschaft, Königtum und Staat*, 7, 34). The crucial text 1 Kgs. 4:7–19 — but others also — indicates more than only "the beginning of the change from a chiefdom to a state" (*art.cit.*, 280–8, esp. 286), but an "early, inchoative state" (Schäfer-Lichtenberger, *art.cit.*, 105, regarding the state under David).

[585]Schäfer-Lichtenberger, "Sociological Views", 99–105.

[586]To use the designation applied by N.Na'aman, "The Contribution of the Amarna Letters to the Debate on Jerusalem's Political Position in the Tenth Century B.C.E.", *BASOR* 304 (1996) 17–27, 22.

[587]N.P. Lemche, "From Patronage Society to Patronage Society", in: V. Fritz, P.R. Davies (eds.), *The Origins of the Ancient Israelite States* (JSOTS, 228), Sheffield 1996, 107–20, 108.

[588]Jamieson-Drake, *Scribes and Schools*, 39–40.

an uninterrupted continuity of settlement on the Ophel Hill from the
tenth to the early sixth century BCE and such an uninterrupted continuity of settlement leaves only a few remains of the earlier building activity.[589] In addition, the data concerning Jerusalem were out-
dated, because in the tenth or early ninth century BCE a new town
was founded[590] having large and impressive *public* buildings.[591] The
building area was restricted to the top of the hill but no houses were
found here.[592] Because of these dominant public structures, Jerusalem
in the tenth and ninth centuries appears to be comparable to Samaria,
the (later) capital of Israel, where similar structures have been found
in the ninth and eighth centuries BCE showing that Samaria was a
capital city.[593] With regard to the archaeological remains that are
usually dated to the tenth century BCE I. Finkelstein (albeit with
some doubts concerning the dating, cf. below) wrote

> I sincerely believe that if these datings could have been proven beyond
> doubt, there would have been no difficulty in demonstrating that in the
> tenth century there was a strong, well developed and well-organized
> state stretching over most of the territory of western Palestine. Check-
> ing the above-mentioned remains and other finds in terms of modern
> socio-political theory would indicate that the execution of such large
> scale building activities would have required an advanced administra-
> tion and a sophisticated system of management of manpower.[594]

---

[589]Na'aman, "The Contribution of the Amarna Letters", 19. Cf. also A.R. Millard, "An Assessment of the Evidence for Writing in Ancient Israel", J. Amitai
(ed.), *Biblical Archaeology Today: Proceedings of the International Congress on
Biblical Archaeology, Jerusalem April 1984*, Jerusalem 1985, 301–12, esp. 305.

[590]Estimated surface area of 32 acres (= 13 hectare); Jamieson-Drake, *Scribes
and Schools*, 161.

[591]H.J. Franken, "The Excavations of the British School of Archaeology in
Jerusalem on the South-East Hill in the Light of Subsequent Research", *Levant* 19
(1987) 129–36; H.J. Franken, M.L. Steiner, *Excavations in Jerusalem 1961–1967,
Volume II: The Iron Age Extramural Quarter on the South-East Hill* (BAMA, 2),
Oxford 1990, 123–5; M.L. Steiner, "The Jebusite Ramp of Jerusalem: The Evid-
ence from the Macalister, Kenyon and Shiloh Excavations", in: *Biblical Archaeology Today, 1990: Proceedings of the Second International Congress on Biblical
Archaeology*, Jerusalem 1993, 625–6; idem, "Re-Dating the Terraces of Jerusalem",
IEJ 44 (1994) 13–20; idem, *Jeruzalem in de Brons- en IJzertijd: De Opgravingen
van de 'British School of Archaeology in Jerusalem', 1961–1967* (PhD dissertation, Rijksuniversiteit Leiden), 75–85; furthermore these data were presented in
M.L. Steiner's paper to the SBL-meeting in Leuven (August 1994), "Jerusalem in
the 7th Century BCE". I am indebted to Dr. Steiner, who kindly put an offprint
of her paper at my disposal.

[592]Steiner, *Jeruzalem in de Brons- en IJzertijd*, 80.

[593]Thompson, *Early History of the Israelite People*, 408.

[594]Finkelstein, "The Archaeology of the United Monarchy", 177. This statement

So, it appears that on the basis of the archaeological data, dated according to the classical chronology, the conclusion of Jamieson-Drake cannot be maintained. Here we come to the second point, namely the dating of the main strata of early Iron II. Finkelstein suggested on the basis of a study of Philistine chronology, re-dating Philistine Monochrome Ware to 1135–1100 BCE and Bichrome Ware to the eleventh until the early-to-mid tenth century BCE,[595] a lowering of the dates of Iron Age assemblages from Megiddo, Beer-Sheba and Arad.[596] As a consequence many finds from the supposed Solomonic era have to be dated later, making the Solomonic kingdom only a chiefdom.

It would run too far in detail to discuss all the arguments put forward and the counter-arguments by other scholars. We will mention two out of several crucial arguments against his thesis here. First of all, the use of dating of some carbonized grain with the help of C^{14} method in Beth-shean (stratum S-2) gives a secure date for this layer and as a consequence a "solid foundation for absolute chronology", in this case also for Megiddo.[597] Secondly, the lowering of the chronology would probably cause no problems in Megiddo, however, the result for Hazor would be a "dense" stratigraphy, allowing for each strata at Hazor a duration of only 25 years.[598] These arguments and others[599] refute in our view Finkelstein's attempt to lower the date of early Iron II finds. For that reason we are inclined to accept the traditional chronology of the early Iron Age and to consider the socio-political

---

is approved by A. Ben-Tor and D. Ben-Ami — making a strong case for the dating in the tenth century, however (cf. below) — in their "Hazor and the Archaeology of the Tenth Century B.C.E.", *IEJ* 48 (1998) 1–37, 36. See also V. Fritz, "Monarchy and Re-urbanization: A New Look at Solomon's Kingdom", in: V. Fritz, P.R. Davies (eds.), *The Origins of the Ancient Israelite States* (JSOTS, 228), Sheffield 1996, 187–95; W.G. Dever, "Archaeology and the 'Age of Solomon': A Case-Study in Archaeology and Historiography", in: L.K. Handy (ed.), *The Age of Solomon: Scholarship at the Turn of the Millennium* (SHCANE, 11), Leiden 1997, 217–251, who states as conclusion (p. 251), "My evidence throughout has been archaeological, and my point simple. We *have* an Israelite state in the Iron IIA period. If we had never heard of a 'Solomon' in the biblical texts, we should have to invent a 10th century BCE Israelite king by another name."

[595] Finkelstein, "The Date of the Settlement of the Philistines", 213–39.

[596] Finkelstein, "The Archaeology of the United Monarchy", 180–85.

[597] A. Mazar, "Iron Age Chronology: A Reply to I. Finkelstein", *Levant* 29 (1997) 157–67, 160.

[598] Ben-Tor, Ben-Ami, "Hazor", 32–3; Mazar, "Iron Age Chronology", 164.

[599] Cf. in addition to the above-mentioned papers, also A. Zarzeki-Peleg, "Hazor, Jokneam and Megiddo in the 10th Century B.C.E.", *TA* 24 (1997) 258–88; D. Oredsson, "Jezreel — Its Contribution to Iron Age Chronology", *SJOT* 12 (1998) 86–101.

structure of the tenth century to be a state, albeit in the sense of a state "still in its formative stage"[600] or an "early state".[601]

Concluding the existence of a "state" during the tenth century does, however, not prove the existence of David, nor Solomon. Whereas the latter's existence is solely to be derived from biblical records, the former's historical existence is attested as the founder of the dynasty *bytdwd* "house of David" in the stele from tel Dan.[602] The mention of David as the founder of the dynasty does not lead to the conclusion that a "United Monarchy" existed,[603] nor does the archaeological data prove the existence of an "golden age".[604] Yet textual data based on old documents from the Solomonic era, like 1 Kgs. 4:7–19, may — as several scholars have suggested[605] — argue in favour of the

---

[600] Ben-Tor, Ben-Ami, "Hazor", 36.

[601] Schäfer-Lichtenberger, "Sociological Views", 105. Cf. also Knoppers, "The Vanishing Solomon", 42–3; W.G. Dever, "Archaeology, Urbanism, and the Rise of the Israelite State", in: W.E. Aufrecht *et alii* (eds.), *Urbanism in Antiquity: From Mesopotamia to Crete* (JSOTS, 244), Sheffield 1997, 172–193; idem, "Archaeology and the 'Age of Solomon'", 243–51.

[602] Knoppers, "The Vanishing Solomon", 39; Dietrich, *Die frühe Königszeit*, 141. For a review of the discussion of this stele, see Knoppers, *art.cit.*, 36–40; Dietrich, *op.cit.*, 136–41. For additional bibliographical information, cf. above, p. 419, n. 351.

[603] Knoppers, "The Vanishing Solomon", 39.

[604] G.W. Ahlström, "The Role of Archaeological and Literary Remains in Reconstructing Israel's History", in: D.V. Edelman (ed.), *The Fabric of History: Text, Artifact and Israel's Past* (JSOTS, 127), Sheffield 1991, 116–41, 139; Fritz, "Monarchy and Re-urbanization", 187–95; Steiner, "Jerusalem in the 7th Century BCE".

[605] Cf. for example Miller, "Separating Solomon of History", 16–7; Na'aman, "Sources and Composition in History of Solomon", 70; Niemann, "Socio-Political Shadow", 280–8. However, the last-mentioned scholar hesitates between a text ("that is the intentions and structures behind it", *art.cit.*, 287) belonging to the time before Rehoboam and Jeroboam I, or one representing a plan for northern expansion after the fall of the northern kingdom. The latter option is suggested by, for instance, P.S. Ash, "Solomon's? District? List", *JSOT* 67 (1995) 67–86; Knauf, "King Solomon's Copper Supply", 174–6; idem, "Le roi est mort, vive le roi!" 88, n. 28. The latter suggests a time of composition during the reign of Josiah, "who wanted (or was wanted by his counsellors) to be the king Solomon was imagined to have been". Yet, in our view clear Deuteronomistic passages in 1 Kgs. 1–11 are critical with regard to Solomon, and the assumption that Josiah wanted to be like Solomon is not warranted. Cf. M.A. Sweeney, "The Critique of Solomon in the Josianic Edition of the Deuteronomistic History", *JBL* 114 (1995) 607–22; G. Knoppers, "Solomon's Fall and Deuteronomy", in: L.K. Handy (ed.), *The Age of Solomon: Scholarship at the Turn of the Millennium* (SHCANE, 11), Leiden 1997, 392–410. See also R. de Hoop, "The Testament of David: A Response to W.T. Koopmans", *VT* 45 (1995) 270–79, esp. 274–6, with n. 27. It was rather David who was the ideal founder of the dynasty, see *e.g.* P.S. Ash, "Jeroboam I

existence of a larger kindom than the territory of Judah alone.[606] The assumption that we might be dealing here with a text going back to the period of Solomon, presupposes some literary activity during that era.[607] The evidence of writing is pointing in that direction indeed[608] and a comparison with other Near Eastern cultures and Jerusalem itself during the Late Bronze suggests that the knowledge of writing cannot be denied to Jerusalem in the tenth century.[609] However, this argument certainly does not mean that the accounts of David and Solomon in the books of Samuel and Kings can be considered as absolutely reliable historical reports. On the other hand, this does not imply that the Deuteronomistic History should be excluded from the historical debate, for "it is nevertheless a history — a meaningful and substantial account of the past".[610]

Criticizing the Deuteronomistic account of the reigns of David and Solomon it is generally emphasized that the Deuteronomistic History presents its material in a theological or ideological fashion. Generally this discussion conveys the idea that the ideological aspect can be intrinsic to an account of some decades or even centuries later, while this ideological aspect would not be intrinsic to a contemporaneous account .[611] E.A. Knauf wrote, for instance,

---

and the Deuteronomistic Historian's Ideology of the Founder", *CBQ* 60 (1998) 16–24.

[606] Cf. Knoppers, "The Vanishing Solomon", 40, who argues with regard to other West Semitic states (like for instance Moab), that "one still can recognize the validity of the more general point, namely, that the leaders of West Semitic states could control territories far beyond the confines of their own capitals".

[607] The use of annals or old documents in the Deuteronomistic History of Solomon is defended by *inter alii* Miller, "Separating Solomon of History", 1–24; A. Millard, "King Solomon in his Ancient Context", in: L.K. Handy (ed.), *The Age of Solomon: Scholarship at the Turn of the Millennium* (SHCANE, 11), Leiden 1997, 30–53; Na'aman, "Contribution of the Amarna Letters", 22; idem, "Sources and Composition in the History of David", 170–3; idem, "Sources and Composition in the History of Solomon", 57–61; Knauf, "Le roi est mort, vive le roi", 81–95; Knoppers, "The Vanishing Solomon", 43.

[608] Na'aman, "Sources and Composition in the History of Solomon", 57–61; Knoppers, "The Vanishing Solomon", 41–2; K.A. Kitchen, "Egypt and East Africa", in: L.K. Handy (ed.), *The Age of Solomon: Scholarship at the Turn of the Millennium* (SHCANE, 11), Leiden 1997, 106–23, 122. See also above, pp. 444–5, n. 440.

[609] Cf. Knoppers, "The Vanishing Solomon", 41–2; Na'aman, "The Contribution of the Amarna Letters", 22.

[610] Knoppers, "The Vanishing Solomon", 43. Cf. also Knauf, "Le roi est mort, vive le roi!" 95: "It requires, however, a critical reading which may not be to everybody's liking and it does not lead further than to reasonable speculation, which all history writing is and which I, for my part, prefer to willful ignorance."

[611] Miller, "Separating the Solomon of History", 15–8 (cf. also his "Response to

> One is thus forced to concede that even the 'story of David's succession' contains some glimpses of real history. This does not imply that one must necessarily defend the character of the 'succession story' as a historical record *by some eyewitness*. This text is neither historiographical in character, nor does it date from the 10th century; it rather is a sophisticated novel from the 7th century ...[612]

Whether Knauf is right in this respect is irrelevant, yet what is at stake here is the general tendency to consider contemporaneous documents more reliable than later texts. However, considering the theological, but especially the ideological features in the text it has to be borne in mind that the original account could have been ideological and theological itself.[613] If in 1 Kgs. 2:1–10, for example, vv. 3–4 is considered a later Deuteronomistic insertion, having a clear theological and ideological purpose, this does not exclude the fact that the pre-Dtr. version (vv. 1–2, 5–10) has also an ideological bias.[614] Illustrative in this respect is B. Halpern's remark,

> There was certainly, on the evidence of texts and of such archaeology as we have, no extensive Davido-Solomonic empire in Syria. In fact, were we to find a monument of Toi of Hamath or his successors, it might even claim hegemony 'unto Israel' in the south, as his own ascendancy over Zobah is at least as likely to have been asserted as David's.[615]

Apparently we have to reckon with an ideological aspect in the text we read, which has not only to be traced back to the Deuteronomistic historian, but eventually even further back to the contemporaneous writer of David's and Solomon's era. Yet, in that case the ideological aspect probably should be labelled as "legitimizing", making use of an ideology in order to legitimize the ruler's position.[616]

Millard", 54–6, esp. 54); Millard, "King Solomon in his Ancient Context", 30–53; Na'aman, "Sources and Composition in the History of Solomon", 80; Niemann, "Socio-Political Shadow", 268–9, 272.

[612] Knauf, "Le roi est mort, vive le roi!" 87 (emphasis mine, RdH).

[613] With regard to the "succession narrative", cf. the survey of recent research on its tendency in W. Dietrich, T. Naumann, *Die Samuelbücher* (EdF, 287), Darmstadt 1995, 191–8.

[614] J.S. Rogers, "Narrative Stock and Deuteronomistic Elaboration in 1 Kings 2", *CBQ* 50 (1988) 398–413; M. Weinfeld, *Deuteronomy and the Deuteronomistic School*, Oxford 1972, 11; 254, n. 1; De Hoop, "Testament of David", 270–9.

[615] B. Halpern, "The Construction of the Davidic State: An Exercise in Historiography", in: V. Fritz, P.R. Davies (eds.), *The Origins of the Ancient Israelite States* (JSOTS, 228), Sheffield 1996, 44–75, 75. Cf. also the studies by T. Ishida referred to below, 613, n. 621, in which a similar recognition of this "early ideological aspect" is found.

[616] Schäfer-Lichtenberger, "Sociological Views", 91, 105.

6.7.5.2   The Ideological Factor

Given the present state of research on David and Solomon, it appears that *grosso modo* they are considered historical figures who reigned in Palestine in the tenth century BCE. Whether the socio-political structure could be defined as a "state" is a matter of dispute, for some scholars are inclined to label it as a "chiefdom". But in both cases it is agreed that the structure tends towards or is still in the transitional phase of becoming a "state", hence an "early state".[617] According to the account of the books of Samuel, the establishment of the monarchy is still in need of legitimation, not only Saul's kingship but also David's position as ruler. Indeed David's position as ruler over Israel and as the successor of Saul is contested and consequently itself in need of legitimation.[618]

The same is true of Solomon, whose position is also in need of legitimation according to 1 Kgs. 1–2, where he is put on the throne by the Jerusalemite élite, Nathan and Bathsheba.[619] His position as ruler is apparently also questioned by his brothers (1 Kgs. 1),[620] by the descendants of Saul and by some of the old military personel of David (Joab), who in all likelihood were not faithful to Solomon.[621] Furthermore, it appears that the tension between the North (Israel) and the South (Judah) which was found already during David's reign persisted and even mounted during the reign of Solomon.[622] Apparently it was still not a matter of course that Israel was ruled from

---

[617]Schäfer-Lichtenberger, "Sociological Views", 99–105. Cf. also Niemann, "The Socio-Political Shadow", 283–5.

[618]In this we differ slightly from Schäfer-Lichtenberger, "Sociological Views", 105, who regards the establishment of the monarchy itself as no longer in need of legitimation. Yet, in our view the legitimation of Saul's kingdom as she describes it ("calling on the will of the deity, by the choice of the people, and by success"; *art.cit.*, 99), returns in a similar fashion in the description of David: calling on the will of the deity (1 Sam. 16:6–13), by the choice of the people (2 Sam. 5:1–5) and by success (1 Sam. 18:7).

[619]Knauf, "Le roi est mort, vive le roi!" 87.

[620]This seems also to be implied by the "apologetic" character of the "succession narrative", if it can be read indeed as a "pro-Solomonic" document; see T.N.D. Mettinger, *King and Messiah: The Civil and Sacral Legitimation of the Israelite Kings* (CB OTS, 8), Lund 1976, esp. 27–32; cf. also Dietrich, Naumann, *Die Samuelbücher*, 191–8, for this interpretation (and deviating ones).

[621]Cf. T. Ishida, "Solomon's Succession to the Throne of David — A Political Analysis", in: T. Ishida (ed.), *Studies in the Period of David and Solomon and Other Essays*, Winona Lake (IN) 1982, 175–87; idem, "The Story of Abner's Murder: A Problem Posed by the Solomonic Apologist", *ErIs* 24 (1993) 109*–13*.

[622]Ahlström, *History of Ancient Palestine*, 487–98, 543–9; Cf. also J.A. Soggin, "Compulsory Labor under David and Solomon", in: T. Ishida (ed.), *Studies in the Period of David and Solomon and Other Essays*, Winona Lake (IN) 1982, 259–67.

Jerusalem by a Judahite, treating the North as a vassal country,[623] and these points seem to have been the most important reasons for the division of the kingdom.[624] It is in this context that we may ask for the function and role of Genesis 49 in its literary and historical context.

The result of the diachronic analysis suggests generally a shift in political conditions and the need for a legitimation of these changes, demonstrated by the following items:

1. Judah's position had to be legitimized among his (older) brothers;

2. the position of Joseph had to be reduced as much as possible;

3. the system of twelve brothers (*viz.* tribes) did not occur in the earlier (pro-Joseph) version but only later in the redactional (pro-Judah) layer;

4. the final version of the Deathbed Episode presupposes the equation of "Jacob" with "Israel", which is not supported by the earlier version.

If in the period of David and Solomon the "unity" of the two entities Judah and Israel was indeed a matter of tension because this unity was not original, this might have required legitimation. As Schäfer-Lichtenberger has argued, one of the characteristics of an early state is the fact that the position of the ruler is based on explicit ideas of legitimation. This certainly can be applied to the "United Monarchy" whose unity was only one or two generations old. Nevertheless the need for legitimation should be applied, in that case, not solely to the ruler, but also to the ruling class (or tribe?).

---

[623] Ahlström, *History of Ancient Palestine*, 490; cf. also the discussion above on מַס עֹבֵד in the North, pp. 548–552.

[624] Ahlström, *History of Ancient Palestine*, 543–9. *Pace* Gelinas, "United Monarchy — Divided Monarchy", 227–37, who apparently is only willing to read the biblical text in a historistic and biblicistic fashion, which forces her either to accept it as eternal truth, or to conclude that the division of the "United Monarchy" must have been fiction. For in the account of 1 Kgs. 11–12, the ideology and theology of the Deuteronomist is apparent in almost every line and the conclusion that this account is not literally historical is thus inevitable. Contrast in this respect D.V. Edelman, "Solomon's Adversaries Hadad, Rezon and Jeroboam: A Trio of 'Bad Guy' Characters Illustrating the Theology of Immediate Retribution", in: S.W. Holloway, L.K. Handy (eds.), *The Pitcher is Broken: Memorial Essays for G.W. Ahlström* (JSOTS, 190), Sheffield 1995, 166–91, who offers a much more sophisticated discussion of the historical background.

Starting now with *item three*, the system of twelve did not exist in the earlier version of the Deathbed Episode. This might be regarded as an indication that the "pro-Judah" redaction made an attempt to legitimize the construction of "great Israel" by the twelve-tribe system. Genesis 49 is part of the larger context of Genesis in which also the birth-story of the tribal ancestors or eponyms is narrated. The origin of the unity of these twelve tribes is projected back in history to the time when the "ancestors" could have been brothers. In that period the promise of the land to their common ancestors is given. This promise is given to Abraham in the North, at Shechem(!) and in the South, at Hebron (Gen. 12:6–7; 13:14–18), and this promise is repeated to Jacob also (35:12). This promise of the whole land might also imply a legitimizing function, because it appears that some parts, belonging to Dan, Gad, Asher and Naphtali, Zebulon and Issachar became only part of Israel after David's rise to power.[625] So, David apparently was able to expand his territory not just into that of Saul, whose was restricted to the Central-Hill-country,[626] but even beyond their borders up to Dan, incorporating also Canaanite strongholds such as Megiddo.[627]

Item two, Joseph's position had to be minimized as much as possible, which indicates that the position of "Joseph" was a threat to "Judah". If our analysis is correct, however, the earliest version would neither reckon with the leadership of Judah (he was even not mentioned) nor with the explicit presence of the other brothers. It might be that Joseph was indeed the name of a ruling dynasty in the north, which might still be reflected in the use of בֵּית יוֹסֵף "house of Joseph" for the northern realm (1 Kgs. 11:28).[628]

Item one, Judah's position among his older brothers was also in need of legitimation. Because Judah has apparently the role of ancestor of the tribe in Genesis, one is inclined to limit this figure of

---

[625] Ahlström, *History of Ancient Palestine*, 278–80; Dietrich, *Die frühe Königszeit*, 198–201.

[626] Ahlström, *History of Ancient Palestine*, map 13 [between pp. 542–3].

[627] Cf. with regard to the plain of Jezreel, where the cities became Israelite after the eleventh century, the following Gal, "Settlement of Issachar", 80–1; Finkelstein, *Archaeology of the Israelite Settlement*, 92–3; idem, "Ethnicity and Origin of the Iron I Settlers in the Highlands of Canaan: Can the Real Israel Stand Up?" *BA* 59 (1996) 198–212, 201; D.L. Esse, "The Collared Pithos at Megiddo: Ceramic Distribution and Ethnicity", *JNES* 51 (1992) 81–103, esp. 88–95, 101–2. See also our discussion of the Issachar-saying above, pp. 546–52.

[628] This usage is known from the *bytdwd* inscription from Tel Dan, where "house of David" refers very likely to the state of Judah headed by the Davidic dynasty. Yet this occurs in an *Aramaic* context; cf. Knoppers, "The Vanishing Solomon", 36, with n. 102.

Judah solely to this role as ancestor. However, we would like to defend another interpretation. "Judah" not solely reflects the ancestor of the *tribe* Judah, but in the narratives of Genesis he might also reflect other *persons*. In the discussion of the different sayings above, we compared several narrated events in Genesis with some stories from the "Succession Narrative" in which it occurs that the brothers and sister in Genesis might be compared — though sometimes in an antithesis — with those in the "succession narrative". First of all this might be argued on the basis of their position within the family; secondly on the role of the other brothers in the Testament and in the narratives in Genesis and 2 Samuel. If we take a closer look at the older brothers, Reuben, and Simeon & Levi, it appears that they also reflect figures in the environment of Solomon. First of all, Reuben, in his act of defilement of his father's concubine, reflects Absalom in his capture of his father's harem (2 Sam. 16:22).[629] Secondly, the rape of Dinah is reflected in the rape of Tamar (2 Sam. 13), whereas the revenge on Shechem by Simeon and Levi is also mirrored in the revenge on Amnon by Absalom.[630] In the case of Genesis 49 it might be that Judah also mirrors two roles, one as the tribe Judah, who receives the promise of leadership; and one who reflects the position of Solomon as a younger brother who nevertheless receives the leadership among his brothers.[631] So it seems that Judah reflects in that case the next brother in line, who will be the successor of David, *i.e.* Solomon. So, it appears that the motif of the "forsaken first-born" in Genesis returns in the succession narrative, although in that case it appears as being settled. So also in that case the book of Genesis, and Genesis 49 especially seems to have an important legitimizing function. It is certainly no coincidence that both parallels from the book of Samuel are part of the "succession narrative", which is considered by some as being apologetic in favour of Solomon.[632] It is this parallel between Genesis, and especially Genesis 49 that gives strength to this argument.

Item four, the equation of Jacob and Israel is not reflected in the earlier version of the Deathbed Episode. It appears that the name

---

[629] Cf. section 6.5.1.3, above.

[630] Cf. section 6.5.1.4, above.

[631] Note that in 2 Samuel it is unclear who *is* the oldest son, because according to 2 Sam. 3:2–5 Absalom does not follow directly after Amnon. However, from six sons mentioned in 2 Samuel 3 only three have a decisive role in the following narrative. In addition to the "forsaken first-born" motif in Genesis it might be pointed out that David was also considered to be the youngest (1 Sam. 16:6–13). Remarkable, however, is the fact that this account can be considered as part of the legitimation of David's kingship (cf. p. 613, n. 618 above).

[632] Cf. above, p. 613, n. 620.

"Israel" belonged to the older version, and the editor was interested to relate those two entities with each other. Relating these two persons with each other, patriarchal or ancestral traditions were merged into one tradition with one common ancestor. In this way Israel became also the ancestor of Judah, where, in all likelihood, the ancestor was originally Jacob.

Summarizing now these points it appears that the reign of Solomon was in need of legitimation. This legitimation was not solely offered at the level of direct indications, but also by means of indirect elements like in narratives concerning a common background in history, the prediction and assignement of rulership by a common ancestor, the promise of the whole land to the common ancestor, etcetera. But this legitimation was also offered by means of narratives concerning the recent past (succession narrative), offering also in that way an apology for his reign.

6.7.6 Before Solomon Was, Joseph Was ...

If we try to describe of the possible historical background to the pro-Joseph version the attempt will perforce be schematic, not because of lack of time or space, but because of the paucity of data. Our findings in the Deathbed Episode can be described as follows. The patriarch in this narrative is solely named Israel, suggesting that he had only one name: Israel. Joseph, who is the second important person on the scene, is considered in this narrative the successor of Israel his father. In this function he is called the "head of the tribe" (47:31), "one above his brothers" (48:22) etc. This indicates that Joseph's position among his brothers — who are anonymous here — is very crucial, he can be considered as the leader of his brothers. Finally, Joseph receives as his father's successor the city of Shechem, which, according to the text of Gen. 48:22, Israel took from the Amorites.

These data from the narrative might be considered as follows. Because, with the pro-Joseph version, we are dealing with a version that is older than the pro-Judah version it is consequently to be dated before the reign of David and Solomon. Probably we have to allow for a hundred years at least ($>$ 1100 BCE), taking into account that immediatly before David a Benjaminite, Saul, was king and reigned in the central hills.[633] In this version Israel is depicted as a person, which

---

[633]It appears to us, in each case, that the reign of Saul and this pro-Joseph version cannot be related with each other. On the other hand it cannot be excluded completely because Joseph and Benjamin were considered sons of the same mother in Genesis. Yet, the utmost that can be derived from this is that (the tribe) Benjamin is apparently related to the North and the house of Joseph, which is

might suggest that he functions here as a kind of eponymic ancestor in the narrative.[634] It is interesting that in this version Israel, Joseph and Shechem are related to each other, because Shechem seems to play a crucial role in Israel's early history although the picture is incomplete. The narrative in Judges 9 suggests the existence of a king in Shechem; Joshua 24, though probably a Deuteronomistic passage, does not presuppose the conquest of the city. Historically even more important is the fact that on the Mernephtah stele (ca. 1208 BCE) Israel is mentioned as a people, not as a polical entity like a country, city-state or the like.[635] Yet from the listing of the stele it might be inferred that "Israel" was found in the vicinity of Shechem.[636] In our view this would argue in favour of linking the "Israel" of Mernephtah with this Israel of the pro-Joseph version, who became the later biblical Israel.[637] However, it has to be emphasized that, in this case, Israel is only a small group (tribe, cf. 47:31),[638] which, apparently, has given its name to a larger entity,[639] namely a twelve-tribe system, even though that system lasted only two generations.[640] So, it appears that our reconstructed version presupposes the existence of a tribe, who had as its eponym "Israel", who regarded Shechem as being a part of its territory, and probably had descendants from (the house of) Joseph in a leading position. However, this is somewhat

---

reflected in the territory where Saul reigned. But also the discrepancy between Saul's "capital" Gibeah and Joseph's city Shechem suggest that these two are not to be viewed on a par.

[634]So, it is not denied that Israel might ever have been a real person, even as the ancestor of a group called "Israel". But with regard to this narrative it is questionable whether Israel, the eponymic ancestor of the tribe, and Joseph, the founder of the dynasty(? see above) are indeed related in the sense the narrative suggests.

[635]Cf. Lemche, *Early Israel*, 430–1.

[636]Cf. *e.g.* De Moor, *RoY*, 180–1; *RoY²*, 274–5; D.B. Redford, *Egypt, Canaan, and Israel in Ancient Times*, Princeton (NJ) 1992, 275.

[637]The link between Mernephtah's Israel and the biblical Israel is almost generally accepted; cf., for instance, De Moor, *RoY*, 111, 180; *RoY²*, 124, 275; Lemche, *Early Israel*, 430–1; idem, *Die Vorgeschichte Israels*, 81–2; Redford, *Egypt, Canaan and Israel*, 269–80; Ahlström, *History of Ancient Palestine*, 60, 286; V. Fritz, *Die Entstehung Israels im 12. und 11. Jahrhundert v. Chr.* (BE, 2), Stuttgart 1996, 73–5.

[638]*Pace* Lemche, *Early Israel*, 430.

[639]Cf. in this respect A. Lemaire, "Asriel, šr'l, Israel et l'origine de la confederation Israelite", *VT* 23 (1973) 239–43. He refers to the fact that in Switzerland (*Schweiz*), the name is derived from one of the cantons (*Schwyz*); similarly in France (< Franks), and the same pattern can be seen in Holland, where the name of a smaller part is often used for the whole country (The Netherlands). See also Ahlström, *History of Ancient Palestine*, 286.

[640]Cf. Fritz, *Die Entstehung Israels*, 121–6.

schematic but, given the available data, it appears that only these vague contours are visible at the hazy borderline between history and pre-history.

6.8 Recapitulation

1. At the beginning of Chapter Six we postulated as a working hypothesis that an ancient version of the Deathbed Episode, favouring Joseph as the successor of the patriarch, was revised in order to legitimize the (recently obtained) leading position of Judah.[641] This working hypothesis explains the different tensions and tendencies in the text quite well. For that reason the hypothesis can be regarded as the key to understanding this difficult episode. The terminology used to discern between these two different layers in the text is based on these two tendencies: we discern a "pro-Joseph" layer and a "pro-Judah" layer.

2. The Deathbed Episode (Gen. 47:29–49:33) has to be read as a whole and it should not be read as two independent entities in which the Testament (Gen. 49:1–28) is separated from its immediate context. This holds true in both cases: in the earlier pro-Joseph layer as well as in the (present) pro-Judah version.

3. The first part of the Deathbed Episode (Gen. 47:29–48:22) is made up of large parts of the so-called pro-Joseph layer. In this version Joseph has to take care of his father's funeral (47:29–31). Then, after the transitional scene (48:1a, 2b), the patriarch, called "Israel" throughout the pro-Joseph layer, meets Joseph's sons (48:8–11). Following this scene Joseph is blessed by his father (48:12, 14aA, 15aA), which, in the first part, ends with Israel bestowing Shechem on his son (48:21–2).

4. The foregoing reconstructed version was then adapted by adding several elements which weakened Joseph's position considerably and supported Judah's preferential status. As added and adapting elements we have to consider — next to the rather neutral introduction of Joseph's two sons by their names (48:1aB–2a) — the adoption of Joseph's sons (48:3–7) and their blessing (48:9bB, 13, 14aB.b, 15aB–20).

   (a) The adaptation of the text left Joseph childless and consequently without inheritance in Israel: his sons were not anymore *his* sons.

---

[641] For the exact wording, cf. above, pp. 455–456.

(b) The important position of Joseph receiving a blessing without his (anonymous) brothers on the scene is glossed over in this way, and Joseph receives a blessing among the eleven other "sons" of Israel (Gen. 49:1–28).

(c) "Israel" has become the "new" name of the patriarch, who is, in the new version, the final one of the three patriarchs in the fixed triplet "Abraham, Isaac, Jacob".

5. The Testament of Jacob (Gen. 49:1–28) is — except for the greater part of the Joseph blessing — the product of the pro-Judah editor. This assignment includes the framework of the Testament (vv. 1–2, 28) as well as all the sayings on Joseph's "brothers".

6. In the Testament, as well as in the first part of the Deathbed Episode, the motif of the "forsaken first-born" is of great importance. This motif in the book of Genesis, legitimizes Judah's position as the younger brother who rose to power over his older brothers.

7. The saying on Judah (49:8–12) must be dated in the period of the "United Monarchy", when the northern tribes (= Israel) were governed by the southern part (= Judah). At that moment the patriarch's pronouncement "your brothers shall praise you" and "your father's sons shall bow down before you" came true.

8. The Blessing of Joseph is for the greater part a substantial element of the pro-Joseph layer. Pro-Judah elements, added later, were intended to "remove" *political* implications of the blessing and not so much the *theological* import. Yet, the earlier version of the blessing clearly supports Joseph's position as the successor of the patriarch. This is also reflected in the idiom of the blessing which is applied in other contexts (Ugarit) specifically to kings.

9. The decease of the patriarch (Gen. 49:29–33) is an adaptation of the earlier report in the pro-Joseph layer of the patriarch's death as described in verse 33aBb. The aftermath as described in Gen. 50:1, simultaneously supports the idea that Joseph was the only one present at the moment of his father's death and consequently supports the pro-Joseph import. The present form (49:29–33) smoothly "includes" the patriarchal line of Abraham, Isaac and Jacob, whereas the tradition of the patriarchal grave is fixed in the south near Hebron.

10. The diachronic analysis differs in several respects from the previous literary critical studies of the Joseph Story. It suggests that we are dealing with only two layers, of which the oldest originated in the North and applies the name "Israel" for the patriarch, whereas the younger comes from the South using the name "Jacob". In an attempt to give a name to our method, it appears that we are close to a Supplementary Hypothesis, though other names are also possible. However, a differentiation based on the DNN El(ohim) and YHWH is impossible at this moment. The present analysis suggests that the classical definition of P in the book of Genesis should be reconsidered.

11. The Deathbed Episode in its present form is the product of the era of the "United Monarchy" and is intended to legitimize the position of (a king of) Judah to reign in "great Israel", the nation consisting of twelve tribes. On the other hand it is also intended to legitimize the position of the reigning king (Solomon) among several "competing" candidates, of whom several were probably older brothers.

12. The pro-Joseph version of the Deathbed Episode originated in the North. It presupposes the existence of a group (tribe) "Israel" in the surroundings of Shechem, in which the "house of Joseph" has apparently a leading role. Given the dating of the pro-Judah layer, the pro-Joseph layer should be dated in all likelihood at the end of the Late Bronze, or the beginning of Early Iron I. This might suggest some sort of relation between the "Israel" of the Mernephtah stele and the "Israel" of the pro-Joseph layer.

Chapter 7

Summarizing Conclusions

7.1 Genesis 49: *Status Quaestionis*

In the description of the *status quaestionis* of Genesis 49 in Chapter
One we identified four main problems in the research of this enigmatic
chapter.[1] First of all, by means of a comparison of several translations of the Hebrew text of Genesis 49 it can be demonstrated that
the translation of this chapter is very difficult because the Hebrew is
in many cases equivocal. Secondly, already in 1753 J. Astruc isolated
Genesis 49 from its context on the basis of the use of different divine
names and this separation has survived — albeit sometimes based on
different arguments — up to the present day. This has resulted in a situation in which Genesis 49 as well as its context (the Joseph Story) are
treated as two completely independent entities, which are discussed
separately. Thirdly, in addition to the literary critical approach of J.
Astruc, the historical critical approach started to question Genesis
49 as spoken originally by the patriarch. This resulted finally in the
theory that Genesis 49 is composed out of several independent oracles
concerning the tribes, a theory that was developed especially by H.
Greßmann. Genesis 49 contained so-called tribal sayings, independent
sayings in oral tradition, expressing something crucial concerning the
tribes. This final classification became the cornerstone of literary critical studies, which separated Genesis 49 from its context. Related to
this discussion is the question of origin of these independent sayings
in Israel's oral tradition. In which historical situation could a certain
saying be pronounced and if several periods are possible, which period
is the most likely one?

  The review of the relevant previous research on the translation
of Genesis 49 and on its origin has lead us to the formulation of the
following desiderata for further research:

1. A correct translation of Genesis 49 is a *conditio sine qua non*.

2. An analysis of the poetic structure, which might give a first
   impression of the text's (in-)coherence. This impression might
   in its turn be helpful to the diachronic analysis.

3. The testing of the definition of the genre of Genesis 49 as a
   collection of "tribal sayings" with the help of (ancient) Near

---

[1] Cf. above pp. 1–7.

Eastern literature.

4. A synchronic reading of Genesis 49 and its immediate context in the hope that certain ideological inconsistencies can be found, indicating a diachronic development.

5. A diachronic analysis on the basis of the foregoing results.

6. These results will finally be interpreted with regard to Israel's history.

In the present chapter we are to infer some conclusions from the previous chapters.

7.2 Genesis 49: Translation and Structure

In Chapter Two we offered a translation of the difficult Hebrew text of Genesis 49. For details the reader is referred to the relevant passages of that chapter. Here we single out one important general aspect of our translation in Chapter Two, namely the rendering of the verbal tenses in the sayings which might give an indication of their purpose. In general it appears that the scope of the sayings is the future of the relevant tribe. In most strophes (fifteen out of twenty) the scope is obviously the future, whereas in only three cases a different interpretation cannot be excluded. In two strophes (one saying: Issachar) the verbs were interpreted in a present sense, although in the second strophe the future seems to be the focus of the saying. This result corresponds at a synchronic level, with the introduction spoken by the patriarch, in which he announces the future to his sons.[2] Some sayings are open to other interpretations and, if separated from their context, may be rendered in a way not directed to the future. However, this holds true only for a small number of sayings. It appears, therefore, that in most cases we are indeed dealing with predictions of the tribes' future.[3]

The fact that most sayings can be read as a kind of prediction should be considered in connection with other features of the text. It is, for example, significant, that most sayings have an identical opening phrase, a nominal clause that might describe a certain state of affairs.[4] In addition it should be noted that the sayings on Reuben

---

[2] For the translation of בְּאַחֲרִית הַיָּמִים as "days hereafter"; cf. pp. 86–7, above.

[3] This conclusion might be contrasted with Holzinger's statement that we are not dealing here with *Weissagungen*; cf. Holzinger, *Genesis*, 256.

[4] It concerns the sayings on Reuben (49:3aA); Simeon and Levi (49:5AB); Judah (8aA, 9aA); Issachar (14A); Asher (20A); Naphtali (21A); Joseph (22a); Benjamin (27A).

and on Simeon and Levi have an identical structure and function, which results in the fact that these sayings are, together with the Judah-saying, firmly embedded in the present context. Furthermore the analysis of the poetic structure of Genesis 49 suggests that both framework and sayings form one well integrated unity and are connected with each other by means of verbal repetition. The use of verbal repetition is noticeable throughout the text, especially in the way the sayings from Zebulun, Issachar, Dan, Gad, Asher and Naphtali are linked together in a kind of chain.[5] For that reason it appears that the fragmentary character of Genesis 49, as it is presented by many scholars, is not as certain as it once seemed to be. Until recently scholars regarded almost every verse of Genesis 49 as an independent saying. Since the text shows much more coherence than has generally been assumed, this argument cannot be maintained any longer. On the other hand, it should be stressed that despite many parallels with the larger sayings, the Joseph-saying has a rather loose place in the whole, while the contents of the saying do not suggest a firm interrelationship with the rest of the Blessing.

7.3   Genesis 49: The Genre

In Chapter Three we discussed the definition of the genre of Genesis 49 in the wider context of (ancient) Near Eastern literature (including the Hebrew Bible). The definition of a "tribal saying" was based on the evidential tribal sayings found in an Arabic satire, which could not be misunderstood. Our sample survey of Near Eastern literature demonstrated that a genre "tribal saying" did exist in the Arabian world and while this genre might have been possible in the ancient Near East though there is no unequivocal evidence for it yet.[6] Yet, when the relevant text had a positive tendency it appeared that the definition "tribal saying" was *not* appropriate and better definitions could be found such as, for instance, "hymn". In the case of clearly negative sayings, which might indeed be called "tribal sayings", metaphors are mostly applied to offend the tribe involved in a stereotypical way. Usually most tribal sayings are concerned with the present: either both the past and the future are absent (in most cases) or they are only there to serve the sayings concerning the present. Thus, next to an independent origin and occurrence of such sayings, we had to conclude that comparable texts occur firmly embedded in

---

    [5]Cf. above, p. 240.

    [6]The different versions of a song, like the song of Heshbon, and the comment in Num. 21:27a suggest that taunt songs on other cities and nations existed, so it might be possible that comparable sayings existed too.

the literary context in which they also originated. This enforces us to conclude that *the coherence of a supposed "tribal saying" with the present literary context might be original.*[7]

Nowadays Genesis 49 is the only text in the Hebrew Bible which is regarded as a collections of "tribal sayings". As a result of S. Beyerle's recent study of Deuteronomy 33 the latter text is to be dismissed as belonging to that genre.[8] Yet our discussion revealed that also with regard to Genesis 49 there is insufficient evidence to uphold the idea that this text is a collection of "tribal sayings", because the essential mocking element is absent in most of the sayings. Furthermore, most of the sayings in Genesis 49 are orientated toward the future in contrast to the real "tribal sayings", which are all concerned with the present. Consequently, the inference to be drawn from these findings is that the use of this genre in the Hebrew Bible may have to be abandoned.

It was concluded in our discussion of Genesis 49 that the term "blessing" for the rendering of בְּרָכָה is inappropriate and "testament-ary saying" or "gift" would probably be better, although this is open to misunderstanding too.[9] Yet the word בְּרָכָה is in this sense not restricted to something positive and can also be used with regard to a negative saying in which the succession is denied to the oldest sons (Esau [Gen. 27: 38–41], Reuben, and Simeon & Levi). In this way the sayings in Genesis 49 can be considered "testamentary sayings" expressing the final will of the patriarch concerning his estate. As such Genesis 49 can also be described as the "testament" of Jacob, suiting the present literary context (the Deathbed Episode) very well. However, the implication is that form critical observations cannot be used any longer as literary critical arguments against the unity of this episode (Gen. 47:29–49:33) and thus against the position of Genesis 49 in its present context.

A study of the "testament" as a literary product in the ancient Near East, revealed that such a document functioned mostly in a court context as a legitimizing or as an apologetic document in which the reign of the current king was justified. The apology was applied mostly in those cases where the king assumed his office in an irregular

---

[7]It has to be stressed that this conclusion is based on both biblical and extra-biblical texts (ancient and more recent Near Eastern), of which were excluded of course Genesis 49, Deuteronomy 33 and Judges 5.

[8]S. Beyerle, *Der Mosesegen im Deuteronomium: Eine text-, kompositions- und formkritische Studie zu Deuteronomium 33* (BZAW, 250), Berlin 1997. With re-gard to Judges 5 it is generally acknowledged that this song does not contain "tribal sayings" in the same form as Genesis 49 and Deuteronomy 33.

[9]Cf. our *excursus*: "What is a blessing?" above, pp. 294–8.

fashion, not being the first in the line of succession. It appears that Genesis 49 has an identical function, legitimizing the position of Judah over his elder brothers. However, although as a testament Genesis 49 suits its present context rather well, this context — the Deathbed Episode — is a similarly problematic text, of which the provenance is also disputed. For that reason a *synchronic* and *diachronic* analysis of the complete Deathbed Episode seemed the only appropriate method to establish the possible process that gave rise to the present form of Genesis 49 and its literary context.

7.4   The Deathbed Episode: A Synchronic Reading

The Deathbed Episode as the final conclusion to the Joseph Story (Genesis 37–50) has to reckon with the purpose and plot of the Joseph Story. This story has *one* plot: the question whether Joseph will be king over his brothers (37:8, 10). This plot has, however, *two* focal points. The first is within the narrative framework and is fulfilled in favour of Joseph. Yet, the second focal point is far beyond the borders of the narrative and awaits the future, where it will be fulfilled in favour of Judah (49:8).

The Deathbed Episode in its present form is composed of four scenes, which are arranged chiastically. The general tendency of the first two scenes appears to be rather favourable toward Joseph. A closer reading demonstrates, however, that the general purport is not as positive as it appears to be. The adoption of Ephraim and Manasseh by the patriarch cannot be considered positive for Joseph, because *his* name is not continued in them, but rather his father's name(48:16). Moreover, the fact that they are equated with Reuben and Simeon should be regarded as an act of putting them aside, comparable to the way these two sons will be excluded (49:3–4, 5–7). In this sense the Testament (Gen. 49:1–28) and the remaining Deathbed Episode (Gen. 47:29–48:22; 49:29–33) cannot be regarded as independent entities. Both function to give a strong foundation to Judah's future position. The Deathbed Episode in its present form weakens Joseph's position, whereas in the Joseph Story his importance is diminished as the instrument by which the nation will be saved. Judah's leadership is proved in the Joseph Story and is confirmed by the patriarch in the Blessing: tensions which might be felt between the Judah-saying and the one on Joseph are eliminated: Judah's blessings are for the future and his future office; Joseph's blessing is for his former office.

However, it is shown that the consonantal text of Gen. 47:31 and of 48:22 has been obscured during the course of transmission. The reading the text seems to hide, which is partly supported by LXX and Peš, points in the direction of an important position for Joseph, which is not in line with the synchronic reading of the Deathbed Episode. Apparently Joseph and Judah are rivals. Some elements, in the texts, point in the direction of Joseph's leadership among the brothers. On the other hand, other elements deny this and ascribe the future leadership among the brothers (tribes) to Judah. These diverging lines seem to contradict each other and might reflect different historical situations. This had to be investigated in the diachronic analysis.

7.5 The Deathbed Episode: Previous Research

The previous research of the Deathbed Episode is marked by the studies of the Joseph Story and depend completely on the results of the research on that narrative. In fact two main approaches can be distinguished, the first one being a literary critical approach in all its divergencies. The second approach put the emphasis on the literary quality of the story despite the recognition of its compositeness. The latter approach in fact marginalizes the reworked parts into some obviously composite passages. The literary critical approaches (Documentary Hypothesis, Supplementary Hypothesis, Traditio-Historical Approach) use stratification criteria like the names of the two "hostile" brothers, Judah and Reuben, as representants of two different layers, and in addition the name of the patriarch, Jacob and Israel; whereas in an earlier part (Genesis 37) the names of the merchants, Ishmaelites and Mideanites, are used as criterion for the identification of the different layers.

Despite all the differences, the stratification of the P-layer in the Deathbed Episode is almost generally regarded as an established fact. Gen. 47:28, 48:3–6, 49:1a, 28bB–33aA.b are ascribed to P, and many scholars who initiated a completely new investigation took the stratification of P for granted, together with the accepted view on Genesis 49. Only Gen. 48:7 and 15–16 are considered problematic passages and the classification differs sharply, while also the attribution of 48:21–22 to a particular source is difficult. Moreover, Genesis 48 is in its entirety is hard to classify and analyses differ between , on the one hand, a general attribution to E (Wellhausen, Noth) and on the other hand, a denial of the occurrence of E-material within Genesis 48, and a distinction of the layers between J and a later addition (Schmidt). In these analyses Gen. 47:29–31 is generally ascribed to J / Judah-(Israel-)layer and therefore within the literary-critical analysis of the Joseph Story it is considered to be one of the most certain classifications.

An evaluation of previous literary critical research disclosed several inconsistencies and methodologically questionable suppositions. To begin with, it has been argued that the use of the names "Jacob" and "Israel" cannot be used as a *principal* argument for discerning different layers within the Joseph Story. Nevertheless, since its use is not consistent it might, on some occasions, betray a certain stratification of the text. Because of this possibility it can only be considered as a supporting argument for the delimitation of different layers. Further, regarding the names of the two "hostile" brothers, Reuben and Judah, it is doubtful whether they belong to two different layers within the text. They are each other's competitors in the narrative, a pattern which continues up to and including Genesis 49. Finally, the existence of the Priestly Document cannot be ascertained since a continuing narrative string is missing. Also the classical delimitation of P in the Deathbed Narrative is open to debate, since there are some verses which are usually considered to be part of other layers, but which could also be assigned to P, or *vice versa*. It appears for that reason that the use of these arguments hampers the diachronic analysis in stead of enabling a solid investigation into the provenance of the narrative.

With regard to its historical setting in life, the Joseph Story has been related to many periods of Israel's history, from the eighteenth century BCE to the Hellenistic period. The former period, together with other attempts to relate the Joseph Story to historical events, is abandoned by most scholars nowadays. Predominantly the Story is considered a kind of political metaphor, reflecting the political situation of the United Monarchy and the later Northern and Southern kingdom. The possibility of an early date (pre-eighth century BCE) for the biblical texts is excluded in advance by some scholars who presume that a national state in Palestine, showing advanced stages in administration and literature, only arose during the eighth century. However, this assumption is questionable and must be disputed since archaeological and textual data may point in a different — and also more differentiated — direction.

7.6 The Deathbed Episode: A Diachronic Reading

The synchronic reading of the Deathbed Episode has revealed that the narrative consists of two traditions which seem to exclude each other. One tradition favours Joseph as the most important son, the successor of his father; the other tradition seems to favour Judah and weakens Joseph's position. In Chapter Six we have made an attempt to establish whether these differences are indeed due to a diachronic process

of the text, and, if so, whether this diachronic process can shed some
light on the historical context in which the text and possible redaction
originated. For that reason it was postulated as a working hypothesis
that an ancient version of the Deathbed Episode, favouring Joseph as
the successor of the patriarch, was revised in order to legitimize the
(recently obtained) leading position of Judah. It was with this hypothesis in mind that the Deathbed Episode was read and questioned to
see whether the different tensions and tendencies could be explained
by it.

We established as parts of the so-called "pro-Joseph" layer[10] several continuous passages. The first, and probably also most important
passage, is found in Gen. 47:29–31. Here Joseph is asked to take care
of his father's funeral in the grave in the land of his fathers. When
Joseph swears to his father to do as he asked, Israel bows down עַל־רֹאשׁ
הַמִּטָּה "before the head of the tribe" as the consonantal text might be
interpreted (supported by LXX and Peš). Then, after Israel sat back
on his bed (48:1aA, 2b), the patriarch meets Joseph's sons and embraces them (48:8–11). Following this scene Joseph is the one who is
blessed when he bows down to the earth (vv. 12, 14aA, 15aA). The
blessing the patriarch pronounces starts with the bestowal of Shechem
on his son, אַחַד עַל־אַחֶיךָ "O One above your brothers" (48:21–2).[11] This
blessing is followed in the present form of the biblical text followed by
the "Testament" in which all the sons of Jacob are present, yet in our
reconstruction the word of the patriarch directed to Joseph does not
suddenly stop but continues in 49:22–26. After this blessing *expressis
verbis*, which was only adapted by some smaller expansions, we find
the final report of the patriarch's decease at the end of the fourth
scene (49:33aBb).

As the elements of the "pro-Judah" layer we found first of all the
introduction of Joseph's sons by means of their names on the scene.
This introduction in fact presupposes the birth-story (Gen. 41:50–2),
which is in its form comparable to other birth-stories in Genesis. Then
at the moment the patriarch is seated he pronounces the adoption of
Joseph's sons (48:3–7) and their blessing (48:9bB, 13, 14aB.b, 15aB–
20). The adaptation caused Joseph to be childless and consequently
to be without inheritance in Israel. The important position of Joseph
receiving a blessing without his (anonymous) brothers on the scene

---

[10]Inevitably some overlap of material between the synchronic and diachronic
reading must be allowed for in this presentation.

[11]In this case "blessing" has also the meaning of "testamentary saying", comparable to our interpretation of בְּרָכָה in connection with Genesis 49 itself; cf. our
discussion above, section 7.3.

is glossed over in this way, it were Ephraim and Manasseh who are blessed. Joseph receives a blessing among the eleven other "sons" of Israel (Gen. 49:1–28). It is, of course, the blessing of Judah that is the focal point of the whole Testament, in this saying the leadership among the brothers is announced and bestowed to the only true heir of the patriarch: Judah (49:8–12). All other sayings, but especially the first two and the tenth on Joseph support the position that Judah receives from his father. Finally by the instruction that Jacob should be buried in Machpela in his fathers' grave smoothly moves the grave of the patriarch from a possible northern location to the south in the surroundings of Hebron.

From a methodological point of view the results of our diachronic analysis might be rather interesting because they differ in several respects from previous studies on the Joseph Story as well as on Genesis 49. It suggests that we are dealing with only two layers, of which the oldest originated in the North and applies the name "Israel" to the patriarch, whereas the younger layer comes from the South using the name "Jacob". Neither a differentiation on the basis of the DNN El(ohim) and YHWH, nor on the basis of the PNN Jacob and Israel is possible at this moment. The present analysis suggests that the classical definition of P in the book of Genesis should be reconsidered in the light of these findings.

Historically it is important to stress that many scholars recognize that the Testament has a kind of legitimizing function and in that case especially the Judah-saying. The United Monarchy, when "all his brothers" and "all his father's sons" could bow down to a Judahite leader, appears to be the most likely period in which this document could have originated. The fact that we are dealing with the socio-political structure of an "early state" in the period under discussion, might strengthen the idea that our document was intended to legitimize the position of the king at that moment. This conclusion corresponds factually with the occurrence of "Testaments" as a literary product in other ancient Near Eastern contexts, where the document was intended to apologize or legitimize the present king.

The pro-Joseph version of the Deathbed Episode originated in the North. It presupposes the existence of a group (tribe) "Israel" in the surroundings of Shechem, in which the "house of Joseph" had apparently a leading role. Given the date of the pro-Judah layer, the pro-Joseph layer should be dated, in all likelihood, at the end of the Late Bronze, or the beginning of Early Iron I. This might suggest some sort of relation between the "Israel" of the Mernephtah stele and the "Israel" of the pro-Joseph layer. It might be that in this way only one saying, though the word "blessing" is more appropriate, originated in the historical context of ancient Israel.

7.7 Epilogue

In the opening paragraph of Chapter One we introduced the *status quaestionis* with a quotation from C.J. Ball's article on Genesis 49 from 1895.[12] With reference to this quotation, the present author has to admit that the text has exercised an absorbing kind of fascination on his mind. Yet it is his sincere wish that after all the pains that have been lavished upon its interpretation in this study, some of the former remaining obscurities might have been cleared up, and that he has produced out of materials, gathered from every possible source, a trustworthy text, and a self-coherent and harmonious interpretation which may carry some conviction to the gentle reader.

---

[12]C.J. Ball, "The Testament of Jacob (Gen. xlix)", *PSBA* May 7 (1895) 164–91, esp. 164.

Indices

Abbreviations

General

adj.	adjective
Akk.	Akkadian
Amor.	Amorite
aor.	aorist
Arab.	Arabic
Aram.	Aramaic
BCE	before common era
BHebr.	biblical Hebrew
det.	determinative
DN(N)	divine name(s)
E	Elohist
Eg.	Egyptian
EHebr.	epigraphical Hebrew
ET	English translation
Eth.	Ethiopic
fem.	feminine
GN(N)	geographical name(s)
Gr.	Greek
Hebr.	Hebrew
hiph.	hiph'il
hithp.	hithpa'el
hoph.	hoph'al
Hur.	Hurrite
imper.	imperative
impf.	imperfective
inf.abs.	infinitive absolute
inf.cstr.	infinitive construct
J	Yahwist
K	Ketib
LBHebr.	late biblical Hebrew
LMHebr.	late Hebrew (mishnaic)
LN(N)	locative name(s)
masc.	masculine
ms(s)	manuscript(s)
niph.	niph'al
NN	*nomen nescio*
n(n).	note(s)
n.s.	new series
OSArab	old south Arabic
P	Priestly document
part.	participle

pass.	passive
perf.	perfective
pers.	person
plur.	plural
PN(N)	personal name(s)
prep.	preposition
Q	Qere
R^{JE}	Jehovist, Redactor J and E
R^{P}	Redactor JE with P
s.a.	*sine anno*
Sem.	Semitic
sing.	singular
subst.	substantive
s.v.	*sub voce*
Syr.	Syriac
TN(N)	tribal name(s)
Ug.	Ugaritic

Bibliographical

AAA.H — Acta Academiae Aboensis, Ser. A: Humaniora (Åbo)

Aalders, — G.Ch. Aalders, *Het boek Genesis opnieuw uit de grond-tekst vertaald en verklaard* (KV),

Genesis, dl. 1 — dl. 1: *Hoofdstuk 1:1–11:26*, Kampen ¹1933; ⁵1976

Genesis, dl. 2 — dl. 2: *Hoofdstuk 11:27–30:43*, Kampen ¹1936; ⁵1976

Genesis, dl. 3 — dl. 3: *Hoofdstuk 31:1–50:26*, Kampen ¹1936; ⁵1976

AB — The Anchor Bible (Garden City [NY])

ABD — D.N. Freedman (ed.), *The Anchor Bible Dictionary*, 6 vols., Garden City (NY) 1992

ABRL — The Anchor Bible Reference Library (Garden City [NY]).

AbrN — *Abr-Nahrain* (Leiden; Leuven)

AbrN.S — Abr-Nahrain Supplement Series (Leiden; Leuven)

AcAL — *Acta Archaeologica Lovaniensia* (Leuven)

ADAJ — *Annual of the Department of Antiquities of Jordan* (Amman)

ADPV — Abhandlungen des Deutschen Palästina-Vereins (Wiesbaden)

ÄA — Ägyptologische Abhandlungen (Wiesbaden)

ÄAT — Ägypten und Altes Testament (Wiesbaden)

AET — Abhandlungen zur evangelischen Theologie (Bonn)

AfO — *Archiv für Orientforschung* (Berlin, Graz)

AfO.B — Archiv für Orientforschung, Beiheft (Berlin, Graz)

AHw — W. von Soden, *Akkadisches Handwörterbuch*, 3 Bde., Wiesbaden 1965–81

Aistleitner, WUS	J. Aistleitner, *Wörterbuch der ugaritischen Sprache*, Hrsg. v. O. Eissfeldt, Berlin 1963
AJBA	*Australian Journal of Biblical Archaeology* (Sydney)
AJBI	*Annual of the Japanese Biblical Institute* (Tokyo)
AJSL	*American Journal of Semitic Languages and Literatures* (Chicago [IL])
ALASP	Abhandlungen zur Literatur Alt-Syrien-Palastinas und Mesopotamiens (Münster)
ALGHJ	Arbeiten zur Literatur und Geschichte des Hellenistischen Judentums (Leiden)
Alt, KS	A. Alt, *Kleine Schriften zur Geschichte des Volkes Israel*, 3 Bde., München 1953–59
Alter, Genesis	R. Alter, *Genesis: Translation and Commentary*, New York 1996
AnBib	Analecta Biblica: Investigationes scientificae in res Biblicas (Rome)
ANEP	J.B. Pritchard (ed.), *The Ancient Near East in Pictures Relating to the Old Testament*, 2.nd ed. with suppl., Princeton (NJ) 1969
ANET	J.B. Pritchard (ed.), *Ancient Near Eastern Texts Relating to the Old Testament*, 3.rd ed. with suppl., Princeton (NJ) 1969
Anton	*Antonianum: Periodicum philosophico-theologicum* (Roma)
AOAT	Altes Orient und Altes Testament (Neukirchen-Vluyn)
AOS	American Oriental Series (New Haven [CT])
AOS.TS	American Oriental Society, Translation Series (New Haven [CT])
Aq	Aquila
ArmB	The Aramaic Bible (Edinburgh)
ARMT	Archives royales de Mari: Transcriptions et traductions (Paris)
ArOr	*Archiv Orientalni* (Prague)
ARTU	J.C. de Moor, *An Anthology of Religious Texts from Ugarit* (NISABA, 16), Leiden 1987
AS	Assyriological Studies (Chicago [IL])
ASOR.DS	American Schools of Oriental Research: Dissertation Series (Winona Lake [IN])
ASTI	*Annual of the Swedish Theological Institute* (Leiden)
ATD	Das Alte Testament Deutsch (Göttingen)
ATD.Erg	Grundrisse zum Alten Testament: Das Alte Testament Deutsch: Ergänzungsreihe (Göttingen)
AThANT	Abhandlungen zur Theologie des Alten und Neuen Testaments (Zürich)
AuOr	*Aula Orientalis* (Barcelona)

AuOr.S	Aula Orientalis-Supplementa (Barcelona)
AmUSt.TR	American University Studies; Series 7, Theology and Religion (New York)
BA	*The Biblical Archaeologist* (New Haven [CT])
BASOR	*Bulletin of the American Schools of Oriental Research* (New Haven [CT])
BASP	*The Bulletin of the American Society of Papyrologists* (New Haven [CT])
BB	Biblische Beiträge (Fribourgh)
BBB	Bonner biblische Beiträge (Bonn)
BDB	F. Brown, S.R. Driver, C.A. Briggs, *Hebrew and English Lexicon of the Old Testament*, Oxford 1907, ^{2}1957
BE	Biblische Enzyklopädie (Stuttgart)
BEATAJ	Beiträge zur Erforschung des Alten Testaments und des Antiken Judentums (Frankfurt aM./Bern)
BEThL	Bibliotheca Ephemeridum Theologicarum Lovaniensium (Leuven)
BEvTh	Beiträge zur evangelische Theologie: Theologische Abhandlungen (München)
BHH	B. Reicke, L. Rost (Hrsg.), *Biblisch-Historisches Handwörterbuch: Landeskunde — Geschichte — Religion — Kultur — Literatur*, 4 Bde., Götingen 1962–79
BHK$^{1/2}$	R. Kittel (ed.), *Biblia Hebraica*, Leipzig 1909; Stuttgart ^{2}1912
BHK$^{3/7}$	R. Kittel, P. Kahle (eds.), *Biblia Herbaica*, Stuttgart ^{3}1937, ^{7}1951
BHS	K. Elliger, W. Rudolph (eds.), *Biblia Hebraica Stuttgartensia*, Stuttgart 1967–77, ^{4}1990
Bib	*Biblica* (Roma)
BibOr	Biblica et Orientalia (Roma)
BibS	Biblical Seminar (Sheffield)
BijbH	A.S. van der Woude (red.), *Bijbels Handboek,* dl. 1: *De wereld van de bijbel*; idem, dl. 2a: *Het Oude Testament*, Kampen 1981, 1982
BiOr	*Bibliotheca Orientalis* (Leiden)
BIOSCS	*Bulletin of the International Organisation for Septuagint and Cognate Studies* (Toronto, etc.)
BIS	Biblical Interpretation Series (Leiden)
BiSt	Biblische Studien (Neukirchen)
BKAT	Biblischer Kommentar Altes Testament (Neukirchen-Vluyn)
BL	H. Bauer, P. Leander, *Historische Grammatik der hebräische Sprache*, Halle a.d. Saale 1918–22 (repr. Hildesheim 1962)

BLGNP	D. Nauta (red.), *Biografische lexicon voor de geschiedenis van het Nederlandse Protestantisme*, dl. 1– , Kampen 1978–
Böhl, *Genesis*	F.M.Th. Böhl, *Genesis*, II (T&U), Groningen 1925
BOT	Boeken van het Oude Testament (Roermond)
BrAMA	British Academy Monographs on Archaeology (Oxford)
Bruno, *Genesis–Exodus*	A. Bruno, *Genesis – Exodus: Eine rhythmische Untersuchung*, Stockholm 1953
BS	*Bibliotheca Sacra* (London)
BSOAS	Bulletin of the School of Oriental and African Studies (London)
BThSt	Biblisch Theologische Studien (Neukirchen-Vluyn)
BZ	*Biblische Zeitschrift* (Paderborn)
BWANT	Beiträge zur Wissenschaft vom Alten und Neuen Testament (Stuttgart)
BZAW	Beihefte zur Zeitschrift für die alttestamentliche Wissenschaft (Berlin)
CAD	*The Assyrian Dictionary of the Oriental Institute of the University of Chicago*, Chicago (IL), Glückstadt 1956–
CARTU	J.C. de Moor, K. Spronk, *A Cuneiform Anthology of Religious Texts from Ugarit* (SSS NS, 6), Leiden 1987
Cassuto, *BOS*	U. Cassuto, *Biblical and Oriental Studies*, vol. I: *Bible*; vol. II: *Bible and Ancient Oriental Texts*, Jerusalem, 1973, 1975
CBET	Contributions to Biblical Exegesis & Theology (Kampen)
CB OTS	Coniectanea Biblica. Old Testament Series (Lund)
CBQ	*Catholic Biblical Quarterly* (Washington [DC])
CBQ.MS	Catholic Biblical Quarterly Monograph Series (Washington [DC])
CML²	J.C.L. Gibson, *Canaanite Myths and Legends*, Edinburgh ²1978
CNEB	Cambridge Bible Commentary on the New English Bible (Cambridge)
COT	Commentaar op het Oude Testament (Kampen)
CPH	*Calwer Predigthilfen* (Stuttgart)
CRINT	Compendia Rerum Iudaicarum ad Novum Testamentum (Assen, Philadelphia [PA])
Cross, *CMHE*	F.M. Cross, *Canaanite Myth and Hebrew Epic: Essays in the History of the Religion of Israel*, Cambridge (MA) 1973
CRRAI	Compte Rendu de la Rencontre Assyriologique Internationale (*inter alii*: Leiden, Paris)
CTM	*Concordia Theological Monthly* (St. Louis [MT])

Dalman, *Hw*	G.H. Dalman, *Aramäisch—Neuhebräisches Handwörterbuch zu Targum, Talmud und Midrasch*, Göttingen ³1938 (repr. Hildesheim 1987)
Davidson, *Genesis 12–50*	R. Davidson, *Genesis 12–50* (CNEB), Cambridge 1979
DBHE	L. Alonso Schökel (ed.), *Diccionario Bíblico Hebreo-Español*, Valencia 1990–4
DCH	D.J.A. Clines (ed.), *The Dictionary of Classical Hebrew*, vol. I–, Sheffield 1993–
DDD	K. van der Toorn *et al.* (eds.), *Dictionary of Deities and Demons in the Bible*, Leiden 1995
Dillmann, *Die Genesis*	A. Dillmann, *Die Genesis erklärt* (KEH), Leipzig ⁴1882
DISO	C.-H. Jean, J. Hoftijzer, *Dictionnaire des inscriptions sémitiques de l'ouest*, Leiden 1965
DMOA	Documenta et Monumenta Orientis Antiqui (Leiden)
DNWSI	J. Hoftijzer, K.A. Jongeling (eds.), *Dictionary of North-West Semitic Inscriptions*, 2 vols., (HdO, 21), Leiden 1995
EA	El Amarna Tablet, according to J.A. Knudtzon, *Die El-Amarna Tafeln*, 2 Teile, Aalen 1964; A.F. Rainey, *El Amarna Tablets 359–379: Supplement to J.A. Knudtzon, Die El-Amarna-Tafeln* (AOAT, 8), Kevelaer, Neukirchen-Vluyn 1970
EAEHL	M. Avi-Yonah, M. Stern (eds.), *Encyclopedia of Archaeological Excavations in the Holy Land*, 4 vols., London 1975–8
EdF	Erträge der Forschung (Darmstadt)
Ehrlich, *RG*, Bd. I	A.B. Ehrlich, *Randglossen zur hebräischen Bibel: Textkritisches, sprachliches und sachliches*, Bd. I, Leipzig 1908
EHS.T	Europäische Hochschulschriften. Reihe 23: Theologie (Frankfurt aM./Bern)
EJ	*Encyclopaedia Judaica*, 16 vols., Jerusalem 1971–2
EPROER	Études préliminaires aux religions orientales dans l'Empire romain (Leiden)
ERC.S	Editions Recherche sur les Civilations, Synthèse (Paris)
ErIs	*Eretz-Israel* (Jerusalem)
ESHM	European Seminar in Historical Methodology (Sheffield)
ÉtB	Études bibliques (Paris)
EÜ	*Die Bibel: Altes und Neues Testament.* Einheitsübersetzung, Stuttgart 1980
EvQ	*Evangelical Quarterly* (London)
EWNT	H. Balz, G. Schneider (Hrsg.), *Exegetisches Wörterbuch zum Neuen Testament*, 3 Bde., Stuttgart 1980–3

Ex	Exegetica: Oud- en Nieuw-Testamentische Studiën (Delft; Amsterdam)
FJB	*Frankfurter Jüdische Beiträge* (Frankfurt)
ForBi	Forschung zur Bibel (Würzburg)
FOTL	The Forms of the Old Testament Literature (Grand Rapids [MI])
Fowler, *TPN*	J.D. Fowler, *Theophoric Personal Names in Ancient Hebrew: A Comparative Study* (JSOTS, 49), Sheffield 1988
De Fraine, *Genesis*	J. de Fraine, *Genesis uit de grondtekst vertaald en toegelicht* (BOT, I/1), Roermond 1963
FrB	*Bibel út de oarspronklike talen op 'e nij yn it Frysk oerset*, Haarlem *s.a.*
FRLANT	Forschungen zur Religion und Literatur des Alten und Neuen Testaments (Göttingen)
FuF	Forschungen und Fortschritte (Berlin)
FzB	Forschung zur Bibel (Würzburg)
GAG	W. von Soden, *Grundriss der Akkadischen Grammatik* (AnOr, 33), 2.Auflage samt Ergänzungsheft (AnOr, 47), Rome 1969
GB	W. Gesenius, F. Buhl, *Hebräisches und aramäisches Handwörterbuch über das Alte Testament*, Leipzig [16]1915
GeoR	*Geographica Religionum* (Berlin)
GerThT	*Gereformeerd Theologisch Tijdschrift* (Kampen)
Ges[18]	W. Gesenius, *Hebräisches und aramäisches Handwörterbuch über das Alte Testament*, 18.Aufl. bearb.u.hrsg.v. D.R. Meyer und H. Donner, Lief. 1– , Berlin 1987–
Ges, *Thes*	W. Gesenius, *Thesaurus philologicus criticus linguae Hebraeae et Chaldaeae Veteris Testamenti*, Bd. I–III, Leipzig 1835–53
GK	W. Gesenius, E. Kautsch, *Hebräische Grammatik*, Leipzig 1909 (repr. Hildesheim 1985)
Grossfeld, *TgOGen*	B. Grossfeld, *The Targum Onqelos to Genesis: Translated, with a Critical Introduction, Apparatus, and Notes* (ArmB, 6), Edinburgh 1988
Gunkel, *Genesis*	H. Gunkel, *Genesis übersetzt und erklärt* (HK, I/1), Göttingen [2]1902, [3]1910
HAE	J. Renz, W. Röllig, *Handbuch der althebräischen Epigraphik*, 3 Bde., Darmstadt 1995–
HAL	L. Koehler, W. Baumgartner, *Hebräisches und aramäisches Lexikon zum Alten Testament*, 3.Aufl. neubearb.v. W. Baumgartner und J.J. Stamm, Leiden 1967–95
Hamilton, *Book of Genesis*	V.P. Hamilton, *The Book of Genesis: Chapters 18–50* (NICOT), Grand Rapids (MI) 1995
HAR	*Hebrew Annual Review* (Columbus [OH])
HAT	Handbuch zum Alten Testament (Tübingen)

Hatch-Redpath   E. Hatch, H.A. Redpath, *A Concordance to the Septu-agint and the Other Greek Versions of the Old Testament (Including the Apocryphal Books)*, 3 vols., Oxford 1897 (repr. Graz 1975)

HdO   Handbuch der Orientalistik (Leiden)

Hecke, *Judah*   K.-H. Hecke, *Judah und Israel: Untersuchungen zur Ge-*
und Israel   *schichte Israels in vor- und frühstaatlicher Zeit* (FzB, 52), Würzburg 1985

HK   Göttinger Handkommentar zum Alten Testament (Göttingen)

Holzinger,   H. Holzinger, *Genesis erklärt* (KHC), Tübingen 1898
Genesis

Houtman, *Der*   C. Houtman, *Der Pentateuch: Die Geschichte seiner Er-*
Pentateuch   *forschung neben einer Auswertung* (CBET, 9), Kampen 1994

HSM   Harvard Semitic Monographs (Atlanta [GA])

HSS   Harvard Semitic Studies (Atlanta [GA])

HThR   *Harvard Theological Review* (Cambridge [MA])

HTIBS   Historic Texts and Interpreters in Biblical Scholarship (Sheffield),

HTS   *Hervormde Teologiese Studies* (Pretoria)

HUCA   *Hebrew Union College Annual* (Cincinnati [OH])

IBS   *Irish Biblical Studies* (London)

ICC   The International Critical Commentary of the Holy Scriptures (Eddinburgh)

IDB   G.A. Buttrick (ed.), *The Interpreter's Dictionary of the Bible: An Illustrated Encyclopedia*, 4 vols. Nashville 1962

IDBS   (ed.), *The Interpreter's Dictionary of the Bible: An Illus-trated Encyclopedia: Supplementary Volume*, Nashville 1976

IEJ   *Israel Exploration Journal* (Jerusalem)

IntB   *The Interpreter's Bible* (Nashville)

JA   *Journal Asiatique* (Paris)

Jacob, *Das*   B. Jacob, *Das erste Buch der Tora Genesis übersetzt und*
erste Buch   *erklärt*, Berlin 1934 (repr. New York *s.a.*)

Jagersma,   H. Jagersma, *Genesis 25:12–50:26* (VHB), Nijkerk 1996
Genesis 25–50

JAOS   Journal of the American Oriental Society (New Haven [CT])

JARCE   *Journal of the American Research Center in Egypt* (Boston [MA])

Jastrow,   M. Jastrow, *Dictionary of the Targumim, Talmud Babli*
Dictionary   *and Yerushalmi, and the Midrashic Literature*, 2 vols., New York 1903

JBL   *Journal of Biblical Literature* (Philadelphia [PA])

JBR	*Journal of Bible and Religion* (Boston [MA])
JBSt	Jerusalem Biblical Studies (Jerusalem)
JCS	*Journal of Cuneiform Studies* (Chicago [IL])
JETS	*Journal of the Evangelical Theological Society* (Wheaton [IL])
JJS	*Journal of Jewish Studies* (London)
JM	P. Joüon, T. Muraoka, *A Grammar of Biblical Hebrew* (SubBi, 14), Roma 1991
JNES	*Journal of Near Eastern Studies* (Chicago [IL])
JNSL	*Journal of Northwest Semitic Languages* (Stellenbosch)
JPh	*Journal of Philology* (London)
JPOS	*Journal of the Palestine Oriental Society* (Jerusalem)
JPS	*The Torah: The Five Books of Moses. A new translation of the Holy Scriptures according to the Masoretic text,* Philadelphia (PA): Jewish Publication Society, ²1962
JQR	*Jewish Quarterly Review* (Philadelphia [PA])
JSNT	*Journal for the Study of the New Testament* (Sheffield)
JSOT	*Journal for the Study of the Old Testament* (Sheffield)
JSOTS	Journal for the Study of the Old Testament Supplement Series (Sheffield)
JSSt	*Journal of Semitic Studies* (Manchester)
JThS	*Journal of Theological Studies* (London)
KaCa	Kamper Cahiers (Kampen)
KAT	Kommentar zum Alten Testament (Leipzig, Erlangen/ Gütersloh)
KBL	L. Koehler, W. Baumgartner, *Lexicon in Veteris Testamenti Libros*, Leiden ²1958
KBS	*De Bijbel uit de grondtekst vertaald; Willibrord Vertaling,* Boxtel 1980
Keel, Uehlinger, *GGG*	O. Keel, C. Uehlinger, *Göttinen, Götter und Gottessymbole: Neue Erkentnisse zur Religionsgeschichte Kanaans und Israels aufgrund bislang unerschlossener ikonographischer Quellen* (Quaestiones Disputatae, 134), Freiburg 1992
KEH	Kurzgefasstes exegetisches Handbuch (Leipzig)
KHC	Kurzer Hand-Commentar zum Alten Testament (Tübingen)
König, *Die Genesis*	E. König, *Die Genesis eingeleitet, übersetzt und erklärt,* Gütersloh ³1925
König, *Wb*	E. König, *Hebräisch und aramäisch Wörterbuch zum Alten Testament*, Leipzig 1910
Korpel, *RiC*	M.C.A. Korpel, *A Rift in the Clouds: Ugaritic and Hebrew Descriptions of the Divine* (UBL, 8), Münster 1990

KTU	M. Dietrich *et al.*, *Die keilalphabetischen Texte aus Ugarit. Einschliesslich der keilalphabetischen Texte ausserhalb Ugarits.* Teil 1, Transkription (AOAT, 24), Neukirchen-Vluyn 1976
KTU²	M. Dietrich *et al.*, *The Cuneiform Alphabetic Texts from Ugarit, Ras Ibn Hani and Other Places (KTU: second, enlarged edition)* (ALASP, 8), Münster 1995
KV	Korte Verklaring der Heilige Schrift (Kampen)
LAPO	Littératures anciennes du Proche-Orient (Paris)
LdÄ	*Lexikon der Ägyptologie*, 7 Bde., Wiesbaden 1972–92
Lett	J.P. Lettinga, *Grammatica van het Bijbels Hebreeuws*, Leiden ⁸1976
Lett¹⁰	J.P. Lettinga, *Grammatica van het Bijbels Hebreeuws*, 10ᵉ herz. ed. door T. Muraoka; met medew. van W.Th. van Peursen, Leiden 1996
Van der Lugt, *SSBHP*	P. van der Lugt, *Strofische structuren in de Bijbels-Hebreeuwse Poëzie: De geschiedenis van het onderzoek en een bijdrage tot de theorievorming omtrent de strofenbouw van de Psalmen*, Kampen 1980
LVT	F. Zorell, *Lexicon hebraicum et aramaicum Veteris Testamenti*, Roma 1955
LXX	Septuagint; edition: *Vetus Testamentum Graecum: Auctoritate Academiae Scientarium Gottingensis edditum*, Bd. I: Genesis, ed. J.W. Wevers, Göttingen 1974
Maher, *TgPsJGen*	M. Maher, *Targum Pseudo-Jonathan: Genesis; Translated, with Introduction and Notes* (ArmB, 1B), Edinburgh 1992
McNamara, *TgNGen*	M. McNamara, *Targum Neofiti 1: Genesis; Translated with Apparatus and Notes* (ArmB, 1A), Edinburgh 1992
Mes(C)	Mesopotamia: Copenhagen Studies in Assyriology (København)
MVEOL	Mededelingen en Verhandelingen van het Vooraziatisch-Egyptisch Genootschap Ex Oriente Lux (Leiden)
MGWJ	*Monatschrift für Geschichte und Wissenschaft des Judentums* (Breslau)
MLC	G. del Olmo Lete, *Mitos y Leyendas de Canaan segun la tradicion de Ugarit: Textos, versión y estudio*, Madrid 1981
De Moor, *RoY* ⁽²⁾	J.C. de Moor, *The Rise of Yahwism: The Roots of Israelite Monotheism* (BEThL, 91), Leuven 1990, ²1997
De Moor, *SPU*	J.C. de Moor, *The Seasonal Pattern in the Ugaritic Myth of Ba'lu according to the Version of Ilimilku* (AOAT, 16), Neukirchen 1971
De Moor, *BCTP*, I	J.C. de Moor, *A Bilingual Concordance to the Targum of the Prophets*, vol. I: *Joshua*, Leiden 1995

MPI	Monographs of the Peshitta Institute (Leiden)
MSSOTS	Society for Old Testament Study Monograph Series (London)
MT	Masoretic Text; edition: BHS
MVÄG	*Mitteilungen der Vorderasiatisch-Ägyptischen Gesellschaft* (Berlin)
NBG	*Bijbel: Vertaling in opdracht van het Nederlands Bijbelgenootschap*, Haarlem 1952
NEAEHL	M. Stern, *The New Encyclopedia of Archaeological Excavations in the Holy Land*, 4 vols., New York 1993
NEB	*The New English Bible with the Apocrypha*, Oxford, Cambridge 1970
NEB.AT	Neue Echter Bibel: Kommentar zum Alten Testament mit der Einheitsübersetzung (Würzburg)
NedThT	*Nederlands Theologisch Tijdschrift* ('s-Gravenhage)
NICOT	The New International Commentary on the Old Testament (Grand Rapids [MI])
NIV	*The Holy Bible: New International Version*, New York 1978
Noth, *IPN*	M. Noth, *Die israelitischen Personennamen im Rahmen der gemeinsemitischen Namengebung* (BWANT, III/10), Stuttgart 1928
NThS	*Nieuwe Theologische Studiën* (Groningen)
OAC	Orientis Antiqvi Collectio (Roma)
OBO	Orbis Biblicus et Orientalis (Freiburg)
OLA	Orientalia Lovaniensia Analecta (Leuven)
Del Olmo Lete, Sanmartín, *DLU*	G. del Olmo Lete, J. Sanmartín, *Diccionario de la lengua ugarítica* (AuOr.S, 7), Barcelona 1996
Or	*Orientalia: Commentarii periodici Pontificii Instituti Biblici*, Nova Series (Roma)
OrAn	*Oriens Antiquus* (Roma)
OTS	Oudtestamentische Studiën (Leiden)
Pardee, UB	D. Pardee, "Ugaritic Bibliography", *AfO* 34 (1987) 366–471
Pehlke, *Gen. 49:1-28*	H. Pehlke, *An Exegetical and Theological Study of Genesis 49:1-28*, Ann Arbor 1985
PEQ	*Palestine Exploration Quarterly* (London)
Peš	Pešiṭṭa; edition: *The Old Testament in Syriac according to the Peshitta Version ... Part I¹: Preface. — Genesis; Exodus*, Leiden 1977
PJB	*Palästinajahrbuch des Deutschen Evangelischen Instituts für Altertumswissenschaft des Heiligen Landes zu Jerusalem* (Berlin)
POS	Pretoria Oriental Series (London)

PredOT	De Prediking van het Oude Testament (Nijkerk)
Procksch, *Genesis*	O. Procksch, *Die Genesis übersetzt und erklärt* (KAT), Leipzig, Erlangen ³1924
PSBA	*Proceedings of the Society of Biblical Archaeology* (London)
QuSem	Quaderni di semitistica (Firenze)
Von Rad, *Erste Buch Mose*	G. von Rad, *Das Erste Buch Mose: Genesis übersetzt und erklärt* (ATD, 2–4), Göttingen ¹²1987
Von Rad, *GSAT*	G. von Rad, *Gesammelte Studien zum Alten Testament*, Bd. II (ThB, 48), München 1973
RANE	Records of the ancient Near East (Wiesbaden)
RB	*Revue Biblique* (Paris)
RechBib	Recherche Biblique (Paris)
*RGG*³	K. Galling (Hrsg.), *Die Religion in Geschichte und Gegenwart: Handwörterbuch für Theologie und Religionswissenschaft*, 6 Bde., Tübingen ³1957–62
RHR	*Revue de l'Histoire des Religions* (Paris)
RIM.AP	Royal Inscriptions of Mesopotamia, Assyrian Periods (Toronto)
RLA	*Reallexikon der Assyriologie*, Bd. 1–, Berlin, Leipzig 1928–
RSP, vol. I–II	L. Fischer (ed.), *Ras Shamra Parallels: The Texts from Ugarit and the Hebrew Bible*, vol. I–II (AnOr, 49–50), Rome 1972–75
RSP, vol. III	S. Rummel (ed.), *Ras Shamra Parallels: The Texts from Ugarit and the Hebrew Bible*, vol. III (AnOr, 51), Rome 1981
SAA	State Archives of Assyria (Helsinki)
SABCP	W. van der Meer, J.C. de Moor (eds.), *The Structural Analysis of Biblical and Canaanite Poetry* (JSOTS, 74), Sheffield 1988
Sam	Samaritan Pentateuch; edition: A. von Gall (Hrsg.), *Der hebräische Pentateuch der Samaritaner*, Giessen 1919 (Berlin 1966)
Sarna, *Genesis*	N.M. Sarna, *Genesis: The Traditional Hebrew Text with New JPS Translation* (JPS Torah Commentary), Philadelphia (PA) 5749/1989
SBL.DS	Society of Biblical Literature: Dissertation Series (Missoula [MT], etc.)
SBL.MS	Society of Biblical Literature: Monograph Series (Missoula [MT], etc.)
SBEsp	*Studia Biblica Español* (Madrid)
SBFLA	*Studii Biblici Franciscani Liber Annuus* (Jerusalem)
SBT	Studies in Biblical Theology (London)

SBTS	Sources for Biblical and Theological Study (Winona Lake [IN])
Scharbert, *Genesis 12–50*	J. Scharbert, *Genesis 12–50* (NEB.AT). Würzburg 1986
Schumann, *Genesis*	G.A. Schumann, *Genesis Hebraice et Graece recognovit et digessit varias lectiones notasque criticas subiunxit, argumentis historico-criticis illustravit et cum annotatione perpetua edidit; Volumen I: Genesin complectens* (Pentateuchus Hebraice et Graece, 1), Lipsiae 1829
ScEs	*Science et Esprit* (Bruges)
ScrHie	*Scripta Hierosolymitana* (Jerusalem)
SCSt	Society of Biblical Literature: Septuagint and Cognate Studies Series (Atlanta [GA])
SDIO	Studia et Documenta ad Iura Orientis Antiqui Pertinentia (Leiden)
Sef	*Sefarad: Revista del Instituto Arias Montano de Estudios Hebraicos y Oriente Próximo* (Madrid)
SEL	*Studi Epigrafici e Linguistici sul Vicino Oriente antico* (Verona)
Van Selms, *Genesis*, I–II	A. van Selms, *Genesis*, 2 dln. (PredOT), Nijkerk 1967
Sem	*Semitica* (Paris)
SGKAO	Studien zur Gesellschaft und Kultur des alten Orients (Berlin)
SHAW.PH	Sitzungsberichte der Heidelberger Akademie der Wissenschaften, Philosophisch-historische Klasse (Heidelberg)
SH(C)ANE	Studies in the History (and Culture) of the Ancient Near East (Leiden)
Simpson, *IntB*	C.A. Simpson, "The Book of Genesis", in: *IntB*, vol. I, New York 1952, 437–829
SJOT	*Scandinavian Journal of the Old Testament* (Aarhus; Oslo)
Skinner, *Genesis*	J. Skinner, *A Critical and Exegetical Commentary on Genesis* (ICC), Edinburgh ²1930
Smelik, *BCTP*, II	W.F. Smelik, *A Bilingual Concordance to the Targum of the Prophets*, vol. II: *Judges*, Leiden 1996
SOA	Sammlung orientalischer Arbeiten (Leipzig)
Speiser, *Genesis*	E.A. Speiser, *Genesis: A New Translation with Introduction and Commentary* (AB, 1), Garden City (NY) 1964
SPIB	Scripta Pontificii Instituti Biblici (Roma)
SSN	Studia Semitica Neerlandica (Assen)
SSS NS	Semitic Study Series, New Series (Leiden)
Stamm, *BHAN*	J.J. Stamm, *Beiträge zur hebräischen und altorientalischen Namenkunde* (OBO, 30), Freiburg 1980
StANT	Studien zum Alten und Neuen Testament (München)

StOr	*Studia Orientalia* (Helsinki)
StP	Studia Pohl (Roma)
StPB	Studia Post-Biblica (Leiden)
SubBi	Subsidia Biblica (Roma)
SVT	Supplements to Vetus Testamentum (Leiden)
SWBAS	The Social World of Biblical Antiquity Series (Sheffield)
TA	*Tel Aviv: Journal of the Institute of Archaeology* (Tel Aviv)
TCS	Texts from Cuneiform Sources (New York [NY])
THAT	E. Jenni, C. Westermann (Hrsg.), *Theologisches Hand-wörterbuch zum Alten Testament*, 2 Bde., München ³1978, ²1979
ThB	Theologische Bücherei (München)
Them	*Themelios* (Leceister)
Theod	Theodotion
ThLZ	*Theologische Literaturzeitung* (Leipzig)
ThQ	*Theologische Quartalschrift* (Tübingen)
ThWAT	G.J. Botterweck *et al.* (Hrsg.), *Theologisches Wörterbuch zum Alten Testament*, Bd. I–, Stuttgart 1973–
ThWNT	G. Kittel, G. Friedrich (Hrsg.), *Theologisches Wörterbuch zum Neuen Testament*, 10 Bde., Stuttgart 1933–79
ThZ	*Theologische Zeitschrift* (Basel)
ThZ.S	Theologische Zeitschrift; Sonderband (Basel)
TJon	Targum Jonathan; edition: A. Sperber (ed.), *The Bible in Aramaic. Based on old Manuscripts and Printed Texts, vol. II: The Former Prophets According to Targum Jonathan*; idem, ... *vol. III: The Latter Prophets According to Targum Jonathan*, Leiden 1959, 1962
TN	Targum Neophyti or Palestinian Targum; edition: A. Diez Macho, *Neophyti 1: Targum Palestinense Ms de la Bibliotheca Vaticana*, Tomo I: Génesis. Edición Principe, Introdución General y Versión Castellana, Madrid/Barcelona 1968
TO	Targum Onkelos; edition: A. Sperber (ed.), *The Bible in Aramaic. Based on old Manuscripts and Printed Texts, vol. I: The Pentateuch according to Targum Onkelos*, Leiden 1959
TOML	A. Caquot *et al.*, *Textes Ougaritiques*, tm. I: *Mythes et Légendes: Introduction, traduction, commentaire* (LAPO, 7), Paris 1974
TPsJ	Targum Pseudo-Jonathan; edition: M. Ginsburger, *Pseudo-Jonathan (Thargum Jonathan ben Usiël zum Pentateuch)*, Berlin 1903
TRE	G. Krause, G. Müller (Hrsg.), *Theologische Realenzyklopädie*, Bd. 1– . Berlin 1977–

TTHLLI	Textwissenschaft, Theologie, Hermeneutik, Linguistik, Literaturanalyse, Informatik (Tübingen)
T&U	Text en Uitleg (Groningen)
TUAT	O. Kaiser (Hrsg.), *Texte aus der Umwelt des Alten Testaments*, 3 Bde., Gütersloh 1982–
Tuch, *Die Genesis*	F. Tuch, *Kommentar über die Genesis*, Halle 1938
TUMSR	Trinity University Monograph Series in Religion (San Antonio)
TynB	*Tyndale Bulletin* (London)
UBL	Ugaritisch-Biblische Literatur (Münster)
UF	*Ugarit-Forschungen* (Neukirchen-Vluyn)
UT	C.H. Gordon, *Ugaritic Textbook* (AnOr, 38), Rome 1965
Vawter, *On Genesis*	B. Vawter, *On Genesis: A New Reading*, London 1977
Vg	Vulgata; edition: *Biblia sacra iuxta Vulgatam versionem*, 2 tomi, ed. R. Weber *et alii*, Stuttgart ²1975
VHB	Verklaring van de Hebreeuwse Bijbel (Nijkerk)
Vrs	*versiones omnes vel plurimae*
VT	*Vetus Testamentum* (Leiden)
Waltke, O'Connor, *IBHS*	B.K. Waltke, M. O'Connor, *An Introduction to Biblical Hebrew Syntax*, Winona Lake (IN) 1990
WBC	Word Biblical Commentary (Waco [TX])
WdO	*Die Welt des Orients* (Göttingen)
Wenham,	G.J. Wenham,
Genesis 1–15	*Genesis 1–15* (WBC, 1), Waco (TX) 1987;
Genesis 16–50	*Genesis 16–50* (WBC, 2), Waco (TX) 1993
Westermann,	C. Westermann, *Genesis*,
Genesis 1–11	1: *Genesis 1–11* (BKAT, I/1), Neukirchen-Vluyn 1974;
Genesis 12–36	2: *Genesis 12–36* (BKAT, I/2), Neukirchen-Vluyn 1981;
Genesis 37–50	3: *Genesis 37–50* (BKAT, I/3), Neukirchen-Vluyn 1982.
WMANT	Wissenschaftliche Monographien zum Alten und Neuen Testament (Neukirchen-Vluyn)
WThJ	*Westminster Theological Journal* (Philadelphia [PA])
WZ(L).GS	*Wissenschaftliche Zeitschfift der Friedrich-Schiller-Universität Jena, Gesellschafts- und sprachwissenschaftliche Reihe* (Jena)
YNER	Yale Near Eastern Researches (New Haven [CT])
ZA	*Zeitschrift für Assyriologie und Vorderasiatische Archäologie* (Berlin)
ZÄS	*Zeitschrift für ägyptische Sprache und Altertumskunde* (Leipzig, Berlin)
ZAH	*Zeitschrift für Althebraistik* (Stuttgart)
ZAW	*Zeitschrift für die alttestamentliche Wissenschaft* (Berlin)
ZBK.AT	Zürcher Bibelkommentare: Alte Testament (Zürich)

ZDPV	*Zeitschrift des Deutschen Palästina-Vereins* (Stuttgart, Wiesbaden)
Zobel, *SuG*	H.-J. Zobel, *Stammesspruch und Geschichte: Die Angaben der Stammessprüche von Gen 49, Dtn 33 und Jdc 5 über die politischen und kultischen Zustände im damaligen "Israel"* (BZAW, 95), Berlin 1965
ZRGg	*Zeitschrift für Religions- und Geistesgeschichte* (Köln)

Index of Authors

Index of Textual References

Index of Greek and Semitic Words

PHOENICIAN
b'l mrp' 213
'z 88
rš't 88
šdy 213

SYRIAC
pr' 187

UGARITIC
ảl 176
ảyl 176
ảrgmn 132
ảṯr 204
ỉbrd 197
ỉbr 197, 198
ỉl ảbk 24
ỉlỉb 24, 204, 206, 208, 211
ỉl 176, 210, 211
ủḥryt 87
'bn 199
'br 198
'lh' ṭb' 213
'y'l 119
bkr 97
brk 191, 206
bt 212
dn 166, 167
ḏmr 202, 203, 204
ḏmrb'l 203
ḏmrd 203
ḏmrhd 203
ḥdy 111
ḥp ym 148
ẓby 100
yqy 133
ybl 139
yqy 134
kbkb 211
lṯr ỉl ảby 206
mlk 208
mlk 'lm 211
mnḥy 132, 138
mrr 191, 206
mṣṣ 76

mt 212
mṯpdm 156
ndr 131, 132
skn 204
'bd 134
'l 91, 190
'ly 133
'tk 210
ġr ‖ gb' 223
prt 189
qb't 76
qdš 204
r'y 203, 211
rpủ b'l 213
rp' 213
rpủ
rpủ 203, 208, 210, 211,
šd 208, 210, 211, 212, 213, 215
šdy' 213
šdrp' 213
šm ỉl 205
šmn 171
šmt 171
ṯd 212
ṯpd 155
ṯpṭ 133
ṯt' 76
ṯr ảbh 206
ṯr ảbk ỉl 206
ṯr ỉl 206
ṯydr 138
ṯyl 138
ṯyndr 131
ṯy 130, 131, 133, 138, 139
ṯr 23, 100, 197, 198,
ṯrr 104

HEBREW
אב 240, 241, 511
בן ‖ אב 94
אבד 160
אבה 111
אביהוד 118, 120
אביו 91
אביטוב 119